Marketing Communications

From Fundamentals to Strategies

Marketing Communications

From Fundamentals to Strategies

Michael L. Rothschild
University of Wisconsin–Madison

D. C. HEATH AND COMPANY
Lexington, Massachusetts   Toronto

Acquisitions Editor   Harry Briggs

Production Editor   Kimberley Rieck Fisher

Designer   Sally Thompson Steele

Production Coordinator   Mike O'Dea

Text Permissions Editor   Margaret Roll

Front cover photo   Ray Ellis/Photo Researchers, Inc.

Back cover photo   Jeffrey M. Dunn

Published simultaneously in Canada.

Printed in the United States of America.

International Standard Book Number: 0-669-07210-9

Library of Congress Catalog Card Number: 86-80486

Preface

*T*his text is an introduction to the management and strategies of marketing communications, for courses in marketing communications or promotional strategies at schools of business. It is designed to follow the decision sequence framework that a manager would follow in developing a communications campaign. To that end, it proceeds from situation analysis, to objectives and positioning, to strategies, to budgeting.

One of my main goals in writing this text was to show students the world of marketing communications as realistically as possible. I have tried to make this text unique by developing a balance of theoretical and practical perspectives. In doing so, the chapters are based on theory and models, and then develop issues with real-world examples from the practitioner's point of view. Chapter topics, chapter features, and extensive visuals and examples have all been designed with this goal in mind.

Research Input

All of these issues—the balance of theory and real-world application, the highly visual nature of the text, the emphasis on topics of managerial relevance—have emerged as a result of extensive research done by D. C. Heath before a single word of the text was written. What has resulted is an attempt to use the marketing concept to develop a text that meets the needs of the instructors, students, and managers who will use it.

The development of this text followed the decision sequence framework that it recommends. Analysis of the marketplace included survey and focus group research; the result of both of these plus other analyses of the market led to objectives and a position that set this book apart in a meaningful and beneficial way. The resulting book is an execution of strategies designed to meet the objectives and position.

Content

The table of contents also follows the basic decision sequence framework. In addition, current issues most relevant to practitioners and not dealt with in competing texts are given special attention. These issues include positioning (Chapter 5), the media plan and scheduling (Chapter 13), sales promotions (Part 6), and the brand name, packaging, and point-of-purchase displays (Chapter 19).

After an introduction to basic definitions, Parts 2 through 8 get students right into the strategic framework they need to learn marketing communications management, beginning with the situation analysis, or assessment of the marketing

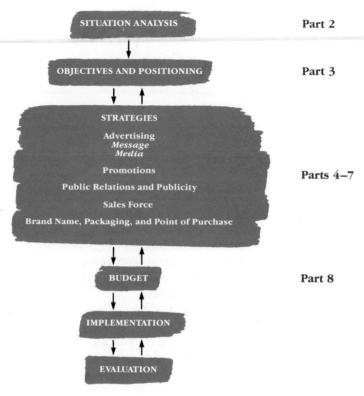

Decision Sequence Framework

communications problems facing the firm (Part 2). Although a solid foundation of consumer behavior theory is discussed here, its coverage is not limited to these chapters. Consumer behavior theory is also introduced and applied, where relevant to other decision making, in Chapters 7 and 8 on message strategies, in Chapter 13 on media scheduling, and in Chapter 14 on promotions.

Setting objectives and positioning (Part 3) are the natural outcomes of the situation analysis and prepare the way for the development of strategies. Chapter 5's section on developing a position presents more detail than is found in other texts.

Parts 4 through 7 deal with the specific message, media, promotions, public relations, selling, and other communications strategies that evolve from objectives and positioning. As mentioned earlier, consumer behavior theory is interwoven wherever it applies directly to marketing communications practice. A unique feature of Part 5 is Chapter 13's up-to-date section on media scheduling and planning, which is strongly based on verbal learning theory and repetition effects.

Part 8 (budgeting) is concerned with evaluating the costs and benefits of the strategies developed in Parts 4 through 7. The objective and task method and payout planning are presented in detail.

While Parts 2 through 8 take the student through the decision sequence framework, Part 9 utilizes this information to examine a number of specific promotional situations. As Parts 2 through 8 examine primarily the promotion of consumer products, Part 9 devotes three chapters to the promotion of retail locations, industrial products, and a variety of services.

Finally, Part 10 concludes with a discussion of social and ethical concerns, a realistic assessment of ad agency careers, and a review of keys to success in advertising and promotions.

Chapter Features

The Inside Outlook To meet my goal of showing the world of marketing communications as realistically as possible, a number of practitioners were asked to write short essays of advice for students. As a result, each chapter has one or two interviews, called "The Inside Outlook," where industry leaders share their knowledge and experience with the reader. Most of these practitioners are senior vice-presidents, or above, in major advertising agencies.

Good Vibrations Case The goal of realism was also reached by means of an ongoing case, "Good Vibrations." Sunkist Soft Drinks, Inc., agreed to contribute the history of the introduction of Sunkist Orange Soda for this text. At the end of Parts 2 through 10, the case shows how the company dealt with the problems it encountered as it progressed through the decision sequence. In this way, the student (who was probably part of Sunkist's original target market) can see an entire set of strategies being developed.

Examples The goal of showing reality was also achieved through a large number of examples. Virtually every strategic issue is followed by at least one example of its real-world execution.

Visuals Since advertising and promotions are visual topics, this text is also visual; it contains over 400 figures and tables, a large percentage of which are ads used as examples of the points made.

End-of-Chapter Materials Each chapter concludes with a summary and discussion questions that review the chapter topics.

Also Available

Instructor's Guide with Test Items This complete teaching resource includes learning objectives, chapter outlines, lecture outlines, teaching topics, discussion question answers, and references. A test item file of 1,500 questions, with about 25 multiple-choice, 30 true-false, and 6 or 7 essay questions per chapter, is also included.

Archive A computerized test item file is available for both Apple and IBM microcomputers.

Advertising: From Fundamentals to Strategies A comprehensive text for courses in advertising is also available from D. C. Heath, with the same features included in *Marketing Communications.*

Acknowledgments

There are, of course, many people to thank for their assistance in this project. And, unfortunately, I must extend apologies to those I am unable to mention; so many people were helpful that it is impossible to list all of them.

Two of my advertising partners, Roman Hiebing, President, and Sheila Dorten, Vice-President and Creative Director of The Hiebing Group, read large parts of the text and gave unselfishly of their time and thoughts to help make this book a reality. In addition, I have learned from them over the years by observing them at work and in my classes. Similarly, I learned from my other three partners, Andy Pellizzi, Art Director; Michael Gramling, Media Director; and Marion Michaels, Account Supervisor. They taught me through their work and through their thoughts when they joined my classes.

Many other practitioners also contributed to this text. Every chapter contains the ideas of practitioners who were willing to share their experiences in order to make the book more realistic. Each of the pieces contributed by these people is special in its view of the advertising world and because it reflects time taken from a hectic schedule in order to help future practitioners become better acquainted with the industry.

Another thread of reality woven through the book is the Sunkist Orange Soda case. Allen Layfield, of Sunkist Soft Drinks, and David Haan, of Foote, Cone & Belding, were very helpful in answering my questions and opening their files so that the case would be as accurate as possible.

Michael Tobin, of Foote, Cone & Belding; William Lynch, of Leo Burnett; Michael Lynn, of J. Walter Thompson; and Scott Cooper and Michael Pratzel, of The Hiebing Group, responded to my requests whenever I needed more materials, another name, or another example.

And, of course, I need to thank all of the other people in advertising from whom I have learned over the years. Some of them were clients with difficult questions; some of them were colleagues at the three advertising agencies for which I have worked who had answers to the difficult questions.

On the academic side there are also many people to thank. Most important are the students. Without their questions it would be easy to be complacent; with their questions it has been necessary to show how theory and reality come together. The book benefits from this interaction; I have tried not to use any theory that did not have a real-world application.

My students have been most valuable in challenging me in a project course that forces them to create an entire advertising and promotions campaign for a real client. The pressure of this task requires answers to problems that do not have easy answers. By searching together, both my students and I have grown. These campaign projects could not have succeeded without help from many companies. Some of those who have contributed are: S. C. Johnson & Son, Oscar Meyer, General Motors, Harley Davidson, Sanna Division of Beatrice Foods, American Family Insurance, Ray-O-Vac, Jockey International, and Northwestern Mutual Life Insurance. These firms helped to create a questioning environment so that answers could be sought.

This text was aided immensely by the critical reviews of several colleagues. I believe that the final version has been improved by their comments, but any errors are mine. Alan Sawyer, University of Florida, was my main sounding board and critic; his unique style was invaluable. Many others read large parts of the draft: Robert Eng, Babson College; Thomas Leigh, Pennsylvania State University; James Merrill, Indiana University; John Perrachione, Kent State University; Len Reid, University of Georgia; Surendra Singh, University of Kansas; Bruce Stern, Portland State University; and Valarie Zeithaml, Texas A&M University. Special thanks go to Frank Pierce, University of Florida, for an especially insightful and thought-provoking review, which was a constant thorn in my side and, as a result, a valued companion during the revisions.

No book can become a reality without an editor and a publisher. Harry Briggs and the D. C. Heath management need to be thanked for giving me enough incentives and threats to keep me going. Harry had the ability to create depression with every phone call; the resultant paranoia led to better work. Paranoia is a great motivator; thanks, Harry. Thanks also to Kim Rieck Fisher, Margaret Roll, Sally Thompson Steele, Mike O'Dea, Barbara Piercecchi, and Sue Gleason for their help in transforming the manuscript into a book, and to Ruth Smith for writing an excellent and thorough instructor's guide.

Several other people also deserve thanks. Michael Houston and Robert Bock helped work out the mechanism to allow me the time to complete this project. Janet Christopher did a superb typing job and kept me on schedule. Tom Genske, Paul Loomans, and Cynthia Socall spent innumerable nights and weekends working on the footnotes, figures, and other details so that I could concentrate on writing.

Most important are the thanks and love I have for the three women in my life, Judy, Jenny, and Beccah. They helped keep my life in the proper balance and wouldn't let me remain a workaholic. It is to them and to Nelly, Sieg, and Milton that this book is dedicated.

M. L. R.

To The Student

*E*very reader of this book has a lifetime of personal experiences with its subject matter. Marketing communications is something that surrounds us all; it is impossible to avoid in our society, and most of us interact with some form of commercial message over a thousand times a day. Given this constant barrage of messages, it is no wonder that each of us is an expert on marketing communications. As with fine art, we may not know much about the subject, but we do know what we like and dislike. Most of us have probably had many animated conversations with friends about good and bad advertising. We also have suffered through the torture of the constant bombardment of jingles that remain firmly embedded in our minds, only to pop out and attack us at some unexpected moment. And who among us has never responded to a price-off deal, a coupon, or the lure of a sweepstakes prize?

These are all the subjects of this text. The topic of marketing communications is familiar—it is not like accounting, calculus, or subatomic physics. Therefore, one task of this text will be to organize the intuitive wisdom held by all its readers. Another task will be to consider why all those ads and promotions exist, and whether they really are as good or as bad as we, as passive observers, might believe. Along the road of organizing our casual observances, we will consider not just the worth of marketing communications to the firm, but also its worth to ourselves as individuals and to our collective selves as a society.

Contents

Marketing Communications

*From Fundamentals
to Strategies*

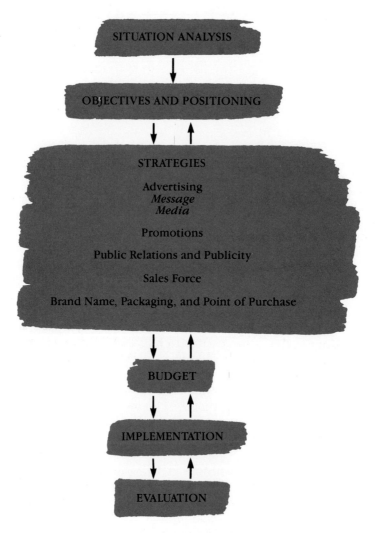

Decision Sequence Framework

Part One
An Introduction
to the World of
Marketing Communications

*A*dvertising is the most fun you can have with your clothes on.[1]

The feelings behind this statement represent those of many people in all areas of marketing communications. If it is necessary to work for a living, then we might as well do something enjoyable; creating and managing promotions is fun. It's challenging. It's hard work. It's stimulating. And it's never boring.

Creating and managing the promotions process are immensely challenging tasks whether they are done from the perspective of the advertising agency, the manufacturer, or the retailer. The business is full of impossible deadlines and lofty objectives, but it is also full of extremely intelligent, talented, and creative people working together toward these goals.

Few people who work in advertising and promotions are neutral about it. Those who succeed thrive on the constant pressure and challenges; those who drop out find the rewards to be insufficient to maintain the constant push; and many who remain would like to leave but find they can't tear themselves away from something they really enjoy doing.

The areas of promotions, communications, and advertising are all part of marketing and will be approached in this text from a managerial perspective, but also from the perspective that this is a fascinating business to be in and a business full of interesting and challenging people.

It is easy to create a controlled, persuasive message; anyone can do it. Most people already have done it by writing a classified ad for the newspaper, by putting up a poster, by asking another person for a date, or by trying to get a grade changed. While it is easy to create a message, it is extremely difficult to create the most appropriate message for the occasion. And while most people have created some type of persuasive message, few have created the particular type of message that is defined as marketing communications. Even fewer have created the most appropriate promotional message for the situation.

1

This text is about the management of marketing communications. As such, its purpose is to aid managers and future managers in communicating more effectively with mass audiences so that a specific behavior (usually purchase, but possibly voting, letter writing, driving more slowly, enlisting in the military, etc.) will result. This book is written to help the reader become more effective and efficient at this mass persuasions task.

Note

1. Jerry Della Femina, *From Those Wonderful Folks Who Gave You Pearl Harbor* (New York: Simon and Schuster, 1970), p. 253.

Chapter 1
An Introduction to the World of Marketing Communications

*T*his first chapter will try to establish a foundation on which the rest of the text can be built. Therefore the topics will include

- A review of some basic marketing so that the concepts of this text can be integrated into the larger marketing function

- The definitions of some key terms so that the reader will understand the language of marketing communications

- A preview of some basic models used throughout so that the development of the text will proceed in an orderly fashion

- An introduction to the structure of the promotions business and the types of people who work in it

A Review of Basic Marketing and Its Relevance to Marketing Communications

Modern marketing communications tools are rarely used in isolation by sophisticated practitioners. These managers know that promotions strategies must be incorporated into the larger marketing function and that the tools discussed in this text make up only a part of the many options available. Because marketing is so pervasive in the development of communications strategies, this text begins with a review of some basic marketing issues.

The marketing concept

One of the key concepts of modern marketing is the *marketing concept*. As described by Kotler in *Marketing Management*, the *marketing concept* is a management orientation that holds that the key task of the organization is to determine the needs and wants of target markets and to adapt the organization to delivering the desired satisfactions more effectively and efficiently than its competitors.[1]

Kotler juxtaposes this with the *sales concept.*

The *sales concept* is a management orientation that assumes that consumers will either not buy or not buy enough of the organization's products unless the organization makes a substantial effort to stimulate their interest in its products.[2]

The sales concept is an internal orientation stressing the capabilities of the firm; the marketing concept is an external orientation focusing on the needs of relevant consumers. These two managerial philosophies have a strong impact on the effectiveness of the firm's communications.

All marketing communications inform and persuade to some degree.[3] At the most basic level all such messages inform the consumer of the brand name of the sponsor; beyond that, some messages become quite complex in the level of information that they make available. All marketing communications also attempt to persuade; advertising, for instance, is an advocacy form of communications that is intentionally one-sided. The firm that pays for the message gets to present its point of view. In some cases the persuasion is mild; in others it may get quite pushy. All messages have some combination of these two elements. Informing and persuading relate to the use of the marketing and sales concept, as can be seen in the following example of two firms that are attempting to introduce new products.

Firm A practices the marketing concept; as a result, its advertising will stress an informative component. Having done prior research, the firm will be able to announce that its new product, strawberry-flavored beer, meets the needs of the marketplace. Consumers will only need minor persuasion to purchase this marvelous beverage because they have already expressed a desire for the product through the firm's research. The firm has responded to marketplace needs and/or wants. Strawberry beer is so successful that after its initial campaign, the firm is able to cut back on its advertising. Repeat purchase levels are high, and the firm has trouble manufacturing enough to keep up with demand.

The management of Firm B, on the other hand, learns that it has excess capacity in several of its brewing plants and decides to manufacture chocolate beer in order to absorb excess inventory of one of its subsidiaries, a cocoa bean plantation in South America. Without researching the tastes of consumers, it begins to produce its own marvelous brew. Chocolate beer, though, does not win over the hearts and minds of U.S. consumers; the advertising and promotions campaign is intensified.

The messages no longer try to inform consumers of the joys of chocolate beer. Now the messages must try to persuade consumers about something that they do not believe, that is, that chocolate beer really tastes great. In addition to a persuasive appeal, the message must be repeated more often because repetition has been found to be an aid in the persuasive process. Promotional tools are also used more extensively; premiums, sweepstakes, and a variety of pricing deals are used to get consumers to try, and then to adopt, chocolate beer. Excessive advertising and promotions are very expensive, and, after a year or two, Firm B decides that the losses are too great. Chocolate beer is removed from the market and becomes another of the many new product failures that come and go each year.

The difficult task of communicating and of managing behavior are made considerably easier if the firm follows the marketing concept. If the good or service does not meet a need, all the firm's horses, men, women, and promotional plans, cannot keep the product alive in the long run. Many types of low-priced poor products are sold once, and advertising and promotions can be very useful in bringing about trial use, but without a good product, repeat usage is not likely to result. Managers have high expectations for the magical qualities of advertising and promotions, but success must begin with the product itself and with a pursuit of the philosophy of the marketing concept. Few products can survive without repeat purchases; these only come in response to a product that meets needs.

The marketing mix

The major strategic tools of marketing can be broken into four classes called the *four Ps:*

> Product
> Price
> Place
> Promotions

(*Distribution* is a more accurate term than *place,* and *communication* is more accurate than *promotions,* but *four Ps* is easier to remember than *two Ps, a D, and a C.* Managers like to develop mnemonic devices to aid memory and learning of their messages. The *four Ps* is such a device; two Ps, a D, and a C just doesn't have the same memorable ring to it.)

The *product* is "something that is viewed as capable of satisfying a need or want"[4]; put another way, it is the bundle of positive attributes that the consumer receives in a transaction. The *price* is what one party to a transaction must give up in order to receive the product. It consists of all the negative attributes or dissatisfactions associated with the transaction; these include monetary price as well as time cost, hassle cost, and psychic cost, among others. *Place* covers all the issues related to the system of distribution. Most relevant to marketing communications is the convenience with which the product can be acquired. It can be positive or negative depending on this convenience. A 24-hour market offers time (and maybe place) utility but charges a higher monetary price. Conversely, a factory outlet may lower its monetary price to compensate for a higher place cost (which leads to a higher payment of precious time) if the outlet is located far from where its customers live.

Promotions (defined in depth later in this chapter) contains the advertising message; this message should emerge as a result of an evaluation of product, price, and place. Consumers are informed of the positive attributes and persuaded that these positive attributes will lead to a positive cost-benefit relation when compared to the price. If the firm stresses a marketing philosophy, it will develop the product, price, and place before it develops promotions. (In this section of this chapter, the word *promotions* is used as one of the four Ps and in this light includes within it advertising, sales promotions devices, public relations, the sales force, and all other ways by which the firm can communicate with its publics. Later in the text, in Chapters 14, 15, and 16, a section on promotions will deal with nonadvertising inducements to behavior such as coupons, samples, premiums, and a host of other devices.)

In considering the relation among the four Ps, the allocation of the firm's scarce resources between product development and promotions development must also be considered. If all the firm's capital is invested in the product, consumers will learn about it very slowly. Conversely, spending too much on promotion may lead to a well-known product that may be inferior or does not keep pace with changes in the marketplace. A balance between product and promotion is, therefore, necessary.

Finally, in the product-promotions relation the manager soon learns that good promotion is the best way to kill a poor product. If the firm promotes well, its prospective consumers will investigate its offering; a poor product doesn't stand a chance under the scrutiny of the careful consumer. Firms have known this fact for a long time, and it is the basis of the marketing concept.

Just as promotions cannot overcome a bad product, it also cannot overcome poor distribution or a high price. If advertising creates excitement but the product cannot be found on store shelves, then the promotions budget has been wasted. Even worse, consumers may have learned not to look for the brand when it is advertised again later. Now the brand is on the shelf but no one cares.

Advertising also cannot overcome an exorbitant price. Awareness can be generated, but if the cost/benefit relation is perceived to be poor, no sale will result. The elements of the marketing mix must work together or the product will not succeed.

The promotions mix

As the firm begins to develop communications strategies, it has a number of alternatives available. These alternatives can be classified in a two-by-two diagram such as that shown in Figure 1.1. The tools are either mass or personal and either paid or free. This book stresses mass and paid forms of communication but will devote some space to the other forms as well.

To be most effective, management must keep control of its message, its form, its time of delivery, and its place of delivery. Management is rightfully concerned that consumers receive the correct message at the correct time, and the firm is willing to pay to ensure its control. A contract is therefore established between the firm and the medium of message delivery. All the tools listed in the left column of Figure 1.1 allow the firm to retain control by virtue of payments made.

The message can be delivered through mass or personal channels, but control over the message and its time and place of delivery must be retained by the

Figure 1.1 *The promotions mix*

	PAID	FREE

MASS	Advertising
	Sales promotions
	  devices
	Packaging
	Brand name
	Point of purchase
	Some publicity
		Public relations
		Endorsements
		  such as
		Consumer
		Reports
		Some publicity

PERSONAL	Sales force	Word of mouth

firm. Content of the message is also most clearly controlled in mass situations where all consumers receive the identical message. Control is slightly less when the message is delivered via the sales force because each salesperson can create an individual message that may stray from the original message designed by the firm. Of course, if the agent strays too far from the original message, the firm may terminate its contract and find someone new to deliver its messages.

Disadvantages of paid media include high cost and low credibility. It is not uncommon for a firm to spend $10 million on advertising and another $30 million on promotions in the first year of a product's life to introduce it. McDonald's spends over $200 million per year to support its products and stores. This is a high price to pay for control, but it is necessary if the firm wants to compete.

While the expenditures just described seem high, the cost per person reached is quite low. The $10 million of advertising may be spent on a series of 30-second television commercials that may cost $100,000 every time one is shown. Each commercial may be seen by 20 million people, though, and, therefore, the cost is only $\frac{1}{2}$ cent per person. This low cost per person results from the large numbers of people reached. The main advantages of mass advertising are the low cost per person and the large number of people reached.

Another key disadvantage of mass media lies in the inability to receive rapid feedback. While the firm can easily talk to 20 million prospective buyers, it has more difficulty in assessing the immediate marketplace response. It may easily take six months for a firm with a new product to know if consumers will accept or reject it; in that time period the firm may spend $20–30 million.

(To get around this expensive problem, firms usually test market their product in a small area and at a much lower cost; there are also sophisticated new product assessment models that help predict success or failure after as short a period as two months. Since this text is concerned only with communications strategies, it will not deal in depth with either of these issues.)

One exception to the problem of fast feedback exists for retailers who learn within a day or two whether their advertising works. Retail advertisers can go to the sales floor and see if the advertised item is moving. The goal of most retail advertising is to create an immediate sales response while the initial goal of new product advertising is to create awareness and knowledge, which are more difficult to assess. Retail advertising will be discussed in Chapter 21.

The following generalizations emerge from Figure 1.1. Paid communications gives the firm control over its message, but these tools have a high total cost and low credibility. Mass communications offer a low cost per person reached and the ability to reach a large audience quickly; these tools do not give any consumer feedback (although the firm can make an expenditure in marketing research to obtain feedback). The generalizations about the rows and columns that were not discussed are the reverse of those discussed. There are texts and courses that deal with both of the top and both of the left cells. This text will be primarily concerned with the top left cell, although there is one chapter devoted to the sales force and one to public relations.

Introducing Some Key Terms

The world of marketing communications uses a vocabulary of its own. Most of these terms will be defined as they are encountered in the various chapters, but a few are pervasive throughout this text and should be introduced here.

Advertising

What is *advertising?* Over the years the scope of this word has changed several times. When advertising agencies were first established in the United States in the late 1800s, their purpose was primarily to act as sales agencies for newspapers and magazines (there were no broadcast media). The generally accepted definition of that time was "keeping your name before the public"; this was consistent with the role of the agency of selling space to firms.

In 1904 the definition was dramatically changed to "salesmanship in print." This changed advertising from an activity geared toward creating and maintaining awareness to one geared toward persuading, affecting attitudes, and influencing behavior. It also changed the purpose of the agency to one of creating and producing advertising rather than just selling space.

In addition to persuading, it was necessary to inform accurately, to reflect the personality of the firm, and to consider how and why consumers responded. The change in definition changed the practice of advertising at a time when many new nationally distributed consumer goods were first emerging. As these goods were sold in a geographic area that was often far from the factory, it was necessary to talk to large numbers of widely dispersed consumers. Advertising was the tool for this task, and the task was captured in the following verse:

> *He who has a thing to sell*
> *and goes and whispers in a well,*
> *is not so apt to get the dollars*
> *as he who climbs a tree and hollers.*

There have been other changes in the definition over the years. One, of course, expanded salesmanship to the realm of the space and time of newer mass communications media. This allowed for inclusion of broadcast media; radio advertising began in the 1920s and television in the 1940s.

In 1964, Alexander, in *Marketing Definitions,*[5] defined advertising as "any paid form of nonpersonal presentation of ideas, goods or services by an identified sponsor." This definition helps to separate advertising from other communications tools. *Paid* separates advertising from public relations, which also uses mass media but does not pay for time or space. *Nonpersonal presentation* separates advertising from the sales force that is also paid for but is personal in its interactions with consumers.

The paid aspect, though, does not always discriminate because many nonprofit organizations, such as the United Way, receive free space or time for messages that are clearly thought of as advertising. In these cases the space or time is paid for by a charitable contribution from the media vehicle; if the time were not donated, it would be sold to another organization or firm. Generally speaking, advertising deals with messages that are paid for and that are sent to a mass audience through an impersonal format.

Advertising is salesmanship, and it is paid for by a firm, a person, or a group with a particular point of view. The message advocates that point of view, and its goal is to create awareness, attitude, or behavior that is favorable to that advocacy position. The message attempts to inform and to persuade; it is intentionally biased, and there is no intent to present a balanced point of view with regards to the product class, brand or other object, service, or issue. Consumers are generally aware of this bias and take this knowledge into account when evaluating messages.

Promotions

Promotions is a catch-all phrase that has become popular as one of the four Ps of marketing (product, price, place, promotions). While the concept of four Ps is a handy way to remember the basic classes of strategic tools, the word *promotions* is less convenient because it has two meanings.

In the context of the four Ps, promotions is an umbrella concept that refers to all of the firm's marketing communications. This includes advertising, sales promotions (the second meaning discussed below), public relations, the sales force, packaging, point-of-purchase displays, and the brand name.

According to Nickels, this *promotions mix* "refers to the particular combination of elements in its promotional strategy"[6]; *promotion* is "the persuasive flow of marketing communications" and *marketing communications* is "the two-way exchange of information and persuasion that enables the marketing process to function more effectively and efficiently."[7] This text will use the term *marketing communications* interchangeably with *promotions* when the latter is being used as this umbrella concept.

There is also a second common use of the word *promotions.* This more narrow use of the word refers to "a direct inducement which offers an extra value or incentive for the product to the sales force, distributors or the ultimate consumer with the primary objective of creating an immediate sale."[8] Samples, coupons, price-off deals, refunds, rebates, premiums, contests, and sweepstakes are all promotions devices aimed at getting a short-run behavior change from the consumer. The narrow use of promotions is discussed in detail in Chapters 17 and 18 and is the concept referred to throughout the text. The broader component that is part of the four Ps will be referred to as the *promotions mix.*

Public relations

The *public relations* component of the promotions mix uses the media to disseminate favorable news about a brand, product, firm, organization, or individual. While it deals with a mass target in an impersonal way, there is no payment to, or control over, the mass media. Public relations aims generally more toward image building and less toward a direct change of behavior. Because public relations messages appear as news stories, they often have more credibility than advertising and may be attended to with more interest and care.

One definition of public relations is that it is "a management function that determines the attitudes and opinions of the organization's publics, identifies its policies with the interests of its publics, and formulates and executes a program of action to earn the understanding and goodwill of its publics."[9] This is an image-oriented definition that aims the tool at many targets besides consumers. As such, public relations has very different purposes than does advertising; public relations is not free advertising.

Sales force

The *sales force* can also be used as a communications tool; its members are paid and deal with consumers on a personal level. Owing to the high cost of interaction, this tool is rarely used to create awareness but is used to develop attitudes and, primarily, to close sales; the sales force is most valuable for high-priced, durable, complex products and services, and in industrial settings. The sales force is a unique communications tool in that it allows two-way interaction between buyer and seller.

Packaging

While the *packaging* serves to protect the product, in the context of this text its role is to provide a last chance to communicate at the time and place of consumer decision making. Recognition of the package should help the consumer recall the key benefits discussed in the advertising.

Point-of-purchase display

As the name *point-of-purchase display* implies, this member of the promotion mix also communicates at the time and place of the final purchase decision. Tools in this category include counter displays, display racks, banners, and in-store and outside-of-store signage.

Brand name

The *brand name* can be used to communicate a benefit through a descriptive title. If the name tells something about the brand, then the work of the other communications tools will be made easier.

Introducing Some Key Models

Throughout this text there will be models to help develop general frameworks for understanding. A few of these will be used quite often and, therefore, should get an early introduction.

The decision sequence model

The first major model represents an annual iterative process commonly used by all major firms as a way to guide the creative process toward managerially sound promotional strategy and execution. This text is vitally concerned with the balance of art and science in marketing communications and, to that end, will use the *decision sequence model* as its major organizing structure. Figure 1.2 shows a

Figure 1.2   Decision sequence framework

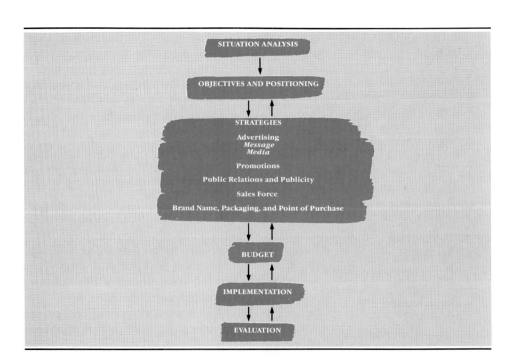

Figure 1.3 *Leo Burnett*
assesses the product

tcudorp.

The first job of an ad agency is to look
at your product in every imaginable way:
frontwards, backwards, sideways, upside down,
inside out. Because somewhere, *right there*
in the product itself, lies the drama that
will sell it to people who want it.
There may be 10,000 ways to bring that
inherent drama to the stage. And given a
world in which "me-too" products multiply
like mayflies, the drama may seem that much
harder to find.
It is.
But every good product has it.
And every good agency finds it.

Please note: The "t" in tcudorp is silent.

Leo Burnett Co., Inc.
33 offices in 23 countries

schematic of the model as it will be used throughout the text. Parts 2 through 8
of the text will each cover a part of the model as it organizes the communications
plan.

The *situation analysis* (at the top of Figure 1.2) is necessary to guide the assessment of the problem. What is the current state of the world in which the firm
must operate? There are numerous areas to investigate in order to have a clear
understanding of how to develop strategy. These will be discussed in depth in
Part 2 of this text. Key areas include:

1. *An assessment of the consumer*   The consumer must be evaluated from at
   least three directions:

   a. *Descriptors*   A target market must be derived so that the most appropri-
      ate segment of consumers can be reached. This classification process
      needs to identify consumers on a number of criteria such as demograph-
      ics, usage levels, and knowledge (to name just a few).

   b. *Perceptions*   In order to communicate with consumers, it is important to
      assess their perceptions of the product, its competition, and the relation-
      ships between the consumer and the product class.

   c. *Processes*   It is also important to learn how consumers process informa-
      tion and make decisions. How involved are consumers in decisions? Are
      brand decisions made in the home or in the store?

2. *An assessment of the product class*   Part of this assessment comes from the
   study of consumer perceptions, but the analyst must also be sure to evaluate
   the attributes and benefits of the product, how well each of the brands performs in these areas, and what uniquenesses are offered. In addition, analysis
   should consider past strategies and market shares for each brand. Leo Burnett
   Co., Inc.'s view of this assessment is displayed in Figure 1.3.

3. *An assessment of the firm*   This evaluation should include corporate goals and philosophy as well as financial and production capabilities and marketing support in terms of distribution and the sales force.

4. *An assessment of the environment*   Analysis here includes factors that impact upon the firm but cannot be affected by the firm. These issues include the economy, seasonality, availability of resources, and legal issues.

Each of these and many other areas will be developed in the situation analysis; this analysis will often result in a fact book of several hundred pages that then provides guidance as the process continues. Having done a thorough evaluation, management will set *objectives and positioning* (Figure 1.2). By doing this it will have a statement of where it would like to be at the end of some period of time. Part 3 of this book will explore how goals should be set and how a position can be established. The objectives and positioning must be extremely precise so that the later strategies can be evaluated for appropriateness. The major value of setting specific objectives and position will be to eliminate poor strategies. *Strategies,* per se, are easy to generate; relevant strategies are a rarer commodity. Good objectives eliminate bad strategies.

The objective is a clear statement of target market, time deadline, and task of the message in terms of marketplace response. This is coupled with a positioning statement that describes how the target should perceive the product relative to the competition. Young and Rubicam, Inc., express this point much more eloquently in Figure 1.4.

Figure 1.4 *Young & Rubicam on the need to set objectives*

**You can really fly
once you know where you're going.**

We believe the sharpest advertising strategies provide the greatest creative freedom. Only when you know exactly where you're going can the imagination soar free, without fear or formulas.
YOUNG & RUBICAM INC.

It is at this point that the art and science of marketing communications meet. Science will have been used to develop a clear picture of the situation and, in turn, will have led to specific objectives. The art of marketing communications then can lead to wonderfully interesting messages. Through the use of the decision sequence the art can be channeled in the appropriate direction so that the captivating message also deals with the relevant problem.

Having specifically defined goals and direction, the next step of the decision sequence is to *develop strategies*. This step is the heart of the text. Part 4 will deal with message strategies, Part 5 with media strategies, Part 6 with sales promotions, and Part 7 with other strategic areas such as public relations, publicity, the sales force, the package, the brand name, and point-of-purchase materials. Each of these areas is developed independently, but there must be coordination across the areas. Having the situation analysis and objectives and positioning to refer to will help create the necessary focus and coordination.

After developing strategies, their worth must be assessed. How much will it cost to execute the strategies and how much can the firm afford in its pursuit of its objective? *Budgeting strategies,* discussed in Part 8, deal with these issues. Human nature seems to lead to grandiose strategies that are generally accompanied by high costs. When costs may exceed the resources of the firm, an evaluation must be made about whether to spend more to meet goals or to scale down the goals.

As strategies are developed, budget constraints must be considered. These constraints often will force the manager to reconsider strategies and objectives. This reconsideration is shown by the arrows pointing upward in Figure 1.2. Because the arrows go in both directions between most pairs of stages, the process is described as *iterative,* or repetitive. Is it possible to develop strategies to meet objectives? If not, then the next planning stage will feature a change of objectives. Is it possible to budget enough to pay for the strategies? If it is not possible, then the next planning stage will feature a change of objectives and/or strategies.

The iterative nature of this model allows continuous updating as new information is received or constraints change. Updating can occur during planning as described above but also as the plan is executed and/or evaluated. While the crux of the budget evaluation should occur as a response to the proposed objectives and strategy plans, budget constraints must first be determined as part of the situation analysis. Managers should assess the possible range of budgets during the situation analysis so that the first attempt in the planning of objectives and strategies will be realistic.

After the planning has been completed, the campaign is produced; then it is *implemented and evaluated* (Figure 1.2). In some cases it will first be used in test markets so that its impact can be evaluated at a low cost. In a test market the firm only needs to invest the media budget in one or a few cities as opposed to the entire geographic target market (often the entire United States). This allows for a relatively low-cost evaluation.

When the test market is deemed to be a success (or often without a test market), the full-blown campaign is implemented in the entire market area. After a period of time (usually 6–12 months) evaluation begins. Often the evaluation research will be a repeat of the situation analysis research so comparisons can be made and success or failure relative to the objectives can be measured. This evaluative research, then, becomes part of the situation analysis for the next time period.

In addition to the points already made concerning the decision sequence, one more remains. This framework helps to bring the often disparate views of the creative strategy into focus by giving guidelines based on research; it also shows the need for creative solutions to business problems.

As Blair Vedder, Chief Operating Officer of Needham, Harper Worldwide has said, "time and time again we have proved that the right proportions of research intelligence and free-wheeling imagination, carefully blended together, produce powerful advertising. Intelligence alone or imagination alone run the risk of producing either dullness on one extreme or embarrassing inappropriateness on the other."[10]

In addition to this general marketplace research, the decision sequence implies the need for other research during each type of strategy development and during early stages of implementation. It is routine in many agencies to test message strategy to see if it reflects the desired position and elicits the desired response from the target market. Media plans are tested less routinely, although it is equally necessary to know if the message is delivered to the target with sufficient impact to meet objectives. Research issues will be considered throughout the text in relevant chapters.

The decision sequence imposes a managerial framework on a process that too often is done by the seat of the pants. It imposes a necessary rigor on a process that should not be left to intuition. It helps management weed out faulty strategy and justify appropriate strategy.

The hierarchy of effects model

The decision sequence model suggests that objectives be clearly defined in terms of the task of the message or the promotion. This task is generally considered in terms of the response sought from the target audience. Although there are many possible responses, these can be grouped into three distinct categories:

Awareness
Attitude
Behavior

Figure 1.5 *Building awareness*

Introducing New Listermint with Fluoride.
For better teeth **and** better breath.

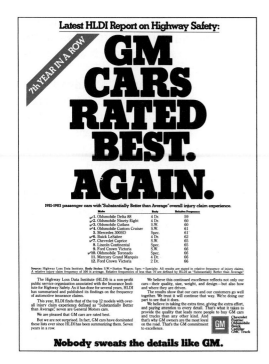

Figure 1.6 *Developing a positive attitude*

Figure 1.7 *Asking for a purchase*

All messages and promotions attempt to influence at least one of these responses. Either the message wants the consumer to become aware (introducing new Listermint; see Figure 1.5), to develop a positive attitude toward something (GM cars rated best; again, Figure 1.6), or to behave toward something (get up to a $20 rebate, Figure 1.7; vote for Pat Quinlin, Figure 1.8).

Figure 1.8 *Soliciting a vote*

The *hierarchy of effects* concept states that consumers must pass through a series of stages from unawareness to brand loyalty. In early models there was a set ordering to these effects so that:

Awareness
↓
Attitude
↓
Behavior

The most appropriate ordering of these components will be considered in the next section and in later chapters. It is important to keep in mind that all responses fit into the three categories. Marketers want to affect what consumers *know, feel,* or *do.*

Involvement

A concept that will be central to virtually all managerial decisions concerning marketing communications is that of *involvement.* In its most basic form, this concept forces the manager to ask if anyone out there in the target market cares about the product or brand. Brand managers (for the manufacturer), account executives (for the advertising agency), or store managers (for the retailer) are vitally concerned with their products and may have difficulty understanding that consumers do not always care which brand they use.

There are basically three levels of involvement:

1. *No involvement*   There is no interest in the product class and no purchase behavior takes place.

2. *Low involvement*   There is enough interest in the product class that the product is used, but there is insufficient interest to cause the consumer to make careful brand choice evaluations.

3. *High involvement*   There is interest in the product class and also enough concern about brand differences to lead to a careful evaluation of the available choices prior to the purchase decision.

The high- and low-involvement categories relate to the ordering of the components of the hierarchy of effects. If there is low involvement, then there may not be enough interest to generate an attitude before trial behavior; instead, a purchase is made but no feeling is established toward the brand until after it is used.

Awareness
↓
Trial Behavior
↓
Attitude
↓
Repeat Behavior

In high-involvement cases, an attitude/feeling develops prior to behavior as was suggested in the prior section.

Stimulus-response model

A fourth model is the *stimulus-response model, S–R.*

The world is made up of stimuli and responses; the evolution of a species of plant or animal is a set of responses to a set of stimuli. On a more mundane level, the responses described in the hierarchy of effects model are the result of a wide range of stimuli. Marketers control a small number of these through the four Ps (e.g., a good product leads to repeat purchase; a high price inhibits trial purchase; a clever jingle enhances the development of awareness, and, if a person sings the jingle enough times, it will lead to a memory trace and may also lead to positive or negative feelings).

When a firm advertises, it is sending a stimulus and seeking a response:

$$S_{\text{Advertising}} \longrightarrow R_{\text{Awareness, Attitude, or Behavior}}$$

Most commonly, advertising creates awareness. Various components of verbal learning theory in psychology suggest ways by which the nature and intensity of advertising will enhance the probability of learning.

$$S_{\text{Advertising}} \longrightarrow R_{\text{Awareness}}$$

Cognitive psychologists complicate the model by inferring that some process occurs within the individual that mediates the simple $S \longrightarrow R$ process. This can be seen as:

$$S \longrightarrow O \longrightarrow R$$

where O represents some process internal to the organism. This reflects a situation where the consumer makes an evaluation in addition to the rote learning described by the $S \longrightarrow R$ model. For an advertiser:

$$S_{\text{Advertising}} \longrightarrow O \longrightarrow R_{\text{Attitude}}$$

Behavioral psychologists put forth a different view of human nature. Their model of operant conditioning asserts that people respond to anticipated consequences of their behavior. In this view

$$R_1 \longrightarrow S \longrightarrow P(R_2)$$

Here a behavior (R_1) occurs and is reinforced by a stimulus (S). If the stimulus is perceived favorably, the probability (P) of a future similar behavior (R_2) occurring is increased; if the reinforcing stimulus is not perceived favorably, the probability of future similar behavior decreases. For example, a consumer goes out and buys (R_1) new strawberry beer (S). When she tries this exotic brew, it brings forth tears of rapture. Clearly she has been positively reinforced, and the probability of making a second purchase of strawberry beer has increased [$P(R_2)$]. Conversely, if her first purchase of chocolate beer led to unusual feelings in her throat and stomach and a strange ringing in her ears, an observer would say that she was punished for her behavior and would predict a lower probability of repeat purchase [$P(R_2)$].

If management feels that its product is good, it also may provide artificial inducements (samples and coupons) for the first behavior to occur so that later repeat purchase can develop more rapidly. Often there are also promotions (coupons, premiums, money refund offers) given along with the product to enhance the probabilities of repeat behavior. These can be seen as

$$S_{\text{Sample}} \longrightarrow R_{\text{Trial Purchase}} \longrightarrow S_{\text{Product}} \longrightarrow R_{\text{Repeat Purchase}}$$

Perhaps use of the product also leads to favorable feelings (attitudes). This would be shown as

$$R_{\text{Trial Purchase}} \longrightarrow S_{\text{Product}} \longrightarrow R_{\text{Attitude}} \longrightarrow R_{\text{Repeat Purchase}}$$

A stimulus-response model that encompasses all of these relations is shown in Figure 1.9.

Figure 1.9 *An overview of a stimulus-response model*

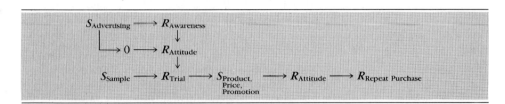

This model will be returned to at various times throughout the text as the various stimulus-response relations are examined. At this point it is important to keep in mind that the advertising or promotions manager is always seeking some type of response and that the firm has control over a set of stimuli. The stimuli that are selected should elicit the response that is sought. Figure 1.9 captures most of the stimuli and responses that will be dealt with in this text.

Schramm's model of communications

Accurate one-way mass communications (the goal of most marketing communications) is very difficult to achieve. To get an idea of this difficulty, gather some friends to sit down with paper and pencil. Now describe Figure 1.10 to them without using your hands and without looking at them. After doing this, consider both the difficulty and simplicity of this task. If you tried, you know how difficult this task was. On the other hand, this was a simple message. You were only sending tangible information; you didn't need to change attitudes or behavior; you didn't need to sell intangibles such as "gusto" (which at one time was found in a major brand of nonstrawberry beer) or "hope." (Charles Revson of Revlon Cosmetics has been quoted as saying, "In the factory we make cosmetics; in the drugstore we sell hope."[11]) How does a firm communicate "gusto" or "hope"? If you

Figure 1.10 *A collection of rectangles*

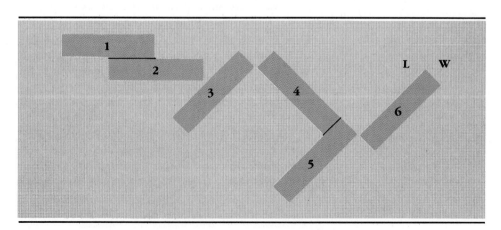

have tried to describe Figure 1.10 to some friends you have discovered the meaning of

> I know you believe you understand what you think I said, but I'm not sure you realize that what you heard is not what I meant.

Schramm has developed a model to show the potential problems associated with one-way communications.[12] Figure 1.11 shows a schematic of this model; a discussion of the linkages shows some problems that a promotions manager must consider.

Figure 1.11 Schramm's model of communications

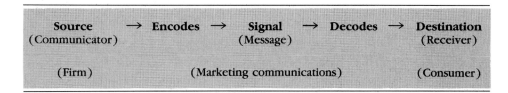

Schramm identifies four problem areas:

1. *Source ⟶ Encodes*   If the source perceives the problem incorrectly and, as a result, develops and encodes the wrong concept, it cannot possibly communicate correctly. A good situation analysis is essential if the sender is to understand the problem properly.

2. *Encodes ⟶ Signal*   The source (advertiser) does not say what it means. Even though the problem is understood, the message strategy is not on target. Internal review of the message should show that it does not meet the objectives and/or position for which it was designed. Such a message will have difficulty in eliciting the desired consumer response.

3. *Signal ⟶ Decodes*   The receiver does not understand the message or does not interpret it correctly. Clarity and simplicity are virtues; be sure that the key selling point is easily understood by the target.

4. *Decodes ⟶ Destination*   The receiver understands the message correctly but either ignores or forgets it. This common problem may be due to a poor media plan. Sufficient repetition of a message enhances learning and inhibits forgetting. If the consumer is not vitally interested in the message (generally the case), he or she will not spend cognitive effort to learn it. The sender must help through sufficient message repetition.

A point that will be stressed often in this text deals with the difficulty of successfully communicating through one-way mass channels. Schramm's model categorizes the key areas; Foote, Cone & Belding, Inc., explains why it feels that these issues are important in Figure 1.12.

The Paradox of Promotions

Having seen some of the potential pitfalls and problems of marketing communications, it becomes difficult to imagine how any firm could possibly succeed in achieving efficient and effective communications. An example will show that although any one message will have little impact, over time a promotional campaign can be very effective and can also be the most financially efficient way to reach a mass audience.[13]

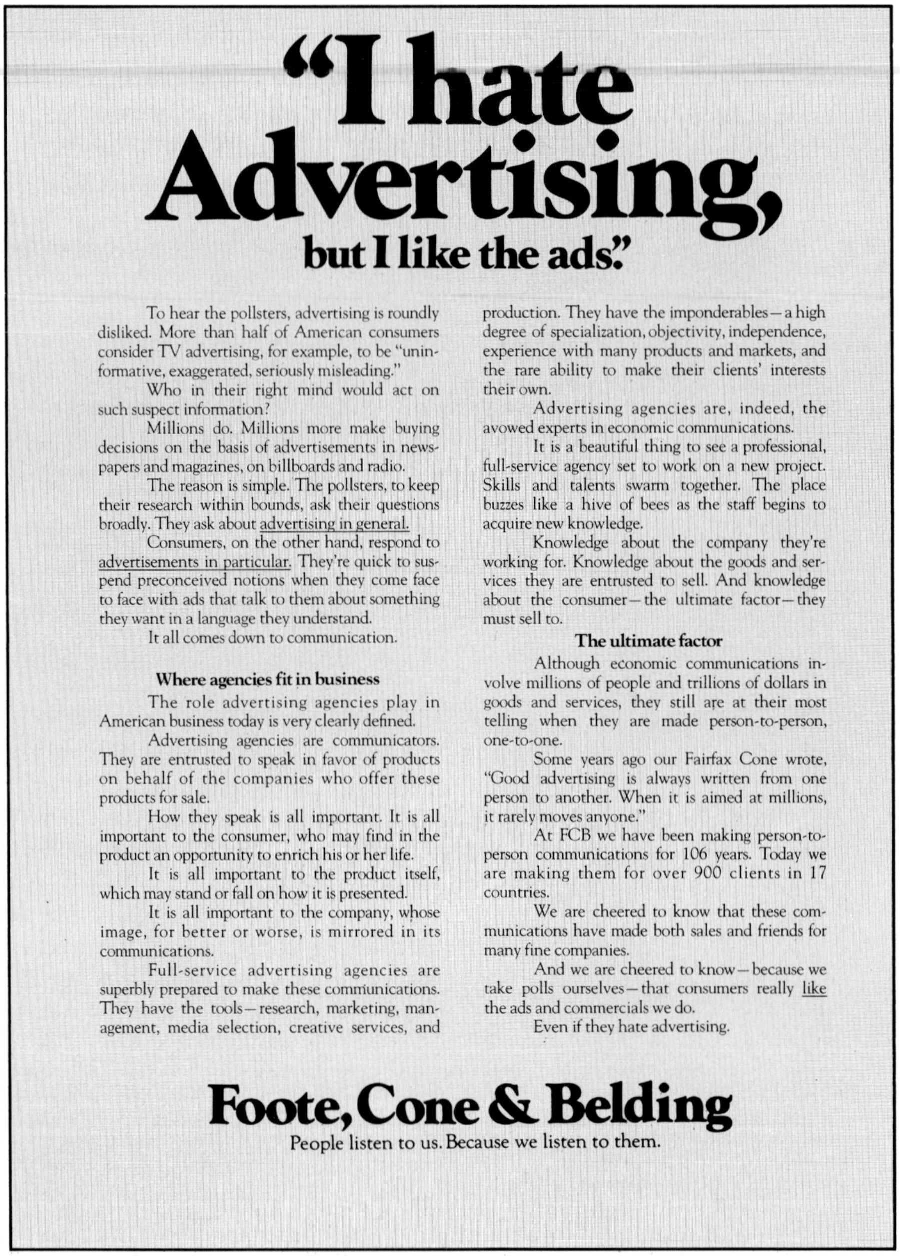

Figure 1.12 *Foote, Cone & Belding on the difficulties of mass communications*

"I hate Advertising, but I like the ads."

To hear the pollsters, advertising is roundly disliked. More than half of American consumers consider TV advertising, for example, to be "uninformative, exaggerated, seriously misleading."

Who in their right mind would act on such suspect information?

Millions do. Millions more make buying decisions on the basis of advertisements in newspapers and magazines, on billboards and radio.

The reason is simple. The pollsters, to keep their research within bounds, ask their questions broadly. They ask about <u>advertising in general.</u>

Consumers, on the other hand, respond to <u>advertisements in particular.</u> They're quick to suspend preconceived notions when they come face to face with ads that talk to them about something they want in a language they understand.

It all comes down to communication.

Where agencies fit in business

The role advertising agencies play in American business today is very clearly defined.

Advertising agencies are communicators. They are entrusted to speak in favor of products on behalf of the companies who offer these products for sale.

How they speak is all important. It is all important to the consumer, who may find in the product an opportunity to enrich his or her life.

It is all important to the product itself, which may stand or fall on how it is presented.

It is all important to the company, whose image, for better or worse, is mirrored in its communications.

Full-service advertising agencies are superbly prepared to make these communications. They have the tools—research, marketing, management, media selection, creative services, and production. They have the imponderables—a high degree of specialization, objectivity, independence, experience with many products and markets, and the rare ability to make their clients' interests their own.

Advertising agencies are, indeed, the avowed experts in economic communications.

It is a beautiful thing to see a professional, full-service agency set to work on a new project. Skills and talents swarm together. The place buzzes like a hive of bees as the staff begins to acquire new knowledge.

Knowledge about the company they're working for. Knowledge about the goods and services they are entrusted to sell. And knowledge about the consumer—the ultimate factor—they must sell to.

The ultimate factor

Although economic communications involve millions of people and trillions of dollars in goods and services, they still are at their most telling when they are made person-to-person, one-to-one.

Some years ago our Fairfax Cone wrote, "Good advertising is always written from one person to another. When it is aimed at millions, it rarely moves anyone."

At FCB we have been making person-to-person communications for 106 years. Today we are making them for over 900 clients in 17 countries.

We are cheered to know that these communications have made both sales and friends for many fine companies.

And we are cheered to know—because we take polls ourselves—that consumers really <u>like</u> the ads and commercials we do.

Even if they hate advertising.

Foote, Cone & Belding

People listen to us. Because we listen to them.

Assume that the firm has been very careful in designing its communications and has appropriately dealt with all the problem issues raised by Schramm. What happens to the message after it is sent? Assume that the target market consists of adult women and consider what happens when they are reached via network television. Assume that the advertising firm chooses a popular program with a rating of 20. This means that 20% of all households with television (essentially all households have television) watch the chosen program. This also means that *roughly* 20% of adult women are in this audience.

Of that 20% whose sets were on the correct channel at the correct time, approximately two-thirds may have been in the room and watching during the commercial. Therefore, 13.5% of all adult women were exposed to the commercial.

If the firm were to call a sample of these women the next day to learn what they recall seeing, it would find that about 20% of those will remember having seen the commercial and can remember something about it. This translates to 2.7% of all adult women.

Of these, about one-third will only remember something irrelevant to the main selling point. Some will remember how cute the baby was or how amused they were when the waiter fell with a tray full of dishes. If two-thirds of these women remember a key message point, the commercial had an approximate impact on 1.8% of all adult women. This is considered a success.

How could the firm possibly be successful if its message has an impact on less than 2% of the target? First, the target is very large (there are over 75 million adult women in the United States); second, the message will be repeated many times during the year.

If the firm buys television programs with undifferentiated audiences during prime time, it can maintain an average rating of 20, and each message transmission therefore will go to the homes of about 15 million adult women. (An undifferentiated audience has no characteristics that make it different from the general population.)

If there is an annual advertising budget of $10 million for the brand, and a prime-time television spot costs $100,000, the firm can buy 100 spots per year.

This will yield 1.5 billion message impressions (15 million women × 100 spots) on the target, or an average of 20 impressions per woman (1.5 billion ÷ 75 million women) over the one-year period.

The cost of all this is $10 million, but the cost per impression per woman is two-thirds of a cent ($10 million ÷ 1.5 billion impressions) and the cost per woman per year is 13.3 cents ($0.0067 × 20 impressions).

While one message transmission is discouragingly weak, eventually the firm can build repetitions of the message. Over time, learning occurs even though few of the respondents actively try to learn the message.

While the cost ($10 million) seems high, remember that 75 million women were each spoken to 20 times; consider the cost of doing this using door-to-door salespersons.

These are the paradoxes of promotions. A single message may do poorly, but over time the effect of repetition is quite strong. The cost of communications to a mass market is extremely high, but the cost per individual is so low that it would be impossible to achieve such efficiency in any other way.

The Cast of Characters in the Ad Agency

Approximately 100,000 people work at more than 8,000 advertising agencies in the United States. In addition, many thousands more work in advertising-related jobs in the millions of firms that advertise their products and services. Others do advertising-related work with the thousands of media vehicles that deliver advertising messages, and still others work in public relations, develop sales promotions materials, do research, or sell something either as a retail or industrial salesperson. See Tables 1.1–1.3.

Table 1.1 Largest U.S. agencies based on world income—1984

World Income rank		Agency	World gross income ($000,000)		U.S. gross income ($000,000)		World billings ($000,000)		U.S. billings ($000,000)		U.S. capitalized fees ($000,000)		Total employees	
1984	1983		1984	1983	1984	1983	1984	1983	1984	1983	1984	1983	1984	1983
1	1	Young & Rubicam	480.1	414.0	323.1	274.4	3,202.1	2,761.4	2,155.1	1,830.1	0.0	0.0	8,418	7,745
2	2	Ted Bates Worldwide	424.4	387.9	263.2	244.4	2,839.2	2,586.1	1,754.7	1,629.0	237.7	185.2	5,345	5,124
3	4	Ogilvy & Mather International	421.0	345.8	270.5	204.1	2,887.9	2,360.4	1,804.3	1,361.4	0.0	0.0	7,428	8,030
4	3	J. Walter Thompson Co.	405.8	368.3	218.2	188.3	2,706.7	2,456.2	1,455.4	1,255.9	0.0	0.0	8,174	7,636
5	6	BBDO International	340.0	292.0	235.0	199.0	2,275.0	1,969.0	1,581.0	1,349.0	242.0	205.1	4,472	4,018
6	7	Saatchi & Saatchi Compton Worldwide	337.5	253.3	157.4	110.9	2,301.7	1,710.6	1,093.3	771.8	0.0	177.2	3,814	1,140
7	5	McCann-Erickson Worldwide	325.2	267.2	118.5	95.4	2,169.4	1,782.2	790.5	635.4	0.0	0.0	6,422	5,962
8	9	Foote, Cone & Belding Communications	268.5	208.4	196.9	158.9	1,802.3	1,405.6	1,324.4	1,075.5	0.0	0.0	5,832	4,468
9	8	Leo Burnett Co.	253.5	216.5	163.2	135.0	1,734.8	1,485.3	1,132.9	914.1	42.0	20.8	3,668	3,461
10	12	Grey Advertising	224.2	183.5	155.1	125.1	1,495.2	1,224.0	1,034.6	839.5	127.4	76.1	4,300	3,908
11	10	Doyle Dane Bernbach International	218.3	197.6	154.1	144.6	1,510.6	1,321.0	1,085.1	970.0	146.9	142.0	3,280	3,365
12	13	D'Arcy MacManus Masius Worldwide	198.6	173.0	106.9	91.6	1,337.5	1,156.5	712.9	610.3	0.0	0.0	3,583	3,626
13	11	SSC&B:Lintas Worldwide	182.9	155.5	62.2	50.8	1,230.3	1,047.5	414.6	333.7	0.0	0.0	3,765	3,705
14	14	Benton & Bowles	159.4	140.1	111.0	98.1	1,129.4	966.3	766.7	649.9	272.3	146.1	2,934	2,973
15	15	Marschalk Campbell-Ewald Worldwide	140.3	126.7	112.1	99.5	935.6	844.9	747.9	663.8	0.0	0.0	1,934	1,851
16	19	Needham Harper Worldwide	114.7	94.2	96.7	77.9	775.0	631.9	655.0	519.9	204.3	121.3	1,293	2,126
17	16	Dancer Fitzgerald Sample	110.4	105.0	109.2	94.1	758.0	726.1	750.2	627.0	0.0	0.0	3,352	3,175
18	18	N W Ayer	104.7	97.4	91.2	83.2	751.7	650.0	652.5	558.0	0.0	68.0	2,300	1,230
19	20	Wells, Rich, Greene	96.3	92.7	94.2	91.0	632.0	608.5	618.0	595.6	0.0	67.0	962	916
20	22	Bozell & Jacobs	94.2	74.4	92.5	73.5	671.0	557.0	660.0	551.0	114.0	86.0	1,550	1,350
21	21	William Esty Co.	78.0	84.8	78.0	84.8	520.0	565.0	520.0	565.0	0.0	0.0	597	636
22	N/A	HCM	75.3	59.9	30.6	28.1	502.0	399.1	204.0	187.1	59.5	43.5	1,329	N/A
23	24	Ketchum Communications	60.9	52.7	53.1	46.8	406.1	368.4	354.1	312.2	83.6	68.7	1,050	1,050
24	27	Backer & Spielvogel	59.3	51.6	59.3	51.6	395.7	344.1	395.7	344.1	4.1	9.2	554	514
25	23	Kenyon & Eckhardt	56.4	60.5	41.3	45.0	376.2	392.2	275.2	289.2	67.1	59.6	2,375	2,319
26	25	Cunningham & Walsh	53.3	52.7	53.3	52.7	370.0	366.0	370.0	366.0	18.8	18.3	600	711
27	29	Campbell-Mithun	45.0	42.8	45.0	42.8	300.3	285.3	300.3	285.3	0.0	0.0	670	660
28	31	Scali, McCabe, Sloves	44.6	35.2	30.5	23.6	307.0	229.2	209.5	158.8	0.0	0.0	635	583
29	28	HBM/Creamer	44.2	43.5	44.2	43.5	294.8	290.0	294.8	290.0	25.3	22.8	653	700
30	32	TBWA Advertising	40.5	35.0	10.9	7.7	270.0	237.2	72.8	51.0	0.0	0.0	523	502

World Income rank 1984	1983	Agency	World gross income ($000,000) 1984	1983	U.S. gross income ($000,000) 1984	1983	World billings ($000,000) 1984	1983	U.S. billings ($000,000) 1984	1983	U.S. capitalized fees ($000,000) 1984	1983	Total employees 1984	1983
31	33	Ross Roy Inc.	37.8	34.1	37.8	34.1	252.0	227.0	252.0	227.0	99.0	80.0	600	516
32	N/A	DYR Worldwide	36.9	29.4	21.3	17.4	246.0	196.0	142.0	116.0	0.0	0.0	693	N/A
33	34	Della Femina, Travisano & Partners	33.0	30.8	33.0	30.8	220.0	205.0	220.0	205.0	23.1	21.4	370	363
34	36	Leber Katz Partners Advertising	32.4	29.2	32.4	29.2	279.3	251.0	279.3	251.0	36.1	31.4	285	300
35	44	Tracy-Locke	32.4	22.8	32.4	22.8	239.8	198.1	239.8	198.1	15.9	45.2	476	341
36	35	Laurence, Charles & Free	32.3	29.3	32.3	29.3	215.0	195.0	215.0	195.0	12.0	10.0	205	197
37	38	Wunderman, Ricotta & Kline	31.2	25.8	23.8	19.2	256.8	215.8	207.8	171.9	0.0	0.0	461	389
38	57	Lord, Geller, Federico, Einstein	29.8	14.4	29.8	14.4	207.2	98.2	207.2	98.2	12.7	12.1	257	198
39	42	Admarketing	28.1	26.8	28.1	26.8	171.3	146.3	171.3	146.3	11.3	0.0	275	275
40	56	Chiat/Day	27.8	14.8	27.8	14.8	226.6	138.4	226.6	138.4	42.8	34.5	300	240
41	41	McCaffrey & McCall	27.5	23.9	27.5	23.9	183.4	159.9	183.4	159.9	0.0	0.0	340	330
42	37	Tatham-Laird & Kudner	27.1	27.0	27.1	27.0	226.0	224.0	226.0	224.0	84.2	85.4	377	375
43	39	W.B. Doner & Co. Advertising	26.9	24.8	26.9	24.8	179.0	165.0	179.0	165.0	27.7	26.2	424	395
44	52	Hill, Holliday, Connors, Cosmopolus	26.3	17.3	22.7	14.6	175.4	115.0	151.5	107.4	93.3	32.6	411	306
45	47	Jordan, Case & McGrath	24.2	21.0	24.2	21.0	165.1	147.8	165.1	147.8	25.3	28.7	205	170
46	30	Geers Gross Advertising	23.8	23.1	23.8	23.1	168.0	165.0	168.0	165.0	10.0	10.4	311	335
47	40	Doremus & Co.	23.5	24.1	23.5	24.1	153.9	158.4	153.9	158.4	51.7	51.9	314	350
48	45	Ally & Gargano	23.4	22.2	23.4	22.2	182.9	174.1	182.9	174.1	31.1	8.7	261	244
49	43	Bloom Cos.	23.1	21.9	23.1	21.9	154.1	146.4	154.1	146.4	0.0	0.0	350	400
50	49	Keller-Crescent Co.	22.5	19.2	22.5	19.2	114.0	96.1	114.0	96.1	50.7	45.8	585	585
51	46	Dailey & Associates	22.2	21.5	22.2	21.5	147.9	143.5	147.9	143.5	0.0	0.0	245	301
52	51	Sudler & Hennessey	20.5	17.5	16.4	13.5	136.7	117.0	109.4	90.0	0.0	0.0	280	265
53	50	Warwick Advertising	20.3	18.9	20.3	18.9	135.0	126.0	135.0	126.0	38.5	36.0	270	270
54	54	Rumrill-Hoyt	18.2	16.2	18.2	16.2	121.6	108.1	121.6	108.1	0.0	43.2	306	241
55	53	MCA Advertising Ltd.	17.6	16.5	17.6	16.5	148.7	137.5	148.7	137.5	9.5	2.6	95	92
56	61	AC & R	16.4	12.9	15.9	12.2	98.7	82.6	94.7	77.5	2.5	2.8	240	207
57	60	Medicus Intercon International	16.2	13.4	6.7	6.0	135.9	117.9	61.1	52.7	42.7	38.0	290	250
58	55	Rosenfeld, Sirowitz & Lawson	15.6	14.8	15.6	14.8	121.5	115.0	121.5	115.0	28.6	26.0	202	202
59	68	Evans Communications	15.6	11.6	15.6	11.6	104.0	77.5	104.0	77.5	29.5	24.0	295	227
60	48	Nationwide Advertising	15.0	20.0	14.3	14.0	100.0	67.0	95.0	69.0	0.0	0.0	290	N/A

Source: Reprinted with permission from the March 28, 1985 issue of *Advertising Age.* Copyright 1985 by Crain Communications, Inc.

Table 1.2 Top 100 advertisers' spending as % of all advertisers'*—1984

| Medium | 100 leading national advertisers | | | $ as % of U.S. measured spending by all advertisers | | All advertisers U.S. measured advertising expenditures | | |
| | Advertising expenditures | | % chng. | | | | | % chng. |
	1984	1983		1984	1983	1984	1983	
Newspaper	$986	$946	4.2	31.2	36.8	$3,161	$2,572	22.9
Magazine	2,210	1,904	16.1	47.3	48.3	4,669	3,939	18.5
Network cable	184	153	20.7	70.2	66.0	263	232	13.4
Spot tv	2,695	2,484	8.5	42.6	44.7	6,323	5,558	13.8
Network tv	6,462	5,207	24.1	75.5	74.0	8,555	7,040	21.5
Spot radio	485	451	7.6	36.4	40.6	1,333	1,108	20.3
Network radio	144	153	(6.0)	53.1	58.0	270	263	2.7
Outdoor	270	292	(7.3)	45.3	53.0	597	550	8.6
Farm pubs.	28	26	7.1	37.9	35.6	73	73	0.7
Total	13,463	11,615	15.9	53.3	54.4	25,245	21,335	18.3

* Dollar figures in millions
Source: Reprinted with permission from the September 26, 1985 issue of *Advertising Age.* Copyright 1985 by Crain Communications, Inc.

Table 1.3 The leading advertisers by rank ($000)—1984

Rank	Company	Advertising	Rank	Company	Advertising
1	Procter & Gamble Co.	$872,000	26	U.S. Government	$287,807
2	General Motors Corp.	763,800	27	American Cyanamid	284,410
3	Sears, Roebuck & Co.	746,937	28	General Mills	283,400
4	Beatrice Cos.	680,000	29	Dart & Kraft	269,200
5	R. J. Reynolds Industries	678,176	30	Colgate-Palmolive Co.	258,731
6	Philip Morris Inc.	570,435	31	Bristol-Myers Co.	258,440
7	American Telephone & Telegraph	563,200	32	Sara Lee Corp.	258,362
8	Ford Motor Co.	559,400	33	RCA Corp.	239,400
9	K mart Corp.	554,400	34	H. J. Heinz Co.	227,286
10	McDonald's Corp.	480,000	35	Kellogg Co.	208,800
11	J. C. Penney Co.	460,000	36	Revlon Inc.	205,000
12	General Foods Corp.	450,000	37	General Electric	202,400
13	Warner-Lambert Co.	440,000	38	Tandy Corp.	190,000
14	Ralston Purina Co.	428,600	39	Nestle Enterprises	186,848
15	PepsiCo Inc.	428,172	40	Warner Communications	181,749
16	American Home Products	412,000	41	CBS Inc.	179,800
17	Unilever U.S.	395,700	42	Mobil Corp.	172,500
18	International Business Machines	376,000	43	American Express Co.	172,100
19	Anheuser-Busch Cos.	364,401	44	ITT Corp.	168,000
20	Coca-Cola Co.	343,300	45	Sterling Drug Co.	166,600
21	Nabisco Brands	334,977	46	Gillette Co.	165,673
22	Pillsbury Co.	318,473	47	Nissan Motor Corp.	164,200
23	Chrysler Corp.	317,400	48	Richardson-Vicks	163,500
24	Eastman Kodak Co.	301,000	49	Quaker Oats Co.	161,300
25	Johnson & Johnson	300,000	50	Gulf & Western Industries	149,249

All of these people are vital links in the marketing communications process. Central to this text are the people who work in advertising agencies. Although there are over 8,000 agencies in the United States, 40% of the total dollar volume is handled through 0.1% of them; these ten largest agencies employ about 17,000 people, mainly in New York, Chicago, Detroit, Los Angeles, San Francisco, and various international offices. Table 1.1 is a listing of the largest U.S. agencies based on world income.

Incidentally, concentration among advertisers is also great; in 1984, the 100 leading advertisers spent $13.5 billion in the nine major media, while the total amount spent on advertising by the 13 million businesses in the United States was estimated to be $25.2 billion. This means that 100 firms (0.0008% of approximately 13 million firms in the United States) spent 53% of the advertising dollars. As can be seen in Table 1.2, this concentration was even greater in television; note that 100 firms spent over 75% of all network television advertising dollars.

There was further concentration among the top 100. The Procter & Gamble Company spent $872 million in 1984; the hundredth largest spender was Van Munching & Co. which spent $58.9 million. Table 1.3 is a listing of the top 100 advertisers of 1984.

Rank	Company	Advertising	Rank	Company	Advertising
51	Chesebrough-Pond's	$145,500	76	Canon Inc.	$100,000
52	Schering-Plough Corp.	144,300	77	Apple Computer	100,000
53	Campbell Soup Co.	142,000	78	Union Carbide Corp.	93,000
54	Mars Inc.	139,282	79	E.I. Du Pont de Nemours	91,000
55	Adolph Coors Co.	138,700	80	Wendy's International	90,833
56	Loews Corp.	137,900	81	S.C. Johnson & Son	90,000
57	Toyota Motor Sales Corp.	137,900	82	GTE Corp.	89,775
58	Beecham Group p.l.c.	137,000	83	Pfizer Inc.	86,400
59	UAL Inc.	136,700	84	Stroh Brewery Co.	85,200
60	American Honda Motor Co.	134,700	85	Hasbro Inc.	83,691
61	Time Inc.	133,900	86	Greyhound Corp.	80,200
62	American Brands	133,000	87	Kimberly-Clark Corp.	80,000
63	Mattel Inc.	132,892	88	Hershey Foods Corp.	79,200
64	Xerox Corp.	127,583	89	MCA Inc.	77,058
65	IC Industries	127,289	90	Grand Metropolitan p.l.c.	76,200
66	CPC International	123,500	91	Noxell Corp.	74,200
67	Levi Strauss & Co.	122,000	92	Mazda Motor Corp.	71,797
68	American Motors Corp.	120,500	93	Wm. Wrigley Jr. Co.	70,400
69	Cosmair Inc.	119,500	94	American Broadcasting Cos.	68,900
70	Jos. E. Seagram & Sons Co.	115,827	95	Delta Air Lines	66,900
71	Batus Inc.	113,400	96	Trans World Airlines	66,200
72	AMR Corp.	110,800	97	Goodyear Tire & Rubber Co.	64,700
73	Clorox Co.	109,600	98	Cotter & Co.	63,900
74	Bayer AG	105,296	99	Eastern Airlines	60,800
75	Volkswagen of America	103,000	100	Van Munching & Co.	58,970

Source: *Advertising Age,* 26 September 1985, p. 1. Reprinted with permission. Copyright 1985 by Crain Communications, Inc. Figures are a composite of measured and unmeasured advertising.

The advertising agency is a service organization that plans, creates, and produces advertising for its clients. It is made up of a number of very specialized individuals, each of whom is involved in a discrete part of this process of creation, and, except for very small agencies, there is a high degree of specialization among the employees. Figure 1.13 shows an organization chart for a typical medium-sized agency. Most large agencies would also have a department for public relations, another for direct marketing, and another for sales promotion, or they would own a subsidiary company for one or more of these functions.

In addition to this structure there is a second type of structure in the agency; in this structure people work together on specific teams to serve specific clients. Any single individual may work on several accounts at the same time and may be on different account teams with different people. As shown in Figure 1.14, each account team is headed by an account executive and has assigned to it one or more media people, writers, artists, and researchers; again, a large agency might also assign public relations or sales promotions people to the team. An account supervisor oversees the work of several account teams, or, if the account is very large and/or important, the supervisor may head a single account team. In addition, large agencies generally have a creative review board made up of a cross section of senior management personnel; this group reviews all creative work before it is shown to a client. The next few pages describe the jobs that are listed on the organization chart.

Account executive

Figure 1.13 Typical advertising agency organization chart

The account executive is the liaison between the agency and the client. The account executive is responsible for leading and coordinating the team's efforts and making sure that the work gets done and, at the same time, explaining and selling

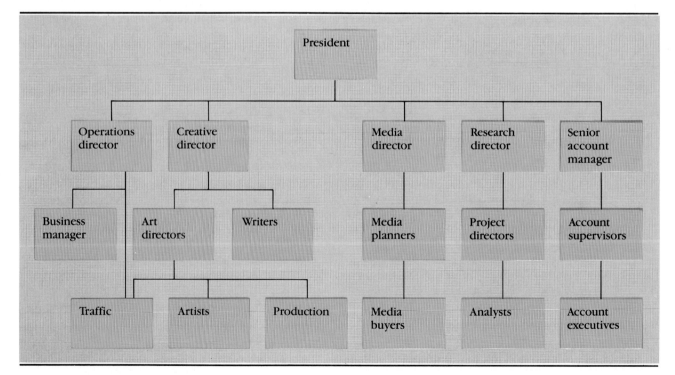

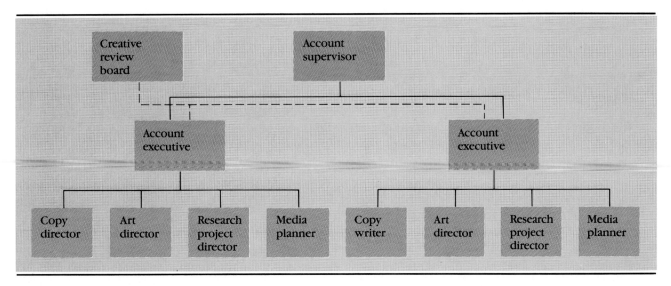

Figure 1.14 *Structure of account teams*

the work to the client. This person needs to know how to be a diplomat, a sales-person, a manager, and a marketing consultant as well as have basic knowledge of each of the functional areas of advertising and marketing.

Research

The researcher is one of the first members of the team to get involved in the project. As was seen in the decision sequence framework, the first step toward good advertising is a good situation analysis which, in turn, is based on sound research. The researcher works closely with the account executive and the client contact person to assess the marketing problems that can be dealt with through advertising; after doing the research, it is reported to all members of the account team for their use. As strategies are developed, the media and/or creative people also may get involved in designing tests of strategies in their areas; again the results are reported to the entire team, but, depending on the purpose of the test, they may not be reported to the client. Often an agency may do its own *copy test* (research to assess message impact) to see if a strategy is on target before presenting the strategy to the client.

Creative

The account team generally has two types of representatives from the creative department; these are the writer, known as a *copywriter,* and the artist, known as an *art director.* These two will translate the research data and statements of objectives and position into the art of the advertisement. They work together to develop a verbal message (*copy*) and a visual message (*layout*) that best communi-

---

Toward the end of each chapter, there will be a section entitled "The Inside Outlook." Each of these will present the thoughts of a leading practitioner who is an expert on the topic of that chapter. In this first chapter, Michael Tobin and Christopher Nelson present their views of the advertising agency –client relationship from the perspectives of the agency and client, respectively.

T·H·E ·I·N·S·I·D·E· O·U·T·L·O·O·K

Michael Tobin

Vice-President–Account Director, Foote, Cone & Belding

Michael Tobin is Vice-President–Account Director at Foote, Cone & Belding, assigned to the S.C. Johnson account. Mike has had a varied career within the realm of packaged goods advertising, working with such clients as Procter & Gamble, Pillsbury, Kellogg, Philip Morris, Kraft, and Star Kist Foods. He has held the position of Vice-President at three of the top ten world-wide agencies, including Leo Burnett, J. Walter Thompson, and Foote, Cone & Belding. His background includes an 18-month stint of international experience in Copenhagen, Denmark, where he had responsibility for Leo Burnett multinational accounts in Scandinavia.

Mike has worked with a wide range of client contacts, on several different levels, representing numerous business styles and philosophies. He has devised an overall approach to working with such clients, which seems to be effective over the entire range.

Good Client/Agency Relationships

For most of its practitioners, agency work is challenging, frustrating, and, most of the time, fun. Because it's a highly competitive, service-oriented business, however, agency people—especially account people—are often entrusted with balancing: (1) a responsibility for keeping large numbers of diverse individuals happy, and (2) their own instinct for self-happiness. The key to this balancing act is in forging and maintaining good client relationships.

The key to such relationships is in managing the "gap." The "gap" has been identified as follows: "When it comes to independent thinking on the part of the agency, client assistant brand managers are often threatened by it, brand managers resist it, group brand managers tolerate it, vice presidents welcome it, and top management demands it." Client structures and personalities vary, but the principle seems to hold, posing the primary challenge to good client/agency relationships.

Agencies generally succeed or fail, based on the quality of the ideas and independent thinking they provide, and management is right to demand it. The generation and exchange of such ideas and thinking usually takes place at the lower levels, however, where distrust and resentment can breed. Agency account managers *must* find ways to get agency ideas heard without alienating their client counterparts.

In my experience, staying within some basic guideposts usually ensures you'll stay somewhere on the road to success in this endeavor.

The Guideposts

1. *Seek leadership equilibrium* Brand managers are intrinsic leaders. Agency account

people also succeed or fail primarily on their leadership skills. Anyone who's ever participated in a task group with two leaders knows the problems. Thus, a good brand manager/account manager relationship must be based on some sense of leadership equilibrium, often achieved by identifying separate areas of leadership responsibility.

Because the brand manager has bottom line responsibility for the business, the agency person must give the most in this mix. Most good brand managers, however, recognize that it's in their own best interest to allow the account manager to manage agency resources—creative, media, etc. Either way, the agency person must exercise this prerogative. I know of no agency manager who has succeeded without doing so.

2. *Provide client "wants" and "needs"* This is a slightly arrogant concept that says an agency must give the client what he wants plus what's really good for his business. Succinctly, it says that where there's a conflict between the way the client and agency view a task, the agency has an obligation to do it the client's way, and to do it, and argue forcefully and persuasively for it, the agency's way.

3. *Seize the initiative for analysis* Though top client management expects it, few brand managers will ask for an independent analysis of the business. Account managers must do this on their own, knowing that better strategic input, copy, and media plans will inevitably result.

4. *Show commitment but not stubbornness* Agency people with "round heels" rarely succeed, but neither do those who constantly have their heels dug in.

5. *Accept "idea-napping"* Finally, know going in that the best of your ideas will eventually become everybody's; as the saying goes, "success has a thousand fathers." Still, people who are consistently "around" good ideas tend to succeed.

T·H·E   I·N·S·I·D·E   O·U·T·L·O·O·K

Christopher Nelson

Product Manager, General Mills

Chris Nelson is a 1972 graduate of the University of Wisconsin–Madison, School of Business with a major in marketing. After several years of business experience, including two and a half years selling with Johnson & Johnson, he returned to school. He received his MBA from Roosevelt University in October of 1977 and joined General Mills in July of 1978. While at General Mills, he has held various assignments including product manager assignments for Monsters, Cocoa Puffs, Golden Grahams, and Buc*Wheats. He is currently Product Manager for Betty Crocker Layer Cakes.

The Client/Agency Relationship

Over the past seven years at General Mills I have had the opportunity to work with several different agencies during seven different assignments. These assignments ranged from new products with limited media expenditures to established brands with multimillion dollar advertising budgets. Despite the variety of assignments, it's clear the best relationship between client and agency is where a true partnership in the business exists.

This partnership can only work if both client and agency clearly understand the objectives set for the brand. These objectives are established by the client and include volume and share as well as financial goals. Accomplishing these objectives demands a good working relationship between client and agency with each party understanding what is expected of it.

Based on my experience at General Mills, there are two major steps I, as a product man-

ager, can take to foster a good relationship with the agency:

1. *Keep the agency informed of ongoing business issues* Since the agency is generally removed physically from the client's office, it must be kept informed of progress toward the accomplishment of the brand's objectives. Ongoing business activities, changes from other functional actions, and competitive actions must be discussed with the agency so it too can have a clear understanding of the environment in which it is working to help accomplish the brand's objectives.

2. *Foster a healthy environment for open communications and innovation* A major function of the agency is to provide advertising to help sell product and accomplish the brand's

objectives. Clearly, an environment fostering open communication will help develop new, innovative, motivating, and effective creative work.

For the agency's part of the partnership, I've felt there are two major responsibilities of the account person:

1. *Knowledge of advertising*   On the surface this may seem rather basic, but the product manager and his brand group depend on the agency to be fully conversant in all aspects of advertising. The most important roles an agency plays for their client are those of media and creative. This includes the planning for both media and creative as well as the actual media buying and creative execution.

   The final creative product that is produced and the associated media plan are vital components of the marketing plans developed to accomplish the strategic objectives.

2. *Good business person*   Again, this may seem rather basic, but it is important not only in

managing the daily activities of the agency functions but in acting as a business consul to the client. When the partnership is working at its best, the agency and client communication is open and candid. The agency must have good strategic marketers and good business people to help the client accomplish the objective laid down for the brand.

In summary, the client/agency relationship is based on a partnership, that is, working together to meet goals set for the brand.

This partnership, to be effective, must have open lines of communication and a complete understanding by all concerned of what needs to be accomplished to meet the objectives set for the brand.

cate the key points established by the account executive. Their job continues until the copy is exactly stated and the layout is clear enough for production to take place.

Media

Many people who end up in account management begin in *media* as trainees. There are huge amounts of data to be massaged in this department so that planners can match the demographics and usage characteristics of the target market against the available ways of delivering the message through magazines, television programs, and other media.

The goal of the media people who work on the account is to deliver the message effectively at the lowest cost to the precise target market while still making the appropriate impact in terms of how often and how frequently the message must be received.

Production

Large agencies have separate departments for print production and broadcast production because these processes differ greatly. The print production department takes the layout and prepares its final form for the printer by putting all the elements of the ad together. It may need to do its own photography, buy available stock photos, or do original art work. It also contracts with printers to set up the appropriate typefaces for the text of the ad and has the type composed in a format for printing. These are then combined onto plates by photoengravers so that printing can take place.

In broadcast production the storyboard (a combination of copy and layout that shows the sequential progression of the commercial) is taken to an outside producer who will design or find a background setting (set) and will recruit appropriate actors. The commercial is shot on film or videotape and is then edited to the proper length and given any added sound and/or visual effects. Most agencies subcontract some or all production work.

Traffic

The process of creating advertising involves many people over a period of time that may cover several months. The traffic department controls the process to ensure that each person along the way meets his or her deadlines and that the media receive the finished work on time. If the April issue of *Reader's Digest* has a closing date of January 15 (so that it can be put together and distributed by March 1), then the creative process will probably start in late October. While it may seem like a lot of lead time, everything is timed to meet this final deadline, and the success of the agency often depends on its ability to do so. More precisely, the agency–client relationship is sure to be put in jeopardy if too many deadlines are missed. (*Too many* may be as low as *one*.)

While large agencies may have many people in each of the job functions described above, smaller agencies may not have anyone in some of the areas and may subcontract specific tasks to other firms. An agency that covers all the areas of creative media and research (except final production) is known as a *full-service agency,* and as part of its complete service, also offers general marketing expertise and may offer public relations, sales promotions, trade show, and package design assistance.

There are also *media buying services* that act as a media department for hire. These services act as a buyer for the agency but usually do not do media planning. They are paid a fee or a commission for their work.

Creative boutiques produce copy and art. They do no research, marketing, or media and may not even be involved in production. Their only function is to create fresh new ideas. Since creative ideas are the heart and soul of advertising, a good boutique can do quite well without incurring the overhead of the other departments. Users of this service need to have done their marketing research homework ahead of time because creativity without marketing constraints rarely sells a product.

A Caution

This text will try to present general models and techniques that can be applied to any mass behavior management setting, but most examples in the major body of the text will deal with consumer goods simply because this is where the bulk of the media dollars is spent. In addition, the marketers and advertisers of these consumer products have the greatest expertise in executing the principles advocated by this text. Readers should learn from the best; in this case the consumer goods marketers, in general, should be emulated.

Chapters 21 through 23 will be devoted to other types of applications such as retailing, industrial sales, professional services, services in general, and public and nonprofit sector ideas and issues. The principles that are being discussed throughout the text will hold in any applications case with little change. There are, though, some important differences across contexts, and it may be clearer to put these issues together in a separate section rather than to interrupt the flow of the main text with side-track discussions of exceptions to the basic frameworks.

Summary

This chapter has laid the foundation upon which the text can build other concepts. Advertising and the rest of the promotions mix are marketing tools to be used in the larger context of the firm, but before beginning to develop promotional strategies it is necessary to establish a tie to marketing.

The decision sequence model provides the major structure that will tie the concepts of the text together. Using this framework, all the decisions that need to be made will relate to a base of logic.

The hierarchy of effects model presents the major classes of responses that can occur when strategies are developed; these are awareness, attitude, and behavior. Their order is influenced by how involved the consumer is with the product—if at all—at the time of the purchase.

Marketing communications offer a number of stimuli to be used to trigger specific consumer responses. The stimulus-response model takes into account the interaction of events and their effect on consumer behavior. In order to market an item effectively, the manager must first select the desired response to the product and then select the appropriate stimuli to increase the probability of achieving that response.

Schramm's model also considers the interactions of sender and receiver but shows how the message transmission can fail. In creating messages it will be important to keep in mind the ways that a failure to communicate can arise.

Finally, the short introduction to the advertising business allowed the reader to get a sense of the structure of the advertising agency. This structure will be expanded as the functional areas of the agency are discussed. This topic will be returned to in the concluding chapter in order to examine job opportunities in the advertising business.

Welcome to the world of marketing communications.

Discussion Questions

1. Should advertising attempt to inform consumers? Why? Always? Should advertising attempt to persuade consumers? Why? Always?

2. How do the philosophies of the marketing concept and the sales concept affect the way advertising and promotions strategies develop? Consider media, message, and promotions strategies in your discussion.

3. There are several ways in which product, price, and place relate to advertising and promotions. Discuss these relationships.

4. What are the advantages and disadvantages of mass and paid forms of communications (compared to personal and free forms)?

5. Define advertising and promotions. How do you think that they differ in the dominant tasks that they are asked to perform?

6. Describe the stages of the decision sequence process. What are some of the virtues of this process for communicators?

7. What are the stages of the hierarchy of effects? How and why does the order of effects differ in high- and low-involvement cases?

8. What is a positive reinforcer? Can a product be a positive reinforcer? Can an advertisement? Support your decisions.

9. Discuss how a message sender and receiver can fail to communicate. Relate the failings to some advertising examples.

10. What is the paradox of advertising?

11. Describe what an account executive, media planner, copywriter, art director, and research project director do.

Notes

1. Philip Kotler, *Marketing Management,* 4th ed. (Englewood Cliffs, N.J.: Prentice-Hall, 1984), p. 31.

2. Kotler, *Marketing Management,* p. 29.

3. Shelby Hunt, "Informational vs. Persuasive Advertising: An Appraisal," *Journal of Advertising* (Summer 1976), pp. 7–8.

4. Kotler, *Marketing Management,* p. 20.

5. Ralph S. Alexander, ed., *Marketing Definitions* (Chicago: American Marketing Association, 1964), p. 9.

6. William G. Nickels, *Marketing Communication and Promotion,* 3rd ed. (Columbus, Ohio: Grid Publishing, Inc., 1984), p. 18.

7. Nickels, *Marketing Communication,* p. 7.

8. Louis J. Haugh, "Defining and Redefining," *Advertising Age,* 14 February 1983, p. M-44.

9. Richard E. Stanley, *Promotion, Advertising, Publicity, Personal Selling, Sales Promotion* (Englewood Cliffs, N.J.: Prentice-Hall, 1982), p. 240.

10. Blair Vedder, "The Research Role in My Company," presentation at the 1982 AMA Attitude Research Conference, Scottsdale, Arizona, February 9, 1982.

11. Charles Revson, as quoted in Philip Kotler, *Marketing Management,* 5th ed. (Englewood Cliffs, N.J.: Prentice-Hall, 1984), p. 462.

12. Wilbur Schramm, "How Communication Works," in *Advertising Management: Selected Readings,* ed. Harper W. Boyd, Jr., and Joseph W. Newman (Homewood, Ill.: Richard D. Irwin; 1965), p. 79.

13. This discussion is based in part on the testimony of Lawrence Light to the Federal Trade Commission, circa 1980.

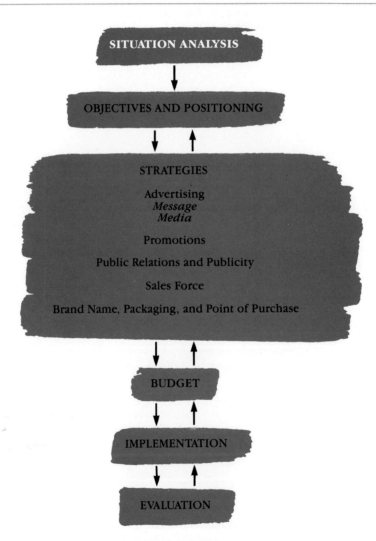

Decision Sequence Framework

Part Two
Situation Analysis and Marketing Research

When Aim toothpaste was developed to take on Crest, what did management need to know in order to position its gel toothpaste appropriately against such a well-entrenched leader? In order for Burger King to attack McDonald's, it needed to know what consumers felt they were not getting. Miller Lite Beer took a discarded product (low-calorie beer) and built a new product category using advertising and positioning. What was in their situation analysis that allowed them to see what no other firm had seen? This part covers these issues. The decision sequence framework and the place of the situation analysis in this framework appear in the figure opposite. As the first step in developing a campaign, the situation analysis is vital. If it is done poorly, the entire campaign can easily go astray.

This part of the text will consider the types of information that a manager should have in order to develop objectives, positioning, and strategy. Included also will be an introduction to the uses of the information, that is, what value is there in having a particular piece of knowledge? In order to show the value of information, some strategies are discussed in this part; this will give the reader a sense of purpose for the concepts of the situation analysis and allow each one to be more easily placed in the overall decision sequence framework. Finally, the part concludes with a discussion of primary and secondary data collection methods and sources; some of the information needed will already be available while other information will need to be gathered by the firm.

Although strategies are introduced here, it is important to remember that in an actual situation analysis, strategies should not be considered. When strategies are considered this early in the process, there is a tendency to jump to conclusions, to not properly assess all options, and to set the wrong objectives. Although past strategies are evaluated in the situation analysis, they should not be carried into the current campaign until after objectives have been set. This orderly progression holds improper strategies to a minimum.

What are the key issues? Each organization puts together its own set, but the basic areas are always the same across product classes and problems:

- The consumer
- The product
- The competition

These are the three key topics that will be most carefully developed in the situation analysis. In addition there will also be an assessment of

- The firm
- The environment

These five areas cover most of the topics relevant to the situation analysis, although some may not be germane for a particular product or service. Initially, it is important to gather every possible piece of information; later, the information is organized into these five headings. As information is collected, a key question to be asked is: "What possible value can this information have for the development of an advertising and promotions campaign?" If there is not an acceptable answer, throw it out. If information has no intended purpose, it has no value and therefore its cost is too high.

Table 1 presents a summary of the key issues to be covered in the situation analysis and serves as a road map for the three chapters dealing with this topic. The center of the marketing world is the consumer; in evaluating the consumer there are three key sets of issues: descriptors, processes, and perceptions. While it is impossible to separate these issues in considering the problems of advertising and promotions, it is useful to be able to separate the issues for the purposes of analysis.

In addition to the subjective perceptions, the product and competition can also be assessed on more objective grounds as seen in the listing in the lower half of the center column of Table 1. The right column shows a list of firm and environmentally related issues to be considered.

It is easy to see from this table that the situation analysis fact book could be several hundred pages in length before any objectives, positioning, or strategies can be considered. The importance of such a thorough analysis cannot be stressed enough. If this task is properly done, the objectives and position will be easily seen. If the fact book is complete it will provide support for the strategies that follow as well as giving ideas and directions for the copywriters, artists, media planners, and promotions and other specialists who get involved in the later stages of the decision sequence. The fact book allows each of these people to jus-

Table 1 Key issues to be covered in a situation analysis

Consumer	Product class, brand, and competition	Parent firm and the environment
Descriptors	Perceptions of	The Firm
Demographics	Attributes	Corporate goals and
Psychographics	Benefits	philosophy
Geographics	Position	Financial resources
Usage level and	Uniqueness	Production
end use	Flaws	capabilities
Time of adoption		Distribution
Information sources	Product life cycle	Sales force
Loyalty	Diffusion of innovation	Product portfolio
Needs/benefits	Past strategies	
Hierarchy of effects	Market shares	The Environment
Reference and		The economy
peer groups		Legal issues
		Middlemen
Processes		Size of market
Consumer life cycle		Growth potential
Involvement		Suppliers and
		natural resources
Perceptions		Societal issues
Likes/dislikes		Seasonality
Important issues		Technology
Problems in category		

tify their decisions to management and the client and also helps to coordinate the various parts of the campaign. Without a good situation analysis there can still be advertising, and some of it may even win awards for its artistic merit. This text, though, is concerned with developing advertising that contributes to brand sales. To make such a contribution there must be a clear set of objectives based on a thorough analysis of relevant problems.

Chapter 2
Describing the Consumer and Defining the Target Market

*I*n order to develop effective marketing communications it is important to have an accurate assessment of the relevant problem(s) and a view of the past, present, and predicted future states of the relevant parts of the world. Without this type of information there is no way to know if proposed strategies are appropriate or if they have the potential to succeed.

This text is strongly rooted in a "management by objectives" perspective, which implies that strategies must be consistent with management objectives. In order to set proper objectives, the firm must first do a thorough situation analysis so that it has a proper understanding of its problems and opportunities.

There was a time in the history of U.S. advertising when agencies did not see the need for this sort of rigorous up-front analysis, but the tide had started to change at least by the 1920s when Claude Hopkins used systematic problem analysis at the Lord and Thomas Advertising Agency in Chicago and wrote a book called *Scientific Advertising*.[1] Hopkins was firmly convinced of the need for problem analysis and insisted his clients pay for such an evaluation before he began to write. He was generally recognized as the most successful (and highly paid) copywriter of his period for the same reason.[2]

Although a thorough situation analysis is now an almost universally recognized concept, it is interesting to note that as recently as the late 1960s some copywriters were still complaining that the need to use such data stifled their creativity. Now there is little opposition to the use of data, although there are different complaints about the volume and value of the data and arguments about its interpretation.

The fact book that emerges from the situation analysis is used by practitioners in all areas of communications from advertising to promotions to packaging. Most advertising professionals who have written their autobiographies or

Figure 2.1 On the importance of the situation analysis

Research provides the stuff that ads are made of: information. Thus it is the most important function of all. Without research the campaign would be without compass and rudder. Without it an advertisement would be empty.—*O'Toole*

You have to know your product so well you could go out and be a salesman for the company pushing the product. What you're trying to do in all of this is to isolate the problem of the company—naturally they wouldn't have switched their advertising to your agency if everything was going along fine. What you're trying to do is to crystallize the problem. Once you arrive at the problem, then your job is really almost over, because the solving of the problem is nothing. The headache is finding out what the problem is.
—*Della Femina*

An ad.-writer, to have a chance at success, must gain full information on his subject. The library of an advertising agency should have books on every line that calls for research. A painstaking advertising man will often read for weeks on some problem which comes up.
—*Hopkins*

Before you start work on a new campaign, study the product, the previous advertising, the competitive advertising, and the research. (This is hard work.)
—*Ogilvy*

Major clients can't survive without research. There's a need to probe, measure, sort, count; to get the facts and turn them into strategy. But you can't print the research. You have to leave room for the magic to happen. Then bring back research to find out if the magic works.
—*Bates*

Learn from the experience of others. You will not always be fortunate enough to have had previous experience with the product you are writing about. In that case, you can seek the help of other people. Talk to friends, family, associates and persons you meet in your daily affairs, or at the luncheon table, or at social gatherings.

Ask questions of people. Have they heard of the product? Where did they hear about it? What do they know about it? What do they think of it? Have they bought it? If yes, why did they buy it? If no, why didn't they buy it? Get their experiences and their viewpoints.
—*Caples*

Research . . . that information-giving, life-giving link between the advertising writers and the advertising readers.
—*Reinhard*

other books related to the field have noted the importance of the situation analysis and up-front research. Figure 2.1 shows a small sample of such statements.

Without good data at the front end it is improbable that the resulting campaign can have much merit. Computer analysts call this *GIGO*—"garbage in, garbage out," and the concept is applicable to marketing communications as well. Therefore, good research will expand the scope of existing knowledge and reduce instinctive biases, and good researchers will provide insightful interpretation of the findings.

This first chapter of the situation analysis section deals with describing the consumer and is divided into two parts. In the first part the consumer is analyzed in terms of demographic, geographic, and psychographic issues. These are known as *enduring variables* because they are constant within the consumer across all products (at any single point in time). These variables are commonly used to provide input for media decisions.

The second part of the chapter analyzes the consumer in terms of usage, benefit, knowledge, and attitude issues. These are known as *dynamic variables* because they differ for a consumer relative to each product (at any point in time). These variables are more commonly used to provide input for positioning and message decisions. Combining these two types of variables, the firm can determine why consumers behave in certain ways toward the product using dynamic variables and then can develop a profile of these consumers using enduring variables.

Describing the Consumer

In all cases of advertising and promotions planning it is necessary to define the most relevant target market and then to develop strategy to best reach and influence that target. Since it is unusual to pursue everyone in the population, segmentation principles are employed; the purpose of describing consumers is to define the most appropriate segments. *Segmentation,* then, is the art of dividing a mass market into identifiable subsets in order to meet the needs of specific consumers and to match the product and the user more clearly. The target market must be selected so that the greatest potential sales can be achieved at the lowest cost.

A quick review of segmentation

The description of the consumer and the development of target segments will be considered simultaneously in this text because they are so strongly interrelated. There are two major reasons to segment a market:

1. It is generally wasteful and inefficient to try to reach or to market to everyone with the same product. Some people are easier to get to than others; given limited resources the manager should pursue the easier and more profitable targets. If the firm has one product, it probably won't appeal to all people, and, therefore, the firm's efforts should be limited to the most likely prospects.

2. All people are not alike but the firm cannot develop separate products for each consumer. Economies of scale dictate that there can only be a small number of variations in the product line (unless the firm is creating designer fashions, original works of art, or a few other unique and high-priced products).

Two unacceptable extremes emerge here: One product for all people and one product for each person are both generally less than ideal. Offering several products for all consumers or one product for a subset are two common segmentation strategies that emerge. These two strategies call for detailed descriptions of consumers.

It should be noted that there are rare cases when the organization must get 100% of the target market to behave a certain way. The Swedish government, several years ago, decided to switch from left-hand to right-hand driving on its roads. To meet this objective successfully, the government needed a 100% market share and needed all behaviors to change at one point in time. Anything less was unacceptable and would have led to undesirable consequences. Consider the chaos if the government would have been happy with a 6% market share or if it would have allowed a build-up of market share over time. While segmentation was not employed in terms of selecting a set of best prospects, segmentation was employed in terms of media and message strategies. Even when the goal was to capture an entire market, segmentation was still relevant in reaching and educating the market.

The concept of segmentation began to emerge formally as a major issue in marketing in the late 1940s. It has become an important issue as a result of three other developments in the U.S. marketplace.

1. *The introduction of the marketing concept*   As firms became more concerned with meeting the needs of consumers, it quickly became clear that not all consumers had the same needs. As segments were defined, different product attributes were developed, and messages discussed differing benefits.

2. *A higher standard of living*   As the economy matured, the population's level of needs was raised. In a developing economy, people need food, food may be scarce, and therefore it certainly is not necessary to advertise its existence. As food becomes abundant, it is prepared with needs other than hunger satisfaction in mind. Marketers can now appeal to the need to receive love and other warm feelings by serving appealing meals or to enhance an ego by being creative in the kitchen. Instead of marketing food, the firm can market creamed onions, and, at a higher level, the firm can intimate the benefits of creamed onions in terms of endearment or self-fulfillment. These higher levels of motives are described by Maslow[3] and can be used to segment markets using differing message strategies.

In looking at product development, the reader can see a great change from the days of Henry Ford, who was reputed to have offered consumers "any color as long as it's black." Now automobiles come in many shapes, sizes, and designs to meet differing needs; clearly, the advertising messages must also differ to capture the benefits of each style or feature.

3. *More competition*   Virtually all product classes have become more competitive during this same time period. One response to this trend has been for firms to find their own niche in the market by catering to one or a few segments. This allows firms to avoid head-on competition by developing their own *position*. While a segmentation strategy advocates going after a particular piece of the market, a positioning strategy advocates the presentation of a unique and meaningful benefit to that segment. The two concepts are strongly interrelated and, often, are mirror images of one another. Positioning strategies need strong support from advertising in order to develop the appropriate image in consumer's minds. This is especially true for the many product classes where there are few true brand differences. Positioning is discussed in depth in the next part of the text.

There are two aspects of segmentation to consider:

1. *Classifying consumers*   This is the task of the situation analysis and will be developed in this section. Here it is necessary to analyze the market and identify potentially profitable pockets. Since some people are more responsive than others, the objective of classification is to find these responsive groups and select them for pursuit. Viable segments must have a sufficient mass of consumers so that it is profitable to appeal to them and must have some identifiable characteristics so that they can be described.

2. *Designing a strategy*   Strategies evolve from the classification process. Advertising and promotions strategies for dealing with segments will be discussed as those sections are presented.

The next few pages will consider many ways of describing and classifying consumers; the variables to be discussed will fall into two broad categories:

- Enduring variables
- Dynamic variables

Enduring descriptive variables

These variables are enduring because, at any given time, they do not change across product classes; they endure with the individual. *Demographic, geographic,* and *psychographic* variables are enduring; they describe the consumer regardless of the product being analyzed. A person's age, for example, does not change as a function of the product class being examined. Be it orange juice or stereos, a 30-year-old male living in Des Moines with an avid interest in tractors will still be 30 years old, living in Des Moines, with an avid interest in tractors. Knowing these things is important in describing consumers and in media selection strategy (as will be seen in later sections) but generally is less important for message strategy than what can be learned from dynamic variables.

Demographic characteristics   These are derived from the statistical study of a population with reference to its size, density, distribution, and vital statistics. The manager would like to describe the target in several ways in order to communicate most effectively. Therefore, the situation analysis is used to generate a consumer profile. Typical demographics include age, sex, income, education, marital status, family size, and occupation. These variables can be easily determined through survey research and are a standard part of almost any such work; for many products demographic data can also be found in syndicated data sources such as Simmons Market Research Bureau (SMRB) or Mediamark Research, Inc. (MRI). (These services are described in more detail in Chapter 4.) Figure 2.2 shows the categories of demographic data available from SMRB and the breakouts of that data.

In addition to considering descriptors of a target market, demographics are examined to note changes in the overall environment. For example, in the recent past there have been major changes in

- The percentage of working women and the role of women in society
- The number of dual income households
- The median age and the numbers of old and young people
- The number of single person households

In recent years there also has been a fragmentation of the United States so that the concept of a melting pot where most attempted to, or were forced to, assimilate into the dominant mass (middle-class white Anglo-Saxon Protestant) culture has changed to a society of special interest groups. This splintering of the whole may be due at least in part to the marketer's notions of segmentation. Certainly politicians have embraced segmentation as they have made promises to many groups each time elections draw near. Special interest groups have learned that there is power in being a vocal segment of the political market; in product marketing the brand manager actively seeks out these segments, and, if they are large enough, develops products to meet their needs.

Demographic trends must be watched and changes anticipated. For example, Procter & Gamble was successful in introducing the first disposable diaper, Pam-

Figure 2.2 SMRB demo-
graphic and geographic categories

Total females	Northeast-marketing
Female homemakers	East Central
Employed mothers	West Central
18–24	South
25–34	Pacific
35–44	County size A
45–54	County size B
55–64	County size C
65 or older	County size D
18–34	Metro central city
18–49	Metro suburban
35–49	Non metro
Graduated college	Household inc $35,000 or more
Attended college	$25,000 or more
Graduated high school	$20,000–$24,999
Did not graduate high school	$15,000–$19,999
Employed	$10,000–$14,999
Employed full-time	$ 5,000–$ 9,999
Employed part-time	Under $5,000
Not employed	Household of 1 or 2 people
Professional/manager	3 or 4 people
Clerical/sales	5 or more people
Craftsmen/foremen	No child in hshld
Other employed	Child(ren) under 2 yrs
Single	2–5 years
Married	6–11 years
Divorced/separated/widowed	12–17 years
Parents	Residence owned
White	Value: $40,000 or more
Black	Value: under $40,000
Other	
Northeast-census	
North Central	
South	
West	

pers, even though the birth rate was declining. One reason for the decline was that more women were working; this information led to the observation that those women having babies wanted convenience so that they would not lose their independence and be tied down.[4] Procter & Gamble was the first company to translate these changing needs into a product, and, as a result, they dominated the product class for many years. Analysis of demographic trends is essential to new product development; this text, though, will key on the relevance of demographic trends for advertising and promotions decisions.

Geographic characteristics For any product with less than national distribution, it is usually a waste of media dollars to advertise in areas where there is no product. (As will be seen in the media section, it is not always a waste to do so.)

Geographics are also important in discriminating between urban, suburban, and rural areas of the country. Many products have greater or lesser usage depending on the level of population concentration; in addition, many media vehicles also have geographic skews. For example, *New Yorker* is an urban-skewed magazine while *Grit* is read mostly in rural parts of the country. An urban/rural skew is affected by the demographics and psychographics of people who live in different places; geographics, demographics, and psychographics, therefore, are probably not independent of one another. This skew affects brand selection as well as media habits and can be seen in regional descriptions as well.

Regions of the country also influence consumption patterns. While it is obvious that climate will influence behaviors (the Sunbelt and Snowbelt states have different needs for air conditioners and snow blowers), regionality influences behavior in more subtle ways. In his book *The Nine Nations of North America,* Joel Garreau[5] presents data that allow a division of the United States into nine regions. While his report seems more anecdotal than factual, it does give some feel about regional differences relevant to geographic segmentation. Figure 2.3 shows Garreau's description of each of the nine regions.

Different regions (or other geographic breaks) can be seen to have greater or lesser levels of consumption of various products and brands. In a geographic segmentation plan, the manager would use these levels of consumption as a basis from which to maintain or build share. In an area of high product and low brand use there would be good opportunities for growth. In an area of low product use, it would be difficult to increase sales for the brand without first changing attitudes toward the product itself. This is generally felt to be a poor investment of advertising dollars.

As with demographics, there are geographic trends to keep in mind. As shown in Table 2.1, there has been a definite shift of consumers and dollars from the Northeast and Midwest to the South, Southwest, and West (the greatest population growth has occurred in California, Florida, and Texas during the past decade). During the 1980s the West's population will grow almost 20% while that of the East is declining. In fact, some major Eastern cities have lost over 10% of their populations during the 1970s. Such shifts will affect media planning but will also affect message strategy because life styles, needs, and outlooks differ in the different regions. Ultimately the greatest use of geographic data will be for

Table 2.1 The imbalance of regional population shifts

Region	1980 population (thousands)	1990 population (thousands)	% change 1980–1990	Net migration (thousands)
New England	12,348.6	12,733.1	+3.11%	+55.4
Mideast	42,237.5	41,312.6	−2.18%	−2,116.9
Great Lakes	41,669.7	42,371.9	+1.69%	−1,828.1
Plains	17,184.0	17,898.6	+4.16%	−284.2
Southeast	52,646.2	60,970.0	+15.81%	+5,162.0
Southwest	21,271.6	26,531.3	+24.73%	+2,947.6
Rocky Mountain	6,551.2	8,598.9	+31.26%	+1,102.1
Far West	32,596.2	38,791.6	+19.01%	+3,503.8
Total United States	226,504.8	249,203.0	+9.72%	+8,541.7

Source: *Sales and Marketing Management, Survey of Buying Power,* 31 October 1983, p. 42.

Figure 2.3 *Capsule summaries of the nine nations of North America*

The Foundry

NATION: Foundry
CAPITAL: Detroit
GEOGRAPHY: Ohio, Pennsylvania, New Jersey, northeastern Illinois, northern Indiana, Michigan (excluding northwest region), New York (excluding Manhattan), southwest Connecticut, northern Virginia, northern Maryland, eastern Wisconsin, northern Delaware, northern West Virginia, and southeastern Ontario.
DESCRIPTION: The industrialized northeast that is losing population, jobs, and investment to the other "nations" is marked by gritty "urban prison camps," decaying infrastruc-

tures, heavy trade unionism, obsolete technologies, and racial friction. "The whole point of living in the Foundry is work," Joel Garreau observes. "No one ever lived in Buffalo for its climate or Gary for its scenic vistas. Work is so central to the Foundry experience, that when people are thrown out of it they literally go crazy."
OUTLOOK: This is the only "nation" on decline, due to soft demand for autos, steel, rubber, and its other major products. It no longer represents "America" in a business or social sense, even though it is home to 90 million people. However, it will bounce back in a different form, probably in the early 21st century, according to Garreau. The Foundry's ma-

Figure 2.3 *continued*

jor asset is water, which gives it a competitive edge over most of the other "nations."

MexAmerica

NATION: MexAmerica
CAPITAL: Los Angeles
GEOGRAPHY: Southwest and south central California, southern Arizona, western New Mexico, southern Texas, southern Colorado, and Mexico.
DESCRIPTION: The southwest "nation" of North America has as its capital the second largest Mexican city in the world. Its language, culture, economics, food, politics, and lifestyle are under heavy Hispanic influence. "There are great numbers of Hispanics in the southwest who can't be told by Anglos to 'go back where you came from.' They *are* where they came from," Garreau said. Houston, which is starting to strongly resemble Los Angeles, is the world's new energy capital, bordering Mex-America on the east. Phoenix is now the 11th largest city in the U.S. MexAmerica is a watershed of the future, but its No. 1 problem is water, most of which is "imported."
OUTLOOK: It is rapidly becoming the most influential of all the nations. If a circle were drawn around Southern California, it would be the 14th wealthiest country in the world. A strong entrepreneurial spirit and "unlimited growth" perspective attract hard-working Anglos and Hispanics. But "northern" influences are creeping in. The southwestern "sombrero, siesta"; the Los Angeles "hot tub, laid-back, flakiness"; and the Houston "all (oil) well, cowboy hat" stereotypes are no longer accurate.

Dixie

NATION: Dixie
CAPITAL: Atlanta
GEOGRAPHY: Georgia, Alabama, Mississippi, Louisiana, Arkansas, Kentucky, Tennessee, North Carolina, South Carolina, southern Virginia, southern Maryland, southern Illinois, southern Indiana, southern Missouri, north and central Florida, eastern Texas, southeastern Oklahoma, southern West Virginia, and southern Delaware.
DESCRIPTION: Dixie is that "forever-under-developed North American nation across which the social and economic machine of the late 20th century has most dramatically swept," Garreau notes. Dixie is an emotion, an idea, a way of life in small towns and cities, calling oneself a "Southerner," the Confederate flag, and waving to strangers. It is knowing where and who you are.

OUTLOOK: No longer predominantly backward, rural, poor, and racist, Dixie is undergoing the most rapid social and economic change on the continent. However, Dixie's growth is all "catch up," since most of its "impressive" growth statistics (per-capita income, for example) are still below the national average. Southern cities tend to annex surrounding towns with industries, thus creating "artificial" population growth. Yet, the people are among the most optimistic about the future. "Dixie isn't the 'sunbelt,'" Garreau warns. "There is no such place as the sunbelt."

New England

NATION: New England
CAPITAL: Boston
GEOGRAPHY: Massachusetts, Maine, New Hampshire, Vermont, Rhode Island, eastern Connecticut, Nova Scotia, Prince Edward Island, Labrador, Newfoundland, and New Brunswick.
DESCRIPTION: With virtually no energy or raw materials, little agriculture, few basic industries, high taxes, and expensive home fuel and auto gas, New England is the poorest of the nine "nations" (poverty is actually chic). The oldest and most civilized Anglo "nation" on the continent has people who are environmentally aware, tolerant, intelligent, political, fair, but somewhat elitist, Garreau notes. They feel "we're all in this together."
OUTLOOK: New England was the first "nation" to enter economic decline and a post-industrial society. It is rebounding thanks to an influx of high-tech industries, the proprietors and employees of which like New England's charm and quality of life. New England is once again a land of pioneers, only this time they're resurrecting a fully depreciated "nation."

Empty Quarter

NATION: Empty Quarter
CAPITAL: Denver
GEOGRAPHY: Wyoming, Nevada, Montana, Utah, Idaho, western Colorado, eastern California, northern Arizona, eastern Oregon, eastern Washington, northwestern New Mexico, northern Alaska, Yukon, Northwest Territories, eastern British Columbia, Alberta, northern Manitoba, north and southwest Saskatchewan, and northern Ontario.
DESCRIPTION: The Intermountain West boasts wide-open spaces, energy (oil, gas, tar sands, oil shale), and minerals (gold, silver, copper, zinc, iron, magnesium, uranium, and

hundreds of others). While it is the largest "nation" in terms of land area, it has the smallest population, which makes it politically weak-voiced. With its pristine environment, it is the true "west." There's plenty of fresh air, but the land is high and dry, and largely government-owned. It's not uncommon for residents to drive 200 miles to see a movie.
OUTLOOK: The future of the Empty Quarter will largely be determined by outsiders: environmentalists who want to preserve its beauty, and the "rape-and-run boys," who want its energy, Garreau said. The people still believe in the "frontier ethic," but this "nation" will undergo radical change over the next 20 years. It's estimated that development of the Overthrust Belt alone could result in one million jobs and eight million additional population.

Ecotopia

NATION: Ecotopia
CAPITAL: San Francisco
GEOGRAPHY: Northwest California, western Oregon, western Washington, western British Columbia, and southeastern coastal Alaska.
DESCRIPTION: The only part of the west blessed with adequate water and renewable resources (and volcanoes). The home of "Silicon Valley," computer chips, aluminum, timber, hydroelectric power, fisheries, bio-engineering, environmentalism, outdoor nature lovers, energy conservation, and recycling. "Quality of life" is a religion in the great Pacific Northwest, which considers the rest of North America "screwed up." Strongly antinuclear, with a penchant for seriously discussing "appropriate technology" and holistic medicine, Ecotopians have as their motto: "Leave. Me. Alone."
OUTLOOK: Ecotopia's economy is interest-rate-based, so it won't explode with opportunity until interest rates fall, Garreau said. Still, the residents will only want clean, high-tech industries, and will cling to the "small-is-beautiful" ideology. Ecotopia is best positioned to exploit the growing Pacific Rim nations. Unlike the eastern part of the U.S. and Canada, which is European-oriented, Ecotopia looks to Asia for its future.

Breadbasket

NATION: Breadbasket
CAPITAL: Kansas City
GEOGRAPHY: Minnesota, Iowa, Kansas, North Dakota, South Dakota, Nebraska, northern Missouri, western Wisconsin, northwest Michigan,

Figure 2.3   continued

western and central Oklahoma, eastern New Mexico, eastern Colorado, western and central Illinois, north and central Texas, southeastern Saskatchewan, southern Manitoba, and southwest Ontario.

DESCRIPTION: The Breadbasket is marked by agriculture and agriculture-related industries and economies. If there is a mainstream America, this is it — conservative, hard working religious residents. "People in the Breadbasket are the ratifiers of social change," Garreau explains. "Ideas still must *play* in Peoria before they become accepted. When the people in Kansas started opposing the Vietnam War, you knew the war would soon be over."

OUTLOOK: This nation works best. It is stable and at peace with itself by virtue of its enviable, prosperous, renewable economy. The Great Plains also have acquired great political power because of the strategic world importance of food. But farmers are being hurt financially by their own productivity: they are 3% of the population yet feed North Americans and millions of others around the world.

Aberrations

EVERY RULE HAS EXCEPTIONS, including the "Nine Nations" theory. Some cities and states in the U.S. simply don't "fit in" with their regions; Joel Garreau calls them "aberrations."

WASHINGTON, D.C.: The atmosphere of this city is directed inward to government, bureaucracies, lobbyists, lawyers, consultants, the news media, and the military. While its interests are not those of average Americans (Washington, D.C. residents like to find out what's going on "out there"), this city refuses to admit it's different, isolated, and a parody of its own institutions. Excluding the poor blacks in the city, the Washington, D.C. area has the highest per-capita income in the U.S., and more psychiatrists per capita than any other U.S. city. After a few years in office, former President Jimmy Carter commented, "Washington is out of tune with America."

MANHATTAN: While residents of the Washington, D.C. area refuse to recognize their uniqueness, people in Manhattan are actually proud of being different—and the rest of America views Manhattan as different. As Garreau observes, "You just don't find transvestite discos in Oklahoma City." In the 1970s, Manhattan considered becoming the 51st state, and many residents still feel civilization ends at the Hudson River. The world, in their view, is divided into two parts: New York and Not New York. With Wall Street, Madison

Avenue, Times Square, Broadway, the United Nations, and three-room apartments with $1,500 monthly rents, Manhattan surely must be considered an aberration.

HAWAII: Many Americans feel Hawaiians are on vacation every day of the year, thanks to a tropical climate, Aloha spirit, and easygoing lifestyle. Hawaii *is* beautifully different, but it also has its problems, among them no energy resources, sky-high prices, racial tensions, and feelings of being isolated—out of sync with the Mainland. It is the only state where whites of European stock (haoles) are a minority; two-thirds of the population is Asian. There are few Hispanics and even fewer blacks. And, while Hawaiians take pride in their cultural diversity, the locals resent the presence of military personnel. "Anglo kids fear the last day of the school year," Garreau notes. "The locals call it 'kill a haole day.' The Japanese and Filipinos encounter similar problems." Hawaii's major industry is tourism, followed by the military and agriculture (the No. 1 cash crop is marijuana).

ALASKA: While Garreau included parts of Alaska in Ecotopia and the Empty Quarter, he feels the state as a whole is an aberration. "Alaskans—whose judgments about anything must be measured against their decision to live in a place where tomatoes won't—think that theirs is a separate nation," he said. Alaskans refer to people from other states as "outsiders," and high-ranking Alaska politicians admit their state would like to secede from the U.S. Due to the influx of tax money from the Alaskan pipeline, the state income tax was eliminated. Alaskans are politically "schizophrenic," Garreau said, pointing out that possession of marijuana is legal there.

The earth is perpetually frozen; garbage is dumped in front yards because the items are too expensive to ship out and too difficult to bury. Despite the mountain snow, Alaska actually receives less rainfall than the Sahara Desert. It has great mineral wealth, but only 1% of the land is in public hands. Alaska has the lowest population age in the U.S., and Anglos are a distinct minority. The Eskimos, in fact, feel more allied with other residents of the Arctic Circle than they do with the U.S. "All you need are heavy boots, a hunting rifle, and a piece of earth-moving machinery and you'll fit right in," Garreau said.

The Islands

NATION: The Islands
CAPITAL: Miami
GEOGRAPHY: Florida south of the Jupiter Inlet, northern Venezuela, northern Columbia,

Cuba, Jamaica, Puerto Rico, Bahamas, Virgin Islands, Dominican Republic, Haiti, and dozens of other smaller Caribbean islands.

DESCRIPTION: This "nation" consists of southern Florida, which looks south for its future, and the Caribbean, which sees Miami as its capital. The major industries are (1) the $55 billion illegal drug trade, (2) trade with the "Latin American Rim," and (3) non-Anglo tourism. The Latin American influence is strong and pervasive. The *Miami Herald* circulates editions in Central America. JC Penney stores in Miami stock fur coats in the summer—for tourists south of the equator who arrive during their own winter.

OUTLOOK: The "weirdest and hardest to track civilization in North America," Garreau calls The Islands. Miami has become a world-class capital with a Caribbean influence, "although southern Florida doesn't want to admit it," he adds. The main point is that southern Florida has very little in common with the rest of the state, let alone Dixie.

Quebec

NATION: Quebec
CAPITAL: Quebec City
GEOGRAPHY: Province of Quebec
DESCRIPTION: The French-speaking area of Canada, steeped in history, tradition, ethnic pride, and a homogeneous culture. It is blessed with plentiful hydroelectric power, prosperous transportation industries, a diversified economy, and a perspective conducive to the acceptance of high technology.

OUTLOOK: Because they've had to struggle to maintain their identity since the first French settlers arrived, the Quebecois feel they've withstood the test of time. "They feel they're not only different from the rest of Canada, but different from the rest of the world," Garreau notes. Fiercely independent, the Quebecois make a habit of saying they want to be "maitres chez nous," or "masters of our own house." While Quebec may never separate from the rest of Canada, the important point is that the people feel they can, and would succeed on their own.

media vehicle selection. If there are geographic skews in product usage, there probably should be similar skews for the vehicles selected as well.

Demographic and geographic information can be easily obtained through survey research and can be cross-tabulated against any number of usage variables. This allows the manager to describe light versus heavy users or users of various competing brands. This information can also be obtained from SMRB or MRI for approximately 450 product classes, the major brands in each product class, and the major vehicles of each print and broadcast medium.

Segmentation has evolved over time. Earliest studies were based on crude geographic variables such as city size, urban/rural location, or region of the country. Then came demographics, which looked only at age or sex or education, and so on; and even more recently came life-style analysis. Now there are complex multivariate methods for segmenting the market. This is partly a result of better statistical methods using more powerful data crunching computers and programs. It is also due to increased sophistication among marketers. Chiefly, however, it is a response to a breakdown in the traditional demographic patterns of the United States. For example, income used to define audiences so that an over-$30,000 household had predictable education and lived in predictable neighborhoods. In 1982, though, one-third of SMRB's blue-collar respondents had such an income. As another example, only 4% of households now consist of a working husband with a nonworking wife and two children living at home.[6] Table 2.2 gives some insights into the present family structure. One in five households now has only one member because divorce rates are high and marriage is occurring later in life.

Because of this breakdown in traditional demographics, there has been a shift to behavioral variables such as those discussed later as part of dynamic segmentation. In addition, tools based on multiple variables such as PRIZM have emerged.

PRIZM[7] is referred to as "geo-demographic" market segmentation and targeting by its parent company, Claritas. Claritas has taken neighborhoods such as the 35,600 residential zip codes in the United States, 68,000 census tracts, and 254,000 block groups and factor-analyzed them to arrive at 40 life-style segments based on 535 variables that key on education, affluence, stage of the family life cycle, mobility, ethnicity, housing, and urbanization measures. Thus, by defining a desired target, a manager can get a listing of relevant zip codes, census tracts, or block groups. This is based on the axiom that "birds of a feather flock together," or, if not together, at least in the same zip code geographic neighborhood. Each market cluster is defined on the basis of the key defining variables. For example,

Table 2.2 The shrinking family

Type of household	Number (millions)	Percent of total
Male head of household, wife present	47.5	57.7
Male head of household, wife absent	1.4	1.7
Female head of household, husband present	1.8	2.2
Female head of household, husband absent	2.6	3.1
Single, never married	10.0	12.2
Divorced people	8.2	10.0
Widowed people	10.8	13.1

Source: Bureau of the Census

No. 24. Young Suburbia

Cluster 24 is the largest ZIP-Market Cluster (5.64% of 1985 U.S. households). It consists of large, young families and ranks second in incidence of married couples with children. Cluster 24s are fairly well distributed across the nation and are strong consumers of family products.

No. 31. Black Enterprise

Cluster 31 is 60% Black with median Black incomes well above average, and consumption behavior to match. The majority of these Blacks are educated, employed, and solidly set in the upper middle class.

No. 30. Blue-Chip Blues

Cluster 30, ranked third in married couples with children, is similar to Cluster 24 on most dimensions, save social rank, its predominant high-school educations and blue-collar occupations being reflected in fewer high-end incomes and lower home values.

No. 19. Shotguns and Pickups

Cluster 19 aggregates hundreds of small, outlying townships and crossroad villages that serve the nation's breadbasket and other rural areas. Cluster 19 leads the nation in mobile homes and shows peak indices for large families with school-age children, headed by blue-collar craftsmen and operatives with high-school educations. Cluster 19s are dedicated outdoorsmen.

No. 13. Norma Rae-ville

Cluster 13s are found throughout the South, with their geo-center in the Appalachian and Piedmont regions. They include hundreds of industrial suburbs and mill towns, a great many in textiles and other light industries. Cluster 13s are country folk with minimal educations. They lead the nation in non-durable manufacturing.

To get a feel for the people in the Clusters, PRIZM literature shows a profile of people living in the clusters most likely to buy an imported sports car (see Table 2.3) and those most likely to buy a power tool (Table 2.4). Each figure shows the top 20 and bottom 20 demographic profile items, product usage profile items, automobile registration profiles, and television shows and magazines preferred (1976–1979). Figure 2.4 shows indices of product usage across the 40 clusters. Such information is invaluable in segmentation work.

The main advantage of PRIZM, though, is in giving a richer profile of potential segments than the traditional single variable descriptions and in giving zip code, census tract, and block group targets at which to aim media vehicles. Being able to tie demographics to small area geographics makes PRIZM a very useful tool.

Psychographic characteristics   These help the manager segment and describe a market based on life-style issues or activities, interests, and opinions (AIO). Life-style analysis and AIO analysis are two terms fairly synonymous with psychographics. In each case data are collected when large numbers of consumers are given a lengthy battery of statements with which to agree or disagree.

Table 2.3 Profile of probable imported sports car buyer

Rank order correlation	Significance Level[a]	Title
		Top twenty positive clusters
0.927	**	% Home values $50–100K
0.903	**	% Professional & technical
0.892	**	% Finance, insurance & business
0.891	**	% Population enrolled in college
0.885	**	% Pop. U.K. foreign stock
0.876	**	white/blue collar ratio
0.861	**	% HH's w/$50K$^+$ incomes
0.828	**	% Pop. 25$^+$ w/4$^+$ yrs college
0.823	**	% Sales workers
0.816	**	% Pop. Yiddish mother tongue
0.805	**	% Home values $100K$^+$
0.786	**	% Pop. 25$^+$ w/1–3 yrs college
0.785	**	% Pop. Russian foreign stock
0.773	**	% HH's w/$30–50K incomes
0.770	**	% Res. 5 yrs ago diff. state
0.753	**	% Pop. Irish foreign stock
0.752	**	% Profess'l & related services
0.732	**	% Housing in multi-units
0.696	**	% HH's w/air conditioning
0.689	**	% Public administration
		Bottom twenty negative clusters
−0.522	**	% Craftsmen & foremen
−0.526	**	% Housing in single units
−0.534	**	% Pop. aged 0–5 yrs
−0.582	**	% Home values $20–30K
−0.585	**	% Vacant of housing units
−0.612	**	% Farmers & farm managers
−0.613	**	% HH's w/< $6K incomes
−0.631	**	% 6$^+$ Person households
−0.634	**	% Farm laborers
−0.640	**	% Nonmetro residents
−0.642	**	% Housing in mobile units
−0.689	**	% Construction
−0.700	**	% Operatives
−0.705	**	% HH's w/$6–14K incomes
−0.734	**	% Res. 5 yrs ago same house
−0.744	**	% Pop. 25$^+$ w/0–8 yrs school
−0.793	**	% Nonfarm laborers
−0.796	**	% Moved in over 20 years ago
−0.876	**	blue/white collar ratio
−0.894	**	% Home values < $20K

Source: *PRIZM, An Introduction* (New York: Claritas Corporation, 1982), p. 22.

[a] Significance indicator:
* Significant at 95% level.
**Significant at 99% level.

Table 2.4 Profile of probable power tool buyer

Rank order correlation	Significance level[a]	Title
		Top twenty positive clusters
0.933	**	% HH's w/food freezer
0.908	**	% Housing in mobile units
0.903	**	% Farmers & farm managers
0.883	**	% Nonmetro residents
0.838	**	% Housing in single units
0.829	**	% Farm laborers
0.730	**	% Construction
0.685	**	% Pop. aged 14–17 yrs
0.677	**	% HH's in mountain
0.645	**	% HH's in West No. Central
0.554	**	% HH's in West So. Central
0.530	**	% Vacant of housing units
0.530	**	% Pop. aged 6–13 yrs
0.511	**	% Home values < $20K
0.472	**	% HH's w/3 or more cars
0.451	**	% HH's w/clothes dryer
0.440	**	% All other industries
0.425	**	% 6+ Person households
0.402	**	% HH's in East So. Central
0.373	*	% 4–5 Person households
		Bottom twenty negative clusters
−0.644	**	% Pop. Russian foreign stock
−0.655	**	% HH's in Middle Atlantic
−0.661	**	% Pop. Austrian foreign stock
−0.668	**	% Housing in 2–4 units
−0.702	**	% Pop. Hungarian foreign stock
−0.712	**	% Units renter occupied
−0.732	**	% Finance, insur. & business
−0.747	**	% Population of foreign stock
−0.753	**	% Pop. Polish foreign stock
−0.756	**	% Fems. age 14+ in labor force
−0.778	**	% Pop. Yiddish mother tongue
−0.783	**	% Pop. Italian foreign stock
−0.784	**	% Pop. Irish foreign stock
−0.785	**	% Pop. Italian mother tongue
−0.820	**	% Clerical workers
−0.859	**	% Central city residents
−0.883	**	% Pop. Cuban foreign stock
−0.888	**	% Housing in multi-units
−0.902	**	avg # HH's per zip
−0.932	**	% HH's w/public sewer

Source: *PRIZM, An Introduction* (New York: Claritas Corporation, 1982), p. 28.

[a] Significance indicator:
* Significant at 95% level.
**Significant at 99% level.

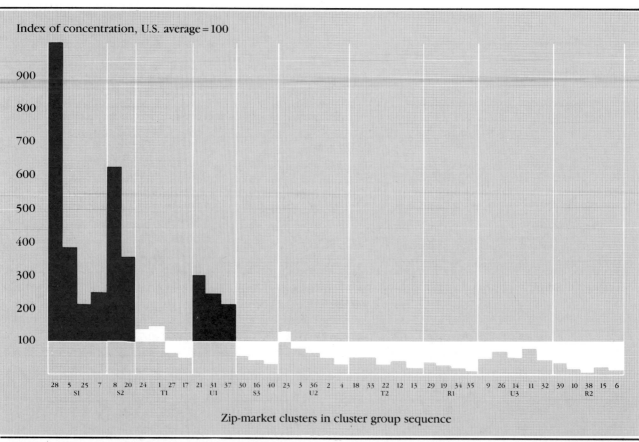

Index of concentration, U.S. average = 100

Zip-market clusters in cluster group sequence

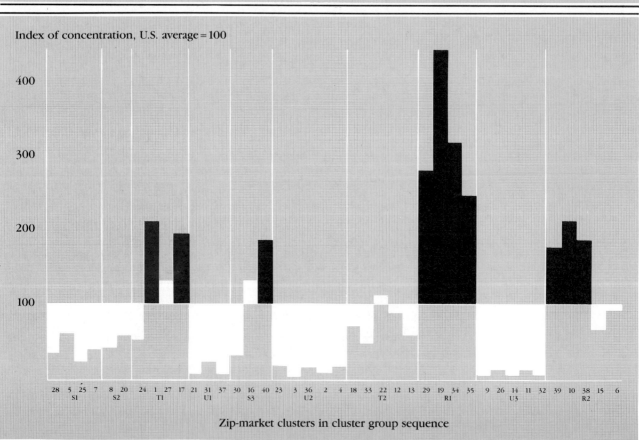

Index of concentration, U.S. average = 100

Zip-market clusters in cluster group sequence

Figure 2.4 (*opposite*)   *Indices of imported sports car purchasers* (*above*)
and power tool purchasers (*below*) *by zip cluster groups*

Based on responses to these items (a sample of such items is shown in Figure 2.5), consumer profiles are developed. The profiles are then correlated with product, brand, and media usage.

Just as demographics does a quantitative analysis of socioeconomic characteristics, so does psychographics provide a quantitative analysis of self-concept and life-style issues. The purpose of this analysis is to provide a more complete and human picture of the consumer for the manager. This verbal snapshot can be used in message strategy to give the writer more insight into the person being addressed and to provide character traits that the target market can better relate to in the commercial.

Unfortunately, psychographic research is quite expensive and is not amenable to cost-saving shortcuts. A battery of items can easily number up to 300, and a sample of 1,000 respondents may be necessary. Cutting the size of either of these lowers the reliability of an instrument that is already questioned by many researchers. The syndicated services such as SMRB have at times attempted to include psychographic variables but have dropped these measures at present. While the concept of psychographics is very appealing, the execution has been disappointing to many researchers. Many others feel that this area is the greatest thing since sliced bread, and they can show numerous examples of successful applications.

For example, compared to the light or nonuser of mouthwash, the female heavy user is more likely to agree to the following psychographic statements:

- I do not feel clean without a daily bath.
- Everyone should use a deodorant.
- A house should be dusted and polished at least three times a week.
- Odors in the house embarrass me.

Figure 2.5   *A sampling of items from a psychographic test*

I like to play poker.
I don't like to take chances.
I like sports cars.
I don't like to fly.
A woman should not smoke in public.
I have somewhat old-fashioned tastes and habits.
I often wish for the good old days.
Young people have too many privileges today.
If Americans were more religious, this would be a better country.
Spiritual values are more important than material things.
I often can talk others into doing something.
A party wouldn't be a party without liquor.
Liquor is a curse on American life.
There are day people and there are night people: I am a day person.
I am a girl watcher.
I like television news programs.
I like to pay cash for everything I buy.
We will probably move at least once in the next five years.
I expect to be a top executive in the next ten years.
I often try new brands before my friends and neighbors do.
Once I find a brand, I like to stick with it.

- The kind of dirt you can't see is worse than the kind you can see.
- Garbage should be put into a garbage bag before it is thrown out.
- I usually keep my house very neat and clean.
- I am a very neat person.
- I usually comb my hair and put on my lipstick first thing in the morning.
- I brush my hair at least twice a day.
- When my hair is clean and combed, I feel more alive.
- When my children are ill in bed, I drop most everything in order to see to their comfort.
- I use one or more household disinfectants.
- Dirty dishes should be washed promptly after each meal.
- It is very important for people to wash their hands before eating each meal.

The profile that emerges here led to Listerine's position in the mouthwash market and has allowed it to keep a dominant share of sales for a long period of time against the competing brands that promote "sex appeal" and "fresh breath." This dominance has continued even after the Federal Trade Commission ruled that Listerine didn't kill germs and forced Listerine to put disclaimers in their advertising. Listerine's strong taste and medicinal package appearance certainly promote their position effectively.[8]

A second example comes from the U.S. Army.[9] When the draft ended in 1972, the Army began to advertise heavily to recruit young adults. Its initial theme was that the Army was a big party with less discipline, no orders, and nice living conditions. Enlistment dropped.

A psychographic study showed that people who thought "the army is a good career for young men" were not party types but rather were conservative people who believed in discipline and were more likely to agree with the following statements than would people who did not think the army was a good career choice.

- We often display the American flag on national holidays.
- American made is best made.
- Communism is the greatest peril in the world today.
- I go to church regularly.
- If Americans were more religious this would be a better country.
- I like to work on community projects.
- I work for the Boy Scouts or other service organization on a fairly regular basis.
- I like to think I am a bit of a swinger (Disagreed).
- I like parties where there is lots of music and talk (Disagreed).
- There are day people and there are night people; I am a day person.
- I would rather spend a quiet evening at home than go out to a party.
- Today most people don't have enough discipline.
- Young people have too many privileges today.
- I work more than 45 hours a week.
- I consider myself a member of the silent majority.
- I have old-fashioned tastes and habits.
- Everything is changing too fast today.
- If I had my life to live over, I would sure do things differently.
- I like to go hunting.
- There should be a gun in every home.

The psychographic data show that the original position was not the best one and that a different one featuring hard work, discipline, and patriotism might be more appropriate. This change was made and enlistments rose. More recently, the campaign shifted to a personal benefit approach (learn a trade; earn money for college). As will be seen in the following pages, benefits are probably even more useful than psychographics. This is not meant to demean psychographics because they can be used in conjunction with a benefit analysis, and perhaps their greatest value is in conjunction with other variables to give additional insight to copywriters.

The enduring variables described above are useful to advertisers in terms of describing key market segments. In later sections this information will be integrated into media, message, and promotions strategies.

Dynamic segmentation variables

These variables are felt to be dynamic because they change with every product class. That is, they are specific to the individual's relation to the product and are not necessarily constant across products. Variables such as level of knowledge, desired benefit, and amount of usage define a precise product-consumer relation and provide specific insights for the advertiser. Where enduring variables provide information that primarily aids in describing the consumer (useful for media vehicle selection), the dynamic variables are more likely to show the advertiser what message and positioning strategies will be most appropriate.

Heavy versus light users   For many products 20% of the users consume 80% of the product. This 80/20 rule holds true across a large number of product classes. Who are these people? Do they differ on demographic or psychographic dimensions that allow the manager to make media decisions? Often heavy users will read related special interest magazines. What are these magazines? Why do these people consume so heavily? What should be said to them?

Several years ago Schaeffer Beer had a fantastic slogan for heavy users. "The one beer to have when you're having more than one." This line pulls no punches. If you're drinking only one, it doesn't matter what you drink, but Schaeffer would like your business if you drink more than one at a time. And heavy drinkers don't stop at one. Or two. Or three.

Miller Lite Beer also aims at this market. Its product is less filling. That means you can drink more at a sitting. That's important to the manufacturer. Heavy drinkers are less concerned with saving calories, so this issue is dealt with to a lesser degree.

Early versus late adopters   Time of adoption of a new product seems to differ on a number of variables that tie to demographics. If consumers differ on demographics (and they probably also differ on psychographics), then message strategies should also differ at different points in the introduction of a new product in order to capture these differences. Early adopters tend to be younger, more venturesome, more cosmopolitan, better educated, and have higher income and greater social mobility than later adopters. In this sense, time of adoption is an enduring variable. Although the specific group of people who adopt early seems to vary by product, their characteristics are remarkably stable. Later

Figure 2.6 *Loyalty and usage levels*

	HEAVY USERS	LIGHT USERS
LOYAL TO US	Reminder advertising	Campaign to increase usage
SWITCHERS	Bulk of budget spent here	Campaign to increase usage
LOYAL TO THEM	Not a good investment	Not a good investment

adopters are much more deliberate in their decision making, more skeptical about new ideas, and have lower levels of education and income.[10]

End use of the product   This is also useful as input to message strategy. For what purpose is the product purchased? Do heavy users use the product differently than do light users? Northwest Fabrics sells materials for sewing and crafts and has identified heavy sewers on a number of dimensions. What is important to them is that heavy sewers use fabrics in much more creative ways than light sewers. As a result the chain now calls itself "The More Ideas Store" to reflect the fact that they can help the (heavy) sewer develop creative new ideas. Television commercials also have reflected this by showing an ever-changing melange of ideas in each 30-second *(:30)* commercial.

Brand-loyal versus brand-switching users   These two groups need to be communicated to in different ways. Loyal users need only be reminded to remain loyal. Those loyal to a different brand are probably not worth pursuing; they will be too hard to capture and the dollars can be better invested in wooing switchers. *Brand switchers* are the best target and provide the best payoff for investments in advertising and promotions. Among switchers, those that are also *heavy users* need the most attention. Survey research should try to identify these consumers and then describe them based on enduring variables as well as needs and benefits sought. Figure 2.6 shows six combinations of loyalty and usage level.

Benefit segmentation   Many of the above issues are really a result of preferences based on product benefits. What do people want from a brand? What are their needs? What benefits are important to them? Haley,[11] in a classic marketing article, presented *benefit segmentation* as the ultimate segmentation device. He showed that the best way to break apart a market is based on the needs and desires of the consumers.

In his paper Haley used toothpaste as an example. Table 2.5 shows the segments he derived based on benefits. The benefits were flavor and appearance of the product, brightness of teeth, decay prevention, and price. He went on to show that a single firm could produce noncompeting brands to deliver each benefit. To do so successfully, though, would require different moods to be developed in the copy and different media to be used to deliver the messages.

In a second article, Haley hypothesized message and media strategy for his four segments.[12] For the social and sensory segments, he recommended a light

Table 2.5 Toothpaste market segment descriptions

Segment name	The sensory segment	The sociables	The worriers	The independent segment
Principal benefit sought	Flavor, product appearance	Brightness of teeth	Decay prevention	Price
Demographic strengths	Children	Teens, young people	Large families	Men
Special behavioral characteristics	Users of spearmint-flavored toothpaste	Smokers	Heavy users	Heavy users
Brands disproportionately favored	Colgate, Stripe	Macleans, Plus White, Ultra Brite	Crest	Brands on sale
Personality characteristics	High self-involvement	High sociability	High hypochondriasis	High autonomy
Lifestyle characteristics	Hedonistic	Active	Conservative	Value-oriented

Source: Russell I. Haley, "Benefit Segmentation," *Journal of Marketing,* July 1968, p. 33.

and superficial tone for short, highly visual messages to be delivered primarily on television; for the worrier and independent segments, he recommended a more serious and intensive tone for longer, more verbal messages to be delivered primarily via print vehicles. His point here was that it is not enough merely to stress the different benefits, but it is also necessary to use different message formats and tones. Figure 2.7 shows two toothpaste print ads that might have been developed based on Haley's recommendations.

Figure 2.7 *Examples of messages derived from benefit segmentation*

Haley's important work is a key to modern segmentation strategy. Many major manufacturers have a brand for each major segment in the market, and each brand can take share from competitors' brands without greatly cannibalizing from the manufacturers' own other brands. Individual brands can speak to different segments of a market by discussing different benefits or different values of the same benefit.

Stage of the hierarchy of effects   Clearly, different messages are needed to talk to consumers who are unaware as opposed to those who are already brand-loyal repeat users. The CAPP model (*Continuous Advertising Planning Program*) was developed for General Motors by John C. Maloney to provide input to appropriate message strategy by pointing out problems in moving consumers through the hierarchy. If a manager assumes high involvement (as General Motors would assume), then the outline of CAPP in Figure 2.8 would be appropriate. After collecting survey research data, the firm might discover a profile such as that shown in Figure 2.8(a). It would interpret this to mean that advertising had done a good job of creating awareness but that few people moved beyond that point. Of those who had, almost all tried and liked the product (since they were repeat users). In Figure 2.8(a), a strategy is needed to develop favorable attitudes and trial because the largest segment in the market has high awareness with weak attitudes.

A very different situation exists in Figure 2.8(b). Here awareness is high, and at one time attitudes and trial behavior were also high. Because repeat purchase behavior is low, the product may be poor. Advertising has created high awareness

Figure 2.8   *Continuous advertising planning program (CAPP) model*

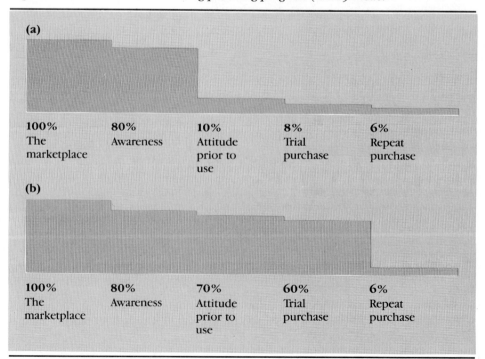

(a)				
100% The marketplace	80% Awareness	10% Attitude prior to use	8% Trial purchase	6% Repeat purchase

(b)				
100% The marketplace	80% Awareness	70% Attitude prior to use	60% Trial purchase	6% Repeat purchase

and contributed to favorable attitudes, and promotions have moved consumers to trial behavior, but repeat behavior did not occur because of a weak product. An alternative explanation is that the advertising oversold the product and led to disappointment.

Maloney's CAPP model can help the manager collect useful segmentation data based on the hierarchy of effects. The appropriate hierarchy should be chosen based on involvement of the target market with the product class. This type of segmentation is necessary for the development of advertising strategy.

For each of the dynamic segmentation variables, it is possible to isolate one or more key groups of consumers. These variables help determine segments based on perceptions and preferences of products and brands, key attributes and benefits, and levels of awareness, attitude, and behavior. Much of the data necessary for assessing these variables is collected using multiattribute attitude models and multidimensional scaling models. These models will be discussed in the next chapter.

After determining these segments, they can be more fully described based on the enduring variables discussed earlier. Based on the dynamic and enduring variables, media and message strategies can be developed.

Haley[13] has also shown that attention, awareness, attitude, and interest all shift more when

1. The message stresses a *relevant benefit*
2. The message is shown to the *proper audience*

Since people screen out most advertising through active or passive perceptual defense mechanisms, it is important to segment appropriately. Therefore, the message must use appropriate media so that a passive consumer is reached (at the lowest cost), and it must use appropriate message strategy to make an impact.

The above discussion has reviewed many of the key enduring and dynamic variables that are used to describe consumers and determine target markets. The remainder of this chapter looks at common strategies of segmentation that have evolved with relevance to advertising and promotions; the chapter concludes with an example of what happens to a product class when segmentation strategies appear.

Common segmentation strategies   Kotler[14] suggests four common strategies that may emerge from a situation analysis:

1. *Undifferentiated strategy*   This is truly mass marketing. At one time Coca-Cola sold one product in one size to all consumers. Figure 2.9 is an example of their advertising at that time. The media plan for such a strategy would be broad and would employ many vehicles to try to reach everyone; the message strategy would probably be bland so as not to offend anyone. Such a segmentation strategy is rarely found today.

2. *Wholly differentiated strategy*   In this case the firm still aims at the entire population but does so either with a variety of products and messages or by tailoring messages without changing products. The current strategies of Coca-Cola are in this arena. There is Classic Coke, New Coke, Cherry Coke, Decaffeinated

Figure 2.9   *Undifferentiated marketing for Coca-Cola*

Figure 2.10   *Example of early Volkswagen advertising-concentrated strategy*

Coke and Diet Coke; each comes in a variety of sizes and containers. Advertising strategies vary for each product and also vary for different targets within the product. Both media and message strategies would be specific and tailored to reach a specific audience.

The strategies of the Swedish government to change driving handedness (discussed earlier in this chapter) would fall somewhere between undifferentiated and wholly differentiated. There was one product for all citizens but there were many message and media strategies to ensure that everyone was reached and understood the issues.

3. *Concentrated strategy*   The firm has one product (as in the undifferentiated strategy) but markets this product to only one segment of the market (which differs from the undifferentiated segment). When Volkswagen first began to sell automobiles in this country in the late 1940s, there was only one product and one target market. Figure 2.10 shows some examples of their early advertising. In their first year in the United States, one Volkswagen was sold.

4. *Partially differentiated strategy*   Over time Volkswagen developed new products and aimed at new markets, but they never covered the whole automobile market. In fact, they still do not cover the whole automobile market. They have specific messages and specific media to get at the several specific targets for their several specific products. Figure 2.11 shows current advertising to support their partially differentiated strategy.

Figure 2.11 *Example of current Volkswagen advertising—partially differentiated strategy*

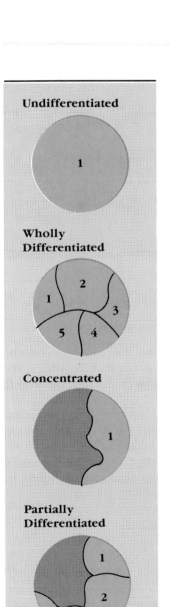

Figure 2.12 *Four segmentation strategies*

Figure 2.12 graphically shows the four segmentation strategies just discussed. The last two are most commonly used by major manufacturers.

The specific and broad media and message strategies discussed here are more commonly referred to as rifle and shotgun approaches. A *rifle strategy* aims a message at a very specific segment. Such a *media* strategy would encourage the use of direct mail, special interest magazines, or specific radio formats; these vehicles reach very specific segments of the market. A rifle *message* strategy would be very specific in its statements, benefits, and advocated position as shown by the example in Figure 2.13. When done well, the rifle approach is superior because it gets the right audience with the least wasted coverage of people not in the target market and says exactly what consumers need to see or hear. The disadvantage is that if the situation analysis is faulty, the wrong message will go to the wrong people. This is therefore a higher risk and higher potential payoff strategy.

A *shotgun strategy* tries for a broader reach or a broader message. A shotgun *media* strategy would use television, general interest magazines, and newspapers because these media generally attract broad ranges of consumers. A shotgun *message* strategy would use a broader, not-too-specific message that would not upset anyone; an example can be seen in Figure 2.14. Such strategies are less risky because they are more certain to cover the relevant segment. Unfortunately, they are also expensive and potentially inefficient. Their value is for products with a fairly broad reach where the high expense can be justified.

In combining media and message, a popular feeling is that *shotgun media* and *rifle message* strategies should be combined. This ensures that the relevant target market will be reached (a wide-reaching shotgun vehicle will get the message to the target but will cost more because nontargeted people are also reached) and that the message will be appropriate. The specific rifle message will be absorbed by the target and will be ignored by those who find it irrelevant.

Good news for the difficult-to-fit, difficult-to-please set: We're introducing a striking new line of young junior jeans. Jeans specifically designed to fit the fashion conscious 10 to 13-year-old who's "too old" for youth wear—and not quite ready for juniors. Come see them at our New York showroom, 131 W. 33rd St., 17th floor. Phone: 212-695-5571. Or at any of the regional markets. We've got the young junior figure figured.

Wilkins Young Junior Rumble Seats

Figure 2.13 *Example of rifle message strategy*

Figure 2.14 *Example of shotgun message strategy*

An example of segmentation strategy's impact on a market

This discussion ends with an example of what happens in a market when segmentation strategies are encountered. This example could occur in virtually any product class; as public sector and nonprofit organizations compete more intensely, the example could occur there also.

Assume a chocolate cake mix market with annual sales of 6 million units. These sales are distributed across six brands, A through F, so that A and B each have sales of 2 million units and C, D, E, and F each have annual sales of 0.5 million units as shown in column 1 of Table 2.6. The characteristics of consumers are such that the users of 1 million units prefer dark chocolate cake, the users of 1 million units like light chocolate cake, and the remaining 4 million units are purchased by consumers who prefer an average amount of chocolate. Figure 2.15 shows a distribution of these users.

At first all firms produce and market the same average chocolate cake mix product aimed at a mass market. This is *undifferentiated segmentation.* For some unknown reason (perhaps they have been around longer), A and B do this best.

Brand C does a situation analysis and learns that a sizeable segment of the market likes dark chocolate cake and that the consumers in this segment would buy such a mix if it were on the market. Having done this *benefit segmentation* analysis, Brand C decides to *reposition* itself in order to find a unique niche. So, C reformulates its brand and begins to advertise "New Improved C with 27% more dark chocolate." C has adopted a single segment strategy of *concentrated seg-*

Table 2.6 Data pertaining to hypothetical chocolate cake mix market

Brand	(1) Original sales (million units)	(2) Sales after new brand C (million units)	(3) Sales after new brand L (million units)	(4) Sales after new brand R (million units)
A	2.00	1.80	1.43	1.33
B	2.00	1.80	1.43	1.33
C	0.50	1.00	(C + L) 2.00	(C + L + R) 2.33
D	0.50	0.47	0.38	0.33
E	0.50	0.47	0.38	2.33
F	0.50	0.47	0.38	0.33
Total	6.00	6.00	6.00	6.00

mentation; since all other brands are average chocolate, C gains this entire segment of the market and loses consumers who do not want dark chocolate. Column 2 of Table 2.6 shows the new market shares.

C finds this strategy to be so successful that it now introduces Brand L, which is aimed at the light chocolate market, and, because this new product is advertised as well, the firm gains another million units of sales. This is now a *partially differentiated segmentation* strategy and leads to sales levels as shown in column 3.

Then C might get greedy and try for a piece of the regular chocolate market also. Management introduces Brand R that only gets 0.3 million incremental units of sales owing to stiff competition. For better or worse, the firm now is employing a *wholly differentiated segmentation* strategy. Annual sales are now up to 2.3 million units, but it is not clear from the limited data if the marginal sales exceed the marginal expense of acquiring them. Before introducing Brand R, management should assess the feasibility of success given the intense level of competition in the regular chocolate segment.

Of course, in the real world things rarely work this well. Competitors rarely sit around and watch while their sales erode. They, too, would develop alternative flavors of cake mix, and the market would become fragmented with many

Figure 2.15 *Distribution of preferences in hypothetical chocolate cake mix market*

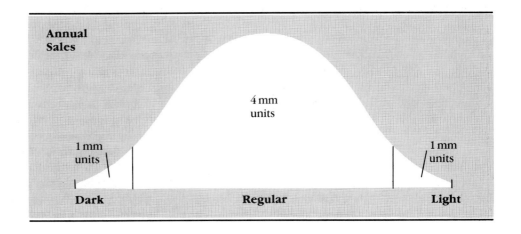

T·H·E   I·N·S·I·D·E   O·U·T·L·O·O·K

Bob Drane

**Vice-President, Marketing Research and Planning,
Oscar Mayer Foods Corporation**

*Bob Drane is a Phi Beta Kappa graduate of Lake Forest College
and the University of Wisconsin, with degrees in English Literature. His work experience includes IBM, The Quaker Oats Co.,
and Oscar Mayer Foods where he is currently Vice-President,
Marketing Research & Planning. He has taught marketing
courses in the University of Iowa Graduate School of Business
and is presently a visiting lecturer at the University of
Wisconsin.*

Dealing With the Return on Investment (ROI) Question

Marketers and their agencies today are confronted by two facts that are shaking the founda-
tions of the advertising industry. The first fact is
that the cost of delivering advertising messages
to target customers is rising more rapidly than
the sales revenue of most companies. The second is that a growing number of in-market sales
tests (e.g., split cable experiments run by BehaviorScan and Ad-Tel) are showing that volume for
many products remains unchanged when advertising levels are doubled or halved.

Taken together, these two facts are forcing
executives charged with bottom line profit responsibility to ask a simple question: "Am I
really getting a decent ROI on my advertising?"

While such a question sends shivers down the
spines of marketing and agency advocates alike,
it's probably the exact spark required to begin
to restore advertising's shaken credibility.

Where the executive's "ROI question" takes
the marketer and his agency is back to their
fundamental challenge: to find and communicate
behavior-modifying messages about their product.

And once this issue of "what's the right message" (rather than "how much to spend") is center stage, the spotlight will inevitably come to
rest where it belongs: on better understanding
and articulating target customer needs.

Here is where the information gatherers in
the organization try (and often fail) to earn their
keep.

What is required of them is a massive data integration exercise that ends with a well-thought-
out profile of potential customer targets and a
set of hypotheses about what it would take to
win each over to the core franchise. In schematic form this might look as follows:

This is the stuff that sharpens strategies and
helps to produce famous advertising messages. It
is also the stuff that is all too often missing in action when campaigns are formulated.

Potential Target	Present Relation to Brand	% HH	Conversion Barriers	Potential Solutions
Untouched	No name recognition No defined image			
Unconvinced	Image but no trial			
Partially in	Light loyals/ switchers			
Core franchise	Heavy loyals			
Rejectors	Negative trial			

Nearly a century ago Mark Twain remarked: "If all the folks who had nothing useful to say stopped saying it, mankind would be well served." He must have been gazing ahead to modern prime time.

Over the next decade as the cost of advertising continues to spiral and its actual impact on volume is revealed through improved measurement, more executives will announce the "ROI question" with more vigor.

The result will either be sharp cutbacks in the use of advertising or a leap ahead in our understanding of customer needs and our ability to produce behavior-modifying messages that pay out at the bottom line.

brands and flavors. This is, in fact, what has happened in many product classes in the past 20 to 30 years. The key to the marketplace changes have evolved from segmentation and the situation analysis that show market potential.

> In the communications jungle out there, the only hope to score big is to be selective, to concentrate on narrow targets, to practice segmentation.[15]

In the hypothetical chocolate cake mix market the situation analysis revealed a need and an opportunity for a new product, which was developed. It was successfully introduced because the situation analysis yielded insight as to advertising and promotions strategy. The target was defined in terms of usage level, current satisfactions (and resulting brand loyalty), knowledge of the product class, and, of course, the benefit sought. The desired target was further described based on geographic, demographic, and psychographic variables. Finally media, message, and promotions strategies evolved.

Summary

It is important to be able to describe the consumer on a number of dimensions for the purpose of developing advertising and promotions strategies. Segmentation is very useful to this end because it helps classify consumers in terms of enduring and dynamic variables. The enduring variables are most insightful for media planning and efficient message delivery systems; the dynamic variables are more likely to be used in the development of positioning strategies and message content. Both classes of variables give the writers and artists, as well as the managers, a clearer picture of the relevant subsets of the market.

Discussion Questions

1. Why is it important to do a thorough situation analysis?

2. What are the major topics to be covered in the situation analysis?

3. Why segment a market?

4. What are enduring and dynamic segmentation variables? Give examples of issues covered in each class of these variables. For what types of strategies does each class of variables provide input?

5. Describe PRIZM. What is its value to marketing communications?

6. What does psychographics describe? What is its value to advertising?

7. If 80% of a product is purchased by 20% of the target market, should you pursue the 20% who are heavy users or the other 80% who may have potential? How would you decide?

8. What are several benefit segments for furniture buyers? Describe possible consumers in each segment as well as potential media and message strategies for each.

9. Why is it useful to segment based on stage of the hierarchy of effects? How would such a classification affect media, message, and promotions strategies?

10. Describe shotgun and rifle differences in media and message strategies.

11. Soon you will be leaving your studies and looking for a job that meets your career goals. It is obvious that you can't pursue all the openings or all the

firms in your field. How will you segment the population of firms that you could pursue? Begin your situation analysis by describing the types of firms that interest you. Consider both enduring and dynamic variables.

Notes

1. Claude Hopkins, *Scientific Advertising* (Chicago: Advertising Publications, 1966). Originally published in 1923.

2. Claude Hopkins, *My Life in Advertising* (Chicago: Advertising Publications, 1966). Originally published in 1927.

3. Abraham Maslow, *Motivation and Personality* (New York: Harper & Row, 1954).

4. Curt Schleier, "The Baby Business: Can You Succeed in a Failing Market," *Product Management* (April 1977), pp. 29–34.

5. Joel Garreau, *The Nine Nations of North America* (Boston: Houghton Mifflin, 1981).

6. "Changing Lifestyles, Changing Media," *Marketing and Media Decisions* (August 1982), p. 62.

7. *PRIZM, An Introduction* (New York: Claritas Corporation, 1982).

8. William L. Wilkie, Dennis L. McNeill, and Michael B. Mazis, "Marketing's Scarlet Letter: The Theory and Practice of Corrective Advertising," *Journal of Marketing* (Spring 1984), pp. 11–31.

9. William D. Wells, *Life Style and Psychographics* (Chicago: American Marketing Association, 1974).

10. E. M. Rogers and F. Floyd Shoemaker, *Communication of Innovations: A Cross Cultural Approach* (New York: The Free Press, 1971).

11. Russell I. Haley, "Benefit Segmentation: A Decision-Oriented Research Tool," *Journal of Marketing,* 32 (July 1968), pp. 30–35.

12. Russell I. Haley, "Benefit Segmentation," *Journal of Marketing* (July 1968), p. 33.

13. Haley, "Benefit Segmentation," pp. 30–35.

14. Philip Kotler, *Marketing Management* (Englewood Cliffs, N.J.: Prentice-Hall, 1984).

15. Jack Trout and Al Ries, *Positioning: The Battle For Your Mind,* 2nd ed. (New York: Warner, 1982).

Chapter 3
Consumer Perceptions and Processes

Marketing communications works in an environment with many other distracting stimuli. In order to ensure that a product has an impact, the manager who deals with advertising and promotions must have a sense of how consumers process information, make decisions, and evaluate alternatives. This chapter considers these issues as they relate to marketing communications.

The first half of the chapter explores processes of acquiring awareness and attitudes with an emphasis on whether or not the consumer cares much about the brand choice decisions that need to be made. Promotional strategies will differ greatly depending on how much consumers care, and, therefore, the evaluation of consumer involvement is a key issue in the situation analysis.

The second half of this chapter examines ways to evaluate consumer perceptions of the product and the various competitors in the product class. Message strategy and positioning are built on the objective of influencing attitudes and perceptions; therefore, the situation analysis must evaluate these areas. The techniques described here consider what is important to consumers in making decisions, how well or poorly the various brands are perceived to perform, and the relative images of the competing brands. The chapter also introduces some strategies that emerge from these evaluations.

Consumer Information Processing

The consumer life cycle

Just as products go through a series of stages, so do consumers. One of the most complete expositions of this concept comes from Howard;[1] it shows how consumers can be described in relation to products. For any product, the consumer goes through a series of stages of information processing and decision making that are described here. Howard calls these

EPS—extended problem solving
LPS—limited problem solving
RRB—routinized response behavior

These stages are similar to those needed to deal with the three levels of innovation suggested by Rogers (discontinuous, dynamically continuous, and continuous innovations) and to those needed to deal with situations eliciting high and low levels of involvement. (Diffusion of innovation and involvement are discussed later in this chapter.)

Consumers may enter EPS and proceed to LPS and RRB because a new product class has appeared on the market or because they are dealing with a product class for the first time. An example of the latter would occur for a couple about to have their first child; these people may have never dealt with baby products before and now must begin to learn about a whole new set of products.

In the case of the new product class, consumers will proceed through stages as the product progresses through the product life cycle (described in Chapter 4). As can be seen in Figure 3.1 *most* consumers are in EPS during the product's introduction, LPS during its growth, and RRB during its maturity. During the introduction, consumers are concerned with what Howard calls *concept formation,* that is, they are becoming acquainted with the new attributes and concepts of the new product. During growth, consumers use these concepts to evaluate alternative brands; Howard calls this *concept attainment.* Finally, in maturity consumers go through *concept utilization* where they make routine decisions with very little cognitive effort.

Each stage requires different types of information processing, and, therefore, each stage requires different types of advertising messages to match the most effective processing style. Table 3.1 shows some differences resulting from processing style. While these processing stages clearly exist, not all consumers go

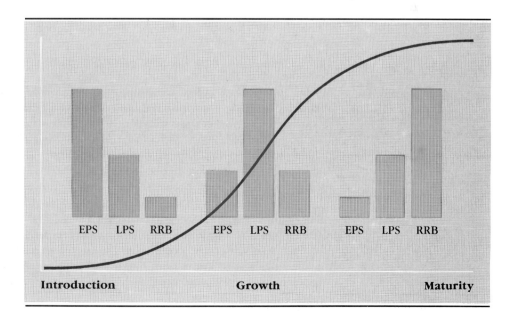

Figure 3.1   Consumer life cycle and product life cycle

Table 3.1 Some characteristics of consumer life cycle stages

Stage	Relevant information in long-term memory	Amount of information	Speed of decision	Locus of search	Concept development
EPS	Little	Lots	Slow	External	Concept formation
LPS	Moderate	Moderate	Moderate	Mixed	Concept attainment
RRB	Lots	Little	Fast	Internal	Concept utilization

Source: From *Consumer Behavior: Application of Theory* by John A. Howard, 1977, p. 13. Reprinted with permission of McGraw-Hill Book Company.

through all stages for all products. The stages are meant to be useful descriptors to aid the manager in intuitively assessing the information needs of consumers.

In EPS the consumer is unfamiliar with even the concept of the product and needs large amounts of information. The information will be sought externally; because the concepts are new, existing memory structure will provide little help. For this reason, too, the decision will be made slowly and carefully. These conditions can best be met by print ads with considerable explanatory copy and with a message approach that tries to tie the new product to existing concepts. (These strategies are relevant to EPS but may be added to or changed when other aspects of the situation analysis are also considered.)

After learning the concepts, the consumer can evaluate and compare brands. In LPS a fair amount of knowledge is available to draw upon, at least in terms of the product class. Brand information is needed; some of this will come from memory, and some from external messages. Many combinations of broadcast or print would be appropriate because either type could present the moderate amount of information needed. LPS would probably be the appropriate level of processing when encountering a new brand with minor changes in an existing product class. Most new brands are of this variety and need to present messages sufficient to allow LPS processing.

Having made a few purchases in the product class, the consumer enters RRB. Now past experiences are sufficient so that external search is really unnecessary. Because the consumer will not be actively seeking information, the marketer must provide messages for passive receipt; these can best be sent using television. Since little information is needed, short repetitive messages are sufficient. RRB would probably be appropriate for a new brand that offers virtually no change from existing brands in the product class, although it would take a few moments of LPS processing to recognize that RRB would be sufficient. The strategies suggested here are expanded upon in the involvement discussion that follows.

The consumer life cycle is an important part of the situation analysis. The manager needs to know how much and what types of information to give consumers. Research should consider where consumers are in terms of their information processing life cycle.

Involvement

This concept was introduced earlier as one of the key threads running through this text. It basically concerns the issue of whether or not consumers care very much about brand choice decisions when purchasing a product. As will be seen, this level of caring or motivation will affect information-processing and decision-making styles. Management assessment of the level of involvement is important so that appropriate advertising and promotions strategies can be developed.

Many definitions of involvement have been put forth in the social psychology and marketing literatures over the past 50 (or so) years. Two of these are especially germane to our purposes. Festinger[2] has defined involvement as "concern with the issue itself," while Freedman[3] defines it as "commitment to a position or concern with a specific stand on an issue."

It would seem that Festinger has defined low involvement, a situation where consumers need to use a product (and therefore have a positive attitude or concern with the issue/product) but do not need to use any particular brand (and therefore do not have a positive attitude or concern with a position or need to take a stand). For example, there are certain societal norms concerning tolerable body odors. People purchase soap in response to these (and other) norms, but the norms don't specify any desired brand choice behavior. While consumers have a commitment toward the product class of soap, they may have no commitment toward a brand and, therefore, may show low involvement. Products for which consumers are more likely to use low-involvement processes are generally low-priced, frequently purchased convenience goods where the available choices are seen to be similar and the cost of a poor decision is low.

A second example concerns the act of voting. People have been taught that they have a civic duty to vote and that the right to vote is a sacred trust. The League of Women Voters urges citizens with a musical jingle, "Don't Forget to Vote." Again, while the issue of voting is stressed, the issue of a particular position is not—the League of Women Voters doesn't say, "Don't Forget to *Think Before You* Vote." Voters will undoubtedly have low involvement in many electoral races. A person may go to the voting booth to cast a carefully thought-out ballot for a Senatorial candidate but may also vote for school board officers without having given the candidates much prior thought.

Freedman's definition describes high involvement. A highly involved consumer carefully selects a brand for some reason: price, style, fuel efficiency, past experience, brand loyalty, etc. This person has a positive attitude toward the brand as well as the product class prior to purchase. Products that generally are more likely to receive high-involvement processing are durable goods, high-priced goods, goods that are unfamiliar to the consumer, infrequently purchased goods, or goods where the choices are dissimilar. If the cost of a poor decision is high, then consumers generally become more involved with that decision.

This concept of involvement leads to two orderings of the hierarchy of effects as shown in Figure 3.2. Note that the hierarchy has been expanded since the earlier discussion; it now includes two behavior cells: trial and repeat purchase. These are distinct types of behavior and require distinct advertising and promotions strategies.

Figure 3.2 shows the distinctions between high and low involvement. In high-involvement cases, attitude precedes trial behavior. This attitude connotes a specific stand and positive feelings toward both the product class and the brand. In low-involvement cases, trial behavior is felt to precede attitude. This indicates

Figure 3.2 *Two orderings of the hierarchy of effects*

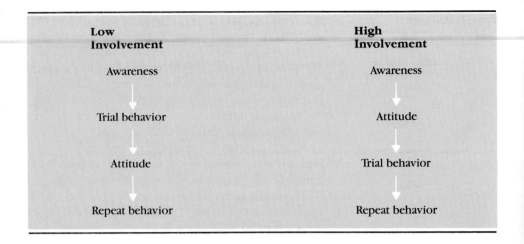

that positive feelings exist toward the product class (because behavior took place) without strong feelings toward the brand. If an attitude is formed, it is after product use rather than as a result of information evaluation.

The distinction being presented here is important for communications strategies. A highly involved consumer is more likely to *actively seek information* and to try to make an optimal decision regarding the product. In the low-involvement case, the consumer will not engage in much information search but rather will *passively receive information.* For this person, several brands may be acceptable, decision making may be satisfying, and behavior may appear to be random. As strategies are developed, the manager must carefully consider involvement. Consumers who are seen to be making thoughtful decisions should be given a different type of information in a different format than consumers who don't seem to care. Table 3.2 summarizes some differences between the high-involvement, active consumer and the low-involvement, passive consumer.

Strategies for high and low levels of involvement

The preceding discussion has dealt with conceptualizing the relation of involvement and information processing. Given a case where advertising and promotions may be called for, the manager must assess whether consumers care about gathering information and making optimizing decisions. This decision is a basic one for all of the strategy development that will follow. This part introduces many of the strategy issues that will be developed in later parts.[4] It will quickly become clear that the strategies for high- and low-involvement cases differ greatly and that a proper assessment of this construct is, therefore, crucial. The discussion of possible strategies will center on the hierarchy of effects model.

In *high-involvement cases* the following process has been hypothesized:

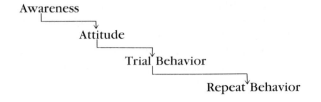

Table 3.2 The high-involvement, active consumer versus the low-involvement, passive consumer

Traditional, high-involvement view of an active consumer	Newer, low-involvement view of a passive consumer
1. Consumers are information processors.	1. Consumers learn information at random.
2. Consumers are information seekers.	2. Consumers are information gatherers.
3. Consumers represent an active audience for advertising. As a result, the effect of advertising on the consumer is *weak*.	3. Consumers represent a passive audience for advertising. As a result, the effect of advertising on the consumer is *strong*.
4. Consumers evaluate brands before buying.	4. Consumers buy first. If they do evaluate brands, it is done after the purchase.
5. Consumers seek to maximize expected satisfaction. As a result, consumers compare brands to see which provide the most *benefits* related to needs and buy based on multiattribute comparisons of brands.	5. Consumers seek some acceptable level of satisfaction. As a result, consumers buy the brand least likely to give them *problems* and buy based on a few attributes. Familiarity is the key.
6. Personality and life-style characteristics are related to consumer behavior because the product is closely tied to the consumer's identity and belief system.	6. Personality and life-style characteristics are not related to consumer behavior because the product is not closely tied to the consumer's identity and belief system.
7. Reference groups influence consumer behavior because of the importance of the product to group norms and values.	7. Reference groups exert little influence on product choice because products are unlikely to be related to group norms and values.

Source: From Henry Assael, *Consumer Behavior and Marketing Action,* 2d ed. (Boston: Kent Publishing Company, 1984) p. 93. © 1984 by Wadsworth, Inc. Reprinted by permission of Kent Publishing Company, a division of Wadsworth, Inc.

Consumers will be motivated to seek and evaluate information actively, and they will try to make an optimizing decision that leads to selection of the single best brand (for their needs) in the product class. Because they are concerned about the decision, consumers develop an attitude prior to behavior. As discussed earlier, products most likely to elicit high levels of involvement are high cost, infrequently purchased, complex, have dissimilar brand choice alternatives, relate to the consumer's central values, elicit feelings of risk, and are visible to others. (At least some subset of these will apply.) While it seems obvious that automobiles and stereos will elicit a highly involved response, it may be less obvious that a mother choosing a fluoride toothpaste (low cost, frequently purchased) for her children may also be highly involved with the decision (because the issue of health care is important). Over time, though, the toothpaste decision becomes routinized, an attitude is formed, and little new processing occurs until new brands become relevant.

Advertising will be the primary tool for generating *awareness* and knowledge. Because consumers are seeking information, messages can be longer and more informative than they would be in the low-involvement case; they will be delivered primarily through print media to allow the consumer to digest the information at a self-controlled pace. The messages do not need extremely high levels of repetition; when people are more interested they learn more rapidly. In high-involvement cases the role of advertising is limited to generating awareness and knowledge. Figure 3.3 is an example of an ad for a product that assumes high involvement; it is information oriented. (While print advertising is appropriate for delivering information, most high-involvement campaigns use broadcast extensively to develop basic brand name awareness and then use print to develop more extensive knowledge.)

Attitude development will need different tools. Advertising is a low-credibility source and has done its job by preparing the prospect for the more credible sources that follow. Higher credibility sources are the sales force and the product trial or demonstration. The latter two allow consumers to become their own source of information; learning can take place through personal observation. Promotional tools have value here because they can help bring the consumer to the retailer so that the demonstration can take place; promotions may not be powerful enough to elicit high-involvement purchase behavior but are useful in getting the consumer to look at the product. Figure 3.4 is an example of a promotion designed to get the consumer to the showroom. Other sources such as word-of-mouth and *Consumer Reports* are extremely valuable but are not discussed because they are not directly under the marketer's control.

Figure 3.3   *Example of an informative ad aimed at high-involvement audience*

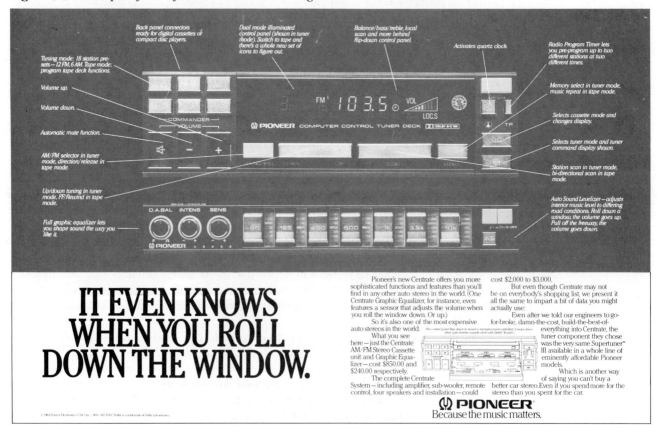

Figure 3.4 *A promotion designed to get the consumer to the retailer*

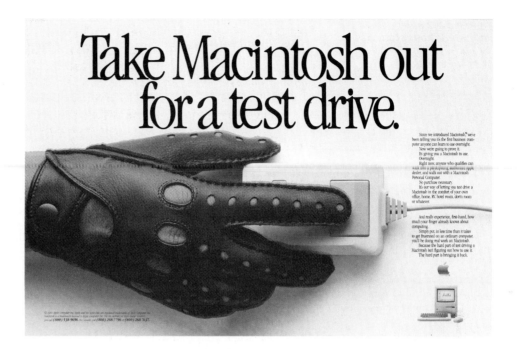

Trial behavior/initial purchase will be primarily a function of perceived product quality after careful evaluation of information. Price-oriented promotions are often used here, but these take a weak second place to the product attributes and benefits unless the price deal is quite extreme.

Long-run repeat behavior is also primarily a function of product quality. Related product issues such as warranty and service become important here.

The roles of advertising and promotion are important in high involvement but are limited to generating awareness and getting the consumer, retailer, and product together. Both of these classes of tools are cost-effective means of transmitting information and preparing the consumer for the next stage in the purchase process. Figure 3.5 summarizes the communication strategies appropriate to each level of the high-involvement hierarchy.

Low-involvement cases are quite different. Theoreticians speculate that in low-involvement cases consumers do not form what has traditionally been considered an attitude until after trial product use has taken place. For this reason the low-involvement hierarchy differs in that

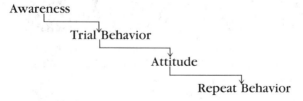

Consumers are typically not highly motivated to seek or process information and are quite happy to select any one of several acceptable brands in the product class. Trial behavior may appear to be whimsical or to be a response to some promotion. Repeat behavior results from a satisfactory trial and from the knowledge that brand loyalty allows the consumer to stop giving further consideration to the

Figure 3.5 Advertising and promotions strategies for each level of the hierarchy of effects

High-Involvement Cases	Low-Involvement Cases
Awareness	**Awareness**
Advertising	Advertising
Primarily print	Primarily broadcast
High information	Low information
Low repetition	High repetition
Longer messages	Shorter messages
Broadcast for basic awareness	Unique selling proposition
↓	↓
Attitude	**Trial behavior**
Personal selling	Advertising
Trial	Promotions to induce trial
Demonstration	Pricing promotions
Promotions to bring consumer to retailer	Packaging
	Point of purchase
↓	↓
Behavior	**Attitude**
Product	Product usage
Price	
Pricing promotions	
↓	↓
Long-run behavior	**Long-run behavior**
Product	Advertising
Warranty	Product
Service	Pricing promotions

product class. Consumers seek low involvement because there are too many trivial decisions to be made in life to get highly involved with each one. How should the manager respond to this situation?

As in the high-involvement case, advertising is the key *awareness* building tool. In low involvement, though, there are many differences in the characteristics of the advertising because consumers are not actively seeking information but rather are passively receiving it. As a result, messages are shorter and have less information. Low involvement implies that consumers learn more slowly and forget more rapidly, and this means that messages must be repeated more often. All of this also means that the messages should key on one (or two) important benefits (often referred to as the *unique selling proposition,* or *USP*). The USP should dominate the campaign, and all messages should stress it. (The USP is discussed in Part 4.) Since consumers are not actively seeking information, this continuity in messages is an aid to learning. Repetition can be further enhanced by repeating the USP within the message. Figure 3.6 is a storyboard for a Butterball turkey commercial. It is extremely single-minded and deals with the USP six times in 30 seconds.

Low involvement also calls for primarily broadcast media. Print media require the consumer to work for information; because consumers will not make

Figure 3.6 *Photoboard for Butterball commercial*

this effort for low-involvement items, broadcast is more appropriate. In broadcast no effort is required of the message recipient; the message just pours out and washes over the consumer. Learning takes place over time as repetitions build up and advertising continues through all stages of the hierarchy to inhibit forgetting. (Print advertising is used in low-involvement cases to deliver coupons but rarely to deliver information.)

Initial *trial purchase* behavior can take place as a result of in-store brand and benefit recognition but is more likely to occur because the consumer can take advantage of a promotion.

Promotions are important to trial behavior because they change the cost/ benefit perception of the brand. In high-involvement cases, price is merely one of many important attributes; in low-involvement cases there is often no single attribute that discriminates between brands, so price can become the overwhelm-

Figure 3.7 Example of advertising and promotions for a brand eliciting low involvement

ing attribute in decision making. Figure 3.7 shows an example of a new low-involvement brand attempting to elicit trial behavior.

Since up to 60% of low-involvement brand choice decisions are made at the purchase location, in-store communications are also important. These include the package and point-of-purchase displays. Both cases provide an opportunity to bring the USP to the point of decision making. To further aid recognition, the package can be shown in the advertising and a prominent scene from the advertising can appear on the package.

Attitude formation is a result of product usage. Advertising and promotions can often elicit a trial purchase of a low-involvement product without much consumer decision making, but attitude and *repeat purchase* are a function of the quality of the brand.

If the brand is acceptable, brand loyalty may result. Loyalty is a form of high involvement because it indicates that a stand has been taken; loyalty is also a convenient device that allows the consumer to avoid further processing for that product class. Advertising strategy here is to encourage loyalty to continue. Conversely, other brands are advertising and promoting to consumers to change their loyalties. This means that the firm will need to continue its own advertising and promotions.

The current high levels of promotion in many product classes may be serving to erode brand loyalty, enchance the value of price loyalty, and lower profits. It's a jungle out there. A strong position, shown through the USP, is a key factor in combating competitive promotions encroachment.

In an interesting experiment, consumers were shown differing amounts of advertising for fictitious brands of detergents and then asked for their feelings toward the brands. When their only cue was advertising, the respondents liked best the brand they had seen most often. Then they were given product samples to use at home. When they were retested, their feelings reflected the quality of the sample rather than the amount of advertising. Again, in the low-involvement case trial behavior can be elicited by advertising (and promotions), but repeat behavior and attitudes will be a result of product quality.

There are, as shown in Figure 3.5, clear differences in the advertising and promotions strategies for high- and low-involvement cases. Again, the importance of assessing involvement in the situation analysis should be apparent.

Changing involvement from low to high

Several other general strategy issues related to involvement can be introduced here and will be useful to consider in the later strategy development sections. A low-involvement strategy different from those described above is to *raise consumer involvement to a higher level.* If this strategy were successful, it would mean that consumers would find fewer brands to be acceptable. In addition, consumers would be more active in their pursuit and evaluation of information and less likely to receive information passively without putting up perceptual defenses. This means that competitive advertising and promotions would have less of the subtle effect associated with passive learning situations.

In order to achieve a higher level of involvement, the brand would need to be linked to some salient and central issue in consumers' lives. For example, cigarettes with low tar and nicotine link themselves to health issues; this heightens involvement and leads to advertising with longer copy. Figure 3.8 displays two cigarette ads. Kent shows a low-information strategy that avoids health issues, while True represents a high-involvement, high-information strategy. Crest also used this strategy of raising involvement when it introduced fluoride toothpaste

Figure 3.8 *High- and low-involvement strategies in the same product class*

in 1960 and, at the same time, made toothpaste a high-involvement product for at least one benefit segment.

It is not always necessary to initiate this strategy; sometimes involvement is changed by some environmental force and responding strategies naturally evolve. For example, consumer advocate Ralph Nader attacked the hot dog industry during the 1970s for using non-nutritional filler ingredients. Oscar Mayer responded with a television spot that showed all the ingredients in their hot dogs. After Nader had tried to raise consumers' involvement toward hot dogs, Oscar Mayer produced a commercial that would help those consumers with high involvement learn more about the brand.

Low involvement for high-involvement products

A different involvement problem occurs in durable goods cases. Here most consumers have high involvement at the time of purchase but do not devote much cognitive effort to the product at other times. For example, if the life of a washing machine is about ten years, then a consumer is motivated to search for and process information for a month or so when the old machine is suffering from a terminal illness and a purchase is imminent. During the next nine years and eleven months, most consumers will rarely seek information regarding this product. The great majority of consumers have low involvement during the great majority of the time, yet there are always a small number of consumers at any time who are buying and therefore are highly involved.

The marketer needs to talk to both groups all the time. Those with low involvement need to be addressed so that the brand stays in their minds to be remembered as a viable alternative when the active search and processing begins. Those with high involvement need to be addressed because they are making their only purchase in a ten-year period; if the firm misses them now, it will be a long time until the next chance comes.

As seen earlier, short, repetitive broadcast messages are most applicable for consumers with low involvement, but longer less-repetitive print messages are appropriate for high involvement. What to do? Clearly the firm must go after both groups. What percentage of the budget goes toward each segment? How should the two campaigns be tied together? These are interesting questions for the reader to ponder. Perhaps they will become easier to deal with after continuing for a few hundred more pages.

Further views of involvement

An interesting extension of the involvement materials comes from Richard Vaughn of Foote, Cone & Belding Communications, Inc.[5] He has added another dimension to the involvement model, as is shown in Figure 3.9. Here consumers have high or low involvement but also engage in thinking or feeling types of processing at each involvement level.

This model has minor inconsistencies with the earlier involvement discussion but adds some interesting ideas, especially for message strategy. Clearly, messages for jewelry and cars should differ; one is a much more emotional decision than the other. While messages differ across products, they can also differ across subcategories and brands; a station wagon message is probably less emotional than a

Thinking ────────────────────▶ Feeling	

1 Informative (thinker)
car house furnishings
new products
 	
Model: Learn-feel-do
              (economic?)
 	
Possible implications
Test: Recall
              Diagnostics
Media: Long copy format
              Reflective vehicles
Creative: Specific information
              Demonstration
	2 Affective (feeler)
	jewelry cosmetics
	fashion apparel motorcycles
	
	Model: Feel-learn-do
	              (psychological?)
	
	Possible implications
	Test: Attitude change
	              Emotion arousal
	Media: Large space
	              Image specials
	Creative: Executional
	              impact

3 Habit formation (doer)
food   household items
 	
Model: Do-learn-feel
              (responsive?)
 	
Possible implications
Test: Sales
Media: Small space ads
              10 second I.D.'s
              Radio: POS
Creative: Reminder
	4 Self-satisfaction (reactor)
	cigarettes liquor candy
	
	Model: Do-feel-learn
	              (social?)
	
	Possible implications
	Test: Sales
	Media: Billboards
	              Newspapers
	              POS
	Creative: Attention

High involvement (top) ▼ Low involvement (bottom)

Figure 3.9   Thinking versus feeling related to involvement

sports car ad. Differences also occur by level of the hierarchy of effects; awareness ads differ from attitudinal ads. One of the interesting research topics currently in vogue concerns measuring the impact of an emotional versus a rational ad. It is felt that emotion and rationality lead to different thinking/feeling responses.

According to Vaughn, Figure 3.9 is intended to be a thought starter rather than a formula for solutions. This is consistent with the situation analysis concept. The manager must have a clear feeling of what is happening in the marketplace and what strategic options are available. Most situations do not clearly fall into one quadrant of Figure 3.9, but an evaluation of the issues is necessary before strategy can be recommended.

The work on involvement and thinking versus feeling has been extended further by Rossiter and Percy.[6] In their work, they consider that advertising has two major tasks: to create awareness/knowledge of the brand and to create attitude/positive feelings toward the brand. Before advertising can be used, Rossiter and Percy feel that the manager must make the following assessments.

1. *Should the advertising be directed toward awareness or attitude formation?*   This derives directly from the hierarchy of effects, and although advertising attempts to do both of these, there generally is an emphasis in one direction or the other.

2. *Should there be a recall or recognition level of knowledge?*   If the advertising is directed toward awareness, then this next issue must also be addressed. If consumers make brand choice decisions in the home, then they must know the brand name and its benefits well. In the home there are few brand cues available to aid the consumer and so the brand must be firmly imbedded in memory. The consumer must be able to recall the brand. This level of learning requires more frequent advertising and in-home promotions such as coupons.

Many consumer decisions, though, are made in the store. In this case a recognition level of learning is sufficient because there are memory cues at the time of purchase. These cues include the package and point-of-purchase materials (e.g., displays, signs). Advertising does not need to create as strong a memory because the cues are available, and promotions are more likely to be in-store (e.g., price-off deals, bonus packs).

3. *Should the advertising be directed toward high- or low-involvement processes?*   This has been discussed.

4. *Should the advertising be informational or transformational?*   Informational messages deal with "reason why"; why should the brand be purchased? Transformational advertising creates brand images and mood. As part of the situation analysis, the manager needs to assess these directions for later strategy. Some products are utilitarian and do not lend themselves to mood creation (oven cleaner, bathroom cleanser); others are essentially parity products and can only be differentiated through mood and image (soft drinks, beer); still others are bought for a variety of reasons and allow many strategies (automobiles are sold because they are safe, economical, and durable, but they are also sold as an extension of the owner's personality or as the image that the owner would like to portray).

From these last two issues, Rossiter and Percy suggest strategies that might evolve. It is clear that a proper situation analysis is important because the following four emerging strategies are quite different from one another.

1. *Low-involvement informational advertising*   Simple problem–solution format with one or two clearly stated, easy-to-learn benefits. It is not important for the message to be well liked.

2. *Low-involvement transformational advertising*   Unique execution of authentic emotion in a message that must be liked. Brand information can be implicit.

3. *High-involvement informational advertising*   Several execution styles can take into account initial and desired future attitudes. These include comparative (us versus them) and refutational (this is what we do well and what we do less well) messages. Benefits must be believable and convincingly stated.

4. *High-involvement transformational advertising*   Audience must identify with the product and like the ad; emotion must be tailored to the target. While proper emotion is vital, it may also be necessary to provide information so that the buyer can rationalize the purchase.

Summary of involvement

It is important to consider information processing styles so that the proper message can be delivered at the proper time. All these issues can lead to different types of strategies across several areas of advertising development.

1. *Frequency of message*   In low-involvement cases, consumers have little motivation to learn advertising messages. Because of this, messages must be repeated often to enhance learning and inhibit forgetting.

2. *Medium used*   Print is preferable for high involvement where information is sought and a self-controlled pace of learning is desired, although the ability of broadcast to intrude is also useful to enhance the build-up of awareness. With passive low-involvement learning, broadcast media are preferred so that messages will, indeed, be received regardless of whether or not they are sought.

3. *Message content*   The multiattribute attitude model (which is discussed next) is useful in showing key issues to discuss; the data generated from this model are especially relevant in high-involvement cases. In low involvement, the message should be kept very simple with a continuity across all messages in the campaign. Learning may need to be assisted by creating interest where none exists. Low-involvement cases may be low because there are no apparent brand differences and no point of inherent drama associated with the product. In these cases, the message strategy must consider ways to create interest through extraneous devices such as animation, music, or humor.

4. *Pricing issues*   Price is a universal high-involvement attribute. That is, almost everyone cares about money regardless of how involved they are with any particular product. In high-involvement cases there are generally several key attributes to consider; therefore, price is only one of several and does not dominate decision making. In low-involvement cases, price may be the most important variable and may dominate decision making. Pricing promotions tend to be much more crucial in low-involvement cases where other attributes may not discriminate among brands.

Consumer Perceptions of the Product, the Competition, and the Marketplace

These areas need to be considered together because the set of competitors is the same as the set of variations of the product being offered in the market. These areas are also interrelated with the consumer because the key issue is the consumer's *perception* of the product and the competition. Reality is not as important as perceptions, and consumer perceptions are more important than those of the firm.

The key issues to be developed here concern consumers' perceptions and preferences of the various brands; these will be a result of the attributes and benefits that discriminate between the brands. There are two useful classes of models or tools available to assess perceptions and preferences

- Multiattribute Attitude Models (MAM)
- Multidimensional Scaling Models (MDS)

Each deals with perceptions and preferences, and each describes consumer attitudes. As attitude models, they fit nicely into the situation analysis because one of the key issues discussed earlier dealt with describing consumers in terms of their place in the hierarchy of effects. These models can add a wealth of information concerning the attitude component of the hierarchy.

The MAM models are known as *composition models* because the data collected by their use allows the manager to *compose* an attitude structure based on the pieces of information gathered through the questioning. The MDS models are known as *decomposition models* because the data, which show an overall attitude structure, must be broken down, or *decomposed,* to find the underlying parts from which the attitude is derived.

Multiattribute attitude models

There are many definitions of attitude in the psychology literature; some cynics say that the number of definitions equals the number of researchers that have worked in the area. One of these definitions is especially germane when considering MAM models. In this definition

Attitude is a measure of
the *perceived value of alternatives*
for purchase or consumption
along *appropriate evaluative criteria.*

This is a measurement-oriented definition and suggests a measuring instrument. It says that

Attitude $= f$(criteria or attributes)(brands or alternatives)

This has been stated as

$$A_b = \sum_{i=1}^{n} (I_i B_{ib})$$

where

A_b = attitude toward brand b

n = the number of attributes

I_i = importance of attribute i

B_{ib} = belief concerning the goodness of attribute i in brand b.

In this model an attitude toward brand b can be calculated by multiplying the importance of each attribute i by its goodness in brand b and summing these scores across the n attributes. Table 3.3 shows fictitious data in the hand-held calculator market. Column 1 shows how important each attribute is to the respondents when they make a hand-held calculator choice decision. Columns 2 and 3 show respondent perceptions as to how well the brand performs with respect to the attribute. Columns 4 and 5 show the multiplication of values in columns 1 and 2, and 1 and 3, respectively. At the bottom of columns 4 and 5 are the summed scores for each brand as derived using the MAM equation.

The multiattribute attitude models were originally conceptualized to allow comparisons of objects based on single scores, and that result can be achieved as shown in Table 3.3. More important, though, is the matrix of data that is generated. The real value of the MAM has become this rich matrix, and as a result the MAM has become a popular situation analysis tool for both manufacturers and advertising agencies.

Table 3.3 MAM data for a fictitious hand-held calculator market

	(1) I	(2) B_A	(3) B_B	(4) IB_A	(5) IB_B
Key attributes	Importance of attribute (1 = not important 10 = very important)	How well brand does on the attribute (1 = very poorly; 10 = very well) Brand A	Brand B		
Number of functions	8	7	9	56	72
Small size	5	9	6	45	30
Amount of memory	9	10	8	90	72
Nice case	4	6	8	24	32
			$\sum_{i=1}^{n}(IB) =$	215	206

The data in Table 3.3 can be simplified and represented as in Figure 3.10. In this figure, the manager of Brand A can see precisely what product and/or communications decisions need to be made. Amount of memory is important and the brand does well; therefore, the manager would stress this in communications. "We know amount of memory is important to you and therefore we have built a calculator with a large memory."

Brand A also does well on its small size, but consumers do not see this as important. The firm would want to take advantage of data that show that A is superior, so the manager would try to make size a more important attribute. "Who wants a large bulky calculator today? Brand A has always been a leader in making powerful calculators that are small enough to take anywhere."

Number of functions seems to be important, but A is perceived poorly in this area. Management has several alternatives available. One is to acknowledge the low level and change it. That is a product decision beyond the scope of this book. A second strategy would be to learn if the number of functions is merely misperceived. It may be that consumers have another brand in mind (the advertising may remind them of Brand C). If A's number of functions is misperceived, then a new communications campaign may move it to the upper left quadrant. A third

	ATTRIBUTE IS IMPORTANT	**ATTRIBUTE IS NOT IMPORTANT**
BRAND DOES WELL	Amount of memory	Small size
BRAND DOES POORLY	Number of Functions	Nice case

Figure 3.10 *Simplification of importance and goodness for Brand A*

alternative is to acknowledge that there are few functions but to change perceptions of the importance of having many functions (which no one ever uses anyway).

The fourth attribute in the example is a nice carrying case. Brand A is perceived as doing poorly here, but consumers do not feel the attribute is important. Therefore, management may do well to ignore this attribute. There is often a tendency to try to do too much in an advertising campaign. The attribute in the lower right quadrant would be a good candidate for deletion.

Boyd, Ray, and Strong[7] have written an excellent paper summarizing the potential communications strategies that emerge from data such as those presented in Table 3.3 and Figure 3.10. They suggest five potential classes of strategy:

1. *Change the salience of the characteristics*   That is, make attributes more or less important as was suggested for size and number of functions in the previous example.

2. *Add new characteristics*   If the brand does poorly in all of the commonly used attributes, it may be time to introduce new ones. Perhaps the brand would do better if advertising stressed the brand's easy-to-read display and how important this is.

3. *Change the brand's image on a key characteristic*   This is similar to alternative two for number of functions; let the advertising change consumers' perceptions as to the number of functions that the brand has.

4. *Change the image of the competition on a key characteristic*   Table 3.3 shows that Brand B's number of functions is seen quite favorably. Can advertising convince consumers that this complexity is obsolete (and that A's lower number and ease of operation are the wave of the future)?

5. *Change the product usage occasion*   Good examples of changing usage occasions can be seen in Chex cereals ads that show the product as a great snack food (when salted and baked), and in Florida orange juice ads ("It's not just for breakfast anymore").

Figure 3.11 shows still another way to present MAM data. Here the importance ratings are on the vertical axis and the goodness ratings are on the horizontal axis. The horizontal lines show the importance of each attribute; on each line the manager can see the distance from each brand to the ideal ($\textcircled{I}$). The more important attributes (which need to be dealt with before the less important attributes) are higher on the vertical axis.

Figure 3.11 presents hypothetical data for the compact automobile market. This visual representation allows the manager to see easily how consumers perceive the firm's brand relative to major competitive brands and to see what strategies could emerge to help the brand communicate to remedy any flaws.

For example, Brand B is perceived as having gas mileage and performance that are close to the ideal. Mileage is important and performance is of moderate importance. Brand B is also closest to the ideal on style and far from the ideal on price and comfort.

How should these benefits be communicated? One way would be to position B as the compact car that doesn't sacrifice style in order to get good mileage and good performance. B costs a little more but it delivers great gas mileage and per-

Figure 3.11 *Fictitious data for compact auto market*

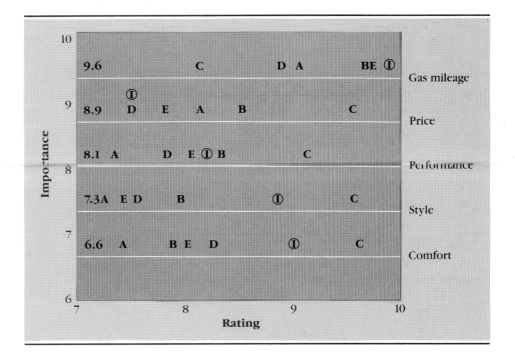

formance in style. Given the Boyd, Ray, and Strong recommended strategies, B should try to increase the importance of style; without style it is merely a high-priced version of E. The presentation shown in Figure 3.11 shows how the firm's own brand does, but without also considering competitors the firm cannot develop a unique position. In B's case, style is a necessary component in order to develop a unique position. Positioning is discussed in detail in Chapter 5.

There are four other brands in Figure 3.11. Given the discussion of MAM to this point, the reader should be able to devise descriptions and strategies for these brands.

Multiattribute attitude model data can also be used to develop benefit segmentation strategies. The MAM figures shown so far have not used benefit segmentation but rather have used aggregate data; this has masked segments that may exist. A population can be divided based on importance values. Some consumers, for example, will feel that style is most important while others will be most concerned with gas mileage. A further segmentation can be based on the location of ideal points. For example, some consumers may want a high level of performance while others may prefer a weaker, less responsive car. So, benefit segmentation can be based on importance of attributes and also on value of ideal points within an attribute.

A clear example of such segmentation would occur in industrial marketing situations where several specialists in a target firm are involved in the decision-making process. Here the most important attributes for the engineer are related to the technical specifications of the product, while the purchasing agent is most concerned with price issues. In such a case the firm can develop a technical ad for engineers and deliver it in *Engineering Digest,* while developing a price/value ad for purchasing agents that can be delivered in *Purchasing Agents Weekly.*

Before you prepare this,

you'll have to prepare for TEFRA.

ADP can help. You already have more than your fair share of jobs. Owner. Chef. Personnel manager. Maitre d'. Yet the IRS would like to give you one more: Super-bookkeeper.
Because to comply with their tip reporting law, the Tax Equity and Fiscal Responsibility Act (TEFRA), you'll need an accountant's knowledge and savvy— and a bookkeeper's patience.
Unless you hire ADP to do your payroll. Our payroll package now includes a TEFRA preparation service. Free. We'll prepare tax allocation reports showing employee hours, gross receipts, declared tips, and shortfalls. We'll also print tip totals on payroll registers, check stubs, and management reports as a running reminder.
At year's end you'll receive signature-ready 8027

forms. Your employees will receive W-2s showing allocation totals, a benefit they're sure to appreciate come tax time. In case of an audit, we'll rush your records, up-to-date and accurate, to your restaurant.
All this, along with our economical payroll services, *at no extra cost.*
Spend your time pleasing customers instead of the IRS. Call ADP toll free at 800-526-7474. In New Jersey, call collect at 201-992-2234 and ask about our payroll services with TEFRA preparation.

WE'RE GOOD, FOR BUSINESS.

ADP The computing company®

Insert local address/phone #

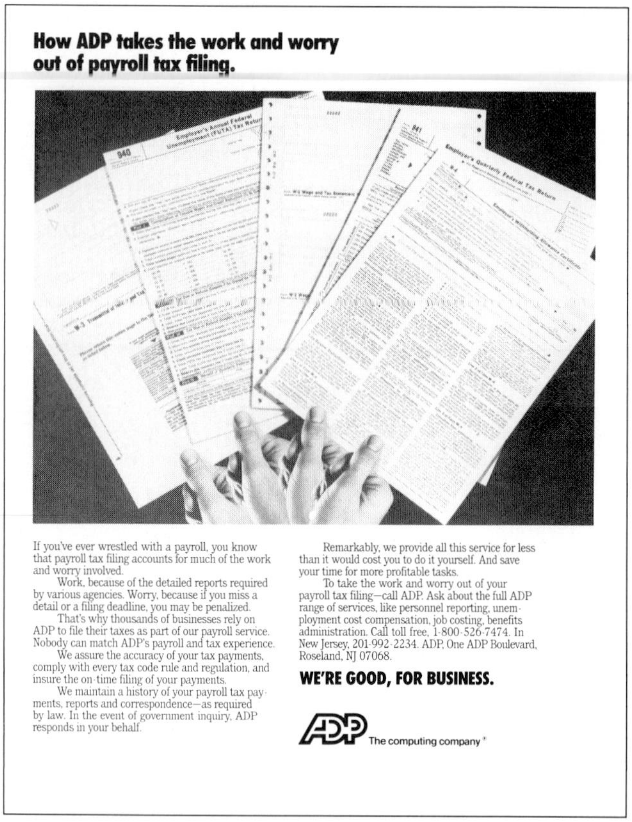

How ADP takes the work and worry out of payroll tax filing.

If you've ever wrestled with a payroll, you know that payroll tax filing accounts for much of the work and worry involved.
Work, because of the detailed reports required by various agencies. Worry, because if you miss a detail or a filing deadline, you may be penalized.
That's why thousands of businesses rely on ADP to file their taxes as part of our payroll service. Nobody can match ADP's payroll and tax experience.
We assure the accuracy of your tax payments, comply with every tax code rule and regulation, and insure the on-time filing of your payments.
We maintain a history of your payroll tax payments, reports and correspondence—as required by law. In the event of government inquiry, ADP responds in your behalf.

Remarkably, we provide all this service for less than it would cost you to do it yourself. And save your time for more profitable tasks.
To take the work and worry out of your payroll tax filing—call ADP. Ask about the full ADP range of services, like personnel reporting, unemployment cost compensation, job costing, benefits administration. Call toll free, 1-800-526-7474. In New Jersey, 201-992-2234. ADP, One ADP Boulevard, Roseland, NJ 07068.

WE'RE GOOD, FOR BUSINESS.

ADP The computing company®

Figure 3.12 Different audiences receive different messages for same brand

Figure 3.12 shows a pair of ads for the same product that ran in different journals for different audiences.

It is easy to see the value of the multiattribute attitude model in the situation analysis, because it provides the manager with such a rich set of data. The key difference between this and other attitude models is the inclusion of the importance dimension. Because no message or campaign can cover all issues, it is crucial to be able to evaluate the importance levels. The following two examples where importance was neglected are instructive.

In 1977, R. J. Reynolds Tobacco introduced Real cigarettes with a large advertising budget. Real was positioned with ad copy stating "nothing artificial added," and "all natural." Research had told management that smokers did not want flavorings or additives, but the research missed a key point. Until they were asked, smokers had never thought about these issues and they really did not care. Real's advertising was based on a unique position that did not solve a problem. The attributes and benefits were not important. The brand went up in smoke because consumers were concerned with low tar information rather than natural tobacco ingredients.

In the second example, a group of investors began a chain of car waxing outlets in the Midwest. These shops used a series of machines, much like a car wash, to give a very nice hard wax shine to cars. No preliminary research was done and the chain never did very well. Later, when research finally was done, two segments emerged. The first segment was small; for these consumers a shiny car was important, no expense was too great, but no impersonal machine was going to massage their precious vehicles. The second, larger segment did not mind if a machine waxed their cars but a shiny car was not important to them and they would not spend the $20 that it cost to get the car waxed. Again, importance was a key issue. An assessment of what was important to consumers would have shown that there was not a large market for the service.

In summary, the MAM is a useful situation analysis tool. It is easy to execute and provides relevant data in several areas:

1. What attributes are important to consumers in their decision-making?

2. How is the firm perceived on these attributes?

3. How are the competitors perceived?

4. What would consumers like from an ideal brand?

5. How can the market be segmented based on importance and ideal point data?

A second set of attitude evaluation models are the multidimensional scaling models. These are considered next.

Multidimensional scaling models

As stated earlier, the MDS models seek overall perceptions and/or preference judgments from consumers and allow managers to decompose the judgments to determine the underlying structure of attitudes concerning the brands in the product class. MDS models have never achieved the popularity of the MAM models but can provide considerable managerial insight. In addition, the issues raised by MDS are central to positioning decisions. This is especially true for those product classes with few real differences between brands. This section will consider both the virtues of MDS and the issues it raises. For our purposes, the latter will be more important.

In an MDS research project consumers are generally asked to give similarity or dissimilarity judgments between different brands in a product class or between brands and ideal points. The similarity judgments are converted by a mathematical algorithm to physical distances; these are then plotted on a map such that the brands which are most similar are closest to each other and the brands that are least similar are furthest apart; this plot is known as a *perceptual map* because it shows physical distance between objects relative to the perceptions in consumers' minds.

Subjects will have completed a fairly simple task; they do not have to deal with attributes or scales, they merely judge the similarity of various pairs of brands. Furthermore, the subjects don't need to judge the amount of similarity between pairs; they only need to judge which pairs were more similar. The mapping attempts to retain the ordering of the pairs of similarity judgments.

In a more specific example, if subjects were asked to judge the similarities of Toyota, Nissan, and Cadillac on a 100-point scale, where 0 is very dissimilar and 100 is very similar, the following judgments might be found:

Pair	Score
Toyota–Nissan	97
Toyota–Cadillac	03
Nissan–Cadillac	05

*Figure 3.13   MDS map
with three objects*

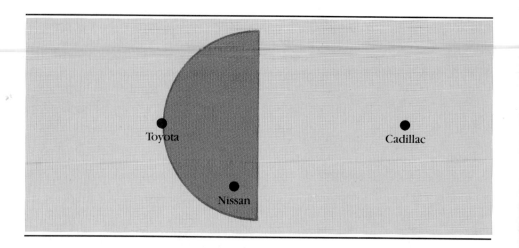

Figure 3.13 shows a physical map of these three brands; the map and the task are both trivial when dealing with three objects. In fact, there are many possible mappings for these data. If Toyota and Cadillac are fixed points as shown, Nissan can be plotted anywhere within the semicircle of Figure 3.13 without violating the ordering of the distances. As the number of objects increases, the number of pairs increases, and the map quickly becomes constrained. With eight objects there is virtually no room for the type of movement seen in Figure 3.13; with eight brands the location of Nissan would be constrained to a single point on the map.

Figure 3.14 shows a map of ten brands in the cigarette market. The generation of such a map and the discussion to this point is fairly straightforward mathematics. What follows is more relevant to the situation analysis and to the decisions that can be made from the situation analysis.

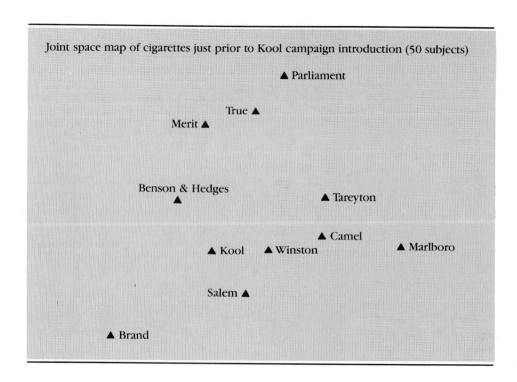

*Figure 3.14   Perceptual
map of ten cigarette brands*

The map in Figure 3.14 needs to be interpreted as part of the situation analysis. The questions that need to be answered are key to deriving value from the map and to developing good positioning and advertising strategy.

1. *What are the major perceptual dimensions underlying this map?*   That is, when smokers were judging the similarities of the ten brands, what were the most important attributes underlying their perceptual decisions? The managerial answers to these questions are subjective and subject to argument. The researcher who generated these data[8] felt that the dimensions were as shown in Figure 3.15. The reader may disagree and may wish to suggest other underlying attributes.

2. *What brands are perceived as similar to other brands?*   This question deals with the issue of substitutability. If a smoker's favorite brand is not available, what brand is most likely to be purchased? Does the brand have a unique position in smokers' minds or will brand switching readily take place? There are mathematical routines known as clustering algorithms that show which brands are seen as most similar, that is, which brands cluster together.

3. *What holes exist in the map for repositioning of an old brand or for a new product introduction?*   That is, what points are there on the map where no competitive brands currently exist? Answering this question does not assure success since there may not be any demand for a brand where the hole in the map exists. Nevertheless, these holes suggest potential opportunities for unique positions and must be explored. If two brands are competing for a position, one may

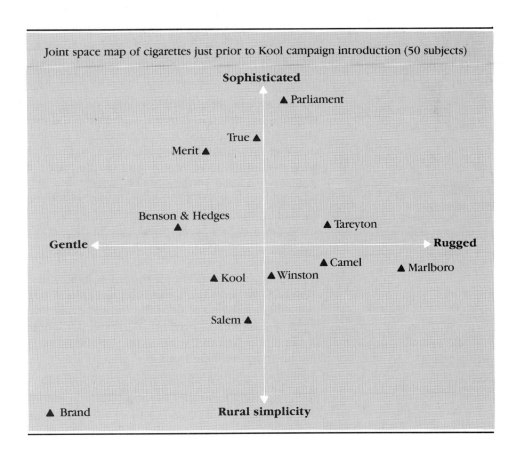

Figure 3.15 *Perceptual map with underlying dimensions for cigarettes*

Figure 3.16 Preference map of cigarette market

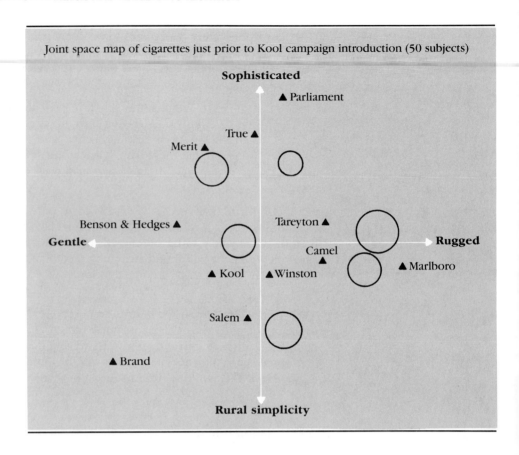

Joint space map of cigarettes just prior to Kool campaign introduction (50 subjects)

choose to reposition where there is a hole in the market. In Figure 3.15, for example, there is a sizeable hole between True, Tareyton, and Benson & Hedges.

4. *Where are ideal points located on the map?*   If smokers could have any product they wished, where would it be positioned? Answering this question usually also shows segmentation data because smokers with different tastes will have different ideals. To collect ideal point data, the researcher asks subjects to compare the similarity of each brand to their ideal brand. Figure 3.16 shows ideal point data for the smokers who judged the ten brands of cigarettes. The circles represent clusters of ideal points; larger circles represent the views of larger numbers of consumers.

Note that an ideal point lies in the area close to the hole previously identified. This indicates that there may be room for a brand to succeed with a position in this area.

Maps based entirely on *cognitive* judgments, that is, on how the consumer *perceives* the world, are known as *perceptual maps.* Maps that also include *affective* judgments, that is, what the consumer *prefers,* are known as *preference maps.* Ideal points indicate preferences; the closer a brand is to an ideal point, the more it should be preferred and the greater should be its market share. Maps with ideal points are preference maps.

5. *Are brand perceptions and the advertising compatible?*   When consumers see cigarette ads do they associate the ads with the correct brands? If the advertising is misperceived, it is, at best, a waste of money. At worst, it is helping a

Figure 3.17 *Perceptions of advertising versus product for cigarette market*

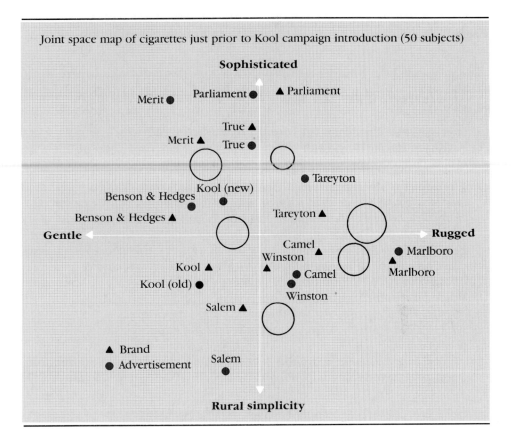

Joint space map of cigarettes just prior to Kool campaign introduction (50 subjects)

competitor. One can see from Figure 3.17 that the Marlboro brand and advertising are seen as extremely similar; that is, there is very little misidentification of the advertising (98% of the identifications are correct). Conversely, Camel advertising is often misidentified. It is correctly identified by only 34% of respondents and is misidentified as Winston by 38% of respondents. This technique used to plot brands versus advertising is called TRINODAL and was developed by John Keon.[9]

In another analysis of the data, Kool is shown as not being close to any ideal point and its advertising is pulling its brand image away from all ideal points. These data were collected when the advertising slogan was "Come up to Kool." Data were again collected six months after the beginning of the new jazz-oriented ad campaign, "There is only one way to play it, Kool" and the accompanying publicity of the Kool Jazz Concerts. Figure 3.18 shows the change in perceptions after six months; this change brings Kool closer to an ideal point and further from Salem. In addition, the new advertising position will continue to pull Kool toward an ideal point. In Keon's study, the data were collected six months after the campaign began; a manager could also, though, collect data from a laboratory experiment where subjects were shown the new campaign in a controlled environment to learn what perceptual movement to expect when the advertising was actually used.

The five questions raised here are important in interpreting an MDS map but are even more important in a general sense in the situation analysis and should be

William D. Wells

Executive Vice-President and Director of Marketing Services, Needham, Harper Worldwide

William D. Wells received an A.B. degree from Lafayette College and M.A. and Ph.D. degrees from Stanford University. He taught in the Psychology Department of Rutgers University and served as a consultant for Benton & Bowles, Inc., and the New Jersey Bell Telephone Co.

He joined the Graduate School of Business at The University of Chicago in 1966 as Professor of Psychology and Marketing. While on the Chicago faculty, he served as consultant to the Leo Burnett Co., Market Facts, the American Dairy Association, WBBM-TV, the law firm Jenner & Block, and the Federal Trade Commission.

He joined Needham, Harper Worldwide in 1974 as Director of Corporate Research and is now Executive Vice-President and Director of Marketing Services in the Chicago Division.

The Creative Leap

According to one popular theory, the left brain thinks orderly, logical, linear thoughts, while the right brain thinks melodies, pictures, diagrams, and signs. Even though this dichotomy is an oversimplification of the way the brain actually works, it is a useful image because it summarizes a phenomenon we all know to be true: People are sometimes logical and sometimes intuitive. And some of us are generally more logical and less intuitive than others.

Most textbooks make it appear that complex marketing and advertising problems are almost always solved by "left-brain" procedures. The problem solver gets a situation analysis, an orderly, logical presentation of the facts, a thorough knowledge of consumer preferences and brand perceptions, and then the one-and-only correct solution pops out, like wheat bread from a toaster. The process is portrayed as more complicated but essentially the same as $2 + 2 = 4$.

That is not the way the real world works.

In the real world, one rarely has time to collect and analyze all the "left-brain" data. A great many important decisions are made under strict deadlines set by schedules and events beyond any researcher's control. And even on those occasions when enough time is available, the data that emerge are always questionable, messy, and subject to a variety of more or less reasonable interpretations.

This means that the "left-brain" work is only the first, and sometimes the least important, step in solving a complex marketing or advertising problem. When all the "left-brain" work has been done, someone must make a creative leap from information to policy. This leap may be a timid, tentative hop, in which case the policy will be thoroughly and literally pedestrian. Or it may be a new creative synthesis of half-formed old facts, new data, semi-knowledge, and dimly perceived ideas. That's where the "right brain" comes in. And that's what's exciting, challenging, demanding, frustrating, and fun.

So don't think that the process of solving real marketing problems is as orderly or logical as the textbooks make it seem to be. This game isn't only for "left-brain" people.

The most interesting part of the work begins when the computer has been disconnected; and it ends (to quote James Joyce) in "the most deli-cate and evanescent of moments when the what-ness of a thing leaps to us from the vestment of its appearance."

The intuitive skill with which that part of the work gets done is what makes the difference be-tween a brilliant solution and a dud.

Figure 3.18 Preference map for cigarette market after advertising change

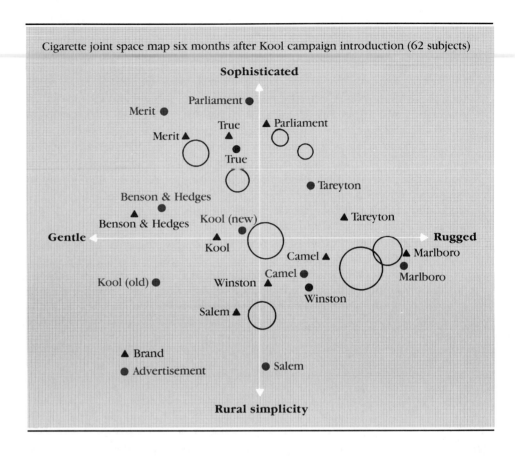

regarded chiefly in the latter context. Most firms never generate MDS data, but these questions should still be asked and answered. Given enough experience in a product class, a manager could create an intuitive map that would be a reasonable approximation of a data-based map. Again the five questions just discussed would be relevant.

Summary

This chapter has focused on two areas of critical importance to strategy development: How do consumers process information and how do they perceive the brands of a product class?

Consumers process information in many ways and for many reasons. One difference in style results from familiarity with the product class. As the consumer learns, there is an ever-lessening need for new information; the more routinized the decision, the less the need also. It is important for managers to assess these information needs.

A more commonly considered variable that influences processing style is involvement. As consumers become more concerned with making optimal decisions, their needs for information grow and they actively seek information by talking to friends and salespersons and by attending to commercial messages. In these cases, messages can be more complex; consumers will possess the material because they have a need to know.

In other cases, consumers may perceive brands as being very similar or may feel that the low price of the product doesn't warrant a careful examination. In these cases, consumers may merely try a brand and then develop an attitude about it based on their use of it. In these low-involvement cases, there is little search for information and most learning is acquired through a passive receipt of information. Advertising and promotions decisions should differ dramatically based on the level of consumer involvement.

In addition, it is important to assess consumers' needs for information and whether there is a strong need to create a mood or feeling for the product. When brands are similar on key benefits, it may be necessary to differentiate based on emotional intangibles. There are also products where brands do differ, but the development of mood or emotion is still key to developing the position and the sale.

Another aspect of information processing that will affect strategy concerns the location where brand choice decisions are made. Some decisions are made in the home and require a strong level of learning because the home environment provides few brand name cues. Other decisions are made in the store; these require a weaker level of learning because the store shelves, displays, and packages provide the cues that aid the memory in retrieving information.

In analyzing information processing it is necessary to consider consumer perceptions of alternatives and the relative importance of each attribute in the makeup of attitudes. These perceptions can also show how brands cluster together, what ideal points exist, and what preferences are not being met by existing brands.

From all of this information the manager can develop benefit segmentation, positioning, and message strategy.

Discussion Questions

1. If you were to develop a preference map for all students graduating with you, what would be the major attribute/benefit dimensions? Where would you place yourself, your competition, and the ideal point(s)? What strategies could you use to make yourself appear more unique and closer to an ideal point?

2. Describe the type of information processing that future employers would use in evaluating students, and list the issues you would need to evaluate before you could begin to develop appropriate strategies.

3. What are the three stages of the consumer life cycle? Describe information processing at each stage.

4. Describe high and low involvement and the way in which information is processed and decisions made for each level.

5. How do attitude and behavior relate to each other at each of the two levels of involvement?

6. How do advertising strategies differ in terms of media and message at each level of involvement?

7. Why would you want consumers to develop high involvement for your brand? How could you make consumers become more highly involved?

8. Why does it matter whether consumers make brand choice decisions in the home or in the store? How would strategies differ in response to each decision-making style?

9. What makes multiattribute attitude models unique (and useful) among all attitude models?

10. Develop a description for each of the brands in Figure 3.11 and then develop a message strategy for each.

11. Describe Boyd, Ray, and Strong's five strategies for changing attitudes.

12. What are the key questions that can be answered with a multidimensional scaling map, and what is their value in a situation analysis?

Notes

1. John A. Howard, *Consumer Behavior: Application of Theory* (New York: McGraw-Hill, 1977).

2. L. Festinger, "Behavioral Support for Opinion Change," *Public Opinion Quarterly,* 28 (1964), pp. 404–417.

3. J. L. Freedman, "Involvement, Discrepancy and Change," *Journal of Abnormal and Social Psychology,* 69 (1964), pp. 290–295.

4. M. L. Rothschild, "Advertising Strategies for High and Low Involvement Situations," in *Attitude Research Plays for High Stakes,* edited by John C. Maloney, and Bernard Silverman (Chicago: American Marketing Association, 1979).

5. Richard Vaughn, "How Advertising Works: A Planning Model," *Journal of Advertising Research* (October 1980), pp. 27–33.

6. John R. Rossiter, and Larry Percy, "Advertising Communications Models," in E. C. Hirschman and M. B. Holbrook, eds., *Advances in Consumer Research,* 12 (1985).

7. H. W. Boyd, M. L. Ray, and E. C. Strong, "An Attitudinal Framework for Advertising Strategy," *Journal of Marketing,* 36 (April 1972), p. 27.

8. John W. Keon, "Product Positioning: Trinodal Mapping of Brand Images, Ad Images, and Consumer Preference," *Journal of Marketing Research* (November 1983), p. 380.

9. Keon, "Product Positioning," p. 380.

Chapter 4
Completing the Situation Analysis

*T*he third and last chapter of the situation analysis deals with a number of disparate areas that do not relate directly to the consumer. These include discussions of the product (other than those related to consumer perception issues), the firm, and the environment. The chapter concludes with a discussion of data collection and research issues relevant to the situation analysis.

The Product

The product life cycle (PLC)

The product life cycle is a view of the changing existence of a brand or product and the stages it goes through from its introduction in the marketplace until it is pulled off the market by its managers. The product life cycle is useful in the situation analysis because its stage should impact on the setting of objectives and the strategies that follow. The discussion here will deal primarily with the relevance of the product life cycle to advertising and promotions decisions.

Many authors have suggested that products and product categories go through four distinct stages of development and that strategies need to consider the relevant stages of the brand.[1] These stages are

Introduction
Growth
Maturity
Decline

Although the cycle will differ by product, by brand, and by market, the underlying concept is universal. In using it, the manager must consider that the product, brand, and market cycles occur simultaneously and that strategy must be developed in the face of possible conflicts in these stages. If the manager makes an improper assessment of the current PLC stage and, as a result, uses the wrong set of strategies, sales may be adversely affected.

Figure 4.1 *The product life cycle*

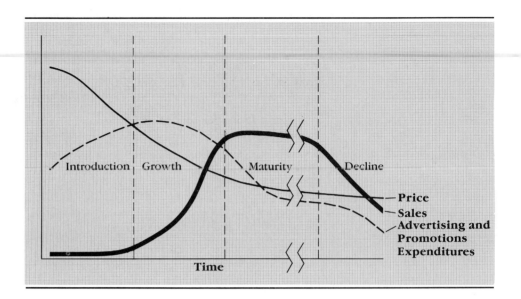

Figure 4.1 shows the generally accepted product life cycle sales curve (bold line) plus commonly prescribed pricing strategies, promotions expenditures, and projected profits. (Most introductory marketing texts cover these issues.) After a slow beginning, sales grow rapidly and then stabilize at some level until decline sets in.

Before discussing strategy, though, another common response function should be considered. Figure 4.2 shows a typical new product introduction sales curve. This figure shows early periods similar to the introduction and growth stages of Figure 4.1 but then shows a decline. Initial trial is artificially high owing to promotions, but then sales stabilize with a lesser number of repeat users. This decline should be shown in the PLC curve and is shown in Figure 4.3, which incorporates features of Figures 4.1 and 4.2. If the decline at the end of initial trial

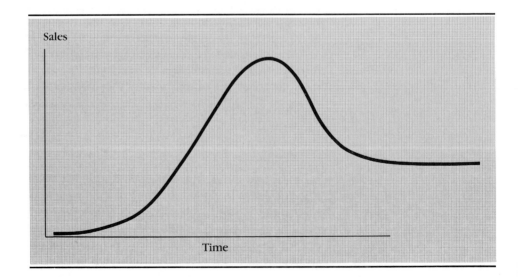

Figure 4.2 *Typical new product introduction sales curve*

Figure 4.3 *Product life cycle reflecting new product sales curve*

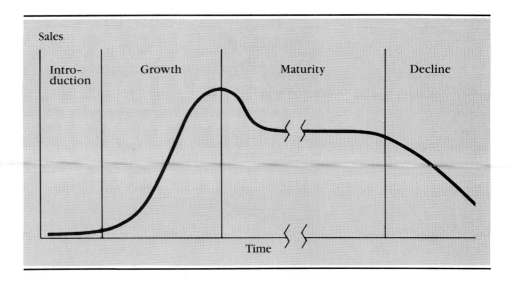

were misread, management would cut back on advertising and promotions support and might eventually kill a good product that was just going through a short-run stabilization process.

Because this text is concerned with management at the brand level, (either at the account management or brand management positions), the following discussion of the product life cycle will primarily consider brand descriptions and strategies at each stage.

Introduction   This stage is marked by low to no sales, low awareness and knowledge, and no attitudes. The strategies discussed below are not offset by revenues, so losses are great. If the brand is also a new product class there will generally be a high price (relative to later stages) and, of course, little competition. Most new brands, though, enter a competitive market and cannot use a strategy of high price. The objectives here are to create awareness and knowledge and to generate trial by innovators.

Advertising strategies should be concerned with creating awareness both for consumers and for the channel members. If the brand is also a new and different product, then message strategy can be directed at generating primary demand; that is, demand for the product class itself. If the brand is a new one in an existing product class, then advertising strategy must also establish a unique position. In either case a heavy media plan is needed to ensure the generation of awareness.

There are also two aspects of promotions to consider. First, new brands generally need to provide a promotional incentive to retailers in order to get shelf space; space is precious and competition for it is fierce. Second, promotions to consumers are less relevant during the introduction because awareness and distribution must be established first.

Growth   The number of users of the brand will be higher during the growth stage than at any other time because many people will try it once; some lesser number will become loyal repeat users. As a result, promotions will be instrumental in maximizing trial in the growth stage. Figure 3.4 shows an ad aimed at generating trial during the growth stage.

Figure 4.4 Ad aimed at getting retailer support

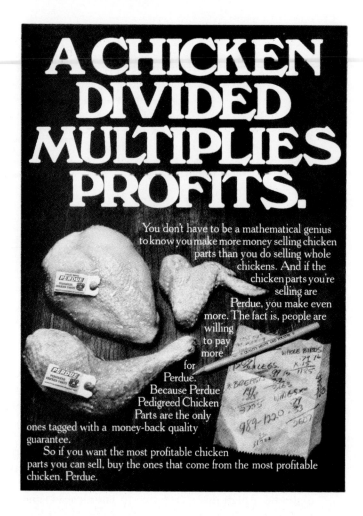

Promotions to the trade are also necessary in order to maintain and expand distribution. Figure 4.4 shows an ad aimed at obtaining retailer support for a new brand.

In the growth stage of the product class, there is first a rapid increase in the number of competitors; in the later stages of growth, there is a shake-out of the weaker firms. At the same time, there is market acceptance of the product leading to rapid increase in product class sales. As competition increases, prices drop. The increase in volume should more than compensate for lower prices and high advertising and promotions expenditures, so that by the end of the growth stage firms are able to show a profit. The profit probably is not great enough to allow for total recovery of early losses; this will happen during maturity.

The firm's objective during its own growth phase is to establish a position among competitors and to gain a high level of trial. The firm must also be concerned with maintaining and increasing retail distribution outlets.

Advertising strategies will key on generating selective demand; that is, demand for the brand. This will require a message strategy that emphasizes a unique position and desired benefits. The media plan can be lighter than during introduction because awareness should now exist. Promotions using samples and coupons are essential in generating high levels of trial.

Maturity Brand sales tend to stabilize eventually. Awareness has reached its limit, those consumers who want to try the brand have done so, and, the brand manager hopes, the stable level of sales is significantly greater than zero.

Product class maturity is typified by a slowdown of growth and a fairly constant level of sales. This means that competition may become very intense because any brand can only increase its sales by taking them from a competitor or by developing new uses, users, or changing the product. Mature product classes are also typically composed of many brands with only minor differences between them; many consumer product classes in the United States are in a mature stage.

The brand's objectives during maturity are to defend its position, take share from the competition, promote new uses and users, and support the retailer.

Advertising strategies are to maintain the position in consumers' minds. Often this means attempting to differentiate on the basis of intangible benefits. In addition, the advertising should stress new uses (as shown in Figure 4.5), new users (Figure 4.6), and new usage occasions in an attempt to increase overall sales of the product class. Developing new uses or new users for the brand is done so that the potential market is enlarged and there is, in effect, a return to the growth stage. Jello is a good example of a brand that has moved in this direction. What was once a mature gelatin dessert has grown in several ways by becoming an in-

Figure 4.5 *Maturity stage—new uses*

Figure 4.6 *Maturity stage—new users*

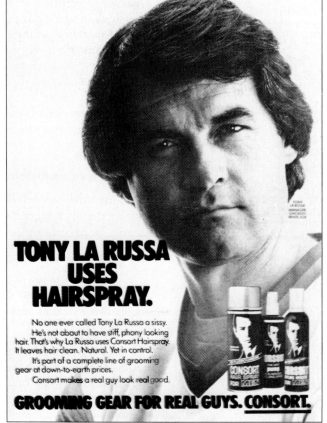

gredient in salads and other types of desserts. This strategy calls for a repositioning along with an entirely different advertising campaign.

Price-oriented promotions are all too common at the mature stage of the PLC, as brands use coupons and price-off deals to break old loyalties to other brands. Unfortunately, over time consumers can become loyal to the lowest price rather than a brand, and all brands in the product class end up promoting on an almost continuous basis. It is important for brands to establish a unique position to ward off these promotions attempts of competitors.

Decline In this stage, sales are in a downturn that is no longer profitable to reverse. The objective of management at this point is to generate as much profit as possible by maintaining the product at the retail level with as little advertising or promotions support as feasible. Sales can often continue in this stage for quite a while and can lead to handsome profits because expenses are kept low.

The strategy here is to do sufficient promotions to the trade to maintain distribution support, but to otherwise cut back advertising and promotions. This strategy is only viable in cases where the firm sees no long-run chances for the brand's recovery. The lack of support recommended here would send an otherwise healthy product into the decline stage. Be careful; do not make decisions on very short periods of data.

In a study reported by Jensen,[2] sales curves were plotted over time for brands in 20 categories that had been introduced during the 1970s. Approximately 80% of the brands conformed to the product life cycle curve. Jensen felt that for most brands the introductory phase of the curve had a modest slope because it occurred during early roll-out when the brand was only in a limited number of markets. As the brands approached national distribution, they also began their rapid climb through the growth phase. This led to a peak and then a drop of about 30% in sales before a stable maturity level was reached. In 60% of the cases, the brand never again reached the peak that it had achieved at the end of the growth phase. Brands do seem to go through a life cycle, and the manager must stay aware of the current stage of the brand because appropriate advertising and promotions strategies differ dramatically between the stages.

Diffusion of innovation

This literature is derived from work in rural sociology and is most commonly associated with Rogers.[3] Although this work was not designed specifically for marketing or advertising problems, it contains several frameworks that are useful for the situation analysis. In marketing this area has been developed most thoroughly by Robertson.[4]

The first framework deals with several characteristics that lead to successful products. While these are most relevant to product design, they are also relevant to marketing communications because the key part of any message is developing appropriate perceptions within consumers. The characteristics are

1. *Relative perceived advantage* A brand must offer some relevant uniqueness in order to be purchased. The situation analysis must find a reason for consumers to want to buy the brand; if no reason can be found, then the brand will have a difficult time. Deriving a relative perceived advantage leads to a positioning strategy.

Squeeze Parkay did poorly when it was first introduced. Although it was the first liquid margarine, research done after its introduction showed that consumers saw no benefit in buying it. Advertising was then created to show that liquid margarine would not cause a corn muffin to crumble when it was spread (as stick margarine would). Liquid margarine was also easier to spread on an ear of corn (stick margarine nearly always falls off the ear). Other benefits were also shown. The campaign showed a relative perceived advantage, and trial usage rates increased.

2. *Compatibility* Products need to be consistent with consumers' values and need to fit into existing behavior patterns. This suggests that a position which is too unusual or unique may drive consumers away. The situation analysis needs to determine the right balance between usefulness and uniqueness.

Microwave ovens were initially shunned by consumers because they were perceived as being too different. Later advertising showed that these ovens were compatible with existing values; the product was still an oven, it just did things faster. Sales improved when a less extreme positioning strategy was adopted.

3. *Trialability* Can the new product be sampled easily? If not, can it be used in some sort of trial? If not, can advertising provide some sort of vicarious substitute for trial? Adoptions will be slow if there is risk involved, but sampling serves to reduce risk. The situation analysis should uncover perceptions of risk; high perceived risk inhibits adoption and must be countered through promotions, personal selling, or advertising.

One strategy used by retailers to induce purchase of videodisc players (remember them?) was to offer consumers a two-week free in-home trial with several discs of the user's choosing. Although this strategy dealt with the issue of trialability and reducing risk, there were still enough other problems (e.g., its lack of perceived advantage over videotape) and the product failed.

4. *Complexity* Is it difficult to understand or use the product? The situation analysis can uncover perceptions in this area and appropriate messages can allay fears. Videotape machines, for example, are extremely complex but have been shown to be simple to operate. Personal computers were scary pieces of technology during the early 1980s. It was not enough merely to produce noncomplex products, but the "user friendliness" needed to be communicated as well to dispel the image of complexity. Figure 3.4 shows a Macintosh computer ad specifically aimed at this problem.

Communications must show that products have an advantage, a compatibility, can be tried, and are not complex. The diffusion of innovation literature is replete with data that relate these variables to successful behavior management.

Another type of classification developed in the diffusion of innovations literature relates to the type of products found at various stages of the consumer life cycle. According to Rogers there are three levels of innovation:[5]

1. *Discontinuous innovation* This level introduces a major change and a completely new product. Examples would include the automobile or the personal computer. These required a totally new set of information and required consumers to engage in extended problem solving to process information.

2. *Dynamically continuous innovation* Here a new product shows change in the product class, is somewhat disruptive to processing, but allows some existing

concepts to be used. The introduction of the first compact car required limited problem solving in order to create a new framework for this new style of automobile. Volkswagen's advertising at the time was disruptive in its approach even though copy was often minimal. The theme was built on the concept that there were important differences between Volkswagen and competitors and that some values needed to be reconsidered. Figure 4.7 shows an ad for a dynamically continuous innovation; it seems to assume that the consumer will engage in limited problem solving.

3. *Continuous innovation*   These new products are least disruptive to consumption patterns because they are merely minor alterations of existing products. Consumers who are using an RRB processing style might briefly go to LPS to assess the new product and then return to RRB; those using LPS would not need to change processing styles. Examples of continuous innovations would be gel toothpaste, menthol cigarettes, or a new model year for an automobile. Figure 4.8 shows an example of an ad for a new brand with minor changes from existing competitors.

The firm should consider the above issues in the situation analysis because these will be useful in examining the pace of the innovation's adoption. The manager needs to assess both the characteristics of the product and the consumer. This has been shown several times in these chapters; the diffusion of innovation literature merely presents a different perspective for this task.

Past strategies

The manager also must be a student of history in order to maximize effectiveness. It is important to study past strategies to learn what has succeeded and what has failed. The decision sequence framework recommends evaluating strategies after

Figure 4.7   Example of an ad for a dynamically continuous innovation

Figure 4.8 *Example of an ad for a continuous innovation*

they have been in use. This evaluation allows the firm to adjust strategies in the short run. In the longer run, the data collected in this way become part of the situation analysis for the following campaign.

After several years of data collection, it is possible to do regression or time series analysis to determine the causality of marketing variables. The more that recent historical data can be analyzed, the more likely it is that past mistakes will not be repeated and that the reasons for success will be uncovered.

In analyzing past strategies, the manager should also consider those of competitors. Past advertising expenditures can be obtained from leading national advertisers. Various services even provide scheduling information and past advertising. These services are discussed under secondary data sources in the media chapters. The situation analysis needs to consider past expenditures, messages, position, media plan, promotions, and changes in sales and market share for itself and its major competitors.

The Firm

Most firms follow the marketing concept and attempt to succeed by assessing and meeting needs. For this reason the situation analysis centers on the consumer and perceptions of the brand and competition. Meeting needs, though, is only a means to an end, and that end is in the corporate goals. In addition, before beginning any communications, the manager must be familiar with the constraints that will be posed from within the firm.

Corporate goals and philosophy

In order to communicate effectively, the manager must be aware of the direction that the firm is taking. Does top management seek short-run profits from the brand in order to fund other projects? Or does top management want to build market share by creating loyal long-run purchasers? Is the goal to create an image for the brand or to also show the parent company in the best light in order to aid other brands held by the firm? If the manager is to get corporate approval for communications budgets, the goals of the communications need to be consistent with the larger corporate goals.

Knowledge of goals and philosophies is especially important during the introduction of a new brand. While most firms see the need to invest in a new brand, each has its own views as to how long it will allow for a brand to become profitable. If a brand must be profitable within two years, there is a lot of pressure to get immediate results; this implies a need for a strong, concentrated promotions effort. If the brand may pay out over a longer period, the promotions effort can be more relaxed and the introductory advertising campaign lengthened.

Some firms regard advertising as an expense in the period in which it is incurred, inferring the need for rapid results. Conversely, most major firms now see advertising as an investment over time. In this case there is less immediate pressure so that the impact of advertising can grow over time. This issue can be very important during periods of economic decline; here advertising is a short-run drain on profits during a time when profits are already depressed. A firm with a long-range vision will maintain advertising during this time because it will be ahead of competitors when the economy turns up again.

Corporate budgeting philosophies differ greatly and reflect the above issues. Some firms budget as a percent of sales and therefore accentuate downturns by cutting back on advertising. Budgets that reflect advertising tasks are more resistant to recessions and seem to lead to better long-run corporate performance. These philosophies are considered in more depth in the chapter on budgeting but are relevant in the situation analysis because the brand manager must know what budget range to shoot for.

Financial resources and the promotions budget

Regardless of philosophy or goals, budgets will be restrained by financial realities. Even though an $80 million advertising and promotions budget would do a marvelous job, there is no need to develop such a campaign if the firm cannot afford to spend over $20 million. It is therefore important to be aware of the financial constraints on the firm as well as the spending philosophy of management.

Atari was sold in July 1984. In September, it was reported that over $300 million of its accounts receivable were uncollectable and that as a result the firm would be doing virtually no Christmas advertising[6] even though it had spent $73 million on media advertising in 1983. In a seasonal business, one missed season can be very damaging, but regardless of corporate philosophy as to the investment merits of advertising, if the resources are not available there are few options. Part of the situation analysis must be to determine financial resources.

Chapter 20 of this text discusses various ways to set spending limits. That chapter will explore the merits of setting the budget as a response to the objectives and strategies that preceded it. While that method (known as the *objective and task method* of budgeting) is preferred, it must be tempered by the realities of available financial resources. Part of the situation analysis must be a consideration of these financial constraints so that the objectives (set in the next stage of the decision sequence) are realistic.

For example, the situation analysis may reveal that brand awareness is very low. This would lead to an objective of high awareness (perhaps 80% among some relevant target market), but when the firm's financial resources are considered, the manager realizes that the budget cannot support a campaign that will raise awareness beyond 50%. This, in turn, means that the manager must set more narrow objectives. These may be to get 50% awareness of the original target market or to redefine the target so that 80% awareness can be achieved within a narrower audience.

While Atari is an extreme example, it is a fact that firms almost never have enough money to fund an ideal campaign. As a result, the manager must have some sense of spending limitations before setting objectives and developing strategies. Remember that in the decision sequence model the arrows go in two directions. Adjustments can be made as the campaign is developed. Consideration of the budget during the situation analysis and foresight in objective setting will minimize the later adjustments needed.

Production capabilities

This is another internal resource area that must be considered. There is little value (and perhaps negative value) in stimulating demand beyond the capabilities of the firm to produce the product. If production is limited, then the advertising should be local or regional. If the advertising and promotions cause consumers to search for a nonexistent product, then it will become more difficult to get them to search a second time. The advertising budget is wasted if sales cannot result; in addition, badwill results if the product cannot be found. At the other extreme there is limited value in advertising to increase demand if the plant is already producing at its capacity.

In addition to Atari's financial difficulties in 1984, they also had a production-related problem. Their major supplier was bought by one of their major competitors so there would be limited product available even if there were an advertising budget.[7] The situation analysis needs to consider production capabilities so that the objectives are of proper scale and so that strategies do not lead to a demand that cannot be met.

Distribution and the sales force

Just as with production, the manager must be careful so that the communications do not outstrip the capabilities of the distribution and sales force systems. If the advertising is too far reaching or too successful, then there may not be sufficient product, facilities to distribute the product, or sales force to assist in its sales. The scope of the plan must be tempered by the capacity of the systems to cope with demand.

On another dimension, the sales force must be considered in terms of its ability to communicate in tandem with the advertising. How do these two forms of communication work together? If the sales force acts primarily as order takers, then the advertising must give information, but if the sales force is involved in problem solving and the development of order specifications, then the advertising may merely create awareness and image.

Product portfolio

A brand manager must be aware of the specific position of the brand if the parent firm has more than one brand in a product class. Procter & Gamble has several detergents that compete with one another, but each has its own special position in the marketplace. While the brands compete, it is best that they take sales from other firms rather than cannibalize one another. It is important to learn how the brand is constrained by its in-house competition before positioning is established.

The Environment

In addition to consumers, products, competitors, and the firm, there are a number of other areas that can influence marketing communications decisions. These are collectively referred to as the *environment* and consist of forces that influence the firm's decisions but that cannot be directly influenced by the firm in the short run. While the firm can have an impact upon the consumer, the product, and the competition, it generally cannot influence the state of the environment. This section considers some of these exogenous variables and the importance of keeping abreast of changes.

The economy

Economic conditions need to be considered at the societal and individual levels in order to assess the real status of the economy as well as consumer perceptions of it. During a downturn households have less disposable income, which means that lower priced brands or those that emphasize a price benefit may do better among certain segments of the population. At the same time, price-oriented promotions will elicit a stronger response.

Changing economic conditions affect middle and lower income families, but may have little or no impact on upper-middle or upper income families. This means that while savings-oriented benefits may be useful for some products they may yield poor results for others.

As the economy becomes more debt oriented, promotions that offer favorable financing may be quite appealing. During times of high interest rates, automobiles are often advertised on the basis of the terms of the finance package rather than the features of the brand, and retailers of durable goods offer terms such as "nothing down, no interest for 90 days." Economic changes cannot be controlled but can be responded to as these issues become more important to consumers.

At the household level, there have been some striking changes in disposable income related to the rising number of dual career households. With over 50% of adult women now working, many more households have incomes of over $30,000 and larger amounts of disposable income. Even though the economy in general may be in a downturn, the impact on these households is less great because of the increased income from the second worker. As a result messages aimed at this group do not need to resort to a price orientation.

It is important to note that loyalty based on price is weak and easy to break because any competitor can offer a lower price. While the economy may occasionally dictate a price-oriented strategy, this is to be avoided in favor of benefit strategies when possible.

Legal issues

A wide range of laws apply to advertising and promotions practices; those that specifically apply to message, promotions, packaging, brand name, and other specific strategies are covered in their respective chapters, but other laws that apply to specific product classes need to be reviewed during the situation analysis. For example, legal restraints govern energy-consuming products, food, loans, tires, automobiles, drugs, tobacco products, toys, children's sleepwear, air travel, and other industries. Advertisers should be familiar with regulations specific to their own products before developing strategies.

Network of middlemen

While this area is not considered environmental from an overall marketing perspective, it is considered here because of its distant relation to consumer advertising and promotions. The retail network needs to be considered from at least two perspectives in the situation analysis. First, the firm may need to develop a separate campaign in order to achieve retail placement of its product. This could include business-to-business advertising (discussed in Chapter 22) as well as co-op advertising and trade promotions (also discussed in a later chapter). If such a campaign were to be developed, the firm would need to assess retailers in a manner similar to the earlier assessment of consumers. That is, the firm should assess relevant descriptors, decision-making processes, and perceptions.

At a second level, retailers need to be evaluated so that the position developed in the advertising is consistent with the image of the retailer. It may be difficult to establish a prestige image for a product if it is primarily sold through discount stores in factory outlet malls. When Jockey International, a manufacturer of men's underwear, began to produce women's underwear, it needed to assess both its own existing channels and retailers as well as those for brands in the new product class. This analysis was necessary so that the new outlets would be consistent with the quality image it wanted to establish for its women's line.

Size of market and growth potential

Before any campaign planning can begin, marketing objectives that deal with sales must be formulated. It would be foolish to recommend an advertising budget of $10 million for a product in a class that only has potential sales of $8 million. While that is an extreme example, it is necessary to evaluate past, present, and predicted sales for the product class as well as the major competitors. If the category is rapidly growing, then it is reasonable to invest in advertising to build share in such a category. Conversely, it will be difficult to justify an increase in advertising expenditures for a product class that is stagnant or decreasing in size.

If the goal of advertising is to achieve a 10% share of market in the first year but the category sales are only increasing by 3%, then the goal will be difficult to achieve because it can only be reached by taking share from competitors. The new brand, though, may have some unique benefit that overcomes prior consumer resistance and dissatisfaction, in which case the goal may be quite reasonable.

Category sales overall may grow and the brand may establish a position that is unique compared to its competitors. Analysis of category size and growth potential must include a realistic appraisal of the impact of the firm's new brand. Similarly, such an assessment must also include the potential impact of a new competitor.

Any assessment of growth potential must also be tempered by potentially misleading information. For example, *dollar* volume of frozen and refrigerated whipped toppings grew 12, 13, and 20% in 1977, 1978, and 1979 and would appear to offer potential to new category entrants. Conversely, *pound* volume increased by 12, 9, and 7% during these years and showed a different trend when inflation was factored out of the growth.

During the same period, shampoo sales increased by almost 10% per year in case volume. Potential entrants were wary, though, because at least part of this increase was due to a large increase in the number of brands, which had stimulated a greater than normal level of trial sales. The market was oversaturated with brands, and the potential for category growth was weak. While these issues may seem to be unrelated to the advertising situation analysis, budget decisions are made, at least in part, as a result of sales projections that, in turn, are dependent on predictions of product class sales.

Suppliers and natural resources

It would be foolish to embark on a major communications campaign if product production were jeopardized by a lack of supply. Sometimes a lack of resources causes a firm to change its advertising in interesting ways. During the energy crisis of the late 1970s, power utilities changed their advertising. They had previously advertised ways to enjoy the bountiful harvest of inexpensive energy, but shifted to a posture of energy conservation. When that campaign led to a surplus of supply, some changed again to show the virtues of responsible consumption.

Societal issues

Marketers respond to changes in society by introducing new products, and advertisers respond by changing media, message, and promotions strategies. Changes in the roles of women, for example, are leading to major changes in message (the portrayal of women) and media strategy (alternatives to daytime television are needed because over half of all women work outside the home). Similarly, a rise in the number of elderly, dual-income households, single households, as well as geographic shifts in population will have an impact on advertising and promotions strategies.

The following pages consider some relevant issues concerning two demographic groups, women and middle-aged/elderly consumers. Such an analysis should be done by the manager for any relevant demographic target. These two discussions are meant to be examples in the use of demographic information; to present profiles for all major demographic groups would fill a separate book.

Women   You've come a long way, baby. Or have you? Clearly advertising has changed since the 1950s when women were shown cleaning the house and waiting on men. Change has occurred very slowly, though, according to Keith Reinhard, chairman and CEO of Needham, Harper Worldwide. He feels that women in advertising do not accurately portray the rapidly changing woman and woman's role in society. If advertising reflects society, there seems to be a lag in the reflection for many manufacturers. In a speech in 1983, Reinhard read from "a loose-leaf diary being kept by Q.T., a visitor to our planet from outer space":

> Arrive safe Earth after bumpy landing [writes Q.T.]. Make way to house here with big box in middle of floor. Much light in box. Strange people live in box. Mostly women. Women make two piles of towels, guess which more white. Or which more soft. Then laugh and laugh when find bottle hiding under towels. Then go to store to pinch tissue. Laugh and laugh again.
>
> Many women take boxes, cans and jars from each other, say "Don't use any more. Big surprise: Use new and improved." Clap hands. Then laugh and laugh some more. Earth women very easily amused.
>
> When you see commercials I beam up, you notice men no work here. Sit all day in breakfast nook eating and drinking "new improved." Different men, but always in same kitchen and always say same thing: Want more "new improved."[8]

Not all advertisers treat women in this way, and Reinhard praised Procter & Gamble for breaking the mold on the outdated formats observed by Q.T. The point to be made here is not that of the role of advertising in society (which will be addressed in the last chapter of this text), but rather the examination of the changing role of women as part of the situation analysis.

As can be seen in Figures 4.9 and 4.10, women now make up over 40% of the work force, and over 50% of all adult women work. As more women work, advertisers need to reconsider media and message strategies. Media needs are changing because women are not only watching less daytime television (they are not home if they are working), but also watching less prime-time television because they need the evening hours to do the household tasks that were formerly done during the day. (Prime-time television usage has decreased less dramatically than daytime usage.) Print usage has also shifted as new magazines have been introduced to cater to working women. These include *Savvy, Self, Working Woman, Working Mother, Ms.,* and *New Woman;* there also has been an impact on the ed-

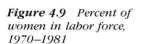

Figure 4.9 Percent of women in labor force, 1970–1981

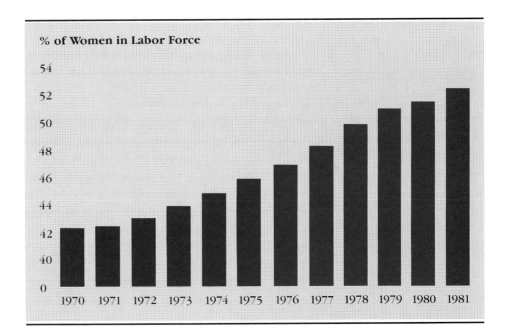

% of Women in Labor Force

Figure 4.10 *Working men and women, 1900–1980*

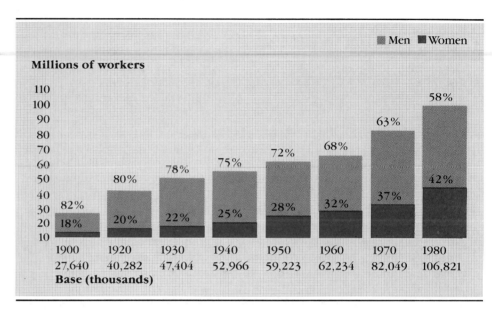

itorial climate of the established women's magazines such as *Ladies' Home Journal, Better Homes & Gardens, Family Circle, Woman's Day,* etc.

Clearly, there is a change in media usage characteristics, but there also needs to be a change in message strategy, as Reinhard pointed out. To make such a change, the manager needs to assess the target market and recognize that not all women work or desire to do so.

Can women consumers be described in ways useful to advertisers? Rena Bartos, Senior Vice President at J. Walter Thompson, has divided women into 4 categories[9]:

- *Career-oriented working women* Twenty-two percent of all women. Median age of 36; 58% attended or graduated college; 50% with children under 18. More likely to be in professional or managerial positions. Brand loyal; interested in style, more likely to have credit cards, buy cars, travel. Heaviest users of magazines and newspapers; lightest users of television. Strongest and most positive self-image; more broad minded and independent. Least likely to be offended by sexual treatments in advertising. A similar group of women is described by Nickles in *The Coming Matriarchy.* [10]

- *Just-a-job working women* Thirty-seven percent of all women. Median age of 36 with lots of 18–24-year-olds working until they get married or have children. Not wedded to careers. More responsive to new products and promotions. More impulsive than the two groups of housewives below and least likely to be brand loyal. More concerned about money than are career women.

- *Planning-to-work housewife* Thirteen percent of all women. Youngest of the four groups. Similar in self perceptions to career woman. Also intelligent, well educated, and aware. Most active consumer; most active user of all media.

- *Traditional homemaker* Twenty-eight percent of all women. Oldest and least educated group. Most likely to be embarrassed by sexy advertising treatments. Thinks of herself as kind, refined, and reserved. Economy minded, rarely buys on impulse.

Bartos feels that women change as consumers as they go through these different stages of life. While the dramatic social change that has occurred is not reflected in most advertising, all four groups are reported to respond most positively to contemporary advertising. Even the traditional homemaker responds negatively to the traditional format of advertising and with empathy to symbols of change. Given the unflattering presentation of women in traditional slice-of-life messages, this is not surprising.

What does this mean for advertising strategy? Bartos does not feel that separate strategies are needed for the same product to appeal to different types of women or to appeal to men versus women, but that advertisers need an awareness of women's perceptions. This point of view is echoed by other advertising professionals who also feel that a single message strategy is sufficient but that it should carry a more contemporary portrayal of women. Minor strategy changes should occur for products that have traditionally advertised to women. Wisk, for example, still uses its "ring around the collar" theme but has dropped the chorus of naggers who sang(?) the theme. As a further change, the woman is not always doing the wash. Men do the wash when the woman is away or when they move away from Mom. In the latter cases the woman always returns to let the man know how to do it right. As Ellen Goodman has pointed out, the woman is still Head Laundress and change comes slowly.[11]

More major changes are occurring in advertising for products that did not aim at women in the past. Auto, finances, and travel are three such product classes. The automakers are starting to realize that 40% of principal drivers are women and that they represent $35 billion of sales per year.[12] The auto messages have not changed much, but the models have. The male role has been split between men and women, and the sexy female role is disappearing. Figure 4.11 shows some examples of this change. Media plans are also changing to include

Figure 4.11 *The changing portrayal of women in automobile advertising*

more women's service magazines and working-women magazines. In terms of the situation analysis it is important to be aware of changes in the perceptions of the target market toward society and advertising as well as toward the product.

Middle-aged and elderly consumers   As shown in Figure 4.12, the number and percent of persons over 55 are increasing and are expected to continue to do so. This means that these people will become a more important segment of the market just because of their sheer size. While many products can be tailored to this group, many firms merely need to redirect messages for existing products.

In 1981 there were about 45 million Americans aged 55 or above (28% of the population); the size of this group was growing twice as fast as that of the

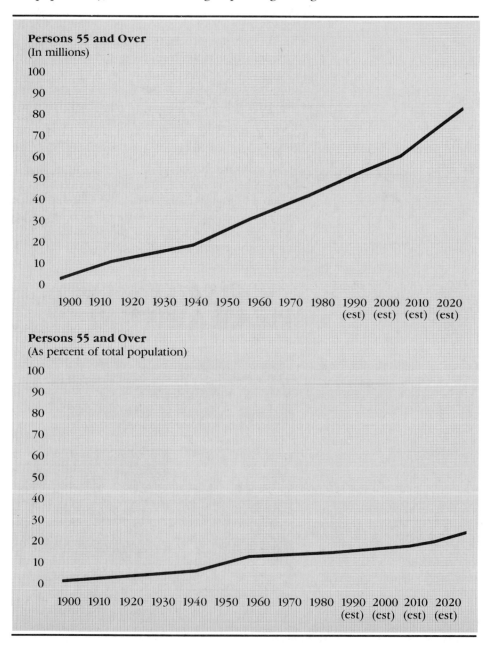

Figure 4.12 *Population trends: persons 55 and over*

Figure 4.13 Some examples of advertising for and by the elderly

Nationwide Insurance

Maxwell House Instant's "Maxine"

Francine Neff for American Express

Joe DiMaggio for Bowery Savings Bank

overall population, and one-third of all households had as their head someone over age 55. Only about 5% of these people live in institutions; most are independent and most are financially stable. For example, they account for 25% of consumer expenditures and bought 24% of new cars in 1982. As a result, Ford now has a Mature Consumer Advisory Board to consider special issues relating to product design, advertising, sales, and service. Although there are no plans to build a car especially designed for the mature market, there have been minor product modifications. While Ford advertises in magazines such as *Modern Maturity,* its advertising did not feature older actors in 1983 (although some competitors did).[13] This is a common response by advertisers; after considering the issue of segmentation, there is media response but no message change. The same response was noted when discussing women. Managers need to consider the trade-offs of obviously pursuing a market (in the message) versus being more implicit (through media planning). As the percentage of over-55s increases, marketers will need to be more responsive to their desires and more cognizant of their changing, more active life styles.

As agencies and manufacturers become more cognizant of this large market, new products are beginning to emerge (salt-free and caffeine-free foods, new lines of makeup, clothes with a fuller cut) and so are a new line of advertising spokespersons (Karl Malden, John Houseman, Clara Peller, Robert Young, Joe DiMaggio). Change is coming slowly as this market is recognized. Figure 4.13 shows some of the emerging new old spokespersons and actors appearing in commercials produced by Ogilvy and Mather.

While the number of elderly increases, so does their vigor and their spending power. The over 55 market has much more disposable income than the under 55 market and is spending it on themselves. This group is also quite active and fit, further enabling its members to remain prime consumers worthy of the attention of advertisers. While there are poor in any age group, the poor among the elderly are particularly helpless; this group represents only a small percentage of the elderly, though. In 1980, only 3 to 4% of elderly lived in poverty (after allowances for food stamps and Medicare were made) according to a Presidential Commission on Pension Policy.[14] If the 1960s was a youth market and the 1970s saw the emergence of women as a new consumer power, then the 1980s may be the decade devoted to increased awareness of the elderly as viable consumers.

People aged 45 to 55 comprise a very strong economic force. As can be seen in Table 4.1, while the 45–64 age group headed 33.6% of households, it had 52.8% of discretionary income in 1979; this imbalance should increase as the population continues to age. This means that marketers need to change their approaches to advertising. The travel industry, for example, consistently shows scantily dressed young adults frolicking on exotic beaches around the world, yet young adults have limited discretionary dollars to spend on travel. Older adults with money may not relate to the models in the ads and may seek different information on different attributes about the same beach area. Traveling is a prime luxury item for people over 45 yet most advertising does not seem to be aimed at them.

All of these societal changes occur very slowly and subtly but need to be assessed in the situation analysis. If the firm does not change its communications to keep pace, it may find an erosion in its share as its target moves away from its position. Communications planning usually occurs on an annual basis, and the situation analysis fact book should also be redone every year; if this is done annually the firm will keep in touch with trends and will be more likely to remain viable.

Seasonality

While many products are bought and consumed at similar levels throughout the year, others have sales periods that peak at certain times of the year. While the firm can attempt to change usage patterns through aggressive advertising and promotions, most such efforts do not succeed. It is relatively easy to change existing brand choice patterns from one brand to another, and it is possible to increase

Table 4.1 Spending power of several age groups

Age of head of household	Millions of households	Percent of total households	Average household income	Percent of total	
				Spending power	Discretionary income
Under 25	5.9	8.1%	$ 8,989	5.3%	1.1%
25–44	27.7	38.0	15,340	42.3	39.0
45–64	**24.4**	**33.6**	**16,619**	**40.5**	**52.8**
65 and over	14.8	20.3	8,063	11.9	7.1

Source: Reprinted from the November 19, 1979 issue of *Business Week* by special permission, © 1979 by McGraw-Hill, Inc.

Figure 4.14 *Seasonality trends: refrigerated and frozen toppings*

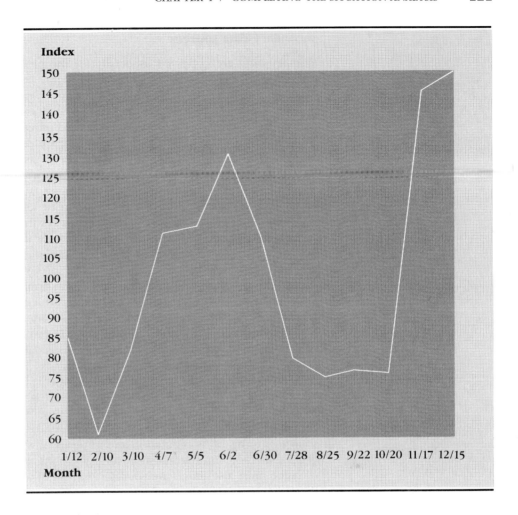

product category sales by introducing a new benefit in a new or existing brand. It is, though, quite difficult to change the seasonality of purchase patterns; it is much easier to study, accept, and plan around existing seasonality.

For example, a large percentage of all toys are purchased between Thanksgiving and Christmas, most motorcycles and boats are purchased during spring and summer, and most refrigerated whipped topping is bought in late spring and during November and December. In each case there is a specific reason for the seasonality, and advertisers can best use their media and promotions dollars by riding along with the patterns. The seasons for whipped topping are seen in Figure 4.14; spring sales reflect the harvest of strawberries and other berries while late fall is a time for holidays and parties. There are sales at other times of the year, but amounts are low and may not warrant the use of a limited advertising budget.

Doing Marketing Research

Given the information needs of the manager, where can help be found? The first response is to go out and collect data. This is an expensive and time-consuming process that may ultimately be necessary; before going in this direction existing data from other sources should be considered.

Secondary data sources

Primary data are collected especially for the problem under investigation. *Secondary data* were originally gathered for some other purpose but may now be useful to the firm. Given the potential savings from using existing data, the latter is clearly the place to start. Generally the best chance for finding useful secondary data exists when the problems are broad and industry relevant; the more specific the problem, the less likely it is that secondary data will be able to answer the questions. It may be, though, that some questions *are* answered and as a result the primary research can move on to other issues or be done at a lower cost. Secondary data can be useful in eliminating issues from a study, and because there are always too many questions that need to be asked, this paring-down process can be useful. For example, in industrial surveys the same attributes keep appearing across industries as the most important ones in the decision-making process. Eventually it is not necessary to ask these important questions.

Secondary data sets have the advantage of saving time and money but have several disadvantages. First, they rarely fit the firm's needs exactly. Problems can arise in the unit of measurement (e.g., data are collected by family but management wants information by individual), classification definitions (e.g., data are collected for age groups of under 21 and over 21 but management wants age groups split at age 30), and age of the data (e.g., census data are collected every ten years and tend to lose their value as they age).

Secondary data also may be of questionable accuracy. Management knows how well its own research department does; it is more difficult to judge others. As firms change advertising agencies, they bring old research to the new agency. How valid are the data? When using secondary data, the manager must judge the source in terms of its reputation and in terms of what can be seen in judging the general method and the questionnaire. Were things done reasonably?

One must also judge the source's purpose. Data are often collected to serve the source's own ends. For example, it is fairly clear that when seven different trade publications all report that they are most often read by top executives, at least six of them are reporting a bias of their method or questionnaire. Generally the biases of research are less clear, but many studies are done to support a point of view rather than to generate objective data. Managers must be able to separate the two. If the data do not suffer too greatly from the above disadvantages, they can fill several useful roles. Such data can serve to state the problem better, can suggest ways of examining the problem, can serve as a source of comparative data, and can solve minor problems. By looking at several studies, the manager will begin to see consistencies and will be able to pull some realities out of them.

Internal information   Secondary data can be available internally (to the firm and/or the agency) or externally. Internal data have the virtues of being cheap and handy. These data exist in many formats

- Sales data
- Salesperson reports
- Warranty cards
- Competitive product evaluations done by some internal office or laboratory
- Old advertising and promotions plans and budgets

Part of any situation analysis should be an analysis of prior campaigns. It has been said in another context that those who ignore the mistakes of the past are doomed to repeat them. Good internal data can answer many questions, but the manager must take care not to rely too heavily on old data. The more the world changes, the less value there will be in the old records.

The internal search for information should encompass each of the four Ps in order to ensure that any communications strategy is consistent with the other efforts of the firm. A formal process for this evaluation is the marketing audit. Figure 4.15 shows a fairly comprehensive list of questions to be used in such an examination. In addition to yielding a wealth of data concerning the firm, the audit also suggests specific problem areas that will need primary research when there is insufficient internal information.

The audit serves as a good way to summarize the types of issues for which data are needed. Note that to do effective advertising the manager must be aware of what is happening in other places in the firm from top management down to the various nonadvertising aspects of marketing. Two items not explicitly listed in Figure 4.15 that need to be considered are the overall corporate objectives for the next year and next five years and the marketing objectives for the same two periods. Advertising must fit into these broader sets of objectives.

External secondary data come from a variety of sources and range in price from free to many thousands of dollars. The sources discussed here are relevant to the situation analysis. Another set of secondary sources relevant to media research will be discussed in that section.

External information sources—government The U.S. government provides more data than anyone could ever use. The problem is finding the relevant information. First on the list are several government censuses. These are done at regular intervals and allow comparisons over time and observation of trends.

The *Census of Population* is taken every ten years and shows the number of inhabitants of cities, states, counties, and Standard Metropolitan Statistical Areas (SMSAs). These geographic areas are further broken out by major demographic, social, and economic classifications.

The *Census of Housing* is also conducted every ten years and shows housing data for city blocks, SMSAs, and states. Data include descriptions of housing (plumbing, number of rooms) and occupancy (demographics).

Business-related census information comes from the *Census of Agriculture, Census of Manufacturers, Census of Retail Trade, Census of Selected Services, Census of Wholesale Trade, Census of Mineral Industries,* and *Census of Transportation.* These censuses give counts of types of businesses, employment, and payrolls by geographic areas.

To help wade through all these, the government publishes the *Bureau of the Census Catalog of Publications,* a quarterly index of available data, and the *Statistical Abstract of the United States,* an annual compendium of thousands of tables from various sources. The *Federal Reserve Bulletin* gives monthly economic and financial information; the *Survey of Current Business* is a monthly statistical summary of business indicators, consumption, and commodity prices. The *Monthly Catalog of United States Government Publications* contains a list of federal publications each month, and the *County and City Data Book* contains a variety of local statistics.

External information sources—industrial A variety of business publications have industry data and occasional special reports. The *Business Periodicals*

Figure 4.15 *Marketing audit questions*

MARKETING COMMITMENT: Corporate culture

1. Does the chief executive believe in marketing planning and is formal planning ingrained with all top managers?
2. Are plans prepared with the participation of functional managers, or dictated by the president?
3. Do you have a coordinated marketing program or an isolated sales department?
4. Are you using the computer as a marketing tool and do your managers understand its capabilities?
5. Do you implement a marketing plan, measure performance, and adjust for deviation?
6. Are all marketing functions under the direction of one executive who reports to the chief executive officer?

PRODUCTS/SERVICES: The reason for existence

1. Is the product/service free from deadwood? Do you have a well-defined, continuous program to weed out unprofitable products and add new ones?
2. What is the life cycle stage?
3. How will user demands or trends affect you?
4. Are you a leader in new product innovation?
5. Do you have a systematic liaison with the research/development group?
6. Are inexpensive methods used to estimate new product potentials before considerable amounts are spent on R&D and market introduction?
7. Are new products introduced with forecasts and budgets?
8. Have you investigated possible advantages resulting from new materials or technology?
9. Do you have different quality levels for different markets?
10. Are packages/brochures effective salesmen for the products/services they present?
11. Do you present products/services in the most appealing colors (formats) for markets being served?
12. Are there features or benefits to exploit?
13. Has the safety of the product/service been brought to a satisfactory level?
14. Is the level of customer service adequate?
15. How are quality and reliability viewed by customers?

CUSTOMER: User profiles

1. Who is the current and potential customer?
2. Are customers younger or older, on average, than those of competitors?
3. Are there geographic aspects of use: regional, rural, urban?
4. Why do people buy the product/service; what motivates their preferences?
5. Who makes buying decisions; when, where?
6. What is the frequency and quantity of use?

MARKETS: Where products/services are sold

1. How is the market shaped; where is the center of gravity?
2. Have you identified and measured major segments?
3. Are you overlooking small but profitable segments of the market in trying to satisfy the tastes of the majority?
4. Are the markets for the products/services expanding or declining?
5. Should different segments be developed; gaps in penetration?
6. Do segments require marketing differentiation?

SALES HISTORY: Previous results

1. How do sales break down within the product/service?
2. Do you know where sales are coming from; segments and customer classification?
3. Are there abnormal cycles or seasonalities and, if so, how do you plan for them?
4. Do sales match previous forecasts?
5. Which territories/markets do not yield potential?
6. Are growth and profit trends reflected?

COMPETITORS: Their influence

1. Who are the principal competitors, how are they positioned, and where do they seem to be headed?
2. What are their market shares?
3. What features of competitors' products/services stand out?
4. What are their strengths and weaknesses?
5. Is the market easily entered or dominated?

PRICING: Profitability planning

1. What are the objectives of current pricing policy: acquiring, defending, or expanding?
2. Are price limitations inherent in the marketplace?
3. Are price policies set to produce volume or profit?
4. How does pricing compare with competition in similar levels of quality?
5. Do you understand how your prices are set?
6. Is the price list understandable and current?
7. Does cost information show profitability of each item?
8. What is the history of price deals, discounts, and promotions?
9. Are middlemen making money from the line?
10. Can the product/service support advertising or promotion programs?
11. Will size or manufacturing process require more volume?
12. Are there cost problems to overcome?
13. Are profitability and marketing cost known by the customer?

Figure 4.15   *continued*

MARKETING CHANNELS: Selling paths

1. Does the system offer the best access to all target markets?
2. Do product/service characteristics require special channels?
3. Have you analyzed each market with a view toward setting up the most profitable type of presentation: direct vs. reps, master distributors or dealers, etc?
4. What are the trends in distribution methods?
5. Do you provide cost-effective marketing support, selling aids, and sales tools?

SALES ADMINISTRATION: Selling efficiency

1. Have you analyzed communications and designed paperwork or computer programs to provide meaningful management information?
2. Are customers getting coverage in proportion to their potential?
3. Are sales costs properly planned and controlled?
4. Does the compensation plan provide optimum incentive and security at reasonable cost?
5. Is performance measured against potential?
6. Are selling expenses proportionate to results and potentials within markets or territories?
7. Are there deficiencies in recruitment, selection, training, motivation, supervision, performance, promotion, or compensation?
8. Do you provide effective selling aids and sales tools?

DELIVERY & INVENTORY: Physical performance

1. Are adequate inventories kept in the right mix?
2. Is inventory turnover acceptable?
3. Do orders receive efficient, timely processing?
4. Are shipping schedules and promises kept?
5. Is the product/service delivered in good condition?
6. Are forecasts for production planning acceptable?
7. How does performance compare with competition?
8. Are warehouses and distribution points properly located?

ADVERTISING: Media program

1. Are media objectives and strategies linked to the marketing plan?
2. What are the objectives of the ad program?
3. How is media effectiveness measured?
4. Is advertising integrated with promotion and sales activity?
5. Is the ad agency's effectiveness periodically evaluated?
6. Do you dictate copy theme and content to the agency?

7. Are you spending realistically, in relation to budget?
8. Do you use trade publications effectively?
9. How do you choose the ad agency?

PROMOTION: Sales inducement

1. Does the promotion support a marketing objective?
2. Was it carefully budgeted?
3. Is it integrated with advertising and selling activity?
4. How is it measured for results?
5. What was the reason for its success or failure?
6. Are slogans, trademarks, logos, and brands being used effectively?
7. Is point-of-sale material cost-effective?
8. Do you have satisfactory displays of products/services?
9. Are you effectively using couponing, tie-ins, incentives, sampling, stuffers, combination offers?
10. How do you evaluate trade shows for effectiveness?

PUBLIC RELATIONS: Prestige building

1. Do you have a clear idea of the type of company you want people to think you are?
2. Do you have a consistent communications program?
3. What kind of ideas and impressions have you created about your company?
4. Do you really know what your image is on a factual basis, or are you relying on customers' letters, salesmen's reports, and publicity in the press?
5. Does your company name, brand, and logo add to or conflict with the image you want?
6. Are you getting a share of favorable, unpaid publicity in editorials of the media?

Index, Reader's Guide to Periodical Literature, Topicator, Wall Street Journal Index, and *New York Times Index* are good guides for specific topic areas. Specific trade publications to pursue include

Advertising Age
AdWeek
Broadcasting
Business Week
Forbes
Fortune
Marketing and Media Decisions
Wall Street Journal

The above often include special issues or articles to summarize industry data. In addition, virtually every industry has several trade publications devoted to it. *Standard Rate and Data Service, Business and Farm Publication Volume* lists over 4,500 trade publications classified in 160 different industry categories and is invaluable for finding industry source materials.

There are also a number of syndicated services available that sell useful marketing-related information. The most well known are *Simmons Market Research Bureau* (SMRB) and *Mediamark Research, Inc.* (MRI).

Simmons Market Research Bureau (SMRB, pronounced "smurb," as in "smurf"; at a recent agency–client meeting, the brand manager wanted to know what smurf data were doing in the research) annually publishes a 40-volume analysis of product and media usage. It covers approximately 450 products and the major media vehicles. Product information is presented for heavy, medium, light, and nonusers and for each of the major brands in the product class. These breaks are cross-tabulated by several demographic variables, media imperatives, and major vehicles. Media and vehicle information also includes accumulation and duplication data to show the buildup of reach and frequency for multiple insertions in the same vehicle or different vehicles over time. (Each of these media terms will be discussed in the media chapters.) Figure 4.16 shows a portion of a page of SMRB data and an explanation of how to read the data. Similar types of data are provided by Mediamark Research, Inc. (MRI); unfortunately, the methods and questions used by SMRB and MRI differ and as a result the data also differ in places. The user of the services will need to decide which seems more appropriate to the firm's needs because there is presently no industry consensus as to rightness. Table 4.2 summarizes information concerning SMRB and MRI.

Sales Management Survey of Buying Power is an annual compendium of market data for states, counties, large SMSAs, and cities. Data include population, retail sales by types of stores, household income, and buying power for the various geographic areas.

Standard Directory of Advertisers gives information by firm on all major advertisers including names of products, managers of the products, and their advertising agencies. The *Standard Directory of Advertising Agencies* gives the names of all senior executives and clients of almost all advertising agencies in the United States. While these two directories may be less useful for a situation analysis, they can be invaluable for job hunting. *Bradford's Directory of Marketing Research Firms* provides similar information for research firms.

Nielsen Product Index collects data every two months on retail movement of grocery products in a large number of categories. Information includes brand

Figure 4.16 *Sample of SMRB data*

Shampoo (for use at Home): Usage (Females)

	Total U.S. '000	All Users A '000	B % Down	C % Across	D Index	Heavy Users A '000	B % Down	C % Across	D Index	Medium Users A '000	B % Down	C % Across	D Index	Light Users A '000	B % Down	C % Across	D Index
Total females	81073[A]	75414	100.0	93.0[G]	100	26485	100.0	32.7	100	30503	100.0	37.6	100	18427	100.0	22.7	100
Female homemakers	74434	68973	91.5	92.7	100	22984	86.8	30.9	95	28539	93.6	38.3	102	17450	94.7	23.4	103
Employed mothers	16753	16321	21.6	97.4	105	6602	24.9	39.4	121	7344	24.1	43.8	117	2375	12.9	14.2	62
18–24	14334[B]	14114[C]	18.7[D]	98.5[E]	106[F]	8582	32.4	59.9	183[H]	4189	13.7	29.2	78	1343	7.3	9.4	41
25–34	17519	17211	22.8	98.2	106	7733	29.2	44.1	155	7603	24.9	43.4	115	1875	10.2	10.7	47
35–44	12488	11921	15.8	95.5	103	4171	15.7	33.4	102	5593	18.3	44.8	119	2157	11.7	17.3	76
45–54	11996	11056	14.7	92.2	99	2828	10.7	23.6	72	5142	16.9	42.9	114	3086	16.7	25.7	113
55–64	10991	9548	12.7	86.9	93	1588	6.0	14.4	44	4332	14.2	39.4	105	3628	19.7	33.0	145
65 OR OLDER	13745	11565	15.3	84.1	90	1583	6.0	11.5	35	3644	11.9	26.5	70	5338	34.4	46.1	203[I]
18–34	31853	31324	41.5	98.3	106	16315	61.6	51.2	157	11792	38.7	37.0	98	3217	17.5	10.1	44
18–49	50029	48544	64.4	97.0	104	22027	83.2	44.0	135	19957	65.4	39.9	106	5561	35.6	13.1	68
35–49	18176	17220	22.8	94.7	102	5712	21.6	31.4	96	8165	26.8	44.9	119	3343	18.1	18.4	81
Graduated college	9131	8518	11.3	93.3	100	3123	11.8	34.2	105	3842	12.6	42.1	112	1554	8.4	17.0	75
Attended college	12426	11555	15.3	93.0	100	5060	19.1	40.7	125	4372	14.3	35.2	94	2123	11.5	17.1	75
Graduated high school	33454	31171	41.3	93.2	100	11654	44.0	34.8	107	12907	42.3	38.6	103	6610	35.9	19.8	87
Did not graduate high school	26062	24169	32.0	92.7	100	6647	25.1	25.5	78	9382	30.8	36.0	96	8140	44.2	31.2	137
Employed	38362	36164	48.0	94.3	101	15155	67.2	39.5	121	14628	48.0	38.1	101	6382	34.6	16.6	73
Employed full-time	29473	27580	36.6	93.6	101	11827	44.7	40.1	123	11006	36.1	37.3	99	4747	25.8	16.1	71
Employed part-time	8688	8585	11.4	96.8	104	3327	12.6	37.4	115	3622	11.9	40.8	108	1635	8.9	18.4	81
Not employed	42711	39250	52.0	91.9	99	11330	42.8	26.5	81	15875	62.0	37.2	99	12045	65.4	28.2	124

A. There are projected to be 81,073,000 females, 18⁺ in the U.S.

B. There are 14,334,000 females 18–24.

C. 14,114,000 females 18–24 use shampoo at home.

D. 18.7% of all female shampoo users, 18⁺, are 18–24.

E. 98.5% of all females 18–24 use shampoo at home.

F. If 100 equals the average incidence of shampoo usage by all females, 18⁺, then the incidence by those 18–24 equals 106. 106 = E/G = 98.5/93.0. That is, women 18–24 are more likely to use shampoo than are all women.

G. 93.0% of all females use shampoo at home.

H. Women 18–24 are almost twice as likely to be heavy users as are all women 18⁺.

I. Women 65⁺ are twice as likely to be light users as are all women 18⁺.

In all cases:

Column A: projected numbers of people (in thousands).

Column B: % of demographic break compared to entire demographic variable (women 18–24 as percent of women of all ages; computed by dividing relevant column A figure by figure at top of column A).

Column C: % of demographic break having a particular attribute (women 18–24 who are users as percent of all women 18–24; computed by dividing relevant column A figure by left most figure in same row).

Column D: Index where 100 is average for attribute shown at top of column (% of women 18–24 who are users divided by all women who are users; computed by dividing relevant column C figure by figure at top of column C).

Source: Simmons Market Research Bureau: Study of Media and Markets

Table 4.2 Marketing/media syndicated data sources

	Simmons Market Research Bureau	*Mediamark Research*
Market data	750 product categories, 3,000 brands, product frequency/volume of use	800+ product categories, 4,000 brands, product and brand frequency/volume of use data
Media covered	TV, cable TV supplements, radio, magazines, newspapers, outdoor, Yellow Pages	• Network TV, cable, pay TV, subscription TV, radio, magazine, newspaper supplements, comics, outdoor, Yellow Pages • Local markets—10 major ADI(s), DMA(s)
Methodology Sample size-derivation	15,000 adults (one per household)	20,000 adults (one per household)
Interviewing technique	Product usage questionnaire hand delivered	Booklet questionnaire hand delivered
Quality control	• In-house sample selection and data processing • Fulltime field region managers	Computer logic editing procedures, field supervision
Data supplied Demographic	All major demographics, media exposure, brand usage, media imperatives, psychographics	All major demographics, brand usage, psychographics
Geographic	Four U.S. regions, 11 Nielsen regions, ADI(s), DMA(s), SMSA(s)	Four U.S. regions, 10 ADI(s), national average, SMSA(s)
Interduplication	Brand usage/media usage	Brand usage/media usage
Format Frequency	Annual report	Twice a year—12-month moving average
Reported on	Hard copy, computer tape for on-line access, special computer tabs, database	Hard copy, tape, database, special runs
Subscriber universe	About 600: Magazines, newspapers, advertisers, advertising agencies, radio, cable services, TV, outdoor, Yellow Pages	About 285: Advertisers, advertising agencies, broadcasters, buying services, magazines
Terms of sale	Annual subscription	One + year subscription
Special features	• PRIZM, Donnelley's geo-demographic clusters, SRI life style segmentation (VALS) • Echo Omnibus recontact survey • Two-year database	• Business-to-business purchase decision making data • Magazine reader action measurement • PRIZM, VALS available in 1983 • Ability to recontact respondents for custom interview

Source: Reprinted with permission from the November 8, 1982 issue of *Advertising Age.* Copyright 1982 by Crain Communications, Inc.

sales, prices, deals, local advertising, displays, and percent out of stock. These data can be purchased by geographic area, county size, and store type for the brand and for major competitors.

There are various consumer panels such as *Marketing Research Corporation of America* (MRCA) that collect purchase information on grocery and beauty aid products. Data are aggregated by brand, variety/flavor, quantity, price, deal, and type of store.

There are many other sources for secondary information. As mentioned above, media-related sources are discussed in the media section. There are also many financially related sources with some relevance to advertising projects. These include *Moody's Industrial Manual, Standard & Poor's Register of Corporations,* and *Thomas' Register of American Manufacturers.* These and many others are described in *Business Policy and Strategic Management* by Glueck.[15] One other useful source is the *Encyclopedia of Associations,* which lists thousands of organizations that have information relating to the topic of their organization (e.g., the Sugar Beet Growers Association) and also have some self-interest in sharing their knowledge.

Primary research

This is not a marketing research text; therefore, the following discussion of primary research deals with the issues of the situation analysis rather than data collection and analysis methods. After having gone through the analysis of secondary data, the manager may still have many unanswered questions. Aside from guessing, the best option available is to collect data specific to the problems.

While every firm and every product has its own unique issues, there is a commonality because all of the problems relate in some way to communications. The research director of an advertising agency was in a meeting with the client to discuss the need for primary research. The client asked if the director had ever done any research concerning employment agencies (the client's business); the research director responded no, but he had done research on semiconductors and the problems were the same.

What are these common problems? Every firm needs to know where its consumers are on the hierarchy of effects according to the CAPP model discussed earlier. This is a basic issue for which secondary sources are generally of little help. To deal with this issue there must be questions related to awareness, attitude, and behavior. The importance of this line of questioning can be seen by returning to Figure 2.8 and its supporting text.

Awareness can be broken down to include

- *Top-of-mind awareness*   What is the first brand mentioned by the respondent when asked an awareness question? This is the strongest measure of awareness.

- *Unaided awareness*   What are all the brands mentioned when a person is asked about a product class? Here the respondent is given no cues. "Please tell me the names of all the brands of color televisions that you can think of." The first response is considered to be top-of-mind.

- *Aided awareness*   Does the respondent recognize the brand name when he hears/sees it? This is the weakest level of awareness. "Here are some brands of dog food that other people have mentioned. Have you heard of any of these?"

T·H·E   I·N·S·I·D·E   O·U·T·L·O·O·K

Jack J. Honomichl

President, Marketing Aid Center, Inc.

Mr. Honomichl is president of Marketing Aid Center, Inc., Scarsdale, New York, a consulting firm he founded in 1978. Previously, he had been Executive vice president, Marketing Information Center (a research subsidiary of Dun & Bradstreet) and held executive positions at Audits & Surveys, Inc., and Market Research Corporation of America. He started his research career with the Chicago Tribune *in 1957.*

Prominent for his writing on the subject of marketing/advertising research and its utilization in the decision-making process, Mr. Honomichl has had over 180 articles published in the trade and academic press. He has been research columnist for Advertising Age *since 1971, and in 1969 he published* The Analyst, *the first trade journal for research professionals. His book,* Marketing/Research People: Their Behind-the-Scenes Stories, *was published in 1984.*

Mr. Honomichl holds a B.S. degree from the Kellogg School of Management, Northwestern University, and an A.M. in the social sciences from the University of Chicago.

Stay Close to the Source

In the early, formulative days of marketing/advertising research, emphasis was on the social sciences. Almost all the survey research pioneers had strong academic grounding in sociology, psychology, or anthropology, etc., and their perspective was humanistic. They wanted to understand behavior, the communications process, the role of symbolism, the dynamics of peer pressure—why some people bought products and why other people did not. This was the intellectual challenge.

A beer drinker knows what it means to belly up to a bar. These research pioneers bellied up to society; they found intoxicating nourishment from getting close to *people*—not respondents, nor numbers, nor graphs or charts.

Moreover, the most prominent researchers in those long-ago days—most notably Alfred Politz and Ernest Dichter—often had intensely personal relations with their clients, and it is no exaggeration to say that many of those clients valued the man and his interpretation more than they valued the data he developed. (If the reader would like more "feel" for the colorful worklife and times of these survey pioneers, I suggest reading the biography of Alfred Politz, which I wrote for *Advertising Age,* 31 October 1983.)

People entering advertising/marketing today will find little of what I have just described; now the emphasis is on a relatively depersonalized, technocratic approach to data collection and analysis. Indeed, it seems, many of today's researchers—and users of research—work at staying away from the *source,* the consumer, instead of getting closer.

There are numerous reasons for this. One has been what some feel to be the prohibitive cost of doing personal, face-to-face interviews door to door. Another has been a rapid—almost frightening—utilization of electronic equipment in data collection. Many aspects of consumer behavior can be "measured" electronically today, and usually faster and at lower cost vis-à-vis traditional methodologies. The dropping cost of computer time makes the processing of vast amounts of data reasonable in cost, and so, in many cases, bulk is equated with quality.

But, most of all, the change is one of attitude; consumers are beans to be counted as fast and efficiently as possible. The elegant processing of data is an end unto itself; the concept of GIGO gets lost in the shuffle, and analysis often is done by people with an accountant's mentality. Newcomers to the field, accordingly, tend to have a systems, statistical, or M.B.A. orientation. Hot new equipment innovations have a Buck Rogers glamour, especially to clients. Exciting graphic presentations can often make shallow, mundane data look impressive, convincing.

So, dear student, it's up to you. If you want to reach out and touch someone with an advertising campaign or a marketing plan, I suggest you do whatever you can to stay close to the source—to have a hands-on relationship with the consumer. Become part of the research process at every stage: Sit and listen carefully in focused group sessions, listen in on pretests of questionnaires, stand in stores—not just for a few minutes, but for hours—watching people buy things, and talk to some right afterwards to learn what you can about their motivations. Listen carefully as friends and colleagues describe the process they went through in buying a new car or choosing a vacation spot. Reconstruct some of the purchase decisions you've made recently, and write down the factors that influenced you.

If you eschew this extra burden on your time and mentality and just naturally drift into the bean-counting/data processing-for-its-own-sake syndrome, you'll get just what you deserve—mountains of numbers, but precious little understanding.

In addition there can be specific knowledge questions such as, "Please describe the concept of resort timesharing." The answer to this question tells the manager how much depth of knowledge exists along with the basic awareness of the product.

There may also be advertising awareness questions. "For which retail stores have you seen or heard stereo component advertising in the past six months?" helps in assessing past advertising impact. Depth can be explored by asking for a description of what was seen or heard.

The attitude component can be easily tapped using the multiattribute attitude model that was discussed earlier. "I am going to read you some features that you might consider when selecting a brand of bubble gum. For each one tell me how important that feature is." These statements are followed by, "For each of these items, please tell me how well Hubba Bubba does and how well Bazooka does."

Behavior questions generally deal with brand selection, amount of usage, and purpose of brand usage. Behavior may deal with the past ("Which brand have you used in the past year?"), the present ("Which brand did you purchase on your most recent shopping trip?"), or the future ("Which brand do you think you will buy on your next shopping trip?"). Brand switching questions are also insightful: "Why did you change brands? What would get you to change brands?"

Behavior questions can also give insight into marketplace potential and market share: "How many pairs of shoes have you purchased in the past year? How many of these were purchased at Kinney's? At Famous Footwear?" etc.

A second set of common questions deals with information sources. This relates to the issue of where consumers go when they need to learn how to deal with a particular problem. At another level, information sources deal with the media and vehicles used by the target market. That is, what is the best way to reach a particular group of consumers. If the target is broad and/or the product class is common there may be answers in SMRB, Nielsen, or Arbitron data (discussed in media), but often the firm's needs differ from what is offered by the syndicated services.

Information that classifies consumers is also important. Here the descriptive questions deal with some relevant subset of the enduring variables previously discussed. In addition, respondents may need to be classified by level of usage or by user/nonuser categories. The questionnaire should cover each of the important areas discussed and contain no extraneous questions; all should be relevant for management.

Research has become a cornerstone of advertising and promotions planning. In addition to the work done in the situation analysis, there are also many later opportunities to do research. Figure 4.17 shows relevant types of work to be done as the firm moves through the decision sequence framework.

The strategy development areas include two classes of research. Developmental pretesting can be done to learn if the basic concepts are on target. Later, final pretesting can be done to see if the finished messages work well in a real-world environment. After implementation, posttesting should be used to determine whether the campaign met its objectives. This posttest will also be a contributing element to the situation analysis for the next year's campaign. The pretest areas of research will be developed in the appropriate section of the text; the posttest is very similar to the situation analysis research described here.

Figure 4.17 Research to be done at each stage of the decision sequence

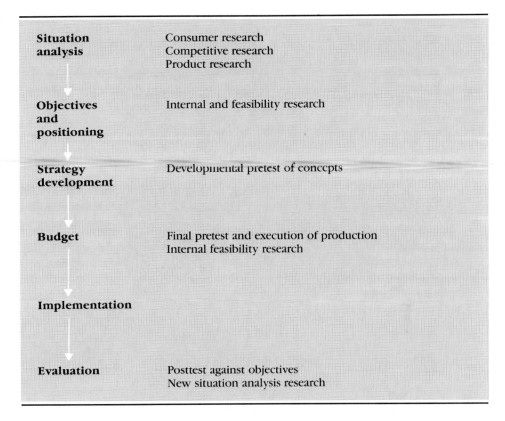

Situation analysis	Consumer research Competitive research Product research
Objectives and positioning	Internal and feasibility research
Strategy development	Developmental pretest of concepts
Budget	Final pretest and execution of production Internal feasibility research
Implementation	
Evaluation	Posttest against objectives New situation analysis research

For most companies, the major research thrust is during the situation analysis stage because this work provides the greatest potential cost-benefit payoff. The information gathered here will set the tone for all of the planning that follows. If an error is made in problem assessment, all that follows will be off the mark. If this upfront work is done well, then the campaign should at least be dealing with the appropriate issues. If there are limited research dollars, this is the place to spend them. To test copy that may not be dealing with the correct problem is foolish; while copy testing is very important, it must take second billing behind the situation analysis research.

Having completed the research, the manager is ready to conclude the situation analysis. At this point, there may be a book of several hundred pages of facts that will be used through all phases of campaign development. To summarize all this, the manager should develop a list of problems and opportunities. Sometimes it is difficult to know whether an item is a problem or an opportunity because every problem creates an opportunity. Be optimistic. See the opportunities that will unfold during the time period of the campaign.

There is a research service that studies dissatisfaction among consumers in many product categories. The Landis Group interviews 1,000 consumers in a product class and then reports the problems and opportunities that emerge, as shown in Figure 4.18. They also report verbatims (the actual wording of the response) as shown in Figure 4.19. Data from these two types of responses can be very valuable in developing objectives and positioning.

Figure 4.18   Detailed dissatisfaction areas for frozen meat entrees (beef, turkey, etc.)

Taste/Flavor Problems	36%	Texture Problems	14%
Flat/tasteless	(7%)	Meat too tough	(5%)
Poor taste	(6%)	Too much gristle in meat	(3%)
Meat doesn't taste as true meat	(6%)	Watery/heavy gravy	(2%)
Artificial tasting	(4%)	Some too dry (meat)	(2%)
Too salty	(4%)	Meat usually too chewy	(2%)
Not fresh tasting	(4%)		
Taste needs to be improved	(2%)	Cost Problems	4%
Miscellaneous taste/flavor problems	(4%)	Too expensive	(2%)
		Small portions for price	(1%)
		For the price they should remove the fat	(1%)
Ingredient Problems	33%		
Less gravy	(15%)	Packaging Problems	4%
Not enough meat	(11%)	Larger packages needed	(2%)
Gravy too watery	(3%)	Put into microwave containers	(1%)
Not enough vegetables	(3%)	Round containers to heat in	(1%)
Too many chemical additives	(1%)	electric frying pan	

Figure 4.19   Complaints, problems, suggestions for frozen meat entrees (beef, turkey, etc.)

Taste/Flavor

"No taste."

"Do not have a natural flavor. All taste like some strange spice has been added and all have the same flavor."

"Salt too much."

"Bland."

"Too much salt.

"It's just not a great flavor, taste a little old."

"Flavor is not real good."

"Dissatisfied because food has no taste like ordinary cooked food. Taste needs to be improved."

"Not fresh cooked turkey tasting."

"Dislike the gravy."

Ingredients

"Put more meat, less gravy."

"Not enough meat."

"Too much gravy, lack of meat."

"Too much gravy."

"Not enough meat, too much liquid."

"Most is gravy which is too watery."

"Too much gravy."

"More gravy than meat."

"Too much soy in meat."

"Too much gravy."

"Not enough meat."

"Too much gravy and not enough solid food."

"Some don't have very much meat in them."

"Not enough meat for my family of four."

Summary

The situation analysis is a systematic gathering of information in a number of key areas; this will be the foundation for the objectives, position, and strategy that follow. Colley has called this the 6M approach to advertising goals.[16]

1. *Merchandise*   What are the important benefits of the products we have to sell?

2. *Markets*   Who are the people we want to reach?

3. *Motives*   Why do they buy or fail to buy?

4. *Messages*   What are the key ideas, information, and attitudes we want to convey in order to move the project closer to the ultimate aim of a sale?

5. *Media*   How can they be reached?

6. *Measurement* How do we propose to measure accomplishment in getting the intended message across to the intended audience?

The 6M approach was suggested in 1961 by Colley to prod advertisers to give more thought to what they were doing, rather than just going out and creating an interesting jingle for people to sing. What he wrote will be discussed extensively in the next section; his work is important in developing a systematic approach to advertising. The first three Ms are the heart of the situation analysis; the next two Ms are the major areas of strategy, while the last M deals with the evaluation of the campaign. Between the third and fourth M, the manager must set some specific objectives to guide the strategy. According to Colley the objective states in a few words

This is the message we want to deliver.
This is the audience we want to reach.
This is the accomplishment we expect to achieve.[17]

On to objectives and positioning.

Discussion Questions

1. How do marketing communications strategies differ for a brand as it moves through each stage of the product life cycle?

2. The diffusion of innovation literature discusses several characteristics that are necessary for a new brand to be successful. Discuss these and suggest strategies that would ensure that consumers perceived the existence of these characteristics.

3. Why is it important to assess the level of continuity of a product innovation?

4. Why should the advertising manager look within the firm when doing the situation analysis? After all, the messages are all directed externally. If the manager looks internally, will this lead to adoption of the sales concept rather than the marketing concept?

5. How can something as large and uncontrollable as the economy have an impact on advertising and promotions strategies?

6. Consider the changing roles of minority ethnic groups in the United States in the past 20 years. How has this changed communications strategies?

7. How should advertisers deal with the seasonality of their products?

8. Define primary and secondary data sources, and discuss the advantages and disadvantages of each.

9. Write a questionnaire that would allow you to assess how you proceed with your campaign to market yourself to prospective employers.

10. Where would you go to look for the following pieces of information? (More than one source may be relevant.)
   (a) Sales of your major competitors at the retail level
   (b) Which of ten local markets would be most responsive to your new product
   (c) The demographic characteristics of heavy users of your product class
   (d) Awareness of your brand
   (e) Major demographic trends in the United States

Notes

1. Chester R. Wasson, *Product Management, Product Life Cycles and Competitive Marketing Strategy* (St. Charles, Ill.: Challenge Books, 1971).

2. William N. Jensen, "Life and Death for Any Product?" *Advertising Age,* 27 October 1980, p. 72.

3. Everett M. Rogers, *Diffusion of Innovations* (New York: The Free Press, 1962).

4. Thomas S. Robertson, "Marketing's Potential Contribution to Consumer Behavior Research: The Case of Diffusion Theory," *Advances in Consumer Research,* vol. XI, ed. Thomas C. Kinnear (Ann Arbor: Association for Consumer Research, 1984).

5. Rogers, *Diffusion of Innovations,* 1962.

6. Brian Moran, "Has 'Crunch' Stolen Atari's Christmas?" *Advertising Age,* 4 September 1984, p. 1.

7. Moran, "Has 'Crunch' Stolen Atari's Christmas?"

8. "Reinhard Urges New, Improved Images of Women," *AdWeek,* 27 June 1983, p. 36.

9. Rena Bartos, *The Moving Target: What Every Marketer Should Know About Women* (New York: Macmillan Publishing Company, Inc., 1982).

10. Elizabeth Nickles, "The Newest Mass Market—Women Go-Getters," *Advertising Age,* 9 November 1981, p. 56.

11. Ellen Goodman, "On Madison Avenue, Woman Is Still Laundress," *The (Madison, Wisconsin) Capital Times,* 4 October 1983.

12. "Women's Market for Big Ticket Items," *Marketing and Media Decisions* (September 1982), p. 76.

13. "Ford Reshapes Cars to Fit Growing Elderly Market," *Ad Forum* (September 1983), pp. 23–24.

14. Jane Bryant Quinn, "The Affluent Elders," *Newsweek,* 4 August 1980, p. 53.

15. William F. Glueck, *Business Policy and Strategic Management* (New York: McGraw-Hill, 1980).

16. Russell H. Colley, *Defining Advertising Goals* (New York: Association of National Advertisers, 1961).

17. Colley, *Defining Advertising Goals.*

BACKGROUND AND SITUATION ANALYSIS[1]

In 1977

the name Sunkist meant oranges and lemons.

Today it means oranges, lemons and carbonated soda as well.

The growth of Sunkist brand orange soda from a test market product in 1978 to the 10th best selling soda in the U.S. in 1981, is little short of sensational. That such a performance should be achieved in the orange flavor category makes the accomplishment astounding. These days, even getting a cola off the ground is a demanding proposition, as Walter Mack, founder of the defunct King Cola Corporation, well knows.[2]

The story of how Sunkist orange soda was developed is presented here as an aid in tying together the concepts of the text. At the end of each major text section there will be a review of what Sunkist did as it relates to the issues of that section.

Background Overview

In the fall of 1977, General Cinema Corporation, the largest theater operator and soft drink bottler in the United States, acquired the rights to use the Sunkist trademark. A subsidiary company, Sunkist Soft Drinks, was formed. After screening a number of advertising agencies, the company assigned Foote, Cone & Belding (FCB) the advertising business, and the project began in early November.

At the start of the project, a product had not been formulated, packaging had not been designed, no research had been fielded; the company was not even incorporated until several weeks after the project had started. Nor were there any Sunkist offices, and only three people were working on the project at that time.

The fundamental challenge was to develop the entire program for introduction into test markets at the end of six months. In essence, Sunkist had to create a soft drink franchising business from the ground up in an extremely short time period.

Key Strategic Concerns

Early in the development process, three key strategic issues were identified. These strategic issues and their resolutions would establish the direction for the creative development work. These issues were

1. How should Sunkist Orange Soda be positioned?

2. To whom should the brand be targeted?

3. How should the advertising establish the brands positioning?

Within these major issues, a number of other important decisions needed to be considered. These included overall corporate and marketing objectives, product development (taste), and packaging design. In addition, Sunkist needed to market itself to local bottlers who, in turn, then needed to obtain retail distribution.

Background

The soft drink market was established at $14 to $15 billion in retail sales in 1977. However, Sunkist analysis of the market indicated that while orange soda was the third largest segment of the total market, it was clearly a distant third with only 7% of the volume. This figure was well behind the colas, which accounted for 65% of dollar volume, and the lemon/lime segment, which had 14%. Moreover, no dominant orange brand (e.g., Crush, Fanta, or Shasta) was advertised and promoted nationally. Orange was a cluttered segment with up to 600 different brands of local and regional entries, and no orange soda had ever been able to penetrate the top ten national brands of soft drinks.

Table S.1 shows the way the U.S. carbonated soft drink market looked in 1977 as Sunkist prepared to enter the business. The only categories that had been advertised and promoted nationally were colas, lemon/lime, and Pepper-type brands.

Table S.1 1977 soft drink market shares by flavor

Flavor	Market share
Colas	62.3%
Lemon/lime	12.3
Dr. Pepper-type	7.7
Orange	7.4
Root beer	5.4
All others	4.9
	100.0%

Fanta was the leading brand in orange sales volume, with Crush enjoying the highest consumer awareness; neither had significant advertising support or national distribution. Table S.2 shows the sales and market shares of the leading brands of orange at that time. The orange soft drink market was a $1 billion retail business that existed only because of consumer demand for the flavor. For that reason, most franchised bottlers in the United States carried an orange in their brand line-up.

Table S.2 1977 estimated sales and market shares of orange soft drink

Major Brands	Estimated Eq. Case Volume	Industry Market Share
Fanta Orange	67 million	1.2%
Orange Crush	63	1.2
Shasta Orange	24	0.4
Canada Dry Orange	22	0.4
Nesbitt's Orange	21	0.4
Nehi Orange	12	0.2
Patio Orange	9	0.2
Suncrest Orange	9	0.2
Welch's Orange	3	0.1
	230 million	4.1%
Other orange	177	3.3
Total orange	407 million	7.4%
Total soft drinks	5.5 billion	100.0%

Primary research

In addition to this secondary data, Sunkist made extensive use of quantitative research. Foote, Cone & Belding's Know the Consumer Program was used intensively and included qualitative and quantitative studies. In total, 18 separate research projects were designed, fielded, and analyzed within three months. This included

- 3 national quantitative user studies
- 320 in-depth consumer interviews
- Diagnostic assessment of advertising components
- 20 focus group sessions conducted consecutively
- Quantitative evaluation of alternative campaigns

General usage findings

A mail survey of 1,200 respondents carried out for Sunkist in late 1977 revealed that

- 95% of all respondents had tried orange soda.
- 67% of adults and 85% of teenagers had drunk orange soda in the past three months.
- Average consumption was 6.5 servings every four weeks, or roughly 1.6 servings per week. While consumption was quite broad, it was also infrequent.
- Consumers of orange soda drank more soft drinks in general than did those who did not drink orange. Orange was used as a change of pace by heavy cola drinkers, but there were few people who drank only orange.
- 70% of orange soda consumers said Crush was either excellent or very good; no other brand scored over 50%.
- Adults felt that orange soda was too sweet, but children thought the taste was fine. Adults also felt that the taste of orange soda was artificial and inconsistent.

Only 24% of people were "regular" orange soda drinkers, and even those people were really only "occasional" users. While a regular cola drinker might consume at least one serving per day, the regular orange drinker consumed only one serving per week. Orange soda was merely an occasional change from colas and it was consumed after activity. The penetration of this segment was limited, and the majority of volume was consumed by children under 12 and members of ethnic groups.

In exploring consumer attitudes toward the major brands and orange sodas, Sunkist learned that the image of the drinker had a strong influence on brand choice for all soft drinks. The soft drink user was not simply buying a product but was also concerned with the perception of the type of person that drank the product. Orange soda was perceived as a drink for children, not teens or adults. Moreover, the orange drinker was viewed as immature, odd, and "dippy." For many teens and adults, the negative social stigma attached to orange soda was so strong that they would not think of drinking orange soda in public.

Findings about Sunkist

In exploring the attitudes toward Sunkist, the research probed for what the name meant to consumers, what they felt about an orange soda with that name, and who they thought might drink it

- The Sunkist name had many positive associations: fresh, healthy, naturally sweet, sunshine, California, beaches, and summertime.
- A Sunkist orange soda would be: natural, less sweet, refreshing, tingly, of dependable quality, and have a fresh orange taste.
- The Sunkist drinker would be: more adult, active, in shape, athletic, tall, tan, blonde, and beautiful.

Therefore, while orange soda was seen as bland, with little potential, the Sunkist name was seen as positive

- 95% thought Sunkist would make an excellent or very good soda.
- 50% felt that a Sunkist orange soda would be better than currently available orange sodas.
- Almost 70% thought that a Sunkist orange soda would taste like real oranges.

Product Development

The research findings confirmed the wisdom of proceeding with the Sunkist orange soft drink project, and product development continued. Sunkist Growers, Inc., and International Flavors & Fragrances, the largest independent flavor development firm in the world, worked as a team to assure product taste superiority.

The final product was a result of seven months of intense development effort by this team and included three comprehensive phases of market testing in 13 major U.S. cities. Sunkist orange soda, a naturally flavored product, enjoyed almost a 2 to 1 superiority over the two leading orange brands in taste tests as the firm prepared to go to market.

Color was also felt to be important and so this factor was also tested in three markets. The final color of the orange soda was the one most preferred by orange soft drink consumers.

At this point Sunkist had a good sense of the current market in terms of size, competitors, consumers, and consumer perceptions. The research showed an opportunity to introduce a new brand successfully and also showed that perceptions of Sunkist and the new product indicated that this brand could be the right one.

Notes

1. This case study was compiled from information provided by Sunkist Soft Drinks, Inc., and Foote, Cone & Belding Communications, Inc., as well as from two published reports: Fred Gardner, "Sunkist: What's in a Name," *Marketing and Media Decisions,* Spring 1982 Special Edition, pp. 149–155; and Gordon Mitchell, "General Cinema's Star," *Barron's,* 10 March 1980, pp. 39–41.
2. Gardner, "General Cinema's Star."

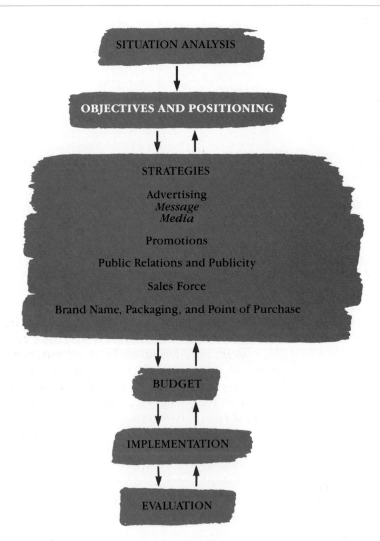

SITUATION ANALYSIS

OBJECTIVES AND POSITIONING

STRATEGIES

Advertising
Message
Media

Promotions

Public Relations and Publicity

Sales Force

Brand Name, Packaging, and Point of Purchase

BUDGET

IMPLEMENTATION

EVALUATION

Decision Sequence Framework

Part Three

Objectives
and
Positioning

*M*ost managers on both the client and agency sides of the business will quickly acknowledge that decisions relating to objectives and positioning are probably the most important ones to be made. Without sound objectives and positions, the strategies that follow probably will not be on target.

This section serves as a transition between the early fact gathering and research that is done in the situation analysis and the later advertising and promotions strategies that follow. In the previous chapter, it was stated that the most cost-efficient research dollars would be spent in the situation analysis; if the problem were not assessed properly, then all that followed might be worthless. The same logic holds in this part. If the data are not properly evaluated, then the objectives and position probably will be incorrectly or incompletely stated, and, again, the strategies will be off the mark.

This sort of precision is discomforting. It is much easier just to go off and be creative. Enjoyable, award-winning advertising can be composed without the nit-picking detail this chapter will require. Unfortunately, advertising is ultimately a business function, and the agency is accountable to the client. Creating exciting words and pictures is not sufficient although this *does* help deliver appropriate messages more effectively. Objectives and positions should give direction to the writers and artists and allow the work produced to be an effective selling instrument. The figure opposite shows the decision sequence framework and the important place that objectives and positioning hold in the sequence.

Chapter 5
Objectives
and
Positioning

Setting Objectives

*S*pecific and measurable objectives are instrumental to sound marketing communications because ultimately the results must be evaluated. If the results of a campaign cannot be measured, how can success or failure be determined? If specific objectives have not been determined prior to development of the campaign, against what will results be measured? So, one purpose of objectives is to give management a goal against which to measure accomplishment. The reverse also holds true in that to measure accomplishment, a firm must have a clear understanding of the specific goals it seeks.

The second purpose of specific objectives is to constrain the strategies that follow. An almost limitless number of strategies can also be devised in the areas of media, message, and promotions, and an almost equal number of inappropriate strategies can be produced. The purpose of an objective is to help eliminate the very large number of poor strategy options; the remaining small number of strategies then will be close to what is appropriate. Making a poor choice from these good strategies will not be too damaging. The key is to eliminate those strategies that have no chance of allowing the firm to meet its objectives.

The more specific the objective or goal, the smaller the number of acceptable strategies; initially, this will make things more uncomfortable for all concerned. Setting sound objectives is an extremely difficult task that must be done well. The objectives must be put in writing and must be agreed to by all concerned parties; the results of the campaign must later be measured against these objectives.

To deal with these difficult issues, Russell Colley wrote *Defining Advertising Goals for Measured Advertising Results*[1] in 1961 as a monograph for the Association of National Advertisers. The acronym of the title, *DAGMAR*, became the name of the model that is most commonly used by managers in setting marketing communications objectives. The book and its model have become a cornerstone of contemporary advertising and promotions planning.

Management by objectives

Before explaining DAGMAR, it would be appropriate to go back one step to the more general literature upon which DAGMAR is based. The *management by objective (MBO)* concept was first presented by Drucker in 1954[2] and had become quite popular when DAGMAR was formulated. The key issue of MBO is a recognition that many firms flounder about without a clear sense of purpose beyond a vague goal of profit and growth. To get past this level, MBO was designed to help management establish clear and measurable goals. Since a significant feature of managing is the ability to achieve results, the results must be assessable against some previously established standard; the objectives must be clear, concise statements of anticipated accomplishments and must have a time component to constrain the period in which the objective is to be met.

Another key aspect of MBO encompasses the relation between the superior and the subordinate persons in the management hierarchy. This dimension of MBO, first advocated by McGregor,[3] concerns the behavioral notion of contract setting. That is, the manager and those being managed develop a commitment based on the goal for the workers that both parties have together developed before beginning. Rewards and punishments are then contingent on performance relative to the goal. Participation in developing the goals tends to legitimize them. This aspect of MBO is important but has been neglected in the DAGMAR model, which is more concerned with the effective statement of goals than the interpersonal relations within the firm or between the agency and client firms. In advertising, this issue is important because goals are often set by the client and then given to the agency. If there are to be mutual benefit and optimal results in the long run, the client and the agency should develop objectives together as suggested by McGregor.

Etzel and Ivancevich[4] have written about the application of the MBO concept in marketing and have derived seven potential benefits:

1. Concrete objectives can direct performance, reduce uncertainty, and serve as an instrument of communication.

2. MBO can point out where greater coordination between managers is required. For example, one marketing unit may have to cut down its request for budget money because another unit needs the money more.

3. MBO can remove performance appraisal from the realm of a superior acting as a judge evaluating subordinates, to a role of counseling and encouraging.

4. MBO can provide subordinates with the latitude and freedom to reach decisions without always checking for approval.

5. MBO can lead to improved planning because the manager knows what his or her objectives are as well as the expectations of superiors.

6. MBO can produce a shift from control over people to control over operations. Managers are evaluated on how well they manage the operation.

7. MBO can generate a more immediate response to deviations from standards because the manager knows the objectives and their priorities.

In order for MBO to work well, the objectives must become more specific as one moves down in the organization. This relationship can be seen in Figure 5.1

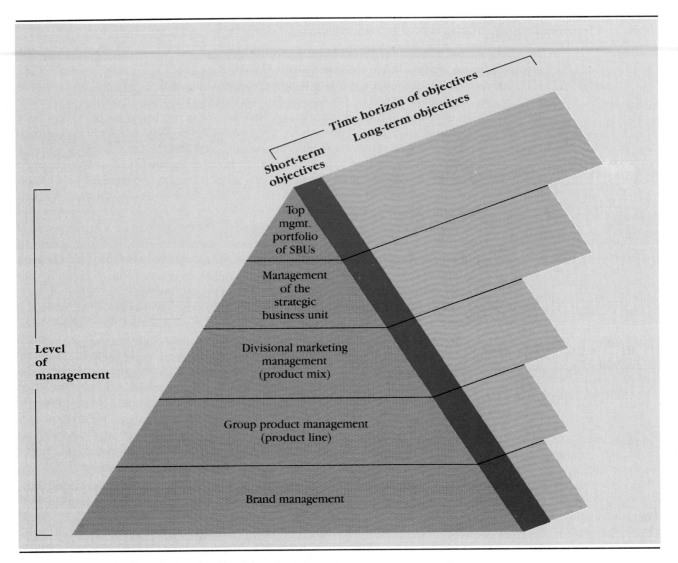

Figure 5.1 *Levels of objectives and relevant time horizons*

in reference to the time dimension, where top management objectives have the longest time horizon and brand managers and advertising account executives have the shortest horizons. The relationship is also evident from an examination of the corporate and marketing objectives of the firm versus the advertising objectives. While the situation analysis shows the broader corporate and marketing objectives within which advertising must fit, this chapter will develop advertising objectives that are quite specific. The media, message, and promotions sections will become even more specific.

The process discussed above is shown in Figure 5.2. Note that

- Organizational objectives give direction to more specific group or division objectives.
- There are contracts for performance based on objectives.
- There is an evaluation of performance.

- The evaluation serves as input to the next time period's objective. This last issue is important because it ties directly to a similar proposed ordering of events in the decision sequence framework.[5]

The following dialogue typifies the objectives and measurement processes of too many firms. Think of how much trouble Alice could have avoided if she had only come along after the advent of MBO.

Alice:	"Will you tell me, please, which way I ought to go from here?"
Cat:	"That depends a good deal on where you want to go to."
Alice:	"I don't much care where—"
Cat:	"Then it doesn't matter which way you go."
Alice:	"—so long as I get somewhere."
Cat:	"Oh, you're sure to do that if you only walk long enough."[6]

DAGMAR

And now, back to DAGMAR. Colley has defined an advertising objective as "a specific communication task, to be accomplished among a defined audience to a given degree in a given period of time."[7]

This definition lends itself to specificity. It has four components that relate to the key issues of the situation analysis. If these four components are carefully spelled out and followed, the ensuing campaign's chances for success will increase dramatically. The four components are discussed in the following sections.

A *specific communications task*   What job shall the advertising perform? Typically any advertising task can be reduced to that of moving consumers to the next level of the hierarchy of effects. Given a segmentation analysis based on level of the hierarchy (as described in the previous chapter and related to the CAPP model), where is the greatest growth opportunity?

Figure 5.2   *The generalized MBO process*

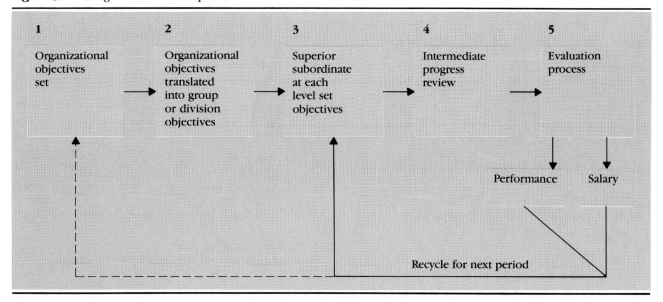

Earlier discussions of the hierarchy reduced it to its three most basic components:

Awareness
Attitude
Behavior

But there have been many discussions where more components or a finer cutting of the components have been suggested. One of the more popular early hierarchy models was presented by Lavidge and Steiner.[8] It has six stages:

Awareness
Knowledge
Liking
Preference
Conviction
Purchase

The first two components relate to the *cognitive* or *knowledge element* of an attitude; the next two components relate to the *affective* or *liking element,* while the final two components represent the *conative* or *action element* of attitude. This model was popular before the notion of a low-involvement hierarchy had been introduced and would need to be restructured in such a case. The more specific component parts are relevant, though, and suggest a broader set of advertising tasks.

A still broader set is suggested by Colley. As shown in Figure 5.3, he suggests 52 tasks of advertising and is careful to state that even this list is incomplete. As

Figure 5.3   *Advertising task checklist*

(This check list is a "thought starter" in developing specific advertising objectives. It can be applied to a single ad, a year's campaign for each product, or it can aid in developing a company's entire advertising philosophy among all those who create and approve advertising.)

To what extent does the advertising aim at closing an immediate sale?

1. Perform the complete selling function (take the product through all the necessary steps toward a sale)
2. Close sales to prospects already partly sold through past advertising efforts ("Ask for the order" or "clincher" advertising)
3. Announce a special reason for "buying now" (price, premium, etc.)
4. Remind people to buy
5. Tie in with some special buying event
6. Stimulate impulse sales

OTHER TASKS: _____

_____

Does the advertising aim at near-term sales by moving the prospect, step by step, closer to a sale (so that when confronted with a buying situation the customer will ask for, reach for or accept the advertised brand)?

7. Create awareness of existence of product or brand
8. Create "brand image" or favorable emotional disposition toward the brand
9. Implant information or attitude regarding benefits and superior features of brand
10. Combat or offset competitive claims
11. Correct false impressions, misinformation and other obstacles to sales
12. Build familiarity and easy recognition of package or trademark

OTHER TASKS: _____

_____

Does the advertising aim at building a "long-range consumer franchise"?

Figure 5.3 *continued*

13. Build confidence in company and brand which is expected to pay off in years to come
14. Build customer demand which places company in stronger position in relation to its distribution (Not at the "mercy of the market-place")
15. Place advertiser in position to select preferred distributors and dealers
16. Secure universal distribution
17. Establish a "reputation platform" for launching new brands or product lines
18. Establish brand recognition and acceptance which will enable the company to open up new markets (geographic, price, age, sex)

OTHER TASKS: _____

_____

Specifically, how can advertising contribute toward increased sales?

19. Hold present customers against the inroads of competition
20. Convert competitive users to advertiser's brand
21. Cause people to specify advertiser's brand instead of asking for product by generic name
22. Convert non-users of the product type to users of product and brand
23. Make steady customers out of occasional or sporadic customers
    Increase consumption among *present users* by:
24. Advertising new uses of the product
25. Persuading customers to buy larger sizes or multiple units
26. Reminding users to buy
27. Encouraging greater frequency or quantity of use

OTHER TASKS: _____

_____

Does the advertising aim at some specific step which leads to a sale?

28. Persuade prospect to write for descriptive literature, return a coupon, enter a contest
29. Persuade prospect to visit a showroom, ask for a demonstration
30. Induce prospect to sample the product (trial offer)

OTHER TASKS: _____

_____

How important are "supplementary benefits" of end-use advertising?

31. Aid salesmen in opening new accounts
32. Aid salesmen in getting larger orders from wholesalers and retailers
33. Aid salesmen in getting preferred display space
34. Give salesmen an entree
35. Build morale of company sales force
36. Impress the trade (causing recommendation to their customers and favorable treatment to salesmen)

OTHER TASKS: _____

_____

Is it a task of advertising to impart information needed to consummate sales and build customer satisfaction?

37. "Where to buy it" advertising
38. "How to use it" advertising
39. New models, features, package
40. New prices
41. Special terms, trade-in offers, etc.
42. New policies (guarantees, etc.)

OTHER TASKS: _____

_____

To what extent does the advertising aim at building confidence and good will for the corporation among:

43. Customers and potential customers
44. The trade (distributors, dealers, retail sales people)
45. Employees and potential employees
46. The financial community
47. The public at large

OTHER TASKS: _____

_____

Specifically what kind of images does the company wish to build?

48. Product quality, dependability
49. Service
50. Family resemblance of diversified products
51. Corporate citizenship
52. Growth, progressiveness, technical leadership

OTHER TASKS: _____

_____

will be seen later, one missing task is to establish the brand's position. This is a key task, but Colley did not include it because his book was printed almost ten years before the concept of positioning was introduced.

A defined audience   To whom shall the advertising speak? The objective must clearly state the target market; often there will be more than one, and different strategies will go against each target. The target should be readily definable based on the situation analysis. It can be based on a combination of dynamic and enduring variables or on either set. As discussed earlier, the best targets are defined on the basis of usage-related, or dynamic, variables and then described on the basis of their enduring demographic, geographic, and psychographic traits.

A given degree of change   How many members of the target or what percent of the target shall be affected? Strategies will certainly differ if awareness is to be raised from 10 to 20% versus from 10 to 90% of the target.

A given period of time   Neither the tide nor the competition will wait. How long will it take to accomplish the change that is proposed in the other three components? An important part of measurement is knowing when to measure. At which point will the goals be met?

An example of an advertising objective that meets all four criteria would be to increase awareness of brand X as a low sudsing detergent (*task*) from 30 to 70% (*amount of change*) within three months (*time period*) among housewives who own automatic washers and have at least two children (*target*).

This statement is very clear, it is measurable, and it eliminates inappropriate strategy. By defining the task, the copywriter knows what needs to be said most strongly. Generating brand awareness requires only a simple message that can briefly grab and hold attention; developing an attitude may require more information; eliciting behavior may call for promotional tools.

Involvement is essential here in eliciting the appropriate hierarchy and strategies. By defining the target, the writer knows something about the type of message that has the best chance of being favorably received and the types of characters to script into the story; the media planner also knows what types of vehicles are most likely to reach the target. The amount of change and time period are also important to the media planner because more people and less time may make the job more difficult. Scheduling decisions concerning repetition will be influenced, as will the mass or personal nature of the message delivery system.

Multiple communication objectives

Despite the amount of labor invested in defining a set of objectives, one set may be insufficient. Different objectives may be needed at different times of the year; this is most likely to occur in the fast-changing world of a new product introduction or for products with severe seasonality.

For example, for a new convenience good introduction, the goal for the first three months may be to generate awareness, the goal of the next three months may be to generate trial, and the goal for the final six months of the first year may be to ensure repeat purchases and the development of loyalty. Because most marketing communications plans cover a one-year period, it will be necessary to set goals to cover that entire year. It is easy to see that this may mean multiple objectives.

With the goals of the previous paragraph established for the first year, there might be a very heavy advertising campaign during the first quarter. In the second quarter, the strategy might show lighter advertising but heavy promotions geared to trial usage (such as samples and print or mail-delivered coupons). The third and fourth quarters would probably show promotions geared to repeat usage such as in-pack coupons and multiple purchase refund offers. In this way the strategies would be consistent with the objectives and the introduction would proceed smoothly while moving consumers through the hierarchy from unawareness to awareness to trial to repeat usage.

Marketing versus communications objectives

One problem that may arise concerns the lack of separation between marketing and communications objectives. Often management will state marketing objectives when asked for advertising and promotions objectives, but these are generally inappropriate. While the marketing goal may be to achieve an 8% market share or $57 million in sales, advertising and promotions alone cannot realistically be asked to meet this objective. Sales will be a function of several marketing variables (product, price, distribution), and communications will have a specific role in moving consumers toward purchase. While there are specific tasks that advertising and promotions can complete and for which success can be measured, the final sale (or repeat sales) should not be the exclusive responsibility of marketing communications.

Advertising can have an impact upon awareness and liking and may even have an influence on trial behavior, but, ultimately, long-run purchase behavior must result from product quality. It is not reasonable to assign a marketing objective such as long-run sales to advertising. It is, though, reasonable, prudent, and necessary to consider the marketing goals when determining communications objectives. Part of the situation analysis should be a review of marketing and corporate objectives.

Until fairly recently, there were two schools of thought regarding advertising and promotions objectives. The Sales School felt that the only meaningful goal was sales and that advertising must directly influence sales. This has become a minority view that is now dominated by the view of the Communications Effects School. The latter perspective posits that the consumer must move through the hierarchy of effects toward purchase and that advertising and promotions work in combination with the other marketing mix variables to achieve sales.

One key objection to this latter perspective is that measurement of tasks is more difficult. Opponents feel that it is easier to measure sales than it is to measure awareness, knowledge, liking, or preference. That is true; one need only monitor inventory or check the cash register to measure sales. This is also illogical because, as stated earlier, communications should not bear the sole responsibility for sales.

Additionally, one must note that the relations between awareness and behavior, or attitude and behavior, are weak. The psychology literature is replete with examples showing the weaknesses of the relations between these pairs of variables. Nevertheless, it is also the case that little behavior occurs without some level of prior awareness.

Benefits of specific marketing communications goals

Colley suggests several benefits of the DAGMAR process:

- People do better work when they have a clear idea toward what they are aiming. Specific goals allow all who are involved with the process to deal with the appropriate issues.

- Goals are critical because advertising and promotions are intangible and the resulting process is amorphous. Because these are so subjective, any opportunity to introduce objectivity must be used.

- As the work of communications is done by more specialists with narrow views beyond their own tasks, it becomes necessary for all involved to be able to see the common goal. The statement of objectives reduces wasted effort and keeps the team on target by clearly showing what needs to be said.

- Being specific allows measurement, which allows a better allocation of budgeted resources. The budget is aided in the short run of the current campaign and is also helped in the long run. By measuring success and failure, the firm gains insight for appropriate budgets in future campaigns.

These four benefits all tie closely to what may be the major reason that Colley wrote his book: to improve the client-agency relation by improving the communications between the two. By carefully spelling out objectives and putting them in writing for all parties to see, there would be increased specificity, clarity, and objectivity in a field where subjectivity and vagueness could easily undermine productivity. To get maximum benefit from objectives they must be put in writing and agreed to by all concerned parties.

Is the target market large enough?

Another benefit of setting objectives is that being specific allows an early assessment of the probability of success of the campaign. Given the marketing objectives, can the communications objectives possibly lead to strategies that will contribute to the marketing plan?

For example, the firm attempts to be as specific as possible in selecting a target market, but the more specific it gets, the smaller is the size of the target. While being specific is a virtue, the firm must also have enough prospective buyers to allow for the possibility of success. Conversely, a vaguely defined target will be larger and allow more room for success; this will be more expensive because more people who are less directly interested will need to be reached by the advertising. What to do?

Assume that the manager for a new brand of strawberry-flavored beer has the marketing objective of achieving an 8% market share by the end of the first year of the brand's life. To simplify the example, assume also that there are 50 million beer drinkers in the United States and that all have the same consumption patterns. This means that 4 million beer drinkers must become regular users of Strawbeery (the registered brand name of new strawberry-flavored beer).

To achieve this goal, the manager will establish a number of advertising and promotions objectives for the first year:

- To achieve 80% awareness of Strawbeery among all beer drinkers within the first three months of introduction

- To achieve 25% trial usage of Strawbeery *among those beer drinkers who are aware;* this goal is to be reached by the end of the sixth month after introduction
- To achieve 40% regular repeat usage of Strawbeery *among those who tried the product;* this goal is to be reached by the end of the first year

If these goals are achieved, there will be approximately 4 million regular repeat users.

Target market	50,000,000 beer drinkers
80% awareness	40,000,000
25% trial usage	10,000,000
40% repeat usage	4,000,000

This plan may work, but it is expensive because the target is large. What happens with a smaller target? Assume that the best target for Strawbeery consists of adult males with blue-collar jobs and a high school education or less. There may now be only 30 million members of the target market, but the increased specificity will allow for a more precise media plan with less wasted coverage and lower costs.

Target market	30,000,000
80% awareness	24,000,000
25% trial usage	6,000,000
40% repeat usage	2,400,000

If the earlier assumptions are correct, the manager cannot meet the goal of an 8% market share with the narrow target because this target will only yield 2.4 million regular repeat users. There are, though, some other considerations. Perhaps the narrow target consists of heavier users (20% of all beer drinkers consume 80% of all beer). If this were true, the firm could achieve an 8% market share of beer sales without having an 8% share of consumers. Perhaps, also, the narrow target market has more involvement with beer and therefore learns faster, thus allowing a smaller budget to do the job.

Or, perhaps, the higher level of involvement will lead to higher levels of trial usage. If the firm needs 4 million regular users and expects 40% of the tryers to become regular users, then it must get 10 million tryers. Given the smaller original target, 42% of those who are aware must try.

Target market	30,000,000
80% awareness	24,000,000
42% trial usage	10,080,000
40% repeat usage	4,032,000

Is it reasonable to expect to achieve a 42% trial purchase rate? Probably not. As will be seen in the promotions section of the text, redemption rates for promotional tools show much lower mean levels of trial.

Can awareness be higher than 80%? Yes, but at great expense. As will be seen in the media section of the text, advertisers can achieve 70 to 80% awareness by pouring enough money into the media plan, but the higher the desired awareness, the less efficient things become. Awareness levels above 80% are difficult to achieve, especially in the first three months of the product's life. Achieving higher awareness will become very expensive.

Can the repeat usage conversion rate exceed 40%? A 40% conversion indicates a well-liked product, inasmuch as many people will take advantage of the trial promotion but will never repurchase at the full price. A rule of thumb is that a 40% conversion means that the new product will succeed. The firm could test market the product to learn how well liked it is and perhaps the conversion rate would exceed 40%. Probably not.

All of this means that a large target is needed if the marketing goal is to be met. It is important to work through the numbers in this way to determine if the objectives are realistic. There is no value to the firm in establishing objectives that are impossible to meet. Perhaps the 8% market share is unrealistic and should be lowered. Perhaps the 8% represents what is necessary for the brand to succeed financially and meet corporate profit goals. If the latter is the case, then perhaps the firm should reconsider the introduction. Ultimately, the communications must tie back to the profitability of the firm, and the return on the advertising investment must be a reasonable one. This is truly a difficult issue and will be tackled again in the budget section of the text. In any case, it is important to examine the advertising and promotions objectives for their feasibility before beginning to develop strategies.

Quantifying objectives

One of the more difficult tasks for a manager to perform is the specific quantification of the objectives, both in terms of amount of change and time period. The task becomes easier over the years as a person gains experience with the advertising process. As noted in the previous paragraphs, there will be hints in the promotions and media sections to give the new manager some feeling about the impact of various strategic tools.

Furthermore, the process of using the decision sequence is an iterative (or repetitive) one. That is, after the situation analysis is completed, the manager will continuously adjust the objectives, strategies, and budget until all three seem reasonable. Working with internal constraints on budget, past experience, and industry data relating to the effectiveness of strategies, the manager will, over time, reach a feasible set of objectives; reasonable strategies and budget will also emerge. Using an iterative process and a sense of reason, attainable objectives *do* get set.

The role of research

The importance of research has been discussed earlier, but this issue is worth repeating with respect to the setting of objectives. A good situation analysis is necessary to establish the benchmarks required for setting objectives. If the firm does not have a clear picture of its current status, how can it develop expectations for the future? This will require primary and/or secondary research.

After completion of the time period set for the objective, additional research must be done to evaluate the success of the campaign. The purpose of this post-research is not just to be self-congratulatory or to allow for the casting of blame on others (although these goals of research are often present); in most cases the firm will need to develop another set of plans for the following year, and the post-test of the first year becomes part of the situation analysis of the second year. By doing this sort of research on an ongoing annual basis, management will stay in touch with the marketplace and continue to set relevant objectives and strategies.

Another research-related issue of relevance to objective setting concerns the need to determine the evaluation methods and terms prior to developing strategy. For example, if the objective is to achieve a specific level of awareness, the methods might include survey research where a sample of the target market is asked to name brands it is familiar with, or the method might include a Burke day-after recall test where the respondents are asked what commercials they saw on television on the previous night. Concerning terms, an awareness test might consider top-of-mind awareness, unaided awareness, or aided awareness, and the subject of the test might be awareness of the advertising, the brand, or the major benefit. These all need to be specified so that the research will measure exactly what the campaign was trying to accomplish. These issues are expanded upon later in the advertising research chapter. Defining awareness was touched upon in the previous chapter.

The issue of measurement is considered to be one of the most challenging when the MBO framework is used in advertising. If objectives are measurable, then success or failure will be apparent, but most responses to advertising are not clearly definable. Awareness, as discussed in the previous paragraph, can be measured in a number of ways, and attitude is even trickier. An attitude is a totally imaginary concept, yet the goal of advertising is often to change an attitude. The paper and pencil tests that are substitutes for attitude must be carefully designed if they are to be useful in the measurement process.

Kleber has written that "any simpleton could write objectives for a production department," but many other areas of the firm deal in intangible output. He calls the advertising and public relations area one of the six hardest to manage by objectives.[9] The issues that he raises are similar to those discussed above.

Introducing strategy

There is a tremendous temptation to introduce strategies during the setting of objectives. The temptation should be resisted. The premature discussion of strategies tends to create tunnel vision when it later actually becomes time to generate strategy. Those strategies that are stated with the objectives tend to have the inside track and are hard to dislodge. Their premature statement tends to give them a false credibility. During objective setting, management should only be concerned with *what* needs to be done, not with *how* to do it.

Colley presents as an example a case of a cooking oil that has as its benefit the fact that it does not begin to smoke until it is heated to some higher temperature than that of its competitors. Research has shown that this is important because smoke leads to a need for more frequent cleaning of the kitchen and is a threat to the cook's ego in that "other people will think I am not a good cook if they see my kitchen filled with smoke." (This was written in 1961.) Lots of interesting strategies can be generated based on that finding, but first the objective must be clearly stated. Colley suggested the following objective:

> To communicate the "no smoke" feature of the brand so that 50% of the housewives who use some kind of product for frying will be aware of the feature within two years.[10]

From this objective, strategies can then emerge and their merits can be discussed. In fact, each part of the objective contributes to the selection of correct strategy, or, conversely, to the elimination of inappropriate strategy.

Knowing the task contributes to media selection: Awareness is most easily generated through television; knowledge is transferred through print media; trial behavior needs promotional tools. A specific task also contributes to the message and should carry over to packaging, brand name, and point-of-purchase displays. The "no smoke" feature in the previous example specifically directs the message strategy.

The target market drives the vehicle selection part of media strategy because different people read different magazines, watch different programs, and so on. Characters in messages should be created to be similar to the target market in demographics and psychographics.

The amount of change and the time period will determine media and promotions scheduling decisions. How often the message needs to be repeated will depend on how quickly and to what extent the change must take place.

Some final thoughts concerning objectives

An advertising goal expresses the communications aspects of the marketing function. The goal is written in measurable terms that include

A task
A target market
A time period
A degree or amount of change

In order to make such a statement, there must first be a thorough situation analysis that leads to a statement of current benchmarks against which change can be measured. All concerned parties should agree to the current state of the world, the objectives to be achieved, and the methods to be used to evaluate later whether the objectives have been met.

Magazine Age has an annual Objectives and Results Competition to judge advertising campaigns against their objectives. Figure 5.4 shows one 1983 winner selected by the American Business Press. The International Paper Company's objective was to increase sales by 400% in 1982 without using a sales force. The firm also wanted 200 inquiries from potential distributors and 500 leads from liquor and convenience store managers. Figure 5.4 shows the print ad that ran in *Modern Brewery Age.* Ads were also designed specifically for *Liquor Store* and *Convenience Store News.* These three vehicles reached the desired targets with very little wasted coverage. Measured results showed that "sales increased by 450 percent. Interest from beer distributors exceeded objectives by 6% and inquiries from retail liquor stores and convenience stores . . . exceeded objective by 10 percent."[11]

By clearly stating its objectives, International Paper was able to measure its results, and its agency, Ogilvy & Mather, was able to home in on the most appropriate strategies while eliminating the myriad poor strategies. Remember that a key benefit of setting specific objectives is that inappropriate strategies are eliminated because they just don't fit the goals.

Figure 5.4 International Paper Company ad for Portacool

Developing a Position

One of the four components of a sound objective is to define the task of the advertising. Many practitioners of advertising feel that the single most important task is to establish the brand's position in the marketplace. This section will discuss the development of positioning strategy based on data generated in the situation analysis.[12]

What is positioning? *Ayer's Dictionary of Advertising Terms* defines it as

the art and science of fitting the product or service to one or more segments of the broad market in such a way as to set it meaningfully apart from competition.[13]

Ries and Trout, who popularized the term through extensive writings, describe and discuss positioning but do not actually define it. For them, the term refers to the image in the mind of the consumer that is created by relating the firm's brand to one or more competitive brands.[14] A brand, therefore, cannot have a position unless it has competitors against which to compare itself.

In order to succeed at a position, the brand must not just relate to the competition, but it must do so with reference to a *unique* and *meaningful benefit*. 7-Up gained market share by positioning itself as the "uncola"; this succeeded because compared to colas it was unique and in the soft drink field the presence or absence of cola was a key discriminating variable for consumers.

In 1982, 7-Up dramatically changed its position relative to its competitors by advertising that it had no caffeine. This was not a unique benefit at the time (RC-100 was first), but it seems to have been a meaningful benefit because within a year all of the major competitors had introduced caffeine-free colas and rendered the position virtually meaningless.

A related issue in the 7-Up no-caffeine position concerns being first with, or preempting, a position. Often a position is not unique but the firm that states it first appears to make it unique. United Airlines, for example, has for years had "friendly skies." Consumers relate friendliness with United and any other airline using this attribute would do less well with it.

A position exploits consumers' perceptions of a unique and meaningful benefit in the product class. Knabler[15] presents four simple but important rules concerning these perceptions in the marketplace.

1. *If consumers aren't users or potential users, they are of no concern to the firm.* Developing the appropriate target market for the position is important. Segmentation and positioning are closely related because the position will rarely appeal to the entire market. Positioning based on benefits really ties very closely to benefit segmentation (which was discussed in Chapter 2).

Calantone and Sawyer[16] examined benefit segmentation and positioning in the banking industry and showed how to derive strategy from the data. They also showed that the benefit segments were stable over a two-year period even though the demographic characteristics of the segment members changed somewhat. This implied that while the message strategy (based on the position which, in turn, is based on benefit segmentation) would hold for a long period of time, the media strategy (based on demographics) would need to be revised periodically.

This stability in attributes and benefits has also been shown in studies by McGraw-Hill. This research has shown that across many industrial research projects, the most important attributes are very similar. Famous Footwear, a chain of shoe stores, in its annual research of its consumer markets, has also found remarkable stability over time, to the point where it now does not feel a need to ask respondents about the importance of attributes.

2. *If the users do not believe that a product characteristic is a benefit to them, it isn't a benefit.* Perceptions are reality. Consumer perceptions dictate consumer behavior, and management perceptions aren't relevant at the point of consumer decision making.

Consumer perceptions are based on benefits, but the firm's perceptions are often based on attributes. Consumers don't buy attributes; they buy benefits. Therefore, the attributes must be translated to benefits in order to develop a meaningful position. In a simplistic example, the automobile has attributes of round wheels, independent suspension (whatever that means), and shock absorbers (whatever they are), but the benefit is a smooth ride. Consumers generally make decisions based on perceived benefits to them, not on attributes.

3. *If the benefit is not important to the user, it isn't important.* Again, the perceptions of the consumer are all encompassing. Importance of the benefit is a key issue in designing positioning and can be determined readily through the multiattribute attitude models discussed in Chapter 3. Using a figure such as Figure 3.11 from that chapter gives a visual representation of importance. The multidimensional scaling models also show importance but do so in a more subtle way because management must derive them from a mapping such as the one shown in Figure 3.15 from the same chapter.

Figure 5.5 *Fictitious data for compact auto market*

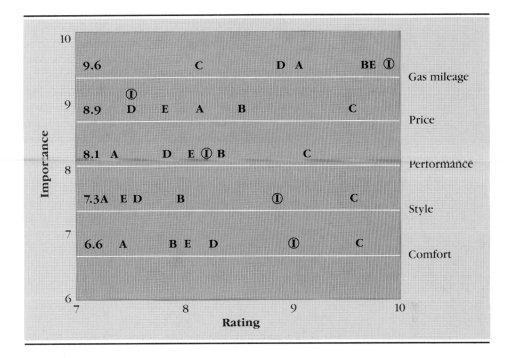

Figure 3.11 is reproduced here as Figure 5.5. From these data one can derive a position for Brand B based on (a) unique meaningful benefit(s). Note that while gas mileage is meaningful, it is not unique because Brand E scores equally well. Note also that while style is a unique benefit of B, it is not very important or meaningful. True uniqueness results for B when gas mileage, performance, and style are combined. Brand B is the only one to offer that combination. Now this dry and sterile position must be brought alive by a big idea that creatively shows the benefits of these attributes.

There is an irony to the issue of selecting important and meaningful benefits upon which to position. The more important an attribute or benefit is to a large number of consumers, the more likely it is that all major brands have that feature, and therefore it is of little value in positioning. As a result, in reality the firm must turn to lesser benefits or unique combinations of benefits (as for Brand B in Figure 5.5 above). The challenge in pursuing this strategy continues when the manager considers that a large portion of advertising is devoted to 30-second commercials in which only limited information can be disseminated.

4. *If the user does not perceive that the firm delivers the benefit, then the firm doesn't deliver.* Once more, perceptions are vital. Returning to Figure 5.5, it doesn't matter that Brand A is felt to be quite stylish by the National Academy of Stylish Automobiles (NASA) or that NASA awarded the brand the 4-Fin Award for "most spiffy design." What matters is that consumers don't have the same perceptions. This is a difficult situation. Not only does the firm need to create a position, but when it does, chances are good that it won't be accepted. Either A can change its style or try to convince consumers that its style is indeed a good one.

The reason that positioning is based on difference, according to Ries and Trout, is that the United States has too much communications noise. There is too much advertising, too much repetition, too much clutter, and there are too many brands. Some figures alluding to this were presented in the introductory section of this text. In order to have an impact, Ries and Trout feel, a message must be tied to something else to which consumers can relate. New messages will be rejected if they differ from existing perceptions; therefore, positioning builds on what exists in consumers' perceptions of the world. Avis tried harder because Hertz was number one. The Avis message built on what existed in consumers' minds and made it relevant to themselves. Volkswagen built its position by acknowledging that other cars were prettier and flashier. Miller Lite acknowledged that other beers had more calories. Miller made less into a virtue, as had Avis and Volkswagen.

These three firms all admitted that consumers' perceptions were correct, but then expanded those perceptions to include themselves. In this way, present perceptions were accepted by the firm as correct and not challenged, but these were then shown to be incomplete; when new information was added, behaviors often changed even though perceptions had not. Consumers did not feel threatened, but their view of the product class had broadened.

Problems created by poor positions

If the position is not appropriate it will lead to later problems. Some potential problems are discussed next. If the firm is not the leader (and most are not), it should not attack the leader's established position. It is hard to beat an estab-

Figure 5.6 Directly attacking the leader

Figure 5.7 Building off the leader's strengths

lished brand on its own merits. Most leading national brands have invested millions of dollars in advertising. It is hard to overtake them by saying, "We are better than Brand X on X's major attribute or benefit." Consumers know and trust Brand X and have less reason to believe the new brand. Let X have its benefits and position; to beat the leader the firm must develop its own niche and its own position. Figures 5.6 and 5.7 show two disparate themes. One attacks the leader; it tries to take away share by being better than the leader at its own game. The other acknowledges the leader and builds its own position relative to the leader's.

Another positioning flaw is the "me-too" position. Some brands claim to be as good as another or to have a trivial—but meaningless—advantage. Why should the consumer switch brands? It may not be sufficient to be an improved version of a succesful brand. How much more of a winning benefit would it take to gain share from a competitor? And if it is successful, how long will it take for the competitor to respond with a "new improved" version? Because the original position belongs to the competitor, it will be tough to dislodge that firm. Again, it is probably wiser to develop a new position. Figure 5.8 is an example of a "me-too" message that may not compel brand-switching behavior.

Ries and Trout[17] warn against a number of other positioning traps. These are discussed next and are followed by recommended strategies.

Figure 5.8   A "me-too" position

The factory trap   Firms often design products to pick up slack production time. These products lead to efficiencies in the factory but may have no market at which to aim. This trap goes back to the difference between the product concept and the marketing concept. If there is no need for the new product, then it is not necessary to devote production time to its manufacture. There must be a perceived unique meaningful benefit. Similar to the factory trap is *the technology trap,* which can lead to the same problems. Just because a new idea is different, takes advantage of a technological innovation, and can be produced does not mean that it is needed.

The everybody trap   Trying to be something for everyone makes it very difficult to have a position. Positioning is, as stated earlier, an outgrowth of benefit segmentation, and as such it ties closely to the basic concepts of segmentation. Few products engage in undifferentiated segmentation, that is, in appealing to the entire marketplace. There are also few positions that are meaningful for an entire market. By trying to be all things to all consumers, the brand is most likely to end up with no position at all and weak sales.

The line extension trap   In this case the new brand attempts to build a position based on the existing position and brand name of another product manufactured by the same firm. In the short run the new brand gains because awareness and distribution come easier if the name is familiar. Over time, though, the name becomes weaker for both the old and the new brand. People are confused about the position of each, and both brands suffer. For example, J. C. Penney and Sears both introduced automobile batteries; one was named the J. C. Penney Battery and the other was the DieHard. Both have the same features, both will last 48 months, yet only one name says something important about the product and only one creates a position. This issue is discussed in more depth in the chapter concerning brand names.

The F.W.M.T.S. trap   This acronym stands for "forgot what made them successful." Often a brand does well with a particular position and then violates its own position; this can quickly turn around a winning campaign and lead to problems. Volkswagen lost ground when it introduced a large, plush car; the concept of a large, plush Volkswagen doesn't fit in people's minds. Avis said it wanted to be number one; again consumers couldn't conceive of this. Avis was liked *because* it was number two and tried harder. Would it try as hard if it were number one? Not according to its ads. Number two tries harder. Changing a successful position has no logic and can be dangerous to corporate health.

One final problem emerges when the original position no longer works and must be replaced. *Playboy* developed a position over many years of presenting a voice on the forefront of a new, more liberal morality. In more recent years, it has been passed by other magazines that were willing to push harder against the borders. As a result *Playboy* was left without its position. Readers detected this trend and began to search elsewhere for tantalizing thoughts and pictures. To pursue new readers, the magazine attempted to change its position to reflect the prevailing fashions, but it met resistance because this market remembered the old position. The magazine's original audience was moving elsewhere but no new audience appeared to subscribe to the altered *Playboy* image. It is very hard to establish two positions in the life of one brand. The more people remember the first position, the more difficult it is to establish a second one.

This point is especially difficult for an image-oriented position such as that of *Playboy*. A real product change can be shown through a new position and new advertising. The cost of this change is high, though. The J. C. Penney Company is spending $1.5 billion to refurbish its stores so that it can change its image. It is also spending many millions in advertising to support the new position. Initial sales seem to be increasing in support of the new position.

Developing positions that lead to strategies

There are several other authors who also have dealt with positioning. The rest of the chapter summarizes ideas that have not been presented earlier. Aaker and Shansby[18] discuss six strategies that should be considered in developing the appropriate position:

- *Positioning by attribute* The most common way to position is to set the brand apart by the attribute or benefit it offers. This can be done by developing a particular niche, by developing a benefit that others have ignored, or by combining two or more benefits.

- *Positioning by price/quality* Products, services, and retailers all can use an image in this area. For some the position is of high price and quality; for others the desired position is low price and adequate quality. In each case "value" must be conveyed in addition to the price/quality relation.

- *Positioning with respect to use or application* Segmentation can be done on the basis of usage occasion, and so can positioning. It is not necessary to capture all usage, but, rather, it is important to dominate some aspect of usage. Rice Chex as a snack food, Arm and Hammer baking soda as a deodorizer, and Jello as an ingredient in many colorful desserts and side dishes all capture one type of product usage.

- *Positioning by the product user* Users can be segmented in many ways as previously seen. Johnson & Johnson at one time positioned its shampoo toward infant/baby usage but gained a large increase in sales when it was repositioned toward adults who wanted a gentle shampoo. They achieved the latter position without losing the original market. Marlboro was originally a cigarette aimed at women, but it became the largest selling brand in the world after it was repositioned against men.

- *Positioning with respect to a product class* Rather than relate to another brand, a brand can position itself against another product class. Parkay doesn't compete with other margarines; its advertising is built on the theme that "the flavor says butter." Amtrak service between New York City and Washington, D.C., has positioned itself against the automobile by showing that the train is cheaper and has fewer hassles from one downtown to the other. Figure 5.9 shows a different ad that positions Amtrak against the airlines but does it from another perspective. In these examples the positioning was against a different product class but one where there clearly was substitutability.

- *Positioning with respect to a competitor* This is a key strategy, according to Trout and Ries, and is similar to the prior strategy except that the product class boundaries are erased. The most successful positions are those that relate to the competition. M&M is a candy that "melts in your mouth, not in your hands"; this sets it apart. "When a candy bar is only a memory, you'll still be eating your

NOT EVERYONE WAS MEANT TO FLY.

Although flying on a commercial airliner is one of the most widely accepted ways to travel, a lot of people still don't like to fly. It makes them feel uncomfortable to be strapped into a seat. To be told when they can get up. And when they can't. To have to wait to be served a drink when they're thirsty. And a meal when they're hungry.

Fortunately, there is a real alternative to flying—training.

A delicious menu is available on most trains.

On a train, you have infinitely more freedom than on a plane. For instance, there are no seat belts. So you can get up and stretch your legs whenever you like. If you're hungry, you can walk into the dining car and order anything from a snack to a full meal on most trains.

We also think you'll find training more comfortable than planing. Our coach seats are wider than the seats most airlines use. So you have more room to stretch out and relax, or get some work done.

Amtrak has improved its on-time record nearly 40%.

Of course, creature comforts aren't the only reasons for traveling by train. Did you know that Amtrak can take you to over 475 different cities and towns. That's more than all the major airlines in the U.S. put together.

Since 1979, we've improved our on-time performance nearly 40%. And, in the last 6½ years, we've rebuilt our entire fleet. Amtrak now offers you some of the newest, most technologically advanced equipment in the world.

So the next time you're planning to travel somewhere, think about taking the train. See how good it feels to fly without leaving the ground.

For information and reservations, call Amtrak or your travel agent.

ALL ABOARD AMTRAK

Figure 5.9 *Amtrak versus the airlines*

Milk Duds"; again the brand is set apart by implicit comparison to competition. Scope's "medicine breath" campaign was successful because it was built with respect to a competitor. Ironically, Listerine also remained successful by building on Scope's medicine breath theme. The two brands truly dominate the product class, having built positions against one another to the exclusion of all other brands.

Ries and Trout also discuss the "ugly" position, the "against" position, and the "uncola" position. In each case these positions for Volkswagen, Avis, and 7-Up, respectively, are built against competitors. They explicitly acknowledge the position attributes of the competition and then build on these for their own ends.

Developing the position from the situation analysis

The brand's position must be built on data gathered in the situation analysis. It is necessary to identify the competitors; these will include all products and brands that are substitutable. Next, one needs to assess these competitors in terms of how they are perceived and what positions they hold. A key part of this is also to determine the underlying attributes and benefits. These data allow a mapping to be generated either using MAM, MDS, or intuitive data as discussed previously in the situation analysis. Analyzing these data leads to the development of the brand's position. Ennis[19] has suggested a three-stage process in this development:

1. *Category positioning*   Here the brand is assessed relative to alternative applications and market potentials. Rather than discussing multiple applications or uses, the brand should seek one role where there is good market potential and stick with that identity. Ennis' example here is of Pillsbury's Figurines. Should this product be positioned as a nutritional breakfast food to compete with Carnation's Instant Breakfast or as a low-calorie snack food to compete with General Mills' Granola Bars? Management should consider the market potential of each alternative, taking into account potential sales and growth of the category as well as the intensity of competition.

2. *Selling positioning*   This refers to the specific selling idea used to market the product to the public and can be broken down further into product-oriented and consumer-oriented positioning concepts. Of these two, Ennis feels that the product orientation is more commonly used because here there is an observable physical difference that can be communicated more easily.

(a) *Product-oriented positioning concept*   These selling ideas are based on a specific attribute of the product and lend themselves to a quick solution for the marketer in search of a position. Unfortunately, such positions also lend themselves to quick duplication by competition. For example, Lipton Cup-A-Soup led to a product-oriented position that achieved rapid success but was quickly followed by Nestle's Souptime. The mere physical attribute of a single-portion serving was too easy to duplicate. When an innovation is easy to copy, the position will be hard to protect without large expenditures for advertising and promotion.

(b) *Consumer-oriented positioning concept*   Selling ideas here are based on consumer perceptions and may avoid all reference to product attributes. This type of positioning is closest to the conceptualization of Ries and Trout and relates the brand to the consumer's unique perspective of the product class. Ries and Trout's examples of Avis, Volkswagen, and 7-Up are classic cases of consumer-oriented positioning concepts. These positions are more difficult to copy because they only exist in the mind. Once the position is established in the mind it is hard to dislodge.

Ennis points out that best of all is a combination that develops a consumer orientation for a physical attribute. His example is of American Optical Company's bifocal eyeglasses in which the bifocal line is eliminated. A product orientation would point out that the line was missing. American Optical, though, pointed out that users looked younger because the bifocal line was missing. The physical attribute was not the primary issue; the benefit of a more youthful appearance was primary and the attribute was merely support for the benefit.

3. *Commercial positioning*   Here the message rather than the product is positioned and the basis is, again, a consumer orientation. The advantage of this class of strategy is that it is based totally in the mind of the consumer and is therefore more difficult for the competition to dislodge. For the same reason, this strategy is most difficult to execute. While most attempts in this direction fail, successes lead to long-term profits.

Marlboro cigarettes has a unique unassailable position although the product itself is essentially generic. Miller Lite Beer has a unique position that competitors have not been able to attack even though there are some who say that light beer

T·H·E I·N·S·I·D·E ° O·U·T·L·O·O·K

William E. Whitney, Jr.

Managing Director, Ogilvy & Mather, Chicago

Bill is a veteran of 28 years in agency account management. He joined Ogilvy & Mather's New York office in 1960 as Account Executive on Lever's Dove Beauty Bar. From 1960 to 1968, he supervised a number of the agency's package goods accounts including Lever and Mead Johnson Nutritionals. He was elected a Vice President in 1966.

In 1968 he became Account Supervisor on the agency's assignments from Sears, Roebuck and Co. He was named Management Supervisor on Sears in 1971 and also assumed management responsibility for the Nationwide Insurance Co. advertising in 1973. He was elected a Senior Vice President in 1971.

In 1976 Bill moved to Chicago as General Manager and one of the founders of Ogilvy & Mather's Chicago office. He has helped that office grow from four to fifteen clients and become the agency's second largest office in the world. He has been responsible for the supervision of account management for all accounts and Chairman of the office's Strategy Review Board. He was named Managing Director in 1981 and a member of Ogilvy & Mather U.S., Board of Directors in 1984.

Before joining Ogilvy & Mather, Bill received a Master's Degree in Marketing from Harvard Business School and worked at McCann-Erickson and McCann-Marschalk for four years on the Coca-Cola and Genessee Brewing Co. accounts. He is a graduate of Amherst College in 1954 with a B.A. in economics.

Objectives and Positioning

In previous chapters in this book, you have read about the importance of an objective and thorough analysis and understanding of the competitive societal and business environment in which products and services seek to compete successfully.

In this chapter you have read about the important task of finding the best positioning for a product, service, or brand and of setting realistic advertising objectives for a brand.

As you study this chapter on positioning and objectives, you might consider some of the things we have learned over the years and from the experience of our offices all around the world. It won't provide you with a pat formula, but it should bring a perspective to your studies from those of us who make advertising that attempts to position products and meet objectives.

Clearly, objectives that are based on sound information are central to any advertising plan or program and, just as clearly, those objectives must be based on the most competitive product positioning, i.e., the positioning that offers the greatest ROI in advertising and communications.

Remember that advertisers do not spend money to *say* something to consumers but to *do* something to them. It may be to change a long-held attitude about a product or a service or brand; it may be to make them aware of a benefit—a benefit they may be unaware of or may have overlooked; or it may be to convince them that one product attribute is more important than another in the selection of a brand or a service.

Today, understanding the consumer goes from demographics, psychographics, and lifestyles to a rounded and well-thought-through understanding of attitudes, values, and aspirations. Remember when you set objectives and position your advertising—and your product—that very few successful products are pushed by the manufacturer: They are pulled by the consumer. Products that are not consumer led will fail.

In today's marketplace the consumer is offered an enormous number of options and alternatives for his or her dollars, time, or attention. The competitive choices are many and are not always conveniently in the same product category. Even if they are, the consumer is often faced with brands that offer familiar or similar benefits.

In the decision process, the consumer reduces the greater number of choices to a lesser number that he or she will consider for purchase to fill a general or specific need or meet general or specific performance criteria.

In order to be among the brands that will be considered, you need to position your product or brand on the basis of the benefits—rational, sensory, or emotional—that you offer, how they separate you from your competition, and what their importance is in the consumers' decision process. The key is to know what the consumer thinks of a brand now and what you want him or her to think of the brand in the future. Advertising is one of the means for getting the consumer to consideration and on to purchase.

And don't forget the competition is doing the same thing.

is merely regular beer that has been watered down, and that many similar brands exist. In both cases the position is based on the commercial position more than on product attributes.

Conversely, there are many other commercial positions that fail because they do not have the right impact on consumers. If the product has a truly unique difference that is difficult to copy, then a product-oriented position is appropriate, but most brands do not offer much of a difference and must, therefore, rely on a consumer or commercial orientation. As David Ogilvy has said, "It isn't too difficult to decide how to position your product. Any intelligent brand manager can do it. But it takes genius to create a *big idea* based on the positioning . . . And a lot of today's campaigns which are based on optimum positioning are totally ineffective—because they are dull, or badly constructed, or ineptly written. If nobody *reads* your advertisement or *looks* at your commercial, it doesn't do you much good to have the right positioning." The message must communicate the benefit creatively.

Another way to tackle the positioning question is presented by Overholser and Kline.[20] From their perspective the key issue is that of *product class definition.* They note that traditional product classes are generally arbitrary and based on ease of data collection for the industry or on some long-forgotten definition. In reality the product class is defined by consumers, based on the choices they consider when attempting to meet needs or acquire benefits. That is, items that are substitutable are in the same product class. As products proliferate, brands compete across traditional product class lines or are so specialized as to define their own narrow product classes. For these reasons, part of the positioning decision is to first define the product class and the relevant competition. This decision then guides the later decisions of target market selection and message strategy.

The concept of defining the product is taken a step further in an article by Bloom,[21] where he discusses what he calls *product redefinition.* For him, Calvin Klein jeans are not blue jeans, they are a sex symbol; Miller isn't a beer, it's blue-collar macho; and the American Express card isn't a piece of plastic to charge purchases, it's a security blanket. Product redefinition stresses the benefit that the consumer pursues rather than the physical attributes of the product. Such redefinition, Bloom feels, leads to better creative strategy.

Positioning refers to the place a brand occupies in the mind in relation to a given product class. This place was originally a product-related concept based on economics work concerning market structure, product class definition, substitution, and competition. The concept now refers to the place that the brand holds in the consumer's mind relative to perceptions and preferences. Given this shift, the term is now important to communications because the perceived position will be as much a result of advertising as of product development. As brands continue to proliferate and there are fewer real differences among them, the brands will need to set themselves apart more on the basis of positioning and will define their product class and competitors on the basis of consumer perceptions and preferences.

As a result, an important part of the situation analysis is a study of perceptions and preferences. This type of research was discussed in Chapter 3 and is done primarily through attitude models such as the multiattribute attitude models (MAM) and multidimensional scaling (MDS). Wind[22] has suggested several strategy issues that emerge. These include:

1. *Consideration of relevant target markets*   The greater the specificity of the position, the more precise must be the target. Most applications of positioning simultaneously examine the perceived relations between brands and various market segments and then target the position to a specific subset of consumers. It is better to dominate a viable portion of a market than to be a little-known brand to all consumers. The latter strategy, which often emerges from trying to be all things to all people, can lead to being second or third best to all people. First place will go to the brand that carefully nurtures a particular target. Being a brand for all consumers means that the brand will come in behind each of the well-positioned brands that are dominating their own small segments of the market.

2. *Consideration of the entire product line*   Most firms offer more than one product and must therefore also position each item so as not to cannibalize its own alternative offerings. Often this is not a severe problem; for example, General Motors' Cadillac is a product quite distinct from the Vega (which no longer exists). As the product line grows, the problem increases, such as when General Motors has a Buick and a Chevrolet (and consumers know that the engines and bodies may come from the same design), or a Camaro and a Chevrolet as well as a Vega. (In 1984, General Motors began to restructure its divisions so that problems such as the Buick-Chevrolet overlap could be eliminated.) Figure 5.10 shows a mapping and clustering of several brands of automobiles. While the map's main purpose is to give positioning guidance versus competitive companies, the threat of cannibalization must also be considered. In Figure 5.10, the different offerings of the Chevrolet division of General Motors cluster separately, although Chevrolet does compete with Buick.

In the automobile example it is easy to make the case that there are specific physical differences that keep Vega, Camaro, and Chevrolet from cannibalizing one another. If the examples were Procter & Gamble detergents, this argument would be more difficult to support, but the brands are still positioned separately so as not to cannibalize. Tide makes clothes white, Cheer makes them whiter than white in all temperatures, and Bold makes them bright. Each has its own position even though they each pursue a similar target market.

3. *Consideration of alternative bases for positioning*   These are similar to those suggested earlier by Aaker and Shansby[23]:

- Position on specific product features ("The new Chevrolet Cavalier. Its new high-compression fuel-injected engine will make it go quicker. So will its new lower price.").
- Position on benefits or needs ("Here comes Bright; a fresh new taste experience that outshines menthol.").
- Position for specific usage occasions ("Weekends were made for Michelob.").
- Position against another brand ("In a side-by-side-by-side test for crisp, clear copies, we [Minolta] tied with IBM and Xerox [shown in visual and copy].").
- Position against another product class ("Our Puerto Rican white rum is smoother than gin or vodka.").
- Position by the product user ("The one beer to have when you're having more than one.").
- Position by price/quality ("Good shoes at great prices.").

The choice of a positioning strategy should be a function of

- *Whether the brand is a leader or a follower*   Ries and Trout's first rule is never to attack the leader. It is too difficult to take on the leader at what it does

Figure 5.10 *(a) Two-di-mensional configuration of brands of automobiles (il-lustrative output); (b) Hi-erarchical clustering analy-sis of 14 automobiles (illustrative output); (c) Two-dimensional configuration of brands of automobiles and their clus-ters (illustrative output of superimposing the results of a hierarchical clustering analysis over the multidi-mensional scaling solu-tion)*

(a)
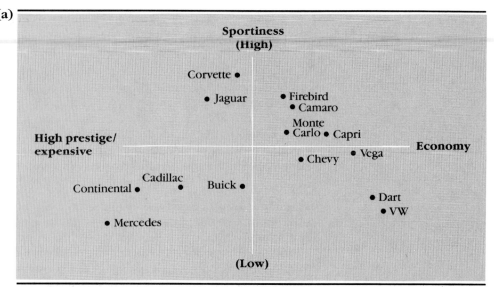

(b)
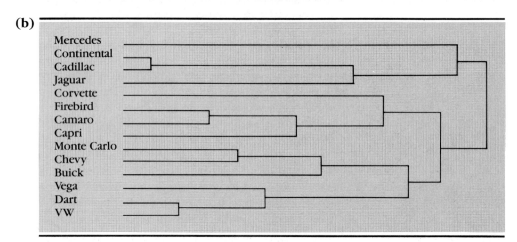

(c)
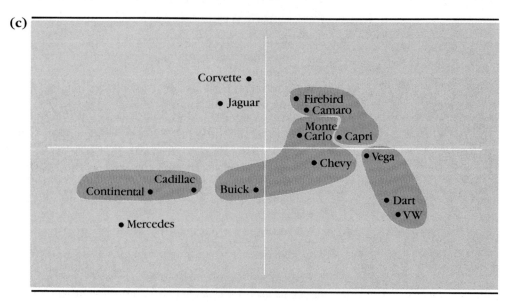

best. The leader doesn't need to attack and can even ignore competition. Often the leader's advertising is generic because it will pick up the largest share of any growth in the product class.

- *The current positioning of competitors and the newness of the brand*   The first to use a position will own it (until that firm gives it up or doesn't properly support it through advertising). Being a "me-too" brand offers no benefit unless there is a price differential.

- *The resources available to communicate the position effectively*   Ries and Trout warn that it is very expensive and time consuming to establish a position. This holds even more strongly when there is a commercial position rather than a product or benefit orientation. Once the position is established, it takes many more dollars to maintain it because success will spawn several "me-too" brands eager to share that success.

Regarding the above points, one can look at the successes of the Philip Morris Company. This chapter has examined three of their big hits:

- *Marlboro*   Originally a weak brand positioned as a woman's cigarette (ahead of its time, perhaps), it was repositioned as a strong macho brand and became the world's largest selling brand. The position wasn't based on any product attribute or benefit, yet it earned a unique spot in male smokers' minds. Philip Morris later came back with a different position to get the women's market through Virginia Slims.

- *Miller Lite*   Low-calorie beer was introduced in 1968 (Gablinger's) and failed; in the early 1970s, Meister Brau Lite was introduced and also failed. When Miller introduced low-calorie beer in 1975, it was positioned as a less-filling but still all-man style beer. Lite was first with a unique position and became very successful. Competitors have failed by attacking the less-filling position and also by returning to the low-calorie position. Miller's success has made it hard for any other brand to compete, and Miller Lite dominates a growing product class that didn't exist until they created it.

- *7-Up*   This brand is also now in the Philip Morris stable, and its most recent positioning strategy has caused retrenchment of the entire soft drink industry. The caffeine-free position has led to many new introductions. By the end of 1983, noncaffeine colas had 8% of soft drink sales, and all caffeine-free soft drinks had over 20% market share.[24]

In addition to the successes, Philip Morris also owns Löwenbräu. Even the best don't always totally succeed. This brand had a great position, "a truly great German beer," when Miller bought it. But Miller decided that it couldn't import it fast enough and started brewing it in the United States. As a result it needed to change its position; it went to "a truly great American beer," but the new position didn't work. Löwenbräu doesn't sound American; its virtue was the aura of an import. Miller has now spent many millions creating a new position, after they lost their original truly great beer position.

Summary

This concludes the setting of objectives and positioning. These important decisions will guide the strategy during the remainder of the decision sequence framework. The decisions made here came directly from the situation analysis research. The key issues concerned:

- Defining the target market
- Defining the relevant stage of the hierarchy of effects
- Defining the key attributes and benefits of the product
- Defining the key competitors

Based primarily on these issues, and to a lesser degree some other issues, the situation analysis has allowed objectives and positioning to be determined. Next the message strategy, media strategy, and promotions strategy will be developed.

Discussion Questions

1. Write a set of objectives and a positioning statement that will guide your strategy during your job search. How can you position yourself in a unique and meaningful way in a product class of thousands of look-alike brands? What unique benefits can you offer an employer?

2. What are the four components of an objective that is derived using the DAGMAR model?

3. Why would a brand need multiple objectives?

4. How can you justify an advertising goal of raising awareness when everyone knows that the real goal of advertising is to sell more product?

5. How can you tell if the target market is large enough?

6. What are the characteristics of a position that will help a brand in a competitive marketplace?

7. Describe a positioning statement for each brand shown in Figure 5.5.

Notes

1. Russell H. Colley, *Defining Advertising Goals for Measured Advertising Results* (New York: Association of National Advertisers, 1961).

2. Peter F. Drucker, *The Practice of Management* (New York: Harper & Row, 1954), p. 60.

3. Douglas McGregor, "An Uneasy Look at Performance Appraisal," *Harvard Business Review* 35 (May–June 1975), pp. 89–94.

4. Michael J. Etzel and John M. Ivancevich, "Management by Objectives in Marketing: Philosophy, Process, and Problems," *Journal of Marketing* 38 (October 1974), pp. 47–55.

5. Etzel and Ivancevich, "Management by Objectives in Marketing," pp. 47–55.

6. Lewis Carroll, *Alice's Adventures in Wonderland* (London: Macmillan, 1877).

7. Colley, *Defining Advertising Goals*, p. 6.

8. R. Lavidge and G. A. Steiner, "A Model for Predictive Measurements of Advertising Effectiveness," *Journal of Marketing* 25 (October 1961), pp. 59–62.

9. Thomas P. Kleber, "The Six Hardest Areas to Manage by Objectives," *Personnel Journal* (August 1972), pp. 571–575.

10. Colley, *Defining Advertising Goals*, p. 41.

11. *Magazine Age*, July 1983, p. 52.

12. This discussion is due in large part to the work of Al Ries and Jack Trout: *Positioning: The Battle for Your Mind* (New York: McGraw-Hill, 1982).

13. *Ayer's Dictionary of Advertising Terms* (Philadelphia: Ayer Press, 1976).

14. Ries and Trout, *Positioning*.

15. William Knabler, "Position Brand in Its Optimal Niche by Finding Benefits That Matter to Buyers," *Marketing News*, 15 May 1981, sec. 2, pp. 14–15.

16. Roger J. Calantone and Alan G. Sawyer, "The Stability of Benefit Segments," *Journal of Marketing Research* 15 (August 1978), pp. 395–404.

17. Ries and Trout, *Positioning*.

18. David Aaker and J. Gary Shansby, "Positioning Your Product," *Business Horizons* 25 (May/June 1982), pp. 56–62.

19. Beavin F. Ennis, "Positioning Revisited," *Advertising Age*, 15 March 1982, p. M-43.

20. Charles E. Overholser and John M. Kline, "Advertising Strategy from Consumer Research," presented at the FTC Hearings on Advertising, October 1971, reprinted in David A. Aaker, *Advertising Management: Practical Perspectives* (Englewood Cliffs, N.J.: Prentice-Hall, 1975).

21. Robert H. Bloom, "Product Redefinition Begins with Consumer," *Advertising Age*, 26 October 1981, p. 51.

22. Yoram Wind, *Product Policy* (Boston: Addison-Wesley, 1982).

23. Aaker and Shansby, "Positioning Your Product," pp. 56–62.

24. *Advertising Age*, 2 January 1984, p. 24.

OBJECTIVES, POSITIONING, AND TARGET MARKET

Objectives

The Sunkist sales goal was to become the best sell-ing carbonated orange soft drink and to be one of the top ten soft drink brands by 1981, and to achieve a 3.5% overall market share by 1985. Table S.1 shows the 1977 market shares of the leading brands and shows what Sunkist would need to do to break into the top ten.

Table S.1 1977 soft drink industry brand shares

	Rank	Brand	1977
	1	Coca-Cola	26.3%
	2	Pepsi-Cola	17.6
	3	7-Up	5.9
	4	Dr. Pepper	5.4
	5	Sprite	3.1
	6	RC Cola	3.0
	7	Tab	2.9
	8	Mountain Dew	2.4
	9	Diet Pepsi	2.3
1981 Objective	10	Sunkist	2.1

Sunkist's advertising goal was to establish its posi-tion. Management recognized that the brand choice decision was a low involvement one and would be based on emotional rather than rational persuasion. The advertising, therefore, should capture the es-sence of people's perceptions of what Sunkist and a Sunkist drinker would be like.

Position

As the research drew to a close, two prospective po-sitions were put forth. Based upon the limited quan-titative research, some advisors concluded that the brand should be positioned as the best orange soda and that this position should be based upon clearly establishing the product's differences and superior-ity. The recommended target was the high orange consumption segment comprised primarily of chil-dren and teens, aged 6–18. These conclusions were soundly based on the research studies that were available.

However, the advertising agency was also con-ducting a lot of research to aid in defining the proper advertising strategy. This work indicated that there was a different and more promising direction. Considering Foote, Cone & Belding findings on top of the basic user studies led to a different interpreta-tion of the results that supported the best orange positioning.

Sunkist had gained some valuable insights into consumer perceptions and attitudes toward orange soda as well as the meaning of Sunkist, the percep-tion of what the product would be like, and who would drink it. These findings were most encourag-ing and indicated that the Sunkist name was the key to unlocking the opportunity for the brand because it took the "dippyness" out of orange and redefined consumer perceptions of the category. With that in-formation the firm faced a decision to position Sunkist as "the best orange" or as a "legitimate major brand alternative."

It concluded that Sunkist orange soda should be positioned as a legitimate major brand alternative, not just as the best orange. While the "best orange" positioning was very reasonable, the "major brand" positioning was more daring and really expanded the brand's horizons beyond the limitations of the orange segment. It was a "bigger idea" that repre-sented significantly greater volume potential. More-over, the Sunkist name was powerful enough to make it possible.

Target market

The target audience grew right out of this positioning. The firm concluded that Sunkist orange soda should be targeted to all soft drink consumers aged 12–34 with emphasis on high consumption segments, not just current orange users. This was consistent with the strategic positioning, and the Sunkist name made it possible because it connoted a more adult orange. As can be seen in Table S.2, the 12–34 age group had the largest number of heavy soft drink users.

Table S.2 Heavy users—soft drinks

Age	Index
18–24	164
25–34	131
35–44	99
45–54	78
55–64	57
65+	36

Source: Target Group Index, Courtesy of Sunkist Growers, Inc.

In DAGMAR terms, the objectives were

1. To create 90% awareness of the Sunkist name and position among soft drink consumers, aged 12–34, within 13 weeks of entering a geographic market.

2. To get 80% trial of Sunkist among those in the target market that were aware (e.g., 72% of the entire target market), within 13 weeks of entering a geographic market.

3. To achieve a 2.1% market share of all soft drink sales by the end of 1981.

173

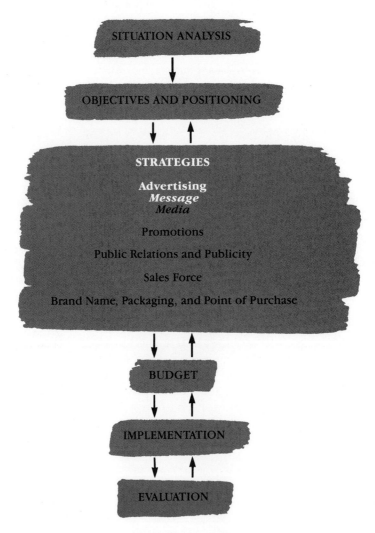

Decision Sequence Framework

Part Four
Message
Strategies

*I*t's not creative unless it sells.[1]

This is the stated philosophy of Benton & Bowles and the unwritten philosophy of most other major advertising agencies, and it should be everyone's guiding star in advertising, for the purpose of advertising is not to entertain but rather to assist in the selling of the product.

Creativity is essential. Without it, the target market will pass over the message and learn more slowly about the product. But creativity for its own sake is insufficient; it must be used to show the unique benefit of the product in a memorable way. By combining one or more benefits in a memorable way, creativity has the chance to help sell the product. Benton & Bowles has said all this very nicely in an ad to prospective clients which is shown in Figure 1.

What happens when creativity is misguided and doesn't show a benefit? A few years ago a wristwatch that was able to show the time in two time zones ran an ad with the headline, "Quick! If it's 10:09 in Tokyo, What Time Is it in Tucson?" This ad may have been creative and may have been unique, but it is not clear that it showed a benefit to many prospective buyers. One response to the question in the headline is: "Who cares?"; this may be followed by a quick page turning. It's not creative if it's not compelling. And it is always dangerous to ask a question that can be answered by "who cares?".

What happens when creativity is misguided and implies the wrong product? An ad for Rauschenberger carpeting may have gone off in the wrong direction when it tried to be cute with the brand name. The headline stated: "Here comes a rauschenberger with the works!" The visual showed a hamburger and pickle on a plate and a soft drink. The copy begins with references to McDonald's. On close inspection the reader can see that there is carpeting inside the hamburger roll, and the copy discusses a new brand of carpeting. Both the visual and the headline

Figure 1 *It's not creative unless it sells*

It's not creative unless it sells.

If anything came out of the so-called creative revolution of the 60's and the recessions of the early 70's, it was a clearer understanding of what advertising is and what it isn't.

By the time those years were over, many advertisers and their agencies had been painfully reminded that advertising was not an art form but a serious business tool. And that "creative advertising" really was advertising that created sales and not just attention.

You might say creativity grew up in those years. And one would think that the mistakes made then would never again be repeated.

Yet here we are, a short time later, and like war and politics, advertising seems to be repeating itself. You need only look at television or pick up a magazine to see the frivolities and ambiguities that are passing as creative selling.

It seems such a pity that many advertisers are still learning—the hard way—what some of us have always known:

Not an entertainment medium.

During those crazy 60's, the ambience of television rubbed off on the advertising message and more and more advertising tried to become as entertaining as the programming in which it appeared—very often at the expense of the selling idea. One can still see a rash of imitative commercials following the advent of popular new television programs and feature films. Extravagant productions featuring everything but a concept are still prevalent. Movie stars and athletes continue to serve as substitutes for selling ideas.

Awards for what.

Awards for creativity conferred by juries of advertising people often have nothing to do with advertising that sells. Certainly, in recent years, the importance of advertising awards has diminished. Their value seems to have decreased in direct proportion to the proliferation of festivals. At the same time, many began to question the worth of honors bestowed out of context of sales results.

But as long as advertising will continue to be written by people, people will continue to give each other awards. And that isn't all bad. George Burns once said of Al Jolson, "It was easy enough to make him happy. You just had to cheer him for breakfast, applaud wildly for lunch, and give him a standing ovation for dinner."

You don't have to be loved.

Criticism of an advertising campaign has little bearing on selling effectiveness. There are many examples of advertising which are disliked by the very people who are reacting to the message.

By the same token, much advertising that is

beloved by the critics and consumers alike fizzles badly.

This is not to suggest that advertising need be grating or irritating or hated to be effective. Wouldn't it be great if we could always write advertising that would win awards, that people would love and talk about, and that would sell the product, too?

But, alas, this magic combination is very elusive. And remember, the main objective is not to win awards, not to get people to love your advertising, but to get them to act upon it. In the process of meeting that objective, you may not endear yourself to some consumers but you may become very popular with your stockholders.

Watch out for distraction.

A selling idea runs a very real risk of being swamped by its execution. It's a cliché of the advertising business, but how many times does someone describe a commercial to you almost verbatim and then fail to remember the product? Humor is most often involved. A good joke, a funny piece of action, a great punch line—all can undermine the strongest selling idea. And yet humor, judiciously used, can uplift a piece of advertising, increasing its chances of being remembered while actually enhancing the selling idea. A good test: Is the humor relevant to the message?

Explore the alternatives.

There is no sure way to sell anything. There are many ways to approach the sale of a product— strategically and executionally. Some ways are better than others and you really don't know for sure which is best until you copy test and market test.

The time is long past when an ad agency can deliver a single advertising campaign to a client without examining and presenting alternatives. Every client has the right to take part in the selection process that an agency goes through in leading up to a creative recommendation.

And the most creative campaign is the one that ultimately proves itself in the market.

Don't overshoot the audience.

A lot of words have been written and spoken about advertising catering to the lowest intelligence level of its prospects. That of course is as untrue as it would be unwise.

But equally ridiculous is advertising that wafts over the head of the prospect. We still see and hear commercials and ads that are so cleverly obtuse that they reflect no more than the private narrow world of their creators. For every potential customer who reacts to such "sophisticated" advertising, there are countless others who just don't get it.

There is no "soft sell."

The one factor that did more to end the creative revolution and topple the "creative crazies" from power was the recession of 1970. It was a very sobering experience for many high-flying businesses and advertising agencies.

Creative philosophies seemed to change overnight. "These are hard times that call for hard sell" became the watchword.

But the truth of the matter is: All times are hard times and all times call for hard sell. Hard sell meaning the presentation of a cogent, persuasive idea, stripped of any distracting or irrelevant elements, that will convince people to buy a product. Is there any other kind?

There can be no doubt that advertising today must be more intrusive, more imaginative, more innovative than it has ever been. In a business riddled with sameness and clutter, there is a great virtue in being "creative."

Yet, if ever a word was subject to misinterpretation and confusion, it is the word "creative."

To some it means advertising that wins awards. To others it is advertising that makes people laugh. And there are those who think to be creative, advertising must be talked about at cocktail parties and joked about by comedians.

But "creative" can also mean dramatically showing how a product fulfills a consumer need or desire. Or it can be something as simple as casting the appropriate person for a brand. A unique demonstration of product superiority can be creative. So, of course, can a memorable jingle.

There are probably as many opinions of what is creative as there are people who conceive and judge advertising.

But no matter what your interpretation of the word, one thing is irrefutable:

It's not creative unless it sells.

That, in six words, is the philosophy that guides Benton & Bowles.

imply a hamburger. The reader needs to stay with the ad for quite a while before learning that the ad is for carpeting.

It is said that the average print ad is looked at for eight seconds. If that were the case, would this ad grab hold of a consumer in the market for carpeting? Probably not. Would this ad grab hold of a consumer in the market for a hamburger? Maybe, but should it? It's not creative if it misidentifies the product class.

This section of the text deals with message strategy. What should be said to consumers so that the objectives set earlier can be met? Liberal doses of art and science must be combined to answer this question. The science of research gives insights into the appropriate attributes, benefits, position, and target market; verbal, visual, and musical arts translate this dry, sterile data into a compelling message.

In addition, the message strategy must fit into the decision sequence framework. Much of the information gathered in the situation analysis will be used here to give insight to the writers and artists who ultimately create the message. Also, the message must help the advertiser to meet its objective (relevant issues here are the *task* of the message in terms of movement along the hierarchy of effects and the *target market* to be pursued) and to meet its position (the *unique meaningful benefit* of the brand). Finally, the message must be consistent with constraints imposed by the media and promotions strategies that are being developed simultaneously. The figure on page 174 shows the place of the message strategy in the decision sequence framework.

The message strategy part will be divided according to the following topics:

1. *The relevance of issues derived earlier from the situation analysis and objectives and positioning*   These issues are generally broken down to include the product, the consumer, and the competition. The writers and artists must immerse themselves in all available information before they can create a message of relevance. In this section the key issues are reviewed from the perspective of their relevance to message design.

2. *Legal constraints*   Many laws govern advertising. Most of them constrain the type and presentation of information in the message. Current regulations, primarily from the Federal Trade Commission, are presented here.

3. *Creativity*   This is an elusive concept and is certainly not the exclusive domain of writers and artists. It is most appropriately discussed as part of message strategy because it is here that the most visible creativity takes place in terms of the creation of the message.

4. *Broad and specific classes of message appeals and execution styles*   Appeals can be product oriented or consumer oriented and they tend to locate somewhere on a continuum of rationality and emotion. Styles include humor, fear, sex, slice of life, documentary, and many more.

5. *Advertising research*   Although extensive research has occurred in the situation analysis, a special class of advertising research must be discussed as part of message strategy. This research deals with the measurement of the message's impact and can take place at several levels ranging from a test of an early creative concept to a test of a finished commercial that is being shown on television. Dependent variables range from awareness through behavior depending on the nature of the objectives.

Note

1. Benton & Bowles, "It's Not Creative Unless It Sells," as seen in *Advertising Age*.

Chapter 6
Inputs to
Message
Strategy

*T*he goal of the message strategy is to develop *a message or a series of messages* that will be *informative and persuasive* in their *compelling presentation* of *relevant issues* to the *target audience.* This concept can be broken down so that its components can be examined.

▪ *A message or series of messages* The messages can be in print and/or broadcast media. There can be one message or a number of messages working together. In many cases it is preferable to have several messages coordinated over time as a campaign. The series could be, as in the case of Miller Lite Beer, a set where each message brings home the same point ("tastes great . . . less filling"), but the story and characters change in order to maintain interest and freshness. Or the series could be used to present different benefits or different products in the line. Figure 6.1 shows a coordinated series of messages for Kodak film that presents both benefits and products. The campaign shows continuity across messages to aid consumer learning. In this case, the media plan also contributes to continuity because the messages were placed as consecutive right-hand pages in major consumer magazines.

▪ *Informative and persuasive* All advertising has elements that are either informative or persuasive.[1] Some is geared to be more of one or the other, but all messages have some of each component. By nature, all advertising tries to persuade the consumer to purchase a particular brand or exhibit a particular behavior. Advertising is advocacy oriented; it does not try to be totally objective, nor should it be so. The advertiser spends money to present a narrow and specific point of view. By nature all advertising also tries to be at least minimally informative. It should at least state the name of the brand; that alone is information. Possibly it is not useful, but it is, nevertheless, information. In a descriptive sense,

Figure 6.1 (opposite) Continuity in a series of ads

180

Figure 6.2 *Example of an informative ad (which attempts to persuade)*

Figure 6.3 *Example of a persuasive ad (with minimal information)*

there certainly *are* ads that fail in one or both dimensions, but in a normative sense all advertising *should* attempt to deal with both dimensions. Figure 6.2 shows an example of a print ad that is highly informative (yet still persuasive), while Figure 6.3 shows an ad that stresses persuasion and has minimal information.

▪ *Compelling presentation* In order for the informative and persuasive dimensions to have an impact, the message must be presented in a way that stops the consumer and holds attention. The world's best new product will go unnoticed (or at least will be noticed more slowly) if it is not presented in an interesting way. Consumers are bombarded with too many messages each day (some estimates are as high as 1,500 messages); in addition, most consumers are not very involved with most products most of the time. This means that in order for a message to have an impact, it must break through a cluttered environment to an often apathetic recipient. While media strategies are useful (high repetition levels), a great deal of creativity is necessary to get the consumer to stop and take note of the message. The devices that command attention, moreover, are overused and are, therefore, by themselves, not compelling. Figure 6.4 shows a compelling presentation for a brand from a low-involvement category. Its headline and visual grab the reader's attention.

Figure 6.4 Compelling presentation for a low-involvement product

- *Relevant issues*   A compelling presentation is necessary to stop the consumer, but relevant issues are necessary to hold the consumer. (There are exceptions. A wonderfully entertaining but totally irrelevant message will also hold the consumer's attention. Such messages may win awards for the client, the writer, and the art director but they don't necessarily sell the product.) Relevant issues deal with consumer needs (ah, yes, the old marketing concept strikes again) and unique benefits (as described in the brand's position or unique selling proposition). The importance of relevance cannot be overstated for a new product's introduction; it is somewhat less important in the maintenance of an existing low-involvement brand.

- *Relevant audience*   Target market is an issue throughout the development of the campaign. In *media* this will be important so that the proper vehicles can be used to reach the target. In *message* the target is important so that it can be represented appropriately by the characters in the story line; demographics and psychographics will be useful here. The target is also important because it gives insight into the relevant issues in the message; benefit segmentation is important for its insights here. Figure 2.7 showed messages for different brands of toothpastes aimed at different targets. The information, the ambience, and the characters of the two messages differ dramatically as a function of the target markets that were developed based on benefits.

Inputs to Message Strategy

The broadest statement concerning the message will be that of the *copy platform*. Here the basic message idea is presented in written form and put into the perspective of the prior situation analysis, objectives, and position. The copy platform will essentially serve as the objective statement for the message section and must therefore be totally compatible with the advertising objectives mentioned earlier.

According to the DAGMAR model, the objective has four components:

- Target market
- Task of the advertising
- Time period within which to accomplish task
- Amount of change to achieve within target

Only the first two of these will be relevant to message objectives; time period and amount of change are more relevant for the media and promotions areas. Although the objectives here will just be concerned with the target and task, it is still necessary to achieve a high level of precision in the objective statement. It will also be useful (and should be required) to justify each of the component parts as they are expanded below.

It is often said that objectives and strategies are the enemies of creativity, that objectives and strategies stifle, restrict, and confine, that strategies should only provide guidelines, and that strategies are straightjackets. These statements almost always come from writers or artists and show a lack of concern for the business of the client and for the ultimate need to influence behavior.

Of course, the complaints are accurate. Objectives and startegies *do* stifle, restrict, confine, and act as straightjackets. That is their purpose. Given the level of competition in most product classes and the perceptual defenses put up by most consumers, it is important to direct creativity. It is important that the creative work be on the mark so that it accomplishes the proper task on the proper target market. This doesn't stifle *real* creativity. *Real* creativity leads to the development of a unique, memorable, forceful message that is *also* consistent with the campaign objectives. Remember, it's not creative unless it sells.

As David Ogilvy wrote, "What you have to say is more important than how you say it. Your most important job is to decide what you are going to say about your product, what benefit you are going to promise."[2]

Ed Meyer, head of Grey Advertising, says, "The stimulation of creative advertising starts with the clear articulation of its objectives."[3]

And Dick Bowan of Marschalk Advertising says, "The trouble with most advertising is that few people ever stop to think through the marketing problem and objectives first."[4]

The rigor imposed by objectives, positioning statements, and strategies is designed to focus rather than constrict creativity. It permits the total creative effort to be directed toward execution rather than toward a search for directions and, ultimately, allows for a measurement of the success of the messages in accomplishing their goals. A nicely written defense of strategies was prepared as an internal memo by Howard Shank of Leo Burnett; it appears as Figure 6.5.

Responsibility for developing objectives and strategy lies with the account management group at the agency, but before execution can be initiated there must be approval from the client. The statement of objectives and strategies should be complete but concise and should show justifications for decisions that emerge from the situation analysis.

Tightly defined strategies also give freedom to copywriters because they know that their work should be judged solely against these preexisting guidelines. This direction should, therefore, be cherished. From another perspective, Norman Berry of Ogilvy & Mather says, "There is nothing, in my view, so stupid, or so wasteful of time, talent and money, as to produce a whole lot of work saying one thing brilliantly, when in fact one should have been saying something else in the first place."[5]

To set accurate message objectives, a quick review of relevant issues may be useful. In terms of the *target market:*

1. *Describe the audience as precisely as possible in relation to demographics, geographics, and psychographics.*   It is not enough to merely pursue "young people"; they must be defined on as many socioeconomic dimensions as possible. Geographics, while imperative for media planning, are useful to message strategy because people differ from region to region or from urban to rural areas, and these differences are reflected in life styles, mannerisms, and clichés used. Life styles are also important in terms of allowing the copywriter and artist to speak to the audience appropriately. In broad terms, psychographics can be very insightful, allowing advertising to fit with consumer's drives, goals, opinions, and interests. Using these data, the copywriter and artist can better understand the message recipient and can create messages familiar to the audience that are delivered by characters similar to members of the audience. Consumers are more likely to accept messages from sources similar to themselves than from a completely different type of person. It is highly unlikely that Boy George, for example, would replace Robert Young as a spokesperson for Sanka coffee.

It should also be noted, though, that celebrity spokespersons are often selected for exactly the opposite reasons. They may be used because they personify the consumer's fantasy life. This fits the consumer's drives, goals, and interests but does not lead to a "similar" type of spokesperson. More on this later.

2. *What is the problem that the brand will solve for consumers?*   A strong statement of needs must be derived from the situation analysis. If the brand doesn't fill a need and, preferably, do so in some unique way, then some uniqueness must be created and communicated. If there is no unique benefit, then a shared benefit must be expressed in a unique way. If neither of these uniquenesses can be communicated, then failure will be imminent.

In terms of the *task:*

3. *Describe the task in terms of the stage of the hierarchy of effects.*   Key issues for the copywriter concern the awareness level of the audience, its knowledge, its past behaviors, and its use of the brand. A new brand needs a different message from one that has been on the market for several years. Still different is the message for an established brand with a new feature. The task must clearly state what action the consumer should take. If the action is cognitive (learning) or affective (attitudinal), the statement should show *what* needs to be learned or liked. If the desired response is conative (action), the statement should describe the action (buy, vote, clip a coupon, send money). The copywriter needs to know what response to solicit.

At a more detailed level, the writer needs to know *how* learning and behavior occur. If the consumer makes a brand choice decision in the home, then the advertising must be strong enough to teach the brand name and key benefits so they can be recalled with no outside memory cues. When the consumer thinks of buy-

Figure 6.5 A few kind words about creative strategy

It seems to be in the nature of creative people to chafe at those little pieces of paper entitled "Creative Strategy."

To watch a lot of creative people react, you'd think those documents were really headed, "Creative Straightjacket." Or, "Arsenic. Take full strength. Do not dilute."

There is, to be sure, some reason for this revulsion. It is not unheard of for writers and art directors to be asked to execute something that should really be called an "*un*creative strategy."

The authors of these papers have been known to be neither creative nor strategic in their thinking and to mask a certified non-idea behind formularized words. If you execute such a non-idea, what you are bound to have is a noncompelling advertisement. No matter how cleverly you write and visualize.

Which is too bad for all concerned.

Especially the client (who may be expected, if presented with too many nonthoughts, to become a *non*client).

Basic truth, you folks: the highest form of creativity in advertising is the setting of *real* creative strategies.

We must never forget it.

It's what built this business.

It's where your future and my future lie.

It's where at least half the joy in our business is found.

It's also where the hardest work is found, I'll admit. But don't forget, you always love hard work. Afterwards.

If you're still with me, I'd like to tell you what a real creative strategy is.

But first, I'll suggest to you some of the things it is *not*.

It is not just a sentence that says, "The advertising will convince people that our product is the (tastiest) (freshest) (mildest) (hardest-working) (classiest) (fastest) product in the store."

It is not the product of logic and analysis alone—although they're part of how you get there.

It is not the province of the client or the account man—although they should be heavily involved.

It is not a jail for creative execution. Rather, if you've got a real creative strategy, it will inspire you to write and visualize at the height of your powers.

It is not aimed at robots but at human beings with hearts and guts as well as brains.

The last sentence is the crux of the matter.

The real creative strategy is the one that relates product to yearnings. Formula to life style. Performance to passions.

If you can look at a thinner cigarette and see it not only as a special cigarette for women but also as a symbol of equality for women, you can create real creative strategies.

If you can look at a bar of soap with pumice in it and see not only an efficient hand washer but also the solution to the problem of "Public Dirt," you can create real creative strategies.

If you can look at a glass of chocolate milk and see it not as just a yummy thirst-quencher or a hunger-fighter but as a cure for a kid's "thungries," you can create real creative strategies. (Some of our smart people did that just the other day.)

Figure 6.5 continued

In all truth, the process that leads to real creative strategies is the process that leads to inventions.

It involves the seeing of old facts in new relationships.

It involves the discovery of needs and wants in people that even the people may not have discovered in themselves. (Hardly anyone knew he needed a telephone until A. G. Bell came along.)

It also involves hard work. As I said before.

When you have a creative strategy problem on your plate, you are confronted by a need to know everything you can get your hands on. About the product itself. About competitive products. About the market: its habits, its attitudes, its demographics. About the advertising history of the category.

You need to study all the research you can get your hands on.

You need to ask questions until people hate to see you coming.

You need, in short, to dig, dig, dig.

The dismal truth is that your chances of finding a compelling creative strategy are in direct proportion to how much information you stuff your head with.

If you are working on a new coffee, say, you will wind up knowing more about coffee than you ever thought you wanted to know.

There is a very good reason why you must do this human sponge act if you are to invent real creative strategies.

Your subconscious mind—where a very important part of the invention process goes on—needs a richly-stocked data bank to do its best work.

The job of your subconscious is to review and re-review everything you know about a subject. It searches, even during your sleep, for new relationships between people and products; searches, as I suggested earlier, for new combinations of old ideas; searches for the new insight that can give even a very old product the right to ask for new attention in the market.

If you stint your subconscious on the input side, it will surely stint you on the output.

Creative strategy goes around in the world under several pseudonyms: basic concept, basic selling idea, product positioning, basic selling proposition.

But whatever the name, the purpose of real creative strategizing is simple and vital: the invention of a big idea.

I said earlier that *this* kind of creative strategy work is the highest form of creativity in advertising.

I believe it wholeheartedly.

I also believe wholeheartedly in the power of brilliant execution.

What I believe in most of all is the synergism you create when you couple a big idea with brilliant words and pictures.

When you can do that regularly, you can't help getting rich and famous. Not to mention happy in your work.

One final thought. If you don't have the habit already, make close business friends of every client, every client service man, every research man you can. Pick their brains. Push them for information. Involve them heavily in your invention work.

Their input can—and very likely will—make all the difference in your output.

Howard Shank / Leo Burnett, Inc.

ing detergent, the name Solo and the benefit of a built-in fabric softener must come to mind. To help the consumer in this memory task, the message strategy may need some special mnemonic devices such as a memorable jingle or an image-evoking analogy. If the brand choice decision is made in the store, then the advertising doesn't need to be as strongly imbedded in memory. There will be memory aids in the store in the form of packages. Here the advertising needs to tie the brand name and benefits to the package so that when it is seen, the package will help the consumer remember the key points. Because memory works differently in these two scenarios, the message strategy should also differ to be most effective.

4. *Describe the task in terms of the audience's involvement.* The amount of information that can be transmitted is in large part a function of how much the audience cares about brand choice decisions within the product class, and different products will elicit different levels of consumer involvement.

Knowing the level of involvement helps determine how much information will be attended to and how aggressively it must be presented. If consumers care about the brand choice decision, they will seek and evaluate information; advertising will be more important and will not need to be shouted out.

5. *Describe the task in terms of the brand's benefits.* Each message must build on the brand's image and must convey the appeal of the brand. Furthermore, the situation analysis must clarify the true appeal of the brand. Is the appeal the tangible benefit of usage or some intangible such as status, gusto, or sex appeal? Most messages should try to convey one issue, so it is essential to determine the single overriding benefit of the brand. This benefit must be explained in terms of its value to the consumer. Remember that products have attributes, but people buy benefits; attributes can be used to explain and support the benefits.

Benefits can be tangible or intangible. The former can be described through rational informative messages; for example, tangible automobile benefits include fuel economy, size, leg room, and styling. Other benefits deal with image and are better described through emotional or transformational messages; intangible automobile benefits include prestige or statements about self (e.g., macho, affluent, or sporty). While knowledge will result more from tangible benefits, attitude will result from both classes of benefits.

Message strategy and execution will differ dramatically depending on the types of benefits being emphasized; sometimes the key selling point may stress one area while the justification for the purchase may really be elsewhere. For example, luxury cars are probably bought on the basis of image/intangible benefits, but the advertising may also discuss tangible benefits of safety or performance to allow the consumer to rationalize the purchase.

As was shown in the situation analysis, level of involvement and type of benefit are not necessarily related. Some low-involvement products are sold on the basis of physical benefits (toilet tissue, oven cleaner, pens), while others are sold on the basis of image benefits (beer, soda, beauty aids). Similarly some high-involvement products also are sold on the basis of physical benefits (personal computers, appliances, stereos), while others are sold on the basis of image benefits (some autos, vacations, clothing).

6. *Describe the task in relation to the competition.* This is an extension of the previous issue and leads to positioning, which, in turn, relates to the *unique selling proposition* or *USP.*

The USP is a concept conceived in the 1960s by Rosser Reeves, a former president of the Ted Bates Agency.[6] His notion was that every ad must have a proposition that sets the brand apart from others. This USP can then be used to tie together all advertising. The USP also can be shown through collateral materials such as point-of-purchase displays and through any promotions being used. Effective advertising sets the brand apart from the competition in some unique, meaningful, and beneficial way.

7. *Describe the desired tone of the advertising.*   This is important because the type of advertising appeals and message formats to be considered will be derived from the statement of tone. Tone deals with the personality of the brand. Is it staid and proper or loose and casual? Implicit here is that certain formats will not be acceptable because they just don't suit the personality of the brand. The personality is a result of distribution and pricing strategies as much as it is a result of the core product being sold.

Some final thoughts on the transition from marketing to message strategy

The statement of message tasks must cover four specific areas:

- Whom to sell
- What to sell
- Support for the selling idea
- Tone of the selling idea

For a message to be effective in accomplishing its tasks it must be:

1. *Attention getting*   It must attract and hold the receiver.

2. *Understandable*   It must use symbols that are common to both the sender and the receiver.

3. *Relevant*   It must arouse basic needs and suggest a way to satisfy the needs.

4. *Acceptable*   It must suggest a solution that is compatible with the receiver.

In developing objectives and tasks, the manager must develop a coordinated campaign, not just one or a series of messages. There must ultimately be continuity across all messages so that consumers can learn more easily. Most preferable is for the continuity to be based on the USP or position. Of lesser value is continuity based on a story line, a character or a message delivery format. This coordination should exist across all messages, across all relevant media, and should extend to packaging, point-of-purchase, and the brand name itself.

Any advertising to be done must follow certain legal guidelines as well as follow the managerial guidelines established earlier. Since most legal issues are concerned with message strategy, it seems appropriate to review them at the onset of message strategy development.

Legal Constraints on Message Strategy

Advertising managers must be aware of the laws that govern their practice. These laws, how they are enforced, and the philosophy guiding them have changed several times in the past thousand years of Western/Anglo civilization; in the United States these changes have come fairly often in the past several decades.[7]

William T. Lynch, Jr.

Vice-Chairman, Client Services, Leo Burnett

Bill has been with Leo Burnett for 19 years and is currently vice-chairman, Client Services, Leo Burnett U.S.A. and a member of the Board of Directors.

Bill's college education began at Loras College in Dubuque, Iowa, where he received a B.A. in Liberal Arts. He then graduated from the University of Iowa in 1966 with an M.B.A. in Marketing.

Since joining Burnett, he has had extensive advertising and marketing experience on a variety of package goods accounts including Procter & Gamble's Secret deodorant, Nestle's Taster's Choice coffee, Pillsbury refrigerated dough products, and all of Kellogg's ready-to-eat cereals.

Strategizing

For those of you who are going to be involved in advertising, I would like to take this opportunity to stress the importance of getting the right strategic objective identified, articulated, and agreed to . . . upfront. Some may disagree with the importance I place on this first step, but as an unknown advertising person once said, "Brilliant execution of the wrong strategy loses to dull execution of the right strategy every time." The right strategy is essential if you expect to develop effective, compelling advertising. It's the foundation for all successful campaigns.

Getting the right strategy begins by trying to determine what is unique or special about each product. This comes from a review of the individual product's attributes, benefits, ingredients, name, image, manufacturing process, heritage, competitive set, usage patterns, and anything else that is necessary to familiarize yourself totally with the product or service you want to advertise.

From this, a formalized copy strategy should be prepared that sets the direction for all other advertising decisions which follow: Who's my target audience? What's the primary product benefit? What tonality do I want the execution to have? What's the desired brand image? It's critical that the agency's account people, the creatives, and the client thoroughly understand, challenge, and ultimately agree on the strategic objective for the advertising, then commit this strategy to writing. A written strategy statement is a good discipline to force concise thinking and articulation. The written document then becomes the guideline for the creatives and the criteria against which all work will be evaluated.

Too often the critical strategy decisions receive the short end of everyone's efforts. Tight timetables, subjective judgments, poor analysis, bad information, or "not wanting to restrict the creative effort" are all too common reasons.

However, if effort isn't spent here and convictions aren't formed about the elements in the strategy, the final work stands a good chance of missing the mark. The work may be judged and selected on executional appeal alone. Don't misunderstand; executional pizzazz has to be pres-

ent, but it will earn you a smile, not a sale, if the message isn't right and motivating to consumers.

Upfront is where the time, effort, analysis, and sweat need to be expended. What can you do about it? A lot. Whether you are a future account executive, brand manager, or a budding creative writer, build sufficient time into the development timetable for this critical step. Ask questions. Force involvement by all key decision makers. Push to find the distinctiveness that separates your product or service from competition. Build that distinctiveness into the strategy rather than relying on execution alone to carry it. Resolve the strategic direction before one minute of creative time is spent thinking execution. The effort at this initial stage will be rewarded by better, more effective advertising.

A short history

During the Middle Ages the legal system was dominated by the church, and sellers had a quasi-moral obligation to stand by the claims that they made concerning their goods. By the sixteenth century this stance was reversed, and the buyer was expected to assume the full responsibility in an exchange. *Caveat emptor,* "let the buyer beware," was the rule, and the difficulty of the obstacles that constrained product examination was not considered in most cases. This stance held until the twentieth century when nationally distributed consumer products began to appear in the United States, and when it became ever more difficult for consumers to assess the goodness of increasingly complex products.

One of the first U.S. laws to deal with honesty in advertising was the Federal Trade Commission Act of 1914. This act established that the FTC, as an organization, policed unfair methods of competition and unfair or deceptive practices in commerce; in 1922 the Supreme Court ruled that deceptive advertising was an unfair trade practice within the scope of the FTC. By 1931 the pendulum had swung in the other direction when the Supreme Court ruled that the FTC could not control false and deceptive advertising unless competition was also injured by the deception.

This ruling led, in 1938, to the Wheeler-Lea Amendment to the FTC Act and legally extended the authority of the FTC. It was now unlawful "for any person, partnership, or corporation to disseminate, or cause to be disseminated, any false advertisement . . . for the purpose of inducing . . . , directly or indirectly, the purchase of food, drugs, devices or cosmetics."

In addition, Wheeler-Lea gave the FTC the power to be proactive rather than reactive. This meant that it could initiate cases rather than merely *respond* to formal complaints. The amendment also gave the FTC the power to issue cease and desist orders and to fine violators up to $5000 per day per incident.

Although given this power, the FTC was a fairly dormant agency until 1971. At that time, Ralph Nader had recently denounced the FTC for squandering its resources on trivia, and a task force from the American Bar Association reported to President Nixon that it agreed with Nader.

During the decade from 1971 to 1980, the FTC's power grew as it pursued corrective advertising remedies and monetary penalties for deceptive advertising, affirmative disclosure of information that an advertiser might not voluntarily give, and, finally, industrywide advertising regulation rules that carried the force of law. (Each of these issues is discussed below.)

To further assist the FTC, Congress passed stronger legislation; in 1973 an appendage to the Alaska Pipeline Bill doubled the fine for violating an FTC cease and desist order to $10,000 per day per incident and gave the FTC more authority to initiate lawsuits.

The FTC Improvement Act of 1975 provided for the development of Trade Regulation Rules (TRRs) that allowed the FTC to establish industrywide rules to define unfair practices before they occurred. Until 1975 the FTC could only proceed on a case-by-case basis, and a recurring improper practice had to be prosecuted each time it occurred; this had been a costly and time-consuming process.

By 1980 Congress felt that the FTC had gone too far in formulating new laws (through TRRs) rather than in making judgments concerning existing laws. It therefore passed a second FTC Improvement Act that limited some of the earlier powers it had granted (e.g., it weakened the impact of the TRR). In addition, new appointees to the FTC also changed its direction so that as of this writing, the

FTC has become a much less aggressive party in the advertising regulation marketplace; it is no longer engaged in rulemaking, and its commissioners have redefined deception to be more limited in scope. (These issues are also expanded below.)

The purpose of this introduction is to show the long history of change in laws and their interpretations concerning advertising and the buyer–seller relation. These changes occur at two levels:

1. Congress writes new laws
2. the Commission interprets the law changes

In the 1970s the changes in both areas were toward a more liberal environment and active FTC. In the early 1980s the changes have been more conservative and have led to a less active FTC. It is unclear what the status of advertising regulation will be when this text is read. This text will discuss the interpretations of both eras to prepare the manager for either eventuality.

Non-FTC regulators of advertising

In addition to the FTC there are two other major regulating agencies of concern and several agencies of lesser concern. The *Food and Drug Administration (FDA)* was formed with the passage of the Pure Food and Drug Act and was strengthened in 1938 through the Federal Food, Drug, and Cosmetic Act. The FDA is concerned with proper package labeling and ingredient listings for food and drugs and with the safety and purity of foods and cosmetics. It isn't directly involved with advertising but does deal with packaging; indirectly there is an advertising involvement when the FTC looks to the FDA for advice in the latter's area of expertise. The FDA has had a major impact on the overall marketing of food, cosmetics, and drugs but a limited impact on advertising, per se.

The *Federal Communications Commission (FCC)* was formed as a result of the Communications Act of 1934 to oversee broadcasting and protect the public interest with regard to broadcast communications. Relative to broadcast advertising, the FCC is concerned with eliminating messages that are deceptive or in poor taste. Most of what the FCC does is concerned with radio and television stations and networks and is therefore only indirectly related to advertising (and not at all relevant to print advertising).

The most direct impact of the FCC occurs when a product is controversial enough to call for equal time allocations. The Fairness Doctrine assures equal time for all major party political candidates and gave equality to antismoking messages relative to cigarette advertising (before broadcast cigarette advertising was banned by Congress in 1970). In most cases the FCC refers problems concerning advertising to the FTC.

In addition to these three regulatory agencies there are others concerned with advertising for specific products or classes of products. The *Department of Energy* is concerned with advertising and package labeling for products that consume energy; the *Postal Service* with direct mail and magazine advertising; *Alcohol and Tobacco Tax Division of the Treasury* with liquor advertising; *Library of Congress* with copyrights concerning advertising; *Civil Aeronautics Board* with interstate air carrier advertising; the list goes on and on.

This section will be concerned with general types of regulations and interpretations that affect message strategy across most product classes. The manager should be aware that there may be specific regulations concerning a particular product or service in addition to the general regulations discussed in this section. Table 6.1 summarizes some of the relevant agencies of concern and their functions.

The FTC

Since the bulk of advertising-related regulation emerges from the FTC, it may be useful to describe how this agency operates. The FTC has two basic levels for dealing with cases. The *staff attorneys and directors* select and investigate cases and, if the data warrant, present the government's case as prosecuting attorneys and advocates of a particular legal position. At a higher level there are *administrative law judges and the five commissioners*. At these levels the complaint is issued, and the judges hear the cases and give opinions to the commissioners who render the FTC's opinion and specific orders. The firm may then appeal the case in a regular court of law.[8]

Table 6.1 Major federal agencies involved in the regulation of advertising

Agency	Function
Federal Trade Commission	Regulates commerce between states; controls unfair business practices; takes action on false and deceptive advertising; most important agency in regulation of advertising and promotion
Food and Drug Administration	Regulatory division of the Department of Health, Education, and Welfare; controls marketing of food, drugs, cosmetics, medical devices, and potentially hazardous consumer products
Federal Communications Commission	Regulates advertising indirectly, primarily through the power to grant or withdraw broadcasting licenses
Postal Service	Regulates material that goes through the mails, primarily in areas of obscenity, lottery, and fraud
Alcohol and Tobacco Tax Division	Part of the Treasury Department; has broad powers to regulate deceptive and misleading advertising of liquor and tobacco
Grain Division	Unit of the Department of Agriculture responsible for policing seed advertising
Securities and Exchange Commission	Regulates advertising of securities
Civil Aeronautics Board	Regulates advertising of air carriers engaged in interstate transportation
Patent Office	Regulates registration of trademarks
Library of Congress	Controls protection of copyrights
Department of Justice	Enforces all federal laws through prosecuting cases referred to it by other government agencies

Source: S. Watson Dunn and Arnold M. Barban, *Advertising* (Hinsdale, Ill.: The Dryden Press, 1978), p. 123.

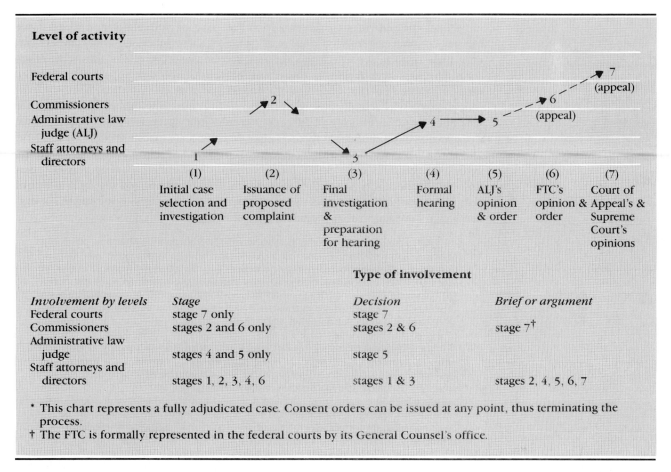

Involvement by levels	Stage	Decision	Brief or argument
Federal courts	stage 7 only	stage 7	
Commissioners	stages 2 and 6 only	stages 2 & 6	stage 7†
Administrative law judge	stages 4 and 5 only	stage 5	
Staff attorneys and directors	stages 1, 2, 3, 4, 6	stages 1 & 3	stages 2, 4, 5, 6, 7

* This chart represents a fully adjudicated case. Consent orders can be issued at any point, thus terminating the process.

† The FTC is formally represented in the federal courts by its General Counsel's office.

Figure 6.6   The FTC case decision process

It is important to note that there are two levels. At one level is the advocacy lawyer and at another level is the unbiased judge. Both reside under the same roof but work independently. Figure 6.6 shows the decision process for an FTC case.

Truth, deception, and unfairness

Until 1983 the FTC had the power to judge deception and unfairness by merely looking at advertising and making a judgment; an ad was deceptive if it had the capacity or tendency to deceive "the ignorant, the unthinking and the unsophisticated"[9] in a material way. At the end of 1983 the Commission made three major breaks with the past:

1. The FTC can no longer arbitrarily judge an ad to be deceptive but, rather, must prove that the ad actually deceived.

2. A "reasonable consumer" must be deceived. This may leave less-than-reasonable (the ignorant, unthinking, and unsophisticated) consumers with less protection.

3. It is not enough merely to deceive; the deception must lead to material injury. That is, the deception must influence consumer decisions.

Under the old rules Crisco was found to have been deceptive in its advertising. Its commercial showed a woman frying chicken in Crisco and claimed that very little oil was absorbed into the chicken because there was almost as much oil in the pan after frying as there was before. Crisco did not account for the melted chicken fat that added to the liquid and that confused the issue of how much Crisco was actually absorbed.[10] The 1970s court ruled there was deception; it is not clear how the post-1983 court would rule. Deception was never shown to have occurred, but the court felt that there was a capacity to deceive.

The third point was designed to prevent FTC lawyers from pursuing trivial cases. For example, in 1975 FTC lawyers tried to make the case that New Dry Ban Roll-On Deodorant was not dry because if a consumer applied enough, it would drip down the side of the person's body. At the time Commissioner Mayo Thompson wrote an opinion that included the following:

> If the American consumer has no more serious problem than the possibility of being deceived [by] his underarm deodorant, he is in much better shape than I had been led to suppose. Even if one believes in the power of television to convince the consumer that wet is really dry and thus the power to sell each potential customer *one* can of the product in question, it would presumably strain the credulity of even the most enthusiastic of TV supporters to believe that *repeat* sales could be won—and market share thus maintained—through the instrument of any such self-evidently false claim.
>
> A customer standing in front of his TV set with a dripping armpit is not likely to go out and buy a second can of the stuff. Put another way, even a confirmed knave does not lie to the customer if the lie is bound to be discovered and one has to have repeat sales in order to survive.
>
> I have grown weary of the kind of literal-minded legalisms we are confronted with in this matter. I think they are too trivial to be worth pursuing. Surely we can find more important work for our legal staff than litigating the questions of somebody's underarm deodorant [claims].
>
> I would dismiss all such cases as having been improvidently brought and direct our lawyers to get on with the serious business of stopping practices that are artificially inflating the prices and/or debasing the quality of the goods and services bought by our 200 million American consumers.[11]

It is not clear how many people need to be deceived in order for deception to have occurred, but the more important issues, such as health and safety, have more strict standards. That is, the court will be more lenient on a case concerning a product such as Ban than one concerning a life-threatening deception.

The three changes made in 1983 may lead to many fewer prosecutions of deception cases, but the manager should still be aware of how deception was dealt with in the past since it is not clear when the legal pendulum may swing back to the point where old deceptions are once again troublesome. While the number of cases may decrease because the standards have been made more rigid, the underlying issues that led to these standards are still the same. That is, most of the laws that emerged during the 1970s still exist, but the standards of enforcement have become more lax. It is important to be familiar with the laws and regulations because they may be enforced more stringently again in the future.

Support for claims   In order to avoid problems it is necessary to have data on file that substantiate any claim made in the advertising, and factual claims must be supported by fact. If Firestone advertises that its tires allow cars to stop 25% more quickly, the company must be able to show this through testing. Deception can occur if consumers interpret the claim to mean that Firestone tires help cars stop 25% more quickly in all cases, but the firm meant that this would occur only in certain situations (e.g., on a wet pavement).

The Firestone ad could indeed be truthful but also could be deceptive or unfair at the same time. The FTC must decide if the message has crossed the thin line between giving information that a reasonable consumer will interpret correctly and being deceptive. In the Firestone case, the FTC found deception.[12]

Substantiation   The FTC can ask any advertiser to substantiate a claim it makes. Until 1983 the firm needed to have the information in its files prior to making the claim. Since 1983 the substantiation research can be done on a *post hoc* basis in some cases. Advertisers must still possess a reasonable basis for making objective claims, but this restriction has also been made more lax.[13]

In any case it is up to the advertiser to be able to prove the truthfulness of a claim; it is not up to the government to disprove its validity. A clear-cut example occurred in the Listerine case. For many years Listerine claimed that its use would help prevent colds and sore throats when, in fact, there was no evidence to support this claim. As a result Listerine was ordered to do $10 million of corrective advertising.[14] (This tale is continued below.)

Reinforcing false beliefs   In the past it was deceptive to reinforce a false belief. For example, a firm's marketing research could show that consumers felt that detergent with red and blue crystals led to cleaner wash. The firm could then add worthless red and blue crystals, show them in advertising, mention their presence, and never discuss their ability to clean. Such advertising has been judged to be deceptive.[15]

Comparative advertising   This form of message is deceptive unless:

1. Its comparisons are factual.
2. The differences shown are statistically significant.
3. The comparisons are on meaningful issues.
4. The comparisons are made against meaningful competitors.

The Kroger Company (a grocery retailing chain) was found guilty of deception in the advertising of shopping basket price comparisons against their competitors because they excluded large product areas such as meat and produce, they showed price differences that were not significant, and they did not select comparison items in a random or representative way. In addition, the person who selected the basket items also set the prices for Kroger products (and therefore knew which products would be compared for advertising).[16]

Endorsements   A person (often a celebrity) who makes a brand endorsement must use the brand, must be qualified to make expert judgments, and must examine or study the product. As will be seen below, those who endorse a product improperly also may be liable if there is a deception.

Demonstrations   A claim that is demonstrated must be accurately portrayed. A classic example of this type of deception occurred in 1969 when Campbell's Soup wanted to show the amount of vegetables in its soup. Because cooked vegetables normally sink in liquid, clear marbles were placed on the bottom of the bowl so the vegetables would lie on the marbles and be seen. This, of course, also gave the impression of more vegetables.[17] The concept of corrective advertising first emerged in this case but was not used here; it was first used in the Profile Bread case (described below).

In a second case, Rapid Shave claimed that it could help shave sandpaper (an analogy for a tough beard). It was actually true that Rapid Shave could help to shave sandpaper, but the demonstration didn't look right when it was filmed, so the firm showed sand being scraped off plexiglas. In the Campbell's case there was clear deception, but in the Rapid Shave case there was an attempt to visually demonstrate a supportive claim.[18] Both, though, were felt to be deceptive.

The issue of demonstrations is a difficult one for food products because many foods dry out under hot studio lights; this makes the food look unappealing. If whipped cream is replaced by shaving cream when the filming is done, the firm is liable to be prosecuted by the FTC.

Penalties for deception   Prior to 1970 if a firm was found to have used deceptive advertising it was given a cease and desist order that said the deceptive message could no longer be used. Violation of a cease and desist order was punishable by a fine of up to $5,000 per day per violation. The order was rarely violated, though, because the deceptive message was rarely still relevant to the firm—it often took several years for the message to be found deceptive through the cumbersome proceedings of the FTC. In 1973 the maximum penalty was increased to $10,000 per day per message, but the cumbersome process remained.

The largest penalty to date has been $1.75 million against *Reader's Digest* for violating a cease and desist order concerning a direct mail campaign. The courts agreed with the FTC that each piece of mail was a violation and that the 17.9 million pieces could have led to penalties of $179 billion. The actual penalty was a bargain at less than 10¢ per piece.[19]

Corrective advertising   After 1970 the FTC began to use corrective advertising as a remedy. In this format, the offending firm is ordered to allocate some amount or percentage of its advertising to messages that correct the deception that was perpetrated earlier. It was hoped that this remedy would erase deceptive memory residuals in consumers' minds and deter potential future wrongdoers.

Wilkie, McNeill, and Mazis[20] summarize the five legal criteria for corrective advertising:

1. *The remedy must be prospective rather than retrospective in nature.*   The remedy should seek to clear up potential future deceptions so that future purchases are based on correct beliefs. Without correct advertising, past false beliefs would exist in the future and therefore a simple cease and desist order is not sufficient.

2. *The remedy must be nonpunitive in nature.*   The FTC's responsibility is to stop unlawful practices rather than to punish. It has been very difficult to specify a level of corrective advertising that would remedy the deception without causing financial harm. The reader will see later in the media section that measuring learning and forgetting is quite difficult. Here is a case where, in addition, one piece of learning should wipe out an earlier piece. As a result, some corrective advertising has been quite mild and has neither caused the deception to be erased across all consumers nor caused sales to change; other cases have remedied the deception in general but have also hurt the firm's sales.

Figure 6.7 Profile Bread script

"Hi, (celebrity's name) for Profile Bread. Like all mothers, I'm concerned about nutrition and balanced meals. So, I'd like to clear up any misunderstanding you may have about Profile Bread from its advertising or even its name.

"Does Profile have fewer calories than any other breads? No. Profile has about the same per ounce as other breads. To be exact, Profile has seven fewer calories per slice. That's because Profile is sliced thinner. But eating Profile will not cause you to lose weight. A reduction of seven calories is insignificant. It's total calories and balanced nutrition that count. And Profile can help you achieve a balanced meal because it provides protein and B vitamins as well as other nutrients.

"How does my family feel about Profile? Well, my husband likes Profile toast, the children love Profile sandwiches, and I prefer Profile to any other bread. So you see, at our house, delicious taste makes Profile a family affair."

(To be run in 25% of brand's advertising, for one year.)

3. *The remedy must bear a reasonable relation to the violation in question.* The FTC order should cover the violation but should not suppress other lawful activities; it should be limited in scope to the violation.

4. *The remedy must not infringe on the First Amendment rights of the firm.* The firm has the right to free (not deceptive) speech and the right to remain silent. Corrective advertising must allow the firm to continue other aspects of its message or to cease advertising if it so wishes. The right to cease advertising in the face of an order to do corrective advertising has not yet been tested in the courts.

5. *The remedy should be in the least burdensome form necessary to achieve an effective order.* Corrective advertising should minimize disruptions and other side effects. This may call for the deletion of a deceptive phrase in some cases but call for a longer explanation in other cases.

Profile Bread was found guilty of deception and ordered to spend 25% of its budget for one year on corrections.[21] Figure 6.7 shows the script of the corrective message; anecdotal data are mixed with regard to the impact of this message, which was designed to undo the deception that Profile Bread was a low-calorie bread.

Ocean Spray cranberry juice was found guilty of deception because it claimed to offer more food energy than orange or tomato juice but failed to say that food energy was the same as calories.[22] Figure 6.8 shows the script of its corrective message; anecdotal data indicate that Ocean Spray suffered large sales losses when the ads appeared.

Figure 6.8 Ocean Spray script

"If you've wondered what some of our earlier advertising meant when we said Ocean Spray cranberry juice cocktail has more food energy than orange juice or tomato juice, let us make it clear: we didn't mean vitamins and minerals. Food energy means calories. Nothing more."

"Food energy is important at breakfast since many of us may not get enough calories, or food energy, to get off to a good start. Ocean Spray cranberry juice cocktail helps because it contains more food energy than most other breakfast drinks."

"And Ocean Spray cranberry juice cocktail gives you and your family Vitamin C plus a great wake-up taste. It's . . . the other breakfast drink."

(To be run in one of every four ads for one year.)

Table 6.2 shows a listing of some early corrective advertising cases. Disclosures range from one corrective ad to a $10 million dollar campaign. The latter case was against Listerine; the penalty was severe because it was felt that the firm had falsely claimed for over 50 years that its product could kill germs that cause colds. It was felt also that a substantial campaign was needed to correct the accumulated misperception. After the corrective campaign began, 42% of Listerine users still believed that the brand was being promoted as effective for colds and sore throats, and 57% of users rated cold and sore throat effectiveness as a key attribute in their purchase of the brand.[23]

Liable parties

In addition to the manufacturer, recent cases have shown that the advertising agency, spokesperson, and retailer can also be liable in cases of deception. For example, the J. Walter Thompson Advertising Agency was liable along with its

Table 6.2 History of early corrective advertising cases

Company	Product	Claim	Order type	Disclosure features
Amstar Corp. (1973)	Domino sugar	Sugar benefits	Consent	25% of ad costs
Beauty-Rama Carpet Center (1973)	Retailer	Prices	Consent	Firm used "bait & switch"
Boise Tire Co. (1973)	Uniroyal tires	Tire ratings	Consent	One ad
ITT Continental Baking (1971)	Profile bread	Caloric content	Consent	25% of one year's ads
Lens Craft Research (1974)	Contact lenses	Medical claims	Consent	Four weeks
Matsushita Electric of Hawaii (1971)	Panasonic TV sets	Hazard ratings	Consent	One ad
National Carpet (1973)	Retailer	Prices	Consent	Firm used "bait & switch"
Ocean Spray Cranberries (1972)	Cranberry drink	Food energy claim	Consent	One of every four ads
Payless Drug Co. (1973)	Motorcycle helmets	Safety	Consent	Equal number to original ads
Rhode Island Carpets (1974)	Retailer	Prices	Consent	Firm used "bait & switch"
RJR Foods Inc. (1973)	Hawaiian punch	Juice content	Consent	Every ad until effects are shown
Shangri La Industries (1972)	Swimming pools	Availability and terms	Consent	25% of one year's ads
STP Corp. (1976)	Oil additive	Effectiveness	Consent	One ad, fourteen media
Sugar Information (1974)	Sugar	Sugar benefits	Consent	One ad, seven media
Warner-Lambert (1975)	Listerine	Effectiveness claim	Litigated	Correction in $10 million of ads
Wasems Inc. (1974)	Wasems vitamins	Vitamin benefits	Consent	One ad, seven insertions
Yamaha International (1974)	Yamaha motorcycle	Motorcycle safety	Consent	Corrective letter

Source: William L. Wilkie, Dennis L. McNeill, and Michael B. Mazis, "Marketing's Scarlet Letter: The Theory and Practice of Corrective Advertising," *Journal of Marketing* 48, no. 2 (Spring 1984), p. 14.

client, Sears, for making unsubstantiated claims for the Kenmore potscrubber dishwasher. In order for the agency to not be liable, it must submit to the client all the claims that are to be made in the ad and get approval of the claims. In addition the agency should exercise care that the client is not providing false claims.[24] (The agency should have these procedures regardless of legal incentives.)

Several cases have made the point that expert spokespersons can also be held liable, although in the cases to date the experts were also owners or partners in the firm. Singer Pat Boone was fined 25¢ per unit of sales of an acne product, up to $5,000. The 25¢ represented his share of revenues from the product. Astronaut Gordon Cooper was fined for endorsing a gasoline-saving device that didn't produce savings. The FTC said that Cooper misrepresented himself as an expert and failed to mention that he had a financial interest in the firm.[25]

In at least one case the retailer also was found equally liable. Pay 'n' Save, a retail drugstore chain, was accused of placing false and misleading advertising for a brand of weight reduction tablets. The FTC felt that Congress should "impose higher obligations on disseminators-distributors of advertising for food, drugs, (medical) devices, and cosmetics (which may carry a potential for injury to health and safety)."[26]

Affirmative disclosure

There are times when advertisers are felt to commit the sin of omission; that is, they fail to give all the important relevant information. In such a case the FTC can require a firm, or all members of a particular industry, to add certain information in a particular format to all messages. Affirmative disclosure is used to bring out information that was never dealt with, rather than dealing with information that was deceptively disseminated.

For example, the FTC proposed a rule that antacid ads should contain warnings of contraindications. There was no implication that there had been a deception, but, rather, that it was difficult for consumers to learn about possible side effects of product usage. For example, Alka-Seltzer contains large amounts of sodium and is therefore dangerous for people on sodium-restricted diets. Older people are most likely to be on such a diet and are most likely to use the product; the FTC staff felt that there was a high level of inadvertent misuse and therefore pressed for hearings on the issue.

The result of the hearings was that the FTC did not pass an affirmative disclosure rule. In fact, after hearings concerning several different industries and the need for more information regarding several products, there has never been such an FTC rule put into operation.

There are, though, other cases of affirmative disclosure. All cigarette advertising has an affirmative disclosure warning in print ads and on the package (because of a law passed by Congress); 1984 legislation made cigarette warnings even stronger.

There are other cases of affirmative disclosure in packaging and labeling. Over-the-counter drugs show extensive information on packages and labels concerning contraindications in accordance with FDA rulings; food products give extensive ingredient and nutritional information on package labels (FDA); appliances and automobiles show energy consumption information on packages and/or stickers, and automobiles show this information in advertising as well (Department of Energy).

Several studies have shown that when presented in an effective manner this information has an impact on awareness but rarely on behavior. Often the information is presented in such a way that even basic awareness has not changed significantly.

While the FTC has not been successful in instituting affirmative disclosure rules, other agencies have done better. This concept must be kept in mind by managers in deciding what information to present for controversial products. Industries that do not voluntarily share relevant information may find themselves facing regulations to do so. This is most likely to occur for industries related to health, safety, or the common good (e.g., energy conservation).

Advertising to special audiences

In addition to special issues, regulators are also more prone to try to protect special audiences that are less likely to be able to fend for themselves. This attitude has most noticeably been held for children and the elderly, and most specifically for health and safety-related products that are aimed at these audiences.

In the case of children, considerable data show that until the age of 8, children have not developed the defenses necessary to evaluate advertising properly, and therefore they accept claims at face value. This has had an impact in two ways. First, young children may not be able to separate programs from commercials. Because of this, programming must show a clear break between itself and commercials (e.g., "Don't go away. Captain Kangaroo will return after these messages.") In addition, commercials that use program characters to sell products cannot be shown during the programs in which these characters appear. Therefore, Fred Flintstone vitamins are not sold during "The Flintstones". Anyone watching Saturday morning television will notice the thin line between program and commercial as characters are merchandised by retailers. Is the Smurf show a 30-minute commercial for all the Smurf products, or is it a legitimate program? The line is crossed in less subtle ways with each passing year.

Second, many people feel that any advertising to children is unfair because children are not skeptical enough to evaluate it properly. From this perspective, no matter how truthful or complete the advertising is, it is deceptive because its audience cannot properly evaluate it. This argument was a cornerstone of FTC hearings to eliminate advertising of sugar cereals to children. The argument was made that sugar cereals are a dental hazard, but that the mere existence of the product and its commercials implied to children that the product was good for them. After all, children would reason, if the product exists and people tell me it is good, then it must be so. This argument did not suffice in this case, and sugar cereal advertising still exists.

In other cases, a similar argument has been upheld. The FTC has obtained a cease and desist order in the following cases.

Euell Gibbons, an advocate of natural foods, was shown eating wild berries from bushes to make the point that Post Grape Nuts are a good natural food. The FTC felt that children would emulate Gibbons and indiscriminately eat wild berries that might be poisonous.[27]

Spider Man was used as a spokesperson to extol the virtues of Hudson Vitamins. The FTC felt that children would believe that vitamins gave super powers and would then take large doses. In reality it was not even clear if children should take any vitamins, although it was clear that the children were not sophisticated enough to make that decision.[28]

Mego International showed a young girl washing the hair of a "Cher" doll. When she finished, her mother gave her an electric hair dryer and the girl proceeded to dry the doll's hair although the sink was still filled with water. The FTC felt that the product was being used in an unsafe way and ordered the firm to stop using the commercial.[29]

In sum, past FTC efforts have primarily been directed against showing situations that may prove dangerous for children and against showing heroes as spokespersons. As with other aspects of this discussion, there is no way to predict what future regulatory activities will be although the general aim is in providing information, reducing deception, and concentrating on cases of greatest potential for harm.

Free speech and advertising

It may seem that if the FTC and other agencies can impose their will over the content of advertising messages either through corrective advertising or affirmative disclosure, commercial speech is not protected by the First Amendment to the U.S. Constitution (which protects free speech). While rulings change over time, as noted earlier, the current interpretation is that truthful ads concerning a legal activity are entitled to First Amendment protection.[30] This means that states and societies cannot bar professionals (e.g., doctors, lawyers) from advertising. This issue is further developed later in Chapter 23.

In addition, ads cannot be restricted by law merely because they are offensive. This means that media under direct government control (e.g., the mail) cannot refuse to send offensive ads. There are, though, regulations concerning how and to whom the material may be delivered.

Advertising placed through privately owned vehicles (virtually all broadcast and print vehicles) is subject to the policies of each vehicle and may be constrained or not accepted because speech is only free in public places. The First Amendment is brought into play when the FTC attempts to constrain advertising because this creates a government restraint on speech that must be judged. Current rulings, then, support FTC involvement on cases of deceptive advertising but are less clear in cases where important information is missing rather than false.

State and local regulations

In addition to federal controls there are also state and/or local controls in most cases. Most of these seem to have fallen by the wayside over the years as a result of Supreme Court rulings (e.g., allowing advertising by professionals) and the advent of more interstate communications (e.g., if a vehicle distributes its messages across state lines it is regulated by the federal government). Most states attempt to regulate deceptive or misleading advertising, but their prosecution records are poor because the charge is generally a misdemeanor and it is hard to gain a conviction.

Self-regulation

In addition to government regulations, the media and advertising industries attempt to control the actions of their members; this is often done to avoid what may be harsher regulation if imposed by the government. Some self-regulation has been discussed, as when a vehicle chooses not to accept certain advertising because it is, for example, felt to be offensive. This form of self-regulation is acceptable to the government.

Other types of self-regulation are seen as restraint of trade and are outlawed by the Department of Justice. In 1983 the Television Code of the National Association of Broadcasters was banned for this reason. This code controlled the number of commercial minutes per hour and also provided input on matters of taste. Hard liquor could not be advertised on television; beer and wine could be shown but not consumed; lingerie could be shown but not on live models. There has been little change in these issues since the code was abolished, but now each network or station can be its own judge and there is no longer any explicit restraint of trade.[31]

The Justice Department outlawed the Television Code because it constrained the supply of commercial time through collusion of networks and stations and as a result caused the price of this time to be higher than it otherwise might be. Other forms of self-regulation that do not restrain trade still exist.

The National Advertising Division (NAD) of the Better Business Bureau (BBB) is the major self-regulator for the advertising industry. It investigates, on average, over 180 cases per year and resolves about 98% of these disputes. In about half the cases the firm is exonerated and in half the firm changes the ad or discontinues it. Since most ads have run their course before the NAD makes a ruling, the issue is often moot.

In the 2% of cases that are not resolved in one of the above ways, the National Advertising Review Board (NARB) becomes a court of appeals. The NARB consists of 50 members of the advertising profession (agency and client) and the general public. If the case is still not resolved, the case is referred to the government for further action. Figure 6.9 summarizes this process from NAD to FTC.

While the NAD and NARB attempt to resolve disputes, neither has any real power except to threaten that the case will be sent to the FTC. In spite of this, these groups have been effective, for the most part, in controlling cases of deception and misleading advertising. At the local level, the Better Business Bureau refers cases to local authorities.

The Lanham Act can also be considered a form of self-regulation. Under this law one competitor can challenge the truth of another's advertising. The virtue of this law is that it can lead to an injunction to remove the offending message within just a few days. This is done as a private lawsuit brought through the civil courts. Suits have resulted in injunctions to restrain advertisers and there have been out-of-court settlements for damages, but no court has awarded monetary damages or mandated corrective advertising as a result of this process.[32] It seems ironic that firms that cry for less regulation at one time would then go to court to get more regulation at other times.

Summary

Legal restrictions to advertising practice change rapidly. The more restrictive climate of the 1970s has become less so in the mid-1980s. While most of the laws and regulations that emerged during the 1970s still exist, the standards for their enforcement have been relaxed. This section has considered the existing laws and their level of enforcement.

It is clear from the above that legal issues are quite important in message development. A lawyer should be involved in creative work before money has been

Figure 6.9 *The NAD/NARB process*

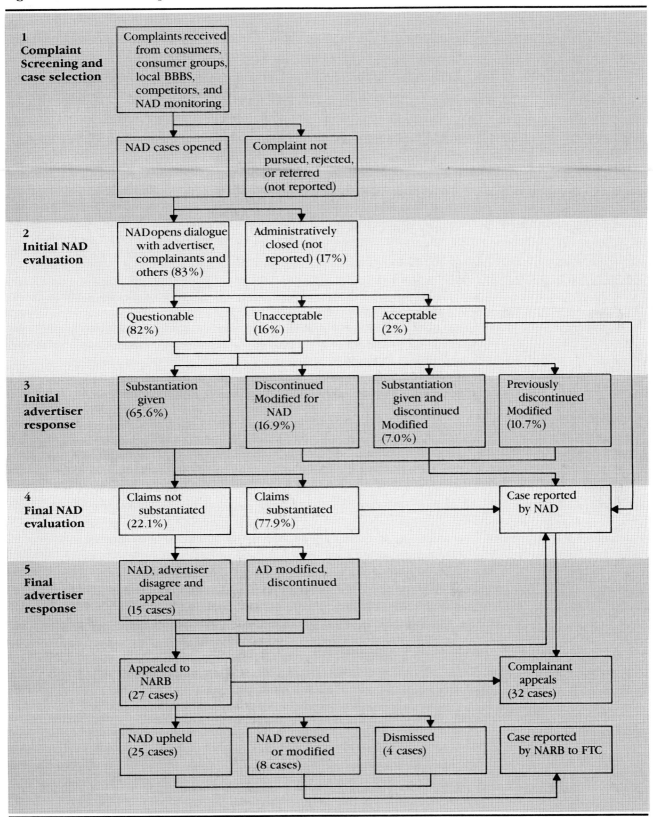

205

T·H·E I·N·S·I·D·E O·U·T·L·O·O·K

Paul Geisler

Vice-President, Kimberly-Clark Corporation

Paul Geisler is a vice-president with the Kimberly-Clark Corporation. He was previously a vice-president, management supervisor, with Young & Rubicam and before that an associate advertising manager with the Procter & Gamble Company. He is a graduate of the University of Wisconsin-Madison.

How to Get the Best out of Your Ad Agency

Study advertising. You can do it every day. Watch TV spots. Read print ads. Ask questions. Follow trends. Observe how people think, talk, feel. By doing these things, you will decipher what makes advertising sell. Clients who both understand and demand effective advertising almost always get it.

Believe in the power of the advertising message. Let your agency know you believe. It's sad that some business people treat the advertising process, and thus their agency, as a necessary evil. In fact, the creative product lends extraordinary elasticity to each advertising dollar—it can make it worth 15¢ if it's bad, $3.00 if it's great.

Be honest. With your advertising, your agency, yourself. Consumers who unmask advertising dishonesty will move with humiliating swiftness to buy your competitor's brand. Be honest about your agency's creative product: It's on strategy or it isn't; it has a focused selling idea or it doesn't; it enhances your product's image or (in your view) it doesn't. I've never known straight talk, delivered with respect and insight, to be unwelcome. And don't fail to be honest about your product's quality. Even great advertising can't sell a lousy-tasting cookie more than once.

Lead and be led. Use your leadership skill to sharply define strategic direction, ensure a deep understanding of what your product truly does for people, and to build a team spirit that brings out the best in everyone working on your business. At the right point, let your agency lead you. After all, the best people in the agency business are very, very good at what they do! Listen to them. Then *make a decision.*

Don't be naive. All creative people are not created equal. If your product is right, your strategy right, your leadership right, and the advertising still isn't right, odds are the creators of it aren't right. Change them. Fast. The people first, the agency if absolutely necessary.

What's the payoff? Advertising that sells, of course. But there's more. In my experience, those who know how to get the best out of their agency usually can get the best out of almost everybody. That's the stuff that leadership is made of. And leadership is the stuff that personal success is made of.

spent on production; the lawyer should constrain the message in the same way as do research and objectives; each of these work to make the advertising correct and appropriate. When a position or benefit is developed, it should be supported in fact; if it is, then there will be little to fear in terms of legal matters. In addition, honest advertising is just plain good business, and regulations, in the long run, protect honest businesses from competitors that are dishonest.

Discussion Questions

1. Before beginning to develop the message strategy, the writers and artists should review the situation analysis, objectives, and positioning statement. Considering all of the components of these areas, which ones are most important? Why? Now that you have finished the situation analysis, objectives, and positioning for your pending job search, describe the components as they are relevant to you.

2. Describe the major areas of concern of the Federal Trade Commission, Food and Drug Administration, and Federal Communications Commission that relate to the topics of this text.

3. Define truth, deception, and unfairness in the context of the FTC.

4. What are the standards of deception that relate to comparative advertising?

5. What is and is not the goal of the FTC when it orders a company to use corrective advertising?

6. How does the advertising industry police itself in terms of deceptive advertising?

Notes

1. Shelby Hunt, "Informational vs. Persuasive Advertising: An Appraisal," *Journal of Advertising* (Summer 1976), pp. 7–8.

2. David Ogilvy, *Confessions of an Ad Man* (New York: H. Wolff, 1964).

3. K. White Sonner, "Strategy Makes for Creative Advertising," *SCAN* 29, no. 6, pp. 16–18.

4. Sonner, "Strategy Makes for Creative Advertising."

5. Norman Berry, "My Creative Philosophy," in *Viewpoint: By, For and About Ogilvy & Mather*, 2 (1980), p. 3.

6. Rosser Reeves, *Reality in Advertising* (New York: Alfred A. Knopf, 1961).

7. The historical section of this discussion is based primarily on Dee Pridgen and Ivan L. Preston, "Enhancing the Flow of Information in the Marketplace," *Georgia Law Review* 14 (Summer 1980).

8. William L. Wilkie, Dennis L. McNeill, and Michael B. Mazis, "Marketing's Scarlet Letter: The Theory and Practice of Corrective Advertising," *Journal of Marketing* 48, no. 2 (Spring 1984), pp. 11–31.

9. Isabella Cunningham and William Cunningham, "Standards for Advertising Regulation," *Journal of Marketing* 41 (October 1977): 92.

10. Joe L. Welch, *Marketing Law* (Tulsa, Okla.: Petroleum Publishing, 1980), p. 84.

11. In re Bristol Myers Co. et al., CCH Para. 20, 900, F.T.C. Docket 8897, April 1975 (D.C.).

12. Paul Blum, *The Research File* no. 6 (March 1978).

13. Richard L. Gordon, "Miller Stands behind Prior Substantiation," *Advertising Age,* 26 March 1984, p. 1.

14. Wilkie, McNeill, and Mazis, "Marketing's Scarlet Letter," pp. 15–17.

15. David M. Gardner, "Deception in Advertising: A Conceptual Approach," *Journal of Marketing* 39 (January 1975), p. 42.

16. Welch, *Marketing Law,* p. 91.

17. Welch, *Marketing Law,* p. 101.

18. Welch, *Marketing Law,* p. 99.

19. Dorothy Cohen, "Each Item in Bulk Mailing Can Be Fined If Offer Violates FTC Order," *Marketing News,* 19 March 1982.

20. Wilkie, McNeill, and Mazis, "Marketing's Scarlet Letter," pp. 11–31.

21. Wilkie, McNeill, and Mazis, "Marketing's Scarlet Letter," p 14.

22. Wilkie, McNeill, and Mazis, "Marketing's Scarlet Letter," p. 13.

23. Wilkie, McNeill, and Mazis, "Marketing's Scarlet Letter," p. 26.

24. Welch, *Marketing Law,* pp. 104–105.

25. Richard L. Gordon, "FTC Hits Astronaut for Deceptive Ads," *Advertising Age,* July 16, 1979.

26. Welch, *Marketing Law,* p. 100.

27. Welch, *Marketing Law,* p. 88.

28. Welch, *Marketing Law,* pp. 88–89.

29. Welch, *Marketing Law,* p. 88.

30. Michael B. Metzger and Barry S. Roberts, "The New Commercial Speech Doctrine," *MSU Business Topics* (Spring 1979), pp. 17–23.

31. "Now That the TV Cable is Dead," *Marketing and Media Decisions* (May 1983), p.72.

32. Debra L. Scammon and Blake Wade, "Lanham Act Provides Quick Relief from Comparative Ads," *Marketing News,* 22 July 1983, p. 8.

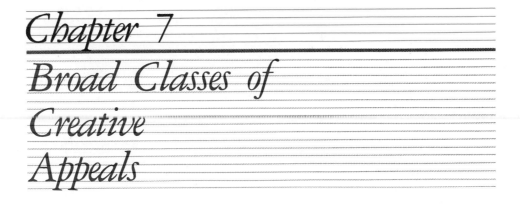

Chapter 7
Broad Classes of Creative Appeals

*U*ntil this point in the text the emphasis has been on marketing and managerial issues that precede the development of strategy. The first chapter of the message strategy section has served as a link to show how these earlier issues relate to the message. Now it is time to develop the message.

In this chapter the creative department and the concept of creativity are introduced. These are important topics because they deal with the core production function of the advertising agency. Agencies are hired because their people have the ability to translate marketing research and objectives into uniquely appealing messages. While the other functions of the agency are also important, the key one is related to creativity.

The Big Idea emerges from the proper mix of marketing, research, and creativity. It is the manifestation of the position into advertising, the creative translation of strategy into a message with a unique perspective.

The rest of the chapter considers broad classes of message appeals and executions. These are divided into emotional versus rational and product-oriented versus consumer-oriented appeals. The Big Idea can come from any piece of marketing knowledge combined with any class of appeal and execution, but it must contain both in a proper balance.

The Creative Department

Occasionally known as the zoo, the creative department is headed by the creative director who is usually a copywriter (or *was* until promoted to an administrative position). The department usually has two major components: the writers and the artists. (The various production facilities, liaisons with outside production vendors, and the traffic department are usually found in the art department of the agency. The traffic department keeps track of all the physical pieces of all the ads and makes sure that all production deadlines are met.)

209

> *"When the day's last meeting is over,*
> *And the V.P.'s have left for the train,*
> *When account men are at bars with the client,*
> *And the space men have switched off the brain,*
> *We shall work, and, by God we shall have to—*
> *Get out the pencils and pads,*
> *For finally, after the meetings—someone*
> *Must get out the ads!*
>
> *Let others have gray suits and homburgs*
> *We'll stick to black pencils and pads,*
> *The life, core and heart of our business,*
> *You're right—it's making the ads."*   —Leo Burnett

Just as the account service person wears a uniform (often a three-piece suit), so too the creative person wears a uniform of nonconformity that expresses creativity. Generally this uniform spills over into the decor of the office that also reflects creativity. Since the process of creation is elusive and fleeting, it is best to develop an environment conducive to it. The individuality of the thinker is therefore seen in the individuality of the thinker's environment. The space where a person spends half the day should be supportive of the activity conducted therein.

Creatives also spend less time interacting with clients and therefore have less need to conform to regular working hours. Agencies are very output and deadline oriented, and some tend to be supportive of unusual work schedules (which do not hamper the overall advertising process). Of course, the unusual schedules are also necessary because all the work can't possibly be done during a normal work day. Leo Burnett, as an advocate of the copywriter in the 1950s, summed up the hours nicely in rhyme. See Figure 7.1 above.

The differences between account management and creatives are much deeper than clothing style or office decor. The two groups really think differently. Whether by temperament or by training, account managers tend to be more logical, organized, and conventional; this helps in data analysis, setting of objectives, and developing positioning statements but generally leads to deadly, boring advertising. Creatives tend to be more innovative and able to see different perspectives in problems; this is essential in translating the formal direction of the campaign into captivating copy and art. Sheila Dorton, Creative Director of The Hiebing Group, explains it this way: "Most account people see black and white while good creatives see an infinite variety of shades of grey. Therefore, leaps of logic—terrifying to account types—are perfectly natural to creatives because they are going from grey to grey, not black to white."[1] Figure 7.2 is included here for those readers who have a need to distinguish between so-called creative and noncreative types.

This distinction is important to realize because the two groups need to work together even though there is often only a grudging appreciation of one for the other (as seen in Figure 7.3). As discussed earlier, the creative work developed at an agency can easily be killed and must be nurtured. Figure 7.4 shows a list of ways to kill ideas.

The creative process exists in all businesses and all departments, but there are few places where the specific charge of the business or department is to be

Figure 7.2 A child's primer to advertising

CHAPTER ONE — "AD-MEN"

this is the first chapter
of a book
by Alan Barzman
illustrated by Gene Holtan
to be published by
somebody like Doubleday

There are two kinds of ad-men. CREATIVE PEOPLE . . . and UN-CREATIVE PEOPLE

CREATIVE PEOPLE are responsible for creating the ads—and UN-CREATIVE PEO-
PLE are responsible for rejecting the ads.

CREATIVE PEOPLE are frustrated because they are not understood.

UN-CREATIVE PEOPLE are frustrated because they are not CREATIVE PEOPLE.

CREATIVE PEOPLE are very insecure . . . and let everybody know it.

UN-CREATIVE PEOPLE are also insecure . . . but keep it a secret.

CREATIVE PEOPLE drink Martinis . . . but prefer Cocoa.

UN-CREATIVE PEOPLE drink Martinis . . . but prefer Gibsons.

Usually CREATIVE PEOPLE are not very tactful. They say things like, "I just got an
extremely great idea," or "I quit!"

UN-CREATIVE PEOPLE are usually very tactful. They say things like, "Frankly I like
it very much, but the Client will never approve it." or "Okay, go ahead . . . but
you're certainly blowing a lot of fringe benefits."

CREATIVE PEOPLE despise what they are doing, but accept it.

UN-CREATIVE PEOPLE love what they are doing, but don't know it.

CREATIVE PEOPLE enjoy playing Tennis, Perquackey and Jacks.

UN-CREATIVE PEOPLE enjoy playing Tennis, Perquackey and the Stock Market.

CREATIVE PEOPLE write speeches about Creativity, which UN-CREATIVE PEOPLE
deliver at Ad Club luncheons.

(CREATIVE PEOPLE eat lunch in their offices.)

CREATIVE PEOPLE have nothing to say to UN-CREATIVE PEOPLE.

Conversely, UN-CREATIVE PEOPLE have lots to say to CREATIVE PEOPLE.

For example: "Now I don't want to tell you how to write the copy because I'm not
'Creative.' But I do think that you should say something about 'this,' and make
mention of 'that,' and get in a plug about 'such,' with reference to 'so,' . . . in
your own inimitable way!"

CREATIVE PEOPLE then write what the UN-CREATIVE PEOPLE are trying to
say . . . and go home and have a cup of cocoa with an olive in it.

Now then. What about that strange breed of ad-man who is one part CREATIVE
PEOPLE, and one part UN-CREATIVE PEOPLE?

We shall deal with him at great length in a forthcoming chapter entitled, "THE
HYBRID AD-MAN" or "WHAT THIS INDUSTRY REALLY NEEDS IS MORE GOOD
NEUTER-CREATIVE UN-PEOPLE!"

---

creative and innovative. In addition to the task of creation, there is the task of interpretation and translation. Writers and artists are the communications middlepersons between the manufacturer and the consumer. And, therefore, the writers and artists are the sales force for the manufacturer; they must personalize the impersonal interaction of the firm with its millions of consumers and also be heard by the consumer in competition with thousands of other vendors who are selling their wares at the same time. To be heard and understood in this situation requires an innovative appeal that must be on target. This is the conflict of the necessary conservatism of management desiring the right message and the necessary innovativeness of the artists and writers desiring to break through and to be heard.

Figure 7.3 *The creative attitude*

Some agencies are "creative"; they stress innovative messages and are dominated by a top management who came from the creative side of the business. There are also "marketing" agencies where the strategy is almost always on target but the creative work is merely a usable translation of strategy to execution. The best agencies are able to achieve a balance between the two extremes and turn out artful executions of appropriate strategy. One of the most difficult tasks of management is to create an environment conducive to all points of view; one way to do this is to acknowledge that *all* departments (management, research, media, copy, art) can and must do their work creatively. Creative thinking cannot be limited to the creative department. The best research, the best strategy, and the best media plans all are the result of creative work.

Creativity

The heart and soul of advertising is creativity. This is what sets apart the great from the mediocre, and it is what sets apart this profession from most others. Few businesses have creativity as their major product, and, as a result, few have as many interesting, challenging, and dynamic people with whom to interact.

What is creativity? In one sense it relates to constructing, building, or creating. In that sense advertising is like many other businesses where a tangible end result is produced in some way. Those people in the agency who are thought of as creative are the ones who produce the advertising. They receive some amount of information and from that they create advertising.

In a more important sense creativity deals with seeing a problem and developing a unique and appropriate solution. Ray Whittier of Young & Rubicam said that "in advertising, the beginning of greatness is to be different, and the beginning of failure is to be the same."[2] Creativity in its most elusive form deals with originating different ideas from the same set of information. In music, art, or poetry, creativity is self-expression; in advertising, creativity is translating information into purposeful music, art, or poetry.

Another definition of creativity is merely "combinations." No idea can come from nothing, just as matter cannot be created from nothing. Creativity is the combination of existing elements into a new form.

Figure 7.4   *Twenty-five ways to kill an idea or, deadly clichés guaranteed to destroy any creative idea*

1. Network will kill it. Let's not spin wheels.
2. Okay, this is safe. No problem with network. But we're not in the business to create commercials that make network censors happy. Let's do it our way . . . and let them kill it.
3. Genius thinking! And at some particular point in time, we may want to consider whether it has practical application. But to meet our immediate objectives, let's talk about an alternate approach.
4. Personally, I love it. But I'm wondering about "Mom" Jones out in Columbus, O. Are we over-reaching her intellect?
5. Using a female spokesperson is fine. But research proves that women listen to men.
6. Using a male spokesperson is fine. But research proves that women listen to other women.
7. Terrific! You've done it again. But let's put this one on the back burner for the moment. It's not killed. Just back-burnered.
8. Okay, this is right on target. But this isn't what the client wants. Shouldn't we be giving the client what he wants? Isn't that why he hired us?
9. Sure, it's a blockbuster concept. But it's outside the client's budget. Period.
10. Well, you've gone the el cheapo route. And there's nothing wrong with that. But if we could find the extra bucks . . . do you think you might develop a really blockbuster concept?
11. Okay, this is what the client wants. But shouldn't we be giving the client what he should have? What he needs? Isn't that why he hired us?
12. It's funny. Very, very funny. But this is serious stuff we're talking about. Are we being too flippant?
13. This is serious stuff we're talking about, sure. But are we being too serious?
14. Somehow, the idea just doesn't . . . work.
15. It's great! But it looks like every other beer commercial.
16. It's great! But it just doesn't look . . . like . . . a beer commercial.
17. Nobody reads long cigaret copy.
18. Okay, we're selling cigarets. But tell the consumers something new and fascinating. They'll read every word.
19. You may be surprised to learn that there is actually intelligent life across the Hudson River. This concept is dumb and cornball. Even for out there.
20. A terrific concept . . . for New York. But let's face it: Omaha ain't New York. Can we have a little less sophistication?
21. What you're saying is provocative. But in today's socio-economic climate, we've got to get back to basics.
22. What you're saying is basic. But in today's socio-economic climate, we've got to be provocative.
23. I'll try to be brief: No.
24. All right, it's not the whole truth. But do we have to advertise what's wrong with our product? Let's focus on the positive.
25. All right, it's not a lie . . . but it's not the whole truth, either. Let's always tell the truth wherever possible.

By C. Richard Williams, Senior copywriter, Sawdon & Bess, New York

All of these definitions imply that creativity is the generation of unique ideas. An idea is nothing more nor less than a new combination of old elements.[3] Powerful advertising is the physical manifestation of ideas presenting old elements (the situation analysis) in new ways.

It is primarily for this reason that manufacturers come to advertising agencies. Agencies produce ideas and creativity. Ogilvy was quoted earlier as having said that *what* is said is more important than *how* it is said. The *what* stems from the situation analysis and the objective and strategy statements, but the *how* represents the creativity and must also be considered as very important. The creativity must always be subservient to the strategy, but either the *what* or the *how* without the other will not produce great advertising.

This is, again, especially important for products where many brands are similar, share the same benefits, and have access to the same information. In these cases the creation of unique ideas becomes dominant. This means that while the advertising promises the same benefit, it does so in a unique way.

That is what makes superb advertising, but that is also what creates risk. Newness is always risky because it is different, and so there are tradeoffs between

Figure 7.5   The pyramid principle

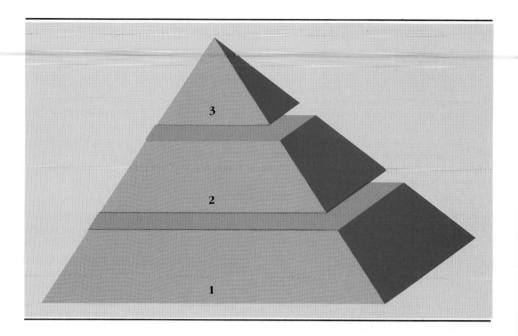

originality and prudent business practices. Prudence leads to sameness and "me-too" advertising; originality leads to risk.[4]

Or, as Keith Reinhard of Needham, Harper Worldwide has put it, "Playing it safe is another way to say imitation, which is the opposite of creation. Imitation is the ability to bring familiar things into familiar relationships over and over again, to the surprise of no one and the advancement of nothing. The best examples of imitating will occur again tonight on your television screens."[5]

The creative process, as ascribed to by the mainstream of advertising professionals, is similar to the decision sequence model that forms the framework for this book. As presented by Baker,[6] the process moves through a pyramid as shown in Figure 7.5. The pyramid principle has three parts that also divide the pyramid into components. Part 1 is the foundation and is the *gathering of information,* part 2 is the *analysis of information,* and part 3 is the culmination, the *idea.* In theory, lots of information leads to a few good ideas.

More detailed is the presentation of Reva Korda, who was at Ogilvy & Mather when she presented the following:[7]

> First you dig *for* all the information you can and then you dig for what you missed the first time.
> Then you dig *through* the information to set objectives.
> Third, you dig for a niche for the brand that differentiates it from all competing brands (i.e. a position).
> This in turn leads to an image of the product that will be easily elicited when the brand name is mentioned.
> And then the creative strategy can be developed. This strategy encompasses the objective, position and image.
> Finally you spread all this out on your desk and stare at it. It's all useless until an idea emerges. Nobody can explain *how* an idea happens; nobody can tell anyone else how to have an idea.

Korda goes on to say that before showing the fragile newborn idea to others, some questions should be answered:

- Is the work on target and aiming at the right strategy?
- Is it clear?
- Is it in good taste?
- Will anybody remember it?
- Is it persuasive?[8]

An advertising idea must lead to a positive response on each of these questions.

But how does creativity occur? How do ideas come? One set of hints comes from Bruce McCallum, Creative Director and Group Head of Ogilvy & Mather, Toronto:[9]

1. *List all the facts.* McCallum feels that the facts should be on paper so they can be easily accessed and not forgotten.

2. *Never say no.* Children, geniuses, and the insane come up with ideas because they haven't learned to think negatively. Critical thinking is a virtue in our society, but it hampers creativity because fragile new ideas are crushed rather than developed. Every idea should be saved. Later some will be enlarged and some rejected. (Incidentally, one of the most important rules for brainstorming sessions is that no one can be critical of anyone else's ideas.)

3. *Quantity of ideas is important.* The more ideas that are generated, the better will be the quality of the best one. Write down every idea without evaluation. This means generating lots of dumb ideas because perhaps one in 20 ideas will have enough merit to be pursued.

- Strive for quantity of ideas. A quality goal leads to evaluation; a quantity goal will lead to quality.

4. *Avoid panic by self-stimulation.* The rational thing to do after staring at a blank piece of paper for a while is to panic. While rational, it may not be too useful. It may be more useful to

- *Go walk in the woods.* Or take a shower. Or do some other mindless task. Or work on something else. If there are enough stored facts, eventually this incubation period will lead to some ideas. If a deadline is approaching, return to a panic state or continue to the next item.
- *Force a relationship.* Since an idea is a new way of seeing old materials, force facts together in new ways or force facts together with new words from the dictionary. Forcing a relationship may trigger useful thoughts.
- *Rewrite the fact sheet without looking at earlier information.* This will bring old facts back to the surface and trigger ideas.
- *Look through a thought-starter catalog.* This may be a book of great ads, some old magazines, a telephone book, or a Sears catalog. Whatever triggers thoughts is fine.

The Big Idea

Although the objectives have been set and the basic strategies agreed upon, the campaign won't be a success without *a big idea.* Earlier, in Chapter 5, it was written that one purpose of specific objectives is to help eliminate poor strategies and that the few which remained would all be close to what would be needed. That is correct, but from among the acceptable strategies the advertiser still needs to strive for greatness.

Sheila Dorton states:

> First, when you're writing copy, don't give up until you've hit "The Big Idea" . . . the one that sets your product apart from its competition, but recognizes and capitalizes on the consumer's current problems, feelings and needs.
>
> This can begin as easily as just putting yourself in the customer's shoes for a while. Try thinking it through like this:
>
> Let's say your product is a car. What's the need it satisfies? Transportation? Of course—but for a housewife that car may fill a need for freedom—or for privacy. The one place where she gets away from the 3-year-old with the runny nose and the husband who's always complaining about the house not being clean enough. For a man, your car may represent status . . . or fulfillment of a boyhood fantasy . . . or a way to say that under his conservative suit and striped tie lies a "free spirit" . . . or the car may represent the only place he's away from the boss, and the whining 3-year-old and the wife who's always complaining about the way grocery prices are rising faster than his salary!
>
> How about insurance? What's the need? Safety, of one kind or another. But down deep it's probably freedom from *worry*. Worry is a *human* emotion . . . the writer can work with that. Safety is antiseptic, sterile.[10]

What is a big idea? To some a big idea is one that stands up to the test of time. For David Ogilvy it's not a big idea unless it could be used for at least 30 years. That's a tough test to pass, but here are some themes that have endured very well over time (although some aren't 30 years old yet).

- The Marlboro man and Marlboro country
- The Jolly Green Giant
- Good to the last drop
- My insurance company? New England Life, of course
- The friendly skies of United Air Lines
- All the news that's fit to print
- When it rains, it pours
- Leave the driving to us
- Baseball, hot dogs, apple pie, and Chevrolet

Ogilvy says that to recognize a big idea five questions need to be answered affirmatively:

1. Did it make me gasp when I first saw it?

2. Do I wish I had thought of it myself?

3. Is it unique?

4. Does it fit the strategy to perfection?

5. Could it be used for 30 years?[11]

To this list Stephen Baker would add that a big idea leads to a sigh and the question, "Why didn't I think of that?"[12] Figures 7.6 and 7.7 show two big ideas from Ogilvy & Mather. Both have achieved bigness over a long period of time, both seem simple, even mundane, and both also contributed to the agency's current stature by helping the brand do well. Dove was separated from all other soaps by promising that it would cream the skin as well as wash it; Hathaway was given a personality through the eyepatch worn by men who modeled the brand.

While it is certainly pleasant to stumble across a big idea, it is a rare and probably hopeless goal for the copywriter who needs to meet daily deadlines. But, as Leo Burnett said, when you reach for the stars, you may not quite get one, but you won't end up with a handful of mud either.

Figure 7.6 *Dove "creams your skin" was a big idea*

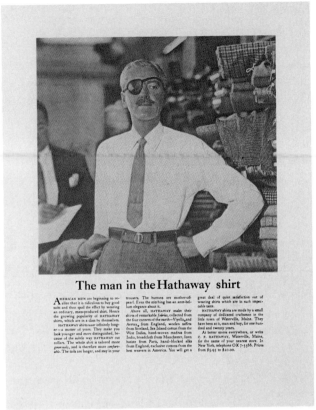

Figure 7.7 *The Hathaway "eyepatch" was another big idea*

Because the need to produce ideas continuously is so strong, some ideas will not yield positive answers to the first and last of Ogilvy's questions, but all advertising should at least draw a positive reaction to the third and fourth questions. Otherwise, as seen in Figure 7.8, the big idea may not be the right idea.

By meeting these criteria the advertising will be "positively good." This term has been ascribed to Joel Raphaelson of Ogilvy & Mather and is useful in situations where the brand is one of several essential commodity items in a product class. In this case it is hard to say that the brand is superior, and, in fact, it is probably not. It may be acceptable to say that the brand is positively good; sales will go to the most appealing presentation of this concept. A big idea can also be derived from such a stance.

Leo Burnett expressed the same views in different ways. For him it was important to find the "inherent drama" of the brand. The way to success was to find the inherent drama and present it. If there was no inherent drama in the brand, then it would be necessary to create it and this could be done through "borrowed interest," a concept that allowed the drama to come from elsewhere. Many of his successes came through animation, as with the Keebler Elves, Charlie the Tuna, and the Jolly Green Giant. In other cases, the inherent drama of the brand was brought to life through a spokesperson such as the Lonely Repairman for Maytag or Morris the Cat for 9 Lives Cat Food. In each case the benefit is not intrinsically interesting and is, therefore, made more so by using borrowed interest.

Figure 7.8   Another big idea?

Often, the big idea isn't the right idea.

At the time, the airplane billboard probably seemed like a big idea.

It was certainly dramatic. It was newsworthy. It broke ground. And it pre-empted the competition.

It was also misplaced, misguided, and mistaken.

That's the way it is with a lot of big ideas. They aren't right because they ignore the marketing need at hand.

They sound big, but do little. They're creatively good but strategically bad.

At Frankel & Company, we don't fall into this trap. When we plan promotions, there's a solid reason behind everything we do.

Whether it's an incentive program for your sales-

people or a traffic-building event for your customers, the tactics we employ *meet your marketing need.*

When we create a promotion for a client, we ask ourselves these questions.

Is it dramatic? Is it newsworthy? Does it break ground? Is it pre-emptive?

Then we ask ourselves—are there sound reasons for doing this? Will the idea solve the marketing problem? Does this tactic bring the strategy to life? Will it meet our objective?

That's how we make sure that our big ideas are the right ideas, too.

For more right ideas, call Bud Frankel at 312-938-3409.

The Marketing Services Agency

FRANKEL & COMPANY

111 East Wacker Drive, Chicago, IL 60601 • 312/938-1900
Sales Promotion • Merchandising • Direct Response

More succinctly, John O'Toole of Foote, Cone & Belding says that, "an advertisement without an idea is like an empty fortune cookie. Life is too short, and space and time too dear, to be filled with empty fortune cookies."[13]

Broad Classes of Message Appeals

The creativity discussed above will lead to many levels of ideas. This and the following sections will discuss these levels. Beginning with broad classes of appeals, the text continues to specific types of appeals and executions of style. These topics should cover the areas of creativity related to message development.

Basically, the broad classes of messages can be emotional or rational and product or consumer oriented. Each of these dichotomies would be more fairly represented as a continuum but then would be more difficult to discuss. Neither the broad nor the specific listings of appeals are meant to be complete, but rather attempt to present most of the major categories of message presentations currently in use.

Rational versus emotional messages

One dichotomy in examining types of messages is between rational and emotional, although most ads probably strive for some sort of balance between the two. The distinction here is an interesting one because it highlights some of the differences between account management and the creative department. This text has largely emphasized the logical process of the decision sequence that leads to ·factual information and straightforward strategy as well as a tendency to produce logical/rational advertising that can be measured by recall or recognition tests.

This, though, may be a great mistake, for the most important unique service of the agency is to provide creativity, which may be best seen in emotional messages. The best advertising represents a mixture of art and science, or sound management and creativity, or rational plus emotional components combined.

Part of the creative philosophy of Needham, Harper Worldwide is to "appeal to both heart and head. No sale is entirely in the mind. All sales are made at least partly in the heart. Effective advertising, therefore, does more than present practical reasons why. It invests the product with real emotional values."[14]

Or, as stated by Hal Riney, Managing Director of Ogilvy & Mather, San Francisco, "I wouldn't attempt to define emotion, beyond the observation that emotions are feelings, and advertising that works is advertising that makes somebody feel something."[15]

One of the really dangerous pitfalls to avoid in designing advertising is that of staying strictly within the narrow guidelines of the strategy to the extent that there is only fact and no feeling. This is not to say that the factual part of the message should stray from the strategic statements; it says that there must also be an investment of feeling and emotion.

Lack of feeling stems from an emphasis on fact but also stems from a need for measurement. Learning of facts can be easily measured but measurement of feeling is more difficult. There is a feeling (which does not yet have enough support to be fact) that the most commonly used advertising effectiveness tests are biased toward rational ads. Because agencies often need to show clients that the ads test well, there is a tendency to produce more rational and fewer emotional messages.

A third reason for a lack of emotion in advertising stems from the type of training that people get. Business schools teach rationality, measurement, and numbers, but advertising that covers only these aspects will not be exciting. (In fairness to almost all other bodies of education, it should be mentioned that they also stress these issues too much; business schools, though, seem to be at the leading edge here and are therefore the worst offenders.) There is much more to advertising than the rational processes advocated in this book and in formal avenues of education. To neglect these in the practice of advertising is to negate the essence of the profession.

A major complaint in advertising is that too many messages are dull. Advertising that is devoid of emotion is likely to be dull. There is a time and place for rational argument as well as emotion; most messages have the capacity to incorporate both, but as more money is spent on research and planning there often is a (perhaps improper) shift to more information-oriented messages in order to use the large set of prepared materials. But advertising must stand out if it is to have an impact, and when differences between brands are minor, emotion is necessary to set the brand apart from others.

Earlier it was pointed out that the two key issues of message strategy deal with *what is said* and *how it is said.* What is said is the rational part of the message, while how it is said deals with the emotion (or lack thereof) that is simultaneously conveyed.

Riney has compiled a number of useful thoughts concerning emotion in advertising.[16] Some of his ideas are presented next.

1. *All advertising has some emotion. Some advertising is all emotion.* The balance of emotional and rational depends on

- The importance of what you have to say—more importance leads to more rationality
- How familiar your message is—more familiarity leads to more emotion
- The number of times the consumer will be exposed to your message—more repetition allows for more emotion

2. *The rational appeal of your advertising is always important; one should seldom depend entirely on emotion.*   Although many decisions are made for emotional reasons, people need a rational one to justify their emotions. Buying an expensive luxury car is an emotional decision, but print ads in this product class also give rational information so that buyers can justify their decisions in terms of brakes, leg room, trunk space, and fuel economy.

3. *If emotion is used, be sure it is relevant to the strategy.*

4. *Television is better at conveying emotion; print is better at rational argument.*   This difference is due to the pace of presentation, the control given to the receiver, and the ability to convey emotion using sight, sound, and motion. It is harder to put emotion into a still picture or a set of words. As a result, many products split the two and use television to show emotion and then justify things with a rational print campaign. To try to do everything in one medium can easily lead to failure. There was a time when many television commercials had an emotional video track with a rational audio track. It didn't work.

5. *A strong emotional element is most relevant in certain situations:*

- When there is nothing of importance to say
- To add interest when there is nothing to say
- To create a difference when the benefit is generic
- To suggest superiority in a subjective area
- To provide continuity across messages in a campaign
- There is no advertising situation where the inclusion of strong relevant emotional appeals will not be beneficial.

The following pages present a discussion of a number of types of appeals that also can be considered as emotional and/or rational. These messages focus on either the product or the consumer as the star. Product-focused messages tend to be more attribute oriented and rational, while consumer-focused messages tend to be more benefit oriented and emotional. These, though, are broad tendencies.

Product-focused versus consumer-focused appeals

Figure 7.9 shows a listing of many of the types of appeals that William Weilbacher of Dancer, Fitzgerald and Sample feels belong to the broad categories of product- and consumer-oriented appeals. Product-oriented appeals tend to be more rational or informative in nature and focus on the attributes of the brand while casting the benefits in a more minor role. This can be seen most clearly in the *product feature appeal.* The stereo ad in Figure 7.10 is characteristic of this type of presentation. Technical products such as stereos, computers, and appliances also often lean in this direction. Little emotion is evident in this verbal and highly informative presentation of technical information. The ad needs a highly involved

Figure 7.9   A list of major headings of advertising appeals

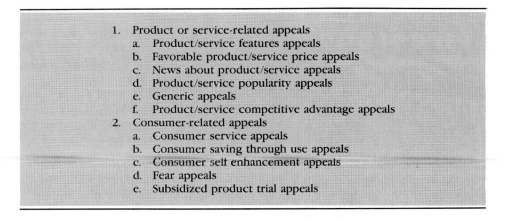

1. Product or service-related appeals
   a. Product/service features appeals
   b. Favorable product/service price appeals
   c. News about product/service appeals
   d. Product/service popularity appeals
   e. Generic appeals
   f. Product/service competitive advantage appeals
2. Consumer-related appeals
   a. Consumer service appeals
   b. Consumer saving through use appeals
   c. Consumer self enhancement appeals
   d. Fear appeals
   e. Subsidized product trial appeals

Figure 7.10   Ad with product feature appeal

THE LONGER YOU OWN IT, THE LESS OBSOLETE IT WILL BECOME.

A lot of stereo equipment starts becoming outdated as soon as you lift it out of the box.

But not Pioneer's SX-60 Receiver. It's been planned for the future, not for obsolescence.

Because it's not just designed to be a stereo receiver, but the control center for the home entertainment system of the future.

The SX-60 has both the performance and features necessary to interface with the video and digital recording hardware and software you will certainly be buying over the next two decades.

To begin with, the SX-60 has the ability to accurately reproduce the wide dynamic range of digital recordings because of its revolutionary Non-Switching, low distortion amp (80 watts per channel into 8 ohms, 20-20,000 Hz with no more than 0.005% THD). Its incredible 95dB signal-to-noise ratio can easily handle the 90dB digital range.

And when the video/audio marriage is consummated, you'll have a receiver that will remain compatible. A video input in the SX-60 enables you to listen to VCR or video disc programs through your stereo system. And a simulated stereo circuit transforms the mono output of video (and AM) broadcasts to create theatre-quality, stereo-like imaging.

The SX-60 features Quartz-PLL digital synthesized tuning that locks in stations and prevents any drift. Plus there are 10 FM and 10 AM electronic station pre-sets and precise digital readout.

As for ease and accuracy of operation, all of the SX-60's circuits are completely microcomputer controlled. Finally, a fluorescent pictographic display provides visual reference to the receiver's vital operating mode.

While this display may give the SX-60 a futuristic appearance today, you can rest assured that 10 or 15 years from now, it will fit right in.

⧉ PIONEER®
Because the music matters.

Figure 7.11 Retailer
price-oriented ad

Figure 7.12 Manufacturer price-oriented ad

reader who is either currently in the market for the product or who is an aficionado.

Favorable product price appeal is commonly used by retailers in announcing sales, weekly specials, or just day-to-day prices. Manufacturers are less likely to state price but may hint at it more implicitly (lowest sticker price of any compact car made in America). Figures 7.11 and 7.12 show retailer and manufacturer price-oriented ads, respectively.

News about product appeal is most commonly used for a new product introduction or a change in an existing product. This appeal also may be used on occasion as a strong statement of an existing benefit that consumers may have misper-

Figure 7.13   *New product news*

Figure 7.14   *New, improved product news*

ceived or toward which they have shown poor awareness. Figures 7.13 and 7.14 show new product news and product improvement news, respectively. Although product news is rare, it should be played up when it exists; Ogilvy is a strong believer in the word "new" and advocates its use whenever possible because it is a forceful word that catches and holds the consumer's attention. The Federal Trade Commission feels that "new" lasts up to six months; after that the word "new" can no longer legally be used.

Product popularity appeal, sometimes known as a *bandwagon appeal,* is an emotional product-oriented appeal that may be useful when there isn't much else to say. "Why not buy our product? Many other people do, therefore it must be good." Figure 7.15 shows an example of an ad that shows the benefit of being part of the group.

A *generic appeal,* also known as *primary demand stimulation,* is often used by the dominant brand in the product class. Such an appeal merely asks potential consumers to use the product and extols its virtues without many specific references to the brand. If the brand truly dominates, it will gain most of the new sales as it builds the product category. Such a strategy would also be useful during the introductory stage of the product life cycle when there are few competitors and the goal is to build the overall product class. There was a time when IBM was

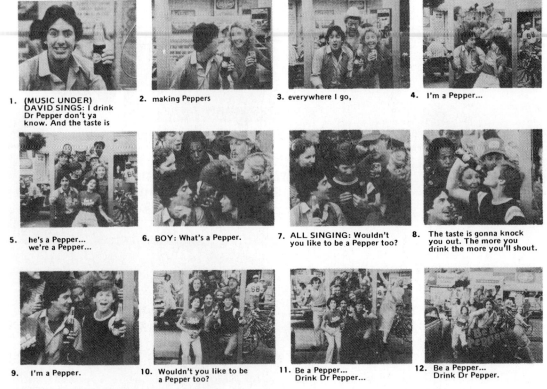

1. (MUSIC UNDER)
   DAVID SINGS: I drink
   Dr Pepper don't ya
   know. And the taste is

2. making Peppers

3. everywhere I go,

4. I'm a Pepper...

5. he's a Pepper...
   we're a Pepper...

6. BOY: What's a Pepper.

7. ALL SINGING: Wouldn't
   you like to be a Pepper too?

8. The taste is gonna knock
   you out. The more you
   drink the more you'll shout.

9. I'm a Pepper.

10. Wouldn't you like to be
    a Pepper too?

11. Be a Pepper...
    Drink Dr Pepper...

12. Be a Pepper...
    Drink Dr Pepper.

Figure 7.15 Bandwagon appeal

such a dominant force in computers that it advertised in this way. A second type of generic appeal would be made by a trade association on behalf of its members. Since most of the manufacturers belong to the association, they will share the benefits of the advertising. Figure 7.16 shows a trade association generic ad.

Product competitive advantage appeal is also referred to as *comparative advertising* and has had a controversial existence. In this type of message the brand is compared to one or more competitors either by name or by innuendo, and comparisons are made across one or more attributes.

For many years advertisers felt that this approach was unwise because it gave free mentions for competitors and because it was in poor taste to disparage the competition publicly. The first fear may have originated with faulty research. If a brand tested a comparative message against a noncomparative approach in a standard copy testing situation, the comparative message would elicit more false mentions of the competitor as sponsor of the message; in the unreal testing situation it would seem that the message gave aid to the competition, especially if respondents were not paying close attention. This happened because in the laboratory test there were no competitive messages.

In the real world of advertising there *are* competitive messages, and so mentioning the competitor has little impact. In fact, the greater the preexisting awareness of the competitor, the less impact there will be on competitor's awareness from comparative advertising. This would suggest that if comparative advertising were done using the leader's brand, there would be little impact on behalf of the leader because that brand already has the highest awareness. Usually comparative advertising is done in relation to the leader because the follower would like to be more closely associated with the leader, or at least thought of in the same mind-

Figure 7.16 Trade
association originated
generic appeal

set. One of the strongest voices against comparative advertising has always been David Ogilvy. Perhaps he has not seen the virtues of comparison because most of his clients are leaders; it is generally accepted that leaders in the product class have the least to gain by comparing themselves to others. Leading brands generally ignore those with smaller market shares.

Since the advent of positioning, which is heavily steeped in building an image at the expense of the competition, there has been more comparative advertising, and recent tests show that the public is not offended by comparisons and, indeed, welcomes intelligent ones.

Social psychology research can offer assistance as to the value of comparative messages. Relevant issues deal with the audiences's initial position and the likelihood of its exposure to subsequent opposing arguments.

- *Regarding the audience's initial position*   If the audience agrees with the presenter's position, then it is best to present a noncomparative message to strengthen prior beliefs and reinforce and enhance current opinion; a comparative message can create doubt among an agreeing audience. This would imply that a market leader (that has the most agreeable audience) should avoid a comparative message.

If the audience disagrees, then a comparative message can increase credibility by appearing to be more objective. Such a strategy would be most valuable for a brand with a small market share and, by implication, a large audience in disagreement with its point of view.

- *Regarding the likelihood of exposure to opposing messages*   If the audience is likely to be exposed to competitive messages, then comparative messages have value because they are felt to inoculate the receiver against the stronger dose of information that will appear in the opposing message. If there will be no opposing message, then there is no need to inoculate.

In the real world of advertising there are, in most cases, competitive messages, and therefore comparative advertising would be an appropriate strategy to consider according to social psychology theory. Comparative advertising would seem to have its greatest potential value when consumers are not loyal, when the market is fragmented, when the brand has a small market share, or when the brand is first being introduced (and has no market share).

In 1972 the Federal Trade Commission took a stand that encouraged the use of comparative advertising as a tool to give consumers more and better information and to aid the competitive marketplace processes. Since that time the use of comparative advertising has steadily increased as have the number of research studies and speeches both for and against the technique. The pros and cons deal with whether the technique helps the consumer, the firm, and advertising in general; the arguments seem to be split fairly evenly. What is of most relevance in this text is what happens to the firm and when is the technique useful. Two sources should be considered.

Graham Phillips, Managing Director of Ogilvy & Mather, New York, has developed a set of guidelines.[17] He feels that comparative advertising *should* be considered when

- *The brand is not the leader*   The smaller the share, the greater the potential. This includes new brand introductions.
- *The benefit is tangible*   Price comparisons work well as do benefits that can be seen visually and/or demonstrated.
- *The budget is lower than that of competitors*

Comparative advertising *should not* be considered when

- The benefit is not meaningful or is based on puffery
- The benefit is subjective, image based on a matter of taste
- There is a high level of satisfaction with the brand being compared.

In addition, the American Association of Advertising Agencies (the 4As) has developed a set of ten guidelines for the proper use of comparative advertising. These are reproduced as Figure 7.17. The 4As feels that comparative advertising is one of many valid techniques that may be properly used or abused.

Figures 7.18 and 7.19 show two examples of comparative advertising. The Blatz beer commercial compares on a more subjective, taste dimension while the Intellivision commercial compares on a more objective, visual dimension. Both seem to follow the guidelines developed by Phillips.

Having finished the product-oriented appeals, *consumer-oriented appeals* can now be considered. This class tends to be more benefit oriented and more emotional. These ads tend to show what's in it for the consumer and feature the

Figure 7.17 *Guidelines for the proper use of comparative advertising*

1. The intent and connotation of the ad should be to inform and never to discredit or unfairly attack competitors, competing products or services.
2. When a competitive product is named, it should be one that exists in the market as significant competition.
3. The competition should be fairly and properly identified but never in a manner or tone that degrades the competitive product or service.
4. The advertising should compare related or similar properties or ingredients of the product, dimension to dimension, feature to feature.
5. The identification should be for honest comparison purposes and not simply to upgrade by association
6. If a competitive test is conducted, it should be done by an objective testing source, preferably an independent one, so that there will be no doubt as to its validity.
7. In all cases the test should be supportive of all claims made in the advertising based on the test.
8. The advertising should never use partial results or stress insignificant differences to cause the consumer to draw an improper conclusion.
9. The property being compared should be significant in terms of value or usefulness to the consumer.
10. Comparatives delivered through the use of testimonials should not imply that the testimonial is more than one individual's thought unless that individual represents a sample of the majority viewpoint.

Figure 7.18 *Blatz Beer storyboard*

1. (Anncr VO): Here's what happened when Jeff Bridge took the Blatz taste test.

2. JEFF BRIDGE: (VO) Oh, give me a break!

3. JEFF BRIDGE: I can't wait to see what that is.

4. (Anncr VO): Ta..da!

5. JEFF BRIDGE: Budweiser. I can't believe that!

6. I picked Blatz over Budweiser and I drink Budweiser constantly and I think Blatz tastes better.

7. I can't believe I'm saying this 'cause...I don't believe these guys on television when they say it.

8. (Anncr VO): What do you say now? JEFF BRIDGE: I can believe it. (Anncr VO): Why now?

9. JEFF BRIDGE: Because it happened to me.

10. (Anncr VO): Taste Blatz yourself.

11. Compare the quality. Compare the price.

12. JEFF BRIDGE: Blatz tasted better.

Figure 7.19   *Intellivision commercial*

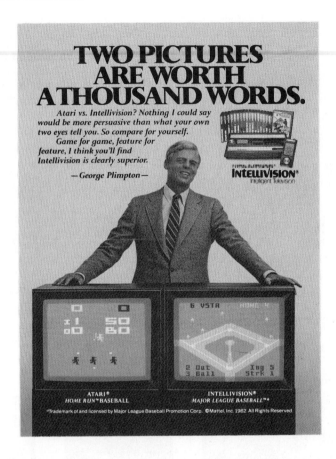

consumer, uses, and advantages more than merely showing the product, as was often done for product-oriented ads.

Consumer service appeals show how to use the product and what benefits will result from its proper use. The product is secondary to the benefit and the impact on the consumer. Figure 7.20 shows a consumer service appeal.

Consumer savings through use appeals don't emphasize price but, rather, emphasize the benefits of getting savings. Where a product-oriented ad would say "our price is . . . ," a consumer-oriented savings ad would emphasize benefits such as "using our new widget will allow you to save $3 per hour" or "with the new framistander attachment, your old widget will run for six more years." Figure 7.21 is an example of a savings benefit appeal.

Self-enhancement appeals present the benefit of improving the user in some way. These are generally emotional ads offering rewards such as sex appeal, love, or respect. Charles Revson of Revlon Cosmetics has been quoted as saying that in the factory they manufacture cosmetics but in the drugstore they sell hope. Beauty aids typically use self-enhancement appeals; so do sports cars; so do cake mixes. The list is endless for this type of appeal, which offers the consumer some intangible along with the tangible product. Figure 7.22 on page 230 shows that the user will be more appealing to other members of the family by using Pillsbury cake mixes and poppin' fresh dough because nothin' says lovin' like somethin' from the oven. Figure 7.23 offers the user a different self-enhancement.

Figure 7.20 *Showing how to use the product*

Figure 7.21 *Savings benefit appeal*

Fear appeals have a long history of use for products that are difficult to evaluate, yet have the ability to save a person from loss of life, limb, or personal property. Product classes that often use fear appeals are tires and insurance; these can be seen in the ads of Figures 7.24 and 7.25. This class of appeal plays on uncertainties that consumers may have: "You may never need this product but when you do, if it's not ours you'll be sorry," "Don't risk skidding in the rain," "Don't leave them unprotected," "You can pay me now or you can pay me later." Often these messages are a combination of long rational arguments combined with emotion-laden statements.

The social psychology literature concerning fear appeals was reviewed by Ray and Wilkie in 1970 for its appropriateness to marketing.[18] They concluded that a high level of fear was too threatening to consumers and as a result, the message would be rejected and avoided. At the other extreme, too little fear would not be recognized and no response would occur. In addition to the level of fear, the writer must also consider the level of anxiety of the message recipient. Anxious people cannot deal with stronger levels of fear appeals so they must get a mild dosage. For example, smokers would be more anxious about cigarette health issues and, therefore, would be most affected by mild fear appeal antismoking

Figure 7.22 *Nothin' says lovin' like somethin' from the oven*

1. (SFX: OF CAN)
P.F.: (ECHO) Let me out!

2. Let's make those Pillsbury Butterflake rolls!

3. (SFX: UNWRAPPING PACKAGE)

4. (SFX: POP!)
(MUSIC: PUNCTUATED)

5. P.F.: (RELIEVED) Whew!

6. I'm Poppin' Fresh, the Pillsbury dough boy!

7. (SFX: WHISTLE)
Okay gang, everyone into the oven.

8. (SFX: APPROPRIATE SOUND EFFECT)

9. P.F.: (SINGS) Oh, a house smells so nice when you bake in the oven --...

10. P.F.(VO): ...a warm kind of smell when you bake in the oven.

11. P.F.: Ah, baking in the oven.

12. Who can ever forget mother's kitchen and the aroma of fresh baking that filled the house?

13. Like today -- when you bake Pillsbury sweet rolls --...

14. ...biscuits,...

15. ...cookies,...

16. ...dinner rolls -- yes,...

17. ...Butterflake dinner rolls -- layered with Grade A butter --...

18. ...all in the dairy case,...

19. ...made from Pillsbury Poppin' Fresh Dough.

20. P.F.: (SINGS) Nothin' says lovin' like somethin' from the oven ... and Pillsbury says it best.

messages. Conversely, nonsmokers would have little anxiety about this issue and could receive strong fear appeal messages to keep them from starting to smoke. How much fear is a "high" level or "low" level? That has not been clearly spelled out and will differ from case to case. The above findings should be useful, though, in considering appropriate strategies.

Subsidized product trial appeals are basically the set of ads used along with the delivery of promotions. Their purpose is to announce that the firm will accept some or all of the financial risk of the consumer's trial purchase behavior. Issues

Figure 7.23 *For a more sensuously attractive you*

Figure 7.24 *Tire ad with fear appeal*

Do you really need a tire this good when the weatherman predicts clear skies?

Uniroyal's Royal Seal is engineered to handle any forecast. Even a wrong one.

The reason is Uniroyal's advanced technology. It enables Uniroyal engineers to achieve an optimum all-weather tread before the first prototype is even produced. It all takes place on a computer screen. And it draws upon the knowledge and experience of millions of consumer and test track miles.

One result is a tread that delivers excellent all-weather traction.

And for added protection

Royal Seal is lined with Uniroyal's patented sealant. It automatically and permanently seals most tread punctures up to 3/16 of an inch in diameter.

There is also the confidence

in knowing Royal Seal is backed by a warranty unsurpassed in the industry. In fact, unlike most warranties this one provides complete coverage against any road hazard damage—glass, nails, potholes or whatever—for 2 years or 30% of tread depth (whichever comes first). If a road hazard makes a Royal Seal unserviceable during the warranty period, Uniroyal will replace it. Free.

Get Uniroyal's Royal Seal. And when the weatherman predicts clear skies, you'll be ready for anything.

UNIROYAL

You may never need a tire this good. Royal Seal.

Figure 7.25 *Insurance ad with fear appeal*

CAN YOU AFFORD TO SURVIVE AN ACCIDENT?

If a serious accident or illness left you disabled, life could be a lot tougher than you think.

Because even after your medical insurance takes care of your hospital and doctors' bills, you're still left with the bills you've always had. Without the salary you've always had.

That's why it helps to know someone with MONY, Mutual Of New York.

At MONY, we can offer you comprehensive disability insur-

ance, tailored to your needs and lifestyle. If you should become totally disabled, it would help replace your lost income.

And, unlike traditional disability plans, MONY will even pay you partial or residual benefits after you return to work, if your earnings are reduced by 25% or more.

Your MONY agent can also offer you an option that adjusts your benefit upward as the cost of living rises.

So call someone at Mutual Of New York about our disability programs. Because it's good to know you'll always have an income you can count on. Even if you're faced with something you didn't count on.

MONY
IT HELPS TO KNOW SOMEONE WITH MONY.
The Mutual Life Insurance Company Of New York
1740 Broadway, New York, N.Y. 10019

T·H·E   I·N·S·I·D·E   O·U·T·L·O·O·K

Burt Manning

Chairman & Chief Executive Officer, J. Walter Thompson U.S.A., Inc.

Burt Manning says he really began his advertising career as a door-to-door salesman. But Burt's training as a copywriter began with Leo Burnett in Chicago, where he worked on everything from Camay to Schlitz. Burt says he learned from Leo, "Make the best possible ad every single time." (A personal credo that could have come from J. Walter Thompson's Stanley Resor as well.)

Burt joined J. Walter Thompson Chicago in 1967. In 1972 he transferred to New York and was subsequently named Executive Creative Director of the New York agency.

Burt's high standards have resulted in creative selling campaigns such as "When you're out of Schlitz, you're out of beer," "The closer you look, the better we look," for Ford, the Marvelous Magical Burger King, and many more.

In June 1977, he was appointed Vice Chairman of the Board of J. Walter Thompson Company, a position he retains.

Creativity in the Advertising Mix

Of all the elements in the advertising mix, creativity is the least quantifiable. Yet it has potentially the greatest leverage on the media dollars spent. The best way to understand the importance of creativity in advertising is to understand what it does for the advertiser.

Creativity first separates the individual advertisement from all the advertisements surrounding it. In the process of doing that, creativity achieves its real goal: to separate the brand in a positive and motivating way from all other brands in the product category.

It may be possible to do something like this through sheer media weight, by simply outspending your competitors. But creativity is usually the least expensive way to make both ad and brand stand out in the crowd. This is not to say it is necessarily the best way. The best way to make a brand stand out is to put a significantly superior or unique product behind it. In

the real world, however, competition and technology virtually force parity upon products in the same category—close similarity in function, quality, price, and often appearance.

Can you give a branded parity product distinction through unique advertising strategy? Sometimes. Still, that is a very limited opportunity. Brands of parity products all marketed to the same group of consumers most likely will have the same advertising strategy, because it is the only one that makes sense. Dishwashing liquids will need to communicate efficacy and mildness, fluoride toothpaste cavity-prevention and taste, sports cars performance and status, and so on.

When brands all have the same essential advertising strategies, what is it that makes one brand's advertising more salient and more effective? It is the creativity with which the strategy has been executed.

When advertising works, it works because it makes something happen inside the consumer. An advertisement is, after all, no more than a set of stimuli intended to evoke a set of desired responses among a specific group of consumers. The effect of a "creative" advertisement is to generate a more intense positive response to the brand than a "noncreative" advertisement. Whether it achieves its ends through the use of words, images, sounds, or music, whether it evokes laughter, fear, shock, or feelings of warmth and tenderness, the creative advertisement stands out in the consumer's mind and makes the brand stand out too.

How do creative people create? Nobody really knows. Nobody really knows where ideas are born; where an unforgettable bar of music comes from; why a felicitous phrase pops into someone's head. No one really knows how some people can put words and pictures and sounds and ideas together in ways that can move millions of other people to think and feel and act.

But we do know the most effective advertising (which I contend is the most creative) always has at least two of three elements and often has all three

Relevance   Surprise   Emotion

Relevance, of course, is strategically, not creatively, driven. But advertising cannot be creative without it. It is based on knowledge; knowledge of what the consumer wants and what the product has to offer. It is present in all but the most dismally poor advertising.

It is the other two characteristics in combination with relevance that distinguish the best advertising. Relevant surprise. Relevant emotion.

Arthur Koestler said that "surprise is at the heart of every creative act." But why does the element of surprise help to make advertising more effective? Consider one dictionary definition: "surprise: to capture unexpectedly."

Advertising that captures the consumer unexpectedly not only gets attention, not only stands out in the mind, it stays in the mind. It is remembered long after the immediate experience has passed. The usual and the expected are barely noticed and quickly forgotten.

Emotion—relevant emotion—is the other element common to the most effective advertising. Advertising that warms or charms or amuses or otherwise stirs up real and positive feelings about a brand is advertising that separates that brand from its competitors. And because purchase decisions are rarely made on a purely rational basis, advertising that adds emotional value to a brand may be the most effective—the most creative—advertising of all.

Figure 7.26 Subsidized
product trial appeal

concerning price-oriented promotions are discussed in Part 6. Figure 7.26 gives an example of a coupon delivered through a print ad; it reduces the product cost through a subsidy from the manufacturer, and the purpose of the ad is to announce that the coupon subsidy is available. Other subsidies would include samples, money refund offers, and premiums.

Summary

The key to the success of an advertising agency lies in the creative department because it is here that the messages are actually conceived and developed. While a full-service agency may provide research, marketing, media, promotions, and public relations assistance, its success is primarily dependent on its ability to produce creative messages.

Creativity is an elusive concept that has been described as "deriving unique ideas as combinations of old elements." Many people can be given a set of information about a product but few will reshape the pieces so that an uninvolved audience will stop and take notice of the result. A creative solution will do this and, at the same time, will present the relevant information. Remember that it's not creative unless it assists the overall process of selling the product.

Most advertising looks like most other advertising; while it may present relevant information it doesn't stand out and it doesn't grab hold of the consumer. This sameness avoids risk and may maintain the status quo but also inhibits the chances for a positive movement. Creative advertising is essential for new product introductions and other cases where the objectives include growth.

One end product of creativity is The Big Idea. This is a concept that can hold attention for many years and can be translated into lots of message executions across all relevant media. The Big Idea expresses the inherent drama of the product either on its own merits or through borrowed interest.

After the situation analysis, objectives, and position are set, there are many dimensions from which to begin developing the message and no simple best way. In this chapter the process of defining the message was begun with an examination of rational versus emotional and product-oriented versus consumer-oriented messages. These broad classifications are important because they tie back to the discussion of involvement and information processing. The entire tone of the message will be determined by the decisions made in these areas. Regardless of the consumer information needs, it is important to remember that no sale is made entirely in the head; emotion and feelings are both important parts of any successful message.

Discussion Questions

1. What is creativity?

2. Why is creativity so elusive?

3. Describe a brainstorming session.

4. What makes an idea big?

5. Should advertising be rational or emotional? Why?

6. Why might a high-involvement brand want to use an emotional message?

7. Which brands benefit most from comparative advertising? Which brands benefit least from comparative advertising?

8. In what ways do product-oriented and consumer-oriented appeals differ?

9. What is the proper level of fear to use in advertising for life insurance?

10. Pick your favorite automobile and breakfast cereal brands. Now go through the list of product- and consumer-related appeals in Figure 7.9 and develop a big idea for each brand for each appeal.

11. Review the situation analysis, objectives, and position that you have formulated so far in your job search campaign. Come up with a big idea for your message strategy. Next develop messages based on the four most relevant appeals (of those discussed in this chapter).

Notes

1. Sheila Dorton, personal communication.

2. David Ogilvy, *Ogilvy on Advertising* (New York: Crown Publishers, 1983), p. 198.

3. Vilfredo Pareto, *The Mind and Society* (New York: Harcourt, Brace and Company, 1935).

4. Norman Berry, "My Creative Philosophy," in *Viewpoint: By, For and About Ogilvy & Mather,* 2(1980), pp. 3–5.

5. Kathryn Sederberg, "Top Agency 'Creatives' Take a Closer Look at Creativity," *Advertising Age,* 4 June 1979, pp. 5–11.

6. Stephen Baker, *Systematic Approach to Creative Advertising* (New York: McGraw-Hill, 1979).

7. Reva Korda, "The Creative Process," in *Viewpoint: By, For and About Ogilvy & Mather,* 3(1979), pp. 9–10.

8. Korda, "The Creative Process," pp. 12–13.

9. Bruce McCallum, "What To Do When You're Stuck for an Idea," in *Viewpoint: By, For and About Ogilvy & Mather,* 1(1980), pp. 30–32.

10. Sheila Dorton, October 1982, presentation at the University of Wisconsin, School of Business.

11. Ogilvy, *Ogilvy on Advertising,* p. 16.

12. Baker, *Systematic Approach to Creative Advertising,* p. 104.

13. Sederberg, "Top Agency 'Creatives,'" pp. 5–10.

14. Needham, Harper & Steers, *Statement of Creative Philosophy.*

15. Hal Riney, "Emotion in Advertising," in *Viewpoint: By, For and About Ogilvy & Mather,* 1(1981), p. 5.

16. Riney, "Emotion in Advertising," pp. 5–13.

17. Graham Phillips, "Naming the Competition in Advertising: Is It Effective and When Do You Do It?" in *Viewpoint: By, For and About Ogilvy & Mather* (Fall 1983), p. 32.

18. Michael L. Ray and William L. Wilkie, "Fear: The Potential of an Appeal Neglected by Marketing," *Journal of Marketing* 34 (January 1970), pp. 54–62.

Chapter 8
Specific
Execution
Styles

Specific Classes of Message Appeal Executions

*H*aving considered emotional versus rational appeals, and product-oriented versus consumer-oriented appeals, the writer can next consider a number of ways to execute these appeals. The following set of executions is by no means complete, nor is each type independent of each of the others. Rather, the listing is designed to describe most of the major, commonly used alternatives. Often two or more execution styles are used together.

In a similar vein, Table 8.1 shows a subjective listing of how execution styles fit with the broader classes of message appeals. There are really no rules governing assignment of execution to appeal; the table instead shows common usages. The reader will note that there are commonly used executions for consumer-oriented emotional appeals and for product-oriented rational appeals.

Table 8.1 Appeals and executions

Appeal	Executions commonly used with the appeal
Product-oriented (Rational)	Slice of life
	Product comparison
	Factual
	Problem–solution
	Demonstration
	News
	Unknown consumer
	Expert spokesperson
Consumer-oriented (Emotional)	Sex
	Music
	Humor
	Animation
	Celebrity spokesperson

Before beginning the discussion of executions, it is useful to reiterate that execution styles are techniques used to enhance strategies. Their purposes are to increase attention, to cut through the ever-present clutter, and to help the consumer learn some vital point about the brand. As such, they should be chosen only *after* the strategy has been developed. To say "let's do a humorous commercial" without taking into account the relevant selling points may lead to humor but probably won't aid the client firm.

Product-Oriented Rational Appeals

Executions in the product-oriented rational appeal cell include slice of life, product comparison, testimonial, and factual.

The *slice-of-life execution* is often disparaged as a boring and unrealistic execution; it is also known as the *problem–solution execution* and the *demonstration execution*, although there are cases of the latter two that are not slice of life. In the slice-of-life style, a character in the commercial encounters a problem in daily life such as static cling, ring around the collar, or a yellow wax buildup on the kitchen floor. In 30 seconds the problem is solved through the use of the brand and an assist from a helpful friend/relative/neighbor/stranger/voice-over; as the commercial ends, the protagonist is generally pleased and relieved. Each vignette is a dramatization with a cast selected to be as similar as possible to the target market (often based on psychographics).

This execution style is frequently maligned for its lack of creativity and emotion, but the style is very effective at making its point. Information is single-mindedly presented, with no distractions to take the consumer away from the key message points. While the slice-of-life approach is not exciting, it does take a lot of creativity to condense reality to 30 seconds.

Reinhard makes the interesting observation that the slice-of-life advertising that is most often maligned isn't really a slice of life, but rather a slice of something else. Good slice-of-life advertising is full of emotion and feeling and presents a vignette to which viewers can relate. It also has believable characters who act in believable ways and recite believable lines. Some of the finest and most emotional slice-of-life commercials were made by Needham, Harper Worldwide for McDonald's and were aimed at families and teens. The slice-of-life commercials that are maligned are unrealistic views of life portrayed through unrealistic conversations. Even though this is true, it *is* difficult to generate a meaningful dialogue about static cling!

The problem–solution execution is closest to the slice-of-life in that it also begins with a conflict that then gets resolved. The slice-of-life ad is set in an everyday situation to which viewers can relate, as in Figure 8.1, while the problem–solution ad may be set in a laboratory or other uncommon environment, as in Figure 8.2. In both slice-of-life and problem–solution ads, the product is the hero and rescues the consumers from a tenuous situation.

However the demonstration is accomplished in one of these two styles, the product is clearly the star of the show. Some of the most spectacular demonstrations are done in foreign commercials to show the durability of pickup trucks (they are driven off cliffs and out of airplanes) and the strength of super glues (the rears of two trailer trucks are glued together and the trucks are driven in opposite directions; they don't separate). Figure 8.3 on page 240 shows an especially captivating execution of a demonstration for a product that would surely keep viewers' eyes glued to the screen.

Figure 8.1   *Slice of life*   **Figure 8.2**   *Problem–solution*

From the demonstration, it is only a short leap to the *product comparison execution* in which the brand and one or more of its competitors are shown as competitors in solving a problem or demonstrating an attribute/benefit. Here one paper towel is more absorbent than another, one car has more trunk room than another, or one ketchup is thicker than another. This execution style was discussed earlier as comparative advertising (see Figure 5.7 for a product comparison message).

Print advertising for new products is at times designed to look like news. The *news execution* style can offer a greater advantage when a brand is truly new or improved. It is often combined with another style (slice-of-life: "Marge, have you seen this *new* fabric softener?"; demonstration: "Watch what this *new* fabric softener can do for you!"). "New" is an attention-getting word and should be used when possible. Figure 8.4 shows a new product execution.

A *reason why execution* may be an extension of news when nothing is really new. Helping people justify a purchase is a worthwhile endeavor when possible, especially given that in many cases it is difficult to come up with a unique reason why. Figure 8.5 gives consumers a reason why to buy. While all rationally based advertising gives a reason why, emotional advertising may also do so. If it is hard

Figure 8.3 *A unique demonstration*   **Figure 8.4** *News execution*

to justify a decision based on emotion, some reasons may also be given. For example, a Porsche is bought for emotional reasons, but advertising gives information to allow the buyer to justify the decision on rational grounds.

The *talking head* may be the extreme in direct sell with no superfluous distractors. In its purest form, there is an extreme closeup of a head delivering the sales pitch. If television can bring the salesperson into the home, this is the clearest example. Most talking heads are not done quite to this extreme, but instead show the spokesperson standing, sitting, or walking, and allow the package and product to be shown. Many commercials have at least a few seconds of talking head, but few are dominated by, or exclusively use, this technique.

The parallel technique in print advertising would be the straight verbal, *factual execution* with little or no visual support. Although straight factual advertising can appear on television, it is much more likely to appear in print. Virtually all advertising is at least partly factual (giving the brand name is a fact), but the factual execution is almost exclusively straightforward fact. One of the most famous print ads of this type is the Rolls Royce ad in Figure 8.6; it was written by David Ogilvy at a time when long print ads were being shunned.

A final execution style that leans toward the rational end of the scale is the *testimonial* or *spokesperson* advertisement. This approach tends toward a factual orientation, but there are many nonfactual examples as well. This format allows a

When to Take Five.

- When you total up your dog's veterinarian bills and discover he's getting better medical care than you.
- When your credit card balance makes you the fourth biggest deficit spender after Argentina, Mexico and Brazil.
- When the number of candles on your birthday cake makes it necessary to blow them out with a fan.
- Whenever you bring work home on the weekend and actually do it.
- When you have a flat and the spare is in the garage.
- When you arrive in Toledo and your bags arrive in Taipei.

- Whenever the car repair bill is under $100.
- When your mother informs you she's taking up break-dancing.
- After taking 1st prize at a costume party and you didn't wear one.
- Anytime on Monday.
- When you discover that the CPA who found all those loopholes for you last year, is working for the IRS this year.
- **After you finish reading all these reasons to take five and you're dying to try a Take Five bar.**
- **When you want light wafers, silky peanut creme, covered with Hershey's milk chocolate...**
- **When you want the richness of a candy bar without the heaviness of one, try a Take Five bar.**

HERSHEY'S
Take Five
light wafer bar • peanut creme • milk chocolate

You earned it.

Figure 8.5 *Reason why execution*

The Rolls-Royce Silver Cloud—$13,995

"At 60 miles an hour the loudest noise in this new Rolls-Royce comes from the electric clock"

What makes Rolls-Royce the best car in the world? "There is really no magic about it—it is merely patient attention to detail," says an eminent Rolls-Royce engineer.

1. "At 60 miles an hour the loudest noise comes from the electric clock," reports the Technical Editor of THE MOTOR. Three mufflers tune out sound frequencies—acoustically.

2. Every Rolls-Royce engine is run for seven hours at full throttle before installation, and each car is test-driven for hundreds of miles over varying road surfaces.

3. The Rolls-Royce is designed as an owner-driven car. It is eighteen inches shorter than the largest domestic cars.

4. The car has power steering, power brakes and automatic gear-shift. It is very easy to drive and to park. No chauffeur required.

5. The finished car spends a week in the final test-shop, being fine-tuned. Here it is subjected to 98 separate ordeals. For example, the engineers use a stethoscope to listen for axle-whine.

6. The Rolls-Royce is guaranteed for

three years. With a new network of dealers and parts-depots from Coast to Coast, service is no problem.

7. The Rolls-Royce radiator has never changed, except that when Sir Henry Royce died in 1933 the monogram RR was changed from red to black.

8. The coachwork is given five coats of primer paint, and hand rubbed between each coat, before nine coats of finishing paint go on.

9. By moving a switch on the steering column, you can adjust the shock-absorbers to suit road conditions.

10. A picnic table, veneered in French walnut, slides out from under the dash. Two more swing out behind the front seats.

11. You can get such optional extras as an Espresso coffee-making machine, a dictating machine, a bed, hot and cold water for washing, an electric razor or a telephone.

12. There are three separate systems of power brakes, two hydraulic and one mechanical. Damage to one will not affect the others. The Rolls-Royce is a very safe car—and also a very lively car. It cruises serenely at eighty-five. Top speed is in excess of 100 m.p.h.

13. The Bentley is made by Rolls-Royce. Except for the radiators, they are identical motor cars, manufactured by the same engineers in the same works. People who feel diffident about driving a Rolls-Royce can buy a Bentley.

PRICE. The Rolls-Royce illustrated in this advertisement—f.o.b. principal ports of entry—costs **$13,995**.

If you would like the rewarding experience of driving a Rolls-Royce or Bentley, write or telephone to one of the dealers listed on opposite page. Rolls-Royce Inc., 10 Rockefeller Plaza, New York 20, N. Y. Circle 5-1144.

Figure 8.6 *Factual, verbal Rolls-Royce ad*

user (who may be an expert or an ordinary consumer) to discuss the merits of, and experiences with, the brand. To have a user or an expert advocate the brand will probably imply a factual underpinning.

A different type of endorsement comes from a *celebrity* who may have no great expertise with the product at all. The messages in these ads may be much less factual and may rely heavily on the celebrity's visibility. In this case, the celebrity is less an endorser and more a borrowed interest appeal.

A fair amount of literature says that celebrities don't do much good in selling products. Attribution theory in social psychology would predict that a celebrity would have low credibility. Consumers will ask themselves why the celebrity is endorsing the product and will respond to themselves that the celebrity is acting that way for lots of money. On the other hand, consumers may feel that an unknown consumer or technical expert is endorsing the product because it is a good product. This feeling is enhanced when the unknown is also an incompetent actor (or an actor good enough to look like an incompetent actor).

From another perspective, the source credibility literature would make some similar predictions. The more credible the source, the greater the resultant attitude change. This would suggest that the expert would be the best spokesperson of the three types. To this, one must also add the notion of involvement and then note that this finding holds only in the high-involvement case. In low-involvement

Figure 8.7 *Predominant uses of different types of spokespersons*

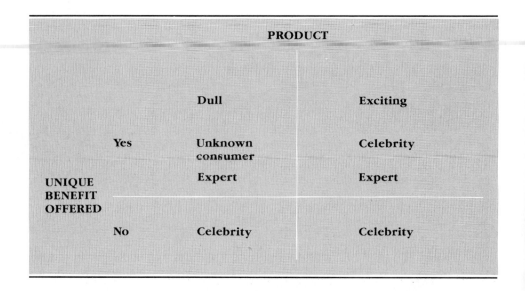

		PRODUCT	
		Dull	Exciting
	Yes	Unknown consumer	Celebrity
UNIQUE BENEFIT OFFERED		Expert	Expert
	No	Celebrity	Celebrity

cases, consumers don't pay attention and probably are equally unaffected by all sources.[1] In actual practice, the purpose of the celebrity may be merely to gain attention for the brand, as has been done successfully by Bill Cosby for Jello and Joe Namath for popcorn poppers.

In some cases it is possible that the celebrities truly are experts or are perceived as heavy users in the product class and therefore are credible sources. This may have been the case for Jackie Stewart and Ford and for a long line of ex-jocks for Miller Lite Beer. Again, the agency and client must be careful in selecting the right celebrity for the endorsement. The wrong celebrity will lack credibility or steal the show from the product. Given the cost of using a true celebrity (the top of the line get close to $1 million for their efforts), care is required here.

After studying 12 years of tests for commercials with unknowns and celebrities, McCollum/Spielman Research, Inc. concluded that, overall, the two types of spokespersons led to similar results in terms of awareness and attitude shifts. More important, they felt that there were well-defined situations for each of the two types of spokespersons. As outlined in Figure 8.7, unknown consumers would do better for unexciting convenience goods of which the brand had a distinct benefit, but that celebrities would do better for more glamorous, exotic products or in cases where there was no real brand benefit advantage.[2] Figures 8.8, 8.9, and 8.10 show examples of unknown consumer, celebrity, and expert spokespersons, respectively.

The "real person" can only appear in drudge product commercials because there would be a lack of consistency in having this person endorse glamour. Furthermore, the "real person" doesn't have the charisma to carry a commercial that doesn't offer an easily perceived benefit, so there must be a clear benefit over which the person can rhapsodize. Conversely, if there is a benefit, there is less need for a celebrity, given that a key value of a celebrity is to hold attention through borrowed interest when no benefit exists.

As pointed out by Bourne Morris of Ogilvy & Mather, use of a celebrity or any other spokesperson is a technique (or execution style), not an idea (or strategy). The objectives and strategies must be developed before the technique is selected. For example, Morris says that Dave DeBusschere, a professional basketball

"Is a big long distance bill the price of friendship?"

"With Sprint, you can't have too many friends."

"Sprint's new volume discounts save me even more.

Sprint keeps finding new ways to save me money. I like that. Now, the more I call, the more I can save on all interstate calls. That's Sprint's volume discounts. That's a smart idea. With Sprint, I save right from the start. And when my bill reaches $25 I save even more. And that's just the beginning of Sprint's volume discounts. Best of all, the discount applies for every call I make that month. Sprint feels if I call more, I deserve more. So, they gave me more... more savings. Good for you, Sprint.

And I save right away.
With Sprint, I can call my family and friends and save every time. In fact I can call anyone out of state and save every time. You'd think something so good would be hard to get. But Sprint wasn't. All I had to do was call up and ask for it. No start-up fee. No monthly fee. As long as I make $5 worth of calls a month.

I save all the time. Even when I'm away.
You probably don't know this but most long distance discount services charge two rates (one low, one higher) depending on where you call. With them you might save only part of the time. With Sprint, I save all of the time. And Sprint gave me a free Travelcode.™ So, when I'm away from home, I can call at Sprint's low rates from almost any phone. And those calls apply toward the volume discounts, too. I've got friends all over the place. But those friendships don't mean big phone bills anymore, because I switched to Sprint. In fact, with Sprint's volume discounts, I can't have too many friends. Call Sprint and ask them more about it. I bet you'll switch, too."

Switch to SPRINT®
800-521-4949

GTE SPRINT®

© 1984, GTE Sprint.
®Sprint is a registered service mark of GTE Sprint Communications Corp. Sprint is an interstate service and is available in most areas.

"Turn the blues and blahs into ooohs and ahhhs."

Know someone who's having one of those days? Send them the new Pick-Me-Up® Bouquet from your FTD Florist. Cheerful flowers in a coffee mug and a reusable tote bag. It's a sure cure for the blues.

Merlin Olsen

Lift someone's spirits with special care.™

FTD and the Mercury emblem are registered trademarks of Florists' Transworld Delivery Association.

Figure 8.8 *Unknown consumer as spokesperson*   **Figure 8.9** *Celebrity as spokesperson*

Figure 8.10 *Expert as spokesperson*

A man in search of an honest car.

Jackie Stewart, three-time world champion driver, now consultant to Ford Motor Company.
Get it together—buckle up.

I've traveled around the world looking for a certain kind of car.
I call it the honest car.
Once, I would have started my search in Europe. Because Europeans had to face crowded roads and high fuel costs sooner than people in other parts of the world.

But things have changed.
Now you also have to look in the U.S., and at companies like Ford.
And what is an honest car supposed to do? In a few words: It's a car that starts, stops and steers.
Of course, this is a terrific oversimplification.

Take the first point, starting.
Some small-engined cars have tended to be cranky starters.
Ford has opted to meet the problem in certain models with electronic engine controls, multiple-port fuel injection and stronger starters.
It took time and money, but it was the responsible way to go.

And then there's stopping.
Stopping quickly, in a straight line, with the car under control, is the name of the game here.
And Ford products undergo extensive testing while striving to improve their braking characteristics.

Ford gets a grip on it.
All Ford cars are equipped with steel-belted radial tires.
But Ford doesn't stop there.

On certain models, tires and wheels are "indexed." Since tires and wheels have a "high" point and a "low" point, these are marked, so "low" and "high" can be matched when tire and wheel are assembled.
A small point, but it is attention to details like these that gives you a rounder tire and wheel combination to help ride quality.

And then there's steering.
In the past, many people were content with cars that emphasized boulevard ride, not handling.
I've been told that you could blame this on a mythical Aunt Minnie. It was said she didn't like cars that responded quickly and accurately to driver input.
But if Aunt Minnie didn't like a responsive car, what was she doing tooling around in that little, quick-on-the-trigger compact?

American drivers like a quick-to-react car.
Not necessarily a sports car. But one that feels like it's being driven by the driver, not some disinterested third party.

An impressive change in one company's cars.
It's a change in aerodynamics, in handling, in quality. In what the engineers call product integrity.
I think someday every good car company has got to have this new approach to building cars.

Ford has it. Now.

FORD · MERCURY · LINCOLN · FORD TRUCKS

Figure 8.11 Relevant celebrity spokespersons

(SFX: RIP, CRASH!) ROCKY: (TO CAMERA) When Joe gets hungry, he gets <u>mean.</u>

JOE GREENE: So I grab myself a Swanson Hungry-Man Dinner. And I feel <u>nice</u>!

VO: A big dinner with all the fixins. And look at all that beef.

OC: Swanson already put the second helping in.

ROCKY: I'm a meat and potatoes man. JOE: Hey! Have a Hungry-Man Entree.

JOE: Just meat and potatoes . . . and <u>plenty</u> of meat!

Swanson Hungry-Man Dinners . . . ROCKY: and Entrees, enough to turn a mean man into a . . . JOE: pussycat!

player, was a good celebrity spokesperson for Swanson Hungry Man Frozen Entrees because he fit the headline, "Got a big man—give him Hungry Man Entrees from Swanson" (Swanson has continued this campaign for several years. Figure 8.11 shows a more recent version with Mean Joe Greene and Rocky Bleier.) Conversely, Peter Sellers failed for TWA. In spite of being a memorable person, he didn't help the firm because the advertising had no big idea behind it.[3]

With the discussion of the various types of spokespersons, the various execution styles have begun to shift from rational, product-oriented appeals to more emotional, consumer-oriented appeals. In addition to the celebrity spokesperson, other creative directions include humor, animation, sex, and music.

Consumer-Oriented Emotional Appeals

Humor vacillates in popularity as an execution style and has long been controversial. One of the strongest statements made against its use came from Claude Hopkins during the 1920s: "People don't buy from clowns."[4] Until recently, Ogilvy also objected to the use of humor in advertising but more recently has said that he has seen research substantiating its use. Probably the biggest questions stem from the facts that good humor is hard to find, that poor humor is of no value at all to the firm, that nothing is funny to everyone, and that even the best joke isn't funny after several repetitions. On the positive side, good humorous messages attract and hold attention. This is positive on the surface, but there are some "buts."

First, it is not sufficient merely to attract attention. Seeing a roller-skating gorilla in a tutu is amusing to some, but unless attention eventually relates to the product sell, it is not worthwhile. Humor is a type of borrowed interest and thus the manager must be careful to ensure that it doesn't create attention for itself rather than for the product.

A second *caveat* concerning humor's ability to attract attention deals with the fact that repetition of the message reduces its ability to hold attention. After all, how many times does anyone want to hear the same joke? This means that a humorous campaign must have more specific executions than a regular campaign. Miller Lite, for example, uses humor to hold attention, and to do so, the company develops a dozen or so spots each year. These spots can be rotated to avoid wearout. The humor in each message also is carefully constructed around the position and benefits of the product. (Sorry to keep using Miller Lite as an example, but they and their agency, Backer & Spielvogel, do good work. Always steal from the best.)

A third warning comes from Michael Ray,[5] who points out that, while humor may attract attention, it does so most clearly when it is novel. If competitors are already using humor, then the novelty of this approach is diminished and should be reconsidered. If the purpose of humor is to attract attention, make sure that the attention ends up on the product, that the humor won't wear out after one or two showings, and that the competition has not already pre-empted this approach.

Some analysts feel that humorous appeals are more persuasive. One justification is that humor distracts and consumers therefore don't put up perceptual defenses, don't evaluate messages as critically, and don't develop counterarguments.[6] Another justification is that humor enhances the credibility of the source.[7] There do not seem to be many data sets beyond these two studies to show that humor is more persuasive than serious appeals. Conversely, the ability of humor to distract may be more of a negative than a positive. If people are absorbed by the humor, they may miss the point of the message.

Finally, it is important to remember that humor is subjective, and that what is funny to some may be offensive or dumb to others. For example, Dick and Bert, a team of comedians who wrote and performed many commercials before they broke up in 1983, wrote a slogan for an Ohio cemetery that said, "conveniently located six feet under Cleveland." To some, this could have been one of the all time great advertising lines. It was rejected by the client.[8]

Humor is a ticklish situation for most advertisers and, in addition, is difficult to execute well. It's easy to fail with humor. Still intent on trying it? Table 8.2 shows some guidelines to consider based on a study of the content of 40 television commercials. Figure 8.12 shows another example of humor in advertising that plays off the benefits of the product and doesn't distract from the selling theme. Something worked to get the message across; the humor probably helped to hold attention so that learning could occur.

Animation is another execution style that is most often used as a device to create borrowed interest. Generally, fictitious characters are created to communicate a dimension or benefit of a product that otherwise might not be interesting. How can canned corn be made different or better than that of the competition? By growing it in the Valley of the Jolly (Ho! Ho! Ho!) Green Giant. How can cookies be made to taste better? By putting the factory in a tree so elves can bake them with elfin magic.

Green Giant vegetables and Keebler cookies both use Leo Burnett as an agency and, as a result, can take advantage of the successful animation techniques

T·H·E I·N·S·I·D·E O·U·T·L·O·O·K

Sheila Dorton

Vice-President–Creative Director, The Hiebing Group

*Sheila Dorton is co-founder, vice-president, and creative direc-
tor of The Hiebing Group, a Wisconsin advertising agency created by and for big city/big agency escapees. Her claims to
fame include being a radio disc jockey at 16; dispensing radio
household hints and recipes despite the handicap of being the
only woman's show hostess in America without two first
names; having Leonard Bernstein sing one of her Bold Detergent commercials on a TV Young People's Concert; and writing
award-winning advertising for a wide variety of clients, including Head and Shoulders Shampoo, McDonald's, Sears, Mr.
Clean, Libby's, Sara Lee, Curad Bandages, Parker Pen, Butter-nut Coffee, and Coors Beer.*

If You Do Your Job Well Enough, Nobody Ever Says
"I Wonder Who Wrote That Great Ad?"
Just "I Think I'll Buy Some of That Stuff!"

Copywriters are, first and foremost, copyreaders.
The best copywriters I know will read anything
readable, including ketchup labels; "Caution"
warnings on cold remedy bottles; even, in a
pinch, the ingredients listed on a bottle of nail
polish. ("Toluene, formaldehyde resin? My nails
need that?")

My own bedside table, for example, is
currently stocked (the only appropriate word
since, like a pantry, I view it as anti-starvation
insurance) with: two Michael Innes mysteries,
And Ladies of the Club, Dickens' *Our Mutual
Friend,* Gail Parent's last novel, Susan Cheever's
book about her writer father; a stack of glitzy
mail order catalogs; and a mini-Matterhorn of
magazines: *Newsweek, Video, Chicago, People,
McCall's, Texas Monthly, Esquire, TV Guide,*

*Vogue, Family Circle, Glamour, Woman's Day,
Vanity Fair, The New Yorker,* and trade
publications such as *AdWeek, Magazine Age,
ADS,* and *Millimeter.* I read at least two
newspapers a day, often three or four.

And everything I read is grist for my copywriter's mill. Because I learn what interests,
what excites, what angers, what motivates people whose lives are quite different from my own.
That's fun (other people's lives are nice to visit
even if you might not want to live there), it's
mind-opening, and it's information I need to do
my job well. Until I know what my target customer *cares* about, how can I expect to make
her care about my product? Until I have some
understanding of her problems, how can I know
how seriously I can *believably* treat the problem

my product's designed to solve for her? (For instance, in her hierarchy of worries, how high does "ring around the collar" rank?)

Good copywriters are television watchers, too. I try to watch all kinds of programming, even shows that don't suit my personal tastes. I began watching MTV when I realized it was probably the greatest current influence on the tastes and fashions of America's young. Now I like MTV. And I learn from it.

I also watch television for the commercials. Not so much my own since the gestation period for a television campaign can sometimes be as long as a year and, by the time one's "born" I'm hatching another. It's the competition that interests me. Competing agencies and competing products. I need to see what they're doing right and to watch for minor copy changes that may signal major strategy shifts ahead.

Good copywriters watch people. People at football games: How do they react when their team's losing? Winning? People in supermarkets: How many women use a grocery list? How many couples shop together? Who makes the purchase decisions? People in shopping malls: Do they browse from store to store? Do they seem happy or grim? Is "malling" becoming a social experience for people in general and teenagers in particular?

And a good copywriter listens. I eavesdrop shamelessly, listening not so much for *what* people say as for the *way* they say it. When I lived in Chicago, I often took the bus or subway when a cab would have been quicker, just so I could hear "PeopleTalk"—a refreshing change from the somewhat insular language of the advertising business. On the bus I could hear secretaries, shoppers, out-of-work husbands, out-of-patience wives, Yuppies, cleaning ladies, kids, and crazies. I still count on PeopleTalk to keep me current on the language as it's really being spoken; to give me a variety of perspectives on specific problems and life in general. PeopleTalk has inspired a fair number of commercials for me; and,

most important, it reminds me exactly *who* I'm writing *to*—puts flesh on the bones of "Target audience: women, ages 18–34, high-school educated," and so on.

Copywriters do a lot more reading, watching, and listening than actual writing. But that's because our job is really *translation*. We're the translators between the sellers and the buyers. The ones who can turn R&Data and ClientSpeak into PeopleTalk. (And translate back the other way, as well.)

A classic Stan Freberg lyric has Betsy Ross complaining "Everybody wants to be an art director, everybody wants to call the shots . . ." She didn't know how well off she was. Because even people who will reluctantly admit they can't draw are totally convinced they can write copy. After all, it's just putting words on paper, isn't it?

No. It's knowing which words to put there.

Table 8.2 Guidelines for creating an effective humorous commercial

	Characteristics associated with	
High performance		*Low performance*
Early brand product category identification		Late brand product category identification
Begin with the *key idea*		"Set the stage" or employ an indirect lead-in
Subtle/light humor—Designed to amuse rather than overwhelm		Bizarre/overdone humor
Relevant humor, well integrated with brand/key idea		*Irrelevant*—Humor for its own sake
Contain a relevant characterization		Contain either an irrelevant characterization or none at all
Satirize or parody familiar/universal subjects—viewer is in on the humor from the beginning		Conceal or delay the "punch line" or source of humor—viewer can't share in the fun
Belittle or kid the *brand* or the *subject matter*		Belittle the consumer

Source: Harold L. Ross, Jr., "How to Create Effective Humorous Commercials Yielding above Average Preference Changes," *Marketing News,* 26 March 1976, p. 4.

Figure 8.12 *Federal Express uses humor effectively*

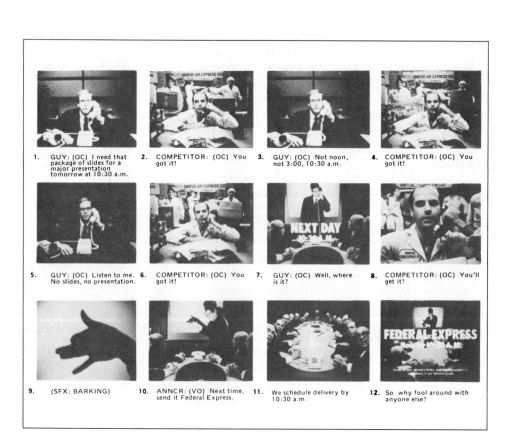

1. GUY: (OC) I need that package of slides for a major presentation tomorrow at 10:30 a.m.

2. COMPETITOR: (OC) You got it!

3. GUY: (OC) Not noon, not 3:00, 10:30 a.m.

4. COMPETITOR: (OC) You got it!

5. GUY: (OC) Listen to me. No slides, no presentation.

6. COMPETITOR: (OC) You got it!

7. GUY: (OC) Well, where is it?

8. COMPETITOR: (OC) You'll get it!

9. (SFX: BARKING)

10. ANNCR: (VO) Next time, send it Federal Express.

11. We schedule delivery by 10:30 a.m.

12. So. why fool around with anyone else?

developed there. Over the years, research has shown the agency that animation works in those cases where borrowed interest is necessary. In addition, it has been found that this style works best when there is a slice of real product (called a beauty shot) and/or real people (often a slice of life) between two pieces of animation. The result is called—at least at Leo Burnett—an animation sandwich. Figure 8.13 shows an example of an animation sandwich.

Figure 8.13 An animation sandwich

1. SPROUT: Mmm! That looks good.

2. BUTTER MAID: It's real butter, Sprout.

3. For the Green Giant's butter sauce.

4. SONG: TASTIN' FRESH AND BUTTERY...

5. TASTIN' GOOD AS GOOD CAN BE.

6. BUTTER UP THEIR APPETITE.

7. THAT GREEN GIANT GOOD-NESS...

8. REALLY SHOWS TONIGHT.

9. (Anncr VO): A butter sauce made with real butter...

10. is why Green Giant vegetables make every meal special.

11. BUTTER MAID: It makes his vegetables taste better.

12. SPROUT: You mean, taste butter.

13. SONG: HO HO HO...

14. THAT GREEN GIANT GOOD-NESS...

15. REALLY SHOWS.

Figure 8.14 Using sex as an element unrelated to the product

Another alternative is the use of an animated figure superimposed on live action. Kellogg's Tony the Tiger has been successful in his interactions with real people in this way.

Though an animation technique has been successful at Leo Burnett, Ogilvy & Mather's research has shown that animation works less well than live action. Perhaps the product and its benefits are key to deciding on whether to use animation or not. These comments all relate to television, where animation is less common; animation is a more common format in print.

Sex appeals in advertising are common, controversial, and used for a variety of purposes. Combined in this category are such diverse executions as the presentation of scantily dressed models of either gender used to get attention, and the implicit or explicit benefit of gaining sexual or sensual attractiveness through use of the product. Isn't this a great book—from fear to humor to sex in only a few pages!

A considerable amount of data point out that the use of sexy elements gains attention for the advertising. An ad such as that in Figure 8.14 will get people to stop and look. On the other hand, recall and attitude scores do less well as a re-

Figure 8.15   *Using sex as an integrated part of the message*

Figure 8.16   *More sex as an integrated part of the message*

sult of this type of ad. In ads where the sexual nature of the material does not relate to the product or its benefits, sex does not help in increasing recall or attitude. Sex, then, is a poor communications tool when it is an unrelated component of the message.

Conversely, ads for products with sexual benefits—such as perfume, beauty aids, and various articles of clothing—benefit from sexual elements. In some cases, the elements are fantasy-oriented and in some they are more explicit, but either way, recall scores are enhanced because there is a logical tie between sex and the product/benefits. In Figures 8.15 and 8.16, the sexual elements relate to the products' major selling points. (Two examples are necessary here since this author believes in equal opportunity voyeurism.) The important point here is that sex, as any other type of appeal, must have a logical tie to the product and benefit if it is to be useful.

Just as sex has been well researched in society in general, it has also been well researched in advertising. Findings show that, for men, sex correlates with nudity, but for women, sex correlates with romance. Therefore, when men are presented with sexy ads, they have much more difficulty in recalling brand names and often cannot even remember the advertised product class. Consistent with this finding, one can find more sexy ads in *Cosmopolitan* than in *Playboy,* according to Yovovich.[9]

There are other demographic differences as well. Johnson and Satow report differences among women on the basis of both age and blue-collar/white-collar backgrounds. These differences are especially apparent for ads that employ sexual fantasy themes to which the different demographic groups can relate more or less well.[10]

Managers should also consider the vehicles used when deciding on the appropriateness of sexual themes. Broad reach vehicles such as television are more difficult to use because the viewer may be in a viewing group with children or the parish priest and may be embarrassed by the material. Magazines can be savored more privately. Similarly, some vehicles such as "Dallas," *Cosmopolitan,* or daytime soaps include an expectation of sex, so sexual ads are more acceptable than they would be in more conservative vehicles. Sexual ads seem to be more or less acceptable based on the viewer's expectation of exposure (or the mindset of the receiver).

Sexual appeals are most appropriate when used in the correct context for the correct audience. Thus, such an execution style is no different from other styles; it must evolve from the objectives and strategies rather than occur for its own sake. One final example is the ad in Figure 8.17 for Paco Rabanne cologne. The ad is sensual, is appropriate to the product, led to a sales increase of 25% in one year, and won several awards for best print advertising during 1981. Who could ask for anything more?

Figure 8.17   Ad for Paco Rabanne cologne

Hello?
You snore.
And you steal all the covers. What time did you leave?
Six-thirty. You looked like a toppled Greek statue lying there. Only some tourist had swiped your fig leaf. I was tempted to wake you up.
I miss you already.
You're going to miss something else. Have you looked in the bathroom yet?
Why?
I took your bottle of Paco Rabanne cologne.
What on earth are you going to do with it...give it to a secret lover you've got stashed away in San Francisco?
I'm going to take some and rub it on my body when I go to bed tonight. And then I'm going to remember every little thing about you...and last night.
Do you know what your voice is doing to me?
You aren't the only one with imagination. I've got to go; they're calling my flight. I'll be back Tuesday. Can I bring you anything?

My Paco Rabanne. And a fig leaf.

Paco Rabanne
A cologne for men
What is remembered is up to you

Table 8.3 Effects of music on recall and attitude

	% Brand recall	% Main idea recall	% Favorable attitude
Jingle with music song	58	46	22
Background music	51	40	19
No music	50	41	19

Music can add emotion and feeling to many products and can help advertising stand out in a cluttered environment. Data from McCollum/Spielman Research, reported by Reinhard,[11] show some tangible benefits of music. In a cluttered viewing setting (a cluttered setting is one where there are many commercials in a row), advertising with music did better than that without music on both brand recall and main ideal recall. Table 8.3 shows these data and also reveals that a favorable attitude test yields little difference and that background music has little impact. The greatest value of music seems to be when it is an integral part of the sell and when it is aimed at straight learning.

The data in Table 8.3 are similar to data for many types of advertising executions. It is easiest to influence awareness but more difficult to change attitudes. Because the main purpose of advertising is to create awareness and knowledge, music is appropriate. It can be used as a mnemonic device to aid learning of the brand name, key benefit, and key image issue.

In addition to Reinhard's paper on music, there is also one by Ed Vick of General Foods and Hal Grant of Ogilvy & Mather.[12] The following findings come from these two papers. Both sets of authors agree that there are a number of benefits to the use of music.

1. *Consumers remember the brand and its promises better.* This point has already been discussed.

2. *Music gets people's attention.* It sets the commercial apart and breaks through the clutter of radio and television. While many commercials drone on, music can break through the boredom factor and gain attention. The manager must be careful that attention is not taken over by the music and that the music focuses attention on the product.

3. *Music helps maintain continuity across messages, years, and media.* Advertising should be single-minded in all its presentations so that consumers will quickly recognize the sponsor and so that the effort needed for learning is held to a minimum. Good music will lend immediate recognition across many settings, yet also lend itself to adaptation. McDonald's "We do it all for you" theme was used in many ways over several years. People immediately recognized it, yet it was flexible enough to be used with many themes and products.

Music also seems less resistant to wearout, so it can perpetuate a campaign theme for a longer period of time than other techniques. Along similar lines, music is remembered long after a campaign ends, so that there are long-lasting benefits from it.

Continuity can also be established from television to radio through music. One media strategy that can be used is to establish an image in television and

Table 8.4 Music can add emotional benefit to the product

Product	Product benefit	Emotional benefit
Diapers	Dryness	"I'm good to my baby"
Vegetables	Taste, nutrition	"I'm good to my family"
Dog food	Taste, nutrition	"I'm good to my dog"
Toothpaste	No cavities	"I'm good to my children"
Mouthwash	Fresh breath	"I'm good to my friends"

Source: Ed Vick and Hal Grant, "How to Sell with Music," *Viewpoint: By, For and About Ogilvy & Mather*, 1 (1980), p. 16.

then maintain it in radio. Music can help in this transference because it stimulates recall of visual images during the radio broadcast.

4. *Music helps differentiate the brand and often adds value to it.* This is especially the case with commodity-like products. When there are few real differences, music can create a difference of feeling, although music won't do well at this task if there *are* real differences. Airlines, for example, have simple promises for similar brands. TWA sings "You're going to love us," while United sings "Fly the friendly skies," Republic sings "Nobody flies our Republic like Republic," and others sing other bland songs. No brands really offer a meaningful difference, and all sing their puffed self-praises. Music can help in this case to establish an identity of feeling.

Music adds emotional benefit to mundane products. As shown in Table 8.4, the product benefit can be enhanced using an emotional benefit. Although this can be done through the use of good copy alone, the addition of music is strengthening.

Vick and Grant have several other suggestions for the use of music.[13]

1. *Show the package and product in use.* A good use of music has the visual track showing product usage accompanied by a related or unrelated musical audio track. This format is common for soft drinks; for example, in 1985, Sunkist, Mountain Dew, Coca Cola, Pepsi Cola, Shasta, Dr. Pepper, and several diet drinks used it.

2. *Put the brand name and promise in the lyrics.* If the firm is going to go to all the expense of writing music and lyrics plus the expense of a media plan, it should at least teach consumers to sing something relevant. Vick and Grant say, "You want to deliver a commercial every time people sing your song."

3. *Make the lyrics simple and clear.*

4. *Don't just have music; also have some nonmusical script.* In animation it was shown that a slice of real product and real people bolstered the animation. So, too, here; there should be a musical sandwich with a spoken slice between the musical opening and closing. This gives the emotion of music plus extra rationale.

5. *The tone of the music should match the brand's and the target market's personalities.*

Figure 8.18   *Sell in the song*

SELL IN THE SONG
USIN' MUSIC IN YOUR SPOT
CUTS THE COPY DOWN A LOT
GIVES YOUR PROPOSITION POWER
WHEN THEY SING IT IN THE SHOWER
USIN' MUSIC IN YOUR ADS
HAVE 'EM DANCIN' CROSS THE LAND
AND YOU'RE STEPPIN' OUT FROM ALL
THEM OTHER BRANDS.

AND WITH A SONG IN YOUR SELL
AND LITTLE SELL IN YOUR SONG
YOU CAN SING YOUR PRODUCT'S PRAISES
ON TV ALL NIGHT LONG
TWELVE WAYS BETTER, FOUR TIMES LONGER,
NEW, IMPROVED AND EVER STRONGER
IT'S THE GREAT AMERICAN SING ALONG
WITH A LITTLE SELL IN THE SONG.

SELL IN THE SONG
SELL IN THE SONG
SELL IN THE SONG

MUSIC DOES IT EVERYTIME
WITH THE VIOLINS UP HIGH
GETS 'EM CRAZY WITH EMOTION
RAISES ALL YOUR SELLIN' QUOTIENTS
KEEP IT SIMPLE, MAKE IT FUN
TELL 'EM THEY'RE THE ONLY ONE
AND YOU CAN SELL 'EM WITH A SONG.

THAT'S WITH A SONG IN YOUR SELL
AND A LITTLE SELL IN YOUR SONG
YOU CAN SING YOUR PRODUCT'S PRAISES
ON TV ALL NIGHT LONG
TWELVE WAYS BETTER, FOUR TIMES LONGER,
NEW, IMPROVED AND EVER STRONGER
IT'S THE GREAT AMERICAN SING ALONG
WITH A LITTLE SELL IN THE SONG.

YOU! WHEN YOU SAY YOU!
CAN SELL 'EM WITH A SONG IN YOUR SELL
AND A LITTLE SELL IN YOUR SONG
LET'S YA SING YOUR PRODUCT'S PRAISES
ON TV ALL NIGHT LONG
MUCH BETTER, FOUR TIMES LONGER
NEW, IMPROVED AND EVER STRONGER.
IT'S THE GREAT AMERICAN SING ALONG
WITH A LITTLE SELL IN THE SONG
TALKIN' 'BOUT YOUR HAMBURGER
YOU CAN SELL 'EM WITH A SONG
SELL IN THE SONG.

TWO ALL BEEF PLOP, PLOP, CHEW, CHEW
ISN'T IT AMAZING WHAT A HOKEY MELODY CAN DO!
Source: Keith Reinhard, "I Believe in Music," presentation of Needham, Harper Worldwide (n.d.).

Music has more advocates than detractors. When used well, it can add tremendous impact to a campaign in terms of increased learning and emotional feeling. Figure 8.18 is an ode to the power of music in advertising. It loses a little without its musical score, but still makes the point.

T·H·E   I·N·S·I·D·E   O·U·T·L·O·O·K

Hank Seiden

Executive Vice-President and Director of Creative Services, Hicks & Greist, Inc.

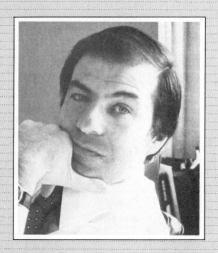

Hank Seiden is a principal in and Executive Vice-President, Director of Creative Services of Hicks & Greist, Inc. advertising agency. Mr. Seiden joined H&G in 1966. Prior to H&G, Mr. Seiden was Senior Vice-President, Creative, of Grey Advertising; Senior Vice-President, Creative Director, Chairman of the Plans Board of McCann-Marschalk, Inc; Vice-President, Associate Creative Director of BBDO. Before launching his advertising agency career, Mr. Seiden was in media promotion as promotion manager of both Redbook *and* Woman's Home Companion *magazines, as well as being national promotion manager of the* New York Post.

Among Mr. Seiden's many awards is the most coveted in the industry, the Gold Key Award, which he won three times for best newspaper, magazine, and television advertising of the year. In addition, he was awarded a Four Freedoms Foundation Award, presented to him by President Kennedy; a special commendation from the police commissioner of the city of New York; and the "man of the year award" from B'nai B'rith.

Hank Seiden lectures at the NYU Graduate School of Business, Bernard M. Baruch Graduate School of Business, The New School Graduate Center, Ohio University, Ohio State University, Temple University, Lehman College, and The School of Visual Arts. In addition, he is a regular columnist for Advertising Age *and was a contributing editor to* Madison Avenue *magazine and* The New York Times Sunday *magazine. He is also the author of one of the largest-selling books on advertising,* Advertising Pure and Simple, *published by the American Management Association.*

Concept and Execution

All good advertising consists of two parts. Concept and execution. All bad advertising consists of one part. Execution. If you have a good concept, you can't possibly have a bad ad, though it may not be great. If you have only execution, you can't possibly have a good ad, no matter how great the execution. What's needed in advertising today—even more than fresh ideas—is a return to what advertising is all about. The basic selling concept, the compelling reason to buy, the unique angle—these are the guts of advertising and the toughest part to formulate. They deserve 90% of the time spent on a commercial or ad. The remaining 10% should be spent on execution, not the other way around. As a matter of fact, the stronger the concept, the less time and effort and money are required for the execution.

Execution is only the craft we use to express the idea. Far from being an end in itself, it is merely the means to the end. And so, as a rule of thumb, I've learned to be guided by this principle: Any execution that enhances, speeds up, and/or makes more understandable and believable the communication of the basic selling idea is a good one; any execution that slows down, confuses, dominates, or subverts the communication of that concept is dead wrong.

The best advertising contains a good concept and a good execution. Good ads and commercials are incisive, simple, and don't waste the consumer's time or the client's money. They're not hard to separate from the crowd. Just look for a commercial that actually sells you something, whether it's oatmeal or a political candidate, by offering you a clear, compelling reason for buying, with a believable execution.

When is an execution believable? When it's inseparable from the concept. When it delivers its message unmistakably, yet remains altogether unobtrusive. When it leaves you completely unaware of its existence as a separate entity. When it does not obscure or overpower the message and is functional to the idea. Good execution is most often brilliantly simple and shockingly inexpensive to produce. Believe me, good execution is the best friend a concept can have.

I have my own test of an execution's worth. I ask myself whether the execution gets the message across faster, more clearly, and more believably than if a stand-up announcer delivered it. If it does, then the execution is a good one. If it doesn't, I get rid of it. Remember, an ad is the sum of its parts:

Ads with bad concepts and bad execution. They're the worst.
Ads with bad concepts and good execution. They're almost as bad.
Ads with good concepts and bad execution. They're inexcusable.
Ads with good concepts and good execution. They're advertising.

Summary

This discussion of execution styles has a certain degree of subjectivity and is certainly not a complete list. Furthermore, each style is examined separately, while in reality the styles are combined in many different and fascinating ways. This aspect of advertising is, after all, the art part and cannot be too neatly examined. To borrow from E. B. White

> Advertising can be dissected as a frog can,
> But the thing dies in the process;
> And the innards are discouraging,
> To any but the pure and scientific mind.

What is crucial here is that almost any style of execution can go with almost any strategy. It is the task of the writer and artist to see the best execution and to develop it so that the correct strategy (developed earlier) is executed in a meaningful, memorable, and unique way. So that there is less risk of turning wondrous art into dissected frogs, this chapter is now brought to a close.

Discussion Questions

1. How do execution styles, classes of appeals, strategies, and objectives relate to one another?

2. Find an example of a print ad and a broadcast commercial for each of the execution styles listed in Table 8.1. Now reconsider each example; does it seem to be appropriate for the product being advertised? What type of appeal would be more appropriate? How does the present appeal enhance what you feel is the brand's position?

3. Continuing your own campaign designed to get you a first job, select three execution styles that you consider to be appropriate and develop the general content that such ads might have.

4. What are the key merits and faults of each of the execution styles listed in Table 8.1?

5. There are at least three types of spokespersons: experts, celebrities, and unknown consumer. Under what conditions would it be most appropriate to use each type? When would each be least appropriate?

Notes

1. Richard E. Petty and John T. Cacioppo, "Central and Peripheral Routes to Persuasion: Applications to Advertising," *Advertising and Consumer Psychology,* Larry Percy and Arch Woodside, eds. (Lexington, Mass.: Lexington Books, 1983), pp. 3–24.

2. McCollum/Spielman & Co., Inc., "The Realities of Real People," *Topline,* May 1981.

3. Bourne Morris, "Will a Famous Personality Help You Sell Your Product Better?" *Viewpoint: By, For and About Ogilvy & Mather,* (Sept./Oct. 1977), p. 11.

4. Claude C. Hopkins, *Scientific Advertising* (Chicago: Advertising Publications, Inc., 1966) (originally published in 1923).

5. Michael L. Ray, *Advertising and Communication Management* (Englewood Cliffs, N.J.: Prentice-Hall, 1982), p. 303.

6. B. Sternthal and C. S. Craig, "Humor in Advertising," *Journal of Marketing* 37 (October 1973), p. 17.

7. C. Gruner, "Effect of Humor on Speaker Ethos and Audience Information Gain," *Journal of Communication* 17 (September 1967), pp. 228–233.

8. Jerry Alder and Janet Huck, "Masters of the Ad Absurdum," *Newsweek,* May 19, 1980, p. 90B.

9. B. G. Yovovich, "Sex in Advertising: The Power and the Perils," *Advertising Age,* 2 May 1983, p. M-4.

10. Deborah K. Johnson and Kay Satow, "TV Ads Sexual Offensiveness Depends on Appropriateness, Audience, Other Factors," *Marketing News,* 24 March 1978, p. 7.

11. Keith L. Reinhard, "I Believe in Music," Needham, Harper & Steers, Inc.

12. Ed Vick and Hal Grant, "How to Sell with Music," *Viewpoint: By, For and About Ogilvy & Mather,* 1 (1980), p. 16.

13. Vick and Grant, "How to Sell with Music," p. 16.

Chapter 9
Advertising
Assessment
Techniques

Research has become one of the cornerstones of modern advertising management. It is a vital force in giving direction to the ultimate strategy of the campaign, and it is regularly used to assess the creative product that finally emerges. Directional research has been discussed at length in the situation analysis of the text and so is only briefly treated here. This chapter is primarily concerned with the research that evaluates the advertising itself. The purpose of the chapter is to expose nonresearchers to important issues in the evaluation of advertising.

It is generally acknowledged in the advertising world that directional and assessment research are very different and that practitioners have *very* different feelings about each type. At this time, most sophisticated advertising people (creatives as well as account managers) agree that research plays an important role in guiding the account team to the most appropriate solutions. For example

> Research is absolutely essential to the creative process. . . . I would encourage and insist on lots of up-front research, perception of product, how people live, how it will translate into their lives. Anything that will provide grist for the creative mill.—John E. O'Toole, President, Foote, Cone & Belding Communications Inc.[1]

> I think people who resist information are pretty narrow. . . . They're risking client dollars. In the 60s creative was on an ego trip. I want to be as knowledgeable as I can. . . . Research can help you break new ground.—Amil Gargano, President, Ally & Gargano Inc.[2]

> Up-front research is very important because all too often what *you* think is perfectly clear, *is perfect mud*!—Tom Dillon, Late Chairman of the Board and Director, Batten, Barton, Durstine & Osborn, Inc.[3]

> The amount of time getting basic background is the most important part of the process of making advertising.—Jerry Siano, Executive Vice President and Corporate Creative Director, N. W. Ayer International[4]

Before I start work on a product or service, I'll take any and all research as a starting point.—George Lois, Chairman of the Board, Creative Director, Lois, Pitts Gershon, Inc.[5]

They're not incompatible things, research and creativity. My God! They're companions. I am damned grateful for research. In no way do I want to expend my creative skill on a false premise, and I really like to find out if people understand me.—William Bernbach, Late Chairman of the Executive Committee, Doyle Dane Bernbach, Inc.[6]

On the other hand, although research *guides* the team to the onset of creative development of the actual message, these same people have strong reservations as to the ability or appropriateness of research in *evaluating* the creative product. For example

Don't depend on post testing. . . . It's wrong to make multi-million dollar decisions on such "faulty evidence."—John O'Toole, President, Foote, Cone & Belding Communications, Inc.[7]

It can be the springboard to doing something innovative and great. But, when it becomes a mandate for everything, a slavish attention to research puts creative in a straight jacket.—Amil Gargano, President, Ally & Gargano Inc.[8]

An advertiser should never be excessively dependent on commercial testing, or substitute it for judgment.—Tom Dillon, Late Chairman of the Board and Director, Batten, Durnstine & Osborn, Inc.[9]

The techniques of pre and post testing are still primitive, and because the same methods are being used, everything has begun to look very much alike and these techniques might very well be restricting creativity.—Jerry Siano, Executive Vice President and Corporate Creative Director, N. W. Ayer International[10]

Scientific prejudgment that tells creative what to do, results in advertising that *kind of works*. It takes ten million dollars and makes it look like one. Everytime at bat you go for a bunt, single, instead of a home run. . . . If all this stuff is so well tested, why is it all so lousy? It's advertising without theatre, excitement, humanity or magic! Marketing men have been trained that advertising is a science. We know that advertising is an art.—George Lois, Chairman of the Board, Creative Director, Lois, Pitts Gershon, Inc.[11]

I don't want the head of research telling me what to do creatively. . . . For there is a tendency on the part of people concerned with precise things, not to understand the nuances of creativity. . . . So I want them to give me the facts, and let me decide, on how best to convey them in the end.—William Bernbach, Late Chairman of the Executive Committee, Doyle Dane Bernbach, Inc.[12]

Even though these quotations may seem contradictory, they are not so at all. These and most other advertisers welcome a clearer picture of the realities with which they must deal. Conversely, measuring the effect of emotion, warmth, and other difficult-to-measure components of a message on consumers' perceptions, preferences, attitudes, and other elusive responses enters the realm of intangible issues and creates uncertainty. When the result of such measurement is reduced to a single numerical score, the whole process may become unreasonable. Even so, advertisers recognize the need for measuring the value of the creative product and would welcome an accurate, reliable, and valid way of measuring creative work.

I am not questioning the advertiser's right to measure. He not only has a right, he has an obligation. He's about to spend 10 million, 20 million, 30 million dollars,

(the numbers are astonishing) on a function of his company that jobs and factories and profits depend on. No enlightened Board of Directors can permit him to
do this without at the very least some supportive measure of its merit.—Shepard
Kurnit, Chairman of the Board, DKG Advertising Inc.[13]

In addition to the perceived accuracy of research at the different stages of the decision sequence, the manager must also consider the cost/benefit relation of the
different types of research. Research done early in the process has the greatest
value because it gives direction to the entire planning process. Without this early
information, it is too easy for the campaign to go off in the wrong direction. If this
happens, it won't matter if the test of the actual advertising is good or bad; if the
advertising is off target, it won't sell the product because it will not be communicating the right information to the right audience. Conversely, if the early research leads the creative team to the appropriate issues, then the advertising
should do reasonably well even without further testing because it is at least dealing with the correct ideas.

The same logic holds within the creative process itself. The most cost-
efficient copy testing research is done early in the developmental process to test
the creative concepts and initial translations of research into advertising. If the
concept is not correct, there is no sense in going through the production process.
Conversely, if the concept is a good one, its execution should be close to correct.

For these reasons, advertisers and agencies tend to spend the bulk of their research dollars at the early stages of the process. This is somewhat misleading,
since it can easily cost $50,000 to do situation analysis research but may cost
only $5,000 to test an ad. Nevertheless, more research is done at the early stages,
as can be seen by the data in Table 9.1. Here, advertisers and agencies were asked
what types of research they did; more participated in the early stages of the decision sequence. Table 9.2 reports on the importance of testing at various stages of
the creative development process. Again, the early stages were felt to be more
important. Figure 9.1 shows the various types of research and how they fit into
the decision sequence framework.

This chapter continues with the discussion of when research should be done.
This is then followed by a discussion of the various dependent variables available
and the appropriateness of each. Next, there is an examination of issues that make
research more or less useful and of the development of an ideal measurement
procedure. Finally, the discussion evolves to a description of the relevant methods for assessing advertising and a brief review of some of the evaluation services
currently available.

This is not a research text, and this chapter is not written for researchers. Its
goal is to make nonresearchers comfortable with some of the issues that surround
the measurement of advertising. As stated previously, the chapter is not concerned with situation analysis issues of research but considers only the actual
testing of advertising.

The testing of advertising is the evaluation of a stimulus (some form of advertising) in terms of the response it elicits (such as awareness, attitude, behavior).
Key issues to be developed are the form the advertising should take when it is
tested and the type of response that should be measured. The major purpose of
testing should be to give feedback to the creative team so that it can benefit and
so that it can create more effective advertising. In reality, research often acts as a
report card (the commercial "passed" or "failed") rather than giving diagnostic or
corrective information. This chapter attempts to show what is happening currently in advertising research.

Table 9.1 Types of research employed

	Total panel			Advertisers			Agencies		
	When developing a new product	Major change in strategy	Routine, ongoing	When developing a new product	Major change in strategy	Routine, ongoing	When developing a new product	Major change in strategy	Routine, ongoing
Precreative idea exploration	62%	60%	28%	53%	55%	20%	76%	65%	37%
Concept testing	68	67	25	64	64	24	73	71	27
Preproduction execution	50	50	28	45	46	25	57	57	33
Recall testing	41	47	66	34	39	66	49	59	65
Advertising tracking	39	45	71	30	43	68	51	47	76
Tracking over time	28	33	62	26	29	60	31	37	63
Store audits	37	25	46	28	23	44	49	29	49
Diary panel	17	10	15	13	6	15	24	16	14

Source: Herbert Zeltner, "Ads Work Harder, but Accomplish Less," *Advertising Age*, 3 July 1978, p. 31. Reprinted with permission. Copyright 1978 by Crain Communications, Inc.

Table 9.2 Importance of various elements in improving advertising effectiveness

	Total panel			Advertisers			Agencies		
	Very important	Somewhat important	Not very important	Very important	Somewhat important	Not very important	Very important	Somewhat important	Not very important
Strength of basic concept	99%	—	—	98%	—	—	100%	—	—
Attention getting device	43	52	4	38	56	5	50	48	2
Visual elements	56	43	—	58	41	—	54	46	—
Copy	72	26	1	66	31	1	81	19	—
Production values	26	65	8	29	63	11	29	67	4
Suitability of medium	59	37	2	64	31	3	52	44	4
Timing of insertion	29	60	6	34	50	11	21	73	—
Lack of clutter	24	57	17	30	53	14	15	63	21
Repetition	50	45	2	44	49	3	58	40	—

Source: Herbert Zeltner, "Ads Work Harder, but Accomplish Less," *Advertising Age*, 3 July 1978, p. 32. Reprinted with permission. Copyright 1978 by Crain Communications, Inc.

Figure 9.1 Research as a part of the decision sequence

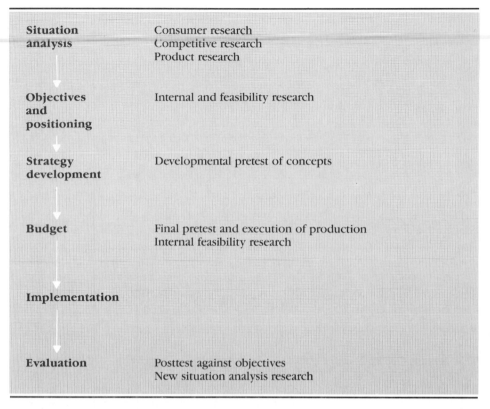

Situation analysis	Consumer research Competitive research Product research
Objectives and positioning	Internal and feasibility research
Strategy development	Developmental pretest of concepts
Budget	Final pretest and execution of production Internal feasibility research
Implementation	
Evaluation	Posttest against objectives New situation analysis research

Pretesting versus Post-testing

All advertising research fits into the categories of pre- and post-testing, and pretesting can be further divided into developmental and final pretesting. These classes correspond to the various stages in the process of creating the advertising as shown in Figure 9.1.

Developmental, concept, or *format, pretesting* is done at early stages of the creative process and is used for guidance to see if the concepts are appropriate to the objectives and positioning statements. Testing at this stage can be artificial. The showing of the messages is in a forced situation, and the messages are in a very rough form; print ads are shown as layout boards, often without complete copy, but with just headline and illustration. Television commercials are shown in animatic form. (Remember, an animatic is a cartoon-like format with limited movement and an audio track.)

The purpose of this early test is to get quick and inexpensive feedback. Often it tests two or more competing conceptualizations to see which is more clear. Questions concern likes, dislikes, points of confusion, and immediate playback; that is, did the subject pick up the key message points, or did the subject learn something different or less relevant?

Television commercials can be tested using animatics that can be produced for about $3,000 and that represent a finished commercial that might cost ten to a hundred times as much. Proprietary tests have shown that the animatic test can predict the future success of the finished commercial fairly well in terms of main idea communication. This format can also give diagnostic insights that allow the commercial to be improved before expensive final production takes place. Animatics represent finished work least well in emotional or image-building messages; their main virtue is in testing informative messages.[14]

Most large agencies have an ongoing laboratory for routine testing of all work in its early stages. Some bring in subjects every day on the assumption that there will always be something to test. This means that the test can be done quickly because there is no time lost in hiring a recruiting service and waiting for subjects; therefore, a diagnostic test can be done and reported in two to three days. This process is also inexpensive because there are no startup costs and because the sample size is small; it is felt that 30 to 50 subjects can give insight into the basic soundness of the approach and to any flaws that might exist in the commercial.[15]

As seen, two major criteria of fast and inexpensive are met. The test must also measure the correct response. An artificial laboratory cannot easily measure sales or memory build-up over time, but it can measure attentiveness, transmission of a key idea, and impact on the consumer's feelings. The first two of these are fairly straightforward and can be dealt with by open-ended questions. The third can be approached through rating scales: "Which of the following adjectives describe the commercial that you just saw?" Generally a set of 20 to 30 adjectives are used, and this set breaks down to three or four key dimensions. In the Leo Burnett lab, there are seven dimensions of adjectives or statements: Entertainment (lots of fun, clever, and entertaining); Confusion (too complex, distracting); Relevant News (gave me a new idea, learned something); Brand Reinforcement (good brand; dependable, reliable brand); Empathy (realistic, acting out what I feel like); Familiarity (done many times, same old thing); and Alienation (didn't demonstrate claims, farfetched, annoying).[16] The dimensions were developed by the Leo Burnett Research Department during the 1970s. Bruzzone Research Company uses four dimensions: Entertaining (clever, imaginative, amusing . . . .), Personal Relevance (interesting, informative, effective . . . .), Dislike (irritating, silly, pointless . . . .), and Warm (appealing, gentle, well done).[17]

These adjective lists are used throughout the testing stages and are useful in developmental pretesting because they show different ways that a consumer can respond to a message. A response can occur because the message is relevant, because it entertains, or because it leaves a warm feeling. Different ads work for different reasons, and it is important to know why an ad does its job and whether the ad is doing what it was designed to do.

The developmental pretest's main purpose is to give feedback to the creative team, to show them that they are on target or why they have erred. Evaluating art is a sensitive process, and measuring feelings is a subtle skill.

At this point in the process, the main concern is the ability to communicate the key issues correctly. For this concern, the forced viewing laboratory is appropriate. Whether the message generates sales or can survive in a competitive environment needs to be tested in different ways.

The *final pretest* takes place after final production or with an almost-finished production that is only missing minor touches, such as color correction. This is the last check before the message is put into a magazine or on television. The most common test here is done in a real situation in which the ad is put on the air in a real market with more controlled competition, noise, and, perhaps, repetition (*field test*). Less common, but still useful, is the more controlled *laboratory test* of the final production work.

At this point, production dollars have been spent, but a final check needs to be made before media dollars are spent. Generally, the final pretest is of a single execution, since one purpose of the developmental pretest was to discriminate between the early conceptual contenders so that only one would remain.

A *field test* (that is, a test of the commercial under natural conditions) has the advantage of being real; there is the opportunity to see the commercial's real-world impact. Conversely, such a test gives the firm less control over the environment; it may snow, the competition may have a sale, important events may change people's moods.

In addition, if the competition knows about the test, it may try to disrupt the process. For example, if B learns that A will be introducing a product that will compete with it, B may offer its product at a considerably lower price in the test market so that A cannot evaluate its advertising accurately. Worse yet (or better yet, depending on whether one is A or B), if A is unaware of B's actions, it will assess the advertising and/or the market incorrectly.

Finally, the field test is usually slower and more costly to execute than the lab test because media time or space must be purchased. The field test is more realistic, though, and this outweighs its disadvantages in certain cases.

One of these cases occurs when repetition of the message is an important part of the test or purchase behavior is the key dependent variable. It is difficult to simulate message repetition in the lab without creating some reactiveness to the setting; therefore, this need leads to real-world tests.

An example of a field pretest was one done by Wisconsin Power and Light, a gas and electric utility; WPL was trying to create more favorable attitudes toward itself during the energy crisis of 1978 by promoting the concept of energy conservation. Before spending a large amount on media throughout its service area, WPL wanted to test its television spots. It did a pre-advertising survey in two of its markets, then placed its conservation campaign in one market, with no advertising in the control market. After 15 weeks, it conducted a post-advertising survey in both markets. From this it learned that attitudes had become slightly less favorable during the 15 weeks in the no-advertising market. At the same time, there was a significant positive change in attitudes in the advertising market. Based on this field pretest, WPL went ahead and aired its conservation campaign throughout its service area. The WPL case is a good example of a field pretest, and it is also a good example of experimental design research (which is discussed below).

The *laboratory test* brings a number of consumers to a central location, where they are exposed to advertising in a controlled setting and are then asked questions or are otherwise observed. The key advantage of this method is the control over the viewing situation. The weather is constant, the competition is constant—all variables are constant unless the researcher wants to change them. This allows for measurement of dependent variables in a situation where it is fairly clear what has caused any change in the variables.

The major disadvantage of this controlled setting is that it is not real. Subjects know they are in an artificial environment and may respond in an artificial manner. It is therefore incumbent upon the researcher to attempt to develop as realistic a setting as possible for both exposure to the message and opportunity to respond.

This discussion has taken a continuous process and divided it into two stages (developmental and final), but there are actually many degrees of completion that can be pretested. These include

1. Drawn storyboard with soundtrack
2. Slides of a drawn storyboard synched to a soundtrack
3. Animatics
4. Photomatics (stills from the actual commercial put on film or tape with a soundtrack)

5. Rough finish of the commercial
6. Finished execution

Comparable levels of finish can be tested for print ads. The choice of level of finish to test depends on several factors:

1. *Type of commercial*   Mood and image messages need to be closer to the end product so that their intent will be communicated. It is difficult to convey the emotion of a commercial through a storyboard. Appetite appeal and other variables dependent on clear visuals also will not test well in their early stages.

2. *Level of risk*   The newer the creative concept, the greater the risk, and the earlier feedback should be acquired. Conversely, the newer the concept, the greater the need to test the finished advertising product. Just as with other business decisions, the greater the risk, the greater the need to put money into research to protect the investment. Doing a new execution of a campaign that has worked well for 20 years will need much less research support and confirmation.

A second risk issue pertains to the media budget that will support the advertising. The larger the percentage of the ad budget that goes into delivering one message, the greater the need for testing. Regardless of the absolute dollar size, if there is one campaign scheduled for the year, it needs to be tested well. Retailers often create a new message every week; in their case, the test is less vital because a bad decision will waste 2% or less of the budget.

3. *Cost*   The major cost of copy testing is not in the test itself but rather in the production of test materials. Later in the production process, the cost of creating test materials increases, and the total amount invested in production is also greater. While the cost of using a storyboard for a test may be a few hundred dollars, the cost of an animatic may be $3,000, and the cost of an almost finished spot may be $100,000 if it is pulled from the actual production.[18]

It is easy to see that there are large tradeoffs here. Early production is inexpensive but may not communicate well; later production is costly but communicates subtle feelings and emotions. The determinant criterion, though, is probably that of risk. A new concept must be tested early to ensure that there are no major flaws, while a minor extension of a current campaign needs much less pretesting.

Post-testing is done after the campaign has been in the field for a while to make sure that it is doing its job in terms of meeting objectives and establishing the position. Post-testing is less likely to be experimental in nature and is usually survey-based. The post-test has two major functions:

1. *To see if the objectives of the campaign have been met*

2. *To act as the situation analysis for the next campaign*   The decision sequence is a repetitive process with many opportunities to adjust as the campaign develops, but it is also important to use the post-test of one campaign as the input to the following year. In this way, the firm's advertising will proceed in a logical way from year to year, taking advantage of opportunities as they occur and adjusting to any new problems that arise.

Given a limited research budget, it would seem that its best allocation would be in the combination of situation analysis/post-test research that gives the firm an annual picture of the marketplace opportunities and problems. The next increment of budget should be spent on developmental pretesting, while the last dollars should be allocated to final pretesting. Of course, the best situation is one in which all types of research can be done because they each deal with different problems. Most large consumer goods manufacturers in the United States do allocate dollars for each phase of research.

Dependent Variables

Having addressed the issue of when to do research, the next question is what to measure in the research. The dependent variable is the response in the stimulus–response relation. Given an advertising stimulus, what consumer response should follow?

The most basic answer to this question is that the response to be measured should be the response specified in the objectives previously specified. While this seems obvious, it is often neglected for two reasons. First, the people working on the advertising forget what the objectives were—or worse, never set any specific objectives in the first place. Despite the publication of DAGMAR years ago, it is still all too common in some organizations for a project to progress without clear objectives and clear dependent variables.

Second, a developmental pretest may not be able to measure all specified responses because the production hasn't progressed far enough to elicit such responses (feelings, emotions). In this case, the test may not relate to the advertising's objectives; nevertheless, there should still be specific testing objectives that should clearly state the relevant dependent variable. In the developmental pretest, the dependent variables are likely to be comprehension, understanding, and lack of confusion, even though the overall dependent variable may be something more subtle, such as feelings or perceptions. This discrepancy is reasonable, given that some level of comprehension must precede the development of feelings.

Dependent variables generally fall into the three levels of the hierarchy of effects, although within each level other variables are of greater or lesser specificity.

Awareness
- learning
- forgetting
- memory
- knowledge (of specific items/issues)
- recall
- recognition

Attitude
- perceptions
- persuasion
- feelings
- preference
- intention to purchase

Behavior
- trial purchase
- repeat purchase
- sales records
- shopping trips

In addition to these traditional measures from the hierarchy, there are also physiological measures that show some type of mental or bodily response rather than a verbal or behavioral response.

Physiological
- brain waves
- galvanic skin response
- pupil dilation response
- eye tracking
- heart rate

Awareness measures learning and/or comprehension of a message. Researchers generally agree that there is a weak linkage between awareness and ultimate sales, but they also agree that some basic learning impact must occur if the ad is to be effective.

The most common test of awareness is day-after recall (DAR): the percentage of people who remember seeing a commercial or ad the day after it was shown. ("Did you watch '*Dallas*' last night?" "Please tell me the names of the sponsors of that show"; "Did you see any commercials for dog food? Which ones?") This sequence establishes that the commercial may have been seen and then asks for unaided recall.

A weaker test of learning would be a recognition test. ("Which of the following brands were advertised on '*Dallas*'? Barfo, Ruff Mix, Doggie Meal or Poochie Chow?"). Recall typically gets an average of 20% correct responses after one day, while recognition typically gets 80 to 90% correct responses.

Recent work by Singh and Rothschild[19] shows that recall may be too difficult a test for low-involvement products. Because consumers don't care about the product, they don't pay a lot of attention and don't show that a lot of learning has occurred. Recognition tests, which are less taxing, show that learning has occurred in spite of recall's lack of ability to tap it.

Recall tests are currently receiving criticism from many directions. A study done by Hubert Zielske at Foote, Cone & Belding[20] shows that recall tests are biased against emotional messages in favor of informational ones. Zielske feels that it is easier to recall information but wonders how one responds to a feeling. Recognition tests show equal levels of learning for both types of messages, but the recall test, which is more prevalent, doesn't show learning of feeling messages as well. Perhaps one reason for lots of dry, boring commercials during the 1970s was because these did better in recall tests and were therefore used more often. Table 9.3 shows this difference for television. While the bias clearly holds for television, a similar test for print showed no difference.

John Andrews of General Foods Corporation has different problems with recall. He feels that recall doesn't measure advertising effectiveness, but rather measures how loud the message shouts; he feels that recall measures the commercial's ability to intrude and impress. This creates an opportunity to be effective but does not ensure or measure effectiveness. In this sense recall is important, but it is not most important.[21]

Another common complaint is that recall often provides a single number: "*X*% of respondents were able to recall the message." The commercial is aired or thrown out based on this number. This is a simple test, and it is easy to digest a single number, but the test takes a creative judgment and reduces it to too simple a format. Over time, writers and artists have learned to make commercials that

Table 9.3 Recognition versus recall for "thinking" versus "feeling" television commercials

Thinking commercials		Proven recognition	Day-after recall	Day-after recall understatement
A		56%	49%	13%
D		32	24	25
E		24	21	13
	Average	37	31	16
Feeling commercials		Proven recognition	Day-after recall	Day-after recall understatement
B		37%	21%	43%
C		36	25	31
F		23	10	57
	Average	32	19	41

Source: From Hubert A. Zielske, "Does Day-After Recall Penalize 'Feeling' Ads?" *Journal of Advertising Research,* February/March 1982, p. 21. © Copyright February/March 1982, by the Advertising Research Foundation.

test well on recall but are not necessarily effective in generating sales. This has created a situation in which management makes a decision based on a single number and creatives write commercials geared to scoring well. Both sides have lost sight of the real goal of the advertising in too many cases.

In a 1977 study, creative directors and research directors of top agencies generally agreed that copy research, especially recall tests, did not lead to the best decisions in cases where commercials dealt with emotional or psychological benefits or where commercials were characterized by visual distinctiveness. These issues were not captured well through verbal tests.[22] These complaints existed in 1977 and still seemed to exist in 1982 when Zielske reported his data.

In spite of these complaints, recall tests continue to be used (probably because they are easy, fast, and inexpensive). In 1979, almost 10,000 commercial tests were done by the major testing firms at an average cost of $3,500 (plus production and media costs). Of these, about one-third were on-air recall tests; it is unclear what percentage of the remainder were also recall tests.[23]

Why were there so many recall tests in the face of so much doubt about their efficacy? There is a need to determine if learning is occurring, because many practitioners feel that learning is the first step toward behavior; also, there is a need to measure learning because many advertising objectives are built around awareness. Testing awareness is important in spite of flaws in the current methods.

Attitude (or feelings or perceptions) is the area that most advertisers want their messages to influence (concurrently with, or in addition to, awareness). Having an impact here is important. Remember that the Needham, Harper Worldwide corporate philosophy says "Appeal to both heart and head." While awareness measures attempt to assess appeals to the head, attitude measures attempt to assess appeals to the heart and head.

An interesting view of this comes from Joel Baumwoll of J. Walter Thompson.[24] He feels that *recall* measures reconstruction of the *stimulus* while *perception* measures the *response* of feeling. Although it is important to know if people

Figure 9.2 *Advertising playback vs. brand perceptions for RCA*

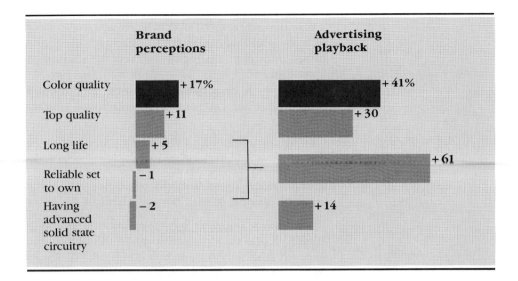

can remember what they saw, he feels that it is equally or more important to learn what people internalize and use from the message. Recall testing causes people to focus on the concrete and verbal elements of an execution while deemphasizing the emotional and abstract elements that can often be effective in producing the desired response. Figure 9.2 shows an example of different findings for the two measures.

The data in Figure 9.2 come from a print ad for an RCA XL100 color television. The brand perception data show the difference between the perceptions of a group who saw the ad and a control group who did not. Their *feelings* about quality changed, but their feelings about reliability did not. The advertising playback data represent recall data from a group exposed to the ad. This group *knew* that the ad said the product was reliable as well as that it had quality. On a knowledge basis, the ad was fine, but on a feelings basis, it needed to be revised. Although the ad *said* reliability and people *learned* reliability, they did not *feel* reliability; they did not assimilate the concept. The attitude measure showed a different effect than did the awareness measure. According to Baumwoll, the difference is between measuring the recall of the stimulus and measuring the response of the consumer.

Behavior is a common measure in a post-test; it is rarely the dependent measure in a pretest because it is a weak response and is hard to elicit. Because it is the last stage of the hierarchy of effects, it is least likely to occur or change from the limited exposure of a copy test.

Principles of Advertising Assessment

Earlier in this text, the point was made that advertising is part art and part science. The following discussion shows that a large amount of judgment is necessary, even where the science of measurement exists. There are few clearcut decisions in this or any other part of advertising. It is important to know what issues are relevant to the decision, and it is important to keep the objectives of the project in mind.

In 1982 the research directors of 21 of the largest advertising agencies put forth a document of nine principles of copy testing. This effort came about because of disagreement over what would make a copy test valid and reliable. If researchers and managers are familiar with these principles and demand their existence from copy testing firms, then the state of the art of copy testing will rise over time.

The nine principles are known as Positioning Advertising Copy Testing (PACT); the principles of PACT state that a good copy testing system has the following attributes.

1. *Provides measurements that are relevant to the objectives of the advertising*

2. *Requires agreement about how the results will be used in advance of each specific test*   These first two principles are related in that the goals of the test must be consistent with the objectives of the advertising.

3. *Provides multiple measurements*   This can be accomplished in two ways. There can be multiple measures of the same item; for example, attitude can be measured using both semantic differential scales and Likert scales. There can also be multiple dependent variables so that the copy test considers both awareness and attitude in the same measure. This latter issue is important because advertising works at several levels of the hierarchy of effects; the measurements must be consistent with the objectives.

4. *Is based on a model of human response to communications that considers the reception of a stimulus, the comprehension of the stimulus, and the response to the stimulus*   Again, PACT considers that advertising works at several levels. To do good copy testing, advertising must be considered in the context of the stimulus–response, involvement and hierarchy of effects models that were presented earlier in this text. Advertising affects the heart as well as the head, and tests must consider both aspects.

5. *Allows for consideration of whether the advertising stimulus should be exposed more than once*   Given the objectives of the campaign, the media budget, the involvement of consumers, and the subtlety of the message, one must consider how often the message should be repeated in the test situation.

6. *Recognizes that the more finished a piece of copy is, the more soundly it can be evaluated and requires, as a minimum, that alternative executions be tested in the same degree of finish*   Test results can vary greatly depending on the level of finish of the commercial. This is especially true for mood/image messages and must be considered in designing a test. This issue is especially important if two messages are being tested so that one can ultimately be chosen to go on the air. In this case, the level of finish must be sufficient to accommodate the one needing the most finish (i.e., in a test of mood versus information, the factual nature of the latter will assure its superiority in a test of rough finishes or animatics, even though it may not be the better message in the finished form).

7. *Provides controls to avoid the biasing effects of the exposure context*   The responses to advertising vary greatly as a function of the way in which the commercial was seen. This means that all competing commercials must be tested in the same context and that more natural viewing situations are to be preferred over artificial ones.

8. *Takes into account basic considerations of sample definition*   This means sampling from the target market in a scientific manner and using a sufficient sample size.

9. *Demonstrates reliability and validity* Reliability means that the test yields the same results each time the same advertising is tested; validity means that the test results should represent actual marketplace performance. Currently, many copy test methods and services cannot show either reliability or validity.[25]

Methods and Services Available

In this final section, a number of copy testing methods are examined. They fall into two basic groups: experimental and survey methods. Within each group are examples of the commercial testing services that are currently available. Their inclusion does not imply an endorsement; they are merely used as examples of the methods.

Experimental or causal design

Generally, the key question in copy research concerns the effect of advertising on consumers. That is, what result is caused by exposure to a particular commercial or ad? These statements imply causality and a sequence of events such that the latter occurs as a result of the former. Research techniques known as experimentation or causal design are used to investigate these relations.

In an experiment, the researcher attempts to control all independent variables that may affect the dependent or response variables. Given this control, one or two independent variables are manipulated while all others are held constant, and the effect on the relevant dependent variable is observed.

In the laboratory, or closed setting, all variables can truly be controlled; here, for example, some subjects see execution A of a commercial, others see execution B, and others see no commercials for the brand; after exposure to the commercials (the manipulated independent variable), subjects are tested for their feelings toward the brand (the dependent variable). In this laboratory situation, all other independent variables (such as price, deals, shelf location, competitive advertising) were either held constant across all groups of subjects or were eliminated (and therefore held constant at a value of zero).

Experiments can also be conducted in the real world; these are known as field experiments and are in an open setting. The same procedures apply (different subjects see different executions of the commercial, and their feelings are tested), but the researcher has less or no control over other independent variables. For example, if the two executions are shown in different cities, then the change in feelings may also be a result of varying prices or competitive advertising in the two cities.

The laboratory experiment creates greater internal validity because of the greater control of the variables. The researcher is, therefore, more able to conclude that the implied causality exists. As a tradeoff, there may be less external validity, or "generalizability," to real-world situations. Conversely, the field experiment has greater external validity because it is conducted under situations that more closely represent reality. In the field experiment, there may be less internal validity because other variables may have had an impact on the causality being studied.

Ideally, one would like to study advertising in a setting that ensures both internal and external validity. Since the two exist so that, in most cases, more of one means less of the other, there are tradeoffs to be made. The choice made must be based on the objectives of the research. Typically, the more finished the production, the more one leans toward external validity. It is important, though, to have a research design that includes adequate levels of both types of validity. If either is completely missing, the experiment will be worthless.

Most copy testing is an experimental design format to investigate causality. Generally the design used is a simple one of

$$X \qquad\qquad O$$

where: X is the *treatment,* or showing of the commercial, and

O is the *observation* or test of the respondent's memory or attitude.

The treatment is followed by an observation. This design is adequate because the observations are usually compared against other observations for other commercials. The schematic shown above is correct for the single commercial, but when the observations are compared to others, the schematic is actually as follows:

$$
\begin{array}{ll}
X_1 & O_1 \\
X_2 & O_2 \\
X_3 & O_3 \\
\;\cdot & \;\cdot \\
\;\cdot & \;\cdot \\
\;\cdot & \;\cdot \\
X_n & O_n
\end{array}
$$

where each commercial $(X_1 \ldots X_n)$ is tested in a similar way, and the impact on subjects is recorded $(O_1 \ldots O_n)$.

Each test is therefore an experiment in which all variables are held constant while only the commercial to be tested changes. In this way, commercials can be compared to one another for their suitability for on-air or in-print usage. This sort of design is the basis for virtually all advertising testing services, as well as for the testing done by the agency itself. The design holds across both lab and field settings. For a more in-depth discussion of causal designs, their merits and potential pitfalls, see Chapter 4 of *Marketing Research* by Churchill.[26]

Field experimental copy testing methods

For the purpose of this discussion, a field setting is defined as one where subjects see a commercial either on television or in print in their own home. Because exposure takes place in a normal viewing setting, the message is generally in a finished format and is being given its final Go–No Go test. The dominant method here is the traditional day-after recall test.

1. *Day-after recall*   In this test, the finished (or almost finished) commercial is shown on air in one or more local markets as part of normal programming. The next day, consumers are called by telephone and questioned as follows.

- Did you see the program?
- What commercials were shown in the program?
- Did you see a commercial for *X*?
- What do you remember about *X*?

By remembering something of relevance, the respondent has shown recall. The commercial's recall score is based primarily on this issue and is compared to scores received by commercials for the same product class, the same brand, or all tested commercials within a selected time period.

The *Burke Day-After Recall Test* airs the test commercial in three or four dispersed markets and then interviews 200 viewers of the program in which the commercial appeared. Recall scores are compared to norms based on demographic respondent groups, on product classes, and on execution styles.

Burke also has a rough commercial test. In this test, the commercial is aired in one city during morning programming. The sample of 150 is prerecruited to watch the program, and the subjects are called the following day for the day-after recall test. Both Burke tests offer limited diagnostic information and are used primarily as a "report card" compared to norms.

The *Gallup & Robinson In-View Test* places all of its commercials in a prime-time program on a UHF channel in several geographically dispersed cities. Six hundred people are prerecruited to watch the program, and a sample of 300 of these is called the next day for a recall test.

2. *Recognition*   The most commonly used test for print advertising in finished form is a recognition test. The *Starch Readership Report* allows an advertiser to test the response to a printed ad in a single issue of a magazine (a concept similar to day-after recall) or to test an ad over time and across several magazines to see how learning changes over time or how effective different vehicles are at delivering the message.

After a magazine has had a suitable time to be read (this varies depending on frequency of publication), personal interviews are conducted with a minimum sample of 100 persons per sex (spread over 20 to 30 urban locations) who acknowledge that they have read some part or glanced through the magazine in question. The interviewer then goes through the issue one page at a time and, for each ad, asks if the respondent remembers seeing the ad. If yes, there are questions pertaining to the headline, illustration, copy, and signature. Respondents are also classified as having

- *Noted*   seen the ad
- *Associated*   read enough to know the advertiser
- *Read most*   read half or more of the written material

Starch reports show percentages for the three classifications of readers and comparisons to norms. In addition, the advertiser receives a labeled ad similar to that shown in Figure 9.3, which reports the data collected for each element of the message.

Laboratory experimental copy testing methods

A laboratory test setting is one that is out of the home. Generally, this will be a theatre, a specially designed room (particularly when dealing with physiological responses), or, less frequently, a mobile unit. Because the setting is already artificial, labs often accommodate unfinished work in more developmental stages. In 1979, approximately 45% of laboratory copy tests were of rough commercials.[27]

Theatre and small group tests   In these settings, subjects are prescreened and invited to a location for the stated purpose of viewing and evaluating pilot television programs. Before viewing begins, subjects are told that there will be

Figure 9.3 *Starch-labeled ad*

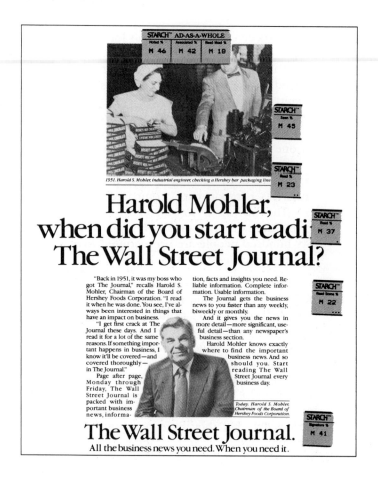

some awarding of prizes and that the subjects should select the brands they would prefer if they were to win prizes in particular product classes. Subjects then view the programs and commercials. After viewing, subjects are told there will be another round of prizes and would they again check their preferred brands. Finally, there is a questionnaire with awareness, attitude, and demographic questions. This is a basic pre–post test:

O X O

where there is an observation both before and after the stimulus is presented.

The *ASI In-Theatre Test* invites a minimum of 250 people to its theatre in Los Angeles. Viewers list the brand choices they would prefer if they won a drawing, and then view a cartoon, a 30-minute program, five commercials, a second 30-minute program, and another cartoon on a movie screen. After the first program and again after the commercials, subjects evaluate what they just saw. Before the final cartoon, subjects fill out another brand choice questionnaire because, they are told, the first questionnaire had an error on it. After the final cartoon, the subjects complete a recall questionnaire.

During viewing, a subset of subjects operate hand-held dials to indicate how interested they are in what they are watching. A second subset wears basal skin response (BSR) devices on one hand to show physiological responses to the stimulus materials. BSR measures emotion but does not indicate if the emotion is positive or negative. A third subset of subjects views the programs and commercials and answers questions. In addition, advertisers can recruit members of the audience for focus group types of in-depth discussions after the above events have all been completed.

AC-T (Advertising Control for Television) is the laboratory procedure of Mc-Collum/Spielman. In this test, approximately 400 respondents (100 from each of four cities) watch a television monitor in groups of 25. Before viewing, they indicate the brand used last in several product classes as a premeasurement. Subjects then see a 30-minute program with seven commercials inserted in the middle; four of these are test commercials, and three are control commercials shown in all tests and used as norms.

Program T_1 C_1 T_2 C_2 T_3 C_3 T_4 Program

where $T_{1 \ldots 4}$ are test commercials

$C_{1 \ldots 3}$ are control commercials

At the end of this program, subjects are given a recall test that provides what McCollum/Spielman call the clutter awareness score because of the cluttered nature of the commercial environment. Next, subjects see a second program, with each test commercial appearing again.

Program T_1 Program T_2 Program T_3 Program T_4 Program

After answering questions concerning the program material, subjects are told there will be drawings for prizes in several product categories and are asked for their brand preferences in each category. Persuasion is measured by the percentage of people who switched brands from the one they purchased last. Other measures of persuasion are used for durable goods, services, and public sector appeals.

Advertising Research Services (ARS) is a third theatre type of test run by Research Systems Corporation. Commercials are tested in four cities on a total of 400 to 600 subjects. Before viewing, subjects indicate brand choices for a prize drawing. This is done by selecting from pictures of packages of the brands, and changes the task from recall-related to recognition-related.

Subjects then watch a 30-minute program with three sets of two commercials each imbedded. After answering questions about the program, there is another 30-minute program with commercials. The test commercial might be any of the 12 commercial slots.

Program T_1 T_2 Program T_3 T_4 Program T_5 T_6 Program

Program Questions

Program T_7 T_8 Program T_9 T_{10} Program T_{11} T_{12} Program

After the second program, subjects are told there will be another drawing and are asked to make brand choices again from the set of package illustrations. Approximately half the subjects are phoned after 72 hours and given a recall test for the 12 commercials. Recall scores are evaluated against product class norms. If diagnostic information is desired, this is done separately from the persuasion and recall tests.

In another use of UPC scanners, *TRIM Inc.* recruits subjects in a supermarket and divides them into viewer and nonviewer groups. Viewers go to a trailer in the parking lot, where they are shown five television commercials before they begin shopping. Both groups are given an ID card to present at the checkout counter and are offered a discount if they present the card. This method allows for a fairly direct link between exposure to the commercial and purchase behavior. Researchers can measure number of purchasers and number of units purchased relative to the control group that did not see a commercial or to other subjects that saw different versions of the commercial. This is not as realistic as *BehaviorScan* or *AdTel* but is much cheaper.[28] *BehaviorScan* and *AdTel* are described in Chapter 20.

In addition to these services which, for the most part, test finished commercials, there are a much larger number of tests done within advertising agencies. Many agencies have developed their own in-house testing services to evaluate concepts and messages in various unfinished stages of production. These are known as *forced exposure* situations and progress as follows.

A group of 30 to 50 members of the target market come to a central location, where they are shown the commercial without program content (i.e., they are forced to watch it). Next, each subject is individually interviewed or given a questionnaire. The questions asked are

1. What do you remember seeing?

2. What was the brand?

3. What did you like in the commercial?

4. What did you dislike?

5. Was there anything that you found hard to believe?

Any specific issues troubling the account team also should be investigated at this point. This type of research gives early feedback so that any negatives can be corrected before a large expenditure has been made on production and media.

One type of pretest for unfinished print ads is known as a *folio test.* The test ad is put into a prototype or dummy magazine. The prototype is given to consumers to examine, with the explanation that it is a new magazine concept that is being tested. Subjects are asked to examine the magazine in their homes for a few days, and then the interviewer returns to discuss the magazine. Questions begin with the editorial content, but then questions about ads are asked in order to measure

- *Attention*   Was the ad seen?
- *Comprehension*   Was the ad understood?
- *Motivation*   Would the reader buy the product?

As with forced exposure, the folio test provides a low-cost way to test unfinished ads before final production.

Physiological measures   Tests with physiological response variables are almost always measured in a laboratory because of the large amounts of sophisticated equipment they require. As electronic circuitry becomes more sophisticated, this will undoubtedly change. For example, Krober-Riel is working with a portable eye movement recording device that allows the researcher to track eye movement as a subject walks down a grocery store aisle.

While physiological measures are not commonly used at this time, their future potential is great. The following discussion highlights a few measures that seem promising. In each case, exposure to an advertising stimulus is followed by a response that can be measured. Since these measures are nonverbal, one must infer learning and feelings or ask additional questions.

Physiological measures are felt to have potential for two main reasons. First, they do not require any mental effort on the part of the consumer. If one accepts low-involvement notions of information processing as valid, then asking questions might lead to heightened involvement and invalid responses. Physiological measures show response without effort, but they don't describe the response; though the researcher can see a response, it is not clear if the response is positive or negative or if any learning, for example, has taken place. The value of the measure is merely in seeing a response.

The second value of physiological measures is that they give an ongoing record of responses. All the measures listed show responses to the stimuli within a brief time interval (brain waves, for example, will change within .3 seconds of exposure). This means that researchers can learn what parts of a commercial are most likely to grab attention; in turn, key message points can be made at these times, or nongrabbing parts of a commercial can be changed.

These measures are, for the most part, involuntary, and they can be taken without asking the subject any questions. Therefore, they have the theoretical virtue of not getting an answer that the subject feels is "proper" or socially acceptable. Brain wave, eye movement, and skin response data are the most commonly used physiological measures.

▪ *Brain waves*   Electroencephalographic (EEG) data can be collected from several locations on the skull, for several electrical frequencies at each location and up to 1,000 times per second for each of these. There seem to be two emerging areas of concentration from this huge mass of potential data.

Occipital alpha activity comes from the rear of the skull (near the occiput) and is in the 8 to 13 cycles per second frequency range (this range is known as alpha). This signal is strongest when the subject is resting and weakest when there is attention to the stimulus. A sudden drop in the strength of alpha indicates an involuntary response to a visual stimulus (such as a scene change in a commercial). Over time (a period usually less than six seconds), alpha recovers to its resting strength; the length of time of the recovery is a function of how interested the subject is in the stimulus. Alpha is negatively correlated with recall; the lower the level of alpha, the higher the level of recall. Since alpha relates to learning and its level can be related exactly to specific scenes, the scenes that do the best job at enhancing learning can be located.[29]

Hemispheric lateralization is concerned with differences in alpha activity in the right and left sides of the brain. It is hypothesized, but not yet shown clearly in advertising, that visual stimuli are processed primarily in the right hemisphere and verbal stimuli primarily in the left. Similarly, the right hemisphere reacts more to emotional messages, while the left is more responsive to logical reasoning. Also, recall is a left hemisphere-dominated task, while recognition is a right-dominant task.[30] If these hypotheses were correct, it would be possible to learn the type of stimulus that dominates at any time in a commercial or print ad and use the more appropriate learning measure.

▪ *Eye movement tracking*   Subjects are asked to look at a print ad or television commercial while a sensor aims a beam of infrared light at the eye. A portion of the light is reflected by the cornea and detected by the same sensor, which electronically measures the angle between the beam reflected by the cornea and

Figure 9.4 *Eye movement tracking*

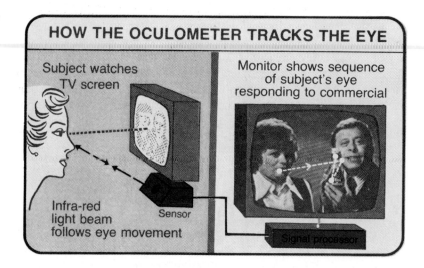

the center of the eye's pupil. This information can be processed to show the exact spot on the ad or television screen where the eye is focused. The data are shown on a second television monitor as a white dot superimposed on the stimulus commercial.[31] This process can be seen in Figure 9.4.

As with brain waves, this process gives a continuous reading of the subject's responses. In this case, the data show *what* is holding attention, while brain waves showed *when* attention was held. A common finding is that subjects focus on the spokesperson rather than the product; this is especially the case for celebrity spokespersons. For print ads, this process can show how much time is spent on each element of the ad from headline and illustration down to logo and slogan, as well as the order in which the elements are considered. It is claimed that the process can pinpoint the exact word upon which the subject is focusing.[32]

▪ *Galvanic skin response (GSR)*   Electrodes are placed on two fingers, and the stimulus is shown. One physiological response to emotion is the activation of sweat glands in the palm. When the sweat glands open, the electrical skin resistance drops, changing the electric circuit between the two electrodes. This change is measured.[33] While GSR had some popularity a few years ago, this seems to have faded; GSR, though, has had several prior periods of popularity and will probably return to popularity again in the future.

Survey and quasi-experimental methods

As was stated earlier, the best way to test the effects of advertising is through an experimental design. In this way, causality can be inferred. Often, it is not possible to set up an experiment, or the issue of measurement is raised after the advertising is already being disseminated. In any case, most advertisers want to know the effect of their campaign after it has been in operation for a while.

The most common response at this point is to do a *survey*. Although a survey can obtain valuable descriptive information, it cannot be used to infer causality. One can ask questions concerning awareness, attitude, and behavior as is done in the situation analysis, but this doesn't directly show that the advertising was effective. There are, though, two techniques that can help to answer the causality question.

Quasi-experiments result in situations where the researcher has no control over the variables and/or is trying to recreate a test situation from post hoc data. This situation works best when the advertising plan differs in different markets and the researcher has other data concerning the makeup of the markets. When this occurs, one can recreate an experimental situation after the fact. Because it was not set up on an a priori basis, this is not a true experiment and is known as a quasi-experiment.

Diary panel and store audit data are two cases of quasi-experiments. In these cases, the researcher has a long series of records and can observe the change in purchases before, during, and after the advertising campaign. After carefully ruling out other hypotheses (the price was lowered; the competition's product was recalled as a result of botulism), the researcher can tentatively infer that the change in sales was due to the change in advertising.

Bruzzone Research Company (BRC) offers a special case of a survey quasi-experiment. BRC mails a questionnaire to 1,000 households across the United States and typically achieves a 50% response rate. Questionnaires consist of a series of photos and scripts of commercials as shown in Figure 9.5. Questions use recognition-based items to measure learning and adjective checklists to measure

Figure 9.5 *Bruzzone Research Company recognition questionnaire*

Please look over these pictures and words from a TV commercial and answer the questions on the right.

(Boy #1) What's this stuff?

(Boy #2) Some cereal. Supposed to be good for you.

(Boy #1) Did you try it?

(Boy #2) I'm not going to try it. You try it.

(Boy #1) I'm not going to try it.

(Boy #2) Let's get Mikey.

(Boy #1) Yeah.

(Boy #2) He won't eat it. He hates everything.

He likes it!
Hey, Mikey!

(Announcer) When you bring brand name home, * don't tell the kids it's one of those nutritional cereals you've been trying to get them to eat. You're the only one who has to know.

Do you remember seeing this commercial on TV?

☐ Yes   ☐ No   ☐ Not sure-I may have

How interested are you in what this commercial is trying to tell you or show you?

☐ Very interested   ☐ Somewhat interested   ☐ Not interested

How does it make you feel about the product?

☐ It's a good product   ☐ It's OK   ☐ It's bad   ☐ Not sure

Please check any of the following if you feel they describe this commercial.

☐ Amusing   ☐ Irritating
☐ Appealing   ☐ Lively
☐ Clever   ☐ Original
☐ Confusing   ☐ Phony
☐ Convincing   ☐ Pointless
☐ Dull   ☐ Repetitious
☐ Easy to forget   ☐ Sensitive
☐ Effective   ☐ Silly
☐ Gentle   ☐ Uninteresting
☐ Imaginative   ☐ Warm
☐ Informative   ☐ Well done
☐ Interesting   ☐ Worth remembering

* We have blocked out the name. Do you remember which brand was being advertised?

☐ Life
☐ Total
☐ Special K
☐ Don't know

Does anyone in your household use this type of product?

☐ Regularly
☐ Occasionally
☐ Seldom or never

T·H·E I·N·S·I·D·E O·U·T·L·O·O·K

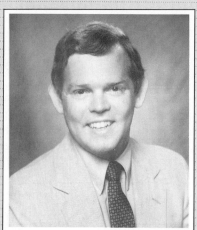

Joseph T. Plummer

Executive Vice-President, Young & Rubicam USA

Joe Plummer is executive vice-president and director of research services at Young & Rubicam USA, and is a member of the board of directors. He is based at Young & Rubicam, New York.

Prior to becoming Y&R's research director in March 1979, Dr. Plummer had been with the Leo Burnett Company in Chicago. He joined Burnett in 1967 as a research analyst and held a succession of research posts until 1974, when he became vice-president of worldwide marketing services and in 1976, senior vice-president and research director.

Dr. Plummer holds a B.A. degree from Westminster College (Pennsylvania) and both M.A. and Ph.D. degrees in communications from Ohio State University.

The Future of Advertising Assessment

"Think of the size of the book that could be written about all we know," said the little boy. "Think," said his father, "of the size of the book that could be written about all we have yet to learn."

When television was new and "clutter" had little meaning beyond the three-year-old's room, advertising "effectiveness" measurement was simple. Simple brand name memorability, for example, may have been meaningful for marketers who hoped to guide consumers to shelves as uncluttered as the airwaves. Competition, not merely for shelf space and immediate sales, but for the more far-reaching objective of the mind and heart of the consumer, has intensified, and overly simplistic memory measures will no longer suffice.

Problems of reliability, resulting in part from shifting program and commercial contexts and varying audience composition, represent only part of the reason to pursue other routes to understanding of advertising performance. The overwhelming need today is to assess each advertising effort on the basis of the objective(s) set for it, rather than on a rigid test measure that assumes all advertising objectives are identical. The more carefully developed objectives often address the emotions and motivation. They are often focused on important communication values such as rapport and empathy with the target consumer on a long-term basis, rather than on stimulation of short-term memory of a claim.

Values instilled by powerful advertising may be viewed in terms of reward—that is, a psychological incentive offered to the viewer for attending to the message. Reward may take the form of a new product or new use information; it may offer entertainment—humor, fantasy, charming characters—or it may simply demonstrate in tone and manner a respect for the consumer as an intelligent human being. Reward frequently and importantly is visible in the dimension of empathy—the capacity for advertiser participation in consumers' feelings, needs, and ideas—a dynamic process in which the personalities of the advertiser, product, and consumer converge and focus on a similar objective. This valuable, supercharged rapport is often achieved with partially nonverbal stimuli, after repeated exposure. Its value to the uniqueness of the brand can be immense and can lead to a growing long-term consumer franchise.

The potential for more accurate assessment of advertising lies in two major directions: augmentation (or replacement) of current methods with practical instruments based on reward theory, and a marriage of high-tech instrumentation with "high-touch" understanding.

The first is already in place in some advertising agencies and is constantly being updated, customized, and improved. The Viewer Reward Profile, for example, utilizes open-ended questioning to help determine the integrity of the commercial structure and flow, the integration of product into the storyline, and perceptions of favorability (or unfavorability) to both product and commercial. Structured questioning—Likert scales—is administered to gauge the degree to which the key rewards are communicated. Immense value has already been derived from the procedure, in terms of assessment and improvement of alternative executions.

High tech may or may not revolutionize advertising assessment, depending on the ability of the technology to facilitate understanding of motivations and reactions.

The Trace system from Market Facts, Inc., measures reaction to commercials with individual, scaled keypads operated continuously as the commercial is shown. The derived response graph is later shown to the audience, superimposed on videotape over the commercial. Verbal reactions are subsequently obtained. The value seems to be not in the technology per se, but in the ability to obtain spontaneous, preverbal response as well as considered, verbal reactions.

Potential for assessment of print advertising and packaging may come from organizations such as the Pretesting Company, which studies line of gaze with a new miniaturized eye camera, freeing the respondent from the unnatural and intimidating "head vice" previously required in eye tracking research.

Changing media patterns will require other innovative research methods. Shorter lengths (5 to 15 seconds) will be all but invisible to single exposure recall and attitude questioning; and appropriate, often customized techniques will be needed. Longer lengths, such as seven- to ten-minute "infomercials," combining interesting usage information with a sales message, will be studied by methods aligned with their specific objectives, not by an all-purpose memory test.

To meet the challenge of understanding and strengthening commercial communication, research methods must be as dynamic and objective-oriented as the advertising itself. Only then will the messages we convey provide maximum reward for both viewer and advertiser.

feelings. This test evaluates the interaction of media weight and message strategy on a *post hoc* (after the fact) basis.

This technique is experimental in the sense that different people are asked about different commercials, but it is quasi-experimental in that it is done without experimental controls. The method provides a check of learning after an extended period of time (most tests only consider one or two exposures, while BRC may test after the message has been on the air for several months), but this feature negates any attempt to evaluate a commercial for a Go–No Go decision.

Because this test is done by mail, and all exposures are achieved through normal channels, the cost is quite low. As with other methods, BRC has extensive norms against which to compare scores.

Econometric or *regression analysis* is also a possible tool for evaluating the impact of advertising. Typically, the dependent variable of sales would be evaluated as a function of a number of advertising and marketing variables. This is certainly not a copy testing procedure, but rather would be used to assess the impact of advertising over time and across markets.

As can be seen, the experimental methods tend to focus on individual messages before they enter the media schedule. The purpose of these methods is to provide diagnostic and or Go–No Go decision data. The survey, quasi-experimental and econometric methods tend to be post-hoc analysis procedures that have great value for the following campaign but little value in making diagnostic or Go–No Go decisions.

Focus groups

One other common technique that is neither experimental nor survey is the *focus group interview*. This method can provide rich supplemental qualitative data to enhance quantitative data, but it can be misleading if used improperly.

A focus group consists of six to ten consumers from the target market, plus a moderator who controls the discussion, asks questions, and keeps the group on task. Its purpose is to generate in-depth discussion at a level that could not be obtained in a standard interview. The ideas should be used to generate hypotheses that then can be tested in large-sample quantitative research, or the in-depth discussion should be used to generate thoughts about why some percentage of a large sample responded in a certain way. Focus groups can be useful to copywriters in terms of generating a long list of product-related ideas to consider.

Because focus groups are often misused, it is important to consider some of their inherent problems.

1. *The data derived from a group are not quantitative.*   At best, the sample size of a group is the number of people in the group. Since groups are so small, this means the sample size is six to ten and not large enough to make generalizable statements about a target market. More realistically, a group should be considered to have a sample size of one, because the thoughts of its members are not independent. Because the members talk to and listen to each other, they influence each other's ideas. This is especially true if there is a dominant personality in the group.

2. *Consumers are experts on consumer products but not on advertising.*   The value of a focus group for advertising is in the ideas generated about the product that will be advertised. Consumers can generate interesting ideas and unique perspectives about a product, and these can then be evaluated for incorporation into

the message. To have consumers sit around a table and analyze advertising is less useful. Advertising can be evaluated more effectively using the methods discussed earlier and then will be quantitatively sound as well. Consumers should be asked to act as consumer product experts, not as advertising experts.

3. *Focus groups have the appearance of reality.*   Since managers can watch the focus group (with real, live consumers), there is a tendency to come away with the feeling that what one lady from Trenton, New Jersey, said represents the thoughts of 20 million homemakers. It is also easier to believe Ms. Trenton than it is to pore over pages of computer printouts.

Summary

It should be clear that research plays a vital role at several stages of advertising development.

First, there is the situation analysis, with its prestrategy research to serve as input to guide the ensuing process. This research tries to define the marketing and advertising problems in terms of the target market, stage of the hierarchy, and importance and perceptions of attributes and benefits. Given limited research dollars, this research gives the best return on dollars spent because it gives the most global guidance.

This work leads to objectives, positioning, and strategy. No matter how good the research, there is a leap at this stage when the situation analysis data are converted to advertising. This leap should be tested to see if the advertising really communicates the benefits and position properly and if the correct image is transmitted. The developmental pretest serves this purpose and provides early feedback before too great an expenditure has been made on production. Research at this stage provides the second-best return on investment.

The next opportunity to do research occurs after production and before the ad is widely distributed in print or broadcast media. The final pretest provides a last check on the work and is an insurance policy against an unwise expenditure of several million dollars in the media plan. This test should be unnecessary if the developmental pretest was done, but it is often done anyway. Given its low cost (several thousand dollars) compared to the media plan, it is a good investment.

Finally, there should be post-testing done after the campaign has been underway for a while. This allows a check to see if objectives are being met and also serves as input to the next situation analysis and campaign. Research is a valuable aid at all stages to show

- What needs to be done to create the best messages
- Whether the new measures meet the objectives

Remember also that there is no ideal measure in reality; rather, there are many tradeoffs to be made between

- time
- cost
- internal validity
- external validity
- a natural setting

And any research that is being considered should be evaluated with respect to

- research objectives
- advertising objectives

- time and budget constraints
- scope of the campaign
- desired response(s)
- target market
- conditions of exposure and measurement

After considering these issues, the most appropriate advertising assessment can be done. Proper evaluation can aid management in selecting the most useful messages for any set of objectives.

Discussion Questions

1. Explain the differences between research used to provide input to creative strategy and that used to evaluate creative strategy.

2. How would you evaluate the job search advertising campaign you have developed for yourself? You have only one shot at your target market, so you need to know that your campaign will attract attention and will be understood correctly.

3. What are the purposes of developmental pretesting, final pretesting, and post-testing? Design a test for each stage for print and for broadcast advertising. What criteria are most important at each stage?

4. What are field experiments and laboratory experiments? What are the pros and cons of each?

5. What is a dependent variable? An independent variable?

6. Consider the nine principles of good copy testing. Why is each of these issues important?

7. Describe a test that would measure learning from a television commercial. From a print ad.

8. Describe a test that would measure persuasion of an audience.

9. Describe a test that would relate behavior to the quality or quantity of advertising that was seen.

10. What are some physiological measures that are currently being used? What does each measure? What problems exist in their use?

11. Describe a focus group. What are its proper uses? What are some of its drawbacks?

Notes

1. Shepard Kurnit, "The Impact of Creative Research on Creativity," speech given at the Advertising Research Foundation's 25th Annual Conference, October 22, 1979.

2. Kurnit, "The Impact of Creative Research on Creativity."

3. Kurnit, "The Impact of Creative Research on Creativity."

4. Kurnit, "The Impact of Creative Research on Creativity."

5. Kurnit, "The Impact of Creative Research on Creativity."

6. Kurnit, "The Impact of Creative Research on Creativity."

7. Kurnit, "The Impact of Creative Research on Creativity."

8. Kurnit, "The Impact of Creative Research on Creativity."

9. Kurnit, "The Impact of Creative Research on Creativity."

10. Kurnit, "The Impact of Creative Research on Creativity."

11. Kurnit, "The Impact of Creative Research on Creativity."

12. Kurnit, "The Impact of Creative Research on Creativity."

13. Kurnit, "The Impact of Creative Research on Creativity."

14. Jack Honomichl, "A 'Rough' Look at Tests of TV Commercials," *Advertising Age,* 14 April 1980, p. 32.

15. Clark Leavitt, "Creative Guidance Research," paper for Leo Burnett Company Inc., File Copy #37.

16. Leavitt, "Creative Guidance," pp. 4–5.

17. "BRC Direct Response Tests of TV Commercials," Technical Memo, Bruzzone Research Company.

18. Valerie Free, "Copy Testing Techniques," *Scan* 27, no. 7, p. 14.

19. Surendra N. Singh and Michael L. Rothschild, "Recognition as a Measure of Learning from Television Commercials," *Journal of Marketing Research* 20 (August 1983), pp. 235–248.

20. Hubert A. Zielske, "Does Day-After Recall Penalize 'Feeling' Ads?" *Journal of Advertising Research* 22 (February/March 1982), pp. 19–22.

21. John R. Andrews, "If Recall's Not the Answer, What's the Question?" Slide presentation given at the Advertising Research Foundation's 26th Annual Conference, March 17–19, 1980.

22. Shirley Young, "Creative Void in Copy Testing," *Scan* 29, no. 2, pp. 8–10.

23. Jack Honomichl, "A 'Rough' Look at Tests of TV Commercials," p. 32; and "TV Copy Testing Flap: What To Do About It," *Advertising Age,* 19 January 1981, p. 59.

24. Joel Baumwoll, Untitled speech for the J. Walter Thompson Company, 1979.

25. "Positioning Advertising Copy Testing (PACT) Report," The PACT Agencies, January 1982.

26. Gilbert A. Churchill, Jr., *Marketing Research,* 3rd ed. (Hinsdale, Ill.: The Dryden Press, 1983).

27. Honomichl, "A 'Rough' Look at Tests of TV Commercials," p. 32.

28. John L. Carefoot, "Scanner-Based Copy-Testing Methodology Links Purchase Behavior to Ad Exposure," *Marketing News,* 17 September 1982, sec. 1, p. 11.

29. Michael L. Rothschild, Ester Thorson, Judith E. Hirsch, Robert Goldstein, and Byron B. Reeves, "EEG Activity and the Processing of Television Commercials," *Communication Research,* April 1986.

30. Herbert E. Krugman, "Sustained Viewing of Television," Paper presented at the Conference Board, Council on Marketing Research, New York, 1980.

31. Peter Gwynne and Charles Panati, "Eye Opener," *Newsweek,* 6 June 1977, p. 74.

32. "Determining How Ads are Seen," *Dun's Business Month* 119 (February 1982), pp. 85–86.

33. Mary Jane Hewett, "Sweaty Palms Test Ad Effectiveness," *Magazine Age,* October 1980, p. 79.

MESSAGE STRATEGY

Advertising That Established Positioning

The company had found in the research that the strength of the Sunkist name by itself conveyed the best product attributes. Therefore, there was an opportunity in the advertising to attack the negative perceptions of the orange soft drink drinker and to build an image for the product as a legitimate major brand. Since the image of the drinker was so important in the soft drink brand decision, the company had to redefine the image of the orange drinker in very positive terms—in Sunkist terms.

Based on this premise, Sunkist developed the brand's copy strategy: *To clearly establish Sunkist orange soda as a legitimate major brand by forcefully using the positive imagery of the name to define the drinker of Sunkist orange soda.*

With the positioning, target definition, and copy strategy set, 600 theme lines, 10 musical arrangements, and over 100 complete campaign concepts were developed. From this, seven campaigns were selected for testing.

In order to isolate the strongest campaign, two testing objectives were set. The first was to determine the ability of the commercial to create brand awareness by measuring its recall/memorability. The second was to access the ability of the commercial to generate trial by measuring persuasion. Two testing services were used. Advertising Research Systems was used for recall/memorability. To measure persuasion, Sunkist used RECAP, which was essentially an in-store, simulated purchase situation.

The testing results were quite positive. The campaign's indexed scores on recall were from 158 to 282 versus a normative index of 100 for all soft drinks. In terms of persuasion, the indexed scores ranged from 271 to 357 versus the index of 100 for a control cell in which trial of the product was measured without advertising.

One clear winner emerged. It was a campaign called "Good Vibrations," which incorporated the melody of the Beach Boys' famous song. This campaign was superior on both recall and persuasion, set a new all-time record for the soft drink category on recall of 61%, and generated 350% more trial than the control cell. Overall, it scored the highest of the seven test campaigns on 10 of 12 measures.

In addition, focus groups indicated accurate playback of the Sunkist commercials. Viewers saw fun and sociable activity on the beach and idealized people drinking Sunkist; they heard the "Good Vibrations" music and accepted its meaning. Focus group members also felt that Sunkist would have a more acceptable orange flavor.

Radio spots were also developed at this time using the same theme. These were essentially the audio track of the television commercial extended to 60 seconds. As with the television, it was important to retain the true California/Beach Boys sound.

Building a Long-Term Equity

With those results in mind, Sunkist thoroughly analyzed all of the copy research and identified seven "building blocks." These were core elements that were determined to contribute to the success of the advertising in testing.

Identifying those elements that were working was important because Sunkist wanted a durable campaign that could be the basis for developing a long-term equity for its name and product. The company was only going to be new in the soft drink business once, and it wanted the right campaign that it could live with for a long time. The building blocks identified were

- beach
- sunshine
- summertime
- idealized youthful people

288

- thirst-generating activity
- unique taste description
- "Good Vibrations" music

These tied closely to what was learned about Sunkist in the early research. The building blocks were used in developing all companion commercials and are represented in all advertising developed for the brand since its inception. Figure S.1 is a photoboard of a commercial used during the introductory period. Figures S.2 (1980) and S.3 (1983) show the continuity of the campaign over the ensuing years.

Figure S.1 *"Scooter"* :30

ANNCR: A new soft drink has come to town

with a taste from Sunkist·

that'll turn you around.

SINGERS: I'm drinking up

good vibrations.

Sunkist·orange taste sensations.

Good good good good vibrations.

Bubbly orange jubilation.

Sunkist·is a taste sensation.

I'm giving out orange vibrations.

Bubbly Sunkist·sensations.

Sunkist·is giving out GOOD VIBRATIONS.

Figure S.2   *"Surf Tube"* :30

(SFX: GUITAR VAMP BUILDS)

(MUSICAL EFFECT)...

...

(MUSIC BUILDS)

(MUSICAL EFFECT)

SINGERS: I'm drinkin' up good vibrations...

...Sunkist® Orange Soda...

...taste sensations.

Good, Good, Good, Good...

...Vibrations. Bubbly orange jubilations. Good...

...Good, Good...

...Good Vibrations.

Figure S.3 *"Windsurfing" :30*

MUSIC: (GOOD VIBRATIONS) Good Good Good

Good Vibrations

Sun and surfing excitation

call for Sunkist®

good vibrations.

Bubbly orange jubilation

Sunkist® Orange Soda

taste sensation

Sunkist® is givin' out good vibrations.

Bubbly Orange

jubilation

Sunkist® is givin' out good vibrations.

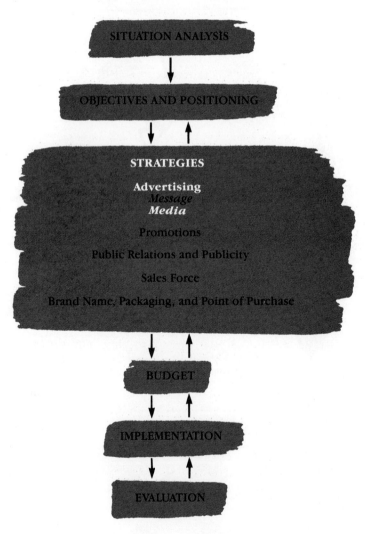

Decision Sequence Framework

Part Five
Media
Strategies

*H*aving completed the situation analysis, objective setting, and positioning, the manager is now in the midst of developing strategy. The major strategic areas of media, message, promotions, public relations, sales force, packaging, brand name, and point-of-purchase decisions are developed simultaneously in different departments of the advertising agency under the coordinating guidance of the account executive and account supervisor. Given the sequential nature of a book such as this, however, these topics are discussed one at a time; message strategy has been considered, and the other strategic topics will follow the media discussion. The figure on the opposite page shows where media strategy fits into the decision sequence framework.

Media planning has changed greatly in the past decade. While the basic decisions remain the same, the tools have become much more sophisticated. The media department, as with much of advertising, has become a fascinating combination of art and science requiring creativity of the same magnitude as that found in message development. While science helps in the evaluation of target markets, vehicles, and learning curves, art is still key in the evaluation of the editorial climate of, and placement within, a vehicle.

Many people say that media analysis and planning are rote and boring. That would seem to be a shallow view of an extremely complex area that has too many unanswered questions at this time. In either case, most students who plan to work in the managerial end of an advertising agency (account executive) will probably start in the media department as a trainee. Given this dominance of entry-level media positions, this section of the text should be relevant to the reader.

The duties of the media department can be divided into three main areas:

1. *Plan* The planning function consists of developing advertising schedules, known as media plans, that will allow the advertising to meet the objectives set earlier.

2. *Buy*   After the schedule has been approved, the vehicles in the plan must be contacted and time or space purchased. Price and other terms are often agreed upon through lengthy negotiating.

3. *Monitor*   The vehicles must be monitored to ensure that purchased space and time are actually received. Print vehicles supply tearsheets to demonstrate execution; broadcast vehicles supply copies of the station log.

This text is primarily concerned with planning; the planning function has become quite complex for there are, in the United States, some 240 million people who receive messages through 18,000 media vehicles concerning 450,000 brand names and services that flow through 1.9 million retail establishments. The yearly cost in advertising dollars is estimated at $40 billion.[1] The amount of data available to analyze all this is quite large, and the number of possible combinations of plans is greater than any media planner could consider. The science of media is making sense of the data; the art is in the decision making that cannot solely rely on quantitative data but must also have a qualitative element. This part of the book considers the art and science of media planning.

The purpose of the media is to deliver the message. While message strategy deals with what to say and how to say it most effectively, the media plan must ensure that the appropriate target market receives the message, that the message is received often enough so that learning takes place, and that the medium is most conducive to learning taking place.

This leads to a statement of goals for the media plan:

1. *To deliver the message to the consumer*   If the message is not seen or heard, it cannot have an impact. The proper vehicles must be used so that the target market is reached. Some consumers prefer magazines to television; some prefer *Playboy* to *Newsweek.* Part of the task is to find the best way to deliver the message.

2. *To maximize reach and/or frequency*   Reach is a measure of the breadth of coverage of the target market; frequency is concerned with the number of times that the message reaches the target market. Given a finite budget, the media planner needs to decide on the appropriateness of trying for reach versus frequency. As the firm tries to reach a larger target, its costs will increase and there will be fewer dollars available to repeat the message. Conversely, if there is a need to repeat the message often (perhaps owing to a low-involvement target market), fewer people can be reached. Nevertheless, the goal is to maximize reach and frequency; if both cannot be maximized, it will be necessary to choose a compromise goal from the two.

3. *To minimize cost*   Media decisions can lead to high expenditures. Within advertising, the media area is where the bulk of the dollars is spent. While management wants to maximize reach and frequency, costs must be contained. This

will temper earlier goals so that the firm does not overspend in achieving adequate amounts of reach or frequency.

4. *To be effective and efficient*   "Effectiveness" and "efficiency" are two common English words that have precise meanings for media planning. *Effectiveness* is concerned with the impact that the media plan has. Given the advertising objectives set earlier (e.g., to achieve 80% awareness among college students within three months), how well will the plan meet these objectives? Will the plan get the job done? *Efficiency* deals with the cost of the plan. The more efficient the plan, the lower its cost. It will become clear that a plan can be either effective or efficient without being both. A plan can meet its objective at a prohibitively high cost or it can be inexpensive but not meet its objective. A good media plan should be both effective and efficient.

To achieve these goals, three sets of decisions need to be made:

1. *The media to use*   The first decision to be made regarding the delivery of the message is media choice. Media is the plural of medium. The word *media* is also used to refer to the department in the agency and to the type of decisions it makes. The major advertising media are radio, television, newspapers, magazines, outdoor, and direct mail.

McLuhan has said that the medium is the *message;* he later said that the medium is the *massage.*[2] This latter thought is key, for, indeed, each medium massages the recipient in different ways and in its own way, therefore, contributes to learning.

For example, Krugman[3] has hypothesized that television washes over people with an endless stream of messages which, in time, lead to passive learning, while magazines need active participation on the part of the recipient. These and many other issues are described in an evaluation of the media and their abilities to massage in different ways.

2. *The vehicle to use*   Vehicle selection is the second decision to be made in media planning. A *vehicle* is a particular offering within a medium. For example, a television vehicle would be a commercial during "Dallas"; a magazine vehicle would be a page in *Newsweek.* After deciding how best to massage the target, the manager must decide which vehicles will give the best match of readership/viewership/listenership with the target market profile. To maximize efficiency and minimize cost, the manager will want to obtain the optimum match so that the desired target is reached and so that those not in the target are not reached. Reaching unwanted persons is referred to as *wasted coverage* and lowers the efficiency of the plan.

3. *The schedule to use*   The third decision to be made relates to scheduling. Scheduling is concerned with the timing of the specific insertions within and across the specific vehicles. How often must the message be repeated before the

desired percentage of the target is aware? Once awareness has been established, how often must the message be repeated so that forgetting does not occur? How should the message be scheduled to take advantage of seasonality in the demand for the brand? How do reach and frequency grow if the message is repeated in one vehicle or if it is repeated across several vehicles?

To deal with these decisions, the manager must keep in mind the specifics of the objectives and position established earlier and the message and promotions strategies being developed simultaneously. If these other components are neglected, there is a high risk of developing an ineffective media plan.

Notes

1. Richard C. Anderson, "Is There a Place for Judgment Decisions in a Computer-Dominated Media World?" Speech to International Advertising Market Seminar, May 1978.

2. Herbert Marshall McLuhan and Quentin Fiore, *The Medium is the Massage* (New York: Bantam Books, 1967).

3. Herbert E. Krugman, "The Impact of Television Advertising: Learning without Involvement," *Public Opinion Quarterly* 29 (Fall 1965), pp. 349–356.

Chapter 10
Media Concepts, Terms, and Secondary Sources

Concepts, Terms, and Measures

*T*he media department has its own language which helps to develop precision in planning and buying. Media textbooks have glossaries of up to 30 pages of short definitions of the hundreds of special words and unique definitions of common words used in this area. In order to be able to work in, or with, the media department it is first necessary to be familiar with a set of media concepts, terms, and measures. In addition, a set of secondary sources and syndicated data services exists to provide specialized data to media analysts, and these sources also have a special language. Without a working knowledge of this language, it is difficult to discuss the major strategic issues of media planning. Without such knowledge it would also be difficult to follow the discussions in the three chapters that follow this one. This chapter is an introduction to the world of media planning and sets the base for the chapters that follow.

Reach and frequency

The most basic terms are *reach* and *frequency*. *Reach* is the percent of the defined target market that is exposed to the message at least once during the relevant time period. Although reach is defined as a percent, the decimal point is typically ignored in calculations and a reach of 80% is said to be an 80 reach.

To plan most effectively, reach should use the target market as a base. For example, a popular network television program may reach 20% of all households in the United States. It may, though, have a different reach for the product's target market, which happens to be households with income over $50,000 per year and who are known to be light viewers of this particular program. Finding specific target market reach is important but often difficult and sometimes impossible. Nevertheless, planning should always be based on the target market desired. Methods for estimating target market reach will be discussed next.

Reach has been achieved if the message gets to the approximate proximity of the audience member (e.g., the newspaper is delivered to the home; the car is driven past the billboard location; the television set is on and tuned to the right channel). Exposure must take place at least once during the time period for purposes of calculating reach. The time period generally used is four weeks; that is, when determining how many people were reached by all messages across all vehicles, a four-week period is used as a unit of measure.

Frequency is concerned with the average number of exposures received by a member of the target market during the relevant time period. Given a budget constraint, reach and frequency are generally inversely related. That is, if the size of the budget is fixed, the planner must sacrifice reach to get frequency, or vice versa. This is a difficult choice because the ideal plan has both sufficient reach and frequency. Campaign objectives will guide the media planner in determining whether to emphasize reach or frequency.

If the goal is to create a broad general level of awareness, then a reach strategy may be preferable; if management is trying to increase learning about a high-involvement product, then less repetition is needed (because people learn more rapidly when they are interested) and a reach-oriented strategy will be appropriate. On the other hand, if management is trying to induce trial purchase of a low-involvement product, then it will want a high level of repetition (because people's mindsets are more changeable when they are less interested in the issue or product) and a frequency-oriented strategy will be appropriate.

Reach and frequency are also inversely related within any vehicle over a time period. As the media planner buys multiple insertions in a vehicle, either reach or frequency will grow at the expense of the other. (This happens within certain limits. Eventually a limit is achieved for reach and then only frequency can increase.) For example, if an ad is put into four consecutive issues of a magazine that is sold primarily through subscriptions, it will primarily hit the same readers each time; reach will therefore not increase much over time, but frequency will increase. Conversely, if the magazine is sold primarily at newsstands, then different people will buy it on different weeks. The lower the readership loyalty factor, the greater the reach and the lower the frequency.

Another example of the reach and frequency relationship comes from television. If time is bought for several days on a daytime serial, the commercial will reach a small but loyal audience. This plan will achieve low reach but high frequency. If time is bought for several days of prime time movies (e.g., "Tuesday Night at the Movies," "Sunday Night at the Movies," etc.), the message will reach a less loyal audience that is attracted to a particular movie rather than an ongoing story. This constantly changing audience will allow the advertiser to build reach but probably not frequency.

A term closely related to reach is *rating.* Rating is a measure of the reach of a television program. The most common ratings are done by the A. C. Nielsen Company and are often used to evaluate the success of a network program. Because the production costs of a program are generally independent of its viewership (i.e., there is no variable cost), the marginal revenues acquired by the higher program ratings are all contribution to the network's or station's overhead and profit.

The rating measures the percent of all households owning a television set (essentially all households) that are watching a particular program. Assuming that there are 80 million households in the United States, a rating of 20 would indicate a viewership of approximately 16 million households. A one point shift in the ratings represents approximately 800,000 households. The amount that a station or network charges for commercial time is largely a function of the size of the audience that it commands.

A second key variable that determines price is the quality of the audience. Nielsen television ratings data can be broken down by various demographic groups as shown in Figure 10.1. Note that the ratings for a program are different for different demographic groups. Ratings are most useful to the media planner if they pertain to the desired target market. Ratings based on all households are not particularly useful if the target market is, for example, teens 12–17. Figure 10.1 clearly shows this discrepancy.

Another term used to indicate the size of a television audience is *share*. Share measures the percent of those television sets *in use* at any time that are tuned to a particular program. For example, assume that at 10 P.M. on a Tuesday evening half of the households in the United States are watching television and that, as in the rating example, 16 million households are viewing a particular program. The program's share is 40 (while its rating is 20) because the base is now 40 million sets in use. Table 10.1 shows the difference between rating and share.

The planner needs to be careful when using information about a program's viewership to differentiate between rating and share. As shown in Table 10.1, the two concepts give quite different values to represent the same viewership profile. The difference between those values increases as the number of television sets not in use increases. For example, the "Johnny Carson Show" usually receives a high share even though its rating is quite low.

Returning to reach and frequency, the planner must also consider *duplicated reach* and *unduplicated reach*. Reach and frequency were straightforward concepts when there was only one message insertion. As soon as more than one purchase is made, the planner needs to evaluate the overlap in reach across these purchases.

If the goal is to maximize reach, then unduplicated reach is desired; that is, each message insertion should reach different people. Figure 10.2 shows a diagram of unduplicated reach and the resultant reach and frequency levels. If the agency bought the late news on both Channel 7 and 9 in New York City, there would probably be pure unduplicated reach because few people will be able to watch both programs at the same time.

In Figure 10.2, 40% of the market (20% + 20%) is reached one time. One way to ensure virtually unduplicated reach is to buy the same time of day simultaneously on all three networks. This expensive strategy is called a *blockbuster* and allows a manager to build reach quickly. Such a strategy could only be justified

Table 10.1 Rating versus share information

	Number of Households (*millions*)	Rating	Share
Program A	16	20	40
B	20	25	50
C	4	5	10
Sets not in use	40	(50)	Not relevant
Total	80	100	100

Figure 10.1 *National Nielsen television demographic ratings data (based on estimates for two weeks ending 24 March 1985)*

HOUSEHOLDS

Rank	Program	% U.S.	No. (000)
1	Bill Cosby Show	27.1	23,010
2	Family Ties	23.5	19,950
3	Dynasty	23.4	19,870
4	Dallas	22.7	19,270
5	A Team	22.0	18,680
6	60 Minutes	21.8	18,510
7	Cheers	21.4	18,170
8	Murder, She Wrote	20.9	17,740
9	Newhart	20.5	17,400
10	Kate & Allie	20.4	17,320
11	Crazy Like A Fox	19.5	16,560
12	Hotel	19.3	16,390
13	People's Choice Awards	19.2	16,300
14	Riptide	19.1	16,220
15	Eye to Eye	18.1	15,370
16	Highway to Heaven	18.0	15,280
16	Night Court	18.0	15,280

WOMEN (18+)

Rank	Program	% U.S.	No. (000)
1	Bill Cosby Show	21.6	19,090
2	Dynasty	21.4	18,980
3	Dallas	20.0	17,750
4	Family Ties	19.3	17,100
5	Cheers	17.3	15,280
6	Murder, She Wrote	16.6	14,700
7	60 Minutes	16.4	14,530
8	A Team	16.2	14,340
8	People's Choice Awards	16.2	14,340
10	Newhart	16.1	14,230
11	Hotel	15.9	14,050
12	Crazy Like A Fox	15.6	13,780
13	Highway to Heaven	15.4	13,660
14	NBC Monday Night Movies	15.2	13,450
15	Falcon Crest	15.0	13,310
16	Kate & Allie	15.0	13,260

WOMEN 18–49

Rank	Program	% U.S.	No. (000)
1	Bill Cosby Show	21.4	11,920
2	Family Ties	20.2	11,280
3	Dynasty	19.5	10,850
4	Cheers	18.4	10,270
5	Dallas	16.2	9,060
6	A Team	15.7	8,730
7	Newhart	15.3	8,510
8	Riptide	15.1	8,450
9	NBC Sunday Night Movie	15.0	8,390
10	Night Court	15.0	8,380
11	Miami Vice	15.0	8,370
12	NBC Monday Night Movies	14.7	8,210
13	Snoopy Gets Married	14.2	7,920
14	ABC Sunday Night Movie	14.1	7,850
15	Kate & Allie	14.0	7,810
16	Hill Street Blues	13.5	7,550

MEN 18–49

Rank	Program	% U.S.	No. (000)
1	ABC Sunday Night Movie	15.7	8,500
2	A Team	15.2	8,200
3	CBS NCAA BSKBL CHMP-SPC-2	14.2	7,660
4	Bill Cosby Show	13.7	7,390
5	Riptide	13.3	7,180
6	Cheers	13.2	7,160
7	Lifes-Embarassing Moments	12.2	6,610
8	Family Ties	12.2	6,590
9	Night Court	12.1	6,540
9	60 Minutes	12.1	6,540
11	CBS NCAA BSKBL CHMP-SPC-1	12.1	6,520
12	Miami Vice	12.0	6,470
13	CBS NCAA BSKBL CHMP TH 1	11.3	6,110
14	Airwolf	11.2	6,060
15	It's Magic Charlie Brown	11.2	6,050
16	Garfield in the Rough	10.9	5,910
17	Hill Street Blues	10.7	5,800
18	Newhart	10.6	5,730
19	Kate & Allie	10.5	5,660
20	Wildside	10.2	5,510
21	Knight Rider	10.1	5,470

TOTAL PERSONS (2+)

Rank	Program	% U.S.	No. (000)
1	Bill Cosby Show	19.3	42,850
2	A Team	16.5	36,710
3	Family Ties	16.2	36,000
4	Dallas	14.3	31,870
5	Snoopy Gets Married	14.0	31,200
6	Dynasty	14.0	31,030
7	Cheers	13.9	31,000
8	60 Minutes	13.6	30,180
9	Knight Rider	13.5	30,110
10	Murder, She Wrote	13.4	29,780
11	Riptide	13.0	28,970
12	It's Magic Charlie Brown	12.7	28,300
13	Romance of Betty Boop	12.6	28,000
14	Highway to Heaven	12.5	27,720
15	Garfield in the Rough	12.3	27,360
16	Webster	12.0	26,730
17	Kate & Allie	12.0	26,710
18	Newhart	11.9	26,460
19	Crazy Like A Fox	11.9	26,420
19	Facts of Life	11.9	26,420

MEN (18+)

Rank	Program	% U.S.	No. (000)
1	60 Minutes	16.6	13,250
2	A Team	16.2	12,940
3	ABC Sunday Night Movie	14.7	11,700
4	Bill Cosby Show	14.1	11,260
5	Murder, She Wrote	13.3	10,640
6	Riptide	13.2	10,520
7	CBS NCAA BSKBL CHMP-SPC-2	12.8	10,250
8	Cheers	12.7	10,110
9	Dynasty	12.4	9,920
10	Dallas	12.3	9,850
11	Family Ties	12.3	9,800
12	Lifes-Embarassing Moments	12.0	9,600
13	Crazy Like A Fox	11.9	9,470
14	CBS NCAA BSKBL CHMP TH 1	11.7	9,360
15	People's Choice Awards	11.3	8,990
16	Wildside	11.2	8,970
17	Newhart	11.2	8,950
18	Airwolf	11.2	8,930
19	Night Court	11.0	8,790

WOMEN 55+

Rank	Program	% U.S.	No. (000)
1	Dallas	28.1	7,650
2	60 Minutes	26.8	7,290
3	Murder, She Wrote	26.5	7,230
4	Dynasty	25.5	6,950
5	Crazy Like A Fox	23.9	6,520
6	Falcon Crest	22.7	6,180
7	Hotel	22.3	6,070
8	People's Choice Awards	22.2	6,050
9	Bill Cosby Show	21.7	5,900
10	Highway to Heaven	21.6	5,880
11	Trapper John, M.D.	20.4	5,550
12	Newhart	18.4	5,000
13	T. J. Hooker	17.7	4,830
14	Magnum, P.I.	17.5	4,770
15	A Team	17.4	4,750
16	Family Ties	17.3	4,720
16	Kate & Allie	17.3	4,720

MEN 55+

Rank	Program	% U.S.	No. (000)
1	60 Minutes	27.7	5,720
2	Murder, She Wrote	22.6	4,680
3	A Team	20.3	4,190
4	Dallas	20.0	4,130
5	Crazy Like A Fox	19.8	4,090
6	Dynasty	17.7	3,650
7	T. J. Hooker	16.7	3,450
8	Highway to Heaven	16.6	3,440
9	20/20	16.3	3,360
10	Bill Cosby Show	16.1	3,330
11	CBS Evening News–Rather	16.0	3,300
12	Hotel	15.7	3,250
13	Trapper John, M.D.	15.2	3,140
14	Detective in the House	15.0	3,110
14	Hardcastle & McCormick	15.0	3,110

Source: A. C. Nielsen.

Figure 10.2 *Unduplicated reach*

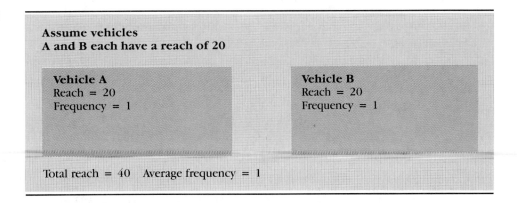

for a new product introduction or where timely information needed to be disseminated quickly to large numbers of people. This strategy is often used by political candidates shortly before an election to ensure high reach along with other frequency strategies.

More commonly, as expenditures increase, there will be more duplicated reach. As duplication is acquired, frequency grows; every time a consumer receives another exposure to the message, the frequency increases. Figure 10.3 shows a diagram with duplicated reach and the resultant reach and frequency levels. In Figure 10.3 the total reach is the sum of the three components (15 + 15 + 5). Average frequency is the weighted sum of the three components divided by the reach.

$$\frac{(15 \times 1) + (15 \times 1) + (5 \times 2)}{35}$$

Generally as multiple purchases are made, duplication will occur. A buy in the May and June issues of *Ladies' Home Journal* will lead to high duplication (and high frequency); a buy in the May *Ladies' Home Journal* and the June *Better Homes and Garden* will yield less duplication; buying space in the May *Ladies' Home Journal* and the June *Hustler* will probably yield little duplication. To learn the approximate levels of duplication across pairs of vehicles or over time

Figure 10.3 *Duplicated reach*

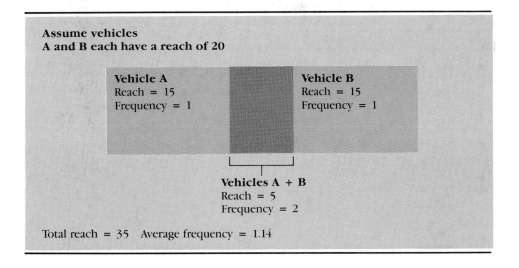

within a vehicle, the Simmons Market Research Bureau or Mediamark Research data are useful.

Returning to frequency, note that it is reported as *average frequency*. The average, as pointed out in introductory statistics, can be a misleading value. A common example relates the case of a six-foot-tall person drowning in a lake that has an *average* depth of two feet. Of course the person fell into the part of the lake that was ten feet deep.

A similar problem occurs when dealing with average frequency. The objective of the media plan may be to get an 80 reach with a frequency of 3 within a four-week period. This calls for an average frequency of 3, and the plan that is developed shows such an average. A detailed examination of the plan shows the following frequency distribution across the target market. Of those who are reached

> 60% are reached one time
> 20% are reached two times
> 20% are reached ten times

While the average frequency is 3, only 20% are reached more than two times. The media plan meets its objective in theory but in reality is unable to do its task. The plan is inefficient for 20% of the market because these people receive more messages than necessary; the plan is ineffective for 80% of the market because these people have not received enough messages for learning to take place.

The above plan had three exposures as its goal in order to introduce another concept. *Effective reach* is a term based on the concept that in order for learning to occur in a low-involvement setting, multiple exposures are necessary. Over time the advertising industry has adopted three exposures in a time period as the minimum needed for learning, and, therefore, advertisers feel that a frequency of 3 is needed for effective reach. This concept helps to explain why many advertising campaigns have a high level of reach but a low level of recall. These campaigns have reach without sufficient frequency and therefore do not have effective reach. As will be seen, one of the most difficult media planning questions concerns the amount of frequency necessary for learning to take place.

In the tradeoffs between building reach and frequency, it is important not to overextend the reach. As reach is built up, there must be sufficient frequency to ensure that learning will occur. Reach without adequate frequency is a waste of money. More on this issue later.

When reach and frequency are combined, the result is the *gross rating point* (*GRP*).

> GRP = reach × frequency

The GRP is a measure of gross media weight for a target market in a geographic area in a time period. The GRP is usually the first number considered in evaluating the media plan.

"Tell me about the media plan."

"We'll get you 300 GRPs per month."

What does 300 GRPs represent? It could be

> 300 exposures to 1% of the target market
> or 3 exposures to 100% of the target market
> or 6 exposures to 50% of the target market

To evaluate the worth of the GRP bundle, the manager also needs to know the reach and frequency levels as well as whether the GRPs are directed toward the general population or the target market. Finally, the objective of the plan must also be considered in order to assess the appropriateness of the GRP level. [To deal with specific targets, a new term that is emerging is *target rating point* (*TRP*). This term will not be used in this text, but remember that GRPs will always relate to the target market.]

To calculate GRPs the earlier formula is made more formal.

$$GRP = \sum_{i=1}^{n} (reach_i \times frequency_i)$$

where *i* are the vehicles, and *n* is the number of vehicles.

Therefore the total GRPs in a plan is the sum of the GRPs for each vehicle, or the reach times the frequency for each vehicle. For example

	Reach	*Frequency*	*GRPs*
Program A	10	6	60
Magazine B	30	4	120
		Total GRPs =	180

Figure 10.4 is useful for approximating the relationship between reach, frequency, and GRPs within television dayparts (time of day), radio, and magazines.

Figure 10.4 *Relation of reach, frequency, and GRPs*

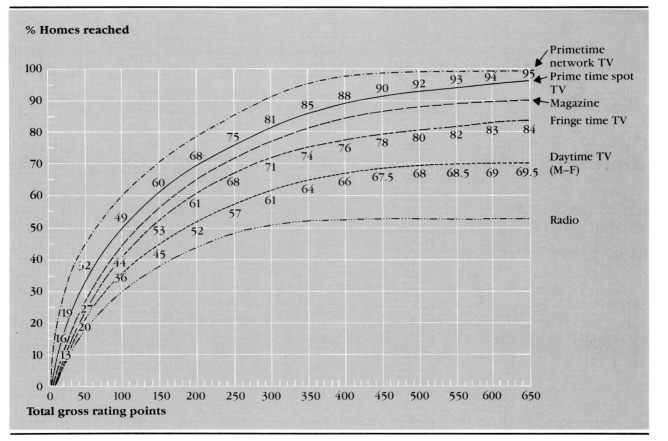

For example, if a plan called for the purchase of 200 GRPs of prime-time network television, it would build approximately a 78 reach and therefore a 2.6 average frequency. A 200-GRPs buy on daytime television would yield a 52 reach with a 3.8 frequency. Knowing how reach and frequency build up is important in estimating the weights needed to meet various learning goals.

Having estimated media weights within a single medium, it may next be necessary to combine weights across media. Figure 10.5 can help with this task. In the previous example, 200 GRPs of prime-time and 200 GRPs of daytime television were bought; these yielded reaches of 78 and 52, respectively. Going to Figure 10.5, the planner can see that the combined reach is approximately 85 (85 is at the intersection of row 78 and column 52); therefore, average frequency for the combined 400 GRPs must be 4.7 (400/85 = 4.7). Although neither Figure 10.4 nor 10.5 is exact, each gives a good approximation for planning purposes.

The next media concept to be discussed is *cost per thousand,* commonly referred to as *CPM.* (The M comes from the roman numeral for thousand.) CPM has traditionally been used for broadcast media although it holds equally well for print. Its purpose is to give added meaning to the cost of an insertion by normalizing for the reach of the vehicle; its formula is

$$CPM = \frac{\text{cost of message}}{\text{number of homes reached } or \text{ circulation}} \times 1000$$

This allows a more precise (but still inexact) comparison between vehicle costs. For example, vehicle A costs $100,000 per insertion and reaches 20 million homes and vehicle B costs $60,000 and reaches 7.5 million homes. Which is the

Figure 10.5 Accumulated reach levels across media

All Media Combinations (Homes and Individuals)																	
REACH	5	10	15	20	25	30	35	40	45	50	55	60	65	70	75	80	85	90
5	10	14	19	24	28	33	38	43	47	52	57	62	66	71	76	81	85	90
10	14	19	23	27	32	36	40	45	50	54	59	63	68	72	77	81	86	91
15	19	23	27	31	35	39	43	48	52	56	61	65	69	73	78	82	86	91
20	24	27	31	35	38	42	46	50	55	59	63	67	71	75	79	83	87	91
25	28	32	35	38	41	44	48	53	57	61	64	68	72	76	79	83	87	92
30	33	36	39	42	44	47	51	55	59	63	66	70	73	77	80	84	88	92
35	38	40	43	46	48	51	53	58	62	65	68	71	75	78	81	84	88	92
40	43	45	48	50	53	55	58	60	64	67	70	73	76	79	82	85	88	92
45	47	50	52	55	57	59	62	64	66	69	72	75	77	80	83	86	89	93
50	52	54	56	59	61	63	65	67	69	71	74	76	79	81	84	86	89	93
55	57	59	61	63	64	66	68	70	72	74	76	78	80	82	85	87	90	93
60	62	63	65	67	68	70	71	73	75	76	78	80	82	84	86	88	90	94
65	66	68	69	71	72	73	75	76	77	79	80	82	83	85	86	88	91	94
70	71	72	73	75	76	77	78	79	80	81	82	84	85	86	87	89	91	94
75	76	77	78	79	79	80	81	82	83	84	85	86	86	87	88	89	91	95
80	81	81	82	83	83	84	84	85	86	86	87	88	88	89	89	90	92	95
85	85	86	86	87	87	88	88	88	89	89	90	90	91	91	91	92	92	95
90	90	91	91	91	92	92	92	92	93	93	93	94	94	94	95	95	95	95
95	95	95	96	96	96	96	96	96	97	97	97	97	97	97	98	98	98	98

Figure 10.6 Calculation of cost per thousand (CPM)

$$CPM = \frac{\text{cost of message}}{\text{number of homes reached}} \times 1000$$

$$CPM \text{ vehicle A} = \frac{\$100,000}{20 \text{ million}} \times 1000 = \$5.00$$

$$CPM \text{ vehicle B} = \frac{\$60,000}{7.5 \text{ million}} \times 1000 = \$8.00$$

better buy? Clearly B is cheaper but A reaches many more homes. Figure 10.6 shows the CPM calculations for each.

Vehicle A is more efficient because it costs $5.00 per thousand people reached (or $1/2$ ¢ per person) while B costs $8.00 per thousand. As before, many other factors must be considered before the manager can be certain that A is the better buy, but clearly it is cheaper than B per person reached.

When computing CPM, it is important to compute for the target market whenever possible. Table 10.2 shows that different vehicles reach different demographic segments and therefore have different cost efficiencies that need to be considered in the media plan. For example, "Happy Days" delivers a broad undifferentiated audience more cheaply than does "All in the Family"; if the planner wants to reach older people (men and/or women), then "All in the Family" is cheaper; "Happy Days" delivers younger people more cheaply. Note that the absolute cost of the spot does not change; the delivered audience changes in size and this, in turn, changes the CPM.

Another concept similar to CPM is *cost per rating point* (CPRP). This is computed as

$$CPRP = \frac{\text{cost of spot}}{\text{rating of show}}$$

Cost per rating point is used to evaluate television costs and is employed less frequently than CPM.

A recently developed concept is *CPM of retained impressions.*[1] While it is too early to judge whether the industry will accept this concept, the logic behind it is certainly appropriate. Basic CPM is important; advertisers care about cost efficiencies, and measuring cost in terms of reach is useful. Advertisers also care about learning and recall; these are a function of message as well as media. A

Table 10.2 CPM differences by demographic groups

	"All in the Family"	"Happy Days"
All households	$ 2.61	$ 1.74
Women 18–49	5.01	2.85
Women 50+	6.58	10.21
Men 18–49	7.17	3.67
Men 50+	10.45	15.59

Source: Foote, Cone & Belding Media Guide, 1976.

Table 10.3 Cost efficiency of selected television campaigns—second quarter 1982

	Average weekly retained impressions (millions)	Average weekly television expenditure (000)	Cost per 1000 retained impressions
Soft drinks			
Coca-Cola	84.2	$ 923	$10.96
Pepsi	82.4	1363	16.54
Dr Pepper	36.6	442	12.08
7-Up	48.5	515	10.62
Mountain Dew	16.6	277	16.69
Tab	18.6	344	18.49
Shasta	10.1	116	11.49

Source: From Steve Raddock, "The Nielsen of T.V. Efficiency?" *Marketing and Media Decisions,* November 1982, p. 70.

good message enhances learning, and a high-repetition media plan also enhances learning. CPM of retained impressions combines these and considers the cost to get 1,000 people to remember seeing the message, or the cost to make an impression that lasts. It combines the weight of the media plan with the quality of the message strategy. Table 10.3 shows some assessments that compare dollars spent and the CPM of retained impressions in the soft drink product class. These data show that 7-Up had the best combination of efficiency and effectiveness in the second quarter of 1982 while Tab was least memorable per dollar spent. Coca-Cola had the greatest total impact in the market even though it was outspent by Pepsi.

Another new measure is *media imperatives.* While this measure is only about ten years old, it has been widely accepted and has shown itself to be a useful and important concept. The media imperatives concept was developed in 1975 by the Magazine Publishers Association as a defensive reaction against the increasing dominance of television. While television was being sold to advertisers as the best medium because of its ability to command huge audiences, magazine publishers were attempting to point out that this quantity of viewers was lacking in quality.

Media imperatives allows planners to compare the users of different pairs of media based on demographics, psychographics (life style), or amount of, and brand of, product usage. For example, while on the average people spend more time watching television than reading magazines, there are key segments for whom the reverse is true. If planners know how segments interact with the major media, they can do a better job of selecting the appropriate medium to reach this segment.

The media imperatives process seeks information from consumers concerning the number of hours per week they spend with a particular medium and then ranks all consumers in terms of heaviness of viewership, listenership, and so on. Next these rankings are divided into quintiles (top 20%, next 20%, and so on) and given labels that describe media habits for a pair of media. Figure 10.7 shows this labeling for users of television and magazines. "Magazine imperatives" are generally in the heavy user quintiles for magazines and the light user quintiles for television; these people spend considerable time reading magazines (compared to

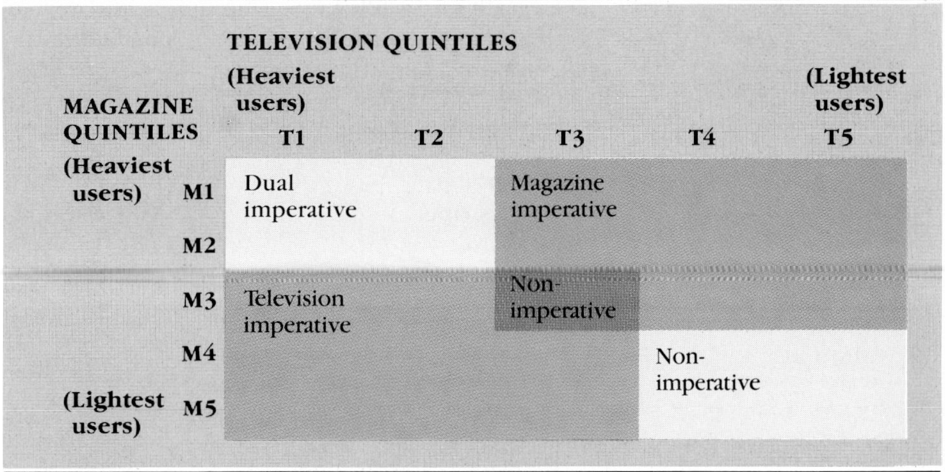

Figure 10.7 Media imperatives for television and magazine

the general population) and little time watching television (compared to the general population).

Data concerning adult women in the United States show that

30% are magazine imperatives
38% are television imperatives
16% are dual imperatives
16% are nonimperatives

The 30% who are magazine imperatives account for 52% of all magazine reading but only 15% of all television viewing; the 38% who are television imperatives account for 56% of all television viewing but only 16% of all magazine reading. Clearly, these groups are different in their media habits.

These women also differ in demographics as can be seen in Table 10.4. This table shows the magazine imperatives group of adult women to be upscale demo-

Table 10.4 Demographics and product usage characteristics of adult women by media imperatives (magazine versus television)

	Imperatives			
	Dual	*Magazine*	*Television*	*Neither*
Total U.S. Women	17.3%	30.8%	39.3%	12.0%
Index	100	100	100	100
18–49 Years	17.8%	36.6%	34.4%	11.2%
Index	103	119	88	89
Attended/graduated				
college	23.9%	46.8%	22.2%	7.1%
Index	139	152	56	57
$15,000 & over	21.5%	43.0%	26.1%	9.4%
Index	125	139	66	75
Employed	17.6%	42.1%	29.1%	11.2%
Index	102	137	74	69

Source: Reprinted with permission from *Magazine Newsletter of Research*, no. 18, published by the Magazine Publishers Association.

graphically; to reach this group, magazines would do a better job. Other demographic groups of adult women and product users might be more skewed toward television or some other medium.

Simmons Market Research Bureau shows media imperatives data for all pairs of the following media:

Magazines	Radio	Outdoor
Newspaper	Television	

Figure 10.8 *Purchases of sporting goods by users of magazines and television*

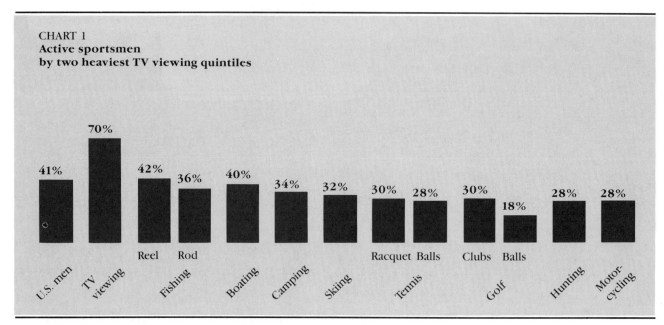

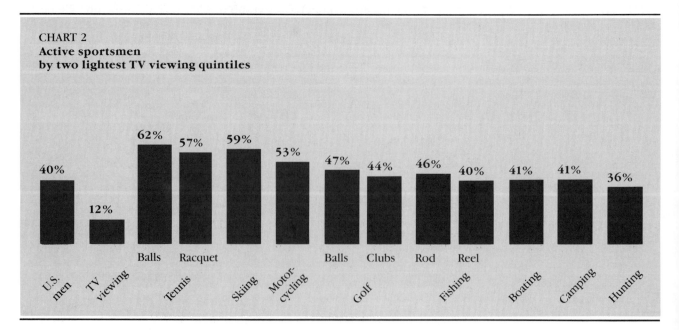

Figure 10.8 clearly shows differences in the purchase of sporting goods equipment by adult men who are in the heaviest and lightest quintiles of television viewing and magazine reading. The heavy readers (37% of men do 12% of all television viewing and 71% of all magazine reading) seem to be disproportionately heavy users of most types of sporting equipment. It would be difficult to reach them through television (although some specific shows may consistently draw these men). Although users of these products will be best reached by magazines, heavy users of other products may be best reached by television. One

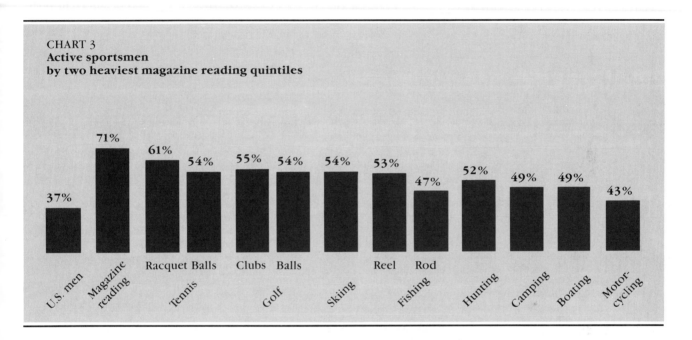

CHART 3
Active sportsmen
by two heaviest magazine reading quintiles

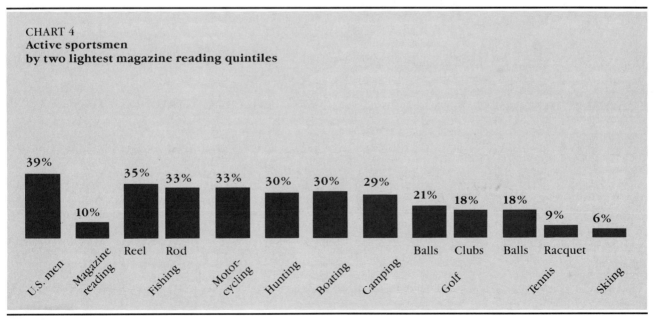

CHART 4
Active sportsmen
by two lightest magazine reading quintiles

medium will not be best for all products or all people, but a media imperatives analysis should help the planner see which media are best for a given situation.

Secondary Sources of Media Information

In order to deal with the vast sea of data available to decision makers, the planner must first learn where to get the data. The next few pages present short descriptions of some of the major services available and the types of data they provide. The purpose of this discussion is not to evaluate the quality of the method; marketplace acceptance of these services will serve as an indication of sufficient quality. Table 10.5 is a summary of the major sources for general marketing media information plus that for each of the four major media.

Table 10.5 Major secondary data sources for media analysis

	Marketing/media	
	Simmons Market Research Bureau	*Mediamark Research*
Market data	750 product categories, 3,000 brands, product frequency/volume of use	800+ product categories, 4,000 brands, product and brand frequency/volume of use data
Media covered	TV, cable TV supplements, radio, magazines, newspapers, outdoor, Yellow Pages	• Network TV, cable, pay TV, subscription TV, radio, magazine, newspaper supplements, comics, outdoor, Yellow Pages • Local markets—10 major ADI(s), DMA(s)
Methodology Sample size-derivation	15,000 adults (one per household)	20,000 adults (one per household)
Interviewing technique	Product usage questionnaire hand delivered	Booklet questionnaire hand delivered
Quality control	• Inhouse sample selection and data processing • Fulltime field region managers	Computer logic editing procedures, field supervision
Data supplied Demographic	All major demographics, media exposure, brand usage, media imperatives, psychographics	All major demographics, brand usage, psychographics
Geographic	Four U.S. regions, 11 Nielson regions, ADI(s), DMA(s), SMSA(s)	Four U.S. regions, 10 ADI(s), national average, SMSA(s)
Format Frequency	Annual report	Twice a year—12-month moving average
Reported on	Hard copy, computer tape for on-line access, special computer tabs, database	Hard copy, tape, database, special runs
Subscriber universe	About 600: Magazines, newspapers, advertisers, advertising agencies, radio, cable services, TV, outdoor, Yellow Pages	About 285: Advertisers, advertising agencies, broadcasters, buying services, magazines
Terms of sale	Annual subscription	One + year subscription

Table 10.5 continued

	Marketing/media	
	Simmons Market Research Bureau	*Mediamark Research*
Special features	• PRIZM, Donnelley's geo-demographic clusters, SRI life style segmentation (VALS) • Echo Omnibus recontact survey • Two-year database	• Business-to-business purchase decision making data • Magazine reader action measurement • PRIZM, VALS available in 1983 • Ability to recontact respondents for custom interview

	Television	
	Network TV *Nielsen Television Index (NTI)*	*Local/national TV combination* *Nielsen Home Video Index*
Media covered	• National network TV • Three national commercial networks, PBS and WTBS "superstation" • Special orders on ad hoc networks put together by syndicators/distributors	Nonbroadcast video: Cable programing, cable originated programing, videotex, teletex, VCR, VDP, interactive services, games/computers
Audience definition	Households tuned to TV by program and individual viewing	Household and individual audience
Methodology Sample size-derivation	• Participants randomly selected from all U.S. housing units—personal contact • 1,250 households with TV meter • 2,400 households with diaries (one per set)	• Participants randomly selected by possession of phone • Sample size varies by market • 20,000+ households in each sweep for cable • Customized format
Quality control	Data checked by editors and/or computers	Data checked by editors and/or computers
Data supplied Time breaks	Average per minute TV households and persons by program	• Average quarter hour household and individual audience • Average per minute household audience
Demographics	All standard demographics	Standard age and sex breaks with combinations
Geographic breaks	Five Nielsen regions	National or custom
Cumulative	• Schedule or program up to four weeks • Other ratings on request	Day part cumulative household or individual audiences up to four weeks
Frequency	• 24 primary reports covering two-week intervals through year • Plus supplemental reports for recaps and detailed demographics	• Four times yearly national pay cable report • Monthly-household audience • Quarterly individual audience—national reports for HBO, CNN, CBN and ESPN
Reported on	Hard copy, tape, on-line database and special tabulations	Hard copy, tape and special runs
Subscriber universe	About 300 clients—advertising agencies, networks, advertisers, TV stations, station representatives, producers/distributors and talent agencies	100+ pay and nonpay cable program services, cable systems, advertising agencies and advertisers

Table 10.5 *continued*

	Television	
	Network TV *Nielsen Television Index (NTI)*	*Local/national TV combination* *Nielsen Home Video Index*
Terms of sale	Custom supplier contract or one + year subscription	Custom contract
Special features	Additional demographics (e.g. pet and late car model ownership)	Custom research on viewer satisfaction indexes and product usage information

	Local TV	
	Nielsen Station Index (NSI)	*Arbitron Co.*
Media covered	All local TV markets (220+) in 50 states	210 local TV markets
Audience definition	Household and individual audience per station/program	Household and individual audience per station/program
Methodology Sample size-derivation	• Participants randomly selected by possession of phone • Sample size varies by market • Each national sweep—75,000 to 100,000—in tab households	• Participants randomly selected by possession of phone • 200 to 2,300 diaries per market • 350 to 500 households metered per market
Interviewing technique	• Viewing data collected via diaries—one per TV • Meters used in top six markets to measure household usage	• One household diary per set for individual viewing • Meter in four major markets to measure household usage
Quality control	Spot checks by editors and/or computers	Manual and computer edit on selected basis
Data supplied Time breaks	Average quarter-hour household and individual viewing for individual stations	• Four-week household totals and program averages, average quarter hour household and audience dayparts totals • Share trend, daily and weekly
Demographics	Standard age and sex breaks with combinations	Standard age and break with combinations, working women
Geographics	• Household audience for metro areas and 205 DMA(s) • Individual audience for DMA, also DMA plus surrounding areas, all U.S.	• Metro, home county, 210 ADI(s), total survey areas • Custom via database
Cumulative	Household cumulative audience reported by daypart—weekly and four-week	Household cumulative audience reported by daypart—weekly and four-week
Format Frequency	• Each market measured four to seven times per year depending on size • Primary and supplementary detailed reports • In metered markets, daily and weekly reports optional	• At least four sweeps yearly • Weekly meter in New York, Los Angeles, Chicago, San Francisco • In metered markets, daily and weekly household reports are available

Table 10.5 *continued*

	Local TV	
	Nielsen Station Index (NSI)	*Arbitron Co.*
Reported on	Hard copy, tape, special runs available, database	Hard copy, tapes, database, special runs
Subscriber universe	2,000+ clients—TV stations, advertising agencies, advertisers, station representatives, producers/syndicators	3,350—advertisers, agencies, TV stations
Terms of sale	Single reports or subscription	One + year subscription, also single reports
Special features, services	• Usage trends, cable penetration, Nielsen plus • Cable penetration • Special area data (e.g. Zips, county-by-county) (Nielsen Plus)	• PRIZM • Direct access to database (AID) • County-by-county report • Network cable report

	Radio	
	Network *RADAR (Statistical Research)*	*Local* *Arbitron Co.*
Media covered	All radio on a national basis including 11 wired networks	256 local radio markets
Audience definition	All persons 12+ years in continental U.S. households	All persons 12+ years in survey area, SMSA and total survey area
Methodology Sample size—derivation	Random digit dial sample of 6,000 combined with 1 million station clearance records	• Participants randomly selected by possession of phone • Sample varies by market between 250 and 13,000
Interview technique	• By telephone • Recall of radio listening—daily calling for a week	• One diary per person • By mail
Quality control	• Monitoring of selected calls • Daily checking of call letter with respondent	Manual and computer edit on selected basis
Data supplied Time breaks	• Dayparts or quarter hours • Average quarter hour, five day weekly, weekend, full week	• Average quarter hour persons/shares/ratings • Time spent listening—special report • Selected dayparts, day combinations
Demographics	Most standard demographics	Age and sex categories with combinations
Geographic breaks	Four U.S. region, 80 ADI(s) market groups	Metro survey area, total survey area, top 50 ADI(s)
Other breaks	• Am/fm, location of listening, TV usage • Network audience to all commercials • Network audience to commercials within programs	• Am/fm home vs. not at home • Average share trends

Table 10.5 *continued*

	Radio	
	Network *RADAR (Statistical Research)*	*Local* *Arbitron Co.*
Cumulative	One-day, five-day weekly, seven-days	• Cumulative listening within selected dayparts • Exclusive cumulatives
Format Frequency	Two measurements and reports per year	One to four times per year
Reported on	Hard copy, on-line access to database, special tabs	Hard copy, database, tape, special runs
Subscriber universe	ABC, CBS, MBS, NBC, RKO, SBN, and NBN, about 35 advertisers and agencies	5,300—radio stations, advertisers, agencies
Terms of sale	Annual contract	One + year contract
Special features	• Multiweek cumulative estimates • Reach and frequency build-up analysis	• PRIZM • Qualidata—for top 10 markets—qualitative product information cross referenced to listening • Coverage—county-by-county radio • Direct access to database (AID) • Special network radio report

	Magazines		
	Simmons Market Research Bureau	*Mediamark Research*	*Mendelsohn Media Research*
Media covered	103 consumer magazines	190 consumer magazines	77 consumer magazines
Audience definition	Total adult (18+) average issue	• Total adult, average issue • Primary and secondary audience	• Average issue, total • U.S. adults with household income greater than $40,000
Methodology Sample size-derivation	• 19,000 individuals • National probability sample from census maps and prelistings. 1,269 interviewing clusters—each in a different census tract or MCD	• 20,000 respondents from national probability sample originating from telephone directories and car registrations • 2,400 interviewing clusters—each in a different census tract or MCD	Sample of 15,000 chosen from Donnelley Marketing computer file plus census and demographic data
Interviewing technique	• "Through the book" issue —specific technique • Conforms to Four A's criteria for syndicated magazine audience research	190 title cards sorted by recent reading	Questionnaire—repeated mailings

Table 10.5 continued

	Magazines		
	Simmons Market Research Bureau	*Mediamark Research*	*Mendelsohn Media Research*
Quality control	• Validation by mail/ telephone of 60% of interviews • Inhouse sample selection and data processing	• Logic editing by computer • Chilton Research does field work and validates 20+% by phone	
Data supplied Demographic	All major demographics plus others	All major demographics plus others	All major demographics plus others
Geographic breaks	Four census regions, 11 Nielsen regions, ADI(s), DMA(s), SMSA(s)	Four U.S. census regions, SMSA(s), 10 top ADI(s)	Eight top ADI(s), Four U.S. census regions, Zip codes
Other	• In same report other major media covered —TV, radio, newspapers, supplements, outdoor, Yellow Pages • Magazine reading days, place of reading, media imperatives, quintiles	In same report other media covered—TV, pay TV, subscription TV, radio, newspapers, supplements, comics, outdoor, Yellow Pages • Where read, reader exposure, reader action, days read, pages opened, reading time	Other media covered in same report, some TV, radio and newspaper
Cumulative	Twelve issues cumulative with tape, any number	Up to 12 issues, more with tape	
Format Frequency	Annual report	• All data annually • Total audience and product usage summary and update semiannually	Yearly report
Reported on	Hard copy, computer tape for on-line access, special computer tabs, database	Hard copy, tape, database, special runs	Hard copy, tape, special tabulations, database
Subscriber universe	600: Magazines, newspapers, advertising agencies, radio, advertisers, cable services, television, outdoor, Yellow Pages	About 285: Advertising agencies, magazines, advertisers, broadcasters and buying services	70: Publications, advertisers and advertising agencies
Terms of sale	Annual subscription	One + year contracts; advertisers may buy book by book	Annual report purchase
Special features	• Available for analysis on PRIZM + Donnelley's • Geo-demographic clusters • SRI life style segmentation (VALS) • Echo Omnibus recontact surveys • Two year database on-line	• Business to business data • Geo-demographic data available via PRIZM • Can recontact respondents for customized interview • VALS	• Assorted publication qualitative data • Geo-demographic data available via PRIZM • Cable TV data

Table 10.5 *continued*

	Newspapers	
	Simmons Market Research Bureau	*Scarborough Research*
Media covered	Daily and Sunday newspapers—79 markets available	Daily and Sunday newspapers—top 100 markets available
Audience definition	Average adult reader "yesterday" and "last Sunday" reader	Total adult (18+) reader
Methodology Sample size-derivation	• Random digit dial • 58,000 individuals	• Random digit dial • 60,000+ sample
Interviewing technique	Telephone	Telephone
Quality control	ARF audit and concurrent monitoring	• 100% field validation of all respondents • Complete computer editing and consistency checks
Data supplied Demographic	All major demographics	All major demographics including recent revisions
Geographic	50 SMSA(s), 39 ADI(s)	Top 50 ADI(s) and top 50 SMSA(s) within those ADI(s)
Other	• Newspaper sectional readership • Cable tv ownership	• Daily—average issue, any daily • Sunday—average issue, any Sunday
Cumulative	• Five issues for dailies (for week) • Four issues for weekends (for month) • With tape, any number	• Daily—two issues, five issues • Sunday—two issues, five issues • Via database, any number
Format Frequency	Annual report (each market is on a two-year cycle)	Annual report (each market on a one-year cycle)
Reported on	Hard copy, computer tape for on-line access, special computer tabs	Hard copy, tape, on-line database, special runs
Subscriber universe	About 140 newspapers and ad agencies	• 160+ newspapers • All agencies may use study
Terms of sale	Biannual subscription	By subscription
Special features	• Data available for geo-demographic clusters • Newspaper Echo Omnibus surveys • Integrated product usage data from SMRB's study of media & markets	• Product data questions from actual respondents • PRIZM and ACORN segmentation analysis • Also offers syndicated local multimedia/market report

Source: *Advertising Age*, 8 November 1982, pp. M10–M11, M16. Reprinted by permission. Copyright 1982 by Crain Communications, Inc.

Simmons Market Research Bureau (SMRB) was described in Chapter 4. In addition to the product usage data described at that time, there are also media and vehicle data. Brand and usage level data are cross-tabulated by several demographic variables, media imperatives, and major vehicles. Media and vehicle information also includes accumulation and duplication data to show the build-up of reach and frequency for multiple insertions in the same vehicle or different vehicles over time. Chapter 4 contains a portion of a sample page and an explanation of how to read the data. Similar types of data are provided by *Mediamark Research, Inc. (MRI)*.

Standard Rate and Data Service (SRDS) provides rate and other information for buying space or time in virtually any vehicle in the United States. The eight-volume set is updated every other month and includes the following volumes:

Network Television
Spot Television
Network and Spot Radio
Consumer Publications
Business and Farm Publications
Direct Mail
Newspaper
Outdoor and Transit

Rate information is quite detailed. For example, for print it shows how rates change with size of the ad, location of the ad in the magazine or newspaper, color usage, number of insertions, and other variables. Network television rate information is not printed but must be obtained directly from the network; often local television rate information is also not shown. Nonrate information includes, for example, for print media the editorial philosophy, circulation, and contact persons of specific vehicles. Many of these issues are discussed in more detail in the next chapter. Geographic information (state, county, city) is also provided concerning populations and aggregate economic data. Figure 10.9 on page 320 shows a sample SRDS page.

Broadcast Advertising Report (BAR) provides competitive spending information for network television. For all brands on network television, BAR shows the programs used, day of week, daypart, number of commercials bought, amount of time bought, and amount spent. This information is useful in analyzing competitive media plans.

BARCUME provides the same information as BAR but does so for local television.

Publishers Information Bureau (PIB) provides BAR-type data for magazines.

Leading National Advertisers (LNA) provides ad spending information for over 30,000 major brands of consumer products in the United States. These data are shown by parent company and major media. The media included are

Network television
Spot television
Network radio
Consumer magazines
Newspaper supplements
Outdoor

LNA information is not as detailed as BAR; rather, it gives summary data for each medium.

Sy Goldis

Senior Vice-President and Director of Media Services, Doyle Dane Bernbach

Sy Goldis is Senior Vice-President–Director of Media Services for Doyle Dane Bernbach. He is responsible for media research, spot buying, estimating, international media, and data/word processing groups, as well as the integration of the personal computer into the Media Department. He has initiated and developed various automated systems to aid in the planning and placement process.

During his 21 years with DDB, Mr. Goldis has been involved with the media planning for every one of the agency's clients, which today include Clairol, GTE, IBM, Joseph E. Seagrams, Mobil Oil, and Volkswagen, to name a few.

Students to Lead Automation Revolution on Madison Avenue

For the advertising student who plans on becoming a media buyer or planner I offer this advice: Learn the rudiments of the personal computer. After that, if you've demonstrated a mastery of your course work and interned in an advertising agency media department, I can safely say that your chances of finding a job will far exceed those of students who did not choose to enhance their educational processes by learning to use the computer and having the foresight to see its future necessity in a broad range of business applications.

I can make this statement because the functioning of the media department is undergoing a change—a change brought about by automation. It will come slowly, but it's happening and nothing can stop it. The emerging media department will require the skills of students well versed in the principles of media planning with an understanding of how to apply the computer to them.

You see, until just recently, the advertising industry has continued to prepare media plans and do the buying in the same time-consuming, inefficient way as it has done for a great many years. However, a new newspaper planning/buying system has been developed with the help of several newspaper representative firms that prom-

ises to revolutionize the media function. I do not use the term revolutionize loosely. Traditionally, the preparation of the media list has been a tedious, grueling process involving eye-straining number crunching, using thick, heavy books crammed with big numbers in small print. These numbers require constant analysis, checking and rechecking, and considerable mathematics.

But the truth is, practically every mathematical application can be handled by existing software programs. So, in the preplanning stage, information and cost per point/space unit files, for example, are available. In addition, different plans with their individual media costs, audience delivery/efficiencies, and qualitative adjustment factors are incorporated. This is true not only for newspapers but for all media.

Such variables as reach, frequency, frequency distribution, product usage, psychographics, demographics, and a host of other qualitative factors can also be worked into the process.

The average media department is now overrun with paper, books, directories, and other vital sources of information that make shelf space a premium and room to move much desired. By bringing automation to the department, this problem can be dramatically eliminated.

Moreover, electronic filing eliminates the possibility of people reinventing the proverbial wheel—which happens all too often in our business when several people work on the same project or something similar in nature. They all need the same information, but no one knows that anyone else has it. So you wind up with four or five people all researching and compiling this information, giving it to their secretaries to type, then proofing it—when all they had to do was access the computer to see if such data had been prepared. As time progresses and more data are stored, chances are that the desired information will be available.

But what good is having a lot of data at our disposal if we don't have the time to make qualitative judgments in assessing the information? After all, this is what our clients pay us to do. Some data require more analysis than do others. Often we need the time to find solutions to questions that don't have hard data to support them. We can make the time available by using the computer technology that exists today.

For example, in its initial field trial, Doyle Dane Bernbach's automated newspaper planning/buying system reduced the time spent preparing the media list and circulation and cost data for 38 markets from 35 to 3 hours. By lightening the time-consuming, labor-intensive burden of buying newspapers, we will create time for media buyers to consider the qualitative characteristics of particular audiences and local marketing conditions.

This is where an understanding of marketing principles is a must. Now that the time spent in preparation has been eliminated by using the computer and related automation, the time saved can be spent creatively in evaluating media choices and strategizing buys. It's a fallacy to think that creativity is confined to an agency's creative department.

I might also add that automating the media department will help the media salespeople and representatives whose job traditionally has been to sell ad space or air time. It frees them up to serve agencies and their clients better by providing viewership and readership data and qualitative information about their magazines, newspa-pers, and television/radio stations and how best to use them.

You as the student embarking on your first job in advertising are ahead of the game if you understand how the computer fits into the media planning/buying process. I do not exaggerate when I say that you who will emerge from college in the next few years will be in a position to help lead the industry into an era of greater efficiency and creativity through the media department. In effect, the media department will become the nerve center for the dissemination of information throughout the agency, and it will be responsible for eliminating the redundant preparation of data in many departments. The functions you perform will have an impact on the account group, broadcast and print traffic, and accounting, because much of the data you generate will be directly applicable to these departments. For example, the amount of time devoted to the preparation of buying authorization documents, with the constant revising, retyping, and proofreading they require as they pass from department to department, will be virtually eliminated. Revisions will be made quickly and easily by means of data and word processing technology, leaving everyone more time to attend to the qualitative aspects of their work.

The agency that does not automate will find itself lacking sufficient time to provide well-thought-out marketing solutions and, thus, will fall behind in its ability to provide maximum service to its clients. Those agencies that have begun the process—one that should take up to two years to effect—will be eager to have your skills.

The advertising student in media today is fortunate in being in the right situation at the right time. For those of you who are able to combine the knowledge acquired in your advertising and marketing courses with solid computer skills and, more importantly, have the ability to apply these skills to day-to-day problem solving, the advertising field offers a great deal of opportunity. For, as automation takes on a bigger role in advertising, fewer positions will remain. Those of you who are reading these words and are prepared to act on them will be the ones to benefit.

320 PART FIVE / MEDIA STRATEGIES

Figure 10.9 *Sample page of SRDS data*

BOAT & MOTOR DEALER'S MARKET MANUAL

BPA

Published annually as 13th edition of Boat & Motor Dealer by Van Zevern Publications, Inc., 340 LINden AVE., Wilmette, IL 60091. Phone 312-251-8301

NOTE: For basic information on the following numbered listing segments 1, 2, 3, 15, see Boat & Motor Dealer listing in this classification.

PUBLISHER'S EDITORIAL PROFILE

BOAT & MOTOR DEALER'S MARKET MANUAL is a reference guide for the marine industry. Editorially it contains the year end statistics on the industry; survey reports on special projects; manufacturer, distributor, association industry address listings for the pleasure boat marine industry. Rec'd 1/5/81.

4. GENERAL RATE POLICY

The regular rates of B&MD apply. Advertising orders are accepted subject to the terms and provisions of the current rate card. Rates and conditions are subject to change without notice. Advertisers in Boat & Motor Dealers' Market Manual are entitled to the frequency rate earned for advertising in B&MD. Market Manual insertions do not count as part of the B&MD schedule except for bulk pages.

ADVERTISING RATES
Effective August 12, 1981. (Card No. 13.)
Card received June 16, 1981.

5. BLACK/WHITE RATES

	1 ti	3 ti	6 ti	12 ti
1 page	1695.	1485.	1375.	1295.
2/3 page	1400.	1110.	1045.	980.
1/2 page	1095.	990.	915.	880.
1/3 page	810.	685.	675.	615.
1/4 page	675.	635.	575.	505.
1/6 page	545.	495.	475.	445.
1/8 page	495.	435.	405.	375.

BULK RATES
Page units only.

24 times	1275.	48 times	1255.
36 times	1265.	80 times	1250.

6. COLOR RATES

2-color standard AAAA colors, per page, extra	250.
Matched colors, per page, extra	300.
Metallic inks, per page, extra	350.
4-color, per page, extra	600.

7. COVERS

	1 ti	3 ti	6 ti	12 ti
2nd and 3rd cover	2545.	2335.	2225.	2120.
4th cover	2595.	2385.	2275.	2175.

8. INSERTS

Complete inserts ready for binding with no back-up required.

4 pages, or less, earned rate, less	15%
6-8 pages, earned rate, less	20%
12 pages, earned rate, less	25%
More than 12 pages, earned rate, less	30%
Standard mechanical and handling charge on all inserts (non-commissionable)	200.
Backup charge, per single page	200.
Per spread insert	225.

9. BLEED

No charge.

10. SPECIAL POSITION

Non-cancellable.
10% of earned black and white rate.

11. CLASSIFIED AND READING NOTICES

BUSINESS OPPORTUNITIES
Per word, per issue (minimum 20.00 net) .... .75
Box numbers 3.50
Closing date is the first of the month of publication.
DISPLAY CLASSIFIED
Per column inch .... 50.

16. ISSUE AND CLOSING DATES

Published annually; issued December.
Closing date November 1.

17. SPECIAL SERVICES

MCC Media Data Form registered 7/14/77
Instant Sales Cards .... 400.

18. CIRCULATION

Established 1969. Single copy 10.00.

B.P.A. 1980 Edition

Total	Non-Pd	Paid
23,627	23,627	...

BOAT & MOTOR DEALER'S SHOW SHOPPER

Published annually by Boat & Motor Dealer, 340 Linden Ave., Wilmette, IL 60091. Phone 312-251-8301

NOTE: For basic information on the following numbered listing segments 2, 3, see Boat & Motor Dealer listing in this classification.

1. PERSONNEL

Publisher—G. Van Zevern.

ADVERTISING RATES
Effec ve August 12, 1981. (Card No. 13.)
Card received June 16, 1981.

5. BLACK/WHITE RATES

	*1 ti	+3 ti	‡4 ti
1 page	1135.	775.	555.
2/3 page	795.	740.	500.
1/2 page	635.	555.	435.
1/3 page	555.	445.	380.
1/4 page	475.	415.	315.

(*) Show Shopper issue only
(+) Show Shopper issue plus Sept. issue and Market Manual issue.
(‡) Show Shopper issue plus Market Manual and Sept. and Oct. issues.

6. COLOR RATES

Single AAAA color, each page	250.
4-color process	500.

8. INSERTS

Available.

9. BLEED

Space and color, extra 15%
No charge for 4-color bleed.

15. MECH REQUIREMENTS

For complete, detailed production information, see SRDS Print Media Production Data.
(Offset)
Binding method: Saddle stitched.

DIMENSIONS-AD PAGE

1	7 x 10	1/3	2-1/8 x 10
2/3	4-1/2 x 10	1/3	4-7/8 x 4-1/3
1/2	3-1/4 x 10	1/4	3-1/4 x 4-7/8
1/2	4-1/2 x 7-1/2	1/4	2-1/4 x 7

16. ISSUE AND CLOSING DATES

Published annually; tied in with the model year Trade Shows, September.
Ads close August 20.

18. CIRCULATION

SWORN September 1981 Convention
Non-paid controlled circulation (daily average) 22,000.

Boating Industry

(incorporating Marine Business)
A Whitney Communications Publication

BPA ABP

Media Code 7 070 1200 1.00 **Mid 002205-000**

Published monthly (except semimonthly in December) by Boating Industry, Inc., a subsidiary of Whitney Communications Corporation, 850 Third Ave., New York, NY 10022. Phone 212-593-2100

For shipping info., see Print Media Production Data.

PUBLISHER'S EDITORIAL PROFILE

BOATING INDUSTRY is edited for the pleasure boating trade. Its editorial concept is designed to provide ideas, suggestions and methods for operating more effectively and profitably. This encompasses information on product trends, selling, merchandising, display, safety, service, repair, legislation, etc. The magazine also provides news of people, products, events and business trends throughout the industry. Rec'd 4/7/77.

1. PERSONNEL

Editor/Publisher—Charles Jones.
Advertising Director/Assoc. Pub.—Hugh Evans.
Adv. Services Mgr.—Carol A. Fleming.
Production Manager—Denise Renfro.

2. REPRESENTATIVES and/or BRANCH OFFICES

New York 10022—Hugh Evans, 850 Third Ave. Phone 212-593-2100.
Braintree (Boston) Mass. 02184—George J. Dob Mehl, 22 River St. Phone 617-848-0660; 749-1987.
Naperville (Chicago), Ill. 60540—Larry Brockman, 441 Aspen Court. Phone 312-420-8410.
Pasadena 91101—Jack Clemens, Dick Railton, Clemens Co., 465 E. Union St. Phones 213-681-8706; 213-792-7064.
Melrose, Fla. 32666—Walt Henderson, P. O. Box 369. Phone 904-475-1588.

3. COMMISSION AND CASH DISCOUNT

15% of gross allowed to recognized advertising agencies on space, color, bleed and position. No commission allowed on cost of art work, engravings, printing, back-up of inserts, or tip-in charges when necessary. No cash discount.

4. GENERAL RATE POLICY

All advertising orders are accepted subject to the terms and provisions of the current rate card. Orders are accepted subject to change in rates on notice from the publisher. However, orders may be cancelled at the time the change in rates becomes effective without incurring a short rate adjustment provided the rate has been earned up to the date of cancellation. Rate holders not accepted.

ADVERTISING RATES
Effective August 1, 1981.
Rates received April 20, 1981.

5. BLACK/WHITE RATES

	1 ti	3 ti	7 ti	13 ti
1 page	2800.	2630.	2415.	2205.
2/3 page	2220.	2130.	2035.	1915.
*1/2 page	1795.	1705.	1570.	1430.
1/3 page	1405.	1340.	1285.	1170.
1/4 page	990.	930.	860.	765.

(*) Island half page, extra 10%.

BULK RATES

13 pages	2020.	36 pages	1915.
24 pages	1965.	48 pages	1860.

6. COLOR RATES

Standard AAAA 2-color, red, blue, green, yellow, per page or fraction	225.
Matched color, per page or fraction	250.
3-color, per page or fraction	575.
4-color, per page or fraction	675.
5th color	200.
Metallic silver	375.

7. COVERS

	1 ti	3 ti	7 ti	13 ti
2nd and 3rd covers	4300.	4050.	3785.	3570.
4th cover	4985.	4720.	4405.	4120.

8. INSERTS

Furnished inserts:

	Per card		Per card
2 pages	2155.	12 pages	14490.
4 pages	3370.	16 pages	19320.
6 pages	8695.	24 pages	23180.
8 pages	11605.	32 pages	30910.

Back-up charges non-commissionable.
1 page or fraction .... 175. 2 pages or fraction .... 225.

9. BLEED

Add 15% to space and color.
No charge for bleed on 4-color and gutter bleed on spreads.

10. SPECIAL POSITION

Yearly contract only available.

13. SPECIAL ISSUE RATES AND DATA

OEM PURCHASER
For boat builders, suppliers and distributors.
Published 6 times a year as part of regular February, March, May, June, August and November issues.
Black/White Rates:

	1 ti	3 ti	6 ti
1 page	1075.	910.	795.
2/3 page	830.	730.	625.
*1/2 page	665.	570.	470.
1/3 page	540.	460.	390.
1/4 page	370.	340.	285.
Spread	1815.	1575.	1455.
Cards	245.	205.	195.

(*) Island half, extra 10%.
Color:
Standard color, per page .... 200.
4-color—not accepted.
Furnished inserts earn 10% discount.
Bleed:
No charge.
Closing date: 25th of 2nd preceding month of publication.
MARINE BUYERS' GUIDE
SHOWTIME SHOWCASE
See separate listings which follow.

13a. GEOGRAPHIC and/or DEMOGRAPHIC EDITIONS

Regional advertising rates based on total insertions run in any 12-month period. Ads for any one or more regions restricted to full page units only. Regional ads not accepted in Marine Buyers' Guide.

Run of book advertising:	1 ti	6 ti	12 ti
Eastern	785.	725.	660.
Southern	810.	750.	680.
Western	480.	450.	410.

Half page 60% of regional full page rate.
Color:
2nd color .... 200. Matched color .... 225.
4-color—Not accepted.
Inserts:
Up to 4 pages, deduct 20% from earned rate.
Over 4 pages available.
Back-up charge .... 75.
Bleed:
Per page, extra .... 35.
No charge for 4-color bleed or gutter bleed on spreads.

14. CONTRACT AND COPY REGULATIONS

See Contents page for location—items 1 through 18.

15. MECH REQUIREMENTS

For complete, detailed production information, see SRDS Print Media Production Data.
(Web offset)
COVERS: SHEET FED OFFSET
Trim size: 8-1/8 x 10-7/8.
Binding method: Perfect.
Colors available: 4-Color Process (AAAA/MPA): Metallic: AAAA red: 3-Color.

DIMENSIONS-AD PAGE

1	7 x 10	1/2	4-1/2 x 7-1/2
2/3	7 x 6-5/8	1/3	4-1/2 x 4-7/8
...	4-1/2 x 10	...	2-1/8 x 10
1/2	3-5/16 x 10	1/4	7 x 2-3/8
...	7 x 4-7/8	...	3-5/16 x 4-7/8

16. ISSUE AND CLOSING DATES

Published monthly; issued on 1st day of issue date.
Closing date 1st of preceding month of publication.

18. CIRCULATION

Established 1929.
Summary data—for detail see Publisher's Statement.

B.P.A. 6-30-81 (6 mos. aver. qualified)

Total	Non-Pd	Paid
23,668	21,796	1,872

Average Non-Qualified (not included above):
Total 5,311

TERRITORIAL DISTRIBUTION 5/81—24,302

N.Eng.	Mid.Atl.	E.N.Cen.	W.N.Cen.	S.Atl.	E.S.Cen.
2,093	3,679	4,410	1,843	4,885	1,069
W.S.Cen.	Mtn.St.	Pac.St.	Canada	Foreign	Other
2,098	730	3,200	123	83	89

BUSINESS ANALYSIS OF CIRCULATION

TL —Total.
1 —Marine retailers.
1-1 —Dealers only.
1-2 —Marinas or boatyards only.
1-3 —Dealers & marinas or boatyards.
1-4 —Other retailers.
2 —Marine wholesalers, distrs. or jobbers.
3 —Marine mftr's. reps.
4 —Marine product mftrs.
4-1 —Boat builders.
4-2 —Other products.
5 —Others allied to the field.

TL	1	1-1	1-2	1-3	1-4	2	3	4
24302	15338	8099	1760	3702	1777	2076	1282	...
4-1	4-2	5						
1852	2610	1144						

(C-C1)

Boating Industry Marine Buyers' Guide

A Whitney Communication Publication

BPA

Published monthly (except semimonthly in December) by Boating Industry, Inc., subsidiary of Whitney Communications Corp., 850 Third Ave., New York, NY 10022. Phone 212-593-2100

NOTE: For basic information on the following numbered listing segments 1, 2, 3, 15, see Boating Industry listing in this classification.
For shipping info., see Print Media Production Data.

PUBLISHER'S EDITORIAL PROFILE

BOATING INDUSTRY MARINE BUYERS' GUIDE is a reference manual of suppliers of pleasure boating products and services. The Guide categorizes the products of marine manufacturers under product headings. Major sections are: Supplier Address Directory, including telephone numbers, sales contact, and general product category; Product Directory listing marine manufacturers (except boat builders); Stock Boat Directory, Trade Name Directory, and Services Directory. Rec'd 4/8/77.

4. GENERAL RATE POLICY

All advertising orders are accepted subject to the terms and provisions of the current rate card. Orders are accepted subject to change in rates on notice from the publisher.
Advertisers in the Marine Buyers' Guide are entitled to the frequency rates earned for advertising in Boating Industry. Regional advertising in Marine Buyers Guide not accepted.

ADVERTISING RATES
Effective August, 1981.
Rates received April 20, 1981.

5. BLACK/WHITE RATES

	1 ti	3 ti	7 ti	13 ti
1 page	2800.	2630.	2415.	2205.
2/3 page	2220.	2130.	2035.	1915.
*1/2 page	1795.	1705.	1570.	1430.
1/3 page	1405.	1340.	1285.	1170.
1/4 page	990.	930.	860.	765.

(*) Island half page, extra 10%.

BULK RATES

13 pages	2020.	36 pages	1915.
24 pages	1965.	48 pages	1860.

6. COLOR RATES

Standard AAAA 2-color, red, blue, green, yellow, per page or fraction	225.
Matched color, per page or fraction	250.
3-color, per page or fraction	575.
4-color, per page or fraction	675.
5th color	200.
Metallic silver	375.

7. COVERS

	1 ti	3 ti	7 ti	13 ti
2nd and 3rd covers	4300.	4050.	3785.	3570.
4th cover	4985.	4720.	4405.	4120.

8. INSERTS

Special discounts available for furnished inserts.

9. BLEED

Add 15% to space and color.
No charge for bleed on 4-color and gutter bleed on spreads.

10. SPECIAL POSITION

Yearly contract only available.

16. ISSUE AND CLOSING DATES

Issued December closes November 1st.

18. CIRCULATION

B.P.A. 1980 Edition
Total Qualified—25,258.

Boating Industry Showtime Showcase

A Whitney Communications Publication

Published twice a year by Boating Industry, Inc., a subsidiary of Whitney Communications Corp., 850 Third Ave., New York, NY 10022. Phone 212-593-2100

NOTE: For basic information on the following numbered listing segments 2, 3, see Boating Industry listing in this classification.
For shipping info., see Print Media Production Data.

1. PERSONNEL

Publisher—Charles Jones.
Advertising Director/Assoc. Pub.—Hugh Evans.
Advertising Service Manager—Carol Fleming.

ADVERTISING RATES
Rates received June 22, 1981.

5. BLACK/WHITE RATES

Fall Showtime Showcase:

1 page	960.	1/3 page	520.
2/3 page	795.	1/4 page	360.
*1/2 page	605.		

(**) Island half, extra 10%.
Winter Showtime Showcase:
(*) Advertisers using Showtime Showcase in conjunction with 3 of the following issues of BI and/or BPN: December, January, February, Marine Buyers' Guide.
(†) Advertisers using Showtime Showcase in conjunction with 2 of the following BI and/or BPN issues: December, January, February, Marine Buyers' Guide.
(‡) Advertisers using Showtime Showcase in conjunction with 1 issue of BI.
(#) Advertisers using Showtime Showcase issues only.

6. COLOR RATES

Fall Showtime Showcase:
Standard color, per page or fraction, extra .... 150.
4-color, per page or fraction .... 375.
Winter Showtime Showcase:
Standard color, per page or fraction .... 200.
4-color, per page or fraction .... 375.

7. COVERS

Fall Showtime Showcase:
2nd and 4th cover ... 1650. 3rd cover .... 1450.

8. INSERTS

Special inserts available.

9. BLEED

Add 15% to space and color. No charge for 4-color bleed.

10. SPECIAL POSITION

Available.

15. MECH REQUIREMENTS

For complete, detailed production information, see SRDS Print Media Production Data.
(Offset)
Binding method: Perfect.

DIMENSIONS-AD PAGE

1	7 x 10	1/2	4-1/2 x 7-1/2
2/3	7 x 6-5/8	1/3	4-1/2 x 4-7/8
...	4-1/2 x 10	...	2-1/8 x 10
1/2	3-5/16 x 10	1/4	7 x 2-3/8
...	7 x 4-7/8	...	3-5/16 x 4-7/8

16. ISSUE AND CLOSING DATES

Published twice a year; in conjunction with the fall and winter trade shows. Closing dates: The Fall Showtime Showcase closes August 10th and the Winter Showtime Showcase closes December 5th.

18. CIRCULATION

SWORN Fall 1981 Convention
Non-paid controlled circulation 16,500

Boating Product News

A Whitney Communications Publication

BPA ABP

Media Code 7 070 2200 0.00 **Mid 002208-000**

Published 8 times a year by Boating Industry, Inc., a subsidiary of Whitney Communications Corp., 850 Third Ave., New York, NY 10022. Phone 212-593-2100

For shipping info., see Print Media Production Data.

PUBLISHER'S EDITORIAL PROFILE

BOATING PRODUCT NEWS is a newspaper edited for the pleasure boating industry. It is designed to provide its readers with new product and industry news briefs, featurettes, staff written columns touching upon various topics, and other industry fare of interest to the man who moves product. Rec'd 9/15/77.

Nielsen Television Index (NTI) and *American Research Bureau (Arbitron)* both provide audience information about local and national television ratings; Arbitron also provides radio data. The information is broken out by various demographic categories and dayparts. All counties that predominantly receive broadcast signals from a particular city belong to a geographic territory known as an "Area of Dominant Influence" (ADI; Arbitron) or "Designated Market Area" (DMA; Nielsen). According to these systems, the United States is divided into about 200 ADIs or DMAs. Figure 10.10 on page 322 shows Arbitron data for Chicago television stations on Wednesdays from 7:30 to 10 P.M. The columns show ratings, share, or thousands of people (as indicated in the headings).

Audit Bureau of Circulations (ABC) is a cooperative association of advertisers, agencies, and publishers with the purpose of verifying and disseminating circulation data concerning magazines and newspapers. Data are broken out by paid/unpaid copies, subscription/newstand prices, and type of edition (regional, demographic); newspaper data are also shown by geographic areas of the market.

The *Advertising Checking Bureau (ACB)* monitors all daily and Sunday newspapers and all major consumer magazines. Information provided includes tearsheets (copies of advertisements—yours or your competitors'), brand name mentions, co-op advertising, schedules, and expenditure reports.

Summary

This chapter has acted as an introduction to the concepts of media planning. Any plan will yield an overall impact that can be measured in gross rating points, but these GRPs must also be broken down in terms of reach and frequency. It is important to know what percent of the target market will be exposed and how often the average person will be reached.

When media are bought, the cost of vehicles must be assessed. One way to compare costs on some constant unit is by using the cost per thousand. CPM shows the cost to reach a standard number of people in the target market. This is useful because each vehicle has its own costs and its own audience size.

Any media plan must be assessed in terms of effectiveness and efficiency. That is, does the plan seem as if it will meet its objectives (and be effective), and will it meet these objectives at the lowest possible cost (and be efficient)? There are many syndicated services available that provide data to assist in the evaluation of effectiveness and efficiency.

Discussion Questions

1. Define reach, frequency, gross rating points, and cost per thousand.

2. How do reach, rating, and share relate to one another in terms of the program's audience and the brand's target market?

3. How do duplicated and unduplicated reach relate to reach and frequency?

4. Discuss effective reach with relation to learning.

5. If you bought 500 GRPs of daytime television, what would be your reach and frequency? What if you bought the same amount of radio? Which is a better buy? Why?

Figure 10.10 *Sample page of Arbitron data*

Weekly Program Estimates | Time Period Average Estimates

DAY AND TIME / STATION	PROGRAM	WEEK-BY-WEEK ADI TV HH RATINGS WK 1	WK 2	WK 3	WK 4	ADI TV HH RTG	ADI TV HH SHR	ADI TV HH SHARE/HUT TRENDS MAY '84	METRO TV HH RTG	METRO TV HH SHR	TOTAL SURVEY AREA, IN THOUSANDS (000's): TV HH	PERSONS 18+	PERSONS 12-24	PERSONS 12-34	WOMEN TOT 18+	WOMEN 18-49	WOMEN 12-24	WOMEN 18-34	WOMEN 25-49	WOMEN 25-54	WKG WMN 18+	MEN TOT 18+	MEN 18-49	MEN 18-34	MEN 25-49	MEN 25-54
		9/26	10/3	10/10	10/17																					
		1	2	3	4	5	6	58	8	9	11	13	15	16	18	19	20	21	22	23	24	25	26	27	28	29
▲ RELATIVE STD-ERR THRESHOLDS (1 σ)	25%	4	4	4	4	3			5		49	64	78	65	50	47	73	50	42	42	47	48	48	55	42	44
	50%	1	1	1	1	-			1		12	16	19	16	12	11	18	12	10	10	12	12	12	14	10	11
WEDNESDAY																										
4:00P- 4:30P (CNTD)																										
WCVB	RITUALS	6		4	5	5	15		6	19	95	111	51	70	86	50	46	34	32	35	9	24	13	9	8	8
	NT LG CHP DY		7			7	20		7	23	150	163	40	47	68	36	15	11	28	38	6	95	38	8	33	33
	--4 WK AVG--					5	16	19	6	20	108	124	48	64	82	46	38	28	31	36	9	42	19	9	14	14
WNEV	NEW MKE DEAL	5	5	5		5	14		5	17	109	130	43	71	93	41	30	26	35	35	3	37	26	17	17	18
	CBS SCHLBRK				5	5	15		5	18	105	133	9	13	94	14	9	3	14	33	10	39	9		9	9
	--4 WK AVG--					5	15	11	5	17	108	130	35	56	93	35	25	20	30	34	5	37	22	13	15	16
WMUR	HART-HART	1			2	1	5		1	3	27	14	6	7	8	6		1	6	6	3	6	6	6		
	NT LG CHP DY		-								6															
	ABC SCHL SPC			1		1	4				27	21	19	19	21	21			21	21	11					
	--4 WK AVG--					1	3				22	12	8	8	9	8		1	8	8	4	3	3	3		
WXNE	DUKE HAZRD-S	1	1	1	1	1	4	4	2	6	32	11	6	8	7	5		2	5	5	2	4	3		3	3
WSBK	HE-MAN UNVRS	3	3	3	1	2	8	9	3	10	59	13	15	16	8	7	8	5	3	3	1	4	4		4	4
WNDS	BRADY BUNCH	-	-	-	-						4															
WLVI	INSPTR GADGT	4	4	3	2	3	10	8	3	10	83	19	31	41	8	6	17	5	4	4	2	11	11	11	7	7
WQTV	STAR THEATER	1	-	-	-				1	2	9	3		1	1							2	1	1	1	1
WGBH	PTV	3	2	2	3	3	8	7	3	9	60	13	2	13	8	8	2	8	6	6	1	5	5	5	5	5
WENH	PTV	-	-	-	-						11	4		1	4	4		1	4	4	3					
	HUT/TOTAL	30	34	34	30	32		33	29		631	498	210	292	347	176	137	105	129	145	49	150	85	51	59	62
4:30P- 5:00P																										
WBZ	LOVE BOAT-S	5	7	7	6	6	18	27	5	16	149	194	75	96	147	70	55	44	45	52	23	47	21	10	14	16
WCVB	SOAP-S	5			4	5	14		6	21	93	121	57	81	79	68	48	47	40	42	6	42	37	14	28	28
	NT LG CHP DY		9			9	25		9	26	201	204	40	66	87	56	33	38	40	51	26	117	42	4	42	42
	SPRTS FILL		5			5	14		6	18	122	123	22	40	50	36	18	24	27	30	16	74	26	2	26	26
	ABC SCHL SPC			5		5	14		7	18	103	117	65	72	76	49	56	36	20	20	18	41	18	8	10	10
	--4 WK AVG--					5	15	14	7	20	112	131	53	72	76	58	44	40	33	36	13	55	31	10	25	25
WNEV	MATCH GAME	6	5	6		6	15		6	16	127	173	17	49	104	40	3	25	37	39	3	69	42	22	29	30
	CBS SCHLBRK				5	5	15		5	16	112	148	1	4	100	17		3	17	42	3	48	14	1	13	13
	--4 WK AVG--					5	15	11	5	16	123	167	13	38	103	34	2	20	32	39	3	64	35	16	25	26
WMUR	HART-HART	1			2	2	5		1	2	34	14	5	8	9	7	2	1	7	7	3	4	4	4	1	1
	NT LG CHP DY		-								6															
	SPRTS FILL		1			1	2				12															
	ABC SCHL SPC			1		1	4				27	21	34	34	21	21	15		21	21	11					
	--4 WK AVG--					1	4		1	2	26	12	11	12	10	9	5	1	9	9	4	2	2	2	1	1
WXNE	DUKE HAZRD-S	2	1	2	2	2	5	5	2	6	40	13	11	17	10	7		5	7	7	2	4	1	1	1	1
WSBK	VOLTRON	2	4	3	2	3	8	8	3	9	75	21	36	37	12	12	26	6	6	6	1	9	9	2	8	8
WNDS	MUSIC MAG	-	-	-	-						1															
WLVI	BRADY BUNCH	4	3	3	2	3	9	8	3	9	77	14	40	46	5	5	16	5	1	1	2	9	9	7	7	7
WQTV	STAR THEATER	1	-	1	1	1	2	2	1	3	13	3		1	1							2	1	1	1	1
WGBH	PTV	4	2	3	4	3	9	8	3	9	73	12	2	12	7	7	2	7	5	5	1	5	5	5	5	5
WENH	PTV	-	-	-	-						10	4		1	4	4		1	4	4	3					
	HUT/TOTAL	35	36	39	34	36		36	33		699	571	241	332	375	206	150	129	142	159	52	197	114	54	87	90
5:00P- 5:30P																										
WBZ	PEOPLES CRT	7	7	5	5	6	14	19	6	15	150	228	24	43	142	45	16	17	38	45	17	87	32	13	28	29
WCVB	TOO CLS CMFT	6	5		6	6	14		6	15	126	142	39	73	95	65	23	39	49	52	33	47	17	13	13	18
	ABC SCHL SPC			6		6	14		8	19	114	136	44	63	78	46	39	27	30	30	32	57	27	13	22	22
	--4 WK AVG--					6	14	15	6	16	123	140	41	70	91	60	27	36	44	46	33	49	19	13	16	19
WNEV	100000 TUNE	8	6	7	7	7	17	18	7	19	146	215	31	40	136	46	17	16	38	44	20	80	28	13	16	25
WMUR	BRNABY JONES	2	1	1	1	1	3	3			32	33	12	12	22	5	10	3	2	2	5	12	1		1	1
WXNE	8 IS ENOUGH	2	1	2	2	2	4	4	2	5	39	19	39	48	16	15	35	14	8	8	10	3	3	2	3	3
WSBK	QUINCY-S	4	5	4	3	4	10	5	4	11	131	185	54	91	91	70	26	39	53	59	44	94	63	35	43	56
WNDS	MORK MINDY-S	-	-	1	-	1	1				11															
WLVI	BRADY BUNCH	4		3	4	3	8		4	10	93	14	22	28	6	5	12	4	5	5	2	8	5	2	5	8
	CARE BEARS		4			4	9		4	11	81	5	12	12								5	5		5	5
	--4 WK AVG--					4	9	11	4	10	90	12	19	24	4	4	9	3	4	4	1	7	5	1	5	7
WQTV	STAR THEATER	1	1	1	1	1	2	1	1	3	16	4		1	2							2	1	1	1	1
WGBH	PTV	4	3	3	4	3	8	7	4	9	71	9	1	9	4	4	1	4	3	3		5	5	5	5	5
WENH	PTV	-	-	-	-						6															
WGBX	PTV	-	-	-	-						2															
	HUT/TOTAL	42	41	42	39	41		43	39		817	845	221	338	508	249	141	132	190	211	130	339	157	83	118	146
5:30P- 6:00P																										
WBZ	LIVE ON 4	9	9	8	9	9	20	20	8	18	208	316	23	49	183	51	8	20	45	63	27	133	42	18	37	38
WCVB	ALL IN FAMLY	8	7	8	8	7	17	17	8	19	159	210	49	93	121	56	23	37	46	60	42	89	47	26	37	49
WNEV	WHEEL OF FOR	9	9	9	9	9	21	24	10	24	196	302	52	73	192	75	32	33	59	67	29	110	41	17	28	37
WMUR	BRNABY JONES	2	1	2	1	1	3	3			33	32	11	11	20	5	9	3	2	2	5	12	1		1	1
WXNE	8 IS ENOUGH	1	2	2	3	2	5	4	2	5	46	21	57	69	15	14	46	14	9	9	9	6	6	5	4	4
WSBK	QUINCY-S	4	4	5	3	4	9	4	4	10	124	152	34	73	79	60	26	37	46	52	41	73	42	18	40	53
WNDS	HPY DAYS AGN	1	-	1	1	1	2				13															
WLVI	THIS WK MUSC	2	3	2	1	2	5	11	2	5	57	13	28	33	5	5	10	3	4	4	1	8	7	3	7	8
WQTV	STAR THEATER	1	1	1	2	1	3	2	2	4	26	8		3	4							4	3	3	3	3
WGBH	PTV	2	3	3	3	3	6	6	3	6	57	17	18	22	6	6	7	2	5	5	3	10	10	10	4	4
WENH	PTV	-	-	-	-																					
WGBX	PTV	1	-	1	1						9															
	HUT/TOTAL	44	44	45	45	44		46	43		928	1071	272	426	625	272	161	149	216	262	157	445	199	100	161	197
6:00P- 6:30P																										
WBZ	EYE NWS EVEN	11	11	12	10	11	23	21	9	20	259	416	50	85	219	88	25	37	69	86	46	197	86	34	70	85
WCVB	NS CTR 5 ERL	11	10	12	10	11	23	28	12	27	232	357	32	97	201	77	16	48	67	86	40	157	66	34	58	74
WNEV	N E NEWS E	7	6	7	7	6	14	16	7	16	137	221	9	26	133	32	5	9	32	42	15	88	27	11	23	31
WMUR	NEWS NINE	2	1	2	1	2	3	3			41	54	11	12	32	5	10	4	2	5	6	22	1		1	1
WXNE	DFRNT STRK-S	3	4	4	3	3	7	5	3	7	71	26	49	59	13	12	27	10	11	11	8	13	11	3	10	11
WSBK	ONE DAY TME	2	3	3	3	3	6	6	3	7	81	84	61	77	52	42	31	38	18	18	18	31	17	17	2	17
WNDS	TV50 NW TNGT	-	-	-	-						2															
WLVI	THREES CMPNY	3	5	4	4	4	8	12	4	9	97	87	53	82	44	42	25	27	33	33	15	43	42	28	26	26
WQTV	MANNIX	2	2	1	2	2	4	2	2	5	35	23		5	9	4		4	4	4	1	14	7	1	7	7
WGBH	PTV	2	2	2	2	2	4	3	3	6	47	39	2	8	9	1	2		1	1	1	29	13	6	13	13
WENH	PTV	-	-	-	-																					
WGBX	PTV	1	1	-	1	1	1				13															
	HUT/TOTAL	47	49	47	48	48		52	47		1015	1307	267	451	712	303	141	177	237	286	150	594	270	134	210	265
6:30P- 7:00P																										
WBZ	EYE NWS EVEN	11	12	13	11	12	23	19	9	19	266	422	50	89	224	89	25	35	73	92	47	197	90	39	71	87
WCVB	NS CTR 5 ERL	10	10	12	8	10	20	24	11	23	211	316	32	90	171	76	18	45	61	77	39	145	69	37	60	73
WNEV	N E NEWS E	6	6	5	5	6	11	13	7	14	117	193	6	21	114	20		7	20	33	12	79	22	12	18	27

BOSTON 51 WEDNESDAY OCTOBER 1984 TIME PERIOD AVERAGES

* SAMPLE BELOW MINIMUM FOR WEEKLY REPORTING
** SHARE/HUT TRENDS NOT AVAILABLE
\- DID NOT ACHIEVE A REPORTABLE WEEKLY RATING
‡ TECHNICAL DIFFICULTY
\+ COMBINED PARENT/SATELLITE
▲ SEE TABLE ON PAGE iv

6. What would be your reach and frequency if you bought both of the media in the previous question?

7. What is the cost per thousand of "60 Minutes"? It costs $190,000 for 30 seconds and reaches 38 million people.

8. What is the major value of the media imperatives concept? What does it mean if a person is a "dual imperatives" with regard to newspaper and radio?

9. Where would you go to get the following information?
    (a) The number of women 18–49 who are heavy users of hot dogs.
    (b) The number of women 18–49 who read *Cosmopolitan.*
    (c) The reach and frequency generated by four consecutive buys in *Cosmopolitan.*
    (d) The number of women 18–49 who watched "Dallas."
    (e) The cost of 30 seconds on "Dallas."
    (f) The cost of a full page of *Cosmopolitan.*
    (g) The past national television schedule of major competitors to your brand of hot dogs. Their local schedule. Their major media expenditures.
    (h) The paid circulation of *Cosmopolitan.*
    (i) Tearsheets of your competitors' print ads.

Note

1. Steve Raddock, "The Nielsen of TV Efficiency?" *Marketing & Media Decisions,* November 1982, p. 70.

Chapter 11
Broadcast
Media

*R*emember, from the introduction to this part, that the medium is the massage. Each massage has different pros and cons and a different impact on the reach, frequency, and timing of the media plan as well as how consumers learn the key message points. Each will have a different efficiency and effectiveness and will be more or less appropriate for a particular task.

• Need to demonstrate how a product operates? Television can do the job best if there is a process or movement. The West Bend Food Preparation System is an example, as in Figure 11.1.

• Need to show appetite appeal and color? Magazines have the most consistent high-quality color reproduction capability (television can transmit great color but not all receivers can show great color). Figure 11.2 showed colorful appetite appeal when it was first printed.

• Need to provide lots of information for people to think about? Print media allow the reader to work at a deliberate and self-controlled pace in order to absorb information. The Merrill Lynch ad in Figure 11.3 would be hard to do in 30 seconds on television.

• Need to make a big impact without saying much? Outdoor advertising can be visual but doesn't allow much in the way of verbalization. Figure 11.4 shows the big impact potential of an outdoor visual message.

• Need to create a mood on a limited budget? Radio can build mood as well as awareness through a catchy audio track. It can also reiterate at a lower cost what has been done earlier on television at a higher cost.

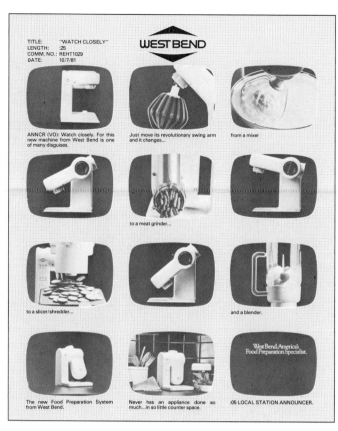

Figure 11.1   TV photoboard of product demonstration

Figure 11.2   Magazine ad showing appetite appeal

Figure 11.3   Magazine ad: high information content

Figure 11.4   Big impact of outdoor

▪ Need to deliver a timely message concerning a sale or a promotion? Local broadcast media can give basic facts, but newspapers can give much more price and availability information as well as deliver coupons. Figure 11.5 shows timely sales information using newspaper.

▪ Need to reach a particular audience? As was seen in the previous chapter, media imperatives often suggest that magazines are more appropriate for certain targets. Figure 11.6 shows an ad directed at media buyers to make this point. Figure 11.7 is a response from Cable Networks, Inc., which also feels that it can deliver the best audience. Figure 11.8 presents the opinion of the Radio Network Association, which also promises to deliver. Clearly, they all agree that reaching a specific audience is important; that point is not in doubt. The media buyer will need to decide which medium (and, later, which vehicle) can best deliver a particular target audience.

These are just a few of the tasks that the media are called upon to perform; it quickly becomes apparent that one medium cannot do everything. Again the

Figure 11.5   *Newspaper ad with timely sales information*

Figure 11.6   *The Magazine Publishers Association sells reach*

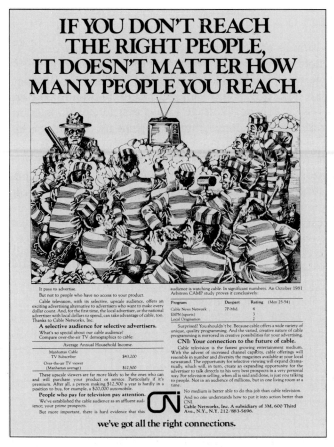

Figure 11.7   Cable Networks, Inc., sells reach

Figure 11.8   The Radio Advertising Board sells reach

manager needs to return to the decision sequence to determine the objectives that are being pursued. This chapter and the next will examine the major media to see how they are qualified to perform certain tasks. To do so, each medium will be examined in terms of the following issues:

General description	Frequency
Strengths	Timing
Weaknesses	Cost
Reach	

Television

A discussion of this medium must be conducted not only in *general terms* but also in terms of *network* versus *local* television. Also, before proceeding, two confusing concepts need to be clarified.

A *television spot* is another name for a television commercial; any paid or public service message can be referred to as a television spot. *Spot television,* though, is another name for local television advertising; local television commercials originate in a single market rather than at the network. In addition to locally sponsored programs, there are local messages during most network-originated shows; these latter messages are generally clustered from 28 to 32 and 58 to 02 minutes past each hour.

Strengths and weaknesses

The major strength of television as an advertising medium is its *intrusiveness.* It imposes itself on the household and is hard to avoid. Television is in virtually every home (98%); the average household has a set in use for almost 50 hours per week or over 7 hours per day. Figure 11.9 and Table 11.1 present additional data on the intrusiveness of television. This heavy usage means that television is good for reaching a broad undifferentiated audience but may yield too much wasted coverage if a narrow target is desired. The broadest reach is generally for prime-time programs (8–11 P.M. in the Eastern and Pacific time zones; 7–10 P.M. in the Central and Mountain time zones), when over 60% of households use television; daytime, sports, and cable shows offer a narrower reach and some ability to segment toward less broad audiences.

Because of its broad reach, television, especially network, offers *good cost efficiencies in terms of low cost per thousand.* While a 30-second spot on a top-rated network program may cost over $150,000[1] (that's right: $150,000 for one showing of one 30-second commercial!), the cost per person reached will be about 1/2¢. The obvious disadvantage here is that network television advertising can lead to extremely high absolute dollar costs. At the time of this writing, the highest single program cost was for the 1986 Super Bowl, which sold for a reported $550,000 per 30 seconds. Given an audience of approximately 90 million

Figure 11.9 *Estimates of households using television, hour by hour, March 1978*

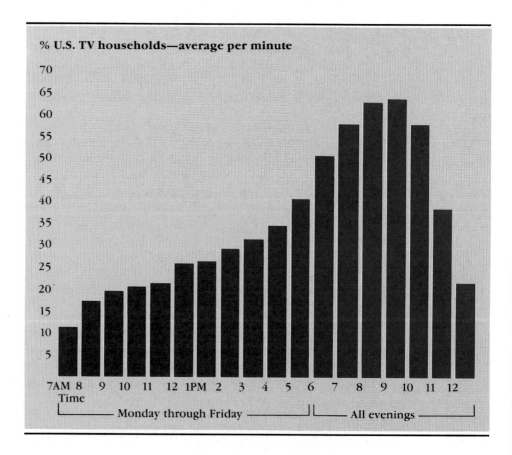

Table 11.1 Some television viewing data (Monday–Sunday 24 hours)

Descriptor	Hours of television viewing per week (hours:min)
All households	51:57
All individuals	30:38
Adult women	35:19
Adult men	29:04
All teens	22:28
Women 55+	42:07
Men 55+	37:11
Women 18–34	31:26
Men 18–34	25:43
Female teens	21:37
Male teens	23:19
Children 2–5	28:20
Children 6–11	26:34

Source: November 1984 National Audience Demographics, Nielsen Television Index.

viewers, the CPM is still at about $6.11 and should be reasonable to a marketer with the goal of achieving high reach to a wide undifferentiated audience. Ultimately, the networks are able to command such high unit costs because they deliver such large audiences; this continues to hold even in the face of lessened network viewing because of cable.

At the other extreme, advertisers were reluctant to advertise on "The Day After," a program about nuclear war. As a result ABC sold spots for $60,000 but the show was seen by about 100 million viewers. Those advertisers who sponsored the show were rewarded with a CPM of $.60; in addition, polls showed that viewers were favorably disposed towards the firms that helped to bring this show to the public.

The rising cost of a network television spot is chiefly due to the laws of supply and demand coupled with government regulation of the industry. Regulations control the number of television stations that may transmit programming over the airwaves; this controls the total supply of air time. (Until recently, the amount of allowable commercial time per broadcast hour had been agreed upon by members of the National Association of Broadcasters, but the Supreme Court has ruled that such controls are illegal. Without controls, the amount of commercial time could rise. If there truly is competition, prices should then drop or at least not rise as rapidly.)

In any case, until now the supply of commercial air time has been closely controlled while the demand for air time has grown continuously as more marketers have sought to advertise on television. Basic economic theory would (correctly) predict rising prices until the supply increased or the demand decreased to some equilibrium. Because neither of these has occurred, price has continued to increase at a rate much greater than that of inflation. (Profits to the networks and stations have also been substantial because their basic costs are fairly fixed and independent from the revenues they receive.)

The high cost of television time (and the profits resulting therefrom) have led to other marketplace changes. Cable television has grown rapidly in an attempt to increase the supply of television time (and to get a share of profits); new magazines have been introduced at a rapid rate in an attempt to capture advertising that couldn't fit on television's limited schedule (and also to garner a share of the profits).

Ultimately, the cost of television advertising will remain high as long as its supply is limited. As alternative media are seen as substitutes, the supply will increase. Recently, there has been a slight erosion of the network monopoly position to cable, but it is too early to tell if the networks will adapt and recover or if the nature of the industry is likely to change significantly.

The adverse supply-demand situation also has created another type of problem for buyers. Because the supply of time is limited, *it is sold quite early relative to when the spot will be aired.* The great majority of network time is sold during the late spring and summer preceding the new fall season of programs. This means that some air time is bought a year before it is to be used and possibly before its program has ever been publicly shown. In one of the more extreme examples of this problem, time for the 1984 Olympic telecasts was being sold in 1982. In a less extreme example, 80% of all network National Football League spots for 1983 were sold by early August of that year.[2] This timing problem is not as severe for any other medium, including local television.

A third recent problem concerns "guarantees." In the past the networks have guaranteed to the advertiser that a certain program would deliver a minimum number of households and a minimum demographic mix. In 1982, CBS dropped its guarantees. This meant that media planners no longer had network assurance that their buys would deliver a specified audience. This, in turn, led to fewer early and more late buys. In 1983 the networks were still debating whether or not to offer guarantees. Certainly this issue is the result of the adverse supply-demand situation. If advertisers continue to buy without guarantees, there will be no reason for the networks to offer them. As long as advertisers feel that the tremendous potential reach of television is worth the price, the cost will continue to escalate.

In its favor, television has the physical capabilities to provide the greatest potential attention levels. Its *unique combination of sight, sound, and motion* gives it tremendous intrusiveness and delivery potential; as such, it becomes the closest representation of an actual salesperson in the home.

In reality television has not achieved this potential. It has become so much a part of daily life that it is easy to tune out even when people are in its presence. As Krugman has pointed out, television is a low-involvement medium; it sends out messages at its own pace, quite independent of viewers' needs and desires. Because the sender sets the pace, the viewer has no control over speed or content of presentation and cannot review it if a point is difficult to grasp. As a result, attention to television, and especially commercials, is generally quite low. These issues all lead to slow learning, low retention, and rapid forgetting. Because of these poor learning curve characteristics, it is usually necessary to use a repetition strategy in order for television to be an effective tool. Repetition, in turn, drives up the cost of using television even further.

Despite its limitations, television's unique use of sight, sound, and motion make it the best medium for a demonstration as well as for conveying a mood, an emotion, or a dramatic event.

Differences between network and local television

There are several key differences between network and local television advertising. The greatest is, perhaps, the placement difference. Network commercials are shown within the program; therefore, they are in a less cluttered setting (e.g., there are fewer messages shown consecutively) and should receive more attention from viewers. In-program breaks are usually shorter and therefore also hold viewers' attention better.

Spot commercials are shown within the program for *locally originated* programming but are shown during the adjacent time periods of *network programs*. These adjacencies (28 to 32 and 58 to 02 past the hour) are generally longer, have more messages and are more likely to be between programs. As a result there is less viewership during these breaks.

People out there in viewer-land seem to know very well when the long breaks are and plan their activities around the time they know exists during a station break. In a study of clutter effects, one subject told the experimenter that the experimental videotape was phony; she knew that during the commercial break of the program shown to her there would be exactly enough time to make a cup of tea. In the experiment the break time had been reduced and she therefore felt sure that the study was about commercials.[3]

Spot television can be purchased in many markets so that the geographic coverage of the message will be equal to the geographic distribution of the product being sold. However, this strategy eventually becomes inefficient because the cost of a network buy equals the cost of a collection of local buys that will, in sum, cover approximately 60% of the U.S. population. If the manager wanted to reach more than 60% of the population, it would be cheaper to buy a network spot (which would cover the entire country). For this reason, messages are sometimes aired in regions where a brand has no distribution.

Conversely, buying local markets gives more flexibility to the advertiser in terms of coverage and weight. Local buys allow the advertiser to advertise more or less heavily in certain markets to reflect competition, market shares, and other influences. There is also another dimension of flexibility available because local television has a fairly short lead time for purchases; this allows the advertiser to update the media plan continuously and to take advantage of changing opportunities such as sales.

In sum, network buys are more efficient than local ones if the target is geographically large enough and may lead to better learning because of less clutter. Local buys offer more flexibility in terms of markets reached, media weights used, and timing. In reality, national advertisers often combine network and local buys in order to take advantage of both, and, as network costs increase, some buyers are shifting more dollars to the spot market.

Given this broad introduction to television, it is now necessary to consider some specific issues.

Reach

Television has the advantage of providing large undifferentiated audiences. In the past, television gave too much wasted coverage if a segmented audience was desired. While these statements still hold for most prime-time network programs, there is some segmentability in terms of news, sports, daytime, and late fringe time (late fringe is the time after prime time). Cable television is also rapidly

Table 11.2 Listing and coverage of cable networks

Program source	Number of households (1000s)	% U.S.	Format
Black entertainment TV (BET)	2102	2.5	Black
Cable Health Network	4600	5.5	Health/sci
Cable News Network (CNN)	15827	19.0	News
Cable News Network II (CNN II)	2500	3.0	News
CBN-Cable	17800	21.4	Various
ESPN	18780	22.5	Sports
Hearst/ABC - Arts	8000	9.6	Cultural
Hearst/ABC - daytime	7200	8.6	Women
Music television (MTV)	7007	8.4	Music
Modern Satellite Network	6567	7.8	Consumer info
National Spanish TV Net[a]	3350	4.0	Spanish
Satellite News CHNL I	3500	4.2	News
Satellite News CHNL II[b]	n.a.	n.a.	News
Satellite Program Net. (SPN)	5200	6.2	Various
Telefrance	8500	10.2	French
USA Network	13000	15.6	Various
UTV (2)	n.a.	n.a.	Retailing
Weather Channel	4700	5.6	Weather
WGN (Chicago)	10939	13.1	Various
WOR (New York)	15493	18.6	Various
WTBS (Atlanta)	23324	28.0	Various
Nashville Network	n.a.	n.a.	Country

Source: From *Adweek,* 1 November 1982, p. 230. Reprinted with permission of *Adweek,* 1982.

[a] Spanish HH/total homes = 25MM
[b] Launch date: February 1983

changing the viability of segmentation on television. Table 11.2 shows a listing of the cable networks and their coverage of the United States in late 1982. It is easy to see that most of these cable networks appeal to specific segments and attempt to attract a narrow audience. This concept of "narrowcasting" (as opposed to "broadcasting") is rapidly changing the reach characteristics of television.

Frequency

Television does not generally induce rapid learning in viewers; the continuous flow of television does not allow the audience to review messages. Therefore, high-frequency schedules are generally necessary. Frequency can be accomplished by buying the same program over many weeks, a number of different programs, or some combination depending on the media objectives. While an advertiser could also buy several messages in the same program, this is rarely done.

Timing

Television offers both excellent and horrible timing. The timing can be excellent because the advertiser knows exactly when the spot will be aired. When air time is purchased, an exact time can be acquired, e.g., between 9 and 9:30 P.M. on

Monday, August 22. Exceptions are described below. This exactness is important in building a learning strategy of high repetition and for transmitting timely information.

In a different use of the word, horrible timing is achieved when purchasing network time since it must be purchased so far in advance of its transmission.

Cost

Because television's virtue is high reach and one of its liabilities is the need for high frequency, the use of television is usually expensive. Nine variables affect the cost of a television spot:

1. *Daypart*   The time of day affects the cost, but probably time and cost are mostly a function of audience size, which changes dramatically during the day. Television dayparts are

> Early morning (6–9 A.M.)
> Daytime (9 A.M.–5 P.M.)
> Early fringe (5–7 or 8 P.M. depending on time zone)
> Prime (7–10 or 8–11 P.M. depending on time zone)
> Late fringe (10 or 11 P.M. to signoff)

2. *Audience size*   This determines the ratings of the program; greater audience size commands a higher price. A difference of one rating point nationally can mean many millions of dollars in gross revenues for the network over the duration of a year.

3. *Quarter of the year*   The fourth quarter (October–December) tends to be most expensive because audiences are somewhat higher and because competition for air time is greatest. Many products have high seasonal sales at Christmas, and this leads to the greatest demand for the limited air time. The third quarter (July–September) is cheapest because viewership is lowest.

4. *Geographic area* (for local television)   Some markets command higher prices even after considering size of the market, number of channels, and disposable income. This may be due to competition. If many local retailers in a market want to buy a limited supply of time, its price will go up. If the market is a popular one for test marketing, this will also drive up prices.

5. *Editorial climate/audience composition*   There is an attempt to charge more for certain programs because it is felt that the quality of the audience is better. ("Better" usually means higher income.) If there are qualitative differences, these are probably due to either program content or editorial climate. Roller derby doubtless has a different audience profile than golf.

6. *Length of the message*   The 30-second spot is currently the industry standard. If a 30-second costs $X, a 60-second will cost about $2X and a 10-second will cost about $.5 to $.6X. In 1985 the networks began to experiment with a 15-second spot.

7. *Preemptability*   The standard contract for purchase of air time exchanges a fixed amount of money for a specific piece of air time. The advertiser can, though, buy *preemptable time* for a lower cost. In this condition another advertiser can buy the same spot later for a higher price. Buying preemptable time may be fine for the firm that merely wants to remind people over a long period that it is still

in the market. Wrigley's Spearmint Gum may choose this strategy knowing that if it loses an occasional spot, not much damage will result. In addition, the lower cost per spot may be appealing.

Even cheaper is an *opportunity buy.* Under this condition, the advertiser tells the network or station that it will buy any/some unsold time (within desired constraints) remaining at air time at a very low cost. Again, this can be useful for a reminder strategy and has the virtue of low cost. Any revenue that the station can get for unsold time is a contribution to overhead and profit because there is virtually no variable cost involved. Unsold air time for Tuesday, March 2, at 4 P.M. cannot be sold on Wednesday, March 3. The perishability of time makes the opportunity buy a good transaction for both parties.

A more expensive buy is one that preempts another purchase of the same time. Sometimes it is necessary for an advertiser to buy time at the last moment when none is available. Buying in this situation becomes more expensive.

8. *Time remaining to air time* As stated above, air time is a perishable product. As a result, unsold air time becomes cheaper as its time approaches. If the media buyer can wait for purchase time, the price will drop. This issue generally holds only for local time because network time tends to sell out early.

This timing issue can lead to ulcers for media buyers. If the buy is made too early it may be too expensive; if the buy is attempted too late, no time may remain.

Figure 11.10 *Networks' 30-second price list: fall 1984*

"60 Minutes" is not only network tv's highest-rated program, it is also its most expensive. According to Advertising Age unit cost estimates, a 30-second spot during the fourth quarter on "60 Minutes" averages $190,000. Closely following "60 Minutes" is ABC's "Dynasty," which averaged $187,000 per 30 seconds. Nearly half of the program's audience is women, 25 to 54, one of the most sought after demographics this fall. — By Verne Gay.
Figures are based on an average of agency figures. Source: Advertising Age.

		7:00	7:30	8:00	8:30	9:00	9:30	10:00	10:30
Monday	ABC			Call to Glory $88,000		Monday Night Football $140,000			
	CBS			Scarecrow and Mrs. King $109,000		Kate & Allie $120,000	Newhart $120,000	Cagney & Lacey $105,000	
	NBC			Tv's Bloopers & Practical Jokes $114,000		NBC Monday Night at the Movies $115,000			
Tuesday	ABC			Three's a Crowd $95,000	Who's the Boss $81,000	Paper Dolls $112,000		Jessie $95,000	
	CBS			AfterMASH $80,000	E/R $80,000	CBS Tuesday Night Movie $100,000			
	NBC			The A Team $167,000		Riptide $117,000		Remington Steele $124,000	
Wednesday	ABC			The Fall Guy $125,000		Dynasty $187,000		Hotel $145,000	
	CBS			Charles in Charge $95,000	Dreams $84,000	CBS Wednesday Night Movie $83,000			
	NBC			Highway to Heaven $85,000		Facts of Life $106,000	It's Your Move $95,000	St. Elsewhere $105,000	
Thursday	ABC			ABC Thursday Night Movie $85,000				20/20 $90,000	
	CBS			Magnum, P.I. $133,000		Simon & Simon $153,000		Knots Landing $135,000	
	NBC			Cosby Show $116,000	Family Ties $106,000	Cheers $120,000	Night Court $102,000	Hill Street Blues $158,000	
Friday	ABC			Benson $95,000	Webster $101,000	Hawaiian Heat $75,000		Matt Houston $88,000	
	CBS			Dukes of Hazzard $88,000		Dallas $143,000		Falcon Crest $121,000	
	NBC			"V" $101,000		Hunter $85,000		Miami Vice $71,000	
Saturday	ABC			T.J. Hooker $82,000		Love Boat $108,000		Finder of Lost Loves $86,000	
	CBS			Airwolf $88,000		Mickey Spillane's Mike Hammer $103,000		Cover-Up $85,000	
	NBC			Diff'rent Strokes $83,000	Gimme a Break $83,000	Partners in Crime $80,000		Hot Pursuit $76,000	
Sunday	ABC	Ripley's Believe It or Not! $73,000		Hardcastle & McCormick $120,000		ABC Sunday Night Movie $140,000			
	CBS	60 Minutes $190,000		Murder, She Wrote $110,000		Jeffersons $113,000	Alice $105,000	Trapper John, M.D. $105,000	
	NBC	Silver Spoons $65,000	Punky Brewster $59,000	Knight Rider $117,000		NBC Sunday Night at the Movies $117,000			

9. *Negotiating*   Given all the above issues, it is no wonder that packages of television buys are negotiated. The larger the package, the greater the room for negotiation; the larger the buying firm, the more leverage it has. Given current supply and demand, though, the networks have the upper hand in negotiations. As cable and other alternatives grow, the balance of power should shift.

Television prices range from $20 (for 30 seconds on a station in a medium to small city; early morning or late night; multiple units purchased) to $550,000 (30 seconds on Super Bowl). Such a range makes television affordable for virtually any budget. Whether or not television is a wise investment and/or reaches the appropriate target market is quite another issue. Figure 11.10 shows the networks' 30-second price list for fall 1984.

Network television costs continue to climb rapidly although economies of scale hold CPM figures close to those of other media; network costs have increased fourfold since 1967. Table 11.3 shows unit cost and CPM index trends for each of the major media using a base year of 1967. These trends will be referred to in the cost section for each medium discussion that follows. Spot television unit and CPM costs are in the middle range across all the major media. Spot prices are, of course, dictated by local market conditions and therefore vary considerably.

Cable television and other entertainment forms that detract from network viewing

The television set that exists in virtually every home in the United States has had a very limited repertoire of uses until quite recently, because it was able only to present audio and visual images of materials broadcast from a small number of other locations. Technological innovations of the past few years have radically expanded the capabilities of the television set; these changes are important to advertisers because they change the size and composition of audiences and because they bring about new advertising opportunities.

Noncommercial competition includes videogames, videocassette players, videodisc players, computer interaction systems and pay-per-viewing television. All of these detract from traditional broadcast viewing and, because they are expensive technologies, generally take higher income households away from the networks.

The greatest detractor from traditional viewing has been cable television, which was in almost 45% of households in 1985.[4] (Table 11.4 shows penetration levels for several entertainment forms that utilize the television set. Table 11.2 showed penetration levels of the major cable networks.) As the number of available channels increases, the networks' share of viewing drops. In a 1982 study by A. C. Nielsen Company in one market, the networks had a 90% share of viewers during prime time in homes without cable. Homes with 12-channel cable systems gave the networks a 74% share; homes with 36-channel systems gave the networks a combined 56% share.[5] Clearly, as cable grows, network viewership will decline. Cable viewers are also slightly more upscale on income and education variables.

In 1983 the networks began to react to this change. They increased their rates! They did so because the laws of supply and demand so dictated; as cable has grown, most of its managers have not documented viewership well, have charged high rates for a supposedly premium audience, and have kept media buyers uneasy. In addition, cable will not offer a national advertising option until

Table 11.3 Media unit cost and CPM trends

Average annual price increases					
	1981	*1982*	*1983*	*1984*	*1985**
Prices:					
Consumer prices	+10.4%	+ 6.1%	+3.2%	+ 4.3%	+5.2%
GNP deflator	+ 9.6	+ 6.0	+3.8	+ 3.8	+4.9
Media cpms:					
Network TV	9.7%	+11.9%	+9.0%	+11.0%	+8.0%
Spot TV	+10.9	+11.2	+8.0	+ 8.6	+6.0
Magazines	+ 8.7	+ 9.0	+8.0	+ 8.1	+6.0
Newspapers	+11.9	+ 9.6	+9.0	+ 8.0	+8.0

Media unit cost** trends (1967 = 100)					
	1981	*1982*	*1983*	*1984*	*1985**
Newspapers	279	308	336	366	395
Magazines	201	219	237	256	274
Network TV	329	365	394	441	476
Spot TV	286	317	342	376	399
Network radio	244	268	300	327	353
Spot radio	215	232	248	268	284
Outdoor	303	330	363	392	416
Direct mail	263	286	290	299	319
Composite	270	297	318	344	369

Media cpm trends (1967 = 100)					
	1981	*1982*	*1983*	*1984*	*1985**
Newspapers	263	288	314	339	366
Magazines	188	205	221	239	254
Network TV	261	292	318	353	381
Spot TV	223	248	268	291	309
Network radio	202	220	244	264	282
Spot radio	182	195	207	221	233
Outdoor	242	262	286	306	322
Direct mail	263	286	290	299	319
Composite	244	267	286	307	329

Source: Prepared for *Advertising Age* by Robert J. Coen, McCann-Erickson, Inc.
* Estimated
** A unit in the various media listed include a single black-and-white page for newspapers, a four-color ad for magazines, 30-second spots for network and spot tv, one-minute spots for network and spot radio, a 100 showing in outdoor (100 GRPs, which is the reach and frequency of x-amount of boards per day), and 25,000 pieces of direct mail.

a cable network is wired into a large percentage of the nation's homes. As a result, demand for cable advertising space has been low and demand for network space has remained high. A second reaction of the networks has been to remove or limit their demographic guarantees (discussed earlier).[6]

Media planners currently disagree widely about the future value of cable as an advertising medium. Some feel that cable will succeed when it becomes adept at "narrowcasting." While the networks "broadcast" to a broad, undifferentiated audience, it is felt that each cable entity should focus on a narrow target market. Narrowcasting would make cable networks similar to most specialty magazines

Table 11.4 Household penetration levels of television technologies

Technology	*% Penetration in 1983*
Basic cable television	37% [1]
Pay cable television	23% [1]
Videogames	18% [2]
Videocassette recorders	7% [2]
Videodisc players	< 1% [2]

Sources:
1. *Marketing and Media Decisions,* June 1983, p. 44.
2. Susan Spillman, "B & B Study Sees Little Videogame Growth," *Advertising Age,* 6 June 1983, p. 20. Reprinted with permission. Copyright 1983 by Crain Communications, Inc.

and radio stations. Such a strategy would also be consistent with current marketing philosophy (segment the market; appeal to one audience). MTV (Music Television) is a successful example of this strategy.[7]

The anti-narrowcasting group feels that this strategy will lead to small audiences; small audiences will lead to low advertising revenues, poor production, and still smaller audiences. This has happened in cases where the target was too narrow or the programming provided no unique benefit. To rebut this the pro-group feels that narrow targets will be of higher quality demographics and the cable networks will be able to charge higher rates to maintain quality production.

Cable has been seen for several years as a major force on the horizon. It is currently still on the horizon, largely because its members have had difficulty in developing an identity and a benefit for advertisers. In 1983, cable received about 2% of the revenues spent on all television advertising.

Cable and other alternative uses of television may ultimately have a profound impact on advertising. The important issues for advertisers will deal with (1) what will happen to the networks in both quantity and quality of viewership; (2) what quantity and quality of audiences can be delivered by alternative media; and (3) what impact these issues will have on other media as well. Technological changes will continue to appear; managers must be able to evaluate these in terms of audience delivery potential.

Radio

Radio suffered a long period of neglect from advertisers in the 1960s and 1970s as television grew and was considered to be the marvelous solution to all advertising problems. As has been seen, television never was able to fill this impossible role as the all-purpose medium; now radio commercial sales are again experiencing rapid growth. Radio can attribute its recent "rediscovery" and regained health to a number of unique attributes.

Strengths and weaknesses

Most of the 8,000 radio stations in the United States deliver *a selective audience of listeners* at a low cost per spot aired. Although major metropolitan areas may have up to 60 AM and FM stations, most listeners are quite loyal and listen to only 4 or 5 of them. This relationship also holds in smaller markets with fewer stations. Given this relation, each station delivers a precise and fairly unique portion of the market and makes radio an excellent medium for segmentation. Cable television is now attempting to build the same types of narrow interest profiles, but radio is years ahead in the art of narrowcasting.

This audience selectivity is closely tied to radio's *low cost per unit of time.* Because radio stations deliver precise segments, the size of the segments tends to be smaller, leading to lower costs. Lower costs, in turn, allow the advertiser to stretch a budget and build high levels of frequency. Most advertisers, then, use radio as a *high-frequency medium.* It is more difficult to build reach because the audience is fragmented, but easy to build frequency toward a precise target.

Figure 11.11 is an ad from the CBS Radio Network directed to national advertisers to convince them of the merits of using Network radio. It will take a few minutes to digest, but it's a good investment of time. Then come back and well put it into a proper perspective.

Welcome back. Now, what can an advertiser get for the two different $30 million media plans? First, television. The ad suggests that an advertiser could purchase three or four 60-second spots in top-rated prime-time network programs per week. Since 60-second spots are rarely purchased, it would be more appropriate to consider this as seven 30-second spots per week. Because a top-rated program has approximately a 20 rating, the firm will be buying approximately 560 GRPs/month. (For a quick review of GRPs, see the previous chapter.) Now go to Figure 10.4; 560 GRPs can be converted to about a 98 reach and a 5.6 frequency for network prime-time television. The firm could buy that every month for $30 million.

Now, radio. The most typical length for radio spots is the 60-second spot. The ad suggests that the same budget would buy 200 60-second spots per week. With an average rating of 1.5 on radio, the firm would get 1,200 GRPs per month. Returning to Figure 10.4, this yields a 55 reach and 21.8 frequency, and, again, that level of radio could be bought every month.

This example points out a key difference between radio and television. For the same budget, television will yield more reach while radio yields more frequency. Which is better? Again the manager must go back to the objectives of the campaign. Radio and television each have their own place depending on the firm's goals.

While frequency and a low level of wasted coverage are benefits, other issues must also be considered. Because there are so many stations, the reach of any one is limited (often a station may have a reach of 1 or 2%) and the audience is fragmented. This means that *the absolute cost to develop reach through radio will be quite high.* As mentioned earlier, radio is not a good reach-building medium.

Another benefit concerns the *great visual enhancement* provided by radio. Anyone who has ever listened to a mystery drama knows that radio allows the listeners' imaginations to create much more suspense than can be created when the visuals are all presented. This point has often been made by the Radio Advertising Bureau when it airs messages on member stations to solicit advertising from local businesses. This campaign has always been clever and has constantly tried to make the point that radio is more versatile than other media, especially television, and that the visuals created in the mind by an audio track cannot be duplicated by actually showing visuals. Figure 11.12 is the script for one of the best of this series and also shows comedian Stan Freberg at his finest.

Figure 11.12 Radio as a visual medium

1st Person:	Radio, why should I advertise on radio? There's nothing to look at no pictures.
2nd Person:	Listen you can do things on radio that you couldn't possibly do on TV.
1st Person:	That'll be the day.
2nd Person:	All right, watch this. Okay, people, now when I give you the cue I want the 700-foot mountain of whipped cream to roll into Lake Michigan which has been drained and filled with hot chocolate. Then the Royal Canadian Air Force will fly overhead pulling a ten-ton marischino cherry which will be dropped into the whipped cream to the cheering of 25,000 extras. All right, cue the mountain.
SFX:	Sound of bulldozers pushing dirt followed by splashing of dirt falling into water.
2nd Person:	Cue the Air Force
SFX:	The sound of planes flying past.
2nd Person:	Cue the marischino cherry
SFX:	Whistling sound of bomb falling
2nd Person:	Okay, 25,000 cheering extras
SFX:	Sound of thousands of cheering people
2nd Person:	Now, you wanna try that on television?
1st Person:	Well, . . .
2nd Person:	See, radio is a very special medium because it stretches the imagination.
1st Person:	Doesn't television stretch the imagination?
2nd Person:	Up to 21 inches, yeah.

Source: Radio Advertising Bureau.

Visuals can be further enhanced by combining radio with television. In a common strategy, an advertiser will establish an image and visuals through television and then continue to air the audio track on radio. This allows the advertiser to build more frequency within the budget while maintaining the visual images in the mind through the less expensive reminder medium of radio.

In addition to the low cost per insertion of radio, there is also a *low cost of production.* Television spots of network quality generally cost between $100,000 and $250,000; radio production seldom exceeds $3,000 and often has no production cost because the announcer merely reads the spot; therefore, the only cost may be the agency's fee to write the script.

Radio provides *good local flavor* because the vast majority of programs are locally produced; only a small percentage have a network origination; these are primarily news and occasional features. As a local medium, it also provides reasonable access and quick turnaround. This means that items of local news value (e.g., special promotions, sales) can be produced and aired quickly.

Radio is much more accessible than television because there generally are more radio than television stations in a market and because radio stations generally accommodate more minutes of commercial air time than do television stations. This accessibility also contributes to the local flavor of radio because it

Figure 11.13 Radio audiences of all U.S. AM and FM stations by hour

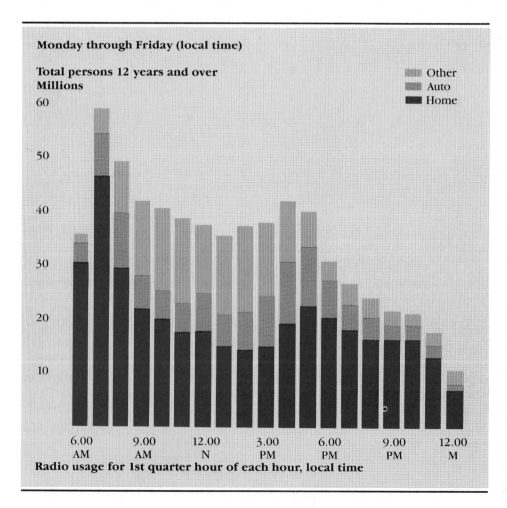

makes radio more available to the low-budget advertiser. Because of its availability, time often can be purchased within a day or two of air time in order to present timely messages.

The easy availability of radio can also be seen as a weakness. Because so much commercial time is available, there is *often a high level of clutter* on radio; this can lead to a weaker learning environment. One reaction of stations to this availability has been to cluster messages; this leads to more commercial-free air time but creates even higher levels of clutter when messages are broadcast. Another response has been for stations not to sell all available time but rather to charge more for fewer minutes. The more effective learning environment may more than compensate for the higher cost to the advertiser, while the higher costs compensate the radio station for the lower number of commercial minutes.

Radio is a low-involvement medium for most people. It is by nature a background companion. While it has been described as an intimate and personal friend, it is not closely attended to. The radio is on many hours each day but generally as background to other tasks. Learning may take place slowly under such conditions, with high frequency being a necessity. Again it is incumbent upon the advertiser to create a message device to capture attention in a situation where normal attentiveness is quite low.

One exception to this normal low attentiveness may occur in large urban areas from 7 to 9 A.M. and 4 to 6 P.M. During these times many inhabitants of these areas go through a strange ritual whereby they lock themselves up alone in a metal box with wheels and slowly follow one another along long ribbons of concrete. During this ritual, their only companion is the radio, and they are, therefore, more attentive to it. Radio stations, having noticed this also, charge their highest prices during these hours when they reach the 95% of automobiles that have radios, and they gain their highest ratings at these times.

Reach

The average home has 5.7 radios, and many commercial establishments have a radio on during business hours. The average adult listens to radio almost $3\frac{1}{2}$ hours per day. Figure 11.13 shows hourly listenership of radio. It would seem that such universal use of radio would make it ideal for creating high reach. As noted earlier, though, listenership is fragmented across many stations, making it difficult to get high reach across a broad, undifferentiated audience. Radio can, though, be used to build reach among specific target markets.

Frequency

Radio's great virtue is in building high levels of frequency at low cost across narrow targets. This has been adequately discussed in the previous pages.

Timing

Radio rates well on the two timing issues considered. Turnaround is generally good in that a spot can be aired within a day or two of its purchase. In addition, when the spot is purchased, the buyer knows when it will be aired in terms of day and daypart so there is no delay in audience receipt of the message as may happen in print.

T·H·E   I·N·S·I·D·E   O·U·T·L·O·O·K

Gordon L. Link

Executive Vice-President, Director of Media Services, McCann-Erickson

Gordon L. Link is McCann-Erickson's Executive Vice-President and Director of Media Services, U.S.A., and the agency's top-ranking media professional in the United States. Prior to joining McCann, Mr. Link had been Vice-President and Director of Eastern Sales for the ABC television network for 14 years.

Mr. Link's association with ABC as one of its senior negotiators interrupted an advertising agency career that started at BBDO in 1960. He went on to Ogilvy & Mather's broadcast department in 1965 and joined McCann-Erickson for the first time later that same year as an Account Supervisor. He was working on the Coca-Cola account when he left McCann in 1970 to work with ABC.

A native of Philadelphia, Mr. Link earned his B.S. from the University of Pennsylvania.

Worldwide Television: Emerging Patterns in the Global Village

Television is the most pervasive medium for advertising communications on a world-wide scope. Although household penetration of television sets may vary from a high of 98% in Canada and the United States to a low of 4% in the developing country of Zambia, McCann-Erickson Worldwide estimates that a global total of over one-half billion households (54% penetration) now have at least a single television receiver.

Despite the relatively advanced age of almost 40 years (positively ancient for an electronically based technology), television is now being buffeted by change and is evolving in a dynamic fashion in all quarters of the globe.

A kaleidoscopic array of newer technological "add-ons" has emerged to transform television from a monolithic and static transceiver of lim-

ited programming (software) to one that offers the ultimate in flexibility and form.

These newer technologies include cable and pay television, videotex, videocassettes, and direct broadcast satellite. All have the common link of the television set as the end-line display device.

The development of these new technologies is not occurring in a single and simple jump across the globe but is, rather, appearing on the world scene as bubbles on the surface of a heretofore quiet pond. These bubbles of development appear first in one locale, then another, then yet another. Each bubble—each coming to fruition of one technology in one place on the globe—leaves a ripple that creates effects in other quarters.

An observer from a single locale can certainly see and measure the effects in that one place. But a single observer can never see the overall fabric of patterns that ultimately evolve. To truly understand what is occurring, and to truly be able to use the experience of one locale to project and predict the transformations that will occur in other places, one needs the facility of global understanding and observation.

McCann-Erickson Worldwide is the premier global advertising agency—with ubiquitous presence across the globe. Based on extensive surveys and reviews across our 112-office system, we have recently concluded a major study of the emerging global patterns of television and television-based technology. This study examined the very fabric of television development in the United States and the world and has uncovered predictability and commonality (and differences too) that transcend the seemingly chaotic patterns of country-by-country variations in the emergence of television-based new technologies.

The changes that are being wrought by technological development will ultimately affect every aspect of marketing and advertising communications.

- Television penetration will increase dramatically on a global scale.
- Suppliers of programming (software) will experience extended growth as the multiplicity of new channels will have to be filled by audience-attracting content.
- Viewer time spent with television will increase as program choices expand.
- Pressures to commercialize television will grow as current levels of commercialization and license fees in noncommercial venues will prove insufficient to support the physical plant and the programming flow that is being created.
- Television's share of worldwide advertising revenues will increase.

- Marketers and agencies alike will have to face the challenges of audience fragmentation, increased creative flexibility, and the negotiating complexities of a vast array of communication channels.
- Sophisticated new approaches in research and in media planning and execution will have to be developed in order to meet these challenges.
- The very structure and functioning of agency media departments will undergo dramatic change in order to provide the new skills and expertise that will be required.

The remainder of this discussion will touch on some of the main points and points of view that we have developed after intensive examination of and reflection about the events that are continually unfolding within the world of television.

Worldwide television share of measured media expenditures now hovers in the high 30% range. This will increase dramatically as the proliferation of new technologies will themselves spur overall television penetration levels to the 50 to 70% range within the next 15 years.

Consumer (viewer) time spent with television averages over four hours per day per adult in the United States, 2.6 hours per day in Europe, and somewhat between these two marks in the rest of the world. As new channels of communication open up, and as viewer-attracting programming becomes available, international "time spent" figures will rapidly expand. The U.S. experience of relatively greater viewing hours among cable and pay cable households should be a replicatible pattern in other situations of increased programming alternatives.

Our studies of international television patterns indicate that the lower non-U.S. levels of "time spent" is related in no small measure to the lower number of stations (broadcast outlets) that are the norm in most areas.

The lower penetration and time spent levels thus appear to us to be more a function of supply rather than lessened demand. (Of course, governmental policies restricting broadcast outlets play a major role in many countries.) As channels of communication increase, there will be a proportionate rise in the levels of "time spent" with television.

Of course, programming development will have to expand to fill the many voids that will be created by a burgeoning of outlets. Advertisers and agencies alike may emerge ever stronger as developers of software—not solely as the actual production agent, but also as the investors who contribute ideas and development monies to those who actually produce the programming. This in many ways is similar to the recent explosion of syndication, particularly first-run syndication, in the United States.

There may also be new opportunities for advertisers and agencies to expand revenue streams (or to develop new ones) by acting as the actual distribution agents for the new program software.

One new commercial communication form and distribution channel will be advertiser-supported videocassettes, whose growth—partially fed by the explosive increase in rentals and the learning curve decline in hardware costs—will accelerate in all quarters during the next ten years. A sidenote of this growth is the increasing diminution of over-the-air and cable broadcast ratings deliveries. Another interesting and possible foretelling aspect of videocassette growth (although not yet applicable in the United States) is the English experience where VCRs have contributed to a halving of the movie theater audience over the last three years.

The current levels of commercialization (or the addition of commercial revenue streams on top of licensee-only noncommercial venues) will have to increase in order to pay for the new programming and perhaps even the physical plant that will be required to provide cable or direct satellite communications. Pressures for this will undoubtedly begin to percolate even in countries with strongly regulated television industries.

Overall, advertising revenues will expand on a global basis because part of the new revenue requirements will be met by expansion of acceptable commercial loads on over-the-air or cable television stations. Much of the world restricts commercial load to "minutes per day." The U.S. approach of "minutes per hour" will slowly expand to other countries as revenue needs expand and as consumer viewing expands because of more attractive programming.

Audiences will become more and more fragmented. The U.S. experience of fragmentation leading to diminished rating deliveries on the part of the more traditional outlets will likely be mirrored in many national scenes.

Audience fragmentation also brings out the potential for more precise targeting opportunities.

However, increased fragmentation also leads to an increase in inadequate audience measurement and the risk of so finely defining an audience that the slightest error results in totally missing the desired prospects. This is the converse of traditional "mass" television whose total reach was always so large that all population segments could at least be touched by advertising schedules.

Media planning and the research that supports strategy and tactic development will grow even more complex. Whole new techniques will have to be developed and tested and implemented in order to stay on top.

There will arise a vastly increased multiplicity of communication channels that will offer the potential of a broad new panoply of creative form and content as narrowcasting to specific demographic and interest groups becomes a reality.

Cost

Issues that determine the cost of a radio spot are similar to those for television:

Daypart (the parts differ from television to reflect heavy listenership during drive times rather than prime time)

Audience size

Geographic area

Editorial climate/audience composition

Length of the message

Preemptableness (not a major issue owing to the availability of radio time)

Radio prices range from $8 for 60 seconds (multiple purchases) in Helena, Montana, to $300 to $400 for 60 seconds (single-unit purchase) in New York City. A 30-second spot costs about 80% of a 60-second spot; therefore 60-seconds are a better buy and are more commonly used. About 95% of all radio advertising is spot. Demand for spot radio, primarily from local retailers, has been flat for several years; as a result radio prices have also been stable. Spot radio now has the lowest CPM index of any major medium (see Table 14.3).

Summary

This chapter has reviewed issues related to television and radio, but these are only one part of the media that need to be considered. The next chapter includes the various print media and a comprehensive summary of all the major media.

Discussion Questions

1. What is the difference between a television spot and spot television?

2. Discuss why the cost of network television has increased so dramatically in the past few years. Now that it is illegal for the National Association of Broadcasters to regulate the amount of commercial time per hour, what do you think will happen to the supply and cost of this time?

3. Describe how consumers typically learn about products through television.

4. Describe the virtues of TV in terms of reach, frequency, timing, and cost.

5. Why would an advertiser ever want to buy a preemptable spot?

6. What impact will cable TV have on advertising in the future?

7. Describe the virtues of radio in terms of reach, frequency, timing, and costs.

Notes

1. "Networks' 30-Second Price List," *Advertising Age,* 11 October 1984, p. 63.

2. James P. Forkan, "Network's NFL Spots Hot Despite Hikes," *Advertising Age,* 8 August 1983, p. 6.

3. Peter H. Webb and Michael L. Ray, "Effects of TV Clutter," *Journal of Advertising Research* 19 (June 1979), pp. 7–12.

4. Don Veraska and Len Strazewski, "Industry works to improve fuzzy image," *Advertising Age,* 5 December 1985, p. 15.

5. Craig Reiss, "New Audience Data Fuel Erosion Debate," *Advertising Age,* 25 July 1983, p. 6.

6. David C. Lehmkuhl, "Television," *Marketing & Media Decisions,* October 1982, p. 86.

7. Roger C. Bumstead, "Cable," *Marketing & Media Decisions,* January 1983, pp. 96–97.

Chapter 12
Print,
Out-of-Home, and
Direct Response Media

This chapter is a continuation of the previous one in that the same format is used to present information about the various media of magazines, newspapers, outdoor, and direct response. While the latter medium includes nonprint alternatives, it is included here for convenience. The chapter concludes with several figures that allow a comparison across media on a number of dimensions.

Magazines

The role of magazines in the media plan is different from that of television or radio because magazines allow for detailed presentation of information that can be perused at leisure. As with radio, the audience for any particular magazine often is specific and, therefore, lends itself to segmentation strategies. Magazines are generally divided into four categories. After considering each of these, the strengths and weaknesses of the medium in general are considered.

1. *General and news magazines*   These magazines (*Time, Reader's Digest*) are high in circulation and tend to reach a broad market. On the surface, therefore, they may seem to resemble television in terms of reach. This is not the case, though, for an advertiser can buy one or any number of parts of the circulation as well as the whole. *Time* and *Newsweek,* for example, each offer about 500 different ways to segment their markets on the basis of profession, income, geographic region, or combinations of these.

An advertiser in *Newsweek* could buy just Kansas City, or just college students, or just physicians in the northern suburbs of Chicago. Figure 12.1 shows some of the parts of *Time* circulation. As the desired circulation decreases (owing to a smaller target market), the overall cost also decreases, but the CPM tends to increase. The increase in CPM is generally a function of the perceived quality of the target audience.

Demographic Editions

TIME Business

Offers the largest all-business circulation of any magazine in the United States. All TIME Business subscribers are individually qualified by industry and job title through completed questionnaires verified by the ABC. Provides in-depth reach to top, middle and technical management readers in all 50 states.

Rate Base: 1,635,000
Rates based on subscription circulation only.
Space available every other week starting with the January 14, 1985 issue. (See page 4, Cycle D.) **Five week closing date** for B&W and B&1C, **seven week closing date** for 4C. (See page 3.)

	Black & White	Black & 1-Color	4-Color
Page	$39,915	$49,895	$62,270
2 Columns	20,005	37,100	40,800
1 Column	15,970	19,960	28,020
1/2 Column	9,980	12,475	NA

See page 28 for Dollar Volume Discount schedule.

TIME Top Management

Circulates exclusively to owners, partners, directors, board chairman, company presidents and other titled officers. Subscribers are 100 percent qualified through completed questionnaires verified by the ABC. Provides highly refined reach targeted to top management nationwide.

Rate Base: 600,000
Rates based on subscription circulation only.
Space available every other week starting with the January 14, 1985 issue. (See page 4, Cycle D.) **Five week closing date** for B&W and B&1C, **seven week closing date** for 4C. (See page 3.)

	Black & White	Black & 1-Color	4-Color
Page	$20,965	$26,200	$32,700
2 Columns	15,725	19,650	26,165
1 Column	8,385	10,480	14,715
1/2 Column	5,250	6,550	NA

See page 28 for Dollar Volume Discount schedule.

TIME Top ZIPs

Circulates to the highest-income postal zip codes ranked by average household income. TIME Top ZIP's circulation has been redesigned to conform with 1980 U.S. Census data. Circulation is distributed in over 2,300 of America's highest income zip codes.

Rate Base: 1,250,000
Rates based on subscription circulation only.
Space available in 1985 issues dated: January 21, February 4, March 4, 18, April 1, 15, 29, May 13, 27, June 10, 24, July 22, August 19, September 16, October 14, 28, November 11, 25, December 9. (See page 4.) **Seven week closing date** for all colorations, full pages only. (See page 3.)

	Black & White	Black & 1-Color	4-Color
Page	$33,965	$42,460	$52,985

See page 28 for Dollar Volume Discount schedule.

TIME Regional Editions

Space available every other week starting with the January 14, 1985 issue. (See page 4, Cycle D.) **Five week closing date** for B&W and B&1C (except for New England Region), **seven week closing date** for 4C. (See page 3.)

NOTE: See pages 19–27 for Rate Computation and page 28 for Dollar Volume Discount schedule. See pages 6 & 7 for map of Regional Editions.

Eastern
Rate Base: 1,570,000
Circulation area: Maine, New Hampshire, Vermont, Rhode Island, Connecticut, Massachusetts, New York, New Jersey, Pennsylvania, Virginia, West Virginia, Maryland, Delaware, District of Columbia, Bermuda, Puerto Rico, U.S. Virgin Islands.

New England
Rate Base: 370,000
Circulation area: Maine, New Hampshire, Vermont, Rhode Island, Massachusetts, Connecticut. **Seven week closing date** all colorations, all units. (See page 3.)

East-Central
Rate Base: 930,000
Circulation area: Ohio, Michigan, Illinois, Indiana, Kentucky, Wisconsin, St. Louis, Minneapolis/St. Paul.

West-Central
Rate Base: 300,000
Circulation area: Minnesota (except Minneapolis/St. Paul), Iowa, Missouri (except St. Louis), North Dakota, South Dakota, Nebraska, Kansas, Montana, Wyoming, Colorado.

Southeast
Rate Base: 505,000
Circulation area: North Carolina, South Carolina, Georgia, Florida, Tennessee, Alabama, Mississippi.

Southwest
Rate Base: 390,000
Circulation area: Louisiana, Oklahoma, Texas, New Mexico, Arkansas.

Pacific Southwest
Rate Base: 715,000
Circulation area: California, Nevada, Arizona, Hawaii.

Pacific Northwest
Rate Base: 190,000
Circulation area: Washington, Oregon, Idaho, Utah, Alaska.

California
Rate Base: 610,000

Northern California
Rate Base: 245,000
Circulation area: California except for counties in Southern California.

Southern California
Rate Base: 365,000
Circulation area: Imperial, Inyo, Kern, Kings, Los Angeles, Mono, Orange, Riverside, San Bernardino, San Diego, San Luis Obispo, Santa Barbara, Tulare and Ventura Counties.

Figure 12.1 *Pages from the Time National Advertiser's Guide*

By being able to purchase specific segments, an advertiser can reduce wasted coverage and/or can send specific and different messages to each target. For example, it is a well-known fact that the people of Wisconsin drink more brandy per capita than the residents of any other state—that is, the fact is well known among the brandy drinkers of Wisconsin and the makers of Coronet Brandy. Coronet has combined media and message strategy to arrive at the ad shown in Figure 12.2. This ad was placed in Wisconsin editions of *Newsweek* and shows how a creative media plan can reach specific segments of a market while cutting down on wasted coverage.

The magazine advertiser can also test messages by sending different versions to different, but demographically similar, geographic areas. Using the same logic, the advertiser can test different media schedules and/or weights.

Finally, there is the opportunity to put a local message into a high-prestige national magazine. In this way Balise Chevrolet of Springfield, Massachusetts, can

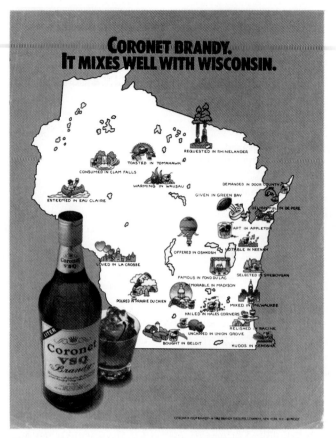

Figure 12.2 *Media plan segmentation in a national vehicle*

Figure 12.3 *Example of a local tag on a national ad*

get good color reproduction, reach its upscale target, and at the same time minimize wasted coverage. In the same vein, a national advertiser can put a local tag on its message to tell its customers where to go to make a purchase. The bottom left corner of Figure 12.3 shows such a tag for the Northwestern Mutual Life Insurance Company. Aside from helping the reader, such a tag provides a boost to the morale of the sales force.

2. *Special interest magazines* There were almost 2,000 consumer-oriented special interest magazines in the United States in 1983. These ranged from *Tennis Today* to *Apartment Living Today* to *Psychology Today,* and perhaps there may even be a *Pigeons Today.* Each is tailored to a specific demographic or life-style segment and thus offers a very specific target market.

3. *Business publications* There are over 4,500 magazines listed in over 160 categories in Standard Rate and Data Service. These narrowly targeted publications deliver specific groups of professionals with narrow and specific needs pertaining to their careers. The magazines are categorized within specific industries (e.g., *Pollution Equipment News, Travel Weekly, Toys, Hobbies and Crafts, Airport Journal*) and by job title across industries (e.g., *Purchasing Management Digest, Marketing News, Mechanical Engineering*).

4. *Farm publications*   As with industrial publications, farm publications are specifically oriented to career interests. There are about 350 journals tailored to every conceivable type of farm and farm product (e.g., *The Peanut Farmer, Pork Challenger, Poultry and Egg Marketing, Spudman, Cow Country*).

Strengths and weaknesses

Magazines, as seen above, generally offer the opportunity to *reach a specific target*. This can happen through a high-circulation magazine that offers many ways to split its readership or through smaller circulation special-interest magazines. As time passes, the computer technology for split runs (e.g., offering different forms of the magazines to different readers) becomes ever more sophisticated. Even smaller circulation magazines are now offering partial circulation rates to advertisers; almost 15% of all magazines now offer split runs. In addition, magazines are also changing editorial content for different targets; for example *Newsweek* runs different regional stories in the East Coast and West Coast editions, and some magazines use a different cover for subscription versus newsstand copies.

The issue of specificity can be expanded; not only can specific audiences be reached, but magazine audiences are more likely to be upscale on demographic and life-style dimensions. Therefore, the media planner can reach specific narrow groups of desirable consumers.

Because each magazine can have a distinct personality, its editorial philosophy can create a *special mood* that may lead to greater receptivity for the advertising. This would be the case especially for products that tie to the magazine's content (e.g., automobiles in *Car and Driver;* running shoes in *Runner's World*).

Magazines also have the advantage of *requiring attention*. A consumer can attend to television or radio in a casual way, but magazines and newspapers require more attention, which should aid learning.

Magazines offer *long life* to ads. When magazines appeal to specific interests, they may be kept for many months or even years. This is especially so for industrial and farm publications. At the very least, though, a magazine generally stays in the home until the next issue replaces it.

Long life means that an ad may be seen several times during its life, and even a brief glance at the ad may be sufficient to create an impression that aids learning or retards forgetting. Omnipresent cigarette ads with virtually no copy build up a low-involvement learning through repeat impressions in magazines. The back outside cover of the magazine is clearly most effective for this strategy because it is the advertising page seen most often. It is not a coincidence that the back outside cover is the most expensive page to purchase.

Long life also means that readers can absorb information at their own pace. Since the message won't disappear in 30 seconds, readers can study and absorb information at their leisure, allowing the advertiser to present more detailed information.

There is, though, also a negative side to individual control of pace: The average print ad is said to be examined for eight seconds. This puts considerable pressure on the advertiser either to transmit information succinctly or to grab and hold the reader. One of the greatest challenges of message strategy is to create a headline or visual that will so captivate the reader that the remainder of the message will also be absorbed.

Another strength of magazines concerns their general *high-quality printing,* especially with regard to color reproduction. This quality makes magazines a natural for conveying the appetite appeal of foods or the brilliance of a photo produced by an advertised camera or film. Neither newspapers nor television can compete in this dimension.

In terms of weaknesses, magazines have two major drawbacks related to timing. First, there is *no control over when the message will be seen* and/or read. This means that there is great risk in attempting to deliver timely messages by magazine. The risk depends on the magazine because the range of readership delay is quite large. For example, 90% of the readership of Sunday supplements (e.g., *Parade* magazine) occurs within one day; 90% of *TV Guide* readership occurs within one week; this percentage occurs within two months for *Reader's Digest* and $2\frac{1}{2}$ months for the women's service magazines (e.g., *Ladies' Home Journal, Better Homes and Gardens*). Magazines do not offer as quick a response capability as newspapers, which are almost always read within one day. Problems arising from uncertainty about timing are most disconcerting during a new product introduction and during the distribution of coupons.

The second drawback concerns the *lead time* needed to place a print ad. For most major publications, a 35- to 90-day lead time is necessary. This lead time reflects when the space must be purchased because the publisher needs notice in order to plan editorial content and printing requirements. There is no problem with space limitations as there is for broadcast; if more ad space is purchased, the magazine is simply made larger.

From these general issues, the planner must pull out the following specific items.

Reach

To reiterate, magazines offer specific reach opportunities to get to car buffs, theatre goers, joggers, Episcopalians, or whatever group is being sought. This also minimizes wasted coverage. If necessary, magazine buys can be accumulated to get broad reach because 90% of adults read magazines. However, magazines are rarely used as the basis for developing a broad reach strategy.

A second reach issue deals with pass-along readership. According to the Magazine Publishers Association, there are about 4.64 adult readers for the average copy of a magazine.[1] MRI data show a similar figure; SMRB a slightly lower figure.[2] More specific pass-along data are given for most major magazines by MRI and SMRB; in any case, readership of a magazine and its ads is far in excess of its circulation.

Frequency

An advertiser's message can be seen several times just because the magazine is read and reread. In addition, the advertiser can buy several pages within the same issue, as Kodak did in introducing a new series of photographic film. Magazines are generally not thought of as frequency generating vehicles; their virtue is more in the area of developing reach among a specific audience. It is in that vein that frequency can also be developed; that is, frequency is developed by reaching specific groups repeatedly over time. A study done by Cahners Publishing Company shows that a second ad in the same issue yields 9% higher readership than the first. The cost of the second ad, even with a quantity discount, would greatly exceed 9% and would be considered inefficient. Therefore, frequency should be built across issues or magazines rather than within an issue.

Timing

Magazines cannot offer specific timing because of the long lead times necessary before publication and because the pace of readership varies with the reader.

Cost

Magazine space availabilities are essentially unlimited. This means that the supply always exceeds or equals the demand and limits the increase in the price of the space. While the supply of television time is limited and demand exceeds supply, this is not the case for magazines; they can expand to fill the needs of advertisers. As a result, magazine rates tend to be fairly nonnegotiable. Rates fluctuate in response to eight variables:

1. *Volume/circulation*   As with television, the main influence on rates is the reach of the vehicle. Circulation is audited for most major publications by the Audit Bureau of Circulation (ABC) and is based on subscription sales, single-copy sales, and copies given away.

2. *Position*   Location can be important within a single page for a less-than-full-page ad or within the entire magazine. Requests for specific positions usually are contingent upon a 10% surcharge when they are accepted; greater additional charges are garnered for the back outside cover (the most expensive location with a 35% premium) and for the front and back inside covers. Specific requests are most commonly made for the top right corner (if the ad is less than full page) of a right-hand page, opposite certain editorial matter or a certain number of pages away from a direct competitor's ad. McGraw-Hill Research reports that ads in the front of the magazine draw 30% more responses than those at the back. They also note that this could be due to the fact that larger ads tend to be in the front of the magazine.[3]

3. *Size of ad*   The larger the message, the greater the cost. Figure 12.4 is from a study by Cahners Publishing Company showing how readership is influenced by ad size.[4] In comparing a full-page to a half-page ad, one can see that the full page garnered 36% more readership (124/91); in a similar study, McGraw-Hill Research reported comparable findings.[5] Other data (from SRDS) indicate that the cost of the average full-page ad is 67% greater than that of a half-page ad. In addition to this added cost, the media planner must also consider the value of the additional 36% of readers. Were they eventually converted to sales that generated marginal profits greater than the marginal cost of the full-page versus half-page ad, or could the dollars saved by running the less-expensive ad be better used to create a response through more repetition of the message? For messages without much information, a series of smaller messages may yield greater learning because of the increased repetition available at the lower price. Getting an incremental 36% readership for an incremental 67% cost is not, in the absence of other information, a good buy. There are, though, many issues to consider in making decisions on how to allocate a limited budget.

Figure 12.4 How advertising readership is influenced by ad size

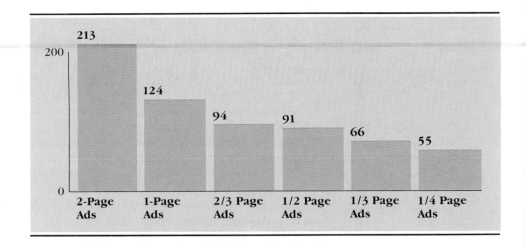

One alternative to a full-page ad is shown in Figure 12.5. Not only does this method save money, but it attracts attention to an unusual advertising format and ensures that the ad is in the midst of editorial content in a two-page spread.

4. *Limited edition*   As discussed earlier, many magazines now offer the opportunity to buy space for less than the entire circulation. By doing so the total cost to the advertiser decreases but the CPM for those reached generally increases.

5. *Bleed and gutter*   These are printer's terms used to describe the three outside margins and the center fold margin of the magazine page, respectively. Because it is more difficult and exacting to print to the edge of the page, there is a cost premium charged for this work (generally 15%). Although bleed and gutter

Figure 12.5 Creatively using small space units

printing look very nice, it is not clear that they enhance readership. Another Cahners study shows 3% higher readership for ads with bleed.[6] This may mean that bleed is an inefficient investment of media dollars.

6. *Color*   Ads can be printed in black and white, black and white plus one color, or four colors (black, red, yellow, and blue). As each color is added, costs go up to reflect printing complexity and effort. Cahners shows that four-color ads get 23% higher *readership* than black and white ads.[7] A McGraw-Hill Research study found 16% more *responses* to a color ad than a black and white ad.[8] The cost of the average four-color ad, though, is 33% greater than a black and white ad so, again, the planner must consider the marginal contribution of the additional readers/responders versus the marginal return of buying a greater number of black and white ads.

In each of these assessments of print format, the value of increased readership or response has shown that smaller, black and white, nonbleed ads may be more efficient. However, there are many other measures of effectiveness such as noting (did you see the ad), attitude (how do you feel about the brand), purchase (did you buy the brand), and others. The results shown on these pages must be put into perspective if the goal of the message is different from mere readership. In assessing any research, the planner must consider the basic objectives of the advertising. For example, food ads must convey appetite appeal; black and white ads may save money, but the impact of the ad may be lessened considerably.

7. *Special paper*   Anything that causes the printer to deviate from the ordinary *run of the press (ROP)* also adds cost to production. Some advertisers feel that an unusual paper stock leads to increased impact; they must pay for this. Often advertisers want to include a coupon or returnable post card with their ad. If it is a separate insert (called a *free-standing insert* or *FSI*) it costs extra.

8. *Quantity of buy*   Quantity discounts are available based on the number of pages bought over some period of time. The larger the buy, the larger the discount.

Rates for magazine ads vary dramatically. The inside front cover of *Reader's Digest,* four color without quantity discounts, costs over $225,000. *Country Folks* (featuring New York State agricultural activities and a circulation of 33,000) offers a full-page ad with two colors for $470. Magazine costs trailed other media during the 1970s owing to a decline in demand for magazine space. As a result costs have only slightly more than doubled since 1967 (as shown earlier in Table 11.3).

Newspapers

As has been seen, each medium has a basic task that it does best (although, rightly or wrongly, it may be asked to do many other tasks as well). Television is best suited for creating basic awareness across large masses of individuals; radio, through frequency, maintains awareness and inhibits forgetting; magazines present detailed information to create in-depth knowledge. The major task of the newspaper is to convey the urgent news of distribution, pricing, and promotions information; that is, what is in stock, what is its price, and what sort of deal is available. The dominant users of newspapers are retailers who have a need to convey this specific type of information.

There are currently about 1,700 daily, 700 Sunday, and 600 weekly newspapers being published in the United States, and the vast majority of these are local. These numbers have decreased as television has increased in prominence during the past 30 years. Total daily newspaper circulation in the United States exceeded 62 million in 1982.

Strengths and weaknesses

Possibly the main strength of the newspaper is in its value as a *catalog to help the consumer shop efficiently.* The newspaper is one of the few media (along with the Yellow Pages and direct mail) where consumers go specifically to look at advertising. Advertisers respond by providing relevant information and also by using the newspaper to distribute coupons. Therefore, the consumer gets information plus incentives to behave.

Newspapers also provide *extensive penetration of the local market.* Most newspapers reach 80% of the households in the market they serve; if there is more than one paper in the market, the combination generally reaches over 80% of the households. Often a two-newspaper market is controlled by one business office so that one advertising purchase leads to space in both papers. An 80% reach for one insertion is high compared to the typical reach in the other media previously examined. This high reach in conjunction with its appeal as a purveyor of commercial information makes the newspaper a powerful advertising tool.

There is, of course, a disadvantage to all this. If the product or retail outlet is aimed at a narrow target, then there may be considerable wasted coverage. This may be somewhat overcome by placing the ad in a specific section, such as the sports or business pages, but the level of segmentation achieved in this way is still poor and newspaper rates are based on total circulation.

A second weakness of newspapers concerns the *poor color reproduction* of the standard run of the press (ROP). This limits the visual persuasiveness of the medium but doesn't seem to hinder it in its main task of providing timely catalog information. One common alternative to the run of the press is the pre-printed free-standing insert (FSI) used by large retailers. The insert allows the advertiser to control the quality of the paper and the printing.

Finally, newspaper advertising is *expensive on a per-unit basis.* In a city where 30 seconds on television may cost $200 to $300 and 60 seconds on radio may cost $20 to $40, a full-page newspaper ad may easily cost $2,000. While the impact of these media differ, it also means that a newspaper wouldn't be appropriate for most frequency-building campaigns. Conversely, the cost may not be excessive given the goal of providing price and distribution information to a large audience within a specific geographic area. In the costs shown here, the CPM of the three media are quite similar because their reach varies so much.

Reach

Newspapers do a superb job of achieving high undifferentiated reach levels in a local market. While overall reach exceeds 80%, reach may exceed 90% among higher income households (e.g., 92% of Wisconsin households with incomes over $20,000 per year read a daily newspaper). In addition to high household reach, it is estimated by the Newspaper Advertising Bureau that each copy is read by 2.1 adults.[9]

Frequency

Eighty-five percent of reading households get home delivery of their newspaper. This means that daily frequency can be accomplished easily. Daily reminders of retail store information may be an effective strategy for building store traffic. Frequency is not built through rereading as n magazines, because the average life of the newspaper is less than one day.

Timing

Newspapers can be current with information because advertising lead time is short (one to two days), and virtually all reading takes place on the day of publication. This makes the newspaper excellent for timely information.

Cost

Newspaper rates are determined based on variables similar to those used for magazines:

> Volume/circulation
> Position
> Size of ad
> Limited edition (some newspapers now offer geographic editions to hit various parts of their market)
> Color
> Special paper (anything other than ROP is extra)
> Quantity of buy

Size of ad had, until recently, been a problem because each newspaper set its own dimensions for the sizes of ads it would accept. In 1981 the American Newspaper Publishers Association accepted a voluntary set of guidelines called the *S*tandard *A*dvertising *U*nit system that suggested 25 size units called SAUs. The SAU guidelines are shown in Figure 12.6. This standardization helps advertisers by allowing one sized ad to be developed for many papers, and helps the newspaper cut down on wasted space and better utilize computerized page-makeup systems.

Another cost consideration for newspapers concerns the source of the ad. Local advertisers get lower rates (up to 40% less) than do national advertisers but are not entitled to an advertising agency discount (15%). A full-page ad in the *Helena Montana Independent Record* costs $766 while the same full-page ad in the *New York Times* costs $23,700 for a weekday morning. Rates have tripled since 1967, but circulation has not kept pace with population changes. As a result newspaper CPMs are now highest of all major media and are accompanied by a decline in advertising lineage. (See Table 11.3.)

Newspaper supplements

Newspaper supplements, the magazine inserts that are distributed with the newspaper, are somewhere between magazines and newspapers. On the national level *Sunday, Parade,* and *Family Weekly* have the largest circulation of supplements (over 50 million combined) and are distributed through a combined total of over 500 local papers. In addition, most major market newspapers have one or more supplements of their own.

The supplements combine some of the qualities of magazines and newspapers. On the positive side, an advertiser achieves strong local market penetration

Figure 12.6 *Sizes of newspaper standard advertising units (SAU)*

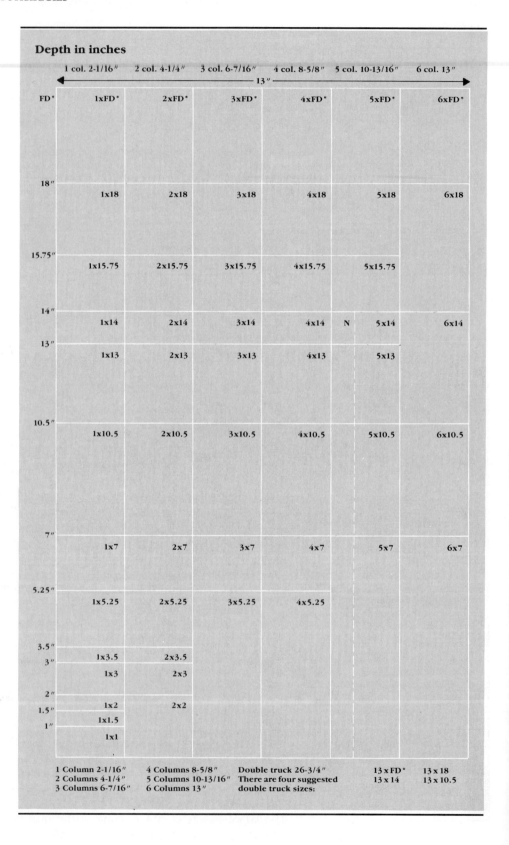

Depth in inches

	1 col. 2-1/16″	2 col. 4-1/4″	3 col. 6-7/16″	4 col. 8-5/8″	5 col. 10-13/16″	6 col. 13″
			◄————— 13″ —————►			
FD*	1xFD*	2xFD*	3xFD*	4xFD*	5xFD*	6xFD*
18″	1x18	2x18	3x18	4x18	5x18	6x18
15.75″	1x15.75	2x15.75	3x15.75	4x15.75	5x15.75	
14″	1x14	2x14	3x14	4x14 N	5x14	6x14
13″	1x13	2x13	3x13	4x13	5x13	
10.5″	1x10.5	2x10.5	3x10.5	4x10.5	5x10.5	6x10.5
7″	1x7	2x7	3x7	4x7	5x7	6x7
5.25″	1x5.25	2x5.25	3x5.25	4x5.25		
3.5″	1x3.5	2x3.5				
3″	1x3	2x3				
2″	1x2	2x2				
1.5″	1x1.5					
1″	1x1					

1 Column 2-1/16″	4 Columns 8-5/8″	Double truck 26-3/4″		13 x FD*	13 x 18
2 Columns 4-1/4″	5 Columns 10-13/16″	There are four suggested		13 x 14	13 x 10.5
3 Columns 6-7/16″	6 Columns 13″	double truck sizes:			

(as in newspapers) with a more quality production (color reproduction and paper more closely resembling magazines). These lead to higher readership and liking scores. Conversely, the only segmentability is geographic; the life of a supplement is only a day or two (as with newspapers), and the closing dates for purchase of space are similar to those for magazines.

Outdoor

Some say that cave drawings were the first signage. More recently, sales messages cut into stone tablets informed traveling Egyptians of places to eat and rest, and signs advertising bordellos found in the ruins of Pompeii closely resemble outdoor advertising. Not only was outdoor the first form of advertising, it was the only visual one until paper and printing became commonly available. In the 1800s lithography made the poster possible for artists such as Toulouse-Lautrec and Manet. As motorization made travel more rapid, the poster needed to grow in size and boldness. What exists now, though, is a direct descendent of what was first used in Egypt 5,000 years ago. Its purpose is also the same: to give a quick piece of information to someone passing by. Although outdoor also includes transit posters (inside and outside the vehicle), mall kiosks, sky writing, and some point of purchase, this section will deal primarily with the billboard since 75 to 80% of out-of-home media are in this dominant format.

Technology continues to make an impact on outdoor advertising in a number of interesting ways (Figure 12.7). Three-dimensional billboards and inflatable

Figure 12.7   Billboards can be larger than life

Figure 12.8 Example of an inflatable display

messages as well as two-dimensional (conventional) billboards with some element appearing to leap off the board toward the viewer are beginning to appear. Inflatables include 30-foot-high beer bottles and 12-foot computer terminals (Figure 12.8).

Other changes include video billboards that show a moving commercial message (these are similar to sports stadium scoreboards that show instant replays). Some of these also have an audio track for use where there is foot traffic; others have the ability to show color. Showing sight, sound, and motion on a 20 by 40 foot screen tends to hold an audience but can only be used where traffic passes slowly and/or has the opportunity to stop.

Another innovation takes advantage of people's having to stop and wait. Supermarkets are experimenting with putting television monitors above checkout counters as point-of-purchase displays. Formats have no sound track but intersperse commercial product messages with trivia quizzes, household hints, and excerpts from TV programs. Response has been positive from consumers and grocers.

Another outdoor innovation presents a billboard or sign in combination with a low-power AM radio message. For example, a "For Sale" sign in front of a house can have the tag line: "Tune your car radio to 1200 AM for more information"; more information can then be given to the listener. The Federal Communications Commission must certify the low-power transmitter; those in use have a signal range of under 300 feet and transmit a message from a continuous loop cassette.[10]

Lighting changes are also having an impact on outdoor. Most viable at this time is backlighting, which allows a much brighter and sharper image on a nighttime billboard than was possible using front lighting. Fiber optics are also on the horizon as a replacement for neon. Fiber optics allow continuous color changes, shimmering light, and more intense light as well as energy efficiency. Somewhere beyond the horizon are three-dimensional holographic messages that can fill up the night sky with a commercial message. The technology exists but the method is not yet commercially viable.[11]

Larger-than-life messages have also invaded sports stadiums, where the latest generation of scoreboards can show commercials between innings or give pitches between pitches. To buy 60 seconds of time for a season of 81 home baseball games costs up to $39,000; in 1982 the CPM, based on attendance, would be up to $27 depending on the stadium.[12] In addition, there is the traditional fixed panel available in various sizes. Table 12.1 shows the costs of buying space for the 1982 season in each major league baseball stadium. CPM ranged from $11.94 in Oakland to $81.54 in Texas. What better place to advertise beer than at a sports event!

And, did you know that the "bullpen" in baseball has advertising ties? In the early days of baseball, most outfield fences featured advertising for Bull Durham Tobacco. Utility players would sit in the shade of this sign until they were called upon to play. Hence the name "bullpen."[13] And that's no bull.

Changing the subject from bulls to cows—it is now possible to rent the side of a cow for an outdoor advertising message. Pick's Farm, near Toronto, Canada, is selling the space on the side of its cows for $500 per side per year. The farm is beside a highway near Toronto's airport so the "mediacows" get a lot of exposure.[14]

Table 12.1 Ballpark figures: the 1982 *AdWeek* Guide

	Rankings for fixed-panel ads (by CPM)		
Team	Estimated 1982 attendance[1]	Prorated dollars[2]	Median CPM
1. Oakland A's	1,379,754	$ 6,588–26,350	$11.94
2. Toronto Blue Jays	1,385,586	8,800–26,400	12.70
3. San Diego Padres	1,025,217	4,080–24,480	13.93
4. Seattle Mariners	876,987	5,060–23,000	16.00
5. Montreal Expos	2,368,440	8,078–72,000	16.91
6. Phila. Phillies	2,632,743	45,334	17.22
7. Baltimore Orioles	1,718,415	17,085–51,254	19.89
8. K.C. Royals	2,275,695	50,000	21.97
9. Milwaukee Brewers	1,770,093	20,350–59,200	22.47
10. Cincinnati Reds	2,003,211	20,700–86,250	26.69
11. California Angels	2,243,295	51,000–73,000	27.66
12. Cleveland Indians	1,134,810	7,800–65,000	32.08
13. N.Y. Yankees	2,663,361	50,000–125,000	32.85
14. Boston Red Sox	1,865,106	25,000–100,000	33.51
15. Atlanta Braves	1,018,170	9,600–64,000	36.15
16. L.A. Dodgers	3,329,019	125,000	37.54
17. New York Mets	1,228,770	27,200–68,000	38.74
18. Chicago Cubs	1,095,849	47,000	42.89
19. Houston Astros	2,277,801	76,500–127,500	44.78
20. Chicago White Sox	1,425,438	18,200–113,750	46.29
21. St. L. Cardinals	1,458,810	69,000	47.30
22. Detroit Tigers	1,828,322	50,000–125,000	47.86
23. S.F. Giants	1,093,743	35,000–70,000	48.00
24. Minnesota Twins	759,861	24,500–61,250	56.42
25. Pitts. Pirates	1,452,978	97,500	67.10
26. Texas Rangers	1,266,435	100,000	81.54

Source: John Grisso, "Baseball Stadiums: Advertisers Are in There Pitching," *AdWeek*, 3 May 1982, p. 18.
1. To arrive at these figures, *AdWeek* computed the average attendance at each team's home games for the past two seasons and multiplied by the 81 home games scheduled for the 1982 season.
2. Some ballparks host only baseball; some offer a year-long menu of sporting and entertainment events. This prorated figure is the cost of buying fixed panels as it relates only to baseball attendance. The range reflects the differing costs of panels of various sizes.

Strengths and weaknesses

Because billboards have a *long life* (they are generally sold in minimum units of one month), it is possible to build *high frequency levels.* People normally pass the same places each day as they go to work, school, shopping, or play. This means that a board can easily be seen 20 to 25 times per month by the same person.

Reach will also be high because an advertiser generally buys several boards in a community and the boards are on duty 24 hours per day. In fact, the standard unit of message delivery is a *100 GRP Showing,* which is a purchase of enough poster panels to deliver gross or unduplicated exposure opportunities equal to 100% of the market population on a daily basis. Such a buy would yield the equivalent of up to 3,000 GRPs over a month. A 50 GRP Showing would generate half the number of exposures but may have more or less than half the number of boards depending upon their locations.[15]

Outdoor is, in most cases, *larger than life* and can therefore have a strong impact. Some of the most creative uses of billboards have resulted from taking advantage of the large size. Graphics can be overpowering and borders can be used to emphasize largeness. In one case the object can extend beyond the frame to show size; in another the product is cut off by the frame to infer size. The size of the presentation makes it valuable for an introduction where strong impact is desirable. Figure 12.9 shows a creative way of going beyond the border in order to make an impact.

Billboards are flexible; they can appear in many places and can be targeted to a mass market by a freeway placement, a neighborhood by a local placement, or a behavioral location by placement near a retail outlet. This flexibility cuts down wasted coverage and, by placement near the retailer, can give the consumer one last message impression while approaching the purchase decision point.

Weaknesses of outdoor are centered on the *limited message possibilities.* In most cases the message recipient has only a few seconds to absorb the message; during that time the recipient may be otherwise occupied with the task of driving, may be forced to look elsewhere (e.g., the road ahead), may be thinking about different issues, and may have no interest in the product being advertised. These combine to make outdoor a challenging medium. How can the firm get its message across when the recipient is otherwise occupied and will be gone in a few seconds?

Figure 12.9 *Creativity in the use of billboards*

Because the length of message is so limited, outdoor generally is used to build awareness and/or image and to complement advertising done in other media. It has been said that a poster is to the eye what a shout is to the ear.[16] That nicely describes how the time limitation affects information processing.

Another weakness (which is being worked on) concerns the difficulty in accurately measuring reach, frequency, and other effects. Recent work with tachistoscopes and eye movement monitors are starting to answer questions in this area.[17]

Reach

Outdoor can be fairly pervasive and can give good, broad reach; geographic segmentation is also possible. To reach other types of specific segments, though, leads to high levels of wasted coverage.

Frequency

Billboards give good repetition possibilities because of their long life and because of the repetitiveness of people's daily travel habits. This high-frequency potential makes the billboard valuable as a supplement to other media during an introduction.

Timing

Most purchases are for a one-month minimum. Closing dates vary from 10 to 60 days prior to posting depending on whether or not the outdoor firm must prepare the posters.

In certain cases, billboards can be made timely through the use of a *snipe*. A snipe is a smaller sheet of paper that can be added to a board. For example, a grocer may have a billboard on a main artery leading to the store and may wish to change specials on a weekly basis on the board. The basic 20 by 10 foot (roughly) board would stay the same but a snipe of perhaps 15 or 20 square feet might be changed as desired.

Cost

Billboard rates are determined by size of board, size of showing, location, duration of buy, and production issues. The cost of outdoor has risen by 360% since 1967 but with a growing population, the change in CPM has been only 280%. Currently, demand exceeds supply of space, and prices are rising rapidly (see Table 11.3 in Chapter 11). In absolute terms, outdoor is expensive (a 100 GRP Showing in Los Angeles cost over $160,000 per month in 1982), but it is difficult to assess value because what it delivers (fleeting message with high repetition to a broad audience) is so different from other media. If it is carefully targeted, the CPM seems to be competitive with other major media.

Direct Response
This medium was formerly known as "direct mail," but it has grown so rapidly into nonmail areas that its name has been changed and made more generic; in fact, since 1981, advertising expenditures on telephone marketing have exceeded those of direct mail (see Table 12.2). As a further sign of change, the Direct Mail/

Marketing Association (DMMA) has changed its name to the Direct Marketing Association (DMA). In addition, *Advertising Age* now has a weekly section devoted to this topic.

The other half of the rapid growth picture for direct response concerns sales. As also shown in Table 12.2 estimated sales volume more than doubled from 1975 to 1981 as sales went from $60 billion to $125 billion. This rapid growth has given legitimacy to an area of marketing that had previously been overlooked and neglected by mainstream advertisers and marketers. During this same time period, 19 of the 20 largest advertising agencies developed internal direct response capabilities.

A third perspective of the size of direct response marketing comes from Table 12.3, which shows the percentage of adults purchasing in this way. Overall, in 1984 over 33% of all adults purchased by direct response. Usage was greatest among women and upscale demographic groups. Those who purchased spent an average of more than $170 each on direct response products during the year. Direct marketing accounted for about 15% of total U.S. retail sales in 1982.[18]

Table 12.2 Making the pitch . . . and the sale

Total estimated direct advertising expenditures (1977–1983)

	$ millions						
	1983	*1982*	*1981*	*1980*	*1979*	*1978*	*1977*
Coupons	**182.1**	127.1	94.6	84.2	72.0	61.0	84.0
Direct mail	**12,692.2**	11,359.4	10,566.7	9,998.7	8,876.7	7,298.2	6,966.7
Consumer magazines	**188.7**	167.0	150.0	135.0	123.0	99.8	86.2
Business magazines	**73.9**	66.0	59.0	53.0	47.0	49.4	49.4
Newspapers	**80.5**	70.6	73.0	60.6	54.4	58.0	42.8
Newspaper preprints	**2,850.0**	2,500.0	2,288.5	2,032.4	1,779.5	1,390.0	1,086.0
Telephone	**13,608.3**	12,935.6	11,467.0	9,845.0	8,555.6	8,555.6	7,699.0
Television	**386.5**	339.0	295.0	253.0	217.0	265.0	340.7
Radio	**37.0**	33.0	29.0	26.0	23.0	N/A	N/A
Total	**30,099.2**	**27,597.7**	**25,022.8**	**22,487.9**	**19,748.2**	**17,777.0**	**16,354.8**

Note: Creative costs not included in any of the above figures.

Estimated total U.S. direct marketing sales volume (1975–1981)

	$ billions
1975	$ 60
1976	$ 75
1977	$ 82
1978	$ 87
1979	$ 99
1980	$112
1981	$125

Source: Reprinted with permission from the April 1984 issue of *Advertising Age.* Copyright 1984 by Crain Communications, Inc. Also used with permission of Direct Marketing Association.

Table 12.3 Percentage of demographic groups ordering mail order items during 1984

	Total U.S. (000)	Any product	Cook books	Book club books	Cos-metics	Rec-ords	Maga-zines	Photo pro-cess-ing	Fruit, cheese spe-cialty foods	Cloth-ing	Needle-craft kits, sup-plies	Sport-ing goods	Tools	Cook-ware kitchen acces-sories	Small appli-ances	Auto acces-sories	Trees plants, seeds
Total Adults	167,727	33.7	2.8	5.7	2.9	3.8	14.2	2.9	2.5	9.5	2.8	1.2	2.2	2.7	1.3	1.9	4.0
Males	79,263	28.2	1.4	4.0	1.3	3.7	11.6	2.5	1.6	5.9	1.0	1.7	2.9	1.9	1.3	2.6	3.5
Females	88,464	38.6	4.1	7.3	4.2	3.9	16.5	3.2	3.2	12.8	4.4	0.7	1.5	3.4	1.2	1.3	4.5
18-24	28,671	28.4	1.7	4.3	3.2	4.2	10.6	2.3	1.5	6.7	2.5	1.3	1.2	2.1	0.4	1.8	1.8
25-34	39,536	37.1	3.3	8.0	3.4	4.7	17.6	4.3	2.9	9.0	3.1	0.9	2.0	3.3	1.2	1.6	3.9
35-44	28,978	37.3	3.3	7.1	2.9	4.0	16.2	3.5	2.8	10.4	3.6	2.0	3.1	3.1	1.6	2.8	5.0
45-54	22,345	37.3	3.7	6.1	2.7	3.7	16.0	2.6	3.0	11.2	2.5	1.5	3.1	2.9	1.6	2.2	5.3
55-64	22,224	34.4	2.6	4.7	2.9	3.5	13.3	2.3	2.5	12.1	2.9	0.8	2.3	2.2	1.5	1.9	4.5
65 or older	25,973	26.7	2.1	2.9	1.7	1.8	9.8	1.3	2.0	9.0	2.1	0.6	1.7	2.3	1.4	1.2	4.1
Graduated college	28,091	43.3	3.5	9.2	2.7	4.7	18.7	3.6	4.2	11.6	3.8	1.8	3.1	3.5	1.8	2.5	5.8
Attended college	28,938	40.5	3.4	8.1	2.8	4.4	18.1	3.7	3.3	12.5	3.9	1.3	2.2	3.9	1.4	2.1	4.9
Graduated high school	65,503	33.9	2.6	5.5	2.9	3.8	14.1	3.4	2.2	9.4	2.9	1.3	2.2	2.5	1.3	1.8	3.8
Did not graduate high school	45,195	23.2	2.2	2.4	2.9	2.8	8.8	1.2	1.1	6.6	1.4	0.6	1.5	1.7	0.9	1.6	2.7
Professional manager	25,845	43.6	4.0	10.0	3.1	5.4	21.4	3.9	4.0	12.4	3.7	1.9	3.4	4.1	1.9	2.6	6.3
Clerical sales	30,895	41.6	3.6	7.5	3.7	4.9	16.5	3.4	3.6	13.0	4.1	1.5	2.5	3.4	1.4	2.4	4.8
Craftsmen foremen	12,629	27.5	1.2	3.3	2.4	2.5	11.6	3.4	1.9	5.5	1.2	1.3	3.2	2.4	0.9	2.8	3.2
Other employed	31,031	29.1	2.5	4.0	2.7	4.2	12.0	2.6	1.8	6.9	1.8	1.4	2.0	2.2	1.4	1.5	2.8
Single	35,557	30.5	2.6	5.0	2.7	4.1	12.1	2.4	2.3	7.5	2.3	0.9	1.4	2.5	0.9	1.6	2.2
Married	103,585	36.1	3.0	6.4	2.9	3.9	15.5	3.3	2.7	10.2	3.1	1.4	2.6	2.7	1.4	2.1	4.8
Divorced/separated or widowed	28,585	29.3	2.4	4.1	2.9	2.8	11.9	1.8	1.7	9.7	2.4	0.5	1.6	2.9	1.3	1.6	3.6
Parents	59,295	35.9	3.0	7.4	3.4	4.4	16.1	3.9	2.5	8.6	3.1	1.4	2.5	2.8	1.2	2.0	4.1
Northeast	38,125	33.3	3.1	6.2	2.6	4.4	13.9	4.3	2.8	9.3	3.3	0.8	2.1	2.1	1.3	1.7	4.1
East central	24,794	35.2	1.9	5.1	2.4	3.9	14.8	3.5	2.1	9.8	2.9	1.8	2.7	2.6	0.9	2.3	4.9
West central	28,511	36.3	2.5	5.5	2.3	3.2	16.2	2.9	2.7	11.4	3.4	1.5	2.6	2.7	1.4	1.6	6.1
South	48,953	29.0	2.9	4.8	3.0	3.1	11.7	1.9	2.2	8.6	2.1	1.1	1.5	2.4	1.2	1.8	3.1
Pacific	27,344	38.7	3.4	7.4	3.8	4.6	16.3	2.0	2.5	9.6	2.8	1.0	2.5	4.2	1.5	2.4	2.7

Source: SMRB Study of Media & Markets, 1984

The rapid growth in direct response can be attributed to a combination of several changes over the past 20 years. The widespread use of credit cards and toll-free 800 telephone numbers provided the technology for growth. Credit ensured that the seller would get paid, and toll-free numbers eased interaction between buyer and seller. At the same time, there was rapid growth in the number of two-worker households. This meant that the household had much more disposable income but much less free time. This combination has led consumers to the convenience of direct response marketing.

Direct response marketing has a history at least as long as that of the United States. Citizens of the colonies purchased many of their goods by mail from Europe, and Ben Franklin published a catalog for mail-order sales of books during Colonial days. Before 1800 the concepts of free trial, no risk offers, and installment payment plans had been well developed. Aaron Montgomery Ward began direct mail sales in 1872 and Richard Warren Sears followed in 1886.[19]

From these humble beginnings, direct response has grown to the volume previously described. Current examples include bill stuffers, computer letters, glossy catalogs, telephone solicitors, late night 120-second television commercials with an 800 number to call, newspaper inserts and coupons, and more. Table 12.4 shows that in spite of all the growth and changes, Sears' and Ward's have kept pace.

Table 12.4 The top 25 direct marketers: Sales volume generated through direct marketing

Company	Sales volume; $ millions 1983	1982
Sears Merchandise Group	$2,092.0	$1,886.6
J.C. Penney	1,652.0	1,537.0
Montgomery Ward (Mobil Corp.)[a]	1,190.0	1,145.0
Colonial Penn Group	615.0	548.0
Spiegel Inc.	512.0	395.0
Fingerhut & Figi's (American Can Co.)	512.0	400.0
Time Inc. (magazines only)	385.0	320.0
Franklin Mint (Warner Communications)	378.0	410.0
New Process Co.	268.0	235.0
McGraw Hill Inc.	254.0	215.0
Columbia House (CBS)	220.0	200.0
Hanover House Industries (Horn & Hardart Co.)	215.0	140.0
L.L. Bean Inc.	205.0	192.0
American Express (TRS Co./merchandise sales only)	180.0	150.0
Herrschners, Brookstone, Jos. A. Bank Clothiers (Quaker Oats Co.)	152.0	120.0
Avon Direct Products	144.0	121.0
Grolier Inc.	135.0	147.0
AT&T Communications	120.0	100.0
Jackson & Perkins, Harry & David's, Bear Creek (Bear Creek Corp.)	111.0	110.4
Wausau Insurance Co.	110.0	—
RCA Direct Marketing	110.0	100.0
World Book Encyclopedia (Scott & Fetzer Co.)	105.0	100.0
New England Business Service	103.0	91.6
Spencer Gifts (MCA Inc.)	101.5	85.0
Amba Marketing Systems (The MacDonalds Co.)	100.0	70.0

Source: Reprinted with permission from the April 1984 issue of *Advertising Age.* Copyright 1984 by Crain Communications, Inc.
[a]Includes Signature Financial/Marketing Services direct marketing sales.

Table 12.5 Comparison of direct response marketing and mass marketing

Direct response marketing	*General advertising and marketing*
▪ Selling to individuals with customers identifiable by name, address, and purchase behavior	▪ Mass selling with buyers identified as broad groups sharing common demographic and psychographic characteristics
▪ Products have the added value of distribution to the customer's door as an important product benefit	▪ Product benefits do not typically include distribution to the customer's door
▪ The medium is the marketplace	▪ The retail outlet is the marketplace
▪ Marketing controls the product all the way through delivery	▪ The marketer typically loses control as the product enters the distribution channel
▪ Advertising is used to generate an immediate inquiry or order	▪ Advertising is used for cumulative effect over time for building image, awareness, loyalty, and benefit recall; purchase action is deferred
▪ Repetition is used within the ad	▪ Repetition is used over a period of time
▪ Consumer feels a high perceived risk—product bought unseen, recourse is distant	▪ Consumer feels less risk—has direct contact with the product and direct recourse

Source: From *Successful Direct Marketing Methods* by Bob Stone. Reprinted with permission by National Textbook Company.

The Direct Marketing Association defines direct marketing as "an interactive system of marketing which uses one or more advertising media to effect a measurable response and/or transaction at any location."[20]

Two key issues separate direct response from other advertising. *Measurable response* means that actual sales figures must be derivable from the effort. Other advertising does not have such a direct tie between stimulus and response. As shall be seen later, the ability to measure responses quickly and accurately is a strong asset to be capitalized upon. This leads to the second issue of an *interactive system* whereby buyer and seller communicate directly. Interaction is common to personal selling but not to other forms of mass communications.[21]

A direct response ad must contain

- A definite offer
- All the information necessary to make a decision
- Specific directions for responding[22]

Such a definition and operationalization clearly distinguish not only the form but also the goal of direct response. While other forms of advertising may have goals that deal with awareness, image, and attitude plus the suggestion of where to go to behave, direct response seeks primarily to sell; while it may also need to create awareness and attitude, this is done simultaneously with the main task of selling. Table 12.5 compares direct response marketing and mass marketing.

There are five major direct response media listed in Table 12.2. These are discussed in order of importance in the following pages.

Telephone

This is currently the area of greatest size and growth, owing to the pervasive nature of the telephone and its ability to allow easy access to the home. Personal sales calls can be made cheaply from a central switchboard; computer calls are even cheaper but yield a lower response rate because they don't allow personal interaction.

While the dominant share of telephone expense is for outgoing sales calls, the use of the incoming toll-free 800 line may generate a larger volume of sales in response to televised messages.

Bob Stone recently discussed telemarketing and offered several examples of why this area of direct response marketing is growing so rapidly:[23]

- Quaker Oats Co., in a four-month promotion for one of its cereals, built a sweepstakes around its toll-free 800 number. The 800 number received more than 15 million calls in that brief span, increasing sales more than 30%.

- Raleigh Bicycles uses telemarketing to reduce the high cost of face-to-face selling and to improve relations with its dealers. In the first year of operation, travel costs were down 50%. Sales, in a single quarter, were up 34% versus an industrywide decline of 10%.

- Scotts Lawn Care uses a hotline to answer customer questions about the proper use of its garden products. Its center takes about 93,000 calls from roughly mid-March to mid-October.

- Valvoline is using telemarketing to differentiate products, improve customer service, and increase productivity. The company receives 90% of its orders by telephone. The average order runs about $10,000!

- Great North American Stationers sells desktop supplies through a telemarketing sales force. In less than 10 years the company grew from annual sales of $25,000 to $14 million.

- American Express catalog sales handles about 1.5 million orders a year. It receives 50% of those by phone. Five years after the telemarketing program began American Express had increased sales from $29 million to more than $115 million.

- B. F. Goodrich Co. uses telemarketing to help establish itself as a leader in the chemical industry because of top-quality service. Its telemarketing program has helped to reduce the size of its field sales force by 25% and cut its sales/ordering costs by roughly $250,000 in one year.

- Montgomery Ward Insurance Group has an outbound telephone selling program that brings in about $150 million worth of life insurance sales a year. In addition, its 800 number is featured in all advertising and policyholder communications. In one year, it received more than 360,000 calls.

Direct mail

Forty-four billion pieces of direct mail were delivered in 1983; most of this volume was third class (often referred to as "junk mail"). There is good junk (interesting to the recipient) and bad junk (irrelevant to the recipient). The sophistication of the firm determines the percentage of bad junk; that is, if the firm segments well and creates an accurate mailing list, then it will minimize bad junk by reducing wasted coverage and by reaching interested buyers. Some practitioners feel that the final sale can be attributed 60% to the right mailing list, 30% to the item offered, and 10% to the copy.[24]

Print

Direct response print includes preprinted inserts appearing in newspapers and magazines, coupons seeking a direct response in these media, as well as ROP ads in the media. Magazines are especially useful because they offer segmented audiences, while newspapers offer the advantage of blanket coverage of an area.

Television

This medium has a small share of direct response because few products are well suited to both the medium and its viewers. The most successful products are in the $10 to $15 range and can be easily demonstrated or explained in less than two minutes. Television is becoming increasingly important in telephone sales by showing merchandise and soliciting the phone response. Cable television, with its ability to segment, is in the forefront of the movement and is leading the way to higher priced merchandise.

Radio

Since radio cannot show the product, it is even more limited as a direct response medium. Furthermore, many people listen to radio while otherwise engaged and are unable to make the required responding phone call or write down a name and address. During the 1950s radio was used extensively as a direct response medium, but now its use is limited.

An aside about direct response lists of names

Lists (used for telephone and mail selling) can be compiled internally from past sales records (often the best source) or rented from firms known as *list brokers.* Rental prices range from about $12.50 to $500 per thousand names although the average is about $50 per thousand; the price depends on the quality of the list. (Is it up to date? How much are members of the list likely to spend? How precise is the segmentation?) There are some 50,000 lists available through the various brokers shown in Standard Rate and Data Service.[25] Lists generally cannot be purchased but can only be rented for a single usage at a time.

Why are you on so many lists? When you return a warranty card after a purchase, you go on the firm's list. They may also sell your name to mail-order companies and list brokers. If you had bought a piece of stereo equipment, you would go on lists for more equipment, other electronics, record and tape clubs, and hi-fi magazines. If you put down your occupation, you will go on an occupation list. The same holds for income, education, and geographic areas.

Your name made all these lists because you bought a piece of stereo equipment. The same thing happens when you register for college, rent or buy a home, join a church, buy a subscription, register your car, get utility service, open a charge account, or donate to a charity. Your name is worth about $4\frac{1}{2}$¢ for each list it is on, so selling it to others is a revenue generator for many organizations.[26]

Strengths and weaknesses

In an ideal world, direct mail and telephoning would offer perfect reach, perfect segmentation, and no wasted coverage. Ideal worlds are few and far between, but direct response still offers the best opportunity to achieve these goals. In striving for perfect reach, the advertiser's CPM of *people reached* goes up dramatically but the CPM of *people who buy* may be the lowest of any medium. *Minimizing wasted coverage and accurately reaching prospective buyers* is a true benefit.

Lists can be very precise and may allow a firm to reach such specific target groups as newlyweds, owners of amphibious aircraft, or dentists in the state of Nevada. Computerized letters can be constructed so that each recipient gets uniquely relevant information. For example, a senator running for reelection could tell his constituents of beneficial acts performed during the previous term. If the senator were instrumental in getting an airport enlarged in one city, that information would be passed on to the voters of just that city but deleted from letters to voters who lived in the new flight paths. Such segmentation using computerized mail has actually occurred in political campaigning.

Finally, computers allow segmentation based on recency of purchase, product class, dollar amount spent, method of ordering, and method of payment, among others. Such analysis offers even more precise segmentation and ever-increasing response rates. Increasing the response rate is important in a field where a 2% response can lead to a profit and is considered a success.

Segmentation is only one area where precise analysis can be helpful. Since direct response is the most measurable of all advertising forms, there is *the opportunity to test media and message strategies scientifically.* For example, "Buy three for $1, get one free" gets a much greater response than "four for $1,"[27] and "50% savings" beats "half off."[28] One of the greatest contributions that direct response has made to the rest of advertising has been its ability to test strategies.

One of the pioneers of the advertising profession as it exists today was Claude Hopkins, who wrote extensively about the virtues of testing strategies using direct mail advertising. His two books, *My Life in Advertising* and *Scientific Advertising* are full of direct response examples.[29] Before Hopkins' career, advertising agencies mainly served as offices to sell media space to advertisers; as he was entering the profession it was changing so that the agency created messages for the advertiser and became an agent of the manufacturer rather than of the medium. As a result little was known about copy strategy; Hopkins was one of the first to realize that messages could be tested and results could be measured.

Another advertising giant who knows this and practices it well is David Ogilvy. Ogilvy started his agency after World War II with $3,000 in capital and built it into a world-wide operation now billing close to $1 billion per year. He has always stated that his first love was direct response and that this was also his secret weapon. Ogilvy has always been a master of innovation and creativity (as was seen in the message strategy part); he was equally adept at direct mail innovation, as the following quote shows.

> Prospects for a new Cessna Citation business jet were surprised when we sent them live carrier pigeons, with an invitation to take a free ride in a Citation. The recipient was asked to release our carrier pigeon with his address tied to its leg. Some of the recipients ate the pigeons, but several returned alive, and at least one Citation was sold—for $600,000.[30]

In spite of its strengths, direct marketing also has several important weaknesses to consider. There is a fair amount of *opposition in the general public* to the basic concepts of direct mail and telephone solicitation; this opposition is based primarily on complaints of devious practices and invasion of privacy. Figure 12.10 shows the top 15 company categories for over 350,000 complaints received by the Better Business Bureau of the United States during 1982. By far the

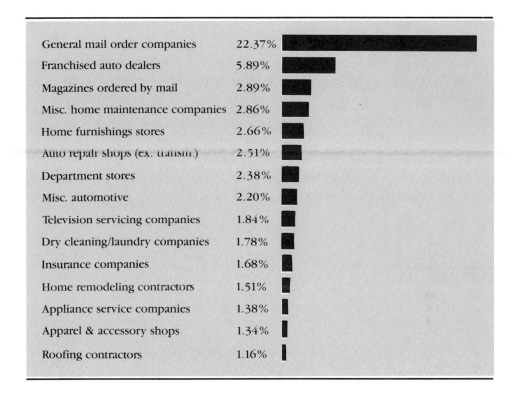

Figure 12.10 *Top fifteen complaint categories by type of business as received by Better Business Bureaus (1982)*

General mail order companies	22.37%
Franchised auto dealers	5.89%
Magazines ordered by mail	2.89%
Misc. home maintenance companies	2.86%
Home furnishings stores	2.66%
Auto repair shops (ex. transm.)	2.51%
Department stores	2.38%
Misc. automotive	2.20%
Television servicing companies	1.84%
Dry cleaning/laundry companies	1.78%
Insurance companies	1.68%
Home remodeling contractors	1.51%
Appliance service companies	1.38%
Apparel & accessory shops	1.34%
Roofing contractors	1.16%

leading category is that of "general mail order companies," and the third category was "magazines ordered by mail." It is hard to create a perspective for these data without more information, but it appears that 0.1% of households sent a complaint about mail orders to the BBB while almost 50% of households made a purchase. Despite this infrequency, direct response marketing has a poor complaint record compared to other industries. Practitioners hope this will change as the industry grows and matures.

The invasion of privacy issue may also be overstated. It is ironic that those who are most vocal about this issue are in the same demographic groups as those who are most likely to purchase by direct response. By purchasing, these people appear on more lists and receive more mail and phone calls. Consumers can have their names removed from mailing lists by filling out a form and sending it to the Direct Marketing Association; few people choose to do this. In fact, more people request to be added to lists than request to be deleted.

Reach

Direct response by mail or telephone has the opportunity to achieve almost perfect reach; lists are available that allow a firm to tailor its mailing to virtually any target. Direct response by other media is only as accurate as each medium itself; magazines offer a good potential for specific reach, while television offers weaker specific reach but greater general reach.

Mail and telephone solicitation also offer controls over the size as well as the quality of the market. The firm can roll out its product as slowly as necessary by controlling its mailing or call schedule.

Frequency

As with reach, frequency levels are dependent on the medium, and, as noted earlier, reach and frequency are often inversely related. Therefore, direct mail is a poor frequency tool but direct response through television does allow for the buildup of frequency. Average frequency for most direct mail offers is one; frequency of actual readership may be less than one because people often throw away direct mail without opening it. Lack of frequency can be a real handicap in direct mail plans because repetition is so important for learning.

Timing

Direct mail offers superb timing (the vagaries of the postal system notwithstanding); so does telephone solicitation. If timing is an issue, the firm can more or less plan for the printed message to arrive on the proper day through the mail. Timing of other direct response media is a function of the capabilities of the medium.

Cost

Direct mail expenditures can be quite high compared to other media, and a CPM of $1,000 is not unusual. Consider that the first class postage is 22¢ for one ounce (postage CPM = $220); add to that the cost of several pages of four-color graphics on high-quality paper. The average direct mail CPM in 1982 was $350; remember that the CPM for a television commercial on the "Super Bowl" in 1986 was $6.11.

While this comparison makes direct mail seem expensive, the *total cost* and *cost per customer who purchased* may be very different. For example, the Merlyn Corporation of Atlanta sent out a direct mail piece with a CPM of $35,000. Total cost, though, was quite low because there were only 12 contacts to be made, and the cost per behavior was excellent because all 12 contacts allowed a follow-up sales call. The direct mail piece was a talking shoe; the shoe was hollowed out and had in it an audio cassette that began by pointing out that the seller had just gotten his foot in the door.[31]

The major costs of direct mail include the rental of the list, production of the mailer, and postage. Costs for the media reflect earlier discussions but are tempered by the realities of direct response. In television, for example, a typical direct response spot would be 120 seconds rather than the more conventional 30 seconds; for a magazine a more expensive FSI returnable postcard might be included with the conventional full-page ad.

Teletext and videotext

These two television formats are currently being used in experimental settings and are predicted to be commonplace by the 1990s. *Teletext* is a one-way communications system that allows a graphic illustration (not a true video image) and/or text to be received on a television set; there is no audio track. Its major use is seen to be for news and classified advertising. *Videotext* is a two-way cable system that allows the consumer to request information and respond to questions (e.g., Would you like to buy this item?). This system also has only simple graphics and no audio but does offer the ability to interact. This interaction makes videotext a prime candidate to be a direct response tool of the future.

Summary

This chapter and the previous one have discussed each of the major media across a number of variables that are essential to decision making. A summary of this work appears in Table 12.6 for television, radio, magazines, and newspapers. This

Table 12.6 Gross media comparisons

	Television	Radio	Magazines	Newspapers
Total population reach (Adults + children)	Very strong	Good	Fair	Good
Selective upscale adult reach	Fair	Good	Very strong	Good
Upscale adult selectivity (per ad exposure)	Poor	Fair	Very strong	Good
Young adult selectivity (per ad exposure)	Fair	Very strong	Very strong	Fair
Cost per 1000 ratios	Fair-Good	Very strong	Strong	Good
National media availabilities + uniform coverage	Very strong	Poor	Good	Poor
Local market selectivity	Good	Good	Poor	Very strong
Ability to control frequency	Fair	Good	Good	Very strong
Ability to pile frequency upon reach base	Very strong	Very strong	Good	Fair
Ability to exploit time of day factors (in scheduling)	Fair	Very strong	Poor	Poor
Ability to exploit day of week factors (in scheduling)	Fair	Very strong	Poor	Very strong
Seasonal audience stability	Poor	Very strong	Good	Good
Predictability of audience levels	Fair-poor	Good	Good	Very good
Depth of demographics in audience surveys	Poor	Poor	Very strong	Fair-good
Reliability and consistency of audience surveys	Fair-good	Good	Fair-good	Good
Ability to monitor schedules	Good	Poor	Very strong	Very strong
Ability to negotiate rates	Good	Fair	Poor	Poor
Fast closing + air dates	Fair	Good	Poor	Very strong
Opportunity to exploit editorial "compatibility"	Poor	Fair	Very strong	Good
Selective ad positioning	Poor	Fair	Good	Very strong
Advertising exposure	Good	Good	Good	Good
Advertising intrusiveness	Very strong	Good	Fair	Poor
Audience concern over ad "clutter"	Very high	High	Almost none	Almost none
Emotional stimulation	Very strong	Fair	Fair	Poor
Sensory stimulation	Fair-good	Fair	Very strong	Fair
Brand name registration	Very strong	Good	Fair	Fair
Product or efficacy demonstrations	Very strong	Poor	Fair	Fair
Ability to exploit attention getting devices	Very strong	Poor	Very strong	Good
Ability to use humor	Very strong	Good	Poor	Poor
Ability to use slice of life approach	Very strong	Good	Poor	Poor
Ability to convey detail + information	Fair	Fair	Very strong	Very strong
Ability to stimulate imagination	Fair-good	Very strong	Fair	Poor
Package identification	Good	Poor	Very strong	Good
Prestige and respectability of the medium	Fair	Fair	Very strong	Strong
Ability to talk person-to-person with audience	Fair-good	Very strong	Poor	Poor

Source: *The Media Book* (New York: Min-Mid Publishing, 1978), pp. 433, 436.

T·H·E   I·N·S·I·D·E   O·U·T·L·O·O·K

Robert Stone

Chairman Emeritus, Stone & Adler, Inc.

Bob Stone is Chairman Emeritus of Stone & Adler, Inc., Chicago. He is also author of Successful Direct Marketing Methods, *co-author of* Successful Telemarketing Methods, *and writer of a feature column on direct marketing that has been appearing in* Advertising Age *since 1967.*

In addition, he has taught direct marketing courses at Northwestern University and the University of Missouri at Kansas City. Bob has won numerous awards including six for the Direct Marketing Association's Best of Industry; he is also a member of the Direct Marketing Hall of Fame.

Direct Response Advertising and Marketing

Advertising and marketing people have lived through two severe recessions over the past decade. And in the process they have felt a growing need for advertising that is measurable and accountable.

Direct response advertising meets that very need, for if it is not measurable and accountable, it is not direct response advertising. Time was when direct response advertising was thought of solely as mail order. Today it is much more. Measurable direct response advertising is used to get inquiries for salespeople, for dealers, and distributors and to drive people into the retail store.

For the year 1984 it is estimated that direct marketing accounted for a total in excess of $200 billion in the sale of goods and services. A review of media expenditures for a recent 12-month period will exhibit the wide variety of media used in reaching this unprecedented sales volume.

Total direct response advertising expenditures (in millions)

Media	For 12-month period
Coupons	$ 127.1
Direct mail	11,359.4
Consumer magazines	167.0
Business magazines	66.0
Newspapers	70.6
Newspaper preprints	2,500.0
Telephone	12,935.6
Television	339.0
Radio	33.0
Total	$27,597.7

Noteworthy is the fact that direct mail, long the number one medium in total expenditures, has been replaced by telephone—the most personal medium there is next to a person-to-person sales call.

This plethora of media opportunities has created a new type of media buyer with different objectives from the general advertising media buyer. This new type of media buyer—the direct response media buyer—is more interested in *responses per commercial* than *reach* when buying broadcast time, and prefers *off time* at lower rates to *prime time* at higher rates. The direct response media buyer prefers *direct response mailing lists*—lists of people who have responded by mail or phone—to *compiled lists* because history has proved that direct response lists pull better.

And when it comes to purchasing print advertising, the direct response media buyer looks for magazines and newspapers with a *direct response atmosphere* created by a goodly number of direct response advertisers. (*TV Guide, National Enquirer, Wall Street Journal,* and *Parade,* for example, are regarded as attractive media for direct response advertisers.)

The rapid growth of direct marketing and the ever-increasing demand for accountable advertising has attracted the attention of major advertising agencies. Whereas a decade ago but a handful of major agencies had a direct marketing arm, today 19 of the top 20 advertising agencies in the United States have a direct marketing unit. And there are scores of smaller agencies devoted solely to direct marketing.

Direct response advertising has grown faster than available talent. And that presents a major problem. But there is a rainbow on the horizon. The universities of this country have identified the need for instruction at the college level and consequently courses and degrees are mushrooming.

Whereas there were practically no college direct marketing credit courses being taught a decade ago, in 1984 there were 59 credit courses being taught, 12 college credit courses in process, and 11 college noncredit courses being taught. The future for college students capable of mastering this unique discipline is bright.

Measurable and accountable advertising: its future seems insatiable!

Figure 12.11   *Evaluation of qualitative media issues*

	Television	Magazines	Newspapers	Radio	Outdoor
Demonstration	1*	2	3	4	5
Elegance	2	1	5	4	3
Features	3	1	4	5	2
Intrusion	1	3	4	5	2
Quality	2	1	5	4	3
Excitement	1	2	5	3	4
Imagination	2	3	4	1	5
Beauty	2	1	4	5	3
Entertainment	1	4	3	2	5
Sex Appeal	2	1	5	4	3
Personal	3	2	4	1	5
One-on-One	1	3	4	2	5
Snob Appeal	3	1	2	4	5
Package I.D.	3	2	4	5	1
Product-in-Use	1	2	3	5	4
Recipe	3	1	2	4	5
Humor	1	4	3	2	5
Tradition	3	1	4	2	5
Leadership	1	2	5	3	4
Information	4	1	2	3	5
Authority	2	1	4	3	5
Intimacy	3	2	5	1	4
Prestige	3	1	5	4	2
Bigger-than-life	2	4	3	5	1
News	2	4	1	3	5
Event	1	4	2	3	5
Impact	1	3	2	4	5
Price	3	4	1	2	5

*1 = most appropriate
 5 = least appropriate

figure comes from *The Media Book;* although it is not a perfect summary of the chapters, it is certainly a useful one.

While Table 12.6 deals primarily with quantifiable issues, Figure 12.11 examines more qualitative areas. In this figure Richard Anderson, former Executive Vice-President and Corporate Director of Media and Programming at Needham, Harper Worldwide, ranks five major media on their abilities to transmit a number of message forms. These two illustrations come together nicely; it is not enough merely to know how well a medium does in terms of building reach; it is also important to know how the medium does in conveying humor or intimacy or any of the other emotions used by advertisers. Together the table and figure summarize the two chapters very well.

Given all these variables, what media do practitioners choose? Unfortunately, there is no simple answer, such as that four out of five media planners recommend dumping the entire budget in network television. The variables interact so that each firm's decision is unique. Table 12.7 shows that the variety of media used varies considerably across the hundred leading advertisers. In spite of the great variety of emphasis, there are some commonalities. Those firms that manufacture products that tend to elicit low-involvement processes generally spend over 80% of their dollars on television while those that tend to elicit high-involvement process generally spend 40 to 60% of their dollars on television. Virtu-

Table 12.7 One hundred leading advertisers' expenditures by media in 1981

	Rank	Company	Total	News-papers	General magazines	Farm publications	Spot TV	Network TV	Spot radio	Network radio	Out-door
Airlines	60	UAL Inc.	57,560.5	33.1	8.1	—	29.1	14.4	14.6	—	0.7
	61	Trans World Corp.	56,486.3	30.7	11.1	—	21.1	26.8	8.4	1.2	0.7
	77	American Airlines, Inc.	44,996.9	44.6	9.7	—	23.2	6.6	15.0	—	0.9
	78	Eastern Air Lines, Inc.	43,622.6	54.3	9.0	—	11.2	4.0	16.0	—	5.5
	86	Delta Air Lines, Inc.	39,954.7	54.2	3.1	—	12.7	0.2	25.8	—	4.0
Appliances, TV, radio	25	RCA Corp.	107,828.2	27.4	25.3	—	11.2	33.6	0.3	1.9	0.3
	42	General Electric Co.	72,749.5	13.8	26.3	—	12.2	41.2	2.7	3.5	0.3
	93	North American Philips Co.	34,152.9	4.1	21.0	0.7	12.8	59.9	—	1.3	0.2
Automobiles	4	General Motors Corp.	335,075.8	19.6	19.5	0.5	4.2	43.8	9.7	1.6	1.1
	6	Ford Motor Co.	264,175.7	12.1	20.8	1.1	8.5	43.1	12.2	1.7	0.5
	10	Chrysler Corp.	182,320.0	17.0	13.8	0.5	9.6	30.1	27.8	1.2	0.0
	33	Toyota Motor Sales, U.S.A., Inc.	91,186.7	12.3	11.1	—	42.4	28.0	4.1	0.2	1.9
	45	Volkswagen of America, Inc.	68,978.7	13.0	35.5	—	19.0	30.8	0.9	—	0.8
	46	Nissan Motor Corp., U.S.A.	68,884.1	12.8	14.3	—	29.0	31.4	11.1	—	1.4
	69	American Motors Corp.	50,150.9	10.4	29.8	—	39.2	20.1	0.5	—	0.0
	72	American Honda Motor Co.	47,846.8	11.0	25.9	1.2	9.5	38.2	11.5	—	2.7
Chemicals	62	Union Carbide Corp.	56,193.6	3.8	0.7	2.6	6.1	75.4	10.3	0.2	0.9
	63	American Cyanamid Co.	54,774.0	0.2	13.8	7.8	17.9	56.0	4.3	—	—
	68	E. I. du Pont de Nemours & Co.	50,487.4	1.6	49.9	6.2	4.3	37.2	0.7	0.1	—
Communications, entertainment	28	Warner Communications Inc.	99,230.5	13.4	21.1	—	16.3	47.9	1.0	0.2	0.1
	32	Time Inc.	91,536.1	19.5	39.8	—	32.8	7.5	—	0.2	0.2
	59	CBS Inc.	57,647.5	27.4	51.4	—	10.6	2.9	0.2	5.7	1.8
	87	Columbia Pictures Industries, Inc.	39,871.1	0.2	3.1	—	6.9	81.8	7.8	0.1	0.1
	92	MCA Inc.	34,311.7	12.0	1.5	—	14.3	52.3	18.8	0.3	0.8
	96	American Broadcasting Cos.	33,485.5	30.7	45.6	—	18.3	—	0.3	3.2	1.9
Drugs	31	Richardson-Vicks, Inc.	93,539.1	0.2	6.6	—	16.2	72.3	2.4	2.3	—
	36	Sterling Drug Inc.	82,787.4	1.1	15.0	—	10.9	66.9	0.9	—	—
	43	Schering-Plough Corp.	69,962.6	0.8	22.4	—	9.7	57.9	1.8	3.9	2.6
	79	Miles Laboratories, Inc.	43,687.7	—	6.9	—	13.0	79.0	0.1	1.0	—
	89	SmithKline Corp.	38,865.5	—	15.0	2.5	12.4	66.5	—	3.6	—
	90	Pfizer Inc.	38,226.1	—	10.9	5.8	1.1	82.2	—	—	—

Table 12.7 *continued*

Category	Rank	Company	Total	News-papers	General magazines	Farm publications	Spot TV	Network TV	Spot radio	Network radio	Outdoor
								% of total dollars			
Food	2	General Foods Corp.	377,690.4	1.6	9.8	—	22.3	63.1	1.7	1.5	—
	8	General Mills Corp.	195,240.3	2.3	7.6	—	42.5	44.3	2.6	0.7	—
	16	Dart & Kraft, Inc.	145,366.7	6.7	21.4	—	30.4	36.7	4.3	0.5	—
	18	McDonald's Corp.	138,148.2	—	0.1	—	54.4	39.2	1.2	2.4	2.7
	22	Nabisco Brands, Inc.	120,983.0	4.9	14.6	—	21.0	49.6	0.2	8.7	1.0
	26	Ralston Purina Co.	103,502.0	1.1	11.2	0.8	17.6	64.5	4.8	—	0.4
	27	Pillsbury Co.	102,355.7	2.1	5.5	—	31.8	57.9	2.3	—	0.1
	29	Kellogg Co.	97,111.3	3.9	5.3	—	17.8	69.3	2.1	1.5	0.1
	37	Consolidated Foods Corp.	81,300.2	3.6	13.7	—	18.5	61.6	2.3	0.2	0.2
	39	Nestle Enterprises	75,167.6	4.1	9.7	—	36.2	46.6	0.4	2.8	3.4
	40	Norton Simon Inc.	73,652.0	13.5	29.2	—	12.2	38.9	1.4	1.4	0.2
	44	Esmark, Inc.	69,523.6	1.9	16.2	—	12.1	67.9	—	1.7	—
	57	Quaker Oats Co.	58,624.7	3.0	13.9	—	24.6	58.3	0.2	—	—
	58	H. J. Heinz Co.	58,407.4	5.1	8.3	—	29.2	57.1	0.2	0.1	4.6
	73	Campbell Soup Co.	47,599.6	9.1	9.7	—	24.7	42.4	5.1	9.0	—
	74	Beatrice Foods Co.	46,567.0	12.3	26.6	2.2	34.0	9.6	10.2	0.5	0.9
	80	CPC International Inc.	42,837.4	3.1	15.5	—	30.5	50.0	—	—	0.1
	88	Morton-Norwich Products, Inc.	39,663.8	4.9	6.7	—	17.7	64.8	—	5.8	0.5
	94	Borden, Inc.	33,875.9	6.7	14.1	—	18.4	52.8	3.0	4.5	
Gum, Candy	49	Mars, Inc.	65,876.8	1.4	2.2	—	48.9	47.3	0.2	—	—
	52	Wm. Wrigley Jr. Co.	62,777.5	—	—	—	21.8	67.2	2.8	8.2	—
	76	Hershey Foods Corp.	45,676.1	4.7	5.0	—	21.5	65.9	1.4	1.5	—
Photographic Equipment	51	Eastman Kodak Co.	65,009.3	3.9	20.4	—	8.6	64.0	1.4	0.8	0.9
	84	Polaroid Corp.	41,049.2	5.6	15.6	—	3.6	73.9	1.3	—	—
	97	Canon U.S.A.	33,205.3	3.0	27.8	—	14.5	50.0	—	4.2	0.5
Retail Chains	11	Sears, Roebuck & Co.	178,171.5	—	33.5	—	7.8	49.4	3.5	5.8	—
	64	K mart Corp.	53,497.3	—	15.4	—	42.6	22.1	14.7	4.9	0.3
	21	J.C. Penney Co., Inc.	47,941.5	—	18.5	—	27.0	53.3	0.7	0.2	0.3
Soaps, Cleaners (and Allied)	1	Procter & Gamble Co.	563,697.4	1.1	6.3	—	22.8	69.8	—	—	—
	12	Unilever U.S.	158,878.8	2.2	10.8	—	27.1	59.9	—	—	—
	35	Colgate-Palmolive Co.	88,920.3	4.2	10.6	—	25.0	54.0	6.2	—	—
	50	Clorox Co.	65,070.5	1.6	8.7	—	11.6	76.4	—	1.7	—
	67	S.C. Johnson & Son, Inc.	51,564.4	2.3	23.9	—	12.4	61.0	—	0.4	—
Soft Drinks	13	PepsiCo, Inc.	157,219.1	1.7	2.3	—	44.4	43.8	7.2	—	0.6
	19	Coca-Cola Co.	134,922.1	3.4	4.1	—	35.4	45.2	9.3	0.5	2.1
Telephone Service, Equipment	7	American Telephone & Telegraph	209,646.4	10.3	16.8	—	28.5	32.9	7.8	3.5	0.2
	53	Int'l Telephone & Telegraph	62,220.3	6.0	14.1	—	44.4	33.8	0.1	0.6	1.0

Table 12.7 *continued*

	Rank	Company	Total	News-papers	General magazines	Farm publi-cations	Spot TV	Net-work TV	Spot radio	Net-work radio	Out-door
								% of total dollars			
Tobacco	3	Philip Morris Inc.	372,971.4	24.3	27.6	—	5.4	26.7	4.8	—	11.2
	5	R. J. Reynolds Industries, Inc.	316,066.3	45.1	28.3	—	9.6	1.1	—	—	15.9
	17	B.A.T. Industries PLC	142,607.0	32.2	42.9	—	5.4	—	—	—	19.5
	47	American Brands Inc.	67,718.9	19.5	51.7	—	1.3	11.9	0.4	0.3	14.9
	83	Liggett Group Inc.	41,614.5	5.9	47.6	—	13.7	25.3	0.6	—	6.9
Toiletries, Cosmetics	9	American Home Products Corp.	190,264.7	0.8	5.4	0.3	21.2	69.1	1.0	2.2	—
	15	Bristol-Myers Co.	151,504.7	1.0	15.6	0.1	7.7	72.6	2.9	—	0.1
	20	Johnson & Johnson	132,568.7	3.5	17.0	0.2	2.9	73.3	2.5	0.6	—
	21	Warner-Lambert Co.	123,250.1	0.5	7.4	—	24.2	62.4	0.6	4.9	—
	23	Loews Corp.	116,384.4	42.6	31.4	—	3.4	1.1	—	—	21.5
	30	Gillette Co.	96,441.0	2.0	9.8	—	8.9	79.3	—	—	—
	41	Chesebrough-Pond's Inc.	73,561.6	3.4	18.1	—	11.1	67.1	0.3	—	—
	48	Beecham Group Ltd.	66,400.8	0.2	8.1	1.1	7.8	82.7	0.1	—	—
	54	Revlon, Inc.	61,972.6	0.7	17.7	—	37.7	39.9	1.0	3.0	—
	85	Noxell Corp.	39,963.1	—	24.9	—	9.2	64.9	0.2	0.8	—
	99	Jeffrey Martin, Inc.	32,246.8	0.2	5.9	—	26.5	42.7	—	24.7	—
Wine, Beer, Liquor	14	Anheuser-Busch Cos.	154,124.3	1.6	4.0	—	20.4	47.8	22.4	2.5	1.3
	24	Seagram Co. Ltd.	114,380.4	11.2	59.1	—	5.6	12.2	0.2	—	11.7
	34	Heublein, Inc.	90,279.5	3.3	16.3	—	32.9	37.3	3.2	—	7.0
	81	Jos. E. Schlitz Brewing Co.	42,763.5	0.9	6.1	—	25.1	42.8	19.5	0.2	5.4
	91	Brown-Forman Distillers Corp.	37,942.4	7.5	45.0	—	20.9	9.7	0.5	—	16.4
	98	Hiram Walker Resources Ltd.	32,525.4	6.4	71.4	—	0.3	—	—	—	21.9
Miscellaneous	38	U.S. Government	78,951.1	11.1	21.6	2.9	8.9	33.7	11.4	9.2	1.2
	55	Gulf & Western Industries, Inc.	61,450.5	8.2	7.6	—	37.7	44.0	1.4	0.7	0.4
	56	Mobil Corp.	60,395.3	14.1	4.0	2.4	55.7	18.8	4.2	—	0.2
	65	American Express Co.	52,794.7	12.2	17.0	—	18.0	48.2	2.7	1.9	—
	66	Greyhound Corp.	52,192.1	4.4	10.4	—	4.5	63.5	16.8	0.2	0.2
	70	Mattel Inc.	48,677.9	4.8	8.5	—	33.0	53.3	—	—	0.4
	75	Kimberly-Clark Corp.	46,344.6	3.6	19.5	0.6	27.9	45.6	1.4	2.0	—
	82	Exxon Corp.	42,482.5	3.6	15.9	—	14.7	57.0	6.9	0.7	0.6
	95	IBM Corp.	33,535.3	13.2	31.8	—	3.0	46.0	4.7	1.3	—
	100	Xerox Corp.	30,336.8	16.6	36.2	—	3.9	38.1	1.0	3.9	0.3

Source: *Advertising Age,* 9 Sept. 1982, p. 12. Copyright 1982 by Crain Communications, Inc.

Table 12.8 U.S. advertising volume: 1981 and 1982

| | 1981 | | 1982 | | |
Medium	Millions of dollars	Percent of total	Millions of dollars	Percent of total	Percent change
Newspapers					
National	2,259	3.8	2,452	3.7	+8.6
Local	14,269	23.6	15,242	22.9	+6.8
Total	**16,528**	**27.4**	**17,694**	**26.6**	**+7.1**
Magazines					
Weeklies	1,598	2.6	1,659	2.5	+3.8
Women's	853	1.4	904	1.4	+6.0
Monthlies	1,082	1.8	1,147	1.7	+6.0
Total	**3,533**	**5.8**	**3,710**	**5.6**	**+5.0**
Farm publications	**146**	**0.2**	**148**	**0.2**	**+1.5**
Television					
Network	5,575	9.2	6,210	9.3	+11.4
Spot	3,730	6.2	4,360	6.6	+16.9
Local	3,345	5.5	3,759	5.6	+12.4
Total	**12,650**	**20.9**	**14,329**	**21.5**	**+13.3**
Radio					
Network	230	0.4	255	0.4	+11.0
Spot	879	1.4	923	1.4	+5.0
Local	3,121	5.2	3,492	5.2	+11.9
Total	**4,230**	**7.0**	**4,670**	**7.0**	**+10.4**
Direct mail	**8,944**	**14.8**	**10,319**	**15.5**	**+15.4**
Business papers	**1,841**	**3.1**	**1,876**	**2.8**	**+1.9**
Outdoor					
National	419	0.7	465	0.7	+10.9
Local	231	0.4	256	0.4	+10.9
Total	**650**	**1.1**	**721**	**1.1**	**+10.9**
Miscellaneous					
National	6,334	10.5	7,067	10.6	+11.6
Local	5,574	9.2	6,046	9.1	+8.5
Total	**11,908**	**19.7**	**13,113**	**19.7**	**+10.1**
Total					
National	33,890	56.1	37,785	56.8	+11.5
Local	26,540	43.9	28,795	43.2	+8.5
Grand total	**60,430**	**100.0**	**66,580**	**100.0**	**+10.2**

Source: *Advertising Age,* 30 May 1983, p. 42. Reprinted with permission. Copyright 1983 by Crain Communications, Inc.

ally all firms (except those excluded by law, such as tobacco, or by convention, such as liquor) spend substantially on television to create and maintain awareness. Products that elicit high involvement transmit information through print media; products with less information tend to devote most of the budget to broadcast. Finally, Table 12.8 shows that in 1982, across all advertisers (not just the largest 100), the largest percent of dollars was spent on local newspaper advertising and that direct mail is growing most rapidly.

Discussion Questions

1. Discuss the virtues of magazines in terms of reach, frequency, timing, and cost.

2. Magazines, radio, cable television, and direct response all offer the ability to segment very precisely. How would you decide which to use?

3. Prime-time television, newspapers, and outdoor all offer the ability to reach a large, broad market. How would you decide which to use?

4. Describe the concept of pass-along readership. What is its importance to an advertiser?

5. Is it better to invest the budget in a few large print ads or many smaller ads? How would you decide?

6. Discuss the virtues of newspapers in terms of reach, frequency, timing, and cost.

7. What is run of press advertising? Why is it becoming less popular?

8. Discuss the virtues of outdoor advertising in terms of reach, frequency, timing, and cost.

9. What is a "100 GRP Showing"?

10. Why has direct response marketing become so popular in the past few years?

11. Discuss the virtues of direct response marketing in terms of reach, frequency, timing, and cost.

12. What are the two major components of direct response marketing that set it apart from all other forms of advertising?

Notes

1. Magazine Publishers Association, *Magazine,* no. 39, July 1982, p. 3.

2. "1982 MRI: Larger Audiences than SMRB," *Marketing & Media Decisions,* November 1982, p. 74.

3. McGraw-Hill Research, "Effect of Size, Color and Position on Number of Responses to Recruitment Advertising," *LAP Report,* no. 3116.

4. Cahners Publishing Company, "How Advertising Readership Is Influenced by Ad Size," *Cahners Advertising Research Report,* no. 110.1.

5. McGraw-Hill Research, "Larger Advertisements Get Higher Readership," *LAP Report,* no. 3102.

6. Cahners Publishing Company, "How Advertising Is Influenced by Bleed," *Cahners Advertising Research Report,* no. 113.1.

7. Cahners, "How Advertising Is Influenced by Bleed."

8. McGraw-Hill Research, "Four-Color Ads Average Higher Readership Scores Than Black and White in 4 Magazines," *LAP Report,* no. 3029.

9. Donald W. Jugenheimer and Peter B. Turk, *Advertising Media* (Columbus, Ohio: Grid Publishing, 1980).

10. "Firm Targets Its Miniature Radio Station at Real Estate Marketers," *Marketing News,* 27 May 1983, p. 4.

11. "Fiber Optics and Other Technologies Add 'Wow Appeal' to Outdoor Ads," *Marketing News,* 22 July 1983, p. 10.

12. John Grisso, "Baseball Stadiums: Advertisers Are in There Pitching," *Adweek,* 3 May 1982, p. 17–18.

13. Bert Randolph Sugar, *Hit the Sign and Win a Free Suit of Clothes from Harry Finklestein* (Chicago: Contemporary Books, 1978).

14. Kevin Quinn, "This Farm Tells Local Advertisers: Hang Your Signs on Our Bovines," *Wall Street Journal,* 27 March 1984.

15. "Larger Than Life," *An Inside Look at Outdoor Advertising* (Rochester, N.Y.: The Gannett Foundation, 1981), p. 14.

16. "Masterwork," *An Inside Look at Outdoor Advertising* (Rochester, N.Y.: The Gannett Foundation, 1981).

17. "The Effect," *An Inside Look at Outdoor Advertising* (Rochester, N.Y.: The Gannett Foundation, 1981).

18. *AdWeek,* 21 February 1983, p. 19.

19. Bob Stone, "The Long Journey from Clocks to Qube," *Advertising Age,* 21 January 1980, p. S–1.

20. Bob Stone, "No Longer Dreary Drudges," *Advertising Age,* 5 July 1982, p. M–27.

21. Stone, "No Longer Dreary Drudges."

22. Stone, "No Longer Dreary Drudges."

23. Bob Stone, "Dial 800-SUCCESS," *Advertising Age,* 23 January 1984, p. M–32.

24. Eileen Norris, "Brokers Making Lists and Checking Them Twice," *Advertising Age,* 16 April 1984, p. M–34.

25. Grey Advertising, Inc., *Grey Matter* 53, no. 1, 1982.

26. Bruce Shawkey, "Mail-Order Peddlers Pan Gold in Them Thar Lists," *Wisconsin State Journal,* 31 July 1983, p. 1.

27. Fred Gardner, "Profile of a Direct Marketer," *Marketing & Media Decisions,* July 1982, p. 42.

28. Roy Beauchamp, "You Could Look It Up," *Advertising Age,* 19 January 1981, p. S–30.

29. Claude Hopkins, *Scientific Advertising* (Chicago: Advertising Publications, Inc., 1966) (originally published in 1923); and *My Life in Advertising* (Chicago: Advertising Publications, Inc., 1966) (originally published in 1927).

30. David Ogilvy, *Ogilvy on Advertising* (New York: Crown Publishers, Inc., 1983), p. 145.

31. Kevin Higgins, "Ad Agency's 'Talking Shoe' Promotion Effectively Reaches Seminar Prospects," *Marketing News,* 19 February 1982, p. 15.

Chapter 13
Vehicle Decisions, Scheduling Decisions, and the Media Plan

*T*his last media chapter covers three important decision areas. The first two, vehicle decisions and scheduling decisions, are two of the three major areas of media decision making. The third topic deals with the development of the media plan.

After the media have been selected based on the criteria established in the previous two chapters, the media planner can make vehicle decisions. These decisions are based primarily on matching the vehicle audience with the target market and finding the best fit to create the appropriate level of reach.

The most difficult of all the media decisions concern scheduling. Since there never is enough information, these decisions are most likely to be based on intuition. Scheduling decisions are important because they influence the speed with which consumers will learn and forget, and the distribution of the media budget over time.

The result of the media, vehicle, and scheduling decisions is the media plan, which is the compilation of all the media-related issues. The plan allows the agency and client to assess the decisions, and, after approval, allows the media buyer to execute the purchases.

Vehicle Decisions

Having completed media decisions, the manager must make vehicle decisions. For example, after selecting magazines as the proper environment for the message, the advertiser next must choose between *Scientific American* and *National Enquirer*. In media selection a choice was made on how best to massage the target market; vehicle decisions consider finding the most similar profile between the target and the vehicles available. Having made a media choice, most vehicles are already eliminated. This part of the chapter will cover matching target markets and vehicles on quantitative and qualitative factors.

Approaches to vehicle selection

There are various ways of allocating media dollars to targets. While each may have its merits, only one can deliver the greatest number of prospects while minimizing wasted coverage. This is the key issue to vehicle selection: maximizing prospects reached while minimizing waste.

The first approach to be considered can be called a *broadside* or *shotgun approach.* Here the marketer spreads media dollars equally across all segments of the population assuming an undifferentiated market. Since this assumption of undifferentiation is rarely correct, it usually leads to less than optimal reach with considerable waste.

An approach that allocates somewhat in accordance with segment strength is *profile matching.* In this approach the marketer allocates media dollars to each segment in proportion to its share of total prospects. If the segment has 30% of prospects, it should get 30% of the budget. The profile of the vehicle selection matches the profile of the target markets.

Finally, there is the *high assay approach.* It suggests going after the best segment as long as it remains best, then going to the next best segment, and so forth. The analogy here is with mining where the vein of purest metal (highest assay) is pursued as long as it remains most profitable.

These three approaches are shown in Table 13.1. The table shows four segments (A,B,C,D), each of which has a population of 100 (column 2) but a varying number of viable prospects (column 3). Assume in this case that each message reaches one person and that the advertiser can afford 40 messages. The broadside approach reaches 10 people in each segment (column 4); it is undifferentiated and as a result reaches a total of 20 prospects (column 5). The profile-matching approach skews the media dollars to segment A in proportion to its percentage of total prospects (column 3 shows that segment A has 45% of prospects; column 6 in turn shows that 45% of the budget is spent on A). This approach is an improvement and reaches 26 prospects (column 7).

The high assay approach mines the richest vein most thoroughly and therefore recommends spending all media dollars on segment A (column 8); this reaches 36 of 40 prospects (column 9). In this example all three approaches could have used the same medium, but within that medium there were vehicles that were more or less effective at reaching the best segment. The main task in vehicle selection is to make this linkage.

Table 13.1 Approaches to vehicle selection

Segment (1)	Population of segment (2)	Number of prospects in segment (3)	Broadside approach Segment reach (4)	Prospects reached (5)	Profile matching approach Segment reach (6)	Prospects reached (7)	High assay approach Segment reach (8)	Prospects reached (9)
A	100	90	10	9	18	16.2	40	36
B	100	60	10	6	12	7.2	0	0
C	100	30		3	6	1.810	0	0
D	100	20	10	2	4	0.8	0	0
Total	400	200	40	20	40	26.0	40	36

Quantitative issues

In the situation analysis the advertiser examined the segments of the market and in setting the objectives, selected the most fruitful ones for pursuit. Now the vehicles must be chosen to deliver the message to these targets. Several secondary sources are useful in this task. SMRB and MRI give demographic information for major network television shows, national newspapers, and national magazines as well as radio and television dayparts and radio formats. Nielsen Station Index (NSI) and ARBITRON provide local market radio and television station demographic information in quarter-hour breaks throughout the day. Nielsen also provides network television information. These are the major sources of information that allow the matching of demographic and vehicle information.

Next the advertiser needs to calculate CPM for the target market for each vehicle under consideration. As shown in Chapter 10, the CPM will vary considerably depending on viewership (or circulation). The differences in target CPM between vehicles must be considered along with the target reach potentials.

A final quantitative decision concerns the ability of the vehicle to build reach or frequency over time. Audience accumulation and duplication data for major national vehicles also can be found in SMRB. As discussed earlier, some vehicles have loyal audiences and build frequency while others have changing audiences and therefore build reach.

Qualitative issues

A much more subjective issue to consider in vehicle selection is editorial climate (sometimes referred to as entertainment climate). This is an important but qualitative decision. For example, assume that *New Yorker* and *National Geographic* deliver roughly the same audience at roughly the same price. Which one should be chosen? Editorial climate suggests that one of these vehicles creates a better environment for the message so that people are more receptive to it. In a more extreme case, people are more likely to read an automobile advertisement in *Car and Driver* than in *TV Guide* while they may be more receptive to ads for blank videotape in *TV Guide*. In another twist of this concept, will people be more receptive to a commercial for bologna while watching "Laverne and Shirley" or "The A Team"? These are all judgment calls after considering the demographic and usage profiles of the viewers/readers.

Vehicles spend many dollars advertising themselves as the most appropriate for reaching the best targets. Figures 13.1 and 13.2 are examples of messages from the vehicle to the advertiser. These messages are, in turn, found in vehicles read by advertising decision makers (e.g., *Advertising Age*, *AdWeek*).

Vehicle decisions are essentially based on two sets of criteria. Quantitative standards allow the planner to compare vehicles based on size, quality of audience delivered, and cost of delivery. Qualitative standards call for an evaluation of the environment within which the message will be placed.

Clearly, vehicle selection is an imprecise art form with lots of room for judgment. To complicate (or simplify) matters, the advertiser may not be allowed to select the vehicle of choice. Network television may be sold in such a way that the advertiser selects demographics and date but the network selects the show to match. This happens when specific shows are unavailable or uncertain. Print allows more precision because the final size of most magazines and newspapers is directly related to advertising volume.

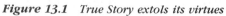

Figure 13.1   *True Story extols its virtues*

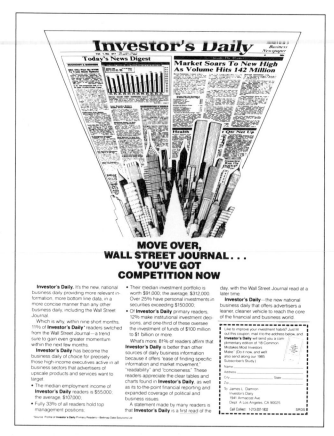

Figure 13.2   *Investor's Daily sells itself*

Precision is also possible in the *unit* of advertising. The unit concerns the size of ad or length of commercial. This decision is, of course, exclusively that of the advertiser.

Scheduling and Planning Decisions

The third major area of media decision making (after the medium and vehicle decisions) concerns scheduling. How often should the message be presented? How much time should be allowed to elapse between exposures? How valuable is a television exposure compared to a magazine exposure? The area of scheduling presents many difficult questions related to how people learn and forget.

Some of the top media decision makers have acknowledged a lack of knowledge regarding these very basic issues. Recent presentations by Priemer[1] and Geis[2] discuss some of the major shortcomings of media research in answering these questions; the topics under discussion in such presentations are primarily in the area of scheduling.

Learning theory

To deal with these problems this chapter first looks at some theoretical work in the verbal learning area of psychology. (An excellent overview of this work was done several years ago by Ray.[3]) Some of the earliest work in this area was done by Ebbinghaus and was first published in 1885. Although the research methods used today are different, his results are still replicated.

In his research, Ebbinghaus used himself as a subject. He gave himself lists of nonsense syllables (three-letter sets of consonant–vowel–consonant) to learn and recorded how many items of the list were learned after each repetition. After learning a list to perfection he tested to see how many items were still recallable after various lengths of time. It's hard to imagine making idle conversation at a cocktail party with a person who spent all day learning and forgetting nonsense syllables, but science has its costs.

Figure 13.3 shows a learning curve typical of that found by Ebbinghaus and many others. Note that the first few repetitions lead to a rapid amount of learning; as repetition increases the marginal amount learned decreases. The data shown in the figure are for individual learning; as a person gets closer to total mastery, the task increases in difficulty. You may have noticed this phenomenon in studying for exams; mastering the last bit of material is difficult. This phenomenon is more pronounced for meaningless nonsense subjects such as accounting and less prevalent for fascinating topics such as advertising and marketing.

While Figure 13.3 shows *individual learning,* the curve also represents the acquisition of a specific piece of knowledge (such as from advertising) across *large numbers of people.* Figure 13.4 shows such data for acquisition of advertising knowledge. Roughly the same curve can be seen. With a small number of repetitions, a large percentage of the target shows awareness. As repetitions increase, the marginal increase in learning decreases. Eventually it becomes quite expensive and time consuming to get awareness among marginal learners. Few advertisers set an objective of getting more than 80% unaided recall of their name within a short time period; to do so becomes too expensive, and the limited budget could be used more productively elsewhere.

Returning to Ebbinghaus, Figure 13.5 presents his forgetting curve, which shows his retention of nonsense syllables over time without rehearsal. Note that a very rapid decay occurs for a substantial amount of material. After 20 minutes, one third of the syllables were forgotten; after one day another third were gone.

Again a personal example can be introduced. Think back to the last time you stayed up all/most of the night to cram nonsense concepts of accounting into your head. As you ran from your room to the exam room you could probably feel the concepts falling out your ears; when you started the exam 20 minutes after studying, too many concepts had already escaped. Again, this is less likely to happen in meaningful courses such as advertising where the material is carefully learned rather than hurriedly memorized.

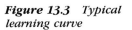
Figure 13.3 *Typical learning curve*

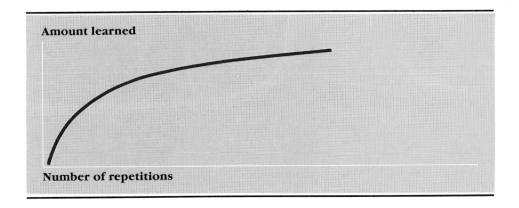

Figure 13.4 *Advertising recall as a function of repetition*

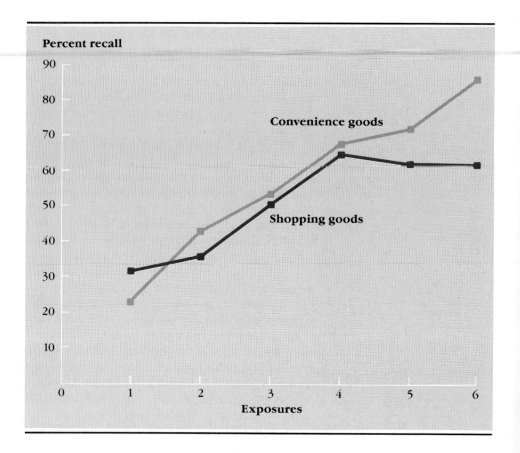

Figure 13.5 *Typical forgetting curve*

Figure 13.5 shows individual forgetting; again, similar data hold across large groups. This raises the questions of how often a message must be repeated in order to ensure learning and inhibit forgetting. An issue to consider here concerns the relevance of the material (e.g., accounting versus advertising courses). For most people (who are not students of advertising), most advertising is not especially important. People do not make a conscious effort to learn it as Ebbinghaus did or as you do. You and Ebbinghaus were motivated to learn; consumers rarely are so motivated.

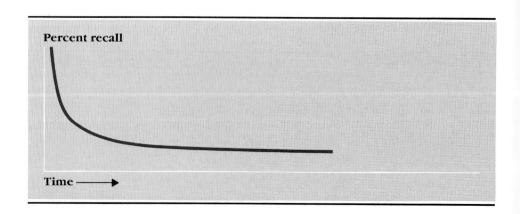

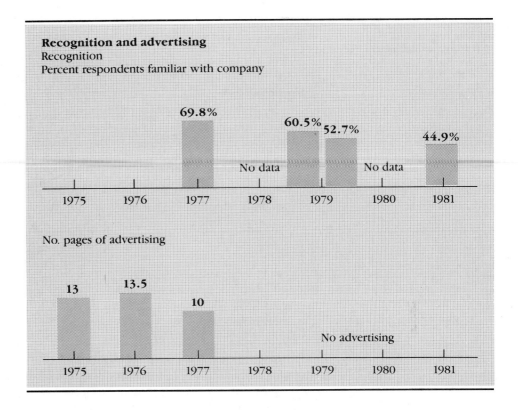

To test forgetting over a longer time period, McGraw-Hill Research did a series of four surveys over a five-year period to learn the drop in recognition for a packaging company. Figure 13.6 shows the advertising schedule for the firm and the recognition over the five following years when no advertising was done. In addition scores on product association and company image also dropped considerably during that time. Several years of low levels of advertising led to high awareness; several years without advertising eroded that base.

The promotions section of this text will deal with providing incentives to enhance learning and behavior. The curves shown here have been optimistic representations of the learning of advertising by the general public without any incentives.

There are some exceptions to consider. Durable, high-priced, high-involvement consumer products and industrial purchasing situations have consumers with an interest in learning who do so quite rapidly and correctly. Figure 13.7 shows data from several experiments where subjects were presented with more meaningful information or had an incentive to learn. Subjects here showed much greater retention of the material, but in no case was recall higher than 42% after three weeks. Even meaningful material is rapidly forgotten although its retention is twice that of meaningless material. One of the tasks of message strategy must be to develop important messages that show why it is in the consumer's best interest to pay attention. A successful message strategy can be invaluable for increasing the efficiency of the media plan.

In a landmark study, Zielske[4] studied the learning and forgetting of advertising in the same research project. He sent messages through the mail to house-

Figure 13.7 Forgetting of meaningful and meaningless materials

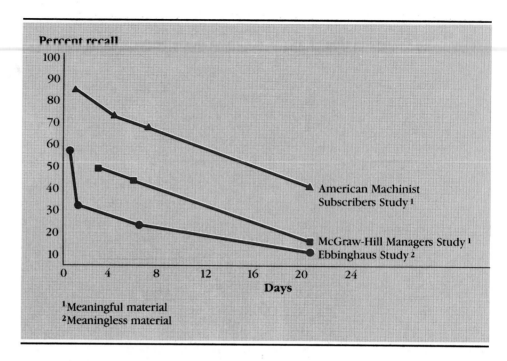

Figure 13.8 Learning and forgetting of concentrated and distributed media plans

wives for a brand of staple food product. Half of the subjects received a message every week for 13 weeks; the other half received a message every four weeks for a year (also 13 messages). Figure 13.8 shows the awareness data for the two groups. Those who saw a message every week reached 65% awareness after 13 weeks but had only 5% awareness after a year. Those who saw a message every four weeks ultimately had 45% awareness after the year.

Which media plan was better? It depends on the firm's objectives. The concentrated approach would be better for seasonal products such as toys where lit-

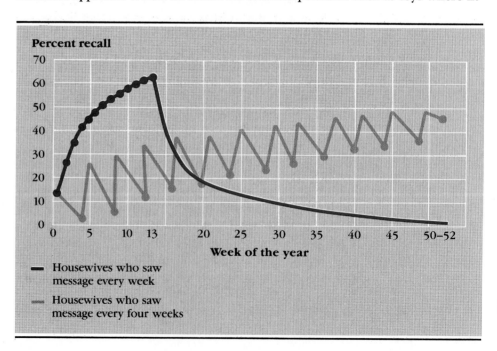

Figure 13.9 Combining concentrated and distributed media plans

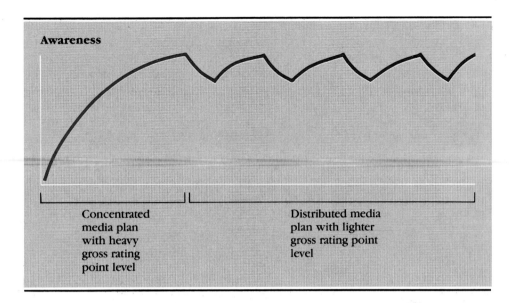

tle awareness is needed after Christmas. It would also be better for politicians who need awareness, attitude, and behavior to peak on one Tuesday early in November. Probably many politicians would be relieved to see these forgetting curves, especially the one showing 5% awareness of campaign promises after one year.

The distributed approach spaced the ads out over a longer period of time and as a result had developed a strong level of awareness by the end of the year. The average awareness over the entire year is also stronger using the distributed approach. This would point to the second approach as being more effective for long-run learning and efficiency of spending.

In a real-world setting, this slow build-up of awareness may not be feasible. Merchants probably won't give the product shelf space for a long time period if it is not selling; therefore, the firm can't slowly introduce the product when the ad campaign begins. On the other hand, if the firm waits for awareness to build before putting the product into distribution, then it will alienate consumers who become aware and look for a nonexistent product. The distributed approach, by itself, has problems.

By combining the concentrated and distributed approaches the firm will approximate the startup and maintenance phases of a typical new product's introductory media plan. Figure 16.9 shows what such a combination might look like. Here there is a concentration of advertising (for about three months) to achieve high awareness rapidly. Then the plan cuts back in frequency to maintain awareness and minimize forgetting. This combination seems to be the most efficient use of limited media dollars—heavy gross rating point levels initially followed by lighter gross rating point levels.

Converting GRPs to awareness

How many GRPs constitute a heavy or light level? David Berger, Vice President and Director of Research at Foote, Cone & Belding, analyzed 14 grocery store new product introductions during the late 1970s; all but one used television as its major medium. He was seeking an answer to the questions "How much do we

Table 13.2 The relation between GRP, reach, frequency, and success in new product introductions

GRP level	Probability of high awareness	Three-month plan	Six-month plan	Possible six-month distribution of GRPs
> 2,500	70%	> 800 GRP/month > 90R; ≈ 9F	> 400 GRP/month > 90R; ≈ 4.5F	600/600/350/350/ 350/350
1,000 – 2,500	33%	3–800 GRP/month > 90R; ≈ 3–9F	150–400 GRP/month 70–90R; 2–4F	500/500/250/250 250/250
< 1,000	0%	< 300 GRP/month < 90R; < 3F	< 150 GRP/month < 70R; < 2F	250/250/100/100 100/100

need to advertise to get high brand awareness?" and "With the amount of advertising we can afford, how much awareness can we expect?"[5]

He found that when assessing cumulative advertising weights over the first three to six months of introduction

- Above 2,500 gross rating points, the likelihood of high awareness is 70%.
- Between 1,000 and 2,500 gross rating points, the likelihood of high awareness is 33%.
- Below 1,000 gross rating points, the likelihood of high awareness is almost nil.[6]

In their present state these statements are too vague. A few assumptions lead to Table 13.2 and findings that are more useful. If high awareness is some level greater than 60% and most dollars are spent on prime-time network television, then Table 13.2 has data for both a three-month and a six-month period to show the bounds of the introductory periods that Berger examined.

Table 13.2 shows that *2,500 GRPs* will yield a high level of reach and frequency for either a three- or six-month period. If "effective reach" is a frequency of at least 3 (as discussed in Chapter 10), then this level of GRPs achieves effective reach. What is surprising at this level is that there is still a 30% probability of *not* achieving high awareness.

At the *1,000 to 2,500 GRP* level there are cases where achieving high awareness would be difficult. Achieving a high level of awareness in three months is a difficult task at any GRP level; as the level decreases to 1,000, the difficulty would increase. Reach levels, though, would be sufficient. In the six-month plan, both reach and frequency levels start to erode. To get 60% awareness with only 70% reach may be difficult because the conversion rate of "reached" to "made aware" needs to be high. This is compounded by frequency levels below those necessary for effective reach. While 200 GRPs per month may maintain existing awareness, this level is probably not sufficient to build awareness.

With under *1,000 GRPs,* Berger feels that the chances for success are nil. Table 13.2 shows that even in a three-month period, frequency will be limited. In a three-month period an advertiser could make a start at creating awareness, but this attempt would not be useful because no funds would remain for the following three months. In six months, the budget is simply spread too thinly.

The issue of converting GRPs to awareness has also been considered by David Olson of Leo Burnett.[7] In his paper he plotted this relation for 124 new products. The data are shown in Figure 13.10 and are consistent with those of Berger. In addition, Olson also shows the relation between awareness and trial for the same products. Figure 13.11 shows these data. By combining the two figures, a manager can get a sense of the high GRP levels necessary to achieve a respectable level of trial purchase.

There is a valuable lesson here; creating awareness is a necessary first step in a new product introduction, but it is expensive. If a firm cannot afford to invest large sums of money in advertising during the initial introductory period, then it should reconsider its options. Berger's and Olson's data show (and other cases will confirm) that inadequate advertising expenditures are wasteful and provide little hope of success.

Figure 13.10   *Converting GRPs to awareness*

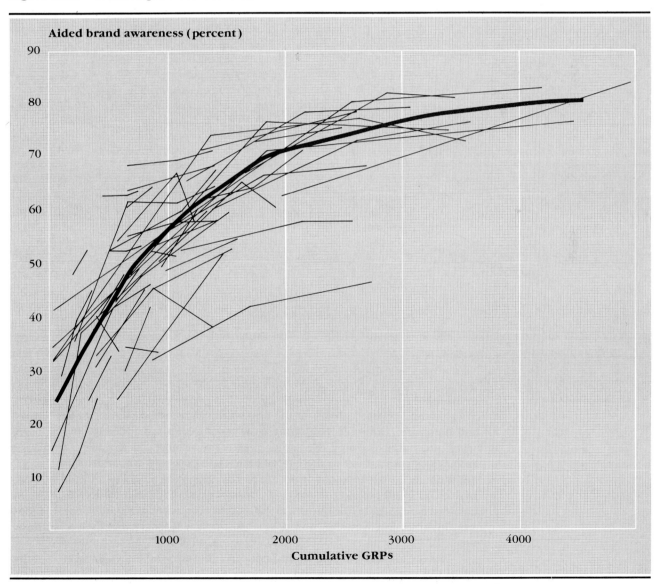

Aided trial (percent)

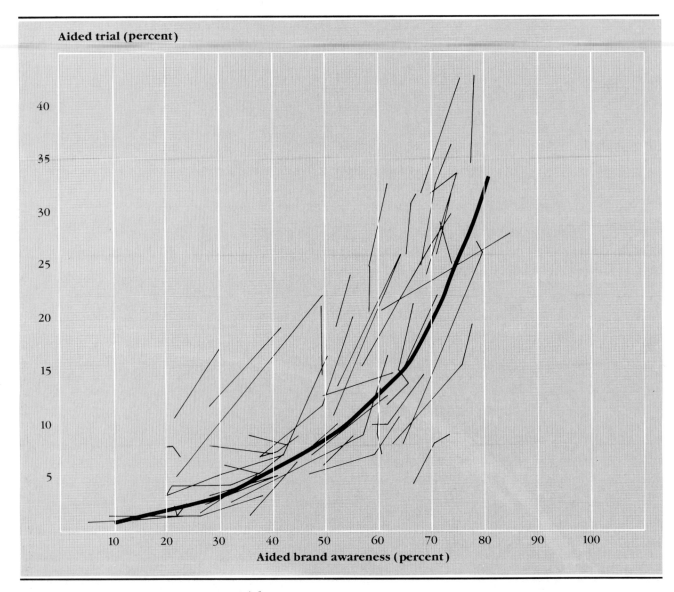

Figure 13.11   Converting awareness to trial

Working with a low budget

There should be alternatives for the firm with a great new idea and limited capital and there are. The most viable one is to reconsider the target market. GRP and reach are based on how the target market is defined. To get 60% awareness among all males 18–49 in the United States will certainly cost more than achieving the same awareness among all males 18–49 in New England. While the number of GRPs will remain the same, the cost per GRP will be considerably less. Or, conversely, a 1,000 GRP budget for the entire United States might buy 2,000 to 3,000 GRP in just New England. A small success will feel better than a large failure.

This means that the firm should not reach beyond the target that can be managed. The media planner should make sure that whenever the firm reaches a person, it can buy enough frequency to create and maintain awareness. If it cannot do that, the money is wasted. It is better off invested in a money market fund or a fast horse. Buying without sufficient frequency is analogous to going halfway to Europe by plane.

More complex scheduling issues

More scheduling information comes from Mike Naples, President of the Advertising Research Foundation. In a recent book,[8] he came to a number of useful conclusions that are consistent with what has been presented above.

1. "One exposure of an advertisement to a target group within a purchase cycle has little or no effect in all but a minority of circumstances." This is consistent with Berger's finding that achieving a low frequency level is a poor investment. Figure 13.12 shows a commonly hypothesized S-shaped advertising response curve. In this figure it is hypothesized that initially there is little impact in response to advertising efforts. With added effort there is an increasing and then a decreasing return. Naples' first point deals with area A of the curve.

2. "Since one exposure is usually ineffective, the central goal of productive media planning should be to place emphasis on enhancing frequency rather than reach." As discussed earlier, repetition leads to learning. Therefore, this important point is repeated here. Slowly build reach as the firm acquires the resources to support the reach with adequate frequency.

3. "The weight of evidence suggests strongly that an exposure frequency of two within a purchase cycle is an effective level. By and large, optimal exposure frequency appears to be at least three exposures within a purchase cycle." This reiterates Krugman's notion of effective frequency and covers the B area of Figure 13.12.

4. "Beyond three exposures within a brand purchase cycle, or over a period of four or even eight weeks, increasing frequency continues to build advertising effectiveness at a decreasing rate, but with no evidence of a decline." This takes the advertiser into the C area of Figure 13.12 as well as a large section of Ebbinghaus'

Figure 13.12 Hypothetical S-shaped advertising response curve

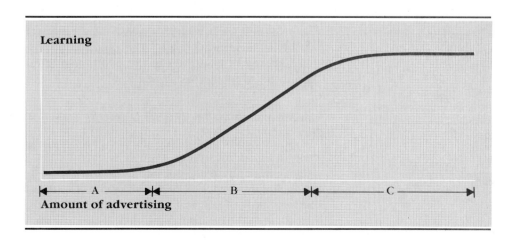

learning curve. Again, after some point it becomes inefficient to try to increase awareness; rather, the media budget should be used for other purposes.

Note that the learning curves in Figures 13.3 and 13.12 differ dramatically. This difference may be a function of involvement: In most learning theory experiments, the subjects are *trying* to learn and, therefore, show some degree of immediate learning. In the real world of advertising, few people are sufficiently interested to learn from the first exposure to a message. This concept may have been best expressed by Krugman in a paper explaining the impact of repetition in advertising. Krugman speculated that the first viewing elicits some cognitive response because the message is novel. In the second viewing, the message is not blocked but its content is evaluated and recognized. The third and subsequent viewings merely remind the viewer of what was previously learned.[9]

Both figures (13.3 and 13.12) show decreasing marginal returns to high repetition levels. Evidence is beginning to emerge that shows that advertisers may be overspending and staying too far in the right end of the C part of Figure 13.12. This overspending may be a conservative reaction to not knowing how much is enough advertising; as a result, managers may overspend to make sure they have bought enough.

Another issue that emerges from Naples' fourth point deals with advertising wearout, or a downturn at the far right of Figure 13.12. Naples writes that he knows of no data to support the idea that there is wearout resulting from too much frequency. This may be overstated. Simon[10] and Calder and Sternthal[11] have found data to support wearout; Axelrod[12] in a review article found mixed data. It is not clear at this time whether or not a manager should consider wearout in developing the media plan.

5. "Very large and well-known brands, and/or those with dominant market shares in their categories and dominant shares of category advertising weight, appear to differ markedly in response to frequency of exposure from smaller brands." This chapter has presented data that show it is easier to maintain awareness than it is to build it. Therefore, a well-known brand would get better efficiencies than the unknown brand. Naples also shows that dominating the total advertising done within any product class leads to greater efficiencies at various frequency levels for the dominating firm.

6. "Perhaps as a result of the different exposure environments of television dayparts, frequency of exposure has a differential effect on advertising response by daypart." This was most clearly shown in Figure 10.4 in Chapter 10.

7. "Nothing we have seen suggests that frequency response principles or generalizations vary by medium." The concept of repetition leading to learning has been shown to be strong in the psychology literature, and Naples has found it also to be strong across all media.

Scheduling and the hierarchy of effects

All of the above discussions of scheduling and planning have considered awareness as a goal. Awareness, though, is only the first component of the hierarchy of effects; what about attitude and behavior? Figure 13.13 shows responses to advertising at different levels of the hierarchy. The data for this figure come from a laboratory study of political advertising and test both high- and low-involvement political races.[13] The data show that awareness increases rapidly as a response to repetition. This occurs in both high- and low-involvement races. The slope is

Figure 13.13 Awareness, attitude, and behavior responses to varying repetitive advertising levels

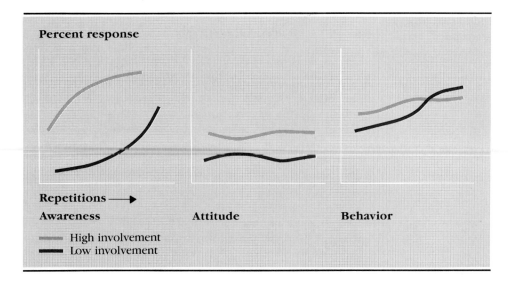

more gentle in the high-involvement races because some awareness already exists, and, ultimately, there is a ceiling effect; it is difficult to raise awareness beyond some level. These awareness data are consistent with the information presented previously.

For attitudinal and behavioral responses, the slopes are different. These slopes are quite flat when compared to awareness. In the high-involvement case, where it is hypothesized that awareness leads to attitude leads to behavior, there is a small amount of attitude change resulting from increasing the repetitions of advertising. There is, though, virtually no change in behavior. This impact had been suggested in earlier discussions of involvement in Chapter 3. In high-involvement cases, advertising can raise awareness and increase knowledge, but there will be only a small impact on attitude and no impact on behavior as repetitions increase.

Low-involvement responses to repetition are quite different. In the low-involvement hierarchy, awareness, it was speculated earlier, leads to behavior which leads to attitude. The data in Figure 13.13 confirm this ordering. There is a strong impact on awareness, a lesser but significant impact on behavior, and no impact on attitude. In low-involvement cases, advertising can influence trial behavior as well as awareness. The data seem to confirm earlier speculation concerning low involvement, that attitude is developed after behavior, possibly as a result of that behavior.

It is interesting to note that in this experiment concerning political advertising, the candidate with the higher repetition level won the election. It didn't matter which candidate dominated the advertising. This powerful advertising effect only occurred in the low-level race. This finding has since been confirmed in econometric analysis of actual voting data. Palda[14] has shown that in low-level elections the amount of money spent on advertising is a strong predictor of the amount of votes received.

Factors that affect scheduling

It is clear that scheduling decisions must be made in light of the advertising objectives and that frequency levels should differ for high- and low-involvement products and for different hierarchical goals. In a recent paper, Ostrow broke

Figure 13.14 *Variables that affect frequency decisions*

MARKETING FACTORS
- Established versus new brand—new needs more frequency
- Brand dominance/share—high share needs less frequency
- Brand loyalty—higher loyalty needs less frequency
- Purchase and usage cycle—longer cycle needs less frequency
- Target group—different groups learn and forget at different speeds

CREATIVE FACTORS
- Message complexity—simple message needs less repetition
- Message uniqueness—uniqueness needs less repetition
- New versus continued campaign—new needs more frequency
- Image versus product sell—image is more tentative and needs more frequency
- Size of message pool—more variety needs more frequency overall
- Size of advertising unit—smaller messages need more frequency

MEDIA FACTORS
- Clutter level—a more cluttered vehicle requires more frequency
- Editorial environment—more appropriate needs less frequency
- Attentiveness of medium—if medium holds attention, less frequency is needed
- Continuous versus flighted—continuous needs less frequency per period
- Number of media used—less media in plan means less frequency
- Opportunity to review—print needs less repetition

Source: Joseph W. Ostrow, "What Level Frequency?", *Advertising Age,* 9 November 1981, p. S-4.

down the factors that affect the frequency decision into three categories: marketing, creative, and media factors.[15] Figure 13.14 shows a listing of issues in each category.

Most of Figure 13.14 is self-explanatory, but a few comments should be added:

- *Message complexity* In evaluating message complexity and frequency, Ostrow's relation is correct, but, generally, simple messages are used in low-involvement cases where learning is slow. Therefore, when the message is simple, high repetition may be called for.

- *Size of message pool* Again Ostrow is correct that more frequency is needed because there are more messages to learn. It is not clear, though, that the brand and its claims also need more repetition. The variety may impede learning of a specific message without impeding the learning of the overall message strategy issues.

- *Size of advertising unit* This may contradict the message complexity issue if size and complexity of message are related.

- *Continuous versus flighted* As discussed in the next few pages, flighting is a strategy to increase repetition when the budget does not allow continuous high levels of repetition. While a continuous plan needs less repetition, it also is not as effective as the higher repetition flighting campaign.

Flighting

Having determined that repetition of messages is important, the next issue concerns the pattern in which to schedule the timing of the messages. Up to this point no pattern has been considered, but rather a constant barrage of messages (except for a heavier constant barrage during an introductory period) has been implied. Figure 13.15 shows five common patterns of presentation. In each part of the figure, the horizontal axis represents time and the vertical axis is the amount of advertising during the time period.

A new media term must be introduced in order to discuss Figure 13.15. The term is *flighting,* and it refers to a nonconstant pattern of advertising weight. The heavy (on) period is called a *flight;* the period of low or no advertising (off) is the *hiatus.* What has been referred to earlier as a *maintenance level* is also referred to as a *sustaining level.* The terms *pulse* and *pulsing* are also used. These last two terms roughly equate to *flight* and *flighting.*

Figure 13.15(a) shows a steady schedule with no flighting. All time periods get an equal share of advertising dollars. The plan might have six messages per day, four messages per week, nine messages per month, etc., but every time period (of whatever duration) would be the same. This has the advantages of neat-

Figure 13.15 *Various types of flighting schedules*

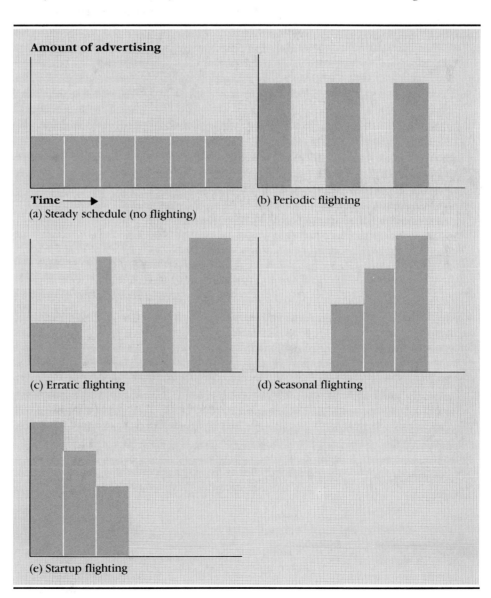

ness and symmetry but otherwise has problems. Given an extremely large budget, a constant level sufficient to maintain learning at all times could be achieved. Given a more moderate budget, the amount of frequency attainable might not be sufficient to get past area A of Figure 13.12. If the marketer tries to advertise continuously, the amount that can be done in any one period may be too little to do much good. The result is a spread-out plan that is likely to become lost in the media noise and clutter and never make an impact. The result is the same as trying to reach too large an audience; the frequency is insufficient to do the job.

There are alternatives. Figures 13.15(b) and 13.15(c) show the same amount of budget used in more concentrated ways through flighting. By not advertising in certain periods, the marketer has more budget available for other periods. These are common strategies used to get more impact from a limited budget. Whenever advertising is scheduled, there is now enough frequency to get into areas B and C of Figure 13.12; whenever there is advertising, there is an impact great enough to break through the clutter and the noise of the environment.

When no advertising occurs there is some slippage in awareness; when advertising reoccurs, awareness goes back up. The mean level of awareness, though, exceeds that obtained by the steady schedule.

Figure 13.16 shows the difference between a flighting and a constant schedule from a field experiment reported by Simon.[16] In this experiment the same advertising budget was spent either as a steady-state schedule (Figure 13.15a) or as periodic flighting (Figure 13.15b). Over a period of one year, the flighting schedule led to 24% greater sales. In addition, Simon reported that the return on the advertising investment was 3.28% for the steady schedule but was 8.54% for the flighting schedule.

Figures 13.15(d) and 13.15(e) show special cases of flighting that respond to marketplace conditions. Figure 13.15(d) shows seasonality. If 90% of the firm's sales occur between Thanksgiving and Christmas, there is no need to advertise in June; if 98% of suntan lotion sales take place between May and August, there is little need to advertise in November. Figure 13.15(e) is derived from Figure 13.9. A new product needs exceptional expenditures in order to develop consumer awareness rapidly. After this goal has been met, then maintenance flighting as in Figures 13.15(b) or 13.15(c) can be instituted.

Media dominance

Given a limited budget and the need to establish sufficient frequency, an advertiser can attempt to dominate a medium or, even more narrowly, a vehicle. By spending a large percent of the budget in one medium or vehicle, the advertiser will establish a high repetition level to the viewers/readers/listeners of that medium/vehicle. This strategy is another attempt to ensure that sufficient impact is achieved toward a particular target. By selecting a particular vehicle and/or daypart, the marketer may produce an even greater impact. At some point, though, the target that receives the message becomes too small to be profitable, so there are tradeoffs to consider between the size of the target and the dominance of the various media reaching that target.

The impact of media dominance combined with flighting can be great. For example, a savings and loan institution in Chicago advertised for one month each year on one radio station. Their limited budget wouldn't make an impact if it were more diffuse. They felt, though, that their strategy was successful and they

Figure 13.16 *The effect of flighting and constant schedules on sales*

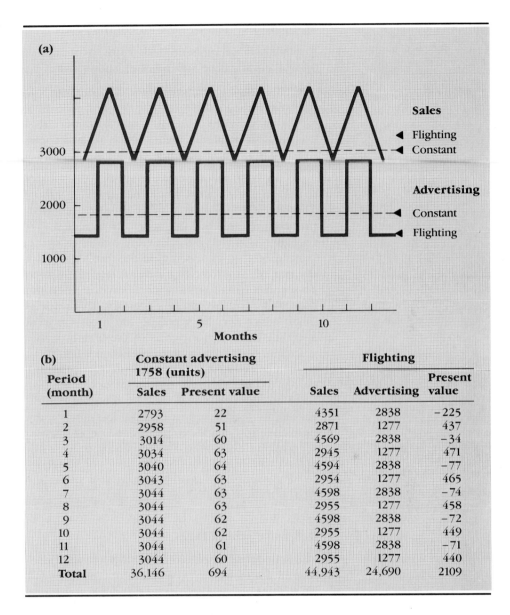

(a)

(b)

Period (month)	Constant advertising 1758 (units)		Flighting		
	Sales	Present value	Sales	Advertising	Present value
1	2793	22	4351	2838	−225
2	2958	51	2871	1277	437
3	3014	60	4569	2838	−34
4	3034	63	2945	1277	471
5	3040	64	4594	2838	−77
6	3043	63	2954	1277	465
7	3044	63	4598	2838	−74
8	3044	63	2955	1277	458
9	3044	62	4598	2838	−72
10	3044	62	2955	1277	449
11	3044	61	4598	2838	−71
12	3044	60	2955	1277	440
Total	36,146	694	44,943	24,690	2109

reported new customers coming in six months after the campaign and saying that they had heard the messages on the radio. This is an extreme example but makes the point that a strategy must be developed so that a limited budget can be used creatively and efficiently to make an impact.

While flighting seems to be a better way to use an advertising budget, there are many unresolved issues concerning the best flighting plan. How long should the flighting and hiatus periods be? How does competition affect this decision? How does involvement affect the decision? These and other flighting questions are product specific and can only be answered by research done by the firm. In addition, if sales drop as sharply during the hiatus as is shown in Figure 16.16, management must be strong in order to accept these temporary setbacks in order to achieve a greater long-run goal.

30-second versus 60-second commercials

Another scheduling issue deals with 30 seconds versus 60-seconds on television. McCollum/Spielman Inc. research shows that

- "30-second commercials yield marginally lower (by about 15%) awareness than 60-second efforts."
- "Two viewings of a :30 (same commercial shown to one audience twice) yield substantially higher levels of awareness and communication than one viewing of a 60-second commercial."[17]

Since a 30-second costs about half that of a 60-second to air, it would seem that greater awareness would be achieved through the use of more 30-seconds. The use of 30-seconds is fairly standard practice now, and the major reason is probably to increase frequency. In a recent study by Singh and Rothschild,[18] recognition as well as recall were examined as measures of awareness, and it was concluded that, depending on the firm's goals, 10-seconds might be sufficient. If the goal of the advertising were merely to create awareness of a brand name, then 10-seconds would be sufficient. However, if claim awareness were also necessary, then 30-seconds would be necessary. This study goes on to suggest that not only might advertisers be spending too much on frequency, but they might also be spending too much in terms of the length of the message. Ogilvy & Mather researchers reached a similar conclusion when they found that four 10-seconds led to greater awareness and brand preference than two 30-seconds. The increased clutter did not seem to have an impact.[19]

McCollum/Spielman Inc. also reported that 60-seconds are more disliked because they tend to repeat material too much within the one spot and that 60-seconds have too much extraneous and unproductive copy. If there is a value to 60-seconds, it lies in being the opening spot for a new campaign or product; that is, it serves as an introduction to a series of 30-seconds that will follow.[20] This tends to be the usage of choice for those few advertisers who actually still use 60-seconds.

Defensive scheduling

The scheduling discussion to this point has been dominated by the assumption that all competitors will tolerate one another and behave in a sporting manner. This is not always the case; it's a jungle out there, and competitors don't always play nicely.

Earlier the point was made that it seems as if many firms are spending more than is necessary to ensure that learning takes place. Often this overspending is a competitive maneuver. For example, if one beer company overspends to buy as much as possible on National Football League telecasts, there will be less time available for competitors. In the fall, this set of vehicles is a primary way to reach heavy beer drinkers. If one firm dominates the buy, it will not only enhance learning for itself (discussed above) but will also enhance forgetting of the competition. For this reason, one firm in a product class may grossly overspend; its overexpenditure can keep a competitor out of a vehicle or lessen its impact considerably.

Beer is a unique product because it is tied so heavily to sports, and fall is a unique season because football is so dominant a sports buy. In other product classes, a strategy of overspending leads to an overspending reaction by competitors. Soon all major competitors spend too much to increase learning, and budgets become bloated from an efficiency standpoint. While defensive scheduling exists to some degree, it is not nearly as bad as the defensive promotions expenditures that are being made. Defensive spending is part of marketing strategy and will be expanded upon in the promotions section of the text.

The Media Plan

At this point the major decision areas of medium, vehicle, and scheduling have been considered. Now the advertiser needs to combine these issues in the media plan. The purpose of the plan is to summarize the various decisions in an orderly way so that they can be evaluated and approved and to guide the media personnel who will need to execute the media decisions. (This portion of the book will also serve as a summary of the media chapters.) To achieve these ends, the media plan should cover the following issues:

1. media problem and situation analysis

2. media objectives

3. media strategies

4. rationale, justification, and coordination

By covering these issues, the media plan follows the decision sequence framework, and the planner is forced to deal with all relevant issues.

Media problem and situation analysis

There are several key areas of the situation analysis done earlier for the overall *advertising* plan that must be reviewed as part of the *media* plan.

Seasonality Products that achieve 90% of their sales in November need little or no media support in July. (There are, though, exceptions to this statement. Often the seasonality of the product has been created over time by the media plan. When the product was first introduced, someone thought that the product would have seasonality; as a result, a seasonal media plan was developed and over time the plan became a self-fulfilling prophecy. Managers must be careful not to create nonexistent seasonality during the early years of a product's life.)

The seasonality decision is much more complex than merely not advertising in July for a November product. The media planner must also consider what value advertising might have when people are not buying. Should some advertising be done in July to create or maintain awareness? Should advertising be done in October to prepare and remind consumers of their November decision? Is advertising done in November too late to influence the buying decision?

These are all issues that the advertising manager for Swift Butterball Turkeys must face, for example, as Thanksgiving approaches. In addition, the manager can consider whether most turkeys are bought in November because that is when people really want to eat them, or because most advertising has over the years occurred in November and has increased the seasonality of demand.

A final seasonality issue concerns competitive timing. Should the advertising for Brand A precede, follow, or overlap that of Brand B. This issue is considered next.

Competition   Part of the situation analysis needs to be a competitive analysis. What media, vehicles, and scheduling have been used in the past by major competitors? This information is available for national brands in LNA, BAR, and BAR-CUME. (See Chapter 10 for a review of these sources.)

In addition, the manager must consider strategic issues such as whether to be reactive or proactive concerning competition. Should the firm try to copy the competitor's media plan, avoid going head on in similar vehicles, or ignore the competition by creating an independent plan?

Geographics   Is there a concentration of a preferred target market in certain cities or regions, or is distribution national? Are consumers urban, suburban, or rural in nature? Should the media plan be primarily national with extra buys in a few key local markets? It is important to match usage patterns and demographics against geographic concentration. In the absence of data collected by the firm, SMRB and MRI would be the best sources to use.

Geographics also need to consider current and future distribution patterns for the product. Generally, the firm wouldn't want to advertise in areas where it has no distribution. One exception: It is cheaper to buy national media than local media if the product is distributed in 60% or more of the United States. This means that the firm's advertising could be seen in up to 40% of the country, but the product would not be available to consumers. A decision has to be made about whether or not this is a good long-run strategy. Other decisions concern the use of regional versus national editions of magazines and network versus adjacent spot buys of particular television programs.

Timing   Related to the timing issue is the question of when to advertise as the product is being introduced into a new market. It takes time for learning to take place and for trial behavior to occur. If the advertising starts before the product is in distribution, then some consumers will be frustrated in their search for a nonexistent product; if the advertising starts when the product has adequate distribution, then the retailer will be frustrated when the product sits on the shelf while consumers go through a learning process. For this reason, marketers try to use a heavy introductory advertising campaign to induce rapid learning followed by a heavy promotions campaign to induce early trial usage. All of this means that the media plan must be coordinated with distribution of the product and with any promotions efforts.

Budget constraints   The issue of budgeting is dealt with later in this text but is relevant to media planning because there is never enough money for an ideal (or, at times, adequate) media plan. Given these constraints, the planner must show creativity in the use of flighting, media and vehicle dominance, and geographic buys.

Media and vehicle selection   This part of the analysis will draw on extensive information presented in the previous chapters. Which media will massage the target in the most appropriate way? Which vehicles will deliver the correct target audience? The situation analysis presents the relevant information so that strategy decisions can be made and justified.

Target market   This issue should have been resolved earlier when the situation analysis was done and objectives were set for the entire campaign. The media plan should use the same target that was defined at that time.

Campaign objectives and positioning   Again, it is important for the media plan to be consistent with the overall objectives. Before the media plan can be developed, there must be coordination with the creative departments. Think of the embarrassment if the creative folk present superb print ads to the client while the media folk present a wonderfully creative way to stretch the budget using daytime and late-night television. Think of how quickly the client would fire the agency. Think of how many persons would lose their jobs. Coordination across the various departments is vital; common objectives help, but good communications are also necessary.

Media objectives

Media objectives should flow from the media situation analysis just as the overall campaign objectives flow from their situation analysis. In addition, media objectives are based on the campaign objectives. Just as in Chapter 5, media objectives should be clear, understandable, and measurable.

The DAGMAR model will again be useful. Target market, time period, and amount of change or achievement will be similar; the task will differ. The tasks of the media plan will be stated in terms of reach, frequency, and GRP. For example, a media objective might be expressed as trying to achieve 420 GRPs per month for a three-month period beginning September 1, with a 70 reach and 6 frequency per month and a target of males 18–25 living in Florida. This media objective would be consistent with an overall campaign objective of achieving 60% awareness among Florida men 18–25 by November 30 and is both implementable and measurable. The media objective must also reflect message objectives and positioning and therefore could be amended with: The message must convey the position that strawberry beer (Strawbeery) is the first sweet light beer. This statement lends further insight for the media strategy that follows.

Media strategies

Decisions concerning media selection, vehicle selection, and scheduling are presented here. This discussion should cover the following issues:

Medium   ▪ Why the selected media are most appropriate for the massage needed

Vehicle   ▪ Why the vehicles selected match up best with the target market
▪ Why the vehicles have the best editorial climate (rather than making specific vehicle choices, the plan will show a number of vehicles that are acceptable)

Schedule   ▪ How learning is assisted and forgetting inhibited
▪ How reach and frequency are built
▪ How accumulation and duplication serve to meet the objectives
▪ How flighting, dominance, seasonality, and geographics are used

This section of the media plan will include graphic displays of media and vehicle selection over the time period of the plan.

Rationale, justification, and coordination

Throughout the plan there must be explanations concerning its value because ultimately it must be sold to the client; the plan must be shown to be better than all possible alternatives. Often alternative plans are also presented to show the client some options and why these options are less satisfactory. Justification should be based on the information gathered and presented in the situation analysis. The situation analysis should contain all information needed for this purpose and should be purged of information not relevant to the plan. Ultimately, the agency may be asking the client to spend many millions of dollars; such a recommendation and subsequent expenditure must be based on the best information possible.

An intricate part of the rationale deals with the balance achieved between efficiency and effectiveness. The plan must be as inexpensive as possible yet it must still meet the media objectives. Achieving either efficiency or effectiveness without the other is less than ideal. To do both with an inadequate budget is a step toward becoming media director and getting a raise. The plan must also show how it is coordinated with message and promotions strategy as well as with other marketing variables.

Budget

After justifying the plan, its costs are presented. These costs need to be itemized by medium and time period. Generally, a very detailed budget will not appear until the plan is approved, but the rough budget should be fairly close to what the actual costs will be.

Example of a media plan

The media plan is merely one part of a larger project. Figure 13.17 presents a media plan for the introduction of an unidentified but real new brand of frequently purchased food product. Note how each of the relevant issues from this part is covered in the fiscal 1986 (F'86) plan.

Summary

The media decisions have now been made. In conjunction with the message decisions, the advertising is now fairly complete. (Only budgeting decisions remain.) The firm has decided what needs to be said, to whom it should be said, and through what mechanism the message should be delivered. The media and message decisions were made together so that the strategies would be well coordinated.

This chapter has reviewed vehicle and scheduling decisions and how to put the media plan together. The vehicle decisions concern, for example, the selection of the specific radio station and time of day, or the specific magazine, edition, and issue. These decisions are made to hit the target market as directly as possible with the least amount of wasted coverage. In addition, decisions are made so that ads will be placed in an environment where the target market will be in a mood receptive to learning the intended message.

The key issue in scheduling deals with repetition. Repetition leads to learning and especially does so in situations where message recipients have low involvement toward the product class.

Figure 13.17 *Fiscal 1986 media plan for introduction of a frequently purchased food product*

_____ Co.

_____

F '86 MEDIA PLANNING
MEDIA OBJECTIVES REVIEW

Marketing Consideration

■ Introduce and grow a new line of _____ . The _____ line will consist of several new varieties of _____ products in addition to the existing _____ entry.

Creative Consideration

■ Emphasize the variety/adult-oriented flavors of the _____ line while expanding on the products "better for you" attributes if and where appropriate.

Communication Goal

■ Generate awareness of and primary demand for _____ .

Target Audience

■ The approved target audience is defined as Adults (both men and women), 18 to 54 years of age.

■ This definition (now including men) moves away from traditional ____ target audiences by focusing on smaller (1–4 member), new and mature households (where the presence of children 12 years old and under is not a factor) with average to above average incomes ($20M+).

  ■ Agreement has been reached that the 55+ years of age segment does not warrant specific media attention. However, plan delivery for the group will be a consideration.

Geography

■ The primary thrust of media efforts will be national to gain and subsequently support distribution and sales in all regions.

■ Additionally, local market efforts may be continued in those markets identified by the client during F '85 planning as deserving special ongoing considerations.

Budget

■ A working media budget of $8.0 million has been established for _____ during F '86.

Seasonality/Timing

■ Year-round, continuous media support is warranted.

  ■ The _____ category is not characterized by any significant seasonal movement skews.

  ■ The _____ category purchase cycle is relatively frequent.

  ■ Year-round continuity will help maximize trial/repeat potential.

■ June 1st, 1985, has been set as the start date for support efforts given product availability projections.

Reach/Frequency

■ Maintain the following delivery levels on an average four week basis

	Introduction	*Sustaining*
National	80–85% R	65–70% R
	4–5X F	2–3X F
Overlay *	85–90% R	70–75% R
(15.4% U.S.)	5–6X F	3–4X F

  * Tentative extra weight in select markets

Figure 13.17   *continued*

_____

F '86 CREATIVE STRATEGY
AND MEDIA PLAN DISCUSSION

- _____ F '86 advertising target will be adults 18–54 who are consumers of _____ .
  - Qualitative research indicates that the new line is particularly appealing to adults, both men and women, on the basis of the adult-oriented flavor profiles of the individual items.
  - Qualitative research further indicates that competitive _____ (particularly other _____ varieties as opposed to _____ varieties) is likely to represent the most lucrative source of volume for the new line.
- The _____ adult dual audience target has implications for both creative and media plan development.
  - Creative will be adult-oriented in tone.
  - Mass target necessitates use of broad reach vehicles or a combination of vehicles whose audience profiles cover the various target sub-segments.
  - Television emphasis to shift from daytime (most efficient daypart for reaching women) to alternative primetime (all-family) and late fringe (working audience) which have been used to a lesser degree in prior years.
  - Print emphasis to shift from a women's service schedule (predicated on a traditional family target) to a more general interest/dual audience-oriented schedule.

_____

F '86 MEDIA PLAN

I. *MEDIA STRATEGY/RATIONALE*

A) *Philosophy*

Use a combination of Network Television and National Magazines to most effectively reach the target audience on an ongoing basis.

- *Network Television* offers broad national reach potential for new creative sales message exposure.
  - A combination of dayparts will be employed to maximize reach levels within the available budget.
- *Magazines* will be used throughout the support period as a supplemental medium to extend the national coverage base. Magazines provide an opportunity to communicate the new creative message to adult readers (who are typically lighter viewers of TV) in an emotionally appealing/involving environment.

Utilize Network Radio to provide additional coverage during key holiday promotion periods. Multiple networks will be used to maximize exposure of the _____ message.

B) *Media Selection*

- *Network Television (30-second units)* is the primary medium:
  - National coverage
  - Reach/Impact (sight, sound & motion)
  - _____'s medium (used continuously for 25 years)
  - Trade merchandisability

Figure 13.17   continued

- *Magazines (Pg. 4/c Bleed)* are the secondary medium:
    - Extend reach in combination w/TV (especially against light TV viewers)
    - Efficient target audience (primary and sub-segments) composition and coverage
    - Editorial compatibility opportunities
    - Regional publications can provide heavy-up in high consumption geographic areas
- *Network Radio (30-second units)* is the tertiary medium:
    - Functions as promotional period heavy-up medium
    - Excellent partner (frequency) to TV (reach)
    - Low creative costs and "Theatre of the Mind" nature of medium allows for creative tailored to specific events and/or times of day, general network formats

C) *Daypart/Vehicle Selection*
- *Network Television*
    - *Primetime (Mon.–Sat. 8–11 pm & Sun. 7–11 pm EST)*
        - Highest adlts   reach potential/unit vs. all dayparts
        - Reaches all family members (women-purchasers/users & men-users/purchase influencers)
        - _____ built its franchise via Prime
    - *Late Fringe (11:30 pm–1:00 am EST)*
        - Less expensive Prime/Adults alternative for continuity
        - Second daypart extends TV reach against Adults
        - Extends reach against working women (qualitatively, a strong target audience sub-segment)
- *Magazines*
    - *Women's Service* publications are recommended for their cost efficiency and good coverage of women (primary purchasers):

▪ Good Housekeeping	"Seal of Approval" quality endorsement
▪ Cosmopolitan	Contemporary book that covers younger segment of target audience
▪ House Beautiful & Creative Ideas	Both books are a little more editorially imaginative vs. other books; good environment for creative message.
▪ New Woman	Very efficient "Working Women's" magazine; good food environment

    - *Dual Audience* publications are recommended for their adult coverage:

▪ Reader's Digest	Largest mass circulation book; excellent and efficient coverage of all demographics
▪ People & US	Contemporary, slightly younger (vs. RD) adult magazines

    - *Men's* publications were recommended to extend coverage of this segment and to help position product as more adult:

▪ Sports Illustrated	"Macho" environment helps to create male appeal/interest in product; male efficiencies
▪ Esquire	Contemporary, somewhat sophisticated magazine extends reach against males 25–34 segment

    - *Epicurean* publications were recommended because of their readers' high interest in quality foods:

▪ Bon Appetit	Cost efficient

    - *Regional* publications are recommended in recognition of _____ determined regional skews.

▪ Southern Living & Sunset	Premiere books of the respective regions; excellent food environments

Figure 13.17   *continued*

- *Network Radio*
  - *Drivetimes (6–10 am & 3–7 pm)* will reach working adults during times of day when lunch and dinner menu planning is occurring and purchase is possible (evening drive)
  - *Housewife (10 am – 3 pm)* will reach women during usage and menu/shopping planning times
  - *Late Nite (7 pm – 12 midnite)* will reach adults during next day menu planning and snack times
- D) *Media Scheduling*
  - *Network Television*

    Advertising will be scheduled primarily August through December to maximize the impact of the _____ introduction by quickly generating high levels of awareness.
  - *Magazines*

    Magazines will be planned September through March (cover dates) with weight relatively evenly distributed on a month-by-month basis.
  - *Network Radio*

    Network Radio will be scheduled prior to key promotional periods (July 4th, Memorial Day and Labor Day) where FSI drops are scheduled.

F '86 MEDIA PLAN
MEDIA DELIVERY
BY QUARTER

F '86

	1985			1986
	AMJ	JAS	OND	JFM
Adults 18–54				
R/F				
GRPs				
Network TV (18–49)	–	85%/4.2X 364	86%/6.3X 540	–
Magazines (18–54)	–	36%/1.2X 44	53%/2.1X 112	51%/1.8X 94
Network Radio (18–49)	41%/3.7X 150	30%/2.5X 75	–	–
Combined	41%/3.7X 150	93%/5.2X 483	93%/7.0X 652	51%/1.8X 94
R with 3+ F	17	63	78	12

Figure 13.17   *continued*

	1985			1986
F '86	AMJ	JAS	OND	JFM
Women 18–54				
R/F				
GRPs				
Network TV (18–49)	–	84%/4.4X	87%/6.4X	–
		373	560	
Magazines (18–54)	–	39%/1.3X	62%/2.4X	58%/2.0X
		49	145	117
Network Radio (18–49)	41%/3.7X	30%/2.5X	–	–
	150	95		
Combined	41%/3.7X	93%/11.6X	94%/7.5X	58%/2.0X
	150	497	705	117
R with 3+ F	17	63	77	13
Men 18–54				
R/F				
GRPs				
Network TV (18–49)	–	81%/4.1X	86%/5.7X	–
		329	494	
Magazines (18–54)	–	33%/1.2X	45%/1.7X	43%/1.6X
		40	79	69
Network Radio (18–49)	41%/3.7X	30%/2.5X	–	–
	150	75		
Combined	41%/3.7X	90%/4.9X	92%/6.2X	43%/1.6X
	150	444	573	69
R with 3+ F	17	63	70	6
Adults 55+				
R/F				
GRPs				
Network TV (18–49)	–	NA	NA	–
		387	596	
Magazines (18–54)	–	35%/2.5X	47%/2.0X	46%/1.7X
		40	91	77
Network Radio (18–49)	41%/3.7X	30%/2.5X	–	–
	150	75		
Combined	41%/3.7X	NA	NA	46%/1.7X
	150	462	596	77
R with 3+ F	17			12

Special Note: Despite minor variations in planning/buying age breaks for the various media, delivery profiles are similar (especially for television) to allow for them to be combined and expressed cumulatively.

Figure 13.17 continued

410

F '86 MEDIA PLAN
QUARTERLY BUDGET RECAP ($000)

MEDIA VEHICLE	1985			1986		
	AMJ	JAS	OND	JFM	TOTAL	% MEDIA BUDGET
Network TV						
Prime	–	1869.6	3132.0	–	5001.6	62%
Late Fringe	–	467.1	797.0	–	1264.1	15%
Total	–	2336.7	3929.0	–	6265.7	77%
Magazines	–	286.1	648.9	608.2	1543.2	19%
Radio	200.0	100.0	–	–	300.0	4%
Grand Total	200.0	2722.8	4577.9	608.2	8108.9	100%

F '86 MEDIA PLAN
MONTHLY BUDGET RECAP ($000)

MEDIA VEHICLE	1985									1986			TOTAL	%MEDIA BUDGET
	A	M	J	J	A	S	O	N	D	J	F	M		
Network TV														
Prime	–	–	–	–	467.4	1402.2	1044.0	1044.0	1044.0	–	–	–	5001.6	62%
Late Fringe	–	–	–	–	166.9	300.3	265.7	265.6	265.6	–	–	–	1264.1	15%
Total	–	–	–	–	634.3	1702.5	1309.7	1309.6	1309.6	–	–	–	6265.7	77%
Magazines	–	–	–	–	–	286.1	261.8	200.0	187.1	227.6	196.9	183.8	1543.2	19%
Network Radio	–	100.0	100.0	–	100.0	–	–	–	–	–	–	–	300.0	4%
Grand Total	–	100.0	100.0	–	734.3	1988.6	1571.5	1509.6	1496.7	227.6	196.9	183.8	8108.9	100%

Figure 13.17 continued

RECOMMENDED MEDIA PLAN (Media Calendar—FISCAL 1986)

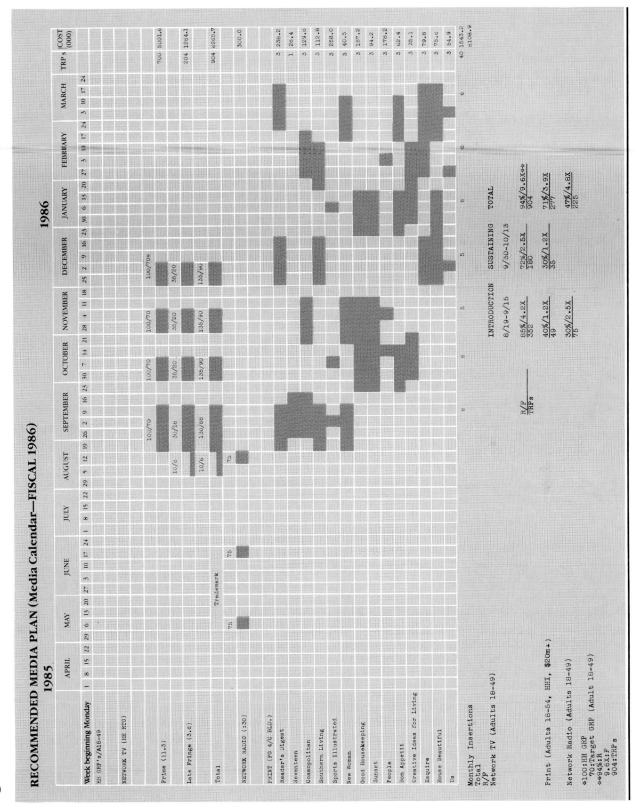

411

Chuck Quarnstrom

Vice-President and Media Director, Leo Burnett

Chuck is a Vice-President and Media Director at the Leo Burnett Company. He has been in the media department at Leo Burnett for 18 years since receiving his B.A. in Communications at the University of Illinois. During this time he has served as media director for a diversity of accounts including The Pillsbury Company, The Keebler Company, The H. J. Heinz Company, Salada Tea, Kimberly-Clark Corporation, Litton Industries, Joseph Schlitz Brewing, United Airlines, and The Green Giant Company. In addition to his agency duties, Chuck has taught an advertising course at Northwestern University.

On Planning and Scheduling Mass Media

A media plan should be a logical but easy to understand statement of how advertisements for a specific product are to be placed in front of the consumers who are most apt to take action. We often forget that the best ideas are usually the simple ones. Like all specialists today, we have our own vocabulary, our own theories, and even our own specialized computer programs to make our task more accurate and more believable to the client.

The media profession is more skilled today—more available research, more available analytical techniques, and hence, more data than we probably need to advise a client on how to invest advertising dollars. This situation is so data intensive that many clients believe that a media plan is the result of "punching a computer" and letting it tell us the answer. Media planning is being perceived as a quantitative "science." A more accurate description would be "pseudo-science."

The more we become blinded by theories and data, the harder it is to keep the advertising role and the product's reason for being in sharp focus. Theories on effective frequency, rates of learning and forgetting, and the importance of a media mix aid us in our thinking. However, these theories are general in nature and should not be universally used to make or judge a specific media plan.

Keep the product and the user in mind above all else. Like a good news story, a media plan should focus on

- who's going to react to the ads
- when are they most apt to do it
- where will the sales come from
- what vehicle will make them act the most
- what have my competitors done and what are they apt to do; can I compete with them; can I be stronger

After the plan is built on these considerations, it should be honed by considering the modern but general media theories. They should be directional tools, not specific laws. After all, if the general theories were absolutely correct and applicable to every product and situation, you wouldn't have to think. The computer would do it. Fortunately, for me and for all your ideas and judgments to come, this isn't and cannot be true.

Therefore, frequency is more important than other variables that use up the budget. This means that when consumers have low involvement and there is not much to say about the product, short messages are better, nonbleed messages are better, and black and white messages are better (in print). The list of variables goes on; sometimes there are reasons to buy less frequency in favor of something else, but frequency is a key issue in scheduling and learning.

In addition, low frequency in a time period is a waste of the budget. Therefore, it is essential to maintain it at the expense of other variables. It is better to pare down the target market so that a smaller market can get effective reach. It is better to flight so that there is sufficient budget to get effective reach at certain times.

Most scheduling decisions deal with creating as great an impact as possible. Without impact there will be no awareness. Consumers who are unaware do not purchase.

Discussion Questions

1. Design a media plan for your find-a-job campaign.

2. Why is the high assay approach likely to lead to the most efficient plan?

3. What are the qualitative and quantitative issues that need to be considered in making vehicle decisions? What secondary sources are most useful in helping to make these decisions?

4. Why is it so expensive to get awareness greater than 80%?

5. How does involvement impact upon learning and forgetting?

6. Give three examples of when a concentrated media plan would be most appropriate and three examples for the proper application of a distributed media plan.

7. Discuss the relationship between GRP level, awareness, trial, and the passage of time.

8. How much advertising is enough? Support your answer as fully as possible.

9. What are three types of flighting schedules and why would you use them?

Notes

1. August B. Priemer, "Are You an Intellectual Eunuch in a Harem of Interesting Ideas?" Speech at Canadian Media Director's Council Annual Seminar, Toronto, 2 May 1979.

2. Robert H. Geis, "How Much We Know," *Advertising Age,* 22 June 1981, p. 58.

3. Michael L. Ray, "Psychological Theories and Interpretations of Learning," in *Consumer Behavior: Theoretical Sources,* eds. Scott Ward and Thomas S. Robertson (Englewood Cliffs, NJ: Prentice-Hall, Inc., 1973), pp. 45–117.

4. Hubert A. Zielske, "The Remembering and Forgetting of Advertising," *Journal of Marketing* 23 (January 1959), pp. 239–243.

5. David Berger, "How Much to Spend," Foote, Cone & Belding Internal Report.

6. Berger, "How Much to Spend."

7. David W. Olson, "Real-World Measures of Advertising Effectiveness for New Products," Speech to the 26th Annual Conference of the Advertising Research Foundation, New York, 18 March 1980.

8. Michael Naples, *Effective Frequency* (New York: Association of National Advertisers, Inc., 1979).

9. Herbert E. Krugman, "Why Three Exposures May Be Enough," *Journal of Advertising Research,* December 1972, pp. 11–14.

10. Hermann Simon, "ADPULS: An Advertising Model with Wearout and Pulsation," *Journal of Marketing Research* 19 (August 1982), pp. 352–363.

11. Bobby Calder and Brian Sternthal, "Television Commercial Wearout: An Information Processing View," *Journal of Marketing Research* 16 (May 1980), pp. 173–186.

12. Joel N. Axelrod, "Advertising Wear Out," *Journal of Advertising Research* 20 (October 1980), pp. 13–18.

13. Michael L. Rothschild, "Political Advertising: A Neglected Policy Issue in Marketing," *Journal of Marketing Research* 15 (February 1978), pp. 58–71.

14. K. S. Palda, "The Effect of Expenditure on Political Success," *Journal of Law and Economics,* December 1975, pp. 745–771.

15. Joseph W. Ostrow, "What Level Frequency?" *Advertising Age,* 9 November 1981, p. S–4.

16. Simon, "ADPULS."

17. "A Perennial Question: 30's vs. 60's," *Topline,* McCollum/Spielman Inc.

18. Surendra N. Singh and Michael L. Rothschild, "Recognition as a Measure of Learning from Television Commercials," *Journal of Marketing Research* 20 (August 1983), pp. 25–248.

19. Kathryn Feakins, ":10's Can Be More Effective Than You May Think," *Ogilvy & Mather: The Research File* No. 11, October 1978.

20. McCollum/Spielman Inc., "A Perennial Question."

Good Vibrations
·THE·SUNKIST·ORANGE·SODA·CAMPAIGN·

MEDIA STRATEGY

With the product development, advertising, and graphics design in full swing, the company turned to developing and selecting initial test markets for Sunkist orange soda. Beginning in May, Sunkist was launched in test for the summer of 1978. The six pilot markets were

- New York, New York
- Hartford, Connecticut
- Winston-Salem, North Carolina
- Texarkana, Texas
- Shreveport, Louisiana
- Rapid City, South Dakota

These six markets consisted of large, medium, and small markets and bottlers, and a diversified geographic configuration. There was also a mixture of Pepsi and Coke bottlers, both publicly held and privately owned; this enabled management to secure a good test reading of the consumer reaction to Sunkist orange soda. The early results were outstanding in both trial and repeat usage, and in the summer of 1978 five more markets were added. By the end of the fall, the test was deemed an unquestionable success with 11 markets under way; in January of 1979, the national roll-out began.

The following pages show the introductory media planning used for these first 11 markets. Later pages show the maintenance plan used in later years.

Introductory Media Objectives

In addition to its messages, Sunkist also used its media plan to reinforce its target market and position. The media objectives were as follows:

- to reach the primary consumers of soft drinks—people 12–34
- to ensure that population segments that were currently heavier orange drinkers were effectively reached; these segments included blacks, Spanish-speaking, and preteens

- to achieve 95% reach of the target audience combined with high levels of frequency against the primary target during the introductory three months
- to provide a media program that would achieve 90% awareness of Sunkist orange soda among the target audience during the introduction

Introductory Media Strategies

In order to meet the above objectives, the following broad strategies were selected:

1. Use television as the primary medium because

   - It is capable of generating broad reach against the brand's target audience.

   - It will provide the opportunity to use sight, sound, and motion to maximize the creative message.

   - It will efficiently deliver the brand's target audience; in addition, program selectivity allows effective coverage of various segments of the target audience.

2. Schedule the majority of television weight in fringe time because

   - In the average U.S. market, fringe time delivers 80% more of the Sunkist target audience per dollar than prime time. While fewer people watch fringe time than prime time, the cost of fringe time is much lower than that of prime time.

   - Fringe-time commercials run in-program rather than between-programs, as is the case during prime time. This means that the viewer should be more attentive.

3. Use prime time during the introductory period because it offers greater reach quickly.

4. Use radio as the second major medium because

   - It is highly efficient against the target audience since it reaches soft drink consumers at 1/2 the CPM (cost per thousand) of fringe television.

   - It is an economical way of building frequency. Owing to radio's cost advantages and selectivity, target listeners reached will hear a message more often.

   - It provides the opportunity to maximize the music, through the use of 60-second commercials, in establishing the brand's identity. Music is an extremely important element of the Sunkist advertising, and it provides a synergistic link between radio and television. The listeners' association of radio with the television commercials helps to further enhance and strengthen the Sunkist beach imagery.

   - Station selection permits the opportunity to heavy-up against specific priority segments within the target market.

   - It reaches a mobile target audience that does a lot of driving, especially during summer months.

5. Utilize media vehicles that maximize the sight and sound required of the Good Vibrations campaign.

   - It was important that the media purchased for Sunkist allow the full utilization of the broadcast executions developed for the brand.

   - The Sunkist advertising was aimed at changing consumer feelings and attitudes toward orange soda by establishing a very positive image of drinkers of Sunkist: young, idealized people in attractive, California beach situations.

   - Proper communications of this identity depended heavily on the visual elements of television as well as the audio of both television and radio to convey the positive energy and enthusiasm of the Good Vibrations music.

Specific media funding was limited only to broadcast. Television and radio provided the best environment for communicating and heightening a dual Sunkist heritage: (1) the Good Vibrations musical heritage, made famous by the Beach Boys and (2) the heritage of Sunkist quality earned over a period of many years. Because the campaign was so heavily based on music, there was not felt to be any need for consumer print advertising other than when needed to deliver coupons or other promotions offers.

6. Use a massive media blitz introduction to establish a universal presence for Sunkist.

   - As shown in Table S.1, 60% of the first year budget for each market was spent during the first three months.

   - During this introductory period, radio commercials were scheduled to run with extremely high frequency to establish the music and popularize it.

Table S.1 Gross rating points desired

	Television	Radio	Total
First 3 months	3,075	1,975	5,050
Next 2 months	1,225	625	1,850
Last 7 months	1,500	—	1,500
Total year	5,800	2,600	8,400

Introductory Media Plan

During the first year of Sunkist's operation, the product was bottled and distributed in 11 markets. Figure S.1 shows the basic introductory media plan. Table S.2 shows the radio buys made in one of the markets, Atlanta, during May 1978; Table S.3 shows

MEDIA SCHEDULE EQUIVALENT TO $20,000,000 NATIONAL PLAN MAY 1978–APRIL 1979

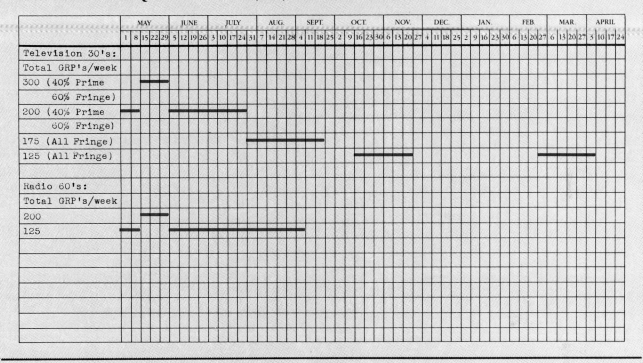

Figure S.1 *Introductory media plan (fiscal 1979)*

the comparable television buys. Local buys during this first year were made at a rate that was equivalent to a national $20 million budget. In later years when Sunkist was introduced into other markets, it was at this same spending level.

Table S.2 Sunkist sample schedule Atlanta market (*Radio GRPs*)

WZGC-FM	15/wk.	3 P.M.–12 mid	38
WKLS-FM	15/wk.	3 P.M.–12 mid	21
WQXI-FM	15/wk.	3 P.M.–12 mid	16
WQXI-AM	15/wk.	3 P.M.–12 mid	15
WAOK	10/wk.	3–7 P.M.	10
			100

Maintenance Media Strategy

As Sunkist achieved wider distribution, its media plan stayed fairly similar in some ways (media and vehicle selection) but changed in others (there was no need for a heavy introductory plan after the first year). The following section details the media plan that was developed for Sunkist orange soda in 1980. Background and rationale are included in order to provide a greater understanding of the media requirements for the brand.

1. Schedule Sunkist orange soda advertising counter to the advertising for Sunkist oranges in order to create greater brand name exposure through the year.

   ▪ Advertising for Sunkist oranges ran during the winter months. Scheduling the Good Vi-

Table S.3 Sunkist sample schedule, Atlanta market (*Television GRPs*)

Station	Time	Programming	Hsld.	Men 18–34	Women 18–34	Teens 12–17	Children 2–11
		Prime Adjacencies					
WXIA	Tues. 8–9 P.M.	Happy Days/ Laverne & Shirley	17	11	16	17	14
	Thurs. 8–9 P.M.	Kotter/What's Happening	18	8	14	18	16
	Fri. 9–11 P.M.	ABC Movie	11	6	9	10	6
	Sat. 9–10 P.M.	Starsky & Hutch	13	9	11	11	12
WSB	Mon. 8–9 P.M.	Little House	19	10	13	13	11
	Sat. 9–11 P.M.	NBC Movie	19	13	14	13	13
		Average:	16	10	13	14	12
		Early fringe					
WTCG	M–F 6–6:30 P.M.	Beverly Hillbillies	6	3	4	8	5
	6:30–7 P.M.	Andy Griffith	8	5	6	10	6
	7–7:30 P.M.	Gomer Pyle	8	7	6	11	7
	7:30–8 P.M.	Hogan's Heroes	7	6	5	8	6
WXIA	M–F 5–6 P.M.	Emergency	7	5	5	6	5
	Sat. 7–8 P.M.	Space 1999	8	7	6	5	11
		Average:	7	6	5	9	7

brations campaign during the summer aided in extending brand name exposure for Sunkist.

2. Spend in accordance with peak sales months.

   ▪ Soft drink seasonality indicated that sales were greatest during the summer months when it was hot and there was a lot of thirst-generating activity going on. Further, students home for the summer added to the number of occasions for drinking soft drinks. Advertising spending would be more effec-tive during this time period, when soft drink sales peak.

3. Concentrate television and radio buys from Wednesday through Sunday.

   ▪ When possible at no greater media cost, spots were placed Wednesday through Sunday. This helped provide exposure when consumers were most likely to make their soft drink purchases—toward the weekend.

4. Run media continuously during the 16-week summer period.

- Soft drink sales peaked during the summer. Concentrating the advertising during this period provided the highest return on the media investment. Running a continuous flight of advertising also helped to maintain and strengthen the momentum and impact of the Good Vibrations campaign. The advertising became more effective as the number of commercial impressions among soft drink consumers increased. A continuous plan allowed frequency to build at a more rapid pace, thus generating faster recall and awareness for the brand.

5. Use of outdoor advertising and other print.

- Outdoor advertising or other print media, in selected situations, provided an inexpensive though less influential form of communication. Bottlers could elect to fund these other media through the use of variable co-op funds. Printed poster materials and newspaper ads were available through Sunkist.

Maintenance Media Plan

The flow chart in Figure S.2 shows the Sunkist maintenance media plan, budgeted at the effective national rate of $12 million during 1980. Every market authorized to run Sunkist television received the plan illustrated unless it was still in the introductory phase. GRPWs are GRPs per week.

GRP Delivery

The following chart shows the total number of Gross Rating Points in the 1980 Sunkist media plan.

Television 30-seconds

Early and late fringe	2,800 GRPs
Radio 60-seconds	1,600 GRPs
Total	4,400 GRPs

Figure S.2   1980 maintenance media schedule/16-week summer program

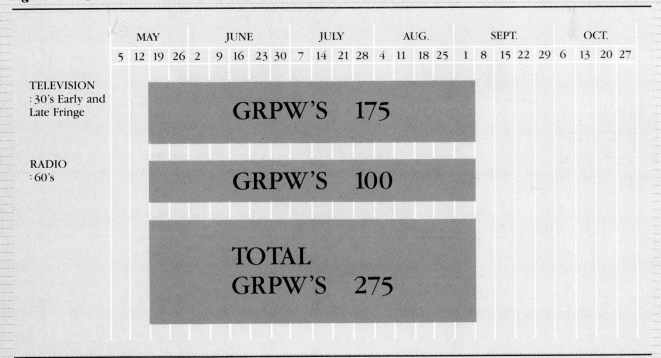

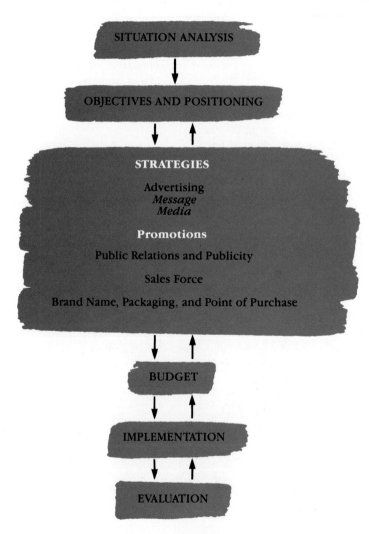

SITUATION ANALYSIS

OBJECTIVES AND POSITIONING

STRATEGIES

Advertising
Message
Media

Promotions

Public Relations and Publicity

Sales Force

Brand Name, Packaging, and Point of Purchase

BUDGET

IMPLEMENTATION

EVALUATION

Decision Sequence Framework

Part Six
Promotions
Strategies

You can work magic with sales promotion when you use it to introduce a new product. There's no better time to measure its effectiveness than during a new product introduction. It actually helps a manufacturer create a new market for the product overnight.[1]

The area of sales promotions is the third major strategic section outlined in the decision sequence. Until now the text has dealt almost exclusively with advertising. To separate advertising from promotions, some practitioners specifically refer to this area as "nonadvertising promotions." Others feel promotions is a catch-all category; if it's not advertising, public relations, or personal selling, it must be promotions. Given the rapid growth of this area and the fact that more dollars are spent here than are spent on advertising, a more precise definition and a close examination are called for.

According to Haugh, *a promotion is a direct inducement that offers an extra value or incentive for the product to the sales force, distributors, or the ultimate consumer with the primary objective of creating an immediate sale.*[2] This essentially states that a promotion is a bribe and that its purpose is to pay someone to behave in a certain way. If the ultimate purpose of marketing is to manage behavior, then promotional tools fit this purpose quite well. It has been said that advertising appeals to the heart and the mind; promotions appeal to the wallet.

The purpose of a promotion is to generate a behavior; the above definition implies a number of different ones. The manager would like consumers to begin using the brand, or to continue and/or increase usage of the brand. The retailer, other middlepersons, and the sales force are being asked to push the brand through the marketing pipeline to the consumer; retailer behaviors will be examined in this part in terms of relevant promotional incentives. Figure 1 shows a list of common promotional objectives. Some of these objectives are offensive (gain trial, gain distribution) while others are defensive (defend share, reinforce image).

Figure 1 *Common pro-*
motion objectives

1. To gain trial among nonusers of the specific brand or product category involved. (This should be qualified by a more specific goal.)
2. To help introduce an improved product or line extension (e.g., new size or new flavor).
3. To increase repeat purchases and/or multiple purchases by current users.
4. To expand product usage.
5. To defend share and usage against competitive threats.
6. To reinforce current advertising positioning and image.
7. To soften the impact of a price increase and reduce temporary sales lag.
8. To gain "cross-item" trial within a given line of products. (For example: In a line of foods available in six flavors, only two flavors are generating the majority of trial for the line and trial of the remaining four flavors is sought.)
9. To synergistically enhance the results of another promotional device (e.g., coupons and recipes).
10. To increase distribution in a given area or during a specific introduction or sales drive.
11. To increase retail trade support and cooperation (increase displays and/or retail newspaper feature-pricing advertising).

Most consumers are constantly bombarded with various purchasing incentives (the average family in the United States receives almost 1,500 store coupons per year[3]), but it is interesting to note that promotions aimed at retailers are even more intensive in terms of total dollar expenditures.[4] The purpose of this two-pronged attack aimed at consumers and middlepersons is to keep goods moving smoothly through the pipeline by using a combination of "push" and "pull" strategies. A *push* strategy provides incentives to middlepersons to buy and resell the product, that is, to push the goods on to the next stage of the pipeline and to the ultimate consumer. A *pull* strategy provides incentives to the consumer to pull the product out of the end of the pipeline at the retailer level. Marketers should attempt to combine the two strategies so that the product will move smoothly from the manufacturer to the consumer.

Dealing with both the middleperson and the consumer does not set promotions apart from advertising; it is their tasks and goals that set the two apart. As noted many times, the goal of advertising is to influence the three levels of the hierarchy of effects, awareness, attitude and behavior, although the major task of mass media advertising is to create awareness and knowledge. The goal of promotions is, very specifically, to induce behavior.

In addition, the time horizons of advertising and promotions also differ. Advertising has both short- and long-range goals. Learning needs to be achieved in the short run to get an initial purchase, but the brand must remain in memory in the long run for future purchases as well; the latter is especially important if the product is infrequently purchased. Promotions, though, have a strictly short-range goal; promotions are used to trigger immediate behavior. As will be discussed later, many problems emerge in the use of promotions; many of these result from the improper use of promotions as a quick fix without a proper regard for long-range drawbacks.

For now it should be noted that promotions and advertising are not substitutes for one another. Rather, they are complementary tools. Advertising aims at creating awareness and knowledge while the goal of promotions is to attain follow-up behavior. Both have an important place in the campaign. Advertising without promotions can lead to less than the maximum possible product usage (especially trial usage for a new product introduction); promotions without advertising can lead to price-oriented behavior where consumers are less likely to develop brand loyalty and less likely to perceive relevant benefit and image issues. The Nielsen Clearing House *Reporter* shows that 59% of consumers redeem coupons for brands they have heard of but never used, but only 36% redeem coupons for brands they have never heard of. Conversely, ad readership scores are 25 to 40% higher for ads with coupons than for ads without coupons.[5]

Promotions, then, need to be coordinated in several ways.

1. There should be coordination of promotions between those directed to middlepersons and those directed to consumers. Without this coordination, shoppers may be looking for a product that is not being stocked by retailers, or retailers may be stocking a product that consumers are not selecting.

2. There should be coordination between promotions and advertising so that awareness of the brand name and benefits exists prior to the promotion. Without this coordination, consumers will have a price orientation rather than a benefit orientation.

3. There should be coordination between promotions and advertising so that the two sets of tools speak with a single voice; that is, so that the benefits and position are consistent across all messages. Without this coordination, consumers must learn two different sets of information and then integrate the two sets.

Earlier it was pointed out that the use of promotional tools is growing rapidly. Figure 2 presents data relevant to this point. The amount spent on promotions clearly exceeds that spent on advertising, and the difference is increasing each year. As a result, in 1981 62% of these dollars were spent in the promotions area. Another result is that 40% of grocer sales are now made with some sort of deal.[6]

Of the promotions dollars, the majority were spent on trade promotions (to middlepersons) although the growth area is in consumer promotions. Of the consumer promotions, the bulk of the executions were on coupons, followed by refunds, price-off packages, and premiums. Figure 3 shows relevant data from a study of 24 consumer product categories in six major U.S. markets.

Figure 2 *Year-to-year growth of advertising and sales promotion ($ billions)*

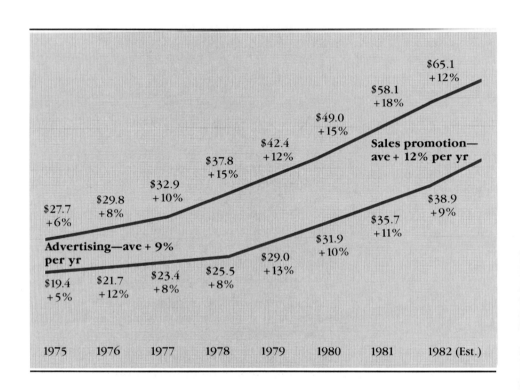

Notes

1. Ed Meyer, "Working New Product Magic," *Advertising Age,* 4 July 1983, p. M-30.

2. Louis J. Haugh, "Defining and Redefining," *Advertising Age,* 14 February 1983, p. M-44.

3. Louis J. Haugh, "Questioning the Spread of Coupons," *Advertising Age,* 22 August 1983, p. M-28.

4. John A. Quelch, Cheri T. Marshall, and Dae R. Chang, "Structural Determinants of Ratios of Promotion and Advertising to Sales," in *Research on Sales Promotion: Collected Papers,* ed. Katherine E. Jocz (Cambridge, Mass.: Marketing Science Institute, 1984), pp. 83–105.

5. Nielsen Clearing House, *NCH Reporter,* no. 1, 1983.

6. Todd Johnson, NPD Research, Inc., "Declining Brand Loyalty Trends: Fact or Fiction?" Paper prepared for the Fourth Annual American Marketing Association Marketing Research Conference, 5 October 1983.

Figure 3 *1982 summary of promotions (based on 6,970 promotions reported over a 12-month period)*

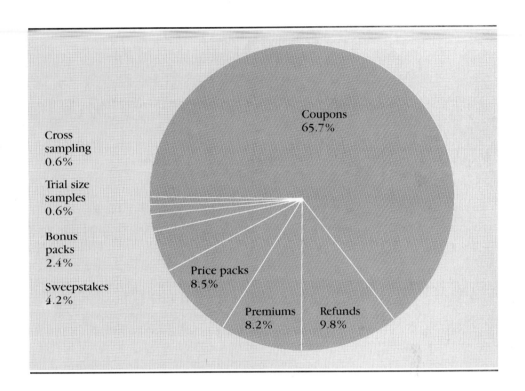

Chapter 14
Consumer Promotions
for New Products

*T*his chapter is the first of two that are devoted to consumer-oriented promotions. The first half is devoted to an overview of consumer promotions. This discussion begins with a review of behavior modification research and its use by marketers. While there are other models of how promotions work, behavior modification seems relevant because it is most effective in low-involvement situations. Promotions also work best when there is low involvement.

The chapter continues with an examination of some of the pitfalls and abuses of promotions. Promotions are misused currently by many firms; this is in part due to the rapid expansion in the area and the need to retaliate against competitors. To use promotions well, the manager must also be aware of potential problems.

The chapter concludes by beginning to examine promotional tools relevant to a new product introduction. Sampling is discussed here; other tools appropriate to a new brand introduction are discussed in the next chapter.

Behavioral Learning Theory

This text has been heavily oriented toward learning theory; so far this has been exclusively verbal learning theory on a cognitive plane. That area of psychology deals with learning and forgetting, and was presented most explicitly in the media scheduling materials (Chapter 13).

$$S_{(\text{Stimulus})} \longrightarrow R_{(\text{Response})}$$

The stimulus of advertising leads to the response of awareness; greater levels of repetition tend to lead to greater levels of awareness, and an absence of messages leads to forgetting.

$$S_{\text{Advertising}} \longrightarrow R_{\text{Awareness}}$$

426

There are also cases where some internal process intervenes and an attitude may result. This is shown by O and is more likely to occur in a high-involvement case.

$$S_{\text{Advertising}} \longrightarrow O \longrightarrow R_{\text{Attitude}}$$

Alternatively, an attitude would result from product use.

$$S_{\text{Product}} \longrightarrow O \longrightarrow R_{\text{Attitude}}$$

Purchase behavior, though, is still missing; it can be introduced by promotions such as samples or coupons.

$$S_{\text{Sample, Coupon}} \longrightarrow R_{\text{Trial Behavior}}$$

A major alternative to this verbal learning model is a *behavioral learning* (or *operant conditioning* or *behavior modification*) model.[1] This model states that future behavior is determined by the rewards and punishments accompanying past behavior. Every behavior (purchase) is followed by a positive reinforcer or a (negative) punishment.

$$R_{\text{Behavior}} \longrightarrow S_{\text{Reinforcing Stimulus}}$$

If the stimulus (product) is favorable, the probability of future behavior (repeat purchase) occurring is increased. An unfavorable stimulus leads to a decreasing probability of future behavior. For example, people continue to see others who are fun to be with and avoid those who make them uncomfortable; consumers continue to buy products that provide a unique benefit and avoid products that do not. Assuming a positive reinforcement of the trial behavior:

$$R_1 \longrightarrow S \longrightarrow > P(R_2)$$

Trial behavior (R_1) leads to gaining a product (S). If the product is good, the probability of repeat behavior is increased $[> P(R_2)]$. In marketing, the behavior is product purchase or use and the reinforcer is the product itself. By introducing promotional tools such as premiums, money refund offers, on-package coupons, or bonus packs, the reinforcer is increased and the probability of repurchase grows.

All of the above can be combined, as in Figure 14.1, to show how advertising and promotions lead the consumer from unawareness to brand loyal purchase behavior.

Of course, all of this is contingent on a good product. Without a good product the firm cannot maintain long-run behavior, although the inevitable failure can be postponed through a continuous infusion of expensive promotional devices.

Figure 14.1 The complete stimulus–response process of marketing

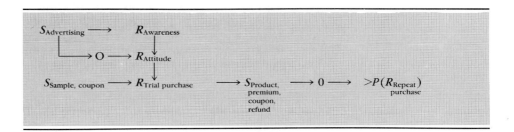

In Figure 14.1 the most vital link is

$$R_{\text{Trial purchase}} \longrightarrow S_{\text{Product}}$$

Here the consumer decides what to do rather than merely receiving messages or coupons; here the product confirms that the behavior of purchase was rewarding. The marketer can advertise, but this is not reinforcing unless the commercial is unusually entertaining or captivating. Coupons also are not reinforcing until they are used to buy a product. Therefore, the marketer must induce trial behavior so that reinforcement can occur. Promotional tools are best for this task.

A second view of the relationships in Figure 14.1 comes from Smith and Swinyard.[2] In a study of the consistency between attitude and behavior, they found that attitudes based on trial behavior predicted future behavior much better than did attitudes based on advertising. In other words, direct experience (product use) is better than indirect experience (from looking at advertising). It is important to induce trial behavior.

A number of concepts in the behavior modification literature help explain how promotions should be used. Shaping is probably the most important.

Shaping

The process of shaping is one where a complex desired behavior is broken down into a series of stages of behavior and the parts are then learned in sequence. In this way a simple behavior is taught; after it is mastered the next step is added. This is continued until the final complex behavior is learned. The series of increasingly complex behaviors is called a series of *successive approximations.*

This process is useful because new, complex behaviors rarely occur by chance and therefore cannot be reinforced. By breaking the behavior into incremental stages, it is easier for one stage to occur, to be learned. Shaping is commonly used in training animals, teaching skills to handicapped persons, and toilet training children, as well as in many situations of programmed learning and formal education. Marketers are beginning to use promotional tools as rewards in new product introduction learning situations.

Shaping is important to marketers because the initial purchase of any new brand involves a complex set of behaviors. To elicit repeat purchase behavior is even more complex. One way to reach this final behavior is through what is known in the behavioral literature as a series of successive approximations. Such a series might begin with the use of a free sample (for a frequently purchased low-priced product). This would lead to the behavior of brand use. A coupon would be included in this sample for a large discount on the first purchase, and in the first purchase the consumer would find a coupon for a smaller discount on later purchases. Each coupon would aid the behavior of purchase and use. As these incentives are reduced, the behavior approximates repeat purchase of the brand at its full retail price. Soon no artificial reinforcers may be necessary. After the appropriate responses of full-price purchase, brand usage, and repurchase have been firmly established, the arbitrary stimulus supports (samples and coupons) are *faded,* or gradually withdrawn, and control is transferred to the brand itself.

In the above example, the sample was given to allow a nonthreatening trial of the brand. The trial was reinforced by a good product and a coupon toward the next purchase. The coupon reinforced further consideration of brand repurchase.

Each ensuing purchase was reinforced by the brand and the enclosed coupon. Each coupon had a lesser value; ultimately, the brand was sufficient reinforcement by itself, repeat behavior was achieved, and the coupons were faded out.

In this series of successive approximations, behavior has gone from no brand usage, to trial without financial obligation, to usage with slight obligation, to repeat usage with full financial obligation. Figure 14.2 summarizes this process. Not only has the desired behavior been accomplished, but the desired behavior is ultimately reinforced by the brand itself and not by promotional incentives.

A common error in the use of promotional tools for shaping purposes is the improper fading out of the incentives. When the promotions are eventually dropped without gradual shaping of appropriate behavior and gradual fading out of incentives, sales may drop as consumers revert to the brand used before the incentives were employed.

A second common error is the tendency to overuse these aids; as a result, purchase may become contingent upon the presence of a promotional tool. Removal of the promotion then leads to the extinction of purchase behavior. If long-term behavior toward the product is desired, promotional tools should not become more important than the brand itself. In a marketing situation, it is important that reinforcement of the purchase come primarily from the brand; otherwise, purchases become contingent upon a never-ending succession of consumer deals.

Figure 14.3 shows how this process was used in the introduction of Solo detergent. Here a sample of the product was mail delivered to the home allowing free trial with no shopping effort. (Product use is one part of the desired complex behavior of brand loyal purchase and use.)

Figure 14.2 *Application of shaping procedures to marketing*

Terminal goal: repeat purchase behavior		
Approximation sequence	Shaping procedure	Reinforcement applied
Induce product trial	Free samples distributed, large discount coupon enclosed.	Product performance; coupon
Induce purchase with little financial obligation	Discount coupon prompts purchase with little cost. Coupon good for small discount on next purchase enclosed.	Product performance; coupon
Induce purchase with moderate financial obligation	Small discount coupon prompts purchase with moderate cost.	Product performance
Induce purchase with full financial obligation	Purchase occurs without coupon assistance.	Product performance

Figure 14.3   Solo shaping process

The sample was large enough for two washes so that some repetitive behavior could occur. Enclosed with the sample was a coupon for the first purchase. This brought the consumer closer to the ultimate desired behavior. Also enclosed was a money refund offer that could only be used if the large-size container of Solo was purchased. This brought the consumer ever closer to habitual usage.

The process shown in the Solo example is a common one. Most samples now include a coupon for the next purchase. In addition, many brands continue the shaping process by including a lower valued coupon on the package that was bought by using the initial coupon.

Three asides: (1) This is an expensive strategy, as will be seen later. (2) The Solo sample pack reiterates the position and benefits of the advertising; to aid learning the sample container looks like the full-sized container. (3) Procter & Gamble (manufacturer of Solo) is a good company to watch when studying how effective marketing should be done.

Viceroy Rich Lights used an interesting variation of the shaping theme. Its three-page magazine spread created awareness of the brand and a sweepstakes. The sweepstakes required consumers to check the number on the game card to see if they were winners. To make this check, the consumer needed to go to the store, pick up the brand, handle it, read it, and search for the matching number which was printed on the package. These were all small steps in the purchase process. If the consumer was a loser (as most sweepstakes players must be), there was consolation in a 25¢ coupon attached to the game card. This allowed players to purchase the brand at a lower price and moved them closer to the desired full-price purchase behavior. Sweepstakes that show winning results on the package of the product have become popular. One reason might be because of the shaping impact. In the Viceroy case, the consumer was moved from unawareness, to awareness, to examining the package, to holding the package in one hand and a coupon in the other. These minor steps move the consumer closer to the actual purchase behavior.

Extinction

Extinction is the removal of a relation between a response and a reward. This is generally accomplished by removal of the reward or by introduction of rewards not related to the response. Removal of the reward would occur if the brand performed poorly; introduction of unrelated rewards would occur if competitive brands were introduced.

In the case of promotional incentives, behavior toward a brand may be based primarily on reinforcement caused by the incentive (e.g., consumers buy the brand because they have a coupon). If this is the case, then removal of the incentive will lead to extinction of behavior. It is important, then, to build behavior toward the brand and its benefits and not toward the promotional incentive. The role of the incentive should be to shape appropriate behavior toward the brand. Extinction, then, may be the result of improper shaping techniques and an over-reliance on incentives that are later removed.

Extinction can be used to explain the two most common errors of shaping. First, trial behavior often occurs primarily in response to the artificial reinforcer (promotion). If the promotion is rapidly removed, then the consumer may not feel any more reinforcement and may stop behaving (i.e., the behavior has been extinguished). It is important to fade out the reinforcers slowly (as in the Solo case) so that consumers have a chance to see that they are being reinforced by the brand itself. A one-shot promotion does not allow the desired consumer-brand relation to develop, and so the desired behavior may quickly be extinguished.

Conversely, if promotions are used for too long a period, consumers become loyal to the deal rather than the brand. As a result, when the promotion inevitably ends, there is no brand loyalty and the behavior is, again, extinguished. This second problem is quite common in product classes where there is a lot of dealing. Consumers become loyal to low price and deals rather than to a brand; in such a case the benefits underlying the various brands become meaningless.

Or, as stated by Robert Klein of Management Decision Systems, "First we teach a consumer how to use coupons and switch brands. Then, when she has redeemed the coupon and proved that she has learned the lesson, she is expected to immediately forget it and become a loyal user of that brand. Of course, that doesn't happen."[3]

The use of promotions by marketers has increased dramatically over the past five to ten years, but there are no generally accepted consumer behavior theories that explain the process. The above discussion of behavioral learning theories is one possible explanation. It seems clear that the task of promotions and the concept of behavioral learning deal with the same basic issue: the management of behavior. Promotional tools are too expensive to allow mismanagement of behavior.

Behavioral learning theory, marketing, and promotions

Marketing consists of a set of tools and philosophies that are intended to aid the firm in managing behavior. The marketing concept is a means to manage behavior, but behavior is easier to manage when consumer needs are met, or, in other words, when behavior is positively reinforced. Promotions tools are a means to manage behavior, but the manager must be careful in combining promotions and product toward the long-run goal of repeat sales and profit (generally). To this end promotions must not overshadow the product.

Behavior modification works best when the subject/patient/consumer works least. In those situations where the consumer is not intent on making the best brand choice decision possible and is dealing with a product class with few brand differences, involvement will be low. Behavioral learning theory and promotions will work best in those cases where brand choices are trivial and consumers don't really care which brand they use.

If the consumer cares, then there will be extensive cognitive processing of information, and promotional tools will have a minor impact. In those cases where promotions do influence behavior, a positive reinforcement must still come from the product itself or repeat behavior won't occur (even with more promotions).

Other consumer behavior theories that relate to promotions

This last issue, whether consumers care, leads to many other psychology theories that have been used to explain why promotions work (or don't work). Sawyer and Dickson have prepared one review of how these theories relate to promotions.[4] They discuss attribution theory as well as several other theories relating to attitude formation, learning and perception; all these theories assume that people care and, therefore, lead to different processes than the uncaring process associated with shaping.

Attribution theory, for example, posits that the consumer asks the question "Why did I just behave the way I did?" If the answer reveals an internal motivation, then the consumer thinks, "I must have made this purchase because I like the brand." If there is an apparent external force, then the consumer feels that this force (e.g., a coupon) caused the decision and that the consumer may not really like the product. Attribution theory predicts that brands which promote will ultimately do poorly because consumers won't repurchase after they have had a promotion. Of course, if the brand is a good one, the consumer can make attributions about the goodness and then repurchase. As stated earlier, the more the consumer cares about the product class, the less will be the impact of the promotion.

In another review of consumer responses to promotions, Gardner and Strang[5] state that the relationships between promotions and attitudes toward the brand are weak. This is consistent with a low-involvement view and a behavioral view, both of which suggest that promotions influence purchase behavior and that later product usage has an impact on attitudes toward the brand.

Using and Abusing Promotions

The above issues raise a major problem in the use of promotions. The ideal use of the promotion is for a new brand introduction. The firm wants to artificially induce trial at this time to show consumers that it, indeed, has a good new product. Without promotional assistance, the brand may build trial very slowly and may not be kept on store shelves by impatient grocers who can sell other brands. The shaping process is useful to establish trial and then to·establish the brand while the deals slowly fade away. It is fairly clear that promotions are quite useful to new brands in these ways.

Unfortunately, many firms keep promotions in use past the introductory period or use promotions as a defensive retaliation against some other promotion. When promotions are used in these ways, they have a reduced chance of returning a profit because sales either are taken from competitors who will, in turn, also retaliate, or are taken from future sales that the firm would normally make anyway at the full price. Many promotions are used in defense against competitors and have no value other than to maintain the status quo.

McAlister[6] has developed a model that can be used by managers to evaluate under what conditions a mature brand should promote. She suggests that there are nine types of buyers for any brand, as shown in column 1 of Table 14.1. She then goes on to hypothesize to which segments the firm should promote. Column 2 summarizes the value of the segment. She feels that it is never profitable to promote to segments 1, 2, and 5 (or when these segments dominate the market) because 1 and 5 do not respond to promotions; the members of 2 are loyal and merely stock up on their favorite brand at a reduced price (stockpile).

Segments 3 and 6 can be profitable if the brand can gain enough from users of other brands to offset purchases by current users who merely buy the brand at a lower price. These segments are favorable for brands with small shares because there will be more users of other brands to draw from and, in the extreme case, is a rationale for using promotions for new product introductions when there are no users of the firm's own brand.

Segments 4 and 7 yield more extreme levels of profit or loss because they stockpile. Again, profit or loss is dictated by current share. In other ways they are similar to 3 and 6, respectively. It is always profitable to sell to segment 8 unless the promotion causes units to be sold at a loss.

McAlister goes on to write that ultimately the profitability of a promotion is dependent upon several factors. One or more profitable segments must exist, and the mix of all customers must be such that profitable segments offset unprofitable ones. As market share grows, so do the unprofitable segments who merely buy the firm's products at a lower price than they normally would if there were no promotion.

Table 14.1 Profitability of promotions when directed to segments with varying purchasing patterns

Segment description	Value of segment to manufacturer
1. Brand loyal— do not use deals	Never profitable
2. Brand loyal— use deals to stock up on favorite brand	Never profitable
3. Brand loyal— but will switch brands in response to a deal	Occasionally profitable depending on market share
4. Brand loyal— stock up on favorite if there is a deal but will switch for a better deal	Occasionally profitable depending on market share
5. Brand switcher— do not use deals and are not loyal	Never profitable
6. Brand switcher— use a deal to select brand to be purchased	Occasionally profitable depending on market share
7. Brand switcher— use a deal to select a brand and stock up	Occasionally profitable depending on market share
8. Will only buy a brand if there is a deal	Always profitable unless product sold at loss
9. Will only buy a brand if there is a deal and stockpile at that time	Always profitable unless product sold at loss

Source: Leigh McAlister and James M. Lattin, "Identifying Substitute and Complementary Relationships Revealed by Consumer Variety Seeking Behavior," MIT Working Paper no. 1487–83. September 1983.

Other factors to consider would include

1. The number of competitors who promote (or the total market share of the promoted brands)
2. The number of units that users will stockpile when they buy a promoted brand
3. The percent of time that the brand is on promotion

Because factors 2 and 3 will vary more for mature brands, the impact of promotions here will be a less clearcut issue than when these are used for new brands.

When promotions are used for mature products, the goal is a response curve as is shown in Figure 14.4(a); this shows new loyal users being brought in by the promotion. What is more likely to happen is shown in Figure 14.4(b) where the promotion attracts deal-conscious shoppers who move on to another deal after this one ends. What is most likely to happen is shown in Figure 14.4(c) where the deal-conscious shoppers of 14.4(b) are joined by the brand's regular users who stockpile when the brand is discounted and then buy less after the deal ends. In 14.4(c) the brand loses money; the larger the starting market share, the larger the potential losses.

Figure 14.4 Possible responses to promotions

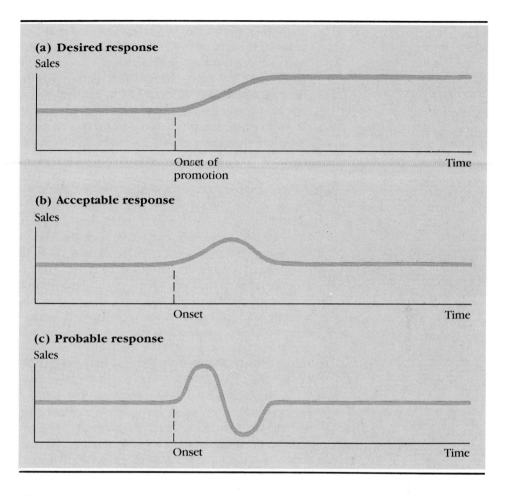

(a) Desired response

Sales

Onset of promotion

Time

(b) Acceptable response

Sales

Onset

Time

(c) Probable response

Sales

Onset

Time

Abusing promotions

Promotions can become similar to a powerful drug with addictive qualities. The first time the promotions drug is used by the firm there is a wonderful glow of increased sales. This soon wears off because the promotions drug only produces short-run sales; soon sales are back to old levels or are only slightly higher, and there is a desire for another quick fix of increased sales. When the anniversary of the first promotion arrives, another hit becomes necessary because sales each month or period often are compared to the same month or period of the previous year.

As the firm becomes more dependent on this drug, competitors see that the firm is increasing its sales so they also develop the habit. Of course, as each competitor starts using these tools, the effects are milder because there are only a finite number of potential sales to be made. As a result, the dosage of promotion increases but the results decrease. While this is happening, profits are decreasing because these are expensive drugs. Ultimately, all the firms in the product class are essentially selling their brands at a reduced price and making a reduced profit. It is by this time virtually impossible for any single firm to cut promotions because consumers are now deal/price loyal rather than brand/benefit loyal; if the firm's promotions were cut, its consumers would go to another brand offering a deal. The above scenario is occurring in several mature product classes where the brands are very similar.[7]

Why does this pattern develop? One reason may be the tremendous pressure on low-level managers to show short-run profits. Turnover at the brand manager level is rapid, and each manager needs to show an impact in order to advance. Because many managers change firms as they advance, they are not around to see the long-run impact of a plan or to reap the benefits of long-run success; therefore, they strive for short-run impact. Promotions are short-run tools when used on established products. Introductory products receive a long-run impact because the promotion helps to establish the franchise by getting the initial trial level necessary to develop repeat behavior.

Retailers also are caught in this spiral. They report that consumers feel cheated by promotions and that the savings are somehow hidden elsewhere in the price. Furthermore, the retailers don't see any impact on their own overall sales because total product class sales rarely increase as a result of promotional strategies. Promotions merely shift sales from one brand to another while increasing administrative work for the retailer.

Is there a way out? When all (or most) firms promote heavily, then no single firm can stop. If one firm stops, it will lose its share to those that continue. This situation is similar to the prisoner's dilemma in which two people are arrested for a crime and are interrogated separately. If neither cooperates, both will go free due to a lack of evidence. If one cooperates he will get a light sentence while the other gets a heavy sentence. If both cooperate, they both will get a moderate sentence. Clearly, neither should cooperate yet if only one chooses a strategy of non-cooperation he will lose.[8]

A similar situation exists for promotional cutbacks. If both (all) firms cut back on promotions, both (all) will enjoy increased profits. If only one cuts back, it will lose share to the other. If neither cuts back, both will lose profits. As with the prisoners, collusion is not a viable strategy. Figure 14.5 outlines the dilemma and shows that the most likely strategy is for all firms to maintain promotions and suffer lower profits.

One alternative is to try to develop a strong position through advertising. If consumers believe there is a unique benefit associated with the brand, they will

Figure 14.5 *The dilemma of cutting back on promotions*

		OUR FIRM	
		Cut back Promotions	Maintain Promotions
ALL OTHER FIRMS	Cut back Promotions	Higher profits for all	Market share goes to our firm
	Maintain Promotions	Market share goes to all other firms	Market share stays constant; profits stay low

be less likely to switch. It is therefore important to build a strong image for the brand and create a niche. The greater the perceived uniqueness, the less will be the impact of a competitive promotion.

Limitations of promotional tools

Promotions cannot build a consumer franchise, cannot overcome product deficiencies, and cannot overcome major marketing errors. In these cases promotions can only forestall the inevitable demise and can only do so at a high price. Recently, a chain of car waxing locations in the Midwest had problems attracting customers and over time became more and more dependent on promotions which, in turn, caused them to go more and more into debt. Research showed there was no real market for the service; people who wanted a shiny car wanted to do it themselves (a very sensual relationship); people who would trust their car to a machine did not care if it was shiny. The operation was being propped up with promotions. Eventually, the promotions could no longer be afforded and the firm was forced to close most of its locations.

Too many promotions weaken the marketing effort, the product, and its image. If the brand is always on sale, its perceived value is lowered; when the product is sold later at full price, this effective price increase is resented. Furthermore, too many deals teach consumers to be price loyal rather than brand or benefit loyal. Ken Roman of Ogilvy & Mather has said that promotions rent customers while product benefits own customers. This is a useful way of contrasting the two sets of strategies.

In many cases, the overwhelming majority of deal users (especially for mature product couponing) are already users of the brand who are getting a discount on what they would have bought at full price. A Nielsen study has shown that 96% of coupon users use coupons for their regularly used brand (as well as for lesser amounts of new brands).[9]

A final limitation occurs when the promotion is too easy for the competition to copy; such a promotion may not even have much short-run value, but rather will immediately lower profits for all competitors. As an example, Republic Airlines in the spring of 1982 introduced its "two for one, pair fare." Within a week Northwest Orient, Delta, Eastern, U.S. Air, and United all had matched the deal in markets where they competed. While Republic's intent was to stimulate traffic during a slow season, the result was that all competitors were giving away seats to existing customers. This promotion was doomed because it was easy to copy and because all brands essentially offered a commodity service.

It is clear that promotions have well-defined uses and misuses which aid in relating to the decision sequence framework. If the campaign objective is to build awareness, advertising is more relevant; a trial behavior objective can be handled by promotions, but attitude and repeat behavior objectives are best handled by product strategies. If the target market is the consumer, the promotion will differ from that used toward retailers. Likewise, promotions strategies will differ for a new brand versus a mature brand trying to keep out the new one; strategies will differ if the new brand is a new offering by the firm or an extension of a family of products that already exist. The strategies that evolve depend on the situation analysis and objectives set earlier and must be coordinated with the media and message strategies being developed concurrently.

This chapter and the next two will examine a number of promotional tools. These have been divided into three categories:

1. Encouraging consumer trial purchase behavior of new brands
2. Encouraging consumer repeat purchase behavior of established brands
3. Inducing the retailer to stock and push the product

It is important to coordinate the relevant areas of this list so that goods will move smoothly through the pipeline. A fourth class of tools, those used to get consumers to a particular retailer, is discussed in the retailing part of this book.

While this text separates promotions into distinct groups based on when they should be used, practitioners seem less concerned with the separations. The text discusses each tool in terms of when it is *most* appropriate. Practitioners often use any tool in any situation if they feel that it will give them an edge on their competitors.

Encouraging Consumer Trial Purchase Behavior for New Brands

Probably the most important use of promotions is in this area. If a new brand does not get large amounts of early trial, it will probably die rapidly. It is estimated that up to 80 to 90% of new products fail within the first year after introduction. Many of these are poor products that do not perform or do not provide any unique benefit, but many are good products that do not have sufficient promotions support. The latter problem means that insufficient trial will occur, and, in the following purchase cycles, insufficient repeat purchase behavior will result.

Figure 14.6 shows a theoretical introductory sales curve for a new, frequently purchased product. Initially there are no sales, but after two to four months, trial sales take off rapidly and peak within six to eight months. This peak is important because in most cases sales in any future period will never again be this high. It is also important because repeat sales will be at some fraction of the peak. If the product is great, 40% of tryers may become repeat users; a higher peak of tryers means a higher repeat level. If the product is a "dog," repeat sales may come in at

Figure 14.6 Theoretical new product introductory sales curve

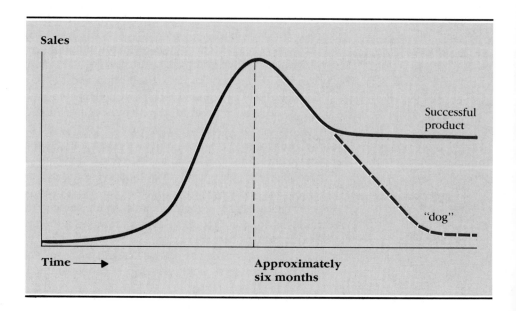

1 or 2% of the peak and building a high peak trial level for a dog probably will not help much.

Promotions are valuable because they can serve to heighten this peak. Even with their high cost, promotions are a good investment at this time because the level of trial is so important in determining the upper bound of the ultimate repeat level of sales. If the new product does not make an impact during this first six- to eight-month period, it may be pulled from shelves by impatient retailers.

Given the high cost of promotions, it is important to have good test market data to show that the product has a reasonable chance of success. Sufficient promotions can drive many poor products to a high level of trial at the six-month point, but poor products do not get repeat purchases and die in the next few months.

Did you ever wonder what happened to that great new snack food that you sampled and then bought, but when you tried to buy more it was nowhere to be found? You may have been one of the three people in the United States who liked the product enough to want to buy it again; as a result it was pulled from supermarket shelves and the manager of the brand developed a new resumé.

Did you ever wonder what happens to 3 million boxes of unbought snack food? Did you ever notice that some large conglomerates that own a snack food factory also own a dog food factory? Did you ever wonder what happened to the 3 million bags of unbought dog food from the brand that failed after introduction? Don't ask!

Three promotional tools are most commonly used in introductory settings:

- Samples
- Coupons
- Money refund offers

Samples

The objectives of sampling are to induce immediate new product trial and to break old loyalties and habits. The best way to get trial use of a new product is to give it away and to deliver it to the consumer. A sample removes all financial risk for the consumer; delivering it also removes any inconvenience.

Since sampling is expensive (probably the most expensive promotion from a sheer dollar investment point of view), it should only be used in certain instances. For example, sampling can rarely be justified for an established brand because the firm would be giving product away to current users.

Sampling is best used by new brands that are clearly superior to the competition. Without this superiority and some unique benefit, the sample merely shows the mediocrity or sameness of the brand and quickly convinces consumers that their current brand is adequate. There is, then, no reason to change behavior. Since most managers feel that their new brand is superior, this issue may require serious soul-searching. The Solo example discussed earlier is a good one. Solo was successful because the sample showed a unique benefit, the combining of detergent and softener into one product.

Sampling is also not recommended for a product that comes in many colors, flavors, shapes, etc., because it is likely that the sample will not be in the correct color, flavor, or shape. Sampling for lipstick or soup can only be done in a situation where the consumer can select a preferred color or flavor. This would be cumbersome but could be done in a retail outlet.

Products with a long purchasing cycle also tend not to sample well because the new brand may be forgotten when the next purchase occurs. Samples work best when they induce immediate purchase behavior.

Throwing out these cases still leaves many products that can benefit from sampling. An area where sampling can help if used properly is one where a modified behavior must be learned. In such a case, a small sample will not allow the consumer to learn how to use the product properly.

When Maxim was introduced as the first freeze-dried coffee, it offered a unique benefit of richer coffee taste over the prior generation of instant coffees. It was, in fact, so rich in taste that much less product needed to be used to make a cup of coffee. Early samples with powder for six cups were not successful. The new product needed a longer period for learning; people used their old behaviors and put too much powder in a cup; this led to a bitter, overly strong taste and the brand was rejected. Later samples offered 25 cups worth of powder; this allowed people more time to get the amounts correct and then they could appreciate the better taste.

Figure 14.7 may be an example of a sample with built-in failure. It shows a sample package of six doses of cold medicine, yet eight doses are needed each day. It would seem that an effective sample should last long enough to get rid of one cold. After six doses the cold may return and show the user that the product really is ineffective. The sample must be adequate in size to show the promised benefit.

If the new product is different or requires different attitudes or behavior, the sample will need to be larger because learning will be slower. If the new product is a minor improvement (e.g., better taste but no change in usage pattern), a smaller sample will suffice. If the new product shows no improvement, don't bother sampling.

Sample delivery methods   Traditionally, sampling has been implemented in four ways:

- Mail
- Door-to-door
- In-store
- On-package

These are reviewed and are then followed by some recent variations on the old themes.

Mail sampling has traditionally been used for small, lightweight products (toothpaste, instant coffee, paper products) or in sparsely populated areas. Lists can be purchased to mail samples to specific demographic groups, but a more likely strategy is to sample entire zip codes. PRIZM data (discussed earlier) allow the use of zip codes to reach demographic or other groups while retaining bulk mailing cost savings.

The above paragraph assumes that the sample is sent out as a unique entity on its own. An alternative approach is to include the sample with other samples and coupons, as would be done in a Carol Wright mailing (Carol Wright is discussed in the next chapter). This approach can only be used for small samples (two applications of a new shampoo can be sealed in plastic wrap; two sheets of a new, more absorbent paper towel can also be sent). A mailing such as Carol Wright is cheaper and easier to execute than a solo mailing but may be lost in the clutter of other samples, coupons, sweepstakes, and direct response offers; it is

Figure 14.7 The sample must be large enough to encourage future behavior

also more limited in size and therefore would have been inappropriate in, for example, the Maxim introduction.

Door-to-door delivery of samples is rarely used any more because it is so labor intensive and, therefore, expensive. It also may be unreliable because the delivery person may steal or throw away the samples rather than deliver them; in addition to other costs, a supervisor must be hired to do spot checking. The virtues of door-to-door sampling were for distributing bulky or heavy items in densely populated urban areas. A good example of a door-to-door sample might have been Solo; it, though, was delivered by mail.

In-store sampling has traditionally been of two types. One is to hire a large number of temporary workers to pass out bite-size samples such as pieces of sausage or pizza. This method is best suited for food products that need to be cooked, kept cold, or in some other way specially prepared for consumption. This method of distribution is also labor intensive and therefore generally limited in usage to the applications discussed.

A second method of in-store sampling is to set up a display from which consumers can help themselves. This method can be used over a wide variety of products and has the advantage of not incurring labor costs. It does, though, have two drawbacks. The first is that while its purpose is to allow consumers to help themselves, the firm does not want people to help themselves too liberally. Second, most merchants are not too eager to give away a product that they are trying to sell. This means that the firm may need to compensate the merchant for lost sales. A workable alternative was presented below in the Manor House example. In cases like these the retailers would generally be paid in some way for lost sales due to the use of the sample coupon.

On-package sampling allows a firm with one or more products to sample its newest product. When Aunt Jemima Pancake Mix introduced its own pancake syrup, it attached sample packs of the syrup onto the box of the mix. This is an inexpensive method of distribution but is also limited in reach. While all the users of the mix were good prospects for the syrup, the sample didn't reach those users who bought a competitive brand of mix or those consumers who used syrup for another purpose.

New variations   In an attempt to control the cost of sampling, new distribution methods have been developed. For example, the cost of rampant oversampling from an in-store display can be controlled by distributing coupons for the sample. Manor House Coffee used such a device during its introduction. It used a newspaper ad with a 39¢-off coupon; this could be used to convert a 39¢ trial package into a free sample. Alternately, the coupon could be used to get a 39¢ price reduction on a regular-size package.

A more complex and expensive sampling process was used by Barclay when it offered smokers a free carton of cigarettes. Distributing the product by mail or door-to-door would incur a great deal of wasted coverage because the percentage of smokers in the general adult population is approximately 32%. Such a plan might also incur the wrath of health groups. In-store free distribution could lead to oversampling by consumers with large pockets. To get around these problems, Barclay offered a free carton to anyone who called a toll-free number. Consumers then received a coupon good for a carton of cigarettes. This promotion reportedly cost Barclay $150 million but also led to high trial usage in a very competitive product class with few brand differences. By giving out 200 sample cigarettes, the firm hoped to establish loyal behavior by the end of the trial carton. This procedure has the obvious problem of being extremely expensive although a firm could give out a less-expensive sample over a less-extensive geographic area. In addition Barclay's advertising campaign began with expensive two-page spreads in newspapers.

By comparison, the Benson & Hedges introduction of Deluxe Ultra Lights, as seen in Figure 14.8, was much more financially conservative. Their sample only gives out two packs of cigarettes per consumer, and their procedure asks the consumer to mail in a response card. Again, in this way only those who want the product receive it and wasted coverage is held to a minimum.

Figure 14.8 Sample for Benson & Hedges DeLuxe Ultra Lights

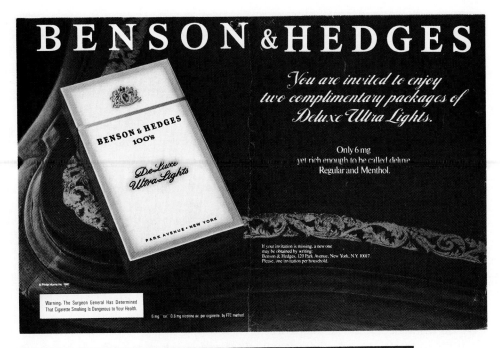

The Barclay and Benson & Hedges samples raise two important strategic issues related to sampling. How large a sample is needed to change behavior? Barclay wanted to create repeat behavior and loyalty before the sample carton had completely gone up in smoke. As stated earlier, a unique product might need a larger sample in order for consumers to learn how to use the product properly. In addition, if the product has little or no uniqueness, then a large sample might be needed so that the old behavior patterns clearly will have been broken by the end of the sampling period. This is a difficult but researchable question that must be considered in conjuction with the return on investment question. How much more behavior must Barclay get than Benson & Hedges in order for their large

Louis J. Haugh

Senior Vice-President, Frankel & Company

Mr. Haugh is Senior Vice-President, Frankel & Company, heading the marketing services agency's East Coast office. Previously, Mr. Haugh had been the founder and a senior member of the Westport Marketing Group, Inc. for more than six years, most recently as managing director.

Prior to joining WMG, Mr. Haugh was senior editor for Advertising Age *where he wrote a regular column on sales promotion. In addition, Mr. Haugh writes for* Nation's Restaurant News *and* Boardroom Reports. *Mr. Haugh joined Crain Communications Inc., publisher of* Advertising Age, *in 1967 as an editor of* Business Insurance *and became editor of* Advertising & Sales Promotion *in 1969. He became senior editor of* Advertising Age *in 1974, after having transferred from Chicago to the New York office. Prior to joining Crain, Mr. Haugh was a general assignment reporter, a financial reporter, and then marketing columnist for the* Chicago Tribune. *Mr. Haugh earned his B.A. and M.A. degrees in journalism/public relations at the University of Wisconsin.*

Promotion

In the more than 15 years we have been commenting on the role of promotion in marketing, there has been a giant swing in the ratio companies invest in consumer advertising, consumer promotion, and trade promotion.

Trade promotion investment has dropped markedly over the last five years, while consumer advertising has remained relatively constant and consumer promotion has increased.

It did not take companies long to figure out that trade allowances were producing little or none of the follow through intended from the trade, i.e., increased feature and/or display support. Manufacturers grew extremely frustrated that the trade moved their allowance monies straight to the bottom line without performance.

Ironically, a major study of promotion allowances offered to the trade found that less than one-third of trade allowance funds were even accepted by the trade.

It became clear in the last several years that excessive dealing, at the expense of advertising, can destroy a brand franchise over the long term. Robert Prentice, a marketing consultant, has actually constructed a grid of success or failure for a brand based upon what he terms are consumer franchise building and nonconsumer franchise building marketing tactics. Suffice it to say that brand sell advertising builds business and promotion activity does not, based on Mr. Prentice's work for the Marketing Science Institute.

Campbell's Soup Company, for one, has taken this message to heart and has built successful franchises for its V-8 and Chunky Soup brands on a strict diet of advertising and consumer promotion but no trade deals, except for line extensions.

For some of its other businesses that have been on an increasing deal diet over the last decade, Campbell's bit the bullet as well. For its flagship business, Red & White Condensed Soup, the company boosted advertising and cut trade dealing, moving from a 60%–40% promotion to advertising ratio to a 30%–70% ratio. According to the company, "we amputated a major peak season trade promotion on one of our leading brands. It hemorrhaged for a few months, but today it's healthier than ever, humming along on a diet rich in advertising, but leaner in dealing."

At the same time, however, some critics have blasted consumer promotion activities, including cents-off coupons and rebates as non-franchise building activities. Based upon a study just completed by Frankel, this does not seem to be the case.

With Perception Research Services, Frankel tracked eye movements of both straight brand sell ads and promotion ads of major brands. The study concluded that promotion advertising had a favorable effect on the image of the brands involved as a result of seeing the promotion offers. Consumers reported their opinion improved 8 to 9 percentage points after having seen the promotion ads as compared to those who saw only brand sell ads.

These consumers responded more positively on rating scales such as "high quality," "brand I would definitely consider buying," "good value for the money," and "company that cares about its customers."

In the past, marketing execs had loved what promotion could do for their businesses, building volume on the short term but feeling guilty for promoting because they were somehow destroying their brands with too much promotion.

It now appears that their worries about consumer promotion destroying their brands are unfounded. Given the tremendous increase in all forms of promotion over the last few years, there is every reason to think consumer promotion will continue to grow over the near term.

promotion to be a good investment? In order to answer this question, management must consider long-run as well as short-run purchase behavior. Clearly the payout period for the Barclay investment will be longer than that for Benson & Hedges. These issues will be considered in more detail in the budgeting chapter.

The second strategic question deals with the wisdom of limited sampling. Two major purposes of sampling are to break old patterns and to create a risk-free trial situation. If the sample is not readily available, will people exert any effort to obtain the sample? Will only a small minority of product users sample the brand? When Tylenol was first introduced, it used a mail response card sampling device similar to that used by Benson & Hedges; how many satisfied aspirin users took the time to respond? Conversely, how many would have tried the sample if it had been sent to them without a request? Again, the manager must ask the return-on-investment question. Is it better to send out few samples to interested consumers or many samples to many consumers with low involvement? The answer is again a function of later short- and long-run behavior.

The answer to these questions is also affected by the advertising campaign. If there is a large introductory advertising budget with a limited sampling plan, then the ad dollars may not have the opportunity to build toward behavior properly. The advertising budget can be considered as a high fixed cost of sampling. If sampling is limited, then that high fixed cost is distributed over too few samples. If this fixed cost is kept low, the image of the brand will not be strongly established in consumers' minds.

In coordinating advertising and promotions, one consideration must be to implement each with the same order of magnitude so that the firm smoothly moves its consumers along the hierarchy of effects to product trial. Minimizing expenditures at one stage may be short sighted if it hinders the long-run goals of the campaign.

Summary

A promotion is an outright payoff for a desired behavior. The manager must consider what behavior is desired and what it will take to get that behavior. Because promotions are expensive and the wrong tool may lead to an inappropriate behavior, the manager needs to consider the stimulus-response relationship in question carefully.

Often the desired behavior is too complex to achieve with a single promotion. In such a case shaping procedures can be used to move the consumer slowly from nonbehavior to repeat purchase behavior. In such cases a single promotion may get a single trial but then the old behavior (purchase of a competitor) may return.

In the past few years, the use of promotions has grown rapidly. With this growth has come inappropriate use and an escalation of defensive promotions to counteract a competitor's offering. As competitors increase their usage, the benefit to any brand decreases as all brands counteract one another. Each stage of stalemate leads to another escalation and further erosion of profits. The best way to avoid this spiral is by having good products with unique benefits.

Sampling is one of the tools used to help introduce a new brand. It allows consumers to try the brand at no risk and clearly shows the benefits of the brand. Sampling isn't used as often as it could be because of its high cost to the manufacturer, but when used appropriately it can be the strongest introductory promotional tool.

Discussion Questions

1. How do promotions and advertising differ? What are the major purposes of each? In what ways should the two be coordinated?

2. List several types of stimuli used by marketers. What are the responses sought by each of these stimuli?

3. What is a shaping process? How does it apply to marketing? Show how you might apply shaping procedures to get consumers to use a new product.

4. Why do one-time promotional events often fail to change long-run behavior? Why do continuous deals hurt brands when the deal is ultimately retracted?

5. What seems to be the natural progression of events as firms in a product class begin to use promotional tools? What can be done to circumvent this sequence?

6. When should promotions not be used? Why?

7. Why is it important to elicit high levels of trial behavior early in the life of the brand?

8. There are four traditional ways of distributing samples. What are the pros and cons of each method?

9. How large a sample should a prospective consumer get? Keep in mind that sampling is extremely expensive.

Notes

1. This section borrows extensively from M. L. Rothschild and W. C. Gaidis, "Behavioral Learning Theory: Its Relevance to Marketing and Promotions," *Journal of Marketing* 45 (Spring 1981), pp. 70–78.

2. Robert E. Smith and William R. Swinyard, "Attitude-Behavior Consistency: The Impact of Product Trial Versus Advertising," *Journal of Marketing Research* 20 (August 1983), pp. 257–267.

3. *Marketing News,* 1 April 1983, p. 4.

4. Alan G. Sawyer and Peter H. Dickson, "Psychological Perspectives on Consumer Response to Sales Promotion," in *Research on Sales Promotion: Collection Papers,* ed. Katherine E. Jocz (Cambridge, Mass.: Marketing Science Institute, 1984), pp. 1–21.

5. M. P. Gardner and R. A. Strang, "Consumer Response to Promotions: Some New Perspectives" in *Association for Consumer Research Proceedings,* eds. M. Holbrook and E. Hirschman, vol. 11, 1985.

6. Leigh McAlister and James M. Lattin, "Identifying Substitute and Complementary Relationships Revealed by Consumer Variety Seeking Behavior," M.I.T. Working Paper no. 1487–83, September 1983.

7. Walter Menzel, personal communication.

8. R. Duncan Luce and Howard Raiffa, *Games and Decisions* (New York: John Wiley & Sons, 1957), p. 95.

9. Nielsen Clearing House, *NCH Reporter* no. 1, 1983.

Chapter 15
More Consumer Promotions for New Products

*T*his chapter continues the discussion of consumer promotions for new products. Sampling was discussed in the previous chapter; couponing and refund offers are examined here. These tools are most appropriate for new products but are often used to build market share for established products or as a defensive retaliation by an established product.

Encouraging Consumer Trial Purchase Behavior for New Brands

Coupons

While sampling is being used infrequently, coupons currently are the most extensively used promotion. Ed Meyer of Dancer Fitzgerald Sample reports that 69% of promotions in 1982 were coupons. The 119 billion manufacturer coupons distributed in 1982 translate to almost 1,500 coupons for each household in the United States. Figure 15.1 shows the sharply increasing use of coupons over the past few years. These figures do not include an unknown number of coupons that are distributed by retailers through their newspaper advertising.

From a different perspective, it is reported that 74% of households use coupons in their weekly shopping. More than a third use more than five coupons per trip; 80% of these coupons came from newspapers, and a third of all coupons are from Sunday newspaper free-standing inserts.[1]

In a recent study, 25 of 40 firms said that couponing was the most important consumer promotion while another 11 firms listed couponing as second most important. Obviously, many people on both sides of the retail exchange think that couponing is important. The next few pages will examine this tool, and then comparisons will be made between couponing and sampling.

What is a coupon? It is money. Firms that print coupons are competing with the U.S. Treasury. Consumers love money and therefore coupons work.

Figure 15.1 *Trend in distribution: billions of coupons*

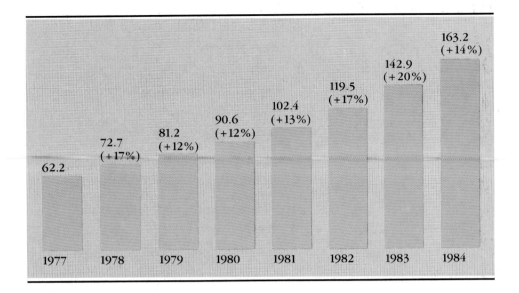

Technically, a coupon is a certificate presented to a dealer that gives the bearer a stated savings on the purchase of a specific product. Logistically, it should give certain types of information. It should state the redemption value, the behavior necessary for redemption (brand involved, quantity or size of purchase required), the expiration date, and instructions to the merchant for redemption and follow-up payback.

Operationally, coupons are delivered to consumers through print media, mail, or on packages. Consumers redeem them for cash savings when making purchases. The cycle is completed when the retailer returns the coupon to the manufacturer. This is done either directly or through a coupon clearing house. As an incentive, the retailer is given 8 to 10¢ for each coupon processed and the clearing house gets an additional 1 to 3¢.

Theoretically, the purpose of coupons is to aid in obtaining consumer trial of a new product; the greater the value of the coupon, the less the risk associated with the trial. In practice, this is not always the case. As is plain to almost everyone, the bulk of coupons are issued for existing brands in mature product classes rather than for introductions. Coupons have become a device to lower the price of a brand temporarily to try to buy some share of the market. Unfortunately for all competitors, such a strategy is easy to retaliate against, and so several firms follow the first with their own temporary price-off deal by using their own coupon promotion. This means that market shares stay relatively fixed, prices are lowered overall, and all competitors are afraid to remove the deal for fear of losing their existing market share. In a mature class, there will be little increase in overall product sales as a function of a price change unless the product appeals primarily to discretionary income. Most couponing at this time seems to be defensive in order to keep existing share of market; any short-run sales increases are at the expense of competitors and/or future sales of the firm's own brand.

Before using coupons, the manager should also consider that

1. The response to a coupon is slower than to a sample. Coupon redemption generally peaks within 90 days although usage will continue for up to six months unless there is an earlier expiration date on the coupon. For this reason coupons

are not as good for the initial trial aspect of shaping as are samples. One consideration here is whether a short expiration date on a coupon will, therefore, speed up its use or cut into the number of redemptions. Figure 15.8 on page 457 shows redemption curves over time for the major distribution media. In 1981, about 75% of coupons had an expiration date.

2. Coupons are less effective without brand name awareness and without adequate retail distribution of the product. A price-off deal on an unknown brand does not instill confidence (or redemption). Redemption of coupons for a known brand has been shown to be over 20% greater than that for an unknown brand.[2] In addition, if product distribution is inadequate, consumers will not be able to redeem coupons and will turn to another brand. It is rumored that Procter & Gamble will not distribute a coupon in a geographic area until the product has 80% distribution in retail outlets.

3. In a recent review of couponing methods, Reibstein and Traver showed 22 factors influencing coupon redemption.[3] While a list of factors can be compiled, the influence of each factor is more difficult to ascertain. It should be noted also that these influencers will vary from product to product and, therefore, will need to be assessed by each firm. Figure 15.2 shows their list of factors.

On the positive side, coupons allow a manager to get some promotional activity at a relatively low cost. Most of the fixed cost of couponing is in the delivery vehicle that simultaneously carries an ad in most cases. A couponing plan, therefore, allows the manager to stretch out a thin budget. In addition, although the response is slower, couponing is faster to implement than sampling, and the logistics are easier to control.

Figure 15.2 *Variables that influence coupon redemption*

1. Method of distribution
2. Product class size
3. Audience reached by coupon
4. Consumer's "need" for product
5. Brand's consumer franchise/market share
6. Degree of brand loyalty
7. Brand's retail availability/distribution
8. Face (monetary) value of coupon
9. Whether new or old (established) brand
10. Design and appeal of coupon ad
11. Discount offered by coupon
12. Area of country
13. Competitive activity
14. Size of coupon drop
15. Size of purchase required for redemption
16. Level of general support for advertising and promotion
17. Consumer attitude and product usage/number of potential users
18. Period of time since the coupons were distributed
19. Growth trend
20. Timing, if brand is subject to seasonal influences
21. Demographics, such as age, family size, annual income and expenditures
22. General level of misredemption in the couponed area

Source: David J. Reibstein, and Phyllis A. Traver, "Factors Affecting Coupon Redemption Rates," *Journal of Marketing* 46 (Fall 1982), p. 104.

Table 15.1 Percent of coupons distributed by media

		1982	1983	1984
Daily Newspaper	*R.O.P. Solo*	23.1%	20.0%	17.3%
	Co-op (All)	15.2	12.2	10.0
	FSI	—	6.4	8.8
Sunday Paper	*Magazine*	6.3	4.9	3.3
	FSI	33.3	36.6	42.7
Magazine		11.4	10.0	8.5
Direct Mail		3.8	4.3	4.4
In/On Pack		6.9	5.6	5.0
	Total	100.0	100.0	100.0

Source: Nielsen Clearing House Group, A. C. Nielsen Company.

Coupon delivery methods   Traditionally, coupons have been delivered in three ways:

- Direct mail
- In-print media
- In/on package

Trends in the use of these delivery systems can be seen in Table 15.1.

Direct mail couponing has grown rapidly in the last few years, primarily through the Carol Wright mailings of Donnelly Marketing. While some manufacturers mail out their own coupons (a *solo* mailing), the bulk of direct mail coupons are sent by local retailers or through a *co-op* mailing where a firm, such as Carol Wright, mails out a packet of coupons for many other firms. Direct mail now accounts for almost 4% of all coupons; the bulk of these are co-op.

Carol Wright, the largest distributor of direct mail coupons, had seven mailings in 1982 averaging over 24 million pieces each. The fall 1982 mailing went to 45 million households; each mailing contained $9.35 of potential coupon savings for a total of over $420 million of redeemable coupons. The CPM of such a co-op mailing is in the $10 to $15 range while a solo mailing can cost from $90 to $130.[4] Figure 15.3 shows part of a Carol Wright coupon mailer pack.

The appeal of direct mail couponing is similar to that of direct mail advertising: The opportunity exists to gain a precise reach. If the firm does its own mailing, it can create its own list; if the firm uses Carol Wright, it loses some reach control but can still specify geographic distribution.

In addition, direct mail coupons are redeemed at a 9% rate;[5] this is much higher than the in-print redemption rate. (See Table 15.2 on page 456 for a comparative summary of coupon delivery systems.) Direct mail offers good coupon impact potential.

Direct mail, though, is a much more expensive delivery system than is in-print. Part of this expense is due to the higher CPM of delivery, but part of the higher cost is due to the higher redemption rate. The issues of efficiency and effectiveness that were so important in media analysis are equally important here. When considering ways to promote, the manager must also remember the goal to be attained and achieve a balance of efficiency and effectiveness.

Figure 15.3 *Carol Wright coupon mailer pack*

Print media are by far the largest delivery system for coupons, accounting for 88% of all coupons. The 88% can be broken down to

Sunday newspaper free-standing inserts:	33%
Solo newspaper	23
Newspaper co-op	15
Magazine	11
Sunday magazines	6

Coupons have a lower average redemption rate in print than in direct mail (3% for daily newspaper; 2% for Sunday paper magazines; 5% for Sunday paper free-standing inserts; 3% for magazine on page; 5% for magazine pop-up)[6], but also have lower delivery costs (solo in local newspaper is up to $8 CPM while national co-op can be as low as $1.50 CPM). Within print, free-standing inserts have the highest delivery costs (CPM up to $12.50) and the highest redemption rates. Figures 15.4–15.6 show examples of free-standing inserts, solo newspaper, and co-op newspaper coupons.

Figure 15.4 Free-standing insert coupons

Figure 15.5 Newspaper solo coupon

Figure 15.6 Newspaper co-op coupons

A *free-standing insert (FSI),* as discussed in Part 5, is an addition to a print vehicle that is not ROP (run of press) and is not bound or attached to the main body of the vehicle. An FSI coupon could be for a single product (solo) or for one or many products being sold by a single retailer or chain (co-op). Currently, the most common type of FSI is the four-color multipage preprinted booklet found in the Sunday newspaper; the largest distributors of these packets are Valassis, Blair, and Product Movers. A firm that purchases space in these FSI packets can gain distribution in virtually all major markets through one buy or can obtain space in almost any desired combination of markets (exceeding some minimum circulation). The space that is bought can be as small as the coupon or as large as the page. Figure 15.7 shows the various spaces offered by Valassis. Price of the insertion is a function of size of space and combined circulation of the selected markets. In 1982, the CPM range was from $2.10 for coupon only to $12.50 for a full page for the network of Sunday newspapers that delivered a circulation of roughly 30 million households. CPM was higher for smaller circulation buys.

Figure 15.7 Valassis space definitions

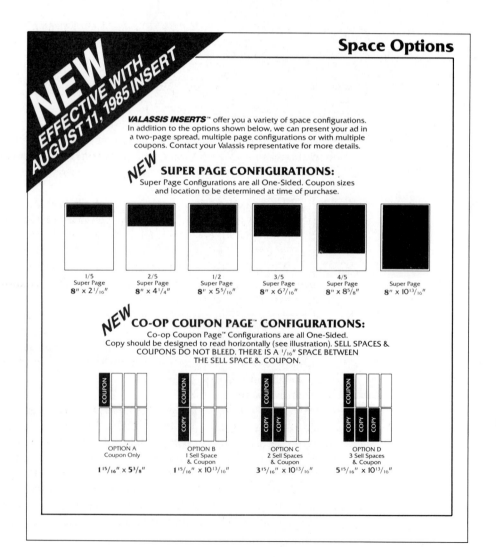

Free-standing inserts are currently very popular. In a 1982 study, half the managers who were asked said that FSI was the most important form of couponing.[7] On a typical Sunday, major newspapers have inserts from all three major coupon distributors. On one Sunday, this led to 52 pages of FSI containing coupons worth $21.86 plus $19.00 of money refund offers, seven sweepstakes, and several self-liquidating (described in the next chapter) and free premium offers.[8] All this for the price of a Sunday newspaper. Quite a bargain for a careful shopper.

A *solo newspaper coupon* is an ROP space ad with a coupon. The cost of inserting the coupon is the same as just running a print ad of the same size. Therefore, if the firm planned to run a quarter-page print ad on the third Wednesday in November in the top 100 markets in the United States, there would be no incremental delivery costs if a coupon were added. There is some synergy here: the coupon has no incremental cost and it increases readership of the ad (as noted earlier). Because many consumers scan the newspaper looking for ads, it is not necessary to buy a large space to surround the coupon. Remember from Part 5 that a strength of newspapers is catalog appeal; consumers go to the newspaper for price and availability information. The manager can take advantage of this behavior when couponing.

Most cities have what is known as a "best foods day," which is usually Wednesday or Thursday. On this day of the week many retailers buy large spaces to advertise their grocery specials. Readership and coupon clipping increase on this day, and there is considerable merit in placing grocery coupons on that day. Marketing Corporation of America is a firm that coordinates ROP coupon buys in many newspapers on "best foods day."

Co-op coupons are shown in Figure 15.6. Here the manufacturer and retailer share the costs and benefits of the coupon. Co-op plans will be discussed in the next chapter as a promotional incentive that the manufacturer extends to the retailer. *Magazine* and *Sunday magazine coupons* are straightforward applications of issues discussed above.

In/on package coupons offer a fair to excellent redemption rate with virtually no cost for delivery. If the coupon is for the next purchase of the same product (product A offers a 25¢-off coupon for the next purchase of product A), it is known as a *bounce-back coupon* and has an average redemption rate of 15%; if the coupon is for a purchase of another product (product A offers a 25¢-off coupon for the next purchase of product B), it is known as a *cross-ruff coupon* and has an average redemption rate of 5%.[9]

In either case the delivery cost is limited to the cost of printing the coupon because it is delivered free with the package. While the cost is right, the reach is limited because the coupon goes only to purchasers of product A. If the coupon is part of a shaping process, then this reach is perfect for the objectives; if the goals are to increase trial or market share, then the distribution vehicle is probably too limiting.

In/on package coupons are also appropriate as a defensive maneuver to keep current customers loyal in the face of a competitive attack. In this case the limited reach is also appropriate. In 1982, 7% of coupons were in/on package. Table 15.2 summarizes the strengths and weaknesses of the three major coupon delivery methods. Over the past few years the redemption rates of the various couponing types have all dropped as the number of distributed coupons has increased. Coupons aren't becoming less effective; there are just too many of them. Consumers' ability to use coupons is more limited than manufacturers' ability to print them.

Table 15.2 Summary of three coupon delivery methods for grocery products

Method	Delivery cost	Redemption rate	Reach	Specificity of target
Direct Mail	Highest	9%	Broad	Some opportunity to be geographically specific
In Print	Cost of space ad	3% (Daily newspaper) 2% (Sunday newspaper magazine) 5% (Sunday FSI) 3% (Magazine on page) 5% (Magazine popup)	Broad	Weak
In/on Package	Virtually free	18% (Bounce back in package) 13% (Bounce back on package) 7% (Cross-ruff in package) 4% (Cross-ruff on package)	Limited to current buyers	Narrow current users

Sources: A. C. Nielsen-NCH Research Report-Coupon Redemption 1983. Dancer, Fitzgerald, Sample-ConsPromo Reports, *Advertising Age.* Reprinted with permission. Copyright 1983 by Crain Communications, Inc.

Figure 15.8 shows Nielsen redemption lag-time data. As can be seen, newspaper and FSI coupons are redeemed most quickly followed by direct mail and then magazine. In/on pack coupons are redeemed most slowly. This information needs to be combined with that of Table 15.2 in selecting a couponing vehicle because timing is generally an important issue in management decision making.

Coupon misredemption (fraud)   As stated earlier, firms that print coupons are essentially printing money; where there is money there is crime, and coupon fraud has become big business. It is not clear how much fraud occurs, but estimates of $350 million per year and 20% of all coupon redemptions have been suggested.[10] The large majority of fraudulent redemptions are from newspaper coupons; direct mail and in/on package are printed in more controlled environments.

There are essentially six ways for fraudulent redemption to occur.

1. The consumer turns in coupons for brands not purchased. Smallest potatoes.

2. The retail clerk slips coupons into the cash register and removes cash. Small potatoes.

3. The merchant redeems coupons for units not purchased with a coupon. In theory, every unit sold by the merchant during a couponing period *could* have had a coupon redeemed; therefore, the fraud is hard to document. Large potatoes.

4. Newspapers and magazines print a few thousand extra of those pages containing coupons. The coupons are clipped and redeemed through a merchant. Large potatoes.

5. The coupons printed in number 4 are redeemed through nonexistent stores. Large potatoes.

Combinations of numbers 3 through 5 lead to large levels of fraud. For example, in 1977 postal inspectors printed a 10¢-off coupon for a fictitious detergent,

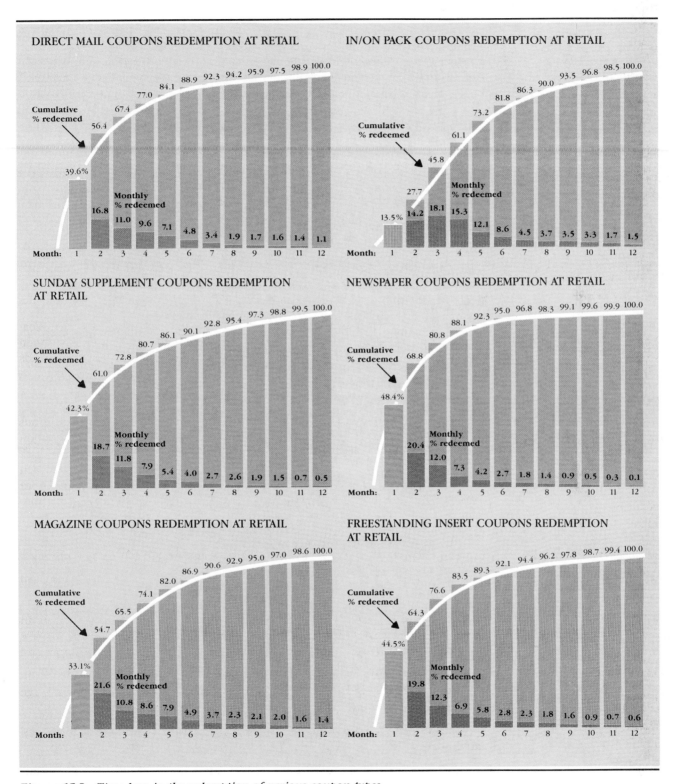

Figure 15.8   *Time lags in the redemption of various coupon types*

Breen, in three New York City newspapers for one day. Twenty-three hundred retailers in 40 states tried to redeem Breen coupons. One merchant submitted 300,000 coupons.[11] Hmmmmmmm!

In 1982 a 25¢ coupon for a fictitious shampoo was printed in newspapers in Detroit and Flint, Michigan. The redemption rate for this brand was 1 to 2%.[12] This is a very high amount given that the average newspaper coupon redemption rate is 3%; it suggests that misredemption may be even greater than 20% of all coupons. All of this also suggests that potential fraud must be a factor in developing couponing strategy and in predicting coupon costs and effectiveness.

Couponing strategy factors   In calculating couponing strategy, the manager first needs to consider the goal of how many coupon usages are desired. From this it is easy to calculate how many coupons need to be distributed. The manager considers the redemption rate for the medium, the potential for fraud, and adjusts these for the value of the coupon.

To predict the cost of the strategy, the manager considers the cost of the delivery vehicle plus the face value of the coupon and the handling costs (currently 8¢ to the retailer plus 2¢ to the clearing house) multiplied by the number of expected redemptions. Having made these calculations, the manager can consider the efficiency and effectiveness of the various alternatives.

The example in Table 15.3 considers the efficiency and effectiveness of four couponing alternatives. As can be seen distributing coupons by run of press newspaper is cheapest, Sunday newspaper FSI is slightly cheaper per redemption than direct mail, and co-op direct mail yields the largest number of redemptions.

Which strategy is best? This depends on the goals of the plan. If the goal is merely to show retailers that the firm is supporting the product, then the cheap-

Table 15.3 Costs and benefits of various coupon delivery systems for delivery of 25 million 15¢ off coupons

	Daily NP-ROP	Sunday NP-FSI	Magazine on page	Co-op direct mail
CPM of medium	$6.70	$2.80	$8.00	$16.40
Total delivery cost of medium	$167,500	$70,000	$200,000	$410,000
Estimated redemption rate	3%	5%	3%	9%
Estimated number of redemptions	750,000	1,250,000	750,000	2,250,000
Estimated number of fradulent redemptions	150,000	250,000	150,000	0
Estimated true redemptions	600,000	1,000,000	600,000	2,250,000
Total cost of redemption (15¢ coupon + 8¢ handling + 2¢ clearing house)	$187,500	$312,500	$187,500	$562,500
Total cost of plan	$355,000	$382,500	$387,500	$972,500
Cost per nonfraudulently redeemed coupon	59.2¢	38.3¢	64.6¢	43.2¢

Source: The format for this table is adapted from Russell Bowman, *Couponing and Rebates: Profit on the Dotted Line* (New York: Lebhar-Friedman, 1980), p. 61.

est plan is the best. If the goal is to maximize coupon users, then the direct mail plan is best.

Or is it? The Sunday FSI is much cheaper than the direct mail; in fact, the direct mail costs 2.5 times as much as the FSI. If the FSI had the same budget, it would deliver about 2.5 million redemptions. In this example, the FSI is the best combination of efficiency and effectiveness but also shows that a clutter strategy is necessary to achieve a goal of a high number of redeemers.

Table 15.3 represents fairly realistic data but should not be used to generalize to other decision-making situations. FSI is not always the best strategy. What can be generalized is the analysis method. In the real world there may be many more choices available including various sizes and colors of ads and various coupon values that can be part of the delivery vehicle. These will influence both costs and redemption rates. The manager also needs to consider the question of how many households redeemed multiple coupons.

Couponing versus sampling

Under what conditions should the firm sample versus coupon? Sampling is a much more effective strategy than couponing, yet couponing was used in 66% of all promotions in 1982 while sampling was used in just over 1% of cases.

One reason for the difference is that sampling is hardly ever used for an existing product while couponing is so used. There are probably ten times more established products than new ones in any given year. Still, an inequity exists; probably the greatest reason for the remainder of the disparity is cost. Sampling is expensive. To sample a new shampoo using a 2-ounce packet delivered by solo direct mail to 40 million households would cost in the range of $15 million. To coupon these same households would cost less than $1 million.

Few companies can afford the luxury of sampling even though the benefits are great. In a study done by Ogilvy & Mather, it was found that 80% of households receiving a free sample used it and that 20% of these users then made at least one purchase. This means that 16% of sampled households made a full-price purchase. This is high when compared to a 4.6% average redemption rate for coupons (across all ways to distribute an introductory coupon). If the same 20% of coupon-using tryers make an additional full-price purchase, that means that 1% of couponed households should be compared to 16% of sampled households. It is clear that sampling is more effective than couponing for eliciting trial purchase behavior.

The cost ratio (15:1) and the benefit ratio (16:1) are similar. It seems that the high cost of sampling is clearly a barrier to the use of an effective tool. To get the same number of tryers from coupons as from samples would require sending coupons to 142 million households. Because there are fewer than 90 million households in the United States, couponing can rarely be as effective as sampling.

Ogilvy & Mather goes on to report that a combination of sample and coupon yields the highest repurchase level. If the sample pack has a coupon for the first purchase, sales increase by another 20% over the initial rate. Therefore, the 16% purchase rate becomes 19.2% ($16 + [16 \times 1.2] = 19.2$). The cost of this additional coupon is relatively low and effective. This combination is advocated by the shaping concept discussed earlier and is now a common strategy among those firms that feel they can afford sampling.

An extension of this comparison of sampling versus couponing comes from Meyer.[13] His data show that sampling to 12 million households leads to almost 2

Figure 15.9 Impact of first 3 months direct mail sample versus direct mail coupon

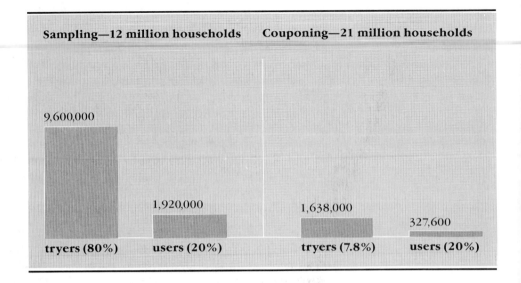

million users while couponing to 21 million households yields only 0.328 million users. This is shown in Figure 15.9. In this example 80% of receivers of the sample use it, and then 20% go out to purchase. In his example, Meyer assumes that 7.8% of households will redeem the coupon. Another 20% then make a follow-up purchase. Trial use of the sample is shown to be much more effective than that of couponing. When high levels of trial are needed in a short time period, sampling greatly outperforms couponing. A high level of trial is necessary to establish an adequate level of repeat behavior; sampling would seem to be a worthwhile investment in many cases because it can ultimately lead to higher levels of repeat purchases.

Why are coupon redemption rates so low when compared to the impact possible from sampling? One reason has been discussed: firms often use coupons in situations where they will be less efficient. A second reason: perhaps the incentive to behavior (10 to 25¢ in most cases) is not sufficient for the complex behavior (clip, save, and use the coupon); this is especially so when compared to a sample (use the product at no charge or effort).

Possibly the main reason that redemption rates are so low is the sheer enormous volume of available coupons. No consumer could possibly use all the coupons received in any time period. A middle-class household must receive hundreds of coupons every week. The figures become more overwhelming for the 40% of households who are heavy readers of newspapers and magazines. In addition, the concentration becomes more extreme when one considers that a few product classes dominate the use of coupons. How much coffee, soap, toothpaste, and breakfast cereal can any household consume? The current low redemption rate for coupons does not indicate that coupons are ineffective. Rather, it is probably a function of the high clutter level that currently exists. Consumers are unable to keep up with the printing presses.

In considering low redemption rates resulting from clutter, the manager must also consider that

▪ There will be some level of wasted coverage in any delivery schedule. The more segmented the product class market, the greater the wasted coverage unless precise direct mail lists are used.

■ Most firms use a frequency strategy such that the number of coupons delivered during any purchase cycle exceeds the number of units purchased by the average consumer. When several firms in the same product class use this strategy, deliveries increase even more.

■ Some 30% of households never use coupons.

■ Many coupons arrive in the home after a purchase has just occurred and are lost/discarded before the next purchase takes place.

Given that the cost of distributing coupons is fairly low, it may be a reasonable strategy to over-coupon greatly and settle for a low redemption rate.

Money refund and rebate offers

A money refund or rebate offer exists when the consumer is given the opportunity to buy X units, mail in some sort of proof-of-purchase, and receive a $\$Y$ refund at some later time. Refunds can be used as a sampling device to minimize the risk of trial behavior (as in Figure 15.14 on page 466), to get consumers to trade up to a larger size (as in the Solo example), or to encourage repeat purchase (send in four proof-of-purchase labels for a $2.00 refund). Refund offers can be used in this last way to encourage a larger trial; in this way the tool is set apart from samples and coupons that generally elicit only one usage or purchase. By encouraging repeat purchases, the refund is a stronger tool for breaking old loyalties.

Refund offers are often misused by firms with established brands if the brands end up merely borrowing future sales from current customers; as with couponing and sampling, refunds have their greatest value when used to reduce risk during the introductory period. In addition, when established brands run a refund or rebate there is a great risk that competitors will match the offer in order to protect their market share. As shown for other promotional tools, when this happens all firms are merely selling their same product with the same market shares but at lower prices.

One example of this occurred in 1981 when Chrysler began to give rebates on its automobiles. It quickly stole customers, but within weeks competitors also began offering rebates. Consumers saved money, but there is no evidence that the market grew or that shares changed.[14] This dysfunctional result is most likely to occur in an oligopolistic industry (one with a few large competitors) where a price decrease is quickly matched by all competitors but a price hike is not. It is therefore difficult to stop a rebate after it has begun.

Once a rebate has begun for a durable good, it is hard for the firm to stop using it. In 1982 General Motors tried to stop its rebate offers, but sales fell by about one-third. Consumers had learned to wait for rebates and therefore would not buy without one. Several months later, GM began to offer discount financing.[15] Rebates are most problematic for durable products where consumers can generally buy a few months earlier or later than they had planned in order to take advantage of a good offer.

One problem with rebates (and other promotions) is that the perception of the true product price can become distorted. Sawyer and Dickson[16] discuss several price perception theories; one of their conclusions is that it is more difficult to change a price that has been constant for a long time than to change one that constantly fluctuates. Similarly, it is difficult to take away a deal after it has been in place for a long time. This is consistent with the behavioral notion of extinction.

THERE OUGHTA BE A LAW!   by Borth

Figure 15.10

Conversely, if there often is dealing and price shifting then consumers are less likely to have a perceived price in mind and will be more willing to accept a wider range of prices.

Redemption rates for refunds are lower than those for coupons even though the payoff is usually much greater. Rates are 1%, 3%, and 5% for print, point-of-purchase displays, and in/on package, respectively. The lower redemption rates may be due to

1. Delayed reinforcement:
   - one to three months delay
2. More effort required:
   - make multiple purchase
   - save proof-of-purchases
   - save cash register receipt
   - save instructions
   - mail

Figure 15.10 shows what may be only a slight exaggeration of the thought processes used by some managers in devising refund offers, while Figure 15.11 may be the refund plan devised by these characters. The ad in Figure 15.11 gives the consumer no hint about how to act to get the $5 refund.

Bowman lists five factors that influence response rates to refund offers:[17]

- *Number of proofs required*   The appropriate number depends on the length of the purchase cycle.

▪ *Cash value offered*   Few people will behave for less than $1, but the ultimate value must be related to the value of the product.

▪ *Media used*   Newspapers and magazines are most commonly used. On package and point of purchase are less popular.

▪ *Expiration date*   Generally, only very short time periods adversely affect response.

▪ *Combination with other promotions*   Coupons or samples help start the consumer toward the multiple purchases necessary for a refund and therefore raise the refund's response rate. Figure 15.12 shows a straightforward, simple refund offer that is helped by an initial coupon offer.

While most consumers are familiar with refund offers, many do not complete the refund task. They start the refund process but get sidetracked along the way.

Managers are becoming (implicitly or explicitly) behavioral in some of the recent variations on the refund theme. Over half of all refund offers in 1982 gave the consumer either a refund of coupons for future purchases or a combination of cash and coupons. In earlier years refunds were strictly for cash. Giving coupons for the refund enhances the probability of repeat usage; redemption rates for

Figure 15.11   *A complicated refund offer*

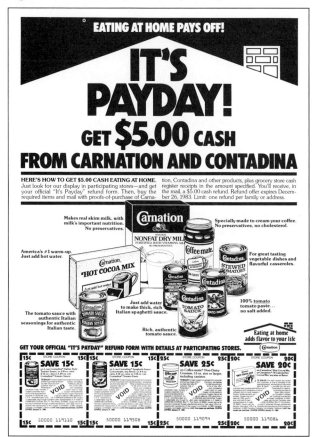

Figure 15.12   *Combination coupon and refund offer*

Peter Consolazio

**Director, Promotions–U.S. Grocery Products,
Quaker Oats Company**

Peter Consolazio is Director, Promotions—U.S. Grocery Products at the Quaker Oats Company, where he has been employed since 1976. Prior to this he held various positions at General Foods Corporation including those of Assistant and Associate Promotion Manager. He has a B.A. and an M.B.A. from Fordham University, New York.

Coupon Promotions

Coupons have been used by many companies for decades. The "New News" today is that the very dramatic growth in the use of coupons, the creative variety in distributing those coupons, and the popularity of coupons with consumers, has resulted in challenging issues for the promotion manager.

A key responsibility is ensuring the delivery of millions (perhaps billions) of coupons efficiently and effectively. Simultaneously, however, the promotion manager must be cognizant of coupon clutter, declining redemption rates, coupon misredemptions, and a decline in the trade's propensity to merchandise a coupon promotion.

Many of these problems are interrelated. For example, coupon clutter is a problem because coupons have traditionally been very successful in achieving manufacturer objectives. Almost too successful—more than 160 billion coupons were delivered in 1984. That certainly means coupon clutter!

Promotion managers must also grapple with the following overall marketing implications related to coupon promotions. If a high coupon redemption rate means more volume sold on the promotion, at what point does subsidization of existing business begin? If almost all brands are delivering millions of coupons, at what level does the trade become unimpressed with "another coupon promotion"? If there are billions of coupons delivered every year and coupon security is low and coupon specific laws and regulations are minimal, what level of misredemption should be factored into the expected coupon redemption rate?

The answer to these questions demands excellent promotion planning. The key to a successful promotion plan is a clear set of promotion objectives and strategies.

Every promotion program, event, or activity (including every coupon promotion) is planned and developed in response to a marketing goal.

Using coupons as a marketing crutch, even if it is an efficient crutch, is probably only a very short term solution. An overall promotion plan and an effective promotion strategy is necessary. Coupons are only one of many promotion "tools."

The promotion planning and development process should use a refined method. The promotion planner must consider the brand's consumer franchise, its demographic profile, competitive brands, other marketing elements (advertising, point-of-sale materials, packaging, trade dealing) and historical promotions.

From the promotion planning process flows a promotion strategy. Since any one promotion event, activity, or program usually is in response to only one objective, it is the collective of all promotions which forms a strategy.

Like almost everything else in the world, a balance is needed. Too many coupons may be just as bad as too few. Tradeoffs are common and there is no single, easy solution.

Sometimes the trade will "demand" an off-invoice, per case allowance exactly when a trial generating direct mail coupon promotion was planned. Sometimes a television commercial will prove to be more beneficial than a comprehensive, on package, label saving, continuity promotion.

Analyze and evaluate your business. Plan, develop, and test your promotion programs, events, and activities in response to specific marketing objectives. Conceptualize a promotion strategy. Recognize that coupons are only one promotion "tool"—use them when warranted.

these coupons reach up to 80%. Figure 15.13 is an example of a refund offer that gives half of the refund in coupons.

A second refund variation is actually a type of sampling. After purchasing a trial package, the consumer is in this case entitled to a 100% refund of the purchase price. Figure 15.14 shows such an offer for Promise margarine. The offer would have been more effective (and induced further shaping) if it had given the refund in coupons to encourage future repeat purchases.

Note that Promise offers *up to* $1.19, depending on what is shown on the cash register receipt. In an earlier use of this strategy, Tylenol offered a constant refund of $1.19 on a package of its capsules. The offer was set at $1.19 because that was the suggested retail price, but some retailers were selling the product at 79¢. This allowed consumers to make a profit by buying Tylenol and dumping it. Be careful when setting up a promotional deal. The consumer is no boob.

Another behavioral twist offers the consumer an extra refund for correctly completing a product knowledge quiz. Here, for a small amount of money, the consumer must spend some time and effort studying the benefits of the product. Such learning will yield a good future return (if the product is a good one).

Still another twist gives consumers a larger refund for a larger number of repeat purchases. This is an inducement leading to repeat purchase, and repeat purchase is generally the firm's ultimate goal. To optimize this strategy, the refund

Figure 15.13   *Example of refund offer featuring coupons*

Figure 15.14   *A refund offer as a sampling tool*

Figure 15.15 *Frequent flyer refund offer*

values should increase more rapidly than the number of purchases needed. For example

3 purchases yield a $1 refund, or 33¢ per package
6 purchases yield a $2.40 refund, or 40¢ per package
9 purchases yield a $4.50 refund, or 50¢ per package

The Wheaties refund offer in Figure 15.13 increases its refund as purchases increase and also increases the refund per package. This increased reinforcement should lead to increased repeat purchase.

One last type of case needs to be discussed as a variant of the refund offer. The refund can be used for an established brand when there is frequent purchasing and the competing brands are similar. In such a case brand loyalty is likely to be low, and an offer that requires several purchases can be useful. For example, airlines that compete between the same cities are perceived as offering very similar service; loyalty is low because travelers choose flights based on convenience of scheduling.

To counter this, many airlines now offer frequent flyer programs such as that outlined in Figure 15.15. In this and competing offers, the flyer gets a free pass after some number of paid flights. This is essentially a refund offer designed to create loyalty; the traveler has been given an incentive to develop brand loyalty. Rather than give a money or coupon refund, the refund is given as a pass. While refunds are most often used to gain initial usage patterns, there are also cases where the refund is appropriate for an established brand.

These examples show effective uses of behavioral models. For the goal of trial, the offer is a complete refund; for the goal of knowledge, the offer is an increased refund for correct quiz answers; for the goal of repeat purchases, the offers are (1) increased for increased purchases and (2) paid off, at least in part, with coupons to be used for future repeat purchases.

When the firm uses promotions, it is buying behavior; it is bribing the consumer. It is important to buy the correct behavior. These examples have shown that *offers can be made specific to the desired goal of the firm.*

Summary

In the last two chapters three introductory tools were suggested that could help to break loyalties to existing brands and start to establish them for new brands. Sampling requires the greatest investment up front but may do the best job of gaining trial users by reducing risk. If a brand has some unique benefit, a sample can clearly show this.

Coupons are a much less expensive device but also have less impact. They are most effective when used in/on package either to encourage repeat of a trial or to defend the brand from competitors.

Refunds are least often used but may be best at encouraging repeat purchases at the time of trial. This can be done by requiring repeat purchases for the refund and by returning the refund in the form of coupons for more purchases.

Discussion Questions

1. Why are coupons such an overwhelmingly popular promotion tool? Explain this, given the fact that redemption rates are low and constantly falling lower.

2. What are the three major methods of delivering coupons? What are the pros and cons of each?

3. Why do you think that FSI coupons have become so popular so rapidly?

4. Describe a bounce-back and a cross-ruff coupon.

5. What are the major ways for fraudulent coupon redemption to occur? What would you do to control this if you were a brand manager?

6. Under what conditions should the firm coupon versus sample? Sample versus coupon? Why?

7. What is the major purpose of a refund offer? How does this set a refund offer apart from sampling and couponing?

8. What are some ways that a refund offer can lead to a greater number of purchases of the new brand?

Notes

1. Louis J. Haugh, "Facts of Redeeming Value," *Advertising Age,* 14 March 1983, p. M-32 and "Consumer's Coupon Clipping Climbs," *Advertising Age,* 11 April 1983, p. 59.

2. Nielsen Clearing House, *NCH Reporter* no. 1, 1983.

3. David J. Reibstein and Phyllis A. Traver, "Factors Affecting Coupon Redemption Rates," *Journal of Marketing* 46 (Fall 1982), pp. 102–113.

4. Russell D. Bowman, *Couponing and Rebates: Profit on the Dotted Line* (New York: Lebhar-Friedman Books, 1980), p. 28.

5. Nielsen Clearing House, *NCH Reporter* no. 1, 1983.

6. Nielsen Clearing House, "Coupon Distribution and Redemption Patterns," 1983, p. 7.

7. Donnelley Marketing, "5th Annual Survey of Promotional Practices," 1982.

8. Dancer Fitzgerald Sample, Inc., *Promotion Report,* March-April 1983.

9. Nielsen Clearing House, "Coupon Distribution," p. 6.

10. Nancy Giges, "New Coupon Trap Set," *Advertising Age,* 12 July 1982, p. M-22.

11. Bowman, *Couponing and Rebates,* p. 89–91.

12. Haugh, "Facts of Redeeming Value," p. M-32.

13. Ed Meyer, "Sampling Builds Business," *Advertising Age,* 12 July 1982, p. M-22.

14. Betsey Hansell, "When Do Customers Tire of Saving Money?" *Advertising Age,* 22 August 1983, p. M-16.

15. Hansell, "When Do Customers Tire?"

16. Alan G. Sawyer and Peter H. Dickson, "Psychological Perspectives on Consumer Response to Sales Promotion," in *Research on Sales Promotion: Collection Papers,* ed. Katherine E. Jocz (Cambridge, Mass.: Marketing Science Institute, 1984), pp. 1–21.

17. Bowman, *Couponing and Rebates,* p. 122.

Chapter 16
Consumer Promotions for Established Brands and Promotions to Retailers

*I*n this the third chapter on sales promotion tools, two major topics are discussed. Consumer promotions for established products are covered in the first half of the chapter. These tools are premiums, contests and sweepstakes, and price-off deals. The first two of these generally are inappropriate for an introduction because they distract the consumer from learning about the product's benefits, while price-off deals may create the wrong price perception for a new product. Each of these tools is appropriate for established brands that need to generate new excitement or protect their shares against a new competitor.

The second half of the chapter deals with promotional tools used by manufacturers to induce behavior from retailers. These fall into three general classes. Buying allowances are essentially pricing deals given to the retailer in return for larger volume purchases; advertising allowances are financial incentives to the retailer to advertise the manufacturer's brand; direct stimulus incentives are additional bonuses given to retailers or salespersons for pushing merchandise. Each of these retailer incentives has a number of variations.

The chapter ends with a short discussion of promotional specialty items.

Encouraging Consumer Repeat-Purchase Behavior for Established Brands

The promotional tools discussed in the previous section have their greatest value for new product introduction periods (i.e., roughly the first six months of the brand's life), although, as seen in some of the prior examples, coupons have become an all-purpose tool used also by mature brands. When these tools and refund offers are used for mature brands, the use is often defensive to hurt the introduction of a competitive new brand. This section examines other alternative strategies for mature brands:

- Premiums
- Contests and sweepstakes
- Price-off deals

These promotions are most appropriate in cases where there is a high brand awareness and where trial has already occurred; these promotions do not induce trial or convey benefit information well. Actually, premiums and sweepstakes often detract from building brand knowledge because the offers discuss themselves rather than the brand's benefits. They try to add value and excitement to the brand but often do so in a way that takes attention away from the brand. Therefore, they may be dangerous in a situation where the brand's position in the marketplace has not yet been firmly established.

Premiums

A *premium* is an extra item of merchandise offered at a low price or free, as an extra incentive to purchasers. Premiums can be effective at increasing sales but can also be distracting from the main purpose of the firm's existence.

To work best a premium must, of course, offer some value to the consumer but, more importantly, must tie to the overall position and communications campaign of the brand. Finally, the firm must be careful not to get into the premium business at the expense of its own original reason for existence.

There are several objectives for which premiums can be suitable:

- To get brand switchers to try the firm's brand
- To get current users to trade up to a larger size
- To increase repeat purchases
- To get a long-run message to the consumer

In the first three cases, the premium provides an incentive for a certain behavior. In the fourth case, the premium is the message. In 1982 over 8% of promotions dollars were spent on premiums.

Executional choices available to the firm are concerned with methods of premium distribution and method of payment.

Methods of distribution *In-package* or *in-store* premiums provide immediate reinforcement to the consumer with no extra effort. Figure 16.1 shows an in-package premium offer for Red Rose tea. This premium encourages repeat purchases since there are 15 different porcelain miniature figures to be collected. The premium was supported by newspaper and television advertising and by FSI coupons, all of which can be seen in Figure 16.1.

The *package* itself can be made into a premium that also provides immediate reinforcement with no extra effort. For example, McDonald's occasionally sells drinking glasses with pictures of its characters along with its soft drinks; dry roasted peanuts occasionally come in a jar suitable for reuse as a coffee table storage unit for future nuts and/or candy; wine occasionally is sold in a decanter that can be saved and reused. Not only is the package an inexpensive premium, but it also saves the cost of the package that otherwise would need to be used. In some cases the premium has a brand logo or other brand reminder that remains in the home for a long period of time. When the premium also ties to the product (wine decanter, nut jar), then it is most valuable to the firm in terms of consumer learning.

Package-carried promotions are also important because they by-pass the retailer. By placing the premium in the package, it is not necessary to get the retailer's cooperation, and the package can announce the premium in conjunction with mass media advertising. The most famous in-package premium program is probably that of Cracker Jack.

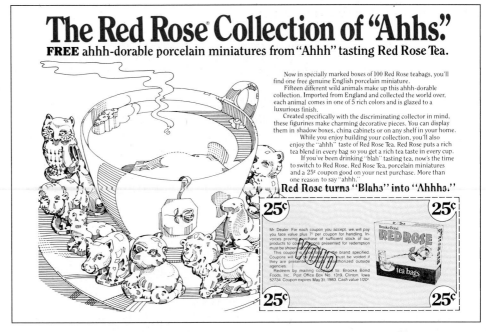

471

Figure 16.1   *continued*

Premiums are also commonly obtained through the *mail.* These would seem to be less valuable from a behavioral standpoint because the reinforcement of the purchase behavior is quite delayed.

A common mail-in offer asks the consumer to send one or more proofs of purchase and possibly some money in order to receive a gift. An example of such an offer is shown in Figure 16.2.

Here the consumer needed to submit five Ralston cereal proof-of-purchases for a free children's ticket on Republic Airlines. While this premium may have sold lots of cereal in the short run, it is not clear how much of it was eaten or if any brand loyal behavior resulted. The deal was so good that many people bought cases of cereal for the free flights and dumped the cereal. Other people did not realize that it was not necessary to eat the cereal and did so for three meals a day, trying desperately to finish off the boxes before the offer expired.

Figure 16.2 *Ralston/ Republic premium offer*

Methods of payment   A premium can be *free* or it can have *some cost.* If there is a cost, it should represent a savings to the consumer from the normal retail price.

Self-liquidating premiums currently are used in about two-thirds of all premium cases. In this mode the cost of the premium to the consumer covers all costs of the premium event to the firm. When all the premium items are gone, the firm has not gained or lost money.

There are, of course, various combinations of distribution and payment that can be used. For example, part of a set of items (steak knives) can be given away free with purchases, and consumers can then mail in for more knives or a holder for the knives at some low cost. The logistics of the deal should be dictated by the desired behavior.

Premiums can be used for high-priced items as well as packaged goods and can themselves be high priced. A condominium in New York City with units selling for $582,000 up to $1.2 million gave away a new Rolls-Royce Silver Spirit automobile (list price $110,000) with each unit purchased. This seemed reasonable to the owner of the building because the automobile was consistent with the image he wanted to create for the building. "I think it will be kind of nice to have all the Rolls-Royces pulling up to the building at night," he said. "It will set the right tone for the place."[1]

The key point in this example is to use a premium consistent with the image of the brand. Marlboro cigarettes also does this with their line of western clothing and paraphernalia. These items fit very well with Marlboro's macho/western image. There are too many examples of other firms using premiums that do not tie at all to the image of the brand. These may help the firm while the premium is available but do not help the brand over the long run.

Savings institutions, as a group, have greatly misused premiums for many years. While giving away toasters, irons, digital travel alarm clocks, boom boxes, kidney dialysis machines, televisions, and blenders offers an additional value to consumers, these items rarely relate to the position of the institution. In addition, these items take the institution away from the business of financial assistance and management and position it in the retail small appliance business. If these institutions insist on using premiums, it would seem more logical to give away, for example, books on money management. Such a premium would enhance the organization's position of helping with financial difficulties. If premiums are not well developed, they take attention away from the firm's products or services.

Sweepstakes, contests, and games

A *sweepstakes* is a game where participants submit their names for a chance consideration of winning a prize but make no payment to enter. The odds of winning any prize must be posted (e.g., the odds of winning first prize in the *Reader's Digest* Sweepstakes are 17.5 million to 1) and winners must be selected by some type of random drawing.

If there is a payment to enter, then a lottery exists; lotteries are illegal in the United States unless you happen to be the government or a church. Until recently, it was not legal for packaged goods to run a sweepstakes because the only way that a person could get a sweepstakes entry was by purchasing the package and this was interpreted as a payment to enter. Now such sweepstakes are legal as long as consumers have the opportunity to enter without making a purchase; consumers may write to the firm for an entry without any purchase obligation.

More recently the Federal Trade Commission has ruled that a "post-win purchase" format is legal. In this format there is an instant winner sweepstakes, but the consumer must submit a proof of purchase in order to claim a prize. Since the element of chance was removed before the purchase was required, the lottery statutes are not violated.

Although the term sweepstakes is occasionally used to refer to all types of price promotions, two other major categories must be considered. In a *contest*, winners are selected on the basis of the skill of their entries (e.g., recipe contests; "25 words or less" slogan contests). Since a contest is not based on chance, entrants may be required to make a purchase to enter. *Games* are sweepstakes with more involved entry systems such as saving game cards to complete a series or a picture.

In terms of legalities, sweepstakes are a thorny marketing issue because there are six federal agencies and 50 states, all with different rules to follow. In some cases, these are quite strict, while others are just unusual (e.g., an animal cannot be given away as a prize in California); additionally, where laws seem equivalent they may be interpreted quite differently. Although there are varying laws, there seems to be a relaxing of enforcement as a result of lawsuits against federal agencies and states brought by companies wishing to use sweepstakes promotions.

Currently, sweepstakes are much more popular than contests as promotional devices; there is a five-to-one ratio of the former to the latter. In addition, the average sweepstakes draws five to ten times as many entrants as does a contest. Finally, the administration costs of the sweepstakes are much lower ($3 versus $350 per thousand entries).

During hard economic times, sweepstakes seem to increase in popularity even though there is little evidence that they have any long-run value to product sales. In 1982, 4% of all consumer promotions were sweepstakes.[2] In 1981 there were approximately 1,000 national consumer sweepstakes and in 1980 over $150 million were paid out in prizes.[3]

In most cases (there are some interesting exceptions shown below) sweepstakes do not add to brand knowledge or position and are therefore poorly suited to an introductory period when advertising space should focus on the brand rather than the promotion. Most sweepstakes, at best, lead to short-run brand switching, and a few may even bring in new product class users during the period of the sweepstakes. After the event is over, though, most consumers return to their original behavior because the reinforcement (the game) no longer exists.

Similarly to premiums, sweepstakes tend to detract from brand image building. The Chaz sweepstakes shown in Figure 16.3 on the following page is an extreme example of this because virtually no space is devoted to the brand. Promotions should aid the brand, not compete with it; when the promotion completely overshadows the brand, appropriate learning cannot occur. A recent *Fortune* article concluded that there is a poor direct relation between sweepstakes and purchases.[4]

It has been said that people never get tired of playing sweepstakes, just as people never get tired of going to Las Vegas. The analogy, though, is a poor one because getting gamblers to participate at the tables in Las Vegas is an end, while the sweepstakes is a means to the end of getting more sales. If the firm appeals to the consumer's gambling instincts without tying this to the brand, then the sweepstakes has been a waste of money and a distraction from the company's real purpose.

As with all promotional tools, there are appropriate times to use this one. Sweepstakes can create involvement in a brand when there is little, and sweepstakes can help the brand shout out that it exists. When the brand has little or nothing unique to say about itself, the sweepstakes can help set it apart (at least in the short run).

New and useful sweepstakes formats

Sweepstakes also can have four other useful and specific purposes that tie to creating specific behaviors. With these four uses, the sweepstakes may even be appropriate as an introductory tool that helps the shaping process. First, some

CHAZ

'Dream Machine' $100,000 Sweepstakes

Grand Prize:
Lotus Turbo Esprit

First Prize: ISUZU Trooper

Plus these Great Prizes

2 *ALPINE* Mobile Cellular Telephones   8 *VITALIZER* Home Exercise Systems

10 Konica FT1 35MM SLR Cameras

10 *ALPINE* Mobile Security Systems

15 *Regency* Programmable Scanners   10 *ALPINE* Car Audio Systems

80 adidas Lendl Warm-Up Suits   5000 CHAZ Invigorating Body Sprays

You may already have won a $50,000 Lotus Turbo Esprit

or any one of more than 5,000 other prizes including an Isuzu Trooper.

© 1985 Revlon Inc.

Enter the CHAZ 'Dream Machine' $100,000 Sweepstakes

There's something about Chaz that just seems to go naturally with fast cars. And vice versa. So it's only logical that the grand prize in the Chaz 'Dream Machine' Sweepstakes should be a Lotus Turbo Esprit.

All you have to do to see if you've won the Chaz Lotus grand prize is scratch off the silver spots on the sweepstakes game piece. Then go to a participating Chaz retailer and see if your number matches the winning number.

If it does, congratulations! But if it doesn't match the grand prize number, it may still match up for an Isuzu Trooper, an Alpine Mobile Cellular Telephone, a Vitalizer Home Exercise System, a Regency Scanner, a Konica 35 MM Camera, an Alpine Car Audio or Security System, an Adidas Lendl Warm-Up Suit, or any of 5,000 other terrific prizes from Chaz.

What if your number doesn't match any winning number? There's the Second Chance Sweepstakes. And it's almost as good as the first chance. If any of the prizes (including the Lotus) are not claimed, you may still be a winner. You'll find the entry blanks for this Second Chance wherever you find the Chaz 'Dream Machine' Display. For details see official sweepstakes rules on back of game piece. You must enter before Aug. 31, 1985 to be eligible.

The Chaz 'Dream Machine' Sweepstakes. The prizes are almost as interesting as the man who wears Chaz.

CHAZ for men by Revlon. Cologne, After Shave, Invigorating Body Spray. From $4 to $9.75.

Figure 16.3   Chaz sweepstakes ad

Enter the CHAZ 'Dream Machine' $100,000 Sweepstakes.

See game card in front of magazine.

You may be a scratch away from a Lotus Turbo Esprit

or any one of more than 5,000 other prizes.

Just scratch off all these silver spots with the edge of a coin.
Then take this card to any participating Chaz retailer.
If your number exactly matches any of the numbers on the Chaz display
you're an instant Chaz "Dream Machine" Sweepstakes winner.

sweepstakes require the consumer to *match the number on the entry with that on the brand's package.* Such a sweepstakes has the advantage of getting the consumer to the retail display, of picking up the package, and of examining it carefully. These behaviors move the consumer closer to purchase. Perhaps the purchase will then be consummated with the additional incentive of a coupon. Figure 16.4 shows such a sweepstakes for 9-Lives cat food.

A second useful sweepstakes format requires the entrant to *answer some brand questions correctly.* Here again there is a behavioral purpose in that either the ad or the package must be read to get the correct answers. Such a ploy is useful for a new brand in order to enhance learning and also to move the consumer toward the appropriate behavior of purchase. Figure 16.5 is an example of a sweepstakes that requires information seeking.

A third good use of the sweepstakes/game is in *building repeat purchases.* To this end the promotion can require that the consumer collects numbers, letters, pictures, or whatever to complete a set. Sweepstakes such as those run by McDonald's and other fast food franchises in the recent past encourage repeat visits to a retail location. They are legal because no purchase is required (even though most people buy when visiting a store).

Finally, a major purpose of the sweepstakes is to help in *building an image.* To this end it must be consistent with the image of the rest of the advertising. In

Figure 16.4 *9-Lives sweepstakes*

Figure 16.5 *Hefty sweepstakes requires information seeking*

Figure 16.6 *True sweepstakes ad*

this way consumers will be reminded of the image even if they are not interested in the sweepstakes. Figure 16.6 shows a sweepstakes ad for True cigarettes. Note the consistency with its long-running advertising campaign.

Sweepstakes can be fun, exciting, and, perhaps, an escape for consumers as shown in Figure 16.7, but for the most part they are not a valuable marketing tool in terms of acquiring or leading to long-run behavior. Consumers cannot be asked to make a *monetary* payment to enter, but they can be asked for a *nonmonetary* payment of effort and/or behavior. If the firm is intent on giving away gifts, it should at least require that consumers learn something relevant to the firm or take some steps toward purchase of the brand. Without this minimal response from the consumer, the sweepstakes is a poor promotional tool.

There are, in sum, several types of sweepstakes:

- *Straight* There is a random drawing for winning entry.
- *Matching* Winners are determined by matching the entry number against a posted number (often shown on the package).
- *Instant win* The player wins or loses immediately by rubbing a covering off the entry blank. This is often combined with a matching process. The instant win game is best from a behavioral perspective because it provides immediate reinforcement.

By ART BUCHWALD

It seems every time the mailman comes, he delivers another large envelope addressed to me announcing that I have either won a GIANT SWEEPSTAKES, or have a CHANCE of winning one if I will just open the letter.

I want you to know that these are not pieces of impersonal junk mail. They are addressed "Dear Art and Ann," and go something like this: "We're happy to inform you that you have almost won a $150,000 solar home, $20,000-a-year for life, a three-month cruise around the world or a Gillette double-edged razor. You do not have to do anything to win one of these prizes except subscribe to Drowning magazine, the new bi-monthly publication devoted to people who can't swim. Even if you don't subscribe to our magazine, you have an opportunity to participate in a drawing for an all-day trip up the Amazon (air fare not included) or a portable screwdriver with your initials on it.

"This is how you can win: Rub the blank white square below. If a buffalo appears in the space, then you are one of the really lucky ones who may be moving into your new solar-heated $150,000 house next month. If a turkey shows up, your name automatically goes into a box for the $20,000-a-year for life annuity. If no animal appears in the white space, YOU HAVE NOT LOST. You are eligible for an oil change at the gasoline station of your choice.

"Wait, there's more. Because we believe Drowning magazine will not only appeal to your desire to learn more about what happens when you sink to the bottom of the sea, we are offering the first one million subscribers a chance to win 1,000 gold-minted coins dredged up from a Spanish galleon which sank off the coast of Florida in 1665. These coins are practically yours if you act NOW.

"Art and Ann, I'll be very hurt if I don't hear from you this week. Love, Judy Hammer."

I must admit that even I get sucked in by this kind of mail, and my wife also gets very excited the day a sweepstakes letter arrives.

The other afternoon when I came home, she couldn't contain herself. "We've just won a three-year-old racehorse," she said, hugging me, "and it will probably win the Kentucky Derby."

"What do we have to do for it?" I wanted to know.

"Nothing," she said, "but take out a health and accident policy which will guarantee us $10 a day for 12 days in any city-owned hospital in the U.S."

"And for that we get a racehorse?"

"We do if our insurance policy number matches the winning number of the Irish Sweepstakes."

"I'm not sure I want a horse," I said. "If he wins the Kentucky Derby, the sportswriters won't give us any peace."

She went through some other letters. "All right, then, how would you like a 707 Boeing jet with leather seats designed by Gucci?"

"That sounds more like it. How do we win that?"

"I'm not sure. All the letter says is 'Dear Art and Ann, You have won a 707 Boeing jet airplane. Please fill out this card and enclose $29.50 for luggage tags. These tags will be placed in a computer, and if your tag is the one selected, the Boeing will be delivered to your hangar or any airline terminal gate that you specify. All cards with checks must be postmarked no later than March 1.'"

"I don't see how the sweepstakes mailers do it," I said. "They give so much and ask so little in return."

My wife agreed: "And people say there is no such thing as the American dream."

Figure 16.7 . . . and there's one mailed every minute

- *Programmed learning* The entrant is required to give correct information and prizes are randomly allocated to correct entries.

By way of further summarizing, the following ideas are adapted from "20 Ways a Sweepstakes Can Help Your Company," a brochure prepared by Louis Scott Associates.[5] These ideas were aimed at industrial marketers but should hold for any firm.

- If the firm does not have anything new to say, a sweepstakes can hold consumers' attention for a while longer until there is something to say. But this cannot be kept up forever.
- A sweepstakes appeals to the imagination; therefore, the prizes should be madcap. A mundane prize will elicit mundane interest.
- Tie the theme of the sweepstakes to the position and/or product of the company, but be careful; tying the electric utility company to the electric chair at the state penitentiary is clever and memorable but may not be fun.

Figure 16.8   On package price-off deal

- Encourage multiple entries. This creates more awareness and interest. Each entry also has the name and address of a prospective customer. Include a box on the entry blank for the entrant to ask for more information.
- Make it easy to enter the sweepstakes. It should be simple and fun.
- Remember that the goal is to increase awareness and interest in the product. Do not let the sweepstakes divert attention from the product.

Price-off promotions and bonus packs

A *price-off deal* gives the consumer a certain amount of money off the regular price of the package and shows this price reduction on the package itself. A *bonus pack* gives the consumer an extra amount of product at the price of the regularly priced package (e.g., four bars of soap for the price of three; 18 ounces of ketchup for the price of 12). In both cases the cost/benefit relation is changed without any ancillary tool such as a coupon or refund offer. In 1982, 9% of consumer promotions dollars were devoted to these types of promotion.

These deals are straightforward maneuvers used as a quick retaliation against a competitor. They attempt to keep current users loyal by rewarding them. They are less useful in bringing in new consumers because they are often not advertised but merely appear on the shelf. As a defensive maneuver, they both attempt to give the consumer more product so that there will be less need to purchase during a competitive introduction or promotion. Figure 16.8 shows the price-off label of a Puff's package opening.

Both types of deals also have an impact on the retailer. The merchant often makes a larger purchase of these promotional items in anticipation of higher levels of consumer demand. In addition the retailer also may give the brand additional or preferred space. The responsiveness of the merchant probably would be even greater if the brands were also advertised.

There are additional advantages to the manufacturer. Because the price off or bonus is controlled in the factory, the firm knows exactly how much stock will be dealt and what time period and geographic areas will be covered. This allows the manager to know exactly what the promotion will cost and to be sure that no fraud can take place. Logistically these deals are also cheaper and easier to administer than other promotional choices. Keep in mind, though, that their target is mainly limited to current users and careful shoppers.

To administer these deals the firm can sell to the retailer at a lower price and allow the retailer to keep the same margin, or it can sell to the retailer at a price that cuts into the retail margin but still offers a volume opportunity. The former yields more reinforcement to the retailer and greater retailer loyalty to the firm. If the purpose of the deal is to increase volume and get extra retail push, the firm should absorb the loss and allow the retailer to keep the standard margin.

Promotions to Retailers

This section examines another important area of promotions by the firm: *promotions to the retailer.* The previous two chapters dealt with tools designed to encourage the consumer to pull the product through the pipeline; this section deals with incentives to get the retailer to push the product, to purchase and stock the product, and to establish positive relations with the manufacturer.

While expenditures on promotions to consumers have been growing rapidly (up 63% between 1976 and 1981), expenditures on promotions to the trade

Table 16.1 Share of promotional dollars: consumer versus trade promotions

	Consumer promotions	*Trade promotions*	*Ratio trade to consumer promotions*
1984	42%	58%	136:100
1983	40	60	148:100
1982	36	64	176:100

Source: Courtesy of Donnelley Marketing. "Seventh Annual Survey of Promotional Practices," 1984, p. 7.

were slowly declining (down 9% in the same period). In spite of these differing trends, trade promotions budgets still greatly exceed those for consumer promotions. In 1982, marketing dollars were split with 45% in media advertising, 29% in trade promotion, and 25% in consumer promotion.[6] Table 16.1 shows the changing relation between consumer and trade promotions in the past few years. For mature grocery products, it is not unusual for up to 70% of sales to the retailer to be on some sort of deal.[7]

It is not clear why the decline in trade promotions is occurring unless it is to create more balance between the two areas of promotions. Trade promotions are vital because it is important to coordinate the pushes and pulls in the pipeline so that goods move smoothly. It is also important to keep on top of the retailer situation continuously; as more products compete for limited shelf space, the retailer will carefully select those brands that provide the greatest margin per unit of area and the most rapid turnover. It is estimated that the average supermarket stocks over 10,000 items, and at any given time the retailer is confronted with over 1,000 promotions offers from advertisers.[8] Given these figures, promotions need creativity to break through the clutter.

Promotions to retailers are also critical because the product cannot be sold to consumers if it is not first sold to the retailer. Any sales projection is limited at the upper end by the distribution of the product. In fact, one of the variables in new product sales projection models is the level of distribution.

The basic goals of retailer promotions are

- To acquire and/or maintain a certain level of distribution
- To maintain and/or expand shelf space
- To acquire and/or maintain more favorable shelf space locations
- To preempt competitive efforts
- Ultimately, to influence consumer purchase patterns

Over the years the balance of power has shifted from the manufacturer to the retailer in most product classes because there are so many similar, mature products competing for limited shelf space. As manufacturers have lost power, they have needed to use more promotions and have eroded their profit base. Conversely, large retailers have recognized their power and have pitted manufacturers against one another by demanding larger allowances. Manufacturers have contributed to the shift by emphasizing short-run objectives that call for dealing.

Promotions to retailers can be broken into three categories:

- Buying allowances
- Advertising allowances
- Direct stimulus of retailer or salesperson

Buying allowances

A *buying allowance* is a temporary price reduction offered to the retailer by the manufacturer. Buy *X* cases and get *Y*% discount. This is the cleanest and simplest way to get the product through the pipeline and onto the shelf. There are many ways of executing a buying allowance, but all revolve around this simple concept, which is essentially a price-off deal for the retailer.

Initially, the purpose of the buying allowance was to help an introductory brand get established, but in the past few years such dealing has become quite indiscriminate. When this happens, retailers will only buy if there is a deal and will not place an order at the normal price. Manufacturers may then raise their wholesale prices so they can deal back to the level necessary to make a profit. In addition, the pipeline loses its smooth flow as sales cease when the deal is retracted.[9]

In theory, when the manufacturer gives the retailer a deal, it should be passed on to the consumer. This seems to be happening less. McKinsey & Company has estimated that as little as 15% of all deals are being passed on to consumers and as much as 50% of retailer profits are from not passing on deals. As manufacturers see less consumer impact from their deals, they are seeking ways to cut back.[10]

Advertising allowances[11]

Another area designed to get the retailer to buy more product is the advertising allowance. *Co-op advertising,* as it is commonly referred to, also has other goals. First, it is a promotional tool that rewards the retailer for buying a specified amount of product; if the retailer buys *X* cases, the manufacturer will pay *Y*% of the retailer's advertising expenses up to *Z* dollars per year. In addition, co-op advertising is an advertising tool aimed at giving the consumer product, price, and location information. As an advertising tool, co-op combines with national advertising so that while the national advertising builds long-run image and attitude, the co-op aims at short-run behavior. Finally, co-op has the long-run goal of developing an ongoing relation between the firm and the manufacturer.

Co-op advertising to consumers   Co-op ads can tend in two directions. One type features the retailer and mentions one or more manufacturers while emphasizing the merits of the location. Figure 16.9 is a straight co-op ad with emphasis on the retailer.

The second type features the manufacturer and lists one or more retailers who carry the product. Figure 16.10 is an example of a manufacturer-oriented ad, known as a *dealer listing ad.* The manufacturer and retailer could also create an ad that has a more even emphasis of each; but such equal emphasis ads are rare.

A major problem with co-op advertising is the resolution of this one-sided emphasis. Both parties are paying some portion of the ads (the percentage split varies based on several factors), both parties have goals that are inconsistent with the other, and both parties want to use the other's dollars for their own ends.

The *manufacturer's objective* is to get the consumer to buy the brand regardless of the retail location. Brand choice is important, but retailer choice is not. The *retailer's objective* is to get the consumer to a specific location to buy something. Store is important, but brand and product choice are not.[12]

It is creatively simple (and simple-minded) to put together a message that emphasizes one party or the other; what is needed is an ad that is balanced if each

Figure 16.9 *Co-op ad featuring retailer*

party is paying 50%. The alternative is for each party to pay a percentage equal to their share of the message. Because both parties enter a co-op deal to stretch their ad budget, one of them will generally be upset by either the financial deal or the layout. Co-op exists, though, because even with its faults there is mutual benefit. Figure 16.11 shows a co-op with equal emphasis on both the manufacturer and retailer.

Co-op has its greatest value to manufacturing firms with specific types of products. For example, it is less valuable for products that have extensive distribution and frequent purchase. If the product is widely available, there is no need to tell consumers where to go; if the product is frequently purchased, consumers already have established purchase patterns. These types of products would be more likely to appear in co-op advertising featuring the retailer and should get a lower percentage contribution from the manufacturer.

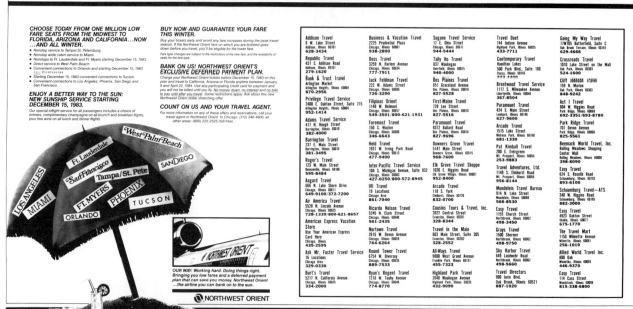

Figure 16.10 *Dealer listing ad featuring manufacturer*

Conversely, co-op is more useful to the manufacturer for infrequently purchased goods where the perceived risk to the consumer is higher. Here the consumer is more likely to move through the high-involvement hierarchy of effects. In such a case, national brand advertising creates awareness and attitude, and then local co-op advertising is an aid to behavior by showing price and location.

Co-op as promotion to the trade   The above discusses the advertising aspects of co-op. As a trade promotions tool, co-op dollars are an incentive to the retailer to purchase more goods from the manufacturer. In this scenario the manufacturer offers the retailer X advertising dollars for every unit purchased within a specified time period. A less behavioral but more common arrangement has the manufacturer offering the retailer $X\%$ of the latter's media cost up to $Y\%$ of the value of the ast year's purchase of merchandise.

Legal issues   Co-op advertising allowances are regulated by the Federal Trade Commission under provisions of the Robinson-Patman Act. The goal of the law is to provide an equal opportunity to all retailers to use the manufacturer's co-op funds and to not allow these funds to be used as discriminatory price discounts. To this end, firms must inform all competing retailers of any co-op offers. It is not enough for the retailer to ask for co-op dollars. A co-op plan offered to one retailer must be offered proportionately to all retailers who compete in a market. Furthermore, if retailer A buys twice as much from the manufacturer as retailer B, then the manufacturer must offer A twice as many co-op dollars.[13]

Figure 16.11 *Example of a 50/50 co-op ad*

In their recent monograph, "Cooperative Advertising: Practice and Problems," Young and Greyser conclude with a set of summary guidelines for marketing managers. Some, such as the need for research and objectives, are not specific to co-op advertising and are discussed elsewhere in this text. Others are specific to co-op and are listed here.

1. For most effective results, use co-op in conjunction with strong national advertising.

2. Do not consider budget decisions between cooperative advertising and (sole-sponsored) national advertising as direct tradeoffs.

3. Assess how important the retailer's efforts are to the brand's success.

4. Assess whether consumers seek product choice information from retailer's or from manufacturer's communications.

5. Emphasize cooperative advertising when a "linkage" with retailer's image in the local market is important.

6. Realize that to be most effective, cooperative advertising must be cooperative.[14]

One other type of co-op advertising is that done by two or more manufacturers with products that are complementary. This is usually done by established brands trying to increase usage by showing new uses for their products. Although the usage shown in Figure 16.12 is not unique or new, it is an example of this type of co-op advertising.

Figure 16.12 Co-op advertising by three manufacturers

Other direct stimulus items

In addition to buying allowances and advertising allowances, the manufacturer can use a number of other tools as incentives to the retailer. Most direct is a cash incentive to the retailer's salesperson in return for sales made. This is essentially a commission from the manufacturer to the salesperson and is known as a *spiff* or *push money* or *p.m.* It is typically used for high-priced goods in a location where several brands compete such as in an appliance or clothing store. The benefit to the manufacturer of a spiff is that it gets to the appropriate party, the salesperson. The detriment to the store is that the salesperson may now sell items that are immediately rewarding rather than those that are in the best interest of the store and/or the customer. In spite of this, the spiff is sometimes also used by retailers to motivate its own salespersons to push hard-to-sell items.

Contests and *sweepstakes* are common incentives for both the retailer and the salesperson and are generally strongly behavioral. Contests are based on selling the most product within a certain period of time or on exhibiting product knowledge by answering questions. Sweepstakes can be separate games just for the trade but can be tied to consumer sweepstakes such as when the retailer associated with the winning consumer also wins.

A creative tie-in of consumer and retailer sweepstakes was recently executed by Velamints. In addition to the fairly routine consumer sweepstakes, there were two parallel ones for the retailer. In the first the retailer got one entry for every four cartons of Velamints purchased or displayed during the sweepstakes period. In the second the retailer won a prize if the winning consumer mentioned that retail location. Both sweepstakes provided proper incentives to stock the product and display consumer entry forms.[15]

In another sweepstakes twist parallel to a type aimed at consumers, retailers and clerks must answer knowledge-based questions in order to be eligible for a drawing. Hanes Hosiery, for example, provided a form with five questions. For two correct answers, clerks received free pantyhose; for five correct answers, names were entered into a drawing. Over 40% of eligible clerks submitted entries. This means that over 40% of the clerks had at least some rudimentary knowledge about the product they were selling.[16]

Retail displays or *point-of-purchase (P-O-P)* materials sometimes can be incentives for the retailer; unfortunately, they also may act as a pain in the neck for the retailer and are often thrown away without being used. Retailers are generally sorely pressed for space so the manufacturer must show the retailer that the P-O-P device will help sales, or at least will not use valuable space that could be generating revenues.

Bettman's review of the consumer behavior literature led him to conclude that most grocery product brand choice decisions are made in store.[17] If this were correct (it will be expanded upon in the discussion of package design), then P-O-P materials would be quite valuable to the manufacturer in terms of increasing brand sales. There are examples of test market situations where relevant P-O-P materials led to brand sales up to 200% greater than those of the control group.[18]

While this type of response would certainly please any manufacturer, it is not clear what the benefit is to the retailer. In most cases, the incremental sales increase is taken from other brands also carried by the retailer. This means that total retail volume for the product class does not change and the retailer's gain is hard to see. For this reason P-O-P must often be accompanied by incentives to the retailer. These could be direct inducements such as the buying allowances described above or indirect inducements such as a consumer-oriented campaign that will bring more traffic to the retailer.

Again, the need for a coordinated campaign can be seen. P-O-P displays are useful as a last reminder to the consumer at the point of decision making but may not be useful without simultaneous incentives to the retailer and/or supporting advertising.

That P-O-P items are rarely used is a point made by Gulledge.[19] He presents several case studies where elaborate displays were used in only 1 to 2% of retail outlets. In one case the manufacturer offered consumers a premium of an inflatable cartoon character and developed a P-O-P display that used the inflatable. When consumer response turned out to be much lower than expected, the firm audited retailers and learned that only 2% of retailers used the display. Most of the inflatables ended up with the children of store personnel. This does not seem to be a unique result; a survey of other manufacturers reveals that most P-O-P creations are never used. While some P-O-P gets more than 2% usage, it has been estimated that only 50% end up being used at all. There are too many brands and too many P-O-P materials to fit them all into the retail outlet. The retailer often requires an incentive to use the P-O-P item.

Related to P-O-P materials is *shelf location*. While this issue does not pertain to incentives to the retailer, it is relevant to in-store communications; to get a desired shelf location, the manufacturer will often need to offer an incentive to the retailer. Is an investment in such an incentive worthwhile? Perception Research Services does extensive package design research and has determined over a several year period that

- Ideal shelf positioning can increase package visibility by over 70%
- Ideal shelf positioning can increase package viewing time by over 200%
- Brands on upper shelves receive 35% greater attention than those on lower shelves
- Doubling shelf facings increases attention by over 30%[20]

It would seem that shelf location and number of facings is important in creating attention at the point of purchase and would be a worthwhile goal in the use of trade promotions.

Dealer aids provide an incentive to the retailer by showing how to manage some part of the retailer's business better. This class of incentives provides help to small businesses in areas such as inventory control, accounting, ad layout, sales force training, etc. In some cases this help comes in the form of an incentive to purchase goods, while in other cases these services are provided by the manufacturer as goodwill.

Promotional Specialty Items

Specialty items are pieces of merchandise to remind someone about something over a long period of time. These items can be directed at consumers, retailers, or sales force and can be used for both new and established products. Typically these items would not be used alone but rather would be in addition to some other tool(s) described earlier. A partial list of specialty items would include

match books	bumper stickers	paperweights	jackets
T-shirts	pens and pencils	stationery	calendars
frisbees	patches	soap	coffee cups
balloons	hats		

The reader can think of many other specialty items without great difficulty.

Items that are left behind can be as ordinary as an embossed pen but often are quite complex. One firm that was trying to sell garbage trucks to a city council left behind one-foot-long exact scale replicas of their trucks with all moving parts (except engine) operational. The John Deere Company has had made up 1-inch perfect replicas of each item in their product line (tractors, backhoes, etc.). These can be put on charm bracelets or worn as pendants; they have also been cast in clear lucite blocks for use as paperweights.

These items have their greatest impact when they are coordinated with message strategy and with the campaign objectives and position. Figure 16.13 shows some examples from the promotional specialities catalog of Sales Guides, Inc. The range of items is limited only by the creativity of the user.

Figure 16.13 Examples of promotional specialty items

Gregory B. DiNovis

Director of Marketing Communications, Eastman Kodak Company

Gregory DiNovis is Director, Marketing Communications for Eastman Kodak Company's Consumer Electronics Division. Since beginning his career with the company in 1969, he has fulfilled a variety of marketing responsibilities in sales, sales training, sales promotion, and marketing planning. Mr. DiNovis planned and implemented the company's sponsorships as Official Photographic Consultant for the 1980 Winter Olympic Games, the 1982 World's Fair, and Kodak's participation in Walt Disney World's EPCOT Center. A native of Queens, New York, he earned a B.S. degree from Western New England College and an M.B.A. from Rochester Institute of Technology.

Trade Promotion or Retail Merchandising Program

Assume you are a consumer goods marketer with a distribution network of wholesalers, specialty retailers, catalog showrooms, and general merchandise retailers. Among the general merchandise accounts are traditional department stores and mass merchandisers. Recognize that competition is intense among these retailers, particularly among the chains that continue to build their own consumer loyalty. You are intent on building and maintaining your brand franchise. You realize the consumer is increasingly price-quality conscious, discriminating in product selection, and making more brand choice decisions in-store. Your mission is to design a trade promotion that strikes a balance among all three stakeholders: marketer, trade, and consumer. Incidentally, you must stay within your budget.

You could employ trade promotion in the narrow sense and offer an off-invoice allowance. Potentially, each member of the distribution net-

work can take advantage of this regardless of their method and philosophy of merchandising. You may even move additional unit volume into the trade over the short term, but what is likely to happen?

Some accounts will order product at their normal stocking level, sustain their retail price, and meet their objectives by pocketing the high retail margin. Not only will you suffer an earnings and revenue reduction but you have not generated a sales increase.

Some buyers will complain that because of their accounting system, their departments do not benefit from off-invoice allowances. Off-invoice allowances accrue to a different bookkeeping account as do cash discounts taken off-invoice for prompt payment of bills. Consequently, executional difficulty may negate the incentive.

Some accounts may be persuaded to stock up based on the off-invoice allowance, but this alone may not motivate a sophisticated merchant. If you want the retailer to stock up and feature the product in a retail advertisement and promotionally display the product in-store, you will be required to provide additional allowances for advertising and display. Do not expect the retailer to chase volume and risk increased operating cost without marketer participation.

Finally, some accounts will tell you that all the trade promotion in the world will not compensate for your responsibility to build the category and build demand with direct-to-the-consumer efforts such as advertising and promotion. If your mix of direct-to-the-consumer effort and direct-to-the-trade effort is heavily skewed to the trade, you can find yourself subsidizing their markdowns—lower and lower retail-price points with negative earnings implications for you.

We view trade promotion in the context of building and of maintaining a trade franchise. It's a long-term view. We recognize that no two retailers and wholesalers merchandise in the same manner. Programs must be tailored to these merchandising needs and be consistent with brand objectives. Strategically, we work to enhance the value to the trade of doing business with us.

This requires providing inducements when appropriate for sell-in, and programs designed to help the trade sell-through to the consumer. These sell-through programs include merchandising aids, in-store display programs, and promotion retail advertising materials. Incentives are provided for promotional display and advertising by the retailer and these incentives are rendered upon proof of performance. Consequently, the sales force is provided the tools to work with the trade in designing individual retail merchandising programs and timing the program to take full advantage of our national consumer advertising and promotion program.

Set specific objectives. What do you want to do? Increase retail advertising by the trade, obtain prime promotional displays, enhance dealer profitability? Approach trade-promotion planning with a strategic view. Balance trade and consumer efforts. Focus on the tactical execution. Measure results against objectives.

Summary

Promotions are important in establishing trial for new products. The firm must get as many tryers as possible so there will be an adequate market share when the brand stabilizes later. Getting introductory purchases is difficult without promotions; getting shelf space for the new product is also difficult without promotions. Again, behavior must be managed to assure its appropriateness.

These chapters have tried to bring some theoretical underpinning to a chaotic area and to show the appropriate uses of promotional tools. While misuse of promotions cannot be avoided when there is competitive misuse, the three chapters have tried to raise issues to allow the best use of promotions in all situations.

Summary of consumer promotions   Figure 16.14 is presented as a summary of this and the previous two chapters. It is a worksheet used at S. C. Johnson to plan consumer promotions. The columns represent marketing objectives and the rows represent available promotional tools. The values at each intersection show how well S. C. Johnson management feels that the tool will do in helping to reach the objective; higher values show that the tool is more likely to be useful. Samples are best for trial; refunds and in/on package coupons are best for building habitual buying behavior; refunds are best at getting consumers to stock up; recipe and public service promotions are best for image building; on/in package coupons are the best defensive tactic; some types of samples and premiums are best at getting retailer support.

Summary of promotions to retailers   A number of promotions have been presented in this section with the underlying theme being that the incentive must tie to appropriate desired behavior. Retailers are offered a large number of incentives by a large number of manufacturers, but only those that elicit desired behavior should be offered. On the other hand only those that can be seen as rewarding will be accepted by the retailer.

The retail travel business (travel agency) receives many incentives and can serve as an example to help summarize this part. This type of business receives many incentives because it is a retail outlet that sells the services of many firms, but many of the services are close to being commodities (i.e., there is great similarity across brands).

Most basic is the commission structure that offers the retailer a direct response to behavior. During the early 1980s, commissions went up because one firm (airline) occasionally tried to increase its market share by raising its commission percentage; this move was quickly countered by all competitors, and the result was a new level of parity with lower profits for each airline. Conversely, the percentages have not come down because each firm is afraid to initiate this change for fear of losing market share. Occasionally one airline attempts this move but rescinds it after a few days when its competitors fail to follow. These actions are typical of the workings of an oligopolistic industry.

In addition to commissions, there are cases of push money being given to sell space on certain routes. Again, a specific behavior is sought from the retailer. In some cases there is a cash override for booking a particular route; in other cases the payoff is made in terms of free passes from the airline. This is clearly an attempt to take share from the competition because it is difficult to convince a traveler who wants to go to New York that the new route to Iowa City is preferable.

For a while airlines that offered frequent flyer incentives to passengers (fly X times on Y airline and receive a pass for a free trip) also gave passes to the travel

Preprinted numbers represent fit, between tactic and objective, for the "average" established package goods product. Use as benchmark for "fit" judgments more specific to each brand.

9 = best fit
1 = poorest fit

Worksheet version

Checklist of tactical possibilities			Mix of objectives / Weighting / Net Fit	Trial (Expanded trial)	Habit (Purchase habit building)	Loading (Pantry loading to increase usage)	Image (Category leadership imagery)	Defense (Defense and retention)	Retail (Retail objectives and getting displays)
THEME INCENTIVES	Premiums	Self-Liquidator		6	6	6	6	3	5
		Continuity		3	7	8	5	4	3
		In-Pack		7	7	6	5	4	5
		On-Pack		8	7	6	5	4	8
		Container		8	6	6	5	4	8
		Near-Pack		7	6	5	5	3	9
	Samples	Media Delivered		8	4	2	3	2	2
		Direct Mail (solo)		8	4	2	5	2	2
		Co-op		7	4	2	3	2	2
		Door Delivered		8	4	2	5	2	2
		Demonstrator Intercept		8	4	2	5	4	9
		Retailed Sample Size		9	5	3	3	5	9
		In/On Pack (Cross Ruff)		8	4	2	4	2	6
	Sweepstakes			4	5	6	7	3	4
	Contests			3	5	6	7	3	4
	Recipe Promotions			8	8	7	8	4	6
	Public Service Promotion			4	5	6	9	2	4
ECONOMIC INCENTIVES	Coupons / Media Del'd / Solo	ROP Newspaper		6	7	5	4	7	5
		Newspaper Insert		7	7	5	5	6	6
		Supplement		6	6	5	5	5	4
		Magazine		7	6	5	6	4	3
		Direct Mail		7	6	5	4	6	4
		Intercept		7	4	5	4	7	9
	Coupons / Media Del'd / Co-op	ROP Newspaper		3	4	4	3	3	3
		Newspaper Insert		4	5	4	4	4	2
		Supplement		3	4	4	4	3	2
		Magazine		5	4	4	4	2	4
		Direct Mail		5	5	4	3	3	2
	Package Del'd	In-Pack (Blind)		1	9	7	4	8	2
		On-Pack flagged In-Pack		3	9	8	4	8	4
	Cross Ruff	Own Brands		7	5	4	5	3	3
		Others Brands		8	5	4	7	3	4
		Store Brands		7	4	3	6	3	5
		Other Institutions		8	4	2	7	2	2
	Refunds	ROP Newspaper		5	7	9	5	7	4
		Newspaper Insert		6	8	8	6	6	3
		Supplement		4	7	8	4	5	2
		Magazine		6	8	7	7	5	2
		Direct Mail		6	8	8	6	5	2
		In-Pack (Blind)		2	9	9	3	5	1
		On-Pack flagged In-Pack		3	8	8	3	7	4
		In-Store		6	9	9	7	7	6
	Off-Labels			7	7	7	4	7	7
	Bonus Packs			6	6	7	6	7	7
	Banded Packs			5	6	9	6	7	9

Figure 16.14 Consumer promotion planning matrix

agency that booked the passenger. This gave excitement to the program for the agent but seems to be waning in its use by the airlines. When used, it is an incentive to the agency to sell the same airline repeatedly.

Numerous contests and sweepstakes are offered to travel agents. Some of these require sales goals to be met, others require an exhibition of knowledge, while still others are based on sheer luck. The first two types are clearly more behavioral. An example of the second type would require agents to read an ad to find the correct answers to the sweepstakes' questions (as in Figure 16.15). This type of sweepstakes requires agents to search their interactive computer ticketing system for information about KLM so that they may have a chance to win. In this way KLM gets the desired behavior (i.e., that agents read and digest relevant information) from many agents while paying off a small subset of the entire group. The KLM sweepstakes go one step further by having a new game with new information to learn every week.

Figure 16.15   A sweepstakes that requires learning from the retailer

Contests can also be tied to P-O-P displays. One airline sent agents buttons to wear that promoted the airline. If the airline's representative came to the agency, all agents wearing the button received a pass. While the buttons probably led directly to few sales, they certainly gave the airline more top-of-mind awareness among its retailers.

While the above are generally incentives to specific behavior, there are also many educational incentives that should probably be classified as dealer aids. In the travel business these include familiarization (fam) trips sponsored by government tourist bureaus, airlines, cruise ship lines, or hotel chains; there are also discount privileges and passes. In each case the purpose is to educate the agent about the merits of a place or service so that the agent can help clients more knowledgeably (and hopefully recommend that place or service).

Each of these promotions is expensive. To maximize the return on the expense, the promotion must be clearly tied to the desired behavior.

Discussion Questions

1. Continuing your job-seeking campaign, consider how you might use promotional tools to increase the responses to the advertising campaign that you designed earlier. Be careful that your offer is realistic given the needs of your target market.

2. What are the major disadvantages to premiums and sweepstakes? What can you do to make sure your brand is not a victim of these problems?

3. What are the major methods of distribution of premiums? What are the pros and cons of each?

4. What are the major methods of payment for premiums? What are the pros and cons of each?

5. What is a self-liquidating premium? How does it work?

6. What makes a sweepstakes illegal?

7. How can sweepstakes be used to increase learning and shape behavior?

8. What is a buying allowance? What does the retailer get? What does the manufacturer get?

9. What is the difference between a co-op and a dealer listing ad?

10. Why is such a small percentage of available co-op money used by retailers? How can this be remedied? What would each party need to do?

Notes

1. Bob Greene, "A Little Something to Sweeten the Deal," *Wisconsin State Journal,* 13 April 1983, Section 5, p. 3.

2. Ed Meyer, "How to 'Play the Angles' and Win," *Advertising Age,* 18 April 1983, p. M-48.

3. Frankllynn Peterson and Judi Kesselman-Turkel, "Catching Customers with Sweepstakes," *Fortune,* 8 February 1982, pp. 84–88.

4. Peterson and Kesselman-Turkel, "Catching Customers."

5. "20 Ways a Sweepstakes Can Help Your Company," Louis Scott Associates, New York.

6. Donnelley Marketing, "5th Annual Survey of Promotional Practices," 1982.

7. John A. Quelch, "Trade Promotion by Grocery Products Manufacturers: A Managerial Perspective," Report no. 82-106, Marketing Science Institute, Cambridge, Mass., 1982.

8. Dancer Fitzgerald Sample, Inc., *Promotion Report,* March–April 1983.

9. Robert G. Brown, "Manufacturers Getting Smeared in the 'Trade Promotions Trap'," *Marketing News,* 4 March 1983, p. 6.

10. Louis J. Haugh, "Trade Dealing Losing Favor," *Advertising Age,* 1 August 1983, p. M-54.

11. Robert F. Young and Stephen A. Greyser, "Cooperative Advertising: Practices and Problems," Report no. 82-105, Marketing Science Institute, Cambridge, Mass., 1982.

12. Robert D. Wilcox, "It's Not Always Cooperative," *Advertising Age,* 6 June 1983, p. M-56.

13. Robert D. Wilcox, "Bending Rules—Unknowingly," *Advertising Age,* 6 December 1982, p. M-52.

14. Young and Greyser, "Cooperative Advertising."

15. William Robinson, "Creativity in Trade Promos," *Advertising Age,* 22 March 1982, p. M-38.

16. Robinson, "Creativity in Trade Promos."

17. James R. Bettman, "Memory Factors in Consumer Choice: A Review," *Journal of Marketing* 43 (Spring 1979), pp. 37–53.

18. "Off-Shelf Displays Perform But When Placed up Front and Used with P-O-P," *Marketing News,* 19 August 1983, p. 4.

19. Larry Gulledge, "Audits Can Salvage Promotions," *Marketing News,* 19 August 1983, p. 4.

20. Elliot Young, "Packaging Research Probes Stopping Power, Label Reading, and Consumer Attitudes among the Targeted Audience," *Marketing News,* 22 July 1983, p. 8.

PROMOTIONS STRATEGIES

Consumer Promotions

Consumer promotions were done through the local bottlers and therefore varied from market to market. Coupons were distributed through local newspaper ads such as that shown in Figure S.1. The figure shown is a page from the Sunkist Marketing Support Materials Handbook. The materials were prepared by Sunkist to maintain the product image nationally, but allowed the bottler to make the pricing decisions based on local needs. Similar ads were available for all container sizes to allow the local bottler

to best meet local conditions. A variation on this offer is the bonus pack shown in Figure S.2. There was no comprehensive promotions plan so that local bottlers could use their own judgment in this area. Note that these materials allowed the local bottler to set both the timing and the price level of the promotion.

Another popular promotion piece during the introductory period was the T-shirt. In some markets these shirts, shown in Figure S.3, were given away as

Figures S.1 and S.2   *Local bottlers can create their own coupon and bonus-pack ads*

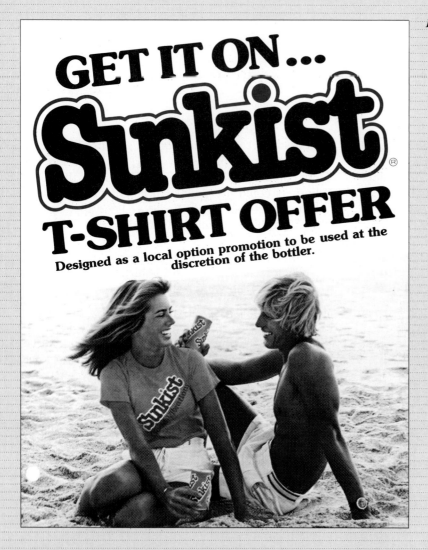

publicity items; 40,000 were given away in New York City alone. In other markets, the shirts cost $3.65 plus a proof of purchase. In either case the shirt was a visual reminder of the brand and exactly showed the package label. Note also the continuity between the television commercial and the tee shirt offer. The themes of California, beach, and beautiful people were carried through all forms of messages.

Trade Promotions

There were two tiers of trade promotions. At one level, Sunkist dealt with the bottlers; at the second, the bottler dealt with the retailer.

Sunkist and its bottlers

These two parties agreed to do cooperative advertising and marketing. Sunkist paid for all advertising during the first 16 weeks of introduction. During the remainder of the first year, the media costs were split 50/50 (and the media plan used was the same as that shown earlier in the media section). If both parties agreed that there should be an additional amount spent for advertising, that would also be split on a 50/50 basis.

The bottler also was required to support all consumer product promotion and sampling (described above) during the first 16 weeks, while Sunkist paid for the incentives to gain retail distribution. Most later promotions to retailers and consumers were split 50/50. Overall, the burden of these expenses fell on Sunkist because the advertising costs during the introductory period were so large.

There was also a sales incentive plan for the bottlers during the first five months in each local market. Bottlers were given sales targets and were then awarded units of drink concentrate as a reinforcement for sales in excess of these targets. The free units of concentrate needed to be used up by the end of the first year. This plan provided an incentive to sell early in the year to get the bonus and provided an incentive later in the year to use up the bonus.

The bottlers and retailers

While the bottler was responsible for doing the work needed to gain local retail distribution, Sunkist assisted with financial support in most cases. Again, there was no national program, but, rather, each local bottler developed the trade promotion that was felt to be relevant to the local market problems. Incentives included price-off deals, co-op advertising allowances and dealer loaders (a gift to the retailer in exchange for the purchase of a certain number of cases or the use of a point-of-purchase display).

A typical price-off deal offered the retailer cases of 12 ounce, 6-pack cans at $6.00 rather than the normal $7.50 price. In some instances this discount stayed with the retailers. In other cities the bottler suggested that the price per 6-pack be lowered from $2.49 to $2.19 for the consumer. With such a retail price change the retailer still got some savings but needed to increase volume to realize much profit.

Note that the bottler can only *suggest* the retail price; it is illegal to *force* a price on a retailer. Some bottlers felt that the best incentive was the price-off deal to the retailer; others suggested that the deal be passed on to consumers in order to provide a dual incentive.

Another price-off deal was used in conjunction with point-of-purchase displays and dealer loaders. Some bottlers offered their retailers a $1.00 discount per case in return for the retailer's use of a point-of-purchase or end-of-aisle display. Some of the displays were in the form of dealer loaders. For example, a summer display might consist of an inflatable raft full of Sunkist drinks. The retailer received a price-off deal for using this display for a specified period of time and then was given the raft as a dealer loader. In general, retailers were most responsive to the most direct price-off deals.

Retailers were also offered price-off deals in return for co-op features in their advertising. In the most straightforward instances, retailers were given case discounts that could be used towards their advertising if Sunkist was featured to some prescribed degree in the ad. In more complex deals, the co-op advertising referred to the T-shirt offer while the in-store point-of-purchase display gave the specific details for the T-shirt. In addition, there could also be some sort of pricing deal for the consumer along with what was needed to ensure retailer cooperation.

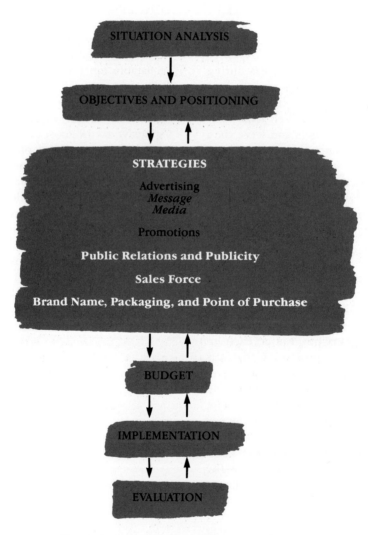

Decision Sequence Framework

Part Seven
Other Marketing
Communications
Strategies

*I*n addition to advertising and promotions, a number of other areas of communications strategy need to be examined. This part considers several of these:

- public relations, publicity, and corporate image advertising as communications tools
- the sales force as a communications tool
- the package, brand name, and point-of-purchase display as communications tools

Just as advertising and promotions were seen to have certain attributes that made them especially valuable to the firm in terms of meeting certain objectives, so too the tools that are explored in this part have particular characteristics that help them fit into the communications mix of the decision sequence.

For example, public relations and corporate image advertising are primarily used to influence attitudes toward the overall organization; the sales force is used to generate purchases in specific cases where a one-to-one interaction is cost-efficient. Packaging, brand name, and point-of-purchase display are ancillary devices to aid learning and to act as a last reminder at the time of purchase, when generally no sales force is available.

Effective communications are difficult to achieve, and the manager should use whatever means are available to reach this end. The decision sequence shows where these tools fit in with the other issues of this text.

Chapter 17
Public Relations, Publicity, and Corporate Image Advertising

The first chapter of this section will examine public relations, publicity and corporate image advertising. These communications tools are generally used to change attitudes toward an organization or issue rather than to directly impact upon purchase behavior. Since they each have different goals that also differ from that of product advertising, their formats and characteristics also differ.

Public relations releases that appear in the media have the characteristics of a news story. This manner of presentation gives credibility to the story and enables it to have greater impact with less frequency than would advertising.

Publicity events often are carefully orchestrated in order to seem spontaneous; other events are straightforward and well publicized in order to bring a target market to a certain location. These events can be behaviorally oriented in that a specific behavior (attendance) is achieved by creating a specific event.

Corporate image advertising has grown in the past few years in response to the firm's needs for disseminating a message that was not being accepted as public relations. As more firms try to use the public relations route more often, a smaller percentage of messages are accepted by the media. Firms have begun to pay for these messages through corporate advertising when they could not succeed through public relations.

Public Relations

The area of public relations is well developed and runs parallel to advertising in the sense that there are entire courses and texts devoted to the topic. Because a great deal of what occurs in these courses and texts is very similar to what has been discussed in the early stages of the decision sequence and in the media and

502

message strategies, it is not necessary to review these issues in detail. As with advertising and promotions, it is necessary to remember to assess the problem through a situation analysis and to set the objectives and position before developing strategies.

Defining public relations

As will be seen, public relations has many definitions and interpretations. One that is *not* acceptable is that public relations is free advertising. Because there are no direct media costs incurred, some feel this tool is free; because there is advocacy communication, some equate the tool with advertising. As will be seen, though, public relations has substantive differences that exceed its superficial similarities to advertising. In most cases, the two tools should complement one another; rarely would they serve as substitutes.

Since any organization that deals with others has, by definition, relations with the public, or public relations, Stanley feels that "public relations is a condition or state of being."[1] By this he means that relations exist, for good or bad, regardless of the desires of management. Given this logic, the firm cannot dictate that there will or will not be public relations (the state of being), but rather can only try its best to manage these interactions through public relations (the strategic tool) so that the state of being will be favorable.

Each public will form its own image, and this image is often referred to as *goodwill;* it is generally in the firm's best interest to monitor and manage this goodwill as well as possible. Out of this comes the concept that

> Public relations is a management function that determines the attitudes and opinions of the organization's publics, identifies its policies with the interests of its publics, and formulates and executes a program of action to earn the understanding and goodwill of its publics.[2]

There are many other definitions[3], but all are basically similar. They use words and phrases such as

- Function of management
- An atmosphere of mutual understanding, respect, and cooperation between an organization and those elements of the public with which it has contact
- Earn public understanding and acceptance
- Evaluate public attitudes
- Public interest
- Communication function
- The totality of an organization's behavior with respect to the society in which it operates

Goodrich, Gildea, and Cavanaugh[4] write that public relations *involves*

1. A planned effort or management function

2. The relationship between an organization and its publics

3. Evaluation of public attitudes and opinions

4. An organization's policies, procedures, and actions as they relate to the organization's publics

5. Steps taken to ensure that policies, procedures, and actions are in the public interest and are socially responsible

6. Execution of an action or communication program

7. Development of rapport, goodwill, understanding, and acceptance as the chief result sought

These authors then continue with a list of eight major *strategic functions* of public relations:[5]

1. Writing news releases, reports, booklets, speeches, trade and general magazine articles, film sequences, radio and television copy, production information, and technical material

2. Editing employee publications, newsletters, annual reports, and other management communications for internal and external audiences

3. Placing client or employer news and features with media editors and others responsible for selecting copy and preparing programs

4. Promoting through special events, such as press parties, open houses, anniversaries, award programs, and institutional films

5. Speaking (also searching for platforms, organizing speakers' bureaus, and preparing speeches for others)

6. Producing brochures, booklets, special reports, and house periodicals

7. Programming (involves determining needs, defining goals, recommending programs, and advising management on special problems of policy when the welfare of an organization is critically affected)

8. Publicizing a company's name and reputation

Similarities to and differences from advertising

It is easy to see from these definitions and functions that the *goals* of advertising and public relations are very different at a basic level. Advertising's goal is to inform and persuade consumers with respect to very specific product offerings (an exception to this is corporate image advertising, which is discussed later in this chapter), while the goal of public relations is to develop understanding, goodwill, and favorable attitudes toward the firm. In other words, advertising (and promotions) work toward fairly short-run sales objectives (especially for consumer convenience products) and long-term learning objectives, while public relations has immediate image and attitude goals that should have some impact on longer range sales objectives.

It is important to note, though, that some public relations has a short-run impact. When a new product is introduced, for example, public relations press releases attempt to build awareness and attitude for immediate trial. Such cases are also geared at creating favorable feelings among retailers and other middlepersons. Each year, for example, the new automobile models are introduced with a fanfare that is part advertising, part public relations, and part publicity. This combination of strategies tries to create awareness among consumers and enthusiasm among dealers. Over the years, many media vehicles have accepted the introductions as somewhat newsworthy and, as a result, have given editorial coverage to these pseudo-news events.

This example makes reference to one of the most important distinctions between advertising and public relations. Public relations messages are inserted in media vehicles as news stories and therefore are *more credible than advertising.* Advertising time or space is purchased and controlled by the firm and is seen by the consumer as an advocacy message; this blatantly self-interested message delivery makes advertising less credible, less sought after, and discounted in terms of its usefulness. These drawbacks, in turn, have led to the need for high-repetition, high-budget strategies so that learning can occur in spite of the low consumer involvement that exists in most cases. Conversely, new product news is interesting to many consumers and is read/viewed by more people.

As news, the public relations story is more credible and more likely to be retained. A large part of this credibility comes from the fact that editorial content is screened by the vehicle; its appearance has the implication of *endorsement by the vehicle* and, as a result, has extra credibility. Donald Levin, senior vice president with Hill & Knowlton, says, "The beauty of product publicity is that you get an editor to endorse a story and that greatly enhances believability."[6]

Related to the news versus advertising dichotomy is the *cost of insertion.* Advertising pays its own way, while public relations stories are accepted with no media cost to the firm. This cost issue is compounded when one considers the need for repetition in advertising. Any possible use of public relations will help to stretch the media budget while also giving extra credibility. There are, though, nonmedia costs involved in obtaining product involvement, as is discussed later.

When Cabbage Patch dolls first came on the market in 1983, Coleco Industries spent almost as much on public relations as it did on advertising. As a result, Nancy Reagan was seen giving the dolls to two South Korean children after their heart surgery, Jane Pauley spent five minutes with a doll on the "Today" show, several women's magazines featured the dolls as Christmas gift ideas, the dolls were featured on the "Tonight" show several times, and Brooke Shields and Catherine Bach were cast as life-size Cabbage Patch Kids on a Bob Hope television special. The result was an early sellout of the 2 million doll stock and lots of sad children who couldn't get one. The value of this program in terms of advertising dollars cannot be calculated.[7]

While credibility and low cost certainly are virtues, there are offsetting issues. When the firm releases a public relations piece, it loses *control of the content, the time of publication/broadcast, or whether the story is used at all.* Advertising offers total control. The message is created and produced by the firm; when time or space is purchased, the firm knows when the message will be delivered. When a vehicle receives a public relations story, it can shorten it, add its own thoughts and facts, change its thrust, delay it until there is room to print it, or throw it in the trash can and ignore it.

This, in turn, raises another issue. In order for a public relations story to be printed, *it must be interesting to someone associated with the vehicle.* Advertising space is purchased and is generally separate from editorial decisions, but the public relations piece must be interesting or useful to an editor as well as interesting or useful to a reader/viewer. Therefore, the public relations story must accommodate at least one more public than does advertising.

Another difference concerns the *types of people* who are likely to manage public relations and advertising departments or agencies. Kotler and Mindak[8] describe the two types as coming from very different cultures in which each has a negative view of the other. Marketers and advertisers are more likely to come from business schools where they are trained to be profit-oriented; generally, they have a narrow training with little background in the arts and humanities; they tend to look down upon public relations people as press agents, flacks, and sponsors of pseudo-events.

Public relations practitioners are more likely to come from journalism schools where they have been trained as writers and have received a wider liberal arts background. They are more likely to have an antibusiness attitude from this environment and to view advertisers as hucksters.

In actuality the two groups are working toward the same goals within the firm; that is, both must communicate with the publics with which the firm deals. Advertisers, though, have trouble seeing that public relations makes a contribution, while public relations people feel that they spend all their time rescuing the firm from the deceptions of the advertisers.

Kotler and Mindak show the types of organizations most likely to use public relations and marketing (it seems that advertising fits their analysis equally well). Figure 17.1 shows what have historically been the types of organizations most likely to use each function. As time passes, though, the members of cells 2 and 3 are likely to join cell 4, while cell 1 members also go to 2 and 3. As this evolution occurs, public relations and advertising people will have an even greater need to work together and speak to one another.

One ongoing argument between the two camps is whether one is a subset of the other or if there is some equality between the two. If the firm has relations with its publics, then advertising is one type of relation and is a subset of public relations. If dominance is measured in size or dollars spent, then advertising is the

Figure 17.1 *Four levels of use of marketing and public relations in enterprises*

Marketing \ **Public relations**	Weak	Strong
Weak	1 Example: small social service agencies	2 Example: hospitals and colleges
Strong	3 Example: small manufacturing companies	4 Example: Fortune 500 companies

more important discipline. One resolution to this discussion is to place both disciplines within the decision sequence framework. Here they are equals, with complementary tasks wherein one or the other is called upon, depending on the objective to be met. In this text, advertising is dominant because the major emphasis is on paid and controlled forms of mass communication. Other texts emphasize public relations.

There are, actually, many similarities between the two tools. Generically, *both share the goal of attempting to stimulate interest* in a target market or public. While the specific interest or response may differ, the goal of stimulation remains.

Both tools also depend heavily on *a strong situation analysis based on research and a precise set of objectives.* It is incumbent in each case to define clearly the target market and the issues that will guide the message.

Both strategies call for *a thorough knowledge of the media.* The strengths and weaknesses of each medium, outlined in the advertising media chapters, is equally applicable to public relations media strategy decisions.

Relevant target markets and publics

One final difference concerns the relevant targets that each strategy class is called upon to reach. Most advertising is directed at consumers. Although this target is often segmented, overall it still represents the single public of consumers. (This discussion does not consider corporate advertising, which uses paid media to do some of the tasks of public relations, but this represents a small percentage of all advertising.)

Public relations is called upon in a greater variety of situations and must communicate to a greater variety of publics. These include "internal" publics of employees, stockholders, suppliers, current customers, and neighbors; "external" publics include the general population, the press, prospective customers, government officials, and educators.[9]

Employees need to receive information about the firm so they can see the results of their efforts and the direction in which the firm is going; they also need to receive information to help their training and morale. These issues can be covered through internal newsletters, magazines, bulletin board notices, pay envelope inserts, annual reports, and handbooks. Most of the major advertising agencies, for example, have periodic newsletters that discuss issues, present awards, and allow employees to present their views (Grey Advertising has *Grey Matter,* and Ogilvy & Mather has *Viewpoint*). If a more personal interaction is needed, there can be social events, orientation meetings, annual reviews, or grievance committees, depending upon the problems.

Stockholders want to learn about their investments. The annual report and annual stockholders' meeting give financial information, but people may want more information concerning the future of the firm and why things went well or poorly. Information can be disseminated through plant tours, films, formal presentations, or meetings with key executives. The latter may be a necessary way of dealing with large shareholders.

Suppliers and customers should receive information that will keep them loyal when things are going poorly. If an identity is created for the firm, these two groups will be more likely to be loyal. Newsletters such as the type sent to employees may be useful so that these publics are aware of what the firm is trying to accomplish and how well it is doing in its endeavors. The firm is dependent upon both suppliers and customers and should maintain open lines of communication with each.

Neighbors include people and organizations that exist in the same geographic locale. This public should be aware of the positive contributions that the firm makes to the community, such as generating income and employment, civic participation, and efforts at controlling pollution. This builds pride in the community and makes things easier during difficult times. Contributions to the community, as well as routine dissemination of information concerning the firm's progress, are necessary.

Marston[10] lists several other external publics that need to be addressed through public relations. Some of these are

- *The press public*   These are the gatekeepers for getting the firm's stories to the general public. A *gatekeeper* is a person who decides which items will pass on to the next level of the public. Gatekeepers should be kept abreast of issues through press kits, press conferences, and interviews. The press needs to be kept interested as well as informed, since it is there that decisions are made as to whether other publics will see a story.

- *The educator public*   These are also gatekeepers for a subset of the general public and should be kept abreast of the firm's events through newsletters, magazines, and cooperative exercises. Some communications are done directly by the firm; for example, *DuPont Magazine* is sent to many educators and has a four-page college supplement. In other cases, trade associations maintain relations with educators to keep them abreast of industry developments and to provide classroom materials. The Leo Burnett Company provides a sample reel of commercials for classroom use; various syndicated data sources provide recently out-of-date books for research projects; Starch/INRA Hooper provides magazine ad evaluations.

- *Civic and business clubs*   These groups can provide a platform from which to present the firm's story to influential members of the community. This, in turn, can be a gatekeeping process to other parts of the community as well as a legitimization process. Offers to speak at luncheons can be a very effective public relations vehicle.

- *The government public*   Many firms and trade associations have professional lobbyists at different levels of government to protect their interests, to ensure that their point of view is understood, and to present their perspective on relevant legislative issues. It is important to keep open lines of communication with both legislative and administrative bodies of the government.

- *The financial community*   It is important to maintain favorable relations with both the banking/lending community and the shareholder community. There are approximately 50,000 publicly owned corporations in the United States that compete for a share of mind among security analysts, brokers, and purchasers. The analyst researches and reports on firms; this person must receive relevant information that will aid the analysis.

The banking community must also be kept abreast of events at the firm, since its interest rates are determined by the level of risk it perceives. A large percentage of the communications with these two groups will be done through corporate advertising rather than public relations.

In addition, the annual report is becoming an ever more popular way of communicating with this public. These reports were originally designed to update current shareholders but are now felt to be the best way of speaking with the financial community. Key items that stock analysts and brokers look for in addition to standard financial information include the direction in which the firm is going, its long-run and short-run goals, and the corporate identity it is trying to achieve. Analysts make judgments on whatever information is available, so the firm should be careful that at least some of the information is provided by itself with its own views and its own accurate information.

Why use public relations?

At this point it may be useful to consider the value of public relations in the communications mix. This tool has its advantages and in some ways provides a unique method for reaching various publics. Goodrich, Gildea, and Cavanaugh[11] suggest several advantages.

▪ *Public relations is inexpensive.* While some cost is involved in putting together the relevant materials, there is no media cost, and in many cases production cost is minimal. This means that public relations can help stretch a finite advertising budget for extra impact.

▪ *Public relations can cut through the advertising noise.* As the level of advertising increases in most product classes and in general, it becomes more difficult for any single brand to stand out. Public relations can offer the opportunity for a supplementary message to be transmitted in a different format and perhaps have a greater impact. While the increase in reach or frequency that comes from using public relations is often negligible, the format change should lead to some effect.

Bacardi Rum cut through the noise of advertising by developing food and dessert recipes using its product. The recipes were then sent with camera-ready photographs and articles to newspaper and magazine food editors. In half a year, this program led to 11 national consumer magazine credits and 4,600 column inches of newspaper space for an estimated 30 million impressions; the company felt that the accompanying rise in sales was due in large part to this public relations campaign. In this well-coordinated effort, there was also a strong impact upon reach and frequency.[12]

▪ *Public relations has more credibility.* The main avenue for public relations messages is through the news media. This legitimization of the message gives it a level of credibility that advertising cannot achieve. These third-party implicit endorsements can be quite valuable. In addition, after a public relations feature has been legitimized by the press, it can then be clipped and used as part of an advertising campaign. This, in turn, lends credibility to the advertising at a low cost.

In another example, Johnson Wax launched a public relations campaign in 1981 to get people to accept the fact that cockroaches existed even in the nicest of homes and that consumers needed to do something about them. Since Raid, a Johnson product, was the product class leader, the company felt that most sales would go to its brand. Johnson developed public service announcements and brochures for distribution through the National Homeowners Association; they got additional air time and press space by disseminating information through home economists. Jane Paley, account executive for the public relations agency reported, "It creates the added allure of a third-party endorsement. When a magazine or newspaper runs an article on how to get rid of bugs and attributes it to Raid, it's almost like them saying 'go out and buy Raid.' You can't beat that kind of endorsement."[13]

- *Public relations can generate sales leads.*   The main goal of a public relations story is image- and attitude-oriented, but a good story can also generate leads. A story about a technological breakthrough that is published in a trade journal is sure to generate sales leads and may be more valuable than any advertising. Such stories also establish the firm as an authority in the field.

- *Public relations may be the only way to get to some publics.*   As seen earlier in the discussion of the various publics, it is necessary to communicate with many targets, and some cannot be efficiently reached by other means. For some groups, any media advertising would lead to too much wasted coverage, and the use of a sales force would be too expensive.

The tools of public relations

Given the tasks and publics that need to be dealt with, what specific tools are available? In a booklet printed by the 4As (American Association of Advertising Agencies), several tools are listed.[14] These can serve as a starter for a narrowly defined public relations program. When moving into publicity tools the list increases:

- *The press release*   This is a statement of facts and/or opinions that the firm would like to see published. It should contain answers to the questions that reporters are trained to ask (who, what, when, where, why, and how) and should perform a useful function for a busy editor by being an aid in the process of collecting news. The release should emphasize facts and be laid out to present the facts. The editor will then take the story and rewrite it as appropriate for the vehicle's own needs.

The release should be on the company's letterhead paper. It should include the name and telephone number of the writer so that the press can easily get more information or clarification. The date and time of release are also important. A story may be sent out for immediate release, or it may be sent in advance of a specific event and held by the press until the release date arrives. Figure 17.2 shows a press release from Foote, Cone & Belding announcing that the CBN Cable Network had awarded its advertising account to FCB.

Before sending out any press release, it is useful to know what vehicles will be most receptive to the story. These vehicles are most likely to be broadcast and print vehicles geographically close to the story and any of the main participants, as well as those vehicles that regularly report on any related trades.

To be ready for the release it is helpful to compile a press list that is up to date and reflects the editorial leanings of the list members. In putting such a list together, the manager might consult *Standard Rate and Data Service* for geographic listings of local vehicles as well as the interest tendencies for both consumer and industrial publications. Other sources include

New York Publicity Outlets
Metro California Media (Public Relations Plus Inc.)
Bacon's Publicity Checker (Bacon's Publishing Co., Inc.)
Ayer Directory of Publications (Ayer Press)

Figure 17.2 *Example of a press release*

NEWS

FOOTE, CONE & BELDING, 101 PARK AVENUE, NEW YORK, N.Y. 10178

CONTACT: Kim Cooper
          CBN Cable Network
          Virginia Beach, VA 23463
          (804) 424-7777

Joyce Harrington
FCB/New York
(212) 907-1555

FOR IMMEDIATE RELEASE

CBN CABLE NETWORK

CHOOSES FCB/NEW YORK

VIRGINIA BEACH, VIRGINIA, April 13, 1983--CBN Cable Network has awarded its advertising account to Foote, Cone & Belding/New York.

In making the announcement, Tim Robertson, group vice president, said, "CBN Cable Network has become a substantial force in the communications industry and we felt it was time to seek an outside agency to expand our marketing impact. FCB has a progressive view of the cable industry, superb creative ability, and they have expressed a strong commitment to CBN Cable by assigning top people from several of their offices to our account."

Mr. Robertson added, "The dynamics that have developed between their people and ours give us the confidence that we will enhance our position in the industry with innovative and aggressive marketing campaigns."

Headquartered in Virginia Beach, Virginia, CBN Cable Network is the third largest cable network in the United States, with over 20 million subscriber homes and an excellent line-up of family entertainment programming.

FCB is developing a national multi-media fall campaign to portray the network's true position as cable's "Family Entertainer."

Billings in the four million dollar range are expected.

Having such a list ensures that the story will at least get wide distribution among editors of relevant publications.

▪ *The exclusive story*   Although the firm generally seeks wide coverage, occasionally there is a reason for offering the story to only one publication. Usually that reason is to increase the detail and coverage given by the one key vehicle. In the advertising industry, the dominant vehicle is *Advertising Age;* by offering its editors an exclusive story, the firm would reach most key executives in this field. In addition, the firm hopes that *Advertising Age* would respond to the offer of exclusivity by giving the story more detailed coverage.

In the case of an exclusive, the firm would contact the vehicle and offer such rights. In order to be worthwhile to the vehicle, the story should be important and might also include an exclusive interview with a senior executive of the firm. Such an exclusive arrangement must not be compromised until at least after that vehicle has run the story. At that point, copyright laws will dictate further publication of the story.

- *Interviews*   There are two types of interviews. In the first case, the firm has an announcement to make or a stand to take. In this case a relevant publication is invited to interview a relevant spokesperson. At the time of the interview, it is helpful to provide the reporter with a fact sheet and/or press release as well as relevant materials such as sample product, sample film, or sample advertising.

  A second case occurs when a reporter calls the firm with questions concerning an issue. Usually this type of interview is done by phone to provide the reporter with facts, background materials, and/or some quotes to be sprinkled into the story.

- *The press conference*   This tool is rarely used in business situations, except in cases of major breakthroughs or emergencies (such as the Tylenol tampering or an airplane crash). It is used in cases when a press release cannot cover all issues or when it is necessary to counter the possibility of negative impressions being formed. It also announces that the story is felt to be important, and this may lead to broader, more thoughtful coverage.

  The timing of the press conference should be such that it coincides with vehicle deadlines. Mornings are best for evening papers and television news; mid to late week is best for the weekly trade publications; afternoons work best for morning papers.

  Press kits should be available and should contain relevant photographs, the complete text of any prepared statement that will be read, biographies of any key individuals, and background fact sheets.

- *The photo and caption*   This release is a simple process for keeping the firm's name in public and for building morale within the firm. Frequent use of this device aids awareness. Examples include

  important anniversaries
  candid photos
  honors and awards
  any special event

- *The by-lined article*   In this case an article is written by someone within the firm and offered to a relevant vehicle for publication. Pieces may originate as internal memos, speeches, training programs, research results, or whatever. The article disseminates a point of view but also shows the expertise of the firm. Both of these results are a benefit to the firm and make this avenue of public relations one that should be pursued whenever possible.

- *Speeches*   Just as with by-lined articles, speeches allow the presentation of a point of view and show the expertise of the firm. There are ample opportunities to speak before industry groups, business luncheons, conferences, colleges, and civic groups. The firm can respond to specific requests on specific topics, or it can solicit engagements. In many cases, the same presentation can be used often so that preparation time is minimized.

  Most speeches also lend themselves to a press release or photo and caption to get further public relations mileage from the event. A press release can cover the highlights of the speech; in either case, the attention will be beneficial to both the firm and the group being addressed.

  Charles Ward, president of a small advertising agency in Houston, asked himself the rhetorical question of whether public relations exposure brought results.

His answer became an article in *Advertising Age* and included the following thoughts.

> The answer is an unequivocal yes. It's fun to have a picture in the paper but the most important motivation is that potential clients see it, they remember it and they ask you to be included in the next agency review or to come by and talk about the next bit of business that becomes available.
>
> Another of our executives, who was well known to the trade media because of various public relations efforts for ourselves and our clients, was named one of the outstanding women in advertising in the Southwest—an honor that resulted in several inquiries from prospective clients.
>
> Because our name is known, introductions and new business calls are easier—and positive publicity enhances the prestige of the agency for existing clients, as well.[15]

Publicity

The previous discussion of public relations primarily concerns the narrow set of communications that are channeled through the press/editorial/news aspects of the media. In addition, the firm can create newsworthy events that are far less formal than press releases, speeches, or news conferences. These are known as *publicity.*

There are no clear sets of definitions of publicity and public relations that show a definite difference between the two. Rather, the distinctions are somewhat vague. Both are concerned with communications between the organization and its publics; neither buy nor control paid media (although publicity can incur large expenses in order to make an impact and often uses paid advertising to announce the upcoming event).

Perhaps one distinction is that public relations creates an impact by proclamation, while publicity does so by deeds. Public relations may work by telling people that the firm is virtuous, warm, and friendly through a press release discussing a corporate contribution in honor of its hundredth year of business; publicity achieves the same end by sponsoring a benefit dance and inviting the public to partake in cake and ice cream in honor of this milestone. (Of course, it will take public relations and/or advertising messages to let people know that they are invited to the celebration.) Given this distinction, the dominant publicity tool is the special event that is done well enough to generate press coverage.

A second distinction that emerges from this is that, in public relations, the firm is beholden to another party (e.g., an editor) to approve the news before it is disseminated, while publicity is controlled by the firm. If the firm wants to have an event, it may do so and can thereby control the amount of impact that it makes.

Goals of publicity

Publicity can be divided in terms of three goals:[16]

- *Merchandising orientation* Events in this class are geared toward direct sales. When a celebrity gives out autographs in the sportswear department of the store, the purpose is to bring in people and generate sportswear sales. When a demonstration of cookware is given, its purpose is to show cooks new product uses so that they will be more likely to buy the product. These events are measured in terms of sales, or at least in terms of traffic count. This class of events is most like promotions since a direct inducement (the event) is given in return for a specific behavior (going to a specific retail location).

- *Entertainment orientation*   These events are aimed at goodwill, awareness, and image. Macy's Thanksgiving parade and July 4 fireworks are entertaining; they also generate lots of media coverage that translates to goodwill and awareness. Though sales measurement is impossible, there is some residual value.

- *Educational or community involvement orientation*   Programs in this class contribute to the quality of life in the community. Sponsoring panel discussions on key social issues or holding a benefit concert for a children's theatre helps the community but also, again, generates awareness and goodwill.

The goals of generating sales, improving the corporate image, and helping the community can each be approached through publicity events. Most events will be geared toward more than one goal; it is important to select the goal carefully so that the event will aid in reaching that goal.

The first goal is similar to promotions in its behavioral orientation; the latter two goals are more similar to public relations in their short-run image-building goals, which may translate to behavior in the long run. In this way, the manager is urged back to the decision sequence framework. Publicity events can be used to generate various types of strong responses but, as with other tools, the desired response must be carefully planned out before events are set. At a more basic level, the manager must first consider publicity in the overall set of communications tools to see if it will best serve the objectives that are set.

As an example, consider how to generate awareness of, interest in, and the behavior of attending a new store opening.[17] These are goals that can be greatly aided by publicity generated through a series of events. In addition to the generic goals stated above, management should also seek press coverage and should focus on creating interest in a quality core of customers.

Having cake and ice cream available at the opening is an event (yawn), but it won't get much press coverage, and it won't discriminate in bringing in key prospects. To get press coverage the store will need something more unusual. A ribbon-cutting ceremony isn't terribly unique but may get coverage if the right person cuts it. The person might be a local dignitary, a noted expert in the relevant industry, or a celebrity.

In terms of generating key prospects, the noted expert probably will do the best job. The expert can be related to some informative theme, interesting demonstrations of new products, or even little-known features of existing products.

If the opening is tied to a theme (other than just saying, "we're open") there should be relevant press releases and press kits so that the local vehicles can do an in-depth story on behalf of the location. By relating to the industry, the firm will appear to be knowledgeable and will start off well toward developing this position.

Another useful position is one of community involvement. Having an opening or new product introduction that ties to a community issue can have a long-run impact on attitudes. For example, when Entenmann's Bakery introduced its product line in St. Louis, it wanted to create a splash. Initially, management thought of making a cake depicting the St. Louis Arch. Later they found that many St. Louis residents were concerned about losing a historic paddlewheel steamer known as the *Admiral.* As part of its introduction, Entenmann's baked a huge cake frosted with a reproduction of the ship. They then sold $1 slices of the cake to help the city raise funds to buy the *Admiral.* The event raised $4,000 and increased support for the project. In addition, Entenmann's got heavy local media attention, including a four-column color photo in a local newspaper.[18]

Publicity events can be part of a year-round program in combination with advertising and promotions. It is important to be visible to consumers; by merchandising, entertaining, and providing community service, the firm can keep its name alive between purchases. This is especially important for durable products and retailers who deal in such goods.

American of Madison is one of the largest electronics, appliance, and furniture retailers in the Midwest. It has grown to its dominant position in less than 15 years through good integration of public relations and publicity combined with heavy doses of advertising and promotions. American is the largest advertiser in its market and a heavy user of promotions (buy a stereo and get a free 10-speed bike; buy a recliner chair and get a free ticket to anywhere that Republic Airlines flies), but it also has continuous public relations and publicity programs.

Its president has a dynamic personality and is a regular speaker at civic organizations and clubs. In addition, the firm takes advantage of its growth by sending out public relations notices with every milestone. As growth continues, the firm keeps adding space onto existing buildings or moving to new larger quarters. Each change is worth public relations and includes publicity events. Other popular publicity events include microwave demonstrations at which the public eats what is cooked, stereo equipment evaluations, and the loan of state-of-the-art electronics equipment to nonprofit organizations with short-term usage needs. The list goes on and on. No opportunity is missed to keep the name before the public through the variety of available communications tools.

One final publicity example covers all three goals of merchandising, entertainment, and community involvement. In August 1983, Coors Beer held its first downtown beach party in Oklahoma City. The event drew approximately 6,000 people, mostly from the relevant 18 to 24-year-old target market, sold 96 kegs of beer in seven hours, and raised over $12,000 for the Oklahoma City Arts Council and Theater Center.

The event was highly publicized through paid media, with approximately one hundred 60-second radio spots and three large-space newspaper ads. There was also strong free public relations through the joint sponsor, KATT, the leading 18 to 24 radio station, and further communications through 1,000 posters in bars, retail establishments, and young adult living complexes. Figure 17.3 shows examples of the stories that appeared prior to the event to publicize it. Because of the large amount of promotion, it was hoped that 3,000 people would attend; in reality, 6,000, or 5 percent of the area's 18 to 24 population, attended.

The event was held on a city street that had been buried under four inches of sand and also had lifeguard towers, a bandstand, and a waterfall. There were dancing, volleyball, sand sculpture contests, tan line contests, and various other events. Coors hats and T-shirts were given away to help serve as a long-term reminder of the event and the brand.

All three network affiliate television stations and both newspapers gave the event extensive coverage and, as a result, Coor's Beer also received a large amount of publicity. Scott Cooper, account executive at The Hiebing Group, the Coors' advertising agency for this event, felt that the event was a good start toward creating a series of events that could be run throughout the summer.[19] Because summer is the heaviest beer consumption period among the 18 to 24-year-old target market, the publicity was oriented toward this heavy usage season.

Figure 17.3 *Several news stories publicizing the downtown beach party*

Downtown location to provide feeling of beach party

Beach bums, bathing beauties and dry-land surfers will converge on downtown Oklahoma City Saturday afternoon for fun in the sand — minus the surf.

The Arts Council of Oklahoma City and the Oklahoma Theater Center will receive proceeds from an unusual beach party sponsored by Coors and KATT radio Saturday from noon to 7 p.m. in the 400 block of W California between Hudson and Walker avenues.

The section will be converted to a beach with truckloads of sand and authentic lifeguard towers.

Participants are encouraged to wear appropriate beach attire and enjoy live music from an outdoor stage.

Food and beverages will be available and a variety of beach activities are planned — including volleyball and sand sculpture contests.

There will be a small admission charge and a commemorative drink cup will be provided.

More information about the party is available by calling the ArtsLine, 236-ARTS.

CALENDAR
Week's best bets

Here are Preview's choices for this week's best bets in entertainment and other cultural events.

THE OK CHORALE, 60-voice men's barbershop chorus, will perform at 6.30 tonight on the campus of Mount St. Mary's High School, 2801 S Shartel. The free, two-hour outdoor concert is part of the Arts Council of Oklahoma City's Sunday Twilight Concert series.

BALLOON RACE AND AIR SHOW will open Saturday at Norman's Westheimer Field. Fifty hot air balloons, two air shows, a fly by and display by members of the Oklahoma Wing of the Confederate Air Force highlight the two-day event. Tickets are being sold at Tinker Air Force Base, Lloyd Noble Center and all OK ticket outlets.

DOWNTOWN "BEACH PARTY" Saturday in the 400 block of W California features tons of sand, music and refreshments from noon until 7 p.m. Novel summertime event will benefit the Oklahoma Theater Center and the Arts Council of Oklahoma City

'BEACH PARTY' SET FOR CALIFORNIA AVE.

A bit of the state of California will be added to California Ave. for an unusual downtown beach party Aug. 27.

That's right. A beach party on California Ave.

Truckloads of sand will be shipped to the 400 block of California Ave., between the Oklahoma Theater Center and the headquarters of the Arts Council of Oklahoma City.

For that special added touch, authentic life guard towers will be set up. Participants will be encouraged to wear beach attire, enjoy live music from local bands, play volleyball and try sand sculpture.

All this is being sponsored by Coors Beer and KATT radio, with proceeds going to the Theater Center and the Arts Council.

Food and beverages will be available. There will be an admission charge, and a commemorative drink cup will be provided.

Oklahoma City Beach Party To Accent Fun in the Sand

Beach bums, bathing beauties and dry-land surfers will converge on downtown Oklahoma City this afternoon for fun in the sand — minus the surf.

The Arts Council of Oklahoma City and the Oklahoma Theater Center will receive proceeds from an unusual beach party sponsored by Coors and KATT radio today from noon to 7 p.m. in the 400 block of W California between Hudson and Walker avenues.

The section will be converted to a beach with truckloads of sand and authentic lifeguard towers.

Participants are encouraged to wear appropriate beach attire and enjoy live music.

Food and beverages will be available and a variety of beach activities are planned, including volleyball and sand sculpture contests.

There will be a $1 admission charge — or a bucket of sand.

More information about the party is available by calling the ArtsLine, 236-ARTS.

A beach party downtown? Yes, Downtown!

The Arts Council of Oklahoma City and the Oklahoma Theater Center will receive proceeds from a unique downtown beach party sponsored by Coors and KATT radio Saturday, August 27th from noon to 7 p.m. on the 400 block of West California Street between Hudson and Walker Avenues.

The block-long party will be converted to a beach scene with truckloads of sand and authentic life-guard towers. Participants are encouraged to wear appropriate beach attire and enjoy live music from an outdoor stage.

Food and beverages will be available and a variety of beach activities are planned including volleyball and sand sculpture contests.

"The California Street Beach Party is a localized version of the beach theme and creates for the Arts Council, the Theater Center, and the two sponsors a unique, mass participation event for the young adult," Scott Cooper, spokesman for Coors said.

There will be a small admission charge and a commemorative drink cup will be provided.

Top local bands will perform at the event.

For more information about the downtown Beach Party, call the ArtsLine, 236-ARTS.

Corporate Image Advertising

A third area of communications that fits with public relations and publicity is *corporate image advertising;* the tie here is that, again, the goal of the message is not in terms of specific product sales, but rather in terms of long-run image and attitude, or in terms of some behavior other than product purchase.

Corporate advertising has evolved rapidly since the late 1970s as an extension of public relations. This form of message distribution has the goals of public relations but uses paid advertising as the means to these ends. By paying for time and space, the firm regains control over the message and its delivery; while the pursuit of public relations attempted to follow the decision sequence framework, lack of control made it difficult to set specific objectives for a specific target market or to pursue a specific position. Corporate advertising allows the firm to regain these controls, but at the expense of a loss of credibility. A key question then, is whether it's better to have a more credible source deliver a one-time message that may not be the proper message to an audience that may not be relevant, or to have a less credible source deliver the desired message to the desired audience as often as the firm desires? The answer may be that it is best to execute both strategies simultaneously.

It is clear that the two functions are closely related. For example, in an informal survey of several Fortune 500 companies in 1984, 21 of 28 reported that the head of public relations also supervised the corporate advertising function.[20]

516

Perhaps the rise in corporate advertising is because of the limited response of the media to public relations. Since the media accept so few stories for dissemination, it becomes incumbent upon the firm to take control of the situation. If the firm has a story to tell, it cannot wait for the media to decide to accept it; corporate advertising provides the opportunity to be more aggressive.

What is corporate advertising? Walter Margulies, chairman of Lippencott & Margulies, has written that[21]

> Corporate advertising is: (a) a legitimate and potentially effective vehicle within a well conceived over-all communications strategy, (b) a costly form of ego self-indulgence by some chief execs who should know better; (c) an "emergency operation" for the company in trouble; (d) "preaching to the saved"—or the ABCs of economics that you may have missed in school; (e) "the fastest growing area of advertising"; (f) the back-burner priority at most major ad agencies; (g) the puzzler ("If it doesn't sell a product, it must be corporate"); (h) an excellent vehicle to help position the corporation for the future; (i) a last resort public relations gimmick; (j) a big waste of time.
>
> It's an indication of the confusion surrounding the nature and function of corporate advertising today that each of the above definitions (and several more) are equally on target.

More concisely, corporate advertising seems to be a catchall category of ads for the benefit of the overall company image rather than for its products. It includes image, financial, advocacy/issue, and special opportunity messages. All of these areas are important because they contribute to the overall image of the firm, and this image ultimately will influence both product purchase decisions and financial/stock decisions. There have been other mentions in this text of the notion that a product is easier to sell when it is well known; this can be extended to include awareness of the parent firm and can be used as one type of support for the use of public relations and corporate advertising.

Similarities to and differences from consumer product advertising

As has been stated, the key difference between the two forms of advertising is mainly in direction. Product advertising can easily be focused on the benefits of a specific brand and is therefore easy to make tangible in its appeal. In addition, the desired behavior is also quite specific and therefore lends itself to a focus. On the other hand, corporate advertising is done on behalf of the firm, with the goal of providing information that will influence images and attitudes. Both the object and the behavior are less tangible to the message recipient.

In addition, corporate advertising differs because the intangibility that is communicated reflects the feelings of the top officials of the firm. Though product advertising decisions are made at lower levels on the basis of the message's ability to sell, corporate advertising decisions often are made at the top. Because it is most difficult to document what should be said, the message tends to follow the instincts and egos of those at the top.

Joseph Bruillard of Bruillard Communications[22] makes this important point very clearly. He writes that both forms of advertising need to get attention, involve the audience, build credibility, and get some action. In addition, corporate advertising needs to present the message the way top management wants it said. The senior officers don't have to like product advertising in order to approve of it; they only need to believe that it will be effective. Corporate advertising must reach top executives at a personal level because this form of communication speaks for these people.

This issue raises complicating factors throughout the decision sequence. In the situation analysis, there will be an extra layer of digging. In addition to the data gathering discussed in Chapters 2, 3, and 4, it is necessary also to review corporate statements such as speeches, annual reports, and so on. Finally, there is a need for a personal touch; to capture the spirit and philosophy of top management, it will be necessary to observe these people and to talk to them. This will provide insights as to the needed aura and tone of the message. Since the message must reflect top management, it must be constructed with them in mind.

Having made this additional assessment, the process will continue through the problem definition, objectives, positioning, and media and message strategies in the same manner as with any other campaign. The strategies will, of course, differ to reflect the differences in the objectives. In reality, the major problem with corporate advertising and public relations is probably related to not using a decision sequence framework. Too often, these messages reflect some issue that is important to the firm but is of no great interest to any segment of the public. These messages often reflect a poor situation analysis, a weak objective, and a message strategy that speaks only to the management group that approved it.

For example, the Greyhound Corporation has used an ad that shows its chairman in front of the Grand Canyon telling the reader that "Some things are timeless." That is certainly true, but so what? What is the problem; what is the objective; who is the target?

Conversely, the Singer Company was much more specific in dealing with a problem of low awareness of Singer's expanded technology. While the firm had been predominantly a manufacturer of sewing machines for many years, these products were now a smaller part of their mix. Its ads tell prospective investors about the firm and the technology it is introducing. The messages are dramatic, purposeful, and are on target in terms of dealing with the problem and the objectives that faced the company.

One measure of the weakness of past corporate advertising comes from a Gallup & Robinson study that showed reader interest in corporate advertising to be 35% below the norm for all advertising.[23] Too much corporate advertising is just not interesting. If there is a difference between corporate and product advertising, it is in the *reality* of poor corporate advertising. The process to be used *should* be roughly equivalent in the two cases. In the past, too much corporate advertising was an ego trip for some senior executive. As the world continues to become more sophisticated and more competitive, this type of justification will become less tolerable. This point will arise in other examples in the chapter.

Goals of corporate advertising

Five classes of goals for corporate advertising are generally acknowledged:

1. *Financially oriented messages* Just as there is competition for product sales, so is there competition in the financial marketplace. If a firm can raise capital at lower costs, it will have an advantage over its competitors and will have more capital to devote to producing a better product.

Corporate advertising can attempt to create awareness of a more favorable image of the firm so it can obtain lower interest rates and so that it can more easily sell its stock offerings. For example, Moore-McCormick is known as a shipping company, but it is also active in the coal industry. If investors became interested in coal stocks, Moore-McCormick would like to be considered. The financial com-

Figure 17.4 Financially oriented corporate ad

munity needs to be kept abreast of the firm's activities and successes; without awareness, investors would take their capital elsewhere.

The firm can have the goal of making investors aware using informative messages, but it must be careful not to tie its message objectives too closely to stock performance. Such a tie could lead to a charge of "touting" by the Securities & Exchange Commission. What can be done, though, is to track awareness and attitudes among the target market; this, though, is an indirect measure of success.[24]

Although there are no data that show any relation between awareness or attitude and stock prices, two studies do show a relation between the amount of corporate advertising done and the price of the stock. These studies show at least a correlation between the two variables; it is not clear, though, if more advertising pushes up stock prices, or if firms that are doing well tend to spend more on corporate advertising.[25]

Advertising directed toward the financial community should provide information because its purpose is to help a decision maker with high involvement; it is therefore analogous to advertising for a consumer durable product, which also provides information. Probably the most useful information is that which is not readily available from other sources. In addition, investors would like to learn about the future plans of the firm. What opportunities and technologies will drive the firm? This is important; to discuss the challenge of tomorrow vaguely will not impress the investment community.[26] Figure 17.4 is one of a series of ads run by ITT that discusses its present and future for the financial community.

2. *Advocacy or issue-oriented messages*   Once again the firm finds itself in a competitive position. Here it needs to compete for attitudes and/or behavior among the general public, or some target such as legislators. The issue may affect the way the firm operates or may concern an issue that reflects how top management feels about some aspect of society.

Sometimes these messages are sponsored by an individual firm, such as when Bethlehem Steel made its views known (see Figure 17.5). Sometimes issue advertising is sponsored by an industry association to speak for all its members; an example of this would be the word to smokers and nonsmokers sponsored by The Tobacco Institute as shown in Figure 17.6. Both of these examples would seem to be cases where the concerned firms wanted to make a public relations statement, but the media would not take the story. As a result, it was necessary to purchase the space to present the point of view.

Figure 17.5   Advocacy ad

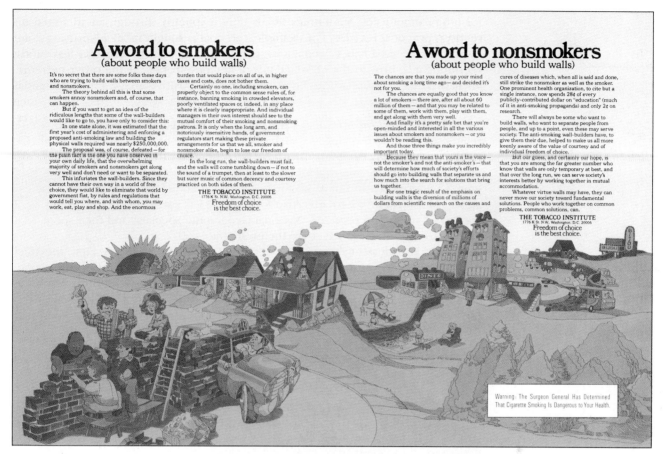

Figure 17.6   Industry association advocacy ad

At this time *advocacy advertising* is practiced by a small minority of firms and seems to be opposed by the large majority. Criticism from executives ranges from the feeling that such advertising is dangerous, to inflammatory, to not disciplined, to not representing the shareholders.[27] Ralph Nader has also written in opposition to "advertorials." He cites misleading and erroneous messages such as the message from one firm which discussed the effects of its alleged pollution control sensitivity. When it showed a picture of the river running by its plant, it used a scene that was upstream from the plant.[28]

Others feel that firms with enough money can buy enough advertising time and space to influence thinking about the priority of public issues. This is probably an overstatement, given the low credibility of advertising, but sometimes the advertising is disguised to appear as news.

There are, though, checks and balances. The *Washington Post,* which carries a large amount of issue advertising because it reaches so many influential leaders, carefully screens each ad for potential libel, truth, and good taste. Such screening is partially done out of self-interest, because the publisher is also liable if the ad is libelous. The press can also reject ads if it desires without violating the First Amendment. The Constitution prevents the government from curtailing free speech but does not control the decisions made by the press.

3. *Recruiting messages*   Again, the firm is in a competitive environment. One goal of corporate image advertising is to present the firm as favorably as possible

for future employees. Sometimes this is done explicitly through an ad aimed directly at potential recruits. For example, this goal is sought in all advertising done by the military and is occasionally sought in specific industry ads. For less subtle recruiting ads, turn to the classified ads of any newspaper. At the other extreme, virtually any corporate ad can be used to create a positive image among potential recruits.

4. *Special situation messages* This class of ads is generally reserved for those related to corporate giving. As such, the most common ones seem to publicize public broadcasting programs that have been underwritten by the firm. These are very indirect image messages because they only mention the firm as the program's underwriter and have no further message about the firm. In 1982, for example, Mobil spent $2 to advertise for every $3 it spent on programming. Gulf spent $4.1 million to produce "National Geographic Specials" and then spent $2.4 million to promote and advertise the programs.

Public broadcasting sponsors generally do so for two reasons. First, they feel that this alternative programming is necessary and good for society, and second, they feel that it helps their image. At the same time, these expenditures reach the appropriate target, because the PBS audience is more likely to be upscale, with higher education and income.[29] Figure 17.7 is a corporate ad for a public broadcasting program.

Figure 17.7 *Corporate ad for public broadcasting*

Figure 17.8   Corporate giving and image ad

While it is not always easy to see a direct tie between corporate giving and corporate image, in some cases, the giving is a direct marketing strategy aimed at building business. In 1983 American Express offered to give one penny for each of its cardholders' transactions and one dollar for each new card to the Statue of Liberty Restoration Project. In three months, American Express had a sharp rise in sales and card applications and donated $1.7 million. Both business and charity benefited. Over several years, American Express has done this in over 30 markets and given to several symphonies, operas, ballets, and track clubs. Figure 17.8 shows an American Express/Statue of Liberty ad.

There are, of course, many other special situations that can be aided with a corporate ad. When the space shuttle was first launched by NASA, many firms involved in the project let the public know this fact. Rockwell, by congratulating America, was also congratulating itself, as shown in Figure 17.9.

5. *General image messages*   In addition to the specific targets and goals mentioned in the above categories, there is also the goal of enhancing the basic image of the corporation. This can be done to establish an identity or position in the public's mind or in those opinion leaders who are in the press and control the dissemination of other news stories. This class of general image messages is by far the largest category of corporate advertising.

The goal of image creation is less defined than any of the prior goals, and it is thus not a coincidence that too many ads in this category turn out to be foggy

Figure 17.9   Rockwell congratulates America and itself after the launching of the first space shuttle

cases of self-puffery. This point was made earlier; it bears repeating because it has been ignored in so many cases. In order for corporate messages to be effective, they must have a specific goal and a specific message. The corporate messages that do poorly are those that have not been based on situation analysis and objectives.

An example of useful corporate advertising comes from Boise Cascade. In 1976 it measured awareness of and attitudes toward itself and began an advertising campaign using ads such as the one shown in Figure 17.10. In 1978 and 1981 it did posttests among opinion leaders and the general public that showed a substantial improvement in awareness and attitudinal perceptions of the company on dimensions such as integrity, credibility, and environmental concern. In 1981 Boise Cascade stopped the campaign; another test in 1983 showed that while awareness had not changed, attitudes toward the company had slipped once again. By mid–1984, a campaign was put back into place. The company felt there was a clear relationship between its corporate advertising and attitudes toward it.

This particular ad also is worth noting because it reflects a trend in corporate advertising to be more visually appealing and to grab the reader's attention. Early corporate messages did not do this and, as a result, were often not read because they did not look interesting. Readers learn about the company; nonreaders don't. As was discussed in the message section, every ad must have a hook in the headline or visual that will grab the reader and bring him into the text. This point is valid for all types of advertising, not just that used for consumer products.

Why does much of corporate advertising do such a poor job?

Answering this question can serve as a summary for much of this chapter. David Ogilvy has written very strong prose damning the poor quality of most corporate advertising.[30] He has written about "the *humbug* in corporate advertising. The

Figure 17.10 Boise Cascade corporate ad

pomposity. The *vague generalities* and the *fatuous platitudes.*" (Italics are his.) He isn't any more charitable about the slogans of these ads either. "Gaseous purple nothings and all interchangeable. The only blessing is that they generally appear at the very *bottom* of the advertisements, under the logotype. Research shows that nobody *reads* bottom lines in advertisements." Ogilvy presents four reasons he believes most corporate advertising is a "flop" (his word).

1. *Corporations fail to define the purpose of their corporate campaigns.*   This point has been made many times throughout this text and holds for any type of advertising. Any message must have a purpose; for corporate advertising, it might be to influence investors, to influence recruits, to take a stand on an issue, or to present an image to some target market. Because the last goal is vague, the firm must define the image that they desire before creating the messages that establish it.

The goal must be defined by the head of the corporation. Without this support, Ogilvy feels that the campaign won't get sufficient financial backing to have an impact. As discussed in the media section, a campaign without sufficient repetition for learning to occur is a waste.

2. *Corporations fail to measure their results.*   Ogilvy reports that a survey of corporate advertisers showed that only one in four measured changes in attitude resulting from these campaigns.

If they had, they might have learned what Yankelovich, Skelly & White found in two studies for *Time* magazine done in 1977 and 1979.[31] The first Yankelovich study showed that firms using corporate advertising had better awareness, more familiarity, and better overall impressions than firms not using corporate advertising. Their second study showed more detail in these attitudes. As shown in Table 17.1, firms with high corporate ad expenditures were perceived more favorably than firms with low expenditures on all ten reported traits. The bottom traits were more current topics; all firms did more poorly on these than on the more traditional topics. This would indicate an opportunity for firms to be more responsive to current events, or it could also indicate that it takes a long time to develop an image on any issue.

3. *Corporations know very little about what works and what doesn't in corporate advertising.*   Firms are beginning to learn what works in brand advertising, but there is much less research done on corporate advertising. Therefore, in addition to not knowing *if* it works, firms know even less about *why* or *how* corporate advertising works.

4. *Very few advertising agencies know much about corporate advertising.*   This fourth point of Ogilvy's article brings the reader full circle. Because corporate advertising is such a small part of most budgets, agencies don't give it enough attention. Neither the firm nor the agency seem to be well versed in how to handle corporate advertising. As an example of spending levels, Table 17.2 shows the corporate and overall advertising budgets of the ten largest corporate spenders. Even these heavy corporate spenders only put a small percentage of their budgets here. To create a better perspective, consider where these ten firms are in the top 100 advertisers shown in Chapter 1.

Table 17.1 Corporate advertisers do better on specific traits used to evaluate a corporation

	Corporate advertising expenditures		Net difference	Benefit of corporate advertising
	High (33) $500,000+	*Low (31)* under $500,000		
Association with specific traits:				
Quality products	39%	32%	+ 7	+22%
Innovative/R&D	34	26	+ 8	+31%
Good financial record	28	21	+ 7	+33%
Competent management	24	18	+ 6	+33%
Responsive to consumers	23	18	+ 5	+28%
Concerned resources	20	14	+ 6	+43%
Honest company	19	16	+ 3	+19%
Responsive to employees	15	10	+ 5	+50%
Truth in advertising	13	12	+ 1	+ 8%
Helps control inflation	6	4	+ 2	+50%
Average (all traits)	22	17	+ 5	+29%

Source: *Corporate Advertising, Phase II.* Yankelovich, Skelly & White, Inc., 1979, p. 9.
Note: Average company scores

Table 17.2 Top 10 leading corporate advertisers

Corporation	1983 Corporate Advertising (000)	1983 All Major Media Advertising (000)
Ford	$44,751	$479,060.0
AT&T	40,770	463,095.5
G.M.	27,857	595,129.5
IBM	20,552	119,222.5
DuPont	9,474	102,637.0
Pfizer	8,400	72,084.3
Chrysler	7,960	230,020.1
GTE	7,954	70,179.9
Amerco	7,942	Not in top 100 advertisers; less than $49,167,000
ITT	6,720	134,229.0

Source: R. Craig Endicott, "Leaders Rebuild Sales, Hike Advertising 10.5%," *Advertising Age,* 14 September 1984, p 1. Reprinted with permission. Copyright 1984 by Crain Communications, Inc.

The poem in Figure 17.11, written by the immortal Anonymous, can serve as a summary of the common pitfalls of public relations and corporate advertising. It captures the essence of what is wrong with these strategic tools when they are misapplied and also ties these tools back to the basics of the marketing concept. If a message is to be read and acted upon, it must show some benefit to the reader.

Figure 17.11 Tell me quick and tell me true

I see that you've spent quite a big wad of dough
To tell me the things you think I should know.
How your plant is so big, so fine, and so strong;
And your founder had whiskers so handsomely long.
So he started the business in old '92!
How tremendously interesting that is—to you.
He built up the thing with the blood of his life?
(I'll run home like mad, tell that to my wife!)
Your machinery's modern and oh so complete;
Your "rep" is so flawless; your workers so neat.
Your motto is "Quality"—capital "Q"—
No wonder I'm tired of "Your" and of "You"!

So tell me quick and tell me true
Less—"how this company came to be"
More—"what it can do for me!"

Source: John Hoefer, "Corporate Institutional Advertising: What's Wrong With It?," Stanford Business School Bulletin, Vol. 42., No. 2, 1974.

T·H·E I·N·S·I·D·E O·U·T·L·O·O·K

Norman Weissman

President and Vice-Chairman, Ruder Finn & Rotman

Norman Weissman, President of Ruder Finn & Rotman—New York, is responsible for guiding the agency's 400-person operating staff based in New York, as well as developing new services for clients.

Mr. Weissman has been with Ruder & Finn since 1956. He was appointed a vice-president of the firm in 1959, and became a senior vice-president in 1962, responsible for the supervision of a group of corporate and industrial accounts. He is also vice-chairman of the agency and a member of the executive committee.

He began his career in 1951 as an editor of Factory *magazine, a McGraw-Hill publication, where he served for four years. In 1955, he was appointed secretary of the Department of Air Pollution Control for the city of New York, where he was in charge of all public relations for this city agency.*

Mr. Weissman received his B.S. degree in English from Rutgers University in 1949, where he was graduated with highest honors. In 1951, he received his masters degree in journalism from the University of Wisconsin.

Rebuilding Tourism in Jamaica

Jamaica is a poor country of the Third World. It is a small nation of a little more than 2 million people. Its major natural resources are bauxite and good land on which everything will grow.

In 1980, Edward Seaga was elected Prime Minister after eight years of the socialist administration of Michael Manley. The country had so suffered during the Manley years that Jamaica's economy was in a shambles at the time Mr. Seaga took over in early 1981. We were retained to help the tourism industry turn around once again. It had fallen on dark days. Visitors to Jamaica had reached pitifully low numbers. Hotels and restaurants were badly in need of repair and refurbishing. There was no food on the shelves of the markets. There was garbage in the streets and a sad, sorry look to everything.

From that point on, an incredibly energetic campaign began. The Jamaica Ministry of Tourism and Tourist Board began having meetings with travel agents in every city of any importance in the United States, and the tourism promotion team made frank statements about the disrepair of the tourist plant and the huge effort that was under way to improve it in time for the next winter season.

Because crime in the streets had been a major reason that Americans stopped going to Jamaica during the country's bad times, we began talking about a new atmosphere in Jamaica where the people were smiling once again. (This was true.) We went to the travel writers of the United States, and we sought to convince them that the country was sincerely interested in U.S. tourists once again and that perhaps people should come back to Jamaica to see for themselves how things had improved since the new government had taken over. We went to the hotel owners, the restaurant owners, the tour operators, and the transportation people on the island, and we pointed out how important it was that they should receive U.S. visitors with enthusiasm and open arms. An entire division of the Jamaica Tourist Board sought in every possible way to encourage the hotels and other facilities to paint and fix up their facilities for U.S. visitors. We began telling positive, nontravel stories in the U.S. newspapers, magazines, and on television—first of all, about how important tourism was for Jamaica since the country could earn from it the foreign exchange it needed so desperately, and, second, what a great advance it was for the free world that a leftist government in the Caribbean had been replaced by a business-oriented prime minister who wanted to build closer ties with the free world. There was an emotional attraction for Americans in this.

An exciting and very different advertising program was launched by Young & Rubicam to encourage Americans to "Come Back to Jamaica," stressing the beauty, friendliness of the people, and variety of tourist attractions. It was an award-winning campaign, and it worked beautifully with the public relations effort.

We concentrated in five cities—New York, Miami, Dallas, Chicago, and Los Angeles—on building regional interest and working with area tour groups and press. We kept the travel trade informed on a moment-to-moment basis on how Jamaica was reenergizing its tourism industry for the various audiences. We even developed a major overseas program designed to attract tourists from England, France, Germany, Spain, Holland, and, finally, South America.

There was enormous cooperation in this effort between the public relations people, the Tourism Ministry of Jamaica, and the hotel,

restaurant, and airline industry of that country. But perhaps the most important factor was the people of Jamaica themselves, who truly did begin welcoming visitors as they had done before.

Today, four years later, Jamaica is considered to be the most successful tourism destination in the Caribbean in terms of growth in this market. The number of visitors has more than doubled since the year we began representing that country. The hotel industry is thriving. More hotels and facilities are being built each year. More airlines and charter groups are including Jamaica in their programs each year, and there are too few airline seats to meet the demand.

To be sure, there have been demonstrations in Jamaica, and short-lived outbreaks of unrest in the heavily populated urban areas. At the same time, public relations has dealt effectively with these, keeping tourism largely unaffected.

It was a lucky thing for Jamaica that such an intensive effort was instituted when it was. Two and a half years ago, the bottom fell out of the bauxite market. Whereas bauxite had been the number one foreign exchange earner for Jamaica for decades, it began to look as if the world no longer was interested in aluminum. Tourism took up much of the slack.

Summary

This chapter presents three areas of marketing communications—public relations, publicity, and corporate advertising. The threads that tie these tools together include a goal of attitude and image development and a nonproduct focal point. The tasks that the tools are asked to accomplish differ from those of product advertising and promotions and, as a result, the tools should be seen as complements rather than substitutes for the major tools discussed earlier in the text.

Even though public relations, publicity, and corporate advertising differ from advertising and promotions, the decision sequence is still relevant.

In order to succeed, the manager must consider the objectives, position, and target market for any problem. After going through this initial analysis, the appropriate strategy can be selected from the entire set of possibilities.

Discussion Questions

1. Compare the goals of product advertising, public relations, publicity, and corporate advertising.

2. How do each of these communications tools differ from product advertising?

3. When would it be more appropriate to use a press release rather than an exclusive story? Why? What about the reverse? Why?

4. Why was the Coors Downtown Beach Party a useful publicity event? What goals did it meet? What other publicity events can you recall? What goals did they meet?

5. Why has the amount of corporate advertising increased so much in the past ten years?

6. What are the traits of poor corporate advertising?

7. Find an example of each of the five classes of corporate advertising.

8. What is an advertorial? Do you feel that firms should be allowed to use their money in this way? Why?

9. Design a public relations release, a publicity event, and a recruiting ad for your career development communications plan.

Notes

1. Richard E. Stanley, *Promotion Advertising, Publicity, Personal Selling, Sales Promotion* (Englewood Cliffs, N.J.: Prentice-Hall, 1982), p. 240.

2. Stanley, *Promotion Advertising.*

3. James G. Engel, Martin R. Warshaw, and Thomas C. Kinnear, *Promotional Strategy* (Homewood, Ill.: Richard D. Irwin, 1983), p. 518; William M. Kincaid, Jr., *Promotion: Products, Services and Ideas* (Columbus, Oh.: Charles E. Merrill Publishing, 1981), p. 324; and J. E. Marston, *Modern Public Relations* (New York: McGraw-Hill Book Company, 1979).

4. Jonathon N. Goodrich, Robert L. Gildea, and Kevin Cavanaugh, "A Place for Public Relations in the Marketing Mix," *MSU Business Topics* 27 (Autumn 1979), pp. 53–57.

5. Goodrich, Gildea, and Cavanaugh, "A Place for Public Relations."

6. Theodore J. Gage, "PR Ripens Role in Marketing," *Advertising Age,* 5 January 1981, p. S-10.

7. "Behind Scenes Look at Cabbage Patch PR," *Advertising Age,* 26 December 1983, p. 2.

8. Philip Kotler and William Mindak, "Marketing and Public Relations," *Journal of Marketing* 42 (October 1978), pp. 13–20.

9. Marston, *Modern Public Relations,* p. 45.

10. Marston, *Modern Public Relations,* pp. 62–76.

11. Goodrich, Gildea, and Cavanaugh, "A Place for Public Relations," pp. 56–57.

12. Gage, "PR Ripens Role," p. S-10.

13. Gage, "PR Ripens Role," p. S-11.

14. Joyce Harrington, *How to Handle Public Relations for Your Advertising Agency* (New York: American Association of Advertising Agencies, 1983).

15. Charles Ward, "Putting PR in the Spotlight," *Advertising Age,* 29 October 1983, p. M-30.

16. William A. Robinson, "Show-Stoppers at Macy's," *Advertising Age,* 26 July 1982, p. M-42.

17. Robert R. Robichaud, "How to Milk Store Opening for All It's Worth," *Marketing News,* 16 March 1984, p. 8.

18. Gage, "PR Ripens Role," p. S-11.

19. Scott Cooper, personal communications, 1984.

20. Norman Weissman, "Capturing Corporate Essence," *Advertising Age,* 23 January 1984, p. M-12.

21. Walter P. Margulies, "A Stepsister to Consumer," *Advertising Age,* 6 July 1981, p. S-2.

22. Joseph Bruillard, "Timely Messages," *Advertising Age,* 29 August 1983, p. M-30.

23. Ed Zotti, "An Expert Weighs the Prose and Yawns," *Advertising Age,* 24 January 1983, p. M-11.

24. B. G. Yovovich, "How to Woo Wall Street," *Advertising Age,* 6 July 1981, pp. S-2–S-6.

25. Zotti, "Prose and Yawns."

26. Zotti, "Prose and Yawns," p. M-11.

27. Cecelia Reed, "Reading the Board Room Message Right," *Advertising Age,* 23 January 1984, p. M-28.

28. Ralph Nader, "Challenging the Corporate Ad," *Advertising Age,* 24 January 1983, p. M-12.

29. Udayan Gupta, "Sponsoring PBS: Selling an Image Tastefully," *Advertising Age,* 24 January 1983, p. M-29.

30. Ogilvy, "Corporate Advertising."

31. Yankelovich, Skelly and White, Inc., *A Study of Corporate Advertising Effectiveness,* 1977; *Corporate Advertising/Phase III,* 1979.

Chapter 18
The Sales Force as a
Communications Tool

Many textbooks deal with the management of the sales force. These books cover a range of topics such as motivating, rewarding, selecting, evaluating, and assigning territories to salespersons. This text will not concentrate on any of these topics; the interested reader is referred to Churchill, Ford, and Walker[1] or Pederson, Wright, and Weitz[2] for these topics. Personal selling has a relatively minor role in this text because the major thrust is in the examination of mass, controlled, one-way communications. This is not meant to lessen the importance or amount of usage of personal selling; quite the opposite is true. Sales management is so important and complex that it has its own texts and courses. Because this text covers the topic of marketing communications, the sales force is examined purely from this perspective. How can the sales force be used as a communications tool? In what situations is the sales force the most appropriate communications tool? How do sales force communications and advertising communications interact?

Some Data on Personal Selling

Personal selling is a vital part of the communications mix. Different estimates show that one and a half to twice as many dollars per year are spent here as are spent on advertising. One estimate, for example, showed that $65 billion per year is spent on personal selling and that about 10% of the U.S. labor force, or over 8 million people, are engaged in sales activities.[3] While these figures are from approximately 1975, they still suggest the enormity of this area.

Another perspective of dollar amounts spent can be seen in Table 18.1, which compares the percent of expenditures for sales force, advertising, and promotions for industrial, durable, and nondurable goods manufacturers. Note that these data are inconsistent with 1982 data presented in Part 6 which show greater expenditures on promotions than on advertising. When the data for Table 18.1 were collected in 1972, the relation was, indeed, as shown. The purpose of

Table 18.1 Expenditures on sales force, advertising and promotions

Sales effort activity	Producers of		
	Industrial goods (%)	Consumer durables (%)	Consumer nondurables (%)
Sales management and personal selling	69.2	47.6	38.1
Broadcast media advertising	0.9	10.7	20.9
Printed media advertising	12.5	16.1	14.8
Special promotional activities	9.6	15.5	15.5
Branding and promotional packaging	4.5	9.5	9.8
Other	3.3	0.6	0.9
Total	100.0	100.0	100.0

Source: Jon G. Udell, *Successful Marketing Strategies* (Madison: Mimir Publishers, 1972), p. 47.
Note: Data are based on the average point allocations of 336 industrial goods producers, 52 consumer durable goods manufacturers, and 88 consumer nondurable goods manufacturers.

Table 18.1 is to show the size of expenditures on the sales force. Since 1972 these expenditures have been increasing more rapidly for the sales force than for advertising in the industrial goods area, according to McGraw-Hill.[4]

Personal Selling versus Advertising

Personal selling activities include industrial selling (one firm selling to another), selling to wholesalers and retailers (one firm selling to middlepersons), and selling to consumers (the agent of the firm selling to the consumer, or a middleperson such as a retailer selling to the consumer). These selling interactions may occur in the office of the buyer or seller, at a retail location, or in the home (or at the front door); they generally occur face to face but may take place over the telephone.

What sets personal selling apart from advertising is that the former usually

1. *Takes place in a one-on-one situation.* This is known as *dyadic* (paired) *communications.* While most personal selling takes place in a one-on-one situation, there are some notable exceptions.

▪ The entire group of people in a large factory that will ultimately be involved in the buying decision process may be invited to an initial presentation of a new piece of machinery so that all the different areas of expertise will be able to provide knowledgeable input into the ultimate buying decision.

▪ A group of potential investors may be invited to a downtown meeting room by Merrill Lynch to learn about its Cash Management Program.

▪ A group of people spontaneously gather around a carnival pitchman who has a never-ending spiel for his veg-e-matic slicer-dicer-chopper.

2. *Allows two-way interaction.* Because buyer and seller are generally facing one another, the salesperson can respond to questions, can clarify difficult concepts, and can overcome objections. In mass communications, the sender does not see or hear the receiver and has no idea how well the message is being received (although the manager has an estimate of goodness from copy testing research). The concept of two-way communications has a key advantage of allowing the sender/seller to assess the message impact and then adjust the message.

This system of feedback can be seen in the diagram of Figure 18.1; the feedback may be verbal in the form of questions and comments but is often nonverbal. Zimbardo and Ebbesen,[5] for example, tell a (perhaps mythical) story of jewelry salespersons who can assess the interest of a customer by watching the dilation of the customer's pupils; greater dilation indicates greater liking. While this may be a little extreme, liking, resistance, and other attitudinal values are transmitted through physical postures and can provide valuable feedback for the salesperson.

In industrial cases where the product is complex and custom designed, the two-way interaction may be a requirement for a sale. Without such an interaction, it would be difficult for buyer and seller to reach an agreement.

3. *Allows an adaptive message strategy*   One of the key benefits of a two-way interaction is the ability of the salesperson to adopt the message to the developing sales situation. This is a unique characteristic of personal selling as a communications tool. An adaptive strategy is also possible because the salesperson can treat each prospect as a unique entity; in advertising, entire target markets receive the same message. The next issue looks at the negative aspects of adaptiveness.

4. *Allows less control over the message content and delivery*   Once an advertising or promotions message is committed to paper, film, or tape, its content is fixed, for better or worse. The manager has no such control over salespeople when they are out on their own. This situation has advantages and disadvantages.

On the positive side, as noted above, flexibility allows the salesperson to answer questions and overcome resistance. On the negative side, the salesperson may make errors, insult customers, make libelous statements about competitors, make unauthorized deals, or err in hundreds of other unique and creative ways. As will be discussed below, a firm can supply audio and visual aids that do have controlled messages and that, as a result, take away some of the opportunity for the salesperson to misstate the pitch; after the canned presentation is made, the salesman is present to answer questions and overcome resistance. In a study by McGraw-Hill, 24% of sales managers felt that their industrial sales force was either "somewhat" or "not at all effective" in conveying exact product and benefit information. This figure was smaller for small firms and larger for large firms.[6]

5. *Has poor reach*   In most cases, mass media advertising is able to reach more people more quickly and at less cost. At times this is not important. If the target market for the product is small, then there won't be any appropriate vehicle other than direct mail that will yield the desired reach without wasted coverage.

At other times the poor reach of the sales force can be a virtue. If a firm needs to recall a defective product, the sales force may be able to disseminate this message to the relevant customers without disturbing others. If the messages

Figure 18.1 *Schematic diagram of two-way communications*

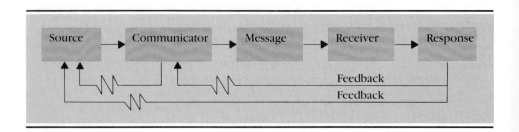

Table 18.2 Strengths and weaknesses of personal selling when compared to advertising

Strengths	Weaknesses
Personal interaction (one-to-one)	Poor reach
▪ Ability to assess others	Poor frequency
▪ Ability to respond	Poor control of message
▪ Ability to adjust message	High cost per impression
Can close the sale	Poor awareness building medium
Good attitude building	because of high cost
Good behavior building	

were in a mass vehicle, it would reach customers that do not need to know about the defect. In the latter case, poor perceptions might result unnecessarily. In this case the sales force can achieve perfect reach.

These uniquenesses of personal selling have both strengths and weaknesses relative to advertising, as can be seen in Table 18.2. One other item that needs to be discussed is cost.

The cost of selling

Cost can be considered from several points of view. First, one can consider the cost per message delivery or call. Advertising delivers messages to large audiences with a CPM as low as approximately $3. This is 0.3¢ per delivery. At the other extreme of mass deliveries, direct mail may cost $1 or more per person; while there are more expensive pieces, these are unusual. Within this range, McGraw-Hill estimates the cost of a "seen" ad in a business publication at 16¢ per person (CPM = $160). This figure takes into account average readership of business magazines and an average "seen" score for ads in these magazines.[7]

Given these benchmarks, what is the cost of a sales call? In 1983 the average cost of a single industrial sales call was $205.40. Figure 18.2 shows the rapid rise in cost over the ten-year period from 1973 to 1983. These figures are only for industrial sales (where the buyer was a firm) and do not include sales to consumers. Figure 18.3 shows 1983 data of average industrial sales call costs for 21 industries. Table 18.3 shows that the cost per call varies depending on the size of the sales force; larger firms have lower costs per call than do smaller firms.

Figure 18.2 *Cost of industrial sales call reaches $205.40*

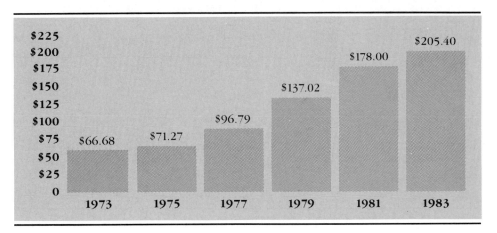

Figure 18.3 *Variations in cost of a sales call found from industry to industry*

SIC*	Industry	Average cost of a sales call	
13	Oil & gas extraction	$165.00	
20	Food & kindred products	$119.20	
25	Furniture & fixtures	$107.30	
26	Paper & allied products	$143.90	
28	Chemicals & allied products	$174.00	
29	Petroleum & coal products	$91.70	
30	Rubber & misc. plastics products	$123.60	
32	Stone, clay & glass products	$175.00	
33	Primary metal industries	$188.80	
34	Fabricated metal products	$225.90	
35	Machinery, except electrical	$221.00	
36	Electrical & electronic equipment	$167.60	
37	Transportation equipment	$227.40	
38	Instruments & related products	$274.90	
39	Misc. manufacturing industries	$229.70	
45	Transportation by air	$194.90	
50	Wholesale trade—durable goods	$71.10	
60	Banking	$202.90	
63	Insurance carriers	$199.60	
73	Business services	$122.80	
89	Miscellaneous services	$328.10	

* Only those SIC groups with five or more responses are included.

Table 18.3 Cost per sales call

Size of sales force	1979		1981	
	No. of companies	Cost of industrial sales Call	No. of companies	Cost of industrial sales Call
Under 10	133	$195.80	100	$285.70
10–25	176	172.81	132	202.70
26–50	137	120.86	113	146.70
51–100	105	122.36	92	144.30
Over 100	210	92.13	145	133.60
Not reported	26	100.88	23	136.70
Average	787	137.02	605	178.00

Source: McGraw-Hill Research Laboratory of Advertising Research.

A second perspective comes from the cost to close an industrial sale. In addition to an increase in the cost per call, there has also been an increase in the number of calls required to close a sale. As can be seen in Figure 18.4, the average number of calls is now 5.5, and as a result the cost to close the average industrial sale is $1,130. Table 18.4 shows the average cost to close a sale in 18 different industries.

Figure 18.4 *Average cost to close an industrial sale increases to $1,129.70*

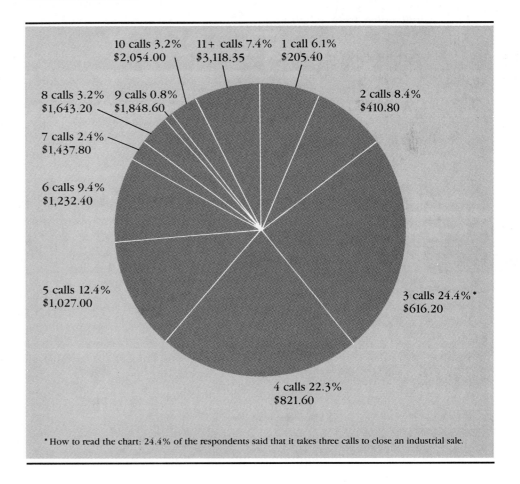

10 calls 3.2%
$2,054.00

11+ calls 7.4%
$3,118.35

1 call 6.1%
$205.40

8 calls 3.2%
$1,643.20

9 calls 0.8%
$1,848.60

2 calls 8.4%
$410.80

7 calls 2.4%
$1,437.80

6 calls 9.4%
$1,232.40

5 calls 12.4%
$1,027.00

3 calls 24.4%*
$616.20

4 calls 22.3%
$821.60

* How to read the chart: 24.4% of the respondents said that it takes three calls to close an industrial sale.

Table 18.4 Average cost to close a sale

SIC	Industry	No. of cases	Average number of calls to close a sale	Average cost per sales call	Average cost to close a sale[a]
25	Furniture & fixtures	9	3.3	$239.90	$ 791.67
26	Paper & allied products	13	4.8	106.20	509.76
27	Printing, publishing & allied industries	7	5.1	66.10	337.11
28	Chemicals & allied products	15	4.9	133.00	651.70
29	Petroleum/refining & related industries	7	5.0	142.00	710.00
30	Rubber & misc. plastic products	12	5.6	98.80	553.28
32	Stone, clay, glass & concrete products	16	4.5	95.30	428.85
33	Primary metal industries	19	3.7	117.90	436.23
34	Fabricated metal products	58	5.0	126.10	630.50
35	Machinery (except electrical)	155	5.9	182.10	1,074.39
36	Electrical & electronic machinery equipment	83	4.9	210.90	1,033.41
37	Transportation equipment	30	6.7	367.20	2,460.24
38	Instruments; photographic & optical goods	31	4.5	150.60	677.70
45	Transportation by air	6	3.0	83.80	251.40
49	Utilities & sanitary services	6	3.5	170.20	595.70
63	Insurance	5	3.6	64.40	231.84
73	Business services	8	4.6	195.00	897.00
75	Automotive repair services	5	4.8	93.80	450.24

Source: McGraw-Hill, LAP Report no. 8052.1. McGraw-Hill Laboratory of Advertising Research.
[a]This is determined by multiplying the average number of calls to close a sale by the average cost per sales call for each SIC.

A third perspective comes from a consideration of the cost of recruiting and training an industrial salesperson. In 1978, *Sales and Marketing Management* magazine found that these costs averaged about $15,500[8], and it was later estimated that this cost would be almost $28,000 by 1998.[9]

Combining Advertising and Personal Selling

To put these costs into the proper perspective, return to Table 18.2 and consider the goals of advertising versus personal selling. While advertising is clearly a cheaper form of message transmission, its main task is to create awareness and knowledge, and it does this work best for frequently purchased, fairly simple products. The sales force is a poor medium for creating awareness because of its high cost. Rather, salespersons should be used to affect attitudes and behavior. Because of these specializations, the two forms work best when advertising creates awareness and then the salesperson follows up with detailed explanations and persuasive arguments. While advertising seems much cheaper, using it exclusively may be a false economy if it cannot do the job assigned to it.

Figure 18.5 shows very nicely the combination of advertising followed by salesperson. If the advertising precedes the salesperson, the selling job is much easier. This point is made in a more objective way in studies by Levitt, Morrill, and Swinyard and Ray. Levitt[10] found that salespersons from well-known companies were more favorably received by potential customers, but customers had higher expectations for the quality of presentation of these salespersons. If the selling firm spent money to create awareness through advertising, it then also needed to spend to get a better trained sales force with better presentation skills and visual aids. The advertising may open the door initially for the salesperson, but the initial advantage disappears without a good presentation. Ultimately, the salesperson must still make the sale. If a salesperson from an unknown firm can get in to see a buyer, that salesperson then has an almost equal opportunity to make the sale. Other things being equal, though, a risky decision is more likely to be made in favor of a well-known company. This is a more residual type of support that advertising can provide for the sales force.

Levitt also found a deterioration of the favorable source effect over time such that if advertising and/or sales calls were not continued, the early favorable position created by advertising would erode to the point where the salesperson from the well-known company no longer held an advantage over the salesperson from the unknown company. This effect is similar to that of the forgetting curves discussed in the media part.

Figure 18.5 Industrial advertising supports the sales force

"I don't know who you are.
I don't know your company.
I don't know your company's product.
I don't know what your company stands for.
I don't know your company's customers.
I don't know your company's record.
I don't know your company's reputation.
Now—what was it you wanted to sell me?"

MORAL: Sales start **before** your salesman calls—with business publication advertising.

McGRAW-HILL MAGAZINES
BUSINESS • PROFESSIONAL • TECHNICAL

Morrill[11] found a similar interaction between advertising and personal selling. He reported that selling costs were from 2 to 28% less when prospects had received advertising messages before the sales force arrived.

In a third study, Swinyard and Ray[12] found value in advertising after the sales call in those cases where a sale was not made. Often the sale is not made because of poor timing, lack of funds, or inaccessibility of decision makers rather than because of a poor or inappropriate product. In such cases Swinyard and Ray feel that further advertising can be useful in leading to future sales.

On another issue, Swinyard and Ray conclude that one personal call is worth four direct mail messages in terms of the impact on behavioral intent. This makes the sales call more effective but, given the relative costs, advertising still may be more efficient. The researchers note, though, that this efficiency may not be realized if the advertising does not provide a mechanism for the sale to be concluded. A big advantage of personal selling is that the one-to-one meeting allows the salesperson to push actively for a conclusion to the interaction, to close the sale, or, at least, to reach some sort of commitment to action. Advertising can only provide a passive meeting with no hard push for a sale.

From another perspective, the manager can consider the reach and frequency capabilities of the sales force when compared with advertising. While cost figures would make it difficult to justify using a salesperson as a frequency building medium, there are also data to show whether the salesperson can build reach very well (aside from cost issues). In a review of 54 studies over a six-year period, McGraw-Hill found that "less than 10 percent of industrial decision makers had been called upon by a salesperson from a specific company about a specific product in the previous two months."[13] This would imply that the sales force is a poor medium for developing reach. One conclusion is that the very specific task of the sales force is to influence behavior by closing sales. Maybe that's why they're called salespersons rather than awarenesspersons.

Applying the Decision Sequence

Having considered the strengths and weaknesses of using the sales force as a communications tool, the strategic uses of this tool and the areas of preferred application are considered next. As with any other tool, it will be used to solve problems and meet objectives. To this end, the sales force will be one of the strategic options found in the decision sequence.

Assessing the situation

Just as there is the decision sequence, which has been used throughout this text as a framework leading to strategies, there is a sales process model proposed by Weitz and shown in Figure 18.6. Weitz calls this model ISTEA, for "impression, strategy, transmission, evaluation and adjustment";[14] although the words differ, the process is similar to that of the decision sequence.

Developing an *impression of the customer* is essentially the situation analysis process. It is essential to learn about awareness, knowledge, attitudes, and past behavior of each prospect as quickly as possible so that the appropriate type of presentation can be made. There is also a large body of literature that discusses the value of similarity between salespersons and customers. While it is not possible to create a new salesperson for each customer, the salesperson should know

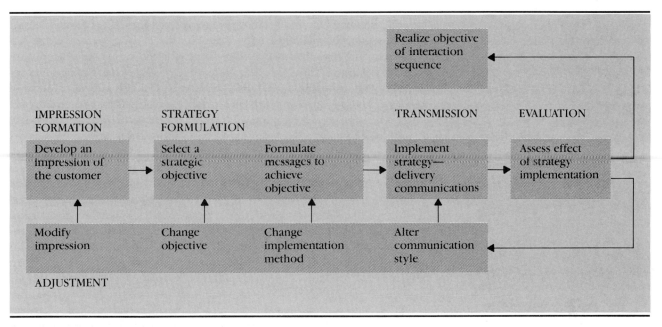

Figure 18.6   Weitz's ISTEA model

what is appropriate behavior in each case. Attempting to make such adjustments is reasonable because most salespersons work in a fairly unstructured environment. Of course it is also important that salespersons learn to make accurate evaluations.

After impression formation, *objectives and strategies* are set. Parallel to the advertising decisions that need to be made, the sales manager must consider both the medium and the message; both of these are affected by the situation analysis.

The salesperson (the medium) should be as similar to the customer as possible; while demographic variables don't seem to be particularly useful, according to a literature review done by Weitz, personality characteristics such as forcefulness and sociability appear to be more influential.[15] In another review, Riordan, Oliver, and Donnelly[16] reached the conclusion that similarity, liking, and perceived expertness are valued traits.

The salesperson's presentation (the message) should also be tailored to the customer. Because the sales force is generally used in high-information situations, the multiattribute model can be useful in suggesting the most important issues to be discussed in terms of strategies. (A review of the MAM model and recommended strategies might be appropriate here. See Chapter 3).

In order for the salesperson to succeed, Weitz suggests that two important communication tasks must be completed and that either one without the other will hamper success. *Impression formation* must be accurate and the *resultant message* must be well presented. The combination of art and science which has been discussed in earlier sections of this text is again important here. Neither an accurate impression without a strong presentation nor a strong presentation based on an inaccurate impression will do the job.

After message transmission, the salesperson will *reevaluate the situation.* In Figure 18.6 this leads either to a realization of the objective (a sale, a promise, a favorable attitude) or to the need for an *adjustment* in one of the areas noted in the bottom cell. Because industrial sales are not realized until after an average of 5.1 calls, adjustments are very likely to be needed.

It would seem that even if the objective were reached, adjustment would be needed because a nonsale objective (such as impression formation) would require more follow-up calls while a sale would lead to calls for repeat sales. One case where a sale is less likely to lead to another sales call is with the retail durable goods sales force. Here the next sales interaction may be 5 to 20 years away, and the flow of Figure 18.6 will indeed end with the top cell.

Weitz[17] points out that the process of Figure 18.6 and the need for well-developed strategies are especially important in the industrial sales case because here both the buyer and seller are highly involved with the decision and both gain from a continuing interaction. Even if the price per unit is low, the order itself is usually large; even if no sale is made on any particular visit, the relationship will be maintained and developed for future calls. Weitz concludes from his research that salespersons who use strategies consistent with the logic of Figure 18.6 are more successful than salespersons who are inconsistent.

In later research, Saxe and Weitz[18] extend these concepts in the development of their SOCO (Selling Orientation–Customer Orientation) scale. Here they show how salesperson communications should relate to the marketing concept as well as to a consideration of important attributes. A purely selling orientation is a short-run perspective geared to gaining an immediate sale. While marketing theory would suggest that this is not the best long-run strategy, the pressures on each salesperson tend to push them to that goal. A salesperson cannot exist solely by building futures; sales must also be gained, although, as will be seen later, the most effective salespersons seem to have a more long-run view and a concern for the best interests of customers.

Conversely, in several situations a customer orientation is clearly called for. These exist when

1. The salesperson can offer a range of alternatives and has the expertise to determine which alternatives will satisfy customer needs.
2. The salesperson's customers are typically engaged in complex buying tasks.
3. The salesperson typically has a cooperative relationship with the customers.
4. Repeat sales and referrals are an important source of business for the salesperson.[19]

As expected, Weitz's data reveal a relation between customer orientation and sales performance across different groups of salespeople. The longer run customer orientation strategy seems more effective even when examined over the short time period of less than one year.

Salesforce aids provided by the firm

While Weitz has shown that consideration of the marketing concept and a solid situation analysis lead to effective communications, other researchers have taken a different tack. For example, Weitz's work suggests that each presentation needs to be tailored to the customer. Such uniqueness puts a great burden on the salesperson, as Jolson[20] has shown in his study of the "canned" versus the "fresh" presentation. The canned presentation is one that is memorized and uses aids such as film, flip charts, and brochures prepared by the company. In the fresh presentation, the salesperson has more freedom to personally describe things. Jolson found that customers learned more in the flexible presentation but showed greater buying intention after a canned presentation. He felt that the canned presentation was especially useful for an unknown firm and/or a weak salesperson. Perhaps what is needed is a situation analysis/impression formation period followed by a canned presentation put together with the specific needs of the customer in mind. That is, the salesperson can use prepared materials, but their use must be tempered by their relevance to the situation.

Interpersonal relations

It is also important to look at salesperson personality variables that seem to relate to success. These would be relevant to both the media and message aspects of the sales force as a communications tool. As noted earlier, one key distinction between the sales force and other marketing communications is the one-to-one relationship that exists here. As a result it is important to consider this dyad, or pairing, of individuals. Several studies have done so across a number of selling situations and product classes.

A study of insurance agents found that successful agents were perceived as expert, similar in outlook and personal situation to the client, and different from the negative stereotype of the agent.[21] In another study, retail paint salespeople were more effective when perceived to have consumption characteristics similar to those of the customer.[22] These findings were also seen in a study of retail music store salespersons. Again, similarity of taste (this time in music) and perceived expertise led to higher sales of a tape machine head cleaner.[23]

In a summary of these and other studies, Riordan, Oliver, and Donnelly[24] concluded that salesperson effectiveness is related to

1. attitude congruence (similarity) on several dimensions
2. the degree to which the prospect's expectations of the appropriate salesperson's roles are fulfilled
3. personality commonalities
4. perceived expertness
5. product usage similarities

These studies were done primarily in retail situations but should hold across other settings as well. The findings are consistent with work in social psychology; people are more comfortable with similar people (although Weitz has pointed out that while this finding holds for personality types of variables, it doesn't seem to hold for demographic variables). Successful salespersons show that they can relate to customer problems and interests, have solved similar problems, and are experts at solving such problems. A visit to virtually any retail outlet that actively uses salespersons will quickly confirm these findings both for good and for poor salespersons.

Interpersonal power

The salesperson–customer relation can also be considered from the point of view of bases of power, as was done by Busch and Wilson.[25] They show that a salesperson can use expert power and referent power in dealing with customers. Expert power exists when the salesperson is perceived to have valuable knowledge or skills; generally this power results after the salesperson shows the knowledge/skill and the customer then acknowledges the expert power. An example of referent power would exist if the two parties both belonged to the same club or came from the same small town. Referrent power results from friendship or sharing of identity; again the power results after the salesperson shows the proper identification. For example, salespeople might say that they had some special training that would establish expertise. There are other less relevant bases of power, but these two seem to have the greatest impact on the attitudes of customers.

Relational communications

Recent work by Soldow and Thomas[26] shows how expertise, familiarity, power, dominance, and other relations may develop between the salesperson and the customer. They suggest that a relation develops through the *form* of a conversation rather than its content.

Their work shows that both parties must reach an implied agreement about who will dominate the relation or if there will be equality between the parties. Without such implicit agreement there cannot be a successful relation; the salesperson must strive for early agreement, or meetings will end fruitlessly. This notion of relational communications would seem to be an important part of the impression formation stage discussed by Weitz.

The salesperson, aware of this need, can attempt to establish a dominant, deferent, or equal relation; the customer will then respond with a signal. This sparring will continue until a relation is established or the meeting is terminated. Without a relation, the true purpose of the interaction (to sell goods) cannot be resolved. As an example, Figure 18.7 shows a dialogue between a soap salesper-

Figure 18.7 Dialogue to be evaluated in terms of relational communications

1. Salesperson: I understand that the Spanish Castle will open in about 90 days. Is that right?
2. Clinton: Well, we hope so. The way delays keep cropping up, we aren't very sure of anything.
3. Salesperson: I can imagine how it must be. But the setting! Why, this is like Shangri-la! Wow!
4. Clinton: It is really a beautiful place isn't it?
5. Salesperson: How many rooms will you have, Mr. Clinton?
6. Clinton: We'll have 150 units. And a lounge. And a coffee shop plus two dining . . .
7. Salesperson: (interrupting) That's a pretty big operation! You must feel right at home—I understand you managed the Cambridge in Los Angeles for several years.
8. Clinton: Yes, that's right. For seven years, to be exact.

9. Salesperson: Nothing like experience, is there? Based on your experience, Mr. Clinton, have you any idea what the break-even point will be here?
10. Clinton: We think we'll make out all right with an occupancy rate of about 60%.
11. Salesperson: That gives you a nice safety factor you can live with. You know, even with your location near the water, you're still reasonably close to the business district, aren't you? I realize you will be a resort, but do you expect to attract businesspeople?

. . . .

21. Salesperson: And check me—the Spanish Castle will be predominantly a resort hotel, but you expect commercial travelers.
22. Clinton: (smiles) Keep your fingers crossed.
23. Salesperson: Hmm. (takes out a pencil) You'll be using about $12\frac{1}{2}$ cases. . . .

son and Clinton, the manager of a new hotel. The following two paragraphs show Soldow and Thomas' evaluation of the interaction.

It appears that the salesperson's first utterance (1) was an attempt to establish dominance. Clinton, however, is reluctant to allow this and, therefore, makes his own bid for dominance (2) by answering with a disconfirmation ("we aren't very sure of anything"). The salesperson defers by indicating support for Clinton's disconfirmation: (3) ("I can imagine how it must be"). The salesperson then changes the subject by talking about the setting. Clinton, by supporting the new topic (4) and hence deferring to the salesperson, provides the basis for discontinuance of the interactants' respective bids for dominance.

Unfortunately, rather than answering the manager's extension (since it was in the form of a question), the salesperson chooses to bid for dominance by changing the topic to number of rooms (5). Had the salesperson pursued the manager's extension, a degree of equality may have been achieved which would have precluded the subsequent bids for dominance. By answering the salesperson's question and extending the topic (6), Clinton provides another opportunity for the salesperson to achieve equality. In addition to interrupting (talkover), the salesperson changes the topic, thereby bidding for dominance (7). If the salesperson had recognized Clinton's willingness either to defer or to achieve relational equality, the interaction could have avoided becoming bogged down in continued dominance negotiation.[27]

Soldow and Thomas go on to suggest that the dialogue in this example probably will stay in a position where both parties try to dominate; as a result the chances for a sale are slight. The point of their work is to show that the salesperson must not allow ego to detract from establishing a relation that can become fruitful. It is not enough to be an expert and to show similarities to the customer; the salesperson must also be able to assess the direction that the relation is taking and to respond accordingly.

Weitz also has proposed a contingency model of salesperson effectiveness that helps tie together a number of the issues discussed above. In this model, shown in Figure 18.8, effectiveness is a result of selling behaviors; this relation is

Figure 18.8 A contingency model of salesperson effectiveness

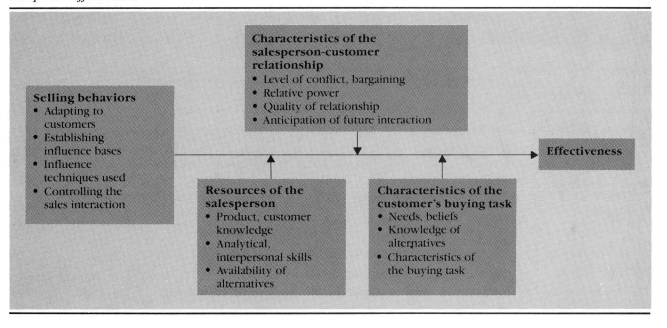

tempered by characteristics of the salesperson–customer relationship, the resources of the salesperson, and the characteristics of the customer's buying task. For the most part, the above issues fit neatly into this framework.

When to Use Salespeople Rather Than Advertising

A basic issue concerns the selection of the most appropriate marketing communications tool for the occasion. In the present discussion, the choices will most likely be between advertising and personal selling in terms of budget allocation. Earlier it was noted that the sales force is a poor tool to use in generating awareness, reach, or frequency. If the market is large, advertising should do the initial job of creating awareness and knowledge. Even for small markets, direct mail advertising will be more efficient at creating at least basic awareness. Only in very limited cases of extremely small markets and complex products would the sales force be the main tool for creating knowledge, and even in these cases some preceding literature would probably be sent to the customer.

In both retail and industrial settings, higher priced and/or more complex *products* are more likely to need a salesperson. Two-way communications are useful in these cases where additional information, reassurance, and the answering of questions are helpful. These products, which may also need the assistance of the sales force, are more likely to need a demonstration or trial; inexpensive products can achieve trial through sampling and couponing. These higher priced, more complex products are also more likely to need follow-up service and user guidance, both of which may be part of the salesperson's duties. Along similar lines there is a need for the development of unique specifications for certain industrial products.

From a *channel of distribution* perspective, there is more likely to be a sales force when the channel is short. This situation exists for manufacturer-owned channels such as for automobiles and for highly specialized types of products. Short channels are more labor intensive and use a "push" strategy to move the product, while longer channels are less able to sustain a sales force and are more likely to use a "pull" strategy based on advertising and promotions. Long channels tend also to lead to a more diffuse set of retailers who are less likely to have an extensive sales force.

From a *pricing* perspective, the sales force is necessary when there is negotiated pricing. Here a representative of the seller must be present to respond to offers. Table 18.5 summarizes conditions when the sales force is more likely to be necessary.

Types of Selling Jobs and Their Goals

Salespersons must play many types of roles, but essentially these fall into three categories. While this chapter emphasizes the problems and opportunities inherent in *creative selling*, an examination of *order taking*, and *missionary selling* tasks and goals is also appropriate. While a salesperson will generally work mostly in one of these categories, some time will be spent in each category.

Creative selling

The *creative selling* process requires the greatest preparation and carries the salesperson through all phases of Weitz's model in Figure 18.6 and the selling process presented next. Creative selling can exist at all levels and with all types of

Table 18.5 When the sales force is a major part of the communications mix

Mix area	Characteristics
Product or service	Complex products requiring customer application assistance (e.g., computers, pollution control systems, steam turbines)
	Major purchase decisions, such as food items purchased by supermarket chains
	Features and performance of the product requiring personal demonstration and trial by the customer (e.g., private aircraft)
Channels	Channel system relatively short and direct to end users
	Product and service training and assistance needed by channel intermediaries
	Personal selling is needed in "pushing" product through channel
	Channel intermediaries available to perform personal selling function for supplier with limited resources and experience (e.g., brokers or manufacturer's agents)
Price	Final price negotiated between buyer and seller (e.g., appliances, automobiles, real estate)
	Selling price and or quantity purchased enable an adequate margin to support selling expenses (traditional department store compared to discount house)
Advertising	Advertising media do not provide effective link with market targets
	Information needed by buyer cannot be provided entirely through advertising and sales promotion (e.g., life insurance)
	Number and dispersion of customers will not enable acceptable advertising economies

Source: David W. Cravens, Gerald E. Hills, and Robert B. Woodruff, *Marketing Decision Making: Concepts and Strategy* (Homewood Ill.: Richard D. Irwin, 1980), p. 384. Reprinted by permission of Richard D. Irwin, Inc.

customers. The salesperson must assess the situation, prepare and make a presentation, and ask for the order. Creative selling is the most complex task, and the goal is to eventually make a direct sale. This type of selling is most often required during an initial buy; that is, when the buyer and seller complete their first exchange.

Order taking

Order taking also occurs at all levels and with all types of customers. It is the easiest of the three tasks because it is most routinized. Here the salesperson sees the customer for an order but doesn't need a significant presentation. This scenario occurs in a well-established buyer/seller relation where the items and quantities don't change much; this exchange is known as a *straight rebuy.* If there are minor product or quantity changes, the exchange is a *modified rebuy* and may require some level of creative selling.

Order taking typically is done by *route delivery salespersons* (e.g., home milk delivery, retail shelf stocking of bread, replenishment of the customer firm's paper supplies). These salespersons often make judgments about the needs of the customer and fill the order.

Wholesaler representatives visit their customers with large lists of goods and record orders that are later filled. This process may include both retailer and industrial customers. Again, little creative selling occurs.

Many *retail clerks* are also order takers who help customers without doing creative selling. At higher priced or higher quality stores the clerks become more involved and are more likely to engage in creative selling. These three types of order takers make sales but don't prepare for the interaction as thoroughly as would a creative salesperson.

Missionary selling

Missionary selling is part of an indirect process where the salesperson prepares carefully and goes through the entire selling process but doesn't ask for the order. These salespeople give information and service but don't sell. An example is the pharmaceutical detail person who visits many doctors, informing them about new drugs and handing out samples, but not taking orders. Sales come later when the doctor prescribes the drug and the pharmacist fills the prescription. The missionary salesperson provides a valuable function by instructing doctors about new drugs, but never makes a direct sale.

Another use of missionary selling can be seen at the Ansul Corporation, the largest manufacturer of industrial fire protection equipment in the United States. Products are primarily sold by over 300 independent distributors throughout the United States. In addition, four national account managers perform missionary selling tasks for customers that meet the following criteria:

- Offer large potential
- Operate numerous facilities that cross Ansul's regional and district sales territories
- Have either centralized purchasing or centralized specification capability

For target customers meeting these criteria (e.g., oil companies, automotive firms, airlines, fast food chains), the national accounts group only tries to get Ansul's products specified by selling the firm's reputation, capabilities, and distribution network. The orders are then taken by the distributors.[28]

The Selling Process The sales process that begins with finding a prospective customer and ends with servicing that customer after the sale is a complex one with many side steps and much backtracking; there are, though, a number of identifiable stages that can be discussed. While the situations vary greatly, the stages seem to remain constant. All three types of selling just discussed follow this sequence although order taking and missionary selling will skip steps. The most commonly used set of stages seems to be the one described by Russell, Beach, and Buskirk[29] and will be followed here. Their seven stages are

- prospecting
- preapproach
- approach
- presentation
- meeting objections
- closing the sale
- follow-up

The parallels between these stages and the components of Weitz's ISTEA model, as shown in Figure 18.6, will become clear.

Prospecting

A salesperson needs to have a list of potential customers to call on and therefore must go through a situation analysis search process to find members of the appropriate target market. The first stage of prospecting is to define the target market. For many industrial products this will be obvious; for example, there may be 73 firms in the United States that use a particular piece of technology in their manufacturing process. These firms comprise a target market list; less obviously, there may be another 2,489 firms with the potential to use the technology if their manufacturing process were slightly altered or if the technology were slightly modified.

After locating a target firm, the industrial salesperson must next find the key people within it who can make decisions and approve funds. This industrial buying process will be examined in the industrial communications chapter later in this text.

For retail salespersons, the target market will be reasonably well defined although it will be larger and more difficult to reach on an individual basis. More appropriately, prospects here will be sought through advertising and the overall image of the retail location.

Prospects can be identified in several ways:

- *Endless chain*   Every prospect is asked for the names of other possible prospects.

- *Coupons and bingo cards*   Every newspaper ad, magazine ad, or direct mail piece can have a coupon for prospects to return for further information and/or a call from a salesperson. A *bingo card* is a free-standing insert to be returned to the magazine publisher that allows the reader to identify one or more advertisers that should get in touch; the names are sent from the publisher to the advertiser.

- *Personal observation*   The salesperson can check listings of new births, business startups, construction sites, or other relevant events for prospects and then contact these individuals or organizations.

- *Centers of influence*   Certain events in this society are recorded by law and become accessible as lists of prospects. For example, each state has a record of automobile sales that are useful to sellers of auto insurance.

- *Cold call*   The salesperson can make calls on a random basis either door to door, by making phone calls, or to firms in a certain geographic area. This way of prospecting is least successful and should be reserved for times when there are absolutely no other available alternatives. Conversely, this method is better than doing nothing and therefore is employed when there are no other leads or if all members of a community (or specific types of members) are eligible to buy the product. The cold call is most appropriate in an unsegmented market.

After developing a list (using any method other than the cold call), the names must be assessed. Pederson and Wright[30] suggest that viable prospects have the following criteria:

- *A want or need that can be satisfied by the product*
- *The ability to pay*
- *The authority to make the purchase*   The prospect must be senior enough to be allowed to make decisions.

- *Accessibility to the salesperson*   Some firms shield decision makers from salespersons.
- *Eligibility to buy*   Purchasers of life insurance, for example, must meet certain health standards.

Given the cost of a sales call, it is important to screen names before calls are made. Just as with advertising and promotions, it is necessary to reach the appropriate target market with as little wasted coverage as possible. The average sales call costs over $200, and that charge applies to cold calls as well as legitimate prospects. Therefore, poor prospects need to be eliminated.

Preapproach

In this stage the salesperson gathers as much information as possible about each specific prospect so the pending presentation can be as relevant and accurate as possible. This includes obtaining data on the dynamic and static segmentation variables discussed in Chapter 2. As with message strategy, the use of an intuitive multiattribute model can be valuable. Static information should be gathered on both the individual prospect and the target firm.

Approach

While the approach is the first meeting of the prospect and the salesperson, lots of earlier work should already have been done; if these earlier stages were not executed well, the salesperson approaches the prospect with a poor chance for success. The goals of this opening approach are to establish contact, make some quick assessments of interest, and set up the continuation of the presentation immediately or at a later time. The approach is vital because the prospect may not have invited the salesperson; setting the wrong tone will lessen the possibility of a sale. While the approach to a first meeting with a new prospect is crucial, the approach to later meetings is much easier because a relation will have been established. The issues of relational communications are germane to the approach; it is at this time that dominance, deference, or equality should be established.

As with an advertising message, the headline is crucial. In this case the approach is the "headline." In some cases, the headline discusses a benefit.

"How long does it take your plant to make an *X*?"

"Our new *Y* will keep your floors cleaner."

"We can help you save money and reduce waste."

In other cases, the headline offers a premium or gift.

"I'd like to give you a sample of our new *Z* to try."

"Here's a model of our tractor for your kids to play with."

Other headlines discuss mutual friends:

"Jack said I should call."

or an introduction of self

"Hi, I'm Mike Rothschild from D.C. Heath, and I've got a marketing communications text you should look at."

or create curiosity

"Do you know that your major competitor increased production by 23% with our new widget-based balancer?"

In many cases the approach and the presentation occur on separate days. Given this luxury, the approach is used to learn more about the customer and the problem; the presentation then builds on this information. If a more rapid impact must be made, then the assessment must be spontaneously integrated into the presentation, which may follow immediately.

Presentation

Having made it past the headline, the salesperson may now continue into the "body copy" and "visuals" of the message. The message strategy should lead to a specific goal; in most cases the goal will be a sale, but often this is not possible and so an alternate goal such as in-depth knowledge or a favorable attitude should be sought. The presentation should continue to the logical conclusion of the goal. Asking for a sale when both parties know the time is not appropriate is awkward; not asking for the sale when the time is right is a waste and will also lead to poor relations. So, the objective of the presentation must be properly determined from the preapproach analysis, and the presentation must be an implementation of strategy that leads to that goal. In this sense, the communications by the sales force are no different than those through mass media.

Meeting objections

An important part of the presentation is the dialogue that develops when the customer has a chance to raise questions and problems. The knowledgeable salesperson will be able to answer legitimate issues but may have problems with false issues that are raised to cover real issues. If the customer cannot afford the product, some other objection may be raised. Solving the problem relating to that issue won't lead to a sale because the true objection still hasn't been uncovered.

In a McGraw-Hill survey of over 1,400 industrial salespersons, price was clearly the dominant objection raised by prospective customers as an obstacle to purchasing.[31] Table 18.6 shows the ten issues raised most often in that study.

Table 18.6 Obstacles encountered by sales people in selling products

Sales obstacles	Mentions #	Mentions %
Price	852	59.9%
Delivery off schedule	97	6.8
Lack of proof that product fills a need	84	5.9
Lack of familiarity with product	59	4.1
Problems with past performance of product	59	4.1
Incomplete product line	55	3.9
Inability to gain confidence or trust	50	3.5
Indifference of customer	46	3.2
Satisfaction with present service	41	2.9
Inability to contact the right person	38	2.7

Source: McGraw-Hill Research 1979 Sales Aids Study. Reprinted by permission of McGraw-Hill Publications Company.

Kincaid notes that if the prospect has been perfectly selected, there should be no objections except for points of information. Therefore, if many objections are raised the salesperson did a poor job of prospecting and preapproach.

Probably the best way to overcome objections is to anticipate them and defuse them in the presentation. For example, if many prospects are concerned that the firm is too small, then the salesperson can defuse this objection in the presentation by discussing the virtues of smallness: "We are able to give more personal service to our customers because we are small."

Closing the sale

Many salespersons find it difficult to close the sale; they are afraid of being rejected and enjoy the safety of the presentation and the discussion that follows. Eventually, though, the meeting must come to an end and the salesperson must ask for the sale.

It is important to look for signals from the prospect that show a readiness to buy. Questions that deal with price, credit, delivery dates, or minor issues such as colors are good indicators. Body language such as leaning forward is also felt to be an indicator of readiness.

When the salesperson feels that the right signals are coming, it is time for a trial closing. If the prospect is agreeable, then the close is completed; if the prospect backs off, then the presentation is resumed with a few more selling points that had been held in reserve.

There are a variety of standard closings. Jacoby[32] discusses 17 of these in a paper that bases the closing styles on theories of social psychology. His list includes

- *Assumed consent*   Assume that the prospect has agreed, and then go on to details such as address, delivery terms, or finance terms. "When would you like delivery?"

- *Closing on a specific objection*   Listen to the objection and then agree to fix the problem and close the sale. "We can easily modify the product to take care of that problem so I guess we've got a deal."

- *Closing on a general objection*   Make the general objection ("I guess I just don't care for it") more specific by asking lots of direct questions about the problem that will force the prospect to agree that the product is good. Then get to the real problem and fix it.

- *The take away close*   After discussing the product, admit to the prospect that it may not be available for various reasons. Scarce items become more desirable.

- *Impending event*   "Buy now before prices go up" or "We're running low on this model and might not get more for a while."

- *Story telling*   Tell the prospect what has happened to similar people who have or have not made the right (purchase) decision in similar circumstances.

- *Special incentive*   "I'll give you another 10% off if you buy today."

- *Puppy dog closing*   It's hard to give back a puppy after it has lived with someone. Similarly, if a prospect is uncertain about a product, allow a trial period prior to the decision. This works well for visible status products such as expensive automobiles. Few people will bring the car back.

- *No risk close*　A money-back guarantee usually works similarly to the puppy dog close. "We'll give you all your money back if you aren't fully satisfied."

- *Delayed/minimized cost close*　"Buy now, pay later" or "No payments for 90 days."

There are other closings as well, but these are some that can be traced fairly clearly to attitude change theories in social psychology.

Follow-up

People are often uncomfortable after making a major decision, be it a consumer or industrial product. A follow-up after the sale allows the salesperson to help by acknowledging the buyer's wisdom. Mailing literature also helps because the buyer needs to feel that the right choice was made. Showing concern at this traumatic time leads to good long-term customer relations and can also lead to extra short-run sales for add-on accessories.

Follow-up should continue until the next purchase period comes up. For some industrial products the salesperson is also a troubleshooter who stays in touch with the buyer in case of problems. "After the sale, it's the service that counts," says one company's advertising. Observers have said about retail automotive sales that the salesperson sells the first car but the service department sells the second.

Another reason for a follow-up call occurs in situations where the salesperson makes the close but the actual, formal sale is drawn up by the firm a few days or weeks later. In such cases the customer can reconsider and have a change of mind. A follow-up call can prevent this reversal.

Characteristics of a Good Salesperson

The preceding discussion covered aspects of the message and its delivery; this section describes attributes of the medium. What types of people are most likely to be successful in delivering the message and obtaining the appropriate customer behavior?

There are many intuitive lists of characteristics of good salespersons, but most lists have three major problems. First, the characteristics would apply to virtually any responsible type of position including President of the United States. Second, finding people who fit the attributes is difficult. Third, the people who fit the descriptors often are not interested in a sales career but would rather pursue something they perceive to be more glamorous. As a result, firms have difficulty finding ideal candidates or selecting them from available pools of potential candidates. Given the high cost of training, this is a major problem for marketers.

The following are some of the characteristics of successful salespersons:[33]

- *Positive attitude, ego drive, self-motivation, and determination*　Successful salespersons believe in their product, themselves, and their ability to make a sale. They are committed to their career, enjoy their work, and show this enthusiasm to customers.

The best salespersons seem to be self-motivated; they don't need a supervisor to push them. This is especially important for a salesperson who must travel a lot

Don Beveridge

President, D. W. Beveridge and Associates

Don Beveridge is president of D. W. Beveridge and Associates, an international consulting firm serving clients in Europe, Australia, and New Zealand as well as in Canada and the United States.

His experiences are extensive. In his career he has held the position of a general manager, Mobil Oil Corporation, director of sales and marketing for Means Services, and he was the founder of the Clean Systems Corporation, for which he is presently Chief Executive Officer.

Don has been featured in business films for Hallmark Cards, Mutual of New York Insurance Company, for 3M, and for the broadcasting industry. At the time of this writing he is one of only 50 individuals awarded the CSP, "Certified Speaking Professional," by the National Speakers Association.

As a seminar leader or convention speaker, Don Beveridge is truly a motivator. He is well known as a dynamic individual who has knowledge, judgment, experience, and an exceptional ability to communicate.

Four Generations of Sales Types

Positioning, market segmentation, market share, and all the other components of a sophisticated marketing plan are addressed in great detail by the major corporations of the world. Unfortunately, what is often considered to be the *un*sophisticated phase of that same marketing plan—skills and capabilities of the salesperson—is delegated to the entry line level manager or, even worse, to a corporate trainer who instructs from the book. The successes of the Xerox Corporation and the continuing selling successes of IBM, even when they lack a technological advantage, are due in large part to new sophistication and a very definite professionalizing of the selling system. Today, selling *is* a science, and the ability to sell efficiently, productively, and pro-

fessionally has long ago evolved beyond the emotional rapport that yesterday's "hustler" perceived to be the cornerstone of the buyer/seller relationship.

In the companies that capture market share there takes place a very rapid evolution in the skills of their sales and marketing personnel. It's a journey through the four generations of sales types with a "home" or skill level quickly established as a third or fourth generation sales type, and discarding of the first and second generation ability level as soon as humanly possible.

The first generation of selling skills is identified as the *Commercial Visitor* level and is recognized by one or more of the following criteria. Commercial Visitors in most cases place an emphasis on, and are desirous of, close, personal, emotional relationships with the clients. It's an antiquated selling ability, but many still utilize the technique.

Their emphasis is to "make the buyer like me," and to become personally involved. They place heavy emphasis on antiquated gift giving, Christmas presents, and theatre or sports tickets. They entertain the secretary and send gifts to the family. Commercial Visitor sales representatives believe subconsciously that they will secure the order because the client eventually feels the business is "owed" to the representatives.

Peer group pressure creates the second group, *Peddlers*. Peddlers are individuals who mentally or physically carry the product to the customer and begin with a product "pitch."

Point by point, feature by feature, their competence in detailing each of their products is without question. If their products are transportable, many have the trunks of their automobiles loaded with samples or models. When one recognizes that the most productive professional sales representatives in the world never sell on the first sales call, it makes somewhat questionable the effectiveness of the peddlers who do.

Professional third or fourth generation salespersons' initial activity is to discover the customer's needs, from the customer's point of view. Their objective is to gain credibility. Their function is to conduct an in-depth customer needs analysis. All of these are mandatory activities that preclude any discussion of product or service.

Third and fourth generation sales professionals cannot sell on the initial sales call because their goal, their objective, is first to identify the customer's needs from the customer's point of view and then to satisfy those same needs profitably with tailored systems rather than isolated products or components.

These third generation sales professionals, the *Problem solvers*, constitute the newer breed of salespeople. They possess all the product knowledge of the peddler. They have the loyalty and commitment of the commercial visitor, but those factors are their foundation or base and are not descriptive of their whole self.

Several other indicators also help formulate the identification of problem solver salespeople. First, they have empathy in depth. Counselor salespersons are so desirous of being of sincere value to their clients that they are motivated to conduct a customer needs analysis with each new client and also annually with all existing accounts. The counselor's needs analysis begins with a questioning exercise of the prospect, incorporating open-ended questions. This type of probing is a fundamental third generation selling technique. Open-ended questions cannot be answered "yes" or "no," and they facilitate the customer's response. It communicates interest and it creates an environment wherein the prospect freely communicates his or her needs.

Problem solvers, however, identify needs from the customer's point of view and will isolate safety, productivity, ROI, profit, decor, sanitation, etc., as the true customer needs, and therefore the "buying motive." They seek to solve real customer problems—to contribute, to deliver value, as well as product. Their empathy causes them to follow this "questioning exercise" with a physical survey, the hands-on, look-see of the client's operation. Most uniquely, this third generation sales type emphasizes solutions to problems, not products, but solutions and systems to solve their customers' problems!

Because expertise is most often a component of their systems and often provided cost free as part and parcel of the sale, the fourth type, the *sustaining resources*, are much in demand. They know the customer's business as well as they know their own. Their credibility is such and their expertise so complete that they regularly receive an invitation to participate in the formulation of the prospect's goal setting, the client's five- or ten-year planning and forecasting activities. This is not blue sky! It's a function many salespeople engage in daily. Their customers' requests are for "help" more than for product.

Factually, these salespersons have fourth generation, sustaining resource type selling skills. At that point their prospects or clients perceive them to be unpaid staff members in the customer's employ. Such a skill, such as identity in the marketplace, provides these sales types a form of invincibility in the eyes of the competitor.

There is a definite method of ascertaining if you or your sales force is perceived by the market to be either problem solvers or sustaining resource level sales types. Monitor a few days' telephone calls to office and salespeople. Determine how many are requesting certain products and determine as well how many, if any, of the customers are requesting help.

A company that receives no customer requests for expertise, for problem solving, and for help has a sales force of commercial visitors and peddlers, and they are in trouble!

and make independent calls. Motivation comes from attitude. If a salesperson enjoys a task, there is inherent gratification in its successful accomplishment. While the firm offers its sales force many tangible motivators, the best salespersons thrive on the task, its challenges, and the good feeling of a job well done.

- *Empathy*   A good salesperson relates to the customer's problems and works to solve them. This customer orientation, as described by Weitz, reflects the marketing concept and the ability to meet needs. It is important to understand the problem from the customer's perspective and to seek a solution. This leads, over time, to a strong trusting relation and long-run success. In this sense, the sales task is an exchange of information and ideas rather than a product pitch. Empathy sometimes will cause the salesperson to advise a customer *not* to buy; this lack of high-pressure tactics will develop a long-run relation.

- *Knowledge*   The best salespersons are extremely knowledgeable about their product and its uses, as well as the customer's needs and problems. This allows them to provide greater assistance than merely selling and allows for an exchange of information. If this knowledge can be used to make the buyer look good, then, again, a long-run relation will be established. In this sense, salespeople are "clearinghouses of information, advisors, relationship builders, problem solvers, customer advocates, deal makers, and, in some cases, delivery or repair persons and installers."[34]

Summary

The cost of supporting an industrial salesperson can easily come to $100,000 per year when salary, commissions, support services, and expenses are considered. John Peters[35] suggests that this can be pared by a few thousand dollars by cutting expenses, but such paring affects morale. The alternative is to increase the productivity of the salesperson by better training, better materials, and/or better support services. This chapter has considered the salesperson as a medium for delivering the company's message.

There are many cases in industrial goods and consumer durable goods when a sales force is necessary to close a sale. When there is a complex good or a high price a salesperson can be useful in overcoming objections and answering questions.

Conversely, for low-involvement products where advertising and promotions combine to elicit trial, the sales force is less valuable. The sales force's high cost makes it inefficient except for special cases; its inability to generate widespread awareness further limits its usefulness.

In situations where it is merited, the sales manager and/or salesperson need to go through a process similar to the decision sequence to assess each prospect and then set objectives and strategies to deal with the prospect. The medium (the salesperson) and the message (the presentation) must be adjusted for each prospect. Over the long run, a customer orientation/marketing concept approach will bring the best results.

Discussion Questions

1. What are the key differences between personal selling and advertising?

2. Why is the cost of a sales call so high? How might it be reduced?

3. How can advertising and personal selling be combined to produce the greatest synergistic impact?

4. What are some key variables to assess in the situation analysis/assessment/impression formation phase of the personal sales sequence?

5. Discuss the value of establishing where dominance lies in a selling situation.

6. Describe the seven stages of the selling process. Describe a situation that you have been in as a customer for each of the seven stages.

7. Describe situations you have been in when a salesperson used each of the types of closing described in the text. Were these successful? Why? Why not?

8. Would you make a good salesperson? Why? Why not? What could you do to improve your chances for success?

9. Develop a sales presentation that takes you from prospecting through follow-up in the job-seeking campaign you have been working on throughout the text. Make sure your presentation is consistent with your advertising.

Notes

1. Gilbert A. Churchill, Jr., Neil M. Ford, and Orville C. Walker, Jr., *Sales Force Management,* 2d ed. (Homewood, Ill.: Richard D. Irwin, 1985).

2. Carlton A. Pederson, Milburn D. Wright, and Barton A. Weitz, *Selling: Principles and Methods,* 7th ed. (Homewood, Ill.: Richard D. Irwin, 1981).

3. Richard E. Stanley, *Promotion: Advertising, Publicity, Personal Selling, Sales Promotion* (Englewood Cliffs, N.J.: Prentice-Hall, 1982), p. 262.

4. McGraw-Hill Publications, LAP Report no. 8013.6, "An Industrial Sales Call Now Costs $178.00."

5. Philip Zimbardo and Ebbe B. Ebbesen, *Influencing Attitudes and Changing Behavior* (Reading, Mass.: Addison-Wesley Publishing, 1970).

6. McGraw-Hill Publications, LAP Report no. 7124, "Sales Force Viewed As Less Than Effective in Communicating Specific Sales Message by One-Quarter of Sales Managers."

7. McGraw-Hill Publications, LAP Report no. 7020.4, "Advertising Supports Personal Selling at Only Pennies per Contact."

8. "Average Cost of Sales Training per Salesperson," *Sales & Marketing Management,* 26 February 1979, p. 66.

9. "How Selling Costs Will Grow," *Sales & Marketing Management,* 10 December 1979, p. 41.

10. Theodore Levitt, "Communications and Industrial Selling," *Journal of Marketing* 31 (April 1967), pp. 15–21.

11. John E. Morrill "Industrial Advertising Pays Off," *Harvard Business Review,* March–April 1970, p. 4.

12. William R. Swinyard and Michael L. Ray, "Advertising-Selling Interactions: An Attribution Theory Experiment," *Journal of Marketing Research* 14 (November 1977), pp. 509–516.

13. McGraw-Hill Publications, LAP Report no. 1029.2, "Fewer Than 10% of Purchase Decision-Makers Are Reached by Salespeople over a 60-Day Period."

14. Barton A. Weitz, "Relationship between Salesperson Performance and Understanding of Customer Decision Making," *Journal of Marketing Research* 15 (November 1978), pp. 501–516.

15. Barton A. Weitz, "Effectiveness in Sales Interactions: A Contingency Framework," *Journal of Marketing* 45 (Winter 1981), pp. 85–103.

16. Edward A. Riordan, Richard L. Oliver, and James H. Donnelly, Jr., "The Unsold Prospect: Dyadic and Attitudinal Determinants," *Journal of Marketing Research* 14 (November 1977), pp. 530–537.

17. Weitz, "Salesperson Performance," p. 514.

18. Robert Saxe and Barton A. Weitz, "The SOCO Scale: A Measure of the Customer Orientation of Salespeople," *Journal of Marketing Research* 19 (August 1982), pp. 343–351.

19. Saxe and Weitz, "The SOCO Scale," p. 348.

20. Marvin A. Jolson, "The Underestimated Potential of the Canned Sales Presentation," *Journal of Marketing* 39 (January 1975), p. 75.

21. Franklin B. Evans, "Dyadic Interaction in Selling—A New Approach," unpublished manuscript, University of Chicago, 1964.

22. Timothy C. Brock, "Communicator-Recipient Similarity and Decision Change," *Journal of Personality and Social Psychology* 1 (November 1965), pp. 650–684.

23. Arch G. Woodside and J. William Davenport, Jr., "The Effect of Salesman Similarity and Expertise on Consumer Purchasing," *Journal of Marketing Research* 11 (May 1974), pp. 198–202.

24. Riordan, Oliver, and Donnelly, "The Unsold Prospect."

25. Paul Busch and David T. Wilson, "An Experimental Analysis of a Salesman's Expert and Referent Bases of Social Power in the Buyer-Seller Dyad," *Journal of Marketing Research* 13 (February 1976), pp. 3–11.

26. Gary F. Soldow and Gloria Penn Thomas, "Relational Communications: Form Versus Content in the Sales Interaction," *Journal of Marketing* 48 (Winter 1984), pp. 84–93.

27. Soldow and Thomas, "Relational Communications," p. 91.

28. H. Doug Plunkett, personal communications, 1984.

29. F. A. Russell, F. H. Beach, and R. H. Buskirk, *Textbook of Salesmanship,* 10th ed. (New York: McGraw-Hill Book Company, 1977).

30. C. A. Pederson and M. D. Wright, *Selling: Principles and Methods,* 6th ed. (Homewood, Ill.: Richard D. Irwin, 1976), p. 217.

31. McGraw-Hill Publications, LAP Report no. 8012, "What Are the Major Sales Resistances Faced by Sales People?"

32. Jacob Jacoby and C. Samuel Craig, *Personal Selling* (Lexington, Mass.: D.C. Heath, 1984).

33. This list draws material from F. Tibbits, Jr., "What It Takes to Make It in Selling," *Sales and Marketing Management* 117 (13 December, 1976), pp. 79–80; Richard E. Stanley, *Promotion;* and John W. Humphrey, "Survey Identifies Tracts of High-Performing Sales Reps," *Marketing News,* 10 September 1983, p. 14.

34. Humphrey, "Survey Identifies Tracts of High-Performing Sales Reps," p. 14.

35. John K. Peters, "Large Field Forces Can Be Efficient—With Sales Data Management System," *Marketing News,* 14 September 1984, p. 16.

Chapter 19
Brand Name, Packaging, and Point-of-Purchase Displays

*T*his is the last chapter dealing with the peripheral tools of marketing communications; its focus will be on three tools that aid the consumer in learning and remembering about the product. The tools discussed in this chapter are brand name, package, and point-of-purchase materials.

As the marketer's world becomes increasingly complex with greater levels of sophisticated competition from brands that are increasingly similar, it becomes more important to utilize every communications opportunity. The brand name is a focal point of every message; it is hard to discuss a brand without mentioning its name. If the name is so prominent, it makes sense to communicate a message using the name alone. An appropriate name can deliver the brand's positioning statement in a word or two.

Packaging and point-of-purchase materials are also important communications tools. Messages delivered through these media will be seen at the time and place of the ultimate purchase decision. These tools are valuable because they are the manager's last shot at making an impact. As brand loyalty decreases, these tools become increasingly crucial.

Brand Name

Names are important. A study done in 80 grade schools in California showed that teachers had preconceived notions of children based on their names and that children named Elmer or Bertha would have grade averages of 1 to 1.5 percent lower based on these preconceptions.

Marketing has similar examples. In the late 1960s the Lipton Company introduced a product they named Pennsylvania Dutch Casseroles. It was a good product; it tested well for taste, convenience, and price; it had a good package and a solid advertising budget. It failed.

The name had not been pretested, but somebody in the company thought it had a nice, homey sound. The name was tested in the post-mortem that followed the brand's death and at that time the company learned that the name *Pennsylvania Dutch* meant little to people outside of Lancaster, Pennsylvania, and that the word *casserole* was a negative word connoting a second-rate meal.

Two years later the same product was introduced using a different name. It became one of the top ten new food product introductions of the 1970s. Its name: Hamburger Helper.

As firms seek a competitive edge, they employ every possible communications tool, and the brand name continues to become a more important part of the product's communication. There are more new product introductions than ever before, the product life cycle gets shorter, competition gets more intense, there are more products on grocery shelves, there are more products being advertised, and therefore the brand name has become increasingly important.

A process for selecting names

McNeal and Zeren[1] collected data from 82 Fortune 500 firms that were major manufacturers of consumer goods in order to learn about the process used in selecting new brand names. Across these firms, six steps emerged as common to the process.

Identifying the objectives and criteria for the brand names This is consistent with the decision sequence; in order to succeed at any task the objectives must be sound. In the case of selecting a brand name, Kathryn Feakins[2] suggests that there are different roles that a name can play. The name can

- position the product
- describe the product
- be arbitrarily associated with the product

As an example, Feakins presented the following table to show examples of each objective in four product classes:

Product class	*Arbitrary*	*Descriptive*	*Positioning*
Beauty aids	Almay	Chap Stick	Cover Girl
Household cleansers	Ajax	Janitor in a Drum	Mr. Clean
Deodorant	Mitchum	Soft 'n' Dri	Sure
Dog food	Alpo	Moist 'n' Chunky	Fit 'n' Trim

Feakins writes that this first issue of brand name objectives is critical to all that follows. A name that positions the brand will aid learning and establish the franchise of the brand in the consumer's mind but can be a problem if repositioning is ever necessary. A descriptive name also aids learning but may limit extensions of the product. For example, Hamburger Helper is descriptive but doesn't work well if the product is reformulated to be used with fish. The arbitrary name doesn't provide any assistance in learning and will need more advertising dollars, but has the virtue of being more flexible if there are line extensions or repositioning tactics. Arbitrary names often are chosen because they are short and easy to pronounce.

Setting objectives will guide anyone involved in the task of generating lists of potential names. Along with objectives, management must develop criteria for the name; these criteria are more general and act as guidelines to creative thinking.

Ogilvy & Mather has composed a list of issues to consider in naming a new product.[3] They say that several important issues relevant to the brand name are that

- *The name should give meaning to the brand.* For example, Mr. Clean tells what the cleanser will do and creates an animated spokesperson to represent the brand.

- *The name should be part of the position.* For example, Campbell's Chunky Soup shows how the brand differs from the competition.

- *The name should be easy for the consumer to use and remember.* For example, Hamburger Helper is descriptive and also presents the position of the brand.

- *The name should show the promise of the product.* No Pest Strip, Die Hard, Roast 'n' Boast, Easy Off, and Beauty Rest all make a promise on behalf of the product.

- *The name should tell the consumer what the product is.* Some poor examples are Fact, Shake, Cue, and Adulton; it is hard to guess what these products are. Some good examples are No Doz, Electra Perk, Tanya, and Slender. See if you can tell what each of the eight products are.*

- *The name should be unique.* It should not allow the consumer to confuse one brand with another. Poor examples are Sinarest, Sineoff, Sinex, Sina Kare, and Sinutab; these all have been over the counter sinus medications at one time or another; their similar names will keep any one from dominating. A more unique name is that of Screaming Yellow Zonkers, although this name fails to meet other earlier criteria.

Many old established products have survived over the years with names that violate the Ogilvy & Mather guidelines (e.g., Michelob, Pall Mall, Chevrolet), but these names were established at a time of simpler communications, a slower pace, and less competition. Now it is important to ensure that the brand name is consistent with these guidelines.

A second important area with regard to the name concerns whether it should be an extension of the existing line (family brand name) or whether it should get its own new brand name. Some guidelines from Trout and Ries are:[4]

- *If the new product has something unique to offer,* give it a new name. Do not diminish the uniqueness by tying it to something else. The tie connotes a similarity that should be avoided.

- *If the new product has more marketplace potential than the old existing line,* give it a new name. The goodness of the new product may be diminished by association with the old.

- *If the new product does not fit the image of the parent company,* give it a new name. Extending the old name in this case would hurt both the new and the old products by confusing consumers.

---

*Fact, Shake, Cue, and Adulton are a low-tar cigarette *and* a toothpaste; a soap; a toothpaste; and a cough medicine, respectively. The well-named products are a stimulant, coffee blended for percolators, a suntan lotion, and a diet drink, respectively.

■ *If the budget for the new product introduction is limited,* consider a line extension name. It is cheaper to create quick awareness with a line extension. This is especially true if the existing line is well known.

■ *If rapid distribution is needed,* consider a line extension. It may be easier to get retailer acceptance of the new product when it has clear linkages to successful existing products.

The last two guidelines advocate a line extension under certain conditions. Note that the benefits in both cases are short run. If a brand offers a unique benefit in the long run, it should have its own unique name to emphasize that benefit. This leads to a last reason for a line extension. If the new product has no uniqueness but is a competent "me-too" product, then a line extension may be useful in creating some identity that it might not otherwise achieve.

Line extensions seem to be increasing in use. In recent years, Procter & Gamble has line extended to introduce

- Spic & Span pine-scented liquid cleaner
- Tide liquid detergent
- Ivory liquid soap
- Ivory shampoo and conditioner
- Crest toothpaste in a pump dispenser
- Folger's instant decaffeinated coffee.[5]

In some cases, these products try to increase the efficiency of advertising by trading off an existing trusted image. In other cases, the products are defensive moves to keep another firm's introduction in check. As product proliferation continues, there is less chance to introduce a unique new brand; in such cases new brands with minor differences may be more likely to trade off existing names and images.

In addition to these criteria put forth by Ogilvy & Mather and Trout and Ries, others have also been suggested. Stern[6] writes that the name

■ *Should be easily pronounced*   People may be embarrassed to ask for something that they may mispronounce.

■ *Should have no negative connotations*   Opium perfume may imply excitement to some but might be offensive to many. It may be that those who would be offended are not in the target market, but this name may lead to strategic problems in the future. Who knows what sort of negative news events could impact on the brand's position.

If the product is to be marketed internationally, there are more potential problems. What does the name mean in other languages? Standard Oil of New Jersey had considered Enco as a brand name until they learned that this name meant "stalled engine" in Japanese. A European sparkling water company found it would have trouble using its name in the United States. Its name is "Pschitt." The "P" is silent.

Moran[7] adds that the name

■ *Should not be a vague concept*   Gillette's disposable razor is named Good News. The name doesn't tie to anything. Almost. It does tie to a packaged cereal and a bra that have the same name.

Table 19.1 summarizes data collected by McNeal and Zeren and shows the criteria actually used by the firm in their study. The list is fairly consistent with

Table 19.1 Criteria used as guides in brand name selection

Criteria	Number of firms using (n = 82)	Per-centage
Descriptive of product benefits	48	58.5
Memorable	38	46.3
Fit with company image and other products' image	38	46.3
Trademark availability	28	34.1
Promotable and advertisable	18	22.0
Uniqueness vs. competition	18	22.0
Length	13	15.9
Ease of pronunciation	12	14.6
Positive connotations to potential users	11	13.4
Suited to package	5	6.1
Modern or contemporary	3	3.7
Understandable	2	2.4
Persuasive	2	2.4

Source: James U. McNeal and Linda M. Zeren, "Brand Name Selection for Consumer Products," *MSU Business Topics,* Spring 1981, p. 37.

the items previously mentioned. The only new issue mentioned in the study was *trademark availability.* This issue will be discussed below.

Generating brand names   Once objectives and criteria have been set, an attempt should be made to generate large numbers of suitable names. Most efforts in this direction are done by brainstorming; several key people get together and create a list by bouncing ideas off one another and building on each other's ideas. A few firms report using computer programs for this purpose also.

In addition, there are consulting firms that specialize in name generation and assessment. NameLab, Inc. of San Francisco, for example, uses staff linguists to compile a lexicon of semantic and symbolic fragments from Greek, Latin, and other root forms of English. These fragments can be combined to form new brand names. This method of name generation is based on an associative model of memory that assumes that learning occurs through a chain of memory links such that a stimulus word leads to a chain of associations. It is important to generate names that bring to mind appropriate symbols, concepts, and images.[8]

Screening or qualifying the potential brand name for appropriateness to the firm's image and/or the image of its products   The large set of names that was generated without critical evaluation is now pared down. First, all names must be checked in terms of the objectives and criteria. Those that remain will be assessed in terms of appropriateness.

One way to do this is by using expert judgment. The list is circulated to internal experts who select and delete names. (These experts may come from the firm, the agency, or may include other trusted individuals. Using the wife of the CEO is probably not a good idea because it is later politically difficult to refuse her idea.) This process leads to a new list that is again judged; the process is repeated until few names remain.

At NameLab, names are chosen because they are memorable or easy to learn and because they contain a number of coding cues. Memorable names are more meaningful and are more likely to be retained. Therefore, One-A-Day is a better name than Theragram-M for a vitamin supplement.

A new name also provides cues in four ways. The cues can be

- *Phonetic*   the name has memorable language patterns of sound and rhythm
- *Semantic*   the name provides a meaning
- *Physical*   the name evokes physical sensations
- *Emotional*   the name evokes feelings[9]

These cues all provide input into the brand's image.

Researching consumers' choices, preferences, and opinions of the remaining names   McNeal and Zeren reported that 89% of the respondent firms conducted some consumer research on names. Generally, consumers were given a choice based on the product concept or the actual product, and asked to select the name felt to be most suitable. In another method, consumers were asked to judge the names on an adjective checklist similar to that used for commercial testing.

Investigating a trademark search for the small number of remaining potential brand users   When a name is selected and used, it becomes a trademark. The firm's rights to this name are derived from commercial usage of the name; the name can also be registered with the U.S. Patent & Trademark Office under the Trademark Act of 1946 (also known as the Lanham Act). While it is not necessary to register a name, doing so gives the firm a stronger legal claim if the name is infringed upon.

Before using a new name it is wise to do a trademark search to see if the name is already being used or registered. If it is, the firm will need to find another name, buy the name from the other firm, or prepare itself for a likely lawsuit.

A new name cannot be registered if it is a generic word (Apple brand apples cannot be registered but Apple brand computers can); if the new mark will cause confusion with an old mark it also cannot be used.

Before a mark can be registered, it must be in commercial use. Many large firms build up a bank of desirable names by using them briefly and thus protecting them for the time when the name is really desired. After registering, the name must be renewed after six years to show active use and then again every 20 years.[10]

Selecting the final brand name   After the above steps have been completed, a name can be selected. The above process should increase the probability of the name being useful to the company. The selected name should be relevant, easy to learn, acceptable to consumers, and legally available.

Packaging

The history of product packaging in the United States parallels the history of retailing; as packaging changes occurred, retailer changes followed. For example, the invention of air-tight containers allowed a change in food storage to occur. This led to the advent of small containers and to the demise of large barrels of products at the retail location. Similar changes occurred during the nineteenth century to make personal interactions between the grocer and consumer less necessary. In 1819 the Underwood Company began bottling jams and pickles; in

1860 Dr. Lyon began to package tooth powder; and in 1899 the National Biscuit Company put its product in a box rather than a large barrel.

Each of these innovations helped to better protect the product and also allowed the manufacturer to deliver a message to the consumer at the retail location without the aid of a salesperson. As the technology improved for protection, preservation, and message delivery, there was more opportunity for self-service and home storage. With the development of refrigeration and the automobile, fewer and larger purchasing trips were possible and markets grew. Again, the trend continued to less retailer personal assistance and more self-service, and, with these trends, there was an increased need for the package to communicate the merits of the brand.

More recently, retailer trends have had a growing impact on packaging and have forced marketers to consider the package as a strategic tool of ever-increasing importance. As the trend to smaller retailer sales forces continues, the package and other P-O-P display items have become more sophisticated tools of communication.

At the same time, the cost of advertising has increased at a rapid rate; this change has also forced marketers to look for alternative forms of communications, and, again, the package has emerged as a logical tool. Because packaging is necessary to protect the product, the media/delivery costs are close to zero. After producing an effective message, the package is an ideal medium to deliver it to the consumer at the time that purchase decisions are being made. While this logic has been accepted for many years for grocery products, manufacturers of other products that come in packages are also beginning to realize the potential of this tool. Housewares, small appliances, toys, games, and many other products are now being sold with little retailer assistance and more reliance on more sophisticated packaging.

The purpose of the package

The purpose of the package is twofold:

1. *Physical*   to protect the product from the environment, to keep all the little pieces from rolling around the floor, and to act as a dispenser for the product

2. *Communications*   to identify the contents, to inform the consumer of attributes, and to persuade the consumer of the benefits

Given these purposes, the marketing department should be as involved as the engineering department in the package design. While physically protecting the product, the manufacturer can, at virtually no cost, also communicate to consumers. While communicating, the package can also attract attention to itself and provide the distinctiveness that should be part of the position. Furthermore, the size of the package can serve to attract new users. For example, as the number of single-person households increases, there is more need for individual serving-sized packages.

At this basic level, the package acts as a substitute for personal selling. It must deliver the product promise and relate itself back to earlier messages seen or heard by the consumer. One way to do this is by being physically different from other packages.

Finally, marketers should ensure that the package is useful. It is all too easy for a stubborn package to send a consumer to another brand. If there are few differences between brands, the convenience of the package may become an important factor. For another viewpoint on this issue, see Figure 19.1, a letter from an unhappy consumer.

In addition to correcting flaws in current packaging modes, marketers also can get involved in new packaging innovations. In a recent article, Margulies described four new technological breakthroughs that should change packaging and communications in several industries.[11]

- *Aseptic packaging* allows milk to be sold without refrigeration while increasing shelf life to 90 days.
- *Wine in pop-top cans* is lighter and easier to handle yet maintains the wine's taste.
- *The retort pouch* allows precooked food to be kept on shelves without freezing and allows opening and closing of the pouch without spoilage of leftovers.
- *Liquid soap in a pump container* reduces waste and minimizes the residue of melted soap bars.

Each of these innovations presents both problems and opportunities. While the new package shows an innovation and sets the brand apart, marketers will need to show that the package is a benefit and not just a change.

Figure 19.1 *Some designs should just be torn asunder*

Mr. Robert D. Stuart
Chairman and Chief Executive
   Officer
The Quaker Oats Co.
Chicago, Ill.

Dear Mr. Stuart:

I am an 86-year-old widow in fairly good health. (You may think of this as advanced age, but for me that description pertains to the years ahead. Nevertheless, if you decide to reply to this letter I wouldn't dawdle, actuarial tables being what they are.)

As I said, my health is fairly good. Feeble and elderly, as one understands these terms, I am not. My two Doberman Pinschers and I take a brisk 3-mile walk every day. They are two strong and energetic animals and it takes a bit of doing to keep "brisk" closer to stroll than to mad dash. But I manage because as yet I don't lack the strength. You will shortly see why this fact is relevant.

I am writing to call your attention to the cruel, deceptive and utterly mendacious copy on your Aunt Jemima butter milk complete pancake and waffle mix.

The words on your package read, "to open—press here and pull back."

Mr. Stuart, though I push and press and groan and strive and writhe and curse and sweat and jab and push, poke and ram . . . whew!— I have never once been able to do what the package instructs—to press here and pull back the son of a bitch.

It can't be done! Talk about failing strength! Have *you* ever tried and succeeded?

My late husband was a gun collector who among other lethal weapons kept a Thompson machine gun in a locked cabinet. It was a good thing that cabinet was locked. Oh, the number of times I was tempted to give your package a few short bursts.

That lock and a sense of ladylike delicacy kept me from pursuing that vengeful fantasy. Instead I keep a small cleaver in my pantry for those occasions when I need to open a package of your delicious Aunt Jemima pancakes.

For many years that whacking away with my cleaver served a dual purpose. Not only to open the damn package but also to vent my fury at your sadists who willfully and maliciously did design that torture apparatus that passes for a package.

Sometimes just for the hell of it I let myself get carried away. I don't

stop after I've lopped off the top. I whack away until the package is utterly destroyed in an outburst of rage, frustration and vindictiveness. I wind up with a floorful of your delicious Aunt Jemima pancake mix. But that's a small price to pay for the blessed release. (Anyway, the Pinschers lap up the mess.)

So many ingenious, considerate (even compassionate) innovations in package closures have been designed since Aunt Jemima first donned her red bandana. Wouldn't you consider the introduction of a more humane package to replace the example of marketing malevolence to which you resolutely cling? Don't you care, Mr. Stuart?

I really am writing this to be helpful and in that spirit I am sending a copy to Mr. Tucker, president of Container Corp. I'm sure their clever young designers could be of immeasurable help to you in this matter. At least I feel it's worth a try.

Really, Mr. Stuart, I hope you will not regard me as just another cranky old biddy. I am The Public, the source of your fortunes.

Ms. Roberta Pavloff
Malvern, Pa.

The package as an aid to learning

A typical nationally distributed grocery product may get 3 to 4 billion exposures per year of its package on the shelves of supermarkets at no cost to the manufacturer (80 million households with one shopping trip per week equals over 4 billion trips). That many exposures of a commercial on network television would cost about $25 million (250 insertions in programs with 20 ratings would yield approximately 4 billion exposures; at a cost of $100,000 per insertion, the total cost is $25 million).

Given that the manufacturer must wrap up all the little flakes of corn or light bulbs to keep them on the shelf, there is virtually no additional cost associated with the communications aspect of the package (other than design costs). The package, therefore, is certainly an efficient way of presenting information.

Bettman[12] has theorized that for many products, consumers make brand choice decisions in the store and that these decisions may be based on recognition of the package. A recent study by the Point-of-Purchase Advertising Institute[13] supports this by showing that 60% of drugstore buying decisions are made in store. Table 19.2 shows these data by major product category. In this table, specifically planned purchases are decided upon before reaching the store while other decisions are made in store. Singh and Rothschild[14] found similar results in

Table 19.2 Amount of prepurchase planning done for drugstore items

Major product categories	Specifically planned	Generally planned	+	Substitute	+	Unplanned	=	Store decisions
Total Study								
Average	41.0%	22.5%		4.0%		33.5%		60.0%
Personal Care	35.3%	24.7%		9.4%		30.6%		64.7%
Magazines/Newspapers/Books/								
Stationery	41.6%	28.6%		1.3%		28.6%		58.4%
Snack Foods	22.2%	23.8%		4.8%		49.2%		77.8%
Drugs/Medicine	51.1%	12.8%		6.4%		29.8%		48.9%
Tobacco Products	66.7%	8.9%		—		24.4%		33.3%
Hardware/								
Housewares	16.7%	40.5%		2.4%		40.5%		83.3%
Prescriptions	100.0%	—		—		—		—
Cosmetics	30.8%	23.1%		15.4%		30.8%		69.2%
Soft Goods/Personal								
Accessories	13.0%	39.1%		—		47.8%		87.0%
Non-Alcoholic								
Beverages	33.3%	11.1%		—		56.6%		66.7%
Alcoholic								
Beverages	80.0%	—		—		20.0%		20.0%
Photographic								
Equipment	70.0%	—		—		30.0%		30.0%
Garden Supplies	50.0%	50.0%		—		—		50.0%
Jewelry	—	20.0%		—		80.0%		100.0%
Automotive								
Supplies	20.0%	20.0%		—		60.0%		80.0%

Source: "Pilot Study Finds Final Product Choice Usually Made in Store," *Marketing News,* 6 August 1982, p. 5.

a pretest; in a study of grocery shopping lists, they found that most consumers wrote down product names but not brand names.

According to Bettman, some brand choice decisions are made in the home prior to a shopping trip. These decisions are based on recall of information about the product because alternative brand choice cues are unavailable; many routinized decisions, based on past experiences, are made in this way. He suggests that other brand choice decisions are made in the store. These occur when certain conditions exist:

1. *When the consumer needs comparative information between brands*   Here the package should show relevant attribute data.

2. *When the consumer has several acceptable brands in mind*   Here the package should aid recognition of the brand and persuade the consumer of the rightness of choosing it.

This latter condition can be enhanced by coordinating the package and the advertising. Bettman suggests that this can be done in two ways to help learning occur.

1. *The advertising should show the package*   In this way the brand information is linked to the visual package; this information will be more easily retrieved from memory when the consumer is in the store and sees the cue of the package.

2. *The package should show a scene from the advertising*   Again, the content of the commercial is brought into the store and the package helps elicit information from memory.

Figures 19.2 and 19.3 show two examples of this from the breakfast cereal product class. The Total package shows the 100% shield; the photoboard scene

Figure 19.2   Total package and photoboard

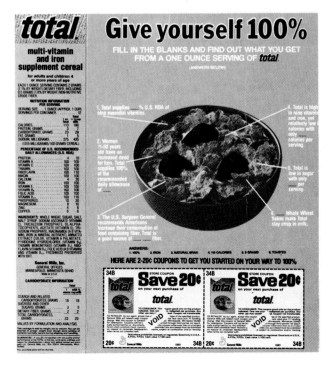

Figure 19.2 *continued*

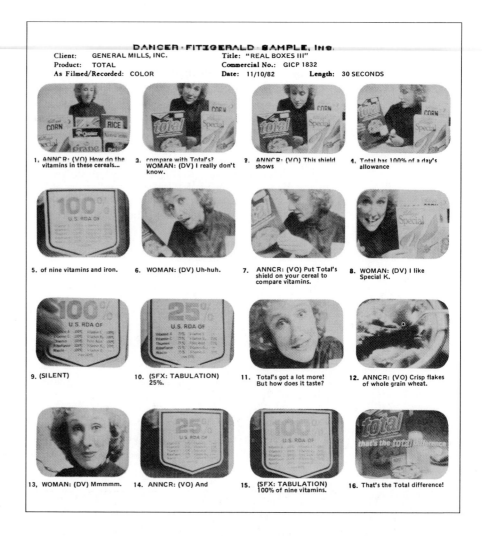

shows the package and the 100% shield with a list of vitamins and minerals. Both clearly complement one another and highlight the brand's position.

The Total package has other notable features. There is no wasted space on this package: The front panel reiterates and reinforces the advertising and also announces two coupons on the back panel. When the consumer turns to the back panel to check on the bounce-back coupon, a short quiz is found. Given typical breakfast table activities, the quiz will be attended to. The quiz can be answered by reading the front of the box or watching the commercial. Again, learning is reinforced through a simple device. Next, one side panel gives required nutritional information, reiterating the brand's position as established on the front and back panels. The second side panel introduces a line extension; Wheat Total is now joined by Corn Total. Finally, at the bottom of the same side panel there is a coupon for a free premium. Offering a booklet on nutrition is certainly consistent with the brand's position. This package has no wasted space; it will be in the home for a couple of weeks, and it will continue to help deliver the brand's message. In addition, it is a vehicle for repeat purchase coupons and for the added reinforcer of the premium.

The Wheaties example combines package and advertising with a contest. The advertising campaign began with athletes singing the praises of Wheaties in television commercials: "Before I ride my racing steedies, I get the eaties for my Wheaties." These musical jingles created top-of-mind awareness of the brand in a memorable way and showed the package. The commercials were followed by a package and contest that aided in home recognition and solidified the memory trace. The back of the package asked users to create new jingles, and this led to countless breakfast eaters (with nothing else to do) sitting at the breakfast table creating jingles. What is important here is not the quality of the jingles, but the reinforcement of the mnemonic device through the package and the contest. This is a creative use of the package to reinforce the commercial.

Figure 19.3   Wheaties photoboard and package

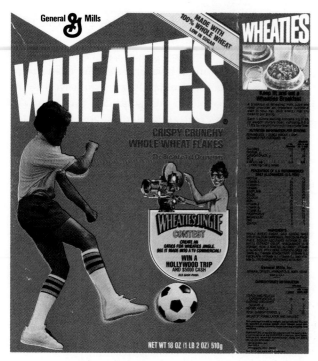

Figure 19.3   *continued*

Criteria for assessing package effectiveness

Considering the above issues leads one to set a criteria for assessing package effectiveness. The following five criteria were suggested by Triestman:[15]

1. *Visibility*   This is the most basic criterion. The package must be seen and must get attention in the store before it can accomplish any of its other tasks. Visibility can be attained through an unusual shape, dramatic coloring, dramatic graphics, or by combining several package facings to create an overall visual image on the shelf that is greater than that of any single package.

2. *Recognition and readability*   The package must easily and quickly communicate brand name, product class, and key selling points. Brand name or visual cue should be large enough for instant identification; the package visual should quickly identify the product. Note that both the Wheaties and Total boxes do this very well. The tie of advertising and package as discussed above is crucial in aiding learning so that recognition will be instantaneous. More and more, the package must be the star of the advertising so that it can do its job at the retail location where there is no sales force support.

3. *Conveying the position/image*   The package must capture the uniqueness of the brand and convey it. This can be a problem if the actual product is small (such as a cosmetic), but the problem can be overcome by a large cardboard backing and blister pack. This form of enlarged packaging was first used to discourage pilfering, but it can also be used to present a message.

The package must give the appropriate cues to the consumer through its shape and visuals. If the package violates perceptual conventions, it won't convey the correct image and will turn away consumers. Soft drinks can physically be stored in containers that look like milk containers but this would confuse consumers—so would chocolate milk in a pink container.

Packaging must convey the correct perceptual cues. This is especially true when the product class features commodity-like brands. Blind taste tests of unlabeled beer, labeled beer, and improperly labeled beer yield very different preferences, yet the only difference between the three is in the packaging. If brands are similar, the package *is* the product; it may be the only distinguishing feature that separates brands.

4. *Aesthetic appeal* The package must look nice to the purchaser and must also look nice in the home if it needs to be displayed. Kleenex, for example, sets itself apart on the basis of many shapes and visual designs in its packaging.

In another example, Stern[16] reports that a roll-on deodorant was tested in consumers' homes to see which combination of color schemes on the container was most preferred. All consumers received the same deodorant, but the color of the package differed across test groups. One set of colors led to favorable responses: it dried immediately; it smelled pleasant; it lasted up to 12 hours. A second set of colors did less well: the product had too strong an aroma and lasted only a few hours. The third set of colors on the container led to an irritating underarm rash and three visits to a dermatologist. There was only one product; the aesthetics of the package influenced responses.

5. *Persuasion* If the package does well on its first four tasks, then it can be called upon to persuade consumers to make a purchase. Having done the first four, persuasion and purchase should naturally follow.

A similar set of criteria has been suggested by Twedt.[17] These criteria compose the acronym VIEW:

- *Visability* Is it easily seen?
- *Information* Does it communicate the proper benefits?
- *Emotional appeal* Does it communicate product personality?
- *Workability* Does the package protect and preserve the product appropriately?

Assessing package effectiveness

Three research methods are commonly used to assess the worth of the package.

Eye tracking studies This method has been discussed as part of copy testing. Its value in package testing is to see where consumers look on the package so that the key verbal and visual information will be presented in the best location and will lead to the easiest sequence of information gathering.

Eye tracking can also be used to determine how consumers respond to an aisle of shelf facings. Does the firm's package attract attention in a cluttered environment? There is now also a two-ounce television camera that can be attached to eye glasses and can follow a consumer's progress through a store, showing eye movement in actual shopping situations.

Tachistoscope This device is used to show a subject a visual stimulus for a very brief time (as little as 1/1,000 of a second). In testing packages, various designs can be shown for varying, but very short, periods of time to learn what items people can identify quickly. The design that communicates in the briefest period of time is felt to do best in terms of visibility, recognition, and/or readability. It should do the best job, therefore, of attracting attention in the cluttered and noisy environment of the retail outlet.

Matched market test   This method of experimentation has been discussed earlier in copy testing and will be expanded upon in Part 8. One example of such a test for packaging would be the case of the three deodorants discussed earlier; similar samples used different packages in this test. More traditional tests would put different package designs in different markets to see which one leads to the best sales response. In such a test, any advertising must also be modified to show the appropriate package being tested in that market. It is necessary to keep all other marketing variables constant across the markets so that the only variable to influence differential sales is the package.

Coordinating brand name, packaging, and the position

This is the tale of how Taster's Choice took control of the freeze-dried coffee market in the late 1960s and early 1970s even though Maxim was the first brand in that new category and spent more on advertising. It serves as a classic example of developing a position in the marketplace and supporting it through coordinated advertising, branding, and packaging. Most of the information reported here comes from the management of Taster's Choice, so the story may be a bit slanted. Regardless of any reporting bias, the end result was a clear market share victory for Taster's Choice.

After a slow start, instant coffees became highly popular in the United States. By the mid 1960s, the concept of instant coffee had been widely accepted and consumers were looking for a better tasting product. Freeze-dried coffee filled this need, and Maxim was the first on the market. Taster's Choice was next, and several others followed.

Maxim held an early market share lead and kept it for several years, but by 1971 Taster's Choice had a 14.5% share while Maxim's share was only 11.5%. In 1970 Maxim's management spent $9.5 million on promotional support while the management of Taster's Choice spent only $8.6 million. Between 1966 and 1970, $24 million was spent on Maxim, and $19 million was spent on Taster's Choice. The following paragraphs describe some decisions made by the two manufacturers of what is essentially a commodity product. First, Maxim.

The name, Maxim, was close to a line extension; it was a spin-off of Maxwell House. Management seems to have been trying to trade off an established brand name, but it is possible that this strategy led consumers to perceive Maxim as being close to existing brands and not as a new and different-tasting product. Initially this gave Maxim a market share lead but much of this lead could have derived from brand switchers going from Maxwell House to Maxim; there may have been a cannibalization problem.

Furthermore, the name Maxim sounded modern and technological. Obviously an attribute of freeze-dried coffee was modern technology, but consumers buy benefits, not attributes. Maxim showed attributes but not the resultant benefits. The benefit of freeze-dried coffee was good taste, not technology. The name did not establish the position; it merely announced a modern product from Maxwell House.

The Maxim package at the time of introduction was a standard instant coffee jar. The lettering and coloring was the same as that of Maxwell House instant coffee; the label said "from Maxwell House." Again there was no differentiation from the old brand; nothing on the package stood out or told the consumer that this was an exciting, new product.

Taster's Choice is made by Nestle. Nestle was not perceived by consumers, prior to Taster's Choice, as having a great deal of competence in the coffee market; Nescafé was never a big mover in the instant coffee market. As a result, the management of the new freeze-dried brand was committed to being divorced from Nescafé as much as possible. This led to a strategy whereby Taster's Choice did not cannibalize, but rather gained from both instant and regular coffee users. The dark cloud of Nescafé had a silver lining for Taster's Choice.

The name and package design tried to establish the benefit of freeze-dried coffee, i.e., good taste. The different name, Taster's Choice, clearly established taste as the prime benefit and positioned the brand far from weak-tasting instant coffees.

The package design further attempted to stress this difference in taste. The jar was not cylindrical, but rather was a masculine shape with large shoulders and tapered waist to connote robustness. The jar was different from others and stood out in ways other than its shape. The label was unique; it showed a man "tasting his choice." The label was also smaller than that of other brands so that consumers could see the actual product. They could see that freeze-dried coffee was not a powder, but rather looked more like little chunks or pebbles. It became apparent to consumers that this brand was physically different from its competitors. As a tribute to Taster's Choice management, Maxim changed its jar and label a few years ago to more closely resemble the Taster's Choice jar.

The result of this positioning battle was a market share victory for Taster's Choice. Figure 19.4 is an intuitive perceptual map of the coffee market of that time which shows Taster's Choice clearly separated from the competition while Maxim was seen as a minor change from other instant coffees. This case clearly shows the importance of good packaging and branding.

Branding and packaging have become important parts of the communications mix. As shopping becomes a more self-service operation, these areas become even more vital. The brand needs a memorable name and package to keep it from

Figure 19.4 *Intuitive perceptual map of the coffee market (circa 1971)*

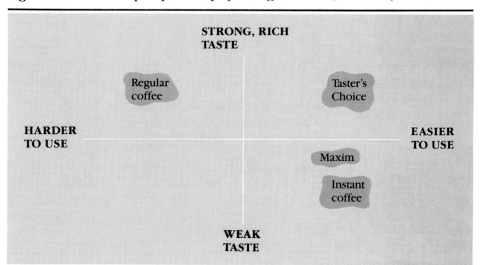

being lost in a sea of other names and packages. All elements of the communications mix must work together. The brand name connotes the position, and the package is the last chance for the manufacturer to talk to the consumer.

Point-of-Purchase Displays

A major purpose of the package is to communicate with consumers at the time and place of purchase. As managers have discovered that the package is an important tool for getting one last message across, they have also become more interested in the value of point-of-purchase (P-O-P) materials.

The world of retailing has changed dramatically in the past decade to the point where there are now few clerks available to help consumers, and most stores are essentially self-service; grocery stores have been this way for quite some time. In addition, retailers are remaining open longer hours, which means that at any given time a shopper is even less likely to encounter a capable clerk. While these trends are purposeful on the part of the retailer, they create problems for the consumer and the manufacturer.

At the same time, consumers also have been changing. They are increasingly looking for sale items and waiting for deals before stocking up. This behavior is a direct result of the growing use of promotions which seems to have taught consumers that everything goes on sale at least once every nine days. In looking for deals, consumers have become very attentive to in-store messages; because there are no clerks to communicate with, point-of-purchase materials have become increasingly important.

Further evidence for the importance of P-O-P is apparent in Table 19.2 earlier in this chapter and in other research done by the Point of Purchase Advertising Institute (POPAI—pronounced "Popeye"). POPAI reports that across a wide variety of product classes, approximately two-thirds of brand choice decisions are made in store. In addition, as seen in Figure 19.5, the influence of P-O-P sources can rival that of mass media advertising for some product classes.

Figure 19.5 *New product information sources*

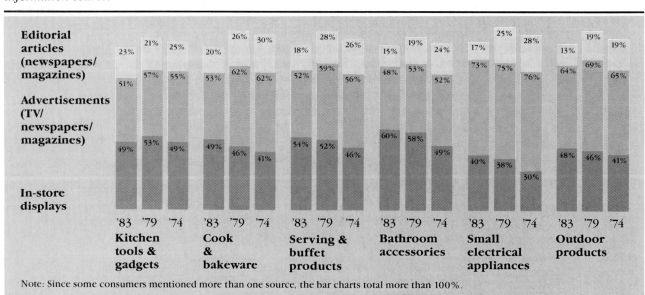

Note: Since some consumers mentioned more than one source, the bar charts total more than 100%.

P-O-P materials have always been important for durable and expensive products because trial and demonstrations are important to learning; more recently consumers have sought out more in-store information for less expensive durable goods as well. These gross patterns of merchandising and shopping all point to an increased need for P-O-P materials.

Manufacturers are beginning to see these trends and are spending ever-increasing sums on P-O-P. In 1983, $6.2 billion were spent on this form of message transmission;[18] while this is much less than what is spent on advertising or promotions, it is much more than the $2.5 billion spent on P-O-P in 1975.[19] On a percentage basis, P-O-P is growing faster than advertising or promotions; on an absolute dollar basis, the growth is slower.

Why use point-of-purchase materials?

There are several reasons to use P-O-P displays and materials:

- *Increased learning*   The above discussion clearly outlines the value of P-O-P for learning. The in-store environment is important because it is the last chance for the brand to make a plea to the consumer; it is the last chance to reinforce the earlier advertising messages and to help the consumer recognize the brand and its key benefits.

- *Increased purchase behavior*   In addition to the impact on learning, there also seems to be a strong impact on purchase behavior. Because a high percentage of food and drug purchases are unplanned, the in-store messages influence behavior. Figure 19.6 and Table 19.3 both show data to support this. In Figure 19.6, Nielsen data show sales increases of 20 to 90% when P-O-P displays are present, depending on the product category. Table 19.3 shows that P-O-P signage can help both advertised and unadvertised products when the message concerns a benefit. The price-oriented P-O-P message only helped in the case of the advertised product.

- *Lower cost*   Except for extreme cases, advertising production plus media costs will greatly exceed those of P-O-P. In terms of CPM, it has been estimated that television advertising is 10 to 100 times as expensive.[20] Given the difficulties

Figure 19.6   *Increase in sales by promotional display.*

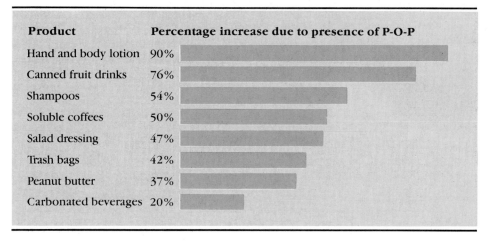

Product	Percentage increase due to presence of P-O-P
Hand and body lotion	90%
Canned fruit drinks	76%
Shampoos	54%
Soluble coffees	50%
Salad dressing	47%
Trash bags	42%
Peanut butter	37%
Carbonated beverages	20%

Table 19.3 Effect of point-of-purchase display on sales

Condition	Average Daily Sales	Change Relative to no P-O-P
Unadvertised — no sign	8.33 units	—
Unadvertised — price only P-O-P	7.42 units	(−11%)
Unadvertised — benefit P-O-P	12.17 units	+46%
Advertised — no sign	9.08 units	—
Advertised — price only P-O-P	10.83 units	+19%
Advertised — benefit P-O-P	13.17 units	+45%

Source: The Point-of-Purchase Advertising Institute *POPAI News* 8, no. 2 (1984), p. 7.

of estimating viewership of an in-store display, these figures should be accepted with caution although the general relation is probably correct.

▪ *Uncontrollable changes in retailers and consumers*   These were discussed earlier. Manufacturers must respond to changes in the retail environment in order to remain successful.

▪ *Easy evaluation of impact*   P-O-P programs can be easily evaluated through matched market or even matched store tests.

Features of good P-O-P devices

A typical supermarket may carry 8,000 to 10,000 items, but the store manager can only use a small number of displays. As a result most displays offered by manufacturers are never used by retailers. What features make a P-O-P device appealing to retailers?

▪ *Monetary incentives*   As discussed earlier in the Promotions part, retailers are more likely to use any device if they are paid to do so. Usually these incentives are given as a discount on some number of cases of the product in return for a specified placement of the P-O-P materials.

▪ *Advertising support*   If the product in question is advertised, it will probably sell better and, again, will be more acceptable to the retailer. In addition, the product will sell best if the P-O-P and advertising are tied together by a common theme.

▪ *Small size*   If the P-O-P doesn't use a lot of floor or shelf space, it will be more likely to be used. Space is a precious commodity; the display that can help sales without using much space has a better chance of being implemented. P-O-P should be designed to fit specific spaces in the retail outlet.

▪ *Eye appeal*   When designing a display, its location in the store must be considered. The P-O-P must fit into the aesthetics of the retail location as well as into the space constraints.

▪ *Traffic shopper*   The P-O-P must be so dramatic that shoppers stop to look at it. For example, the 1983 POPAI Display of the Year Award was given to Pepsi Cola. Figure 19.7 shows the display; it is a six pack of Pepsi that seems to fall off the shelf but is mounted on a battery-operated mechanical arm that causes it to tilt forward off the shelf and then pull back. Surprised shoppers run to the display

***Figure 19.*7** *Pepsi Cola point-of-purchase display*

to try to catch the six pack, which seems as if it is about to fall off the shelf. In test market, the display increased sales by 14 cases per week.

▪ *Easy to set up*   If the P-O-P device is difficult to put together, it has a poor chance of being used. The P-O-P should be easy to assemble, or the manufacturer's sales force or representatives should set it up. The retailer doesn't have the time or interest to devote to the P-O-P unless there is some incentive to do so.

▪ *Tie to other items*   Another incentive to the retailer is for the product in question to tie in with other products sold by the retailer. In this way the retailer may get increased sales of other products along with the increased sales of the P-O-P product. An example would be a P-O-P display for shortcake that includes coupons for concurrent purchases of strawberries and heavy cream. In this way the space given to the P-O-P not only sells its own product but helps the retailer sell two other products.

▪ *Save retailer labor*   One value to a retailer is for the P-O-P to help reduce work. Some displays are designed to keep the product lined up more neatly; a display that keeps 97 shades of lipstick in order is useful; so is a gravity-loaded dispenser for single cans of soft drink.

▪ *Market the P-O-P*   Devices that just show up in the mail are less likely to be used than those that are delivered personally. In the latter case a persuasive appeal can be made to the retailer to show how the display can benefit both parties. The retailer must be sold on the idea of using a particular P-O-P.

One of the most difficult problems in using a P-O-P device is in getting the retailer to accept it, because there is strong competition among manufacturers to get a device onto the retail floor. Those that win will have some appeal to the retailer, and the best appeal is the expectation of increased sales and revenues. To this end, 80% of P-O-P materials are given to retailers at no charge while the remainder are sold at a low cost, given away with some minimal purchase, or sold to the retailer at full price. Displays similar to the one in Figure 19.7 were sold by Pepsi to retailers at a cost of $10 to $25.

Types of P-O-P devices

The range of potential in-store advertising materials is quite broad. Some of the more common types are

1. *Outside signs* that tell the consumer that the brand is sold at that location. Soft drinks, beers, and cigarettes are strong users of this display form as shown in Figure 19.8.

2. *Window displays* that show a simulated product usage situation or merely show the product. Department and specialty stores commonly use this type of display; an example can be seen in Figure 19.9.

3. *Counter displays* that allow self-service for small, light items. These are commonly seen above checkout counters of supermarkets for cigarettes, gum, candy, and magazines. Figure 19.10 shows an example.

4. *Display racks* that hold and show products at the end of the checkout counter or at the end of a grocery aisle. Figure 19.11 shows an example.

Figure 19.8 *Outdoor retail displays*

Figure 19.9 Retail
window display

Figure 19.10 Checkout counter display

Figure 19.11 End-of-aisle display

T·H·E   I·N·S·I·D·E   O·U·T·L·O·O·K

Herbert M. Meyers

Managing Partner, Gerstman+Meyers Inc.

*Herbert M. Meyers has been a specialist in marketing-related de-
sign for major corporations since 1955. Born in Germany, Herb
Meyers graduated from Pratt Institute and gained substantial experience as Design Director at Mead Packaging and International Paper, and as Vice President at a major design firm.*

*In 1970, he joined Richard Gerstman to form
Gerstman+Meyers Inc., New York. The firm specializes in package and corporate identification design and currently employs a
staff of 45 marketing and design specialists servicing over 100
clients internationally, including Ralston Purina, Pillsbury,
Nabisco, Johnson & Johnson, and Eastman Kodak.*

Changing the Package

One of the first marketing decisions the graduated marketing student may very likely face
when entering the "real world" of consumer
product marketing could easily be a packaging
decision. At that time, you may find that packaging is a complex and multifaceted area, offering
both opportunities and perplexing problems.

This is especially true if the product is a leading brand among many competitive brands, each
offering strong product characteristics. The decision you are facing may be in connection with a
new line extension or a slumping sales curve—
at any rate, your decision may well be whether
to retain the current package; whether to modify
it slightly; or whether to redesign it completely
to gain the desired marketing advantage.

It is an old idiom among marketing people
and package designers that the first thing the
new marketing or product manager does upon
being appointed to his or her position is to redesign the package. It is hard to resist the temptation of making an immediate splash as "the

new cat in the old yard" by changing the most
visible part of the assignment—the package. But
the danger of doing so without careful planning
is greater than you might realize. Whenever design decisions have to be made with regard to
the packages of major, well-established brands,
the equity that the packages have built over the
years in the consumer's mind must be carefully
weighed.

Some packages yield more easily to change
than others. The packages of such products as
cereals and pet foods, which are often closely related to the changing advertising themes for
these products, tend to undergo frequent and almost casual package design changes. Children's
cereals, in particular, are frequently tied directly
to Saturday morning television cartoons or to
computer games, both of which are in a constant
state of flux.

Beauty aids packages rise and fall with the
popularity of their products among male and female consumers. These packages sell images that

ride the crest of current fashion trends. Since fashion changes frequently, the packages change just as frequently.

But some packages defy change, running the risk of losing current users. Budweiser found out that even the minutest change on their can or bottle label is detected and viewed with suspicion by the frequent beer drinker, the brewer's most valuable asset. Chanel perfume would surely lose its loyal following if the square bottle, the diamond shaped stopper or the starkly simple black & white graphics were suddenly altered.

But there are also exceptions—sometimes surprising ones—that defy preconceived notions. When Coca-Cola changed its packages dramatically—design changes that anticipated the replacement of the then predominant "hobble skirt" glass bottle with the now totally accepted cans and plastic bottles—the Coca-Cola management was convinced that it had to make this drastic move away from the traditional package. They were right.

When Gerstman+Meyers Inc. recently redesigned a major packaging line for the cough/cold remedy market, we were dealing with a traditionally uninvolved consumer/user. Much to our client's surprise, consumer tests clearly isolated the most dramatic package design change as the clear winner—an opportunity that the company could not ignore. They went along with the difficult choice of reintroducing the line with completely new packaging graphics.

So when you enter the "real world" with your first job, beware of the temptation to become an instant hero at your company by making dramatic packaging changes. While package design improvements are certainly an opportunity with great potential that should be explored, make sure that you have thoroughly researched all roads leading to the best marketing solution before you make a move in any direction.

Be cautious of major packaging changes or introducing new packaging methods for products that are established or traditional in the market. Explore design modifications before you consider dramatic packaging changes. But if your planning and careful research indicate that a major package design change is your best opportunity to reach your marketing goal, then follow the courage of your conviction.

In any event, remember when it comes to package design, an ounce of careful preplanning will be worth a pound of potential trouble.

5. *Banners, posters, streamers, strips, and shelf talkers,* can be used anywhere in the store from the front window to the empty space above the shelves to the shelf itself. The shelf talker is a small sign attached to the grocery shelf at the brand's location.

In addition to these fairly traditional P-O-P displays, several new formats are either emerging or being tested for future use. While their purpose is to increase the manufacturer's sales, they also help increase the retailer's sales.

Displays are becoming more sophisticated in several ways. Motion displays have been shown to improve sales more than static displays. Motion holds attention and can be used in many ways. One place for motion is in the air space above the shelf; mobiles and giant product replicas can attract attention. The unused air space above the shelves is considered to be the last frontier of the retail outlet.

Shopping carts also can act as P-O-P displays. The outside front display can be seen by shoppers coming toward the cart. The inside front and the baby seat are seen by the user of the cart. Each of these spaces is now being rented by retailers to advertisers.

In-store broadcasting includes both audio and visual messages. In both cases, short commercial messages are interspersed between pieces of trivia and homemaker hints. The audio tracks can interrupt the store's background music system for several minutes of each hour. Video displays can be shown on television monitors that hang over checkout counters and give shoppers something to look at while waiting in line. In each case, the retailer gains revenues by allowing advertising into the store.

The computer age has also reached point-of-purchase displays. Mannington Mills has a computerized display in floor covering retail outlets to help consumers pick out appropriate patterns and colors. The terminal asks consumers eight questions about decor and then displays up to ten appropriate Mannington styles. When idle, the terminal beeps to attract customers. The cost to Mannington was $8 million for 700 units. On the other hand, the terminal helped customers better than did salespeople who were not able to remember the entire product line as well. It also encouraged salespeople to sell Mannington versus its competitors and helped to close sales on the customer's first visit.[21]

Shopping bags can be imprinted with ads and coupons. Redemption rates for these coupons has been around 6%. It has been speculated that the response rate is low because shoppers want to save whole bags for collecting garbage. As a result, some retailers are adding sheets of coupons to grocery bags with ads printed on the bags.[22]

The retail outlet is the last chance to make the sale and innovators are trying to capture every possible sale. The purposes of point-of-purchase displays are

1. To remind the consumer of the brand
2. To stimulate impulse purchases
3. To get extra shelf space for the brand

Summary

Brand loyalty is decreasing and brand proliferation is increasing. The number of retail clerks is decreasing and the cost of communications is increasing. The tools presented in this chapter help counteract these deteriorating forces by increasing the opportunities to communicate at a relatively low cost.

In order to be successful, these tools must tie into the decision sequence framework by being consistent with the objectives and position set earlier as well as the strategies developed for the other elements of the communications mix.

Selecting an appropriate name can go a long way toward establishing the position of the brand. Because the name appears in all communications, a meaningful one can help to establish the brand's identity at virtually no cost. Conversely, a nondescriptive name means that all other communications must work that much harder to achieve learning. Any brand with an arbitrarily chosen name can still become a success, but a name that fits the brand's position can aid learning significantly at a cost that is not appreciably different from the name that doesn't help.

Similarly, a brand with a poor package can also succeed, but the cost of a good package is quite low when compared to the cost of advertising. The package can communicate the brand's key benefits and does so at the time of purchase. If the advertising and package are well coordinated, the package will appear in the ad and a scene from the ad will appear on the package. In this way, the package can act as a memory cue to recall even more information about the brand.

Continuing in the same dimensions, the point-of-purchase display offers the same benefits as the package. P-O-P is a low-cost way to repeat a key aspect of the sales message one last time at the place where the consumer decision is made.

All three of these tools (brand name, packaging, and P-O-P) are often overlooked by managers in favor of more conventional advertising strategies. While advertising is generally a necessary component of the communications plan, the tools presented in this chapter are efficient low-cost items that need to be considered along with traditional advertising.

Discussion Questions

1. What unique assets do the brand name, packaging, and point-of-purchase materials each bring to the communications mix?

2. What attributes should a brand name have in order to best aid learning of its brand's position?

3. Look through a current Sunday newspaper FSI and find five new products. Assess their names with regard to the criteria discussed in this chapter. If a name does not meet the criteria, come up with a better one.

4. When should a new brand have a new name? Under what conditions is a line extension appropriate?

5. How should advertising and packaging be coordinated to assist learning?

6. What are the major criteria for evaluating the communicability of a package? Find packages for five products that are less than six months old and assess their packages on these criteria.

7. Why has there been such a great increase in the use of point-of-purchase materials in recent years? Do you feel that these retailer and consumer trends will continue or reverse themselves in the next few years?

8. What makes a P-O-P device stand out in a busy retail environment? Consider these criteria when you next go to some retail outlets. Were there any useful devices in these stores? Why were they useful?

9. Select the durable product class of your choice and design a computer-based P-O-P display that helps consumers learn more about one particular brand.

10. Returning one more time to your career-seeking communications plan, consider whether there would be any value in using the tools of this chapter in your campaign. Justify your decision to use or not use each set of tools.

Notes

1. James U. McNeal and Linda M. Zeren, "Brand Name Selection for Consumer Products," *MSU Business Topics* 29 (Spring 1981), p. 35.

2. Kathryn Feakins, "What's in a Name," *Ogilvy & Mather: The Research File,* no. 17, March 1980.

3. Ogilvy & Mather, "What Ogilvy & Mather Has Learned about Introducing New Products," audiovisual presentation, undated.

4. Al Ries and Jack Trout, *Positioning: The Battle for Your Mind* (New York: McGraw-Hill, 1982).

5. Laurie Freeman, "P&G Brands Shift Gears," *Advertising Age,* 1 October 1984, p. 1.

6. Walter Stern, "A Good Name Could Mean a Brand of Fame," *Scan* 31, no. 2, p. 4.

7. Dennis J. Moran, "How a Name Can Label Your Product," *Advertising Age,* 10 November 1980, p. 53.

8. NameLab, Inc., Informational Booklet, San Francisco, Calif., 1982.

9. NameLab, Inc., p. 4

10. NameLab, Inc., "Everything You Need to Know about Trademarks," Informational Booklet, San Francisco, Calif., 1983.

11. Walter P. Margulies, "What's New on the Outside," *Advertising Age,* 21 March 1983, p. M-14.

12. James R. Bettman, "Memory Factors in Consumer Choice: A Review," *Journal of Marketing* 43 (Spring 1979), pp. 37–53.

13. "Shoppers Buy Sweets Because of In-Store Influences," *POPAI News* 8, no. 5, 1984, p. 1.

14. Surendra N. Singh and Michael L. Rothschild, "Recognition as a Measure of Learning from Television Commercials," *Journal of Marketing Research* 20 (August 1983), pp. 235–248.

15. Joan Triestman, "Packaging Impact at the Point of Sale," Presentation at the Fourth Annual Marketing Research Conference, 1983.

16. Walter Stern, "Design Research: Beauty or Beast," *Advertising Age,* 9 March 1981, pp. 43–44.

17. D. W. Twedt, "How Much Value Can Be Added through Packaging," *Journal of Marketing,* January 1968, pp. 61ff.

18. *POPAI News* 8, no. 2, 1984, p. 4.

19. "P-O-P Volume up in 1975," *Advertising Age,* 15 March 1976, p. 4.

20. "Consumer Product Marketing: The Role of Permanent Point-of-Purchase," *POPAI News* 6, no. 2, 1982, p. 5.

21. Lawrence Stevens, "A Computer to Help Salesmen Sell," *Personal Computing,* November 1982, p. 62.

22. Anna Sobczynski, "Inside the Store, the Selling Never Stops," *Advertising Age,* 15 March 1982, pp. M-30–M-34.

OTHER MARKETING STRATEGIES

Sales Force Aids

In order to increase distribution, Sunkist needed to establish relations with a large number of local bottlers; the bottlers, in turn, developed retail distribution in conjunction with the business-to-business advertising described later in this text. To assist the sales force, Sunkist put together a sophisticated multimedia package of slides and film to introduce the bottler to the company. There was also print advertising support in relevant trade publications.

The sales presentation essentially covered all the issues discussed earlier in this text. It started with a review of the market and the research that had been done concerning market potential and perceptions of the Sunkist name. This was followed by a discussion of Sunkist's objectives and marketing strategy. Next the product, packaging, and advertising were presented, and the results of the first months in the test market were reviewed. Finally, the presentation discussed how Sunkist would support its bottler partners. Except for this last item, all issues in the presentation were consistent with the materials presented elsewhere in the case, and therefore most of these items do not need to be repeated.

In presenting their marketing strategy to prospective bottlers, the firm pointed out that

1. The Sunkist name would be the cornerstone of all marketing efforts

2. The firm wanted to develop the strongest bottling network in the industry

3. Strategy would be based on

- The most thoroughly researched new product entry in the history of the soft drink industry
- A dramatically better product
- Outstanding packaging
- Superior advertising
- Aggressive spending on advertising and promotion

By the time that Sunkist made these claims, they had data to support each one; this certainly helped the sales force to gain bottler support.

After presenting the product, package, and advertising, Sunkist concluded with its proposal for establishing relations with local bottlers. Their goal was to provide a profitable business proposition for both Sunkist and the bottler. This would result from the prior work done by the company to develop a sound product and the flexibility of local strategies that each bottler would provide.

Sunkist had already assumed all up-front development risks, it pointed out; in addition it paid for 100% of media costs during the first 16 weeks and 100% of vending and distribution incentive programs. Local bottlers needed to agree to a co-op advertising plan after the sixteenth week and needed to take care of promotions efforts and consumer sampling as necessary.

Brand Name

Selecting a brand name was never an issue after General Cinema Corporation bought the rights to the Sunkist name. The name was the only established item when Sunkist soft drinks was formed in 1977. It was reassuring to see the consumer research strongly support the name decision.

The Sunkist name had been selected originally because

- The name itself had a rich heritage
- In the citrus fruit category, it stood for goodness and quality
- It was perceived as a standard of excellence.

During the situation analysis, the name had been tested, yielding the following results.

- When orange drink users were asked about a new Sunkist product, 2 out of 3 said they would buy Sunkist.
- More than half said they would prefer Sunkist to their current orange soda.

Packaging

The Schecter Group, one of the largest package design companies in the United States, was selected to develop the graphics for Sunkist orange soda. The packaging objective was to clearly position Sunkist against the top soft drink brands. Further, a high-quality brand image had to be communicated; this meant that impact and outstanding shelf visibility versus major soft drink brands had to be produced.

After several months of design work, several candidates were put into test markets. Figure S.1 shows three of the designs that were tested. This test showed that the name probably should be shown on a diagonal and have a contrasting outline.

One design was clearly preferred in the tests. It gave consumers the impression of

- A high-quality product
- A good orange flavor
- Something good to drink when thirsty
- Something everyone in the family would like

As can be seen by Figure S.2, both the time-honored Sunkist heritage and the on-shelf merchandising impact set forth in the original design objectives were achieved. Figure S.3 shows the on-shelf impact of the Sunkist package next to the leading competitors.

Point-of-Purchase Materials

A variety of P-O-P materials were made available for bottlers to use at their discretion. These included store door decals, window banners, shelf talkers, and carton stuffers. Each offered a variety of sizes and visuals, as can be seen in Figure S.4. There were also panel menus, drink cups, and wall clocks for restaurants, a variety of display racks for retailers, vending machine identification stickers, and bumper stickers.

Figure S.1   Three test package designs

Figure S.2   The winning design

Figure S.3   The winner and its major competitors

Figure S.4   Some of the P-O-P materials available to retailers

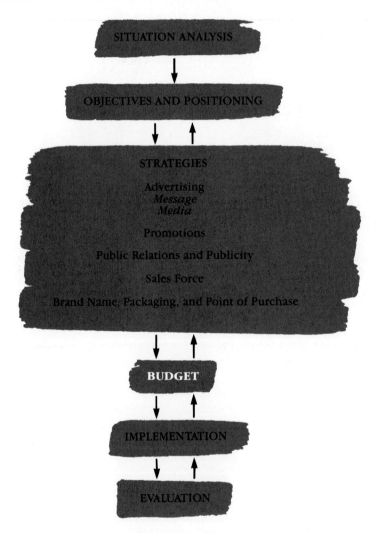

Decision Sequence Framework

Part Eight
Budgeting
Strategies

Now that all the strategies have been set and seem appropriate to meet the earlier objectives and positioning, it is time to consider the cost of the plans. This is not the first time in the planning process that the budget has been considered; potential budgets were examined in the situation analysis (Chapter 4). At that time it was necessary to get a feeling for the financial constraints of the firm.

During the situation analysis, the manager assessed the firm's communications-related problems such as the target market, the product, and the competition. At the same time, the manager also did an internal evaluation of the firm and its resources. Included here were financial issues that would influence the pending objectives. There would be no value in setting an objective of "creating awareness among 90% of all adult men in the United States" if the company could only afford to get 30%. In this early analysis, the budget drives the objectives and, indirectly, the strategies, by setting some broad ranges within which the manager must operate. While this early constraint is not the best way to set the budget, it is a reality of corporate life that such limits do exist. Chapter 20 discusses such constraints in the section entitled "Predetermined Budgeting Methods."

Later in the chapter, there is a more extensive discussion of a budgeting method that is more precise and that occurs after strategies have been set; this method is described under "Strategic Budgeting." In reality, sophisticated managers take a two-step approach to budgeting; first, a ball-park estimate of possible spending is derived during the situation analysis, and then the precise budget is developed after strategies are set.

The figure opposite shows the decision sequence with the budget following the strategies. Note, once again, that the arrows of the decision sequence go in both directions so that the objectives and strategies can be adjusted to reflect both budgeting problems and opportunities.

Chapter 20
Budgeting
Strategies

Advertising and promotions have been undertaken because of some problem in the marketplace that needed to be remedied. The problem was assessed, goals to deal with the problem were set, and strategies to meet the goals were determined. If these stages were dealt with correctly, then justifying the budget will be a reasonable task. The expenditure is necessary because the problem was important, the goals were reasonable, and the strategies were appropriate.

Often, top management says something like "We'll spend whatever it takes to solve this problem." When they find out what it really will take, these grandiose objectives need to be scaled down. Initial vagueness leads to extra work; getting an early ball-park budget range is a useful strategy for planners.

In the objectives part of the text, it was stated that it is important to obtain agreement on objectives before beginning to plan strategy. The value of this agreement becomes more apparent when the budget is considered. Generally, if the budget is not approved, strategies must be changed. If the proposed strategies were well thought out, efficient, and effective, then a budget cut will necessitate a change in objectives. Instead of 80% awareness, the goal may become 60%; instead of a 7% market share, the goal may become 5%.

As the goals change, so does the profit potential. Each set of strategies should be accompanied by a payout plan to show the relation between the budget and ultimate profits. This is difficult to do with something as amorphous as advertising, but is necessary. The budgeting process, therefore, has an impact upon all parts of the decision sequence. It forces management to plan carefully and to be specific; it also provides a yardstick against which to measure performance, for ultimately there must be accountability, and the advertising investment must be profitable within a stated period.

This part of the text considers several common methods of developing advertising and promotions budgets and develops an in-depth example of a method that is consistent with the decision sequence framework.

Predetermined Budgeting Methods

Although it is important to the budget to determine objectives and strategies, many firms do not follow this procedure. Consequently, several alternative budgeting processes are commonly used; these all have the common feature that the budget is determined independently from the other components of the decision sequence. In spite of this omission, there are some virtues in these methods. These alternative budgeting processes are discussed next and are followed by a more strategically oriented process.

Affordable method

In this method, the firm spends what it can. After figuring all other expenses and a desired return on investment, leftover capital can be devoted to advertising; there is no analysis in this method of the task that advertising is to perform. Firms that use this method do not hold the marketing/advertising function in high esteem, and a budget based on this method reflects the fact that the firm places little value on or has little knowledge of advertising. Often firms with no advertising experience begin the process in this way to keep from getting hurt by poor predictions. However, they usually get hurt by underspending.

A scenario for developing a budget using this method might proceed as follows: Top management asks the advertising manager how much is needed for the following year. The ad manager, knowing the company's philosophy, calls the comptroller and asks for an estimate of what will be available in the next year. The comptroller says $1.5 million, so a request goes to top management for a $1.5 million advertising budget for the following year. Since this amount is affordable, the budget is approved.

Of the four methods to be discussed, this one shows the least managerial insight into the advertising process. If the firm felt some need to show an advertising presence in the marketplace but had no idea about the relation between advertising and sales, then perhaps the affordable method is an adequate one. Most product sales fluctuate in response to the marketplace; therefore, advertising has a potential impact, and the affordable method is too imprecise.

Percentage of sales method

When using this method, the firm is stating that the advertising budget is determined by sales. These sales may be past (the 1987 advertising budget will be based on the level of sales achieved in 1986) or future (the 1987 budget is based on the best estimate of 1987 sales). In any case, a change in the level of sales leads to a change in the level of advertising.

Does this seem a little strange? For several hundred pages, this text has dealt with a stimulus–response model, which hypothesizes that advertising leads to sales. Now management is determining its advertising budget level on the basis of sales; this says that sales lead to advertising.

While the logic of setting budgets in this way is theoretically questionable, the method does have some merit and is better than the affordable method. If the firm has no idea about the effects of advertising, then the percentage of sales method provides a hint of what spending level might be appropriate. Each year, Schonfeld and Associates publishes a report of advertising-to-sales ratios for 245 Standard Industrial Classification (SIC) codes and, in addition, *Advertising Age* publishes the advertising-to-sales ratios of the top 100 advertisers; these provide some insights, as can be seen in Tables 20.1 and 20.2.

Table 20.1 1982 Industry advertising-to-sales ratios

Industry	SIC no.	Ad dollars as percent of sales	Ad dollars as percent of margin	Annual growth rate (%)	Industry	SIC no.	Ad dollars as percent of sales	Ad dollars as percent of margin	Annual growth rate (%)
Agriculture Production-Crops	100	2.1	8.9	4.9	Metal Cans & Shipping Cont	3410	4.2	19.5	-1.6
Agriculture Production-Livestock	200	.9	4.0	14.0	Hardware NEC	3429	8.0	17.1	-0.8
Metal Mining	1000	.8	4.1	18.8	Heating Equip & Plumbing Fix	3430	2.2	5.8	5.9
Copper Ores	1021	.3	7.5	-19.0	Solar Energy Equip & Comp	3437	1.8	4.0	22.8
Lead & Zinc Ores	1031	N/A	N/A	N/A	Fabricated Struct Metal Prod	3440	N/A	N/A	N/A
Gold & Silver Ores	1040	.1	.2	-0.3	Mtl Doors-Frames-Mold & Trim	3442	1.0	3.5	-3.6
Misc. Metal Ores	1090	N/A	N/A	N/A	Fabricated Plate Work	3443	.1	.7	3.3
Bituminous Coal & Lignite Mn	1211	.2	.8	24.1	Sheet Metal Work	3444	.6	2.2	16.6
Crude Petroleum & Natural Gas	1311	.1	.3	10.7	Prefab Metal Bldgs & Comp	3448	1.3	5.6	5.1
Drilling Oil & Gas Wells	1381	.5	1.2	-6.9	Misc Metal Work	3449	11.3	50.2	7.6
Oil-Gas Field Exploration	1382	.2	2.7	-100.0	Bolts-Nuts-Screws-Riv-Washrs	3452	.4	1.5	-0.7
Oil & Gas Field Services NEC	1389	1.2	3.2	20.3	Metal Forgings & Stampings	3460	2.2	9.1	-4.1
Misc Nonmetallic Minerals	1499	.1	.4	11.3	Ordnance & Accessories	3480	2.3	6.6	15.7
General Building Contractors	1520	1.2	10.4	-7.9	Valves & Pipe Fittings Ex Bras	3494	1.0	3.7	6.4
Operative Builders	1531	1.9	16.5	4.8	Fabricated Metal Prds NEC	3499	.3	1.0	-4.4
Gen Bldg Contractors-Nonres	1540	.5	4.7	1.7	Engines & Turbines	3510	1.8	6.5	-1.1
Construction-Not Bldg Constr	1600	2.1	16.0	7.8	Farm & Garden Machinery & Eq	3520	1.4	6.4	-4.1
Construction-Spl Contractors	1700	.1	.6	.6	Constr Min Mat Handl Eqp	3530	1.2	4.3	3.6
Food & Kindred Products	2000	4.2	13.1	11.3	Construction Machinery & Eqp	3531	.9	4.9	-1.6
Meat Products	2010	3.1	29.1	4.3	Oil Field Machinery & Equip	3533	.5	1.2	5.3
Dairy Products	2020	4.3	15.8	10.0	Hoist-Indus Cranes-Monorail	3536	.7	2.5	-2.6
Canned-Preserved Fruits-Vegs	2030	4.8	14.4	11.9	Indl Trucks-Tractors-Trailers	3537	1.3	9.6	-11.3
Flour & Other Grain Mill Pds	2041	2.1	10.7	11.1	Metalworking Machinery & Eqp	3540	5.1	16.2	-1.6
Wet Corn Milling	2046	.4	3.1	-34.2	Special Industry Machinery	3550	1.8	5.1	2.8
Prepared Feeds for Animals	2048	7.8	30.6	9.9	Pollution Control Machinery	3558	.4	1.3	-12.8
Bakery Products	2050	1.7	3.8	-4.2	General Industrial Mach & Eq	3560	.9	3.1	3.3
Cane Sugar Refining	2062	.3	2.1	2.3	Office Computing & Acctg Mch	3570	1.6	3.0	10.7
Beet Sugar	2063	.1	.4	-6.0	Electronic Computing Equip	3573	.8	1.4	11.6
Candy & Other Confectionery	2065	6.1	15.9	8.8	Refrig & Service Ind Machine	3580	1.4	5.4	-0.6
Fats & Oils	2070	N/A	N/A	N/A	Elec & Electr Mach Eq & Supp	3600	1.3	4.4	6.8
Malt Beverages	2082	7.0	23.2	13.7	Elec Transmission & Distr Eq	3610	.8	2.6	2.7
Distilled Rectif Blend Bevrg	2085	7.9	17.8	9.3	Electrical Industrial Appar	3620	.8	3.0	1.3
Bottled-Canned Soft Drinks	2086	5.7	11.5	7.7	Industrial Controls	3622	1.1	3.2	5.3
Food Preparation NEC	2099	1.4	4.2	11.3	Household Appliances	3630	2.5	9.6	4.1
Cigarettes	2111	3.7	13.1	10.2	Electrical Lighting-Wiring Eq	3640	2.0	5.8	4.7
Cigars	2121	2.8	5.1	7.4	Radio-TV Receiving Sets	3651	4.0	11.0	9.5
Textile Mill Products	2200	1.2	7.9	-0.6	Phonograph Records	3652	13.0	39.3	20.1
Knitting Mills	2250	1.6	6.7	-0.2	Tele & Telegraph Apparatus	3661	1.5	5.0	1.1
Floor Covering Mills	2270	1.2	5.7	7.1	Radio-TV Transmitting Equip-AP	3662	1.3	4.2	6.4
Apparel & Other Finished Pds	2300	2.8	9.3	9.0	Electronic Components & Acce	3670	.9	2.9	4.7

Industry	SIC	Ad $ as % of sales	Ad $ as % of margin	Annual growth rate
Lumber & Wood Products	2400	.3	1.4	-11.1
Wood Buildings-Mobile Homes	2450	1.0	5.4	-5.4
Household Furniture	2510	1.7	5.9	4.4
Office Furniture	2520	1.6	4.6	10.0
Paper & Allied Products	2600	1.2	6.0	-3.0
Convert Paper-Paperbd Pd NEC	2649	3.6	7.2	10.2
Paperboard Containers-Boxes	2650	N/A	N/A	N/A
Printing Publishing & Allied	2700	3.5	10.2	6.0
Newspapers: Publishing-Print	2711	1.6	3.9	9.3
Periodicals: Publishing-Print	2721	3.5	8.8	1.0
Book: Publishing & Printing	2731	4.6	8.3	6.9
Commercial Printing	2750	.3	.8	8.1
Manifold Business Forms	2761	.7	1.9	-1.2
Greeting Card Publishing	2771	2.9	5.3	14.5
Service Indus for Print Trde	2790	.7	2.3	13.1
Chemicals & Allied Prods	2800	1.2	4.5	6.0
Indl Inorganic Chemicals	2810	6.1	17.5	-15.5
Plastic Matr Synthetic Resin	2820	.7	3.2	-1.3
Drugs	2830	8.2	14.1	8.1
Soap & Other Detergents	2841	6.8	17.6	7.5
Perfumes Cosmetics Toil Prep	2844	8.4	14.5	7.1
Paints-Varnishes-Lacquers	2850	2.5	7.8	10.9
Industrial Organic Chemicals	2860	.7	3.3	8.7
Agriculture Chemicals	2870	8.2	9.4	30.8
Misc Chemical Products	2890	2.2	6.2	1.4
Petroleum Refining	2911	.3	1.5	3.3
Paving & Roofing Materials	2950	1.6	8.1	-3.8
Rubber & Misc Plastics Prods	3000	2.0	8.8	.3
Fabricated Rubber Prods NEC	3069	.9	3.0	13.6
Misc Plastic Products	3079	2.0	7.2	.9
Footwear Except Rubber	3140	3.0	7.9	5.9
Leather Goods NEC	3199	8.3	24.5	5.5
Flat Glass	3210	.7	.7	-8.6
Glass Containers	3221	2.6	12.3	2.2
Cement Hydraulic	3241	.0	.2	-10.7
Structural Clay Products	3250	1.4	5.1	10.5
Pottery Products NEC	3269	.4	1.4	9.3
Concrete Gypsum & Plaster	3270	.5	2.8	-7.3
Abrasive Asbestos & Misc Mining	3290	1.9	7.1	1.7
Blast Furnaces & Steel Works	3310	1.3	5.4	2.2
Iron & Steel Foundries	3320	N/A	N/A	N/A
Prim Smelt-Refin Nonfer Mtl	3330	.3	1.9	-7.5
Second Smelt-Refin Nonfer Mt	3341	.2	5.7	-21.6
Rolling & Draw Nonfer Metal	3350	1.1	3.5	7.8
Misc Primary Metal Products	3390	.3	1.3	12.9

Industry	SIC	Ad $ as % of sales	Ad $ as % of margin	Annual growth rate
Semiconductors & Rel Devices	3674	2.0	5.6	11.4
Electronic Components NEC	3679	1.0	2.4	8.2
X-ray, Electromedical Apparat	3693	1.3	2.0	17.5
Electrical Machy & Equip NEC	3699	5.4	15.4	3.2
Motor Vehicles & Car Bodies	3711	1.7	11.8	7.0
Truck & Bus Bodies	3713	N/A	N/A	N/A
Motor Vehicle Parts-Accessor	3714	.9	3.7	4.9
Motor Homes	3716	1.6	10.3	9.9
Aircraft & Parts	3720	2.1	5.5	10.7
Aircraft	3721	.3	1.8	-2.3
Aircraft Parts & Aux Equip	3728	.4	1.4	5.2
Ship-Boat Building & Repairing	3730	.8	8.7	2.4
Railroad Equipment	3740	.5	1.5	-1.5
Motorcycles Bicycles & Parts	3750	2.3	12.7	8.9
Guided Missiles & Space Vehc	3760	.4	1.9	3.7
Travel Trailers & Campers	3792	.7	3.8	-1.5
Engr Lab & Research Equip	3811	1.5	3.4	7.2
Measuring & Controlling Inst	3820	.8	2.5	7.1
Industrial Measurement Instr	3823	2.0	4.6	4.2
Elec Meas & Test Instr	3825	1.6	4.3	6.6
Optical Instruments & Lenses	3830	5.8	11.8	4.6
Surg & Med Instruments & App	3841	1.2	2.7	8.7
Ortho-Prosth-Surg Appl & Supp	3842	1.0	2.9	8.6
Dental Equip & Supplies	3843	1.6	3.9	-6.4
Photographic Equip & Suppl	3861	3.7	7.4	8.9
Watches Clocks & Parts	3870	2.1	9.6	-21.2
Jewelry-Precious Metals	3911	5.0	12.4	7.1
Silverware-Plateware	3914	2.3	6.3	12.6
Musical Instruments	3931	2.4	9.8	-23.2
Toys & Amusement Sport Goods	3940	10.5	24.8	14.0
Pens-Pencil & Oth Office Mat	3950	5.9	14.9	9.2
Misc Manufacturing Industries	3990	3.8	10.3	9.7
Railroads-Line Haul Operating	4011	.5	4.5	2.9
Intercity & Rural Hywy Trans	4131	2.9	7.7	9.1
Trucking-Local & Long Distance	4210	.6	2.9	12.3
Water Transportation	4400	1.8	5.6	-4.0
Air Transportation-Certified	4511	2.0	15.1	14.6
Pipe Lines Ex Natural Gas	4610	N/A	N/A	N/A
Transportation Services	4700	2.6	9.5	8.0
Freight Forwarding	4712	N/A	N/A	N/A
Telephone Communication	4811	2.0	4.5	24.4
Telegraph Communication	4821	N/A	N/A	N/A
Radio-TV Broadcasters	4830	3.5	8.7	7.4
Communication Services NEC	4890	1.8	4.7	23.0
Natural Gas Transmission	4922	.0	.0	36.0

Legend: SIC - Standard industrial classification. N/A - No data available for this value. NEC - Not elsewhere classified. Ad dollars as percent of sales - Ad expenditures/net sales. Ad dollars as percent of margin - Ad expenditures/(net sales—cost of goods sold). Annual growth rate of advertising dollars.

Table 20.1 continued

Industry	SIC no.	Ad dollars as percent of sales	Ad dollars as percent of margin	Annual growth rate (%)
Natural Gas Transmis-Distr	4923	.2	.8	10.7
Water Supply	4940	N/A	N/A	N/A
Sanitary Services	4950	.3	1.0	-5.2
Whsl-Autos & Parts	5012	1.2	4.7	9.8
Whsl-Lumber & Constr Matl	5030	.0	.3	10.5
Whsl-Sporting & Recrea Goods	5040	1.5	6.2	9.1
Whsl-Metals & Minerals	5050	.5	2.1	26.3
Whsl-Elec Apparatus & Equip	5063	.2	.9	5.7
Whsl-Elec Appliance TV & Radio	5064	7.6	20.4	18.0
Whsl-Electronic Parts & Equip	5065	2.1	7.9	-4.8
Whsl-Hardwr Plum Heat Equip	5070	3.9	35.5	5.5
Whsl-Machinery & Equipment	5080	1.3	4.7	9.3
Whsl-Scrap & Waste Materials	5093	N/A	N/A	N/A
Whsl-Durable Goods NEC	5099	3.1	10.0	10.3
Whsl-Drugs & Proprietary	5120	.5	3.6	31.8
Whsl-Groceries & Related Pds	5140	.2	1.5	1.9
Whsl-Petroleum & Petro Pds	5170	.1	1.0	-6.7
Whsl-Nondurable Goods NEC	5199	.6	5.4	1.3
Retail-Lumber & Bldg Mat	5211	2.7	22.6	14.2
Retail-Mobile Home Dealers	5270	1.3	7.3	.4
Retail-Department Stores	5311	3.0	12.7	9.2
Retail-Variety Stores	5331	2.4	9.0	5.9
Retail-Grocery Stores	5411	1.3	5.6	6.7
Retail-Auto Dealers & Gas Stat	5500	1.3	5.0	7.0
Retail-Apparel & Acces Store	5600	2.8	7.4	8.6
Retail-Womens Ready To Wear	5621	2.5	7.9	6.3
Retail-Shoe Stores	5661	1.6	4.1	10.9
Retail-Furniture Stores	5712	7.2	18.7	1.6
Retail-Hshld Appliance Store	5722	5.7	20.5	16.0
Retail-Eating Places	5812	3.3	16.2	10.0
Retail-Drug & Propriet Stores	5912	1.8	7.2	11.7
Retail-Jewelry Stores	5944	6.3	14.6	8.9
Retail-Sewing & Needlework	5949	3.5	6.9	13.3
Retail-Mail Order Houses	5961	15.7	35.9	3.9
Retail-Auto Mdsng Mach Oper	5962	2.8	8.5	17.2
Retail-Fuel & Ice Dealers	5980	.6	3.1	20.6
Retail-Stores NEC	5999	2.9	8.8	10.9
Savings & Loan Associations	6120	.5	2.1	10.2
Personal Credit Institutions	6140	1.6	4.2	22.5
Business Credit Institutions	6150	.2	.3	2.1
Finance-Services	6199	2.3	12.2	6.0
Security & Commodity Brokers	6200	.5	6.3	12.6
Insurance Agents Brokers	6400	1.1	5.1	13.0
Real Estate	6500	3.0	10.3	-0.2
Operators-Nonres Bldgs	6512	1.9	5.0	9.1
Operators-Apartment Bldgs	6513	1.6	3.6	8.7
Lessors of Real Property-NEC	6519	2.3	4.4	18.5
Subdivid Develop Ex Cemetery	6552	1.9	7.9	4.3
Oil Royalty Traders	6792	.0	.0	-100.0
Patent Owners & Lessors	6794	7.7	22.4	32.9
Real Estate Investment Trust	6798	.8	1.7	6.9
Investors-NEC	6799	.0	.0	9.5
Hotels-Motels	7011	2.5	9.4	7.7
Serv-Personal	7200	6.6	21.5	9.8
Serv-Linen Supply	7213	.5	1.6	7.1
Serv-Advertising Agencies	7311	.2	1.9	4.3
Serv-Clean & Maint to Bldg NEC	7349	.4	2.1	7.5
Serv-Computer & Data Process	7370	1.2	3.5	10.1
Serv-CMP Program & Software	7372	.8	3.4	14.5
Serv-Data Processing Svcs	7374	1.0	2.3	8.5
Serv-Computer Rel Svcs NEC	7379	2.3	4.3	37.6
Serv-Research & Developmnt Lab	7391	.5	1.7	-16.4
Serv-Mgmt Consulting & PR	7392	.2	.5	3.7
Serv-Detective & Protective	7393	22.5	-4.2	0.0
Serv-Equip Rental & Leasing	7394	2.7	4.2	2.8
Serv-Business Services NEC	7399	3.0	12.8	4.4
Serv-Automotive Repair & Ser	7500	2.5	6.0	10.5
Serv-Motion Picture Productn	7810	6.4	27.3	7.1
Serv-Motion Picture Theatres	7830	3.3	19.3	9.3
Serv-Racing Incl Track Oper	7948	3.9	19.6	11.5
Serv-Misc Amusement & Recrea	7990	4.7	16.0	17.3
Serv-Nursing-Person Care Fac	8050	1.7	9.1	11.4
Serv-Hospitals	8060	.3	1.2	-1.7
Serv-Educational	8200	4.6	11.5	17.7
Serv-Engineering & Architect	8911	.4	1.8	1.4

Legend: SIC - Standard industrial classification. N/A - No data available for this value. NEC - Not elsewhere classified. Ad dollars as percent of sales - Ad expenditures/net sales. Ad dollars as percent of margin - Ad expenditures/(net sales-cost of goods sold). Annual growth rate of advertising dollars.

Source: Schonfeld & Associates. Reprinted in *Advertising Age*, 15 August 1983, p. 20. Reprinted with permission. Copyright 1983 by Crain Communications, Inc.

Primary business	Rank	Company	Ad spending	Sales*	Ads. as % of sales
Airlines	59	UAL Inc.	$136,700	$ 6,967,599	2.0
	72	AMR Corp.	110,800	5,353,721	2.1
	95	Delta Air Lines	66,900	4,684,000	1.4
	96	Trans World Airlines	66,200	2,049,361	3.2
	99	Eastern Airlines	60,800	4,363,898	1.4
Automotive	2	General Motors Corp.	763,800	69,355,600	1.1
	8	Ford Motor Co.	559,400	36,788,000	1.5
	23	Chrysler Corp.	317,400	17,239,700	1.8
	47	Nissan Motor Corp.	164,200	N/A	N/A
	57	Toyota Motor Sales Co.	137,900	N/A	N/A
	60	American Honda Motor Co.	134,700	N/A	N/A
	68	American Motors Corp.	120,500	4,215,191	2.9
	75	Volkswagen of America	103,000	N/A	N/A
	92	Mazda Motor Corp.	71,797	N/A	N/A
	97	Goodyear Tire & Rubber Co.	64,700	7,091,500	0.9
Chemicals & petroleum	27	American Cyanamid	284,410	2,686,959	10.6
	42	Mobil Corp.	172,500	25,574,000	0.7
	78	Union Carbide Corp.	93,000	6,766,000	1.4
	79	E.I. du Pont de Nemours	91,000	24,486,000	0.4
Electronics & office equipment	18	International Business Machines	376,000	27,371,000	1.4
	24	Eastman Kodak Co.	301,000	7,118,000	4.2
	37	General Electric	202,400	25,968,000	0.8
	38	Tandy Corp.	190,000	2,344,527	8.1
	64	Xerox Corp.	127,583	5,584,800	2.3
	76	Canon Inc.	100,000	1,260,000	7.9
	77	Apple Computer	100,000	1,187,859	8.4
Entertainment & communications	33	RCA Corp.	239,400	9,164,000	2.6
	40	Warner Communications	181,749	1,726,784	10.5
	41	CBS Inc.	179,800	4,295,600	4.2
	50	Gulf & Western Industries	149,249	4,867,000	3.1
	61	Time Inc.	133,900	3,067,353	4.4
	89	MCA Inc.	77,058	1,381,170	5.6
	94	American Broadcasting Cos.	68,900	3,708,000	1.9
Food	4	Beatrice Cos.	680,000	9,832,000	6.9
	10	McDonald's Corp.	480,000	8,071,000	6.0
	12	General Foods Corp.	450,000	6,876,040	6.5
	14	Ralston Purina Co.	428,600	4,980,100	8.6
	21	Nabisco Brands	334,977	3,950,400	8.5
	22	Pillsbury Co.	318,473	4,344,500	7.3
	28	General Mills	283,400	5,094,500	5.6
	29	Dart & Kraft	269,200	7,129,000	3.8
	32	Sara Lee Corp.	258,562	6,631,000	3.9
	34	H.J. Heinz Co.	227,286	2,661,700	8.5
	35	Kellogg Co.	208,800	1,789,600	11.7
	39	Nestle Enterprises	186,848	5,100,000	3.7
	49	Quaker Oats Co.	161,300	2,586,000	6.2
	53	Campbell Soup Co.	142,000	3,345,000	4.3
	65	IC Industries	127,289	3,874,900	3.3
	66	CPC International	123,500	1,815,300	6.8
	80	Wendy's International	90,833	944,768	9.6
Gum & candy	54	Mars Inc.	139,282	N/A	N/A
	88	Hershey Foods Corp.	79,200	1,892,506	4.2
	93	Wm. Wrigley Jr. Co.	70,400	417,206	16.9

Primary business	Rank	Company	Ad spending	Sales*	Ads. as % of sales
Miscellaneous	26	U.S. Government	$287,807	$ N/A	N/A
	43	American Express Co.	172,100	10,449,000	1.6
	86	Greyhound Corp.	80,200	2,757,000	2.9
	87	Kimberly-Clark Co.	80,000	2,655,400	3.0
Pharmaceuticals	13	Warner-Lambert Co.	440,000	1,910,000	23.0
	16	American Home Products	412,000	3,435,900	12.0
	25	Johnson & Johnson	300,000	3,735,900	8.0
	31	Bristol-Myers Co.	258,440	3,148,800	8.2
	45	Sterling Drug Co.	166,600	1,187,897	14.0
	48	Richardson-Vicks	163,500	N/A	N/A
	52	Schering-Plough Corp.	144,300	1,075,700	13.4
	74	Bayer AG	105,296	3,638,700	2.9
	83	Pfizer Inc.	86,400	2,150,200	4.0
Retail	3	Sears, Roebuck & Co.	746,937	35,885,000	2.1
	9	Kmart Corp.	554,400	20,329,000	2.7
	11	J.C. Penney Co.	460,000	12,963,000	3.5
	67	Levi Strauss & Co.	122,000	1,912,417	6.4
	98	Cotter & Co.	63,900	1,653,199	3.9
Soaps & Cleaners	1	Procter & Gamble Co.	872,000	10,240,000	8.5
	17	Unilever U.S.	395,700	3,606,000	11.0
	30	Colgate-Palmolive Co.	258,731	2,342,678	11.0
	73	Clorox Co.	109,600	N/A	N/A
	81	S.C. Johnson & Son	90,000	N/A	N/A
Soft Drinks	15	PepsiCo Inc.	428,172	6,706,600	6.4
	20	Coca-Cola Co.	343,300	4,566,400	7.5
Telephone	7	American Telephone & Telegraph	563,200	N/A	N/A
	44	ITT Corp.	168,000	6,685,000	2.5
	82	GTE Corp.	89,775	13,421,882	0.7
Tobacco	5	R.J. Reynolds Industries	678,176	10,216,000	6.6
	6	Philip Morris Inc.	570,435	10,034,000	5.7
	56	Loews Corp.	137,900	5,603,354	2.5
	62	American Brands	133,000	3,064,900	4.3
	71	Batus Inc.	113,400	6,211,078	1.8
Toiletries & Cosmetics	90	Grand Metropolitan p.l.c.	76,200	2,040,000	3.7
	36	Revlon Inc.	205,000	1,728,914	11.9
	46	Gillette Co.	165,673	1,102,400	15.0
	51	Chesebrough-Pond's	145,500	1,479,521	9.8
	58	Beecham Group p.l.c.	137,000	1,023,500	13.4
	69	Cosmair Inc.	119,500	N/A	N/A
	91	Noxell Corp.	74,200	N/A	N/A
Toys	63	Mattel Inc.	132,892	697,123	19.1
	85	Hasbro Inc.	83,691	560,787	14.9
Wine, Beer & Liquor	19	Anheuser-Busch Cos.	364,401	6,501,200	5.6
	55	Adolph Coors Co.	138,700	1,262,903	11.0
	70	Jos E. Seagram & Sons	115,827	1,752,000	6.6
	84	Stroh Brewery Co.	85,200	1,600,000	5.3
	100	Van Munching & Co.	58,970	350,000	16.9
		TOTALS	22,504,512	508,670,720	4.4

Source: Reprinted with permission of *Advertising Age.* Copyright 1985 by Crain Communications, Inc.
*All sales and earnings figures are for the latest fiscal year.
Note: Some private companies will not divulge sales figures; estimates were obtained where possible.

More insight is provided by Farris and Buzzell[1] in their analysis of *advertising- and promotions-to-sales ratios (A&P/S)* of over 1,000 firms. Their data suggests that the *A&P/S ratio is higher* (e.g., a greater percentage of sales revenue is used to support advertising and promotions) when

- *The product is standardized rather than produced to order.* A standardized product can be described to many people at once and lends itself to advertising; a customized product needs personal interaction and a sales force.

- *There are many end users.* Advertising is most efficient when used to communicate with mass audiences.

- *The typical purchase amount is small.* Expensive purchases involve more risk, and, therefore, consumers will seek information from sources other than advertising.

- *Sales are made through channel intermediaries rather than direct to users.* The more direct the relation between manufacturer and end user, the more money is spent on a sales force rather than advertising. This relation may be tempered by the relation between length of channel and number of end users. A firm selling bubble gum to 20 million children, therefore, would be more likely to use advertising rather than its own door-to-door sales force.

- *The product is premium priced.* A prestige product needs advertising to reinforce the idea of high quality. Premium quality provides an appealing message that makes the advertising task easier.

- *The manufacturer has a high contribution margin per dollar of sales.* A higher gross margin allows more room for advertising and larger budgets using the affordable method of budgeting. Industries with higher gross margins may also attract more competitors, which in turn increases the need for more advertising (and ultimately reduces profits).

- *The manufacturer has a relatively small share of the market.* Economies of scale allow larger firms to realize more efficiencies in their advertising budgets by gaining quality discounts. They get more sales per dollar spent and have more bargaining power with media vehicles.

- *The manufacturer has surplus production capacity.* A firm operating at peak capacity has little incentive to spend money on advertising. A firm with idle capacity needs to increase demand, and one way to do this is through advertising and promotions.

- *A high proportion of the manufacturer's sales come from new products.* Products in the early stages of the life cycle require more advertising support because more consumer learning must take place and trial usage must be encouraged.

- *The product is differentiable.* A brand with some unique difference will want to communicate this point through advertising.

If all competitors in an industry use the same data about advertising-to-sales ratios, and all have information such as that provided by Farris and Buzzell, then the percentage of sales method has the advantage of creating stability in the industry. If all firms end up with similar ratios, then market shares may stabilize. That's fine if the firm already dominates the market, but most firms don't, and in a free enterprise system, a firm just can't count on all its competitors to be passive in their approach to advertising. There's always some aggressive son-of-a-gun out there who wants to increase market share!

The percentage of sales method also doesn't work well for new brands because managers must overspend in these cases in order to make an impact. As noted by Farris and Buzzell, efficiencies are available to the large spenders; the new brand must spend at a higher rate in order to catch up. Also, because the new brand has no prior sales, it must use industry data that are probably inappropriate for a new brand. These issues are explored later in a discussion on budgeting for new products.

One advantage of the percentage of sales method is that the firm won't spend beyond its means. Because advertising is based on sales, the ad budget will go up only when sales have gone up and there are sufficient revenues to cover the increased expenses. When times are good, this works well because it allows the firm to be aggressive in its growth. This method has a tendency to exaggerate cycles in sales patterns.

This exaggeration also can become a disadvantage during a recession or other downturn. As sales decrease, so will advertising, and that may be exactly the opposite of what should be done. When sales decrease, the firm may need to advertise more to break the downturn in the cycle. Cahner's research shows that firms that continue to advertise during a recession end up in better shape than their nonspending competitors when the recession ends. Figure 20.1 shows data

Figure 20.1 The role of advertising in uncertain times

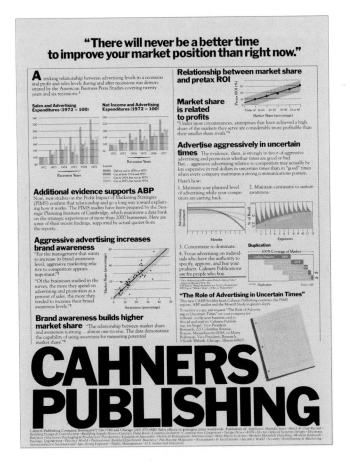

to support this point. The percentage of sales method may lead advertisers to exactly the wrong strategy during a sales decline. This point of view is also expressed by Nicholas Rudd, a senior vice president at Young & Rubicam, who said, "It's pretty well established that many of the successful companies during hard economic times increased advertising. They did not cut back."[2]

As shown throughout this text, advertising and promotions should be used to deal with specific problems and to do specific tasks. The percentage of sales method allocates a predetermined amount for advertising that is independent of tasks. It may be too little to do the jobs that need to be done, but it is equally likely that it is too much. In either case, this method is not likely to lead to an optimal budget.

Competitive parity method

In the *competitive parity method,* the firm matches the advertising levels of its competitors such that the advertising and promotions share equals market share. If the firm has an 8% market share, it will try to spend 8% of all the advertising and promotions dollars spent by the same set of competitors. This is another conservative way of developing an advertising budget and doesn't take into account the unique abilities or problems of the firm. Again, if most competitors use this method, it is likely to promote stability in the industry and to prevent advertising wars. Again, it doesn't take into account the notion that advertising should deal with specific problems and that budgets should be designed to deal with these problems. And again, this method protects the position of the leader by encouraging stability.

The competitive parity method also doesn't consider the unique advantages of the firm. The firm came into being initially because some group of people felt that it could provide some benefit in the marketplace. Competitive parity in essence negates this uniqueness by encouraging the firm to try to be like its competitors. It further assumes no special efficiencies resulting from good or bad advertising; it assumes that all advertising has the same impact. When these assumptions are made, it is only a short leap to copying media plans and developing look-alike advertising.

One result of this method can be advertising wars. If more than one firm in an industry uses this method, then any increase in advertising by one firm will be matched by at least one other. If the first firm increased its budget in order to try to increase market share, it will probably not have been successful after other firms retaliated. If any firm persists in trying to buy market share, the ensuing battle can become costly to all and reduce overall industry profits. Peckham found competitive parity models to be a prevalent part of the budgeting process in the majority of packaged goods that he studied,[3] so this model may prevail. Many product classes today exist in an oligopolistic situation of a few large competitors, and the competitive response to any increase in advertising is responded to much like a lowering of price. That is, competitors quickly follow, equilibrium is maintained, but profits are lower. Because competitors can follow easily, it is not necessarily in any firm's best interest to increase its budget.

It is difficult for the consumer to see the competitive parity process in action for advertising, but it is easy to observe for promotions and pricing changes. In the early 1980s, the major car rental firms all gave away large amounts of premiums in an attempt to maintain parity with the first firm that used this strategy. After the mass giveaways ended, industry analysts felt that market shares had stayed constant and that profits had declined. Similar strategies seem to emerge annually in the airline industry during the doldrums of January and February.

The percent of sales and competitive parity methods are not the most appropriate methods for developing the actual budget. They are, though, useful during the situation analysis when ball-park budget levels need to be determined so that feasible objectives can be set. These two methods are reasonable in terms of showing the advertising planners what the feasible levels of advertising will be. If there is merit to these conservative procedures, it is for that purpose. The budgeting that needs to be considered during the situation analysis was discussed in Chapter 4.

Weilbacher[4] calls the previous three methods "rules of thumb" and includes others such as standard expenditures per unit sold or case sold. Rather than allocating by percentage of sales revenue dollars, the allocation is based on units sold. In a 1974 article, San Augustine and Foley[5] showed that these rule-of-thumb methods were the most commonly used among leading advertisers. Now, more than ten years later, it would be interesting to redo that study to see which methods are currently most popular. During that ten-year period, the objective and task method seems to have become more popular.

Strategic Budgeting

This section considers the *objective and task method* and *payout planning*. Both of these topics attempt to relate the budget more closely to the actual communications events in which the firm is engaged.

Objective and task method

While the previous methods set the budget and then consider the marketing problems, the *objective and task method* sets the budget as a result of the relevant objectives and strategies. As shown in the decision sequence, it is necessary to

- Define advertising and promotions objectives as specifically as possible using the DAGMAR model
- Outline the strategies and tasks necessary to meet the objectives
- Estimate the cost of performing each task

This is the process used for the objective and task method of budgeting. The budget is the total cost of all strategies needed to meet all objectives; as a result, the budget cannot be set until after planning occurs, but the budget reflects the problems to be faced and is not arbitrary in size.

This process leads to budgets that best allow objectives to be met, but there is no test to see if the budgets are affordable or if the expenditures are the best that the firm can make. To make this determination, the objective and task method must be accompanied by a payout plan and a determination of return on investment.

An example of the objective and task method

Earlier in this text, objectives were set for a new brand of strawberry beer, known as Strawbeery. The objective was to acquire an 8% market share by the end of the first year. It was assumed that there were 50 million beer drinkers in an undifferentiated market, and, as a result, the firm wanted 4 million of them to become loyal Strawbeery drinkers.

To reach this objective, three goals were also set:

- 80% awareness (40 million beer drinkers) within three months of introduction
- 25% trial usage by those who are aware (10 million beer drinkers) within six months of introduction
- 40% repeat usage by those who try (4 million beer drinkers) within one year from the start of the introduction

How can the firm get and maintain 80% awareness? It will need media and message strategies. The media plan in this example will be a simple one that uses only network television. (In reality, it would probably also use spot television and outdoor ads. Perhaps there would be a small amount of radio and print.) During the first three months, the plan will have 800 GRPs per month to raise awareness quickly to 80%. This translates to a reach of almost 90 and a frequency of almost 9 and means that most of the target audience will receive slightly more than two messages per week. According to Berger, this should give Strawbeery a good chance to meet its 80% awareness objective. (If the concepts discussed in this paragraph seem foreign, you should review Chapter 13. While you're doing this, consider how quickly you can forget important information and how difficult it is for advertisers to get consumers to learn their claims!)

For the remaining nine months of the year, the media plan will be cut back to 240 GRPs per month. This will be executed in a flighting plan of three weeks of 80 GRPs and one week off. Reach will be close to 80, and frequency will be approximately 3 times per month. Over the 12-month period, each member of the 80% of the target market will receive approximately 57 messages. Total GRPs for the year equal 4,560. Figure 20.2 shows the year-long media and promotions plan.

Figure 20.2 Strawbeery media and promotions plan

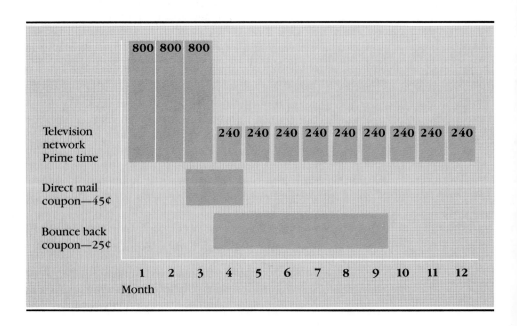

To further simplify the example, all network television buys are on programs that have a 20 rating for our target market, and each spot costs $100,000. Therefore, each rating point costs $5,000. Because the ratings are for our target market, a rating point equals one GRP; because Strawbeery needs 4,560 GRPs, the cost for the media plan is $22.8 million ($5,000 × 4,560 = $22.8 million); this expenditure should allow development and maintenance of 80% awareness.

Note that although each person in the target market receives approximately 57 messages, more than 57 spots are purchased. Each spot reaches only 20% of the target and the goal is 80%, so 228 spots must be purchased (57 × 4 = 228). Each spot costs $100,000, thus the cost of the media plan is, again, $22.8 million.

Now that awareness is taken care of, Strawbeery's brand managers must meet the objective of trial. Considerable trial will occur as a result of the heavy advertising plan, but it can be enhanced using promotions. Again, in an attempt to keep the example simple, assume that only coupons are used. There will be a co-op mailing of 50 million coupons, each worth 45¢ on the purchase of a six-pack of Strawbeery. Given a 9% redemption rate, this will lead to 4.5 million trials. The cost of this promotion will be $3.25 million according to data provided in Chapter 16. This expenditure should lead to achievement of the goal of gaining 25% tryers from those who are aware of the product.

Finally there is a need to retain 40% of the tryers as repeat users. Advertising can generate awareness, and promotions can generate trial, but only a good product can maintain repeat purchase. In an early test market, it was determined that people go bananas over Strawbeery, and 40% of those who tried it made a repeat purchase during the test. Nevertheless, the brand manager is nervous and includes a bounce-back coupon on the first 20 million six-packs, for redemption with purchases made during the second and third quarters of the brand's introduction. This 25¢ coupon costs $910,000 as 2.6 million are redeemed (supporting data come from Chapter 17).

In this example, a series of objectives was set. Next, strategies were developed to meet each objective. Finally, the cost to execute each strategy was determined. This led to a budget of approximately $27 million. The brand manager of Strawbeery will submit this budget to the management of the firm.

While it looks as if the budget will be sufficient in terms of allowing the objectives to be met, it is not yet clear if this is a good investment for the firm. In fact, setting a budget to meet objectives may not be sufficient. Ultimately, the goal will be profit oriented, and the budget must serve this end. If the cost of meeting objectives is so high as to prevent profit, then a reevaluation must be made. The payout plan is an aid at this point.

Payout planning

The payout plan is used in conjunction with budget-setting methods to assess the investment value of the advertising and promotions. This is a projection of future revenues generated and costs incurred and typically is done for a two- or three-year period. Its purpose is to show what level of expenditures need to be made, what level of return might be expected, and what time period is necessary before the return will occur. These issues are of special concern with a new product for which initial sales are often low while initial expenses are quite high. How long will it take to recover the initial expenditures? Most firms have guidelines that set criteria for these issues. They will state the return on investment that must be

Table 20.3 Three-year payout schedule for Strawbeery

	YEAR 1 (Millions)	YEAR 2 (Millions)	YEAR 3 (Millions)
Strawbeery Sales (cases)	30.96	54.50	57.23
Contribution to profit and/or advertising (@ 40¢ per case)	$12.38	$21.80	$22.89
Advertising and promotions expenses	$26.93	$15.12	$15.88
Profit/(loss)	($14.55)	$6.68	$7.01
Cumulative profit/(loss)	($14.55)	($7.87)	($.86)

foreseeable before the project begins and the period of time that the firm is willing to wait for this return.

Table 20.3 shows a three-year payout schedule. These figures show clearly that Strawbeery will suffer large losses in the first year, especially in the first quarter, when expenses are greatest and sales are close to zero. In the second half of the first year, sales have become established as tryers become repeaters. The figures for the second and third years assume no promotions and a continuation of advertising at the levels set in the second half of the first year. Both sales and expenses are assumed to go up at a rate of 5% per year in the second and third years. It is also assumed that there will be a 40¢ per case contribution to profit or advertising expense.

Though it was clear from the objective and task example that Strawbeery would meet its goals, it is equally clear from the payout plan that the expenditure is not a sound one. The large losses of the first year are not recouped by the end of the third year. Although Strawbeery will turn a cumulative profit in the fourth year, that is not adequate if the payout guidelines of the firm call for payback in three years.

It is probably risky to use a period longer than three years, because competitors can retaliate by then and the firm's competitive advantage may disappear. If Strawbeery were successful, there might be several other strawberry beers by then. Or there might be banana beer. Or prune beer. . . .

Sensitivity analysis

At this point the expenses are too great and/or the sales develop too slowly. Adjustments now need to be made to objectives and/or strategies to see if a revised plan can lead to a three-year payback. What would happen if advertising were cut back during introduction? During the $2\frac{1}{2}$ years of maintenance? Could a less expensive flighting plan be used? Are the sales projections too conservative? If there is a 40% loyalty factor, will sales grow faster than 5% per year? Is there seasonality that would allow media cutbacks at some time of year?

These questions are part of a *sensitivity analysis* that must be done to see if costs can be cut without interfering with sales. Any cutback runs a risk of hurting the brand, but some cuts are more threatening than others. Cuts during the first half year are especially risky because repeat behavior can only be as good as initial trial levels. If the product is good, it is essential to achieve a high trial level from which to build repeat purchases.

Figure 20.3 *Advertising is an investment in the future*

If the budget were trimmed during the sales promotions, for example, this might have a major impact on the future stream of sales. If this $.86 million cut were in the co-op coupon mailing, responses would be almost 1.2 million less and repeat users would be .48 million less (1.2 million × 0.4 conversion rate to repeat usage). Since each repeat user was assumed to drink 50 six-packs per year, this would also cut sales by 15 million cases and revenues by $6 million during the final 2.5 years of the three-year payout plan. Clearly the cut of $.86 million in the initial couponing would be harmful.

Conversely, a minor cut in the maintenance media plan could be spread over a long period and probably would have a negligible impact. If the second- and third-year media plans each were cut by 3%, the $.86 million deficit would disappear. There would be an average of 76 GRP less per month; this would hardly be noticeable.

The two suggested cuts are extreme examples, but they show the need for careful analysis in adjusting the strategies in response to budgetary constraints. By using the objective and task method in conjunction with the decision sequence and payout planning, the manager can make adjustments in strategies and see the potential impact on both sales and budget. This method allows the manager to vary strategy, sales, or costs and then see the impact on the other two variables. Such an analysis is usually done in planning to allow the manager to try to adjust the initial plan to see if it can be done even better.

Using a payout plan has a more subtle advantage as well. Managers who consider the payout plan and/or return on investment calculations are implying that advertising is an investment rather than a variable cost that is fully depleted in the current period. This thought process is useful because it takes into account the lagged effects of advertising (discussed below) and the need for repetition in learning and forgetting. In order to assess advertising properly, it must be treated as an investment with future value to the firm. Figure 20.3 speaks to this point.

Some complicating factors

It was stated several times that the Strawbeery example was a simplified one. What are some of the factors that complicate the budgeting process?

1. *More media and more promotional devices* In a real case, there would probably be several media and more than one promotional device, as well as advertising and promotions to the trade. Each medium would have several vehicles, and each vehicle would have its own set of costs and efficiencies. And, to complicate things further, different messages in the campaign pool would also have different efficiencies.

The discussion has assumed that all creativity in messages, media, promotions, and elsewhere is equal. This, of course, is not the case. An exciting message execution can change the amount of budget needed. A well-targeted media plan will have less waste and will do a better job. These issues are especially important in comparing campaigns but have less value in the assessment of a single campaign.

2. *Interactions with other marketing variables* The impact that advertising and promotions can have is certainly tempered by the quality of the product; that is obvious. It may be less obvious that distribution and pricing can also have a great impact. The intensity of advertising will need to be adjusted to reflect the breadth of *distribution;* the narrower the geographic area of distribution, the harder advertising will need to work, all other things being constant. The effectiveness of advertising is also influenced by the depth of distribution coverage within any area. The easier it is for consumers to find the product, the easier it will be for advertising and promotions to do their jobs. And, as pointed out earlier, the more direct the channel, the less the need for advertising.

Pricing and promotion interact because most promotions are in essence changing the price or the cost/benefit relation. Therefore, the pricing strategy will help determine how well the advertising and promotions can do. Although pricing is not a decision made by the advertising manager, it will affect the feasibility of the advertising decisions and the payout plan because it has an obvious impact on sales and profits. As discussed earlier, firms that charge higher prices than their competitors usually also have larger advertising budgets.

Likewise, the *product* impacts on the feasibility of the advertising plan. While the sheer power of dollars invested in advertising and promotions can influence awareness and trial, the payout plan and repeat purchase objectives cannot succeed without a good product.

How should the budget be adjusted to compensate for the quality of the product? If the product is mediocre, the trial to repeat conversion rate will be lower and therefore the budget must be higher so that more people will try it.

Other qualities of the product and price also affect budgeting decisions. As seen in the situation analysis discussion, products that are more complex, that offer a more discontinuous innovation, or that require consumers to engage in more extended problem solving will probably require relatively larger budgets and will yield relatively longer payout periods. Some products move through the life cycle rapidly and therefore require large expenditures early to build trial quickly (for example, snack foods), while other products diffuse slowly and should get larger expenditures in later years (for example, a pharmaceutical product will be adopted slowly because doctors want to observe its success rate and unknown side effects).

3. *Interactions with marketplace variables*   The *intensity of competition* will probably be the greatest marketplace influence on budget. More competition will mean more noise in the market and the need for a larger budget in order to be heard.

Competition can also be measured in terms of similarity of offerings. Brands that have highly substitutable competitors will need more support. If there are no unique attributes on which to differentiate, the firm must advertise more to make its presence felt and/or be aggressive in its use of promotions. Commodity-like products (such as beer and laundry detergent) are less efficient in their use of advertising as a result.

Government regulations can also influence budget efficiencies. Image-oriented products that cannot advertise on television (such as cigarettes and liquor) may have less efficiency as a result. Other product-specific regulations may have similar effects.

The degree of *segmentation* will affect efficiencies. More narrow segments are harder to reach and may lead to wasted coverage in the vehicles used. This will lead to a high budget. If there are several segments to be reached, then each may need its own set of objectives, strategies, and budgets.

4. *Time*   The length of the planning period will affect the budget and payout plan. One example of this results from the demands placed on brand managers. Because managers tend to control a brand for only a short time (two or three years), their goal is to succeed within that span. This means that strategies are developed that may cut budgets to show short-run profit although the strategy may hurt the brand in the long run. Similarly, the overuse of promotions leads to short-run sales although this may erode the long-run franchise.

In a more abstract sense, planners should consider the long-run and short-run effects of advertising. Long-run effects are also known as *lagged effects* or cumulative buildups over time. Lagged effects occur because it takes time to learn and forget. There are also effects of trial behavior that lead to later repeat purchases and effects of word of mouth. All these issues develop over time and lead to an advertising impact in periods of time that occur after the advertising was placed.

Each case is different, but it is clear from both behavioral science and econometric research that advertising effects do build up over time. For example, Palda[6] showed that advertising was a losing proposition in the period in which the dollars were spent, but the cumulative effect over time made advertising a good investment. While this relation may not hold in all cases, it is clear that the effects of advertising do not just take place in the period of expenditure. Budgeting decisions need to take a long-run perspective to account for the future impact of current actions. In this sense, advertising should be considered an investment and not a variable cost. The ad in Figure 20.4 illustrates this point.

Budgeting for New Products

As was seen in the Strawbeery example, the first few months of a product's life require a different budget from that of an established product. A large budget is needed to give the new brand strong initial visibility because it is necessary to achieve high initial awareness and trial. In addition to the high stakes that result, there is also more risk with an unproven new product and less information upon which to base budgeting decisions.

To achieve success, Peckham[7] has suggested that, as a rule of thumb, the new brand should be spending at a rate double that necessary to maintain the desired

The Man Who Sold Chewing Gum

An Ad Age Parable

It was common knowledge among his colleagues that William Wrigley, Jr. attributed the success of his chewing gum empire to constant and forceful advertising.

Once he was traveling to California on the famous Super Chief with a young accountant from his firm. As they were reviewing the figures for a quarterly statement, the young man said, "Sir, Wrigley's gum is known and sold all over the world. We have a larger share of the market than all of our competitors combined. Why don't you now save the millions you are spending on advertising and shift those dollars into the profit column for next quarter?"

Wrigley thought for a moment and then asked, "Young man, how fast is this train going?"

"About sixty miles an hour," replied the young accountant.

And Wrigley asked, "Then why doesn't the railroad remove the engine and let the train travel on its own momentum?"

Media moral: Advertising promotion is the fuel that provides your momentum. Keep it going in Advertising Age. It is must reading for 180,000 important people... in good times and bad.

Advertising Age
The International Newspaper of Marketing

NEW YORK: Gerry Byrne • 708 Third Avenue • 212/986-5050
CHICAGO: Bill Kanzer • 740 Rush Street • 312/649-5304
LOS ANGELES: Ben Malkin • 6404 Wilshire Blvd. • 213/651-3710

P.S. Call one of the above and ask to see the exciting new study that demonstrates how advertising helps sell advertising.

Figure 20.4   *An Ad Age parable*

market share. For example, the Strawbeery payout plan shows first-year expenditures that are twice that of the second and third years. It takes a much greater expenditure to build market share than it does to maintain it. If it takes $14 million to maintain an 8% market share, it will probably take approximately a $28 million expenditure to build to that level.

It is important also to develop sales as quickly as possible and to achieve as high a level of trial as possible. Sales need to be developed quickly, or retailers will not maintain the shelf space. Trial rate needs to be high because the stable sales level will be at some lower level. In the Strawbeery example, 40% of tryers became regular users; the higher the initial trial rate, the greater the number of regular users, as can be seen in Figure 20.5. The need for both timeliness and intensity will demand a large initial budget.

Developing Insights into How Much to Budget

Having examined four methods of budgeting and several variables that complicate the process, it is next necessary to consider some ways of collecting data to evaluate the budget. Field experiments, econometrics, management science models, and expert opinion all can help toward this end. While research studies on copy, media, and promotions have led to a body of knowledge relating these areas to various dependent variables at the individual and short-run levels, there is a

Figure 20.5 *Theoretical sales curve for new convenience good introduction*

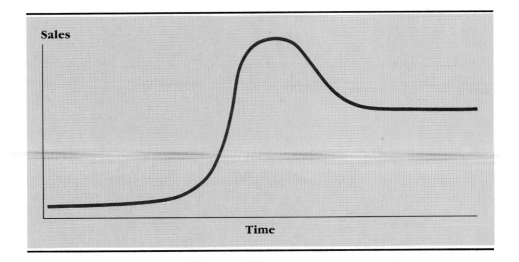

much more limited set of findings that can be used for more long-range budgeting decisions.

In the objective and task example, it was fairly easy to compute appropriate introductory budget levels. In the first quarter, the desired response was awareness; in the second it was trial. Budget levels become less easy to set in later quarters as lagged effects (effects of advertising in one period on sales in later periods), decay effects (such as forgetting), repeat sales, competitive responses, and other less direct effects of the advertising come into play. Nevertheless, budgets must be set.

If the advertising budget is too small, then awareness will slowly erode over time among those who are not brand loyal (usually a large majority of any market). Over a longer period, sales will also erode and may be difficult to recapture in the face of strong competition. Conversely, a budget that is too large will drain profits from the firm or will use marginal funds in ways that do not allow other projects to be developed.

Leaky bucket model

Figure 20.6 *The leaky bucket model*

A simple way to consider advertising budgeting is via the leaky bucket model, as shown in Figure 20.6. In this view, advertising leads to a reserve of goodwill, which is built up over time. The flow of advertising can be regulated as it enters the bucket; too strong a flow causes waste since the bucket can only hold so much. As advertising levels build up, an upper level of impact is approached (as shown in Figure 20.7) and diminishing returns result. Too weak a flow causes the level in the bucket to go down. Because some level of goodwill and sales remain in the absence of advertising, the hole in the bucket is not at its bottom. To complete the analogy, during introduction, the faucet is opened wide to allow for a buildup of goodwill.

Sales response model

There are intuitive and data-based models of advertising that are similar in concept to the leaky bucket model. Figure 20.7 reintroduces the S-shaped response curve that was discussed in the media part. In the *A* range of budgets, there will

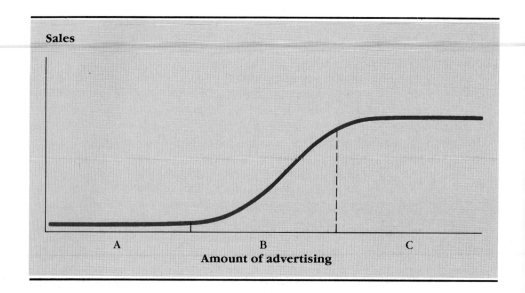

be little response to advertising, although some sales will result from the effects of the product's existence. With a national product, several million dollars may be required to get past *A* during the introduction and some lesser number of millions required to keep from sliding back to *A* after the brand has been established. For example, Paul Luchsinger of Welch Foods, Inc., felt in 1977 that the minimum entry fee for use of network television was at least $1 million.[8] In more current dollars, that translates to almost $3 million; keep in mind that this is just for network television and for maintenance of an established product.

Similarly, the hierarchy of effects and learning theory data both suggest that awareness precedes behavior and that some repetition is needed for awareness. Once learning has taken place, a maintenance budget is necessary to retard forgetting. These all suggest the need for advertising at greater than a threshold level.

At the other extreme of Figure 20.7 is a saturation level of advertising (the *C* range), at which the sales response approaches its upper limit. For various reasons (most likely resulting from competition), there is an upper level beyond which it is almost impossible to gain additional sales. To keep increasing the advertising budget in the face of diminishing returns will merely decrease profits.

Aaker and Carman[9] suggest two reasons why firms might overspend and present data to suggest that many firms currently may be overspending on advertising. The first reason to overspend concerns the reward structure of organizations. Agencies reward account executives for building their accounts. Likewise, brand managers are rewarded for increasing sales; it is more likely that sales will increase if advertising is increased than if it is decreased or kept the same. Both classes of middle to lower levels of managers, therefore, are given at least implicit pushes in the direction of trying to increase their budgets. Second, managers don't know the marginal response to advertising, and this is difficult to determine. Therefore, again, the safest strategy is to increase advertising.

After reviewing a number of field experiments, Aaker and Carman found that, generally, neither a decrease nor an increase in budgets led to a significant change in sales. The test periods were for up to two years and indicated that the

Figure 20.8 *Results of Budweiser advertising level experiment*

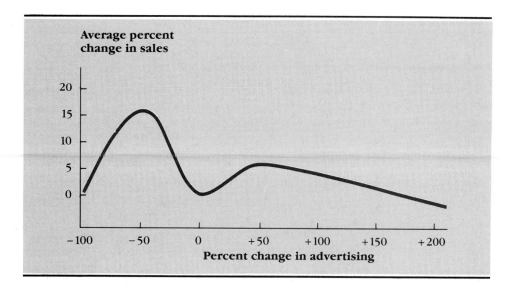

firms may have been operating in the *C* range of Figure 20.7, where the response to advertising would be fairly unrelated to changes in advertising expenditures.

Aaker and Carman's study included a review of work by Rhodes[10], Haley[11], and Ackoff and Emshoff.[12] It should be noted that the reported experiments were not on random products, but rather were done because someone suspected that overadvertising existed. It is likely, though, that there is a significant amount of overspending on advertising in the marketplace because there is generally an absence of good advertising information.

In one of the most well-known field experiments of budgets, Budweiser tested levels of advertising that ranged from no advertising to 200% increases in advertising over the company's current budget and found that a 25% decrease in the budget led to a 50% increase in sales. As a result of these and other experiments, Budweiser decreased its advertising budget from $1.89 to $.80 per barrel, while annual sales went from 7.5 million to 14.5 million barrels, and market share increased from 8.1 to 12.9%. All of this occurred between 1963 and 1968. While the per-barrel budget decreased dramatically, the actual budget decreased by a smaller amount because of the sales increase. Nevertheless, this shift allowed profits to increase dramatically.[13]

In this experiment a 25% decrease in the budget led to a large increase in sales. While firms often overspend, it is unusual for a change to be so dramatic. The study shows that experiments can be used to show advertisers if their current spending levels are appropriate. Figure 20.8 shows the results of this test of different advertising levels.

It is interesting to note that although there are some data to support the concept that firms may be overadvertising, a recent survey of over 1,000 advertising managers showed that about 60% planned to increase their budgets in the following year (1984), and only 6% planned to decrease the budget.[14] Table 20.4 shows in more detail that the larger advertisers were much more likely to increase their budgets. These largest advertisers are most likely to be in the *C* range of Figure 20.8 and, as a result, are most likely to receive the least return on their investment. The small advertisers can probably benefit most yet are least likely to make

Table 20.4 Plans to increase or decrease the advertising budget

Consumer Advertising Budget Plans for 1984
Does your company (or division or group) plan to increase or decrease the total advertising budget in 1984?

	Total Percent	Responses by Total Ad Budget Range					
		Under $500,000	$500,000- $1 Million	$1 Million- $2 Million	$2 Million- $5 Million	$5 Million- $10 Million	Over $10 Million
Number of respondents	284	44	34	37	56	33	80
Increase	61.3%	36.4%	55.9%	59.5%	62.5%	66.7%	75.0%
Decrease	6.3	9.0	0.0	8.1	7.1	6.0	6.3
About the same	32.4	54.6	44.1	32.4	30.4	27.3	18.7

Business-to-Business Advertiser Budget Plans for 1984
Does your company (or division or group) plan to increase or decrease the total advertising budget in 1984?

	Total Percent	Responses by Total Ad Budget Range					
		Under $500,000	$500,000- $1 Million	$1 Million- $2 Million	$2 Million- $5 Million	$5 Million- $10 Million	Over $10 Million
Number of respondents	503	215	142	74	56	6	10
Increase	56.5%	48.4%	57.0%	60.8%	73.2%	83.3%	80.0%
Decrease	8.5	9.8	8.5	6.8	8.9	0.0	0.0
About the same	35.0	41.8	34.5	32.4	17.9	16.7	20.0

Dual (Consumer plus Business) Advertiser Budget Plans for 1984
Does your company (or division or group) plan to increase or decrease the total advertising budget in 1984?

	Total Percent	Responses by Total Ad Budget Range					
		Under $500,000	$500,000- $1 Million	$1 Million- $2 Million	$2 Million- $5 Million	$5 Million- $10 Million	Over $10 Million
Number of respondents	268	58	56	46	46	31	31
Increase	64.3%	39.6%	67.9%	69.5%	60.9%	71.0%	93.5%
Decrease	4.5	5.2	5.3	2.2	6.5	6.4	0.0
About the same	31.2	55.2	26.8	28.3	32.6	22.6	6.5

Source: From "What National Advertisers Are Planning for 1984" by Wally Wood, *Magazine Age*, January 1984, pp. 22–26. Reprinted with permission of *Magazine Age*.

this investment. These results are consistent regardless of the type of advertising to be done.

Next, the *B* range of Figure 20.7 must be considered. Several pleasant events occur in this range. The effects of repetition can begin to be felt here as the advertiser makes enough of an impact to break through the noise in the environment and starts to have enough repetition for learning to occur and be maintained. The advertiser also is now in a range where economies of scale in media buying can be enjoyed. On the other hand, the amount of advertising is not so great as to be dysfunctional. Although diminishing returns have started to set in, the advertising is still worthwhile.

Economist model

Economists also would recommend a point in the *B* range. *Marginal analysis* says that the firm should continue to increase its budget as long as the last dollar spent generates more than itself in sales revenue. The concept of marginal analysis recommends looking at the margin, or edge, of spending. That is, what is the impact of the last dollar spent, or, if less money were spent, what is the impact of the last dollar spent in a lesser plan?

Figure 20.9 shows that the optimal level of advertising is at *A* *, for here total profit is maximized (the difference between sales and advertising is greatest). At higher levels of spending, the total profit begins to drop. The sales curve in Figure 20.9 looks similar to the S-shaped response curve of Figure 20.7; *A* * is in the area of diminishing returns but is still in the *B* range. Theoretically, advertising should be increased in the area of diminishing returns until these returns have decreased to the point where the next dollar spent does not generate an amount of revenue equal to itself.

In reality, it is extremely difficult to do marginal analysis of an advertising budget, but it is worthwhile to know what to look for and at what area in the sales curve to aim. Just in case things weren't complex enough, it is important to keep in mind that all sales responses to advertising do not occur in the same period as the advertising (the effects may lag) and that sales also occur as a result of product, price, and distribution.

Marginal analysis should also include an examination of the marginal contribution of advertising versus other marketing variables. For example, is it more profitable to spend the last marketing dollar on more advertising or on lowering prices? (The manager probably should be thinking in terms of marginal millions of dollars if the product is in national distribution.) In a larger sense, all allocations of marketing dollars occur at least implicitly by marginal analysis. When the brand manager brings the budget to the head of the marketing department, the

Figure 20.9 *Marginal analysis of advertising, sales, and profit*

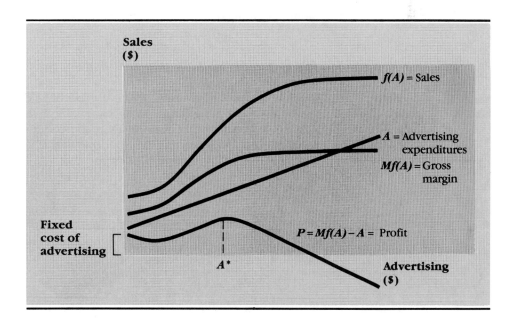

brand will be competing for scarce dollars against all other brand managers, and the department head must decide which allocation of dollars will give the firm the greatest profit. At this level of budgeting, the objective and task method and payout plan become tools that allow the brand manager to present the case to top management in a more effective manner.

Field experimentation

To obtain inputs for marginal analysis, the manager needs data. A common way to get such data is through a field experiment. In this research method, the manager uses different advertising campaigns in different matched markets and observes the results. *Field* refers to the real world (as opposed to a laboratory); *experiment* refers to the method of exposing different groups to different stimuli.

The sophistication of field experiments for budget testing has increased dramatically in the past few years because of several dramatic technological changes. The two most important developments are related to the use of cable television and the use of UPC (universal product code) scanners in grocery and drug stores.

Cable television allows precise control over, and accounting of, what messages are being sent into any particular home. While most cable systems do not take advantage of that potential, some systems do so in conjunction with market research firms. Cable systems can be split up so that a specific message can be sent into a specific home. This means that an advertiser can split a market and send test commercial A to half the homes and test commercial B to the other half. The advertiser also can test various frequency levels of a commercial to develop the best media plan. This arrangement allows comparative tests to be done in a single market; in the past, such a test required two or more matched markets which, in reality, were rarely truly equivalent.

After sending test messages to specific homes, the advertiser can do recall or attitude tests with the knowledge of which homes received which message and with the comfort of knowing that both commercials were seen in the same program environment.

While recall tests are possible in this setting, they are not common because the second technological development, the UPC scanner, makes even more valuable data available. UPC equipment allows the grocer to keep close control over inventories and gives consumers a detailed cash register receipt. The equipment can also be used by manufacturers to monitor sales of their product in response to various advertising, promotions, or pricing deals. There are several marketing research companies that analyze UPC data. To do so is a more sophisticated way to audit store sales, but combining cable and UPC creates a whole new way of testing.

Consumers can be given plastic identification cards with their own codes, which can also be read by a scanner. With this linkage, a researcher can determine what commercials were seen by a person and what subsequent purchases that person made. This allows control of the stimulus commercial, knowledge of competing commercials, and observation of consumer responses. To add sophistication, advertisers can also buy split runs of newspaper ads and place magazine ads by zip codes in certain markets.

Two firms currently offer this combination of split cable control and UPC identification. *BehaviorScan,* owned by Information Resources, Inc. and *AdTel,* owned by Burke Marketing Services, have somewhat similar systems. Both firms have invested heavily in a small number of markets in various parts of the United States and have built systems as described above. Currently, these systems are used predominantly for new product testing because of their high cost to firms (approximately $150,000 for two markets), but some copy testing also has been done. This type of system certainly gives the best reading of the ultimate advertising–sales relation, and as costs come down, they will be used more. When more is learned about this relation, budgeting should become a more precise process.

Little[15] has suggested a modification of the straight experiment such that only a small subset of markets receive experimental budget treatments, and most markets receive the budget that the manager would normally use in the absence of research. Then, half the test markets receive some budget that is below the normal amount, while the other half of the markets receive a budget considerably above the normal amount. Choosing the amount of change to test can be difficult; it must be great enough so that a response in sales will be observable, yet not so great as to make it infeasible as an implementable strategy. Such a strategy is also difficult to implement if there is a sales force dependent on the advertising; no salesperson would want to be in the market receiving a decreased level of spending.

Figure 20.10 shows several possible results of such a test. If the budget increases and sales stay relatively constant (as in *A*), then there is no merit in an increase; this action will merely reduce profits. Conversely, an increase in budget may lead to a large increase in sales (as in *B*); if this occurs, management must do a marginal analysis to see if the increase in sales revenues offsets the increase in advertising costs.

Similarly, a budget decrease can also be analyzed. If (as in *C*) a decrease in budget has little impact on sales, then profits can be increased by cutting the budget, as in the Budweiser case. The manager must be careful, though, to watch this situation carefully over time. While this decrease may not affect sales in the short run, there may be a slow deterioration in memory and eventually in sales over the long run.

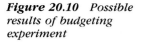

Figure 20.10 *Possible results of budgeting experiment*

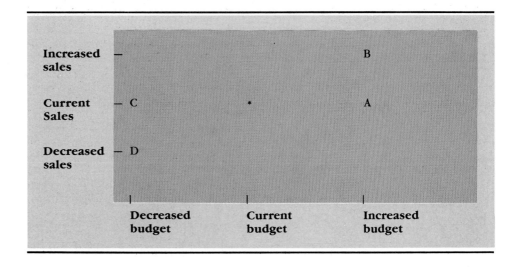

Finally, a decrease in budget may lead to a decrease in sales (as in *D*). Marginal analysis will show if the budget savings are more than offset by sales revenue losses. Again, this situation must be observed over time so that greater slippage does not occur in the longer run.

Computer simulation models

While there are many models in this class, one of the most well known is the BBDO (advertising agency) NEWS (New product Early Warning System) model. It has been used since the late 1960s to provide managers with forecasts and diagnostic information regarding new product strategies. In a recent report,[16] NEWS predicted market shares for 20 new products and was within a mean of 0.9 market share points across its 20 predictions.

Table 20.5 shows its predictions for the first 12 months of Strawbeery.[17] It shows that awareness peaks at greater than 80% (due to the addition of the coupon on top of the media in the third month), but that trial develops more slowly than expected. Market share fails to reach the desired 8%. (In NEWS, "repeat" users have made one purchase beyond "trial" while "users" repeat more than once.)

Perhaps of even greater value is the sensitivity analysis provided by NEWS. It shows that Strawbeery's failings are due to weaknesses in converting trial to repeat and repeat to loyal usage. Even though trial failed to meet the objective, awareness and trial are still above average for tests done by NEWS (due to advertising and promotion); repeat and usage are below average (due to product quality). The product idea seems more appealing than the product itself; perhaps that is a fitting analysis for strawberry-flavored beer.

NEWS represents a class of models that is based on quite sophisticated mathematical formulations that can recreate the marketplace processes quite accurately.

Table 20.5 Response values as predicted by ®NEWS

Period (month)	Aware (%)	Trial (%)	Repeat (%)	Users (%)	Cases (000)
1	42.6	6.4	0.0	6.4	798.1
2	64.8	12.1	2.6	8.3	1991.8
3	83.7	16.4	5.5	9.1	2948.7
4	79.9	18.1	7.7	7.7	3251.8
5	76.9	18.8	8.8	6.8	3135.2
6	74.5	19.6	9.2	6.5	2930.5
7	72.8	20.5	9.6	6.3	2791.7
8	71.4	21.5	10.1	6.1	2708.2
9	70.3	22.5	10.6	6.1	2651.0
10	69.5	23.6	11.1	6.0	2610.3
11	68.9	24.7	11.6	6.0	2581.0
12	68.4	25.8	12.1	6.0	2560.0
Summary				6.8	30958.1

Source: Personal communications with Ed Brody, Vice-President, BBDO. ®NEWS is a registered trademark of BBDO, Inc.

This concludes the discussion of budget setting. The remainder of the chapter deals with another financial issue of advertising: what is the financial arrangement between the agency and the client?

Agency Compensation

Advertising agencies were originally agents of media vehicles and were paid a commission to sell space in magazines and newspapers (there were no broadcast media then). In the late 1800s, the commission rate of 15% of media cost was established somewhat arbitrarily.

Over time, the function of the agency changed so that it became more involved in the creation and production of the advertising as well as its placement, and it eventually became the agent of the advertiser. While this transition took place, the 15% commission remained in place, and it has remained in place in a majority of cases ever since. Times change though, and the pure commission form of agency compensation is losing its dominance.

As can be seen in Table 20.6, the straight commission format was used by 68% of advertisers in 1968, but by only 52% in 1983. The straight fee for service format is gaining most rapidly in popularity, with various combination commission fee structures lagging behind.

There are several methods available by which agencies can be compensated for their work. The Association of National Advertisers believes that three criteria should be used in selecting a method

1. It should be fair to both sides so that both can make a fair profit.
2. The fees should be simple to understand.
3. The plan should be easy to administer.[18]

In addition, the system must be in the best interest of both parties so that they can work together with trust and respect for one another. There must be an incentive for the agency to work hard on the account and for the client to feel a sense of value. In relation to this last point, 75% of advertisers now audit the accounting books of their agencies, and 6% audit the profitability of the agency on their account.[19]

Common compensation methods

In the *straight commission* method, the agency receives 15% of the fees charged by the media vehicle. That is, if the cost of a media insertion is $100, the agency gets $100 from the client, keeps $15, and sends $85 to the vehicle. In other words, the agency gets *15% of the gross fee.*

Table 20.6 Preferred advertiser/agency compensation methods

	1976	1979	1983
Straight 15% commission	68	57	52
Commission/fee combination	15	18	19
Straight fee	17	25	29

Source: *Advertising Age,* 25 April 1983, p. 3. Reprinted with permission. Copyright 1983 by Crain Communications, Inc.

$$\$100 - (15\%)(\$100) = \$85 \qquad (15\% \text{ of gross})$$

Sometimes the commission is referred to as 17.65%. This is actually the same because it is *17.65% of the net fee.* In this case, the agency gets a bill for $85 from a supplier, adds on its commission, and bills the client for $100.

$$\$85 + (17.65\%)(\$85) = \$100 \qquad (17.65\% \text{ of net})$$

In most cases, agencies also add a commission onto final production costs. In a 1981 survey, 94% of agencies and 87% of advertisers felt that it was proper to mark up production costs in this way.[20] It is conventional for the *media* to bill the agency for the $100 and allow it to keep 15% of the gross charge, but the convention for *production vendors* is to bill the agency for $85, which the agency marks up by 17.65% of the net charge. Large agencies are more likely to mark up production costs than are smaller agencies. Large clients are more likely to pay a lower percentage, and small clients, a larger percentage.

In a simple example, the agency might place $3 million in television and receive $450,000 in commissions. At the same time, the agency might pay out $300,000 in production costs; in addition it must pay its overhead, including salaries, and make a reasonable profit.

As expenses mount, agencies have needed also to charge commissions on production to come out ahead. For example, in 1973, the cost to produce six 30-second Midas Muffler commercials was almost $110,000 (without agency commission) while the cost of a network 30-second was about $40,000. In 1983 these six commercials cost over $410,000 (again before commissions), and the cost of the average network 30-second was $85,000.[21] This means that it took almost twice as many media insertions in 1983 as it did in 1973 to cover the production costs.

Does this commission system lead to a fair return for the agency and a fair expense for the advertiser? As seen in Figure 20.9, there is a trend toward dissatisfaction. Advertisers feel the commission is too high in cases where the agency produces one or a few messages and then places them many times over several years. In this case, the agency is rewarded for spending, and encouraged to spend, large sums of money on media. On the other hand, agencies feel that the commission structure is unfair if they must produce many messages for many vehicles and no single message runs very often. This often occurs with industrial and retail clients. The commission system also doesn't work well for noncommissionable media, such as direct mail specialty advertising or special projects such as promotions and public relations.

One solution is to pay a fee for services rendered. With a *fee system* the agency charges the client firm for all services performed. Fees are charged for all time spent on client work, and all expenses are billed either at cost or, more often, at cost plus 17.65%. All overhead charges are built into the fee structure. The commissions received from the media are used against the client's account or are returned to the client.

Somewhere between these two methods is the *combination of commissions and fees.* Here, the advertising work done for commissionable media is compensated for by commissions, and all other services are billed on a fee basis. Typical services would include research, special presentations, training the sales force, promotions, and public relations. Table 20.7 shows a listing of several areas of costs and who generally pays these costs.

Table 20.7 Expenses paid for by agency or client

What expenses are appropriate client expenses? (Marked up either 15% or 17.65%)

	Advertisers	Agencies
Production of finished commercials	87%	94%
Production costs (composition, engravings, etc.)	86	90
Production of collateral materials	85	85
Production of prints, duplicate tapes	71	89
Finished art, photos done outside	80	89

Expense items most widely viewed as normal agency "absorbs" (Percent agreeing)

	Advertisers	Agencies
Legal review and clearance	71%	29%
Rough storyboards	68	29
Rough art, preliminary photos	67	26
Network negotiation	52	56
Auditioning, signing commercial talent	41	39

Who should pay research expenses?

Advertisers: Should be charged to client . . .

	Charged at cost	Marked up 15%	Marked up 17.65%	Should be absorbed	Could go either way
Concept testing marketing	41%	9%	16%	12%	22%
Concept testing advertising	33	8	15	21	23
Copy testing, rough	31	—	12	38	19
Copy testing, finished	37	10	21	13	19
Post-testing (recall, awareness, purchase, etc.)	35	15	21	10	19

Agencies: Should be charged to client . . .

	Charged at cost	Marked up 15%	Marked up 17.65%	Should be absorbed	Could go either way
Concept testing marketing	25%	1%	44%	5%	25%
Concept testing advertising	23	3	37	8	29
Copy testing, rough	30	3	29	11	27
Copy testing, finished	27	3	47	2	21
Post-testing (recall, awareness, purchase, etc.)	24	2	53	3	18

Source: *Advertising Age*, 18 May 1981, pp. 63 ff. Reprinted with permission. Copyright 1981 by Crain Communications, Inc.

T·H·E I·N·S·I·D·E O·U·T·L·O·O·K

Lewis G. Pringle

**Executive Vice-President
and Executive Director, Marketing and Strategy,
Batten, Barton, Durstine & Osborn, Inc.**

Lew Pringle, executive vice-president, member of the board of directors and account management committee, is the executive director of marketing and strategy at BBDO. Dr. Pringle joined BBDO as an associate research director in 1968 and was elected a vice-president the following year. In 1971 he was appointed director of the Marketing Sciences Department. In 1973, he became a part-time consultant to the agency while teaching marketing and econometrics at the Carnegie-Mellon University in Pittsburgh.

Dr. Pringle rejoined BBDO in a full-time capacity in 1974 and was appointed director of management information services and international research in 1975. He was named director of research services and elected a senior vice-president and member of the board of directors in 1978. He was elected executive vice-president in 1981. In 1984, he was made a member of the account management committee and was named executive director, marketing and strategy.

A 1963 graduate of Harvard College in chemistry, Dr. Pringle received his M.S. and Ph.D. degrees from the Sloan School of Management at M.I.T., specializing in O.R. and statistics.

Profit Counts

Perhaps the single most important problem facing senior marketing management today is its relative inability to deal with financial issues the way its counterparts in other disciplines are rountinely able to do.

Almost everyone in a typical business organization has a well-developed capacity to argue on behalf of his or her capital expenditures through the use of tight logic, ample data to support the cause and desired effect, *and,* importantly, straightforward capital budgeting analysis. In other words, almost anyone can provide an analysis of the type that chief financial officers and CEOs are trained to respect.

But—*not* marketing people. In general, we are not well trained in financial matters. And, worse still, we *believe*—and have been told over and over again—that *our* discipline, unlike any other, cannot be reduced to the same rigorous, objective basis as can, for example, a plant replacement investment.

The facts, however, do not support this belief. It is in fact true that, within surprisingly tight bounds, most marketing and advertising expenditures *can* be treated as capital investments and *are* amenable to such ordinary financial tools as discounted present value analysis and/or computation of internal rates of return.

Perhaps we don't use these methods because they are not part of our experience or because we feel that they aren't "realistic" in marketing or, simply, because we don't know how. Whatever our reason, as marketing professionals, we're clearly missing the boat.

The plain truth is that senior corporate management typically relies on certain well-established methods to help it allocate resources across competing demands for funds in a firm. Marketing stands alone in not playing by these generally accepted rules.

We *could* do so—and quite easily. All that is really required to take full advantage of capital budgeting methods is a reasonably precise understanding of what an incremental dollar, invested in a specific marketing instrument (e.g., consumer advertising), will yield in terms of profit or contribution.

Is this kind of understanding *beyond* our current ability? Absolutely not. A few organizations do it routinely. And, as is often the case when firms enjoy competitive advantage, they're not announcing their activities to the world.

How *can* one relate marketing expenditures to sales? With scanner technology. With econometric modeling of historic data. And with carefully designed and controlled marketplace experiments.

Take just modeling alone and consider some of the general principles that have been made clear to us through our own work in this area. For example, most companies overspend on new products and underspend on established brands. Also, there are very few situations in marketing where "expert" subjective judgment can't be improved upon through analysis—*even* though the analytically disinclined will loudly disagree.

At BBDO we have, through modeling, advised clients in areas of budget optimality, timing, allocation of fixed resources across media, brands, and alternative marketing instruments. We've found this work useful in better understanding the forces that *really* drive a business, in developing plans, in establishing decision criteria for market effectiveness testing, and in the critical and objective evaluation of alternative marketing programs. We estimate the short-term and long-term (carry over) effect of advertising. And we do it all with a view toward providing senior management with an objective, financially sound recommendation about where its cash resources can be applied with maximal long-term, discounted impact on the bottom line.

In short, my advice to anyone contemplating a career in marketing today is simple. Develop your skills in finance and the quantitative tools that support expertise in this area. Many of your marketing colleagues will think you've taken leave of your senses. But the *boss* will understand.

Other lesser used compensation methods include

- Some of the methods mentioned on page 630 plus a *retainer* that ensures the agency of some minimal monthly income from the account.

- *Completion billing* whereby the agency submits a proposal plus a cost estimate ($\pm 10\%$) for all work and is paid in accordance with its estimate. This method is commonly used with a fee system to contain costs within some predetermined range.

- A *bonus* based on the profitability of the brand for the client. This is not common but provides interesting incentives to the agency. Other methods give the agency an incentive to maximize media expenditures and/or work. A bonus based on the client's profits provides an incentive to minimize costs while maintaining effectiveness. This method should lead to greater cooperation between client and agency.

Summary

To compute the budget, it is necessary to state (1) the problem, (2) the communications objectives that will lead to a solution to the problem, and (3) the strategies needed to meet the objectives. Having made those statements, it is not so difficult to price the strategies; the sum of these costs becomes the proposed budget. Next this budget must be evaluated to see if it is a good investment for the firm to make in an absolute sense and also relative to other ways in which these limited dollars could be spent.

This budgeting method is the objective and task method; it has the virtue of fitting into the decision sequence framework that has been used as an overall planning model throughout the text. This budgeting process, therefore, complements the managerial processes that have been suggested to derive the advertising and promotions strategies.

Alternative budgeting methods are more intuitive and are not based on the needs of the communications problems. While these rule-of-thumb methods may lead management in the proper direction, there is no reason to believe that the resulting budgets will be appropriate for the problems at hand.

While data in this chapter show that the relation between advertising and sales is sometimes hard to assess, advertising does have a clear and important role. It builds awareness of, knowledge of, and favorable feelings toward the firm. At times it may even lead directly to sales.

Discussion Questions

1. Why does budgeting occur twice in the decision sequence? Describe the two ways in which the budget influences the planning process.

2. What are the three common predetermined budgeting methods? Describe each and discuss the pros and cons of each method.

3. Under what sorts of conditions will a firm need to devote a larger share of its revenues to advertising and promotions?

4. Describe the objective and task method of budgeting. What advantages and disadvantages does it have when compared to the other budgeting methods

discussed in the chapter? How does this method relate to the decision sequence framework?

5. What is the value of the payout plan in the budgeting process?

6. What is a "lagged effect"? Why are lagged effects important in assessing the value of an advertising and promotions plan?

7. Why is it more difficult to budget for new product introductory campaigns?

8. Why does a low level of advertising lead to a weak sales response (as shown in the *A* part of Figure 20.7)? Why does a high level of advertising lead to a weak sales response (as shown in the *C* part of Figure 20.7)?

9. What is the theoretically best level of advertising spending? Why is it difficult to apply this theory?

10. Assume that you are a manager who has just received data showing that, by increasing your budget, your sales go from * to *A* in Figure 20.10. What would you do? What would you do if sales went to *B*? to *C*? to *D*?

11. Now that you have finished planning your career search communications plan, you need to see if you can afford it. How will you make this assessment? Did you consider budgetary issues during your situation analysis? Did this influence the development of your campaign? How?

Notes

1. Paul W. Farris and Robert D. Buzzell, "Why Advertising and Promotional Costs Vary: Some Cross-Sectional Analyses," *Journal of Marketing* 43 (Fall 1979), pp. 112–122.

2. Theodore J. Gage, "Budgets: Figuring with Intuition," *Advertising Age,* 13 April 1981, p. S-4.

3. James O. Peckham, Sr., "The Wheel of Marketing: Analysis and Interpretation of What Generally Happens to Consumer Sales of Branded Food Products, Household Needs, Toiletries, and Proprietary Drug Products When a Series of Marketing Action Takes Place Based on the Nielsen Retail Index Data," (Chicago: A. C. Nielsen Company, 1972).

4. William M. Weilbacher, *Advertising* (New York: MacMillian Publishing Co., 1979), pp. 103–104.

5. A. J. San Augustine and W. F. Foley, "How Large Advertisers Set Their Budgets," *Journal of Advertising Research* 15 (October 1975).

6. Kristian S. Palda, *The Measurement of Cumulative Advertising Effects* (Englewood Cliffs, N.J.: Prentice-Hall, 1964).

7. J. O. Peckham, "Can We Relate Advertising Dollars to Market Share Objectives?," in *How Much to Spend for Advertising?* ed. M. A. McNiven (New York: Association of National Advertisers, 1969), p. 30.

8. "How Many Ad Dollars Are Enough?" *Media Decisions* 12, no. 7 (July 1977), p. 59.

9. David A. Aaker and James M. Carman, "Are You Overadvertising?" Working Paper, University of California–Berkeley, rev. 1982.

10. Reg Rhodes, "What ADTEL Has Learned," Paper presented to the American Marketing Association, New York Chapter, 22 March 1977.

11. Russell I. Haley, "Sales Effects of Media Weight," *Journal of Advertising Research* 18 (June 1978), pp. 9–18.

12. Russell L. Ackoff and James R. Emshoff, "Advertising Research at Anheuser-Busch, Inc. (1963–68)," *Sloan Management Review,* Winter and Spring 1975.

13. Ackoff and Emshoff, "Advertising Research."

14. Wally Wood, "What National Advertisers Are Planning for 1984," *Magazine Age,* January 1984, pp. 22–26.

15. J. D. C. Little, "A Model of Adaptive Control of Promotional Spending," *Operations Research* 14 (November-December), pp. 1075–1098.

16. Lewis G. Pringle, R. Dale Wilson, and Edward I. Brody, "NEWS: A Decision-Oriented Model for New Product Analysis and Forecasting," *Marketing Science,* 1 (Winter 1982), pp. 1–29.

17. Thanks to Lewis G. Pringle and Edward I. Brody of BBDO for their assistance in the NEWS analysis of Strawbeery.

18. Paul Pease, "The Misunderstood Money Side of Client–Agency Relationships," *Scan* 27, no. 12, pp. 9–11.

19. "Clients Continue Shifting from 15%," *Advertising Age,* 25 April 1983, p. 3.

20. Herb Zeltner, "Sounding Board: Clients, Admen Split on Compensation," *Advertising Age,* 18 May 1981, pp. 64 ff.

21. Kim Foltz, with Marilyn Achiron and Connie Leslie, "Goodbye, Mr. Whipple," *Newsweek,* 26 March 1984, p. 63.

Good Vibrations
·THE·SUNKIST·ORANGE·SODA·CAMPAIGN·

BUDGETING STRATEGY

Budget

There was a $20 million national equivalent budget allocated during the introductory period in each market. This meant that the impact in each market was equivalent to what it would have been with a national budget of $20 million. Sunkist began in only six markets in early 1978, added five markets later in the year, and then continued to roll out across the United States in the following year. Because entry into each market was dependent upon establishing relations with a bottler, it would have been difficult to develop a national campaign during introduction. In later years, there was a national media plan. Table S.1 shows the budget allocation for the $20 million plan.

Sunkist realized that the brand needed heavy investment spending and therefore established a long-term payout schedule. In 1979 there were sales of $9.6 million, with losses of $10.8 million. These figures were, respectively, $21.5 and 11.7 million in 1980, and $33.7 and 4.7 million in 1981. With each passing year, sales went up dramatically and losses declined. Introductory expenses were quite high and lasted for several years as the gradual roll-out progressed. The 1981 corporate annual report stated that a profit was shown in the last quarter of that year.

Table S.1 Media dollars by advertising period (000)

	TV	Radio	Total	%
First 3 months	$ 8,195	$3,071	$11,266	60
Next 2 months	2,940	1,246	4,186	22
Last 7 months	3,330	—	3,330	18
Consumer media totals	$14,465	$4,317	$18,782	100
Contingency			1,000	
Trade			50	
Production			150	
Total			$19,982	

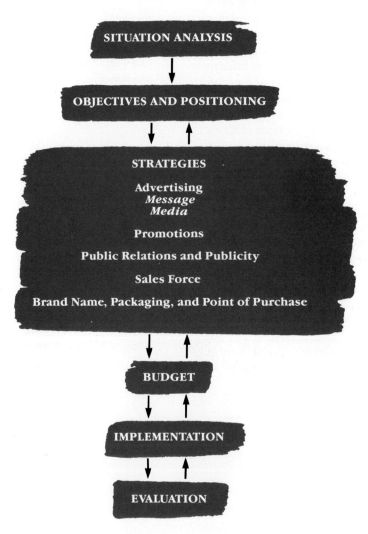

Decision Sequence Framework

Part Nine

Retail,
Industrial, and
Services Marketing

*T*his text now departs dramatically from the course it has taken to this point. Each of the prior parts has examined one aspect of the decision sequence so that the reader has been taken through the construction of an entire campaign. In doing so, there have been discussions of the situation analysis, the setting of objectives and positioning, the development of several classes of strategies, and the determination of the budget.

Throughout this process, almost all examples have come from the area of consumer products. This bias was not meant to reflect the distribution of advertising and promotions dollars in the real world, for such a bias does not exist; rather, this bias was selected for other reasons.

1. Consumer product advertising, in general, is more likely to be developed in a manner consistent with the decision sequence framework advocated here. Other areas are just beginning to discover and use this rigorous and rewarding process; in making this discovery, these organizations are closely examining consumer goods' successes and failures in their own search for models.

2. It seemed cleaner to be consistent in the examples and to avoid an overwhelming number of "yes, buts." "Yes, buts" are often used when there are exceptions to general statements; in this text the use of primarily consumer goods examples avoided this to some degree.

After collecting "yes, buts" for several hundred pages, it is now appropriate to unleash them all at once. This section is devoted to the broadening of the applications of advertising and promotions into other areas. As will be seen, though, the similarities across the areas to be discussed are much greater than the differences. In any of the areas to be explored in this section, the best advertising and promotions will result if the decision sequence is used.

This means that any organization should use the decision sequence frame-work and should carefully assess its problems in terms of a target market, its own product or service, its competition, its environment, and its own internal con-straints. This assessment should lead to a statement of objectives based on the DAGMAR model; the objectives need to specify the type of response desired by the organization.

All communications are a result of the desire of an organization to elicit some response. All responses fit into some level of the hierarchy of effects so that awareness, attitude, and/or behavior are sought. In virtually all cases the organiza-tion should also seek to establish a unique position in the minds of its target mar-ket for itself, its product, its service, or its idea. Success is more likely if members of the customer target audience can be shown the unique benefit of responding to the selling organization. While the specific objectives and position will be unique to each organization, the need to set objectives and establish a position is applicable to all.

These basic issues should be common to any organization, but often they are not recognized. Those observers who see differences at these levels of the deci-sion sequence often see that many organizations, through choice or ignorance, do not go through these vital steps. Some other observers say that retailing, indus-trial marketing, nonprofit marketing, or services marketing is basically different from consumer products marketing. It is true that there are differences in strate-gies and execution styles, but these should emerge from a proper use of the deci-sion sequence and not because the underlying communications process differs.

The same holds true for the use of strategies. Media, message, promotions, public relations, sales force, and brand name are all relevant communications tools. What will differ will be the relationship among them; some are more rele-vant to some organizations while some will never be useful to a particular organi-zation. This, though, was also the case between products that elicit high versus low levels of involvement or between new and established brands in the same product class.

A virtue of the decision sequence is its robustness across varying cases and its ability to help guide management to the most appropriate strategies. The prior several hundred pages of text should therefore be equally useful to any type of organization that has a need to communicate with its publics and target markets.

The next three chapters will be devoted to looking at differences across orga-nizations and problems that would cause managers to make different assessments or select different strategies from those discussed in the prior chapters. To that end, the first chapter deals with issues relevant to retailers; the next chapter deals with business-to-business marketing communications; and the third chapter is concerned with retail, professional, and nonbusiness services. The major value of these chapters should be in raising issues of concern for the situation analysis so that the strategies that follow will be based on the most relevant variables.

Chapter 21
Communications for
Retail Marketing

*H*aving just made the point that retailer problems may differ from those of product advertisers, it should next be pointed out that there are a large variety of retailer types and that different types of communications solutions will need to be found for these differing types.

Describing Retailing and Retailer Activities

Kotler defines *retailing* as "the activities involved in selling goods or services directly to final consumers for their personal, nonbusiness use," and a *retailer* or *retail store* as "any business enterprise whose sales volume primarily comes from retailing."[1] As a rule, retailers provide the basic services of creating time and place utility (access to goods at a time and in a place that is convenient) and assuming a risk of ownership (they will lose money if they cannot sell what they have bought). Their profit is derived by making good decisions concerning utility and ownership, by pricing correctly to cover these risks, and by providing appropriate ancillary services such as the provision of information and knowledge. It is clear from this description that advertising and promotions will play a key role in the retailer's success or failure.

The retailer must make some target market aware of

- The existence of the location and its hours of operation
- The type of goods and services provided
- The price of the goods and services

In addition, the retailer may want to create a unique position and to advertise to form this image. Finally, advertising and promotions may be vital to the sale of product that was overbought and now looms as a large potential loss if it cannot be sold.

This description emphasizes some of the pros and cons of retailing and *retail advertising.* While product advertising tries to create awareness and a favorable image that will ultimately lead to a sale, the focal point of the retailer is to make a sale. This is where the consumer and product interact and where the exchange occurs. Ultimately, the product lives or dies on the basis of retailers' actions in most cases.

From another perspective, this is an area where one can truly see the difference between good and bad advertising. A good product and price-oriented retail ad in the Friday newspaper will lead to sales on Saturday. The copywriter can go to the store or to the cash register and see if the ad worked. One problem discussed in earlier chapters was the general difficulty of measuring the value of advertising. This is not a problem for retailers. The response will be quite clear and easy to measure if the ad is specific in terms of product and price.

Key differences from product advertising

Before examining differences that occur at various stages of the decision sequence, more general differences between retail and product advertising and promotions should be considered:

1. *Immediacy*   As discussed above, retail advertising and promotions should have a quick impact that can be easily seen and measured. In addition, retail planning in general seems to have a more short-run horizon so that yesterday's problems lead to today's advertising and tomorrow's solutions. Product manufacturers expect to build up many repetitions over a long period before seeing any response to advertising; if retailers don't get immediate action, they know the ad failed.

2. *Product versus location*   The manufacturer advertises a product and doesn't care where it is purchased; the retailer advertises a location and doesn't care what is purchased. While that is a generalization, it is useful within broad limits. Of course, the retailer would rather sell a high-priced item on an older model that has been discontinued, but given an inventory of several thousand items, any sale will do. A sale here is always better than a sale there. This issue was discussed earlier as a problem with co-op advertising, because the two (supposedly) cooperating parties have different goals for their advertising. Co-op advertising is reexamined later in this chapter.

The issue of competing goals is only resolvable in the case of a franchise operation (such as a fast food chain) or an exclusive dealership (such as an automobile retailer). Here both parties have a stake in the same products and the same locations. As a result, retail advertising in these cases differs from that of independent retailers.

3. *Breadth of product line*   This issue relates to the prior one. The manufacturer has one or a fairly small number of products to advertise compared to the retailer, who may need to balance advertising across thousands of products. In the latter case, the only constant is the store itself. If the retailer is not careful, the advertising will become fragmented and without focus. While product advertising is likely to have continuity across messages, retail advertising can easily take on the tone of today's products and not build a store image that helps with the next day's products.

4. *Geographic coverage*   The majority of retailers are single-unit establishments, while the majority of products are sold regionally or nationally. Retailers have the advantage that they can more accurately tailor their message to their target; their disadvantage is that there are fewer efficiencies to be gained from large media buys. Even though network television provides large reach efficiencies over a collection of local buys, few retailers (e.g., Sears, Penney's, K-mart, Safeway, the large fast food chains) have the size to take advantage of this opportunity.

Types of retailers

Another area to consider before beginning on managerial issues concerns the various types of retailers. Kotler lists several classification schemes that need to be considered:[2]

1. Amount of service

   - self-service
   - self-selection
   - limited-service
   - full-service

2. Speed of inventory turnover

3. Size of profit margin

4. Size of store

5. Breadth of assortment

6. Autonomy of retailer from manufacturer

7. Proximity to other retailers

Each of these variables will have an impact on the type and frequency of the advertising and therefore will need to be considered in the situation analysis. Figure 21.1 summarizes Kotler's categorizations and shows examples of each.

Relating retailing to advertising

A more useful categorization scheme concerns advertising and comes from Johnson, who organizes retailers into three groups and then describes each of them:[3]

1. *Retailers who will advertise*   These retailers are characterized by having one or more of the following characteristics:

- *Need a large volume of customers or large volume per customer*   These stores have a large inventory to turn over or have a low margin per item. Advertising and promotions are used to bring in more customers. Examples are supermarkets and drugstores.

- *Traffic is irregular or infrequent*   These stores sell items not used in daily activities, so that advertising must be used to keep awareness high. This, in turn, will promote usage when the appropriate events occur. Florists, travel agencies, and shoe stores are good examples of this type.

Figure 21.1   Several ways to classify retail outlets

CLASSIFICATION OF RETAILERS BASED ON THE AMOUNT OF CUSTOMER SERVICE

Decreasing services ──────────▶ Increasing services

	Self-service	Self-selection	Limited-service	Full-service
Attributes	Very few services Price appeal Staple goods Convenience goods	Restricted services Price appeal Staple goods Convenience goods	Small variety of services Shopping goods	Wide variety of services Fashion merchandise Specialty merchandise
Examples	Warehouse retailing Grocery stores Discount stores Mail-order retailing Automatic vending	Discount retailing Variety stores Mail-order retailing	Door-to-door sales Department stores Telephone sales Variety stores	Speciality stores Department stores

DIFFERENT WAYS TO CLASSIFY RETAIL OUTLETS

Product line sold	Relative price emphasis	Nature of business premises	Control of outlets	Type of store cluster

Speciality store
Department store
Supermarket
Convenience store
Combination store,
   superstore, and
   hypermarche
Service business
	Discount store
	Warehouse store
	Catalog showroom
		Mail-and-
		telephone-order
		   retailing
		Automatic
		   vending
		Buying service
		Door-to-door
		   retailing
			Corporate chain
			Voluntary chain
			   and retailer
			   cooperative
			Consumer
			   cooperative
			Franchise
			   organization
			Merchandising
			   conglomerate
				Central business
				   district
				Regional shopping
				   center
				Community
				   shopping center
				Neighborhood
				   shopping center

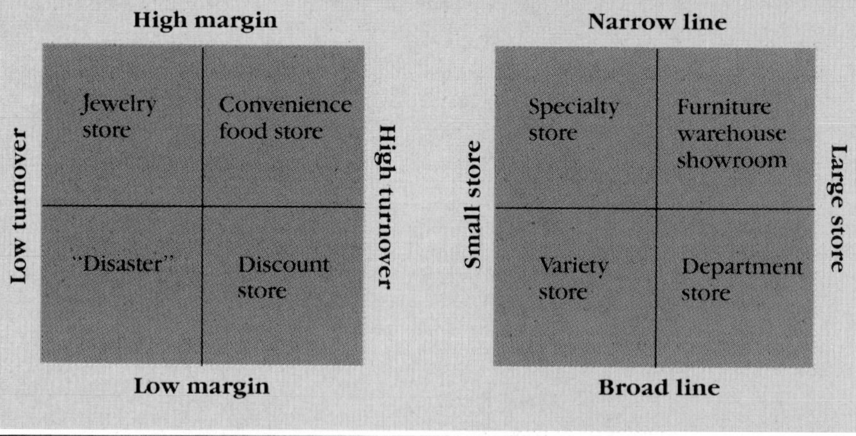

High margin

	Jewelry store	Convenience food store	
Low turnover			High turnover
	"Disaster"	Discount store	

Low margin

Narrow line

	Specialty store	Furniture warehouse showroom	
Small store			Large store
	Variety store	Department store	

Broad line

▪ *Poor location*   Because there may be less walk-in traffic, advertising will be necessary to let customers know about the retailer's existence. Examples could come from virtually any class of retailer where one objective is to keep cost down by choosing a low-overhead location. As a result, the store is out of the mainstream of traffic and unknown by most people. Retailers who must advertise for some other reason anyway (perhaps because of infrequent usage) can select a less well-known location and maintain location awareness through advertising.

- *High-cost items*   These goods may take lots of deliberation before the purchase is made. Image advertising is important here in helping customers select a retailer for these important decisions. This category correlates highly with the infrequent purchase category. Examples include furniture, appliance, and jewelry stores.

- *Strong competition*   Across all the above, another issue is level of competition. Highly competitive classes will need to have increased advertising.

2. *Retailers who may advertise*   This group of retailers is not as likely to advertise as the first group.

- *Small, neighborhood store*   These stores are comfortably successful with steady volume coming from the neighborhood. Advertising will begin or increase if the owner aspires to more growth or volume than the neighborhood can provide. Examples in this class include bakeries, bookstores, dry cleaners, and hair styling salons.

- *Drop-in places*   Customers drop in on impulse and there are lots of short visits. Advertising can increase the number of drop-ins by making the location more top of mind. Ice cream parlors are an example of this class.

- *Special problem to be solved*   Employment agencies, insurance agents, and movers are infrequently used but require considerable thought and/or planning. Advertising keeps awareness up and provides an image for the selection process.

- *Narrow target market*   Hobby shops, nurseries, and veterinarians are used by a small segment of the population; as a result, any advertising will result in large amounts of wasted coverage.

The four "may advertise" categories all deal in products or services used by a small number of people, either because of geographics, infrequent usage, or narrow targets. In each case advertising would be wasteful unless the market is increased in some way.

3. *Retailers who may not advertise*   Johnson feels that this group is categorized by existing heavy daily traffic. Why advertise if the volume already exists? This category consists of needed goods and services. Once a traffic pattern and volume have been established, advertising isn't necessary. Gasoline stations depend on repeat business from people moving in set patterns; repair services rely on wear-outs, break-downs, and obsolescence. Once volume is established, good service will keep it.

Types of advertising used by retailers

Retail advertising basically falls into two classes. *Product advertising* provides price and availability information on one or more products carried by the retailer and has short-run, sales-oriented goals; *retailer image advertising* develops the position of the retailer without giving a great deal of product information and has a more long-run attitude goal. The two classes cannot easily be combined in one message, but two campaigns can be run simultaneously. Often the long-run position is developed on television while the product and price information is presented through the newspaper. Figure 21.2 shows an example of an image-oriented retailer ad.

Figure 21.2 *Image-oriented retailer ad*

Figure 21.3 *Regular price-line advertising*

Mandell suggests that advertising for products sold at retail can be subdivided into three levels of price and immediacy:[4]

▪ *regular price-line advertising*   This type of advertising is closest to the image message and is least immediate. It shows items from the product line of the retailer to let consumers know about breadth and depth. Because the prices haven't been cut, there is less urgency in the message. These ads will also feature the position or atmosphere of the store to develop long-term attitudes. Figure 21.3 is an example of regular price-line advertising.

▪ *sale advertising*   These messages are more immediate and feature reduced prices for a limited time period. Since the regular period ads have little urgency, intermittent sales are needed to urge customers to visit the store. Sales can extend a selling season by offering merchandise before or after the normal season (winter jackets go on sale in August and March), or they can bring customers to a department that is doing poorly. Figure 21.4 is an example of sale advertising. Too frequent use of sales has taught consumers to wait; this leads to slow periods between sales and more sales to pick up the slack. This vicious pattern tends to make discount merchandisers out of too many retailers. The final impact of frequent sales is to erode the quality position that may have been developed earlier as more and more of the budget is put into sale advertising.

Figure 21.4   *Sale advertising*

Figure 21.5   *Clearance sale advertising*

- *clearance advertising*   This class has the most immediate and least image-oriented advertising. Its purpose is to clear the store of merchandise that couldn't be sold in any other way and, as a result, may not be considered desirable. The message of this advertising is that the consumer can now buy at the absolute lowest price. As consumers learn this, they begin to pass up regular sales and wait for clearance sales; retailers, in turn, have ever more frequent clearance sales. Figure 21.5 is an example of a clearance sale ad.

There is also another separation of advertising types within sale and clearance advertising. The sale can be for a department or product type, or it can be storewide. When there is specificity and a narrow offering, the ad can more easily be coordinated in its appearance and theme (as in Figure 21.6); a storewide sale

Figure 21.6 *Sale for a narrow range of products*

Figure 21.7 *A storewide sale*

is more difficult to tie together unless the store itself offers a specialized range of products. Figure 21.7 shows an ad for a storewide sale of many unrelated items; this ad must work harder to keep the reader's attention.

Using the Decision Sequence for Retail Advertising

The purpose of this chapter is to discuss issues that should be considered that set the retailer apart from the manufacturer. Possibly the clearest way to accomplish this task is to consider each stage of the decision sequence. In doing so the reader should keep in mind that most of what was covered earlier in the text will also be relevant to the retailer.

Situation analysis

The basic issues of the situation analysis have not changed. The firm must have information about its target market, competitors, offerings (products and services), and internal constraints.

Target market (trading area)   Determination of trading area is important in establishing geographic segmentation because any advertising messages delivered outside the trading area represent a waste of money. The size of the trading area will vary depending on a number of factors and needs to be considered in media planning; the more unique the retailer or the product line carried, the larger the trading area. The only Jaguar dealer in Joplin will have a trading area covering the entire metro market and can therefore use local media with little wasted coverage; the only Famous Footwear retail shoe store in Fresno will have a small trading area that may cover only a five-mile radius around the store.

The shoe store has a small trading area because there are many similar shoe stores and few people will drive far for the distinction of trading with a particular shoe retailer. Famous Footwear is aware of this and therefore does very little advertising when it first enters a market; it waits until it has enough locations so that the advertising is not wasted. In 1972, when the company first entered the Chicago market, it did little advertising except in regional editions of newspapers; by 1983, it had 12 stores in the area and was covered by local newspapers and television. At that time, it was able to do efficient advertising because the combined trading areas of all the stores covered most of the Chicago market. Geographic coverage is important to a retailer in determining if advertising dollars can be efficiently spent.

Johnson suggests five categories of stores that give insight into the size of the trading area. Figure 21.8 shows this categorization scheme; its key value is in assessing trading area size for media selection. Frequent trips are made to stores

Figure 21.8   Classifying retailers by type of visit

1. **Short-Trip Stores**
   In the neighborhood
   Visit one or more times a week
   Little shopper effort
   - Reminder advertising
   - Announcements of special offerings as direct to customer as possible
   Bakery
   Drugstore
   Dry cleaning
   Food ship (supermarket)
   Gasoline station
   Laundry
   Meat market

2. **Drop-By Stores**
   Along the way
   Visit weekly to monthly
   Minor shopper effort
   - Reminder advertising
   - Frequent announcements of special prices
   - Presentations of new merchandise
   - Notices that describe seasonal appropriateness of goods or service
   Bookstore
   Card shop

   Car wash
   Fast-food outlet
   Photographic supply dealer
   Soft-frozen dessert stand

3. **Special-Trip Stores**
   A distance away
   Visit weekly to several times a year
   Medium shopper effort
   - Frequent notices of special opportunities to save
   - Presentations of new merchandise
   Apparel store
   Florist
   Men's shop
   Pet grooming
   Handicraft store
   Hardware store
   Music store
   Restaurant
   Variety store
   Travel agent
   Shoe store

4. **Excursion Stores**
   Remote
   Visit once a year or once in a lifetime

   Maximum shopper effort
   - Maintain constant advertising
   - Periodic announcements of special prices, deals, or offerings
   Bridal shop
   Caterer
   Do-it-yourself home service
   Furniture store
   Jewelry store
   Painting and wallpaper store
   Photographic studio
   Upholstering shop

5. **Call-Up Stores**
   As handy as the phone
   No shopper effort
   Infrequent face to face contact
   - Constant availability advertising
   Floor service
   Interior decorator
   Painting, interior and exterior
   Paperhanging
   Piano tuning
   Plumbing
   Trucking and cartage

with small trading areas; efficient vehicles would include neighborhood newspapers, direct mail, and door stuffers. The special trip and excursion stores cover a wider trading area and can utilize more traditional local media.

Target market (consumer characteristics)   The issues here are quite similar to those discussed in Chapter 2 concerning segmentation. Advertising strategy needs to be based on typical demographic, psychographic, media, and product usage characteristics.

Product line, competition, and position   Again, the basic issues will be familiar. Specific to retailing, the firm should study its own and its competitors' depth and breadth of product line, the ancillary services of each, the location and trading area of each, the pricing strategy of each, and the perceptions of quality and value of products.

Dealing with these issues leads to data that can be used in positioning the store. In order for the store to succeed, it should have its own unique identity that is tied to the benefits the store offers. Because the retail business is very sale oriented, managers can easily get wrapped up in selling merchandise in the short run with no thought given to a long-run position. The position is important in creating an image for consumers but also gives direction to management across a wide range of issues, such as store ambiance, sophistication of clerks, and quality of product.

Other issues   There must be sufficient inventory before advertising is begun. Bringing consumers to a location for a nonexistent product is damaging to goodwill. Consumers feel deceived and don't come back. Of course, the alternative of excessive inventory is also not pleasing. From an advertising point of view, insufficient inventory is worse; the advertising manager should check that this condition does not exist.

One other issue to investigate concerns the availability of assistance for the retailer. Manufacturers will contribute up to 100% of media costs for their products; some also provide message strategy and finished art work. The retailer must be aware of what sources are available so that proper objectives can be set. Conversely, the retailer must evaluate co-op offers to ensure that they are consistent with the desired objectives and position.

Research   A number of secondary sources are available to help evaluate the retailer's trading area. The *Sales Management Survey of Buying Power* gives detailed local area information on various consumer variables. *Arbitron* gives local radio and television usage information; there are also relevant trade journals, such as *Progressive Grocer* or *Shopping Center World,* as well as state and local government statistics. In addition, local organizations (chambers of commerce; newspapers) often conduct local retail research that is then made available.

Ultimately the retailer may want information that is more specific. Two types of studies are commonly used:

▪ *In-store research*   In this type of survey, customers who buy and who do not buy are compared with one another on issues such as perceptions of the store and its merchandise. Such a questionnaire can be given to consumers as they are leaving the store. Obviously buyers are more satisfied, but what else can be learned? Why did buyers buy? Why were nonbuyers (walkers) not able to find what they wanted? Which group shops more? Buys more? What issues are important to each group (using a multiattribute model format)? Do different departments have different success rates? What is the store's trading area?

- *Marketwide research*   The in-store research speaks to a small part of the community—those who go to the store. What about everyone else? A second survey can be done among the general public. This survey should measure awareness of, attitudes toward, and shopping behavior for the retailer and several major competitors. From this information, the manager can learn if the store is converting awareness to sales, what its present position is compared to competitors, the size of its market share, and what percentage of tryers become loyal users. By combining the information from these two studies, the retailer can gain useful information for its advertising plan.

Objectives

In setting objectives, the retailer should use the DAGMAR model, which suggests that tasks are set in terms of awareness, attitude, or behavior. These basic responses can be made more specific in terms of retail problems.

Awareness   Customers need to be aware of the store's existence and the types of products it carries and/or services it provides. To that end, the retailer needs to communicate the arrival of new merchandise and the types of brands available. Branded product advertising may be supported by co-op dollars; private labels will be advertised less because of a lack of co-op support.

A key area of awareness advertising is in the announcement of sales. These special events require immediate behavioral response and therefore need strong awareness-building advertising. Because many consumers watch for sales, the job of creating sale awareness is probably easier than that of creating awareness for a new product.

Attitude   Advertising also can convey the long-term image that the retailer desires. This goal can be met through a separate image-building campaign that avoids the day-to-day product and price issues. Along with this image advertising, each daily ad should also reflect the store's position in its overall makeup and slogan. Because many stores in any area carry the same basic products, it is important to create some uniqueness that brings in a particular target market. Figures 21.9 and 21.10 show ads for two retailers; they both carry the same product lines but create very different images in their ads.

Behavior   Retail messages that are meant to create awareness also have the goal of eliciting behavior, for it is not sufficient to have consumers merely know that a sale exists; they must also come and make purchases. Manufacturer's product messages are more awareness oriented because promotions and retailer messages will be used to influence behavior. An ad for a sale contains the promotion; the prices being announced should elicit behavior.

More specifically, there are several behavior goals that can be sought; for example, bringing in new customers and getting old customers to increase their purchases. Promotions and publicity events are useful for bringing in new customers, and increased traffic means greater volume. A steady program of messages is necessary to keep old customers; without a constant effort, they will slowly drift to more aggressive retailers.

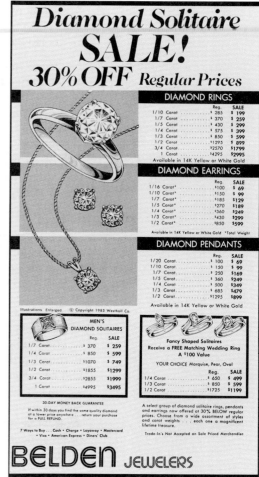

Figures 21.9 and 21.10   *Two different retailer images*

Efficiency   Bovee and Arens suggest three additional objectives of retail advertising:[5]

▪ *To reduce sales expenses*   Preselling through advertising makes the salesperson's job easier and enables one person to deal with more customers because each interaction will take less time.

▪ *To curtail seasonal peaks*   If demand is not constant, then there will be times when salespersons are idle or when lighting and heat are being consumed but no customers are present. Advertising and promotions can generate traffic during the slow periods.

▪ *To accelerate inventory turnover*   Rapid sales of stock generally leads to greater profit through greater volume, and creative retailers continuously dream up new gift-giving holidays to help move inventory during slow periods. There are very few periods of the year when there is not some holiday or special event looming on the horizon.

Timing   A final issue related to objectives is the time period within which the objective should be met. Where product objectives are stated in terms of months or years, retailer goals generally are in terms of days or weeks.

Media strategy

Media planning is somewhat different for local retail advertising than it is for that of national products. The differences are the result of two issues. First, the *trading areas differ;* most retailers are in one or a few markets, and few are national. The choice of media and vehicles is different as a result. Trading area within a city should also be considered. If the retailer does not serve the entire city, then electronic media may yield large levels of wasted coverage. Newspapers, though, may allow for geographic split runs. Outdoor, neighborhood papers, and direct mail will also yield less wasted coverage. Budget constraints call for careful coverage to reach the most appropriate target market.

Second, the *immediacy of retail advertising* suggests that scheduling should be more intense when it announces a specific buying event; there should therefore also be more periods of no advertising in between the intense periods of activity. Because retailers generally work with limited advertising budgets, a pulsing strategy of intensive frequency followed by a hiatus may yield the best return. Food retailers use this strategy by advertising most heavily on a single day of the week that precedes the heaviest buying days.

The key issue for retail media planning seems to be in media selection. The following discussion highlights this issue but does not review the pros and cons of each medium. For such a review, return to Chapters 11 and 12.

Print media   Retailing and newspapers grew together for over a century, and each helped the other. Growth, though, has slowed in recent years as advertisers have begun to put more dollars into other alternatives. In spite of this slowdown, about 60% of retail advertising dollars still go to newspapers, and 85% of newspaper revenues are served from local advertising. In 1982 income from retail ads was $15 billion while $3 billion were generated by national advertisers.[6]

To combat the increasing strength of other media, newspapers have improved their printing facilities to allow for better reproduction and have also increased their acceptance of free-standing preprinted materials. Newspapers are now at the point where they often have several preprints per night and occasionally have ten or more in a Sunday edition. These preprints allow the retailer to have more control of the printing process and to achieve better color reproduction on a better quality of paper. Preprints also allow the retailer to be set apart from the clutter of the rest of the paper and to make a more dramatic impact on consumers. Because the newspaper is seen as a buying catalog by many, the use of preprints has been positively accepted by consumers. With increased sophistication, retailers are setting a consistent tone in their preprints, which also gives them a unique identity that consumers seek out. The key benefit of the preprint is to be set apart from the clutter that typically exists in the newspaper.

A second trend in newspapers has been the recent increase of neighborhood shopping guides. These free papers are delivered to all residences in an area and survive on advertising revenues alone. Their greatest value is to small retailers with limited trading areas. Large retailers are also beginning to use the "shoppers" because they provide close to 100% coverage of their geographic area. An extension of this concept has been the local coupon book/magazine/newspaper that makes no pretension of news but is just a delivery medium for advertising and coupons. One response of traditional newspapers has been the zoned edition, whereby an advertiser can buy one or more regional zones of the circulation area. While this concept is not universal for ROP, it is more common for preprinted inserts.

It is estimated that about 10% of local advertising goes into local magazines or local editions of national magazines. Both of these opportunities are fairly recent arrivals on the media scene and offer the retailer the opportunity to do image advertising in vehicles with more status and better reproduction capabilities than is found in newspapers. Both of these types offer awareness and attitude building but, because of their long lead times, are not viable vehicles for sale or merchandising messages. Up-scale retailers with up-scale targets are the most likely users of these vehicles. Between these magazines and the shoppers' guides, the traditional newspaper is finding itself in a squeeze for revenues.

Broadcast media   Radio and television are rapidly gaining usage among reers, to the point where slightly over 10% of retail ad budgets (or $3–4 billion in 1982) goes to each of the two broadcast media. These figures do not include the huge national and regional television budgets of chains such as Sears, K-mart, Penney's, and Safeway. These dollar levels mean that retailers are a dominant force in radio while they still make up only a small percentage of television advertising revenues.

The reasons for the rapid increase in broadcast usage are threefold:

1. *The need to establish an image*   Retailers have recently discovered the virtues of positioning and image building and feel that television is the best medium for this task; radio is a low-cost alternative that can also contribute to the image. Until recently television was used mostly by heavy discounters to scream out price information and by department stores to send out vacuous messages of warm feelings. Now retailers are finding their niche and sending specific positioning messages.

2. *Viable transmitter of sale information*   Retailers are beginning to use television and radio for the announcement of special prices and sales. At one time it was felt that broadcast media couldn't do this job because of the limited information that could be given in 30 or 60 seconds. Now the feeling is that less information can be given than in newspaper, but the ability to increase the frequency of the message makes up for this. In addition, technological developments allow the retailer to produce a high-quality spot quickly enough to contain timely pricing information.

3. *Increased co-op dollars for television*   Manufacturers are also in the process of reevaluating where retail media dollars should be spent. At one time they generally insisted on newspaper advertising, but now they allow much more television. Between 1981 and 1983, the number of co-op television advertising programs more than doubled, from 400 to 900.

At the same time, large retailers have increased their television expenditures by large amounts. In 1982, Federated Department Stores spent nearly $25 million on television, Dayton-Hudson spent $20 million, and Batus (owner of Gimbel's, Saks, and Marshall Field), spent $15 million.[7]

Currently, strategies are still evolving but seem to combine image and price, with different advertisers favoring one or the other issue. Frequency is still increasing, especially in the use of radio.

Another new strategy favors the "infomercial," which has minimal hard sell, but rather presents general product information. These messages are more likely to be 60 seconds or longer and to be on cable. Many relate to fashion and beauty aids. By providing this information, the store develops an image of helpfulness that they hope will lead to greater sales.

Direct mail   This area is growing rapidly across most types of firms, and retailers are no exception. The features of the medium allow timely delivery of high-quality printing to a select target market.

In a study of the effects of a direct mail catalog sent out by a discount chain, Bellenger and Pingry[8] found that almost 30% of 1,400 shoppers in the chain's store bought something that they had read about in the catalog. While most of these people were regular users of the store, 7% of the sample bought something they had seen in the catalog even though they had not previously been in the store. It is not clear how many of these people would have shopped anyhow or how many would have come in response to some other form of advertising, but it seems that the catalog did have a positive influence. The whole area of direct marketing is a retail concept and is discussed in more detail in Chapter 12.

Outdoor   This medium can create awareness of a narrow and specific piece of information, and therefore has limited value to the retailer who wants to transmit lots of product and price information. Its main value is in a general image sense, unless the billboard is close to the retailer and can be quickly updated to reflect specials. On-premise signs have this virtue, but they may be "preaching to the faithful," since they are only seen by the store's shoppers.

Yellow Pages   This medium is favored by retailers because it has a long life and is seen by consumers who are definitely shopping and actively seeking information. Good yellow-page advertising is very information oriented, as are the ads shown in Figure 21.11. While this medium is useful to retailers, it is also very expensive. The manager needs to consider the efficiency of the yellow pages before making such a buy.

Co-op advertising revisited

In Chapter 16, *co-op advertising* was treated as a promotional device to be used by manufacturers in order to elicit appropriate behavior from retailers. Now co-op is examined from the retailer's perspective. For retailers, co-op advertising relates to the media, message, and budget decisions. Co-op allows the media plan to be stretched further, but the retailer may lose the choice of medium; co-op may give the retailer professional messages but may not say what the retailer wants; co-op certainly helps stretch the budget, but because it is rarely free, it must still be assessed for its value and appropriateness.

The magnitude of the potential of co-op makes it a key issue in retail advertising. As shown in Table 21.1, up to 80% of a store's advertising budget can come from co-op dollars, though an average contribution may be closer to 50%. It is estimated that $5 billion are spent each year in co-op arrangements while another $2.5 billion are offered by manufacturers but not accepted by retailers. Given this abundance of dollars, the retailer should only use advertising that clearly is useful.

Figure 21.11 Information-packed yellow pages retailer ads

Points in favor of using co-op Co-op advertising has several important benefits:

- *Stretches the budget* Co-op allows retailers to do a lot more with their budgets than they otherwise could. For example, the manufacturer may pay for half of all advertising that features the product, up to 5% of the value of goods bought by the retailer from the manufacturer. In this case, if the retailer bought $100,000 of goods, $5,000 would be available for co-op advertising.

  The budget can be stretched further in a dealer listing ad or group program commercial. Here the advertiser pays half, and all listed retailers split the other half. In this way the retailer might pay 5% of a full-page ad that lists nine competitors. This concept raises questions for retailers: Is it better to buy a 1/10 page ad alone or a full-page ad with nine competitors? Is it better to buy one full-page ad alone or ten pages with nine competitors? Put even more severely: How will the store do if it buys one ad during the time that nine competitors are listed ten times?[9] Given the nature of learning and the need to make an impact, cooperation can have its merits.

- *Creates a national tie to quality products* Co-op advertising shows off high-quality merchandise, and these products can act as magnets in drawing customers to the store.

- *Good looking ads and artwork are supplied* Often the quality of the ads supplied by the national manufacturer will exceed the quality of local production. The nice-looking artwork also helps to bring in customers.

Table 21.1 Allowances for co-op advertising in various businesses

Product category	Number of contracts included in survey	Proportion of advertising costs paid by manufacturer						Proportion of purchases used as basis for accumulation of co-op advertising credits (up to proportion indicated)									Fixed Amount Per Unit
		Below 50%	50%	60 to 70%	75%	80%	100%	1% or less	2%	3%	4%	5%	6% to 9%	10%	Over 10%	No Limit	
Appliances	61	0	23	1	22	0	15	1	7	8	7	17	0	0	0	1	4
Hardware, garden and farm supplies	47	0	34	2	0	5	6	1	6	6	2	1	0	4	2	13	2
Automotive (cars and supplies)	58	2	37	1	1	0	17	6	5	0	0	7	1	0	0	7	18
Heating, electric, lighting and plumbing supplies	11	0	9	0	2	0	0	1	1	1	0	2	0	0	0	2	1
Floor coverings, furniture, and household goods	67	0	40	13	2	0	12	2	7	12	6	17	3	7	1	5	1
Office equipment and supplies	9	0	3	0	0	0	6	0	0	2	0	3	0	1	1	0	1
Builder's hardware, paint, and building materials	54	0	40	4	1	0	9	6	4	9	1	5	4	3	2	10	1
Luggage and leather goods	9	0	7	0	0	0	2	0	2	1	0	6	0	0	0	0	0
Photographic equipment and accessories	7	0	1	0	0	0	6	0	0	0	3	1	2	2	0	0	1
Watches	14	0	11	2	1	0	0	0	0	0	0	7	0	5	2	0	0
Apparel	21	1	18	0	0	2	0	0	8	4	4	4	0	1	0	0	1
Miscellaneous	23	2	13	0	1	0	7	3	1	1	4	3	0	7	4	3	1
All trade categories	381	5	236	23	30	7	80	20	41	44	27	73	10	30	12	41	31

Source: From William Haight, *Retail Advertising: Management and Technique.* Copyright 1976 by Scott, Foresman and Company. Reprinted by permission.

Note: In this analysis of a representative group of manufacturers' contracts in several important product lines, when the same company offered different types of contracts for several lines, each contract was included. Contracts were *not* selected on the basis of a true probability sample; hence the table does not necessarily represent the relative preponderance of the various types of contracts. It does reflect the general practice in the different product groups current in 1973 and 1974. The figures for the proportion of purchases used as basis for accumulation do not equal the total number of contracts analyzed, due to options in some plans and an absence of information in others.

• *Provides leverage with local vehicles*   The local advertiser who uses a lot of co-op dollars will have more power in dealing with the local media. This power can lead to a more favorable rate structure. This means more advertising for the dollar. This means more sales. This means more co-op dollars. . . .

But every silver lining has a cloud or two   Co-op advertising also has a few drawbacks:

• *Different goals*   This is the key to problems with co-op advertising. The manufacturer wants to feature the product while the retailer wants to feature the location; when this conflict is resolved, then co-op can work well.

• *Manufacturer restrictions*   In some cases co-op funding may be spent throughout the year, but some funding comes with restrictions that it be spent for specific events. In addition, there may be restrictions on the message to the extreme that the manufacturer will send an ad to the retailer that is ready for the newspaper. In such a case, the retailer has no control over the store's advertising; this often results in a message in which the product dominates, but it may also lead to a message strategy inconsistent with the retailer's position.

In an equally bad case, the manufacturer's message may lack creativity and, when used by several retailers, may give competing stores the same look and feel. While the retailer is trying to set the store apart, the manufacturer may be striving to get look-alike messages across several stores. It is not clear what percent of unused co-op dollars are not spent because the retailer feels hasseled or pushed in the wrong direction, and what percent is unused because the retailer is not aware of its existence. While the retailer may have no choice when using the manufacturer's message, the manufacturer usually is careful to stipulate in what sorts of ways the product message may be used.

Message strategy

Before people go shopping, they often look through the newspaper for ideas, for sale items, and for product availability. These people are involved, are looking for information, and need to be helped. Others are not currently in the market but may be some day. These people are less involved, yet they still glance through the ads to see what is happening and what is on sale. Both types of consumers are reading the same ads, and each consumer at some time falls into each category.

In the first case, the retailer should emphasize price and product selection, while in the latter case, the emphasis is more on image. Should an ad stress price and product, or image? It would seem that the deciding factor should be frequency of purchase, such that stores which get lots of repeat visits by the same consumers will stress product availability and price. Grocery and drug stores would be examples of this type of store; their ads are generally long lists of products at special prices with only marginal attempts at image building. Consumers probably visit a grocery store on the average of at least once per week or a drugstore at least once a month.

Conversely, an appliance or furniture store gets infrequent visits by any one person, and at any time most people are not in the market for these types of products. As a result, the advertising should have somewhat more of an image tone to it. Care must be taken not to stray too far from product and price information, though, because current sales are the key to retailing, and product/price information is essential to current sales.

Having considered this dichotomy, the manager must develop a balance between long-term, less involving, image-oriented messages and short-term, more involving, product/price-oriented messages. If the retailer carries products that generate their own manufacturer-based advertising, then at least part of the longer term strategy will be done for them. Similarly, if the manufacturer has a well-developed co-op program, there is a good chance that this will cover some of the long-term image strategy.

If the retailer's image and position are closely tied to that of the products being carried, then the manufacturer's advertising will help the retailer and allow the latter to concentrate on short-term messages geared to immediate sales. Often, though, the manufacturer's advertising will be inappropriate or inadequate for the retailer's needs. Three classes of retailers can be reconsidered from this perspective:

1. *Exclusive dealerships and franchises* The local Oldsmobile dealer, Wendy's franchise, or K-mart outlet each receive extensive support from their parent company; this builds the position, image, and long-term attitude. Because the local outlet is a manifestation of the parent, there is little need for the local advertising to deal with image. The retailer can, therefore, concentrate on product availability and price advertising, as is done in the K-mart newspaper preprinted insert shown in Figure 21.12. Figure 21.13 shows the photoboard of a more image-oriented corporate television spot. The two messages are quite different in their orientation and immediacy but have the common thread of the gold medal and the slogan to tie them together.

Figure 21.12 *K-mart pre-printed newspaper insert*

Figure 21.13 Photoboard of K-mart corporate television commercial

2. *Retail businesses that sell branded merchandise*   The local hardware, clothing, appliance, stereo, food, or drugstore are all examples of this class of retailer. These products often receive their own advertising for their own image, but that image may not be useful to the retailer. Often these products are sold at competitive retail outlets and then become even less useful in terms of developing a retailer image. In these cases the retailer will need to do local image advertising in addition to availability and price advertising. Figure 21.14 shows an example of an ad that attempts to create image for the retailer beyond that of the product.

An alternative is to use the image of the product and build from it to enhance the image of the retailer. This strategy is often used by retailers that carry top-line brands and want to create a similar image for themselves. Figure 21.15 shows one retailer's attempt to build from a brand to enhance its own image.

3. *Local business without national ties*   Local retailers that carry primarily unbranded goods or services or that carry their own goods—such as restaurants, florists, meat markets, banks, plumbers, and craftspersons—fall into this class. These retailers get virtually no outside assistance in co-op image building and must therefore develop their own. These merchants, then, have the most difficult

Figure 21.14 *Building a retailer position when competitors carry the same brands*

Figure 21.15 *Building a retailer position by tying to a manufacturer's brand*

Figure 21.16   Building a position for a local retailer without any manufacturer ties

task, because they must do both short-run and long-run messages without any assistance. As will be seen below, these merchants also have the smallest volume and can least afford this dual campaign concept. Savannah Oak, a local furniture manufacturer, has dealt with this problem through a creative direct mail campaign that deals with position, product, and price in each message. Figure 21.16 is an example from their mail campaign.

Being creative with a limited budget   While there certainly are many very visible chains and franchise organizations that spend megabucks on their advertising, these are the exceptions. The great majority of retailers fall into the latter two groups of the above classification scheme and are working with very limited budgets. Too many of these retailers are single-minded in their pursuit of short-run goals and thereby don't build their own positions. This means that they must compete on price, and price is an easy attribute on which competitors may retaliate. Over time, a well-developed position can be much more valuable.

In a similar vein, too much retail advertising looks the same. Not only does it not pursue a position, but it uses the same scenes, props, sterile models, and dull copy as the competitors. Advertising should look unique so that, when a consumer sees it, there is instant recognition of the retailer.

Given a limited budget, a retailer should develop consistency across messages so that an impact can be made even when shoppers are not actively in the market. Message consistency should be a minimum goal of advertising; beyond that, it is important that this consistency point to a unique position in the marketplace that can establish a long-run image.

Issues relevant to retail message strategy   A message is a message, and the issues discussed in Chapters 6 through 8 generally apply here. The following items seem to pertain more specifically to retail advertising.

1. *Messages have a short life and rapid impact*   Aside from any image considerations, retail advertising must be designed to trigger an immediate sale. Ads are primarily in newspapers and have a short life; sales are announced one day and end a few days later. Messages that generate a rapid response often use terms such as "limited supply" or "today only."

2. *This immediacy calls for a copywriting style that grabs the reader:*

- *a dominant headline*   Show a benefit and a reason for acting today.

- *a specific and complete presentation*   This is important in listing the brands and products, the prices, the claims, and the terms of the sale. Vagueness is less likely to generate interest; the consumer may not make a special trip if it is not clear whether the merchandise and price are appropriate. Consumers who read retail ads are looking for information that can help them make the best decision.

3. *Include the name and address of the store*   These may be the two most important pieces of information, because a purchase cannot occur if the consumer doesn't know where to go. Included in this issue is name clarity. Local radio advertising has a tendency to be "cutesy"; this often leads to messages that leave the listener with the thought, "Gee, that was a clever message; I wonder who it was for." The message in either print or broadcast must clearly state the name and address of the sponsor. Broadcast messages should repeat this information several times.

4. *Advertise the right product at the right time*   The right product is one that consumers want; advertising poor products is a poor investment in advertising because it probably won't lead to many sales. The right time is when the product can be used; this means selling bathing suits in June and snow shovels in December.

Unfortunately, inventories tend to build up for poor products and at the wrong time of year, so it may be necessary to occasionally advertise these also as part of a clearance sale. In general, though, advertising works best when it deals with good products during peak selling periods because consumers will be more responsive and markups can be greater. Too many clearance sale ads may lead to an undesirable store image and develop buying patterns built around these sales.

Promotions and special events

In earlier sections of this text, promotions and special events were dealt with in separate chapters. This was done because, for manufacturers, the goal of a promotion is an immediate sale, while the goal of a special event is more likely to be long-range image building. For retailers, the two strategies are more likely to have the same goal, and that goal is likely to be an immediate sale. This is not always the case, but the majority of retail special events are held at the retailer's location in order to draw in more shoppers. The goals of these two strategy classes are so similar that many writers lump the two together and write about retail promotions without any distinction between them.

As with other issues, the bulk of information to be considered here has been presented in earlier sections and can easily be reviewed. The relation between manufacturer's and retailer's promotions is strong, because the bulk of manufacturer promotional activities is run through the retailer and has an impact on what the latter does. If the manufacturer uses a coupon, it must be redeemed through a retailer; a price-off deal must be posted by the retailer, a special package (with extra contents or a premium) must be given shelf space by the retailer.

In these ways, the manufacturer's promotion becomes the retailer's promotion, and most retail promotions are a response to a manufacturer's promotion. While many manufacturer's promotions are rejected by the retailer (the retailer refuses to pass on savings that are made available), many others are forced upon the retailer (the retailer has little real choice when a manufacturer distributes a coupon).

Should the retailer use a particular promotion?   Lack of faithful cooperation may result because it is not always clearly in the retailer's best interests to promote. Chevalier and Curhan discuss five questions that the retailer must evaluate in order to assess the impact of the promotion on profit.[10]

1. *What change is there in margin per unit when the product is sold on promotion to the consumer by the retailer?*   While the retailer sells more units at a lower price, total revenues and total profits may suffer. The concept of price elasticity is relevant here. If the price is lowered, sales may increase sufficiently so that total revenue increases; the retailer must question if the price change is sufficiently meaningful to cause large changes in purchase behavior across the target market?

2. *What change is there in margin per unit when the product is sold on promotion to the retailer by the manufacturer?*   When the manufacturer offers a deal to the retailer, it should be sufficiently large to offset any of the losses that the retailer will suffer by using the deal. If the manufacturer's deal saves the retailer $100 in wholesale purchases of Brand A, but the retailer then loses $200 because consumers switched from high-margin Brand B to low-margin Brand A, there is no savings for the retailer.

3. *What loss is suffered by the retailer when consumers switch from a regular brand to a promoted brand?*   Though a good deal helps the manufacturer sell more product, the retailer must assess if these additional sales in Brand A come from units of Brand B and C that could have been sold at full price, or if the sales of Brand A went to new consumers who made a special trip to the retailer. It is

probably more common for the increase in sales of A to come at the expense of sales of B and C; this may lead to an overall loss of revenue for the retailer.

4. *What loss is suffered by the retailer if consumers stockpile the brand when it is on a special deal so they can avoid buying it at full price?*   This issue hurts the manufacturer because it steals future full-price sales, but it also keeps future sales from the competition; this tradeoff may be acceptable. The retailer, though, loses both ways. It doesn't matter whose future sales have been eroded; the loss of any future sales of any brand hurts the retailer.

5. *What additional purchases will the consumer make after going to the retailer to purchase sale units of a particular brand?*   Retailers often feature several products as loss leaders so that consumers will come to the outlet to buy regularly priced items as well. This is the greatest benefit to the retailer, but its value is difficult to calculate.

The above five issues must be assessed in order to determine if using a particular promotion is worthwhile. While this is one way to make the assessment, another completely different assessment can be based on the competitive marketplace. What will the competition do? If the retailer refuses the promotion, will a competitive retailer use it and take away sales? Are sales at a slight loss better than sales lost to the competition? Marginal analysis would suggest that if the revenue generated covers variable costs (the cost of the product) and makes a contribution to fixed costs (store overhead), then the promotion should be used even though it is not profitable. Buyer behavior analysis would suggest that if a lost customer might be lost forever, then the retailer should go to great lengths (losses) in the short run to keep the customer in the long run.

The above discussion assumes that retailer promotions are instigated by manufacturers. While this is not always the case, most retail promotions are in some way subsidized by the manufacturer.

Other options available to the retailer   The following set of promotional tools are the ones most commonly used by retailers. Their major goal is to direct consumers to a particular location rather than to sell a specific product or brand. The basic considerations of these tools have been discussed in Chapters 14 through 16.

▪ *Coupons*   This is the most common device used by retailers of frequently purchased products. The coupon will be for a specific product but will also be redeemable only at the retailer's own locations.

There are variations on this basic theme. Retailer B may advertise that it will accept any store coupons from Retailers A and C (or any others as well). This immediately negates the key value of the coupon to Retailer A because the purpose of the coupon was to create something exclusive. In fact, there is nothing to keep B from advertising an ongoing policy that it will always accept competitors' coupons. This is an inexpensive way to lessen the efforts of competitors.

A second variation is for a retailer to offer double value (sometimes even triple value during a price war) on manufacturer coupons redeemed at that location. Now that Brim coupon worth 50¢ is worth $1.00 at B's location; that Wheaties coupon for 15¢ is worth 30¢. The purpose of couponing is to influence store loyalties in one direction or another. To that end, these variations should do as well as the main theme.

Figure 21.17   Retailer bounce-back/cross-ruff coupon

Another type of coupon is the on- or in-pack bounce-back coupon, which is used by manufacturers to enhance repeat purchasing. This can also be used by retailers, as is shown in Figure 21.17. This item is a Pizza Hut place mat that helps introduce a new product and also enhances store loyalty. The coupon requires another visit to Pizza Hut. If the place mat is used during lunch, it is a bounce-back coupon for a future purchase of the same meal; if it is used for dinner or evening traffic, the coupon becomes a cross-ruff for a different item in the product line.

Some retailers advertise weekly and therefore can continuously work on loyalty by always using coupons. Others advertise infrequently but still want to create loyalty over time. To do this, one ad can carry several coupons that are redeemable at different times. In Figure 21.18, Crandall's Restaurant has two coupons good in April/May and two for June. This provides an inducement to go back over time; by July, Crandall's hopes its new clientele will have it in mind and will return without a coupon.

▪ *Price-off deals*   These have been discussed in Chapter 16; in most cases, a price-off deal is used because the manufacturer gave a purchase discount to the retailer with the understanding that it be passed along to the consumer. Price-off deals can be advertised specials as in the ad shown in Figure 21.18 or can be unannounced specials that are found while shopping. If the purpose of the deal is to bring in shoppers, it seems obvious that it should be advertised.

▪ *Premiums*   Again, the purpose is to increase sales at a location. Ideally the premium should tie to the type of retail location and type of customers desired; in reality, most premiums don't do this. When the premium is tied in to the store, the store's image and position are enhanced. Unrelated premiums enhance the ability to make an immediate sale but don't help the long-run image.

Figure 21.18 *Using coupons to develop behavior over time*

- *Games and sweepstakes* These tools are very effective in bringing in traffic in the short run but do very little for long-run loyalty. Once the customers are brought to the store, something must keep them coming back in the future. Games alone won't do it because ultimately this expensive promotion must end. Customers who are being reinforced only by a game won't become loyal to the location.

- *Special events* Items in this category are limited only by the imagination and budget. They include fashion shows, demonstrations, personal appearances by celebrities, equipment testing, lectures, films, and many other events that bring people to a location. This class of strategy has become well accepted by many retailers as a legitimate device for increasing sales. Anticipating extra customers, these stores also gear up with extra floor help and special sales of items related to the event in order to increase the probability of making a sale. After all, the event should be a means to a sale and should not be the end of the process.

Empty or unrelated themes don't help sales, although they may be just as expensive as a relevant event. The best ideas relate to the uniqueness and benefit of the store and its merchandise. In addition to this issue, Estes lists several other reasons that some events fail; the issues often tie back to the decision sequence:[11]

1. *Off target*   This was discussed in the previous paragraph. Target to the proper audience; make the event relevant to the store, to the target market, and to selling merchandise.

2. *Not enough advertising support*   How can anyone come if they are not aware of the event?

3. *Poor management support*   It must be realized that special events need to tie to sales and need to be supported throughout the store. A special event must be seen as an investment and not merely an expense.

Several of the above devices can be combined with each other and with other devices to gain the benefits of each and a synergistic result:

1. *Coupons and rebates/price-off and rebates*   The retailer and manufacturer can work together to create a strong package by combining two pricing deals. In such a case the retailer would have a price-off coupon while the manufacturer would have an additional money refund or rebate offer. This strong appeal will draw customers to the location with the aid of manufacturer financing.

2. *Coupon and point-of-purchase display*   Either of these devices alone helps to generate sales, but the effect of both together is even better. This can be seen in the Taster's Choice data shown in Figure 21.19.

3. *Publicity event and pricing deal*   The event is useful for bringing people to the store but doesn't ensure a purchase. The pricing deal increases the probability of a purchase.

Figure 21.19   The effect of coupons and P-O-P on sales

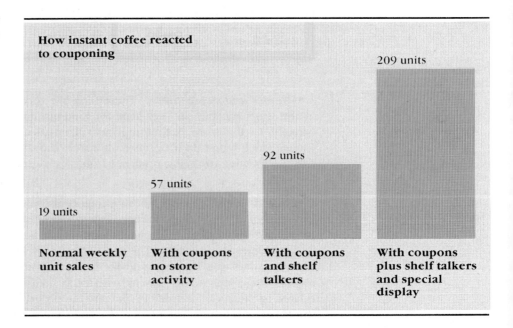

4. *Publicity event and sample*   Again, the event brings people to the retail location. Once they have arrived, there is a perfect opportunity to expose them to a new product. A sample at the buying site can then be converted to a trial purchase.

Store atmosphere, layout, and display[12]

Once inside the retail location, the shopper receives continuous messages at three levels. *Store atmosphere* is the overall setting of the store, its design, lighting, fixtures, color, and sound. These are developed to convey a mood or feeling that separates the store from others that sell similar merchandise. The more similar the product offerings of competitors, the more important it is to create a unique environment.

By going into any large shopping mall and walking from one clothing store to another, a shopper can easily experience atmosphere differences. One store will be brightly lit with neatly lined-up pastel plastic racks and pastel walls. Another will be in seeming disarray, with loud rock music and strobe lights. A third will have a wood decor, soft lights, and soft music. Each type of atmosphere is aimed at a particular target market, and each serves as a screen to tell shoppers whether or not they will feel comfortable in the store and what type of merchandise they might expect.

"Establishing a mood of shopping ambiance has never been more important than it is now," says Lois Patrich, vice president of sales promotion and advertising with Carson Pirie Scott & Co., a Chicago-based retailer. "Department stores have always had a preponderance of merchandise that you can get at any store. How then does a retailer get a customer to buy at his store? By creating a shopping atmosphere that will motivate him to buy and one that he wants to come back to."[13]

Store layout is the arrangement of merchandise to facilitate shopping. The layout tells consumers how to proceed through the store and what pace is expected. An open layout invites shoppers to browse. A cluttered layout sends a signal of busyness and rushing.

An effective layout maximizes customer exposure to merchandise and keeps the customer in the store longer. Studies show that the longer the customer is in the store, the more money is spent. The layout also should have the high-margin merchandise in the high-traffic areas and the most desired merchandise in the back so that consumers must walk past many other goods. In a supermarket, for example, the meats, dairy products, and produce have the greatest constant demand and are placed at the perimeters so shoppers will need to pass other products to get to them.

Merchandise display refers to the organization of goods at a specific place in the store's layout. Displays communicate at still another level to attract attention to the product, enhance product appeal, and increase the shopper's propensity to purchase. While these tasks might lead the display design in one direction, the display also needs to be consistent with the store's atmosphere.

I. Magnin & Company opened a career woman's clothing shop as a special area in 1979. While the rest of the store atmosphere was based on modernistic chrome elements, this space was decorated with antique furniture to convey a warmer feeling. In addition, the store showed a commitment to this target market by sponsoring a series of career woman seminars; the proceeds from the series were used to finance scholarships for women entering business. In this way, atmosphere, display, special events, and publicity were all tied together to reach a specific target.

Sales force

The sales force has declined in recent years in its value as a communication tool for retailers. In many situations, the salesperson has been deemphasized or completely eliminated in favor of a self-service operation. This is in response to a number of factors.

- Advertising presells the consumer.
- Sophisticated point-of-purchase displays serve as in-store information sources.
- The cost of maintaining a sales force is quite high.

In spite of these issues, there are circumstances when a sales force is useful and necessary. For high-priced (e.g., major appliances), complex (e.g., electronics) or difficult to assess products (e.g., fashion merchandise) there is merit in a high-quality sales force. Though these products could be sold on a self-service basis, Rosenbloom suggests several reasons why the sales force is a good investment:[14]

- *Increasing the percentage of shoppers who buy* While many shoppers are just browsing, many would buy if they had adequate information. The sales force can help by giving confidence as well as information to the consumer and by convincing the shopper to buy here and now rather than there or later.

- *Increasing the average purchase size* Because the cost of selling is fairly fixed, if the purchase size increases, so does profit. The sale can be increased by a salesperson who suggests related items and accessories. *Add-on* or *suggestion selling* requires effort on the part of the salesperson, but should be done when the shopper is in a buying frame of mind.

- *Building store loyalty* A good, caring sales force can breed loyalty, especially since these virtues are so rare. Merchandise doesn't vary that much across similar stores, but the sales force can vary and can give customers a reason to return. When merchandise is similar, it is the service that separates one store from another.
Gulliver's Travels is a travel agency with the slogan "Where all our clients are giants." It sells exactly the same product line as all other agencies but has grown rapidly since its inception because its agents care about the customers' needs and make them feel special. As a result clients are loyal and spread the word to others, and there has never been a need for advertising.

- *Enhancing store image* Retailers spend many dollars on all other communication aspects from advertising to in-store materials to special events so that a favorable image can be built. All of this money cannot do the job if the sales force doesn't also fit the image. The sales force is the most direct contact that the shopper has; retailers must train these salespersons to have pride in the store and to have an interest in the well-being of shoppers.

To accomplish all of the above, the sales force must attempt to meet needs in terms of the merchandise that the shopper is looking for, as well as in terms of the information and counseling that may be an unspoken need.

Budget

As was noted earlier in the Budgeting part, there are several budgeting methods:

- Affordable
- Percentage of sales
- Competitive parity
- Objective and task

The first three methods are arbitrary, and the fourth is based on problem solving. Retailers seem to be less sophisticated in managing advertising in general than are consumer goods manufacturers, and this becomes quite evident in the budgeting process. For retailers, the three arbitrary methods seem to dominate, and this tendency becomes more pronounced as the size of the retailer decreases.

This is unfortunate, because retail managers have much better information than do their consumer goods counterparts in terms of the effect of advertising. Retailers get rapid feedback on how well their advertising works by watching the next day's store traffic. Given this ability to collect data, retailers should become more task oriented in their advertising.

Assessing the advertising–sales relation   There are problems in drawing precise relationships, even in the retail situation. First, not all sales result from advertising; sales can also occur because people happen to have a need, go to a store, and make a purchase. It is therefore necessary to establish benchmarks on how many sales take place without advertising. This can be done with an historical analysis (what happened last week, last month, or last year when no advertising took place) or with a matched market study (if the retailer has stores in several distinct media coverage areas). This analysis would be helpful in determining a base sales level for an established store but is less useful for a new or rapidly changing store.

A second problem arises in measuring the effect of advertising on the sales of nonadvertised merchandise bought by people who first responded to the ad. Because of this confounding issue, the manager should measure total store traffic or total store sales as well as sales of advertised merchandise during the time period in question.

The budgeting method most commonly used by retailers seems to be the percentage of sales method, because it allows the manager to have a frame of reference in dealing with a vague but important problem. Table 21.2 shows the average percentage of sales dollars spent on advertising across a number of retail classifications. Across these classes, the 25 largest general merchandisers spent 2.96% of sales, while the 25 largest grocery retailers spent 1.01% of sales during 1981.[15] Table 21.3 shows the sales revenues and advertising expenditures for these large retailers during 1981. Half of these retailers spent more on advertising than did the 100th largest national manufacturing advertiser of 1981.

Co-op aids to the budget   Another method for budgeting that is available to retailers is a subset of the affordable method. Retailers can advertise on the basis of available co-op dollars. In such a scenario, the retailer's budget would be determined by the co-op programs made available by manufacturers. For many small merchants with limited sales revenues (and income), this method dominates their advertising strategies. If this approach is used, the retailer must be careful to create some consistency across ads because each co-op offering will feature a different product with a different message style. The greater the percentage paid by

Table 21.2 Average percentage of sales invested in advertising by type of outlet

Class of business	Average percentage of sales invested in advertising
Appliance, radio, television	2.4
Auto dealers	0.8
Bakeries	0.6
Barber and beauty shops	2.9
Bookstores	1.7
Camera and photographic supply stores	3.0
Children's and infant's wear stores	1.3
Department stores	2.4
Discount stores	2.4
Drugstores	
Chains	2.0
Independents	1.6
Dry cleaners	3.8
Farm and power equipment dealers	0.5
Florists	1.6
Funeral services	2.9
Furniture stores	4.1
Gasoline service stations	0.8
Hardware stores	1.7
Hotels	2.6
Insurance agents, brokers	1.1
Jewelry stores	4.1
Laundries	2.1
Men's wear stores	2.9
Motels	1.4
Motion picture theaters	6.2
Music stores	3.1
Paint and wallpaper stores	1.4
Real estate	
Subdividers, developers, builders	4.1
Agents, brokers, managers	6.0
Restaurants	2.0
Savings banks (mutual)	1.0
Savings and loan associations	2.2
Sporting goods stores	1.6
Supermarkets	1.1
Tire dealers	2.2
Travel agents	5.0
Variety stores (limited price)	1.2
Women's wear stores (specialty stores)	2.8

Source: Courtesy of the Newspaper Advertising Bureau.

the manufacturer, the less the control retained by the retailer. In this way, the retailer will have the feeling of an advertising budget, but there will be little retailer identity and even less retailer image buildup. The retailer that falls into this trap meets the objective of the manufacturers; some co-op is useful, but there also must be some control at the retail level.

Image versus sales As retailers become more competitive, it becomes more difficult and costly to create a position based on price; some other image needs to be created to avoid constant price competition. This logic leads to large expendi-

Table 21.3 Advertising and sales data for largest retailers, 1981

Sales rank	General merchandisers	Advertising	Sales
1	Sears, Roebuck & Co.	$829,000,000	$18,229,000,000
2	K mart Corp.	349,000,000	16,527,000,000
3	J.C. Penney Co.	355,000,000	11,860,000,000
4	F.W. Woolworth Co.	181,000,000	7,223,000,000
5	Federated Dept. Stores	188,800,000	7,067,700,000
6	Montgomery Ward & Co.	180,000,000	5,743,000,000
7	Dayton-Hudson Corp.	103,000,000	4,942,900,000
8	Wickes Corp.	60,000,000	4,100,100,000
9	May Dept. Stores	97,500,000	3,149,800,000
10	Household Merchandising	40,000,000	2,911,100,000
11	Carter Hawley Hale Stores	74,900,000	2,870,700,000
12	Associated Dry Goods Corp.	182,000,000	2,751,200,000
13	Allied Stores Corp.	120,000,000	2,732,700,000
14	R.H. Macy & Co.	127,000,000	2,656,700,000
15	Rapid American Retail Group	18,500,000	2,646,900,000
16	Batus Retail Group	60,000,000	2,617,100,000
17	Wal-Mart Stores	36,000,000	2,444,900,000
18	Zayre Corp.	60,000,000	1,797,100,000
19	Tandy Corp.	20,000,000	1,691,000,000
20	Belek Stores	25,000,000	1,365,000,000
21	Mercantile Stores Co.	25,100,000	1,269,500,000
22	Melville	17,000,000	1,060,100,000
23	SCOA Industries	18,400,000	1,057,600,000
24	Service Merchandise	15,000,000	1,027,100,000
25	G.C. Murphy Co.	20,000,000	817,800,000
	Total	$3,211,200,000	$108,359,000,000

Sales rank	Grocery retailers	Advertising	Sales
1	Safeway Stores	$160,000,000	$16,580,300,000
2	Kroger Co.	131,054,000	11,266,520,000
3	Lucky Stores	53,500,000	7,201,000,000
4	American Stores Co.	79,750,000	7,119,650,000
5	Great A & P Tea Co.	82,650,000	6,226,755,000
6	Winn-Dixie Stores	49,900,000	6,200,167,000
7	Southland Corp.	34,250,000	5,734,160,000
8	Jewel Cos.	60,800,000	5,310,000,000
9	Grand Union Co.	64,300,000	4,290,000,000
10	Albertson's	19,650,000	3,480,570,000
11	Supermarkets General Corp.	38,000,000	2,998,500,000
12	Dillon Cos.	21,300,000	2,494,578,000
13	Publix SuperMarkets	18,300,000	2,375,803,000
14	Stop & Shop Cos.	32,000,000	2,205,385,000
15	Petrolane	18,400,000	1,878,085,000
16	Giant Food	16,500,000	1,735,600,000
17	Fisher Foods	13,900,000	1,555,425,000
18	Waldbaum	12,800,000	1,416,589,000
19	Pantry Pride	13,300,000	1,225,263,000
20	First National	16,000,000	1,174,800,000
21	Borman's	10,900,000	1,061,840,000
22	Cullum	9,500,000	974,934,000
23	Weis Markets	7,400,000	756,800,000
24	Food Town	6,400,000	666,848,000
25	Schnuck's	6,500,000	650,000,000
	Total	$977,054,000	$96,579,572,000

Source: Louis J. Haugh, "The Big Five-Oh—What They Spent," *Advertising Age*, 1 November 1982, p. M-28. Reprinted with permission. Copyright 1982 by Crain Communications, Inc.

Roman Hiebing

President, The Hiebing Group, Inc.

Roman Hiebing is president of The Hiebing Group, a consumer advertising, marketing, and consulting agency that has over the years provided full-service capability to a diverse clientele. These have included package goods companies such as Kimberly-Clark and Coors, and retailers such as McDonalds, Northwest Fabrics, and Famous Footwear.

Roman received his graduate degree in marketing and advertising from the University of Wisconsin, where he wrote his Masters thesis, "Territorial Marketing in Restaurant Franchising," a portion of which was published in Restaurant Business. *This thesis was the basis for the Brat und Brau chain of restaurants he founded in 1969. In addition to his work in the agency and restaurant business, Mr. Hiebing teaches advertising and marketing in the Schools of Business and Journalism at the University of Wisconsin.*

Prior to opening his own advertising agency, Roman spent seven years with the Leo Burnett Company in Chicago working on such accounts as Kellogg's, United Airlines, Kentucky Fried Chicken, and Pillsbury.

Retail Marketing Versus Package Goods Marketing: There Is a Difference

Having been heavily involved in both package goods marketing and retail marketing, I believe that retail marketing is every bit as complex and demanding as the marketing of package goods, if not more so. In package goods marketing, primary focus is on the product. In the marketing of a single retail outlet, regional chain, or national retail franchise, the retail marketer must be concerned not just with the product being sold (the marketer usually has a multitude of products to prepare and/or sell), but also with the people who are selling it and the place from which it is being sold.

Further, in package goods marketing, one has more direct control and can more easily standardize the product. In retail marketing, not only

is it difficult to standardize the product, but it is very difficult to control and standardize the location, and most difficult to standardize the third element—store people performance. This operations segment of retailing has a tremendous impact on sales and profits. For example, it's been my experience that a good store manager can generate an incremental 5% to 25% in sales and a doubling of these percentages in incremental profits.

A major difference between retail and package goods marketing is time. It seems in retail marketing that one has so little of it because everything moves so fast. Both product movement and feedback are immediate. An ad supporting a weekend promotion is run on Friday, and the results are in by Monday. If the promotion did not sell, one must adjust quickly, finding out why it didn't work, and be back in the marketplace with a promotion that does sell.

In retail marketing, because of the instant feedback, there appears to be a more common tendency to overreact or react too quickly. If sales don't respond to a marketing effort, there is a tendency to "shoot from the hip" in solving the problem rather than first clearly documenting what the problem really is and then using a disciplined approach in taking action. Similarly, in an attempt to quickly "fix" sales, there can be an overreaction—scrapping an entire in-place retail campaign when possibly it might have been just one element of the program that needed attention, such as media weight or product inventory.

To market both package goods and retail outlets effectively, there is a need for a quantifiable data base, yet there does not normally exist an ongoing reporting system that provides retailers with an accurate measure of sales performance versus the competition. Unlike for most package goods products, there are no Nielsen, SAMI, or BehaviorScan data available. To fill this void, the more sophisticated retailers have developed their own tracking system to measure on a consistent basis not just behavior in terms of visits and purchases, but also consumer awareness and attitudes for the major competitors in the same retail category. It is my strong belief that, without this type of systematic primary research, no retailer can become or remain a sales leader.

Although all national marketers acknowledge that regional differences affect consumer response, retail marketers, more than package goods marketers, must recognize the need to tailor campaigns to fit the specific marketplace. For example, in retail marketing, if sales are down, one does not just move against a national problem, but must also review the problem on a market-to-market basis because some markets will be doing well and others very poorly for a variety of reasons. Not stopping there but digging deeper, one will find not just a down market problem, but also individual store problems within the market, with some very poor performers pulling down the overall market response. Accordingly, because many of these local market and individual store problems and opportunities stem from less than national causes, such as seasonality, increased competition, local consumption, and media habits and operations, they must be dealt with on a more localized basis.

Related to this issue and based on previous research I undertook among restaurant franchisers, it has been found that franchisers varying their marketing approach by market experienced greater success than those franchisers applying the same marketing approach on a national basis and to all local markets. Beyond theory, and in my actual working with Kentucky Fried Chicken and McDonald's, it has been proved to me again and again that a disciplined territorial approach to retail marketing is most effective. This is particularly true when implemented as a three-tier marketing program incorporating a national plan, local market plans, and individual store plans—all integrated to leverage each other, but with built-in flexibility to realize the potential of the local market and respond to individual store needs.

tures in revamping the atmosphere of the store and then leads to further expenditures on advertising to deliver the message of the new atmosphere and image.

For example, Sears began to spend $1.7 billion during a five-year period beginning in 1984 to upgrade the convenience and attractiveness of its stores. Penney's plans to counter with $1.5 billion in similar expenditures over the same five-year period. To support the in-store changes, Sears is spending large sums on image advertising; $35 million will be spent in 1984 just to build image for the apparel lines. These messages have no price references; they are solely image—predominantly television—and are supported by additional price-oriented newspaper messages.[16]

Charity messages versus advertising Retailers seem to be hit with a constant stream of "advertising" requests by charities trying to raise money. These range from ad books to calendars to door prizes to raffles to community messages ("Gulliver's Travels reminds you that this is save-a-butterfly month, so drive carefully and watch out for all the little monarchs.") Rarely can these messages be considered a good advertising investment, because the media, message, and target market are all constrained in the request. This may seem like a minor issue, but it is not. A day rarely goes by when a retailer is not asked to participate in this type of advertising; the retailer should consider these as requests for charitable donations, should act accordingly, and should note in the accounting records that a charitable donation was made.

How much to advertise While a text cannot recommend exact spending levels, there are several variables that influence whether the retailer will need to spend more or less. Bovee and Arens suggest the following.[17]

- *Stores in less favorable locations need to advertise more.* The more visible the store is, the more traffic it will draw just from passersby.

- *Stores that are new, expanding, or changing their position need to advertise more.* These stores need to create awareness before behavior can follow.

- *Stores with strong competition need to advertise more.* It is harder to develop and hold share of mind in a highly competitive environment.

- *Stores that stress price need to advertise more.* It is easy for competitors to attack this position; therefore, the store must constantly maintain itself through more advertising.

Summary

While retail advertising and promotions need to be planned using the decision sequence, and the same basic issues are encountered as in product advertising and promotions, there are some strong differences. Regardless of these differences, good advertising and promotions can occur when the basic models are followed. It is true that retail advertising is more immediate, that location is being sold rather than product, that the line of goods is broader, and that the geographic coverage area may be very limited.

These issues do not need to lead to poor strategy; poor strategy is more likely to be a function of inattention to the basic issues of advertising. This chapter has shown that retailers' problems are the same as those of consumer product advertisers. It is necessary to create awareness, attitude, and behavior toward a relevant target market. Everything else can be subsumed within these issues. What has been discussed here should fit into the broader models presented earlier.

Discussion Questions

1. How do the goals of retailer advertising differ from those of product advertising? Discuss other differences between the two.

2. What variables make a retailer more or less likely to advertise?

3. Discuss the differences between product and image advertising as they apply to retailers. Consider both media and message strategies.

4. Discuss the key situation analysis issues that a retailer must consider before beginning to communicate. How will these issues affect the communications that will follow?

5. How has the relationship between retail advertising and newspapers changed?

6. Why has the use of television changed so much in retailers' media plans?

7. What are the pros and cons of co-op advertising for retailers? How could the cons be diminished?

8. What is the virtue of positioning for retail message strategy development?

9. What are the positive and negative ways in which manufacturer promotions impact upon retailers?

10. How can store atmosphere and the sales force be used to enhance the retailer's image?

Notes

1. Philip Kotler, *Marketing Management,* 5th ed. (Englewood Cliffs, N.J.: Prentice-Hall, Inc., 1984), p. 565.

2. Kotler, *Marketing Management,* pp. 565–567.

3. J. Douglas Johnson, *Advertising Today* (Chicago: Science Research Associates, 1978), pp. 115–117.

4. Maurice I. Mandell, *Advertising* (Englewood Cliffs, N.J.: Prentice-Hall, 1984), p. 531.

5. Courtland L. Bovee and William F. Arens, *Contemporary Advertising* (Homewood, IL: Richard D. Irwin, 1982), p. 643.

6. Morris Saffer, "Sample the Media Mix," *Advertising Age,* 16 January 1984, p. M-48.

7. Jack Myers, "Advertisers Spread their Sales on TV," *Advertising Age,* 25 July 1983, p. M-28.

8. Danny N. Bellenger and Jerry R. Pingry, "Direct-Mail Advertising for Retail Stores," *Journal of Advertising Research* 17 (June 1977), pp. 35–39.

9. Robert Wilcox, "Standing Upright by Listing," *Advertising Age,* 15 July 1982, p. M-26.

10. Michel Chevalier and Ronald C. Curhan, "Retail Promotions as a Function of Trade Promotions: A Descriptive Analysis," *Sloan Management Review* 18 (Fall 1976), pp. 19–32.

11. Anne Estes, "How Retailers Promote, Entertain," *Advertising Age,* 16 April 1981, p. 48.

12. Bert Rosenbloom, *Retail Marketing* (New York: Random House, 1981), pp. 233–258.

13. Anna Sobczynski, "All the Store's a Stage, Promos are the Actors," *Advertising Age,* 2 November 1981, p. 5–18.

14. Rosenbloom, *Retail Marketing,* pp. 308–12.

15. Louis J. Haugh, "The Big Five-Oh—And What It Spent," *Advertising Age,* 1 November 1982, p. M-28.

16. Jill A. Fraser, "Retailers Dress for Success," *Scan* 32, no. 4 (May 1984), pp. 9–11.

17. Bovee and Arens, *Contemporary Advertising,* pp. 652–658.

Chapter 22
Communications for Business-to-Business Marketing

This is the second chapter dealing with uses of advertising and promotions in nonconsumer product situations; this chapter deals with communications in business settings.

According to the Industrial Marketing Committee Review Board:[1]

- *Consumer goods* are "destined for use by the individual ultimate consumer and in such form that they can be used by him without further commercial processing."

- *Industrial goods* are "used in producing consumers' goods, other business or industrial goods and services, and/or in facilitating the operation of an enterprise, may include land and buildings for business purposes, equipment (installation and accessory), operating supplies, raw materials, and fabricated materials."

There are also goods that can be in either class depending upon their usage. Industrial goods include those used in the production of other goods (such as raw materials or component parts) as well as those used to conduct business (such as machinery or office supplies). These goods are purchased by firms for the use of the firm; consumer goods are purchased by people for the use of people. Table 22.1 shows the stages in the production chain where different actions add value to the product. The five stages to the left of the arrow all have industrial buyers who purchase finished or unfinished products.

(The terms *industrial marketing* and *industrial advertising* are in the process of changing to *business-to-business marketing* and *business-to-business advertising*. There are some who feel that the old terms had negative connotations and that the new have an aura of professionalism that was lacking. The two sets of terms really have the same meanings and can be used interchangeably.)

Table 22.1 Stages in the production chain

First stage	Second stage	Third stage	Fourth stage	Fifth stage	Consumption
Raw materials extraction	Material processing	Manufacturing of parts and subassembly	Final assembly	Distribution and after-market	Wholesale and retail sale to household consumers

Source: B. Charles Ames and James D. Hlavacek, *Managerial Marketing for Industrial Firms* (New York: Random House, 1984), p. 19. Reprinted with permission of Random House, Inc.

End users include middlepersons and industries; the three specific types of persons that are generally addressed are purchasing agents/buyers, engineers/technicians, and managers. Generally, their purchases deal with more complex products and/or with larger volumes of goods than in consumer situations. These traits describe, but do not define, industrial marketing; these descriptors lead to the result of more complex buying situations and the need for more detailed information for buyers.

To complicate things even more, there are cases where key influencers and decision makers are outside the buying firm. For example, if Firm A is building a new plant and buying lighting devices, a key influencer may be the architect who is designing the building. Firm A will also want to buy a fire prevention and extinguisher system; key influencers here may be the local fire marshall or an insurance appraiser. Companies that want to sell to Firm A need to communicate with several people who are not employed by A.

Because of these complexities, a salesperson is often required to act as the primary direct agent of the selling firm; this puts advertising in a more secondary communications role than it is in the marketing of most consumer products. The role of advertising is further limited by the fact that, for many industrial goods, there are a limited number of buyers, and they may not be efficiently reached through advertising. Given these constraints, what are the goals of advertising in an industrial setting?

Goals of Industrial Advertising

The basic goals are the same as those stated for consumer products: to generate awareness, favorable attitudes, or purchase behavior. With the limited impact that advertising can make, the emphasis is primarily on the development of awareness and knowledge; in this sense, the goals will be similar to those for high-involvement durable consumer products.

- *The first goal is to increase awareness and knowledge of the product, the selling firm, the capabilities of both, and, if possible, to create a favorable attitude and image.* Industrial advertising, until recently, was dominated by very dry, sterile copy and poor visuals that stressed a presentation of information with little regard for art or aesthetics. If there was any visual of note in this type of ad, it was the inclusion of a well-endowed woman who had no relevance to the message but who was thought to be able to capture the attention of readers.

In the late 1970s and early 1980s, industrial goods advertisers took a cue from consumer goods advertisers and began to create more visually appealing

Figure 22.1 An ad that assists in the creation of awareness and knowledge

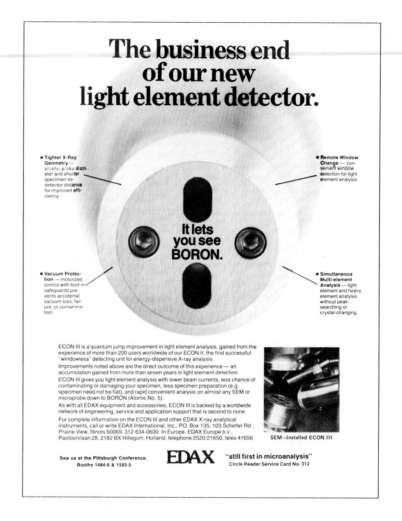

messages in which the visual had specific relevance. As art found its way into industrial advertising, irrelevance had a chance to grow; the result was often vacuous advertising that missed on the important dimension of giving product information. Although such ads might lead to awareness because of their interesting visual look, they fall short in delivering information. Figure 22.1 uses an interesting visual; it also delivers both awareness through its visual, and knowledge through its relevant and interestingly developed copy.

▪ *The second goal of business-to-business advertising is to make the salesperson's job easier and to lower the cost of selling.* It was reported in Chapter 18 that the average cost of an industrial sales call in 1981 was $178, and that it took an average of 5.1 calls to close the sale. Given these figures, advertising has the potential to play a vital role in controlling costs. Any aid that can be given to the salesperson will lead to savings, since it was also shown that the cost to reach a prospect through advertising is approximately $.16. If advertising performs its first task well (i.e., creating awareness and knowledge), then there will be an impact in this second area as well, because advertising can create a favorable environment for the salesperson.

To further expand upon this goal, advertising can reach people within a buying firm who will influence a decision but who may never meet with the salesperson. The purchasing process in many firms is quite complex, and the salesperson probably will never have the opportunity to meet with all the influencers. Well-placed advertising can help by reaching and speaking to these people.

The limited discussion so far should have generated many thoughts about the uniqueness of the industrial setting. As noted previously, the earlier advertising concepts are generalizable, and the basic strategies are the same, but there are some specific issues concerning the industrial setting that need to be considered.

Uniqueness of the Industrial Setting

Many differences between the consumer goods and industrial goods markets need to be considered in the development of a comprehensive communications plan. These issues can be broken into five classes for ease of presentation:

- Market-related
- Product-, price-, and distribution-related
- Buyer-related
- Promotions-related

The first four sets determine the last and are discussed here from a situation analysis perspective; the promotions issues are saved for later and considered from a strategies perspective.

Market-related issues

These issues deal with the types of firms that are being marketed to, and with other broad issues.

Size and concentration of market   For most industrial products, the target market is concentrated and quite small. The size of the market can range from less than 50, in the case of the manufacture of boilers for nuclear reactors, to several million, for the sale of paper clips. Even a market of several million is small, though, when compared to a consumer products market. Within this range, an active base of 4 to 5 thousand customers is considered quite large, and 100 to 250 major customers may account for over half of the firm's sales.[2]

The need for mass media advertising can be quite limited with markets as concentrated as these; as a result, firms emphasize personal selling, direct mail, catalogs, and limited-circulation trade publications. Only firms such as Xerox or Federal Express have a product or service line that appeals across many markets and therefore warrants space in consumer publications or time on television. Their large targets of professional buyers are also private consumers; firms such as these are willing to pay for the wasted coverage of consumer vehicles in order to reach their targets in this way. Federal Express, for example, began to advertise in consumer media in the 1970s; within one year, their sales increased by 40%. Because it was difficult for them to determine the appropriate decision maker, they felt that consumer media would be sure to hit the right person. The firm was willing to absorb a high CPM in their target market in order to reach these people with the best message.

Each customer is large   This is another uniqueness of the business market-place. Because each prospective customer firm is large relative to a private consumer, it is dealt with carefully; this calls for the presence of a knowledgeable salesperson and personal touches not available through advertising.

Derived demand   The demand for all industrial products is derived from demand at the consumer levels. Without any demand for consumer products, there would be much less need for industrial products. For example, if consumers conserve energy, there is less demand by utilities for the boilers made by Combustion Engineering (CE), and, in turn, CE will purchase smaller quantities of the parts needed to make the boilers. This means that firms planning their advertising and sales programs need to be cognizant of consumer trends.

Poor secondary data sources   While consumer product manufacturers have SMRB and many other syndicated services available, there are few such services for industrial goods. This means the firm must do more of its own research or deal with more uncertainty. There is, overall, less information about how industrial marketing works and what is happening with regard to any specific industry. There are, though, some sources available, and Table 22.2 on pages 684–685 shows a listing of some of these, along with the types of data provided. While data exist, they are in most cases general and not very useful for marketing communications decisions.

Segmentation   This issue has been discussed at length in Chapter 2; it is one of the cornerstones of modern marketing. A firm cannot sell the same product in the same way to all its customers, nor should it attempt to do so.

There are many ways to segment an industrial market so that firms with the best sales potential will be targeted and so that appropriate advertising and other communications planning will occur. Bonoma and Shapiro[3] suggest a five-stage approach that proceeds from the most broad to the most narrow segments.

In this approach, segments are first created on three company variables (descriptive variables, operating variables, approach to purchasing), then on situational factors, and finally, on personal characteristics of the individuals involved in the process. It is not necessary to use all five sets of issues; depending on the product and the manufacturer, one or more levels should be analyzed. The more general levels will be more useful to advertising, while the more specific levels will provide insight to the salesperson.

Descriptive variables are similar to the demographic variables used in consumer goods marketing. These include *type of industry, company size,* and *geographic location.* This information can be collected from external sources and is useful to firms that sell goods (such as office supplies) to a wide range of other firms. Media and message strategies will reflect the customer type of industry, while the latter two variables (size and location) will influence salesperson call patterns.

Operating variables are slightly less broad and include the customer's *technological sophistication, past usage status* (product and brand usage), and *capabilities in operating, technical, and financial areas.* The first and last of these refer to the customer firm's expertise; these will influence the level of detail and sophistication, and the issues covered, in messages delivered through salespersons or less personal means. Some firms need technical assistance; others don't. Some firms are willing to pay for financial assistance; others don't have this need.

Users differ from nonusers in some way that made them first becme   users; in addition, users obviously have more knowledge and expertise concerning the product being sold. Knowing which competitor has dealt with the customer in the past allows the selling firm to develop a positioning strategy.

Purchasing approaches examine the way in which a customer firm makes its decisions. This includes *formal organization of the purchasing function, internal power structure, nature of existing organizational relationships, general purchasing policies,* and *purchasing criteria.* These issues are important to advertising decisions so that the influencers from each department (e.g., purchasing versus engineering) are reached; the salesperson needs this information to find the key persons during the sales call. Materials are prepared to show the expertise of the selling firm; it is then necessary to find prospect firms that are structured in such a way that there is a match with this expertise. Each prospect firm has an area of dominant influence that must be found. The selling firm must use its strengths so that it establishes relations with firms where the powerful members appreciate these strengths.

As part of the customer firm's organization, the selling firm must determine if there is centralized or decentralized buying. This is especially important when the buyer has multiple locations. Is the product specified and bought at the corporate headquarters, specified and bought locally, or a combination of the two?

Situational factors deal with the specific purchase occasion being considered and concerns *urgency of the purchase, specific application of the product, size of order,* and *size of a particular part of an order.* A selling firm can use benefit segmentation on these variables. For example, Firm A may specialize in rapid turnover and delivery; it charges more than B, but it is also faster, and so buyers go to B if there is lead time but go to A when pressured. As a result, each firm has a unique position. This is often a way that small firms can prosper against much larger competitors.

Product application can also be used to segment. Computers, for example, have a myriad of users; sellers can segment on their expertise in terms of how the equipment will be most useful. In a different example, some suppliers can provide economies of scale for certain volumes of purchase; they need to seek buyers who purchase in that volume range, and they need to communicate their expertise in that volume range.

Personal characteristics of decision makers attempts to segment at the finest level, that is, by the individual decision makers within the firm. These variables include *buyer–seller familiarity, buyer motivation, individual perceptions,* and *risk management strategies.* While these variables were not judged as overly used by Weitz (see Chapter 18), they are available for consideration. Also, given that firms have, on average, five persons involved in the decision, it may be difficult to develop useful profiles on each one and then to segment on the basis of this information.

Product-, price-, and distribution-related issues

Generally, the products sold to business also differ from those sold to consumers. That boiler sold by Combustion Engineering is a good example (although maybe a little extreme) for the issues that tie in here.

Highly technical, complex and high-priced products   Decision makers need a great deal of information and will go through a long, thoughtful decision-making process. These products are infrequently purchased, and those involved

Table 22.2 A selection of data sources for use in industrial market analysis

Source	Title of publication	Type of Data	Application	Frequency of publication	Comments
Federal Government	*Census of Manufacturers* (U.S. Dept. of Commerce)	General data by 4-, 5-, 7-digit SIC on value added, employees, number of establishments, shipments, and materials consumed. Data shown by region, state, employment size, etc.	Provides comprehensive data to determine potential by area and for specific industries.	Every 5 years	Broadest array of industrial data; based on a census, may be dated.
	Annual Survey of Manufacturers (U.S. Dept. of Commerce)	Based on a sample of firms: yields current 4-digit SIC data similar to the *Census*.	Similar to the *Census*.	Annually	Less comprehensive and detailed than the *Census*, up to date.
	County Business Patterns (U.S. Dept. of Commerce)	Statistics on number of establishments and employment by 4-digit SIC for all counties in the U.S.	Used to estimate market potential by region: evaluate industry concentration by region.	Annually	Provides effective estimates of potential if number of employees is correlated to industry demand.
	Standard Industrial Classification Manual (U.S. Bureau of the Budget)	Complete description of the SIC system. Describes all 4-digit industries.	Used to evaluate possible industrial users based on products they produce.	Every 5 years	Lists each 4-digit SIC category and its primary products.
	U.S. Industrial Outlook (U.S. Dept. of Commerce)	Overall view of over 200 4-digit SIC industries with past and future growth rates in shipments and employment.	Project future market concentration and potential.	Annually	Reasonably current data; provides useful look at growth prospects in selected industries.
	Current Industrial Reports (U.S. Dept. of Commerce)	Series of over 100 reports covering 5000 products; usually based on 3-digit SIC, but may use 7-digit codes. Shipment and production data provided.	Provides in-depth analysis of potential by specific industry.	Monthly to Annually	Very timely data; published 4–8 weeks after data are collected.
	A Guide to Federal Data Sources on Manufacturing (U.S. Dept. of Commerce)	Describes nature and sources of all federal government data related to manufacturing.	A quick guide to locate appropriate government data.	Annually	Valuable source document for understanding government statistics.

672

		Type of data varies, but usually provides individual company data such as SIC code, number of employees, products, and address.	Useful for defining specific potential customers by state and region.	Usually Annual	Provides data on firms of all sizes. Particularly useful when markets are concentrated in a few states.
State, Local Government	State and Local Industrial Directories				
Trade Associations	For example: National Machine Tool Builders Association, Glass Container Manufacturers Institute, Iron and Steel Institute, Rubber Manufacturers Association	Sales history of the industry: industrial, financial, and operating data.	Provides an evaluation of past and present growth potentials by industry.	Usually Annual	May provide useful industry data not contained in other sources, i.e., average age of equipment, etc.
Trade Publications	For example: *S&MM* "Survey of Industrial Purchasing Power"	Number plants and shipments by SIC code by county; county percentage of total U.S. shipments by SIC category.	Provides a ballpark estimate of market potential by state and county.	Updated Annually	Very timely source for quickly assessing potential by county and state.
	Iron Age: "Basic Marketing Data on Metal-Working"	Census of metalworking industry. Data on plants and employees on a regional basis.	Quick estimate of potential for the metalworking industry.	Annual	Useful for easy estimation of potential for a particular industry.
Private Industrial Directories and Research (Fee) Companies	For example: *Predicasts* (Predicasts, Cleveland, Oh.)	Growth forecasts and market outlook for various industries by SIC.	Can be used to extrapolate potential estimates for the long run.	Quarterly	Up-to-date information on growth trends by 7-digit SIC.
	Dun's Market Identifiers (Dun & Bradstreet, N.Y.)	Data on 3.5 million corporations relative to company SIC, address, locations, sales, and employees.	Provides an evaluation of potential sales by individual company.	Continuous file	Timely information on specific firms can be obtained quickly.
	Standard & Poor's Industry Surveys' Basic Analysis (Standard & Poor's Corp., N.Y.)	Data on major industries and companies.	In-depth data on specific companies.	Weekly	Timely, general data on major industries.

Source: Michael D. Hutt and Thomas W. Speh, *Industrial Marketing Management* (New York: The Dryden Press, 1981), pp. 108–109. Copyright 1981 by CBS College Publishing. Reprinted by permission of the Dryden Press, CBS College Publishing.

with the purchase will probably need to learn new information each time they purchase. This does not mean that there are no frequently purchased products but, rather that, compared to consumer goods, the products are more complex and technical.

Products are more likely to be made to specifications   If the product is specially designed, there is more likely to be prepurchase technical consulting on the part of the salesperson as well as more postpurchase follow-up. While advertising can create knowledge about the selling firm's skills, it cannot aid in this individualized work. This is another point showing the need for a sales force.

Price may be established through negotiations or competitive bid
Consumer products generally have a fixed price that the buyer can accept or refuse, but as the products become more expensive, there is room for negotiation (e.g., automobiles, real estate). Negotiated or bid prices are the norm for industrial products; this means that the sales force is, again, vitally important. Given an interactive pricing process, the selling firm must have an agent available to negotiate with the buying firm and, again, the role of advertising is limited. The more individualistic the pricing, the greater the need for a salesperson.

The channel is generally short and may be direct   Consumer products often go through several middlepersons before reaching the user. This removes the manufacturer from the consumer and increases the need for advertising to communicate the firm's point of view. Industrial products generally have shorter channels, and often the manufacturer sells directly to the user firm. The more direct the process, the less the need for advertising and the greater the need for a salesperson. This situation results because most manufacturers sell to a small number of other firms. The smaller the target market, the more direct will be the channel of distribution.

Buyer-related issues

The types of buyers and the buying process evolves directly from the types of firms and types of products that exist in the industry. Understanding the internal buying processes of a firm is essential in developing a coherent communications plan.

Professional buyers   While most households have a person in charge of buying, this is not the major task of that person's life. Conversely, an industrial purchasing agent is trained to make evaluations based on much more detailed information than is available to the consumer. This detail is necessary because an error of a fraction of a cent can change the cost of a large shipment by many thousands of dollars. Given this need for detail, decisions tend to be heavily rational rather than emotional or whimsical.

The buying center or decision-making unit (DMU)   Although the buyers are professional, they rarely act alone. A major difference from consumer purchases concerns the complexity of the buying unit. A study by *Purchasing Magazine* of 603 chemical industry purchasing executives showed that the purchasing agent acted alone in only 13% of all cases. The average number of people involved was 5 and ranged up to 50.[4] Other studies show that, typically, four departments and three management levels become involved in each industrial purchasing decision. In addition, these people may be geographically dispersed over several plants and offices.

Given this complexity, it is important to know who is in the DMU, what roles they have, and who are the key influencers. Typically, the process evolves as shown in Table 22.3; engineers begin the process by identifying the problem and setting technical standards; purchasing agents negotiate with suppliers and eventually recommend one; and finally, management makes a decision. This process is well summarized by Haas:

> Although there is no single format dictating how industrial companies actually purchase goods and services, there is a relatively standard process that is followed in most cases. This process is as follows: (1) a department discovers or anticipates a problem in its operation that it believes can be overcome with the addition of a certain product or service; (2) the department head then draws up a requisition form describing the desired specifications she feels the product or service must have to solve her problem; (3) the requisition form is then sent by the department head to the firm's purchasing department; (4) based on the specifications required, the purchasing department then conducts a search for qualified sources of supply; (5) once sources have been located, proposals based on the specifications are solicited, received, and analyzed for price, delivery, service, and so on; (6) proposals are then compared with the cost of producing the product in-house in a make or buy decision: if it is decided that the buying firm can produce the product more economically, the buying process for the product in question is terminated; however, if the inverse is true, the process continues; (7) a source or sources of supply is selected from those who have submitted proposals; (8) the order is placed, and copies of the purchase order are sent to the originating department, accounting, credit, and any other interested departments within the company; and (9) after the product is shipped, received, and used, a follow up with the originating department is conducted to determine that department's level of satisfaction or dissatisfaction with the purchased product in terms of the problem faced for which the product was purchased.[5]

Knowledge of the general flow of this process is important for advertising so that appropriate messages will reach appropriate influencers. To do this, the selling firm could put a technical message about its product benefits in *Engineering Digest,* it could put a message showing the on-time delivery record and potential savings of the product in *Purchasing Agent's Digest,* and it could put a message showing increased profits with less pollution in *Management Digest.* Each message would be tailored for a specific influencer's needs and perspective.

Table 22.3 Key decision-process influences by decision phase

Decision phase	Prime influence	Secondary influence
1. Initial	Engineering	Purchasing
2. Determine type	Engineering	Production
3. Draw up specs	Engineering	Production
4. Evaluate sources	Purchasing	Production
5. Select supplier	Purchasing	Corporate management
6. Determine amount	Corporate management	Purchasing and production
7. Final authority	Corporate management	Purchasing

Source: Gary L. Lilien and M. Anthony Wong, "An Exploratory Investigation of the Structure of the Buying Center in the Metalworking Industry," *Journal of Marketing Research,* vol. 21 (February 1984), p. 6.

Buying situations   To further complicate the above issues, there are three types of buying situations with differing levels of complexity. Table 22.4 shows the stages of the buying process that are gone through at each level.

These levels of complexity reflect the fact that firms have differing levels of experience with different types of purchases, and that these levels change over time for any particular purchase. The three levels are: *new purchase, partial or modified rebuy,* and *full or straight rebuy.*

- *New purchase*   This situation deals with the first purchase of a product. Because it differs from anything previously purchased, the decision will be a complex one requiring lots of information. There will be an exploration of alternative solutions and an evaluation of alternative suppliers. The situation is the equivalent of *extended problem solving* (EPS) discussed in Chapter 3.

   The seller firm needs to get involved as early as possible so that the problem will be structured in such a way that the seller firm will be perceived as most likely to provide a successful solution. In these cases, there will be seller firms that are "in" with the purchasing firm and others that are "out." Each of these will need to use different strategies in order to be successful. Table 22.5 summarizes these strategies.

- *Partial or modified rebuy*   In this situation, the firm now has experience with the product but feels that improvements could be made. This means that a more limited search of alternatives needs to be made; basic product knowledge exists, but there is some dissatisfaction. Problems could relate to product, pricing, or service, for example. The parallel processing situation for consumers is *limited problem solving* (LPS).

- *Full or straight rebuy*   Now the firm is happy with the product, and there is no need for further evaluation; expedience suggests a simple rebuy from the same

Table 22.4 Complexity of the process by type of buying situation

	Awareness of problem	Product for problem	Search for suppliers	Take bids	Give order	Buy	Evaluate ⟶
Full rebuy (Office supplies, raw materials)					START	STOP	
Partial rebuy (New Communication System)		START ⟶					⟶ STOP
New purchase (Communications/Data System)	START ⟶						⟶ STOP

Purchase Stage

1. The stages involved in the purchase *expand* as problem familiarity decreases, solution cost increases.
2. The number of individuals involved in the buying center increases as problem familiarity decreases.

Source: Thomas V. Bonoma and Benson P. Shapiro, "Industrial Market Segmentation: A Nested Approach, Working Paper no. 83-100, Marketing Science Institute, Cambridge, MA, February 1983. Used also with permission of Allyn and Bacon Publishers.

Table 22.5 Marketing strategies for different buying situations

	Supplier status	
Buying situation	***In supplier***	***Out supplier***
Straight rebuy (Full rebuy)	Reinforce buyer-seller relationship by meeting organization's expectations.	Convince organization that the potential benefits of reexamining requirements and suppliers exceed the costs.
	Be alert and responsive to changing needs of customer.	Attempt to gain a position on organization's preferred list of suppliers even as a second or third choice.
Modified rebuy (Partial rebuy)	Act immediately to remedy problems with customer.	Define and respond to the organization's problem with existing supplier.
	Reexamine and respond to customer needs.	Encourage organization to sample alternative offerings.
New task (New purchase)	Monitor changing or emerging purchasing needs in organization.	
	Isolate specific needs.	Isolate specific needs.
	If possible, participate actively in early phases of buying process by supplying information and technical advice.	If possible, participate actively in early phases of buying process by supplying information and technical advice.

Source: Patrick J. Robinson, Charles W. Faris, and Yoram Wind, *Industrial Buying and Creative Marketing* (Boston: Allyn and Bacon, 1967), pp. 183–210.

supplier. The consumer information processing stage that is most similar is *routinized response behavior* (RRB). The buying firm will gladly stay at this level until a problem occurs. An "out" seller will need to convince the buyer that it can provide better product, price, or service if it would like a piece of the business. If this happens, the buying firm will return to a modified rebuy stage in order to reevaluate the present and prospective sellers.

It can be seen that the industrial buying process is an extremely complex one, with highly involved members attempting to make rational choices after evaluating large amounts of information. This is because the decisions may involve large dollar amounts, very sophisticated products, and/or infrequently made purchases.

Advertising and Promotions-Related Issues

All of the above issues influence advertising promotions. The remainder of the chapter deals with the advertising and promotions that emerge from these issues; this reflects the reality that the strategic changes emerge from the situation analysis. The reader should keep in mind that the goals of industrial advertising are to create awareness and knowledge and to make the salesperson's job easier by preceding a visit to the prospect.

Advertising—media

The mix of media and vehicles differs between an industrial and a consumer product. Because of the smaller targets, the broad vehicles used for consumer products are generally not appropriate and, if used, would in most cases yield a high level of wasted coverage and inefficiency. For this reason, the primary business mass media are trade publications and direct mail.

Figure 22.2 shows the relative cost-effectiveness and reach of various tools used for industrial communications. This figure, from Ames and Hlavacek, shows that as breadth of coverage increases, cost per contact decreases; of course, *total cost* goes up at the same time. While these relations are important to keep in mind, it is more important to meet the objective at hand with regard to a particular target market.

Figure 22.2   The industrial promotional mix

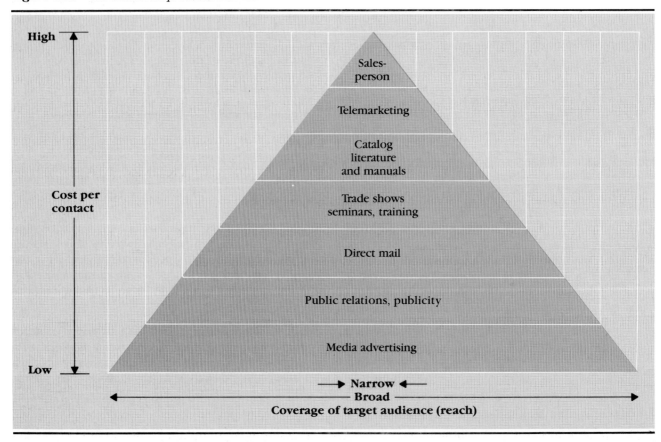

Table 22.6 The value of trade publications advertising

Ad size classification	Average cost of an industrial advertisement in a trade publication	Average number of inquiries generated by ad size	Average cost per inquiry by ad size	Average cost of same size ad in a general business publication
1 page advertisements	$2,064	119	$20.44	$20,202
2/3 page advertisements	1,565	103	17.45	14,948
1/2 page advertisements	1,186	101	14.14	12,043
1/3 page advertisements	842	82	11.37	7,599
1/4 page advertisements	656	92	7.97	N/A

Source: Cahners Publishing Company, *What is the Average Number of Inquiries Generated by Ad Size?*, *What is the Cost of an Average Inquiry by Ad Size?*, and *What is the Average Cost of an Industrial Advertisement as Compared to a General Business Publication Advertisement by Size Classification?* Cahners Advertising Research Reports no. 250.1, 250.2, and 540.2 (Boston: Cahners Publishing Company, 1977).

Trade publications   Over a seven-year period during the 1970s, more than 60% of industrial advertising budgets went to the over-3,000 trade (or business) publications listed in *Standard Rate and Data Service*.

These publications come in two types, known as horizontal and vertical publications. A *horizontal publication* deals with a particular job function without discriminating by industry type (e.g., *Purchasing Magazine*). A *vertical publication* covers a particular industry but does not discriminate by job title (e.g., *Chemical Week*). An advertiser chooses between horizontal and vertical depending upon the product and its market. For example, computer software that helps assess payout periods of new equipment would apply across industries and wouldn't be of much interest to an engineer. Therefore, ads might be placed in *Purchasing Magazine*. Conversely, a piece of equipment that is used to maintain chemicals at a very specific temperature would be of little use to someone in computer or furniture businesses. Therefore, ads might be placed in *Chemical Week*.

The goal, as with consumer messages, is to reach the most people in the target market at the lowest cost. Business publications are, for the most part, narrow vehicles that reach a specific target market at a relatively low cost. While the CPM of these publications is generally higher than that of consumer publications, the total cost is much less because of the much lower circulation. In addition, the value of the publications is high because the ads *are* read. Both the editorial and advertising content are important to the readers, as can be seen in a Cahner's study which showed that 89% of readers read ads regularly, 1% never read ads, and 54% read ads as much as editorial content.[6]

Table 22.6 shows that, although industrial publications reach a limited audience, they elicit a fair number of responses and, therefore, have a low cost per inquiry. This table is similar to others in the media chapters in that it suggests that buying several small-space ads is more effective than buying fewer large-space ads. Figures 22.3 and 22.4 reiterate the information presented in Table 22.6.

Direct mail   In the previously cited study of media allocations, almost 15% of budgets went to direct mail advertising. This percentage is probably too low, because the amount spent on industrial direct mail doubled between 1976 and 1980.

Figure 22.3   *What is the average cost of advertisements in specialized business magazines vs. general business magazines by size?*

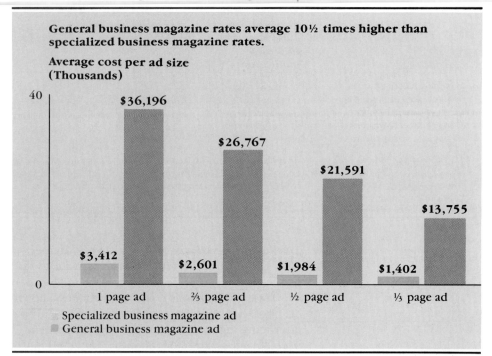

General business magazine rates average 10½ times higher than specialized business magazine rates.

Average cost per ad size (Thousands)

Specialized business magazine ad
General business magazine ad

Direct mail works well because industrial marketers generally have a fairly good sense of their targets; because these targets are small, direct mail is affordable, even though its cost per unit is much greater than that of trade publication advertising. In addition, direct mail allows a lot of flexibility in tailoring the message to the needs of the seller and the prospect. Because the message may be quite long and involved, direct mail is, again, a very appropriate delivery tool.

This form of advertising is a very well-accepted medium and is used extensively by buyers as an information source. In a 1982 survey, 60% of executives said they *preferred* to hear about new products by direct mail, another 21% found direct mail annoying, but half of these wanted to continue to receive it. In a 1980 study, industrial buyer respondents "read or scanned" at least three-quarters of the direct mail sent to them.[7] Given these data, it is clear that direct mail can serve to create awareness and knowledge.

Direct mail can also lower the cost of selling because it includes a cheap mechanism for identifying prospects. By enclosing a return postcard in the mailing, the seller gives prospective buyers the opportunity to identify themselves. These prospects then become viable candidates for a salesperson to call upon.

Mailing lists can be purchased from companies that specialize in this service (for example, R. L. Polk and Company, Dun and Bradstreet, National Business Lists) or from trade publication subscriber lists. The cost to rent such a list starts at about $30 per thousand names and increases as the criteria for the list become specific.

Consumer media   Surprisingly, 10% of the average industrial advertising budget is spent in consumer media. About three-quarters of this is spent in general news magazines such as *Time, Newsweek,* and *U.S. News and World Report.* As

Figure 22.4   *What is the average number of inquiries generated by ad size?*

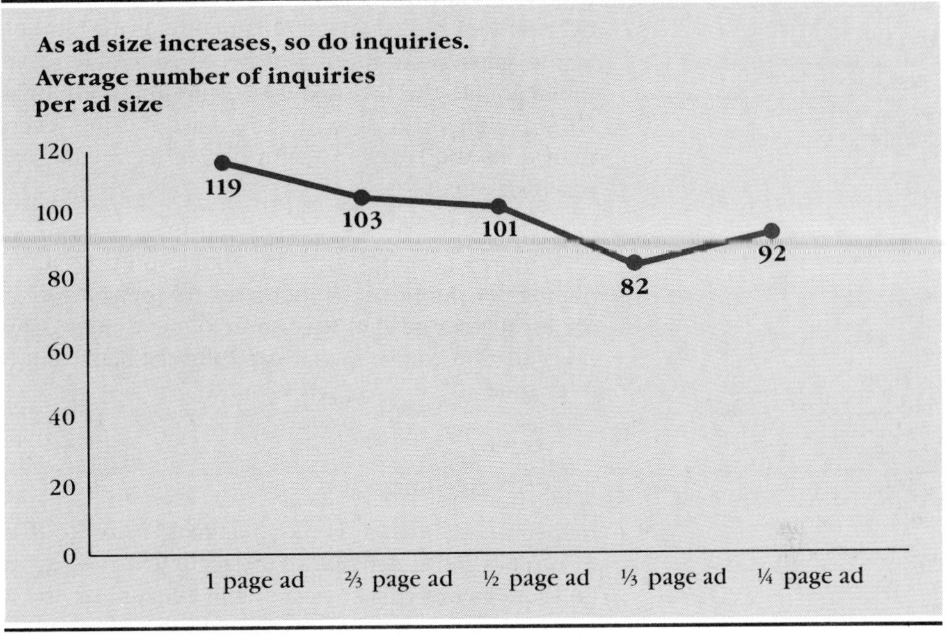

As ad size increases, so do inquiries.
Average number of inquiries
per ad size

120	
100	119
80	103 101
60	82 92
40	
20	
0	

1 page ad   ⅔ page ad   ½ page ad   ⅓ page ad   ¼ page ad

stated earlier, if the product being sold has a wide, general market, then consumer media may be appropriate. Industrial decision makers are also consumers of personal products and users of consumer media, so it can be logical to pursue them in this way. If the product has a target of a few hundred decision makers, this is probably not efficient, but if the product can be used in millions of offices, stores, and factories (e.g., a postage meter), then it may be reasonable to advertise it in consumer publications. *Newsweek* has a circulation of about 5 million and perhaps half of these readers might, at some time, be in a position to influence a postage meter purchase decision. Furthermore, *Newsweek* and other consumer publications have a number of segmented editions that allow the reader to isolate the business community. Finally, there is value in using consumer media because (1) it is less likely that a competing message will be present, and (2) the reader will be in a different environment that may make him more receptive to the message.

Catalogs   This medium is especially important for a firm that uses independent distributors rather than its own sales force, or for a firm with an extensive list of standard products. The catalog may be one of many used during a distributor's sales rounds; it helps ensure that this independent salesperson will accurately represent the firm in a situation where the firm may be competing for the distributor's as well as the buyer's share of mind. The catalog may also be one of many held by a prospective buyer and thus must be both accurate and persuasive in the absence of a salesperson.

To cope with these two types of situations, the firm often puts its catalog into a loose-leaf binder so that it can be easily updated, and it publishes its prices on separate pages from the rest of the catalog, because this is the item that changes most frequently. It is also a good investment to make the catalog visually appealing, because it may be the sales representative of the firm at times.

Reach   Ogilvy & Mather[8] suggest concentrating messages in the top two publications of any industry or job classification. They feel that this strategy will get over 80% of the coverage obtained by using all the publications in a classification; at the same time, there will be considerable savings. By using the less popular publications, the firm would get limited additional reach and erratic frequency. Other studies also show that the *cost* of using several publications increases faster than does the *reach*. As with consumer media planning, it is wasteful to try for too high a reach.

Frequency   Along with the above, putting an equivalent budget into a small number of publications increases frequency. Most industrial publication readers are loyal (they read at least three of every four issues) but are pressed for time. In this situation they may not carefully read any single ad but will learn the message over time.

Advertising—message

Industrial advertising is more difficult to write than is consumer advertising because it is more demanding of accuracy. It is easier for consumer advertising to be vacuous but still be acceptable because, in the absence of facts, it can still appeal on some emotional dimension. In addition to this difference, industrial advertising is generally less profitable to the agency because the media budget is smaller and is more likely to be fragmented across more vehicles. The result is more work for less money.

On the positive side, agency–client relations tend to be less volatile and more stable. An industrially oriented agency can spend less time and money pitching new accounts because it is less likely to lose the ones it has. While the monetary value of this stability is difficult to assess, it must be considered somewhere in the agency's financial equation.

What to say   The readers of industrial advertising tend to be professional decision makers who are looking for information that can be useful. It is therefore necessary to develop messages that show benefits related to the most important attributes.

In a 1979 study, McGraw-Hill[9] asked over 1,400 salespersons to rate a list of attributes on their degree of importance in their customers' decision making. The results are shown in Figure 22.5. Quality was the most important product attribute, while integrity and reputation were the most important company characteristics. Durability, the next most important issue, is closely related to quality. Note that price is less important than seven other issues. The most tangible and important issues are quality, durability, reliable supply, prompt delivery, and technical assistance. These are issues that can be spoken to in advertising. While cost is always important, it seems to be overshadowed by other benefit issues.

Integrity and reputation are more difficult to advertise per se but seem to improve, in part, as the amount of advertising increases. As noted by Levitt and reported in Chapter 18, in the absence of other information, the firm's perceived reputation improves if it has advertised.

In a more detailed study of important attributes, Sibley[10] broke down the issues by buying department and found a different set of priorities for different areas within the buying firm. Table 22.7 shows these rankings by department. This

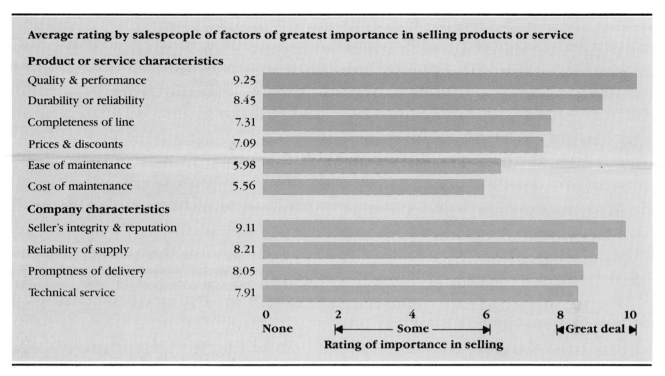

Average rating by salespeople of factors of greatest importance in selling products or service

Product or service characteristics

Quality & performance	9.25
Durability or reliability	8.45
Completeness of line	7.31
Prices & discounts	7.09
Ease of maintenance	5.98
Cost of maintenance	5.56

Company characteristics

Seller's integrity & reputation	9.11
Reliability of supply	8.21
Promptness of delivery	8.05
Technical service	7.91

0 None   2   4   Some   6   8   Great deal   10

Rating of importance in selling

Figure 22.5 *Product and company characteristics that are most helpful in selling products*

level of detail is necessary if ads aimed at different job titles are going to be put into different trade publications or mailings, as discussed earlier in this chapter.

Note that in both Figure 22.5 and Table 22.7 the potential customers feel that the selling firm is as important as the firm's product. As Doug Plunkett of the Ansul Corporation has stated:

> Industrial customers buy "relationships" or "business partners" as much as products. When a manufacturer purchases a new milling machine or computer system for example, they often need to know that the selling company has the resources and service capabilities to continually support the equipment over time. The buyer and seller often establish a long-term relationship to ensure that the equipment can continually be upgraded or improved as new technology becomes available.[11]

The data in Figures 22.5 and Table 22.7 reiterate the importance of the multi-attribute model (MAM), which was first introduced in Chapter 3. By learning what is important, it is possible to design messages to deal with these issues. The reader should note that the data presented in these figures represent averages across large samples and may not be correct for any specific individual product.

In looking at industrial advertising, good ads win out over bad because they deal with important benefits in specific ways. Buyers act out of self-interest, and advertising must therefore appeal on this ground. Ads that are specific in terms of quality, reliability, delivery, etc., are relevant and will be read. To this end, the ad in Figure 22.6 will be of mutual benefit to both buyer and seller.

Rational versus emotional messages   It is generally felt that rational messages are most appropriate in industrial cases. While this is correct, the emotional element of decision making should not be ignored. Messages should probably key on rational issues, especially when the firm has a clear benefit and position in the marketplace; in addition, though, emotional issues should also be used.

***Table 22*.7** Ranking of importance factors by various departments of the buying firm

Accounting Department 1. Offers volume discounts 2. Regularly meets quality specifications 3. Is honest in dealing 3. Answers all communications promptly 5. Has competitive prices 5. Handles product rejections fairly 5. Provides needed information when requested (such as bids)	***Manufacturing Engineering Department*** 1. Delivers when promised 2. Is honest in dealing 2. Provides products during times of shortages 4. Regularly meets quality specifications 5. Can deliver quickly in an emergency

Production Control Department
1. Can deliver quickly in an emergency
2. Ships products when wanted (for example, move-
   up and/or pushback deliveries if necessary)
3. Regularly meets quality specifications
4. Willing to cooperate in the face of unforeseen
   difficulties
4. Helpful in emergency situations
	Quality Control Department
	1. Regularly meets quality specifications
	2. Is honest in dealing
	3. Allows credit for scrap or rework
	3. Provides products during times of shortages
	5. Has a low percentage of rejects
	
	Special Machinery Engineering Department
	1. Provides products during times of shortages
	2. Regularly meets quality specifications
	3. Has a low percentage of rejects
	4. Delivers when promised
	5. Is honest in dealing

Purchasing Department
1. Regularly meets quality specifications
2. Advises of potential trouble
2. Is honest in dealing
2. Provides products during times of shortages
5. Willing to cooperate in the face of unforeseen
   difficulties
5. Delivers when promised
5. Provides needed information when requested
   (such as bids)
5. Helpful in emergency situations
	Tool Design Department
	1. Is honest in dealing
	2. Has technical ability and knowledge
	2. Handles product rejections fairly
	2. Allows credit for scrap or rework
	2. Invoices correctly
	2. Provides products during times of shortages
	2. Answers all communications promptly

Source: From Stanley D. Sibley, "How Interacting Departments Rate Vendors." *National Purchasing Review,* August/September/October 1980, p. 11. Reprinted with permission of National Association of Purchasing Management.

Note: Duplicate numbers indicate ties in rankings. A standard product was defined as having three or more of the following characteristics: (1) low unit cost, (2) little additional information required, (3) few people involved in the purchase, (4) short commitment (one year or less) to the product, and (5) little or no supplier modification of the product needed before use.

Emotional issues are generally more subjective by nature; these would include the image of the firm and product, the size of the firm, and its reputation. While buyers do not acknowledge the impact of emotional issues, they do exist and they do have an impact.

How to say it   As suggested above, it is important to show a benefit and to be specific in its presentation. Several industrial advertising presentation formats are suggested in the Ogilvy & Mather booklet, "How to Create Advertising that Sells"[12] and in David Ogilvy's book, *Ogilvy on Advertising:*[13]

▪ *Testimonials*   Experts in the field who are users of the product are very credible spokespersons. The more well known they are, the better the ad should do. Figure 22.7 is an example of a testimonial format.

▪ *Case histories*   This format is a third-person version of a testimonial and is also very credible. It is important to provide specific details of how well the product did for the customer firm in the case. Figure 22.8 shows such a case, with specifics of the benefits to the customer firm and, by implication, to other future buyers.

Figure 22.6   Highly informative ad with specific benefits for the reader

Optimal Chromatography

No. **3** IN A SERIES

Selecting columns to improve your HPLC results.

A new and practical approach.

We call it Optimal Chromatography. In theory, it applies to every HPLC application. In practice, it makes column selection easier and separations more effective. Here's how.

The tetrahedron illustrates the concept.

From an initial separation, most HPLC analyses can be improved for any one of four objectives: speed, resolution, load, or sensitivity. Each is represented by a vertex on the chromatographic tetrahedron. This reminds us that each objective requires a different combination of column and instrument conditions. The key is knowing which requirements you need to achieve your separation objective. That's where Beckman comes in.

Your optimal column source.

Beckman offers more than 100 columns to meet your specific application needs. For research, methods development, or quality control. From micro to semi-prep. And our proprietary stationary phase chemistries—21 in all—help you optimize sample selectivity, too. Whether it's for amino acid analysis or fast protein LC. Drug assays or carbohydrate separations.

Beckman/Altex columns give you reproducible, reliable results—as documented in hundreds of recent articles by independent scientists. And Beckman has over a decade of experience matching those columns to our customer's needs and objectives. Try us. You'll find that Beckman/Altex columns really can help optimize your chromatography.

Put Optimal Chromatography to work in your lab.

Columns are only one of the ways Beckman helps you get the most out of every separation. Our full line of HPLC systems, components, and accessories is designed with one goal in mind: to help you achieve optimal results.

For complete information on Optimal Chromatography and Beckman/Altex columns, send for your free catalog. And watch for other ads in our Optimal Chromatography Series.

Beckman Instruments, Inc., Altex Scientific Operations, 1716 Fourth St., Berkeley, CA 94710. Phone: 415/527-5900. Offices in major cities worldwide.

BECKMAN

Optimize from the start.

For most initial analyses, select Beckman Ultrasphere™ 150 x 4.6mm columns. These columns feature a minimum count of 9750 plates! That's better efficiency than most 300mm columns—and you'll get twice the speed using 50% less solvent. Once your initial separation is complete, adjust your solvent so that the first peak of the critical pair has K'=2-4. Then optimize for speed, resolution, load, or sensitivity.

Optimize for speed.

When speed is of the essence, use Beckman 3 micron, 75 x 4.6mm Ultrasphere columns for simple isocratic separations. For faster methods development and scouting procedures, use repeated fast isocratic separations. Also, be sure your system has a fast time constant, otherwise apparent efficiency will decrease rapidly.

Optimize for resolution.

When resolution is more important than speed, use a longer column and a shallower gradient with a low dead-volume flow cell to minimize band broadening. Beckman 250 x 4.6mm Ultrasphere columns are ideal for high resolution separations. They give you a 29% increase in peak capacity compared to 150mm columns.

Optimize for load.

Laboratory prep-scale applications require increased column diameter.
Beckman 10mm diameter columns are packed with exactly the same media as our analytical and micro columns. So you can easily scale-up your separation to semi-prep simply by equalizing the linear velocities.

Optimize for sensitivity.

For highest HPLC sensitivity, use microbore (≤ 2mm) columns and a fine-tuned LC system. Beckman/Altex microbore columns consistently improve sensitivity up to 10X that of 4.6mm ID columns.
Microbore columns require highly stable, low flow rate conditions. To fine-tune your system for low flow rate operation, contact Beckman about their complete line of microbore columns, pumps, and detectors with flow cells optimized for high sensitivity HPLC.

Figure 22.7   Testimonial ad for an industrial product

Only $695

"I would have paid a lot more for a fraction collector that does what Cygnet does. But I didn't have to."

ISCO's new Cygnet was exactly the full-featured fraction collector Dr. Lowell Satterlee was looking for. It collects 100 fractions (up to 25 ml each) by time, drop, or volume. For more information write Isco, Box 5347, Lincoln, NE 68505, or phone [800]228-4250.

ISCO

▪ *Demonstrations*   Here, the format shows what the product can do without the specifics of a case history or testimonial. The dramatic demonstrations used by Goodyear in Figure 22.9 clearly show the strength of their stretch film.

▪ *News*   Industrial readers look for new product information; if there is news, it should be clearly announced, as in Figure 22.10.

▪ *Generic product class information*   The firm can position itself as an expert in its field by providing product class information without specifically discussing the brand. By presenting information such as that shown in Figure 22.11, the firm provides a service to potential buyers and positions itself as well. This type of ad often has a long life and could end up being hung in dealer offices as a reference work.

Throughout all of these ad types, it is important to develop and maintain a consistent position and advertising format. In this way, buyers will more easily learn what the firm stands for, and each ad will have a greater impact because it will be easily recognizable.

Promotional materials

When promotional tools are discussed in an industrial context, several areas dominate. One is the catalog, which has been classified in this text as a media tool (often a subset of direct mail). The others are trade shows, specialty items, samples, and pricing deals.

Figure 22.8   *Case history ad for an industrial product*

Figure 22.9 *Demonstration of the strength of Goodyear stretch pallet film*

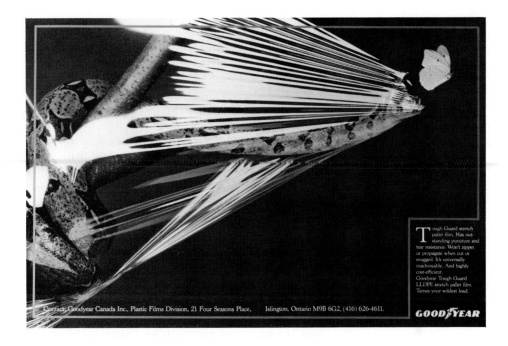

Figure 22.10 *Newsy ad for an industrial product*

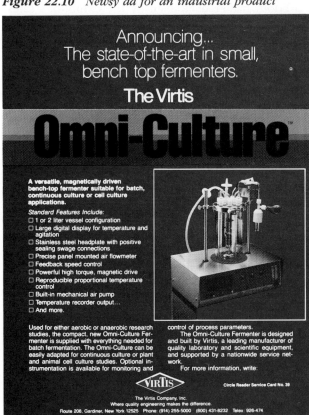

Figure 22.11 *Generic product class information ad*

Trade shows   Approximately $10 billion were spent on over 9,000 trade shows in 1983.[14] This area of promotions was a sleeping giant for many years; until recently, shows were not used appropriately as marketing tools. The emphasis was on show biz, scantily dressed women, and lots of glitter. But, just as other areas of communications have become more sophisticated, so has the trade show.

Many firms now recognize the potential for making an impact through this vehicle. While the cost of the average trade show exhibit (including personnel, travel, etc.) was about $50,000 in 1983 (some exhibits cost over $200,000),[15] most trade shows and conventions drew from 2,000 up to 80,000 prospects who were interested enough to give up their time to be at the show. These figures lead to an estimate that the average cost per prospect contacted at a show is about half of the cost of an industrial sales call.[16]

Because these prospects have made an effort to be at the show, they are felt to be of better quality than those reached through initial sales calls. To this point, over 60% of trade show contacts make a purchase (average value of $225,000) within a year of the show, and over 70% of prospects feel that they are influenced by trade shows.[17]

- ***Objectives for a trade show exhibit***   Just as with other communications tools, specific goals should be set for the use of a trade show. The most common goal of exhibiting seems to be to get sales leads for the sales force to pursue. Along with this, a goal is to give product information to prospects, with special emphasis on new product introductions. These goals are consistent with the needs of the trade show audience; 50% of these people go to see new products, and the top five reasons for attending are information related.[18] In addition, 83% of attendees who stopped at a booth hadn't been seen by the exhibitor's sales staff during the preceding year.

Because there is such a strong opportunity for prospective customers to gather information, the unspoken rule of trade shows seems to be to avoid the hard sell. In this way, attendees are not intimidated and can shop freely for information. Making a sale is definitely a secondary goal. In fact, some shows do not allow selling.

Given these goals, the trade show falls neatly between advertising and sales calls on the hierarchy of effects and should fall between these elements in a chronological fashion as well.

- ***Before the show***   Any exhibit should be preceded by direct mail or trade journal advertising to announce the firm's presence at the show. These messages should also state what will be shown in the exhibit in order to increase interest. As with other messages, the ad preceding the show and the show itself should fit the position of the firm. In addition to creating prior awareness, the firm can call key prospects and set up appointments to discuss the new products. Most attendees appreciate this courtesy (as well as the implication that they are important) and keep their appointments.

- ***After the show***   One of the greatest flaws in the use of the trade show is a lack of follow-up. After attendees have come to a booth, exhibited interest, and left their name, it is a terrible waste not to pursue them. Each attendee should get a thank you note immediately and a sales call within two weeks; some firms try to ascertain the prospect's buying schedule and time the sales call to precede the predicted purchase date. In either case, every lead should be followed up.

- ***Picking a trade show at which to exhibit***   There are almost 150 different sporting goods trade shows in which a firm could participate. While some firms exhibit very often (for example, 3M participates in about 600 shows per year), most firms participate in only a few shows. It is estimated that 50,000 companies took part in at least one of the 9,000 shows that took place during 1983.[19] How does a firm pick its shows?

Dickinson and Faria[20] surveyed over 600 firms and learned that the key attributes in show selection were

1. the proportion of decision makers among visitors to the show
2. the proportion of visitors who are in the target market

Figure 22.12 shows the top 15 attributes that emerged from this study, the number next to each item shows its ranking. Four classes of criteria also emerged, as shown in the figure. The quality of the audience seemed to be most important.

In addition, the firm can do a cost/benefit analysis for each prospective show by comparing the total predicted cost (including personnel and travel) against the predicted number of target market decision makers that will attend. This can be done for all shows being considered for the upcoming fiscal year. It can also be done retrospectively; in this case, the firm can compare costs with sales that developed from leads gained at a show. This post-hoc analysis then provides input for the following year.

▪ *A summary of trade show benefits*   Given the above discussion, the benefits of the trade show are that it

1. is less expensive than sales calls
2. brings in prospects with an interest in learning
3. brings in prospects that the sales force doesn't reach
4. is an easy way to learn about the competition
5. builds the mailing list
6. can capture trade press publicity
7. is a good way to introduce new products
8. is a way to find middlepersons (who also go to trade shows to seek out new clients)

Figure 22.12   Trade show selection criteria

Audience Quality
- Proportion of decision makers among visitors (1)*
- Proportion of visitors who are in your target market (2)
- Show limited to specific types of exhibitors (8)
- Number or percent of new contacts last year (9)
- Screening of visitors (14)

Audience Quantity
- Number visiting exhibits (3)
- Extent of promotion by show organizers (5)
- The show's audience size in past years (6)

Display Location
- Booth position/location on floor (4)
- Ability to specify/negotiate booth size, location, etc. (7)
- Aisle traffic density (13)

Logistical Aspects
- Easy registration or preregistration (10)
- Security (11)
- Easily available moving in/out assistance (12)
- Move in/out facilities (15)

*numbers in parentheses indicate rank order of criteria

9. can be used to show equipment that is too bulky or complex to take around on individual sales calls

In spite of these benefits, there are many firms that stay away from trade shows. Their main reasons are that the shows aren't useful and that they divulge information to competitors. The shows aren't useful when the exhibits are based on glitter and irrelevancies. Firms that use shows as a communications tool and plan their message find success.

It is true that competitors will learn about the firm's innovations, but this is more than offset by the number of prospects that also learn. Firms that use a show to introduce a new product find that the favorable exposure more than off-sets what competitors will learn. Is the best defense a good offense? It seems so in this case.

Specialty items   This is the old standby of industrial promotions based on the logic that it is important for the prospect to have something with the firm's name on it. As a result, firms send out, or salespersons leave behind, large numbers of calendars, paper weights, pens, hats, etc. The best items are those that tie to the product and its benefits.

Samples and pricing deals   If the product is small enough, a sample can be given to the prospect. This might be a 55-gallon drum of industrial cleanser or a case of a new type of typewriter ribbons. As with consumer products, the best way to show the merits of a new product is to let the prospect sample it. Of course, this works less well when the product is a piece of construction equipment.

Pricing deals are also similar to consumer promotions, and are widely used. Because a large number of sales are based on negotiated prices, deals are inevitable.

Sales force

Table 22.8 shows that prospects feel that the salesperson is the most important source of information that the firm can provide. Sources of greater importance than the salesperson are all within the buying firm.

In spite of this importance, there is not much to present at this point of the text that has not been presented previously in this chapter or the one concerning the sales force. To summarize a few key points

1. The salesperson must be aware of the complex buying process and the various persons that are involved in it. Table 22.9 summarizes the types of influencers and the role that the salesperson should take in dealing with each; it would be unusual for a sale to be made after dealing with just one person in the buying firm, except in the cases of simple products or a straight rebuy situation.

2. The salesperson's role is a much more complex one here than in the retail situation; there is work to be done before the sale in providing information, helping to draw up specifications, and, in general, acting as a consultant to the buying firm. After the sale, there is more work in follow-up service and maintenance. Once a relation has been established, the salesperson is a key link between the two firms and acts in a much broader role than merely that of selling the product.

3. The actual sale is likely to be negotiated with regard to price, product specifications, finance terms, delivery terms, and service. Balancing these issues while creating a profitable situation for the seller, maintaining a cooperative situa-

Table 22.8 Perceived importance of sources of information

Source of information	Mean[a]	S.D.
Information systems department	5.011	1.257
The using department	4.688	1.406
Top management	4.213	1.528
Salespeople from manufacturer	3.862	1.454
Actual terminal operators	3.767	1.543
Sales literature	3.446	1.504
Colleagues in other companies	3.220	1.505
Rating services	2.848	1.672
News stories in trade publications	2.684	1.424
Trade association data	2.510	1.478
Trade shows	2.473	1.513
Advertising in trade publications	2.290	1.290
Outside consultants	2.090	1.489
The purchasing department	1.675	1.086

Source: Rowland T. Moriarty and Robert E. Spekman, "Sources of Information Utilized During the Industrial Buying Process: An Empirical Overview," MSI Report no. 83-101, Cambridge, MA, 1983.

[a] Measured on a scale ranging from 1 = not important to 6 = very important.

tion with the buyer, and letting the buyer feel that the deal is a good one can be a difficult task at best.

4. The salesperson's ultimate objective is to make a sale. While this may not be the objective on any single visit, it is the ultimate goal. The sale may be indirect, as in the case of a pharmaceutical retailer, but over time, the salesperson's territory must show product usage. In giving out information and service, the ultimate goal of behavior must be remembered. This sets sales force communications apart from other forms of communication that stress awareness, knowledge, and attitude. The goal of behavior is easier for the salesperson to reach (and is reached at a lower cost) if it is preceded by a coordinated effort of advertising, trade shows, and other devices that are aimed at lower levels of the hierarchy of effects.

5. An important part of any salesperson/prospect interaction is the establishment of a relation that clearly shows which party dominates. If the issue of control is not established, the relation will center on this fruitless issue, and the more relevant issue of selling product will not be reached.

6. The most important attributes to discuss relate to product quality, performance, durability and reliability, and reliability of supply. These are concrete issues to be discussed during the presentation. Less tangible is the firm's integrity and reputation, which are probably better dealt with indirectly or at least in a nonboastful manner. Both the rational and emotional issues have value in decision making and should be recognized.

Budget

As discussed in Chapter 20, there are a variety of methods of budgeting for advertising and other forms of communications. These include arbitrary methods such as affordable, percentage of sales, and competitive parity, and the more strategically oriented method of objective and task. For consumer products, there is a trend toward the objective and task method; firms are learning the value of this budgeting process and are adopting it.

Table 22.9 Marketing strategy for different buying influencers

Buying influence	Effects on buying	Appropriate marketing strategy
Purchasing Agent, Buyer	Handles requisitions from the plant, maintains personal library of supplier's catalogs. Does some discretionary purchasing, especially when delivery is critical. Usually honors sources recommended by key plant personnel.	See them regularly. Keep them informed if you see others in the plant. Keep them supplied with new product and price information. Offer them a benefit on every call. Allow them to pave the way to other buying influences in the plant.
Production Manager, General Foreman	Usually confined to specific production operations such as assembly, finishing, etc. Can describe specific problems in detail.	Sell brand superiority, depth of your inventory, delivery, and your potential for contributing to productivity of production people and equipment. Leave catalog, put him on general mailing list. Call only when you have a real constructive offering.
Plant Controller, Head Bookkeeper	With purchasing department, interested in terms of sale or systems contract.	Be fully prepared with terms stated simply. Come armed with benefits offered over and above those of terms to impress him with value added.
Director or Vice-President of Engineering	Concerned with product or process improvements. Generally involved with future changes, seldom with immediate needs. Searches continually for new, improved products. Relies heavily on his library of suppliers. Also relies heavily on technical aid from vendors. Strong influence on OEM and MRO product type and brand selection.	Responds favorably to outside help in the form of new, potentially useful data and technical counsel. Offer him your complete catalog. Offer him technical capabilities via your own experts. Personally introduce new improved products regularly. Put him on your general mailing list and keep him supplied with your latest complete catalog.
Plant Manager, General Manager, Vice-President of Operations, Vice-President of Manufacturing	Key buying influence on larger plant expenditures. May direct vendors to key personnel and problem areas in the plants.	Receptive to constructive information. Often easier to reach than floor personnel. Contact periodically if possible with your management, to demonstrate your interest in serving, to sell your firm's capabilities, and to probe prospect's problems and plans. Keep him informed on important product breakthroughs.

Source: "Finding the Real Buying Influence," *Industrial Distribution* 67 (June 1977).

Industrial advertisers seem to be lagging in this area, as they were seen to be lagging in other areas of advertising strategy. In a 1978 study of British industrial firms, 28% of respondents used a budgeting method that was related in some way to percentage of sales, 68% used a method that was fixed or unknown, and 4% used some "other" method that may have included objective and task. While the data are not current and come from another country, they do show a lack of managerial insight into the budgeting process.

It may be that managers do not see industrial advertising as important enough to merit the effort. After all, industrial advertising budgets are typically quite small compared to the sales force budget. Table 22.10 on page 697 shows the size of the ad budgets in 1980 for 483 surveyed industrial firms. Note that almost half of the firms spent less than $100,000 on advertising, and only about 1% spent over $3 million per year. These are extremely low budgets when compared to those of consumer goods marketers and are also extremely low compared to the firms' own sales force budgets.

This lack of strategically oriented budgeting is unfortunate because it is often the key to profitability. In many cases, the amount spent and the allocation of marginal dollars are more important than the message strategy, but it is this latter topic that receives the largest share of management thought. Spending too much on communications is a waste because there is a large area of diminishing returns where extra dollars spent are not a wise investment. At the other extreme, there must be some threshold of spending before which any returns will be seen. This issue was discussed in Chapter 20 and is important. To deal with it, management must consider both marginal analysis and the objective and task method.

Combining marginal analysis and the objective and task method

Given the information presented in this chapter plus that of Chapter 20, what are the most appropriate ways of allocating limited communications dollars?

If the objective is awareness, then the strategy will be heavily oriented toward advertising. Beyond this, the manager needs to consider the CPM for actual target market prospects. Because there will be targets with differing job functions, cost will need to be considered for each target. A second complicating factor concerns the amount of information needed and the best presentation format. As complexity increases, the message will be delivered first by journal advertising, then direct mail, then trade show, then sales call. Each level is capable of presenting more detail. If the information is too complex for advertising, then the cost-efficiency of this medium is overwhelmed by its lack of effectiveness.

The cost of a journal ad is approximately $.16 per person who can recall some element of the message. This unit cost may be $2 for direct mail. A trade show will cost $70 to $80 per prospect, while a sales call is almost $200. It is easy to see absolute cost differences but difficult to assess effectiveness.

The manager must also consider marginal costs. At what point is it a better investment to increase awareness, increase knowledge, or try to close a sale? The marginal cost of trying to make one more person aware will almost always be less than the marginal cost of trying to close one more sale, but the marginal revenue from the sale is much greater. There must be tradeoffs as management moves prospects along from awareness to knowledge to behavior, there must be objectives to obtain this movement, and there must be proper usage of the different tools at the different stages.

The sales force is more appropriate for complex products, small target markets, high prices, direct channels, individually specified products, and negotiated prices. Under these conditions, more explanation is needed, and the firm is more likely to need its representative to interact with the prospect. In these cases, the firm must be prepared to pay a high communications price. Given these cases, advertising and other tools can still be used to lower sales costs by delivering lower cost messages to the prospect.

Fred C. Poppe

Chairman and Chief Executive Officer, Poppe-Tyson, Inc.

Fred Poppe started his advertising agency career in the mailroom of Fuller & Smith & Ross. Following a stint as advertising manager of Yale & Towne's Philadelphia Division, he spent seven years at G.M. Basford Company, where he was a group account supervisor. He formed Complan, Inc., the predecessor of Poppe-Tyson Inc., after having served as Executive Vice-President in charge of client services at T.N. Palmer & Company.

He received his degree in economics from Princeton University. Earlier, he studied engineering at Brooklyn Polytechnic Institute. He is former international president of the Business/Professional Advertising Association and once served as president of its New York Chapter. In 1967 he was voted "Agency Man of the Year" by B/PAA New York. In 1983 Fred won the G.D. Crain Award and was elected to the Advertising Hall of Fame. In 1984 he was named B/PAA's "Communicator of the Year."

His book The 100 Greatest Corporate and Industrial Ads, *published by Van Nostrand Reinhold, is considered a classic in the business.*

Over his span of 30 or so years in the business-to-business advertising profession, it's been estimated that Poppe has been responsible for the placement and purchase of more than $150 million worth of corporate and industrial magazine space.

Writing Engaging Ads Is What It's All About

With all due respect for things such as good market research, beautifully developed media strategy, and well-engineered promotions, I would like to suggest that the crux of the communications business is the ad professional's ability to create outstanding advertisements.

We all know the basic rules for producing good industrial and business ads. They are the identical rules we follow for producing consumer print ads. Essentially all you have to do is write a real stopper of a headline (if it contains a user benefit in it, all the better). Add to it a large and exciting illustration using a photograph rather than art. Then tidy it up with clear, easy-to-read typography in 10 point or more for the body copy. Put it all together, and you should have an adequate advertisement.

As you thumb through magazines, you'll pass by hundreds of perfectly good, professionally done ads. You don't have to spend much time looking at business-to-business advertising to realize that there are a plethora of just plain good ads that obey all these rules.

But they just sort of lie there. The best you could say about them is that there is nothing wrong with them.

However, there are a few—all too few—that instantly pop off the page and grab you. They do more than stop you. They *insist* you read on. By some magic they *engage* you—make you like the advertiser and its product. They literally force you to get his or her message. In our shop, we call this ability to convert a lazy thumber into an addicted reader *engagement,* and I categorize these exceptionally done ads as *engaging.* They engage your intellect and your curiosity. Perhaps they tickle your funnybone. Whatever, they absorb you totally.

Almost every engaging ad has its common denominator—"human interest." By this, we do not mean "humanitarianism," but rather basic human interest. Intrigue the reader, and 80% of the battle is won.

A great headline will always stop a reader. A good headline to a construction supervisor or foreman may not necessarily pertain to the job interests of a chemical engineer. Yet great construction ads that score high in general business magazines are read just as much by chemical engineers and steelmakers as they are by the construction workers they are addressed to. The reason is simple. When a well written "engaging" ad is produced, its human interest is high.

This is true in consumer ads as well. The construction foreman will read a great scaffolding ad because its headline appeals to him, just as a great cigarette ad headline might also pique his interest. He's the same guy, whether he buys industrial or consumer products. So the same ad technique will work with him if it's "engaging" enough.

Let me give you some examples. In an Otis escalator ad we wanted reader involvement. Lots of human interest. To obtain it, we literally had to build a tree house, stick a bunch of kids on it, then photograph the whole bit showing an Otis escalator running right up the tree. Difficult? You bet! But did that ad ever Starch! And what did it? *Engagement.*

The Otis J Series escalators are designed to meet your needs and your budget...for almost any kind of project you want to build.

Atlas Copco makes portable rotary compressors. You see them every day on construction sites all over the city. And most compressor manufacturer advertisements show them at these "on-the-job" applications. Not Atlas Copco! Their compressor is really quiet. To brag about it—and show off this unique product advantage—we photographed an Atlas compressor in a savings bank, of all places! Now, that was no easy bit of logistics. But the readership and inquiry response from this engaging ad (top, page 706) proved it was well worth all our efforts.

Here's one more. Abex Corporation markets its well-known railroad brake shoes under the brand name "Tiger." What better way to illustrate its wares than to photograph a live tiger? You can't go to "Rent-a-Tiger," so we sent a

crew to Madison Square Garden one early Sunday morning to take a thousand or so pictures of a Ringling Brothers tiger named Tarus. We almost lost a photographer, a client, and one timid copywriter. But the finished product was an engaging, two-year, four-color campaign that constantly dominated the market's three railroad publications insofar as readership was concerned. We could have taken the easy way out and used stock shots or a stuffed tiger, but then the ads (below) wouldn't have been so engaging.

In our shop, when a writer comes up with an ad that meets all the dictates of our copy platform and selling proposition but lacks that extra engagement quality, we just send it back to the drawing board and tell the writer to work on it until he or she can come up with that extra ingredient that will really engage the reader. Sometimes it's the headline that needs help, often times it's coming up with a bright idea for the visual, but whatever it is, it takes lots of time and lots of extra thought. It's never easy. The more engaging the ad, the harder it will be to produce it.

Table 22.10 Industrial advertising budgets, 1980

Amount	Percentage of Companies
Less than $100,000	49.1%
$100,000–$499,999	34.4
$500,000–$999,999	6.4
$1 million–$2,999,999	5.6
$3 million–$4,999,999	0.8
$5 million or more	0.4

Source: B. Charles Ames and James D. Hlavacek, *Managerial Marketing for Industrial Firms* (New York: Random House, 1984), p. 249. Reprinted with permission of Random House, Inc.

Summary

This chapter considered key issues that differentiate consumer goods and industrial goods advertising and promotions. Some of these key differences relate to the uniqueness of the industrial setting. These include market differences (a small number of buyers may make large purchases; the buyers are often directly contacted by the manufacturer), product differences (often these are highly complex and high-priced; often these are made to the individual buyer's specifications, and the prices are individually negotiated), and buyer differences (there are usually several professionals working together to pool their expertise).

The decision-making process is a complex one that can benefit from several types of seller communications. Advertising can serve to introduce the product and the company; trade shows can be used to increase a prospect's knowledge, while salespersons are used to answer questions, determine specifications, negotiate price, and close the sale. Each of these communications tools provides more specific information to a narrower target at a higher cost per contact.

As the messages are developed in each of these cases, it is important to keep in mind that several departments of the buying firm are usually involved and each has different informational needs. Engineers can be most concerned with product specifications, purchasing agents with pricing issues, and management with reliability of the selling firm.

In sum, business-to-business communications call for careful planning in dealing with a complex process. There may only be a small number of buyers and each decision may be worth a great deal; as a result, each interaction is for greater stakes and has greater risk attached.

Discussion Questions

1. What are some differences between consumer and industrial products?

2. Discuss the major differences between buyers and markets in consumer and industrial settings.

3. What are some of the major differences between consumer- and industrial-oriented communications? Be sure to discuss differences in goals, and how the communications are a result of the differences in products and settings.

4. How would communications differ if the buying situation was a new purchase, modified rebuy, or straight rebuy?

5. Describe the relationship between business-to-business advertising and the sales force in terms of efficiency, effectiveness, and how the two interact.

6. What are horizontal and vertical publications? When is each one more appropriate to the media plan?

7. Why would an industrial advertiser want to use consumer-oriented media?

8. What seem to be the most important variables for buyers across large numbers of industrial purchasing situations?

9. Under what conditions are trade shows an appropriate part of the business-to business-communications task?

10. Reconsidering your job search campaign: Would this campaign be most appropriately classified as a consumer or industrial campaign? Is it necessary to change anything (if you felt your campaign was not consumer)?

Notes

1. Industrial Marketing Committee Review Board, "Fundamental Differences between Industrial and Consumer Marketing," *Journal of Marketing* 19 (October 1954), pp. 152–158.

2. B. Charles Ames and James D. Hlavacek, *Managerial Marketing for Industrial Firms* (New York: Random House, 1984), p. 21.

3. Thomas V. Bonoma and Benson P. Shapiro, "Industrial Market Segmentation: A Nested Approach," Working Paper no. 83-100, Marketing Science Institute, Cambridge, Mass., February 1983.

4. "Purchasing Magazine's Readers Have Something to Tell You about Chemicals," (New York: *Purchasing Magazine,* 1965), Report No. 10A.

5. Robert W. Haas, *Industrial Marketing Management* (Boston: Kent Publishing Company, 1982), pp. 84–85.

6. Haas, *Industrial Marketing Management,* p. 280.

7. Ann Helming, "Direct Mail Leaves Its Indelible Stamp," *Advertising Age* 14 June 1982, p. M-12.

8. Ogilvy & Mather, *How to Create Advertising That Sells* (New York: Ogilvy & Mather, 1981), p. 11.

9. McGraw-Hill Publications, LAP Report no. 8010.2.

10. Stanley D. Sibley, "How Interfacing Departments Rate Vendors," *National Purchasing Review* 5 (August-September-October), p. 11.

11. H. Doug Plunkett, personal communication, 1985.

12. Ogilvy & Mather, *Advertising That Sells,* pp. 10–11.

13. David Ogilvy, *Ogilvy on Advertising* (New York: Crown Publishers, Inc., 1983), pp. 137–142.

14. John R. Dickinson and A. J. Faria, "Trade Show Organizers, Take Note: Exhibitors Rank Participation Criteria," *Marketing News* 18, no. 5, 2 March 1984, p. 3.

15. Dickinson and Faria, "Trade Show Organizers, Take Note."

16. Trade Show Bureau, "Trade Show Exhibit Cost Analysis," Research Report Number 7, August 1980.

17. Joanne Cleaver, "You Don't Have to Be a Star to Be in This Show," *Advertising Age* 14 June 1982, p. M-8.

18. Trade Show Bureau, "The Trade Show Audience," Research Report Number 3, April 1979.

19. Dickinson and Faria, "Trade Show Organizers, Take Note."

20. Dickinson and Faria, "Trade Show Organizers, Take Note."

Chapter 23
Communications for Services Marketing

*T*his chapter is the third to look at advertising and promotions applications in situations that do not feature consumer products. The focus here will be on intangibles, with an emphasis primarily on services, but with some examination also of the advertising of ideas and issues. Mass-marketed retail services (such as banking, lodging, entertainment, and travel), are considered as are professional services (such as health care, accounting, legal services, and dentistry), and public sector and nonprofit services (such as education, urban mass transit, arts, postal service, and libraries). Idea and issue advertising is done to a large degree by nonprofit and public sector organizations and will cover cases such as anti-smoking, pro- or anti-nuclear arms stances, pro- or anti-abortion stances, the 55 MPH speed limit, and the saving of some part of the environment.

The use of advertising, promotions, and marketing is quite recent in most of these areas, so it will be interesting to see some of the applications that have emerged. The chapter will consider what a service is, how it differs from a product, the relevance of these differences for the topics of this text, and what sorts of strategies are currently developing in the area of services advertising.

This chapter differs from the two previous ones in its organization. While those chapters consider all aspects of the decision sequence, this one focuses primarily on situation analysis issues. There are many differences between services and products, and even more differences between the variety of available services. After these issues are resolved, the remainder of the decision sequence falls into place similarly to the objective and strategy issues of the other chapters.

What Is a Service?

A simple and straightforward definition of a *service* in the context of marketing comes from Judd[1]; he defines a service as an object of a transaction that does not entail the transfer of ownership of a tangible commodity. That means that, when air travel is used, a service is purchased; the buyer receives nothing tangible (except perhaps a meal and a drink, but certainly not an airplane or a soft reclining chair), but has engaged in a transaction and received something of value.

A more complex and complete definition is put forward by Uhl and Upah:

> A service is any *task (work)* performed for another or the *provision of any facility, product or activity* for another's *use and not ownership,* which arises from an exchange transaction. It is *intangible* and *incapable of being stored or transported.* There may be an *accompanying sale of a product.*[2]

This is a very useful definition because it leads to the examination of some specific service-related issues. This in turn leads to a discussion of differences between services and products, and to a discussion of the impact that these differences make on advertising and promotions. Uhl and Upah give examples of the components of their definition:

- *Task or work*   physical labor, such as automobile repair, or mental effort, such as accounting services

- *Provision of a facility*   rental of a hotel room or admission to a park

- *Provision of a product*   rental of a car

- *Provision of an activity*   right to view a concert or attend a class

- *Use and not ownership*   restricted usage rights specified in the transaction contract

- *Intangible*   lacking physical properties, although some intangible services provide a tangible accessory, such as a consultant's report, a souvenir, or a ticket

- *Incapable of being stored*   services produced and consumed simultaneously; the producer or facility can be maintained, but the service perishes instantly. An airplane has a long life, but a flight from Tedium to Apathy that leaves at 3:15 P.M. on July 3, 1986, can only be consumed by people who are in Tedium at the appropriate time. An empty seat on that flight cannot be stored for a later sale.

- *Incapable of being transported*   Very few services can be produced in one place and consumed elsewhere. A person in Monotony at 3:15 P.M. on July 3, 1986, cannot use the flight to Apathy that leaves from Tedium.

Exceptions to the non-transportability rule exist through telecommunications; students can be in Tedium and can interact with a lecturer in Apathy, or they can watch a concert on closed-circuit television. Some would argue that the service has been changed when it is transported, but this is as close as a service can get to being transported while it is being produced.

- *Accompanying sale of a product*   Most products are sold with some service, and most services are sold with some product. When a bar of soap is sold, the price covers the service of getting the soap to the right place at the right time; the buyer does not need to go to the factory. At the other extreme, there is the concert, which has no physical product except for a ticket and whatever is bought separately at the performance. Often, product and service are presented and purchased together as in a restaurant or an automobile repair shop. This chapter deals with cases where the service component is dominant.

Differences to Note
in Promoting a
Service

Intangibility

A product can be seen, touched, smelled, poked, and kicked before it is purchased, and it can be easily shown in advertising. Because a service is *intangible,* the specific execution that is being purchased cannot be evaluated before it is consumed. A consumer can buy a bar of soap with reasonable certainty that it will be like the one bought by friend Joe last week. The consumer does not have the same certainty with a service. After using his new soap, Joe went to a restaurant and a concert; the food was well cooked in the restaurant, and the band was really cookin' at the concert. What will happen this week? Will the same chef be there? Will the band have an off night? By the time the consumer learns the answers to these questions, purchase and consumption will already have occurred.

Intangibles are more difficult to assess and as a result may need more advertising. Intangibles, though, are more difficult to portray in advertising and, as a result, often are shown through tangible surrogates. As in Figure 23.1, air travel cannot be shown, but a plane can be shown, and information about schedules and the plane can be given.

Figure 23.1 *Air travel*
service advertising

Because services are intangible, they are judged by what consumers *can* see. Hotels are judged by their lobbies and gardens, airlines by their equipment and flight attendants. These are what are shown in ads. Some services can be assessed more easily. Entertainers and sports teams present themselves through records, films, and broadcast media so that consumers will want to attend their events.

Uhl and Upah suggest that service organizations can be assessed through several tangible areas:

- Physical facilities or equipment
- People
- Organizational capability (e.g., financial stability and resources)[3]

Intangibility leads to three other differences of note.

Inability to store the service

Because there is nothing tangible, there is nothing to store. Because the service only exists as it is being produced, it must also be consumed at the same time or it will be forever lost to consumers. Some products (tomatoes, strawberries) perish quickly, but none perish instantaneously; some products (fashion or seasonal clothing) lose value over time, but these can be saved to be sold later at a lower price.

Some services are wasted if not consumed when produced (an empty seat at the ballet or on a bus represents wasted production); other services cannot be produced in the absence of a consumer (the dentist cannot fill a tooth without the presence of a patient). The elapsed time of nonconsumption cannot be recovered in either case.

This level of perishability suggests the need for strong promotional strategies based on pricing. Most products are manufactured with low fixed costs and high variable costs; the material cost is variable because it is only incurred each time a unit is produced. Most services, though, have a high fixed cost and low variable costs; the cost of flying a plane from Monotony to Tedium is fixed (almost) regardless of whether it is full or empty, and very little extra variable cost is incurred for each additional passenger.

Along with the above, the manager must consider the economic theory that the firm should continue to produce as long as it can cover its variable costs and make a contribution toward fixed costs. Since services have very low variable costs, they should use very volatile promotional/pricing strategy. If the coach fare from Monotony to Tedium is $217 but the variable cost per passenger is $17 (cost of a meal plus the marginal increment of fuel needed for an additional passenger), then the manager could lower the price to $18 and still be contributing to fixed cost and profit. The brand manager for Dial soap has much less leeway. While the price of a bar of soap to the retailer may be $.20, the variable cost of materials and production may be $.17.

The point of all this is that the service cannot be saved, so it must be sold or lost. The lowest acceptable price is one which exceeds variable cost. The manager should plan promotions with this in mind. When theatres offer student rush tickets, and when airlines offer discount standby seats, these organizations are recognizing the perishability of their service and responding with promotional strategies. They are probably not pricing as low as they could, though, because they don't want to teach customers the value of waiting until the last minute when making a purchase.

Inability to transport the service

Again, a lack of tangibility leads to another difference between products and services. If it isn't tangible, how can it be transported? The producer or the factory can be moved, but the service, which perishes as it is produced, cannot be transported. This means that the supplier of a service can only serve those in a limited geographic area who can travel to the producer's location. Alternatives are to create more production locations (H&R Block has tax offices, and Holiday Inn has hotels across the United States) or to put the producer on wheels (the Ringling Brothers Circus, touring companies of Broadway shows, symphonies, bookmobiles, and Michael Jackson concerts are examples of this strategy).

In the great majority of cases, a service is provided to a limited geographic area, and the providers are local retailers. As retailers, these service organizations deal with many of the same advertising problems as do retailers of products; for purposes of advertising, the most important similarities will lie in the areas of media planning, because all local retailers have similar geographic constraints.

As with many retailers, in order for a service to be competitive, it must be available so that the consumer does not need to travel far to obtain it. Once travel becomes an issue, customers will be lost to more conveniently located competitors. Many services have learned this, and, as a result, suburban movie theatres, branch banks, and satellite medical facilities have proliferated in recent years. As this increase in locations has taken place, a problem of quality control has arisen as the next key difference to consider.

Quality control

When products are manufactured, standards are set that can be easily measured; in a mechanized assembly line, both the manager and consumer can have some confidence that the products coming off the line will be within certain tolerances. Services, though, are discretely produced by different individuals who may easily vary from management and consumer expectations. As more locations are needed, it becomes more difficult for management to control quality; managers are needed for each location, and *their* quality must also be controlled. This point is made by James Schorr, executive vice-president of Holiday Inns:

> Well, I suppose a major difference between product marketing and service marketing is that we can't control the quality of our product as well as a P&G control engineer on a production line can control the quality of his product. When you buy a box of Tide, you can reasonably be 99 and 44/100% sure that this stuff will work to get your clothes clean. When you buy a Holiday Inn room, you're sure at some lesser percentage that it will work to give you a good night's sleep without any hassle, or people banging on the walls and all the bad things that can happen to you in a hotel.[4]

The quality is difficult to control because the manager must deal with independent, free-thinking people as opposed to machines. Robert Catlin, senior vice-president of N. W. Ayer ABH International reflects on this issue:

> There is also a tremendous difference in quality control between the two. When I was working on products, I knew exactly what the product was made of and, as a consequence, what it would do. So as I was trying to develop the appeals, the thrusts, the strategies to communicate to the consumer, I knew that every product that I was dealing with, every unit of that product, predictably would do certain things.

In a service business, you find that you're dealing with something that is primarily delivered by people—to people. Your people are as much of your product in the consumer's mind as any other attribute of that service. People's performance day in and day out fluctuates up and down. Therefore, the level of consistency that you can count on and try to communicate to the consumer is not a certain thing.[5]

Managers can respond by standardizing the product element of the offering and by having very careful training programs for the personal element. The result of this standardization yields some degree of quality control. When people travel, they seek out McDonald's and Holiday Inn because they have faith in what has been standardized. Some unknown competitor may be much better, but it may also be much worse. Advertising such as that in Figure 23.2 for Holiday Inn stresses standardization and even guarantees it. This assurance of quality is an important attribute in service selection and is often a key element of service advertising.

Managing demand

Product marketers for the most part attempt to maximize demand and are able to manufacture enough during periods of low demand so they can meet demand during peak periods. Because they are able to accumulate an inventory, they can advertise and promote to take advantage of seasonality and can maximize sales when demand is greatest.

Service marketers cannot do this. Because there is no inventory, the firm has a more limited sales capacity. A hotel with 100 rooms can only accommodate 100 groups of people. If the hotel is in the Caribbean and is fully booked during January, February, and March, there is no value in advertising for more business during that time. What it needs to do is to convince people to come during other months when there is slack capacity. The advertising task, then, is to shift demand to other months, or to increase demand during these off-season months, or, perhaps, to lessen demand during the peak season.

It is much easier to influence a brand choice decision in a situation where a consumer is already prepared to act (as in the product purchase case) than it is to change a person's basic purchase behavior (as when the hotel tries to get a person to go on vacation in April, May, or June rather than in January, February, or March). This, though, is a common problem for services with periods of slack demand. Figure 23.3 is an ad for a hotel that is trying to build its traffic during a nonpeak period. Most urban hotels have their greatest demand during the work week and need to cover their overhead on the weekends. Note the strong promotions orientation in the attempt to change a basic behavior.

One of the more extreme cases of trying to shift demand to a slack period was attempted by Sunrise Hospital in Las Vegas. While their patient count was quite high on Monday through Friday, their census was down on weekends. Because their fixed costs were very high, they were suffering large losses every weekend. To turn this around, they advertised that patients who had elective surgery on weekends would be eligible to win a cruise for two and that there would be a weekly drawing. Innovative and strong advertising and promotions such as this are needed in order to break existing behavior patterns.

Slack demand for a service provider means that costs are incurred that cannot be recovered; excess demand means that potential revenues are lost forever. Shifting demand can help resolve both cash flow problems, but this is a difficult advertising and promotions task.

YOU DON'T GET THIS GUARANTEE FROM ANY OTHER HOTEL CHAIN.

HOLIDAY INN° "NO EXCUSES" ROOM GUARANTEE

- Your room will be right.
- Or we will make it right.
- Or that night, you stay free.

DEAR GUEST:

Thank you for choosing a Holiday Inn® hotel. We want you to feel welcome and comfortable. That's why we give you this "No Excuses" room guarantee.

- Your room will be right. It will be clean, everything will work properly, and you'll have enough of everything you need.
- Or we will make it right.
- Or we will refund the cost of your room for that night.

"No Excuses!" if you are not satisfied with your room, call the manager on duty who will make every effort to correct the problem, or move you to another room. If these efforts are not satisfactory, and you believe the problem is serious enough to warrant a refund, you must discuss the problem with the manager and ask for a refund request card. If you have any question or problem obtaining this card or a refund call 800/238-8000 and ask for Guest Services.

Again, thank you for giving us the opportunity to take care of you. I hope you will have a pleasant stay.

Sincerely,

JAMES L. SCHORR
President, Hotel Group,
Holiday Inns, Inc.

YOU'LL FIND IT IN EVERY HOLIDAY INN ROOM.

Figure 23.2   Holiday Inn ad guaranteeing its quality control

SPIRITED WEEKENDS, SPLENDID PRICES.

$45 SINGLE OR DOUBLE | $50 SINGLE OR DOUBLE

Fri. or Sat. or Sun. or any combination. Taxes excluded. Free parking. Good through 12/30/84. Under 18, free in parents room. Subject to availability. Cannot be combined with other discounts. Reservations at least 24 hours in advance.

Whether it's fine shopping or fine arts, autumn weekends in Milwaukee are made to order. Especially at the Marc Plaza in the heart of Milwaukee.

Stroll to the renowned Grand Avenue Mall. Spend the evening with the Milwaukee Symphony or Milwaukee Repertory Theatre. And enjoy dining and nightlife at a singularly grand hotel.

The Marc Plaza. City pleasures have never come at such a pleasing price. Reservations: 414-271-7250. Outside Wisconsin, 1-800-558-7708.

From basketball to Beethoven, drama to dancing, Milwaukee has a multitude of fine weekend offerings. And the best way to enjoy them is to stay at Milwaukee's premier hotel.

Blocks from the Art Museum and the Performing Arts Center, the Pfister has a number of its own prime attractions. 4-star dining. Sophisticated nightlife. And a grand elegance that time has left untouched.

Weekends at the Pfister. Everything's remarkable but the bill. Reservations: 414-273-8222. Outside Wisconsin, 1-800-558-8222.

The Marc Plaza Hotel

The Pfister

M I L W A U K E E

Figure 23.3   Trying to shift demand to slow period

James Schorr of Holiday Inn puts it this way:

> In the process of learning differences about the hotel business, there have been a lot of surprises. I came in believing the classical marketing tactics and I've learned that only about half of the so-called classical beliefs are immutable truths. For example, I was taught by Procter that in marketing you fish where the fish are: In periods of high consumption, that's when you advertise the most.
>
> Well, that's ridiculous in this industry. For example, in periods of high consumption, I'm full. I don't have any rooms to sell. This is not the time that I want to spend all my marketing money. Yet, classical theory would have me spend 40% of my marketing effort in that three-month period to stimulate that activity; I have a capacity problem, so I don't spend any of my marketing funds during that period of time.[6]

The most common response to fluctuations in demand for a service is to use price deals. Utilities, phone companies, movie theatres, airlines, hotels, and sports events all use pricing and promotions to generate revenues that contribute to fixed costs and profits. For example

- Phone rates are lowest between 11 P.M. and 8 A.M.
- Movie theatres have lower prices in the afternoon.
- Sports events run most of their promotions on weekdays.
- Airlines promote most heavily in September, October, January, and February.

These promotions are designed to attract consumers who would otherwise not use the service or to increase usage by present consumers. The promotion has failed if it shifts current users from a high-rate period to a lower rate period to such a degree that there is now slack demand during the high-priced period. It has also failed if most of the people who have shifted to the lower priced periods were formerly higher priced customers.

Types of demand

Kotler[7] has written about eight states of demand that a marketer needs to manage. While several of these are familiar from product advertising, others are unique to services. First, the states that are familiar:

1. *No demand* There is no interest in the product. This state exists for firms that do not research the marketplace before developing their great new product idea. Often the response of marketers to this situation is to develop a hard sell, and often the result is failure. This state appears with some regularity in nonprofit marketing in cases such as birth control in developing countries or the 55 MPH speed limit. The marketing of ideas or issues often deals with this state of demand. Advertising requires considerable information and reasons why when there is no demand.

2. *Latent demand* There is a need for a product or service that does not exist; when the product is introduced, it is a success because of good research, faith in the marketing concept, and awareness-building advertising.

3. *Faltering demand* A formerly successful product or service is faced with declining demand because new products have passed it by or its quality has declined. Here a product revision is needed before advertising can be useful. Amtrak, after a long decline period, is now doing well because it updated its rolling stock before beginning its advertising push. Figure 23.4 shows an Amtrak ad that announces the refurbished service.

Figure 23.4 Amtrak ad announcing improved service

4. *Full demand* Supply and demand are fairly equal and are at a level of full production capacity. There is no need to do much except to keep careful watch of the situation so that things do not deteriorate and so that competitors do not gum up the works.

These four states are old friends and have been examined in this and other marketing management texts. The next four states are less common or, if common, are not issues of concern to product marketers. They are, though, of interest to service marketers.

5. *Irregular demand* The patterns of demand are inconsistent with the patterns of supply. This state has been briefly examined above and results from some cyclical buyer behavior. Either supply or demand patterns need to be shifted. It may be very difficult to change demand patterns that have evolved over many years and that reflect other forces in society.

Major league baseball, as one example, is played primarily at night on weekdays because the target market must work all day; even with this shift in supply, demand must still be altered through promotions. Perhaps if there were a smaller supply of weekday games, the demand for the remaining games would increase.

6. *Overfull demand* Demand continuously exceeds supply. Product-based firms can expand their production capabilities, but this may be more difficult for a service. If a highway or bridge is overcrowded, it may not be possible to expand the supply of available space. The same holds for beach space. By attempting to satisfy excess demand, the quality of the service diminishes (who wants to go to an overcrowded beach?); by increasing the supply, the quality may also diminish (if H&R Block continues to hire more tax advisors, will the last one hired be as good as the first one?).

7. *Unwholesome demand* Any level of demand is felt to be excessive and should be eliminated. Public sector and nonprofit organizations often take it upon themselves to deal with unwholesome demand. Both the Surgeon General's Office and the American Cancer Society feel that there is unwholesome demand for cigarettes; many groups feel there is excessive demand for street drugs, and Ground Zero sees an unwholesome demand for nuclear arms. Many advertising campaigns have, over the years, attempted countermarketing, but few have succeeded. This text has shown that advertising is a weak tool in changing behavior; in the cases shown here, the behavior is very strong and as a result, advertising is a weak force with a difficult task.

Cases of unwholesome demand reduction are rarely found in the private sector, although there are some services that help individuals stop smoking or overcome drug dependencies. Figure 23.5 is an ad for such a service, while Figure 23.6 is an ad that tries to change behavior without the aid of any explicit service.

8. *Negative demand* Most potential consumers dislike the product and might even pay to avoid its use. Some of these services have societal value, even though the individual may not wish to participate (e.g., the armed forces); other services are avoided even though they have value to the individual who should receive them. The ad in Figure 23.7 for dental services presents one such example. Even though most people know that dental work is good for them, they still avoid it.

Marketing is concerned with the management of behavior. In product-related cases, the goal is generally to manage with the intent of maximizing purchases. In the realm of services, behavior may need to be managed in more complex ways that include decreasing and shifting the demand.

Figures 23.5 and 23.6   Alcoholism and anti-drug abuse ads

Private Sector
Services

This chapter is devoted to services, issues, and ideas; the next section looks at a number of types of private sector services and organizations, and considers the roles of advertising and promotions in each. This section is organized according to a typology suggested by Nickels.[8]

Convenience services

When a service is based on convenience, it is offering time and place utility as its unique benefits. This means that it is offering more locations, more favorable locations, more hours, or more favorable hours than its competitors. For example, 24-hour convenience stores (PDQ, Stop 'n' Go) don't offer a great selection or low prices; they offer availability, and they charge a premium for it. While they sell products, they charge for a service (convenience).

Banks, over the years, have become ever more sophisticated in offering convenience. They have gone from banker's hours (10 A.M. to 3 P.M., Monday through Friday) to extended hours (8:30 A.M. to 6 P.M. plus half of Saturday) to 24-hour automated tellers. Having mastered time utility, they are also working on place utility. At one time, banks had one central location; they then went to multiple branches and then to additional convenience locations through the use of automated tellers. Most recently, banks are experimenting with telephone funds transfers in order to give the ultimate in place utility: a bank location at every telephone. Figure 23.8 shows an ad for such a service. It combines the convenience services of an Apple Computer and the financial services of the Chase Bank of New York combined to offer 24-hour banking service in the customer's own home—the ultimate in time and place utility. In the food store and banking examples, some firms choose to position themselves in terms of convenience while others develop a position based on a wide product line ("everything you need under one roof"; "full service banking"), and still others compete on price ("never undersold"; "free checking").

Shopping services

Retailers in this area provide intangible services that are difficult to evaluate on quality prior to usage. These services (such as beauty and hair styling salons, appliance and automobile repair shops, restaurants, and travel and real-estate agencies) can either position themselves on some specialization or on the vague attribute of quality. Because an empty promise of quality is not likely to be believed on its own merits, it is useful to offer some unique benefit also.

Figure 23.8   24-hour, in-home banking service

Figure 23.7   Attempting to deal with negative demand for dental services

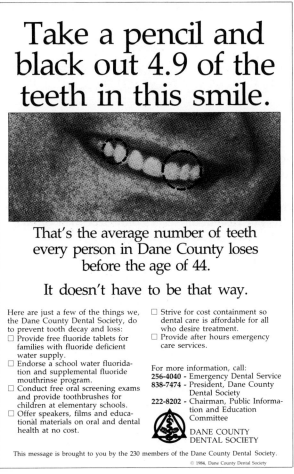

Figure 23.9 *A specific service offering develops uniqueness*

Often this benefit promise is based on the firm's size, but size alone may not be a virtue to a consumer. Size, though, often connotes quality; if we've fixed 73 trillion television sets, we must have some quality.

Other aspects of service may be more marketable: Our travel agency has special knowledge about cruises; our realtors are experts on the West Side of the city; our restaurant serves only Szechuan Chinese cuisine; we repair only foreign cars, so we know them better.

It is easy to create vague advertising that promises intangible quality; it is more useful in the long run to develop some specificity along with the quality, as in Figure 23.9. Over time a service business grows through repeat customers and word of mouth; quality is accepted as time passes. Initially a position based on a unique service benefit is more believable.

Professional services

This area covers a wide range of services that include those of doctors, dentists, lawyers, accountants, architects, and financial counselors. For all but the last of these, strong anti-advertising regulations were written into the statutes of each professional governing body (e.g., American Medical Association, American Bar Association) until 1977. In that year, the U.S. Supreme Court ruled that it was illegal for professional societies to keep their members from advertising.

Even though it then became legal for professionals to advertise, few did so during the remainder of that decade. The primary reason for this lack of advertising was peer pressure; those who advertised were unofficially censured by their colleagues; in many cases, those who advertised also saw their practices grow. With time, more professionals started to advertise in response to competitive pressures to survive. By 1984, for example, about 25% of dentists were advertising, and advertising by large medical clinics was becoming commonplace.

Anti-advertising forces feared that advertising would be deceptive, unprofessional, price-oriented, and would hurt the credibility of the profession. A 1984 study of the medical profession found these fears to be unfounded.[9] There have been few complaints in any of these areas.

What has happened has been that advertising has not had an impact on price (as had been feared), but rather, consumers have become better informed, and service providers have become more specialized within their fields. As with product marketing, the onset of competition leads to advertising, and this is followed by segmentation, specialization, and positioning. All of this is happening slowly, but the trends are in these directions.

Recent studies show that consumers are not offended by professional advertising, and that service providers are slowly accepting advertising. It is interesting to note that, in one proprietary study, lawyers were less trusting of each other than were CPAs in terms of the use of deceptive advertising. Why don't lawyers trust each other? A much more sensible perspective was taken by the health-care professional who wouldn't use deceptive advertising because he knew the need for repeat business.

The greatest need for advertising exists among young professionals who want to start their own practices. They can hardly afford to wait for someone to see their shingle, so they are the group most likely to advertise. Advertising may not be enough. One dentist who moved his practice from Maine to Maryland advertised to his new constituency. Not much happened except that his colleagues harrassed him. The story became newsworthy, and the dentist was interviewed on television; after this, his business grew rapidly.[10]

When the Supreme Court decision was first passed down, the professional societies hoped that their members would advertise only their location, hours, and specializations; it was hoped that price and comparative messages would be avoided. For the most part, that has been the case, and advertising has been fairly bland but informative.

Advertising is now becoming more marketing- and research-oriented. One study showed that the most effective medical message stressed quality of care. The second most important attribute was professional image, followed by distinct specialty and convenient location. Less important issues dealt with fast service and extended hours.[11] This listing would imply a move toward image advertising because the most important attributes are intangible. Ogilvy & Mather, though, suggest a benefit orientation with emphasis on developing a bond of trust. The message should be done with quality and should not use humor.[12] While these Ogilvy & Mather recommendations were made for financial services advertising, they should hold for other professional advertising as well. Figure 23.10 is an example of a professional service ad that combines a tangible benefit and distinct service with the intangible of image and trust.

As with most areas that are just starting to use advertising, there are lots of low-budget operations in the professional services. In 1983, 64% of single and

Figure 23.10 Image and benefit combined in a professional services ad

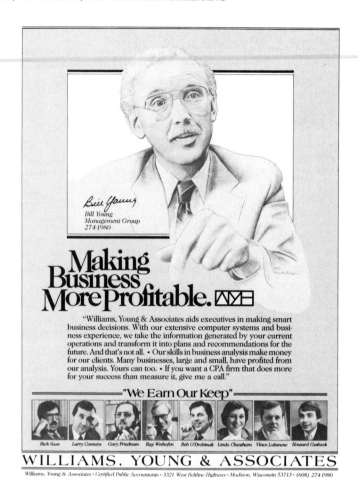

group medical practitioners spent less than $15,000, and 76% created their own ads without the use of advertising professionals. The most commonly used medium was the yellow pages (37%), followed by newspapers (19%), direct mail (15%), and neighborhood shopping guides (11%).[13]

These numbers should change rapidly in the medical profession, where there is a national cry for cost containment. This should lead to a more competitive environment followed by more advertising to try to gain a larger market share in a smaller market. This has begun to happen in Madison, Wisconsin, where four large clinic systems are competing aggressively to win market share. Total advertising expenditures of these four clinics was expected to exceed $600,000 in 1984 in a rapidly changing market. In addition, these clinics are expanding their locations and extending their hours to create more time and place utility. At this time, they have not begun to specialize or position themselves; each is going after the large mainstream market. Nationally, in 1983, less than 10% of medical advertising dollars went to television. This percentage will be much larger in the next few years for the competitive Madison market.[14] As with many topics, Art Buchwald gets in the last word on the advertising and promoting of medical services. Figure 23.11 is his message in this area.

An area of professional services that differs greatly from those discussed above is that of financial counseling. It differs because advertising has been used

By ART BUCHWALD

An Associated Press item says that now that doctors have been given permission to advertise, they have gone one step further and are hiring press agents to get their names in newspapers and to arrange interviews on radio and television. One plastic surgeon who was mentioned in the news story said he knew at least 25 physicians who had retained publicity agents, and he insisted there were hundreds more who had hired someone to flack for them.

I don't see anything wrong with it.

MY FRIEND, Carl Bromberg, whom I consider one of the best press agents in the business, thinks that publicizing doctors will not only be financially rewarding for anyone in the public relations business but will also be challenging and exciting work. He told me:

"This is big stuff. We're going to have to think up items that the gossip columnists will take."

"Such as?"

"Something like, 'What well-known movie queen has stars in her eyes, thanks to Hollywood's new hot plastic surgeon, Dr. Cromley Barton, who, when last seen at Cedars of Lebanon Hospital, was lifting body parts belonging to the wife of a top studio producer?' or 'Everyone at the UCLA Medical Center is still talking about the standing ovation Dr.

George Catheter got last week on his smash kidney-stone operation in the main UCLA Hospital Theater.

"'Everyone who is anyone in the urology world was at the sellout opening. At a post-operation party at the Beverly Wilshire, Dr. Catheter said he thought it was the best thing he'd ever done, but hoped he wouldn't be typed as just another kidney-stone surgeon.

"'I'm getting a lot of offers, but I really have my heart set on removing a prostate.'"

"That's good," I said, "even Rona Barrett would use that one."

"Wait," Bromberg said, taking notes out of his pocket, "I've got more. Listen: 'Dr. Clem Dumbarton, the multi-millionaire orthopedist, has just bought a 120-foot yacht which he says he hopes, for tax reasons, to turn into a hospital ship. Dr. Dumbarton told friends he plans to do all his slipped-disc and tennis-elbow operations at sea, outside the three-mile limit, so no one can sue him for malpractice.'

"And here's one you'll like," continued Bromberg, "it's in the form of a press release:

"'Dr. Rudolf Koenig, the jet set's favorite psychiatrist, announced at a press conference at Studio 54 that he would no longer take patients who want to tell him their dreams. Dr. Koenig said it takes too much

time, and that if you've heard one dream, you've heard them all.'

"'Dr. Koenig, who gets $150 for a half-hour session, also said that because of the heavy demands on his time he would no longer take neurotic or psychotic patients.

"'It's a question of priorities, Dr. Koenig said, adding that as a doctor he wants to devote more time to appearing on television talk shows.

"'Dr. Koenig won an Emmy for his outstanding performance on the Today Show, and he has been honored by the American Psychiatric Association for a recent profile done on him in People magazine.'"

"That's a beautiful press release," I told Bromberg.

"**MEDICINE** is a whole new ball game," he said. "I know many doctors, good people in their fields, who don't think they need a press agent. But they're finding out that when people have an appendectomy, they want a 'name' physician to do it.

"No one is going to be impressed if you say you had surgery by somebody who hasn't at least been on the Johnny Carson show.

"I had one doctor who came to me, and he was barely making $100,000 a year. I got him on the cover of Parade magazine, and now he owns his own hospital and shopping center in New Jersey."

Figure 23.11   *"Hyping of a surgeon" is flack gold mine*

for years and because competition is even stronger than it is in the other service areas. In recent years, Congress has deregulated large parts of the American financial system so that bankers, brokers, insurance companies, and retailers are all competing.

Yes, retailers. Sears, the world's largest retailer, owns Allstate Insurance, Dean, Witter Reynolds (brokerage company), and Coldwell Banker (the largest independent real-estate organization in the United States). Sears is moving toward other financial services as well. As seen in Table 23.1, bankers and brokers are aggressively competing through advertising for investment dollars. (Note that the data in Table 23.1 covers only a six-month period.) As Sears gets more involved, the competition undoubtedly will become more intense, and advertising budgets will probably continue to increase.

Table 23.1 Top 10 financial services advertisers, Jan.–June, 1983 ($000)

Company	Total	Magazines	Newspaper supplements	Network TV	Spot TV	Network radio	Spot radio	Outdoor
1. BankAmerica Corp.	9,640.3	2,412.6	—	305.8	2,625.7	—	3,684.0	612.2
2. Merrill Lynch & Co.	7,698.6	2,268.7	61.2	4,258.7	766.3	—	343.7	—
3. Citicorp	6,757.0	1,051.1	47.0	1,823.6	3,623.0	—	207.6	4.7
4. Prudential-Bache Securities	5,848.8	2,670.1	—	984.8	2,193.9	—	—	—
5. First Jersey Securities	5,595.0	823.4	—	1,134.2	2,298.5	—	1,338.9	—
6. First Interstate Bancorp	5,124.7	819.6	—	762.4	3,095.7	—	286.1	160.9
7. EF Hutton Group	4,938.9	2,258.6	77.6	1,853.8	131.7	259.2	358.0	—
8. Great Western Savings & Loan	4,299.5	201.7	—	—	2,844.2	—	1,253.6	—
9. Manufacturers Hanover Corp.	3,661.4	1,796.4	61.2	—	1,402.4	—	400.2	1.2
10. Smith Barney Harris Upham & Co.	3,042.0	73.7	—	2,855.1	—	—	113.2	—
Total	**56,606.2**	**14,375.9**	**247.0**	**13,978.4**	**18,981.4**	**259.2**	**7,985.3**	**779.0**

Note: Includes banks, brokerage houses, savings & loan associations, mutual fund groups, credit unions. Does not include newspaper or direct mail expenditures.
Source: Cara S. Trager, "Bankers Bring Home the Bacon—Electronically," *Advertising Age,* 13 February 1984, p. M-11. Reprinted with permission. Copyright 1984 by Crain Communications, Inc.

The problems and issues facing financial professionals are similar to those facing other services, but the stakes are greater because there are national advertisers competing with local retailers. If the locals are to survive, they will need to create a unique position and offer unique benefits that the large firms cannot match. The local services will also need to be creative in their media and message strategies because they certainly can't match the spending levels of their larger competitors.

Public Sector and Nonprofit Services, Ideas, and Issues

As can be seen from its heading, this section lumps together a wide variety of topics that have some common points separating them from other topics dealt with elsewhere. The topics in this section are all outside the private sector, and all deal with intangibles. These common points provide the basis for a coherent framework, because the manager of each organization is still interested in eliciting responses that are part of the hierarchy of effects, and wants to do so through the use of communications tools.

This chapter earlier discussed differences between products and services that make the communications task more difficult. The present section builds off this list by acknowledging these issues and adding others that need to be considered when communicating nonbusiness services, ideas, or issues. This section deals with a very diverse set of organizations, and therefore all the items presented in the following list will not always be relevant. The manager should, though, consider each item as part of the situation analysis and discard those that do not apply.[15]

Weak personal benefits

A basic thrust of all successful advertising is that it shows a benefit to the message recipient. If the consumer purchases a product or service, benefits are expected. The task of showing a benefit may be more difficult when the message is soliciting funds to save the seals, asking people to drive 55 MPH, or asking people not to litter. In the first case, behavior results in having less money; if there is a benefit, it is to an environment perhaps 5 thousand miles away. In the second case, the driver arrives later and feels foolish (fuelish?) as other cars speed by; the benefit of greater fuel reserves is difficult to see or personally appreciate. In the third case, the good citizen now has a dripping Popsicle stick to carry around and, again, no easily perceived benefit. If people are going to change their behavior, there must be some personal reinforcement. In the above cases, the reward is a good feeling that comes from being a good citizen; does that outweigh the inconveniences? The types of campaigns that appear in the nonbusiness arena have difficulty in succeeding because communications cannot overcome the perceived lack of reward. It is much easier to perceive the benefits of a new shirt.

The person who pays for the service may not receive it

In the private sector, a person buys a bar of soap and pays for it, but many public services are paid for through taxes and donations that come from one group of people to assist another group. Raising taxes to pay for better schools is often accomplished through a referendum that may need advertising support. Here, all taxpayers are asked to spend more so that the children of a select group can receive a better service. This is another case of lack of reinforcement for the majority of taxpayers, and therefore the referendum advertising must show voters a personal benefit. Many school bond drives have failed recently because voters are looking out for their own wallets rather than for the education of a few, or for the less tangible long-run benefit to society of better schools.

Is there any demand for the service or issue?

In the private sector, a large percentage of new products fail because they do not meet a need. Many public sector campaigns are the result of inner-oriented thinking, but failure is difficult to measure owing to public funding and no sales criterion. Whatever happened to the $2 bill or the Susan B. Anthony silver dollar? It is hard to elicit behavior for ideas and services that have little following or need.

Primary versus selective demand

Truly new products are rare and, as a result, most private sector advertising is aimed at switching a consumer from one brand to another (selective demand) rather than at getting adoption of a new concept (primary demand). As has been noted before, eliciting selective demand is much easier, for it requires a minor behavior shift compared to that needed for primary demand. Many public service and nonprofit campaigns attempt to elicit a new type of behavior, such as using a seat belt or turning down the thermostat at night. New behaviors are hard to develop through advertising. Even promotions fail in the long run if there is no perceived benefit.

Nonmonetary price

Price is generally thought of in monetary terms because that is dominant in the purchase of products. Nonmonetary prices also exist in any transaction, but they become most noticeable in the nonbusiness arena, where there may not be any monetary price. Often the nonmonetary price is extremely high. Joining the military requires the high price of four years of one's life (the cost may be much higher during a war); this is a time and opportunity cost. Driving 55 MPH also requires a time payment. There may be inconvenience costs (what to do with that Popsicle stick), psychic costs (the fear of giving blood), hassle costs (dealing with a bureaucracy in order to get food stamps), embarrassment costs (what if my neighbor sees me using food stamps and learns how poor I must be), and others. The communications problems were already difficult because of a lack of reinforcing benefits; now it is clear that the cost to be paid may also be very high.

Extreme levels of involvement

Compared to private sector products, involvement levels may be much higher or much lower in the nonbusiness sector. For example, while most people have high involvement toward an automobile purchase, they may have even more involvement with joining the military or having their children bused to school. At the other end of the spectrum, people may have low involvement toward an orange juice or facial tissue brand choice decision, but may have even less involvement toward preventing forest fires or supporting the arts. Perhaps there is a continuum of involvement levels, as shown in Figure 23.12.

Figure 23.12   A hypothetical continuum of response involvement levels

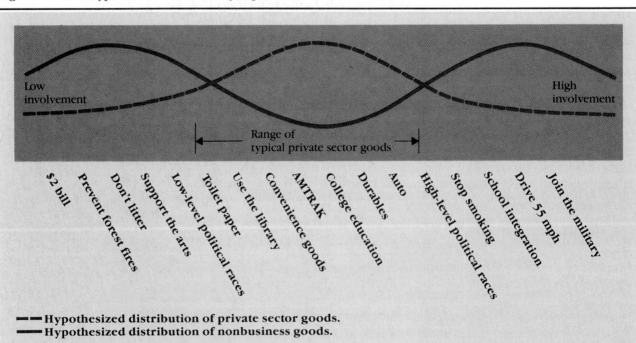

Appealing to all segments

Most private sector product and service brands have very specific target markets and are considered successful with a 6 or 8% market share. In the public sector, there are cases when the entire population is in the target market (for example, when Great Britain converted to decimal currency). This means that management cannot be selective in pursuing the most appropriate target but must also get to hard-to-reach and antagonistic targets. In other cases, management will need a 50.1% market share in order to succeed (for example, in a state referendum ballot). It was shown in the media chapters that it is very difficult to reach an entire population; sometimes the entire population must not only be reached but must have its behavior changed as well.

To make things even more pessimistic, the relevant target segment may consist of those who are most negative about the issue at hand and those whose involvement with this negative attitude is greatest. For example, anti-smoking messages are directed at those who smoke and are least likely to respond to the message. This is very different from private sector efforts to get the most positive segment to make a minor shift to another brand or to greater usage.[16]

Table 23.2 on page 728 looks at four examples that consider the above issues. Some are felt to have a reasonable shot at success given a good communications strategy; others will have difficulty.

An aversion to advertising

The above-listed issues are all environmental and often beyond the control of the marketing manager. There are also internal problems that need to be considered. Although their numbers are decreasing, some members of nonbusiness organizations are anti-marketing and anti-advertising. Fortunately, their numbers are decreasing rapidly as they see their competitors using advertising successfully. (Most organizations have competitors. If they are not competing for sales, they are competing for share of mind, discretionary leisure time, charitable dollars, or city, state, or federal funds. When competition is considered in this broad a framework, then marketing becomes a necessary and pervasive management philosophy.)

Inadequate budgets, public service advertising (PSA), and the Advertising Council

In addition to the difficulties described above, most nonprofit organizations do not have sufficient budgets to properly develop a media plan with adequate reach and/or frequency. In such cases, the organization may get assistance from the Advertising Council and media at the national level or from agencies and media at the local level. At either level, creative and production work are donated by advertising agencies, and time or space is donated by vehicles. One mechanism available for this purpose is the *PSA*, or *public service advertising*.

The Advertising Council is a nonprofit group that began as the War Advertising Council during World War II in order to rally support for the purchase of war bonds and for the conservation of scarce materials. After the war, the council changed its name and objectives and began to work for a wide range of nonprofit and public sector organizations. Currently, the Advertising Council receives about a half billion dollars per year in donated media time and space for the

Table 23.2 Four nonbusiness communications cases consider some difficult problems

Case	Situation involvement	Enduring involvement	Benefits/ reinforcers	Costs	Cost/ benefit	Preexisting demand	Segmen- tation	Conclusion
Military Enlist- ment	Very complex High cost	Little past experience Cultural values	Personal intangibles	Several years of one's life Personal rights	Very good for some segments	Fairly high	Very specific and limited	Marketing communica- tions can impact
55 mph speed limit	Low Little interest	Central Beliefs	Few personal benefits Weak societal benefits	Time Ego/macho	Poor	Virtually none	All drivers	Low likelihood of marketing communica- tions impact
Anti- litter	Low Little interest	Past non- reinforcing experiences	Few personal benefits Moderate societal benefits	Inconve- nience	Poor	Low	All members of community	Short-run impact possible Long-run impact difficult
Voting	High to low— depends on race	Central beliefs Pressure to behave	Good citizenship	Time inconve- nience Infrequent/ Low	Favorable for voting Less favorable for analyzing issues	Moderate	All citizens 18 years of age and over	Short-run impact likely Long-run impact not necessary

Source: Michael L. Rothschild, "Marketing Communications in Nonbusiness Situations or Why It's So Hard to Sell Brotherhood Like Soap," *Journal of Marketing* 43 (Spring 1979), p. 17.

roughly 25 campaigns in which it participates; in addition, it solicits volunteer agencies to aid in the creation and production of the campaigns.

To be accepted, a campaign must be

- In the public interest
- A project that easily lends itself to advertising
- Timely
- Noncommercial, nonpartisan, nonsectarian, and nonpolitical
- National in scope but relevant at local levels

The same sorts of financial and time donations are made by agencies and vehicles at local levels, but the criteria of the Ad Council do not necessarily apply (although campaigns that are noncontroversial have the best chance at getting air time).

There are some who view PSAs as part of the "you get what you pay for" syndrome. That is, if an agency is donating time and materials to produce advertising, it will not donate its best talent. While many PSAs are well done and thoughtful, many others are off the mark and not at all useful. For example, at the height of concern about drug abuse in the late 1960s and early 1970s, about 50 organizations were producing anti-drug abuse advertising, but there was no coordination to produce consistent advertising to deal with unified objectives. One message was a 60-second closeup of an arm receiving a shot of heroin. It was felt from retrospective testing that this commercial actually taught children how to inject themselves. While this was an extreme case, a client with no money has less control over the final message that is produced.

In addition, these spots are generally shown at odd hours or placed near the back of a magazine. One study concluded that only about 10% of televised PSAs were shown during prime time. While stations must do some showing of PSAs in order to justify their existence to the Federal Communications Commission, they do not need to do so at any particular time. Stations need to document that they do work in the "public interest" when they get their licenses renewed, but given the choice between donating time and selling it, most opt for the latter at those times when their rates are highest.

Are PSAs useful? In spite of the above problems, they almost always are. There are a few exceptions when a message has a negative impact, but usually the effect is positive, and any positive effect is better than nothing. Over the years, there have been some strong successes at the national level, such as in in creating awareness of the need to prevent forest fires ("Only you can prevent forest fires"), to prevent crime (Figure 23.13), and to support the United Negro College Fund ("A mind is a terrible thing to waste"—Figure 23.14) as well as innumerable local successes.

In most cases, it is hard to say if the same goals would have been met better through paid advertising. In at least one case, the answer was clearly in favor of paid advertising. Job Service of Wisconsin (the state employment agency) had used PSAs for many years but was unhappy with the results. They did a pilot project in 1977 in which there was a pre- and post-test on several key dependent variables. After 16 weeks of 250 GRPs per week across all media, they found that awareness among the general public was up 11% and among employers was up 15%. Intent to use Job Service doubled among the general public and actual usage by employers increased by 10%. The big difference was not due to the message, but rather due to a paid media plan that ensured that messages were shown when the target was watching.

One of the big advantages of paid advertising is that the manager has control over the message and its delivery. This control is, to a large extent, forfeited by the use of PSAs; managers of nonprofit organizations need to be aware of this and consider the tradeoffs if paid advertising is feasible. If it is not feasible, then PSAs are certainly better than the alternative of doing nothing.

Finally, the manager must also consider the long-run implications of using paid advertising. Once an organization pays, can it get free PSAs in the future? Many organizations fear this and therefore avoid trying paid advertising. There is a real tradeoff of efficiency and effectiveness here. How much effectiveness (having an impact) can be sacrificed for efficiency (saving money)?

Figure 23.13 *Ad for crime prevention*

Figure 23.14 *Ad for the United Negro College Fund*

If PSAs are going to be part of the organization's strategy, then it is important to maximize the potential for their use by local vehicles. It should be recognized that every vehicle receives many more requests for PSA messages than it can possibly use in the limited time or space that it donates. The messages most likely to be used are those that are

- Close to the Advertising Council guidelines
- Of good technical quality
- Broadcast- or print-ready (in an appropriate technological format)
- Of local relevance and with a local tie or tag
- Of interest to the editor or station manager

The use of marketing and advertising in nonbusiness situations has grown tremendously in recent years. Table 23.3 gives a partial list of application areas. The column labeled "social marketing" deals with issues and ideas; the "nonbusiness organizations" column deals with services. Most of the services are important to society but are not tackled by the private sector because they can not generate a profit or because they are too complex to deal with for profit (e.g., police and military services). Others compete with private sector organizations and

T·H·E I·N·S·I·D·E O·U·T·L·O·O·K

William D. Novelli

President, Needham Porter Novelli

Years of working on consumer products—on both the client and ad agency sides—have given Bill Novelli a keen understanding and appreciation of marketing.

Now, as president of Needham Porter Novelli, he's putting marketing to work for a variety of clients: corporations, trade and professional associations, government agencies, social and health organizations, and developing countries.

Bill began his career as a marketing manager for Lever Brothers in New York, then went to Wells, Rich and Greene as account supervisor on several national brands. Following that, he served as director of advertising and creative services for the Peace Corps and ACTION.

He teaches an M.B.A. course in marketing management and a graduate course in communication at the University of Maryland.

Advertising and Promotions for Public Sector and Nonprofit Services

The same combination of discipline and creativity that makes marketing useful in the private sector also makes it attractive to managers of public sector and nonprofit organizations.

Marketing, whether commercial or social, is concerned with behavior. Persuading the public to buy a particular product—say, "Brand X" toothpaste—is a tough, competitive job. But marketing social services (which usually means social *change*) is even more complex and difficult.

A number of general problems confront managers who attempt to transfer approaches used to sell corn flakes and laundry detergent to promote concepts such as family planning, smoking cessation, and blood donation.

The systematic marketing process is similar: recognize audience wants, expectations, and sat-

isfactions/dissatisfactions; analyze and plan program objectives; utilize a full, integrated marketing mix; and continuously track and respond to consumer and marketplace action.

But there are also differences—many in the areas of advertising and promotions—between commercial and nonprofit service marketing. These include: audience segmentation, the "product" benefits that may be available, the often diminished role of advertising in the communication mix, and the selection of motivational appeals.

Part of the difficulty is the lack of resources. While nonprofit/social organizations may utilize marketing's "four Ps" (product, price, promotion, place), frequently they also face the "four Ls" (low visibility, lamentable budgets, little research, and lack of continuity).

But the future for nonprofit marketing appears bright. The application of this ordered, effective discipline for the promotion of social issues, ideas, and causes is likely to grow. Increased competition among organizations (e.g., hospitals, HMOs), reduced social service budgets, and broader familiarity with marketing should contribute to this growth trend.

As nonprofits become more adept at marketing, it will probably be extended into new sectors of society. There may also be a smaller countertrend, with some social organizations abandoning marketing as ineffective or unworkable. These are most likely to be agencies that incorporate marketing into their structure at a low level; this limits the chances for success. Other reasons for failure may include the adoption of marketing jargon and cosmetics, without actually grasping the full marketing model. Fragmented, piecemeal application, low budgets, untrained personnel, and tackling of social behaviors that are highly resistant to change are other probable reasons why nonprofit marketing can fail and be discarded.

One of the earlier criticisms of marketing public sector and nonprofit services—that it was unethical and manipulative—seems to be waning. However, as marketing continues to enter new social arenas, this criticism may continue to be heard.

Today, there appear to be two pressing needs to strengthen nonprofit marketing and increase its acceptance and growth. The first is improved training of managers. Social organizations do not yet have the marketing tradition to serve as training grounds for newcomers entering the field. Managers who transfer their skills from commercial companies often have a solid hold on marketing but not on the differences in nonprofit/social marketing. They also must learn the structure and process of nonprofit organizations. Still, the best training for social marketers at this stage appears to be the commercial marketing world.

The second pressing need is for a thorough review of nonprofit marketing as it is now practiced. A systematic analysis is needed to determine the general state of the art, which public and nonprofit organizations are implementing marketing fully, and with what results; which elements or patterns are common to these marketing organizations, and whether these successes can be exported to other nonprofits.

In the meantime, the profession continues to grow as a branch of the marketing tree and as a useful process for social change.

Table 23.3 Nonbusiness causes and organizations using marketing and advertising

Sample social marketing causes	Sample nonbusiness marketing organizations
Stop smoking	Churches
Consumer information	Public schools
Racial harmony	Associations
Environmental protection	Unions
Yearly checkups	Charities
Fasten seat belts	Boys and girls clubs
Support ERA	Government agencies
Eat a balanced diet	Museums and symphonies
Save fuel	Arboreta
Save water	Cooperatives
Stay in school	Public day care centers
Support your local police force	Theater groups
Don't take drugs	Public universities
Support the charity of your choice	Public hospitals
Buy bonds	Fraternities
Give blood	Sororities
Use mass transit	Social clubs
Consumer education	Political parties
Learn about free enterprise	Cities
Give to the college of your choice	Countries
Practice birth control	Police departments

Source: Adapted from William G. Nickels, *Marketing Communications and Promotions,* 3d ed. (Columbus, OH: Grid Publishing, 1984), p. 432. Reprinted by permission of John Wiley & Sons, Inc.

are approached in ways very similar to private sector service advertising (e.g., universities, hospitals, museums, symphonies). Still others were at one time in the private sector but were not able to succeed, so the government acquired them (e.g., urban mass transit in most cities, interurban passenger train service). Some of these organizations generate revenues in excess of costs in some areas of their operations, although they are still nonprofit (museum gift shops, symphony record sales).

It is clear from this list that, in spite of the potential difficulties in using advertising, many organizations attempt to do so. In using advertising, the manager must keep in mind that this task will be quite difficult for two very different reasons. The target may be very involved with the issue and, as a result, will be difficult to influence. At the other extreme, the target will have no interest at all in the issue and will also be difficult to influence. In either case, the benefits may be perceived as weak, the price may be perceived as high, and there may not be any pent-up demand with regard to the service or issue.

Summary

Marketing and advertising have been used by some services for many years; for others, these tools are new. In either case, there are special problems to consider when dealing with intangible items of exchange; advertising and promotions are more difficult to use successfully in the area of services.

Intangibility means that it is more difficult to show the benefit in advertising. Instant perishability calls for volatile pricing promotions to maximize purchases at the time of production. A lack of inventory buildup capability means that demand patterns may need to be changed so that consumers use the service at less preferred times.

In addition to these problems, nonbusiness services may also suffer from an offering that has no direct personal benefit but high personal monetary and/or nonmonetary cost. The service or idea may need to be advertised with a limited budget or through public service announcements. In either case, it is difficult to get an adequate media plan.

While all these issues do not confront every service manager in every situation, they do appear often enough that the manager should consider them in any situation analysis. The purpose of this chapter has been to raise issues for consideration during the situation analysis for a service. Once past the situation analysis, the manager should seek the appropriate objectives and strategies in the same way as would any other manager, keeping in mind the relevant constraints.

Discussion Questions

1. What is a service? What issues are raised by this definition that complicate the advertising development process?

2. Collect ads for five services. What is the intangible service that is being offered? What is shown in the advertising?

3. How should the issue of intangibility influence price-oriented promotions strategies?

4. How does quality control differ for services versus products? How is this difference reflected in advertising strategies?

5. How do media and message strategies differ for services in terms of managing demand?

6. What are some dimensions upon which services are segmented? Give some examples of firms that fit into each segment.

7. Consider public sector marketing from the point of view of behavioral learning theory. Discuss the problems that many public sector organizations have in offering positive reinforcers to their target markets.

8. Why is it difficult to manage behavior in cases of extremely high or extremely low levels of involvement?

9. What is a PSA? What are the positive and negative issues associated with its use?

Notes

1. Robert C. Judd, "The Case for Redefining Services," *Journal of Marketing* 28 (January 1964), pp. 58–59.

2. Kenneth P. Uhl and Gregory D. Upah, "The Marketing of Services: Why and How Is It Different?," in *Research in Marketing,* vol. 6 (Greenwich, Conn.: JAI Press, 1983), p. 237.

3. Uhl and Upah, "Marketing of Services," p. 240.

4. Gary Knisely, "Greater Marketing Emphasis by Holiday Inns Breaks Mold," *Advertising Age* 15 January 1979, p. 47.

5. Gary Knisely, "Service Business Is People Dealing with Other People," *Advertising Age* 14 May 1979, pp. 57–58.

6. Knisely, "Holiday Inns," p. 47.

7. Philip Kotler, "The Major Tasks of Marketing Management," *Journal of Marketing* 37 (October 1973), pp. 42–49.

8. William G. Nickels, *Marketing Communication and Promotion,* 3d ed. (Columbus, Ohio: Grid Publishing, Inc., 1984), pp. 412–454.

9. *Marketing News,* 8 June 1984, p. 1.

10. *Wall Street Journal,* 30 November 1977, p. 1.

11. *Marketing News,* 8 June 1984, p. 1.

12. Ogilvy & Mather, *How to Create Advertising That Sells,* (New York: Ogilvy & Mather, 1981), pp. 12–13.

13. *Marketing News,* 8 June 1984, p. 1.

14. Marion Michaels, personal communication.

15. Michael L. Rothschild, "Marketing Communications in Nonbusiness Situations or Why It's So Hard to Sell Brotherhood Like Soap," *Journal of Marketing* 43 (Spring 1979), pp. 11–20.

16. Paul N. Bloom and William D. Novelli, "Problems and Challenges in Social Marketing," *Journal of Marketing* 45 (Spring 1981), pp. 79–88.

Good Vibrations
· T H E · S U N K I S T · O R A N G E · S O D A · C A M P A I G N ·

BUSINESS-TO-BUSINESS ADVERTISING

When Sunkist orange soda became a reality, there were no local bottlers, and there was no retail distribution. This changed rapidly after the initial research showed the potential for success and after the first five markets showed actual market acceptance. Figures S.1 and S.2 show the early trade advertising done in trade journals such as *Beverage World*.

Both ads discuss the continued success and growth as Sunkist truly became a national brand. Over the years, the trade ads always stressed some aspect of the continual growth and success of the brand in order to gain bottler and retailer support. Examples of some of these later trade ads can be seen at the end of Part 10.

Figure S.1 and S.2   Trade advertisements

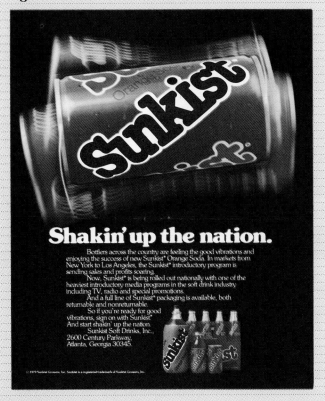

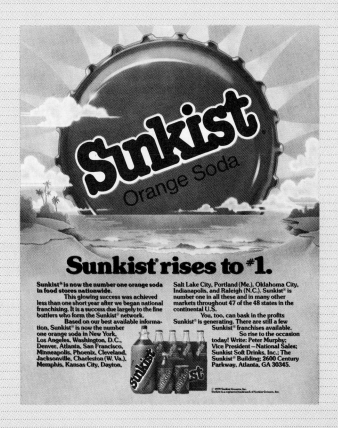

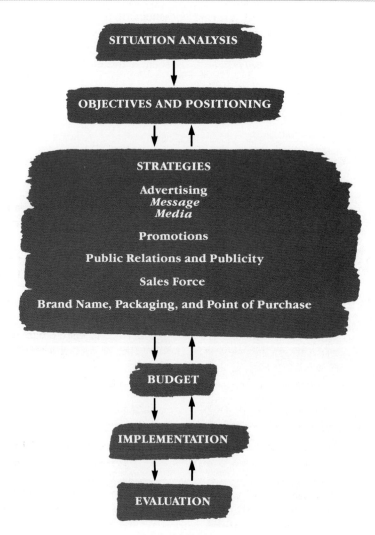

Decision Sequence Framework

Part Ten
Concluding Issues Concerning Marketing Communications

*T*his part covers three important but divergent topics in an attempt to bring closure to the text. Although the text has a managerial perspective, it is necessary to put the practical issues into a societal context. The first chapter topic deals with this area. It shows that, in most cases, the decisions made by managers in their own self-interest are also societally useful decisions. By applying the marketing concept, the firm will make a satisfactory profit by meeting needs.

Future managers need to recognize that their actions and the collective actions of all other advertising managers can have peripheral effects on society at large. In addition, since advertising is such a visible part of the firm's activities, advertisers are often blamed for all of the firm's negative effects and, indeed, for any perceived ills of capitalism.

Societal issues are examined from two perspectives:

- economic arguments
- consumer decision making arguments

The first of these deals with the impact of advertising on prices and levels of competition; the second deals with advertising's ability to manipulate and deceive consumers, and to offend the general public.

The second topic is an exploration of job possibilities related to advertising and how to pursue them. This topic should be read in conjunction with the related part of Chapter 1 before starting a job search.

The text concludes with a short summary of some of the key topics presented in the previous chapters.

Chapter 24
Concluding Issues Concerning Marketing Communications

Advertising and Promotions in the Context of Society

This text has considered one view of advertising—that advertising is a tool of management which should be used as efficiently and effectively as possible to aid the firm in reaching its goals. In the private sector, these goals generally are related to sales and profits; in nonbusiness settings, the goals may relate to other behaviors such as donating money, voting, writing letters, or supporting the organization in some other way.

There are other views of advertising that consider its impact on society and the economy. From these views come arguments that the social and economic costs of advertising are high and that to merely consider the value of advertising to the firm is too narrow. Few people would advocate abolishing advertising entirely; most recognize its value to society but feel there are some associated costs. In fact, many studies have shown that most people in our society regard advertising as an item of low importance or salience to them and one toward which they have fairly neutral feelings. Advertising and promotions are part of their daily lives, and they are not overly concerned about the presence of these tools. This section examines some of these issues and considers some relevant arguments on either side of the issue.

In order to consider the value of advertising outside the firm, the observer must first consider advertising's context. Advertising is most often used in capitalist societies where people are rewarded for their abilities rather than their needs and where firms strive to gain an advantage in the marketplace that can lead to profit. In this context, advertising is a tool of the firm to be used for its own ends and not specifically for the good of society. In spite of this, it may be that the best means to that end are to serve members of society; the marketing concept states that the best means to long-run success are by meeting the needs of consumers. Therefore, any societal good that comes from advertising is a result of management behaving in its own best long-run interests. This is similar to most individual behavior; people generally behave in their own best interests.

One view of the development of advertising in the United States is based on self-interest. Norris[1] suggests that firms began to advertise around 1900 so that they could gain more control in the marketplace. Prior to this time there was little advertising, little branding, and little demand for specific brands. As a result, products were sold as commodities, and price and profit were determined by the distributors and retailers. If brands were asked for by name by consumers, the firm got more power in the channel of distribution, and this, in turn, allowed the firm to raise its price and increase its profit. As new national brands emerged, they were given an identity through advertising and, therefore, kept separate from other brands. Advertising motivated consumers to request a brand by name and gave power to the manufacturer.

Over time, though, product classes that yielded a high profit were most likely to draw competitors; these competitors would compete on price, and high profits would vanish. New brands then were introduced with some differential advantage, which would again give a firm some monopoly power, the ability to raise its price, and higher profits.

As brands emerged, profit structures changed constantly. Unique brands could charge a higher price, while brands in undifferentiated markets were forced by competition to charge a lower price. Advertising helped the firm discuss its unique advantages and helped to create differences. When this occurred, there was a clear benefit to both the firm and society if the improved product met a need and succeeded.

The differences may be minor or nonexistent, and the benefit to society questionable. If the Bayer Aspirin Company is the only firm to sell Bayer aspirin, if this brand is unique because people have learned to trust it, and if this results in a monopolistic situation that allows the firm to charge a higher price, then there may be a social cost. If the free market process allows consumers to reject high-priced Bayer aspirin in favor of low-priced Walgreen's aspirin, then is there societal harm? Only those people who saw a value in Bayer would pay for it, and the marketplace would determine if a high-priced Bayer aspirin would survive.

The goal of advertising and promotions is to help sell more product; informing consumers is a means to that end. In the early 1900s, firms saw advertising as a tool to increase their own market power; current advertisers have the same goals. Because there is freedom of entry to markets, many firms advertise, and the competitive actions of the various brands prevent any single brand from achieving sufficient dominance to totally dictate price. Advertising was first used to separate the brand from competitors through differentiation, but it is advertising that allows firms to be competitive, because this is the least expensive way to communicate with a mass market.

Economic arguments about advertising

The previous few paragraphs reviewed some of the reasons that a firm would use advertising. These are economic reasons why the firm should advertise; they lead to direct arguments based on an economic foundation as to why advertising is bad for society, even though it may be good for the firm.

Advertising leads to higher prices   Higher prices may be a goal of the firm, but this goal only exists if higher prices lead to higher profits. In general, prices can only be easily raised in a monopolistic situation; in most other cases, a unilateral price increase will lead to a decline in sales. Competition keeps prices low and so firms attempt to create a middle ground of monopolistic competition. Here, there is some generic product class competition, but the brand creates some differentiation and uniqueness for itself to avoid a purely competitive pricing situation.

If the firm is, indeed, able to create a situation in which there are no identical substitutes, then it will be able to charge a slightly higher price and establish brand loyalty. Loyalty comes about because the brand is unique; anyone who desires exactly what the brand offers can buy only that brand. The more that consumers perceive the brand as unique, the greater the potential for a price differential. If the brand can easily be replaced by others, then it will have little price advantage.

If the product *truly* differs, then advertising's contribution to the higher price is slight. Advertising informs consumers about the unique product, but it is the virtues of the product that allow the price to remain higher than it might otherwise be. Monopolistic competition allows prices to stay high; the creation of this situation is a combination of product development and advertising. The situation can only succeed for the firm if the product is perceived to meet a need and does so in a unique way. This reiterates the value of positioning to the firm.

Advertising can also lead to a higher price if there is no *real* product difference but *perceptions* of difference or goodness are created. In the extreme case, commodities can be branded, given an image, differentiated, and sold for a higher price. Is beer with "gusto" worth a higher price? Is beer that is endorsed by ex-athletes worth a higher price? Are aspirin with the Bayer label worth a higher price? Are these brands really different? Do people perceive a difference worth paying for? If there is no difference, why do people keep buying a more expensive brand? Are consumers stupid? Is advertising *that* powerful? It is the admitted goal of advertising to attempt to create differentiation. It can succeed only if consumers agree that there is a difference worth paying for. Marketers are responsible for prices, but so are the consumers who pay the prices when lower priced but slightly different alternatives exist.

There are other pricing issues. Advertising has a cost that must be absorbed, and, therefore, total cost to the firm is higher with advertising than without it. It is argued that advertising increases volume so that the total cost is spread across more units. The resulting cost per unit is lower because of economies of scale on other fixed and variable costs. A rational manager will not continue to advertise if advertising does not lead to greater sales or greater profits. Therefore, advertising may lead to higher unit cost in the short run, but in the long run, this won't happen because the manager will act out of self-interest. The cost of advertising can only be absorbed if there is excess production capacity to absorb the cost. If the plant is running at maximum capacity, then advertising cannot lead to lower unit costs, and the firm may cut back on its advertising.

If the market for the overall product class can grow, then advertising can contribute to that growth without leading to higher prices; if the market cannot expand, then advertising increases total cost without increasing sales, and this cost may lead to higher prices. This scenario holds for the overall product class but may not hold for any specific brand that will use its advertising to gain market share (and therefore increase its own sales).[2] Over all brands, the average price may be higher because advertising costs need to be absorbed somewhere. For a mature product class with no growth, advertising can, then, lead to higher prices and/or losses for some brands. Because it is illegal for brands to act together, each will advertise to increase its own share, and this cost of advertising will lead to higher prices. This cost exists because brands compete and therefore advertise more than if they did not compete. The alternative is for brands not to compete, but this would probably raise prices even more, for then there would be a monopoly or a cartel.

If advertising has the task of informing consumers, and if that task needs to be done, then the cost of advertising must be compared to the cost of a sales force, or sky-writers, or whatever the alternative communications tool may be. In this context, advertising is the most efficient tool and raises prices the least. Or, advertising may be said to lower the total cost of marketing from whatever it would be in the absence of advertising. When it is said that advertising raises prices, part of the answer must be "compared to what?" Since rational managers strive to minimize their costs, it can be said that advertising raises costs less than alternative tools.

There does not seem to be clear evidence that advertising leads to higher prices; there are two scenarios when it might (for monopolistic competition and a mature product class), and there are two scenarios when it may cause prices to come down (for strong competition and a growth product class). Figure 24.1 shows a case where advertising can lead to lower prices.

Figure 24.1 Does advertising lead to higher prices?

Advertising creates a barrier to entry   In order for a new brand to be introduced nationally, it may easily have a first year advertising budget of $10 to $20 million (plus a promotional budget of $20 to $40 million if the brand sends out samples). That is certainly a formidable barrier and will keep many firms out of a market. In addition, existing brands may promote extensively during the new brand's introduction in order to maintain loyalty toward their own brands. High costs may be coupled with low initial sales for the new brand in this scenario.

Given the nature of learning and forgetting (as discussed in the media chapters), the firm also will need to continue to spend several million dollars per year to maintain the brand after it is established and the market is stable; if the market is volatile, much more may be needed. McDonald's, for example, spent over $80 million in 1983 for network television alone and over $193 million across all media; most of that was to maintain existing products. Table 24.1 shows total advertising expenditures for the 50 most advertised brands in the United States from 1980 to 1983. Repetition leads to learning and inhibits forgetting, but the need for repetition may be a barrier to entry. If there is a barrier, then there will be less competition, and monopolistic pricing is more likely to result.

Table 24.1 Top 50 millionaire brands, 1980–1983

Brand name (parent company)	Classification	Total annual advertising expenditures			
		1983	1982	1981	1980
1. Sears (Sears, Roebuck and Co.)	Retail	$537,130,000	$556,068,000	$505,372,000	$474,390,000
2. K mart (K mart Corp.)	Retail	383,459,000	325,302,000	301,096,000	274,495,000
3. Penney's (J.C. Penney)	Retail	341,990,000	288,563,000	269,621,000	249,754,000
4. Ford (Ford Motor Co.)	Cars, trucks	304,768,000	253,733,000	223,505,000	197,763,000
5. AT&T/Bell (AT&T)	Communications	303,709,000	161,756,000	171,783,000	91,707,000
6. Chevrolet (General Motors)	Cars, trucks	208,334,000	185,170,000	156,465,000	138,741,000
7. McDonald's (McDonald's Corp.)	Restaurants	193,358,000	163,206,000	138,046,000	130,862,000
8. Wards (Mobil Corp.)	Retail	178,239,000	167,878,000	170,940,000	166,600,000
9. Nissan (Nissan Motors)	Cars, trucks	139,529,000	111,258,000	82,529,000	65,711,000
10. Budweiser (Anheuser-Busch)	Beer	131,782,000	104,897,000	67,037,000	49,032,000
11. Miller (Philip Morris)	Beer	125,028,000	113,276,000	86,108,000	76,239,000
12. Kellogg's (Kellogg Co.)	Cereals	116,470,000	96,530,000	90,696,000	77,785,000
13. Chrysler (Chrysler Corp.)	Cars	115,541,000	101,983,000	81,515,000	57,035,000
14. Kraft (Dart & Kraft Inc.)	Cooking, dairy, prepared foods	109,875,000	107,051,000	96,902,000	77,785,000
15. Purina (Ralston Purina)	Pet food, supplies	107,628,000	94,605,000	63,905,000	78,824,000
16. Honda (Honda Motor Co.)	Cars, cycles, garden equip.	103,843,000	83,172,000	52,140,000	36,557,000
17. IBM (Intl. Business Machines)	Office machines	103,358,000	46,424,000	31,215,000	24,427,000
18. Dodge (Chrysler Corp.)	Cars, trucks	102,957,000	65,376,000	67,067,000	50,271,000
19. Toyota (Toyota Motors)	Cars, trucks	96,019,000	118,036,000	121,232,000	91,707,000

Table 24.1 continued

Brand name (parent company)	Classification	Total annual advertising expenditures			
		1983	1982	1981	1980
20. Kodak (Eastman Kodak)	Cameras, office machines	90,585,000	61,987,000	65,126,000	54,400,000
21. Burger King (Pillsbury Co.)	Restaurants	89,377,000	65,165,000	48,797,000	45,075,000
22. Pepsi-Cola (PepsiCo)	Soft drinks	86,110,000	65,984,000	53,751,000	55,001,000
23. Pontiac (General Motors)	Cars	73,420,000	53,658,000	48,698,000	36,664,000
24. Coca-Cola (Coca-Cola U.S.A.)	Soft drinks	73,061,000	55,611,000	46,879,000	44,988,000
25. Atari (Warner Communications)	Games, home electronics	72,694,000	86,338,000	30,660,000	7,597,000
26. Mercury (Ford Motor Co.)	Cars	71,724,000	39,115,000	45,107,000	45,534,000
27. Marlboro (Philip Morris)	Cigarettes	70,590,000	75,865,000	59,356,000	48,678,000
28. Mattel (Mattel Inc.)	Games	70,405,000	85,064,000	41,782,000	25,436,000
29. Texas Instruments	Office machines	67,864,000	18,745,000	10,762,000	4,794,000
30. Players (Philip Morris)	Cigarettes	65,448,000*	—	—	—
31. Bright (R.J. Reynolds)	Cigarettes	63,276,000	20,143,000*	—	—
32. Oldsmobile (General Motors)	Cars	61,868,000	55,782,000	52,062,000	41,673,000
33. Eastern (Eastern Airlines)	Passenger travel	61,527,000	51,234,000	43,486,000	40,182,000
34. Commodore (Commodore Intl.)	Office machines	61,221,000	15,610,000	1,228,000	163,000
35. Buick (General Motors)	Cars	60,759,000	48,503,000	45,216,000	39,931,000
36. Delta (Delta Airlines)	Passenger travel	60,627,000	45,653,000	39,772,000	34,897,000
37. American Express (American Express)	Financial, travel	60,068,000	54,362,000	47,310,000	37,723,000
38. Volkswagen (Volkswagenwerk A.G.)	Cars, trucks	59,259,000	64,599,000	50,476,000	46,063,000
39. Michelob (Anheuser-Busch)	Beer	57,813,000	53,597,000	44,847,000	33,623,000
40. GE (General Electric)	Major appliances	57,691,000	40,675,000	69,998,000	71,896,000
41. Xerox (Xerox Corp.)	Office machines	57,655,000	41,734,000	29,532,000	21,148,000
42. Tylenol (Johnson & Johnson)	Medicines	56,847,000	43,987,000	36,766,000	26,495,000
43. General Motors (General Motors)	Corporate, parts	56,203,000	61,465,000	35,211,000	39,554,000
44. United Airlines (UAL)	Passenger travel	54,017,000	60,455,000	47,497,000	47,377,000
45. Canon (Canon U.S.A.)	Cameras	52,469,000	42,551,000	33,225,000	28,244,000
46. Wendy's (Wendy's International)	Restaurants	52,205,000	33,412,000	26,375,000	20,555,000
47. RCA (RCA Corp.)	Communications	51,374,000	32,736,000	57,687,000	31,695,000
48. Kentucky Fried Chicken (Heublein)	Restaurants	51,326,000	44,059,000	36,551,000	30,998,000
49. Coors (Adolph Coors Co.)	Beer	51,205,000	28,179,000	29,819,000	24,738,000
50. American (American Airlines)	Passenger travel	51,103,000	51,564,000	45,661,000	41,958,000

Source: From *Marketing & Media Decisions* (July 1984), pp. 56, 58. Reprinted with permission of Decision Publications, Inc.

*New product in year first shown.

This scenario is supported by data that show a correlation between amount of advertising and amount of profit.[3] Work that supports the barrier-to-entry hypothesis assumes that high levels of advertising by established brands reinforces existing brand loyalty and in this way makes it difficult for a new brand to succeed without an inordinately large introductory budget. The correlations cannot show causality, though, so it may be that firms with the greatest profits can afford to do the most advertising. By investing in advertising they are able to generate more profit. Therefore, advertising leads to profit, and profit leads to more advertising. Firms that are reluctant or unable to invest in advertising are left out of this upward spiral and fall behind.

Advertising may make it difficult for a new brand to become established, but if there were no advertising, it would be virtually impossible for a new brand to succeed. Advertising is clearly the least expensive way for a brand to create awareness and knowledge. While advertising is a barrier to entry, it is also a necessary element, and its value probably outweighs its costs.

Howard Morgens, former president of Procter & Gamble, is quoted by David Ogilvy as saying, "We believe that advertising is the most effective and efficient way to sell to the consumer. If we should ever find better methods of selling our type of products to the consumer, we'll leave advertising and turn to these other methods".[4] While advertising has a cost and acts as a barrier, it does its job more efficiently for the firm and for society than would any alternative tool.

Advertising leads to market concentration   Some observers feel that if advertising is a barrier to entry, there will be less competition and more concentration within a product class. This would give consumers less choice and would lead to higher prices.

Concentration can also result when there is enough demand to support only a small number of brands. This could be remedied by increased demand, which leads to increased revenue or decreased costs (such as advertising).

Market concentration could result if each competitor decided that the way to increase its own market share was to increase advertising or promotions. If all or most competitors adopted this strategy, then the effect of each of the campaigns may offset one another and merely lead to lower profits for all firms. Over time, lower profits can lead to some competitors leaving the market; this would therefore result in greater concentration. Again, the alternative to this scenario is collusion, which is also not desirable. Given the fact that there are diminishing returns to advertising as expenditures become very large (discussed in Chapter 20 on budgeting), it is not clear that firms would continue to increase their spending into the range where profits were so adversely affected.

Although concentration seems to be increasing among a small number of brands for many product classes, there are few data to suggest that advertising is the cause. Simon[5] suggests that concentration is more likely to result from mergers and acquisitions. In another analysis, Telser[6] shows that, in most industries, the top four companies do not retain their same positions for long periods. If there were concentration, then there would also be long-term stability among the product class leaders.

Advertising leads to product proliferation   Other writers suggest that advertising leads to the opposite of market concentration—that is, product proliferation. As a result of their ability to use advertising, firms are able to succeed in in-

Figure 24.2 Advertising can help new product introductions

troducing new brands; some say that there are therefore too many brands with meaningless differences on the market and that these brands exist because of clever advertising.

It is ironic that some critics of advertising are upset because there are too many brands, while others are upset because there are too few brands. Even though there is little evidence that advertising helps to promote innovation and new brands, without the opportunity to advertise, the risk of a new product introduction would be too great for most firms, and there would be much less incentive to attempt to be innovative.

Without advertising, it would be difficult to tell consumers that a new brand exists and also difficult to show the unique benefits of the new brand. Figure 24.2 helps clarify this point. Without promotions, it would be difficult to get new product trial up to a satisfactory level.

Arguments relevant to consumer decision making issues

The above arguments are concerned with the economic impact of advertising in terms of prices, profits, and competition. It is also important to consider issues that relate to the impact of advertising on consumer processes.

Advertising manipulates consumers so that they buy products they don't need This argument seems to be made most strongly by those with the least direct experience with advertising. This text has stressed the weak and limited impact of advertising, even though it is clearly the goal of advertisers to persuade and to stimulate demand. There are many issues wrapped up in this topic.

A central point in marketing is that of *meeting needs;* it is felt that the keys to long-term success are assessing and meeting needs. If firms attempt to sell products that consumers don't need, then they are not working in their own self-interest. Between 1970 and 1979, there were almost 6,700 new grocery products introduced; less than 100 of these (about 1.5%) reached annual sales of $15 million.[7] This is ample evidence that advertising is not able to sell products that people don't want. Figure 24.3 deals with the topic of selling products that no one needs.

A second issue is the definition of needs. Maslow[8], in his book *Motivation and Personality,* describes a hierarchy of needs that begins with physiological and safety needs and then moves on to the need for love and belonging, self-esteem and status, and, finally, self-actualization, or inner satisfaction. Given this hierarchy, it is clear that people buy products they don't need; for their only true needs may be for food, shelter, and safety. People could survive without having any other needs met.

Figure 24.3 Does advertising manipulate consumers?

BLOOM COUNTY   **By Berke Breathed**

Figure 24.4 *Does advertising cause penguins to buy products they don't need?*

Is this the way that appropriate needs should be chosen? Some would argue for such a classification scheme. Others would want more control over the list of what is needed. They may want to outlaw cars with large engines, processed food with sugar in it, or videotape machines. Of course, other people might decide that people don't need ice cream or color television or any automobiles (or tomato scramblers, as in Figure 24.4 above). Both groups are right—these products aren't needed—but who will make the choice of what will be offered on the market in a free country? In a capitalist economy, these decisions are made by consumers who vote by buying or not buying, and most new products fail because of this system of voting.

The view that advertising causes people to make poor choices emerges from economics and, within economics, from utility theory. Although current utility theory allows for intangible values, classical utility theory did not. Here, economic man made rational decisions based on perfect information and attempted to maximize the utility of tangible issues. Such a person would not buy a Cadillac instead of a Chevette because the latter would serve the basic purpose of transportation equally well. The wide range of goods and services that go beyond basic needs is testimony to the failure of classical utility theory. It is equally rational for a person to buy a Cadillac if there is a need to have comfort, to show material success, or whatever. It is folly for one person to impose a notion of rationality on another in terms of purchase decisions; we all have our own personal set of needs at the time of purchase.

Consumer behavior theory is also useful in considering the question of *manipulation*. To consider this issue, involvement and trial versus repeat purchases must be considered, as in Figure 24.5. As has been discussed in several places, a consumer with low involvement may be influenced in terms of trial purchase behavior by advertising and promotions. These tools are most potent when the consumer isn't particularly involved in brand choice but does use the product. Most people use bar soap and orange juice but aren't very concerned about brand choice. Consumers watch television without paying much attention and do learn the primary points of an advertising message over time; consumers do use coupons, samples, and other pricing deals. It is fair to say that these tools can have an impact on initial purchase behavior for a new brand or product that elicits only a low level of involvement. Figure 24.6 is another view of how this process operates.

Figure 24.5 Do
advertising and promotions
manipulate?

	INVOLVEMENT LEVEL	
PURCHASE STAGE	Low	High
Trial	Advertising and promotions have strong impact	Advertising and promotions have weak impact
Repeat	Behavior due to goodness of product	Behavior due to goodness of product

The tools of advertising and promotions have much less impact in other cases. Products that elicit high levels of involvement are considered quite carefully by consumers; the more care that is given, the less likely it is that communications tools will have an impact. Here advertising serves mainly to create awareness, knowledge, and a favorable image. Promotions need to be quite extreme in order to have much influence (e.g., a rebate of several hundred dollars).

In considering repeat behavior, the case for manipulation is even weaker. While people may buy an inexpensive, frequently purchased product once without much consideration, it is doubtful that repeat purchase would occur in this way. How many people will buy the same brand a second time if it is unsatisfactory the first time? It is this question that brings out the balance of the marketplace.

Very few firms can survive by selling inferior goods on a one-shot basis. It is more efficient for the firm to build repeat purchases through a good product so that advertising and promotions expenses can be cut. There will always be a few disreputable merchants who succeed by selling inferior goods (often through direct mail or telemarketing so that they cannot easily be found), but these are the exception. Most firms succeed by offering a better product that meets needs.

The above arguments look at potential manipulations that move people between brands. It is also necessary to consider the more global issue of whether entire classes of products succeed through advertising. Do people buy products they don't need because of advertising? This question was considered earlier in the definition of needs.

This issue can also be considered in terms of *whether advertising mirrors and follows society, or leads and changes it.* This is a difficult issue to resolve, but it would seem to be in the firm's best interest to follow rather than lead society. It is expensive to set trends; it is easier to follow and take advantage of opportunities.

In March 1984, there was little demand for boy's gymnastics classes, and it would have been very difficult for any single gymnastics facility (or the U.S. Gymnastics Association) to create a societal trend toward the use of such facilities by boys.

In July of that year, the U.S. men's gymnastics team won several dramatic medals in the Olympics; millions of parents and children saw these events, and

Figure 24.6   Another view of the power of advertising (Reprinted by permission of Newspaper Enterprise Association, Inc.)

© 1979 by NEA, Inc.

"... And upon being taken to a supermarket, you will remember and demand that brand. When I clap my hands you will awake ..."

gymnastics immediately became an "in" sport for boys. Gymnastics classes became popular, and advertising told people where to sign up.

Did advertising lead or follow society? Advertising in March got little response; in August the response was overwhelming. Did consumers buy something they didn't need? Given the state of values in August 1984, consumers bought a service that filled a specific need. Did consumers buy inferior products? Some probably did; in some cases, facilities of little merit opened up to take advantage of consumers. These did not get much repeat usage because parents moved their children to better facilities. In this way, the marketplace continuously adjusts to the conditions of society.

An offshoot of this issue is that *advertising has led to an artificially high standard of living.* In the aggregate, it is probably true that advertising acts to some degree as a catalyst that accelerates forces that exist on their own in Western societies. One measure of success in these cultures is related to material possessions. Advertising provides constant reminders of this and continuously suggests new badges of material acquisition. As such, advertising reflects the majority's value structure and, again, follows rather than leads society.

Perhaps the best way to summarize this issue is by quoting that successful marketer, Anonymous: "The best way to kill a bad product is to advertise it." A bad product can survive until consumers find out about it, try it, and see how poor it is. Products survive through repeat purchases and fail without sufficient repeats. Likewise, products that do not meet any need will also fail. Therefore, it is far easier for marketers to follow rather than lead society.

Advertising doesn't provide consumers with sufficient information
There are several responses to this argument. The first addresses *how much information is enough, what type of information should be given, and who*

should make these decisions concerning sufficiency. The issue of sufficient information is similar to that of meeting needs; who will set the standards of what products we need, and who will set the standards of how much information we need?

Although advertising is criticized for not giving enough information, various studies have shown that consumers don't make "better" decisions just because they have more information. When Jacoby gave consumers large amounts of information in a laboratory experiment, their decisions got "worse" in terms of selecting a "best" brand on certain criteria. He found that it didn't help to give them too much information; they suffered from "information overload" and responded more poorly.[9]

In a different study, Houston and Rothschild[10] found that consumers could process more information than they had been given in the past (they were not given as much as Jacoby gave), but they did not change their decisions. Although subjects showed that they had learned the new information, they did not use it to make a "better" decision.

It is true that advertising does not provide complete information. Advertising is a form of advocacy and should not be expected to provide full information. In several European countries, the government and various public interest groups feel that consumers should have more information, so they supplement advertising with their own public service messages, which appear in a format similar to that used by *Consumer Reports*.

In the United States, the FTC has tried to create an environment whereby more information is given in advertising for certain products, but the results have not been dramatic. Cigarette ads have health information, but per capita consumption of cigarettes did not drop during the first decade when this information was given. The FDA requires extensive information on the packages of various food and drug products, but research consistently shows that knowledge levels are quite low for nutritional information or safety information.

The low-information argument is most often presented against television advertising. It is true that limited information is given in this medium; this is at least in part a constraint of the medium. The consumer cannot control the pace of information and has low involvement for the message in most cases. As Ray pointed out in FTC hearings[11], people rarely turn on their televisions and wait for commercials when they are seeking product information. If they actively seek information, they go to print media or unbiased sources.

The main value of most television advertising is to create brand awareness so that the brand will be considered when a purchase is made. There are, though, high-information messages; these primarily occur for high-involvement type products and are usually delivered in a print format.

It is certainly true that advertising does not provide *complete* information, and it would never be in the advertiser's best interest to do so, because it would be expensive and might be self-defeating. It is less clear if consumers need, or would use, more information than they currently have; studies in this area generally show that high levels of information are either not used or do not lead to better decisions.

Another side of this issue can also be considered; that is, *is advertising too persuasive?* Again, this is a major purpose of advertising; its goal is to persuade. If persuasion is not acceptable in advertising, is it more acceptable elsewhere?

Politicians, lawyers, clergy, and teachers all are professional persuaders; most people use persuasion many times each day. Is persuasion, per se, bad? Probably not. Why is persuasion in advertising worse than that in other contexts? Of all groups of persuaders, advertisers are among the most candid in stating their goals and tactics; consumers understand that commercial messages are biased and persuasive, and they are able to deal with advertising from that perspective. Are other groups of persuaders as candid in stating their goals?

Advertising misleads, deceives, and is full of lies There was a time when this statement was, unfortunately, true in many cases. Now many groups watch for this type of advertising; the government watches through the eyes of the FTC, and competitors report infractions to the NARB. (These agencies were described in Chapter 6.) This does not mean that there is no false advertising; it means that there is very little in an industry that generates over $45 billion of messages each year. The worst cases now exist at local levels, in direct mail, and in back-of-the-book magazine ads. These areas are least observed by regulators, may fall between the jurisdictions of the various agencies, or may just not be worth the time and expense necessary for prosecution. National advertising in major media is, on the whole, remarkably clean; cases that emerge are noteworthy because they are exceptions.

In a study by Jacoby[12], subjects were shown commercials, noncommercial messages (e.g., PSAs), and programming (e.g., news, comedies, adventure shows). Over 80% misunderstood something that they saw. Interestingly, there was more miscomprehension of program than of commercial content. As has been shown throughout this text, it is very difficult to communicate accurately; if deceptive advertising is to be judged, it should be on the basis that some percent of all messages will be misperceived. The percent of cases of intentional deception seems to be quite low.

One area of exception may be advertising done by the U. S. government. U. S. savings bonds are sold as a way to build personal security but are poor investments compared to what is on the market. The military sells the glory of their life style, but there is no warning that it may be hazardous to one's health. There is no federal agency responsible for the truthfulness of advertising done by the government. A second exception, political advertising, is discussed below.

Advertising is offensive and tasteless For the most part, advertising is just innocuous. In an attempt to break through the noise, some messages do offend some people. This issue, though, is a highly subjective one.

For example, a lot of advertising has sexual connotations. (Is advertising leading or following society?) Most of it is aimed at specific target markets who are not offended; problems occur when people who are not in the target market see the message. Few people in the target market for Calvin Klein jeans were offended by its advertising featuring Brooke Shields; those who were most likely to be offended were not in the target market and were probably offended by the concept of tight jeans and a society that has a need for this product. Perhaps the offending party is the media planner who sends the message to the wrong audience; perhaps the offender is the target market that responds to the message and gives license to its presence; perhaps it is the message itself that is offensive.

Figure 24.7   Can any gun advertising be tasteful?

The same people who may be offended by the Calvin Klein ad might find the National Rifle Association advertisement in Figure 24.7 to be acceptable. Others would have the opposite reaction. Everyone is able to find some advertising that is offensive, but only a very small part of advertising is created with no attempt at being tasteful. Perhaps a larger percentage aims close to the boundaries of good taste in order to grab attention.

In the past there have always been groups that have challenged certain advertising on the basis of taste, but these have never been very successful in bringing about changes in advertising. Advertising, for the most part, reflects the tastes of the relevant target market, and any changes occur as the target changes. For example, when the feminist movement began in the early 1970s, its advocates complained about the tasteless and offensive portrayal of women as second-class citizens in advertising. Messages did not change in response to these complaints but did begin to change in the early 1980s because, by this time, a sizable part of some relevant target market held the same feeling.

Advertising is generally responsive to the masses but is less responsive to minority opinions. Again, it reflects society but doesn't lead it. When an issue is tasteless to the point where sales are affected, then messages change. Because it is impossible to placate all tastes, the majority view of the target market dominates. This means that, in the mid 1980s, sexual innuendos are acceptable, but the portrayal of women as airheads is less acceptable.

Is advertising for political candidates useful to the democratic process? It is estimated that over one billion dollars was spent on political advertising in 1980 and again in 1984. Of this amount, each major party candidate for president received $40 million from the federal government. Both John O'Toole, chairman of the board of Foote, Cone & Belding, and David Ogilvy, founder of Ogilvy & Mather have been outspoken opponents of the use of advertising in the political arena.

O'Toole feels that advertising shouldn't be used in political races for several reasons.[13]

▪ When people buy a low-priced product, they can refuse to repurchase it several weeks later if it is no good; when people buy a high-priced product, they usually get a warranty. Neither safeguard holds in the political arena. If a candidate sells himself or herself with misleading advertising, the voters have little recourse but to live with the poor product for two, four, or six years.

▪ Product marketing attempts to shift market share by a few points; the advertiser knows that deceptive practices used today to gain a point will come back to haunt the firm tomorrow. Therefore, ethical practices are in the firm's best interest. Political brands win the entire product class, and all competitors are then put out of business for several years. This puts enormous pressures on candidates and creates the temptation to deceive. O'Toole cynically questions the use of deception: "Why not? If you win, who can take it away from you? If you lose, what does it matter?"[14]

Ogilvy is even more outspoken: "There is one category of advertising which is totally uncontrolled and flagrantly dishonest; the television commercials for candidates in Presidential elections."[15] Ogilvy and O'Toole both point out that the federal agencies which oversee advertising have no control over political advertising; as a result, many political messages are used that would never be allowed by the FTC or the NARB. Political advertising is considered "protected speech" under the First Amendment to the Constitution and therefore is not subject to stringent review. Spero concluded that political advertising is "the most deceptive, misleading, unfair, and untruthful of all advertising . . . the sky is the limit with regard to what can be said, what can be promised, what accusations can be made, what lies can be told".[16]

In addition to misleading message strategies, the media plans are also designed to persuade rather than inform. Candidates typically budget so that there is extremely high repetition of short television spots. In this way they have reduced complex issues to banality at best. When these messages are repeated inordinately, they begin to take hold.

The $40 million that each major party candidate for president receives from the government is spent in approximately two months (Labor Day until Election Day) and therefore would translate to an annual budget of $240 million. By comparison, in 1983, only five of the brands listed in Table 24.1 spend more than that amount. When a short message of little substance is repeated that often, it is clear that the goal is not to inform, but rather to persuade.

T·H·E   I·N·S·I·D·E   O·U·T·L·O·O·K

John O'Toole

Former Chairman, Foote, Cone & Belding Communications, Inc.

John O'Toole graduated from Northwestern University in 1951 with a degree in journalism. He promptly enlisted in the Marine Corps, was commissioned, and served in Korea with the 1st Marine Division.

He joined the copy department of FCB/Chicago in 1954. During the next ten years he worked on virtually every account in the office as copy supervisor or associate copy director. In 1964, he moved to FCB/Los Angeles as creative director and in 1967, he returned to Chicago as creative director there.

In May, 1969, Mr. O'Toole was named president of Foote, Cone & Belding Advertising and in June 1970, president of the parent company, Foote, Cone & Belding Communications, Inc. He became Chairman of the Board on January 1, 1981.

Mr. O'Toole was 1984/85 chairman of the American Association of Advertising Agencies, having served as the previous year's vice chairman and chairman of the A.A.A.A. Image of Advertising Committee. He has also served as chairman of the National Advertising Review Council.

In 1981, his book, The Trouble with Advertising, *was published by Chelsea House Publishers.*

Advertising in Society

Advertising's role in society is of lesser magnitude than its visibility. And therein lies some of its problems.

Its role is as an expediter. In a mercantile society based on a free marketplace, individuals have always sold what they grow or make by means of information and persuasion—salesmanship, in other words.

Mass production of goods, mass markets, and mass communications were brought together, with all the attendant efficiencies, wealth, and jobs, by advertising. It expedited the function of salesmanship by adapting it to the paid time and space of mass communications media.

This view of advertising's role is relatively recent. It began in 1904 when Albert Lasker of the Lord & Thomas agency began changing the generally accepted definition of advertising from "keeping your name before the public" to his new vision of its function, "salesmanship in print." Part of this vision was the equation of an advertisement with a personal salesperson making a call on an individual prospect. The preparation, the techniques, the strategies of a personal sales call became those of an advertisement. Identifying the prospect, appealing to him personally, persuading him—all these became part of the role, multiplied by the millions of impressions made daily by the media.

That role necessitates high visibility, and high visibility calls attention to abuses, excesses, and ineptitude. Abuses, in the form of false or misleading ads, are increasingly rare as a result of the effectiveness of industry self-regulation. Excesses, however, do not seem to be diminishing as the volume of advertising grows. Television clutter irritates the public as more and more commercials are crammed into the same amount of time. And ineptitude will be with us until there is enough objective evidence to convince the most recalcitrant that advertising that consumers say "insults their intelligence" is not as effective as advertising that pleases them.

Thus, it is incumbent upon all of us who practice this craft to be constantly aware of its high profile, to recognize that advertising is an "uninvited guest" whose presence is suffered as long as it behaves itself, to understand that advertising's role in society—as crucial as it may appear to us—will be played by something else if we fail to observe advertising's responsibility to society.

An information-oriented goal would lead to less repetition of longer messages. Longer messages would allow for the development of issues and for a substantive point of view to be presented. Furthermore, if the goal were to reach all voters, then candidates could do so through a reach strategy. The present strategies are very frequency oriented; such a strategy assumes a low-involvement electorate that can be easily persuaded.

Fortunately, all of this is balanced by data that show little impact of advertising in high-level races (high involvement). This means that most of the money spent on advertising in presidential elections is wasted. In low-level elections, there is much less involvement and therefore the impact of advertising can be much greater; in low-level races, though, the candidates rarely have enough money for a high-repetition campaign. However, data across a number of low-level races do show a positive impact of advertising on voting patterns.[17]

Political advertising is felt by many to be a misuse of advertising and a perversion of politics. While advertising has made a societal contribution in many areas outside of the private sector, the political arena is not one of these.

Summary of societal issues

O'Toole has written a contract to define the relation between advertisers and consumers. It makes the point that advertising is a persuasive selling tool, but that it will be used as honestly as possible. Consumers already understand it, and all advertisers should be bound by it:[18]

> I'm an advertiser. You're a consumer. I'm going to communicate to you through advertising. Now, advertising, as we both know, is salesmanship functioning in the paid space and time of mass communications media. That's all it is. Like any salesman, its purpose is commercial. It's going to present products and services in their best light. It's not going to tell you what's good about the other guy's product or service. There are plenty of ways for you to find out about that (see my competitor's contract under separate cover). It's going to be corny at times; maybe there'll be a little too much of it now and then. We're all human.
>
> But I promise you this. My advertising won't lie to you, and it will not deliberately try to mislead you. It won't bore the hell out of you or treat you as though you were a fool or embarrass you or your family. But remember, it's a salesman. Its purpose is to persuade you to trade your hard-earned cash for my product or service.
>
> In return for your putting up with all this, I'm going to support those newspapers and magazines and radio stations and TV programs you like so much. I'm going to pay for music, situation comedies, news, stories, movies, variety shows, football games, cartoon shows and reportage on every aspect of life you may be interested in.
>
> In the process you'll get a lot of important information to help you make informed choices. And you'll get what those lawyers call "puffery." You'll get news about new products you'll like, and you'll be persuaded to try some you'll never buy again. That's the way it goes.
>
> What do you say? Is it a deal? Great. I'm glad we understand each other.

It is important to think about these issues that tie advertising to society; a person entering the business of advertising can expect to be attacked from time to time by people who feel less favorably about it. The previous discussion has considered many issues that confront advertisers and has tried to analyze them from the standpoint of the firm. What is rational behavior for the firm is usually behavior that is also favorable to society. Some excesses occur when all competitors act in their own best interest, but when they all do so, the result is neither in their nor society's best interest. One way to remedy this flaw is to allow collusion, but such a remedy would create more problems than it solves, for the result would be monopoly power. Clearly, the competitive nature of free enterprise does not work perfectly, but it seems to be a lot better than the next best alternative.

Jobs in the Advertising Business

As this text reaches its end, you may be thinking that the ad biz seems like it might be a nice place to work. Interesting people. Challenging problems. Glamour. Wealth.

There are about 150,000 students per year who take an advertising course, and many of them also want to get into the business; many of them would like to work for the same few well-known top agencies. Each of these agencies gets hundreds of unsought applications every month for positions that usually do not even exist.

Seem tough? It is. Getting into the advertising business is very difficult and very competitive. Most advertising agencies don't recruit on college campuses and most, except for the very largest, don't have formal training programs. They don't need to go through these processes because they get so many unsolicited applications.

In addition, starting jobs in advertising pay poorly compared to alternative positions. A person with a bachelor's or master's degree could expect to start at $3,000 to $5,000 per year less in advertising than in some other type of marketing position. It gets worse: The hours are long and the work is demanding; if you can't hack it, there are hundreds of resumes coming in behind you.

On the positive side, the work is very challenging and the people are very interesting. No one ever died of boredom at an ad agency, although many have left with ulcers and other stress-related illnesses. A good person advances very rapidly, either within the agency or by switching agencies.

What are the attributes of a good person? They will, of course, vary between jobs and across agencies, but agencies look for people who are assertive, confident, smart, have good interpersonal and good writing skills, are hard working, and are experienced. The stress is great, and those who thrive on pressure will excel; others drop off quickly. Figure 24.8 may describe the type of person who will succeed in advertising, even though the message in it was written 1,300 years ago.

Still interested? Your first task is to develop a campaign to market yourself. Start with a situation analysis: What jobs could you qualify for? What jobs would you like? What size agency do you want? With what type of client do you want to work? A good source for assessing agencies is the *Standard Directory of Advertising Agencies.* This book, also known as the Redbook, lists all agencies in the United States, their key personnel, and their clients. Other sources are *Advertising Age* and *AdWeek,* two trade papers that list jobs and have related articles.

Next is the setting of objectives and position. You need to define your target market of relevant agencies that are most likely to meet your career objectives. This list should reflect some thought because there are more agencies than anyone could pursue. Geography will serve as a first cut, then some more specific career thinking is necessary.

Most important will be the position you want to assume. Your target assumes that you are one of many thousand commodity-like brands in the product class of

Figure 24.8 On coping with pressure

or the world is like an olive press, and men are constantly under pressure. If you are the dregs of the oil you are carried away through the sewer, but if you are true oil you remain in the vessel. □ To be under pressure is inescapable. Pressure takes place through all the world: war, siege, the worries of state. We all know men who grumble under these pressures, and complain. They are cowards. They lack splendor. □ But there is another sort of man who is under the same pressure, but does not complain. For it is the friction which polishes him. It is pressure which refines and makes him noble.

—St. Augustine
First Archbishop of Canterbury
Seventh Century, A.D.

recent college graduates. How can you develop a position that shows that you can bring some unique benefit to a prospective employer? If you can't answer this question, then there is no need to continue; someone else will, and they will have your job.

Once you have a position, the battle is half over. The other half is developing strategies so that the target market is aware of your position and wants to talk to you. You want a job that places a premium on creativity; you can show your creativity in the media, message, and promotions strategies of your job-seeking campaign. What will you say? How will you say it? How will you get that message to the right person? What incentive can you give so that the message will be read and you will get an interview? One prospect delivered pizzas to important people with his resume taped on to the slices. What will you do to make an impact?

In any case, it is important to consider a job search as the execution of a promotions plan; it is essential to develop a relevant position and strategies to match. Without doing this work, your interview could turn out like the one in Figure 24.9. The examples just given were offbeat and may be inappropriate for you but are used to make the point that a unique strategy is necessary to cut through the noise of thousands of other competitors. This first campaign may be your toughest one. (For more help, see the discussion questions at the end of each chapter that relate to this problem.)

Figure 24.9   *Are you hiring?*

Someone called yesterday and opened up with "Are you hiring?"

"Hiring what?"

"You know, *hiring*. I just graduated from college."

"What do you do?"

"Anything."

"Well, are you in account service or media or art or copy?"

"Art, I guess."

"Illustration?"

"No."

"Art director?"

"No, kind of design."

"You're a designer?"

"I think so. I want to be in commercial art, so I was just going through the Yellow Pages here and your name was the first. *Are* you hiring?"

"No." I got out the Yellow Pages and gave her the names I knew were respectable.

That sort of job applicant is not the kind you feel guilt about. You can't feel guilt about rejecting a job applicant who doesn't know anything about your business. I don't think it's unfair to ask that a job applicant understand how your business works and be able to articulate a preference for this or that position. "Are you hiring?" is a long way from that.

And there's no guilt attached to rejection of people switching careers, who think they'll take a swing at advertising.

"Well, I was selling furniture and I get along real good with people. I'd be good at taking them out to lunch and golf and all. And I could sell clients on stuff. I sold a lot of furniture."

There's no guilt about these well-intentioned job seekers because your normal applicant conversation is Greek to them, something you notice right away.

"What part of the agency are you interested in?"

"Selling."

"Selling?"

"You know, selling products and stuff. I'd be good at thinking up slogans and things."

"Oh, you want to be a copywriter?"

"No, I want to *sell* stuff."

No, the ones you feel guilt about are the advertising graduates. They've majored in your business. For four years they have thought about you, how on this day they would march to their reward, as did their fellow graduates in engineering and teaching and business and journalism and all the others who learned a trade they could practice with some result right out of college.

In walks a clean-face, excited and educated. You are the reason for all his effort. You fill in the face in his interview fantasy. You make worthwhile his perseverance and sacrifice in the name of your business. He studied you, probably knows more history of your business than you do. He could have studied anything, but he decided to be like *you.*

By Jim Albright

What are the possible jobs to go after?

There are at least five paths to pursue; these go in very different directions but allow a person with experience to move from one career path to another.

1. *Work for an advertising vehicle* such as *Time,* The American Broadcasting Company, or one of the thousands of other local and national vehicles that are listed in *Standard Rate and Data Service.* Most of these jobs involve selling space or time to advertising agencies, manufacturers, and retailers. From such a sales position, a person can move to marketing and advertising management or laterally to the media department of an agency. Having spent time interacting with many media departments should help open agency doors if the agency is your ultimate goal.

At the local level, these vehicles offer other opportunities because many provide production and creative services to small retail clients. As a result, there are opportunities to combine creativity, advertising management, and selling all in one position.

2. *Work for a manufacturer* such as Procter & Gamble, General Motors, or one of millions of other manufacturers. Those that advertise are listed in the *Standard Directory of Advertisers* along with the names of their key marketing and advertising personnel. Starting positions would be in sales, sales management, or brand management, and could lead to positions in advertising and marketing management. A lateral move to an agency would be to an account executive position; such a move would come fairly easily for a brand/product manager who would have spent many hours dealing with an account executive counterpart in the past. Many agency people recommend this route and feel that a few years of manufacturer experience is very useful training. As can be seen in Table 24.2, there is a lot of overlap in duties between the agency's account manager and the manufacturer's product/brand manager.

3. *Work for a retailer* such as Marshall Field, I. Magnin, Saks Fifth Avenue, or one of the thousands of other retailers who are large enough to have their own advertising staff. While many large retailers (e.g., Sears, K-mart, Penney's) use advertising agencies, and many small retailers get their work done locally by a

Table 24.2 Time spent on marketing tasks: account manager vs. product manager

Account manager		Product manager
25%	Creative strategy & development	5%
20%	Media	5%
15%	Strategic & marketing planning	15%
20%	Advertising & marketing, research & analysis	15%
5%	Sales promotion & packaging	20%
5%	Pricing & financial planning	15%
5%	Sales & sales analysis	15%
5%	Research & development, product development	10%
100%		100%

Source: Tom Schwarz, *Advertising Age,* 18 August 1980, p. 36. Reprinted with permission. Copyright 1980 by Crain Communications, Inc.

freelance writer or artist, there are many others who do their own work. These retailers have established their own agencies inside the corporate structure. They offer good training because the work is very specific, sales-oriented, and replete with deadlines. Many advertisers feel that this environment also is a good training ground for agency work. The types of positions mirror those in an agency and offer many lateral move options as a result.

4. *Work for a firm that does ancillary activities* such as marketing research, promotional specialties, package design, public relations, or direct response marketing. Each of these areas is growing rapidly, so that many large agencies have an in-house staff for some or all of these services. Growth, though, is so rapid that many successful firms specialize in one of the services with great success. These firms have sales positions and account management positions that allow a person to be heavily involved with advertising and promotions. These positions also allow for significant interaction with agency, manufacturer, and retailer personnel so that lateral movement to these areas is possible.

5. *Work for an advertising agency.* For many people, a job in advertising means the glamour and pressure of an advertising agency; others are more specific and would only want to be at a top, well-known shop in New York or Chicago. While there are over 8,000 agencies in the United States, the opportunities are limited because 95% of the agencies have only a few employees. At the other extreme, ten agencies employ 17,000 people and do 40% of all advertising volume. At one end, there are many leads but few jobs, and at the other end there are few leads in control of many jobs.

The various positions in an agency are described in Chapter 1 and are not repeated here. Business school majors are most likely to end up in account management, media, or research; journalism majors are more likely to end up in media or copywriting. Jobs requiring special training such as graphic arts or production will draw their entry level people from places where such training is acquired.

While most agencies offer informal training, a few have formal training programs. Other agencies offer summer internship programs that may lead to entry level positions upon graduation.

Another way to enter the agency business is through the mail room or as a receptionist. In many agencies, these positions are filled by extremely talented men and women who are waiting for an opening in the department for which they have training. Given the high level of turnover in agencies, a person is likely to stay in these low-level positions for six to nine months. During that time, the agency can evaluate the person in terms of enthusiasm, dedication, and other personality traits, and management will already know the person when an opening appears. If the person doesn't move out of the mail room after a couple of openings have come and gone, this should be interpreted as a strong signal to look elsewhere.

What do advertising positions pay?

Table 24.3 shows some salary information from 1981 and 1983. The data are high and low figures with no mean or median data provided. Most observers feel that agency starting salaries are lower than those in other industries but that good people catch up quickly and great people are rewarded very well. The figures also do not reflect profit-sharing and retirement packages.

Table 24.3 Up and down the ladder. Average highs and lows of ad agency salaries

	1983		1981	
Creative	*High*	*Low*	*High*	*Low*
Creative director	$150,000	$75,000	$85,000	$60,000
Assoc. creative director	85,000	65,000	65,000	50,000
Copy supervisor	75,000	50,000	60,000	45,000
Sr. copywriter	75,000	50,000	50,000	35,000
Copywriter	45,000	25,000	25,000	18,000
Jr. copywriter	16,000	14,000	12,000	10,000
Art				
Exec. art director	200,000	110,000	125,000	85,000
Group creative director	85,000	60,000	70,000	50,000
Art director	65,000	30,000	50,000	25,000
Asst. art director	25,000	14,000	20,000	12,000
*Account**				
Sr. vp-mgmt. supervisor	130,000	40,000	150,000	52,000
Vp-mgmt. supervisor	75,000	45,000	77,000	38,000
Acct. supervisor	58,000	25,000	65,000	27,000
Acct. exec.	40,000	15,000	49,000	15,500
Asst. acct. exec.	29,000	14,000	30,000	15,000
*Media***				
Sr. vp-media director	125,000	50,000	100,000	50,000
Vp-assoc. media director	100,000	32,000	65,000	32,000
Media supervisor	35,000	20,000	35,000	20,000
Media planner	30,000	12,000	25,000	12,000
Media buyer	25,000	12,000	25,000	12,000

*Figures represent absolute, not average, highs and lows, hence the discrepancies from 1981 to 1983
**Figures for 1983 and 1982; figures for 1981 not available

Source: *Advertising Age,* 2 January 1984, p. M-17. Reprinted with permission. Copyright 1984 by Crain Communications, Inc.

Need more advice?

In 1982 *AdWeek* asked a number of established professionals for advice they would give to newcomers. Figure 24.10 is a sampling of their responses. In addition, the next section summarizes some of the key issues presented in this text. These should be liberally sprinkled into the midst of most job interviews.

Keys to Success in Advertising and Promotions

As with most things in life, there are a few keys that increase a person's chances for success. Most important are good luck and good timing; being in the right place at the right time compensates for the absence of many skills, and, at least in the short run, being lucky may win out over being good.

In addition to, or instead of, the above, there are some other helpful ingredients to help push the neophyte advertiser up the ladder of success. Being able to recall the key models and concepts of this text (at the right time and place) will

Figure 24.10   *Agency people offer some advice to the industry's newcomers*

Gabe Massimi

Vice-Chairman/Creative Director, Burton-Campbell Inc., Atlanta

Don't go directly from college into advertising. Get another job first. The agency business takes a very good understanding of people. Get a job where you brush elbows with the public—even work in a gas station. Just so you know what it's like to provide a service for payment.

Mary McInerny

Senior Art Director, Grey Advertising Inc., Los Angeles

Have pride in what you do. Never look down on any job or anybody no matter how small.

Hal Hayes

Executive Vice-President, Cunningham Root & Craig, Los Angeles

Ten years ago I would have said, "Go to New York." Not any more. L.A. is on a par, as are Chicago and San Francisco. From a marketing point of view, my advice would be to get on a piece of packaged goods business. If you can learn to handle the volume of information generated and hammer it down into a point of view that results in great advertising—not just pap—you will be able to handle any other product category and do the same thing.

Robert Bloom

President, The Bloom Agency, Dallas

It is important to know that the agency business is very segmented. The day of the generalist is gone. Most who want to get started in the business don't understand the high degree of specialization. The skills needed for marketing differ from those needed for media or creative. They may have to get supplementary education in some areas and not others.

John Doman

Vice-President/Management Supervisor, TBWA Advertising, New York

I would suggest he work at being observant. There are ideas to be gotten from everything he reads, sees and hears. Output comes from input.

Roger Livingston

President, Chiat/Day Livingston, Seattle

I think the best, most lasting experience a young person in advertising can have is to somehow work in close association with one of the few geniuses in the business. I can't think of a better place to start than being in close proximity to the Bill Bernbachs, David Ogilvys or Carl Allys. How you get those jobs are sheer dumb luck. I feel technique is never a substitute for genius. Qualities like integrity and style are every bit as important as understanding an ASI report. Having an opportunity to work with those who can see through the smoke and who have insight and understanding is a priceless experience.

Larry Jennings

President, Jennings & Epstein, Atlanta

I would advise them to go to New York. That's where the best advertising agencies are. I'd say go to a top New York agency's training program (which are rapidly diminishing) to get well-grounded experience. Then I would suggest getting three to five years experience on the client side. After that, work for a medium-sized agency in any satellite community in the country for 10 years or so. By that time, they'll be ready to find a partner and open up their own agency. The best advice is never work for someone else—but you have to before you reach that goal.

Michael Hooper

President, Ralph Kent Cooke Inc., Los Angeles

I'd encourage him to get a master's degree. Then start to work in either New York or Chicago with a large national agency. Get as much experience as possible on various accounts—and the most important thing is not to feel he has to be the president of a company.

Ray Trapp

President, Keller-Crescent/Southwest, Irving, Tex.

Become well-read, well-rounded and get worldly experience. The sensitive and intuitive nature of a true ad person requires receptivity. To capitalize on this, one should strive to gain every experience—from literature and from activities which enhance one's openness to life.

Robert Woodworth

Vice-President Director of Media Services-Western Region, McCann-Erickson, Los Angeles

This industry is one which works on personal attainment. It demands an exceptional slice of one's personal life. The agency business requires much more commitment than many other occupations.

Roger Myers

Executive Vice-President/Creative Director, Burch Myers Cuttie, Inc., Chicago

The best advice I could give is not prepare for advertising at all. Prepare to observe, think critically, and above all, make up your own mind. The best advertising people know when they are right even when other advertising people try to convince them that they're wrong. Experience things, develop tastes, and pay attention to trends but don't conform to them.

Figure 24.10 continued

Arthur Lubow

Account Executive, William Altman Agency, New York

Make sure you work for people who are self-assured, courageous and smart.

Ann Iverson

Senior Vice-President/Director of Client Service, Ogilvy & Mather, Houston

You've got to work darn hard. One way to succeed is to do more than is expected. Don't be political. Be a good listener, and study. You never stop learning in this business.

Richard O'Connor

Vice-Chairman/Chief Executive Officer, Campbell-Ewald, Detroit

I would encourage them to go into the agency business with one caution—how can they deal with intangibles? If they can handle the intangibles—working with ideas rather than size and dimensions—it's a marvelous business to be in.

Hank Goldberg

Account Supervisor, Beber Silverstein Masciovecchio & Partners, Miami

There are so many skills needed for this business. I would say that

discipline and the ability to listen are two very important attributes. I would tell him to keep thinking even after the job is finished. Even if he has a successful campaign, it doesn't mean it's ever over with. I'd tell a newcomer to have all the fun he can.

Phil Payne

Executive Vice-President, Doe-Anderson Advertising, Louisville

The first thing I'd advise would be to get a degree in anything but advertising. The second thing would be to read everything you can get your hands on—the broader range of subjects the better. And the last would be to get a job where you can learn how to sell a product. Once you know how to sell something and you're able to deal with different situations, you'll be ready to do well.

John Littlewood

Senior Vice-President / Creative Director, NW Ayer, Los Angeles

Because the industry is so volatile—with changes in accounts, etc., happening overnight, the important thing I would tell a young person would be: Never take yourself too seriously. You have to be able to step back and laugh at yourself.

Martin Solow

President, Durfee & Solow, New York

Go off and become a human being. The good agencies create ads that talk to people. The bad agencies (and there are many more of them) talk in superficial terms. God help us all if everyone begins to think the same way.

Hugh Wells

Executive Vice-President/Creative Director, NW Ayer, Chicago

My first advice would be to find a way to work with the best people as early as possible and learn what they know. Secondly, I'd say, keep your eye on the ball—ignore fads, politics and other diversions. Making great advertising is the only sure-fire success formula.

Ron Kaatz

Senior Vice-President/Director of Media Resources & Research, J. Walter Thompson Co., Chicago

To recognize that calling meetings and saying "it's never been done before" rarely produced a great marketing or creative idea.

help in organizing problem situations. To this end, these keys are quickly summarized here. Keep them in mind for that day when you are invited to a planning meeting and Ms. Big asks you for your feelings on the matter (whatever it is).

The decision sequence framework

There is no need to show this framework again, but it is useful to reiterate the value of having a planning model. All too often there is the temptation to begin planning strategy without first properly assessing the situation and setting realistic objectives. This management-by-objectives concept has been universally praised but is sometimes forgotten by practitioners under the pressure of getting something done quickly. An assessment doesn't always need to be 500 pages long, but some thought has to be given to the constraints of the problem.

The hierarchy of effects

All communications attempt to elicit some type of response, and all responses fall into one of three classes: awareness, attitude, or behavior. The order of these elements may vary between situations, but the elements themselves don't change. Any message or piece of strategy usually should influence only one type of response. To attempt to do too much at once leads to confusing messages. Part of any situation analysis should be to determine what type of response is sought and what sequence of responses exists.

Stimulus-response

In a more general sense, the world is made up of stimuli and responses. Marketers control some stimuli (S) and attempt to elicit some response (R). Without a good sense of the exact response that is desired, it will be difficult to select the most appropriate stimuli.

Multiattribute model (MAM)

This model has many varieties in theoretical research, but there are two basic concepts that the practitioner should keep in mind. First, what are the most important attributes for the consumer relative to a particular product class or problem (and what are the least important attributes)? Second, how well does the firm and its major competitors do on each of these attributes? These data allow the manager to speak to the key issues, to fix important product problems, to position the brand in a competitive marketplace, and to generate a relevant message strategy.

Use of behavioral sciences and research

As the field of advertising becomes more and more sophisticated, there is a greater emphasis on the use of research, a greater level of borrowing from the behavioral sciences, and less inclination to make "seat-of-the-pants" decisions. The hierarchy of effects and MAM models were only the first; practitioners are searching for other useful models as well.

Learning theory models come in two classes. *Verbal learning* deals with how cognitive concepts are developed. Repetition and clutter are important to media planners, and come from learning theory. *Animal learning* looks at behavioral concepts (there is now also a new field of *cognitive behavioral learning*). Promotions strategies aim at changing behavior and are becoming more sophisticated in the proper use of reinforcers and shaping procedures.

Information processing models are important because they deal with how, and how much, information is sought and received, with how these processes differ in active search and passive receipt, and with how decisions are made in the presence or absence of information. Knowing how to present information properly so it can be easily learned is vital to message development.

Involvement models remind the manager that all responses are situation-specific. Many communications decisions are greatly affected by how much consumers care about the decisions they need to make. In low involvement, the consumer needs to use a product but doesn't care much about the particular brand being used; in high-involvement decisions, brand choice is important. Managers

Mike Rogers

Executive Vice-President, Foote, Cone & Belding

Mike Rogers is executive vice-president and an executive creative director of Foote, Cone & Belding.

Mike describes himself as a "care-aholic." He cares a little too much . . . a little too intensely.

Sometimes that creates problems. Other times it creates advertising that wins awards and turns businesses around.

Where Does Honor End and Foolhardy Begin?

That's what defines agencies . . . good, bad, or mediocre.

Talent doesn't define which agency is which. Honor does. Strategy is shaped by it. Creative is made, bent, or broken by it. And so is agency morale.

Too much honor can lose business for an agency. A lack of honor can save a piece of business. (And sad though it may be—it can save it for a long, long time.)

Honor can make you personally very satisfied and "honored." Or it can put you on the beach like a piece of flotsam. Unemployable.

Honor, my friend, is an issue you'll have to get down in the mud and wrestle with about two or three times a year for your entire career.

Yet, as important as it is, I don't think there's a university in the world that teaches a course on it.

Now you sit there and think "piece of cake." And I say to you: Oh, really?

You're a creative person. You're working on a fast food account. You have a wonderful campaign that the client loves, but the name of the restaurant doesn't come in till the sixteenth second in the commercial. McCollum/Spielman research says that those campaigns that break through the clutter use the client's name (in audio and video) in the first seven seconds.

Client believes research. You take the position that to use the client's name that early ruins the idea. The research folks don't think so. The client doesn't think so. You refuse to change it. The client says "I want it changed."

Whatcha goin' to do?

Are you foolhardy?

Or are you honorable?

Put on both hats for a minute, and you can clearly argue both sides.

OK. Now you're the account person. The client corners you and says: "I know your creatives have their egos pretty involved in this. I hope you are seeing things a little more clearly. I would also hope that back within the agency you, of all people, will fairly represent our point of view. I'm counting on you."

You are only human. You know that you can "make it" with this client if you fight for him. You know you may be "dead" with this client if you don't fight for him.

What cha goin' to do?

Are you foolhardy?

Or are you honorable?

Now if you're looking for the correct answer to the puzzles I've posed, guess what . . . . you will be looking for the rest of your life.

Because these questions go on and on and there is *no* training in how to deal with them.

Yet these questions . . .

1. When is it right to resign a piece of business?

2. How hard do you let people fight internally?

3. How hard do you fight for strategy?

4. How much do you back creative?

5. How much money do you spend developing creative?

and hundreds of other questions like them determine what kind of agency you are. What kind of advertising person you are.

So what are you goin' to do?

must assess the product class in terms of price, complexity, and frequency of purchase and must assess consumers in terms of past experience with the product. These issues influence media, message, and promotions decisions.

Setting objectives

Any objective should have four components: task, time period, target market, and amount of desired change. The more specifically the components are stated, the more limited will be the choice of available strategies. One purpose of *sound* objectives is to drive away unsound strategies. The purpose of *specific* objectives is to ensure that all parties are going in the same direction and not working toward different ends.

Positioning

The best way to develop a long-run franchise for a product or service is to make it unique. Positioning helps develop this uniqueness in terms of meaningful benefits and major competitors. Sound positioning also drives away unsound strategies. Because there are many more potentially poor than potentially useful strategies available to the manager, it is nice to have at least two tools that will help keep away some of the poor strategies.

Message strategy

There is always a target market. Talk to a single person in that target about the benefits and unique position of the brand. Develop the Unique Selling Proposition (USP) so that the entire campaign is built on these unique benefits that the brand offers.

Media strategy

The three key media decisions are media selection, vehicle selection, and scheduling. These decisions are made with an eye toward a message delivery system that assists learning and retards forgetting for a specific target market.

Promotions strategy

Through the use of promotions tools, the firm can buy behavior from consumers, retailers, or the firm's own sales force. It is important to coordinate the push of the middlepersons and sales force with the pull of consumers. The timing of the message delivery and the USP of the message itself also need to be coordinated.

Other strategic elements

Again there must be coordination among the various elements in terms of timing (the advertising should precede the sales force) and message strategy (the package should show a key scene from the advertising and the advertising should show the package). All elements should tie to the basic objectives and position (the brand name should communicate the key benefit).

In this way, all elements of the communications package can tie together and can tie to the basic problem, the target market, the objectives, and the position. It is important for all elements to be coordinated, for this makes learning easier on the part of the consumer. By tying the elements to the problems and objectives, the strategies can be justified. It is much easier to sell the plan to upper management or to the client if all the decisions can be justified. It is even easier if these people have given earlier approval to the problems and objectives statement.

Ethical behavior

It is possible to simultaneously make a profit and practice ethical behavior. In fact, the two go hand in hand to develop a long-term relation with consumers. In order for mass communications to survive and grow as an institution in our society, it is incumbent upon the members of the field to exhibit proper behavior. There will always be a few who are scorned by their peers and by consumers for trying to make a quick buck at the expense of others. Don't let it be you. It's just as easy to succeed with virtue as it is to go the other route.

In Conclusion

Each year the business of marketing communications grows and becomes more important to the firm. Mass communications have become more important because retail selling has become ever more automated and self-service oriented; there are fewer clerks, and they seem to be less informed. With these trends, nonpersonal communications become more important. Consumers need information before shopping and while shopping, but there are fewer personal interactions that yield this information.

In addition, the world continues to become more competitive as new brands continue to be introduced. Competitors are getting more sophisticated, and the failure rate of new products continues to be quite high. As a result it becomes more difficult to succeed, and it becomes more necessary to be equally sophisticated.

It is no longer enough to be merely creative or to buy some vehicle space; it is necessary to be very systematic as well. For a firm to succeed in its communications, its leaders must have a knowledge of both managerial and behavioral sciences. This text has attempted to provide a general framework for such knowledge that will serve managers in communicating in various ways to various types of people with regard to a variety of problems.

Welcome to the world of advertising and promotions! It really *is* the most fun you can have with your clothes on.

Discussion Questions

1. Discuss the relationship between the self-interests of the firm and the interests of the larger society. When do these move in the same direction? In different directions?

2. What value is there to individual consumers or to a collective society in having brands that are differentiated solely on image? Brands that are differentiated on minor but real differences?

3. Should advertising attempt to persuade? Is it necessary to do so in an honest manner? How would your answers differ from the point of view of society versus that of the firm?

4. Does advertising lead to higher costs? When would it? When would it not?

5. Does advertising keep new brands out of a market? Why yes? Why not?

6. Does advertising lead to market concentration or brand proliferation? Under what conditions would each of these occur?

7. Under what conditions might advertising manipulate consumers? Consider high and low involvement, and trial and repeat purchases.

8. Develop a scoring system to decide if any particular ad is offensive or tasteless.

9. Do you think that there should be political advertising? Would you leave it as it is now or would you change it? If you would change it, discuss your changes.

10. Overall, does advertising make a positive, a negative, or no contribution to society? Defend your answer.

Notes

1. Vincent P. Norris, "Advertising History—According to the Textbooks," *Journal of Advertising* 9 (1980), no. 3, pp. 3–11.

2. Jean-Jacques Lambin, "What Is the Real Impact of Advertising?" *Harvard Business Review,* May–June 1975, pp. 139–149.

3. William S. Comanor and Thomas A. Wilson, "Advertising, Market Structure and Performance," *Review of Economics and Statistics* 49 (November 1967), pp. 423–440.

4. David Ogilvy, *Ogilvy on Advertising* (New York: Crown Publishers, Inc., 1983), p. 206.

5. Julian L. Simon, *Issues in the Economics of Advertising* (University of Illinois Press, 1970), pp. 221, 240–241.

6. Lester G. Telser, "Some Aspects of the Economics of Advertising," *Journal of Business* 41 (April 1968), p. 169.

7. Bob Stone, "Package Goods: A New Frontier," *Advertising Age,* 25 July 1983, p. M-42.

8. A. H. Maslow, *Motivation and Personality* (New York: Harper & Row, 1954).

9. Jacob Jacoby, Donald E. Speller, and Carol Kohn Berning, "Brand Choice Behavior as a Function of Information Load: Replication and Extension," *Journal of Consumer Research* 1 (June 1974), pp. 33–42.

10. Michael J. Houston and Michael L. Rothschild, "Policy-Related Experiments on Information Provision: A Normative Model and Explication," *Journal of Marketing Research* 17 (November 1980), pp. 432–449.

11. Michael L. Ray, Testimony to the FTC concerning advertising for over-the-counter drugs, Proceedings Docket no. 215–51, p. 2935, Washington DC, 24 March 1977.

12. Jacob Jacoby, W. D. Hoyer, and D. A. Sheluga, *The Miscomprehension of Televised Commercials* (New York: American Association of Advertising Agencies, 1980).

13. John O'Toole, *The Trouble with Advertising* (New York: Chelsea House, 1981), pp. 35–40.

14. O'Toole, *The Trouble with Advertising,* p. 37.

15. David Ogilvy, *On Advertising,* p. 209.

16. Rudolph Spero, *The Duping of the American Voter* (New York: Lippincott & Crowell, 1980).

17. K. S. Palda, "The Effect of Expenditure on Political Success," *Journal of Law and Economics,* December 1975, pp. 745–771.

18. John O'Toole, *The Trouble with Advertising,* pp. 28–29.

THE RESULTS

Figure S.1 shows the planning calendar that was followed by Sunkist during the half year preceding the product's introduction. Sunkist orange soda was introduced into test markets on May 15, 1978. By every measure the brand was an enormous success.

Tracking

A tracking study was conducted at 4, 8, and 13 weeks:

■ *awareness* Virtually everyone in the target audience (94%) was aware of Sunkist orange soda after 13 weeks of advertising. In addition, 83% of the target was able to identify the Good Vibrations themeline as belonging to Sunkist. By comparison, 93%, 85%, and 50% were able to identify Coke, Pepsi, and 7-Up themelines, respectively.

■ *trial* Three out of four people in the target audience had tried the brand after 13 weeks, and one out of two among the total population had tried it.

Figure S.1 *Sunkist's pre-advertising planning calendar*

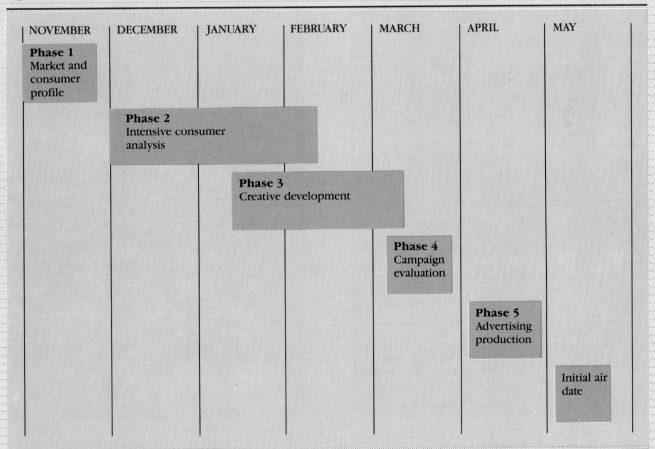

■ *repeat purchase* Eight out of ten tryers were repeat purchasers.

■ *positive purchase interest* Seven of ten people who were aware of Sunkist but had not yet tried it intended to do so.

Sales

The brand's sales and share achieved a level three times the objective. In fact, the business was so strong that the five-year share objective of the market plan was achieved in 13 weeks in introductory markets.

By 1979 Sunkist had distribution in 50% of the United States and was the nation's largest selling orange soda. It had a 25% market share, followed by Orange Crush with 18%, Nehi with 5%, Shasta with 4%, and Fanta with 2%.

In 1980, distribution grew to 85% of the United States and there were over 300 affiliated bottlers. In a survey, consumers were asked, "If you were going to open a grocery store tomorrow, what five brands of carbonated soft drink would you carry?" Sunkist was the fourth most mentioned brand behind Coke, Pepsi, and 7-Up. The results were used in the trade ad in Figure S.2. During 1980 Sunkist became the first orange soda to become one of the top ten selling soft drinks. This fact also was reported in a trade ad (Figure S.3).

Figure S.2 *Top five requested brands*

Figure S.3 *Top ten best selling brands*

Continued expansion in 1980 led to fountain sales (shown in the trade ad in Figure S.4) and the introduction of Diet Sunkist (shown in Figure S.5). While regular Sunkist was aimed at the 12- to 34-year-old market, the diet drink was aimed at the 35- to 49-year-old market. Later research showed that 66% of Diet Sunkist purchasers were new users of the brand.

Marketing and Media Decisions selected Sunkist as one of its "15 Top Marketing Successes of 1980." As can be seen in Table S.1, while industry growth between 1980 and 1981 was less than 3%, Sunkist growth was over 19%. During 1981, distribution of regular Sunkist reached 93% of the United States and Diet Sunkist reached 64%. For the first time, national media buys now were made to take advantage of the wide distribution.

Finally, a 1984 study of the Good Vibrations campaign showed that Sunkist's awareness and memorability were higher than many brands that spent up to five times as much on advertising. Table S.2 shows that Sunkist was third, behind Coke and Pepsi, on three major measures of awareness, although it was eighth in terms of advertising expenditures in the previous year.

This advertising efficiency and effectiveness can be attributed to the careful research that had been done seven years earlier and the fact that the resulting campaign had not been changed during those seven years. As a result, a powerful brand image that was meaningful to the target had been developed. While many brands of soft drinks used a beach image during the seven-year period, Sunkist now owned this image; two-thirds of all consumers linked this image to Sunkist.

Figure S.4 Introduction of fountain Sunkist

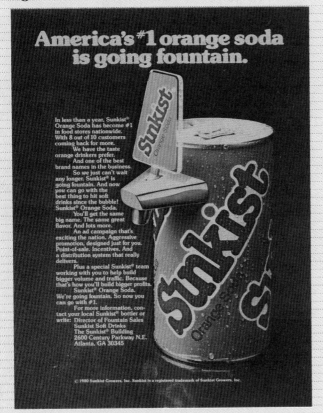

Figure S.5 Introduction of Diet Sunkist

Table S.1 Top 10 soft drink brands (1980–1981)

Brand	1981 market share	1981 Cases (000)[a]	1980 Cases (000)[a]	1981 Brand Growth
Coca-Cola	26.5%	1,495,000	1,452,000	3.0%
Pepsi-Cola	19.5	1,100,000	1,045,000[b]	5.0
Dr. Pepper	4.9	277,000	301,300	(8.1)
7-Up	4.9	275,000	296,000	(7.4)
Tab	3.5	196,000	175,300	11.8
Mountain Dew	3.2	178,970	169,000[b]	5.9
Sprite	3.0	168,500	153,400	9.8
Diet Pepsi-Cola	3.0	168,000	150,960[b]	11.1
Royal Crown Cola	2.7	152,000	164,400	(7.5)
Sunkist	*1.7*	*98,000*	*82,200*	*19.2*
Top 10	72.9%	4,108,470.0	3,990,460	2.96%
Other brands	27.1%	1,524,315.1	1,488,370	2.42%
Total industry	100.0%	5,632,785.1	5,478,830	2.81%

Source: *Beverage World* estimates based on industry contacts.
[a]Eight-ounce equivalent cases
[b]Revised 1980 cases

The Sunkist story has shown the development of a disciplined, complex, and successful campaign. Sunkist followed a decision sequence framework, did rigorous up-front research, and set objectives and positioning; the company then was able to coordinate the development of product, advertising, promotions, package, and other communications elements. The budget for this project was high, but that alone cannot ensure success. Success was a result of extreme diligence in the development of all aspects of the campaign, seeing what none of its competitors saw in the marketplace, and then being able to find a creative way to communicate the product to the public.

Table S.2 1984 Evaluation of Sunkist advertising

Brand	Unaided brand awareness	Unaided advertising awareness	Correct themeline identification	1983 advertising expenditures ($ millions)
Coke	84%	74%	92%	47.8
Pepsi	77	75	71	34.0
Sunkist	*51*	*43*	*72*	*4.1*
Sprite	41	24	N.A.	22.0
Dr. Pepper	40	23	38	8.3
Mountain Dew	26	18	26	9.8
Crush	20	14	25	4.5
7-Up	15	5	63	23.7

Figure Credits

CHAPTER 1 **1.3** Leo Burnett U.S.A.; **1.4** Young & Rubicam; **1.5** Listermint with Fluoride. Warner-Lambert Co./Consumer Products Group; **1.6** Reprinted courtesy of General Motors Corporation; **1.7** Reprinted courtesy of Eastman Kodak Company; **1.8** William Allerton & Associates, Inc./Media & Political Consultants; **1.10** Trustees of the University of Illinois. *The Process and Effects of Mass Communication* edited by Wilbur Schramm; **1.12** Foote, Cone & Belding.

CHAPTER 2 **2.2** Simmons Market Research Bureau: Study of Media and Markets; **2.3** © 1981, Joel Garreau, from the book *The Nine Nations of North America,* published in paperback by Avon Books; **2.4a,b** Claritas, L. P., Alexandria, VA; **2.5** © American Marketing Association. Reprinted from William D. Wells, *Life Style and Psychographics,* Chicago: American Marketing Association, 1974; **2.7a** Colgate Palmolive Company; **2.7b** Courtesy of Lever Brothers Company; **2.9** Courtesy of the Coca-Cola Company; **2.10–2.11** Volkswagen of America, Inc.; **2.12** Philip Kotler, *Marketing Management Analysis, Planning and Control,* 5th ed., © 1984, p. 252. Adapted by permission of Prentice-Hall, Inc. Englewood Cliffs, NJ; **2.13** Wilkins Industries; **2.14** Reprinted courtesy of Eastman Kodak Company.

CHAPTER 3 **3.1** From *Consumer Behavior: Application of Theory* by John A. Howard, 1977, p. 13. Reprinted with permission of McGraw-Hill Book Company; **3.3** Reprinted permission of Pioneer Electronics (USA) Inc.; **3.4** The "Test Drive A Macintosh" ad is provided courtesy of Apple Computer, Inc.; **3.6** Swift and Company; **3.7** Courtesy of The Procter & Gamble Company; **3.8a,b** Lorillard, Inc. **3.9** Reprinted from the *Journal of Advertising Research,* © Copyright 1980 by the Advertising Research Foundation; **3.12** Automatic Data Processing; **3.14–3.18** Perceptual Preference Maps adapted from Keon, *Journal of Marketing Research,* November 3, 1983, p. 385. Copyright © American Marketing Association.

CHAPTER 4 **4.1** Adapted from *Dynamic Competitive Strategy and Product Life Cycles* by Chester R. Wasson. Challenge Books, 1974, p. 3; **4.4** Perdue Farms Incorporated; **4.5** © 1984 Polaroid Corporation; **4.6** Courtesy of Alberto-Culver Company and the Chicago White Sox; **4.7** Hattori Corporation of America, Consumer Electronics Division/Bentley, Barnes & Lynn, Inc. Advertising Agency; **4.8** Advertisement reproduced by permission of American Home Products Corporation, owners of trademark Anacin 3® © 1985 Whitehall Laboratories; **4.11** © Volvo Corporation of America; **4.15** *How to Prepare and Use Marketing Plans for Profit* by Hal W. Goetsch, Reprinted by permission of American Marketing Association; **4.16** Simmons Market Research Bureau: Study of Media and Markets; **4.18–4.19** Oscar Mayer & Company.

CHAPTER 5 **5.1** Yoram Wind, *Product Policy* © 1982, Addison-Wesley, Reading, Massachusetts. Reprinted with permission. **5.2** From *Defining Advertising Goals for Measured Advertising Results* by Russell H. Colley, New York: Association of National Advertisers, Inc., 1961, pp. 67–68; **5.3** From "Management by Objectives in Marketing: Philosophy, Process and Problems" by Michael J. Etzel and John M. Ivancevich in *Journal of Marketing,* 38, October 1974, p. 50; **5.4** Reprinted by permission of International Paper Company. All Rights Reserved; **5.6** Nabisco Brands, Inc.; **5.7** George A. Hormel & Company; **5.8** Medley Distilling Company, Louisville, Kentucky. Agency: Menaker & Paul, Inc., Chicago, Illinois; **5.9** AMTRAK; **5.10** Yoram Wind, *Product Policy,* © 1982, Addison-Wesley, Reading, Massachusetts. Reprinted with permission.

PART 4 **1** Reprinted with permission by Benton & Bowles, Inc.

CHAPTER 6 **6.1a-d** Reprinted courtesy of Eastman Kodak Company and Ingvild–Ford Models; **6.2** Courtesy Pontiac Motor Division, General Motors Corporation; **6.3** Courtesy of Pierre Cardin Men's Cologne; **6.4** General Foods Corporation/Post® Grape-Nuts®; **6.5** Howard Shank, Retired President, Leo Burnett Company; **6.6** "Marketing's Scarlet Letter: The Theory and Practice of Corrective Advertising" by Wilkie, McNeill and Mazis in *Journal of Marketing,* 48 (Spring 1984), p. 18; **6.7** "Marketing's Scarlet Letter: The Theory and Practice of Corrective Advertising" by Wilkie, McNeill and Mazis in *Journal of Marketing,* 48 (Spring 1984), p. 13; **6.8** Ocean Spray Cranberry, Inc.; **6.9** Reprinted with permission from *Journal of Advertising,* Vol. 13, No. 2 (1984), p. 64.

CHAPTER 7 **7.1** Reprinted courtesy of Leo Burnett Company, Inc., Chicago; **7.2** A Child's Primer to Advertising by Alan Barzman. Reprinted with permission of *Magazine Age,* April 1980; **7.3** © 1982 STANMACK. Reprinted from *Adweek* Magazine; **7.5** From *Systematic Approach to Creative Advertising* by Stephen Baker, 1979, p. 2. Reprinted with permission of McGraw-Hill Book Company; **7.6** Lever Brothers Company; **7.7** C. F. Hathaway; **7.8** Frankel & Company; **7.10** Reprinted permission of Pioneer Electronics (USA) Inc.; **7.11** Firestone Tire & Rubber Co., Akron, Ohio; **7.12** Courtesy of Atari (U.S.) Corporation; **7.13** Litton Microwave Cooking Products; **7.14** Young & Rubicam, NY, and General Foods Corporation; **7.15** Courtesy of Dr. Pepper Company; **7.16** Florida Department of Citrus; **7.17** "Slugging It Out Fairly in Comparative Advertising" by Leonard S. Matthews, *Advertising Age,* July 11, 1983, p. M-36. Reprinted with permission by *Advertising Age.* Copyright 1983 by Crain Communications, Inc.; **7.18** G. Heilman Brewing Co., Inc.; **7.19** Copyright Mattel, Inc. Used with permission; **7.20** Rose Holland House Inc.; **7.21** Lennox Industries & American Gas Association; **7.22** The Pillsbury Company and Leo Burnett U.S.A.; **7.23** Courtesy of Revlon, Inc.; **7.24** Uniroyal Tire Division; **7.25** Courtesy of The Mutual Life Insurance Company of New York and The Marschalk Company, Inc.; **7.26** Courtesy R. T. French—Household and Toiletry Products.

CHAPTER 8 **8.1** Courtesy, Andersen Corporation, Bayport, MN; **8.2** Courtesy ITT Corporation; **8.3** Loctite Corporation—Worldwide producer of Specialty Chemicals; **8.4** Courtesy Lederle Laboratories, 1984; **8.5** Reprinted by permission of copyright owner, Hershey Foods Corporation, Hershey, Pennsylvania; **8.6** Courtesy of Rolls-Royce Motors Inc.; **8.8** GTE Sprint Communications Corp.; **8.9** Ford Motor Company; **8.10** Florists' Transworld Delivery Association; **8.11** Courtesy of The Campbell Soup Company; **8.12** Reprinted with permission of Federal Express Corporation. All rights reserved; **8.13** Courtesy of The Pillsbury Company and Leo Burnett U.S.A.; **8.14** Selby Industries Inc., Richfield, OH; **8.15** Courtesy of Pfizer Inc.; **8.16** Soloflex Inc.; **8.17** © Paco Rabanne Parfums; **8.18** Lyrics from "Sell in the Song" from Keith Reinard's speech "I Believe in Music." Courtesy of Needham, Harper Worldwide, New York.

CHAPTER 9   **9.2–9.3** United States Postal Service; **9.4** Advertisement used with permission of Royal Doulton USA Inc.; **9.5** Saatchi & Saatchi Company PLC, London; **9.6** Eastern Airlines, Inc.; **9.7** Toshiba America, Inc., Copier Products Division; **9.8** Volkswagen of America, Inc. and Doyle Dane Bernbach Advertising; **9.9** Heublein Inc.; **9.10** Carillon Importers, Ltd. New York, NY; **9.11** Reprint permission granted by Olympus Corporation, Consumer Products Group; **9.12** Young & Rubicam; **9.13** Courtesy of Lever Brothers Company; **9.14** Volkswagen of America, Inc.; **9.15** Cuisinart and Geers Gross Advertising; **9.16** Courtesy of Nocona Boot Company; **9.17** Reprinted courtesy of Eastman Kodak Company; **9.19** Courtesy of Jaguar Cars Inc.; **9.20** The Maytag Company, Newton, Iowa; **9.21** © 1985 Polaroid Corporation "Polaroid"®; **9.22** Reprinted by permission of Canon U.S.A., Inc.

CHAPTER 10   **10.1–10.4** Courtesy of Wisconsin Power & Light Company; **10.5** The Pillsbury Company and Leo Burnett Advertising; **10.6** Courtesy of AT&T; **10.7** Samsonite Corporation, Denver, Colorado; **10.8** Mannington Mills, Inc., Salem, NJ; **10.9** Armstrong World Industries, Inc.; **10.10** Courtesy of Congoleum Corporation, Resilient Flooring, Kearney, NJ; **10.11** The Stouffer Foods Corporation; **10.12** Canon U.S.A., Inc.; **10.13** Courtesy of N.W. Ayer and John Deere & Company; **10.14** Courtesy of The Campbell Soup Company; **10.15** © NIKE, Inc. Courtesy Wieden & Kennedy, Inc.; **10.16** NYNEX Corporation; **10.17** Food and Wines from France, Inc.; **10.18** Excelsior Fitness Equipment Co.; **10.19** From *Contemporary Advertising* by Bovee and Arens, 1982, p. 379. Reprinted with permission of Richard D. Irwin, Inc.

CHAPTER 11   **11.1** Courtesy Rocky Rococo Corp.; **11.3** Courtesy Rocky Rococo Corp.; **11.4** Courtesy Rocky Rococo Corp.; **11.5** The Pillsbury Company and Leo Burnett U.S.A.; **11.6** Courtesy of W. A. Taylor & Company, importer and marketer of Drambuie Liqueur; **11.8** From *Contemporary Advertising* by Bovee and Arens, 1982, p. 412. Reprinted with permission of Richard D. Irwin, Inc.; **11.9** From *How To Advertise* by Kenneth Roman and Jane Maas, 1976, pp. 79–81, St. Martin's Press, Inc., New York. Copyright © 1976 by Kenneth Roman and Jane Maas; **11.10** Reprinted by permission from *Advertising Writing: Putting Creative Strategy to Work,* Second Edition by Hafer and White; Copyright © 1977, 1982 by West Publishing Company. All rights reserved; **11.12** From *Radio Plays The Plaza* by Ross and Landers, Radio Advertising Bureau, New York, 1969, p. 29.

CHAPTER 12   **12.3** Reprinted with permission of Dow Jones & Company, Inc. and BBDO; **12.4** "How the Oculometer Tracks the Eye" by Harry Carter from *Newsweek,* June 6, 1977. Reprinted with permission of the publisher; **12.5** Bruzzone Research Co.

CHAPTER 13   **13.1** Nielsen Television Index—A. C. Nielsen Company; **13.8** Simmons Market Research Bureau: Study of Media and Markets; **13.9** As reprinted from Standard Rate and Data Service, December, 1981; **13.10** Arbitron Ratings Company.

PART VI   **Fig. 1** From *Couponing and Rebates: Profit on the Dotted Line* by Russell Bowman, Lebhar Friedman, 1980; **Fig. 2** From *Advertising Age,* August 22, 1983, p. M-31. Reprinted by permission of *Advertising Age.* Copyright 1983 by Crain Communications, Inc.; **Fig. 3** From "How to Play the Angles and Win" by Ed Meyer, *Advertising Age,* April 22, 1983, p. M-48. Reprinted with permission by *Advertising Age.* Copyright 1983 by Crain Communications, Inc.

CHAPTER 14   **14.8** Reprinted by permission of Philip Morris Incorporated.

CHAPTER 15   **15.3** Donnelley Marketing, a D & B Company; **15.9** From "Sampling Builds Business" by Ed Meyer, *Advertising Age,* July 12, 1982, p. M-22. Reprinted with permission by *Advertising Age.* Copyright 1982 by Crain Communications, Inc.; **15.15** Midway Airlines, Inc.

CHAPTER 16   **16.2** Printed with permission of Ralston Purina Company; **16.3** CHAZ for Men advertisement courtesy of Revlon, Inc.; **16.8** Courtesy of The Procter & Gamble Company; **16.10** Northwest Orient Airlines; **16.11** Courtesy of North Shore Computers, Inc. Milwaukee and Madison, WI; **16.12** Reprinted by permission of Hershey Foods Corporation and Kitchens of Sara Lee.

CHAPTER 17   **17.1** From "Marketing and Public Relations" by Philip Kotler and William Mindak, *Journal of Marketing,* October, 1978, p. 14; **17.2** Press release courtesy of Foote, Cone & Belding; **17.5** Bethlehem Steel Corporation; **17.6** The Tobacco Institute; **17.7** Exxon Corporation; **17.8** Courtesy of American Express Travel Related Services Co., Inc. Copyright 1983; **17.9** Rockwell International; **17.10** Boise Cascade Corporation; **17.11** Reproduced from Volume 42, No. 2 of the Stanford Business School Alumni Bulletin. Copyright 1973 by the Board of Trustees of the Leland Stanford Junior University. All rights reserved.

CHAPTER 18   **18.1** From *Promotional Strategy, Managing the Marketing Communications Process* by James F. Engel, Martin R. Warshaw and Thomas C. Kinnear, 1979, Richard D. Irwin, Inc. Reprinted by permission of the publisher; **18.2** McGraw-Hill Research "Laboratory of Advertising Performance" Report 8013.7; **18.3** McGraw-Hill Research "Laboratory of Advertising Performance" Report 8052.2; **18.4** McGraw-Hill Research "Laboratory of Advertising Performance" Report 8051.2; **18.5** Reproduced with permission from McGraw-Hill Publications Company; **18.6** From "Relationship Between Salesperson Performance and Understanding of Customer Decision Making" by Barton A. Weitz, *Journal of Marketing Research,* 15, November 1978, p. 502; **18.7** From "Relational Communication: Form Versus Content in the Sales Interaction" by Gary F. Soldow and Gloria Penn Thomas, *Journal of Marketing,* 48, Winter 1984, pp. 89–90; **18.8** From "Effectiveness in Sales Interactions: A Contingency Framework" by Barton A. Weitz, *Journal of Marketing,* 45, Winter 1981, p. 90.

CHAPTER 19   **19.3** Published courtesy of General Mills, Inc.

CHAPTER 20   **20.1** Cahner's Publishing Company; **20.3** Courtesy of Crain Communications; **20.4** Reprinted with permission of *Advertising Age.* Copyright Crain Communications, Inc.; **20.8** Reprinted from "Advertising Research at Anheuser-Busch, Inc. (1963–1968), by Russell L. Ackoff and James R. Emshoff, *Sloan Management Review,* Spring 1975, p. 9, by permission of the publisher. Copyright © 1968 by the Sloan Management Review Association. All rights reserved; **20.9** David A. Aaker/John G. Myers, *Advertising Management,* © 1975, p. 52. Reprinted by permission of Prentice-Hall, Inc., Englewood Cliffs, NJ; **20.10** Reprinted with permission of *Advertising Age.* Copyright 1983 by Crain Communications, Inc.

CHAPTER 21   **21.1** Philip Kotler, *Marketing Management Analysis, Planning and Control,* 5th ed., © 1984, p. 252. Adapted by permission of Prentice-Hall, Inc., Englewood Cliffs, NJ; **21.2** Saks Fifth Avenue; **21.3** Toys "R" Us; **21.4** Creative Field's, Inc./Marshall Field's Chicago; **21.5** The International Home; **21.6** Herman's Sporting Goods, Inc.; **21.7** Used by permission of Somerville Lumber and Supply Co., Somerville, MA; **21.8** From *Advertising Today* by J. Douglas Johnson. © 1978 by J. Douglas Johnson. Reprinted by permission of the publisher, Science Research Associates, Inc.; **21.9** Courtesy: Fortunoff Fine Jewelry & Silverware, Inc.; **21.10** Belden Jewelers; **21.11** Courtesy of Fitchburg Plumbing, Inc., Benjamin Plumbing Inc., Lichtfield Plumbing, Blied Plumbing Co., Inc.; **21.12–21.13** K Mart Corporation; **21.14** Photo: Russ Fischella, Art Director: Zoe Architect; **21.15** Saks Fifth Avenue; **21.16** Savanna Oak Furniture, Madison, WI; **21.17** Pizza Hut, Inc.; **21.18** Crandall's.

CHAPTER 22   **22.1** Ad provided courtesy of EDAX® International; **22.2** From *Managerial Marketing for Industrial Firms,* by Charles B. Ames and James D. Hlavacek, Random House, 1984, p. 253; **22.3–22.4** CARR Reports, Cahners Publishing Company, Newton, MA; **22.5** McGraw-Hill Research Laboratory of Advertising Performance; **22.6** Reprinted by permission, Altex Division of Beckman Instruments, Inc. a SmithKline Beckman Company; **22.7** ISCO, Inc.; **22.8** Omaha Public Power District; **22.9** Goodyear Canada, Inc.; **22.10** The VirTis Co., Inc.; **22.11** Normark Corporation; **22.12** "Trade Show Organizers Take Note: Exhibitors Rank Participation Criteria" by John R. Dickinson and A. J. Faria, *Marketing News,* Vol. 18, No. 5, March 2, 1984, p. 5. Reprinted with permission; **22.13** Otis Elevator Company; **22.14** Atlas Copco Rotec Inc.; **22.15** Reprinted by permission of Abex Corporation, an IC Industries Company.

CHAPTER 23   **23.1** Midway Airlines, Inc.; **23.2** Used by permission of Holiday Inns, Inc.; **23.3** Courtesy Marcus Hotel Corporation; **23.4** Amtrak Systemwide Advertising: Near San Luis Obispo, California, National Magazine; **23.5** Madison General Hospital; **23.6** Courtesy of The Advertising Council; **23.7** Dr. Michael L. Pugh, Dane County Dental Society; **23.8** Advertisement used is by permission of The Chase Manhattan Bank, N.A. Spectrum is a registered service mark of The Chase Manhattan Corporation; **23.9** Courtesy Avis Rent A Car System, Inc.; **23.10** Advertisement developed by Williams, Young & Associates, CPA's and Woodland Marketing, Madison, Wisconsin, 1985; **23.11** Reprinted with permission of the author; **23.12** From "Marketing Communications in Nonbusiness Situations or Why It's So Hard to Sell Brotherhood like Soap" by Michael L. Rothschild, *Journal of Marketing,* 43, Spring 1977, p. 14; **23.13** Courtesy of Pennsylvania Committee for Effective Justice and the Ketchum Advertising/Pittsburgh; **23.14** This illustration courtesy of The Advertising Council.

CHAPTER 24   **24.1** Reproduced by permission of the American Association of Advertising Agencies Inc.; **24.2** Reproduced by permission of the American Association of Advertising Agencies Inc.; **24.3** Reproduced by permission of the American Association of Advertising Agencies Inc.; **24.4** © 1984, Washington Post Writers Group, reprinted with permission; **24.6** Newspaper Enterprise Association, Inc.; **24.7** National Rifle Association of America; **24.9–24.10** Reprinted with permission of *AdWeek,* 1982.

COLOR INSERT   Plates 1–2 Courtesy RCA/Consumer Electronics Division; Plates 3–7 Reproduced through courtesy of American Express Travel Related Services Company, Inc. Copyright: 1985.

Index